AMERICAN
JEWISH
BIOGRAPHIES

AMERICAN JEWISH BIOGRAPHIES

By Lakeville Press, Inc.
Murray Polner, President

A Lakeville Press Book

Facts On File, Inc.
460 Park Avenue South
New York, New York 10016

AMERICAN JEWISH BIOGRAPHIES

Library of Congress Cataloging in Publication Data

Polner, Murray.
 American Jewish biographies.

 1. Jews in the United States—Biography. 2. United States—Biography. I. Title.
E184.J5P625   973'.04924 [B]   80-27105
ISBN 0-87196-462-7

Printed in the United States of America
10 9 8 7 6 5 4 3 2 1

Preface

American Jewish Biographies contains biographical profiles of men and women who have distinguished themselves either in American life or American Jewish life. We have made no value judgment about their lifework. The criteria used are that they are alive, are citizens of the United States and consider themselves Jewish. In our view, those selected for inclusion have made a permanent contribution to life in this country or are identified with a significant event, issue or movement.

In compiling any bibliographical reference volume it is hard to decide who is to be included and who omitted. Many of the entries are self-evident while others may prove surprising. In each instance we have also considered the effect the individual has had on American or American Jewish society, broadly defined, and whether the person has received considerable public attention because of his or her achievements. If readers believe someone we have omitted deserves inclusion in any subsequent volume, they are invited to write the publishers.

American Jewish Biographies was researched and written by a bevy of journalists and writers. We would especially like to thank Myra Alperson for her research, editing, and her general contributions to the project. In addition, Elliot King provided valuable assistance. And finally, an appreciation to the distinguished historian, Dr. Henry L. Feingold, for his Introduction to this volume.

Introduction

If there is a commonality in the millenial history of the Jews, it is their experience of living perpetually among others while trying to maintain their own distinctive culture. What to give to the host society and what to retain for themselves is a basic conflict in all Jewish communities in the diaspora. The Jewish presence in America, which began formally in September 1654, when 23 Jewish refugees from Recife sailed into the harbor of New Amsterdam, marks a new and different page in that long history. America has been a post-emanicipation, intensely secular society and resolving this basic conflict has required a new formula.

Unlike prior settlement experiences in Jewish history, in America Jews were "present at the creation." They were among the first settlers to realize the hope of America. They contributed notably to the ethos and vital commerce that, over a century later, led to the establishment of the Republic. Boundaries were still flexible enough to make room for this inconspicuous minority—less than 2,000 souls during the colonial period—who prayed privately, pioneered in commerce and strongly supported the separation from England, Whereas their religion made them pariahs in the Christian world of Europe, in the colonies the Congregational (Puritan) obsession with the Old Testament made Jews desirable models. The high level of tolerance for the "people of the book" set the terms for a very favorable American-Jewish transaction that continues to this day. Jews who accepted the tenets of the enlightenment with alacrity felt at home in a modern nation, the first child of that enlightenment.

Yet while Jews came early to American society, they would never be precisely of it. They continued to adhere to a preexisting millenial religious civilization, a separate historial stream, whose events, symbols and myths shaped part of their group identity. From that vantage the American experience was merely another diaspora in a history full of diasporas. Unlike that of other immigrant groups who, having left their territorial space, also abandoned their culture, the Jewish group identity was more a thing of the spirit and could not easily be shed. More than anything, that internalized identity, divorced from any specific territory, accounted for the different terms Jews came to in acculturating themselves to American society. Robert Parkes, a noted sociologist who wrote in the 1920s, believed that if one wanted to know what America was all about, one had merely to observe American Jewry. In the way they acted out the success ethos and in the superabundant energy and talent that America's openness released in them, Jews were prototypically American.

At least part of that energy and the uncanny ability to retain some form of separate group identity can be traced to the continuous flow of Jewish immigrants to these shores until 1921. Immigration has been the most central fact of the American Jewish experience, since, in order to survive as a distinct community, American Jewry has been dependent on biological and cultural supplementation from abroad. The periodization of American Jewish history, which is based on three major waves of immigration, is a recognition of that fact. The Sephardic Jewish culture, established by Jews migrating originally from the Iberian peninsula, would have vanished without the timely arrival of a second wave of Jewish immigrants from central Europe, beginning in earnest in 1820. This group too eventually required supplementation. It came from the Jews of eastern Europe—about two and a quarter million of whom sought a haven in the United States after 1881. Most contemporary American Jews trace their ancestry to this last great wave of immigration. The distinctive political culture of today's Jewish community, its general style and the way it now comes to terms with its religion are rooted in this group. The arrival of this group in such great numbers allowed American Jewry to generate a distinctive culture and gave it the numerical strength that is important in a democracy where major decisions are reached by counting heads.

It is not possible to understand the dynamics of American Jewish life without referring to the three waves of immigration superimposed on top of each other. The diversity of cultures created so sharp a conflict that sometimes it seemed as if not even the common religious bond would be sufficient to keep the various groups from tearing each other apart. The division of American Judaism into three branches reflects this diversity. The Reform branch was originally anchored in the German-Jewish migration; the Conservative branch was the most ethnic, and served as a halfway house for eastern European immigrants; the Orthodox branch remained for those who wished to retain more of the religious culture. These religious divisions aggravated deeper class and national divisions that also could be traced to the waves of immigration they belonged to. So distinct did these divisions become that in the early decades of the twentieth century it was difficult to speak of the existence of only one Jewish community. The conflict between German Jews, who were sometimes called "uptown," and eastern European Jews—"downtown"—was in fact a reflection of the conflict between Teuton and Slav in the larger society. Paradoxically, Jews were fighting battles and retaining loyalties to two national cultures—Germany and Russia—that had rejected them. For several decades the residual influence of these cultures helped keep American Jewry divided, but gradually the common experience of the immigrants and their children in America furnished a base for developing a more unified Jewry. In the period after World War II the old divisions became merely memories. Swelled in numbers by an infusion of survivors of the Holocaust—17% of the Jewish population in the United States in 1950 was foreign born—American Jewry nevertheless faced the future as Americans.

The class and cultural diversity that was the hallmark of American Jewry in the first half of the twentieth century sometimes concealed experiences which the various groups had in common. All three groups had undergone the immigration experience; all shared a loyalty to Judaism even while they approached the tenets of the faith differently; all made the concern for and nurture of beleaguered Jewish communities abroad a basic preoccupation; all held philanthropy, the sacred obligation to give what one had been fortunate enough to receive, as a cardinal tenet; and most importantly all shared in common their remarkable economic achievements in the new society.

Jews produced a commercial elite in each of the three periods of their history in America. For most Americans the upward mobility phenomenon has been overstated. The story of America has not been so much a "rags to riches" tale as one in which some went from comfort to wealth. However, in contrast to other subgroups, the Jews actually did act out the American success story. Horatio Alger, the tutor in the Joseph Seligmann household whose success stories so moved America, was not a myth but a reality in American Jewish homes. For the Sephardic Jews of the colonial and national periods, commercial success was achieved by what one historian called "courageous enterprising." That meant pioneering in new, risky businesses, like the fur trade, or the making of castile soap or spermaceti candles. It also involved partaking in ocean commerce. Natural factors, such as storms, and the fact that it was carried on outside the laws of the mercantile system imposed by Britain on the colonies made ocean commerce very risky indeed. The German Jews were represented first by the rustic Bavarian Jewish peddlers, who traveled the roads of America selling their notions until they amassed sufficient capital to become storekeepers. They used merchandising to establish themselves economically. Jewish storekeepers filled the merchandising vacuum between the urban centers of the eastern seaboard and the sparsely settled interior. In a few cases the success story was remarkable. It went from peddler to resident merchant to a department store owner and, finally, to commercial banker.

But such success stories, which make up the background of the popular book *Our Crowd* by Stephen Birmingham, were actually rare. For most German Jews of the 19th century, success meant simply achieving a firm foot hold in the middle class. (There were other conduits to business success for German Jews, including mining, meat packing, ranching and small manufacturing.) Only a small and unrepresentative minority, aided by a parallel development in Europe, entered into banking. Nor did this phenomenon sustain itself. Today most of these banking houses—Kuhn-Loeb, Bache and many others—are no longer recognizably Jewish.

The eastern European Jews, who formed a commercial elite for the third time in the American-Jewish experience, settled into a society and economy that still held out special rewards for those daring to be commercial enterprisers. But it was also an economy that had become more consolidated and offered less opportunity for small businesses. With the exception of the garment industry and some facets of the second-hand business, no single business accounted fully for the rise of the eastern European Jewish business elite.

Two researchers speak of the phenomenon of the "egg-head millionaire," those whose fortunes were made by coupling a profession, such as chemistry or engineering, with normal business acumen. Jewish prominence in the nascent plastic manufacturing and air conditioning industries as well as in hundreds of different kinds of consulting businesses is evidence of this phenomenon. Interestingly, succeeding generations chose not to confine themselves to achievement exclusively through business. Instead they entered the professions, especially the independent professions—medicine, law and accounting—in disproportionate numbers. Others avoided business altogether because of their socialist principles and devoted their energy and talent to the Jewish labor movement. The men who came to lead this movement were no less remarkable than the enterprising Jews who formed the business elite. Without the initial success in business that helped establish a viable economic base, much of what makes the Jewish community distinctive—its theater, its press, its far-flung educational system, its overriding concern for Jews abroad and its support of Israel—would not have been possible.

Sociologists undoubtedly have their explanations for the abundant drive to achieve that has characterized so much of American Jewish life. Some historians are fond of the image of a suppressed steel coil pentup for centuries in the ghettos and released when the enlightenment broke down its walls. However, in America there were at least two additional circumstances that need to be considered. It was not one Jewish community that achieved remarkable success but three different ones at three different periods in the development of American. The only thing they shared in common was their Judaism; so one can assume that their search for excellence and mastery, whether in business or the professions or the arts, was somehow rooted in the Judaic religious culture. Aside from the fact that it was Jews who were doing the achieving, there was also something Judaic in the will to master knowledge that was often behind the success story of the achiever. The second circumstance was related to the nature of American society. If American society had not been open and free and full of promise, no motivation, no matter how intense, would have mattered. It was America's receptivity to talent, no matter what the source, that released Jewish drive and genius. That achievement has been as consistent a thread in the American Jewish experience as had been the comparative openness of American society. From the outset the American-Jewish transaction has been a mutually advantageous one. Jews have played an important role in pushing the American economy and culture forward, and they have been able to do so because America has offered the free environment for a full expression of Jewish talent.

Yet after we are all through theorizing about the source of the remarkable Jewish achievement in America, we are compelled to return to the thousands of individual biographies in which the real story lies. Reading them makes a shambles of our abstract theories regarding "middle man minorities," or the "levantine" tradition among Semitic people, or any other theory used to explain American Jewish success. Each biography, we note, is different, and each achiever finds a different reason for his success. Some find it in caprice, some in hard work, a few trace it to their Judaic upbringing. Many simply do not know, and some few do not care.

This book is a collection of over 400 biographies of select Jewish achievers in all fields of endeavor. It is designed not as inspirational literature but as a guide through the labyrinth of the American Jewish success story. It serves at once as a personalizer of that story and a "finder's guide." That such a guide is required is itself the most certain sign that we are dealing with no ordinary group. It is designed for the general reading public, but it will be especially useful to Jews and others who habitually pose the question, "Is he or she Jewish?" Not so long ago, to have posed that question would have been considered gauche. But today, when the acculturation process has placed the future of all subcultures in doubt, the question is increasingly posed openly and unabashedly. Members of such groups want to know their achievers because, indirectly, they serve as evidence that the culture which they cherish is worth retaining. The question is at once a sign that such group feeling still exists and yields a response which enhances that feeling. For American Jews there is a special reason why a knowledge of the achievers is important. It serves to balance all those negative images that a Jew must still contend with. These brief biographies will confirm that his culture contains values which are cherished by society at large and which encourage excellence. It is something that American Jews are in danger of forgetting. For that reason alone this book is a valued addition to the personal library shelf.

Henry L. Feingold

CONTENTS

AMERICAN
JEWISH
BIOGRAPHIES

ELIE ABEL

b. October 17, 1920
Journalist

Elie Abel can truly be termed the dean of American journalists. In the forefront of both broadcast and print journalism as a diplomatic correspondent for nearly 30 years, in 1969 he became dean of one of America's most prestigious graduate schools in the field—and his own alma mater—the Columbia School of Journalism. Since 1979 a professor at the journalism school of Stanford University, Abel remains one of America's premier political commentators.

Elie Abel was born in Montreal to Jacob, a printer, and Rose (Safetsky) Abel. While still an undergraduate at McGill University in Montreal, where he received a B.A. degree in 1941, he became a school news reporter for *The New York Times*. Upon graduation he reported for the *Windsor* (Ontario) *Daily Star*. He then enrolled in the journalism school at Columbia, earning his M.S. degree in 1942. After three years' service in the Royal Canadian Air Force, he was hired by the *Montreal Gazette,* quitting only a few months later and using a Pulitzer Traveling Fellowship received at Columbia to become European correspondent for the North American Newspaper Alliance reporting on the Nuremberg war crimes trials. In 1947, while visiting the Soviet Union and Poland, he was arrested by paranoid security police for allegedly spying and returned to the United States. During the next two years, he worked in New York as UN correspondent for the Overseas News Agency.

Abel joined *The New York Times* in 1949. He initially reported from Detroit and Washington and was then sent abroad to Europe and India. In 1955 he covered the historic Geneva summit conference and the following year headed the prize-winning team of reporters that documented the 1956 Hungarian uprising.

After leaving the *Times* in 1959 to become Washington bureau chief for the *Detroit News* for two years, during which he covered the Kennedy-Nixon campaign, Abel joined NBC as its State Department correspondent. In

1964 Abel became NBC's diplomatic correspondent and from 1965 to 1967 headed the network's London bureau before returning to New York to anchor the network's news series. During his tenure at NBC he covered the 1964 Goldwater-Johnson presidential campaign, disarmament talks at Geneva, several NATO conferences and the funerals of Sir Winston Churchill, John F. Kennedy and Konrad Adenauer. He also headed the reporting team that covered the initial Vietnam peace talks in Paris and hosted a weekly radio series of news interpretation programs called *The World in Washington,* for which he won the 1967 Peabody Award. The following year he anchored a special TV series called *The Campaign and the Candidates,* which took an in-depth look at that year's presidential campaign.

Three books have come out of Abel's travels and reporting career, all explorations of some of the most crucial events of the last several decades. *The Missile Crisis,* (New York, 1966) is an analysis of the threatened nuclear confrontation in 1962 between the Soviet Union and the United States over the placing of Soviet missiles in Cuba. *Roots of Involvement: The United States in Asia 1784–1971,* co-authored with newsman Marvin Kalb (New York, 1971), focuses primarily on contemporary American intervention in Indochina starting in the 1950s, although some background material is provided. Abel co-wrote *Special Envoy to Churchill and Stalin, 1941–1946* (New York, 1975) with Averell Harriman as a memoir of Harriman's diplomatic efforts to relieve the building Cold War pressures.

In 1969 Abel, who became an American citizen in 1952, left daily newspaper and television reporting to assume the deanship at Columbia. Although ostensibly a radical change in lifestyle, the new post offered Abel many of the same challenges reporting had provided. He stated in an interview:

> The [journalism] business is changing very fast. I think it's hard at this point to see where it will be ten years from now [but] a school with the resources of Columbia ought to be out exploring new patterns of journalism and working as closely as possible with newspapers, radio and television to help prepare young people. I think

we need to develop new sensitivity and above all the capacity to present a story that is of some significance with all the skill and talent we can find.

Abel remained at Columbia for 10 years, when he was invited to become a professor at Stanford University, where he has taught since 1979.

MORRIS B. ABRAM

b. June 19, 1918
Lawyer

The careers of Morris B. Abram—human rights activist, attorney and former American Jewish Committee president—seem better suited to three men than to one, and the path he took to achieve them is even more remarkable. A product of the South, Abram has been in the forefront of national and international movements to seek freedom and equality for all people.

Morris Berthold Abram was born in Fitzgerald, Georgia—a small town and the seat of Ben Hill County, located in the Georgia woods near the Omulcgee River. His father, Samuel, was a Russian-born storekeeper, and his mother, Irene (Cohen) Abram, was the daughter of a physician and granddaughter of Elias Epstein, one of the earliest southern Reform rabbis.

Growing up Jewish in Fitzgerald—a Protestant fundamentalist-dominated southern town—meant that early on Abram had to contend with being in a minority. And being a Jew in the years following the infamous Leo Frank hanging (in which a young Atlanta Jew was falsely accused of murdering a young woman) made Abram doubly committed to assuring that such an event could never happen again—not to Jews, nor to the other oppressed southern minority, blacks. Abram was also deeply influenced by another local immigrant Jew, Isaac Gelders, a Dutch Jewish socialist with a profound attraction to populism.

While a teen-ager, Abram occasionally offered sermons on Rosh Hashana and Yom Kippur and even led services at several bar mitzvahs, since the town did not have a rabbi. These activities must surely have made him feel somewhat estranged from his peers. "If one is a Jew and lives in a small Southern town, one is bound to realize early that a minority group has a different position than a majority," he told the magazine *Atlanta* in 1966, recounting his youthful experiences. "It was the overwhelming white Protestantism that pervaded the town. Any Jew would have been admitted to that white Protestantism structure had he wanted to be identified with it, but if you had any sense of your own worth, of your own identity, you didn't want it."

Abram attended the University of Georgia, where he graduated in 1938 with a B.A. degree summa cum laude and Phi Beta Kappa. Two years later he received his Doctor of Law degree from the University of Chicago Law School. Awarded a Rhodes Scholarship to Oxford University, where he earned both a bachelor's and a master's degree, he later joined the Army Air Corps. Following his discharge in 1945, he became a member of the United States prosecution staff at the Nuremburg war crimes trials and in 1948 was assistant to the director of the Committee for the Marshall Plan.

Thereafter Abram continued to focus his energies on the defense and expansion of human rights. In the 1950s he helped develop a large middle-income housing project for black families in Atlanta—the first of its kind—and ran, unsuccessfully, in a 1954 Democratic primary for Congress. He served as United States representative to the United Nations Commission on Human Rights and as the first legal counsel to the Peace Corps after its establishment under President John F. Kennedy and participated in the efforts to draw international attention to anti-Semitism in the Soviet Union. In 1964 and 1965 he drafted international conventions designed to set standards on racial and religious discrimination around the world. He also conducted a 14-year struggle against Georgia's county-unit election system, which discriminated against city voters. The legal principle that evolved from the resulting decision—which he won in the Supreme Court in 1963—established the one man-one vote rule and played a crucial role in the reapportionment of Congress and many state legislatures.

In 1963 he went home to Georgia to act as attorney for five black and white youths detained without bail in an Americus jail under the threat of execution for allegedly inciting a revolution. Abram's injunction successfully challenged the constitutionality of Georgia's inciting-to-revolution and related unlawful assembly laws, and the defendants were freed.

In 1964 he was elected the 13th president of the American Jewish Committee, one of the nation's pioneer human rights agencies. In this capacity he traveled to Jewish communities around the world, publicizing especially the needs of those experiencing political or other forms of oppression. Four years later he became president of Brandeis University but left after two years to run for the Democratic senatorial nomination in New York state, which he lost. In 1970 he coauthored *How to Stop Violence in Your City* (New York).

Abram has been an active trial and appellate attorney and a partner in the New York law firm of Paul, Weiss, Goldberg, Rifkin, Wharton and Garrison. Nevertheless, in 1975 he went on a leave of absence to serve as chairman of the Moreland Commission investigating the scandal-ridden nursing home industry in New York State. "It's going to better the lives of the old people in the nursing homes," said the lifelong reformer after his appointment was made public.

Abram fell victim to leukemia in the mid-1970s. Although his illness, which was widely publicized, nearly proved fatal, he refused to succumb. After unsuccessful treatment in New York, Abram traveled to Israel, where the treatment he received has led to an apparently complete remission.

Since the late 1970s Abram has attacked the system of quotas in schools and in the marketplace, as harmful to all Americans. "Racial quotas," he says, are "an attempted rape of the 14th Amendment."

For further information:
Abram, Morris B. *The Day Is Short.* New York: 1982.

BELLA ABZUG

b. July 24, 1920
Attorney; former congresswoman

Since rising to prominence as a leader in Women Strike for Peace during the 1960s, Bella Abzug has been an outspoken advocate of a wide range of liberal causes. The former New York City congresswoman has fought for civil rights, the Equal Rights Amendment, nuclear test ban treaties, programs to aid the elderly, improvements in living conditions for the urban poor and middle class, and a host of other projects. An avid supporter of Israel, Abzug has been active in Jewish movements since her youth.

Bella Savitzky was born in the Bronx to Emanuel, who had emigrated to New York City after the outbreak of the Russo-Japanese War in 1904, opened a butcher shop and settled on Ninth Avenue in Manhattan, where he named his shop "The Live and Let Live Meat Market," and Esther Savitzky. Her rearing was typical of Russian Jewish families in that era: kosher food was eaten exclusively, and Yiddish was commonly heard in the home and on the streets. As a young girl she joined Hashomer Hatzair, a Zionist youth organization. Later she attended Hunter College, where she was elected president of the student council and received a B.A. degree in 1942. She then studied evenings at the Jewish Theological Seminary. For a brief period she also taught Hebrew at the Kingsbridge Heights Jewish Center in the Bronx.

In 1947 she received a law degree from the Colum-

bia University School of Law (where she had been an editor of its prestigious *Law Review*) and then specialized in labor and housing law and civil liberties. An early feminist and political activist, she married businessman Martin Abzug and then, seven months pregnant, defended Willie McGee, a black tried for rape in 1950 in segregated Mississippi. During the McCarthy era of blacklisting and heresy hunting, when many lawyers were reluctant to get involved, she offered her legal services to civil service employees threatened by the Wisconsin senator and his allies.

In the 1960s during President Lyndon B. Johnson's Great Society years, Abzug was instrumental in writing legislative proposals later included in the Civil Rights Act of 1964 and the Voting Rights Act of 1965. She became director of the anti-war Women Strike for Peace (1961–70). In the late 1960s, she helped spearhead the "Dump Johnson" movement and then became active in the 1968 presidential campaign of Senator Eugene McCarthy. She was a founder of the reformist New York City political organization, the New Democratic Coalition.

Abzug was first elected to Congress in 1970, representing New York City's 19th district. As she remarked after being cited by *Ms.* magazine in 1980 as a "Woman of Courage.":

> When I was elected to the House in 1970, I was only the second woman in the history of our nation to serve in Congress. I was lonely and an oddity, a woman, a Jew, a New York lawyer, a feminist, a Nixon opponent from way back, a peace activist who passionately opposed American involvement in Indochina and just as strongly favored aid to democratic Israel.

An anomaly, she exhibited from the start a crusty independence, a fierce passion for social and economic justice, an indomitable opposition to the war hawks of both major political parties. She was an early critic of the Vietnam War, despite some constituents' fears that her opponents in Congress would retaliate by reducing aid to Israel. In the House of Representatives she forcefully backed mass transit, peace, women's rights, environmental protection, programs for the elderly, assistance to Israel. As early as 1972 she introduced formal impeachment charges against President Richard M. Nixon. A few months before, she had parried Vice President Spiro Agnew's insensitive comment on the floor of the House that before long she would be wearing hot pants in the House. Abzug replied, "Hopefully, by 1972 hot pants and President Nixon and Vice President Agnew will be out of style." And in 1975 she protested publicly against the United Nations' "Zionism equals racism" resolution at the International Women's Conference in Mexico City and again at a women's session in Copenhagen in 1980.

In 1976 she left Congress to run for the senatorial nomination in New York State and barely lost to Daniel Patrick Moynihan. She has, however, remained in the public eye. In 1979, serving with a White House women's advisory group, she incurred the displeasure of President Jimmy Carter with her outspoken criticism of his allegedly negative attitude toward feminism and was dismissed. In March 1980 she was the featured speaker at a mass rally in Washington, D.C. to protest any reimposition of the draft and in May 1981 was among those at a huge gathering in front of the Pentagon to speak out against United States intervention in El Salvador and massive cuts in domestic aid programs. The gathering was sponsored by the People's Anti-War Mobilization.

Abzug's passion for civil rights is matched only by her passion for feminism. After she arranged to have Rabbi Sally Priesand, the first ordained woman rabbi in the United States, invited to offer the opening prayer at the House of Representatives, she told an interviewer, "Rabbi Priesand was the first Jewish woman to do so and the first woman to do so. I felt that two movements had merged and come of age."

Abzug has been a long-time member of the liberal Americans for Democratic Action, which consistently awarded her 100 percent ratings on her voting record in Congress; B'nai B'rith; the National Organization for Women; the League of Women Voters; and the National Urban League.

MARTIN ZAMA AGRONSKY

b. January 12, 1915
Radio and television newsman

Martin Zama Agronsky, a journalist for more than four decades, has hosted a weekly evening news discussion program over the Public Broadcasting Service (PBS) since 1971. He has a distinguished record in commercial as well as public broadcasting and has won the Peabody Award and Heywood Broun Award for radio reporting and the National Headliners Award for television reporting.

Martin Agronsky was born in Philadelphia to Isador Nathan and Marcia (Dvorin) Agronsky. After obtaining a B.S. degree from Rutgers University in 1936, he worked for a year as a reporter for the *Palestine Post* in Jerusalem. From 1937 to 1940 he was a free-lance writer and contributed to various magazines and newspapers. He was a foreign correspondent for NBC from 1940 to

1943, during which time he was stationed in Europe and the Pacific. From 1943 to 1964 he was a Washington correspondent for CBS radio and television, where he was an outspoken opponent of McCarthyism, and from 1964 to 1973 he was a Paris correspondent and bureau chief for CBS.

Agronsky hosted *The Martin Agronsky Evening Editorial*, a half-hour discussion program on national and international issues, from 1971 to 1976. He conducted the first presidential interview ever granted public television when he interviewed President Gerald Ford at the White House in 1975. Since 1976 Agronsky has hosted two Washington-based public television news programs, *Agronsky at Large* and *Agronsky and Company*, in which major public issues are discussed and debated intelligently and rationally.

Agronsky won an Emmy Award for his television documentary "Justice Black and the Constitution" in 1966 and a Venice Film Festival Award for "Polaris Submarine," a documentary about undersea voyages.

JACOB BERNARD AGUS

b. November 8, 1911
Rabbi; scholar

A leading Conservative rabbi and scholar in the philosophy of Jewish history, Jacob Agus has also been a powerful force in the movement toward ecumenism in his home base of Baltimore, Maryland and among different international religious movements. While continually examining and emphasizing the evolution of a Jewish identity within a Conservative framework, Agus also supports the concept of "trialogue"—communication among Jewish, Christian and Muslim groups.

Jacob Bernard Agus was born in Swislocz, Poland to Judah Leib, a rabbi, and Bela (Bereznitsky) Agushewitz. He came to the United States with his family in 1927 and was naturalized two years later. He graduated from the Talmudic Academy in New York City in 1929 and studied at the Isaac Elchanan Yeshiva and Seminary. Ordained a rabbi in 1935, he also studied at Yeshiva College, where he received a B.A. degree in 1933. In 1936 Agus entered Harvard University to study history and philosophy of religions. He received an M.A. degree there in 1938 and a Ph.D. the following year.

His first rabbinical posts were at congregations in Norfolk, Virginia and Cambridge, Massachusetts from 1936 to 1940, followed by appointments in Chicago (1940–42) and Dayton, Ohio (1942–50). In 1950 he became spiritual leader at Temple Beth El in Baltimore, eventually becoming permanent leader and in 1980 rabbi emeritus. In Baltimore the Conservative movement evolved from a tentative grouping of 90 members to a thriving congregation of 1,100 families. Modification of certain Orthodox traditions, such as permitting men and women to sit together in synagogue and to drive on Shabbat, were among the controversial issues that Agus saw from inception to acceptance. The trend since the mid-1970s for women to seek rabbinical ordination is one that Agus says he favors but only "when the time is right, when the rabbi can be accepted by her congregation." He notes, however, that the concept of Bat Mitzvah is still relatively new and that the overall interest of women in aspiring toward a more advanced religious education is also recent.

Still, to Agus, some important things about the Conservative movement are significant and need to be recalled. For example, its pro-Zionism has been a permanent factor. Says Agus, "Forty or so years ago, the reform movement was not committed to Zionism, and the Orthodox were divided pro-Zionist and independent." But from its inception, he told the *Baltimore Jewish Times,* Conservatism stressed the spiritual national character of the Jewish people.

Agus is a prolific writer, whose contributions to Jewish history and philosophy include eight books, articles in major Jewish and secular journals, and entries in several encyclopedias. The last include the *Encyclopaedia Britannica,* for which he was consulting editor from 1957 to 1969; *Encyclopedia Americana,* for which he wrote an article about modern Jewish philosophy; and the *Yiddish Encyclopedia.* He was consultant to historian Arnold Toynbee on Jewish history and ideas.

Three of Agus's major books are *Modern Philosophies of Judaism* (New York, 1941), an examination of non-Orthodox Jewish philosophies; *Guideposts in Modern Judaism* (New York, 1954), a collection of essays treating modern Jewish thought; and *Jewish Identity in an Age of Ideologies* (New York, 1978), which scrutinizes the reactions of Jewish intellectuals to the many ideologies since the French Revolutionary era. The latter book centers entirely on the nature and scope of Jewish identification in the modern era.

Agus combined his congregational duties and personal scholarship with teaching positions at Temple University, Dropsie College and the Reconstructionist Rabbinical College, all in Philadelphia, and he has lectured widely to Jewish and non-Jewish audiences in universities and institutes across the United States.

His belief in ecumenism is underscored by his involvement at the St. Mary's Ecumenical Institute in Baltimore, where he teaches advanced courses in Judaic thought; his role as board member at the predominantly black Morgan State University and at the Baltimore National Council on Christians and Jews; and his participation in interfaith conferences in the United States, South America and Cambridge, England. He belongs to the Trialogue, sponsored by the Kennedy Institute of Ethics at Georgetown University in Washington, D.C.

For further information:
Agus, Jacob Bernard. *Banner of Jerusalem.* New York: 1946.
———. *Dialogue and Tradition.* New York: 1971.
———. *The Evolution of Jewish Thought.* New York: 1959.
———. *The Meaning of Jewish History.* New York: 1964.
———. *The Vision and the Way.* New York: 1966.

SHANA ALEXANDER

b. October 6, 1925
Journalist

Shana Alexander, an author and journalist who first gained recognition as a reporter for *Life* magazine in the 1950s, has played an important part in advancing the role of women in the field of communications. Starting out in the 1940s, she quickly earned respect as a serious and thoughtful reporter and commentator. One of the first journalists to experiment with the first-person column, Alexander has also held positions in radio and television, including that of "liberal" commentator for the very successful CBS *60 Minutes* television program.

Shana Ager was born in New York City to Milton, a songwriter, and Cecilia (Rubenstein) Ager, a film critic. Her great-aunt was Anzia Yezierska (1885–1970), the well-known immigrant Jewish writer of short stories about life on the Lower East Side at the turn of the century. She attended Vassar College from 1942 to 1945 and upon graduation embarked on a journalism career.

She worked at the newspaper *PM* from 1944 to 1946, at *Harper's Bazaar* from 1946 to 1947 and at *Flair* from 1950 to 1951. She joined *Life* magazine in 1951, where she reported for 10 years and was a staff writer from 1961 to 1964. In the early 1960s she was a pioneer in journalism with her sassy, meditative first-person column. In her book *The Feminine Eye* (New York, 1970), she later compiled some of her witty and honest *Life* pieces.

She was an editor at *McCall's* magazine from 1969 to 1971 and in 1971 became a radio and television commentator for CBS news, a job that lasted a year. From 1972 to 1975 she was a contributing editor for *Newsweek* magazine and from 1975 to 1979 a commentator on *60 Minutes,* where her task was to joust with conservative James Kilpatrick on a variety of public issues from the death penalty (which she opposed) to the Equal Rights Amendment.

In addition to *The Feminine Eye,* Alexander has also written other books, such as *Shana Alexander's State-by-State Guide to Women's Legal Rights* (New York, 1975); *Talking Woman* (New York, 1976), a collection of her pieces, mostly from *Life, Newsweek* and CBS; and *Anyone's Daughter* (New York, 1979), a recapitulation of the Patty Hearst trial in which the author tries to demonstrate that it was essentially a sympathetic story about Patty and her mother—and, by extension, about all American mothers and daughters.

Alexander is the recipient of many journalism awards, including the 1969 Golden Pen award from the American Newspaper Womens Club, the 1973–74 Matrix award from the New York Chapter of Women in Communications, the 1976 Spirit of Achievement award from Albert Einstein Medical College and the Creative Arts Award from the National Women's Division of the American Jewish Congress.

For further information:
Alexander, Shana. *A Woman of My Generation.* Boston: 1982.

WOODY ALLEN

b. December 1, 1935
Actor; director; writer

Many people believe that Woody Allen is the greatest comic genius of this era. His *schlemiel* personality, the highly intellectual misfit who always gets the short end of the stick, rivals Chaplin's "little tramp" character for humor and pathos.

Allen Konigsberg was born in New York City. His parents, Martin and Nellie (Cherry) Konigsberg, were Orthodox Jews. His father had a plethora of short-lived jobs, while his mother kept the accounts in a flower shop. According to Allen, he hated Hebrew school and his attitude toward public school was even worse. He just wanted to be left alone, and he spent hours locked in his room after school practicing conjuring tricks. He also wanted to write and at age 15 began selling jokes under the pseudonym "Woody Allen" to Earl Wilson and other newspaper gossip columnists.

After mention of his name in a Wilson column, Allen got a job at the age of 15 in the office of a press agent as a free-lancer, writing quips for attribution to the press agent's clients. After graduating from Midwood High School in 1952, he began working the next year for the Sid Caesar television show as a comedy writer and later, until 1961, for Art Carney, Jack Paar and Garry Moore. At the same time, within the space of one year, he was expelled from New York University and the City College of New York for low marks and poor attendance. He contends that the expulsions were the best thing that ever happened to him.

In 1961 Allen walked away from a $1,700 a week job writing for the *Garry Moore Show* and began a career as a performing comic. He tried to model himself on Mort Sahl and Bob Hope, comedians who used their natural voice and relied on great phrasing. He also tried "to do what was funny." Allen's humor ranges from sexual exaggeration to wild fantasy and surrealism. A typical Allen gag goes like this: "On my wedding night my wife stopped in the middle of everything to give me a standing ovation." Another story takes place during a dream that he is going to be lynched by the Ku Klux Klan: "I saw myself as a kid again. Goin' to school. Swimmin' at the old swimmin' hole. Fryin' up a mess of catfish. Goin' to the General Store. And I realized it's not my life. They're going to hang me in two minutes and the wrong life is passing before my eyes."

In 1965 Charles K. Feldman, a Hollywood producer, after seeing Allen's nightclub act, hired him as a screenwriter for the comedy film *What's New Pussycat?* starring Peter Sellers. The film was a huge commercial success, but Allen was unhappy over his lack of artistic control. He decided that to be happy in films he had to be the director. In almost a warm-up exercise, Allen took a grade-B Japanese spy thriller, added himself as the narrator and inserted inappropriate dialogue. The result was *What's Up Tiger Lily?* (1966).

In 1967 an Allen play, *Don't Drink the Water,* starring Lou Jacobi, was the surprise hit of the Broadway season. He repeated his stage success in 1969 with *Play It Again, Sam,* a parody of the Humphrey Bogart-style movie. Allen starred in the 1972 movie version of the play.

Since 1969, with the release of *Take the Money and Run,* Allen has written and directed nine feature films and starred in most of them. The early films, like *Take the Money and Run* and *Bananas* (1971), are disjointed comic romps held together only by Allen's zany vision. With *Sleeper* (1973) and *Love and Death* (1975), discernable themes and obvious genre parodies (of science fiction and Tolstoy's *War and Peace)* became more evident in his work. In *Manhattan* (1979) and *Stardust Memories* (1980), Allen, without relinquishing the comic elements, became more introspective and autobiographical.

In 1977 Allen released what many believe is his best film to date, *Annie Hall*. This film chronicled the bittersweet relationship between the comic Alvy Singer, played by Allen in a role loosely based on his life, and Annie Hall, played by former Allen girl friend Diane Keaton. A mix of typical Allen humor and irony, *Annie Hall* won an Academy Award for best picture and best screenplay. Allen won an Oscar for best direction, and Keaton won an Oscar for best actress.

Critics have often examined Allen's relationship in his films to his fellow Jews. One critic, writing in the *New Jewish Times*, defended his work. "But better Americans should think of Jews as ludicrous than demonic. As long as America laughed, the Jew was safe." But to Pauline Kael of *The New Yorker*, he is indeed a Jewish creator, but instead of the redeemer, Allen is the anti-hero, the quintessential self-hating Jew. Writing about *Stardust Memories* in the October 27, 1980 issue, she comments:

> . . . for [Allen] Jewishness means his own kind of schlumpiness, awkwardness, hesitancy . . . in Woody Allen's films Jews have no dignity. That's just about how he defines them and why he's humiliated by them. . . . The Jewish self-hatred that spills out in this movie could be a great subject, but all it does is spill out.

Allen has sought to define his attitude in an interview in the November 1980 *Saturday Review*. Asked if he views himself as a Jewish filmmaker, he said: "Not really. I draw my ideas from everything I've done and everything that interests me. . . . You can have 600 jokes in your film and if two gags are Jewish, the picture will be perceived as a Jewish comedy. This is a false perception, I think."

In 1978 Allen took a completely different tack. *Interiors*, which he wrote and directed but did not act in, was a somber drama that portrayed the breakdown of a middle-aged, upper-middle-class woman and its impact on her family. It starred E.G. Marshall and Geraldine Page. Despite Allen's departure from comedy in this film, *Interiors* was a box-office success.

Allen returned to theater writing with his play *The Floating Light Bulb* (1981), a gentle comedy about a lower-middle-class Brooklyn family in 1945 whose teenage son—modeled on Allen's youth—is an aspiring magician. The play opened at the Vivian Beaumont Theater as part of the Lincoln Center Theater Company, Lincoln Center's first attempt at repertory theater. Allen is a member of its board of directors.

In addition to his work in films and theater, Allen writes short pieces, many of which appear in *The New Yorker* magazine. He has published three collections of these sketches: *Getting Even* (New York, 1971), *Without Feathers* (New York, 1976) and *Side Effects* (New York, 1980).

For further information:
Hirsch Foster. *Love, Sex, Death and the Meaning of Life.*
   New York: 1981

ROBERT B. ALTER

b. April 2, 1935
Professor; literary critic

Robert B. Alter, professor of Hebrew and comparative literature at the University of California at Berkeley, is perhaps the preeminent contemporary literary critic of Judaica and of 19th-century literature as well. A specialist in modern Jewish fiction, he has written dozens of articles for the *New York Times Book Review*, the *Times Literary Supplement* and *Commentary* magazine, as well as several very important books on Jewish, English and American literature.

Robert Bernard Alter was born in the Bronx, New York City to Harry, a salesman, and Tillie (Zimmerman) Alter. He received a B.A. degree in English from Columbia College in 1957, where he was graduated summa cum laude. He obtained an M.A. degree in 1958 and his Ph.D. in 1962, both in comparative literature, from Harvard University. In 1962 he joined the English Department at Columbia University as an instructor and in 1964 was made assistant professor there, a position he held until 1966. A year later Alter joined the faculty at the University of California at Berkeley as an associate professor of Hebrew and comparative literature. In 1969 he was made a full professor, and since 1972 he has been chairman of the Department of Comparative Literature.

From 1965 to 1973 Alter was a book review columnist for *Commentary* magazine, and since 1973 he has been a contributing editor for *Commentary*. He has also been a contributing editor for *Tri Quarterly* magazine since 1975.

Among the articles Alter has written for *Commentary* are "Israeli Writers and Their Problems," "Poetry in Israel," "Malamud as Jewish Writer" and "New Israeli Fiction." Alter has also written about Jewish literature in several books. In *After the Tradition: Essays on Modern Jewish Writing* (New York, 1969), Alter focuses on the meaning of tradition in Jewish literature since the Holocaust by examining works by Eli Wiesel, Saul Bellow,

S.Y. Agnon and Bernard Malamud, among others. He studied individual Jewish writers, like Gershom Scholem and Osip Mandelstam, in *Defenses of the Imagination: Jewish Writers and Modern Historical Crisis* (Philadelphia, 1977), which approaches Jewish writing as resulting from the predicament of the 20th century.

A subject of major interest to Alter has been biblical narrative. In many articles he has demonstrated how the application of literary scholarship can result in a deeper appreciation of the Bible, not only as a work of literature but as a religious document as well. In a *Commentary* article entitled "Biblical Narrative," on which he elaborated in *The Art of Biblical Narrative* (New York, 1981), he says:

> Language in the biblical stories is never conceived as a transparent envelope of the narrated events, or as an aesthetic embellishment of them, but as an integral and dynamic component—an insistent dimension—of what is being narrated. With language God creates the world; through language He reveals His design in history to men. There is a supreme confidence in an ultimate coherence of meaning through language which informs the biblical vision.

Alter believes that while 19th-century American fiction was influenced by the constantly expanding frontier, 20th-century fiction has been profoundly affected by World War I and the subsequent wars. He points to writers like Norman Mailer and Joseph Heller, who explore the impact of modern mechanized warfare on individuals and groups in their fiction. He notes that Saul Bellow is an example of one writer who sees historical forces as threats to the integrity of the individual and the survival of society.

Alter therefore feels that American Jewish writers should be deeply rooted in their culture. In a 1961 *Commentary* essay, he mockingly wrote that the contact of most American Jewish writers with their culture consists of "an acquaintance with gefilte fish and crass *bar mitzvahs,* a degree of familiarity with overstuffed Jewish matriarchs and a mastery of several pungent Yiddish sayings for the male organ."

And in a 1981 *Commentary* article, "Deformations of the Holocaust," he argued—to much criticism in the magazine's letters column—that Jews were over-reacting to that event and that care should be taken to avoid both over-exploitation and making it the centerpiece of Judaism. He urged that attention also be paid to Judaism, history, and Hebrew and Yiddish literature.

In other areas, as in *Fielding and the Nature of the Novel* (Cambridge, Mass., 1968), Alter argues that Henry Fielding's fictional representation of reality reflected a structural unity and a moral point of view. And in *Partial*

Magic: the Novel as a Self-Conscious Genre (Berkeley, Calif., 1975), the author writes that realism is not the exclusive aim of the novel. In this book Alter traces the novel from Cervantes to Nabokov, drawing attention to the authors' fiction rather than their realistic depictions.

For further information:
Alter, Robert B. *A Lion for Love: A Critical Biography of Stendhal.* New York: 1979
———. *Modern Hebrew Literature.* New York: 1975.

IRVING AMEN

b. June 25, 1918
Painter; printmaker

Irving Amen, a woodcut artist of international repute, expresses a spiritual attitude toward life in his works. Using symbols of the solar system, Amen communicates the interrelation of all life and the creative force and energy that binds together everything in nature.

Irving Amen was born in New York City to Benjamin, a butcher, and Bessie (Glusack) Amen. Amen was drawn to art during his youth and studied at Pratt Institute in New York from 1933 to 1935 (and until 1939 he studied at Pratt from time to time); at the Art Students League, also in New York, from 1946 to 1948 (where he studied wood engraving with Fritz Eichenberg); and at the Academie de la Grande Chaumiere in Paris from 1949 to 1950. He also studied classical art in Italy in 1953 and produced woodcuts on the country. One work, *Piazza San Marco #4,* is on permanent display at the Smithsonian Institution in Washington, D.C. Between 1942 and 1945 Amen served in the U.S. Army, directing a mural project for the Third Army Air Force.

In his youth Amen was interested in art for its own sake. During the 1930s he became a social-conscience artist, doing lithographs on subjects such as unemployment, the Depression, the struggle against fascism and, in general, inhumanity. When he returned from World War II in 1945, however, he was disillusioned with easy utopian solutions. "I needed a philosophy that had hope for the future and gave a reason for our being here." Thereafter he became interested in abstract art, and in 1958 he had a show at the Krasner Art Gallery in New York City.

Amen designed a peace medal to commemorate the end of the Vietnam War and was commissioned to design stained glass windows depicting the 12 tribes of Israel for Agudas Achim Synagogue in Columbus, Ohio. He did the illustrations for *Gilgamesh,* an ancient Baby-

Ionian epic originally written on cuneiform tablets. In 1960 Amen (whom Jacob Kainen, curator of the Graphic Arts Division, Smithsonian Institution, described as "the visionary poet who does not forget that he is also a wood-cutter and a designer") was elected a fellow of the International Institute of Arts and Letters.

Using oil, etching and woodcuts, many of his works deal with the quest for peace; some feature traditional Jewish themes, such as a woman lighting the sabbath candles; and others have no relation to Jewish subjects. His work, which frequently includes Jewish symbols, is in the permanent collections of many museums, including the Metropolitan Museum of Art, the Jewish Museum, the Museum of Modern Art, the Library of Congress, the Bezalel Art Museum in Jerusalem, the Victoria and Albert Museum in London and the Bibliotheque Nationale in Paris.

Amen's art reveals an optimism about life and a belief in the interrelationship of everything in the world. His works often have lines that travel from the background to the foreground—lines which, he says, are "energy rays that emanate from God and tie all of us together." He says he tries to communicate to people through his art. "A true woodcutter," whose draftsman's line is "peaceful and imaginative," wrote Kainen in 1960. In his art he is not just building a form or creating a pretty picture, he is trying to be explicit about his philosophy through symbolism. Amen says his philosophy is colored by his Jewish background. For him, God is timeless, limitless and all-powerful. Kainen wrote in 1960 that Amen's themes are the "poor and lonely . . . human vulnerability . . . Jews . . . memories of Europe."

For further information:
Amen, Irving, with a preface by Jacob Kainen. *Irving Amen Woodcuts 1948–1960.* New York:1960.

ANTHONY G(US) AMSTERDAM

b. September 12, 1935
Law professor

Anthony G. Amsterdam, one of the nation's most distinguished law professors and the major attorney in legal efforts to outlaw capital punishment in the United States, teaches at New York University's School of Law. An expert in constitutional law, he is also considered by many to be the preeminent theorist of clinical instruction in law schools. He is also the winner of numerous awards granted by law associations and his views are respected and valued in and out of the courtroom.

Amsterdam was born in Philadelphia to Gustave, a lawyer and corporate executive, and Valla (Abel) Amsterdam. He received a B.A. degree from Haverford College in 1957 and a law degree in 1960 from the University of Pennsylvania, where he was editor in chief of the law review. From 1960 to 1961 he served as a law clerk to Supreme Court Justice Felix Frankfurter.

In 1962 he began his teaching career as a law professor at the University of Pennsylvania, a position he held until 1969. From 1969 to 1981 he taught at the Stanford Law School in Palo Alto, California. There he developed what he terms a "new model" curriculum, establishing clinical instruction as one major component of the law school teaching program. Clinical instruction involves simulated legal work culminating in the representation of real litigants and field work. It involves students in clinics handling such areas as civil rights, criminal, welfare and juvenile law cases. Since 1981 he has taught at New York University, a school he chose to join because of its clinical programs.

Amsterdam is convinced capital punishment should be banned. In *Stanford Magazine* he wrote: "Our children will cease to execute murderers because executions are a self-deluding, self-defeating, self-degrading, futile and entirely stupid means of dealing with the crime of murder and because our children will prefer to be something better than murderers themselves."

A professor and active litigant, he bridges a traditional gap in legal education. "Each time I handle a case, I find myself asking, 'Did I prepare my students for something like this?' " he once told a reporter. Thus evolved the Amsterdam teaching technique: To prepare his Stanford students for the kind of courtroom work Amsterdam often found himself handling, he created advanced criminal law seminars, in which 12 students had to take on actual prosecution and design their own defense cases from pre-trial processes to courtroom maneuvers.

Amsterdam has worked on hundreds of civil liberties cases, many of them without receiving any fee, and has served as a consultant to many government commissions, including the 1968 Commission to Study Disturbances at Columbia. He is a trustee of the Center of Law and Social Policy and the American Civil Liberties Union.

Winner of the 1973 Lawyer of the Year award (given by the California Trial Lawyers Association) and the first Earl Warren Civil Liberties Award of the American Civil Liberties Union (1973), Amsterdam has also received awards from the National Legal Aid and Defender Association (1972 and 1976).

In his most famous case, which resulted in the Supreme Court ruling in *Furman* v. *Georgia* in 1972, three black men had been convicted and sentenced to death under state law, one for murder and the other two for rape. The Court decided that in this case the death sentence was cruel and unusual punishment under the 8th and 14th Amendments.

In addition, Amsterdam has been involved in such famous cases as those of Ernest Miranda—in which the Supreme Court ruled that the police must inform a suspect under interrogation of all his rights—and Gary Gilmore, who was executed by a firing squad in Utah in 1977, the first person to die following the 1972 *Furman v. Georgia* ruling.

MARC ANGEL

b. July 25, 1945
Rabbi

Rabbi Marc Angel is spiritual leader of Congregation Shearith Israel, a Spanish-Portuguese synagogue on New York's Upper West Side founded in 1654 by 23 Jews who landed in New Amsterdam from the island of Recife, Brazil. He has become well-known as a leading educator and lecturer in Sephardic culture and history and as the preeminent American scholar of Sephardic life in the United States.

Marc Dwight Angel (the "Dwight" is for former President Eisenhower, a hero to Angel's parents) was born in Seattle, Washington to Victor, a grocer, and Rachel (Romey) Angel. His grandparents were immigrants from the Greek island of Rhodes and from villages near Istanbul, Turkey. Angel's upbringing included a strong emphasis on the history and folklore of his Sephardic ancestors. He pursued these interests and eventually became both a rabbi and a respected leader in the Sephardic community.

He attended Yeshiva University, graduating with a B.A. degree from Yeshiva College in 1967. In 1970 he was ordained a rabbi, and in the same year he received both an M.S. degree from Yeshiva University's Bernard Revel Graduate School and an M.A. degree in English literature from the City College of New York. He received a Ph.D. from Yeshiva in 1975. Even before ordination, however, he was appointed assistant rabbi at Shearith Israel in September 1969. He became head rabbi in 1977.

As a leader of the Sephardic Jewish community, Angel feels a strong responsibility to this American minority within a minority. There are, he wrote in a publication called *Sephardinews,* many Sephardim in the United States—some are here for as long as 300 years—from regions and countries including North Africa, Turkey,

Iraq, Bulgaria, Greece and Israel. Their history and traditions are different from those of the Ashkenazic Jews, but being outnumbered and traditionally ignored by their East European counterparts, they have had to struggle especially hard to preserve their folkways. For example, the Sephardim have a language of their own— Ladino, a Spanish-based "hybrid" that is parallel in function to the Ashkenazic Yiddish—and a rich and vast musical heritage. As a result of efforts by Angel and other young activists in the Sephardic movement, a new awareness of Sephardic culture has risen among Jews in general—not only Sephardim. In addition to *Sephardinews,* which is published by the American Sephardic Federation in New York City, Hofstra University has developed Project Sepharad in its Division of Continuing Education, offering a wide selection of courses and lectures. Numerous books about Sephardic Jewish communities in the United States have recently been published. They include two books by Angel, *The Jews of Rhodes: The History of a Sephardic Community* (New York, 1979) and *La America: The Sephardic Experience* (Philadelphia, 1982), the story of the New York Sephardic community in the early 20th century told through *La America,* a newspaper, and its editor.

Angel has spoken out forcefully against what he interprets to be discrimination and denigration of Sephardim by Ashkenazic Jews. Writing in the *Jewish Post and Opinion* on March 27, 1981, he pointed to numerous statements complaining of the large number of "Oriental" Jews in Israel and the fact that their greater birthrate will enable them to become a majority. "We need to recognize that whether our recent background was in Morocco or Turkey or Yugoslavia or Poland, our people go back to Abraham, Isaac and Jacob. And we all share the same destiny."

In addition, Angel is founder and director of Sephardic House, a national organization based at Shearith Israel. In 1980 it published *Studies in Sephardic Culture* (New York), which includes a collection of essays, an extensive bibliography and a Ladino-English dictionary; and *Rabbi David de Sola Pool: Selections from Six Decades of Sermons, Addresses and Writings* (New York).

WALTER ANNENBERG

b. March 18, 1908
Communications executive

In addition to presiding over a huge communications network that includes radio and television stations and *TV Guide* magazine, Walter Annenberg has served as the U.S. ambassador to Great Britain and been an active philanthropist.

Walter Annenberg was born in Milwaukee, Wisconsin. His parents, Moses "Moe" Louis, a businessman, and Sadie (Friedman) Annenberg, moved to Great Neck, New York and sent their son to the Peddie School, a private college preparatory school in Hightstown, New Jersey. At school Annenberg was involved in sports and was voted the best businessman of his class. Upon graduation he attended the Wharton School of Finance of the University of Pennsylvania for one year in 1927 and then joined his father's business organization as an assistant bookkeeper in 1928.

"Moe" Annenberg had emigrated from East Prussia to Chicago in 1885. After a period of extreme poverty, when he peddled groceries, tended bars and cleaned stables for a living, he joined the Hearst-owned *Examiner* in Chicago in the circulation department. By 1920 he was the general circulation manager for all Hearst newspapers in the United States. Then, on his own initiative, he expanded into the horse racing information field and gained control of the *Racing Form* and the *Morning Telegraph,* the two most influential newspapers in the field. In 1936 he bought the *Philadelphia Inquirer,* the oldest continuously published daily newspaper in the United States. By then he was reputedly the wealthiest man in the country. However, he was indicted, convicted and jailed in 1940 for income tax evasion. He died in 1942, and Walter became president of Triangle Publications, his father's holding company.

In contrast to his father's flamboyant style, Annenberg has led a life of discreet wealth. In 1945 he purchased WFIL, a radio outlet in Philadelphia, and two years later gained control of a television station, also in Philadelphia. Soon he owned stations in five cities. In 1953 he initiated his most successful project, the immensely popular magazine *TV Guide*. In 1957 he purchased a second daily newspaper in Philadelphia, the *Daily News.* Even so, a critical biography—*Annenberg* by Galton Fonzi (New York, 1970)— charged that the *Philadelphia Inquirer* was biased in its news coverage to reflect the publisher's vast financial interests and his hardline personal opinions. By 1969 Triangle Publications was larger than the New York Times Company and the Chicago Tribune Company.

President Richard Nixon appointed Annenberg ambassador to Great Britain in 1969, since Annenberg had been a strong supporter of and contributor to the Nixon candidacy. Before assuming the ambassadorship, he resigned as president of Triangle Publications but remained as chairman of the board of directors. He divested the company of its daily newspapers and its radio and television outlets but retained its magazines and cable television interests.

Annenberg is the chairman of a number of foundations and trusts bearing his name. He is the founder and president of the Annenberg School of Communications of the University of Pennsylvania and is a patron of the Philadelphia Orchestra and the Philadelphia Art Museum.

Annenberg has also been active in Jewish affairs. He is an honorary alumnus of the Hebrew University of Jerusalem, was awarded the Humanitarian Award of the Federation of Jewish Philanthropies and is on the board of overseers of the Albert Einstein College of Medicine, affiliated with Yeshiva University. In 1967 he contributed $1 million dollars to the Israel Emergency Fund. He also donated $2 million to the Mount Sinai School of Medicine.

ALAN ARKIN

b. March 26, 1934
Actor; director; writer

Alan Arkin ranks among the most versatile performers in films and the theater today. As actor, director and writer, he has developed unpredictable if admirable techniques and a steadfast refusal to be stereotyped.

Alan David Arkin was born in New York City to David I., a teacher of industrial drafting, and Beatrice (Wortis) Arkin, who taught emotionally disturbed children. When he was 12, Arkin moved with his family to Los Angeles, where his father hoped to become a scenic designer in Hollywood. Arkin acted as a teen-ager and, after attending Los Angeles City College from 1951 to 1952 and Los Angeles State College the following year, was one of less than a dozen males to attend Bennington College (1953–55) on a special drama scholarship created to cast men in plays opposite Bennington women. Leaving Bennington without a degree, Arkin settled in New York City, where he acted in small theaters and sang with a folk trio, The Tarriers (1958–59).

Arkin's first break was a regular spot with The Second City, an improvisational troupe in Chicago. In the fall of 1961 Second City came to New York and played on Broadway and in Greenwich Village for more than a year. Largely as a result of the troupe's New York success, Arkin won the lead role over 706 candidates as the Jewish adolescent in the Joseph Stein play *Enter Laughing.* The play, which opened at the Henry Miller Theater in New York on March 13, 1963, was based on Carl Reiner's autobiographical novel. It is the story of David Kolowitz, a young delivery boy who dreams of becoming an actor. Arkin's performance won him a Tony Award. In 1964 he had his next Broadway success in Murray Schisgal's *Luv*.

Arkin's film debut as the whacky Russian sailor, Lieutenant Rozanov, who leads a group of lost comrades into a small New England village where they create utter chaos, was in *The Russians Are Coming, The Russians Are Coming* (1966). His performance won him a Golden Globe Award and an Academy Award nomination. The string of films that followed—several major features and a few well-known short films—display Arkin's versatility. They include *Women Times Seven* (1967); *Wait Until Dark* (1967), in which he plays a psychopathic killer; *Inspector Clouseau* (1968), with the late Peter Sellers; *The Heart Is a Lonely Hunter* (1968), in which Arkin stars as the deaf-mute in the film adaptation of Carson McCullers' novel; *Popi* (1969), in which Arkin portrays a Puerto Rican father; *Catch-22* (1970), in which Arkin plays Yossarian in the film version of the Joseph Heller novel; *The Last of the Red-Hot Lovers* (1972); *Freebie & the Bean* (1975); *Rafferty and the Gold Dust Twins* (1975); *The 7% Solution* (1976) in which Arkin plays Sigmund Freud to Nicol Williamson's Sherlock Holmes; *The In-Laws* (1970); *The Magician* (1979), in which Arkin stars in a story based on Isaac Bashevis Singer's novel *The Magician of Lublin;* and *Simon* (1980).

His well-known short films, based on Second City roles, are *I'm Me,* in which Arkin plays a Puerto Rican dropout approached by a social worker to try to find work; and *The Last Mohican,* in which Arkin claims to have drawn on his recollection of his grandfather to play an elderly Jewish vendor. He and his wife, actress Barbara Dana, who met when Arkin played in *Enter Laughing,* co-starred in a series of spots for public television's *Sesame Street.* In the late 1970s Arkin made his first appearance in made-for-television drama with the title role in "The Defection of Simas Kudirka," (CBS), a dramatization of a true story about a Lithuanian sailor who defected to the United States, and "The Other Side of Hell," (NBC, 1969), the story of an auto mechanic hospitalized for antisocial acts who becomes a fighter for hospital improvements.

Arkin has directed several plays, including Jules Feiffer's *Little Murders* and Neil Simon's *The Sunshine Boys*. He has also written three books: one for children, *Tony's Hard Work Day* (New York, 1972); a science fiction novel for adults (Arkin sold stories to *Galaxy* magazine when he first arrived in New York), *The Lemming Condition* (New York, 1976); and *Halfway Through the Door* (New York, 1979), an account of how he found himself spiritually through yoga. In addition to writing, acting

and directing, he has recorded children's songs with a group called The Babysitters.

STANLEY ARONOWITZ

b. January 6, 1933
Sociologist; labor organizer

Although recognized as an important sociologist specializing in the history of the American labor movement, Stanley Aronowitz considers his work as a labor organizer, a leader in the anti-war movement of the 1960s, the director of numerous programs for disadvantaged youth and adults, and a community activist wherever he has lived to be his most significant achievements.

Stanley Aronowitz was born in New York City to Nathan, a reporter, technical writer and nonprofessional engineer, and Frances (Helfand) Aronowitz. Raised in the Bronx, he attended the High School of Music and Art, graduating in 1950. After a few months at Brooklyn College, he left to work. From 1952 to 1960 he was a steelworker in New Jersey. His experiences provided his grounding as a labor activist and a political reformer within the existing system. In 1960 he became a full-time trade union organizer with the Amalgamated Clothing Workers and the Oil, Chemical and Atomic Workers.

His work with the ACW took him to the South, where his efforts focused as much on desegregating southern unions and obtaining the civil rights of black workers as on improving working conditions as a whole for everyone. Aronowitz also became deeply involved in northern urban movements and fought *against* urban renewal in some cities on the premise that it destroyed the fabric of viable neighborhoods by building impersonal, high-rise projects devoid of any sense of human needs.

In the mid-1960s Aronowitz resumed his education and at the same time became active in youth and job development programs in New York City. He also joined the burgeoning anti-war movement and was one of the founders in 1965 of the National Committee to End the War in Vietnam. From 1967 to 1968 he was supervisor of employment programs for the Manpower and Career Development Agencies with the City of New York. In 1968—the same year he received his B.A. degree from The New School—Aronowitz became the associate director of Mobilization for Youth, an agency that sought jobs for young people and that was supported with federal and private funding. Two years later, as director of planning, he helped implement programs at Park East High School, an experimental public school in East Harlem that sought to enhance the educational process by giving students work experiences in the community. The highly successful program became the basis for a system-wide program to afford qualified high school students the opportunity to combine academics with work.

Aronowitz was at Park East only two years, however. In 1972, while pursuing graduate work in sociology, he used his experiences there to try a similar program on the college level. Named assistant professor at the experimental college within Staten Island Community College, he taught sociology and urban affairs. The following year, as Director of Youth and Community Studies programs, he established a liaison between the college and three New York City communities—Bedford-Stuyvesant, Flatbush and the Lower East Side—where the high school dropout rate and youth unemployment were epidemic. He eventually had 125 young people attending classes who would ordinarily not have fit into any kind of educational setting.

In 1975 Aronowitz completed his Ph.D. at the Union Graduate School, a cooperative program run by colleges and universities in which the student pursues independent studies and attends classes at a variety of campuses or private tutorials. The following year he was invited to become visiting professor of history at the University of California at San Diego and at the University of Paris at Vincennes. (The Vincennes campus is an experimental college that developed as a result of the French student movement and actively solicits attendance by French workers and other nontraditional students.) In 1977 he received a permanent appointment at the University of California at Irvine to teach comparative culture and social sciences. In 1979 he was visiting professor of political science at Columbia University. That year he also taught a course on the problems of the contemporary labor movement at the School for Democratic Socialism.

Despite his academic commitments, Aronowitz has remained active in urban affairs and in reform politics. One of the founders of the New York City-based Center for Workers Education and the Bronx-based Metropolitan Urban Research Center, he has also become involved in community organizing in and near Los Angeles, especially as new problems have developed with the increased urbanization of southern California.

A member of the American Civil Liberties Union and the New American Movement, Aronowitz has contributed many articles to *The Nation, Newsday* and other periodicals and is the author of four books on different aspects of American social and political life, especially within the working class. They are *False Promises: The Shaping of American Working Class Consciousness* (New

York, 1973), *Food, Shelter and the American Dream* (New York, 1974), *Class, Politics and Culture* (New York, 1981) and *The Crisis in Historical Materialism* (New York, 1981). His essays have appeared in *The Revival of American Socialism*, George Fisher, editor (New York, 1971), and *Law Against the Reader* by Robert Lefrant (New York, 1971).

KENNETH J. ARROW

b. August 23, 1921
Economist

When Kenneth Arrow received the Nobel Prize in Economic Sciences in 1972, he was the third American to be so honored since the prize was created in 1969. He was recognized for his contributions to equilibrium theory and welfare theory as well as for his development of a mathematical model that illustrates the disparities in governments advocating different economic systems. His personal economic view is one of moderation in approaching a troubled economy, and he has often been consulted for advice by private corporations and federal agencies.

Kenneth J. Arrow was born in New York City to Harry I. and Lillian (Greenberg) Arrow. He attended New York City public schools and graduated from Townsend Harris High School, a selective public school for boys, in 1936. He received a Bachelor of Social Sciences degree from the City College of New York in 1940 and an M.A. degree from Columbia University in 1941. After serving in the U.S. Army Air Forces from 1942 to 1946, he became research associate in economics for Cowles Communications and taught economics at the University of Chicago from 1947 to 1949. At the same time he continued graduate work and completed his doctorate at Columbia in 1951. Arrow joined the faculty of Stanford University in 1949 and attained the rank of full professor by the time he left in 1968 to teach at Harvard. After six years at Harvard he was named James Bryant Conant University Professor. Arrow left Harvard in 1979 to return to Stanford, where he was appointed Joan Kenney Professor of Economics and Research.

Concurrent with his teaching, Arrow has also been a consultant for the Rand Corporation since 1948. He is a Democrat and so has been frequently consulted by Democratic Party officials for guidance. He has also published many books, including technical economic studies focusing on industrial production, management and fiscal policy.

Arrow's specialty is mathematical economics and

what he called the "impossibility theorem." Insofar as his lifework with the former is concerned, he concentrates on abstractions instead of the more pragmatic and hard-headed approach to economics taken by many economists today. All the same, his theoretical approach, keyed to mathematics, pioneered in suggesting general techniques for understanding complicated questions, such as trying to prognosticate about future economic trends and sketching what he terms "a risk-bearing" way of looking at the economy—that is, comprehending the meaning and implications of assuming risks. As for his "impossibility theorem," Arrow has sought to demonstrate that it is impossible to have an error-free system of choosing alternatives and making choices in any society, even in a democratic one.

Since becoming a Nobel laureate, Arrow has been a frequent public commentator on American economic policy. After Ronald Reagan was elected president in 1980, Arrow openly criticized many of the policies implemented by the new administration. For example, while he supported some personal tax cuts and the concept of budget-pruning, he objected to the huge, regressive three-year plan of annual 10 percent tax cuts because of the enormous deficits that would result. He felt that while changes in economic policy were needed, the "shock treatment" approach touted by some government officials was impractical. In addition, he felt that high unemployment was insupportable because in the long run it would lead to a decrease in production, which had the potential to create irreversible damage to the economy. Arrow felt that economic decisions coming out of Washington were motivated by political considerations rather than practical ones.

For further information:

Arrow, Kenneth J. *Essays in the Theory of Risk-Bearing.* New York: 1971.

————. *Social Choice and Individual Values.* New York: 1951; New Haven: 1970.

ISAAC ASIMOV

b. January 2, 1920
Writer; scientist

Isaac Asimov may be the most popular science fiction writer in America today and one of the most prolific writers in the world. In the past 30 years he has written at least 219 books, ranging in subject from science textbooks to science fiction, from historical works for children to a popular guide to the Bible.

Isaac Asimov was born in Petrovichi, USSR. In 1923 his parents, Judah and Anna Rachel (Berman) Asimov, emigrated to Brooklyn, where they opened a candy store. Isaac was a brilliant student in school and an insatiable reader. However, science fiction was the only pulp fiction his father would allow him to read. He graduated from Boys High School in Brooklyn in 1935 and enrolled in Columbia University the following year as a chemistry major.

Asimov received his B.S. degree in chemistry from Columbia University in 1938, and in 1941 he completed his M.A., also in chemistry. During World War II he served as a chemist at a Naval Air Experimental Station and served in the United States Army from 1945 to 1946. He was discharged with the rank of corporal.

In 1949, after he completed his Ph.D. in chemistry at Columbia University and a short stint of postdoctoral research, he began to teach at the Boston University Medical School. Six years later he was made an associate professor, a rank he still holds today, although he no longer actively teaches.

Asimov submitted his first story for publication to *Astounding Science Fiction* in 1938. It was rejected. Just four months later, after 12 more rejections, Asimov's story "Marooned Off Vesta" was at last accepted for publication in *Amazing Tales.* It was an inauspicious start to an amazingly productive career.

Asimov published his first science fiction novel in 1950. *Pebble in the Sky* (New York) was about the time travels of one Joseph Schwartz following a nuclear accident. Later that same year Asimov published *I Robot* (New York), about the adventures of the robot psychologist Susan Calvin. In *I Robot* Asimov's ability to create completely new and believable worlds became evident. This skill reached its fullest flower in the *Foundation Trilogy* (New York, 1966), which chronicled the decline and rebirth of an intergalactic empire. The *Foundation Trilogy* received the Hugo award for the best all-time science fiction series, and some critics consider it the finest science fiction ever written.

It is impossible to list all of Asimov's works. As an example of the breadth of his interests, he has published a chemistry textbook, *Biochemistry and Metabolism* (New York, 1952); a popular history of science, *The Words of Science and the History Behind Them* (New York, 1959); a history book for teen-agers, *The Greeks* (New York, 1965); and *Asimov's Guide to the Bible* (New York, 1968).

A self-described "non-observing Jew," Asimov has also published his memoirs, *In Memory Still Green,* 1920 - 1954 (New York, 1980) and *In Joy Still Felt,* 1954 - 78 (New York, 1980). In the latter, for example, he discusses love, fame, book reviewers, and science fiction.

In the Beginning (New York, 1980) deals with the first 11 chapters of Genesis in an effort to reconcile scientific findings and revelation. In the book, subtitled *Science Faces God in the Book of Genesis*, Asimov examines each biblical verse line by line and offers a scientific interpretation of the passage.

ED ASNER

b. November 15, 1929
Actor

Ed Asner is an actor of considerable range, depth and versatility. Best-known for his starring role as the hard-outside, soft-inside city editor on the long-running CBS-TV series *Lou Grant*, Asner has acted in Shakespearean plays and contemporary films. His television persona has served him well: Like Lou Grant, Asner has become identified with important public issues about which he has strong opinions.

Edward Asner was born to Morris, who immigrated from Lithuania, and Lizzie (Seliger) Asner, who was born in Russia, in Kansas City, Missouri. He was raised in an Orthodox household, the youngest of five children. "My father was a scrap iron dealer," he said in 1973. "That's one of several euphemisms my brothers taught me when we moved to a middle-class WASP neighborhood. Sometimes he was called a junk man."

Asner attended the University of Chicago for two years and sold encyclopedias, drove a cab and performed other odd jobs to finance his education. He was also involved in college dramatics and appeared as Thomas a Becket in T.S. Eliot's *Murder in the Cathedral*. In 1951 he was drafted into the Army, assigned to the Signal Corps and sent to France (where, incidentally, he managed a basketball team that went on to become the second highest rated Army team in Europe). After his service, Paul Sills of the University of Chicago brought Asner back to perform with the Playwrights Theater Club in that city. He moved to New York in 1955 and acted in several off-Broadway productions, including *Three Penny Opera,* in which he played Mr. Peachum for nearly three years. He performed Shakespeare briefly at Stratford, Connecticut in 1959 and appeared on Broadway in the short-lived *Face of a Hero*, starring Jack Lemmon, in 1960.

In 1961 he moved to California and began his TV career. Asner's big break came in 1970. when he received the role of Lou Grant in *The Mary Tyler Moore Show*. He played a somewhat self-destructive, ill-tempered director of WJM-TV—the mythical Minneapolis news sta-

tion—a part for which he was awarded three Emmys. When the show ended its long run in 1977, Asner's role became the basis for the spin-off *Lou Grant*. In the interim Asner's career had also included roles in the television mini-series *Rich Man, Poor Man* and *Roots* and in several films, where he often played police officers or criminals.

Lou Grant was a perfect vehicle for Asner, who has expressed his concern about the overall lack of integrity on television. By contrast, his show reflects Asner's actual social concerns. Episodes centered on such controversial topics as Vietnam veterans' readjustment problems, alcoholism and the question of a court's right to make a reporter turn over his notes.

Asner is not silent about what he sees as the childish content of the rest of television. "I used to be proud of the quality of television, but that's no longer the case. Television today is more noisy and moves more rapidly. It reflects the increasingly electric pace at which we all live," he said in 1979. "With the exception of 'Lou Grant,' 'Family' and 'Little House on the Praire,' no fully developed human beings exist [presently] on television."

In 1957, while in New York, Asner fell in love with Nancy Lou Sykes, an Episcopalian. They delayed marriage for two years for fear than an intermarriage would anger Asner's parents. They were wed in 1959 in a civil ceremony, and they have raised their three children as Jews.

In recent years Asner has used his visibility to voice his personal views on political and social issues. He is an active participant in several civil liberties organizations including SANE, Common Cause, Americans for Democratic Action and the liberal Committee for an Effective Congress. In 1982, for example, he took a public stand in opposition to U.S. growing involvement in El Salvador. When criticized for identifying himself as the President of the Screen Actors Guild—he was elected in 1981—he apologized, but only for not stating that the affiliation was for identification purposes only. Otherwise, he said, he would continue opposing U.S. military intervention in Central America. More significantly, he took a strong stand in his capacity as President of the S.A.G. on behalf of a merger of his union with the Screen Extras Guild. The film industry in the 1980s was faced with the highest unemployment and the lowest per capita income within the labor movement, asserted actors of all views. Consequently, the S.A.G., affiliated with the AFL-CIO, took the position that only a unified entertainment union could hope to cope with the power of the distant conglomerates that now controlled the film industry.

Asner also lends his name frequently to a wide variety of Jewish causes. In 1979, he hosted a PBS series on Jewish holidays produced by Mississippi Educational Television.

ARNOLD "RED" AUERBACH

b. September 20, 1917
Basketball coach

While Arnold "Red" Auerbach was coach of the Boston Celtics in the National Basketball Association, his team won 10 Eastern Division titles in a row and an unprecedented nine world championships in 10 years. This record is unparalleled by any coach in any major sport in America.

Arnold Jacob Auerbach was born in the Williamsburg section of Brooklyn to Hyman, an immigrant from Russia who operated a drycleaning store, and Marie (Thompson) Auerbach. He was nicknamed "Red" early in his childhood because of his auburn hair.

At Eastern District High School in Brooklyn, Auerbach was a varsity guard in basketball, president of the student body and maintained a high enough grade point average to be named second team All-Scholastic. Upon graduation in 1936 he entered Seth Low Junior College, then a Brooklyn affiliate of Columbia University, on an athletic scholarship. After one year he transferred to George Washington University in Washington, D.C. During his senior year he led D.C.-area scorers with a 10.6 average. At George Washington he learned the fast break that was to become the trademark of Auerbach-coached teams in future years. Auerbach received his B.A. degree in physical education from George Washington University in 1940 and an M.A. degree from the same university in 1941.

From 1941 to 1943 Auerbach taught history and hygiene at Roosevelt High School in Washington, D.C., where he also coached basketball and baseball. In 1943 Auerbach joined the U.S. Navy. As an ensign he directed the intramural sports program at Norfolk (Virginia) Navy Base. He mustered out of the Navy with the rank of lieutenant in 1945 after serving as the rehabilitation officer at Bethesda (Maryland) Naval Hospital.

In 1946 Mike Uline organized a professional basketball team in the Washington, D.C. area called the Washington Capitols. The team was associated with the Basketball Association of America, the forerunner of the NBA. He asked Auerbach to coach the team, and Auerbach agreed, using players he had known in the Navy. He led the team to an .817 winning percentage, still unsurpassed in basketball history, and the Eastern Division title.

Auerbach left the Capitols after three seasons and started the 1949 season at Duke University in an advisory coaching capacity. He finished the year as coach of the Tri-Cities Iowa entry in the newly formed National Basketball Association. He left Tri-Cities at the end of the season, when the owner traded a player without consulting him.

Auerbach then joined the Boston Celtics, which had finished in last place in 1950. For the first six years that Auerbach was with the team, it hovered near the top of the league, never failing to win at least half of its games. In 1956 Auerbach drafted Bill Russell, the star of the University of San Francisco team. With the addition of Russell, a defensive genius, the Celtics began its unparalleled record of 10 division titles and nine world championships in 10 years. Auerbach turned over the Celtics coaching reins to Russell in 1966, becoming the team's general manager and vice president. He is currently the general manager and president of the Boston Celtics.

The Celtics teams under Auerbach were known for their speed, defense and teamwork. Auerbach looked for balanced scoring from his players and shunned the "star" system. He was also a severe disciplinarian. His coaching record was remarkable. In two decades his teams won 1,039 games. No other coach in the NBA has ever approached that mark. Auerbach was inducted into the Basketball Hall of Fame in 1969 and has traveled around the world for the U.S. State Department as "basketball's ambassador."

"Red" Auerbach is a practicing Jew and a member of the B'nai B'rith sports lodges in Boston. He has won a number of B'nai B'rith sportsman trophies. He has written two books: *Basketball for the Player, the Fan and the Coach* (New York, 1953) and his autobiography, written with Paul Sann, *Red Auerbach: Winning the Hard Way* (New York, 1967). His sporting philosophy can be summed up in a few words: "I was convinced that through proper application you could make your body do a great deal more than it seemed capable of doing."

RICHARD AVEDON

b. May 15, 1923
Photographer

Richard Avedon is the international superstar among fashion and portrait photographers. He is probably the highest paid photographer in the world today and has been setting trends and breaking rules since he was a novice looking for work in the 1940s. Long interested in poetry and literature—he aspired to be a poet before he ever held a camera—today Avedon is a poet through his camera.

Avedon was born in New York City to Jacob Israel and Anne (Polonsky) Avedon. His father was a Russian-Jewish immigrant who spent part of his childhood in an orphanage and eventually opened a dress business called Avedon's Fifth Avenue. As a boy, Richard, the older of two children, kept a scrapbook of the photography of Edward Steichen, Cecil Beaton and Martin Munkacsi—three fashion and celebrity photographers who were his earliest role models.

At DeWitt Clinton High School in the Bronx, then a school for gifted students, Avedon read poetry (he especially loved Sandburg, Eliot, Yeats, Jeffers and Mac-Leish) and co-edited its literary magazine with a classmate named James Baldwin. He dropped out of Clinton to study literature in extension courses at Columbia University and photography at The New School in 1940–41. However, his studies were aborted by the war, and between 1942 and 1944, he served in the merchant marine, where he took identification photos for personnel at its branch in Sheepshead Bay, Brooklyn.

After the war Avedon got his first job photographing for Bonwit Teller and, upon showing his portfolio to *Harper's Bazaar* art director Alexey Brodovitch, was accepted for a staff job at *Jr. Bazaar* in 1945.

His career from then on was meteoric. He is said to have revolutionized fashion photography and made it into a highly evolved art form; an examination of fashion photography after Avedon confirms his influence. What made Avedon unique was his transformation of fashion photography from being static and two-dimensional to being rhythmic and vibrant. He took models out of the studio; attempted to put motion into his photographs; experimented with unusual props; and inserted a human, down-to-earth quality into a photographic form that had been highly stylized. His fame was so great that in 1957—Avedon was only 34—Paramount made the Fred Astaire-Audrey Hepburn motion picture *Funny Face* based on Avedon's career. Astaire played a high-fashion photographer named Richard Avery, and Avedon was the film's visual consultant.

Avedon photographed for *Harper's Bazaar* from 1946 to 1965, then for *Vogue* from 1966 to 1970. He has also contributed to *Life, Look, Graphics, U.S. Camera Annual* and the famous 1956 exhibition "The Family of Man" at the Museum of Modern Art in New York.

Avedon also collaborated with writers Truman Capote and James Baldwin in compiling dramatic essays with photography as statements about their world. Avedon and Capote published *Observations* (New York, 1959). In 1964 he and Baldwin wrote *Nothing Personal* (New York), an intermingling of photographs and text reflecting the "state of the world" at that time. For Baldwin, a black man, it was dismal; for Avedon, a poet, a photographer and a Jew, it was a world of contradictions and pain.

Avedon has always used photography as an art form, a way to experiment with images. Avedon the portraitist gained notoriety with huge exhibits at the Minneapolis Institute of Arts in 1970 and at New York's Marlborough Gallery in 1975. Outsized enlargements of celebrities in ultra-fine detail against a stark white background were shocking to many viewers, who rejected the "imperfections" of their heroes. That exhibit also included seven controversial photos of Avedon's father taken between 1969 and 1973, when Jacob Avedon was dying of cancer. *Rolling Stone* magazine followed in 1976 with a major feature of Avedon's photos called "The Family"—a collection of those people chosen by Avedon as being most influential in the United States at the time, in the wake of Vietnam, Watergate, and the Bicentennial and just prior to the presidential election.

Needless to say, Avedon's daring innovations and his perceptions—due, he said in a 1975 interview, to his being nearsighted—have earned him many awards, among them the Highest Achievement Medal, Art Directors' Show, 1950; and One of the World's Ten Greatest Photographers, *Popular Photography*, 1958. His books are *Portraits* (New York, 1976) and *Photographs 1947–1977* (New York, 1978).

ALBERT S. AXELRAD

b. October 22, 1938
Rabbi

Service and activism have been the code words in the career of Rabbi Albert S. Axelrad, who has brought his concern for Jewish tradition to college campuses, synagogues, hospitals, camps and prisons, primarily in the Boston area. A prolific writer and frequent lecturer, and director of the Hillel Foundation at Brandeis University since 1965, he has extended his focus beyond the limits of Jewish concerns to include the American civil rights movement, nonviolence, fair housing, abortion law reform and amnesty for draft resisters.

Albert Sidney Axelrad was born in Brooklyn to Max

a businessman, and Rebecca (Brody) Axelrad. A graduate of Yeshiva of Flatbush in Brooklyn in 1956, he entered Columbia University, where he majored in sociology and received an A.B. degree in 1960.

While still an undergraduate, he was research assistant at the Bureau of Applied Social Research at Columbia. He served as Jewish chaplain at the Hillside Medical Center in Queens, a psychiatric hospital, from 1962 to 1965, and at Bellevue Hospital, the Federal Detention Center in New York City and the New York University Center for Physical Rehabilitation, all in 1963. His first professional affiliation with the B'nai B'rith Hillel Foundation began in 1962, when he served as assistant to the director at the City College of New York from 1962 to 1965. From 1963 to 1965 he also served as congregational rabbi at Temple Beth David of the South Shore in Canton-Randolph, Massachusetts. In 1965 he received an M.A. degree in Hebrew literature from Hebrew Union College-Jewish Institute in New York. He was ordained the same year.

Axelrad then went to Brandeis as Hillel director. But this was only one of several concurrent posts. He was also Hillel counselor at Wellesley College from 1965 to 1969, taught philosophy and religion at Pine Manor Junior College from 1971 to 1972 and lectured at the Brandeis University Institute for Adult Education in 1976 and 1977. He has served as rabbi at Temple Beth Elohim in Acton, Massachusetts (1972 to 1975) and Temple Shalom Emeth in Burlington, Massachusetts (1975 to 1977) and has counseled in a wide range of social service settings and in Jewish summer camps.

Axelrad co-founded the Havurat Shalom Community Seminary in Somerville, Massachusetts and in 1974 joined the Advisory Board and National Executive Committee of Breira, eventually presiding over the Boston region. He also joined the North American Advisory Committee of Interns for Peace, an international organization that involves Jews from around the world and Israeli Arabs in community work in Arab villages within Israel. In addition, he is a long-time member of the Jewish Peace Fellowship, which seeks to protect the legal rights of young male Jews who cannot in good conscience serve in the military.

An activist in the movement to enable Soviet Jews to practice their religion freely or to emigrate if they so desire, Axelrad visited the Soviet Union in 1978 and has written extensively about his experiences meeting Russian Jews, including some "refuseniks." In 1979 he founded Greater Boston's Jewish Hospice Movement, an organization that focuses on the problems of the dying. He is a member of the War Resisters' League and the Fellowship of Reconciliation.

Despite his many activities, Axelrad has found time to write articles that have appeared in such Jewish periodicals as *Jewish Currents, Sh'ma, BaMakom, New Outlook, Conservative Judaism, Present Tense, Moment* and others, as well as in *The New York Times,* the *Boston Globe* and *Esquire* magazine. Axelrad has contributed to such books and pamphlets as *The Jewish Catalogue: A Do-It-Yourself Kit* (Philadelphia, 1973, 1977 and 1980), *Jewish Radicalism* (New York, 1973), *Contemporary Jewish Fellowship in Theory and Practice* (New York, 1973) and other publications.

Axelrad has also lectured at many universities, women's groups, synagogues and other organizations. Using Jewish fundamentals as a starting point, he has a list of topics ranging from domestic issues in American Jewish life—such as intermarriage, the influence of spiritualistic cults on young Jews and the Jewish counterculture—to international topics, including the 1972 Munich massacre of Israeli athletes, Jewish nonviolence in a violent world and the problems of Jewish radicals in their feelings toward Israel and Zionism.

Much admired at Brandeis, Axelrad was honored in 1975 for his 10 years' service there. Afterward, *The Jewish Advocate* summed up his career and his dedication:

> We have seen him on picket lines, late at night in a state prison under siege, . . . calling for administration coolness in a black student takeover, stoutly affirming the wisdom of performing marriage ceremonies for unconverted parties, defending Black Panther hyperbole and eschewing the conventional establishment Jewish position on the Middle East as he speaks, writes and organizes for disengagement and rapprochement between Arab and Jew. . . . Albert Axelrad continues to enrich the Greater Boston community, as he challenges, probes and energizes that of the campus. We keenly anticipate decades more of his presence among us.

LAUREN BACALL

b. September 16, 1924
Actress

Lauren Bacall, who was originally thought of as "Bogey's baby," has starred in over 20 films since her first movie, *To Have and Have Not.* She has since become an outstanding actress, on the stage as well as in films, winning a 1970 Tony Award for her performance in the Broadway musical *Applause.*

Betty Joan Perske was born in New York City to William, a salesman who was born in Alsace, and Natalie (Weinstein) Perske, a New Yorker of German-Rumanian ancestry. She was 6 when her parents divorced, and she was raised by her mother, who took the name "Bacal." The actress later changed the spelling.

A wealthy uncle helped support Bacall's education at a private boarding school, Highland Manor in Tarrytown, New York. She then attended Julia Richman High School in Manhattan. From the time she was 12, she wanted to become an actress, and in 1940, after graduating from high school, she enrolled at the American Academy of Dramatic Arts. She supported herself by ushering at Broadway theaters, where she dreamed of seeing her name in lights.

Fashion magazine editor Diana Vreeland spotted Bacall during her Broadway debut in a walk-on part in 1943 and made her a successful high-fashion model. Bacall's face, on the cover of *Harper's Bazaar* in March 1943, caught the eye of Mrs. Howard Hawks, wife of the powerful director. Hawks gave Bacall a new name—she still doesn't like the name "Lauren"—signed her to play opposite Humphrey Bogart in *To Have and Have Not* (1944) and launched a huge publicity campaign, capitalizing on her sensual "come-on expression," which was promptly dubbed "The Look."

During the shooting of the film, in which Bacall delivers her famous line to Bogey, "If you want anything, just whistle," Bacall and Bogart fell in love. They were married on May 21, 1945. "He was too old for me, he'd had three wives, he drank, he was an actor and he was goyim," she writes in her autobiography. But, "no one has ever written a romance better than we lived it." Bacall, who usually played the smart-alecky, witty, cynical woman, starred opposite Bogart in *The Big Sleep* (1946) and *Key Largo* (1948). They had two children and lived in California until his death in 1957.

Bacall often complains that her roles in films—which include *Confidential Agent* (1945), *Dark Passage* (1947), *Bright Leaf* (1950), *How to Marry a Millionaire* (1953), *Murder on the Orient Express* (1974) and *The Fan* (1981)—never allowed her to demonstrate the depth of her acting ability. But her Broadway roles in *Goodbye Charlie* (1959), *Cactus Flower* (1965) and especially *Applause* (1970) won her the respect and critical acclaim that she had never received for her film acting. In 1981, after an absence of more than 10 years, Bacall once again proved her "Showwomanship," as she starred in an updated Broadway version of *Woman of the Year*.

Bacall, who was married to actor Jason Robards from 1961 to 1969 and with whom she had one son, is winner of the American Academy of Dramatic Arts Award for Achievement (1963) and the Hasty Pudding's Woman of the Year Award (1967). Bacall was cited in 1966 by the women's division of the Anti-Defamation League of B'nai B'rith for her efforts to "strengthen democracy."

The sultry, husky-voiced Bacall, described by one reporter as "a leggy blonde huntress whose cat's eyes never blinked before Bogart's scowls," modestly writes in her best-selling autobiography, *Lauren Bacall by Herself* (New York, 1979), that she's "just a nice Jewish girl from New York."

BURT BACHARACH

b. May 12, 1929
Composer; pianist

Burt Bacharach's songs have become among America's most successful and popular tunes and Bacharach one of America's best-known composers. With such hits to his credit as "Raindrops Keep Fallin' on My Head," "Alfie," "Twenty-four Hours from Tulsa," "Walk on By" and many more, Bacharach—in partnership with lyricist Hal David—has created a rich and unique musical genre.

Burt Bacharach was born in Kansas City, Missouri to Bert and Irma (Freeman) Bacharach. His father was a clothing buyer in Missouri who later became a successful men's fashion columnist. His mother was a portrait painter and amateur singer who encouraged her son's musical talents.

Shortly after Bacharach's birth, the family moved to Kew Gardens in Queens, where he was raised. He studied music as a youngster and attended McGill University in Montreal for three years. After World War II, Bacharach played boogie-woogie music at Veterans Administration hospitals and jazz in the Catskills, and during his own military service from 1950 to 1952, he toured Army bases as a concert pianist. Equally interested in popular American styles and classical music, Bacharach then spent several years studying composition, first at the Mannes School of Music in New York City, then privately with two of the most prominent composers of the time—Darius Milhaud, who was at the New School for Social Research in New York, and Henry Cowell in California. From them he learned the avant-garde forms, which included the constantly changing rhythms and harmonies that would become his trademark.

But Bacharach was personally inclined toward lighter, more popular music, and after working for several years as a free-lance accompanist—including stints with Vic Damone, Polly Bergen and others—he set out in 1956 to write songs. In 1957 he met Hal David, seven years older than he, and in collaboration they wrote two songs that became instant hits. Their first, "The Story of My Life," was performed by Marty Robbins; the second, "Magic Moments," was recorded by Perry Como. Bacharach toured abroad with Marlene Dietrich on and off from 1958 to 1961 and then returned to song writing.

In 1960 he had met Dionne Warwick, a young black singer with a group called the Gospelaires. The quality and range of her voice were such that she could interpret the Bacharach-David songs with an ostensible ease and feeling that few others had been able to duplicate. In 1962 Bacharach, David and Warwick signed a contract with Scepter Records, and from then on they recorded a regular string of best sellers, starting that year with the album *Don't Make Me Over* and the hit single "Walk on By." That same year Bacharach wrote the first of his numerous film scores, *The Man Who Shot Liberty Valance*, and through 1966, with David doing the lyrics, he also composed *Wives and Lovers, Send Me No Flowers, What's New, Pussycat?* and *Alfie.* In 1965 the pair wrote another of their all-time hits, *What the World Needs Now.*

In 1967 Bacharach composed the music for *Promises, Promises,* a Broadway play by Neil Simon, which premiered the following year to enthusiastic reviews and featured another Bacharach hit, "I'll Never Fall in Love Again." In 1969 he received two Grammy awards, one for his score for the film *Butch Cassidy and the Sundance Kid,* the other for his work on *Promises, Promises.* That year he recorded the album *Reach Out,* in which he sang his own songs, demonstrating his fine presence as a musical performer and interpreter, if not a brilliant singer, of his own music.

In 1970 and 1971 Bacharach—who according to one critic had earned the distinction of being America's only songwriter who was also a sex symbol—performed in his own television specials, the second of which earned him an Emmy Award. Then, in 1973 he and David joined forces once more to compose the score for *Lost Horizon,* a film directed by Ross Hunter. The film was a critical failure, but the music was widely praised. Since then, Bacharach has become a prominent nightclub performer, having successfully accomplished the transition from composer and accompanist to featured soloist.

Bacharach arranges and orchestrates all his own work and is so prolific and versatile that music historian David Ewen has referred to him as the "Leonard Bernstein of popular song." Indeed, Bacharach's style synthesizes the styles and rhythms of progressive jazz, soul, rock and bop with the experimental forms of contemporary classical composers. His music is impossible to categorize, but his contributions to the American song form are significant, as jazz critic Leonard Feather has written: "More

than Lennon and McCartney, more than any other writer or pair, this team [Bacharach and Hal David] has succeeded in drawing the popular song away from the dreary, old 32-bar format and away from the verse-and-chorus tradition."

RALPH BAKSHI

b. October 26, 1938
Film animator; director

Ralph Bakshi's ability to weave grotesque, feature-length animated adult fantasies has distinguished him as one of America's most talented, original and controversial cinema artists. With such productions as the X-rated *Fritz the Cat* —an extension of a popular "underground" comic book character of the 1960s—his own futuristic science fiction narrative *Wizards* (1977) and the 1978 adaptation of the popular Tolkien elves-and-hobbits fantasy *Lord of the Rings,* Bakshi has elevated the cartoon medium to a serious art form.

Ralph Bakshi was born in Haifa, Palestine, to Russian immigrant parents, who moved to the United States one year later. They settled in the working-class Brownsville neighborhood of Brooklyn, and his father supported the family by working as a sheet-metal laborer and dock worker. According to interviews with Bakshi, growing up in Brownsville was extremely rough and culturally desolate; to "escape," he created fantasies that became the source material for some of his later work. A talent for drawing was recognized by a perceptive teacher at Thomas Jefferson High School. Bakshi thus transferred to the High School of Industrial Art in Manhattan (now the High School of Art and Design), and when he graduated in 1956, he received a top award for cartooning.

Although he preferred news cartooning, Bakshi landed a job as an opaquer with CBS Terrytoons at $400 a week—a high starting salary at the time. He eventually became an animator and studio head in the production of children's cartoons, remaining until 1966. He then became director of the New York City-based Paramount cartoon department, but when the studio closed within eight months, he sought other avenues for his work, since he found children's cartooning stifling and unsatisfying, albeit lucrative.

Bakshi soon found a mentor in Steve Krantz, a producer of children's shows who was willing to underwrite an adult cartoon. In the fall of 1969 he thus began *Fritz the Cat,* an animated adaptation of the raucous and satirical comic book world of cult-hero and illustrator Robert Crumb. The story combined some explicit sexuality and very serious social commentary beneath its convoluted veneer, where the urban setting (Bakshi often used authentic film backdrops on which his animated creatures would be superimposed) was populated by an array of "animals," who were surrogates for typical "low-life" types found in most cities. *Fritz* made a triumphant debut at the Cannes Film Festival in France in 1972 and was a box office hit in the United States. It also established Bakshi as a formidable new talent.

His next project one year later was *Heavy Traffic,* a surrealistic tale of one man's fantasies—perhaps Bakshi's. Here, he magically combined live and animated sequences including backdrops of photographs and paintings, set to the hard rock music of the era. In 1975 Bakshi completed *Coonskin: Homage to the Black Man,* a personal story of his perceptions about black life in America, using updated versions of the Joel Chandler Harris creations Br'er Rabbit, Br'er Fox and Br'er Bear to tell his story, combining pathos and satire, and using well-known black American actors to do the voice-overs. The exaggerated features of his characters and the stereotypes he chose to emphasize were harshly criticized as racist by the Congress for Racial Equality and other black organizations, and except for limited museum showings, the film was not commercially released. Bakshi's efforts to mollify protesting groups by explaining that the story was merely a reflection of his own youthful experiences in Brownsville were futile.

He thus turned to more ostensibly innocuous themes. *Hey, Good Lookin',* Bakshi's version of *American Graffiti,* told of growing up in lower-class Brooklyn in the 1950s. Completed soon after the furor over *Coonskin,* it was never released. *Wizards* (1977), set in the far future, was an anti-war fantasy pitting good (elves and fairies) against evil (human mutants). *Lord of the Rings* (1978) was an ambitious attempt to re-create a major portion of the Tolkien fantasy and represented new advances in the art of animation. Bakshi first filmed his story on location in Hollywood and Spain with live actors, then employed 600 animators to retrace the movements. The artistic influences of Goya, Breughel, Wyeth and other artists pervaded the film. *American Pop* (1981), using many of the same techniques, is Bakshi's version of the history of popular American culture through its music, spanning from 1910 to the present and encompassing influences as diverse as the immigrant experience and Hell's Angels. Like many of his previous works, *American Pop* was a critical and popular success.

Bakshi's art is frequently compared with Walt Disney's, although in fact the two are light years apart in every respect. While Disney's work has almost always been lightweight, often moralistic and escapist, and predominantly geared for juvenile audiences, Bakshi seeks to recreate honest adult experiences—even if they are not agreeable to look at or hear—through his animation. He has said: When I fantasize my characters that way, it's closer to the truth than you might imagine. . . . I'm not ashamed of them. I love them because they're true. Because I'm working in animation, it comes out more exaggerated than what might be enacted in real life. Blacks, Jews, Italians, are not generally caricatured, mainly because it's not supposed to be liberal or nice to do it. But if I find reality in the stereotype, I'm going after it, pleasant or not. And he is downright serious that the content should be substantial. Sex in his work is not there to titillate but is integral to his stories. He explained once that after *Fritz* he had been offered "million-dollar deals for pornographic cartoons" but turned them down. Instead, he said, "I see myself doing an animated version of *Midnight Cowboy* or *The Grapes of Wrath.*"

RICHARD J. BARNET

b. May 7, 1929
Political analyst

Richard Barnet, senior research fellow at the left-liberal Institute for Policy Studies, an independent research center in Washington devoted to the study of public policy, is one of the country's most articulate critics of the conduct of American foreign affairs.

Richard J. Barnet was born in Boston, the son of Carl J., a leather manufacturer, and Margaret (Block) Barnet. He earned his B.A. degree from Harvard in 1952 and his law degree from Harvard Law School in 1954. He then served in the Army as a specialist in international law from 1954 to 1957.

During the Kennedy administration (1961–62), he worked in the Arms Control and Disarmament Agency in the State Department and as a consultant to the Department of Defense. In 1963 he left federal employment to co-found the Institute for Policy Studies. Among other projects, it sponsors critical examinations of the assumptions and policies that define American posture abroad and at home. It also attempts to develop alternative strategies. Barnet was a co-director of the Institute from 1963 to 1978, when it was a major critic of both the Vietnam War and the successful American effort to depose President Salvador Allende Gossens of Chile in 1973.

Barnet's major theses concerning world affairs include a number of principles. He has urged that Soviet isolation be ended and the United States be encouraged to sell them the technology necessary for the Soviets to exploit their own oil resources; that both sides recognize that there is no alternative to detente or a non-confrontational relationship; that a mutual freeze on new nuclear arms be established; that there be a major diplomatic attempt by nonaligned countries to get the USSR to leave Afghanistan and that the superpowers establish ground rules against intervening in the Third World; that the United States aggressively explore technological advances in alternative energy sources and promote energy conservation as a way of avoiding war. It is high consumption of oil in the United States, he says, that makes the question so vital.

Barnet's articles have appeared in such major publications as *Harper's, The Washington Post, The New York Times Magazine, The New Yorker, Foreign Policy, The New York Review of Books* and *The New Republic*, among others. He has also written widely for limited circulation and scholarly journals.

His first book, *Who Wants Disarmament?* (Boston, 1960), was an analysis of the politics of arms control policy. *The Lean Years—Politics in the Age of Scarcity* (New York, 1980) was serialized in *The New Yorker*. It is a pessimistic look at what he believes to be our dwindling natural resources and depletion of existing energy supplies and the way the world is beginning to respond militarily, economically and politically. In it he related the saga of the oil companies since the 1973–74 oil crisis and considered energy alternatives to OPEC oil. He also detailed how the major American grain firms contribute to higher prices and maldistribution of food; how private interests waste water, control the aluminum supply and rely on foreign-owned minerals; and the way joblessness often results from these machinations. The book won the University of Missouri Business Journalism Award in 1980.

In *Real Security: Restoring American Power in a Dangerous Decade* (New York, 1981), Barnet insists that nuclear superiority, even if possible, is no assurance of world peace and that the more the superpowers maintain bloated military budgets and accelerated arms races, the greater the possibility of conflict. Instead, Barnet calls for arms control negotiations between East and West on armaments, both conventional and nuclear, and a reduction of U.S. dependence on foreign oil.

For further information:
Barnet, Richard J. *The Economy of Death*. New York: 1969.
————. *The Giants: Russia and America*. New York: 1977.
————. *Intervention and Revolution*. New York: 1968.

————. *Roots of War*. New York:1972.
Barnet, Richard, with Muller, Ronald E. *Global Reach: The Power of the Multi-National Corporations*. New York: 1974.

SALO BARON

b. May 26, 1895
Historian; professor

One of America's most prolific and brilliant scholars of Jewish social history is Salo Baron, who was the first historian on an American university faculty to teach Jewish studies. His affiliation with Columbia University for close to four decades set a precedent for the establishment of Jewish studies departments on college campuses across the U.S., many of which are directed by Baron's former students.

Salo Wittmayer Baron was born on May 26, 1895 in Tarnow, Austria, to Elias and Minna (Wittmayer) Baron. He moved with his family to Vienna at the beginning of World War I and attended the University of Vienna, where he received a Ph.D. in philosophy in 1917, a Doctor of Political Science in 1922 and a law degree in 1923. He also studied at the Jewish Theological Seminary in Vienna and was ordained a rabbi in 1920, when he was awarded a Master of Hebrew Literature degree.

By 1920 he had gained recognition as an insightful and original scholar of contemporary Jewish issues. His first published work, *Die judenfrage auf dem Wiener kongress*, explored the Jewish question as it was raised in the Congress of Austria in 1882, which proposed vast restrictions on Jewish rights, later compounded in subsequent congresses.

Even as he began publishing, Baron also began teaching, spending 1919 through 1925 as a history lecturer at Vienna's Jewish Teachers College. In 1926, at the invitation of Rabbi Stephen Wise, he came to the U.S. as a visiting lecturer at the Jewish Institute of Religion (JIR) which Wise had founded in 1922. The following year he joined the JIR as professor of history and acting librarian, and from 1928 to 1930 he headed the JIR's Department of Advanced Studies.

The JIR was then one of the most innovative centers for reform Jewish learning in America, offering studies in secular history and issues as well as Jewish theology. As such, it became a source for major American universities to seek Jewish scholars. In 1930, Columbia University lured Baron to its campus, offering him the newly-created Miller Foundation chair of Jewish History, Literature and Institutions. In this capacity he embarked on one of the most distinguished teaching careers in Columbia's history and produced a steady output of scholarly works on Judaism. These included his best-known work, the 15-volume *A Social and Religious History of the Jews* (New York, 1937), which was published in a second edition with the first two volumes appearing in 1952 and the fifteenth in 1973. Baron's approach to Jewish history differed from that of his predecessors in a consideration of trends of Jews as a people rather than in a concentration on the contributions of individual Jewish leaders. He was drawn to explore the effects of cross-fertilization of other cultures on developing Jewish communities and was as concerned with the rise of Jewish learning and life in the Jewish Diaspora as well as in Israel. Thus he published such studies of Jewish life in America as the three-volume *The Jewish Community: Its History and Structure to the American Revolution* (Philadelphia, 1942); *The Jews of the United States, 1790-1840: A Documentary History,* which he co-edited with Columbia colleague Joseph L. Blau (New York, 1963); and, *Steeled by Adversity: Essays and Addresses on American Jewish Life,* edited by his wife, Jeanette Meisel Baron (Philadelphia, 1971).

But Baron's learning extends from ancient Jewish history to the contemporary experiences of the Jewish people. With Blau he co-edited *Judaism: Postbiblical and Talmudic Period* (1954) and in 1972 his *Ancient and Medieval Jewish History: Essays* appeared, edited by Leon Feldman (New Brunswick, New Jersey). He also wrote *From a Historian's Notebook: European Jewry Before and After Hitler* (New York, 1962) and *The Russian Jew Under Tsars and Soviets* (New York, 1964 and 1976). Baron contributed the section on "The Modern Age" to *Great Ages and Ideas of the Jewish People,* edited by Leo W. Schwarz (New York, 1956). His section explored the rise of the liberal-reform and conservative movements, American Jewry, the founding of Israel, and the concept of contemporary Diaspora Jewry, as well as the revival of Hebrew as a living language in preserving Jewish culture and the role of Yiddish.

But the books mentioned above are only a partial listing of Baron's writings, and they only represent one facet of his career as scholar and teacher. At Columbia, in addition to teaching, he also directed a Center of Israel and Jewish Studies from 1950 until 1968, when he became director emeritus, and he is a member of the American Academy for Jewish Research, of which he was also president from 1940 to 1943, 1958 to 1963, 1965 to 1967 and 1969 to 1971. He also belongs to the American Jewish Historical Society, the American Historical Association, the Society for Biblical Literature and the Conference for Jewish Social Studies.

Baron also lectured at the Colgate-Rochester Divinity School in 1944, and was visiting professor at the Jewish Theological Seminary of America from 1954 to 1972, Hebrew University in Jerusalem in 1958, Rutgers University from 1964 to 1969 and Brown University from 1966 to 1968. He was trustee of the Jewish Institute of Religion from 1937 to 1955, president of the academic council of Hebrew University from 1940 to 1950, and member of the board of governors of Tel Aviv University since 1968 and of Haifa University since 1970.

But if one thought encompasses the totality of Baron's career, it is perhaps found in an essay he wrote in 1963 for *Columbia College Today* and which later appeared in the Bulletin of the National Foundation for Jewish Culture, of which he was one of the first members of the Board of Directors. In the essay, entitled "The Problem of Teaching Religion," Baron begins by discussing the relation of religion and history, which he calls "one of the basic conflicts of our age."

"Most religions derive from certain revealed texts that contain eternal truths," he writes. "History, however, is a discipline that men have devised to look at themselves, past and present. What it regards as 'truth' is determined by very high, but human, standards of evidence." The "chasm between faith and reason," which results from the study of certain ancient or medieval religious texts, presents major problems which "even the most secularist of students of the history of religion cannot entirely evade," Baron says. What makes the study of Judaism different from the study of other religions, he suggests, is that "in the progress of time [it] has increasingly become an historical religion, in permanent contrast to all natural religions."

Baron believes the study of religion should be treated in the same way as other disciplines in liberal arts colleges. "It should be taught with the same objectivity, methods and open-mindedness that are demanded of the investigation of other phases of civilization. Of course, every discipline has its own peculiarities," he adds, "But a serious scholar of religion will not place the peculiarities of his discipline in an uniquely elevated position, fenced off from normal approaches to it by spiritual presuppositions." In this last sentence, Baron displays the universalist approach which characterizes his dedication to scholarship and, in particular, to a lifetime in the pursuit of a greater knowledge of and ability to interpret Jewish history.

For further information:
Baron, Salo. *Modern Nationalism and Religion.* New York: 1947.
———. *Violence and Defense in the Jewish Experience.* Philadelphia: 1977.

————. *World Dimensions of Jewish History*. New York: 1962.

Baron, Salo, ed. *A Documentary History of American Jews*. New York: 1954-.

Baron, Salo, with Kahan, Arcadius. *Economic History of the Jews*. New York: 1975.

Baron, Salo, ed., with Nagel, Ernest, and Pinson, Koppel S., *Freedom and Reason: Studies in Philosophy and Jewish Culture, in Memory of Morris Raphael Cohen*. New York: 1951.

Baron, Salo, ed., *Jewish Social Studies*. New York: 1939-.

————. *World History of the Jewish People*, vols. 14-20. New York: 1957.

LEONARD BASKIN

b. August 15, 1922
Artist

Artist Leonard Baskin, who works in a variety of media, is one of the leading representatives of anti-abstractionism in American art. Drawing on his Jewish roots, he approaches his sculpture and his graphic work as a moralist and humanist. His busts of major American leaders, including Franklin Delano Roosevelt and John F. Kennedy, are internationally known.

Leonard Baskin was born in New Brunswick, New Jersey to Samuel, an Orthodox rabbi, and May (Guss) Baskin. He moved with his family to New York in 1929. Until his 15th year he was trained intensively in the Talmud. He also attended the Educational Alliance on the Lower East Side of Manhattan as a boy. When he was 15 and in the Federal Art Project at the Educational Alliance, he was sculpting a 250-pound chunk of marble he had stumbled on near the East River. The school featured as teachers or students many sculptors who would one day become eminent, among them Jo Davidson, Jacob Epstein, Philip Evergood and Louise Nevelson. Baskin was certainly aware of them. But more significant to his life was when he studied sculpture in his adolescent years with Maurice Glickman, who had a marked influence on him.

By 1940 his work was entered in an exhibit, and he won Honorable Mention for the Prix de Rome. He then studied art at New York University and Yale and served in the Navy during World War II. In 1949 he earned a B.A. degree from the New School for Social Research. Baskin has since studied in art academies in many countries, including Italy, where he was drawn to the sculpture of the Renaissance and its emphasis on the body, a primary theme of Baskin's work and reflected in his many explorations of the human and animal body. Humanity is his consuming interest and at the very heart of his art and his passion.

He has been exhibiting his sculpture since 1939 and had his first important one-man show in 1951. He took up print making in 1949 and since 1953 has given major one-man exhibitions all over the country. His works are in the permanent collections of many major American museums, including the National Gallery of Art, the Metropolitan Museum of Art, the Museum of Modern Art, the Whitney Museum of American Art and the Boston Museum of Fine Arts.

Baskin, who was apparently influenced in his early years by Ben Shahn, has taught print making and sculpture at Smith College in Massachusetts. He is the recipient of many awards, including the Purchase Prize of the Library of Congress, the Purchase Prize of the Brooklyn Museum, a 1953 Guggenheim Fellowship, the Ohara Museum Prize in Tokyo and the International Prize in Engraving at the Bienal in Sao Paulo, Brazil.

His fascination with woodcuts is well-known. In 1952 he began with a series of woodcuts called *Man of Peace* and ended with *Saturn* in 1970. They were eight feet high and more than three feet wide and explored such themes as *Everyman, Angel of Death, Hydrogen Man, Torment* and many more. Wood, he argued, and the trees from whence it derived, was "a natural vehicle for giant prints." He also saw the woodcuts as a "kind of ambulatory mural. They are insistently black, complexly cut, and reasonably successful in causing alarm, misgivings and exaltation." Above all, he admired wood engravers and both mourned their passing and hoped for their rebirth among younger artists. "To engrave even a small block needs hours of continuous, eye-wearing, hand-swelling labor," he stated in admiration of those craftspeople.

His themes are often animals and people. By way of explanation he once defined himself as a "moral realist." In 1959 he deplored a "Man incapable of love, wanting in charity and despairing in hope. . . . In this garden I dwell, and in limning the horror, the degradation and the filth, I hold the cracked mirror up to man." Then followed what he described as "lunatic war and deadening alienation, of gross national debauchery" and the defilement of our environment with "pestilential chemicals." Even so, Baskin believed man to be "collectively redemptible." Still, his pessimism is evident in the way he fashions his subjects:

> pot-bellied and right-assed . . . spent and bewildered, frail and human. . . . I have fashioned a secret cemetery of dead men. . . . My work, a large part of it, has thematically dealt with the duality of tyrant and tyr-

annized, expropriator and the expropriated, the powerful and the flayed victims of oppression, the arm of power.

Baskin is also famous for his "desire to print books [which] derives from [William] Blake." Book illustration, he believes, should act as a partner to the text, "should extend implications, deepen tragedy, heighten insights." Presently he is involved in a "colossal" 20-year project, begun in 1970, to illustrate all of Shakespeare's plays, in 37 folio volumes. "One must set before one tasks one cannot easily realize"—he quotes the obscure Frankish Rabbi Judah ben Samuel—"and this is a tenent I hearken to. . . . Man's survival is the paradigm, our esperance and our fulfillment as life-filled creatures forcing earth to bloom and to yield peace."

The massive project was interrupted briefly for several other tasks, notably his illustrations in *The New Union Haggadah* (New York, 1974) and in David Rosenberg's *Chosen Days: Celebrating Jewish Festivals in Poetry and Art* (New York, 1980), in which he portrayed Esther, Isaac, Jeremiah, Judith and other Biblical personalities.

In addition, Baskin has occasionally been drawn to poster art, marked by his blending of his individual style, his craftsmanship and his keen awareness of graphic arts and typography, exemplified by his impressionist red and black print of Sitting Bull in 1971.

For further information:
Baskin, Leonard. *Baskin Sculpture, Drawings & Prints.* New York: 1970.
———. *Figures of Dead Men.* Amherst: 1968.
———. *Five Addled Etchers.* Hanover, N.H.: 1969.
Dante Alighieri, with drawings by Baskin, Leonard. *The Divine Comedy.* New York: 1969.
Homer, with drawings by Baskin, Leonard. *The Iliad.* Chicago: 1962.
Jaffe, Irma B. *The Sculpture of Leonard Baskin.* New York: 1980.
Swift, Jonathan, with drawings by Baskin, Leonard. *A Modest Proposal.* New York, 1970.
Utley, Robert M., with drawings by Baskin, Leonard. *Custer Battlefield National Monument.* Washington: 1969.

DAVID BAZELON

b. September 3, 1909
Judge

The insanity defense was controversial when formulated and may well remain one of the thorniest legal issues in American jurisprudence for decades. Its use was in part pioneered by Appeals Court Judge David Bazelon, who, in developing the so-called "Durham Rule" in 1954, upheld the right of defendants claiming mental illness during the commission of a crime to plead for rehabilitation instead of punishment. Bazelon has similarly used his judicial powers on behalf of often-oppressed groups, including the mentally disabled and homosexuals. He has thus become known as one of the greatest human rights advocates sitting on the American bench today.

David Lionel Bazelon was born in Superior, Wisc. to Israel Bazelon, a grocer, and Lena (Krasnovsky) Bazelon. Israel died when David, the youngest of nine children, was two years old, and the family moved to Chicago, where Bazelon attended public schools and graduated from Senn High School in 1926.

In order to attend college, Bazelon spent a year working at odd jobs, including movie usher and store clerk. He enrolled at the University of Illinois in 1928, but after one year transferred to Northwestern University, where he completed a B.S.L. degree—a bachelor's degree in law—in 1932. In 1932 he was admitted to the Illinois bar and entered private practice for the next three years. In 1935 he joined the Chicago office of the United States Attorney, where for five years he worked primarily on tax cases. During that period Bazelon also became prominent as a tireless and outspoken worker with the Independent Voters League. His political work overlapped into the early 1940s, when he resumed private practice as a senior partner with the Chicago firm of Gottlieb and Schwartz.

Bazelon returned to public law in 1946—this time for good—when President Truman appointed him assistant attorney general of the United States, heading the Justice Department's lands division. The following year he headed the department's office of alien property.

An expansion of the federal appeals court in 1949 created 27 new judgeships, and in October of that year, Truman nominated Bazelon for a seat in the Appeals Court for the District of Columbia. Confirmed for that lifetime appointment in 1950, Bazelon at the time was the youngest man to sit on the federal appellate bench. By 1962, however, his seniority earned him the post of chief judge.

As a jurist, Bazelon has shown a consistent sensitivity to individual needs and differences. In formulating the Durham Rule, which allowed the not-guilty-by-insanity defense, stating the "accused is not criminally responsible if his unlawful act was the product of mental disease or mental defect," he paved the way for vigorous criticism from opponents of the defense who argued that criminals acted out of free will. Indeed, the ruling as stated was officially adopted only in the American Virgin Islands and has remained a "guideline" in 25 states. Yet by virtue of Bazelon's position, the Durham Rule took on major significance in subsequent criminal trials, even being discussed in the 1982 defense of John Hinckley, Jr., the accused would-be assassin of President Reagan who was found not guilty due to mental incompetence.

In 1965 Bazelon also anticipated what later became (and has remained) a heated equal-rights issue when he ruled that the federal government could not fire an employee just because he was homosexual. But he has also gone beyond the bench in his participation in human rights efforts. From 1964 to 1966, for example, he was an advisor for the Cardozo Project in the District of Columbia, which supervised school integration. And he has both taught and published widely on various issues concerning law and mental illness, juvenile crime, and mental retardation and related issues. From 1957 to 1959 he was a lecturer in law and psychiatry at the University of Pennsylvania and from 1960 to 1961 was Sloan Visiting Professor at the Menninger Clinic in Topeka, Kan. Bazelon was Regents Lecturer at the University of California at Los Angeles in 1964, and from 1966 to 1975 he was clinical professor of psychiatry in social and legal aspects at George Washington University. He has been a lecturer in psychiatry at Johns Hopkins University School of Medicine since 1964.

Many of Bazelon's decisions have had long-term effects on American life. A 1970 ruling favored the effort of environmentalists when he pressured the Department of Agriculture to discontinue the use of DDT. And another ruling that year upheld the constitutionality of 18-year-olds' right to vote.

LEONARD I. BEERMAN

b. April 29, 1921
Rabbi

In addition to being one of America's most outspoken leaders in the Reform Jewish movement, Rabbi Leonard I. Beerman has also developed a national reputation for his efforts to halt the expansion of nuclear armaments. A lifelong civil rights and anti-war activist, he was one of the founders in 1980 of the Interfaith Center to Reverse the Arms Race.

Leonard Irving Beerman was born in Altoona, Pennsylvania to Paul, a salesman of ladies' garments, and Tillie (Grossman) Beerman. He attended Pennsylvania State University, where he received a B.A. degree, Phi Beta Kappa, in 1942, and Hebrew Union College-Jewish

Institute of Religion in Cincinnati, where he was ordained and received a Master of Hebrew Literature in 1949. He spent 1947 to 1948 at Hebrew University in Jerusalem and completed a doctorate at Hebrew Union College in 1974.

Immediately following ordination in 1949, Beerman became spiritual leader of the Leo Baeck Temple in Los Angeles. In the course of his service there, he spoke out in support of a wide range of civil liberties and rights issues that he considered essential not only to Jewish well-being but to the preservation of equality for all people. He is on the National Advisory Council of the Emergency Civil Liberties Committee, the executive board of the Jewish Peace Fellowship and is a member of the Human Subjects Committee of Cedars-Sinai Medical Center and the Committee of 100 for National Health Insurance.

During the late 1960s Beerman participated in peace rallies that were held to protest the escalation of the war in Indochina. At that time he met Dr. George Regas, a minister at the All Saints Episcopal Church in Pasadena. Their friendship formed the foundation for a unique alliance between their two congregations to explore the expansion of the peace movement on a larger scale. In October 1979 they co-sponsored an interfaith conference attended by more than 1,000 participants whose aim was to organize a mass movement to reverse the arms race. At its core was the conviction that the religious community was the best vehicle to promote nuclear disarmament and to confront increased government involvement in the proliferation of nuclear weapons. The success of the conference led in 1980 to the formation of the Interfaith Center to Reverse the Arms Race. Housed in the All Saints Church, the center publishes the *RAR newsletter,* has a Speakers' Bureau to train individuals on how to present issues before groups and has initiated networking among congregations throughout southern California and across the country to lobby for arms control legislation. It has also developed a clearinghouse and resource center with a range of audiovisual and printed materials that document the history of the peace movement and the need for nuclear disarmament.

In a joint statement he wrote with Dr. Regas in the first *RAR newsletter,* Rabbi Beerman asked:

> How can we affirm the sanctity of life if we're using the bulk of our resources in pursuit of death and taking from our society and the world the instruments that can enhance life? There's a fundamental contradiction there that the religious person in a moment of truth must face. . . . The war system is deeply embedded in us, but deeper in us is something greater. It is the instinct for survival, the instinct to make the world beautiful for our children,

the instinct to heal the wounds and not the lacerate the human family, the instinct to feed and not to steal from the hungry, the instinct to do something with hope and heart and love in it, something more than the beastly.

In 1982, Rabbi Beerman became one of the leaders of the Nuclear Freeze mass movement, emphasizing as he always does, the Judaic quest for peace. "The destruction of European Jewry by the Nazis provides a model for destroying the human race. That is why we Jews have a unique duty to warn that this planet can be transformed into a crematorium," he told representatives of 10 New York Reform Synagogues in a conference on nuclear disarmament in 1982.

DANIEL BELL

b. April 10, 1919
Sociologist

Daniel Bell is one of America's most persuasive social critics, and his book *The End of Ideology*, a collection of Bell's most important essays of the 1950s, has become a classic in contemporary social thought.

Born in New York City to Benjamin and Anna (Kaplan) Bolotsky, both garment workers, Bell spoke only Yiddish until he was 6 years old. A precocious child, he read Karl Marx and John Stuart Mill by the age of 13. At 15 he began to deliver street-corner speeches for Norman Thomas, the perennial Socialist candidate for president. In 1935, at age 16, he enrolled at the City College of New York, where he met Irving Howe, Seymour Martin Lipset, Irving Kristol and other young scholars who were to make their marks on American intellectual life. He received his Bachelor of Social Science in 1938.

Upon graduation Bell enrolled at Columbia University and also became a contributor to *The New Leader* magazine. He was medically exempt from World War II. During 1945 he served as the managing editor of *Common Sense* magazine. In 1945 he was appointed a lecturer in social sciences at the University of Chicago. Not totally satisfied, he left the university in 1948 to become the labor editor of *Fortune* magazine but retained some ties with the academic community as a part-time lecturer at Columbia. In 1952 he published his first book, a *History of Marxian Socialism in America* (New York), and in 1955 he edited *The New American Right* (New York), a collection of essays about political shifts in post-World War II America.

In 1956 Bell took an 18-month leave of absence from *Fortune* to help organize the Congresses on Cultural Freedom in Europe. He still chairs the American Congress

for Cultural Freedom. In 1958 he resigned from *Fortune* and, after a year as a fellow at the Center for Advanced Study in Behavioral Sciences at Stanford University, became an associate professor of sociology at Columbia University in 1959 and completed his work for his Ph.D. He was appointed full professor in 1962. From 1959 to 1969 he chaired the Department of Sociology at Columbia.

In 1960 Bell published *The End of Ideology* (New York). It consisted of 16 essays written over the preceding 10 years about such subjects as the declining militancy of the American labor movement, the failure of American socialism and the impact of ideology on social behavior. He defined ideology as the conversion of ideas into social levers and claimed that Nazi and Soviet atrocities dealt a death blow to the old ideologies. Ideology, he wrote, had lost its power to persuade, because people felt revulsion at the horror of Nazi and Communist excesses in the name of ideology. The book was hailed as a major contribution to the study of change in a complex society. In 1965, with Irving Kristol, he founded *Public Interest* magazine, a neo-conservative quarterly intended to continue the dialogue on social issues that Bell had written about earlier.

Like many young intellectuals in the 1930s, surrounded by millions of unemployed people and massive labor unrest, Bell had felt that socialism was the only answer to America's economic woes. However, after the war, Bell began to reconsider his position, sympathizing increasingly with the liberal capitalist system. Lately, he has argued that the traditional class structure of society—with its upper, middle and lower classes—is no longer valid and that the true division of society is between those who have access to information and technology and those who don't. He argues that those who have access to information, through computers, microchips and other technological breakthroughs, will control society socially and economically.

In 1970 Bell moved to Harvard University to explore his interest in the use of sociology for social prediction. He wrote *The Coming of the Post-Industrial Society* (New York, 1973) and *The Cultural Contradictions of Capitalism* (New York, 1976), an analysis of the success and failure of the capitalist system. In *The Winding Passage: Essays and Sociological Journeys* 1960–1980 (Cambridge, Mass., 1980), he propounds the thesis that Marxist class analysis is increasingly incapable of understanding capitalism. More central than class in the contemporary period are traditional power rivalries that follow ethnic, national and religious allegiances.

Bell is currently chairman of the publication committee of *Public Interest* and a member of the editorial boards of *American Scholar* and *Daedalus* magazines. He is the vice president of Social Sciences of the American Academy of Arts and Sciences and a fellow of the American Sociological Association. He is also a member of the Council of Foreign Relations and the Century Association.

SAUL BELLOW

b. June 10, 1915
Novelist

Among Saul Bellow's notable literary legacies is the originality and imagination with which he has related the saga of the Jewish love affair with America. After Bellow received his Nobel Prize for Literature in 1976, not for a specific work but for the aggregate of his contribution to American writing, Rabbi Eugene Borowitz, Reform Judaism's prominent thinker and intellectual, praised him for being "One of the most profound and thoughtful Jewish religious thinkers of our time."

Solomon Bellows was born in the French Canadian town of Lachine, near Montreal, to Russian-born parents, Abraham, a businessman, and Liza (Gordon) Bellows, who had emigrated from St. Petersburg two years earlier. The family settled in Chicago in 1924, where Bellow (who dropped the last *s* and changed "Solomon" to "Saul" when his first work was published) attended the University of Chicago from 1933 to 1935 and received a B.S. degree in anthropology from Northwestern University in 1937, graduating with honors. He briefly did graduate work on scholarship at the University of Wisconsin but dropped out, commenting that "every time I worked on my thesis, it turned out to be a story."

The bent for fiction carried Bellow to the New Deal-sponsored WPA Writers Project, where he wrote short profiles of midwestern poets and writers. He served in the merchant marine during World War II and then published his first novel, *The Dangling Man* (New York), in 1944. The story of an isolated young man awaiting army induction that never seems to happen, it signaled the beginning of a lively, popular and much-acclaimed career as a fiction writer.

Bellow's next book, *The Victim* (New York, 1947), told of the interaction between a rootless anti-Semite and a secure though neurotic Jew. *The Adventures of Augie March* (New York, 1953)—which won the first of his three National Book Awards—was Bellow's first long novel and reflected a sense of affirmation of American values. It was followed, however, by a morose novella, *Seize the Day* (New York, 1957), which focused on a pathetic "loser" who cannot seem to get a grip on his life. In *Herzog* (New York, 1964) the Jewish-Canadian protag-

onist dominates a book that speaks for many intellectuals insistent on remaining outside any defined tradition, including Judaism. *Mr. Sammler's Planet* (New York, 1970) revolves around a Polish-Jewish immigrant, blind in one eye, who roams Manhattan's heavily Jewish Upper West Side neighborhoods. *Humboldt's Gift* (New York, 1975) is an ironic portrait of the American Jewish poet, the flamboyant and tragic Delmore Schwartz, as seen through the narration of a Bellow-surrogate named Charlie Citrine.

Bellow has visited Israel on a number of occasions and served as *Newsday's* special correspondent during the Six Day War in 1967. In the autumn of 1975 he visited Israel as a guest of Jerusalem and later published his favorable reflections on the trip in *To Jerusalem and Back* (New York, 1978), which had been serialized a year earlier in *The New Yorker*.

Bellow's seeming ambivalence toward his Americanness and his Jewishness has been displayed over the years, especially when he is pigeonholed as an "American Jewish writer." In fact, he once commented that "The concept of my being an American Jewish novelist is accurate only insofar as it is true that I am an American and a Jew and a writer. Over the years I have been faintly amused at the curious linkage of Bellow, Malamud and Roth. Somehow it always reminds me of Hart, Schaffner and Marx."

Despite the reservations ("My culture, my language, is American," he stated on yet another occasion. "I can't reject sixty years of life in America"), many critics persist in detecting in his novels and their characters the drama of Jewish life in this country. What sets Bellow apart is, as Irving Howe commented, "the fiction of urban malaise, second-generation complaint, Talmudic dazzle, woeful alienation and dialectical irony . . . fiction in which the Jewish world is not merely retained in memory . . . but is also treated as a portentous metaphor for man's homelessness and wandering."

Bellow was the first American to win the Nobel Prize for literature since John Steinbeck in 1962. The judges specified *Henderson the Rain King* (New York, 1959), a romantic tale of a millionaire on an African safari, as "the writer's most imaginative expedition." However, in all his works the judges found "exuberant ideas, flashing irony, hilarious comedy and burning compassion."

Today, Bellow, whose work has appeared in many of America's finest literary journals, is a professor of English at the University of Chicago and a member of its Committee on Social Thought.

For further information:
Bellow, Saul. *The Dean's December*. New York: 1982.

BARUJ BENACERRAF

b. October 29, 1920
Scientist

Harvard scientist and professor Baruj Benacerraf received the 1980 Nobel Prize in physiology for his research in immunology. His discoveries concerning the role of genetic makeup in determining the ability of an animal to create antibodies to counterattack invading germs has led to a better understanding of the workings of the human immune system, especially in disease. In a 1980 interview Benacerraf said he believed he was the first Sephardic Jew to win the Nobel Prize.

Baruj Benacerraf was born in Caracas, Venezuela to Abraham and Henriette (Lasry) Benacerraf. After attending the Lycee Janson in Paris, where he received a baccalaureate degree in 1940, he came to the United States and completed a B.S. degree at Columbia University in 1942. He was naturalized the following year. In 1945 he received his M.D. from the Medical School of Venezuela and spent one year as an intern at Queens (New York) General Hospital.

After service in the U.S. Army from 1946 to 1948, he began a research career at the Columbia University Medical School in 1950 and then spent six years at the National Center for Scientific Research at the Hospital Broussais in Paris. Returning to the United States, Benacerraf was appointed assistant professor of pathology at the New York University School of Medicine from 1956 to 1958, associate professor from 1958 to 1960 and full professor from 1960 to 1968. For the next two years he was chief of immunology at the National Institute of Allergy and Infectious Diseases of the National Institutes of Health in Bethesda, Maryland and in 1970 was appointed the Fabyan Professor of Comparative Pathology at Harvard University's Medical School. In 1980 he was also named chief executive officer of the Sidney Farber Research Institute at Harvard Medical School.

Benacerraf has served on advisory boards for many American and international medical organizations and is a fellow at the National Academy of Sciences and other related organizations. He has also lectured widely in the United States and abroad. His other prizes include the 1974 Rabbi Shai Shacknai prize of Hebrew University and the 1976 T. Duckett Jones Memorial Award of the Helen Hay Whitney Foundation.

But his crowning achievement—the Nobel prize—represented recognition for lifelong work, which continues. He won for his discoveries of "genetically determined structures on the cell surface that regulate immunological reactions," it was announced in Stockholm by the prize committee. In conjunction with Stanford University scientist Hugh McDevitt, he defined the "histocompatability complex," a group of genes instrumental in building an organic immune system. He first discovered genes in this complex in experiments on guinea pigs and mice, and it was on the basis of this work and how it relates to the human being's ability to fight cancer and other diseases that he was chosen to receive the Nobel Prize.

PAUL BERG

b. June 30, 1926
Scientist

Paul Berg, a 1980 Nobel Prize-winning chemist, is the first person to use the new science of genetic engineering to construct a "recombinant DNA molecule," an accomplishment that has led to dramatic new insights in genetics as well as a whole range of possibilities in disease prevention and cure (especially in cancer). Berg also won the prestigious Lasker Award the same year.

Paul Berg was born in New York City to Harry, a manufacturer of fur coats and collars, and Sarah (Brodsky) Berg. His parents were immigrants from Kiev. After completing high school in 1943, he served in the United States Naval Reserve from 1943 to 1946 and pursued studies at the City College of New York and later at Brooklyn College. He transferred to Pennsylvania State University, which had a superior microbiology department—by then he was almost certain of his career goal—and earned his B.S. degree in 1948. In 1952 he received a doctorate from Case Western Reserve University in Cleveland, Ohio. During his last two years there, he was an NIH (National Institutes of Health) Fellow.

From 1952 to 1953 Berg was a postdoctoral fellow at Copenhagen University in Denmark and from 1953 to 1954 a postdoctoral fellow at Washington University in St. Louis. From 1954 to 1957 he was the American Cancer Society scholar at Washington University as a researcher in microbiology, and in 1955 he was promoted from assistant professor to associate professor of microbiology.

Berg moved to the Stanford University School of Medicine in 1959 as a full professor of biochemistry and was department chairman from 1969 to 1974. In 1970 he was appointed to the endowed chair as Sam, Lula and Jack Willson professor. He has guest-lectured widely in universities and research institutions in the United States and Israel. As early as 1959 he was recognized as a promising researcher when he received the Eli Lilly prize for biochemistry. Since then, and leading up to the Nobel and Lasker prizes, Berg has received many additional awards and honors, including California Scientist of the Year from the California Museum of Science and Industry in 1963.

Berg's receipt of one-half of the Nobel Prize for chemistry (the remaining half was shared by two other scientists) honored his studies of the biochemistry of nucleic acids with a focus on recombinant DNA. Beginning in 1971 he designed some of the first experiments in gene splicing between different animal species, which included splicing one animal cancer virus into the genetic material of another organism that could then be reproduced.

At the same time, Berg, who has often been called the "father" of gene splicing, has been conscious of the hazards of his research and the controversy over the possibility of negative effects of genetic manipulation. He thus spearheaded a movement within the scientific community and the federal government to draft strict guidelines to monitor gene research and to prevent dangerous accidental or deliberate abuses.

GRAENUM BERGER

b. April 21, 1908
Jewish organization executive

Graenum Berger, communal executive and institutional and communal planner, has spent his adult life working for the organized Jewish community. However, he will be best remembered for having raised the issue of saving the beleaguered Falashas, or black Ethiopian Jews, from extinction and then having openly challenged American Jewry and Israel to pay heed to the issue and avert pending disaster by helping rescue them.

Graenum Berger was born in Gloversville, New York, the son of Isaac, a leather dealer, and Bascia (Cohen) Berger. He received a Bachelor of Arts degree from the University of Missouri in 1930, where he chaired the Jewish Student Organization. In 1932 he studied at the Graduate School of Social Work in New York, earning a certificate.

Following service as the executive director of the Jewish Community Center of Staten Island in 1932-38, he became a consultant for the Federation of Jewish Philanthropies of New York from 1949 until his retirement in 1973, engaging in studies for the YM-YWHA on budgeting, site selection and building construction. He consulted on Jewish-sponsored camps, education, and the chaplaincy in the armed forces. He also taught so-

cial work part-time at Yeshiva University and CCNY between 1945 and 1947, at the Columbia University Graduate School of Social Work between 1939 and 1949 and at Yeshiva University's Wurzweiler School between 1965 and 1966.

In 1955 his life was drastically altered when, during a trip to Israel, he sighted several black children on a village street not far from Tel Aviv. He had never seen a Falasha, let alone known of their long history as Jews in Ethiopia. "I didn't know what a Falasha was," he said. "I made inquiries. Who is doing what for them in Ethiopia?" He learned that very little was being done to save them from extinction. In Israel and in the Diaspora, the issue was rarely if ever raised. "I've always been concerned with the welfare of the Jewish people, wherever they are," he says. In 1965 he visited Ethiopia and saw their difficult position in that nation.

To save them and to have them be given the right to leave Ethiopia and depart for Israel, Berger began speaking and writing extensively on the subject. He organized the American Association for Ethiopian Jews (AAEJ) from his home in Pelham, New York in 1974. Within a number of years the cause had become very popular among many American Jews. A West Coast office opened in Contra Costa, California, and branches were established elsewhere.

Soon the AAEJ gave up trying to persuade the Israelis and the organized American Jewish community to defend the Falashas, and it went public. Charging repeatedly that the Israelis under the Labor Party had rarely if ever shown any interest in their plight, the association organized speaking tours of Falashas in this country and in Canada, issued articles and press releases criticizing Israel for lack of interest and American Jewish groups for unquestioningly following the lead of Israel. In 1982 it published an advertisement listing the names of several dozen Falashas who it charged had died in Ethiopia. Stung by these allegations, Israel insisted that the Begin administration was trying to save Falashas in what it asserted was an extremely delicate diplomatic situation; U.S. organizational reactions varied, from those that sent representatives to Ethiopia to judge for themselves to those that rejected Berger's charges as extreme and unproven.

Some critics of Berger also said that civil war in Ethiopia meant merely that Falashas had been caught in a cross fire of opposing forces, that they suffered no more than did other, non-Jewish peasants, and that the Ethiopian government was the main deterrent to emigration by Falashas to Israel. Nor did they accept his charge that Israel had done little to rescue them. Charges and counter-charges of "racism" and "fanaticism" have also been raised.

All the same, Berger's primary thesis remains as he stated in 1980: "It is time to end the callous disregard of our black brothers in Ethiopia. The clock is running out for them—and for us." To pleas that he remain silent because of "secret" negotiations, he responds by calling for changes in the "current Jewish policy of neglecting their rescue by the admonition to secrecy" and simultaneously castigating "some Israeli leaders, in strategic positions, who don't want them."

For further information:

Berger, Graenum. *Black Jews in America: A Documentary with Commentary.* New York: 1978.

———. *The Jewish Community Center as a Fourth Force in American Jewish Life.* New York, 1966.

———. "The Tragedy of Ethiopian Jews. *Present Tense,* Spring, 1978.

Rosenblatt, Gary, and Alloy, Michael. "Fighting for Falashas." *Baltimore Jewish Times,* February 20, 1981.

ABRAM BERGSON

b. April 21, 1914
Economist; professor; government consultant

Abram Bergson is perhaps America's foremost expert on the Soviet economy. A professor of long standing at Columbia and Harvard, he has been a U.S. government consultant for more than 40 years.

Abram Bergson was born in Baltimore to Isaac and Sophie (Rabinowits) Bergson. He attended public schools in Baltimore and graduated from Johns Hopkins University, where he received an A.B. degree in 1933 and was a member of Phi Beta Kappa. He pursued graduate study at Harvard University and completed a Master of Arts degree in 1935 and a Ph.D. in 1940. From 1940 to 1942 he was assistant professor of economics at the University of Texas. At the same time he joined the Office of Strategic Services in Washington, D.C. By the time he left in 1945, he was chief of the Russian Economic Subdivision. During the summer of 1945, he was a member of the American Reparation Delegation in Moscow.

From 1946 to 1956 Bergson was on the faculty of Columbia University and attained the post of full professor of economics at his departure. Since 1956 he has been professor of economics at Harvard University and was named George F. Baker Professor in 1971. Bergson has also been an executive committee member of Harvard's Russian Research Center since 1956. From 1961 to 1964 he was director of the Regional Studies Program —Soviet Union and from 1964 to 1968 was director of

the Russian Research Center, a post he resumed from 1977 to 1980. Bergson has also been a consultant for various federal agencies. He was a member of the Social Science Advisory Board of the U.S. Arms Control and Disarmament Agency from 1966 to 1973 and was its chairperson for the last two of those years. Since 1948 he has been a consultant for the Rand Corporation.

Bergson is the author of eight books—one of which he coauthored—and has edited two more. His work is universally considered to be very erudite and detailed and geared toward advanced students rather than a lay audience. His first book, *Structure of Soviet Wages* (Cambridge, Mass., 1944), a detailed study of wage inequities in Russia, is full of statistics but relatively thin in emotional analysis and is difficult to comprehend if one does not already have some grounding in the subject. Similarly, *Soviet National Income and Product in 1937* (New York, 1953) is a highly technical monograph for specialists. Bergson's subsequent books—including *Soviet National Income and Product,* 1940-1948 coauthored with Hans Jeymann Jr. (New York, 1954); *Real National Income of Soviet Russia* (Cambridge, Mass., 1961); *The Economics of Soviet Planning* (New Haven, Conn., 1964); and *Planning and Productivity Under Soviet Socialism* (New York, 1968)— delve into particular aspects of the Soviet economy. The more recent works focus specifically on the effects of Stalinism in the long-term economic slowdown.

He has long sought to explore the prospects of the economy in the USSR for the coming years. Stressing national income and consumption, he concluded that the economic slowdown, begun under Stalin, would doubtless continue and that per capita consumption would also decline. The book, *The USSR and the Eighties* (New York, 1978), Bergson's contribution to a NATO symposium, first touched on the implications of the Soviet economic failures—the possibility that "the leadership might find it expedient at some point to curtail defense outlays." He also raised the issue of the advanced age of the Soviet leaders and wondered "how, as time passes, the newer figures that emerge will grapple with underlying forces of economic retardation which their predecessors have found so intractable and constraining."

Bergson has also focused on how the health or defects in the Soviet economy affect the West, which is the subject of his most recent work, *Productivity and the Social System—the USSR and the West* (Cambridge, Mass., 1978). And in 1982 he returned to one of his persistent themes and told *Newsday* that the Soviet Union's economy was sagging at so swift a pace that its next group of rulers might have to slow the rate of military spending. This decline in the economy, he said, was far more dramatic than specialists had earlier predicted. "The economic problems seem so severe and deeply entrenched that the Soviets might even be compelled to limit their defense buildup," reported Bergson. "I have resisted this argument over the years. Certainly the economic slowdown during Brezhnev's time has not affected the defense buildup until now. But the pressures are so great now . . . that some degree of austerity here will be difficult to avoid." And in *The Wall Street Journal* in 1982 he continued stressing that theme: "Whether the Russians will be able to finance this program [their military buildup] much longer in the face of mounting economic stresses is an interesting question, but Western credits can only make it easier for them to do so."

Bergson's articles on economics have appeared in scholarly journals since 1936, and since 1956 he has been called upon regularly by the U.S. Congress to testify on foreign policy matters.

For further information:
Bergson, Abram. *Essays in Normative Economics.* Cambridge, Mass.: 1966.
Bergson, Abram, ed. and contributor. *Soviet Economic Growth: Conditions and Perspectives.* Evanston, Ill.: 1953.
Bergson, Abram with Kuznets, S.S. (co-editor and contributor) *Economic Trends in the Soviet Union.* Cambridge, Mass.: 1963.

WILLIAM BERKOWITZ

b. June 28, 1924
Rabbi

Rabbi William Berkowitz, who presides over one of America's most active Conservative congregations, has been a pioneer in the education of Jewish adults and in the advancement of interdenominational and interfaith dialogue.

William Berkowitz was born in Philadelphia to Albert Lewis, a teacher and writer, and Pauline (Obod) Berkowitz. After serving in the U.S. Navy during World War II, he received a B.S. degree from Temple University. He then pursued rabbinical studies at the Jewish Theological Seminary of America and received his Master of Hebrew Literature degree in 1952. A year earlier he became associate rabbi at Congregation B'nai Jeshurun, New York's oldest Ashkenazic synagogue, on Manhattan's Upper West Side. In 1960 he became its chief rabbi.

Innovation and outreach have been essential components of Berkowitz's leadership from the beginning. In 1951 he founded the Institute of Adult Jewish Studies to provide instruction to adults seeking to further their education in basic Jewish values and traditions. The institute evidently filled a need, for it eventually expanded to include several divisions and a wide range of course offerings. Today these may include Hebrew and Yiddish language courses; Jewish history and philosophy classes; and a diverse selection of special seminars with titles like "Is the Media Anti-Jewish?" "How to Mediate as a Jew," "Judaism and Psychiatry," "Judaism and the Unexplainable: Healing, Parapsychology and the Occult" and "Biblical Games of Power."

One of Berkowitz's major accomplishments is the creation of "Dialogue," a lecture forum series also begun in 1951. For terms of eight weeks at a time, Berkowitz holds weekly evening discussions with eminent leaders in politics, the arts, journalism and other areas. His guests are among the most prominent in their field at the time, and the series' reputation is such that each interview invariably attracts an audience of several thousand. In the autumn of 1981, for example, the guests included playwright Arthur Miller, journalist and human rights advocate Jacobo Timerman, novelist Chaim Potok, violinist Itzhak Perlman and conductor-composer Leonard Bernstein. Berkowitz is the questioner at each session —sometimes the devil's advocate. Transcripts from the "Dialogue" series have been collected into five books, which are widely used in adult education classes, and recorded interviews are rebroadcast over the radio.

In 1962 Berkowitz founded a religious day school at B'nai Jeshurun. He has also sponsored a variety of alternative religious services designed to reach out to Jews who otherwise might not attend. These include a women's minyan, a family service, a beginner's service, a Chasidic minyan, and a Havurah-style service. His prerecorded High Holiday services are broadcast to hospital patients and people who could otherwise not go.

Berkowitz has been president of the Jewish National Fund since 1977 and has been active on the boards of many Jewish organizations. He is a regular columnist for the Seven Arts Feature Syndicate and has published articles in *The New York Times,* Jewish periodicals and the Yiddish press.

For further information:
Berkowitz, William, ed. *Conversation With.* New York: 1975.
———. *Heritage and Hope.* New York: 1965.
———. *I Believe.* New York: 1961.
———. *Let Us Reason Together.* New York: 1970.
———. *Ten Vital Issues.* New York: 1964.

MILTON BERLE

b. July 12, 1908
Comedian; actor

In 1948 a new technology called television entered the lives of millions of Americans, and with it came a new folk hero, Milton Berle. As host of the *Texaco Star Theater*, "Uncle Miltie," as he came to be known, became a regular Tuesday night fixture in homes across the country. He brought his vaudeville background to the new medium and for the next seven years was its first superstar, as audiences numbering in the millions came to adore his frenetic ad-libbing, his endless supply of jokes, and his manic and often unpredictable behavior before the television camera.

Milton Berle was born Milton Berlinger to Moses, a painter and decorator, and Sarah (Glantz) Berlinger in New York City. Raised in a Jewish working-class neighborhood on West 118th Street in Harlem (one of his close neighbors was the late comic George Jessel), Berle was entered by his mother in a Charlie Chaplin look-alike contest when he was 5. He won—and so began his career. His mother, who called herself Sandra, was the archetypal stage mother—laughing and clapping loudly on cue, thrusting her son into the limelight at every occasion. She joined him briefly in a vaudeville act, "Milton and Mom," and for a while even included her little daughter to form "Mama, Milton and Baby Roz." But mostly Berle performed solo.

Berle acted in many silent movies made by Biograph Studios in Fort Lee, New Jersey, which was easily reached in those days by a ferry from 125th Street. At 13 he appeared in a Chaplin short, *Tillie's Punctured Romance*. He entertained World War I troops. Later he became a performer in many legitimate theater productions (including *Earl Carroll, Vanities, Life Begins at 8:40, Ziegfeld Follies, See My Lawyer,* his first dramatic endeavor, and more), radio programs for CBS and NBC (*Rudy Vallee Hour, Three Ring Time, Stop Me If You've Heard This One, Shell Chateau* and, finally, *The Milton Berle Show*) and talkies (*New Faces of 1937; Tall, Dark and Handsome,* 1941; *Sun Valley Serenade,* 1946; and others). He was therefore no stranger to the American public when he began his television career.

But television transformed Berle. His popularity put him on a par with Babe Ruth, Joe DiMaggio and Joe Louis, and he was Grand Marshall of the Thanksgiving Day Parade in New York City in 1949. On the Tuesday nights that "Uncle Miltie" was on, many nightclubs and restaurants closed. People uncertain about the worth-whileness of owning a television would flock to appli-ance stores to watch Berle. He was a legend: His ratings were higher than those of such 1970s heroes as "The Fonz" or Farrah Fawcett-Majors. His salary was astro-nomical for the era (his 1946 pre-television income was $710,000—paltry by today's superstar standards). When his show went off the air after seven seasons, Berle had already been dubbed "Mr. Television." His tremendous success spurred Berle to comment in *Milton Berle: An Autobiography,* written with Haskel Frankel (New York, 1974), "It took me 35 years in show business to become a star overnight."

He was the very first variety show host—"Charlie Guinea Pig," he would write in his autobiography—and the expectations for him were high. In the beginning he fulfilled them, but later American audiences grew tired, and a rival inspirational show, *The Fulton Sheen Hour,* soon commanded more attention. ("Sheen has better writers than I have," quipped Berle.) In 1955 Berle's show was canceled and although he retained a lucrative 30-year con-tract with NBC, Berle was a "has-been" at age 47.

Repeated attempts to return to television through the late 1950s and 1960s, including once even a bowl-ing show, were received unenthusiastically. He contin-ued to appear in cabarets and nightclubs, a few films (*It's a Mad, Mad, Mad, Mad World,* 1962; *Where Angels Go, Trouble Follows,* 1968; *Lepke,* 1974; and others) and plays (*The Goodbye People* and Neil Simon's *The Sunshine Boys*), but by the 1960s and early 1970s, his drawing power had waned markedly.

Berle's autobiography reveals many of the details behind the performer. The impact of early and intense fame took a toll on his ego ("You take a kid at the age of five . . . and make him a star—everybody catering to him . . . and it's a miracle if the kid doesn't grow up to be a man who believes he's Casanova and Einstein and Jesus Christ all rolled into one"), and he became known as a tyrant to those who worked with him in television (a popular nickname—for his sardonic humor as well as his temperament—was "King Leer").

Despite Berle's failure to make a significant come-back on television, his seven-year reign as "Mr. Tues-day Night" from 1948 to 1955 marked him as possibly the most powerful influence on the new medium. On March 26, 1978 NBC honored him with a special, "A Tribute to Mr. Television." *TV Guide* (March 31, 1978) summed him up succinctly in its listings the week of the show: "What Henry Ford did for the automobile, Mil-ton Berle did for television."

For further information:

Berle, Milton. *Laughingly Yours.* Edited by S. Sylvan Simon. New York: 1939.

———. *Out of My Trunk*. Garden City, N.Y.: 1945.
———. *Earthquake*. New York: 1959.

CARL BERNSTEIN

b. February 14, 1944
Journalist

Carl Bernstein became a national hero when he and fellow *Washington Post* reporter Bob Woodward untangled modern journalism's most famous investigative news story—the Watergate cover-up. For their political reportage, which set off a constitutional crisis and the subsequent resignation of President Richard M. Nixon in 1974, the two earned every major journalism award, including the 1973 Pulitzer Prize for the *Washington Post*.

Carl Bernstein was born in Washington, D.C. to Alfred David, a labor union official and Sylvia (Walker) Bernstein, also a labor leader. Because of a passion for newspaper work, he applied for a copyboy's job at the *Washington Star* when he was only 16. Before long he was promoted to city desk clerk and telephone man. Meanwhile, he attended the University of Maryland part-time between 1961 and 1964, though he never received a degree. In 1975, he briefly attended Boston University.

In 1964 he quit the *Star* and joined the Elizabeth (N.J.) *Daily Journal*, where his piece on the massive November 1965 New York City blackout earned him first prize in the 1965 New Jersey Press Association competition. Two years later he returned to Washington, but this time to the *Post*, where he was assigned to the police, court and city hall beats. Frustrated and restless, he sought work at *Rolling Stone* only a few weeks before the momentous break-in at the Democratic National Committee's headquarters in the Watergate complex on June 17, 1972.

He and Woodward drew the assignment early on, when it was seen as simply another minor burglary. They were both young and relatively new. Bernstein's forte as a reporter was his meticulous attention to detail, his extraordinary patience in ferreting out scraps of often apparently unrelated information and then fitting them together, his excellent sources developed on his earlier beats and his ability to write quickly and clearly. Initially, the print and electronic media paid little attention to the crime and conspiracy. Yet with astounding regularity the two reporters began publishing startling stories in the *Post* involving minor actors at first but before long drawing closer and closer to the oval office

in the White House. Eventually, they received the highest accolade from their competitors in the media: Vast attention was turned toward the crime, primarily because Bernstein and Woodward and their editors refused to drop the story.

In their book *All the President's Men* (New York, 1974), they tell "the story behind the story." It was transformed into a film starring Dustin Hoffman as Bernstein and Robert Redford as Woodward. Their second collaborative book, *The Final Days* (New York, 1976), focuses on Nixon's final 15 months as president. While they refused to cite specific sources, they did reveal a president badly damaged—emotionally and politically—by the scandal, the discovery of the secret tapes and the ensuing impeachment hearings.

Since 1980 Bernstein has worked for ABC News, first as Washington bureau chief and from 1981 as an investigative reporter and producer based in New York City. He married the writer Nora Ephron on April 14, 1976.

LEONARD BERNSTEIN

b. August 25, 1918
Conductor; composer; pianist

Leonard Bernstein was once described as a "restless maestro," and that characterization seems appropriate, given his extraordinary ability to move easily into different roles as conductor, composer of classical and popular music, television performer and even as academician. In fact, few American-born musicians have been as creative or successful or as willing to experiment as he.

Leonard Bernstein was born in Lawrence, Massachusetts to Samuel, a beauty-supply and hair-goods businessman, and Jennie (Resnick) Bernstein. From the age of 10, when his aunt gave his family her piano, he was fascinated by the instrument. In spite of his father's reluctance to have his son become a musician—his mother provided him with the necessary family support—Bernstein persisted throughout his adolescence, playing in dance bands and giving piano lessons. Before long he was studying with a well-known Boston piano teacher and majoring in music at Harvard, where he received his B.A. degree in 1939 and performed and wrote for a wide variety of theatrical and musical activities. Moreover, he met the composer Aaron Copland and the conductor Dmitri Mitropoulos while yet a student, the former—according to a memoir written by Bernstein's younger brother—a source of much influence on him, especially because of the uniquely American quality of his compositions, and the latter because of his work as guest conductor of the Boston Symphony. Mitropoulos dubbed the young man a "genius boy" and urged him to study music more intensively at the Curtis Institute of Music with Fritz Reiner, then the conductor of the Pittsburgh Symphony. In 1939 Bernstein earned his diploma from Curtis.

Especially significant for him were the summers of 1940 and 1941, when he worked at the Berkshire Music Center in Massachusetts with Serge Koussevitzky and the Boston Symphony. In 1942 he went back as Koussevitzky's aide and then, armed with the maestro's strong recommendation, became Artur Rodzinski's assistant conductor with the New York Philharmonic. Finally, on November 14, 1943 Bernstein's life changed dramatically. The permanent conductor Bruno Walter became ill, and—without rehearsing—Bernstein was pressed into service as his substitute, leading the orchestra in Strauss's *Don Quixote* and the prelude to *Die Meistersinger*. His movements while conducting were dramatic and showmanlike, and the response from the critics and the press was astounding: A star was born. Two New York newspapers even carried front-page stories on the event.

That same year he offered his *Jeremiah* symphony, the first of many to come and which won the New York Music Critics Circle Award. *Jeremiah* was a blending of biblical themes with melancholy yet inspiring music for soprano. He has also written *Kaddish* and in 1952 a one-act opera, *Trouble in Tahiti*. In 1982 he composed a piano piece for the Van Cliburn Competition called "Touches," which he expects to enlarge into a sonata; a divertimento written for the Boston Symphony's centennial; and a "Musical Toast" to the memory of Andre Kostelanetz.

He also composed *Halil*, nocturne for solo flute, string orchestra and percussion, which received its premiere in New York City in 1982 and afterward was performed by Jean-Pierre Rampal and the Israel Philharmonic. Following a guest appearance with the Israel Philharmonic in 1976 in Tel Aviv, Bernstein was asked by the parents of Yadin Tanenbaum, a 19-year-old flutist killed in the Yom Kippur War in 1973, to write a work in honor of their son. "I never knew Yadin Tanenbaum," said Bernstein, "but I know his spirit." The result is *Halil*, which he has dedicated "to the spirit of Yadin and his fallen brothers." Overall, he is a "modern" composer without the dissonance found in the works of so many contemporary composers.

Bernstein has also been an eminently successful and much-sought-after conductor.

In 1945 he took control of the New York City Symphony and began playing the music generally shunned by the major musical organizations—modern composi-

tions by Bartok, Stravinsky, Hindemith, Prokofiev, Copland, etc. He then succeeded Mitropoulis at the New York Philharmonic in 1958, staying until 1966, when he was named "laureat conductor." His broad interests have led him to guest-conducting positions with the Israel Philharmonic in 1947 and again after the 1967 Six Day War, when he led the orchestra at the Hebrew University on Mount Scopus. In Vienna he led the Vienna Philharmonic in Beethoven's nine symphonies, telecast to large audiences by the Public Broadcasting Corporation; in the interim he conducted in Rome, Paris, Boston, Washington, New York and, once again, in Israel.

And he has turned increasingly to operas. He conducted the orchestra at La Scala (his initial appearance was in 1958 in Milan in Cherubini's *Medea*). Since then, in addition to Wagner's *Tristan und Isolde* in Munich in 1981-'82, he has also conducted at the Metropolitan and Vienna opera houses. It may be, as Martin Mayer wrote, that his "significant contribution to the musical life of his time has been as a conductor of other men's music."

Bernstein is also widely known for his popular music. *Fancy Free* (1943), the ballet that was ultimately transformed into *On the Town* (1944), was his first, followed by such theatrical musical scores as *Wonderful Town* (1953), *Candide* (1956), *West Side Story* (1957) and *Dybbik* (1974).

Always associated with liberal and humane causes in the non-musical world, he once played host in 1969 to guests at his home to solicit funds for the protection of the civil liberties of the Black Panther Party. For this he was widely mocked as an example of "radical chic." In 1980, however, FBI documents made available under the Freedom of Information Act revealed that J. Edgar Hoover, the late FBI director, had ordered anonymous letters to be mailed to Bernstein's guests to oppose the alleged support for the Black Panthers among some Jews and to outline "the Black Panther Party's anti-Semitic posture." The letters were mailed on February 27, 1970. In response, Bernstein said in 1980: "None of these [FBI] machinations has adversely affected my life or work but they did cause a good deal of unpleasantness."

Bernstein has also taught. Between 1951 and 1954 he was a professor at Brandeis University. And in 1982 he became the first fellow of Indiana University's new Institute for Advanced Study. In announcing the fellowship the university dean of the School of Music said that Bernstein's "presence on campus as he completes an important composition would have a profound effect on our entire academic community."

For further information:
Bernstein, Leonard. *Findings.* New York: 1982.
Bernstein, Burton. *Family Matters: Sam, Jennie and the Kids.* New York: 1982.
Mayer, Martin. "The Blinding Facility of Leonard Bernstein." *Esquire,* February 1967.

ROBERT BERNSTEIN

b. January 5, 1923
Publisher

In addition to being the president of Random House, one of the most respected publishing houses in the world, Robert Bernstein is a leading American human rights activist. He has constantly exhibited an acute sense of concern for the rights of individuals both in America and abroad, in Communist as well as non-Communist nations.

Bernstein was born in New York City, to Alfred, a textile converter, and Sylvia (Block) Bernstein. He attended the Lincoln School in New York City and graduated in 1940. He then enrolled at Harvard University and received a B.S. degree in 1944. Prior to his graduation he had enlisted in the United States Air Force and he subsequently served until 1946.

After his discharge, Bernstein began working as the general sales manager for Simon and Schuster, the New York publishing house. In 1957 he moved to Random House, becoming its president in 1966. Under his leadership, Random House has become one of the most important book publishers in the world.

Bernstein served as the chairman of the Association of American Publishers from 1972 to 1973. In 1973 he also was the chairman of the Association's Soviet-American publishing relations committee which resolved copyright disputes between the two countries.

Bernstein has long been involved in the struggle for human rights and civil liberties. He is chairman of the American Helsinki Watch Committee, a citizens' group that monitors Soviet compliance with the Helsinki accords which guarantee basic standards of human rights among the signatory powers. He is also an American delegate to the international meetings which periodically check on compliance to the agreements. He is especially interested in the fate of Soviet Jews and monitors their struggle as well. In 1976 he served as chairman of a committee on international freedom to publish. And, in addition to his activities in the right-to-publish field, he is on the national advisory board of Amnesty International and the board of directors of the International League for Human Rights.

However, Bernstein is not simply concerned with human rights abroad. He has also taken an active role in insuring that our civil liberties are not abridged in America. Besides his publishing program at Random House—they have accepted books which the government sought to quash, such as Frank Snepp's *Decent Interval* (New York, 1977), an account by an ex-CIA operative about the agency's machinations—Bernstein won the Florence Lasker award of the New York Civil Liberties Union. He has initiated a citizen's CIA watchdog committee of distinguished citizens to safeguard civil rights and civil liberties and prevent future domestic abuses by the CIA.

Jacobo Timerman has said that it was Bernstein who urged him to complete his powerful book, *Prisoner Without a Name, Cell Without a Number* (New York, 1981)—which caused a furor in this country with its details of torture and widespread disregard for human rights—about his ordeal in an Argentine prison, where he was incarcerated for 20 months, tortured, denounced for being a Jew and a Zionist, stripped of his citizenship for criticizing the government in his Buenos Aires newspaper *La Opinión,* and deported to Israel.

Moreover, Bernstein is very concerned with education affairs for the disadvantaged. He is a member of the board of directors of the predominantly black Tougaloo College in Tougaloo, Mississippi. He also serves on the board of directors of the Dr. Seuss Foundation for children's literature and is a trustee of the State University of New York at Purchase.

The thread which binds all of Bernstein's widespread and diverse activities is his profound belief that people need to be protected from authoritarian *and* totalitarian rulers everywhere in the world.

BRUNO BETTELHEIM

b. August 28, 1903
Psychoanalyst; professor of education

Bruno Bettelheim, child psychologist and scrutinizer of social behavior under stress, has built his reputation upon empirical examination of his subjects, whether in schools for emotionally disturbed children, in the kibbutz or in Nazi concentration camps.

Bruno Bettelheim was born in Vienna to Anton and Paula (Seidler) Bettelheim. He was schooled in Germany and Austria and graduated from the Reform Realgymnasium in Vienna. In 1938 he received his Ph.D. from the University of Vienna in psychology and philosophy and underwent psychoanalysis, all the while working as an educator and psychologist. Unfortunately, the German absorption of Austria—the Anschluss—occurred the same year, and Bettelheim was sent to Dachau and Buchenwald concentration camps for one year. The Nazi policy of the "final solution" had not yet been formulated, and like many other dissidents and Jews, Bettelheim was allowed to leave. In 1939 he reached the United States.

His reputation, however, preceded him, and that year he was hired by the Progressive Education Association as a researcher at the University of Chicago. He remained there until 1941, when he shifted to nearby Rockford College to teach psychology. It was during that time that his article "Individual and Mass Behavior in Extreme Situations" was published in the *Journal of Abnormal and Social Psychology* (1943), in which he sought to use his concentration camp experience to analyze the impact of extraordinary tension upon people and how they coped.

In 1944 he joined the faculty of the University of Chicago as an educational psychologist and was simultaneously appointed as director of the Orthogenic School at the university, a school for emotionally disturbed youngsters of normal intelligence. *Love Is Not Enough* (New York, 1950) and *Truants from Life* (New York, 1954) dealt with his experiences with the school's pupils. In the former, he brought to bear the discipline of abnormal psychology on rearing disturbed children in a suitable and loving milieu; in the latter he described four cases in which such children were restored to a more normal existence.

He has also conducted major studies of the effect of communal child rearing, such as in the kibbutz. His book *Children of the Dream* (New York, 1969) studied youngsters raised in an egalitarian collective setting in Israel. He was deeply impressed with the significance of living and sharing as opposed to the individualism practiced elsewhere among urban and suburban families. "Absent are the frustrations. . . . In their place are deep, permanent, extremely meaningful and mutually satisfying attachments of the youngsters to each other," he wrote in an earlier article in *Commentary* on the subject. Some critics, though, argued that Bettelheim's study was marred by his sketchy knowledge of both Israeli society and the Hebrew language and his lack of data about less successful communal child rearing in Israel. In general, however, the critical reception here and in Israel was positive, and it opened up new areas and questions concerning communalism as a way of life.

To explore how children perceive the world about them, he has in recent years looked at how they learn by means of examining what they hear and what and how

they read. *The Uses of Enchantment* (New York, 1976) explores the impact of traditional fairy tales on young minds. Many of the Grimm brothers' stories tend to be macabre and violent. Bettelheim claims that children can absorb the gruesomeness of these tales without developing morbid sensibilities and that modern attempts to dilute the stories and give them happy endings are less than useful. *On Learning to Read,* with Karen Zelan (New York, 1982), looks at the processes children undergo as they not only master simple reading techniques but also learn to read creatively.

Perhaps his most provocative thesis deals with the victims of the Holocaust. In 1962 he delivered the Eighth Annual Rosenwald Lecture of the American Council for Judaism, "Freedom from Ghetto Thinking," in which he posed this question: "Since we are not Zionists . . . what exactly is the meaning of being a Jew?" To Bettelheim, it meant shunning "ghetto traditions" such as moving into Jewish suburbs or attending parochial schools or "when German Jews objected to the true stories being circulated about their mistreatment." He then turned to the Holocaust, stating that most of those [Jews] who adhered to their ghetto thinking perished, because they sought to "ingratiate" themselves "with a mortal enemy by denying his lash's stings," while those who did not—who were assimilated or acculturated or who took the Nazis more seriously—often escaped, as he did. And why, asked Bettelheim, didn't those victims of the camps he had experienced really believe Hitler meant what he said?

> The vast majority of my fellow prisoners were not Jews but German gentiles. Beholden to ghetto thinking; only what happened to the Jews counted; they were not interested in what happened to the gentiles. But lacking interest they could not learn from it. Those Jews who were interested and learned from it were able to save themselves. . . . it was not a shunning of violence that explains Jewish suffering under the Nazis, but rather an inability to act in self-defense . . . *as a Jew.*

He pursued this theme in *The Informed Heart: Autonomy in a Mass Age* (Glencoe, Ill., 1960), asserting that Jewish victims frequently failed to resist. "They could have marched as free men against the SS, rather than to first grovel, then wait to be rounded up for their own extermination, and finally walk themselves to the gas chamber," he wrote. And in "The Ignored Lesson of Anne Frank" in *Surviving and Other Essays* (New York, 1979) he criticized the Frank family for "passively" hiding. Why, he asked, didn't Anne's father "at least" kill some Nazis? Jews, he concluded, "could at least have died fighting as some did in the Warsaw Ghetto."

For further information:

Bettelheim, Bruno. *Dialogue with Mothers.* New York: 1962.

———. *The Empty Fortress: Infantile Autism and the Birth of Self.* New York: 1967.

———. *Freud and Man's Soul.* New York: 1983.

———. "Does Communal Education Work? The Case of the Kibbutz," *Commentary,* February 1962.

THEODORE BIKEL

b. May 2, 1924
Actor; folk singer

Theodore Bikel, an accomplished actor in theater, films and television and a folk singer with a vast multiethnic repertoire, has also helped keep alive the spark of Yiddish folk culture and music. Fluent in five languages, he has performed in Yiddish and Hebrew to audiences throughout the world.

Theodore Bikel was born in Vienna. He learned Yiddish and Hebrew in the home of his parents, Josef and Miriam (Riegler) Bikel, and German in the Vienna public schools. His family fled Austria after the German take-over in 1938. They settled in Palestine, and his father eventually became the director of the Israeli public health service.

Bikel lived on a kibbutz, where he was the librarian and staged pageants for the community. After four years on the kibbutz, he left to study acting at Habimah, the Hebrew national theater in Tel Aviv, in 1943. After 18 months, during which he received only one small part, he left Habimah and formed the Tel Aviv Chamber Theater with a few other young actors. He stayed with the Chamber Theater for two years. In 1946 he left Palestine to study acting at the Royal Academy of Dramatic Arts in London.

In England he received a number of small roles in plays and films. In 1949 a part in the play *You Can't Take It with You* led to his being cast by Sir Laurence Olivier as Mitch in the London production of *A Streetcar Named Desire.* This, in turn, was followed by a part as a German soldier in the Humphrey Bogart film, *The African Queen.*

Bikel moved to the United States in 1954. He made his television debut on the *United States Steel Hour* in 1956, and then in 1957 he played in the *Hallmark Hall of Fame* production of "There Shall Be No Tomorrow." Bikel won an Oscar nomination for his role as a humane southern sheriff in *The Defiant Ones* in 1958. He has also appeared in *My Fair Lady* in 1964 and as the Soviet submarine commander in *The Russians Are Coming, The Russians Are Coming* (1966).

In addition to his work on stage and in films, Bikel is a well-known folk singer. His most popular albums include *Folksongs from Israel, Jewish Folksongs* and *Folksongs from Just About Everywhere.* He has also compiled a book of folk songs, *Folksongs and Footnotes: An International Song Book* (New York, 1960). He also specializes in singing songs smuggled out of the USSR, songs sung by generations of Russian gypsies.

Bikel has been active in Jewish affairs and politics. He founded the arts chapter of the American Jewish Congress in 1961—the same year he became an American citizen—and served as a national vice president of the American Jewish Congress from 1963 to 1970. In 1970 he became chairman of its governing council. In 1968 Bikel was a delegate to the Democratic National Convention. He is a member of the Academy of Motion Picture Arts and Sciences and the Academy of Television Arts and Sciences. He joined Actors Equity Association in 1961 and served as its president in 1973. Bikel once summed up his personal philosophy by saying:

> If I am a universalist—and I believe myself to be one—I derive my general standard from a particularist experience. For, above all, I am a Jew. Spiritually and culturally to be a Jew is to be a man on the road from Jerusalem to Jerusalem. Jerusalem is my hope and inspiration.

J. DAVID BLEICH

b. August 24, 1936
Rabbi; attorney

Although to most Jews the traditions of the Orthodox end of the spectrum are dated and inappropriate, Rabbi J. David Bleich has developed expertise in ancient Jewish law and shown how the theories of the Rabbinic scholars are precisely attuned to modern life. He is a major theorist on some of the very complex bioethical issues that concern scholars who perceive changes in the way humans live in the age of gene splicing, artificial organs and respirators. His focus has been to assure that respect for life from a Judaic perspective does not waver in the midst of scientific and technological advances.

J. David Bleich was born in New York City to Manning and Beatrice Bleich. Ordained at Mesivta Torah Vada'th in 1957, he received a B.A. degree from Brooklyn College in 1960. He completed an M.A. degree from Columbia University in 1968 and a Ph.D. in philosophy from New York University in 1974. He began teaching philosophy as an instructor at Rutgers University from 1962 to 1963, at Hunter College from 1962 to 1969 and at Stern College for Women from

1965 to 1972. From 1972 to 1978 he was an assistant professor at Stern and from 1974 to 1975 a guest professor at the University of Haifa.

Bleich was appointed "Rosh Yeshiva," or director, of Rabbi Isaac Elchanan Theological Seminary of Yeshiva University in 1969. Bleich distinguished himself as an expert in the interpretation of Halakha, or Jewish law, as it applies to aspects of daily living and to larger life problems from a Jewish philosophical perspective. He was a fellow at the Hastings Institute for Society, Ethics and the Life Sciences from 1974 to 1975 and became a regular contributor to many journals on Halakhic and bioethical issues.

Bleich's publications include *Providence in the Philosophy of Gersonides* (New York, 1973), *Contemporary Halakhic Problems* (New York, 1977) and *Bircas haChammah* (New York, 1980). The last-named book explores the Blessing of the Sun, a Jewish ritual that occurs at 18-year intervals, always on a Wednesday morning, and is based on an ancient tradition formulated by the Sages of centuries ago. He is also contributing editor at *Tradition* magazine and *Sh'ma* and is on the editorial board of *Jewish Life.* His articles have appeared in these magazines and in the *Encyclopedia of Bioethics, The Hospital Physician, Jewish Observer, Judaism* and many other publications.

An example of his work is an article he wrote in *Judaism,* "'Halakhah as an Absolute," in which he debates with scholar Dr. Robert Gordis on the relationship between Halakhah and modern times. Whereas Gordis perceives a tension between the two and suggests that the individual not let the demands of Halakhah interfere with the demands of contemporary life, Bleich contends that similar tensions have always existed. But instead of working against each other, he suggests that "it is not the function of Halakhah to seek an accommodation with society but to refine and purify it." He adds that "Halakhah has never been in conflict with technological, economic or structural advantages of any 'contemporary' society," although at times "it has had to accommodate 'new external conditions—social, economic, political or cultural'—but always on its own terms and on the basis of its own categories." He further discusses such issues as women's rights, polygamy as an ancient and accepted practice, and the process by which an ancient sacrificial requirement was eliminated, in the context of the eras in which these ideas were important and the motives behind them.

His deep concern for human beings and the humane implications of Halakha, led him to write *Judaism and Healing: Halakhic Perspectives* (New York, 1981). Bleich makes the case for not telling every terminally ill patient of his or her impending death because of the "possibil-

ity of adverse reaction," which could bring on premature death. "Accordingly," he comments, "in this, as in other areas of Halakhah, the possibility of hastening death in at least some patients must be the determining factor."

Since 1979 Bleich has also been a visiting professor at the Benjamin N. Cardozo School of Law of Yeshiva University.

HERBERT L(AWRENCE) BLOCK

b. October 13, 1909
Political cartoonist

Herbert L(awrence) Block, famed editorial cartoonist for the *Washington Post* since 1946, is one of this country's most influential, most persuasive and most passionate political commentators. Three times a winner of the Pulitzer Prize for editorial cartooning, Block, who uses the signature "Herblock" on his daily cartoons, which are syndicated throughout the United States, once remarked that he only tries to present "the right things effectively."

Herbert Block was born in Chicago, the youngest of three sons of David Julian, a chemist, and Tesse (Lupe) Block. He began to draw while still very young. When he was 12 he won a scholarship and studied in evening art classes at the Chicago Art Institute. In 1929, after 2 years at Lake Forest College in suburban Chicago, he started work at the *Chicago Daily News,* where for 4 years his cartoons appeared daily on the editorial page. He adopted "Herblock" as a pseudonym at the suggestion of his father. In 1933 he went to the Newspaper Enterprise Association in Cleveland, Ohio, where he stayed for 10 years. In 1943 he joined the Army, drawing cartoons for the Information and Education Division until he was discharged 3 years later and went to work for the *Post.*

Essentially a fair-minded liberal, Block has tried to mock politicians, corporate leaders and tyrants of all nationalities. Described years ago by poet Carl Sandburg as "a pictorial historian of current events," Block won his first Pulitzer Prize in 1942 for a cartoon entitled "British Plane," which depicted a German soldier in occupied France scanning the sky for an RAF bomber while French people watch. He won another Pulitzer Prize in 1954 for a cartoon based on Stalin's death, in which he portrayed the Soviet leader as an ally of the culture of death. The grim reaper is depicted as leading Stalin as he clutches the communist's bloody sickle. The caption read: "You were always a great friend of mine, Joseph." Block's indignation at the actions of Senator Joseph McCarthy and Richard M. Nixon led him to excoriate them in his cartoons as amoral bullies. In one famous drawing he depicted the insatiability of the out-of-control worldwide arms race.

Herblock on All Fronts (New York, 1980) takes a retrospective look at the 1970s, with a focus on the Camp David negotiations and subsequent exchanges between Israel and Egypt, government corruption, and the 1980 presidential primaries. According to *Publishers Weekly* (October 8, 1980), "Herblock's fertile imagination and skillful pen find ever new visual metaphors to portray global tragedies along with the ironies, absurdities and everyday frustrations which beset most citizens."

Block, Herbert L. *The Herblock Book*. Boston: 1952.
———. *The Herblock Gallery*. New York: 1968.
———. *Herblock's Here and Now*. Boston: 1955.
———. *Herblock's Special for Today*. Boston: 1958.
———. *Herblock's Special Report*. New York. 1976.
———. *Straight Herblock*. New York: 1964.

BARUCH BLUMBERG
b. July 28, 1925
Physician; anthropologist

Nobel Prize winner Baruch Blumberg is both a medical doctor and an anthropologist with a unique grounding in scientific research and clinical medical practices around the world. His discovery of a protein in the Hepatitis B virus, which he isolated in the blood of Australian aborigines, research that began in 1963, led to his development of a vaccine for the disease.

Baruch Samuel Blumberg was born in New York City to Meyer, an attorney, and Ida (Simonoff) Blumberg. Educated at Yeshiva of Flatbush in Brooklyn, where he received intensive training in biblical studies in Hebrew and in Talmudic reasoning—"at an age," he later wrote, "when we could hardly have realized its impact." He graduated from Far Rockaway High School in Queens and enlisted in the U.S. Navy in 1943. He completed college through the Navy, studying physics at Union College in Schenectady, New York. He received his B.S. degree in 1946. After briefly studying mathematics at Columbia University, he switched to medicine and received his M.D. in 1953 from Columbia's College of Physicians and Surgeons.

Blumberg's education at Columbia combined intensive basic science and research in its first two years with an unusual experience in applied medicine for several months during the third and fourth years. Under the auspices of a professor of parasitology, Blumberg was sent to an isolated mining town near Surinam, where he helped deliver babies, performed clinical services and undertook a range of health surveys in the region. As a result of his experiences in the area, whose residents came from a range of backgrounds—including indigenous Indians, Africans and some Chinese, Jews and Hindu Indians—Blumberg became fascinated with the different responses of these people to environmentally caused infections and other health problems. His first published article (as a coauthor) was based on this research and eventually led to his studying biochemistry at Oxford University, where he completed a doctorate in 1957. In the interim he served an internship and residency at New York City's Bellevue Hospital from 1951 to 1953 and spent the following two years on research fellowships at the College of Physicians and Surgeons and at Goldwater Memorial Hospital.

After completing his doctorate, Blumberg became chief of the Geographic Medicine and Genetics Section of the National Institutes of Health based in Bethesda, Maryland. His work required him to travel extensively, and during his seven years at NIH, he visited areas in all parts of the world studying social behavior and susceptibility to disease. These travels not only nurtured an interest in anthropology but underscored a focus on the human aspect of disease. Concurrent with his research, Blumberg was also attending physician at the clinical center of the NIH, and for two years (1962 to 1964) he taught clinical medicine at Georgetown University in Washington, D.C.

In 1964 Blumberg joined the Institute of Cancer Research in Philadelphia, where he started a program in clinical research and eventually became associate director and senior member. As with his earlier work, Blumberg retained a strong consciousness of the human end of his work and recruited an international and versatile staff to develop research and clinical programs. He joined the faculty of the University of Pennsylvania as professor of medicine at its medical school in 1970 and as professor of anthropology in 1975. In 1977 he was named University Professor of Medicine and Anthropology.

Blumberg's receipt of the 1976 Nobel Prize in Physiology of Medicine was for "discoveries concerning new mechanisms for the origin and dissemination of infectious diseases." He had discovered a new "infectious agent associated with hepatitis B." In his Nobel lecture, delivered on December 13, 1976, Blumberg said ". . . it is now possible to begin the design of control measures for this disease. . . . The role of the virus in the life of insects in which it is found is not known, but may be profound; and there may be other effects on the ecology that are not now obvious." As of now, his hepatitis vaccine, co-developed with Dr. Irving Millman, is undergoing field trials.

Blumberg, who is on the editorial board of *Medical Biology* and the advisory board of *Perspectives in Biology and Medicine,* has published more than 300 articles in a wide range of scientific journals.

BEN ZION BOKSER

July 4, 1907
Rabbi; author

Rabbi Ben Zion Bokser, spiritual leader of the Forest Hills Jewish Center congregation in Forest Hills, Queens since 1935, is author of many highly acclaimed books on Judaic literature, ritual, belief and Jewish mysticism.

Ben Zion Bokser was born in Lubuomi, Poland to Elie Morris, a businessman, and Gittel (Katz) Bokser and immigrated to the United States in 1920. He received his B.A. degree from City College of New York in 1929 and was ordained as a rabbi by The Jewish Theological Seminary of America in 1931. He earned his M.A. and Ph.D. degrees in Jewish Studies from Columbia University in 1931 and 1935, respectively.

Before coming to Forest Hills, Rabbi Bokser was a rabbi at Congregation Kehillat Israel in the Bronx from 1931 to 1932 and led a congregation in Vancouver, British Columbia, Canada from 1932 to 1933. He has been an editor on the NBC radio program *The Eternal Light,* sponsored by the seminary, since 1950. He is also a member of the Conference on Science, Philosophy and Religion.

Rabbi Bokser has published many books, emphasizing his belief in and exploration of faith and the Judaic traditions, including *Pharisaic Judaism in Transition* (New York, 1935), which was his Ph.D. thesis on Rabbi Eliezer ben Hyracanus of the Talmudic period; *The Legacy of Maimonides* (New York, 1950), an introduction to the medieval Jewish philosopher that places him in the context of his times; *The Wisdom of the Talmud* (New York, 1951), a short, popular introduction to the history and contents of the Talmud; and *From the World of the Cabbalah: The Philosophy of Rabbi Judah Loew of Prague* (New York, 1954), a series of lectures delivered at The Jewish Theological Seminary of America based on an examination of the original writings of Rabbi Loew, who lived during the 16th century.

Bokser has also written *Judaism:Profile of Faith* (New York, 1963), which discusses religion and science, the Jewish concept of God and man, ethics, prayer and other subjects in terms of Scripture. In *Judaism and the Christian Predicament* (New York, 1966), he deals with the differences between Jews and Christians in areas such as the Bible, religious history and the nature of religious experience; and in *Jews, Judaism and the State of Israel* (New York, 1973), he examines the intimate relation between Jews and the land of Israel.

In the end, however, Bokser's significance lies in the scholarly scrutiny he brings to Jewish spirituality. In *Abraham Isaac Kook: The Lights of Penitence, the Moral Principles, Lights of Holiness, Essays, Letters and Poems* (Ramsey, N.J., 1978), he probes the mind of one of Judaism's great teachers of religion and faith. And in *The Jewish Mystical Tradition* (New York, 1981), he continues to probe the world of Jewish mystics, those writers and religious thinkers whose deepest urges were not sated by materialism or more conventional practices. Using representative excerpts, Bokser tracks mysticism, which he defines as "the quest for the ultimate meaning of life," through the Bible, the Talmud and the Kabbalah and through such Hasidic teachers as Rabbi Hayim of Valazhin and Rabbi Abraham Isaac Kook. Mysticism, he concludes, can help overcome the "spiritual decadence in Judaism which has alienated some of the most sensitive children of our people."

HYMAN (HARRY) BOOKBINDER

b. March 9, 1916
Lobbyist; public official

Hyman Harry Bookbinder, Washington representative of the American Jewish Committee, has a long and distinguished career of service to American and world Jewry, human rights and the labor movement, both inside and outside of government service.

Hyman Bookbinder was born in New York City to Polish immigrant parents, Louis, a shomaker and shoe merchant, and Rose (Palger) Bookbinder. He attended Thomas Jefferson High School in the East New York section of Brooklyn, graduating in 1933. He then attended the City College of New York and received a Bachelor of Social Science degree in 1937. Afterward, he worked for the Amalgamated Clothing Workers of America until 1943. He served in the U.S. Navy from 1943 to 1945 and upon his discharge took a job as economist and research director for the union. From 1940 until 1947 (except for the war years), Bookbinder also did graduate work in economics, social science and political science at New York University and the New School for Social Research. From 1950 to 1964 he held a series of positions, including legislation representative, with the AFL-CIO.

Bookbinder was appointed executive officer of the President's Task Force on Poverty in 1964 and served as assistant director of the Office of Economic Opportunity from its inception in 1964 to 1967. His responsibility was that of marshaling private resources to assist in the war on poverty. During that time he also held the post of special assistant to Vice President Hubert Humphrey.

Bookbinder joined the American Jewish Committee in 1967. As Washington representative of the AJC, he maintains liaison between the committee and the White House, agencies of the federal government, the Congress, foreign embassies and Washington representatives of other religious, civil and human relations agencies. He chairs a coordinating committee of delegates of all Jewish agencies in Washington and has moderated an AJC-sponsored radio program called *Washington Scene*. .

In 1980 President Carter appointed Bookbinder to serve on the U.S. Holocaust Memorial Council, of which author Elie Wiesel is chairman. On his return from Auschwitz and other death camps in 1980, he said: "I tell students that their generation will not ever have the same excuse some in my generation invoke, that they 'did not know.' We all know now, and we must act."

Bookbinder's often-stated views include the fact that American Jews, as a small minority, must seek out coalitions with like-minded groups in order to flourish here. Constituting 3 percent of the population, Jews in America "know full well that no Jewish view of public policy can prevail unless there are at least 51 percent of the people who, in the final analysis, agree with such a Jewish view," he remarked in late 1981, after the Reagan administration won the battle to sell AWACS planes and other arms to Saudi Arabia. Jews, he went on, are to be found on all sides of public life, but whatever power they have is hardly monolithic. The vote against AWACS, he added, was not because of Jewish power but rather because many Americans had legitimate doubts about its wisdom. Yet American Jewry found itself the victim of a possible anti-Semitic backlash, from President Reagan's harsh remark about not allowing another country to determine this country's foreign policies to the public statements of three former American presidents urging that the sale be ratified. Bookbinder observed:

> It was presumably proper for industry to express its views; it was perfectly understandable that Saudi Arabia itself would spend lavish sums on the highest-priced lobbyists and lawyers; it was okay for 21 other Arab embassies to express their views; it was only natural that Mobil and other oil companies would expand their "public ser-

vice" advertising programs to promote the AWACS sales. . . . then just as surely Americans concerned with the very security of their co-religionists in Israel. . . . are no less entitled to freedom of advocacy.

Bookbinder served as Chairman of the United Jewish Appeal's Government Division from 1965 to 1967 and received a special citation for distinguished service. In 1977 the National Conference of Christians and Jews presented him with its National Brotherhood Citation "for the depth of his understanding of the meaning of justice and equality." In May of 1978 fellow-liberal Vice President Walter Mondale said:

> I've been in Washington a long, long time. I've seen them all; and there is no one, representing any group or any organization, in any aspect of American life, who does it with more brilliance and more decency, and who deserves our respect more than that remarkable human being, Hyman Bookbinder.

DANIEL J. BOORSTIN

b. October 1, 1914
Historian; educator; author

Daniel Boorstin, a major American historian with a serious interest in technology and its promises, is the 12th librarian of Congress. But perhaps more significantly, he is also the recipient of the most prestigious prizes for his works of history—the Bancroft Prize, the Francis Parkman Prize and the Pulitzer Prize for History.

Daniel Boorstin was born in Atlanta, Georgia to Samuel Aaron, a lawyer and Dora (Olsan) Boorstin, Russian immigrants. When Boorstin was 2 years old, his family moved to Tulsa, Oklahoma, where he graduated from Central High School in 1930. He attended Harvard University, where he studied English history and literature under the famed scholar F. O. Matthiessen. His senior essay won the Bowdoin award when he graduated in 1934.

Upon graduation, Boorstin won a Rhodes scholarship and studied at Oxford. He worked in political science with the highly esteemed Harold Laski and won the Jenkins prize and the Younger award for academic excellence at Oxford. He continued his studies in England at the Inner Temple in London and received high honors when he completed his B.A. degree in jurisprudence in 1936 and a Bachelor of Civil Law degree in 1937. While enrolled as a student at the Inner Temple, he was admitted to the bar in Great Britain in 1937, and was one of the first Americans to qualify to practice law in England. In 1940 he became a Doctor of Juridical Science.

From 1938 to 1942 Boorstin was a tutor in American literature and history at Harvard University and Radcliffe College. In 1942, after acceptance into the Massachusetts bar and rejection for military service because of medical reasons, Boorstin served for a short time in the Lend-Lease Administration in Washington, D.C.

Convinced that he was unsuited for government work, Boorstin left Washington and taught for two years (1942-44) at Swarthmore College. In 1944 he joined the faculty of the University of Chicago. There he taught political science in an interdisciplinary program. He became an associate professor of American history in the university's graduate program in 1949 and was promoted to full professor in 1956. In 1968 Boorstin was appointed Preston and Sterling Morton Distinguished Service Professor of American History, the highest award the University could bestow on a faculty member. The following year he was named Director of the National Museum of History and Technology of the Smithsonian Institution, a role he held until 1973, when he became Senior Historian. In that job he was advisor on all Smithsonian projects. Two years later he assumed his role at the Library of Congress. He was the museum's director from 1969 to 1973 and in 1973 was appointed the institution's senior historian. In 1975 Boorstin became the librarian of Congress, a position he currently holds.

Boorstin's first book, *The Mysterious Science of the Law* (Cambridge, Mass., 1941) was an exploration of the philosophical and historical basis of the work of the English philosopher Sir William Blackstone. His major work is a three-part opus, *The Americans,* for which he was awarded the Bancroft Prize. In the first part, *The Colonial Experience* (New York, 1958), Boorstin examines four settlement experiments: the Puritans in Massachusetts, the settlers in Georgia, the Quakers in Pennsylvania and the planters in Virginia. He concludes that the communities that succeeded were those that abandoned ideology for pragmatic responses to pressures presented by the environment. He continues this anti-ideological bent through *The National Experience* (New York, 1965), which won the Parkman Prize, and *The Democratic Experience* (New York, 1973), which brought him the Pulitzer Prize. He sings the praises of those whom he sees as the builders of America, the doers. He believes that the people who shaped the country were those who had "a love affair with their illusions." He concluded, however, that technology was homogenizing America.

Boorstin is a ground-breaking social historian, less interested in the politics of the times than in an integration of the economics, culture, politics and changing physical environment. He stands with a small group of historians trying to preserve traditional cornerstones.

Often likened to Edmund Burke, Boorstin has been called the "historian of goods and services."

For further information:
Boorstin, Daniel J. *The Decline of Radicalism.* New York, 1969.
———. *Democracy and Its Discontents.* New York, 1974.
———. *The Exploring Spirit: America and the World, Then and Now.* New York, 1976.
———. *The Genius of American Politics.* Chicago, 1953.
———. *The Lost World of Thomas Jefferson.* New York, 1948.
Boorstin, Daniel J., ed. *An American Primer.* Chicago, 1966.
———. *A Lady's Life in the Rocky Mountains.* Norman, Oklahoma, 1960.
———. *The Republic of Technology.* New York, 1978.

VICTOR BORGE
b. January 3, 1909
Entertainer

Victor Borge, often dubbed the "unmelancholy Dane," is credited with creating a unique brand of solo musical comedy combining an inimitable skill at playing piano with astutely selected satirical (or just plain farcical) commentary. He is one of the most successful and original performers of the genre—perhaps the only one—and has been a regular feature of the American cultural scene since he emigrated to the United States in 1940 to escape the threat of the Nazis.

Borge Rosenbaum was born in Copenhagen, Denmark to Bernhard, who was first violinist with the Danish Royal Opera Orchestra, and Frederika (Lichtinger) Rosenbaum, a pianist. With such extensive musical exposure, it was natural for Borge to study music, and after beginning with the violin, he switched at age 5 to the more comfortable piano. At age 9 he entered the Copenhagen Conservatory on scholarship and made his professional concert debut when he was 13 (although at least one account places it five years earlier).

Borge began concertizing extensively in Denmark and then throughout Scandinavia. But along with his playing, he began to add commentary, which soon became an essential component of his performances. A natural comic, he made his professional comedy debut in 1932 and soon developed a lucrative club career. He turned much of his commentary-with-music toward political targets, most notably Adolf Hitler.

Throughout the 1930s Borge became involved in stage, film and radio as well as music and writing and thus was known as the "Danish Noel Coward." But toward the end of the decade, it became clear to him that the Danish Jewish community could be in serious trouble—and Borge, who had earned prominent billing on the Nazi blacklist, more than most. In 1940 he managed to catch a ship from Finland and arrived in the United States. He was "penniless and unable to speak English," although he had developed contacts with Americans in the performing arts as a result of his renown in Scandinavia. He was naturalized in 1948.

Having taught himself English by watching movies, Borge secured a contract with the *Kraft Music Hall* radio program in late 1941 and remained for 54 consecutive weeks. He soon developed the same act for American audiences that he had had in Denmark, spoofing the mannerisms of serious classical performers, improvising themes from well-known musical works, perhaps beginning a waltz by Chopin and, without changing a beat, turning the piece into a Mozart minuet.

Yet Borge's musical integrity has always been on a high level, and he has guest-conducted such symphony orchestras as the Amsterdam Concertgebouw, the New York Philharmonic, the London Philharmonic and others.

In 1953 he made his Broadway debut in a one-man show, *Comedy in Music,* at the Golden Theater. A smash hit, it ran for 849 performances. He has since returned to Broadway several times and performed frequently on television as a guest star on regular shows or on specials of his own.

Borge has been knighted by the Danish, Swedish, Norwegian and Finnish governments and is a member of the President's U.S. Holocaust Council. He is also co-founder and national chairman of Thanks to Scandinavia, an organization created in 1963 to provide scholarships for Scandinavians to study in the United States and to honor the role played by Scandinavians who gave refuge to Jews during the Holocaust.

In 1971 Borge coauthored with Robert Sherman *My Favorite Intermissions* (New York), a collection of anecdotes opening with an "Overture," ending with an "Underture," and in between wittily describing the achievements and antics of the greatest operatic and symphony composers.

EUGENE B. BOROWITZ

b. February 20, 1924
Rabbi; theologian; teacher

The subtitle of *Sh'ma,* the magazine Rabbi Eugene B. Borowitz founded in 1970, is a "journal of Jewish responsibility." That slogan summarizes Borowitz's work

as a Reform rabbi and theologian, author and teacher since his ordination by Hebrew Union College-Jewish Institute of Religion in 1948.

Eugene Borowitz was born in New York City, the son of Benjamin, a garment factory superintendent, and Mollie (Schafranik) Borowitz. He earned a B.A. degree from Ohio State University in 1945 and a Bachelor of Hebrew Literature from Hebrew Union College-Jewish Institute of Religion in 1945. He received a master's degree and doctorate in Hebrew literature from HUC-JIR in 1948 and 1952, respectively, and a Ph.D. in education from Teachers College, Columbia University, in 1958.

Borowitz served as assistant rabbi for Shaare Emeth Congregation in St. Louis (1948–50); as a U.S. Navy chaplain (1951–53); and as rabbi of the Community Synagogue, Port Washington, New York (1951–53).

But it is as a teacher and author that Borowitz is most widely known. From 1957 to 1962 he was the Union of American Hebrew Congregations' national director of education for the Reform movement. Since 1962 he has been professor of education and Jewish religious thought at HUC-JIR's New York City campus and has been visiting professor at Temple University, Princeton, Columbia University, Woodstock College (a Jesuit school of theology in New York) and the Jewish Theological Seminary.

A prolific author, Borowitz has written 9 books and has contributed nearly 100 articles to religious and secular journals and anthologies, writing on theology, Jewish ethics, the Jewish legal process, religious education, social responsibility and the tension between the modern world and tradition.

Borowitz's work in Jewish theology attempts to integrate the concepts and practice of personal autonomy into an understanding of God's covenant with humanity in general and with the people in particular. He is a major contemporary Jewish theologian, attempting to explicate the idea that a covenantal partnership between God and Israel contains obligations on both sides of the contract.

He is a political liberal, frequently speaking out on social issues and on the relationship between Diaspora Jews and Israel, and was significantly involved in the now-defunct liberal Jewish group "Breira," the Hebrew word for "alternative."

In *A New Jewish Theology in the Making* (Philadelphia, 1968), Borowitz summarizes the major Jewish theological positions of the contemporary era and seriously looks at conventional theology and its implications for contemporary Jewish practice.

The Mask Jews Wear (New York, 1973), Borowitz's

most popularly oriented book, and winner of the 1974 Jewish Book Award in the area of Jewish thought, questions the manner in which American Jews have dealt with American society—dealing with assimilation, self-hatred, the concept of Jewish peoplehood and the relationship of the American Jew with Jewish tradition. We wear a series of masks that help us be comfortable as Americans, he says, but these masks prevent us from understanding our essential Jewishness.

Reform Judaism Today (New York, 1978) is a three-volume statement of Reform Jewish ideas and practice. Based partly on the statement "Reform Judaism, a Centenary Perspective," a major manifesto of Reform Jewish principles published in 1976 by a Central Conference of American Rabbis committee for which Borowitz served as chairman and a principal author, the work attempts to define the current position of the Reform Jewish movement. Borowitz presents the alternatives in the movement, a case for covenantal theology and supports Reform Judaism's embrace of Zionism and a return to more meaningful Jewish practice. He supports the current trend toward the observance of the traditional Jewish rituals as a positive component of what makes Jews Jewish.

Borowitz frequently participates in national and international Jewish and non-Jewish religious gatherings. He served as the first Jewish president of the American Theological Society and has been chairman of the Hebrew Union College faculty, president of the Jewish Book Council and vice president of the Religious Education Association of America.

But it is as editor of *Sh'ma* that Borowitz has become influential among the American Jewish community at large. The pamphlet-sized magazine, published every two weeks from September through May, serves as a forum on social ethics and liberalism in Jewish affairs. Issues of *Sh'ma* are theme-oriented and contain short—often diverse—articles from theologians, Jewish communal workers, rabbis and involved laypersons on topics as varied as Israel-Diaspora relations, energy policy, current trends in the Jewish community, ecumenical relations, Jewish feminism, ritual and even the effect on Jews should Israel no longer exist.

For further information:

Borowitz, Eugene B. *Choosing a Sex Ethic.* New York: 1969.
———. *Contemporary Christologies: A Jewish Response.* Ramsey, N.J.: 1980.
———. *How Can a Jew Speak of Faith Today?* Philadelphia: 1969.
———. *A Layman's Introduction to Religious Existentialism.* Philadelphia: 1965.
———. *Modern Theories of Judaism.* New York: 1981.
———. *Understanding Judaism.* New York: 1979.

RUDY BOSCHWITZ

b. November 7, 1930
U.S. senator; businessman

When Rudy Boschwitz won the U.S. Senate seat from Minnesota in 1978, the novelty was not so much that he was a Jew but that he was a Republican. To win, the millionaire businessman-turned-politician combined the same astute sense of timing, strategy—and humor—to break the strong Farmer-Labor-Democratic hold in Minnesota that he had also used to build his huge and successful business. In the Senate he has been an aggressive advocate of the largely agricultural interests of his home state and of American Jews and Israel.

Rudy Boschwitz was born in Berlin to Ely, a stockbroker, and Lucy (Dawidawicz) Boschwitz. In 1935, sensing the threat posed by the ascendancy of Adolf Hitler, the family emigrated to the United States and settled in New Rochelle. Boschwitz attended Johns Hopkins University in Baltimore from 1946 to 1948 and New York University, where he received a B.S. degree in business in 1950 and a Bachelor of Laws in 1952. After serving in the Army for two years, he practiced law for another two and then in 1956 moved to Wisconsin, where he joined his brother's plywood business. Seven years later he moved to Minnesota, where he founded a retail store for do-it-yourself homeowners, stocking paneling, lumber and assorted building items, called Plywood Minnesota. It was one of the first of its kind and became a huge success. By the time Boschwitz entered public office, Plywood Minnesota had 63 franchises throughout the Midwest, and the young businessman was a multimillionaire and public figure, known because of television advertisements in which he plugged such deliberately ridiculous slogans as "Keep Bullfighting Out of Minnesota" and "Unite the Twin Cities—Fill in the Mississippi."

Boschwitz's humorous campaign ploys were part of an astute publicity strategy as he became increasingly active in statewide Republican politics. From 1968 to 1978 he was a delegate to the Minnesota Republican Convention, and in 1972 and 1976 he represented Minnesota at the Republican National Convention. In 1978 Boschwitz seized the opportunity to run for office—his first bid—against Wendell Anderson, the former governor of Minnesota. Anderson had maneuvered himself to the Senate nearly two years earlier (when then-Senator Walter Mondale became vice president) by resigning from the state seat and arranging with his successor to appoint him as Mondale's replacement. Anderson's move sat poorly with Minnesota voters, and the heavily Democratic state voted overwhelmingly for Boschwitz, as much for the latter's own campaign as in protest against the former's indiscreet use of political power.

Once in the Senate, Boschwitz joined the Foreign Relations; Budget; and Agriculture, Nutrition and Forestry committees. He also became a member of the Select Committee on Small Business—an area perfectly suited to his expertise. He has always been a fiercely independent Republican, generally liberal on social issues, conservative on fiscal ones. He advocated the Reagan policy of reduced governmental bureaucracy and endorsed the concept of the Kemp-Roth proposal for massive across-the-board tax cuts.

As a Jew, Boschwitz belongs to a new breed of Jewish politician in the Senate—including Warren Rudman (New Hampshire), Edward Zorinsky (Nebraska), Carl Levin (Michigan) and others—who were voted in not because they had heavily Jewish constituencies in their home states, but on other merits. Nonetheless, he has been one of Israel's most vocal advocates in the Senate, and in June 1981, after the Israeli air force bombed the Osirak nuclear reactor near Baghdad, Iraq, Boschwitz counted himself among the supporters of the controversial attack, remarking that "they [the Israelis] probably did us a favor." In 1981 he voted against the sale of AWACS and other arms to Saudi Arabia.

Although he is a Reform Jew, Boschwitz has been a prominent contributor to the ultra-Orthodox Lubavitch House in St. Paul, an activity attributed to his interest in preserving and expanding Jewish cultural and spiritual life in America. He has also been state chairperson of the Minneapolis Jewish Fund and is active in other state organizations, including the Minnesota Kidney Foundation, the Minnesota Mental Health Association and the American Cancer Society.

LEON BOTSTEIN

b. December 14, 1946
Educator; college president

Leon Botstein, who rose to prominence at age 23, when he was named president of the small, experimental —and then-failing—Franconia (New Hampshire) College, has since become one of America's leaders and innovators in higher education. A Harvard-trained historian and a musician, Botstein has also published widely in professional journals and popular magazines, written music criticism and conducted several small orchestras in New England.

Leon Botstein was born in Zurich, Switzerland to Charles and Anne (Wyszewianski) Botstein. Both parents were physicians who had been refugees from Poland. Raised in New York City, he attended the selective public High School of Music and Art, graduating in 1963, and the University of Chicago, from which he received a B.A. degree in 1967 with special honors, which included a Danforth Fellowship, a Woodrow Wilson Fellowship and the Howell Murray Award granted by the University. In 1968 he received an M.A. degree in history from Harvard University and has pursued doctoral studies there in 19th-century social history.

From 1968 to 1969 Botstein was both a Harvard College tutor and a university teaching fellow. He also lectured in history for a semester at Boston University. In 1969-70 was a special assistant to the president of the New York City Board of Education.

In 1970, when it became known that Franconia College was seeking a president, Botstein (whose wife was a daughter of a Franconia trustee) applied for and got the job. By then, Franconia, which had been founded as a kind of alternative, experimental school in the early 1960s, had had three presidents, five business managers, four admissions directors and a history of drug raids and friction with the surrounding community. Botstein seized the opportunity to use Franconia as "an educational laboratory for developing tools and techniques with far greater resources" than were immediately available and succeeded within three years in strengthening the academic curriculum, leading to accreditation, and in raising enough money to build new dormitories, a student union and a library. The public was invited to share in campus events and to use the library. Enrollment, which had declined, grew significantly.

After five years, Botstein left Franconia to take over Bard College in Annandale-on-Hudson in upstate New York. Like Franconia, a small, experimental college, but with a far older tradition, Bard provided Botstein similar opportunities for innovation. But by now the trend was toward a return to traditional modes of education, and one of Botstein's singular moves at Bard was to institute a compulsory and rigorous writing program for incoming freshmen prior to the beginning of the semester. He also required that "scientific literacy" be an integral component of the undergraduate program, but he also suggested in an article in *Harper's* magazine, "A Proper Education" (September 1979), that undergraduate training programs for prospective doctors and lawyers include grounding in "the philosophical, historical and cultural implications of those professions, even if it delays degree attainment."

Since 1979, in addition to his Bard post, Botstein has been president of Simon's Rock Early College in Great Barrington, Massachusetts, an experimental school offering a college-level program to pre-college age teen-agers.

For further information:
Botstein, Leon. "Are You Better Off at Harvard?" *The New York Times Magazine*, April 17, 1977.
————. "Children of the Lonely Crowd." *Change*, May 1978.
————. "Hannah Arendt: The Jewish Question." *The New Republic*, October 21, 1978.
————. "A Proper Education." *Harper's*, September 1979.
————. *Diploma Madness: Higher Education and the American Intellectual in Crisis.* New York: 1982.

BALFOUR BRICKNER

b. November 18, 1926
Rabbi

Rabbi Balfour Brickner, spiritual leader at New York City's Stephen Wise Free Synagogue since 1980, has devoted his career as a social activist to furthering civil rights for all people and particularly to supporting liberal and humane causes within the Jewish community. A prolific writer and a forceful speaker, he has traveled widely within the United States and abroad to speak on behalf of such causes as freedom of choice in abortion, the need for interaction with Christian organizations and the teaching of Judaism to non-Jewish students and teachers.

Balfour Brickner was born in Cleveland, Ohio to Rabbi Barnett and Rebecca (Aaronson) Brickner. He served in the Navy between 1943 and 1946 and graduated from the University of Cincinnati in 1948 with a B.A. degree in philosophy. He then followed his father into the Reform rabbinate after ordination by Hebrew Union College-Jewish Institute of Religion in 1952. Brickner served as rabbi to Temple Sinai in Washington, D.C. between 1952 and 1961. Between 1957 and 1961 he was the Jewish Chautauqua Society resident lecturer at American University in Washington. Rabbi Brickner hosted a weekly radio program, *Adventure in Judaism,* which won the Ohio State Award for outstanding religious broadcasts in 1965, 1966, 1967 and again in 1968. In 1968 it also won the Religious Heritage

Foundation award. He is co-chair of the Martin Steinberg Center of the American Jewish Congress. In 1980 he returned to the pulpit as rabbi at the Stephen Wise Free Synagogue.

As co-director of the National Commission on Social Action of the Union of American Hebrew Congregations, a position he held between 1961 and 1978, Brickner took part in many of the progressive movements of the day, including the civil rights movement. He points out, for example, that during his travels through the American South from 1961 to 1964, he "enjoyed the hospitality of the region's finest jails" as he was actively involved in the movement to secure civil rights for American blacks. In addition, he was a founder of Clergy and Laity Concerned about Vietnam and visited Saigon as a member of a fact-finding mission organized by the Fellowship of Reconciliation. He wrote the pamphlet "Keeping Mercy for Thousands," a study guide on amnesty for draft resisters. In recent years he has worked actively for women's rights, serving on the Executive Board of the National Association for the Repeal of Abortion Laws (NARAL) and helping to found Religious Leaders for a Free Choice.

Brickner was also past national director of the Department of Interreligious Affairs of the UAHC from 1961–1980. He is also a member of the steering committee of the International Jewish Committee for Interreligious Consultation, "an agency whose purpose is to meet periodically with representatives of the World Council of Churches and the Vatican's Committee on Catholic-Jewish Relations for the purpose of joint consultation and action." He also co-directed an annual seminar in Israel for Christian scholars. He is the author of *An Interreligious Guide to Passover and Easter* (New York, 1968) and a study guide entitled *Jesus Christ Superstar* (New York, 1978).

A supporter of Israel, Brickner nevertheless regards creative Jewish life in the Diaspora as vital. In an article ("Aliyah: Do We Really Mean It?" *Dialogue*, Summer 1980), he wrote, "I refuse to think of myself as a Crypto-Israeli—a person living an ersatz or pseudo Jewish life here in Galut. . . . I do not believe I am living in exile." He concludes, "There is an American Jewish community to be built and preserved alongside of Israel. That too is a commitment and a promise." He opposes Israel's policies of expansion into lands occupied by Palestinians and is a member of American Friends of Peace Now, an anti-expansionist Israeli organization. He also publicly supported Breira (Hebrew for "alternative"), a group that sought to take much the same position in the United States in the late 1970s.

In "Am I Still My Brother's Keeper?" (*Present Tense,*

Summer 1979), Rabbi Brickner reaffirmed his commitment to liberalism. "It is in the Jewish self-interest to see conservative forces curbed," he writes. "Historically when a society turns right, things go wrong for Jews." And he concludes, "Our nation is at a real crossroads. Either our institutions, religious and non-religious return to and rehabilitate the rational, the thoughtful prophetic demand to 'reason together' and to 'pursue justice' or we could find ourselves drawn back into a dark age of obscurantism and regressive social tyranny." For this reason Brickner is especially wary of the Moral Majority, a right-wing Christian movement of the 1980s, which claims to support Israel but which espouses causes that he believes are potentially very damaging to Jews and other Americans. In succeeding years, he began to assume a leadership role as a Jewish liberal, in distinction to the many rabbis and prominent laypeople who had ceased stating their views publicly except on matters directly concerning Israel or Jewish life. In 1981, for example, Brickner's synagogue voted to oppose the reinstatement of the draft and to support instead, a volunteer military and if necessary, the right of conscientious objection for young Jewish males who will not bear arms. In 1982, his synagogue played host to nine other reform synagogues in a mass meeting—the first of its kind among religious Jews—re-emphasizing Jewish objections to the nuclear arms race. The Jewish community, said Brickner, "will not remain silent."

For further information
Brickner, Balfour and Albert Vospan. *Searching the Prophets for Values.* New York: 1981.

DAVID BRODER

b. September 11, 1929
Journalist

Pulitzer Prize-winning journalist and columnist David Broder is one of the most widely read, influential and respected political commentators on the contemporary scene. His column, which appears in more than 300 newspapers throughout the nation, reflects his obsession with finding the story behind the story and detecting future trends.

David Broder was born in Chicago Heights, Illinois, the son of Albert, a dentist, and Nina (Salzar) Broder. He earned his B.A. degree at the University of Chicago in 1947 and an M.A. degree in 1951 from the same school. After graduating he served in the Army for two years, and then in 1953 he found his first newspaper job on the *Daily Pentagraph* in Bloomington, Illinois. From 1955 until 1960 he worked for the *Congressional Quarterly* in Washington, D.C. Broder then spent five years as a reporter for the *Washington Star* and was hired in 1966 by *The New York Times'* Washington bureau. That same year he left for the *Washington Post*, where he has since been a reporter, associate editor and now regular columnist.

A pragmatic liberal, Broder is best-known for the incisive manner in which he tries to determine the shape of things to come. Duke University political scientist James David Barber wrote that the reason Broder "is so highly valued among his colleagues in the press" is essentially because "he is a natural-born and thoroughly cultivated reporter, a diligent picker through the vagaries of real life in search of patterns, a highly curious and indefatigable inquirer."

Broder's method is that of a scholar, although he is capable of angry passion, as when he complained bitterly in 1975 about the public's treatment of Vietnam combat veterans. He is also skeptical about the viability of American political institutions, as evidenced in his book *The Party's Over: The Failure of Politics in America* (New York, 1972), a penetrating look into the state of political life before Watergate. Above all, his columns and writings are the reflections of his continuous and intense effort to comprehend political life. In *Changing of the Guard: Power and Leadership in America* (New York, 1980), Broder detected a major change underway "as great as, if not greater than, any in history." The change he predicted was the coming of new people to authority—people of all political persuasions and of every race and ethnic group—younger generations whose common experiences included civil rights marches, Vietnam and Watergate rather than Munich, World War II and Korea. Broder generally likes and respects the young and is optimistic about the future. "It was surely no mistake to take to the streets to protest segregation. If the Vietnam War was not immoral, as they claimed, it was surely unwise and the protests they organized against it helped push American politics back toward sanity." He went on to predict that the coming 20 years will involve "rehabilitating and repair" instead of negativism and cynicism.

In addition to his career in journalism, Broder has continued his education in the field of political science. He was a fellow at the Institute of Politics at the John F. Kennedy School of Government of Harvard University from 1969 to 1970. In 1973 he divided his time between Yale University and the Indiana University as a Poynter fellow. He is also a fellow of the Institute of for Policy Science and Public Affairs at Duke University.

Broder has received considerable recognition for his accomplishments as a journalist, winning the American Newspaper Guild awards for excellence in 1961, 1973 and 1974 and the Pulitzer Prize for his commentaries on American politics in 1973.

For further information:
Broder, David, and Hess, Stephen. *The Republican Establishment*. New York: 1967.

EDGAR BRONFMAN

b. June 20, 1929
Industrialist

In the tradition of the Rothschild and Montefiore families, Edgar Bronfman has coupled great wealth and exceptional business acumen with an active concern for and involvement with the Jewish community. President of Distillers Corporation, which owns the giant Joseph E. Seagram and Sons, the largest distillery in the world, Bronfman is also president of the influential World Jewish Congress.

Edgar Miles Bronfman was born in Montreal, Canada. His parents, Samuel (a liquor businessman) and Saidye (Rosner) Bronfman, were descendants of immigrants from Bessarabia, Russia. In his youth, Edgar often worked at odd jobs to earn extra money. He recalls that if he asked his father for money, he would have to explain why he needed it, but if he earned it on his own, he could use it as he liked with no questions asked.

Bronfman attended Trinity College School and, after three years at Williams College, graduated with honors from McGill University in Montreal with a B.A. degree in history in 1951. He considered careers as a rabbi, a lawyer and a Wall Street broker but ultimately joined the family business. Samuel Bronfman acquired Joseph E. Seagram and Sons in 1927 and founded Distillers Corporation in 1928. It grew during the prohibition period as it plied "rum row" between the United States and Canada. After prohibition was repealed, the company continued to grow, and by 1940 it was the largest distiller of spirits in the United States and eventually became, under the elder Bronfman, the world's largest distillery corporation.

The younger Bronfman was appointed director of the Canadian operations of Distillers Corporation in 1953. He soon departed for the United States, however, and became a naturalized American citizen in 1955. In 1957 he assumed control of the company's American interests and under his aegis a new corporate headquarters, the

Seagram Building designed by Mies van der Rohe, was built on Park Avenue in New York. He embarked on the most ambitious marketing program ever undertaken by a distiller of spirits and expanded the firm's holdings both in the United States and overseas. Following American drinking trends closely, he introduced bottled cocktails and began importing wines and liqueurs. The American subsidiary of Distillers Corporation grew to account for 86 percent of its total market. Meanwhile, Bronfman began to invest in Israeli orange groves and supermarkets in Canada, partly as a business venture and partly as philanthropy. By 1969 the Bronfmans were the largest landowners in Canada.

In 1967 Bronfman began to invest as well in the entertainment field. That year he gained control of MGM studios but was forced out in a bitter corporate fight in 1969. In 1971, when Bronfman's father died, he assumed complete control of the family firm. By the mid-1970s the corporation controlled at least 39 distilleries and 18 wineries around the world. It had become the largest importer of wines in the United States and manufactured at least 114 different brands of alcoholic beverages.

But the firm has moved beyond liquor, too. In 1981 Bronfman had Seagram sell Texas Pacific (a Texas oil firm his father had purchased in 1968 for $50 million in cash) to the Sun Company for $2.3 billion. In the deal, the liquor magnate's company kept non-American properties in his native country, a gas field in the Gulf of Thailand and other rights to offshore drilling and exploration near Spain and in the North Sea.

Bronfman has used his corporate power as a platform for his personal views on Israel. He has been sharply critical of Israel's settlement policies on the disputed West Bank. "There is disappointment in a country [Israel] which is less than what the original Zionists envisioned —an Israel which we wanted to think of as the embodiment of Jewish ideals: fairness, justice, wisdom," he wrote in the World Jewish Congress publication, *News and Views,* in 1979. During the war in Lebanon in June 1982 he said: "Out of this war Israel must finally face the Palestinian problem. . . . It must look for new openings to make peace with the Arabs rather than war on them."

In addition to his role at WJC, Bronfman is active in many other Jewish organizations. He has also been chairman of the American section of the World Jewish Congress and served on the executive committee of the American Jewish Congress, the American Jewish Committee, the economic development committee of the New York Federation of Jewish Philanthropies and the national committee of the Anti-Defamation League.

He is a member of the board of trustees of Mt. Sinai Hospital and Medical School in New York City, and in keeping with his deep interest in Israel, Bronfman is a director of the American Technion Society and a member of the executive board of the Weizmann Institute of Science in Rehovot, Israel.

MEL BROOKS
b. June 28, 1926
Comedian; actor; director

Mel Brooks has created a unique brand of comedy, which American audiences either love or despise. Drawing often on Jewish vaudeville tradition or on Jewish jokes, he creates scenarios that are zany and hysterical, often of questionable taste, and that combine parody with parodies of parodies to such an extreme that any connection with reality is not only somewhat remote but is often utterly lost. Only Brooks could get away with a Yiddish-speaking Indian (in his film *Blazing Saddles*) or direct the first silent movie *(Silent Movie)* since they were put in mothballs nearly 50 years ago.

Melvyn Kaminsky was born in the then largely Jewish Williamsburg section of Brooklyn. His father, Maximilian Kaminsky, a process server from Danzig, died suddenly of a kidney disease when Brooks was 2½ years old, leaving Brooks with a sense of loss that he readily admits persists in his adult life. His mother, Kate (Brookman) Kaminsky, a garment worker from Kiev, raised Brooks and his three older brothers. "My mother had this exuberant joy of living and she infected me with that," he once remarked. "She really was responsible for the growth of my imagination."

As the spoiled baby in the family, Brooks enjoyed clowning from an early age, making him a problem pupil at P.S. 19. After graduating from high school in 1943, he attended Brooklyn College for a year and then joined the Army. After his discharge in 1946 Brooks played the drums, a talent he had developed in high school, at nightclubs and resorts in the borscht belt—the Catskill Mountains resort hotels. It was during this time that he changed his name in order not to be confused with the well-known jazz trumpet player, Max Kaminsky. He worked for a while as the social director of Grossinger's in 1948 and got his first chance to do comedy when a regular comic at a small Catskills hotel became ill.

In 1949 Sid Caesar, an old friend, asked Brooks to write comic sketches for the television series *Broadway Revue*. A year later Caesar's *Your Show of Shows* featured Brooks as a writer and, occasionally, as a performer.

Your Show of Shows, now regarded by nostalgia buffs as a classic, ran for four years and was followed in 1954 by *Caesar's Hour.* Both shows were written by the same team: Carl Reiner, Imogene Coca, Mel Tolkin, Howie Morris and Mel Brooks. "We wrote things that made *us* laugh . . . not what we thought the audience would dig . . . what really collapsed us, knocked us down on the floor and made us spit and laugh so we couldn't breathe —that went into the script," Brooks said, addressing the American Film Institute in 1977.

In 1960 Brooks recorded the first of a series of hit records with Reiner and Mel Tolkin in which Brooks plays the part of a 2,000-year-old man with a Yiddish accent, who has seen everything but is impressed by nothing. According to Brooks, the reason for the success of his collaboration with Reiner and Tolkin is that they all share the same background, the second generation-Russian-Ukrainian-Jewish cultural heritage.

Brooks has worked on several Broadway shows, including *New Faces of 1952* and *Shinbone Alley.* He created and collaborated with Buck Henry on the writing of the long-running (1965–70) television spy spoof, *Get Smart,* starring Don Adams as the incompetent Agent 86.

Brooks's first film project, a cartoon short called *The Critic* (1963), and his first major feature film, *The Producers* (1968), a show business farce starring Zero Mostel as producer of a pro-Nazi play turned musical comedy, won him Academy Awards. His second major film, *The Twelve Chairs* (1970), a comedy about greed in Communist Russia, and then *Blazing Saddles* (1974), a satire of Hollywood westerns, established Brooks as a cult-hero to many, especially to younger audiences. In a review of *Blazing Saddles,* a *New York Times* critic wrote that Brooks "specializes in the humor of affront—affront to civilized sensibilities, good taste and common sense." And comedy writer Mel Tolkin once told an interviewer, "Half of Mel's creativity comes out of fear and anger. He doesn't perform, he screams."

Over the years Brooks has developed a mini-"repertory company" of actors who regularly appear in his films. They include Madeleine Kahn, Gene Wilder, Marty Feldman, Harvey Korman and Dom DeLuise. Other films by Brooks that capture his manic humor are *Young Frankenstein* (1974), a parody of 1930s horror movies; *Silent Movie* (1976), a string of silent gags linked with captions; *High Anxiety* (1977), a spoof of Hitchcock thrillers; and *History of the World, Part I* (1981), in which Brooks accomplishes in a two-hour romp what scientists claim took billions of years to evolve.

A rarely seen serious side of Brooks is as the producer of the film *The Elephant Man* (1980). Starring

John Hurt and featuring Brooks's wife, actress Anne Bancroft, the award-winning film tells the true story of John Merrick, a 19th-century carnival "freak" in England who is ostracized by everyone except a doctor who perceives Merrick's humanity beneath his deformity.

ART BUCHWALD

b. October 20, 1925
Social and political satirist

Art Buchwald is one of the keenest and funniest of contemporary political satirists. His nationally syndicated column has become something of an institution and is read regularly by many government officials and millions of Americans. He seems to have an unerring knack for pointing out the absurd and the ridiculous in American life.

Buchwald was born in Mount Vernon, New York to Joseph and Helen (Kleinberger) Buchwald, who were involved in clothing manufacturing. His mother died soon after he was born, and until his father could care for him and his three sisters, he lived in the Hebrew Orphan Asylum in New York and in five foster homes. "I think that's where all the humor comes from—a defense from the hostility," he says. When he was 16 he returned to live with his father. Buchwald grew up in Queens and attended P.S. 35, Jamaica High School and Forest Hills High School. However, he never graduated from high school. In 1942, on his 17th birthday, Buchwald enlisted in the U.S. Marine Corps. He was assigned to the 4th Marine Air Wing and spent most of his three-year service in the Pacific theater, where he edited the base newspaper at Eniwetok. He also did public relations for Special Services.

After his discharge in 1945, Buchwald attended the University of Southern California. On campus, he edited the humor magazine, wrote a column for *The Daily Trojan* and produced a variety show. In 1948 he left for Paris, where he became the French stringer for *Variety*, the Hollywood trade paper, for $8 a week, but as he said, he "got to go everywhere."

In 1949 he sold a column he had been experimenting with, which contained offbeat information about Parisian night life, to the entertainment editor of the European edition of *The New York Herald-Tribune*. Called *Paris After Dark,* it became a regular feature in the newspaper. By 1951 the column had become mainly interviews with celebrities living in Paris. The next year the column began appearing in the United States, first under the title *Europe's Lighter Side* and then *Art Buchwald in Paris.*

Buchwald published his first book, *Paris After Dark* (New York), which is based on the columns, in 1950. Since then he has published 20 volumes, primarily collections of his columns. In 1958 he published his only novel. Called *A Gift from the Boys* (New York), it is the tale of a mob leader who is deported to Sicily.

In the mid-1950s Buchwald returned to the United States and set his comic sights on Washington. His column was syndicated nationally by *The Los Angeles Times* syndicate and now appears internationally. Buchwald is widely respected for his fairness in skewering men in power with good-natured but sharp-pronged humor. Centered in Washington, he is well aware of their frailties, their lack of knowledge and their blunders, characteristics too often hidden from public view by public relations specialists and friendly journalists. Along the way he has poked fun at every administration and at many in the nation's capital, from congressmen to the Pentagon's generals. "I thank Ronald Reagan, James Watt, Al Haig and all the others in Washington who made this possible," he said in 1982 after receiving the Pulitzer Prize for distinguished commentary. "I used to be funny," he continued, "but everything is so wild now that all I'm doing is reporting. I mean look at the Falkland Islands. . . . I should have made that up."

A typical example of his humor is his fantasy about the FBI so totally infiltrating the U.S. Communist Party that they are its only members, and the party is therefore being funded by the government. Of course, with trained FBI agents as members, the party becomes much more efficient in its operations. Another mocked—always with humor, yet seriously—Senator Barry Goldwater's hawkish recommendations for Vietnam in 1964. And still another depicted President Lyndon B. Johnson as a gunfighter seeking a military solution to Southeast Asia. Nothing or no one—from Richard Nixon to Yasir Arafat—is exempt from Buchwald's bite.

Buchwald also won the French Grand Prix de la Humor in 1959. Lately he has been complaining that it is much harder to write political satire. Politicians, he says, are too funny in their own right.

JOSEPH BULOFF

b. December 6, 1907
Actor; director

Joseph Buloff, who has produced, directed and acted in more than 200 plays, is a legend in both the English- and Yiddish-speaking theater world. He won the 1973 "Obie" award as best actor for his role in the Yiddish play *Hard to Be a Jew* and has won acclaim for many English-speaking parts, including Pincus Pine on the television program *The Goldbergs* and the peddler Ali Haakim in the Broadway show *Oklahoma* (1943).

Joseph Buloff was born to Benjamin, a furrier, and Sarah (Rotlast) Buloff in Vilna, Lithuania. He was separated at 14 from his family during World War I, when the Russian army came marching through his village. His father was killed in the war. He fought during the war for the German, Polish, Lithuanian, and Red and White Russian armies—whoever gave him a gun and fed him.

In 1918 he joined the Vilna Troupe, a Yiddish company that toured Poland and with which he worked for a decade and became a star. "We did Moliere as no French troupe ever did. We worked off each other like acrobats. . . There is a certain magic that happens when actors work together for years," he told the *New York Post*. "It was a great event in Yiddish. No, the greatest," he repeated years afterward. The Vilna Troupe, he has stated, was the model for the famed Moscow Yiddish Theater and the Habima in Tel Aviv.

In 1928 Buloff went to the United States and joined the Chicago People's Institute as a director and teacher of acting. Two years later he joined Yiddish Art Theater of New York and made his New York City debut as Sam Stern in *Don't Look Now* (1936). He appeared in several other Broadway productions, including *To Quito and Back* (1937), *The Man from Cairo* (1938), *Morning Star* (1940) and *Spring Again* (1941), before attracting widespread attention in the popular musical *Oklahoma* (1943), playing Ali Haakim for four years in the original Broadway production.

Buloff's comic versatility and gift for mimicry have enabled him to break down the barriers of language and appeal to the audience's sense of humanity, regardless of the language in which the play is performed. "I do a play in English and make some money and then I do a play in Yiddish and lose it," Buloff once told a *New York Post* reporter. "But I always had a sentiment for the Yiddish language and the culture; it was what I was raised in as a child and all that remains of my family besides the memory of it."

Among his many successes are *The Fifth Season*, a 1975 Yiddish musical comedy about the garment center, in which he plays Max Pincus, the gentle and hopelessly out-of-date senior partner in a dress firm, who dances, shrugs and, in a drunk scene, trips all over himself. Buloff has also appeared in the Yiddish version of *Death of a Salesman* (1949), in which he played Willy Loman in the Buenos Aires, Brooklyn and Israeli productions.

In 1940 Buloff made his motion picture debut in *Let's Make Music* and has since appeared in *They Met in Argentina* (1941), *To the Victor* (1948), *Somebody Up There Likes Me* (1956), *Silk Stockings* (1957) and *Reds* (1981). He has also appeared on various television programs, including *Ben Casey* and *The Untouchables*. Buloff has directed many plays, including *Mrs. McThing* (1952), and has performed in plays all over the world.

Buloff and his wife Luba Kadison, a Yiddish stage actress who also came from Vilna, created while yet in Europe *The Chekhov Sketchbook*, three one-act plays based on the Russian writer's short stories. Buloff played the lead in each play, which premiered while they were in Russia. The show has been performed on many occasions over the years, most recently in 1980. In the one-act play *The Music Shop*, a critic wrote that Buloff "plays his comic talents like a virtuoso" as he "raises exasperation to an art."

ARTHUR BURNS

b. April 27, 1904
Economist

Arthur Burns has been a major formulator of American economic policies since the mid-1930s. Active on the federal level since the days of Franklin Delano Roosevelt's New Deal, he has remained a steady and influential —and mostly conservative—voice throughout changes of administrations. As chairman of the Federal Reserve Board from 1970 to 1978, Burns helped stave off several major financial crises that directly threatened the well-being of the United States.

Arthur Frank Burnseig was born in Stanislau, Austria (now in the Ukrainian Soviet Socialist Republic), to Nathan, a house painter, and Sarah (Juran) Burnseig. His surname was shortened when the family immigrated to the United States in 1910. The Burns family settled in Bayonne, New Jersey. After graduating from Bayonne High School in 1921, Burns attended Columbia University. He earned his way through college with a collection of odd jobs—waiter, salesman, post office clerk, seaman—and was graduated Phi Beta Kappa in 1925, with both A.B. and A.M. degrees in economics. In 1934 he was awarded his Ph.D. by Columbia.

In 1927 Burns joined the faculty at Rutgers University in New Jersey. He remained there until he returned to Columbia as a visiting professor in 1941. He was named a full professor three years later.

Besides teaching and government service, Burns is known for his affiliation since 1930 with the National

Bureau of Economic Research, an organization largely devoted to statistical research in the social sciences. Under its sponsorship, he published his first book, *Production Trends in the United States Since 1870* (New York, 1934).

Burns was chief statistician for the Railway Emergency Board in 1941. In the years following he was a consultant to various government bodies. In 1953 President Eisenhower named him chairman of the Council of Economic Advisers, a post he held until 1956. When President Nixon appointed him in 1970 to head the Federal Reserve Board, Burns was serving as a counselor to the president with cabinet rank and had a long tradition of government service behind him.

An expert on business cycles, Burns has had the chance to test his theories as few professors have. Both President Eisenhower, after Korea, and President Nixon, after Vietnam, were faced with the difficulties of reorienting economic resources to peacetime goals.

For the eight years he served as FRB chairman, Burns saw inflation as the root of American economic problems. "I cannot stress too strongly the importance of being cautious in launching new federal programs with potentially large budgetary impact," he told the Senate Banking Committee in 1976. In 1970 Burns used his Federal Reserve power to prevent monetary panic when Penn Central went bankrupt by assuring federal loan support. He did the same in 1975 when New York City was on the brink of fiscal disaster.

Burns' policies reflect what in the early 1980s has been called "Reaganomics." He supports lower corporate taxes as a means of generating productivity and therefore employment and investment. He advocates cuts in inflationary federal spending programs, and he proposed a controversial salary differential for teenagers seeking jobs.

The conservative philosophy sometimes caused rifts with President Nixon and even more so with President Carter, who named G. William Miller to succeed him as chairman in 1978. Burns, noting that the continued presence of a former chairman on the board might create tension, resigned in 1978 from the remainder of his term as a governor, which would otherwise have expired in 1984. In 1981 he was named United States ambassador to West Germany.

For further information:
Burns, Arthur F. *Business Cycle in a Changing World.* New York: 1967.
————. *Frontiers of Economic Knowledge.* New York: 1975.
————. *Reflections of an Economic Policy Maker: Speeches and Congressional Statements.* Washington: 1978.

Burns, Arthur F. and Samuelson, Paul A. *Full Employment, Guideposts and Economic Stability.* New York: 1967.
————and Mitchell, Wesley C. *Measuring Business Cycles.* New York: 1946.

GEORGE BURNS

b. January 20, 1896
Comedian; actor

In his autobiography, *The Third Time Around* (New York, 1979), comedian George Burns recounts his reaction to being offered the role of God for a new movie when Burns was 84. "I wondered, 'Why would they pick me to play God?' " he wrote. "Then I realized it made a little sense. I was the closest one to His age. Since Moses wasn't around, I suppose I was next in line." Indeed, at an age when many performers have long since packed in the greasepaint and retired to the golf course, Burns, who began his career at age 7 and was best-known for his nearly 30-year collaboration with his wife, Gracie Allen, refused to retire and at age 80 won his first Oscar for *The Sunshine Boys*.

Nathan Birnbaum was born on the Lower East Side of Manhattan to Louis Phillip and Dorothy (Bluth) Birnbaum, both immigrants from Eastern Europe. His father, who was very religious, worked initially as a pants presser in a sweatshop but later turned toward the synagogue, where he was a *mashgiach*, or supervisor of *kashrut*, and part-time cantor. Burns was the ninth of 12 children, and after his father died in 1903 his mother took a job in the garment industry, and those children who could worked to help support the family.

Even Burns joined in, forming a musical group with three friends called the Peewee Quartet. Singing in their own neighborhood, in a nearby Irish neighborhood and on the Staten Island Ferry, they accumulated a modest amount of money, which, according to Burns, was often stolen by older Jewish boys. His success with the quartet was such that after the group won first prize in an amateur contest at a local Presbyterian church, for which he got a watch, he was ready to convert. Burns said, in response to his mother's query about why he didn't want to be Jewish anymore: "Well, I've been a Jew for seven years and never got anything. I was a Presbyterian for one day and I got a watch." When the watch broke, Burns became a Jew again.

He also took odd jobs over the early years to help his family, selling newspapers and shining shoes. He quit school in the sixth grade. By the time he was in his mid-teens, Burns had begun performing in vaudeville theaters as a trick skater and comedian. He says that he began using a cigar—a constant companion throughout his career—in his acts when he was 14, because it gave him something to hold onto when he was scared. He eventually married a woman named Hannah Siegal, who was his partner in a Latin dance act. Little is written about his first wife, however.

Burns's life changed in 1923, when he met Grace Allen, an Irish-Catholic teen-ager of 17, who had heard he was looking for a new partner. The two soon began performing together and three years later were married. For six years they performed a stand-up comedy routine for the B.F. Keith theater circuit. But their big break came in 1930, when they entered radio, first for the BBC in London and later in New York on the *Eddie Cantor Show*, the *Rudy Vallee Show* and the *Guy Lombardo Show*. Radio multiplied the audiences for Burns and Allen, and their fame grew nationwide. In 1932 they left vaudeville for good when the Columbia Broadcasting System (CBS) offered them their own program, which was broadcast for 18 years, usually earning ratings among the 10 most popular shows. They also made a few films together during this period, beginning with a one-reeler in 1929 called *Lamb Chops*. They made 14 short films and about a dozen features in total, concluding in 1939 with MGM's *Honolulu*.

In 1950 Burns and Allen moved from radio to television, still with CBS, first with a biweekly show and later with a weekly program. These shows, as with their radio series, had Gracie playing a fuzzy-brained but lovable wife to George's raspy-voiced straight man. George, often seeming a bit beside himself with Gracie's antics, would often address the audience directly when the situation comedy seemed to be getting too insane for him to handle. By show's end, however, all would be resolved—until next week. The show aired until 1958, when Gracie retired, and George had his own program, *The George Burns Show*, for one year after that. He became an investor in and producer of several network comedy series, but when his television career ended, he turned to nightclub work, which continued even after Gracie's death in 1964.

Burns' return to film acting in 1975 was unplanned. A film version of Neil Simon's Broadway play *The Sunshine Boys* was about to begin shooting, with Walter Matthau and Burns' close friend Jack Benny cast as two aging vaudevillians—based on the real-life performers Smith and Dale—who have not spoken to each other for years but have been invited to perform together for a television retrospective on American comedy. However, Benny died shortly before shooting began, and Burns was called in as a last-minute replacement. Like the play, the film was a hit, and in 1976 Burns won the Academy Award as Best Supporting Actor.

But his film career was only beginning. In 1977 he had a small part in *Sergeant Pepper's Lonely Hearts Club Band*, which was followed by starring roles in *Oh, God!* in 1978; *Just You and Me, Kid*, with Brooke Shields, in 1979; and *Oh God!—Book 2* in 1980. He also teamed up with veteran actors Lee Strasberg and Art Carney in *Going in Style* (1979), a comedy about three old men who connive to pull off a series of daring robberies.

In his "third wind" as a movie star, Burns has made commercials and had a television special. He has also written two other books prior to *The Third Time Around—I Love Her, That's Why!* (New York, 1955) and *Living It Up* (New York, 1975).

While many people still react with amazement that Burns has carried on an active career with such vigor into his eighties, Burns seems to have taken it all in good stride and with continued good humor. After all, he wrote, he was born singing (he says he remembers the moment of birth), and it was only after he completed two choruses of "Red Rose Rag" that the doctor slapped him to shut him up. With this record, why should he stop?

ABE BURROWS

b. December 18, 1910
Playwright; director

As a successful Broadway writer and director during the 1950s and 1960s, Abe Burrows became known as a "play doctor" for his ability to collaborate with other writers, directors or producers in the creation of several of America's finest Broadway productions. His own first Broadway effort as librettist for *Guys and Dolls* in 1950 established him as one of the theater's most sought-after writers.

Abram S. Burrows was born in New York City to Louis, who ran a wallpaper and paint business, and Julia (Salzberg) Burrows. Raised in Manhattan and Brooklyn, Burrows graduated from New Utrecht High School in 1927 and spent two fruitless years as a premedical student at the City College of New York. He then took business courses at the School of Finance at New York University and from 1931 until 1934—when he was fired—worked as an accountant with a Wall Street firm. He later compared his brief career in the financial world with the theater. "I didn't know when I joined Wall Street in 1929 that I was really working on a flop show," he wrote in *Honest, Abe: Is There Really No Business Like Show Business?* (Boston, 1980).

During the mid-1930s Burrows worked in a series of odd jobs but also began seriously refining a talent for performing comedy skits that he had developed as a student. After several successful stints at borscht belt hotels, by the late 1930s he began writing for radio shows, including *This Is New York* (CBS, 1938–39), *Texaco Star Theater* (CBS, 1939) and *The Rudy Vallee-John Barrymore Program* (NBC, 1940). He then moved to Hollywood and from 1941 to 1945 wrote sketches for a popular radio comedy series called *Duffy's Tavern,* which started on CBS and then moved to NBC. There he became part of a large group of primarily Jewish comics from New York City who were creating a new American subculture that was to have enormous impact on all the arts, but especially in television, theater and cinema. Burrows in particular became known for the parodies of popular songs that he improvised, one of the most famous being "The Girl with the Three Blue Eyes." In 1950 he made a recording of many of these so-called pianologues, called "Abe Burrows Sings."

But it was as a writer of comic sketches that Burrows excelled, and after writing for several other radio programs, he finally had one of his own in 1947 for nearly a year. Burrows was also involved in television during the new medium's infancy; he briefly had his own show, *Abe Burrow's Almanac,* on CBS in 1950 and soon after became a regular panelist on many of the most popular programs on the air.

His Broadway debut with *Guys and Dolls* represented an auspicious new direction for him. The libretto he wrote for the musical, which was based on an old Damon Runyon story and directed by George S. Kaufman, made the difference between the show's being merely a collection of songs with nothing to tie them together or a complete theater piece, where the performers become dynamic and believable because something real is happening to them. Burrows won both a New York Drama Critics award and a Tony award for his writing.

Burrows subsequently went on to direct as well as write. His next major success was *Can-Can* in 1953. In 1956 he wrote the screenplay for *Solid Gold Cadillac.*

But it was with *How to Succeed in Business Without Really Trying* (1961) that Burrows, as director and coauthor, did his greatest work. It earned him both a Pulitzer Prize and Tony award. His subsequent theater work has included directing *What Makes Sammy Run?* (1964), a musical adaptation of Budd Schulberg's novel of the same name, as well as the American version of *Cactus Flower* (1965) and *Forty Carats* (1968). In the early 1970s several other shows he directed were not successful.

Burrows' role as "play doctor" in many shows is widely known but was not extensively documented until the publication of his autobiography. In the case of *Guys and Dolls,* for example, he added several subtle touches that, combined, made the show what critic John Lahr called in a 1980 review "arguably the century's finest musical." One of them included the casting of Stubby Kaye in the role of Nicely-Nicely Johnson; in the original Runyon story, Nicely-Nicely was a skinny chap, but since the casting of Kaye by Burrows, he has traditionally been portrayed by an overweight actor. And it was also Burrows who cast Sam Levene in the lead role of Nathan Detroit, which meant that although the show was a musical, Detroit has only one song, since Levene was tone-deaf. In ensemble pieces Levene was ordered to mouth the words in order not to throw the songs off balance.

Honest Abe provides interesting insights into Burrows' accomplishments in films, television and on Broadway. But away from the world of entertainment he was harrassed by politicians. In fact, he was a victim of the House Un-American Activities Committee during the hysteria of the red scare of the 1950s. Twice he was called on to testify and Burrows graphically describes those fearful days in his book. By the late 1950s though, the inquisitors had vanished into well-deserved oblivion, and Burrows' reputation as a librettist, director, author, comic and American remains unsullied.

CORNELL CAPA

b. April 10, 1918
Photographer

"Concerned photography" and "Cornell Capa" are virtually synonymous. Capa has been a major influence in the international community of photographers for over 30 years. As a photographer himself, as the friend and colleague of many outstanding photojournalists, and as a leader among photographers, Capa has been a major force in turning "picture taking" into an important political and artistic medium and in bringing it to wider audiences.

Cornell Friedmann was born in Budapest. He set out to study medicine in Paris in 1936 but switched to photography after working as his brother's darkroom assistant there. Robert, five years older than Cornell, had distinguished himself as a photographer during the Spanish civil war and later became a prominent war photographer. (Robert Capa was born Andre Friedmann in Hungary but changed his name in Paris for professional reasons.)

Cornell came to New York in 1937, still working as his brother's assistant and doing some of his own photography. He became a staff photographer for *Life* magazine from 1946 to 1954, then helped form the photographers' cooperative Magnum, through which he continued to carry out assignments for *Life* as well as projects of his own.

In 1954 Robert Capa was killed in Indochina, the first correspondent to die in the field. His death affected Cornell deeply and was, in fact, a turning point in his life. Out of a desire to preserve his brother's work and that of other photographers killed in action or on other kinds of assignments, Cornell Capa began to actively collect and publish the works of photojournalists. His commitment to turning photography into a means of exposing the problems of oppressed people around the world was manifested in his personal work as well.

In 1966 his activities, which were shared with other photographers, culminated in the establishment of the International Fund for Concerned Photography and led in 1967 to a major exhibit at New York's Riverside Museum called "Concerned Photographer." That exhibit, which was followed by "Concerned Photographer 2," brought together the works of such major photographers as Andre Kertesz, Robert Capa, Marc Riboud, Roman Vishniac, Bruce Davidson, Gordon Parks, Donald McCullin and W. Eugene Smith. The success of these two landmark exhibits, which traveled widely, planted the seeds for the project that would become the International Center of Photography, paralleling the tremendous resurgence of interest in photography.

Meanwhile, Cornell Capa continued to produce photoessays for books and magazines, some touching on difficult and serious themes. Some of his books include *Retarded Children Can Be Helped*, text by Maya Pines (Manhasset, N.Y., 1957); *Savage Kinsman*, with Elizabeth Elliot (New York, 1959); *Farewell to Eden*, with Matthew Huxley (New York, 1964), an examination of Peruvian Indians whose lifestyle was threatened by missionary efforts to convert them; and *Margin of Life* (New York, 1974), an examination of poverty and hunger in El Salvador and Honduras. Capa has edited numerous additional books in which his work has also been included. He has organized many exhibits and participated in three films related to his photographic work.

Cornell Capa's complete devotion to photojournalism and his many excursions into controversial territory with his camera have earned him several awards. They include the Overseas Press Club Award nomination (1956), for his essay "Peron's Argentina"; Page One Award Citation (1956), for "Retarded Children's Essay"; Robert Leavitt Award (1968), from the American Society of Magazine Photographers, for his overall contributions to photography; and the Morris Gordon Memorial Award (1972), by the Photographic Administrators Inc.

Capa has also lectured throughout the United States on "Concerned Photography" and was responsible for coordinating a series of "Sight & Sound" lectures for *Scholastic Magazine* based on the work of eight photographers who were part of the two original exhibits. They narrate the lectures.

Capa's many endeavors in diverse areas of photography have not blunted his consciousness of his Jewish heritage. In 1954 he and Alfred Eisenstadt photographed a major essay on Judaism for *Life* magazine's series "The World's Great Religions." He has edited two books about Israel—*Israel: The Reality* (Cleveland, 1969) and *Jerusalem: City of Mankind* (New York, 1974)—and directed exhibits at the Jewish Museum in New York based on the two books.

Capa's life has been full and active. With his founding of the International Center of Photography in New York City in 1974 (he is its executive director), Capa realized a years-long dream to create a forum where photographers could assemble and a museum where photography was not a secondary consideration, but the whole reason for being. It has been a huge and important success. With the International Center possibly Capa's crowning achievement, he is probably the individual most responsible for establishing photojournalism and other types of photography (he does not disparage art photography—quite the opposite) as a serious communications medium.

For further information:

Capa, Cornell, ed. *The Concerned Photographer 1*. New York: 1969.
———. *The Concerned Photographer 2*. New York: 1972.
———. *Jerusalem: City of Mankind*. New York: 1974.

ROGER CARAS

b. May 24, 1928
Author; naturalist

Roger Andrew Caras is an expert on wildlife and conservation and is perhaps America's most popular authority on pet life. A former motion picture executive, he is the author of numerous books on humane treatment of animals and has starred on radio and television programs about animals.

Roger Caras was born in Methuen, Massachusetts to Joseph Jacob, an insurance executive, and Bessie (Kasanoff) Caras. After spending a year at Northeastern University from 1948 to 1949, and a year at Western Reserve University from 1949 to 1950, he transferred to the University of Southern California, where he received his B.A. degree in cinema in 1952.

Before Caras began devoting all of his time to writing and teaching about animals, he had a successful career in the motion picture industry. From 1955 to 1965 Caras worked as assistant to the vice president of Columbia Pictures Corporation. In 1965 he was appointed vice president of Stanley Kubrick's Polaris Productions, a position he held until 1968.

Having always been interested in and knowledgeable about animals, Caras lectured at colleges about wildlife and conservation, the environment, geography and natural history from 1955 to 1965. He was science editor at the Armed Forces Radio and Television Service from 1963 to 1968 and since 1978 has lectured at the University of Pennsylvania's School of Veterinary Medicine.

Among Caras's many books on animals are *Venomous Animals of the World* (New York, 1974), a lively survey of poisonous animals, their venom and venom apparatus together with numerous bite and sting stories; *A Zoo in Your Room* (New York, 1975), which gives advice on choosing and keeping small animals and focuses on conservation and humane treatment of pets; and *The Forest* (New York, 1979), a narrative essay that presents the interdependence of over 80 species of plants and animals in a typical North American upland forest. The book also reveals the fragility of life from the perspective of a hemlock tree in a northwestern coniferous forest.

In *Death as a Way of Life* (Boston, 1971), Caras examines the human past as hunter and killer by tracing its history from killer of animals—because of economic necessity—to contemporary hunting, which Caras regards as a murderous activity. Caras argues that there is no such thing as a dangerous wild animal, but rather only a potential menace in *Dangerous to Man, Wild Animals: A Definitive Study of Their Reputed Dangers to Man* (Philadelphia, 1964). His theme is the absolute need to practice conservation and preservation of animals. Other books he has written include *North American Mammals* (New York, 1966), a guide for readers to help them identify mammals, and *The Custer Wolf* (Boston, 1966), a fictionalized biography of a wolf that ravaged South Dakota between 1910 and 1920, written sympathetically from the wolf's point of view.

Caras, a staunch defender of the rights of animals,

has starred on the CBS radio show *Pets and Wildlife* and has been animal correspondent for CBS radio and ABC-TV. He is associate curator of rare books at the Cleveland Museum of Natural History, a member of the advisory council of the Arizona-Sonora Desert Museum and Zero Population Growth. He is vice president of the zoo and wildlife committee of the Morris Animal Foundation and vice president of the Humane Society of America.

He received an award in 1977 from the Hai-Bar Society in Israel (which has developed a preserve in the Negev Desert for animals mentioned in the Bible) for his humanitarian efforts and is a member of the Outdoor Writers Association and the Authors League. He is also a contributing editor to *Geo* magazine, a columnist for *Ladies Home Journal* and since 1975 has been an adjunct professor of literature at Southampton College.

SHLOMO CARLEBACH

b. 1926
Rabbi; singer

In the mid-1960s, when many young people were looking toward the counterculture for role models, a most unlikely one emerged in the form of an Hasidic rabbi. The charismatic Shlomo Carlebach—armed with guitar, the message of Hasidism and an appealing alternative lifestyle—began a movement to draw young people toward a joyous and traditional Judaism. Today the "Singing Rabbi" continues his work, traveling around the world to bring his highly spirited form of Jewish life to Jewish youth.

Shlomo Carlebach was born in Berlin, the son of Rabbi Naphtali Hartwig and Paula (Cohn) Carlebach. He is descended from a line of distinguished Hasidic rabbis and scholars and traces his ancestry to Rabbi David ben Shmuel Halevi, a 17th-century commentator on the Shulchan Aruch. In 1939 the family left Berlin to escape the Nazis and settled in New York, where the young Carlebach studied at Mesivta Torah Vada'ath, Beth Midrash of America, Lakewood Yeshiva in New Jersey and Columbia University. He also assisted his father, who had a small but active congregation, Kehillath Jacob, on Manhattan's West Side.

Carlebach emerged as an anomaly during the turbulent years of the mid-1960s, when student movements on college campuses across the country rose to protest the mounting war effort in Vietnam. Carlebach seemed one more "cult figure," yet he introduced traditions that had a firm historical foundation and then combined them with contemporary popular trends. Wearing Hasidic garb, espousing health foods and admitting philosophical agreement with certain Eastern religious beliefs and lifestyles then in vogue, he began to perform widely before young audiences, singing Hasidic melodies (or updated, "neo-Hasidic," versions), Israeli songs and popular American folk ballads. He appealed equally to religious and nonreligious groups and created two communal headquarters for his worldwide movement, the House of Love and Prayer—one in Los Angeles, the other in Israel. Also in Israel, in Modiin, he established a settlement designed to follow his views, and to support itself, it distributed health food throughout the country.

Carlebach's is an updated form of Hasidism, one that blends the richest traditions of service to God with joy and piety with the contemporary striving for individual fulfillment that characterizes many of his followers. This revivalist rabbi, far from keeping his distance from his "holy little brothers and sisters," creates a mood of camaraderie with them. His eyes rolling and crying "Gewalt!" ["Oh my God!"], he leads his disciples in celebrations of the Divine composed of chanting, storytelling and dancing that create a mood of overwhelming unity between Jew and Jew, between Jew and God. The yearning for ecstasy, for "experience," that Carlebach discerns in the Jewish soul he seeks to harness in God's service, acting, in fact, as a missionary with music as his medium. Full of an undifferentiating type of love for all Jews, he himself has described the type of harmony that he seeks to implement in his music: "To you, young people . . . who are so near to me. Your striving is my striving. Your struggle is my struggle. Together let us find our way to the Ribono Shel Olom, our Father in Heaven, to study His Torah, to keep His commandments and, above all, to be His friends." To this end, and not simply for his own benefit, he travels widely in America, in Israel and in Europe. "The world is my headquarters," he declares.

Although the intellectual content of his message has come in for criticism, and despite a touch of showmanship, the authentic nature of his ardor—his love for God, for the Jewish people and for all people—and its beautifully easy expression in song is beyond question. He is the composer of over 250 songs and two of his recordings in particular—*Songs of My Soul* and *Haneshomoh Loch* (1959)—are especially popular.

For further information

Carlebach, Shlomo, *Encyclopedia Judaica*. Jerusalem: 1971.
C. Sonnenfeld, "My Encounter with the Hippie Rabbi."
    Jewish Digest. July 1972.

SOL "CHICK" CHAIKIN

b. January 9, 1918
Labor leader

Sol Chaikin is president of the International Ladies Garment Workers Union (ILGWU) and one of labor's most articulate leaders. The ILGWU is well-known in the history of American labor struggles, and Chaikin leads a union of diminishing size in a battle against the invasion of cheap imported goods or those manufactured in states with "right-to-work" laws, where employees are largely nonunion.

Sol Chaikin was born in Harlem Hospital in Manhattan, the son of Russian immigrants Sam and Beckie (Schechtman) Chaikin, both garment workers—he a cloakmaker and active in the union and she a dressmaker. Chaikin was the sole surviving child, his two brothers having died in early childhood, one at the age of 4 and the other at the age of 9. Following his birth the family moved and lived in Brownsville in Brooklyn for five years and then settled permanently in the East Bronx.

Chaikin attended Townsend Harris High School (a secondary school for gifted young men), and then attended City College of New York, majoring in political science and economics. He left in 1938 without a degree to attend St. Lawrence Law School, where he earned a Bachelor of Laws degree in 1940 and was named to the school's Dean's List.

He was in law school during a time when labor unions were making great legislative and organizational advances, such as the enactment of the National Labor Relations Act and the Fair Labor Standards Act and the formation of the Congress of Industrial Organizations (CIO). "It was an exciting time for unions and somehow the thought of becoming a lawyer didn't appeal to me," he said. "My father was an active member of the ILGWU so I became interested in the problems of workers and the ways in which unions could help. I wanted to participate actively to make life better for those whose lives were difficult." David Dubinsky, the ILGWU president, knew Sam Chaikin, so Sol Chaikin wrote to him for an interview. "Both my parents were in the ILG, you know. I came by my interest legitimately," he has stated. In the years after he was hired, and until he was elected president in 1975, Chaikin served as organizer, business agent, head of the Southwest and Northeast ILGWU, vice president and general-secretary-treasurer. He is also a vice president of the AFL-CIO.

Before and shortly after World War II, most of the ILGWU members were Jewish, with large numbers of Italian-Americans having a separate local. Today, many members are black and Hispanic, and some four out of five are women, many of them heads of families. All the same, the ILGWU remains a union led by white men. "We have difficulty getting people out of the rank and file," Chaikin has said in defense of the union, citing the fact that many of its female members are otherwise occupied as heads of families, while talented nonwhites tend to leave for better-paying jobs elsewhere. One critic of the ILGWU, Stanley Aronowitz, has remarked, though, that the union's leadership has done little to remedy the situation. The ILGWU, he stated in late 1981, has "permitted manufacturers to contract work all over the world as long as they maintain showroom operations in Manhattan."

Other critics have pointed to the ever-growing problems of the ILGWU, such as the designer-jeans fad, which has meant very few jobs for union members, since production has been centered in foreign countries at much lower wages. In an effort to counter this, Chaikin has advocated what he describes as market sharing—that is, restricting the amount of imports of clothing, with this percentage to be parceled out among nations willing to sell their goods to the U.S. market. Even so, while he censures firms that have fled abroad, he also defends their activities because of the high cost of competing with cheap foreign labor. "It's a tough industry," he remarked to *The New York Times* in late 1981. "It's a crapshooter's game. Nickels and dimes mean a lot because so many people are at each other's throats for a share of the consumer's dollars." Yet Chaikin remains secure in his position and in his frequently expressed faith in his ability "to make life better" for the membership.

Chaikin's book *A Labor Viewpoint: Another Opinion* (Monroe, N.Y., 1980) deals extensively with what W. H. Newman of the Graduate School of Business of Columbia University described as "the second tier of the U.S. labor force, those who are often minorities at the low end of the wage-scale. For them, marginal employment is an experience—not a statistic." The book also emphasizes Chaikin's strong belief in human rights and the need to link free labor unions with free human beings everywhere.

A member of the Trilateral Commission and the Council on Foreign Relations as well as the United Nations Association, Chaikin is equally active in Jewish civic and communal affairs. He is a trustee of Brandeis University and a member of the Board of Directors of the Israel College of Fashion and Textiles in Israel. He has been active with the Workmen's Circle and the National Committee for Labor Israel. In 1977 he was awarded the Histadrut Humanitarian Award and the following year was asked to represent the U.S. government at the funeral of former Israeli Prime Minister

Golda Meir. And following the 1977 breakthrough in Egyptian-Israeli relations, Chaikin represented the AFL-CIO on a trip to Egypt in January 1978 to speak with that nation's union leaders.

For further information:
Chaikin, Sol. "Our Illegal Workers." *The Brandeis Quarterly,* May 1981.

JEROME CHARYN

b. May 13, 1937
Novelist; educator

Although the writing style of Jerome Charyn has occasionally been compared to that of Saul Bellow and Bernard Malamud, and even James Joyce, in fact, he has evolved a quite unique fiction that combines fantasy with a macabre vision of the urban scene and the people who inhabit it. He also has a mystical conception of Jews as symbols of all people and of the dilemmas that are the components of their lives.

Jerome Charyn was born in New York City to Samuel, a furrier, and Fannie (Paley) Charyn. After graduating from Columbia College with a B.A. degree Phi Beta Kappa in 1959, he was a recreation leader for the New York City Parks Department. From 1962 to 1964 he taught English at two of New York City's prestigious public high schools, the High School of Music and Art and the High School of Performing Arts, and in 1965 was a lecturer at the City College of New York. From 1965 to 1968 he was an assistant professor of English at Stanford University, returning to New York to become an assistant professor at Herbert Lehman College of the City University of New York from 1968 to 1971. He was promoted to associate professor in 1971 and has been a full professor since 1978.

In *Once Upon a Droshky* (New York, 1964), Charyn attempted to create a vision of the heyday of the Lower East Side through the reminiscences of several now-elderly men who convene regularly in Schimmel's, a Second Avenue cafeteria. While the idea seemed credible, critics felt Charyn fell short of his goals and that his images were closer to an "animated cartoon." His next novel, *On the Darkening Green* (New York, 1965), fared little better among critics. This time he portrayed an Italian Catholic named Nick Lapucci, a worker at a home in the Catskills for Jewish delinquent boys during World War II and his deepening understanding of the suffering of the Jewish people throughout history but especially at the time depicted in the novel. Yet Charyn appeared to be finding his "voice" in his writing as he developed an ear for language and a flair for the bizarre in creating unlikely, yet somehow plausible, characters and situations. (In New York, as one realizes through reading Charyn's work, anything can happen.)

Thus, in *Going to Jerusalem* (New York, 1967), Charyn contrives a world championship chess match between a 6-year-old genius and an ex-Nazi; and in *Blue Eyes* (New York, 1974), the first in a trilogy about a Jewish cop named Manfred Coen, he creates a detective mystery in which Coen must deal with increasingly absurd characters and events as he seeks to penetrate the white slave market in New York City.

The critical response to Charyn's works has invariably been mixed, from those reviewers who cannot tolerate the outlandishness of his themes to those who revel in his originality and his creativity with language. Acknowledging this paradox, the American Academy and Institute of Arts and Letters awarded Charyn the 1981 Richard and Hilda Rosenthal Foundation prize for "an American work of fiction published during the preceding 12 months *{Darlin Bill: A Love Story of the American West}* which, though not a commercial success, is a considerable literary achievement."

Charyn's stories have appeared in *Commentary, Mademoiselle* and many other publications and collections. He was co-editor of *The Dutton Review* from 1970 to 1972 and has been editor of *Fiction* since 1972.

For further information:
Charyn, Jerome. *American Scrapbook.* New York: 1969.
———. *The Education of Patrick Silver.* New York: 1976.
———. *Eisenhower, My Eisenhower.* New York: 1971).
———. *The Man Who Grew Younger.* New York: 1967.
———. *Marilyn the Wild.* New York: 1976.
———. *Pinocchio's Nose.* New York: 1982.
———. *Secret Isaac.* New York: 1978.
———. *The Tar Baby.* New York: 1973.

LEO M. CHERNE

b. September 8, 1912
Management specialist

As executive director of the Research Institute of America, an organization devoted to helping businessmen understand the increasingly complex regulatory world, Leo M. Cherne is an influential management specialist and economist. Under his leadership, the institute publishes a wide variety of analytic economic books and newsletters that provide information on tax laws and recommendations for making investments.

Leo Cherne was born in the Bronx to Max and Dora (Bailin) Cherne, who owned a printing and stationery store. During high school Cherne sang with the Metropolitan Opera Company, a job that enabled him to save enough money to go to New York University. After graduation in 1931 he obtained his law degree from New York University Law School in 1934. He worked with the law firm of Blau, Perlman and Polakoff from 1934 to 1936, the year he was admitted to the New York bar. In 1967 he was awarded a Doctor of Laws from Pace College and NYU Law School, his alma mater.

In 1936, after answering an advertisement in the New York *Law Journal,* Cherne was hired by Whitgard Services, a publishing house, where he edited *The Payroll Tax-Saving Service,* a text that offered information on social security legislation. Cherne, immediately recognized by his colleagues Edward Whittlesey and Carl Hovgard for his editorial skill, changed the publication so that it offered specific data on concrete cases. The result was the very successful *Social Security Coordinator.* Not long after Cherne was hired, Whittlesey sold his share in the business to Cherne. Whitgard Services was renamed the Research Institute of America. Under Cherne's leadership, the institute has grown in the ensuing years into one of the world's largest private management organizations. Among the publications it issues are *Executive Wealth, Tax Guide, Lawyer's Tax Alert, State Planner's Alert, Federal Action Coordinator* and *The Law and You.*

During the late 1930s Cherne edited such publications as *The Federal Tax Coordinator* and the *Business and Legislative Report,* which helped businessmen confused by the avalanche of new regulations created by New Deal legislation.

In 1939 he published his first book, *Adjusting Your Business to War* (New York), a direct, unemotional depiction of what might happen to business on M-Day, "that day without date when the United States goes to war." The book, which created much controversy in Washington—it was called "a blueprint for Fascism" by the *Annals of the American Academy of Political and Social Science*—was used as a basis for discussion in the Senate. In his second book, *M-Day and What It Means to You* (New York, 1940), he again examined, this time in question-and-answer format, the relation between war and business and between national defense and private enterprise. In *The Rest of Your Life* (New York, 1944), Cherne predicted what the postwar world would be like—the domestic and international problems, the psychological reaction of war veterans, the prospects for housing and unemployment.

Cherne turned increasingly to foreign affairs after World War II. He was a strong backer of South Vietnam's assassinated President Ngo Dinh Diem (and later a supporter of the Vietnam War). In an article in the *New York Times Magazine* in 1961, he praised President Diem as one who was readying his countrymen and women for democracy, although Communist subversion and violence, he wrote, were creating major problems for the Saigon government.

Cherne is chairman of the International Rescue Committee, a group founded in 1933 to assist refugees who become exiles because of political, religious or racial persecution. He has also lectured on economics at the New School for Social Research from 1946 to 1952 and has been active in many governmental organizations. He advised General Douglas MacArthur on taxation and fiscal policy for occupied Japan in 1946. He was a member of the U.S. Advisory Commission on International Education and Cultural Affairs from 1971 to 1976, the President's Foreign Intelligence Advisory Board from 1973 to 1977, and the Panel on International Information, Education and Cultural Relations from 1974 to 1975. He has been chairman of the Citizen's Commission on Indochinese Refugees since 1978.

He is also a sculptor of note. His bronze portraits of John F. Kennedy, Lyndon B. Johnson, Abraham Lincoln and Boris Pasternak are on permanent exhibit at various sites, and his other works hang in such places as the Smithsonian Institution, University of Bahia, Brazil and the American Academy of Arts and Letters.

In 1981 the Reagan administration named Cherne vice chairman of the Foreign Intelligence Advisory Board in an attempt to improve "the quality and effectiveness of intelligence available to the United States."

PHYLLIS CHESLER

b. October 1, 1940
Psychologist; author

The author of the controversial study *Women and Madness* (New York, 1972), which explored how women defying the roles they were expected to play often tended to develop mental disorders that psychologist Phyllis Chesler claims were reinforced by psychiatrists, Chesler has since become a major feminist theorist on the role of men in society and on changing definitions of motherhood.

Phyllis Chesler was born in Brooklyn to Leon and Lillian (Hammer) Chesler. She received a B.A. degree from Bard College in 1963, and an M.A. degree in 1967 and a Ph.D. in 1969, both from The New School for Social Research in New York City.

Early in her career Chesler distinguished herself as a dedicated and meticulous researcher and a social activist. In early 1965 she was a research associate at Yeshiva University, where she developed and administered parent interviews for the newly begun Headstart Project. From this work she developed lectures on the problems of education and community mental health in disadvantaged urban neighborhoods. For one year (1965–66) she was a researcher at the Institute for Developmental Studies at New York Medical College, where she used some of her Headstart experience to explore the verbal and cognitive abilities of disadvantaged children. Additional research positions, undertaken concurrently with graduate studies, took her through studies of psycholinguistics at The New School and clinical evaluations of narcotics addicts and psychiatric patients at Metropolitan Hospital, a municipal hospital that serves primarily the residents of East Harlem. She was an intern at the Department of Psychology and Psychiatry at Metropolitan Hospital in 1968 and at the Washington Square Institute for Psychotherapy and Mental Health in 1969.

In 1969 Chesler became an assistant professor of psychology at the College of Staten Island, a branch of the City University of New York. At the same time she pursued a wide range of independent projects leading to the publication of her books, which won her a national reputation.

In *Women and Madness*, which was first serialized in *Ms.* magazine, Chesler contended that the psychiatric establishment was responsible for perpetuating the passive roles that women were expected to play. Those who rebelled were considered peculiar, even mentally disturbed. Many women in the burgeoning feminist movement cheered the book, although others—and male critics as well—lambasted what they felt was its shallowness. Nonetheless, it served as an important springboard for discussion and led to some reconsiderations of the aims of psychotherapy and psychiatry in their approach to women seeking help and support.

Chesler's second and third books—*Women, Money and Power*, with Emily Jane Goodman (New York, 1976), and *About Men* (New York, 1978)—once again explored the social stereotypes of men and women in American society. The latter book also drew on historical themes in poetry, mythology and art to examine the evolution of the "patriarchal consciousness." Chesler's critics already had their ammunition ready. *Women, Money and Power*, a study of 12 "smaller" male powers (such as physical force, technology, the military and others) dominated by a 13th force (money), was seen as a repetition of earlier work by such feminist theorists as Kate Millett and others. *About Men* was considered poorly conceived.

Yet Chesler's books sold well in the United States and were popular in European women's movements. *Women and Madness* was translated into German, Dutch, French, Italian, Hebrew and Danish; *About Men* was translated into German and Dutch.

Chesler's own life changed dramatically in 1978, when she became a mother. At 38, considered "old" to have her first child, she was nonetheless doing what many professional women of the 1970s have done in delaying childbirth. A diary she kept during pregnancy, shortly after childbirth and during the first months of raising her child became *With Child: A Diary of Motherhood* (New York, 1979). Unlike her other books, it was a personal and moving account of her observations, her worries and the common experiences she found herself sharing with other mothers.

In her new life Chesler began to change her direction away from the "movement" and more toward the concerns of daily life, although she remains deeply involved in researching female psychology and women's historical roles in magic and medicine. She has also written about the Middle East and has been working on memoirs on that subject.

In addition to her books, Chesler has published studies that have appeared in professional journals and popular articles for such publications as *Mademoiselle, The Village Voice, Psychology Today, New York* and *Ms.* She has also lectured extensively at colleges throughout the United States and overseas, exploring such themes as women as political prisoners in Latin America, feminism and Judaism, issues in feminist theory, and obscenity —the degradation of women versus the right of free speech.

ARTHUR A. CHIEL

b. December 16, 1920
Rabbi; historian

Arthur A. Chiel is a distinguished rabbi and historian. Known especially for his original research on Canadian Jewish history, he is currently head of Congregation B'nai Jacob in Woodbridge, Connecticut and an editor of *Conservative Judaism* magazine.

Arthur Chiel was born in Taylor, Pennsylvania to Solomon, a rabbi, and Frieda (Binik) Chiel. He received his B.A. degree from Yeshiva University in 1943 and his rabbinical ordination from the Jewish Theological Seminary in 1946. From 1944 to 1949 he was religious director at New York City's 92nd Street YMHA and YWHA and studied intergroup relations on an Ameri-

can Jewish Congress fellowship awarded him by the late Rabbi Stephen S. Wise.

In 1949 Chiel became a Hillel director at the University of Manitoba (Canada), where he also established and taught in the Department of Judaic Studies. In 1952 he helped organize Winnipeg's new Rosh Pina Congregation, where he served as spiritual leader until 1957. During this period he took on an assignment from the Canadian Jewish Congress to survey the work of the American Jewish Joint Distribution Committee in Europe, North Africa and Israel. In the eight years of his stay in Canada, Chiel lectured widely about his original research in Canadian Jewish history, a subject about which he wrote two books, *Jewish Experience in Early Manitoba* (Toronto, 1955) and *The Jews in Manitoba* (Toronto, 1961), which won the Canadian Jewish Congress's H. L. Caiserman Award.

While Chiel has written articles on subjects generally overlooked in American Jewish historiography— such as essays on Ezra Stiles, Francis Salvador and Juda Monis—few historians had concentrated on Canada's Jews, and his books are landmarks. *The Jews in Manitoba,* his major work of history, is both workmanlike and path-breaking. Basing his study on newspapers, documents and often-obscure secondary material, in addition to interviews with Jewish pioneers in the province, Chiel saw the Jewish community in a larger historical context rather than merely as an isolated phenomenon. He demonstrated how the community had developed a rich and variegated cultural life, both secular and religious. Describing its characteristics as "dynamic" and "consistently intense," he explained its emergence by pointing to the fact that the East European Jews who came to Manitoba created their own institutions and were not dominated by an earlier generation of wealthier, more established German Jews. Then, too, Chiel emphasized the "multi-ethnic character of the province" and how that fact "encouraged" Jews "to preserve their own heritage."

In 1957 Chiel became head of the Genesis Hebrew Center in Tuckahoe, New York and program editor of the *Eternal Light* television program, a position he held until 1962. During that time he also lectured at the Jewish Institute of Religion. In 1960 Chiel received his Doctor of Hebrew Letters degree from the Jewish Theological Seminary. Since 1962 he has been the congregational rabbi at B'nai Jacob Synagogue in Woodbridge, Connecticut.

In 1969 Chiel led the first United Synagogue Youth tour, which included visits to Jewish communities in Russia and Rumania. It was the first tour in which an official United States Jewish youth organization made direct contact with Jews behind the Iron Curtain. That same year he received a Merrill Research Grant from the National B'nai B'rith Hillel Foundations for a study of the Judaic and Hebraic contents in the papers of Ezra Stiles, a Protestant clergyman and president of Yale University from 1778 to 1795.

When he was honored by the New Haven Division of the Anti-Defamation League of B'nai B'rith in 1978, Chiel was praised for his "belief that human beings are inherently good. He has given of himself to an incredible degree in his personal attempt to create a climate where a world of ethical justice flourishes within the true spirit of Judaism."

Chiel has written extensively for *Judaism, The American Jewish Historical Quarterly, Jewish Spectator, Jewish Frontier* and *The Canadian Jewish Historical Journal.* He has also contributed to the *Encyclopedia Judaica* and the *Standard Jewish Encyclopedia* and writes a weekly column called "Looking Back" in the Connecticut *Jewish Ledger.*

Among his many activities, Chiel has been a founding member of the New Haven Commission on Equal Opportunities, a visiting lecturer at Fairfield University and president of the Connecticut Valley Rabbinical Assembly.

For further information:
Chiel, Arthur A. "Dostoyevsky's Anti-Semitism." *Conservative Judaism,* Summer 1977.
———. "Ezra Stiles: The Education of an 'Hebrician.' " *American Jewish Historical Quarterly,* March 1971.
———. "Francis Salvador: Jew, Gentleman, Revolutionist." *American Jewish Historical Quarterly,* Spring 1976.
———. "Judah Monis, The Harvard Convert." *Judaism,* Spring 1974.

NOAM CHOMSKY

b. December 7, 1928
Linguist; political writer

Noam Chomsky, one of the world's leading authorities in linguistics, has produced a seemingly endless string of books in his field and has become an articulate spokesman of critical political-historical commentary. Calling himself a "revisionist" historian, Chomsky has spoken out against the state of Israel and has focused on the shortcomings of his own country. He was one of the most ardent, effective and early opponents of the Vietnam War.

Avram Noam Chomsky was born in Philadelphia to William and Elsie (Simonofsky) Chomsky. His father, a professor at Dropsie College in Philadelphia, was one of the major influences on Chomsky's life. "My father worked in medieval Hebrew grammar and his main study was a book on a medieval Hebrew grammarian named David Kimhi," he once said. He became interested in Semitic languages, and at the University of Pennsylvania, from which he received a B.A. degree in 1949, he did his M.A. thesis on the related subject "Morphophonemics of Modern Hebrew" (1951) and his doctoral dissertation on "Transformational Analysis" (1955), a study of Semitic languages. He also taught Hebrew at the Mikve Israel School in Philadelphia.

When he was first hired to teach at the Massachusetts Institute of Technology in 1955, he was made a professor in the Research Laboratory of Electronics, because at the time there was no linguistics department. He has since become Ferrari Ward Professor of Linguistics in a formally established Department of Linguistics and Philosophy. He also served as a research fellow at the Institute for Advanced Study at Princeton in 1958–59 and at the Center for Cognitive Studies at Harvard in 1964–65.

When Chomsky entered linguistics in the 1940s, linguists were focusing on the specific roles of individual parts of language. By the time Chomsky finished his doctoral thesis, his critique of accepted method and theory had developed along two lines. First, he said, externally imposed structural rules provided little or no understanding of how a child learns language. Second, such rules do not adequately explain certain observed features of language, such as "creativity," which allows the formation of entirely new sentences of any length or complexity. Chomsky put stress on developing rules that would reflect such mental processes as nearly as possible. His revolutionary syntactic theory and concept of "transformation," by which he examines the way speakers "generate" sentences from the rules they possess, has remained central to linguistics since its acceptance in the early 1960s.

Instead of supporting the accepted stimulus-response view of language acquisition, which was rooted in the notion of the mind as a "tabula rasa," or blank tablet, Chomsky believes that certain ordering principles, or underlying mental processes in the human mind, serve as prerequisites for learning. He shifted the goal of linguistics from the classification of elements (into sounds, words and sentences) to the development of a set of grammatic rules that would account for the infinite ways sentences are constructed. His work has therefore had profound impact on psychology and the new field of psycholinguistics. He has challenged psychologists to develop new and richer theories of language learning and of learning in general.

Despite this preeminence in linguistics, Chomsky's fame in the larger world has arisen as a result of his political writings, most notably his sharp censure of Israeli and American policies. He has put himself at odds with the mainstream of his co-religionists by his searing criticism of Israel and its policies toward the Palestinian Arabs. He has, for example, repeatedly and severely criticized Israel for rejecting Palestinian claims to statehood and scorned the Camp David agreement, arguing, as he did in *Peace and the Middle East* (New York, 1974), that its fatal flaw was in permitting Israeli rule over more than 1 million Arabs on the West Bank and Gaza.

In 1980 he wrote a foreword to Robert Faurisson's privately printed book *Memoirs in Defense Against Those Who Accuse Me of Falsifying History; the Question About the Gas Chambers* (Lyons, France, 1980). The author, a Lyons (France) University lecturer, had been suspended in 1978 after saying "Hitler never ordered nor admitted that anyone be killed because of race or creed." Chomsky said in late 1980 that he had not read the book and did not endorse its views. "I addressed myself solely to the civil liberties issue. An author should have his rights of publication protected, regardless of his views." Critics on the left and right, however, scoffed at his explanation and denounced him for defending an apologist for Hitler.

Chomsky was also an outspoken and prominent critic of U.S. intervention in the Vietnam War, denouncing its policies as unjustified imperialist and cruel in numerous articles, many of which appeared in *The New York Review of Books*. He was also a supporter of Resist, the nationwide movement that bitterly opposed the drafting of young men for military service. Following the war he continued to criticize the drift of American foreign policies, notably citing the slaughter of East Tinians by Indonesia and the acquiescence and silence of the United States because of its fear of offending anti-Communist Indonesia. In *Towards a New Cold War* (New York, 1982), a collection of essays, Chomsky takes aim at the Reagan administration. Relating internal to external policy, he condemns revisionist books defending the war in Vietnam, discusses the harmful impact of CIA and FBI surveillance on peaceful domestic groups and asks why the United States deems it necessary to go to war to protect natural resources belonging to other nations and whether other nations have a reciprocal right to natural resources located in the United States. In addition, he asks whether the United States and the USSR are not acting similarly when they attempt to repress opponents and dissidents in their spheres of influence.

He traces his political leanings back to his mother's immigrant family. He Said:

> The whole family was very much a part of that radical Jewish working class milieu of the 1920s and 30s. That was a very big formative influence on me personally. It was a very unusual culture which I don't think exists anymore, a mixture of a very high level of intense intellectual life, but at the same time it was really working class.

For further information:
Chomsky, Noam. *American Power and the New Mandarins.* New York: 1969.
———. *Aspects of the Theory of Syntax.* Cambridge, Mass.: 1965.
———. *Cartesian Linguistics.* New York: 1966.
———. *Language and Mind.* New York: 1968.
———. *Logical Structures of Linguistic Theory.* New York: 1975.
———. *Problems of Knowledge and Freedom.* New York: 1971.
———. *Rules and Representation.* New York: 1980.
———. *Sound Pattern of English.* New York: 1968.

STANLEY FRANKLIN CHYET

b.. April 2, 1931
Rabbi; historian

Stanley F. Chyet has long concentrated on American Jewish history. As a university professor of American Jewish history and as an editor, he has produced and caused to be produced scholarly, serious historiography.

Stanley Franklin Chyet was born in Boston, the son of Jacob and Beatrice (Miller) Chyet. He earned his B.A. degree from Brandeis University in 1952 and a Bachelor of Hebrew Literature from the HUC-JIR in New York City two years later. In 1957 he was both ordained and granted a Master of Hebrew Literature degree from HUC in Cincinnati. In 1960 he earned his Ph.D. at the same school. Shortly after receiving his doctorate he began teaching at Hebrew Union College. In 1969 he was named Professor of American Jewish History, associate director of the American Jewish Archives and associate editor of its semi-annual journal of the same name. In 1976, he moved to Los Angeles to the newly-opened branch of the HUC and two years later became director of its Edgar F. Magnin School of Graduate Studies.

Much of Chyet's reputation as a serious scholar of American Jewish history is derived from his book *Lopez of Newport* (Detroit, 1970), which deals with Jewish society in Colonial and Revolutionary Newport, Rhode Island. *His Lives and Voices* (Philadelphia, 1972) is an anthology of American Jewish reminiscences mirroring the years between the mid-19th to the mid-20th centuries. For many years he taught at HUC and was associate editor of *American Jewish Archives*, a semiannual devoted to reflecting how diverse individuals of Jewish origin saw and experienced America in their lifetimes. He was editor of *Essays in American Jewish History* (Cincinnati, 1958) and contributed a biographical sketch of Jacob Rader Marcus. It served as a Festschrift to mark the tenth anniversary of the founding of the American Jewish Archives (the institution as well as the journal) on the HUC campus under Dr. Marcus' direction. His article "Reflections on Southern-Jewish Historiography," in *Turn to the South,* edited by Nathan M. Kaganoff and Melvin I. Urofsky (Charlottesville, Virginia, 1979) concludes with an appeal that "historiographically Southern Jewry—a group whose communal roots go back to at least the early 1700s—has had to endure something of a shadow existence since the Civil War. It is time for true Southern-Jewish historiography to begin taking shape."

Chyet's translations of modern Hebrew poems have also appeared in various publications. Among the Israeli poets he has translated are Haim Gouri, Ya'ir Hurvitz, Abba Kovner, Tuvia Ruebner and Natan Zach. His own lengthy poem "Seven Poems for Nahum N. Glatzer" [an eminent scholar and editor] appeared in *Texts and Responses: Studies Presented to Nahum N. Glatzer,* edited by M. A. Fishbane and P. R. Flohr (1975), and was prefaced by Chyet's personal note reflecting his love for Judaica: "The feeling which Dr. Glatzer gave me then about the Hebrew Bible as a living moving force, a force which had something deep and important to do with *me,* with my own life and sensibilities—that feeling has remained with me." And in his poem "Be Wise, Solomon," Chyet wrote: "My advice to you, Solomon: rule over mercy/Sacred Cows make the best sacrifices—that is my theory of kingship/Leave your son psalms and graves."

For further information:
Chyet, Stanley F. and Marcus, J.R. *Historical Essay on the Colony of Surinam, 1788.* Cincinnati: 1974.
———— and Gutmann, J. *Moses Jacob Ezekiel: Memoirs from the Baths of Diocletian.* Detroit: 1975.
———— and Herscher, U.D. *On Jews, America and Immigration: A Socialist Perspective.* Cincinnati: 1980.

JILL CLAYBURGH

b. April 30, 1944
Actress

Tall, slinky, blond Jill Clayburgh is an actress who, more than most others, has come to represent the modern woman. For her role as Erica, a wife who rediscovers her identity after being deserted by her husband of 17 years, in Paul Mazursky's 1978 film *An Unmarried Woman,* Clayburgh received an Oscar nomination and the best actress award at the Cannes Film Festival. She is now considered one of the most talented performers in American films.

Jill Clayburgh was born in New York City to Albert Henry and Julia (Door) Clayburgh. Her parents were assimilated Jews and a friend of the young Clayburgh described her home as un-Jewish in style or practice. The actress's mother had been secretary to producer David Merrick before her marriage; and her father, vice president of the Bancroft Bookcloth Company, is the son of opera singer and New York socialite Alma Clayburgh.

Growing up on Manhattan's Upper East Side, Clayburgh loved the fantasy of movies and the theater. She went to Manhattan's private and prestigious Brearley School and later to Sarah Lawrence College, from which she obtained a B.A. degree in 1966. She majored in philosophy, religion and literature. A roommate who was an aspiring actress convinced Clayburgh to spend a college vacation as an apprentice in summer stock at the Williamstown Theater Festival in Massachusetts. Her one-line part in Shaw's *Man and Superman* signaled the start of her career.

While still in college Clayburgh co-starred with her friends Robert De Niro and Jennifer Salt in her first film, *The Wedding Party,* which was independently produced by another friend, Brian De Palma. After college she studied acting in Manhattan with Uta Hagen and then moved to Boston, where she joined the Charles Playhouse and worked in both the children's and adult companies. She appeared in *America Hurrah,* whose cast included another unknown, Al Pacino.

Clayburgh and Pacino moved to New York and appeared on a double bill of playlets by Israel Horovitz that opened in January 1968 at the off-Broadway Astor Place Theater. These were followed by a series of off-Broadway plays, minor roles in nighttime television programs and a year-long stint in daytime soap opera.

Her Broadway debut took place in October 1970 in *The Rothschilds,* a hit musical about the Jewish family that became the wealthiest bankers in Europe. After playing a "panned" Desdemona to James Earl Jones's Othello at the Mark Taper Forum in 1971, and the role of Naomi in the film *Portnoy's Complaint,* based on the Philip Roth novel, Clayburgh returned to Broadway in 1972 to perform in Bob Fosse's musical *Pippin.* As Catherine, the conniving young widow who tries to persuade Pippin, Charlemagne's son, that marrying her will make him happy, she proved she had a good singing voice. Clayburgh next appeared on Broadway in 1974 in Tom Stoppard's play *Jumpers.*

The roles that followed were generally mediocre, and it was not until *An Unmarried Woman* that Clayburgh had the opportunity to prove the depth and breadth of her ability. As Erica she attained stardom, and with few exceptions, she was praised by critics for a flawless performance. Even the usually caustic critic John Simon wrote, "The actress exudes a wealth of inner activity and an ample repertoire of fascinatingly changing expressions, better than any kind of static, conventional prettiness."

Clayburgh's next role was a dramatic departure from the very "New York-ish" Mazursky film. In *Luna,* directed by the Italian Bernardo Bertolucci, the actress played an opera singer who has a semi-incestuous relationship with her son, a marked contrast to her role as nursery-school teacher in ner next film, *Starting Over.*

In another film, *It's My Turn* (1980), Clayburgh portrayed a successful career woman who faces a quandary shared by many high-powered "liberated" women when she realizes that her over-achieving life is empty without personal intimacy and emotional commitment. Directed by Claudia Weill, the film received mixed reviews, but Clayburgh proved once more her ability to adapt to new roles and to assume a greater complexity of character.

ALEXANDER COHEN

b. July 24, 1920
Theatrical producer

In the tradition of P. T. Barnum, and rivaled today perhaps only by David Merrick, Alexander Cohen has brought glamour, innovation and an appealing air of eccentricity to the art of theatrical production and promotion. One of Broadway's great experimenters, Cohen is responsible for importing some of the most significant foreign plays and actors to Broadway and since 1966 has produced the lavish annual Tony Awards ceremonies honoring outstanding accomplishments in theater.

Alexander Henry Cohen was born in New York City to Alexander Henry, a clothing manufacturer and financier, and Laura (Tarantous) Cohen. His father died while Cohen was very young, and through an uncle he received his introduction to theater, attending plays weekly. The producing "bug" hit him early on, and after attending private schools in New York City and studying at New York University and Columbia College, he used a family inheritance in 1941 to buy the Red Barn summer stock theater in Long Island, which he redecorated and promoted. Unfortunately, the Red Barn failed, but Cohen was not discouraged. Even then, risk taking was one of his greatest attributes, and a theatrical failure—Cohen would have many in his career —would only impel him to try something new; he would certainly not give up. Not even when, in the same year, he took over the Daly Theater—a Shubert house—and lost $16,000, a substantial sum in those days. But he also had his first taste of success in 1941 when he became co-producer of the hit Broadway show *Angel Street.*

However, America's entry into World War II cut short not only the show's run but Cohen's career as well. In 1942 he served in the Army infantry but was discharged the following year with leg injuries. Returning to New York, he joined the public relations department of the Bulova Watch Company and so distinguished himself in promotion that within two years he was a vice president of advertising. Although he remained at Bulova for five years more, Cohen's heart was in theater, where he maintained a steady involvement. Finally, in 1950 he became a full-time producer, and although nine years would pass before he had a major hit, he instituted a range of successful promotional gimmicks that not only set him apart from other producers but stimulated audience growth. For example, in 1959 he devised "Nine O'Clock Theater," in which the shows he presented—in this case usually solo or small ensemble productions without an orchestra or the other trappings of large shows—would not begin until 9:00, one hour later than most Broadway curtain times, on the premise that theatergoers should eat dinner without rushing. Under this rubric he produced such shows as *At the Drop of a Hat* with the comic duo Flanders and Swann; (1959), *Hamlet* (1964), *At the Drop of Another Hat* (1966), *Anna Christie* (1977), *Helzapoppin'!* (1977) and others. When *The Pajama Game,* one of the musicals he produced, was trying out in New Haven, Cohen arranged special bus tours from New York, and when French singer Yves Montand arrived for a New York engagement, Cohen had the water fountains spouting champagne on opening night.

The range of Cohen's productions includes Shake-

spearian drama, Neil Simon plays, avant-garde repertory and cabaret acts, on and off-Broadway and in London.
In 1959, as part of the "Nine O'Clock Theater" series,
Cohen was responsible for introducing two young comedians new to New York to the Broadway stage. Mike
Nichols and Elaine May, still in their twenties, presented *An Evening with Nichols and May*—a series of
improvised satirical skits based on audience suggestions
—to critical raves and had a successful and profitable
run. Other notable Cohen productions include *Good
Evening,* a comedy revue featuring the British pair Peter
Cook and Dudley Moore; productions of *School for Scandal, Hamlet* with Richard Burton and Chekhov's *Ivanov,*
all directed by Gielgud; solo performances by Maurice
Chevalier, Marlene Dietrich and Victor Borge; the Sherlock Holmes-based musical comedy *Baker Street* (1965),
the Trevor Griffiths play *Comedians* (1976), which Mike
Nichols directed, and *A Day in Hollywood/A Night in the
Ukraine* (1980), a comedy revue imported from England.
For the Royal Shakespeare Company in London, Cohen
has produced Harold Pinter's *The Homecoming,* Peter
Schaffer's *Black Comedy,* Jules Feiffer's *Little Murders* and
Peter Ustinov's *The Unknown Soldier and His Wife.* In
London he has presented Lauren Bacall in the musical
Applause, Arthur Miller's drama *The Price,* Neil Simon's
comedy *Plaza Suite,* the musical *1776!* and other Amer-
ican imports.

Among Cohen's most publicized flops of the 1970s
were the revival of *Hellzapoppin'!* (1977) in which he
and star Jerry Lewis had a major falling out when the
show closed in out-of-town previews, and *I Remember
Mama,* the 1979 Richard Rodgers musical starring actress
Liv Ullman.

He is annually the center of attention when he produces the televised Tony Awards presentation, in which
representatives from all on-stage and behind-the-scenes
phases of theater production assemble for ceremonies.
At this event, Cohen is reputed to be his most energetic
and eccentric, requiring even camera technicians working on the broadcast to wear black tie or long gowns.

There is, in short, little Alexander Cohen touches
that does not, by virtue of his presence, become interesting.

ARTHUR A. COHEN

b. June 25, 1928
Author; publisher

Arthur A. Cohen, a pioneering publisher and the
author of four critically acclaimed novels, is a Jewish
scholar of the first rank who has also made great contributions to secular intellectual life in America. In both
his fiction and nonfiction, theological, philosophical
and spiritual issues are the focus of his work, as Cohen
seeks to turn his personal explorations of the meaning of
Judaism into a broader context of universal struggle and
self-discovery.

Arthur Allen Cohen was born in New York City to
Isidore Meyer, a clothing manufacturer, and Bess Marion
(Junger) Cohen. He attended Cherry Lawn School in
Darien, Connecticut and Friends Seminary in New York,
where he edited the school paper. Cohen was raised in
an unobservant Jewish home where, despite a strong
cultural education, he nevertheless felt unfulfilled. In
fact, while at the University of Chicago, where he studied philosophy and comparative religion, he made his
first tentative steps toward Christianity. In a 1959 article written for *Harper's* magazine entitled "Why I Choose
to Be a Jew," Cohen said that his parents, concerned by
his interest in Christianity, rushed him to a rabbi, the
late Milton Steinberg. It was through study and reflection with the scholar that Cohen returned to Judaism,
but with a new sense of commitment that would propel
him even further than he first thought.

After receiving his B.A. degree in 1946 and his
M.A. degree from the University of Chicago in 1949,
Cohen studied medieval Jewish philosophy at the Jewish Theological Seminary of America in New York for
the next three years. The pressure exerted by seminary
instructors upon him to become a rabbi, however, pushed
him in still another direction—publishing.

In 1951 Cohen and Cecil Hemley founded Noonday
Press, the first of his publishing enterprises. Five years
later he sold his share to Hemley and started Meridian
Books, which specialized in high-quality paperbacks.
He was its president until it was absorbed in 1960 by
the World Publishing Company. Cohen then served as
editor at several publishing houses until 1974, when he
founded and became president of Ex Libris Publishing
Company.

Meanwhile, beginning in the late 1950s, he was
establishing a reputation as a brilliant essayist on the
subject of Jewish identity, especially that of the American Jew. He also began to write and edit longer books
on Judaic history and tradition. His first two books,
Martin Buber (New York, 1958) and *The Natural and the
Supernatural Jew: An Historical and Theological Introduction* (New York, 1963), explore aspects of existential
dogma. The former captures Buber's longing for tran-
scendence of doubt, while the latter asserts that the role
of Judaism is not to be the creator of culture, but its
critic. In *The Myth of the Judeo-Christian Tradition* (New
York, 1970), Cohen tries to disprove the existence of a
common tradition between Judaism and Christianity.
He says that meaningful dialogue can be conducted

only on humanistic, not theological grounds. In *If Not Now, When—Conversations Between Mordecai M. Kaplan and Arthur A. Cohen*, the author challenges the Reconstructionist interpretation of Jewish life in a dialogue with the Jewish movement's founder.

Cohen has also written *Sonia Delaunay* (New York, 1975), a study of the Parisian avant-garde artist, and the text for the pictorial work *A People Apart: Hasidic Life in America*, with photographs by Philip Garvin (New York, 1970). He has edited numerous books, including *The Anatomy of Faith: Theological Essays of Milton Steinberg* (New York, 1960), *Arguments and Doctrines: A Reader of Jewish Thinking in the Aftermath of the Holocaust* (New York, 1970) and *The Jew: Essays from Martin Buber's Journal Der Jude* (Alabama, 1980).

Religious and spiritual themes have also been central in Cohen's novels, even when not explicitly part of the story line. Each novel has an element of fantasy to it that boils down to a crisis of identity—perhaps similar to the crisis Cohen experienced as a young college student seeking to find out who he was as a Jew and as a man. In *The Carpenter Years* (New York, 1967), an unhappy accountant named Morris Edelman leaves his family—and his Jewishness—behind when he becomes Edgar Morrison, marries a Christian woman and resettles in a small Pennsylvania town, taking a job in a local YMCA, only to find out 20 years later that his son, now a Ph.D., will be coming to town for an interview for a teaching job. As the novel is constructed, a meeting between father and son is inevitable—the book opens at this juncture in Edelman/Morrison's life—and he must finally confront the ambivalences he has kept hidden throughout the years. *In the Days of Simon Stern* (New York, 1973) has a blind Jewish scribe narrating the tale of a poor boy from the Lower East Side who becomes a millionaire and benefactor to poor Jewish survivors of the Holocaust. The protagonist in *A Hero in His Time* (New York, 1976) is an undistinguished Russian-Jewish artist who, for no reason he can fathom, is appointed by the Soviet government to attend a conference in New York City and, while there, to perform some jobs for the KGB. Cohen's most recent novel, *Acts of Theft* (New York, 1980), takes its main character, Stephen Mauger, an artist and collector, to Central America, where he discovers—and sacks—an ancient Mayan site. He runs into conflict with a local art expert and must consider the ramifications of what he has done, both physically and spiritually, to the historic ruins. Despite the variety of locales and actions, Cohen's novels focus on how so-called ordinary men in extraordinary situations confront their consciences in order to discover what is right and moral in life—themes that parallel his theological studies.

An art collector himself, Cohen is the author and editor of several books on art and has contributed essays to many books and journals. Above all, he has remained on a steady course of self-discovery as a Jew and as a writer of his own time. As he once commented, his earliest work was involved in "formulating basic footwork, sign posts, guidelines . . ., but as I gained assurance in my command both of the material of Jewish history and my stylistic ability to reformulate and express, I have found myself moving against the harder and more unyielding issues: God and theodicy, Jewish life after the holocaustal *tremendum* and the founding of the Jewish state, meaning and death."

For further information:
Cohen, Arthur A. *The Holocaust as Tremendum.* New York: 1981.
Cole, Diane. "Profession: Renaissance Man, Arthur A. Cohen." *Present Tense,* Autumn 1981.

BERNARD L. COHEN

b. June 14, 1924
Physicist

Physicist Bernard Cohen has been one of the moving forces in the development of safe nuclear energy and one of the most outspoken supporters of its use for peaceful purposes. A professor at the University of Pittsburgh since 1958, he has been closely involved in public debates concerning nuclear power and has written three books directed toward students and nonprofessionals that explain what atomic energy is and how its development will benefit contemporary society.

Bernard Leonard Cohen was born in Pittsburgh, Pennsylvania to Samuel and Mollie (Friedman) Cohen. He attended the Case Institute of Technology, where he received a B.S. degree in 1944, and the University of Pittsburgh, where he completed a Master of Science degree in 1948. His Doctor of Science degree came from Carnegie-Mellon University in 1950.

From 1950 to 1958 Cohen was engaged in cyclotron research at the Oak Ridge National Laboratory. He then joined the faculty of the University of Pittsburgh, where he became professor of physics and of chemical and petroleum engineering. From 1958 to 1978 he was also director of the Scaife Nuclear Laboratory.

As an ardent nuclear power advocate and one of America's most prominent specialists in the field, Cohen has often become involved in controversial and emotional debate. He feels that most people are misinformed about the radiation risks in nuclear energy and have let themselves be influenced by individuals who not only do not understand the true nature of nuclear power but do not want to know that it is not as dangerous as alleged.

For example, in a January 1977 article in *Family Health,* he criticized consumer advocate Ralph Nader, whom Cohen claimed had taken information about the toxicity of plutonium totally out of context from a federal government report in order to argue against nuclear power reactors. In fact, Cohen wrote, Nader used as his example a scenario that described the worst possible outcome of a nuclear accident, which, according to the study, had a "less than once-in-a-million-year risk of occurring, and that would be if all United States power were nuclear."

Cohen has also addressed many of the public fears about nuclear energy in such general-interest publications as *National Review* and *The Los Angeles Times.* In *Commentary* (November 1978) he concluded that nuclear wastes were "far less dangerous than coal-burning wastes on every count," and "there has never been a fatality or disabling injury due to nuclear wastes, and there probably never will be." His books on the subject are *Heart of the Atom* (New York, 1967), which is geared for a high school-level readership or for nonscientists; *Concepts of Nuclear Physics* (New York, 1971), a college-level text; and *Nuclear Science and Society* (New York, 1974).

Cohen has also published nearly 200 scientific articles and more than 125 abstracts, and he has participated in several hundred colloquia and seminars on various facets of nuclear physics and related subjects. He has worked in almost every major nuclear physics research institution in the United States, including the Brookhaven National Laboratory, the Los Alamos Scientific Laboratory, Massachusetts Institute of Technology and about six others.

His involvement with scientific education includes membership on the National Council of the American Association of Physics Teachers (1975–78); the American Physical Society Panel on Public Affairs (1977–80); and the American Physical Society, Division of Nuclear Physics, of which he was the chairman in 1974–75. Cohen was chairman of the Division of Environmental Sciences of the American Nuclear Society in 1980–81.

In early 1981 Cohen received the Tom W. Donner Prize in nuclear physics from the American Physical Society. He was so honored for "pointing the way to some basic issues in nuclear structures and reactions: to our understanding of low-lying collective states, the occupation of single-particle levels, and the mechanisms of direct reactions."

For further information:
Cohen, Bernard L. "Are Nuclear Side Effects Hazardous to Your Health?" *Family Health,* January 1977.
———. "The Case of the Breeder Reactor." *National Review,* September 16, 1977.
———. "Hazards from Plutonium Toxicity," *Health Physics,* 32, 359 (1977).
———. "High Level Waste from Light Water Reactors," *Review of Modern Physics,* 49, 1 (1977).
———. "Perspective on Occupational Mortality Risks," *Health Physics,* 40, 703 (1981).
———. "A Tale of Two Wastes." *Commentary,* November 1978.

GERSON DAVID COHEN

b. August 26, 1924
Rabbi; Conservative leader

Gerson D. Cohen has been one of America's major Conservative leaders and scholars for many years. He was thus the ideal choice to become the fifth chancellor of the Jewish Theological Seminary of America in New York City in 1972, succeeding such distinguished early scholars as Louis Finkelstein, Cyrus Adler, Solomon Schechter and Sabato Morais. A respected teacher and writer, Cohen is also the Jacob H. Schiff Professor of History at the seminary.

Gerson David Cohen was born in New York City, the son of Meyer, an insurance agent, and Nehama (Goldin) Cohen, a Hebrew teacher. He received his B.A. degree from City College in 1944 and his Bachelor of Hebrew Literature degree in 1943 from JTSA. In 1948 he was ordained a rabbi and ten years later earned his Ph.D. in Semitic languages from Columbia University. He is married to Naomi (Wiener) Cohen, a professor of history at Hunter College in New York City.

Before becoming chancellor, Cohen was librarian from 1950 to 1957 and visiting professor of Jewish literature and institutions at the seminary from 1957 to 1972. He was also Gustav Gottheil Lecturer in Semitic Languages at Columbia University from 1950 until 1960 and from 1963 to 1970 was a full-time faculty member at Columbia University with the title of professor of history and director of the Center of Israel and Jewish Studies.

Among his numerous scholarly works are a critical edition and commentary of Abraham Ibn Daud's *Book of Tradition* ("Sefer Ha-Qabbalah") a history of Jews and Judaism written in 12th-century Spain; (New York,

1967), *Reconstruction of Gaonic History* (New York, 1972); and "Major Trends in Modern German Jewish History," an introduction to the *Leo Baeck Institute Yearbook*, Volume 20 (New York, 1975). A folio of Salvador Dali prints, Aliyah (New York, 1968), contains an essay on Aliyah by Cohen as the text accompanying the 25 lithographs that comprise the work.

Cohen was named to the United States Holocaust Memorial Council in May 1980 by President Jimmy Carter. The council is mandated to establish a memorial/museum in Washington, D.C., an educational and research foundation and a Citizens Committee on Conscience.

In the JTSA he is a strong backer of ordaining women as rabbis within Conservatism. In 1977–78 he presided over the "Commission for the Study of the Ordination of Women as Rabbis" within the Conservative movement, and under his leadership the group concluded, "The ethical arguments coupled with the absence of halakic counterarguments . . . constitute a strong case for the training of women as rabbis at the JTSA."

Cohen has also been in the forefront of those non-Orthodox leaders who insist that their religious rights in Israel be protected. When in 1981 Prime Minister Menachem Begin was urged by three Israeli Orthodox parties to revise the law of Return, whereby Jews can become citizens upon arrival, and to limit further the rights of non-Orthodox Jews in return for their political support in forming a Likud (Begin)-dominated government, Cohen protested publicly, calling the suggested restrictions "a religious affront to the overwhelming majority of the Jewish people." And in a private meeting with Prime Minister Menachem Begin, he cautioned that the proposed bill—since withdrawn—will "cause a rift in the international Jewish community."

Cohen is also a powerful defender of the rights of students and residents of the Morningside Heights neighborhood, which includes the seminary, Columbia University and Barnard College, to study and live in peace without fear of street violence. "It is the duty of spokesmen of religious traditions and institutions to speak out on evils of society," he wrote in "Religion's Business," *Conservative Judaism* (Summer 1976), but "I have watched a city permit lawless throngs to run riot and wreak havoc on business with impunity. . . ."

For further information:

Cohen, Gerson D. "Israel:Anticipation and Reality; The Meaning of Israel in the Perspective of History." *Conservative Judaism*, Spring 1973.
———. "Jewish Identity and Jewish Collective Will in America from an Historical Perspective." *Conservative Judaism*, Summer 1974.

NAOMI W. COHEN

b. November 13, 1927
Historian; educator

Naomi W. Cohen is a historian, whose area of specialization is 20th-century American history and American Jewish history. An educator with many years of service at Hunter College of the City University of New York, she has an active interest in furthering Jewish academic scholarship in the United States.

Naomi Weiner was born in the Bronx to Louis, a customer peddler, and Mary (Halkin) Weiner. She attended New York City public schools and earned her B.A. degree from Hunter College in 1947 and her Bachelor of Hebrew Letters from the Jewish Theological Seminary in 1948. In 1949 she earned her M.A. degree in American history from Columbia University and then received a Ph.D. in American history there in 1955.

Cohen's greatest contribution to American Jewish life is her scholarship in American Jewish history and her dedication to teaching. Her field of concentration is the impact of emergent Jewish life in America, from the Spanish-Portuguese period to the end of the Second World War. She joined the history faculty at Hunter College as an assistant professor in 1962, became an associate professor in 1968 and has been professor since 1973.

As a historian, she hews to a traditional role—namely, producing exhaustively documented studies that attempt to set out everything that happened. Above all, her efforts have allowed readers to sense the enormous amount of material—mainly primary sources—available to serious scholars of American Jewish history. When she began her labors, that history was too often marred by hagiography; her books were reconfirmation that the study of the American Jew had vast potential for scholarly scrutiny.

Her major work, *Not Free to Desist* (Philadelphia, 1972), was based largely on untapped archival material of the American Jewish Committee. It told that organization's story against the background of U.S. foreign policy. "Patterned on European Jewish models," she wrote of the AJC, it was "nurtured in an American matrix." Thus, she lays out its efforts—since 1906—to support human rights, due process and individual achievement because it thought that not only did such actions help Jews here and abroad, but they also reflected American ideals of seeking to help oppressed peoples everywhere.

Her other publications include "Ambassador Straus in Turkey" (*Mississippi Valley Historical Review*, March

1959), "An American Jew at the Paris Peace Conference of 1919" (in *Essays on Jewish Life and Thought,* New York, 1959) and "Abrogation of Russo-American Treaty of 1832" (*Jewish Social Studies,* January 1963). Her books are *A Dual Heritage* (Philadelphia, 1969) and *American Jews and the Zionist Idea* (New York, 1975). *A Dual Heritage* is the biography of Oscar Straus, a former U.S. ambassador to several European countries during the presidential administrations of Grover Cleveland through Warren G. Harding.

Naomi W. Cohen is married to Gerson D. Cohen, chancellor of the Jewish Theological Seminary.

LAURIE COLWIN

b. June 14, 1944
Writer

Laurie Colwin is a popular and respected short story writer and novelist whose work falls under the genre of the comedy of manners. Through her ebullient style and perceptive observations, she attempts to portray the mood of contemporary times.

She was born in New York City to Peter and Estelle (Wolfson) Colwin and grew up in Chicago and the suburbs of Philadelphia. After graduating from high school in 1962, she attended Bard College for one year, majoring in English. She later studied at Columbia University from 1965 until 1968 but did not earn a degree.

From 1965 to 1968 she also worked as a part-time "gofer" for Sanford Greenberger Associates, a literary agency. Between 1969 and 1970 she worked in Viking Press's subsidiary rights department. From 1971 to 1972 she was a reader at G. P. Putnam's and from 1972 to 1977 was on the editorial staff of E. P. Dutton.

Colwin began publishing short stories in *The New Yorker, Redbook* and *Cosmopolitan* toward the end of the 1960s. In 1974 she published a collection of 14 short stories in her first book, *Passion and Affect* (New York). The stories, praised for their quality of grace and understatement, deal with people who are unsuccessful at communicating with others and even at understanding themselves. Colwin seems to enjoy the emotional excitement and idiosyncratic behavior of her characters. One example is a character who loves his job, his house and his family and develops an obsession with exterminating water rats in the inlet where his children swim during the summer. Some of Colwin's stories focus on sexual anxiety and the problems certain people have in understanding, controlling or enjoying their sexual impulses and feelings. Colwin seems to say that love strengthens some people but destroys others who cannot bear its painful aspects.

Colwin's next book, *Shine on Bright and Dangerous Object* (New York, 1975), studied the progression of emotions that a 27-year-old widow experiences as she passes through grief, shock, anger, apathy, fatigue, confusion and passion. Her next novel, *Happy All the Time* (New York, 1978), traced the romantic journeys of graduate students in Cambridge, Massachusetts who have become professionals in New York City. A 1970s comedy of manners, the book examines friendship, marriage, love and morals in the modern world. A *New York Times* critic described it as "a perfectly-executed souffle" that has "a bright, deft, epigrammatic style."

Colwin's book *The Lone Pilgrim* (New York, 1981) is a collection of 13 stories about love. With a keen eye for the accoutrements of the modern lifestyle, she catalogs endless details of fashion styles, interior design, nicknames, diet fads and hobbies. She writes about love with a defiant belief in romanticism. In the story "Intimacy," Martha falls in love with William "as easily as you slide off a warm rock and into a pool of clear, sweet water." In "Saint Anthony of the Desert," the narrator experiences love as "being pulled out of my old self and becoming a new creature."

The winner of the O.Henry Short Story prize in 1977 for her story "The Lone Pilgrim," Colwin is one of the most promising younger writing talents in America today.

BETTY COMDEN

b. May 3, 1919
Actress; songwriter

Betty Comden—lyricist, author and performer, and half of the famous and gifted Broadway songwriting team of Comden and Green—once remarked about her long collaboration with Adolph Green, "If I am ever without Adolph, it will simply be because he has been run over by a truck."

Betty Comden was born in Brooklyn to Leo, a lawyer, and Rebecca (Sadvoransky) Comden, a schoolteacher. Raised in Brooklyn's Crown Heights neighborhood, she attended the Brooklyn Ethical Culture School, Erasmus High School and New York University, where she majored in drama and received a B.S. degree in 1938. She met her future collaborator while looking for an acting job in the theater.

Comden and Green began working together in 1939, when they, Judy Holliday and two other aspiring actors wrote and performed a cabaret act called "The Revuers" at the (Greenwich) Village Vanguard. In 1944, after Judy Holliday departed for Hollywood to become a film star, Comden and Green were invited by Leonard Bernstein to write the book and lyrics for a full-length show based on the ballet *Fancy Free*. It opened on Broadway the same year. But their best work was probably in *On the Town* (1944) whose signature tune, "New York, New York," has remained one of the best-known songs in musical comedy.

Among the many Broadway shows the collaborators have worked on are *Wonderful Town* (1953), *Say Darling* (1958), *Do Re Mi* (1960), *Hallelujah, Baby!* (1967), *Bells Are Ringing* (1968), *Applause* (1970), *On the Twentieth Century* (1977) and *A Party with Betty Comden and Adolph Green* in 1958 and again in 1977. Their film credits include *Barkleys of Broadway* (1949), *Singin' in the Rain* (1952), *The Band Wagon* (1953) and *Auntie Mame* (1958).

Comden and Green have won many awards, including Tony awards in 1953 for *Wonderful Town,* in 1968 for *Hallelujah, Baby!* and in 1970 for *Applause.*

Comden attributes the success of her partnership with Green to the fact that "We don't ever remember who thought up what line" and describes their work process as "mental radar." Once asked what is the cement of their relationship, she responded, "sheer fear and terror."

BARRY COMMONER

b. May 28, 1917
Biologist; environmentalist

Barry Commoner, biologist, ecologist and educator, actively supported the cause of ecology long before preserving the natural surroundings became a major national issue. A long-standing opponent of nuclear power, overpopulation, industrialization and the power of corporations, Commoner brought his scientific expertise into the political arena in 1980, when he became the presidential candidate for the newly created Citizens Party.

Barry Commoner was born in Brooklyn to Isidore, a Russian immigrant tailor, and Goldie (Yarmolinsky) Commoner. Interested in nature since his youth, he developed a strong curiosity about biology at James Madison High School, graduating in 1933. He majored in zoology at Columbia University, where he supported liberal causes, including that of the Spanish Loyalists, and obtained a B.S. degree in 1937.

After receiving his M.A. degree from Harvard University in 1938, Commoner worked as an assistant in biology for two years while pursuing a doctorate, which he was awarded in 1941. From 1942 to 1946 he served in the United States Naval Air Force. In 1947 he joined the faculty at Washington University in St. Louis, where he established a reputation as an entertaining lecturer and a thorough scientific researcher. He helped found the St. Louis Committee for Nuclear Information, serving as its vice president from 1958 to 1965 and its president from 1965 to 1966. From 1965 to 1969 he was chairman of the botany department, which, under his direction, took important steps in the development of techniques for the early detection of cancer.

In the early 1950s Commoner expressed shock at the indifference of government officials to the dangers of radiation fallout and the presence of strontium 90 in the atmosphere caused by nuclear bomb tests. Pollution of air and water by chemical fertilizers, detergents, insecticides and other harmful substances has continued to be one of his major concerns.

With chemist Linus Pauling he led a worldwide effort to halt open-air testing of nuclear weapons. With anthropologist Margaret Mead he helped organize the Science Information Movement. *Time* magazine described him as "the Paul Revere of Ecology."

A lucid speaker and writer, Commoner, since 1979 a professor at Queens College of the City University of New York, has expressed his views at many conferences and symposia, in numerous articles and in his books *Science and Survival* (New York, 1966), *The Closing Circle* (New York, 1971) and *The Poverty of Power* (New York, 1976).

"The proper use of science is not to conquer nature but to live in it. We may yet learn that to save ourselves we must save the world. . . . We may yet discover how to devote the wisdom of science and the power of technology to the welfare and survival of man," he wrote.

In his articles, books and lectures, Commoner emphasizes the importance of protecting the environment. He stresses the dangers of nuclear power, overpopulation and the corporate power that overlooks the needs of individuals, especially "the price gouging and super profits of the oil companies—abetted by . . . the greed and stupidity of the auto industry . . . the poisoning of our air, food and water—profits before people; the export of jobs—by the 'patriotic' corporations," read one of his Citizen Party ads.

AARON COPLAND

b. November 14, 1900
Composer; conductor; critic; performer

The impact of Aaron Copland, often referred to as the "dean of American composers," on the creation of a truly American musical form is extraordinary. Although trained in Europe, Copland was one of the first American composers to incorporate indigenous American folk tunes and themes—as well as Hebraic themes—into his own work. His output has been voluminous: Copland has composed for virtually every music form available, from instrumental solos to operas and ballets, and he has been a seminal influence on generations of younger American composers.

Aaron Copland was born in Brooklyn to Harris Morris, a department store owner, and Sarah (Mittenthal) Copland. He was the youngest of five children. He not only received a Jewish education but was also the first in his family to study music seriously. After hearing his first concert, a Paderewski recital, at age 13, he began studying music with Victor Wittgenstein and Clarence Adler and later studied harmony with Rubin Goldmark. Upon completing Boys High School, he devoted himself full time to music and began to develop a personal style that embraced many of the new musical forms of the European modernists. He broke with Goldmark and departed for Paris in 1921 to study with Boulanger at the Fontainebleau School.

In Paris Copland flourished. In additon to developing under Boulanger, he met and was influenced by composers like Stravinsky, Hindemith, Prokoviev, Schoenberg and the French Six, and the conductor Koussevitsky. He also came into contact with expatriate black American jazz composers and performers. Jazz later became a familiar idiom in Copland's work.

Copland returned to the United States, and in 1924 his first compositions for piano ("Cat and Mouse" and "Passacaglia") were performed at a concert of the League of Composers. Two months later, his Symphony for Organ and Orchestra premiered in New York City, with Boulanger as soloist and Walter Damrosch conducting. That year he received a Guggenheim Fellowship (he was the first composer to do so), which he used in part for a residence at the MacDowell Colony. His orchestral piece *Music for the Theater*, written at MacDowell, made Copland famous in 1927, and he became the United States representative in a festival of the International Society for Contemporary Music in Frankfort. In 1929 he wrote his most striking work on a Jewish subject, the trio *Vitebsk: Study on a Jewish Theme*, with its sharp, unadorned Hasidic flavor.

Copland composed music for almost every type of performance. His ballets based on Americana include *Billy the Kid* (1938), *Rodeo* (1942) and *Appalachian Spring* (1944). He has written chamber music; choral works; operas, including *The Second Hurricane* for children; orchestral music, including three symphonies and many other pieces; piano solos and duets; and vocal solos. The Copland signature was usually a combination of jazz rhythms, modern experimental forms and, frequently, derivative folk sources. Many of Copland's works use themes from American folk songs, such as the Shaker tune "Simple Gifts" in *Appalachian Spring* (for which he was awarded a Pulitzer Prize in 1945) and the cowboy songs "Git Along Little Dogie" and "Old Chisholm Trail" in *Rodeo*. The Latin American Influence surfaced in many pieces following his travels in Mexico and South America, especially in *El Salon Mexico* (1936). But historical American themes are also a Copland trademark, reflected in compositions like *Lincoln Portrait* (1947) and *The Red Pony* (1948), both for orchestra; *Twelve Poems of Emily Dickinson* (1948–'50) and *Old American Songs, Two Sets,* vocal music (1950, 1952); and the opera *The Tender Land* (1954). Blues forms appeared in later works.

During the 1930s Copland became concerned with making modern American music accessible to audiences. His adaptation of popular songs and styles certainly helped. But in addition to composing, he also became a major administrator in music and was actively involved in early television programming on music. Some of the positions he has held include active membership on the board of directors of the League of Composers from its inception, founder of the Copland-Sessions concerts in New York (1928–31); director of the American Festivals of Contemporary Music at Yaddo in Saratoga Springs (1932); organizer of the American Composers' Alliance (1937). He headed the composition department at the Berkshire Music Center at Tanglewood from 1940 until 1957, when he became chairman of its faculty; he retired in 1965.

"I think of my music as Jewish," he told Curt Leviant, an interviewer, "because it's dramatic, it's intense, it has a certain passionate lyricism in it. I can't imagine it written by a goy." His composition *In the Beginning*, written in 1947, has no Jewish themes, but its subject, the Genesis story, is one of the main motifs of Jewish history.

In addition to his early Guggenheim Fellowship and the Pulitzer Prize, Copland has received many other awards and honorary doctorates, including membership in the American Academy of Arts and Letters (1954), an honorary doctorate from Princeton (1956) and the Presidential Medal of Freedom (1964) from President Johnson. In 1981, Queens College of the City University of New York named its School of Music after him.

For further information:
Copland, Aaron. *Copland on Music.* New York: 1963.
———. *Music and Imagination.* Cambridge: 1952.
———. *New Music.* New York: 1969.
———. *What to Listen for in Music.* New York: 1964.

HOWARD COSELL

b. March 25, 1920
Sportscaster

Obnoxious, arrogant and abrasive are only a few of the adjectives commonly used to describe Howard Cosell. What makes Cosell particularly distinctive is that he has risen above them to become America's best-known and most successful sports commentator, whose roost for nearly 30 years has been the ABC radio and television network. His presence combines the showman's panache with the integrity and independence of a man who not only sincerely loves sports but especially prizes the human spirit behind it.

William Howard Cohen was born in Winston-Salem, North Carolina to Isadore and Nellie Cohen. He was raised, however, in Brooklyn, where his Polish immigrant father was an accountant for a chain of clothing stores, and where Cosell developed his love of sports. At Alexander Hamilton High School, he ran track and was sports editor of the school newspaper. Even then he set his sights on becoming a reporter. But to please his parents, after graduating from New York University in 1940 with a B.A. degree in English, Phi Beta Kappa, he studied law and was admitted to the New York bar in 1941. During World War II he served in the U.S. Army Transportation Corps and then opened a private law practice in New York City, where he distinguished himself as an outstanding negotiator, whose clientele included show business and sports figures—among the latter, Willie Mays.

From these early contacts Cosell began to make inroads into broadcast reporting, which had remained his dream. In 1953 he was invited by the program manager at ABC to host a series of Saturday afternoon radio programs (without pay) in which Little Leaguers were introduced to professional baseball stars. (Cosell had been active in forming a local Little League.) He was so successful—and so thrilled with the work—that three years later he signed a full-time contract with ABC.

Cosell's career snowballed. Beginning with a nightly half-hour sports show, *Focus,* from 1956 to 1958, he moved on to cover heavyweight boxing matches for the next seven years. During this period Cosell gained notoriety when he became the outspoken defender of an up-and-coming young black boxer named Cassius Clay who, for reasons of cultural heritage and pride, elected to change his name to Muhammad Ali. In 1967, when the New York State Boxing Commission stripped Ali of his title because of the boxer's refusal on religious and moral grounds to be inducted into the U.S. Army,

Cosell publicly denounced the commission's move, calling it an outrage and a flagrant violation of Ali's Fifth and Fourteenth Amendment rights. His own refusal to be cowed by negative public sentiment at the time—he was deluged with hate mail—was ultimately vindicated by Ali's triumphant return to boxing and the worldwide popular acclaim that followed.

Cosell has always gone beyond mere reportage in his sportscasting. He was one of the few sports journalists to interview Tommie Smith, a black American athlete in the 1968 Mexico City Olympics who participated in a "Black Power" demonstration, and provide a sympathetic perspective on the then-controversial action. Again, during the 1972 Olympics in Munich, Cosell infiltrated the Olympic Village to provide comprehensive coverage of the events following the tragic massacre of 11 Israeli athletes by Palestinian terrorists. For these journalistic "tours de force" and for his overall approach to his work—in which sports becomes a symbol of all human effort, individually and collectively—Cosell has become known as the "conscience of sports." And in recognition of his achievements, he was named Broadcaster of the Year by the International Radio and Television Society in 1974 and was the first television sports journalist to be named Poynter Fellow at Yale several years later for his contributions to media.

Cosell admits that he is controversial. "That is because I don't believe in the sports syndrome that dominates this country," he told *The New York Times* in 1981. "The sports syndrome is so deeply ingrained in the American psyche that it is frightening. Fan violence in recent years demonstrates that some pathetic people feel that they have rights beyond those of ordinary citizens."

Since its inception in 1971 Cosell has been ABC's commentator for *Monday Night Football,* and in 1977 he joined *ABC's Monday Night Baseball.* He regularly comments on championship boxing matches and ABC specials. In 1981 he produced and hosted a monthly half-hour sports magazine program that became weekly in 1982. Meanwhile, he remains a strong radio presence, hosting *Speaking of Sports* 10 times weekly plus a Sunday night program called *Speaking of Everything.*

If Cosell seems a ubiquitous television presence, the reality is quite simple: He is. In addition to his regular sports coverage for ABC, he has guest-hosted for the major talk shows and has appeared in many variety specials and television series, including *The Odd Couple, Laugh-In, Bob Hope Specials, The Flip Wilson Show* and many others. He has also been featured in two Woody Allen films, *Bananas* and *Sleeper,* and a Walt Disney movie, *The World's Greatest Athlete.*

Cosell has produced several television documentaries

that reflect his concern for the human element: the fallibility, the conflicts, the courage, the mystique—which combine to create the magic in sports. "A Look Behind the Legend" examined the life and career of Yankee hero Babe Ruth; "Run to Daylight" profiled football coach Vince Lombardi; and "One Hundred Yards to Glory" chronicled the successful struggle of a small southern black college to create a top-notch football team.

Cosell has written two books that document his career and his experiences in sports. They are *Cosell* (New York, 1973) and *Like It Is* (New York, 1974).

PAUL COWAN

b. September 21, 1940
Writer

Paul Cowan represents a new breed of Jewish-American journalists and authors who, nurtured on the ideals of the 1960s, have used intense self-examination to create a more meaningful life around them. An active member of the Jewish Havurah movement in New York City, Cowan describes the progression of his writing, from civil rights and anti-war activist days to the articles and books he has published on ethnicity, as a "personal spiritual adventure story."

Paul Cowan was born in Chicago to Louis G., a radio broadcasting executive, and Pauline (Spiegel) Cowan. Paul's father changed his name from Cohen to Cowan, according to the writer, "because he hated *his* embittered, unloving Orthodox father." Brought up in a New York home that celebrated Christmas instead of Hanukkah and having attended Choate, an Episcopalian prep school, Cowan cannot remember knowing anyone who kept kosher or observed the Sabbath when he was growing up.

Having worked on his high school newspaper, Cowan spent two years between high school and college, from 1958 to 1960, as a journalist. He wrote obituaries, wedding announcements and the like for the *Quincy* (Mass.) *Patriot Ledger* and was a fiction reader and fact checker for *Esquire* magazine.

Cowan was graduated from Harvard University, with a B.A. degree in American history and literature in 1963 where he had written for the *Crimson*, the school paper. He did graduate work in political and social thought at the University of Chicago from 1964 to 1965. From 1962 to 1964, while Cowan was still a student, he became active in the civil rights movement and began writing political articles for *Esquire* and *Dis-*

sent. One of Cowan's pieces caught the eye of Jack Newfield of *The Village Voice* in 1965, the year Cowan began his long writing career with the iconoclastic New York City weekly newspaper.

After returning from Ecuador in 1967, where he was a Peace Corps volunteer for a year, Cowan continued writing articles for the *Voice*, *Ramparts* and other publications. In 1970 he published his first book, *The Making of an Un-American* (New York), which expressed his disillusionment with cold-war America and with the "melting pot" theory, a feeling that had developed while he was in the Peace Corps.

In 1972 Cowan published his first Jewish article, "Jews Without Money Revisited," in the *Voice*. While he had intended that the article, which focused on the Lower East Side in Manhattan, would be about Jewish socialism, it turned out instead to be about Jewish poverty. "I discovered," Cowan says, "that people with whom I previously felt very distant—old Jews surviving on incomes of about $4,000—had some connection to me." Cowan slowly started developing an interest in Judaism, celebrating Hanukkah and Passover seders with his family. With a group of other assimilated Jews who were interested in learning about their religion, Cowan developed a Havurah or informal congregation on the West Side of Manhattan. The Havurah started a school for children, which involved parent participation and increased Cowan's Jewish consciousness.

In 1973, the year Cowan became a staff writer for the *Voice*, he published *State Secrets* (New York), with Nat Hentoff and Nick Egleson, which examined and bitterly condemned the illegal operations of the FBI and grand juries in domestic surveillance and persecution of anti-war dissenters. He also continued writing articles on Jews in New York City and "Conversos," hidden Jews in Portugal. Cowan says that he was surprised when his father, who had always seemed uninterested in Judaism, urged him to write an article on religious Jews. In 1978, two years after his parents died in a fire, Cowan published a piece, "Orthodox in New York," in the *Voice* as "a form of mourning." The article, which Cowan says helped him "recover a part of my own lost past," received a huge number of reprint requests from readers who also felt a tremendous gulf between their own lives and their cultural and religious history.

Among Cowan's other major interests are ethnicity, about which he wrote *The Tribes of America* (New York, 1978). And he has written sympathetically about the Lawrence, Massachusetts textile workers strike in 1912 and the high price in suffering paid by immigrant workers.

He is involved in the National Havurah Summer

Institute, which offers summer courses in different Jewish subjects at the University of Hartford, and is working with a group of other West Siders in Manhattan to use the Anshei Hesed synagogue as their center.

For further information:
Cowan, Paul. "Wanderings in America." *Present Tense,* Winter 1981.

LAWRENCE CREMIN

b. October 31, 1925
Educator; historian

Dr. Lawrence Cremin, president of Teachers College, Columbia University since 1974, and its Frederick A. P. Barnard Professor of Education, is one of America's foremost scholars in the history of American education as well as a distinguished educator in his own right. He is the author of a major history of American education and the winner of the 1981 Pulitzer Prize for History for his book *American Education: The National Experience (1783–1876)* (New York, 1980).

Lawrence Arthur Cremin was born in New York City to Arthur T., the founder and director of the New York Schools of Music, and Theresa (Borowick) Cremin. Educated at the exclusive but public Townsend Harris High School for gifted boys, he graduated with a B.S.S. degree from City College of New York in 1946 and received his M.A. degree and Ph.D. from Columbia University in 1947 and 1949, respectively.

Cremin's affiliation with Teachers College as instructor and eventually professor of education began in 1949. From 1952 to 1959 he was associate editor of *Teachers College Record* and has been on the editorial boards of *History of Education Journal, Sociology of Education, School Review, International Review of Education* and *Yearbook of Education.* Currently he is on the editorial boards of *American Journal of Education, History of Education, Journal of Family History* and the *World Book Year Book.* Cremin was appointed to the history department of Columbia University in 1961.

Although he has remained primarily at Columbia University, Cremin has also taught summers at Harvard (1957, 61), Stanford (1973), the University of California at Los Angeles (1956), the Bank Street College of Education (1959–60; spring semester), and the Seminar in American Studies at Salzburg, Austria (1956). In 1966 he was Sir John Adams Memorial Lecturer at the University of London, and in 1972 he was Cecil H. Green Visiting Professor at the University of British Columbia.

Cremin's greatest contributions have been his books on the history and theories of education. *The Transformation of the School: Progressivism in American Education (1876–1957)* (New York, 1961) traces the genesis of the progressive movement in schooling from its inception just after the Civil War through its flowering and ultimate fragmentation and collapse after World War II. It won the Bancroft Prize in American History in 1962. *American Education: The Colonial Experience (1607–1783)* (New York, 1971), the first of a projected three-volume history of American education, starts with a description of the intellectual heritage from which early ideas and attitudes arose and proceeds to analyze the development of an educational system in America in concert with social, political, religious and cultural changes, both in the United States and in England. It includes discussions of the impact of the 1689 revolution and other political upheavals. Cremin uses a biographical style, selecting important figures of the time and using them as focuses around which to describe other events. They include Erasmus, Sir Thomas More, John Locke, Cotton Mather, Benjamin Franklin and Thomas Jefferson.

In the Pulitzer Prize-winning *American Education: The National Experience (1783–1876),* the second of Cremin's histories of American education, he discusses the impact of urbanization, national expansion, churches, newspapers, institutions and societies, government, factories and family on the growth of schools and colleges. Essentially, the book is a history of American society seen through its educational systems, with a focus on how changing values led to the establishment of "alternative" schools, especially church-sponsored parochial schools.

Cremin is the author of five additional books and edits *Classics in Education,* a series published at Teachers College. Many of his works express his belief that the best education occurs in a liberal-minded society. Much of the thrust of Cremin's multivolume history of American education lies in portraying educational development in a very broad context in which the rise of the popular press, Mormonism, slavery, religion and other phenomena are seen as contributing significantly to American schools.

Cremin was a Guggenheim Fellow in 1957 to 1958 and a fellow at the Center for Advanced Study in the Behavioral Sciences from 1964 to 1965. In addition to the Pulitzer Prize, his awards include the American Educational Research Association's Award for Distinguished Contributions to Educational Research (1969), New York University's Award for Creative Educational Leadership (1971), Columbia University's Butler Medal (1973) and the College of the City of New York's Townsend Harris Medal (1974).

Cremin is on the boards of trustees of the Children's Television Workshop, the Spencer Foundation, the Carnegie Foundation for the Advancement of Teaching and the Rockefeller Archive Center. He has held several positions within the United States Office of Education and is a member of the Educational Advisory Board of the John Simon Guggenheim Memorial Foundation. He is also a member of the Academic Board of the Melton Research Center of the Jewish Theological Seminary of America, a program dedicated to research in and service to Jewish education.

For further information:
Cremin, Lawrence. *The American Common School*. New York: 1951.
———. *The Genius of American Education*. Pittsburgh: 1965.
———. *Public Education*. New York: 1976.
———. *Traditions of American Education*. New York: 1977.

MARVIN DAVIS

b. 1925
Industrialist

Although he shuns publicity, Denver-based oil executive Marvin Davis has been one of America's newsworthy businessmen of the 1980s. Not only is he America's most successful independent oil wildcatter (one who explores new and untapped oil reserves)—in 1980 his company drilled more wells than Exxon—his ventures also include bank ownership and massive real estate holdings in Denver, as well as the landmark purchase in 1981 of 20th Century Fox.

Little is known of Davis's background. His British-born father, Jack Davis, was a garment manufacturer in New York who eventually founded his own company in the Midwest. Marvin Davis studied engineering, according to one report, at Syracuse University and New York University and joined with his father in 1945. But the phenomenal growth of the Davis Oil Company lies squarely in the lap of the son, whose aggressive strategies in oil exploration, drilling and commerce led to its multimillion-dollar growth and expansion throughout the Midwest and abroad. Over the years Davis developed a reputation as a workaholic with a "frontier ruthlessness" that made him difficult to work for. But he is also known to amply reward his top engineers with percentages of profits made when they locate and tap new oil sources.

Davis became a public figure in the late 1970s when he began to significantly expand his business "empire" in and beyond Denver. He became Denver's most important builder and holder of real estate, in partnership with friend and attorney Myron Miller, including the construction of the city's largest development, which encompassed a shopping center and building complex, as well as the Metro National Bank. In 1977 he tried unsuccessfully to purchase a floundering baseball team, the Oakland Athletics, which he hoped to bring to Denver, but the deal fell through two years later when the team's owner, Charles Finley, could not sever his contract with the Oakland stadium. Davis made history again in March 1981, when he negotiated to buy 20th Century Fox, abruptly withdrew his offer a few weeks later, then just as suddenly reappeared and bought the movie conglomerate for $700 million that June. Earlier he had also bid unsuccessfully to purchase the *Denver Post*.

Easily one of America's richest men, Davis is active in Denver philanthropy and once contributed $5 million toward a study of aging. Nonetheless, he remains a deliberately private figure who is known to make his family his priority.

LUCY DAWIDOWICZ

b. June 16, 1915
Historian; author

Although the Holocaust has been the focus of many books, articles, plays, films, museum exhibitions, television programs and discussions in recent years, probably no exploration and analysis has been as thorough as Lucy Dawidowicz's monumental and award-winning *The War Against the Jews 1933–1945* (New York) published in 1975. With this work, Dawidowicz established herself as a major scholar of the Holocaust era.

Lucy Schildkret was born in New York City to Max and Dora (Ofnaem) Schildkret. She attended Hunter College, where she received a B.A. degree in 1936, and two years later pursued her love for Yiddish culture as a research fellow at the Yivo Institute for Jewish Research in Vilna, Poland. She had come from a nonreligious household in the United States and attended synagogue for the first time in her life in Vilna.

On the eve of the Second World War, and at the urging of the U.S. government, Dawidowicz returned to New York, where YIVO—The Yivo Institute for Jewish Research—was eventually reorganized. From 1940 to 1946 she was assistant to the research director of YIVO. When the war ended, however, she returned to Europe for the American Jewish Joint Distribution Committee to minister as best she could to the shattered concentration camp survivors. Then, back home again in 1947, she researched the information John Hersey required for *The Wall* (New York, 1950) his novel of the Warsaw Ghetto. She was also by then a research analyst and later research director for the American Jewish Committee, a post she retained until 1969, when she joined the faculty of Yeshiva University. At Yeshiva she was Paul and Leah Lewis professor of Holocaust studies from 1970 to 1975 and Eli and Diana Zborowski professor of interdisciplinary Holocaust studies from 1976 to 1978.

In 1967 she edited *The Golden Tradition: Jewish Life and Thought in Eastern Europe* (New York), a volume that sought to preserve the best writing and memoirs of that past world. She contributed an extensive introduction, brilliantly written and shining with insights and originality. In 1975 her book *The War Against the Jews 1933–1945* (New York) was published. Her thesis was that the Nazi "final solution" was more than a vendetta by European thugs and anti-Semites; it was instead the culmination of authoritarian and despotic ideology—the destruction of the outsider, the unspeakable alien Jew. The book is a work of synthesis, derived from source material in six foreign languages. She treats many phases of the period in an almost passionless voice, but one filled with poignant horror.

In 1976 she edited *The Holocaust Reader* (New York), which deals with the historiography of the period. Even so, she is very much against what she refers to as "The Holocaust Industry," which she describes as the vulgarization and sadomasochism she detects in the unprecedented outpouring of books and films on the subject. "It is important to know about the Holocaust, to talk about it," she says. "That's what I've tried to do. On the other hand, you have to put it in the perspective of all of Jewish existence." The central motif in Judaism, she goes on, is the concept of redemption.

> The enormity is not in our suffering but in their evil. It is their history, *goyische* history, that stands outside of what has been normative human experience—even for evil doing. If the old moral positions are no longer valid after the Holocaust, it is not our problem. It's their problem. If only they would realize it.

All the more justification for *The Holocaust and the Historians* (Cambridge, Mass., 1981), in which she attacks those spurious historians who have denied that the Nazis murdered 6 million Jews.

In addition to her teaching at Yeshiva, Dawidowicz has guest-lectured at Stanford University, Bowdoin College and Syracuse University. In 1981 she was visiting professor of Jewish civilization at Stanford. Her articles have appeared in such publications as *Commentary, The* (London) *Times Literary Supplement, The New York Times Book Review, Salmagundi, Jewish Social Studies, Midstream* and many others.

She was a Guggenheim Fellow in 1976. In 1978-79 she was named a member of the President's Commission on the Holocaust.

For further information:
Dawidowicz, Lucy. *The Jewish Presence: Essays on Identity and History.* New York: 1977.
Dawidowicz, Lucy, co-editor. *For Max Weinreich on His Seventieth Birthday: Studies in Jewish Languages, Literature and Society.* The Hague, Netherlands: 1964.

MIDGE DECTER

b. July 25, 1927
Writer; editor

Writer and editor Midge Decter, one of the significant figures in the neo-conservative movement, is a frequent contributor to *Commentary* and other well-known magazines as well as a prominent publicist and personality. She has written three books that focus on social movements of the 1960s and 1970s and has become a leading spokeswoman against affirmative action.

Midge Rosenthal was born in St. Paul, Minnesota to Harry, a merchant, and Rose (Calmenson) Rosenthal. She attended the University of Minnesota from 1945 to 1946 and the Jewish Theological Seminary of America from 1946 to 1948. After she completed her education, she began writing and combined her career with work as an editor. She worked as assistant editor at *Midstream* magazine from 1956 to 1958, as managing editor of *Commentary* from 1961 to 1962 and, in the following years, as editor at CBS's Legacy Books, *Harper's* and *The Saturday Review.* From 1974 until 1980 she was an editor at Basic Books.

In 1971 Decter published her first book, *The Liberated Woman and Other Americans* (New York), a collection of articles written between 1958 and 1971 for various publications. The book is divided into three sections, "Being a Woman," "Being an American" and "Being a Liberal." Exploring the emergence of the women's liberation movement, Decter is highly critical of its motives. Her other essays were critical of political trends, such as the popularity and impact of the Kennedys. In her second book, *The New Chastity and Other Arguments Against Women's Liberation* (New York, 1972), Decter claims that women's real difficulties stem not from their alleged oppression, but from their unprecedented amount of freedom and wide range of choices. A commentator wrote, "Every critic requires its Midge Decter, the citizen not easily buffaloed, who keeps asking embarrassing questions." However, others claimed that she focused too much on fringe elements of feminism and not enough on its overall effect on "average" women. Her third book, *Liberal Parents, Radical Children* (New York, 1975), raises the question: What has gone "wrong" with children? She contends that the young have become self-indulgent and irresponsible because of liberal child-rearing practices of the 1950s and 1960s.

Elsewhere, in a *New York Times* article, she charged that affirmative action caused a loss of self-esteem in its beneficiaries. She also wrote that it was both illegal and a new departure in American history. The latter assertion was promptly challenged by black Howard University professor Martin Kilson, who wrote that Decter would find it hard to uncover many, if any, "Irish, Polish or Jewish Americans . . . who would claim damage to self-respect owing to politically induced benefits like well-paid civil service jobs and multi-billion dollar contracts."

Decter has become associated in recent years with a group of disaffected liberal Democrats now known as neo-conservatives. Along with husband Norman Podhoretz, editor of *Commentary* magazine, as well as with editor Irving Kristol, sociologist Nathan Glazer, philosopher Sidney Hook and others, Decter was involved in early 1981 with the founding of the Committee for the Free World. "Our aim is to alter the climate of confusion and complacency, apathy and self-denigration, that has done so much to weaken the Western democracies," read her committee's policy statement. It declared its aim of battling "the rising menace of totalitarianism." In 1981 the organization published a full-page advertisement in *The New York Times* defending the Reagan administration's policy in El Salvador.

Decter's work as executive director in this organization reflects one aspect of her commitment to neo-conservative principles. Her positions are sympathetic to conservative policies that generally support spending cuts in many American social programs; a very strong military establishment; and a positive stance toward Israel.

ALAN MORTON DERSHOWITZ

b. September 1, 1938
Lawyer; civil libertarian

Alan M. Dershowitz, Harvard Law School professor, attorney and author, is the consummate civil libertarian and one of the nation's significant defenders of individual freedom. "I'm certainly a civil libertarian," he says, "although I don't like that term. I prefer to think of myself as an advocate for human rights."

Alan Dershowitz was born in Brooklyn, the son of Harry and Claire (Ringel) Dershowitz. He attended Yeshiva University High School and graduated from Brooklyn College in 1959, earning his B.A. degree. In 1962 he received a Bachelor of Laws degree from Yale Law School (he had been editor in chief of the *Yale Law Journal*) and became a law clerk at first to Chief Judge David Bazelon of the United States Court of Appeals (1962-63), and afterward to Supreme Court Justice Arthur Goldberg (1963-64) and then a part-time criminal defense attorney.

Dershowitz's deep interest in freedom led him to become Anatoly Shcharansky's American lawyer. Shcharansky is the Soviet Jewish dissenter who was arrested and held incommunicado since early 1977, charged with treason by the USSR. Dershowitz sees his defense as consistent with his belief in the right of dissidents to leave any country. "Maybe as a Jew I overvalue the right of emigration," he once said, "but to me there is no more important right than to leave a place that is treating you badly or that you perceive is treating you badly. This has been the one right that, when exercised, has permitted the survival of my people. When it has been denied, as in Nazi Germany and the Soviet Union, it has caused the destruction of my people."

Dershowitz's deep concern for civil liberties has led him to defend people and causes of all ideological views. He successfully defended actor Harry Reems, *Deep Throat's* male lead, against obscenity charges. "It was an attempt to expand the conspiracy law into the area of First Amendment expression beyond any reasonable scope," he told the *Harvard Law School Bulletin* in the summer of 1978. Thus whenever he believes human rights are threatened, "I try hard to balance my attack, right and left—for every attack on the Soviet Union, there's one on Chile. For every attack on a right-wing repressive government, there should be an attack on a left-wing repressive government."

At home he has defended the right of American neo-Nazis to march and speak in Skokie, Illinois; and of two Stanford University faculty members, one left and the other right, both punished for their views and actions. He also wrote an influential Supreme Court memorandum in favor of Allen Bakke's reverse discrimination complaint charging that the University of California at Davis Medical School had discriminated against Bakke because he was white. His name has been associated with such well-known First Amendment cases in recent years as *Titticut Follies* (about a Massachusetts mental institution), the Pentagon Papers, *Hair* and *I Am Curi-*

ous, Yellow (a film accused of being pornographic). He also defended a young Jewish Defense League member who was accused of murdering a young woman in the bombing of impresario Sol Hurok's office. Despite his serious misgivings about JDL's acceptance of violence, he took the case. Ultimately the case was dismissed, and Dershowitz won, describing it as "a legal tale of intrigue and pathos" in the April/May 1976 issue of the *Civil Liberties Review*. In his book, *The Best Defense: The Courtroom Confrontations of America's Most Controversial Lawyer of Last Resort* (New York, 1982), Dershowitz's tactic of challenging government prosecutors in trials is evident in his discussions of his defense of nursing home "czar" Bernard Bergman and in his attack on those who "entrapped" the J.D.L. in the bombing of Sol Hurok's office. The system, he writes, "depends on a pervasive dishonesty by its participants" including a "cheat elite" of judges and district attorneys who deliberately distort the law to send alleged felons to prison. Thus, lawyers such as himself are justified in using the Constitution and every "fair and legal" technique to save their clients. And, finally, he asserts that "defending the guilty and despised—even freeing some of them—is a small price to pay for our liberties."

For further information:

Dershowitz, Alan M. "Civil Liberties in Israel," in *Israel, The Arabs and the Middle East*. New York: 1972.

———. "Due Process of Law in the Trial of Soviet Jews." *Israel Yearbook on Human Rights*. Tel Aviv: 1975.

———. *Fair and Uncertain Punishment*. Report of the Twentieth Century Fund Task Force on Criminal Sentencing. New York: 1976.

ISAAC DJERASSI

b. July 27, 1925
Physician; researcher

With the receipt in 1972 of the Albert Lasker Award, the most prestigious honor in American medicine, Isaac Djerassi was recognized for his total dedication and brilliance as one of America's most distinguished cancer researchers. His pioneering modes of leukemia treatment —including methods of platelet transfusion and controlled high dosages of methotrexate, a standard cancer drug—have contributed to significantly higher survival rates among leukemia victims and other cancer sufferers.

Isaac Djerassi was born in Sofia, Bulgaria to Rahamim and Adela (Tadjer) Djerassi. His father was a prosperous merchant. In 1943 he was deported with his family by the Nazis and was about to be transported to a concentration camp, but the surrounding Bulgarian community protested and stopped the transports. The Djerassi

family remained in Bulgaria, and from 1944 to 1949 Isaac Djerassi studied at the Sofia University medical school. His M.D. degree, which he received in 1952, came not from Bulgaria, however, but from the Hebrew University in Jerusalem, where he studied for one year and interned for another.

Djerassi came to the United States in 1954—he was naturalized eight years later—and joined the staff of the Children's Hospital Medical Center in Boston, where he specialized in cancer research for the next three years. Focusing on leukemia treatment, he devised a technique of transfusing massive quantities of platelets from cancer-free donors to stop his patients' bleeding, which until then had been uncontrollable. The success of this technique led to his receiving his first major honor, a first prize for research at the Sixth International Congress of Hematology in Boston in 1956. The practice he developed has since become a standard form of therapy for leukemia and related diseases.

Djerassi next spent three years as a research associate in the Pathology Department of the Harvard University Medical School perfecting his work in platelet transfusions. He then moved to the University of Pennsylvania, where he was an assistant professor of pediatrics from 1961 to 1969, and the Children's Hospital of Philadelphia in 1960, where he focused on the use of methotrexate, a well-known cancer drug that had nevertheless been ineffective in leukemia treatment. Djerassi experimented on ten leukemic children with doses 20 to 30 times the usual amount, by having the substance injected into the bloodstream through continuous dripping.

The ten children immediately had remissions, but to avoid dangerous side effects from deliberate overdoses, Djerassi stopped the treatment for several weeks, then resumed it in even greater amounts—from 100 to 200 times the usual dose. However, these dosages were given for one or two days only, in order to avoid the possible negative consequences of long-term treatment. Ultimately, through constant monitoring, he was able to determine a proper schedule for administering methotrexate and for following up with another drug, citrovorum factor, which was designed specifically to counteract the toxic effects of methotrexate.

Djerassi expanded his research to other forms of cancer when he moved to the Mercy Catholic Medical Center near Philadelphia in 1969 as its director of Research Hematology and Oncology and director of the Division of Pediatric Hematology. Within a short time there he achieved important successes in treating osteogenic sarcoma—a highly fatal form of bone cancer often requiring amputation—and lymphosarcoma. He also used methotrexate to extend the life expectancies of pancreatic cancer victims and breast-cancer patients.

In addition to chemotherapy, Djerassi has experimented successfully with new forms of immunotherapy. Although still in the experimental stage, his work in injecting patients with lymphokines, molecules produced by the human body's own immune system, has elicited positive results.

The Lasker Award is but one of numerous honors accorded to Djerassi. Others include the Golden Plate Award from the American Academy of Achievement and the Super Achiever Award of the Juvenile Diabetes Association, both in 1977. He has also participated in conferences, seminars and task forces in the United States and abroad, including a 1974 international symposium on leukocytes in Jerusalem and a symposium in 1976 at the Weizmann Institute in Rehovoth.

E.L. DOCTOROW

b. January 6, 1931
Writer; editor

E.L. Doctorow, a novelist who has written important fiction on contemporary social and political themes filtered through his creative imagination, is also a teacher of writing and a former publishing executive.

E(dgar) L(awrence) Doctorow was born in the Bronx, the grandson of immigrants from Russia and the child of first-generation David and Rose (Levine) Doctorow. His father barely eked out a living selling radios, records and musical instruments; his mother taught piano. Doctorow attended the prestigious Bronx High School of Science, graduating in 1948, and then matriculated at Kenyon College in Gambier, Ohio, receiving his B.A. degree in 1952. For a year afterward he studied for—but never received—his M.A. degree at Columbia University. Drafted, he served in the Army between 1953 and 1955 in the Signal Corps and, once discharged, went to work as a reader for Columbia Pictures. He also began writing seriously.

Welcome to Hard Times (New York, 1960), his initial novel, relied on the mythology of the West as it told a story of the callous and savage destruction of a town, a pusillanimous mayor and a local prostitute. *Big as Life* (New York, 1966), his second work, was a science fiction tale, in which two huge and naked figures are introduced into New York City and frighten New Yorkers. Several critics believed Doctorow was using the figures as a symbol for the atom bomb, but he said nothing on the matter other than to assert that as a writer he preferred "ambiguity."

As he was writing fiction, Doctorow was also working as a full-time book editor, at first for the New American Library (1959–64) and later as editor in chief for Dial Press (1964–69), where his writers included Richard Condon, James Baldwin, Howard Fast and Norman Mailer.

In 1971 he published *The Book of Daniel* (New York), a roman a clef, though Doctorow has vigorously denied that was his intent. The book deals with the execution of the accused Jewish atomic "spies" Julius and Ethel Rosenberg and the devastating impact it had on their two small sons. Doctorow described the Rosenberg execution as "a major political crime in the 1950s." The novel reveals a sense of the fury and indignation that take hold of "Daniel" (a portrait of the younger son) as a witness to the murder of his parents by indifferent, insolent and ruthless institutions. Yet through it all there is also evidence of Doctorow's gently ironic tone.

Ragtime (New York, 1975), his next novel, was a gift of his "marvelous imagination." It is a book populated by now-dead historical figures—Harry Houdini, Sigmund Freud, Carl Jung, Emma Goldman, Teddy Roosevelt, Henry Ford, Woodrow Wilson, J.P. Morgan, Booker T. Washington and Albert Einstein—together with wry observations about their accomplishments and the consequences of their lives on America's 20th century. For example, Doctorow writes that after Freud spent time in the United States in 1906, "at least a decade would have to pass before [he] would have his revenge and see his ideas begin to destroy sex in America forever." Throughout *Ragtime* real and imaginary people and events come into contact with one another, as if by design. What Doctorow seemed to be saying was that the real hero was the pre-technological era before World War I ("America's privileged childhood," commented a reviewer), before corporate control, the films and the motor car dramatically changed this country.

Doctorow has since resigned from book publishing to write. He has been a writer-in-residence at the University of California at Irvine and teaches at Sarah Lawrence College in Bronxville, New York. He has written a play produced by the Yale Repertory Theater. Doctorow also lends the use of his name and presence to aid in the growth and development of the Ben Gurion University of the Negev in Israel.

ALEXANDER DONAT

b. April 19, 1905
Publisher; author

From the ashes of his own experience as survivor of the Warsaw Ghetto and five concentration camps, Alexander Donat founded in 1975 the Holocaust Library, a publishing house designed to provide a legacy of the past for future generations of Jews. Though small, the library has already proven instrumental in the creation of Holocaust studies courses across the U.S.—a learning process Donat feels must take place so that no one ever forgets what happened to the Six Million.

Alexander Donat was born in Warsaw, Poland, on April 19, 1905, to Herman, a businessman, and Fanny (Machlis) Donat. He attended a Polish "gymnasium"—primary and secondary school combined—but when he completed his studies, he was, as often happened to Jewish students, denied a diploma which would have enabled him to enter the university. He thus went to Paris as did other Polish Jews, where he studied chemistry during the day and worked as a typesetter at night.

Two years later, Donat returned to Poland following the death of his father. This time he was accepted at the Warsaw University and finished his chemistry studies. But a decision to change careers led him to forego final exams, and Donat never received a degree.

His new career was as a journalist. Using his chemistry background, Donat started writing articles on popular scientific issues. As his skills improved and he became better known, he began to edit, and in 1935 to own and publish, a major Polish-language daily newspaper called *Ostatnie Wiadomosci (The Latest News)*. In the interim, over a four-year period, he also published a series of more than 200 titles of Yiddish works in paperback—the first "pocket" books ever published, Donat claims —including biographies, novels and short story collections. The newspaper, which Donat published until September 1939, had a special purpose beyond mere news reporting; it was one of the few dailies to avoid the rampant anti-Semitism that was commonly found in most other mass circulation Polish newspapers reaching the general public.

When World War II began in 1939, Donat had to give up publishing. With his wife, a pharmacist, and his young son, he was confined to the Warsaw Ghetto. Two weeks before the Ghetto was wiped out in 1943, the Donats gave their son to a Catholic family, and shortly after were deported together to the Maidenek concentration camp. Eventually they were separated. Donat went to five different camps while his wife—whom he was told had been killed—survived two years at Auschwitz and a later period at Ravensbruck. Liberated at Dachau, Donat returned to Warsaw, where he was reunited with his wife and with his son, who had been placed in a Catholic orphanage and baptized. "It was so unusual to find your whole family again—a one in a million chance," Donat said. The family remained together in Poland for six months and, in 1945, emigrated to New York. Donat returned to his earlier profession, printing, while the family adjusted to its new life.

Donat spent much of the next 30 years building his business, but at the same time an urge grew, rising from his experiences as a survivor and his past career as a journalist, to preserve the memory of the Holocaust so that future generations of Jews and non-Jews would never forget it.

Thus, in 1975 Donat turned over his printing firm to his son and, in turn, took office space at the company to found the Holocaust Library as a non-profit publishing venture. As president and chairman, he organized a board of advisers—all survivors, including Elie Wiesel—to supervise and select works to be published. Some were diaries or reprints of earlier publications of Holocaust experiences, others original, contemporary works.

Included among them was Donat's own memoir, *The Holocaust Kingdom,* which recounted his ghetto and camp experiences, and *The Death Camp Treblinka: A Documentary,* a compilation of statistics, trial transcripts, biographies, photos and other data describing the "hell" that Treblinka was. And among the Holocaust Library are such books as *The Politics of Rescue* by Henry Feingold, an account of how the Roosevelt administration dealt with Europe's Jews; *With Raoul Wallenberg in Budapest* by Per Anger, a memoir of the Swedish aristocrat who helped rescue Jews in Hungary; and *The Black Book* by Ilya Ehrenburg and Vasily Grossman, the controversial account, prepared in 1946 and suppressed in the Soviet Union, of the Nazi extermination of 1.5 million Russian Jews.

In 1980 the Holocaust Library received recognition for its efforts in the form of the prestigious Thomas-Carey Award sponsored by *Publishers Weekly.* The award is remarkable, says Donat, in that for the first time in its 42-year history, it went to a small and relatively new publishing house.

In addition to his work with the library, Donat is a special advisor to the U.S. Holocaust Memorial Council.

NORMAN DORSEN

b. September 4, 1930
Lawyer; civil libertarian

Norman Dorsen has had many roles—professor, author, attorney, organization leader—and he has used all of them to advance the cause of civil liberties.

Norman Dorsen was born in New York City to Arthur Dorsen, a pharmacist, and his wife Tanya. He attributes his interest in civil liberties to the example of fairness shown by his parents in his youth.

Dorsen was graduated from the the prestigious Bronx High School of Science and received his B.A. and a Phi Beta Kappa key from Columbia in 1950. Three years later he got his law degree from Harvard, magna cum laude. He soon got a close look at the potential power of government over the individual when he served as an aide to attorney Joseph Welch at the Army-McCarthy hearings in 1953.

He won a Fulbright Scholarship and spent two years (1954-56) studying international economics at the London School of Economics. In 1956, he returned home and served as a law clerk on the U.S. Court of Appeals. The next year he clerked for Justice Harlan on the U.S. Supreme Court.

Dorsen briefly entered private legal practice, but in 1961 joined the faculty of the New York University Law School, as a specialist in constitutional law. His responsibilities also included direction of the Arthur Garfield Hays Civil Liberties Program, an intensive program for select law students.

Dorsen has edited or authored several books discussing the strains placed on civil liberties by government and society. They include *Political and Civil Rights in the United States* (1967 and 1976 editions), *Frontiers of Civil Liberties* (1968), *The Rights of Americans: What They Are— What They Should Be* (1971), and *None of Your Business: Government Secrecy in America* (1974). He has published numerous articles in professional and mass market periodicals.

Dorsen has also frequently testified as an expert on constitutional law before Congressional committees, where he has advocated the equal rights amendment and warned about the dangers of excessive government secrecy on many occasions.

Long a member of the Board of Directors of the ACLU, Dorsen was named its general counsel in 1969. In that role, he successfully argued the Gault case before the Supreme Court, which established due process rights for juveniles accused of delinquency. Dorsen became the fifth chairperson of the ACLU in 1976. He played a major role in organizing the 1978 National Convocation on free speech and has devoted much attention to improving the organization's finances. He has said he would like the ACLU to cooperate more with other organizations with similar goals.

In his role at the ACLU, Dorsen encouraged the organization to take a leading role in defending the right of neo-Nazis to march in Skokie, Illinois, to fight draft registration, to continue to battle against all government encroachments on such acts as the Freedom of Information law and to fight any efforts to strengthen the roles of the CIA and other intelligence agencies within the United States.

KIRK DOUGLAS

b. December 9, 1918
Actor

Having starred in some 60 films, 20 of which he produced, Kirk Douglas has a well-deserved reputation as a consummate actor and producer. In his long career he has been nominated for three Academy Awards as Best Actor—for *Champion, Lust for Life* and *The Bad and the Beautiful.*

Issur Danielovich was born in Amsterdam, New York to Harry, a businessman who had immigrated from Russia, and Bryna (Sanglel) Danielovich, who had also come from Russia. Interested in acting from his earliest years, he performed in school and at St. Lawrence University, where he joined the school's theater group before graduating in 1939 with a B.A. degree.

Then he headed toward New York City, studying at the American Academy of Dramatic Arts from 1939 to 1941, finally making his Broadway debut in 1941 in a small role as a singing Western Union messenger in *Spring Again.* Following several other bit roles, he joined the Navy. After service in the Pacific, he was discharged in 1944 and returned to the theater in New York.

By now he had changed his name and, following a long-established pattern among actors, was recommended for a Hal Wallis film by a onetime acting school fellow-student, Lauren Bacall. The picture, *The Strange Loves of Martha Ivers,* involved only a small role and was followed by other minor roles in films. By 1949 his big break came, when he was cast as the ambitious and cruel boxer Midge Kelly in *Champion.* The critics raved and saw in his performance a wickedness they loved. Indeed, it was just that wickedness that made him so famous.

In *Detective Story* (1951) he played a New York detective who hated lawbreakers. In *Ace in the Hole* (1951), he gave a stunning performance as an amoral reporter. In *Along the Great Divide* (1951), he was a sheriff who cared not a whit for justice. Soon he began to shift roles, and in *Gunfight at the O.K. Corral* (1957), *Cast a Giant Shadow* (1966; about an Israeli war hero), *Heroes of Telemark* (1965) and *The Fury* (1978), he played powerful personalities. In all, he has been the meanest of gunfighters, the toughest of warriors, the most aggressive of lovers and even—as in *Lonely Are the Brave* (1962), about an anarchist cowboy in the contemporary Southwest, or in *Spartacus* (1960), about a Roman slave revolt —the most principled of men.

Douglas, who describes his craft as a combination of "passion and discipline," has produced many films— including *Seven Days in May* (1964), the story of an attempted military coup in the United States; *Lonely Are the Brave* (1962); *Summertree* (1960) and *Spartacus* (1960)—as president of the Bryna Production Company, named after his mother. He has visited Israel several times and co-starred with Elizabeth Taylor in the television dramatization of "Victory at Entebbe," about the daring Israeli rescue raid on Uganda's Entebbe airport in July 1976.

The actor's dedication to his craft is apparent in more than just the vast number of films he has made. He was the first American to make an independent movie in Israel. (*The Juggler,* 1953), the first Hollywood star who went to do an art film in French (*Act of Love,* 1953) and the first major performer chosen for the well-known Stanley Kubrick anti-war film (*Paths of Glory,* 1958).

Despite his fame and success, Douglas has told reporters that, in a way, he is a failure—he wanted to be on stage, not a movie star. Even so, he received the New York Film Critics award in 1956 for *Lust for Life* (1955) and the 1967 Cecil B. DeMille Award for contributions in the entertainment field. He has also been the recipient of the Man of the Year Award from the Beverly Hills Jewish Council and was awarded the Medal of Freedom in January 1981 by President Jimmy Carter.

"Acting is hard work," he once told a reporter in 1978. "It's exhausting. But to retire? To stop? No, to me to retire is to die."

ELIZABETH DREW

b. November 16, 1935
Journalist

For more than 20 years, writer and television commentator Elizabeth Drew—dubbed "the American Boswell" by Dan Wakefield, the writer—has been observing Washington and interpreting it for the American public. Beyond the mechanics and maneuverings, "there is a very human side to being a politician," she said in an interview, "and these human relationships and the different ways they work are important to understand." Three books, many magazine articles and participation in television programs on politics attest to Drew's ability to sort out and analyze the human element within the front-line and behind-the-scenes complexities in the nation's capital.

Elizabeth Brenner was born in Cincinnati, Ohio to William J., a furniture manufacturer, and Estelle (Jacobs) Brenner. Her fascination with Washington politics began during a summer internship with the Democratic Sen-

ate Campaign Committee in 1956, while she was a student at Wellesley College. She graduated from Wellesley with a B.A. degree, Phi Beta Kappa, in 1957 as a Durant Scholar, having majored in political science and minored in history. After working briefly in Boston, in 1959 she returned to Washington, where she began working for the *Congressional Quarterly.* By 1964, when she left to free-lance, she was a senior editor. She became Washington editor for *Atlantic* in 1967, focusing on subjects of a political or social nature, such as hunger in America, government commissions and others. She developed a reputation for impartiality, incisiveness and inside sources, along with extraordinary energy and sharp insights.

In 1973 Drew left *Atlantic* to become a contributing editor for *The New Yorker,* one of the most influential magazines in this country. There she published excerpts from a journal she began keeping that year. The series evolved into her first book, *Washington Journal: The Events of 1973–1974* (New York, 1975), which traces the first inklings of scandal in the Nixon administration with Watergate to its ultimate disintegration and Nixon's resignation.

Drew's next journal, also serialized in *The New Yorker,* became her second book, *American Journal: The Events of 1976* (New York, 1977), which explores the Bicentennial. Her third book, *Senator* (New York, 1979), chronicles in meticulous detail 10 days in the life of John Culver, then a Democratic senator from Iowa. To write the book, Drew spent virtually every moment she could with Culver—in conferences, committee meetings, debates, visits home to Iowa. She would later observe, "I knew from my experience that Senators and members of Congress lead very hectic, pressured lives. But I must say I had no idea how demanding those lives were until I started the book."

From the vantage point of *The New Yorker,* Drew's views—generally liberal—spread, and soon she was appearing regularly on educational television. From 1971 to 1973 she moderated a weekly interview program for the Public Broadcasting System called *Thirty Minutes With . . .,* which originated from the Washington public television station WETA. Her interviewees included Edmund Muskie, George McGovern, Ted Kennedy, Indira Gandhi, King Hussein and staffers with the Nixon administration. She has since also appeared on *Agronsky and Company* for PBS and occasionally on *Meet the Press* (NBC), *Face the Nation* (CBS) and as a political commentator for the Post-Newsweek station in Washington, WTOP. Drew gained national attention as one of the questioners in the first Carter-Ford debate in 1976. Besides her books and articles for *The New Yorker,* Drew has contributed articles on various aspects of political life in Washington to *The Reporter, The New Republic, The New York Times Magazine* and *Atlantic.*

In *Portrait of an Election: The 1980 Presidential Campaign* (New York, 1981), she followed the Reagan-Carter-Anderson competition, drawing heavily upon unpublished memorandums and exclusive interviews. She wrote: "I tried to look at the election from different angles of vision: to see the principal participants coping with a variety of situations; to listen to the strategists as they groped their way along; to understand as much as possible about human nature in these circumstances; and to learn as much as possible about the rich subject of the Practice of Politics." And in early 1982 she returned to the Reagan administration—one year later—in *The New Yorker* and concluded that the president was "ideological" and "combative" rather than the amiable conciliator many thought him to be.

She is one of the few correspondents to win major awards in both print and broadcast journalism. They include the 1970 Award for Excellence from the Society of Magazine Writers, the 1973 Wellesley Alumnae Achievement Award, the Alfred I. duPont-Columbia University Award for broadcasting (1973) and the 1977 Woman of the Year in Communications award from *Ladies Home Journal.*

RICHARD DREYFUSS

b. October 29, 1947
Actor

From the time he began acting in Hebrew school plays, Richard Dreyfuss knew he wanted to be an actor; by age 30 he was an American cinema star, a veteran of the stage and an Oscar winner. Best-known for his comic roles in such films as *The Apprenticeship of Duddy Kravitz* and Neil Simon's *The Goodbye Girl,* Dreyfuss is also an accomplished performer of dramatic repertory.

Richard Stephan Dreyfuss was born in Brooklyn to Norman, a lawyer, and Gerry Dreyfuss. He spent his early years in Bayside, Queens. Dreyfuss's parents displayed the same daring that would later mark his own career. In early 1956 they sold all their possessions and took the family—Dreyfuss is the second of three children —to Europe for six months. On their return they bought a car with whatever money remained and drove to California. The family settled in Los Angeles, where Dreyfuss's father eventually became a restauranteur.

Dreyfuss's career took shape during his student years at Beverly Hills High School, when he began to act professionally at the Gallery Theater in Los Angeles. He enrolled at San Francisco State College as a theater arts major in 1965 but was forced to transfer to the political science department after he feuded with one of his professors. In 1967 he succeeded in obtaining conscientious objector status with his local draft board and, to fulfill his two-year requirement of alternative service, he dropped out of college and worked as a file clerk on the night shift at Los Angeles County General Hospital. He also got himself an agent at that time and began to act in minor television roles and in such forgettable movies as *The Runaways* (1968) and *Hello, Down There* (1969).

From 1969 to 1971 Dreyfuss lived intermittently in New York, where he performed in a series of unsuccessful off-Broadway plays and one Broadway show, *But Seriously,* which closed after two days. He also acted with the Los Angeles-based New Theater for Now from June 1969 through May 1970. In early 1972 he toured nationally in *Time of Your Life,* starring Henry Fonda, with the Center Theater Group in Los Angeles. He then appeared as Baby Face Nelson in the film *Dillinger,* which was released in 1973.

Dreyfuss's "break" occurred that year, when he appeared at the Mark Taper Forum in Los Angeles as Bill Walker in George Bernard Shaw's *Major Barbara.* On the basis of that role, he was offered the part of Curt Henderson in *American Graffiti,* an off-beat comedy about high school students in the 1950s that was to be directed by a young filmmaker named George Lucas. (Lucas would later become internationally famous for *Star Wars* and *Raiders of the Lost Ark.*) In *American Graffiti* Dreyfuss played a precocious and witty intellectual in his class who, unlike his classmates, was bound for an Ivy League school and a life quite different from theirs. Dreyfuss's subsequent roles have ranged from light comedy to increasingly bleak drama, allowing the actor to display his versatility in capturing different kinds of characters, human problems and themes.

In *The Apprenticeship of Duddy Kravitz* (1974), based on Mordecai Richler's novel of the same name, Dreyfuss portrayed an 18-year-old lower-middle-class Jew from Montreal during the 1940s, whose ambitions to "make it" blind him to the hurt he often inflicts on people around him. In *Jaws* (1975), directed by Steven Spielberg, he was Matt Hooper, an ichthyologist who participates in a frightening shark hunt. One of Dreyfuss's few failures was *Inserts* (1976), in which he portrayed a filmmaker during the 1930s who is unable to get work and thus turns to making pornographic films as "art." *Inserts* received an X-rating—and a drubbing by movie critics—but Dreyfuss claims that it contains much of his finest acting.

Dreyfuss rebounded from the disappointment with *Inserts* to play an aspiring actor in *The Goodbye Girl* in 1977. In that film, he has newly arrived in New York to pursue his career and discovers that the apartment he has rented is already occupied by a young divorcee and her daughter who have no idea that a new tenant is due. Dreyfuss's comedic performance opposite Marsha Mason earned him the Academy Award for Best Actor, and from then on he became one of Hollywood's most marketable performers.

Commanding huge salaries, Dreyfuss went on to appear in Steven Spielberg's science-fiction fantasy *Close Encounters of the Third Kind* (1978); *The Big Fix* (1978), in which he plays a hippie-turned-private investigator; *The Competition* (1981), in which he is a young pianist vying for a serious performing career; and *Whose Life Is It, Anyway?* (1981), an adaptation of Brian Clark's play about a bedridden sculptor who has been paralyzed from the neck down following a car crash. *Whose Life* represented one of Dreyfuss' greatest challenges. He is a very physical actor given to mime and comic dialect, and here had to cope with a different, almost totally cerebral, approach to acting. In the film he challenges everyone around him––his universe is now mostly peopled by doctors and nurses in the hospital that has become his home—to allow him to die, since living as he does, he claims, is worse than death. Dreyfuss's performance was highly praised and represented a new maturity in his career.

Dreyfuss returned to New York in 1981 to perform in a festival of one-act plays and appeared off-Broadway in *The Lady and the Tiger*. He remains a devotee of theater as well as film.

PETER DRUCKER

b. November 19, 1909
Economist; management consultant

Although the name "Peter Drucker" is hardly a household word, his work has become a staple in many U.S. government agencies, corporations, business schools and libraries throughout the United States and abroad. An influential management consultant, economist and former professor, Drucker's impact on up-and-coming managers and business students continues to be felt. He has written more than two dozen books and has been credited with saving several large corporations, including General Motors, with his management input and guidance.

Peter Ferdinand Drucker was born in Vienna to Adolph Bertram, a lawyer and college professor, and Caroline (Bond) Drucker. Following graduation from high school in Vienna, he studied law in Germany at the University of Hamburg and the University of Frankfurt, where he received a Doctor of Law degree in 1931. Before graduating he had become a staff writer for the Frankfurt daily newspaper *General Anzeiger,* and afterward he became its foreign and financial editor.

When Hitler rose to power in 1933, Drucker left Germany, settling first in London for four years, where he became an economist in an international banking firm, then moving to the United States in 1937 as a newspaper correspondent for several British publications and as an advisor to British banking firms in America. He was naturalized in 1943.

His first book, *The End of Economic Man* (New York, 1939), was published two years after his arrival in the United States. It compared the challenge of totalitarian systems with less efficient democratic systems. Drucker also began publishing economic analyses of wartime Europe for major American publications, including *New Republic* and *Harper's Magazine,* thus establishing a firm reputation for himself.

The role of industrial society in war and peace preoccupied Drucker in the early 1940s, and his subsequent books, including *The Future of Industrial Man* (New York, 1942), alerted society to prepare for postwar economic crises. He urged large roles for business in government and highly structured management and worker roles within corporations. Such books as *The Concept of the Corporation* (New York, 1946), *The New Society* (New York, 1950) and *The Practice of Management* (New York, 1954) examined changing modes of production and the new roles people would play as new economic systems emerged. Among other ideas, Drucker stressed American involvement in investment overseas in developing countries in exchange for raw materials, a practice now widespread.

In addition to his writing, which continued throughout the 1950s, 1960s and 1970s, Drucker also began a long academic career, teaching first at Sarah Lawrence College in Bronxville, New York (1940–42); Bennington College in Vermont, where he taught political science and philosophy (1942–49); and New York University, whose faculty he joined in 1950, retiring as Professor Emeritus in 1971. Since then, he has been Clarke Professor of Social Science at the Claremont Graduate School in California and writes six columns annually for *The Wall Street Journal.*

He has published a number of articles commenting on potentially serious problems. In *The Wall Street Journal* (December 9, 1981), he wrote that "the independent pension system faces a severe crisis in the next few years. Some of these funds are in no better shape than Social Security." And in *The Public Interest* (Spring 1981), he argued that teaching "business ethics" in universities runs the risk of allowing it to become an all-purpose rationalization for anything the corporation chooses to do. Thus, he argues, corporate apologists can justify Lockheed Aircraft's bribes in 1975 to a Japanese airline to obtain orders for its troubled L-1011 airliner on the grounds that the orders received resulted in saving thousands of jobs at Lockheed. Still, Drucker contends that corporate executives need only choose between right and wrong; everyone knows the distinction. And he counsels "right behavior," by which he means that executives must "set the tone" for their subordinates.

Drucker is a member of many management organizations, including the International Academy of Management, the American Academy of Management and the British Institute of Management. His many prizes include the Wallace Clark International Management Medal for 1963; the Gold Medal for the International University for Social Studies in Rome and the Hegemann Prize (Germany). He holds honorary doctorates from Pace College (New York), Nihon University (Tokyo) and Wayne State University (Detroit).

For further information:
Drucker, Peter. *The Last of All Possible Worlds.* Novel. New York: 1982.

LEON EDEL

b. September 9, 1907
Biographer

Leon Edel has devoted his career to portraying the lives of others. He is the biographer of Henry James, James Joyce, Henry David Thoreau and Willa Cather. He is also the editor of the works of Edmund Wilson and was once described by a *New York Times* critic as "a scholar in the great tradition of diligence and responsibility." His five-volume respectful edition of *The Life of Henry James,* which he researched for more than 20 years—and which a *Times* critic called "magisterial"—won the 1963 National Book Award and the 1963 Pulitzer Prize for biography.

Born in Pittsburgh, Pennsylvania to Simon and Fannie (Malamud) Edel, Joseph Leon Edel moved with his family to Yorkton, Saskatchewan, in Canada, where his father owned a general store in a remote mining region. Secluded as it was, Yorkton, a frontier village, was

"cosmopolitan, steeped in a nostalgia for European culture," Edel told James Atlas in 1980. From 1923 to 1927 he attended McGill University in Montreal, where he majored in English and founded the *McGill Fortnightly Review,* which played a large role in modern Canadian literature, especially in poetry. He earned his B.A. degree in 1927 and his M.A. degree the next year. It was while doing graduate research, also at McGill, that Edel became interested in Henry James and was deeply influenced by James's faith in literature as a means of personal freedom. His two dissertations for his Doctor es Lettres, granted by the Sorbonne in 1932, were *Henry James: Les Annees Dramatiques* and *The Prefaces of Henry James,* a study of his plays.

Edel spent four years abroad, from 1928 to 1932, and then returned to Canada to work for the *Montreal Herald* as a reporter. Two years later he went to New York to become United Nations correspondent for *PM.* Until 1943 he held a variety of other jobs, including broadcasting and other news work, free-lancing and tutoring. He served in the U.S. Army from 1943 to 1947. During the following years he wrote and taught at a number of universities such as New York University (1950–66), Indiana University (1954–55) and in summer sessions at Harvard (1952), Princeton (1953) and the University of Hawaii (1955).

In 1945, while he was in Zurich, Edel visited the grave of James Joyce and spoke with Joyce's widow and others who knew him during his last days. From their accounts he drew up notes for his book *The Last Journey* (New York, 1947).

Back in the United States, Edel then embarked on documenting and editing the five-volume works of Henry James. He gained access to James's works from the James family and also edited *The Complete Plays of Henry James* (New York, 1949), *The Ghostly Tales of Henry James* (Camden, N.J., 1949), *The Complete Tales of Henry James* (New York, 1963 to 1965) and *The Diary of Alice James* (New York, 1964).

Edel later undertook to edit the extensive journals of literary critic Edmund Wilson, whose long life and career paralleled major events and trends of the 1920s, 1930s, 1940s and beyond. Edel's work, like his earlier volumes on Henry James, Joyce and others, is meticulously assembled so that readers get the best and the most thorough of what is available. Of Wilson's collected journals, Edel has thus far edited *The Twenties* (New York, 1975) and *The Thirties* (New York, 1980), which included a preface quite critical of Wilson's psychological weaknesses.

A true believer in biography—"[it] has replaced fiction; the interest in personality is unprecedented," he said in 1980—he is intrigued with biographical narrative and totally immerses himself in the subjects, trying to establish motives and how the people's lives related to their works. His other works include *Willa Cather: A Critical Biography* (New York, 1953), *Literary Biography* (New York, 1959), *The Psychological Novel* (New York, 1959), *Henry David Thoreau* (New York, 1959) and *Bloomsbury* (New York, 1979).

For further information:

Edel, Leon. *Henry James: The Conquest of London 1870–81.* Philadelphia: 1962

———. *Henry James: The Master 1901–1916.* Philadelphia: 1972.

———. *Henry James: The Middle Years 1882–95.* Philadelphia: 1962

———. *Stuff of Sleep and Dreams: Experiments in Literary Psychology.* New York: 1982.

———. *Henry James: The Treacherous Years 1895–1901.* Philadelphia: 1969.

———. *Henry James: The Untried Years (1843–70).* Philadelphia: 1953.

PAUL R. EHRLICH

b. May 29, 1932
Geologist; biologist; evolutionist

Paul Ehrlich, an entomologist, or insect biologist, who teaches at Stanford University, is a major leader in the international crusade for population control and ecological sensitivity to exploitation and destruction of plant and animal species. He is author of many books, including the best-selling paperback *The Population Bomb* (New York, 1968), which warns of the mounting crisis of a population multiplying faster than the available food supply.

Paul Ralph Ehrlich was born in Philadelphia to William, a salesman, and Ruth (Rosenberg) Ehrlich, a public school Latin teacher. During his childhood his family moved to Maplewood, New Jersey, where he was graduated from Columbia High School in 1949. He received his B.A. degree in zoology from the University of Pennsylvania in 1953 and M.A. and Ph.D. degrees in the same subject from the University of Kansas in 1955 and 1957, respectively. During his studies he participated in surveys of biting flies on the Bering Sea, insects in the Canadian Arctic and Subarctic, and parasitic mites. He joined the staff of Stanford University as an assistant professor of biology in 1959 and was promoted to full professor in 1966. Since 1976 he has been Bing Professor of Population Studies.

Most of Ehrlich's field work with insects has been done in Stanford's Jasper Ridge Biological Experimental Area and in the Rocky Mountain Biological Laboratory at Crested Butte, Colorado. One of his favorite projects is to control butterfly caterpillars with ants, a natural enemy, instead of with pesticides. He has also done field work in Africa, Alaska, Mexico, Australia, the South Pacific islands and Southeast Asia.

It was while Ehrlich was in India in 1966 that he began to understand the problem of overpopulation "emotionally." Ehrlich strongly believes that people must stop thinking of the Earth as a frontier to be exploited; rather, it is a "spaceship"—a phrase coined by architect R. Buckminster Fuller—with a limited carrying capacity. Erhlich forecast in a 1967 article published in the British magazine *New Scientist* that "somewhere between 1970 and 1985 the world will undergo vast famines." He urged that the United States reduce population growth at home by imposing luxury taxes on diapers and baby food and that it should only send food to countries that can become self-sufficient, unlike India, which is "hopeless." "The cancer must be excised," he said. "The operation may seem brutal and callous and the pain may be intense. But the disease is now so far advanced that only with radical surgery does the patient have any chance of survival."

In *The Population Bomb,* which was based on his lectures and articles, Ehrlich wrote, "the birth rate must be brought into line with the death rate or mankind will breed itself into oblivion." He emphasized that if the present rate of growth remained constant, the result would be enormous overcrowding and serious political and economic consequences as well as human misery. When Ehrlich aired these views he found a receptive audience among people who wanted scientific justification for their empirical views. After a publicity tour for the book, thousands of supporting letters poured in, their writers alarmed at overpopulation and seeking remedies.

A long-time pessimist about humanity's ability to survive because of its continued destruction of flora and fauna, Ehrlich and his wife, Anne, a biology research associate at Stanford, argue in *Extinction: The Causes and Consequences of the Disappearance of Species* (New York, 1981) that, as he stated on a tour following publication, "today, humanity has become a major agent of extinction . . . no longer are more species being created than are going extinct each year, and the planet's stock of biological resources is now diminishing rapidly." Species should be preserved, he asserts in *Extinction,* because of compassion; because they have a right to live; because of their beauty, worth or interest; because of their economic value; and because other species are essential parts of ecosystems that benefit mankind.

Ehrlich has written many books on the relation of population pressures to sociopolitical events, crowding in human populations, butterfly evolution and selective changes in natural population of water snakes. In *Population, Resources, Environments: Issues in Human Ecology* (San Francisco, 1970), he analyzed overpopulation and its demands on food resources and environment. In *Ark II: Social Response to Environmental Imperatives* (San Francisco, 1974), he criticized Western industrial society, recommending strong central planning of consumption and resource use. He discussed the correlation between race and intelligence, which he does not believe exists, in *The Race Bomb: Skin Color, Prejudice and Intelligence* (New York, 1977). His other books include *How to Be a Survivor* (San Francisco, 1971), *Man and the Ecosphere* (San Francisco, 1971), *Human Ecology: Problems and Solutions* (San Francisco, 1973) and *The End of Affluence: A Blueprint for the Future* (San Francisco, 1974).

He is a member of the International Association for Ecology, founder and president of Zero Population Growth Inc. and is on the editorial boards of *Systematic Zoology* and the *International Journal of Environmental Science*.

IRA EISENSTEIN

b. November 26, 1906
Rabbi

Ira Eisenstein is descended from an important line of Jewish scholars and married into another. As the recently retired leader of the small but influential Reconstructionist movement and immediate past president of the Reconstructionist Rabbinical College in Philadelphia, Eisenstein was responsible for promoting the Reconstructionist philosophy and assuring its survival through education.

Ira Eisenstein was born in New York City, the son of Isaac, a businessman, and Sadie (Luxenberg) Eisenstein. His paternal grandfather, Judah David Eisenstein (1854-1956), was a prominent American encyclopedist and author, as well as the founder of the first Hebrew Society in the United States, the Shoharei Sefat Ever, in 1880. Eisenstein was educated at Columbia University, where he received a B.A. degree in 1927 and a Ph.D. degree in 1941. He pursued rabbinical studies at the Jewish Theological Seminary of America in New York and was ordained in 1931.

Eisenstein's career as a Jewish leader began the year before, when he became executive director of the Reconstructionist Society for the Advancement of Judaism in New York City. Reconstructionism was founded by Mordecai Menahem Kaplan, Eisenstein's father-in-law,

in early 1922 in the United States, with the establishment of the Society for the Advancement of Judaism. It is a branch of the Jewish religion that believes that Judaism must transform itself from a philosophy directed at other-worldly pursuits to one that can assist individual Jews to attain salvation in this life. Each person should decide which rituals or mores he or she chooses to practice. The following year he became the SAJ's assistant leader. In 1933 he went on to become its associate leader, and by 1945 he was spiritual leader of the congregation. In 1954 Eisenstein moved to Chicago, where he headed Anshe Emet, a Reconstructionist congregation. He returned to New York five years later to assume the presidency of the Jewish Reconstructionist Foundation and to become editor of *Reconstructionist*, the organization's publication. He headed the Reconstructionist Rabbinical College in Philadelphia from 1968, assuming the leadership of Reconstructionism from Mordecai M. Kaplan. He retired in 1981.

In addition to teaching at the college, in 1951 Eisenstein lectured at the Jewish Theological Seminary, where he was visiting professor of homiletics. He is the author of many books that explore aspects of Jewish life from a Reconstructionist viewpoint: *Creative Judaism* (New York, 1936 and 1953), *What We Mean by Religion* (New York, 1938 and 1958), *The Ethics of Tolerance* (New York, 1941) and *Judaism Under Freedom* (New York, 1956). He is editor of *Varieties of Jewish Belief* (New York, 1966) and co-editor of *Mordecai M. Kaplan: An Evaluation* (New York, 1952) and five prayer books.

Eisenstein's thinking in these works is directed toward the creation of viable, self-sustaining contemporary Jewish communities in free societies and a more egalitarian determination of Jewish mores in Israel. His writings emphasize the theme that the purpose of religion is serving people, and not people serving religion. He objects to the dominance of religious theocracy in making decisions for Jews and calls instead for Jewish reconstruction—hence the name—in which members formulate their own rules based on contemporary needs. These communities do not renounce Judaic tradition, however; rather, they insist that Judaism is a culture and a way of living as well as a religious faith and is therefore, in Kaplan's phrase, a religious civilization. On the occasion of Kaplan's 100th birthday in 1981, Eisenstein wrote in celebration: "the cause was the survival of the Jewish people, physically, spiritually, culturally. From *heder* [religious school for children] to Yeshiva, from public school to university, from the Jewish Theological Seminary to the Reconstructionist Rabbinical College, he clung to his single purpose, the reconstruction of Judaism for the 20th century."

With his wife, Judith Kaplan Eisenstein, Mordecai Kaplan's daughter, Eisenstein has written five cantatas based on Jewish themes. He has also contributed to *Tradition and Contemporary Experience: Essays on Jewish Thought and Life,* edited by Alfred Jospe (New York, 1970).

He is a member of the Rabbinical Assembly of America, which he headed from 1952 to 1954, and the National Advisory Committee on Education of Hadassah. He received an honorary doctorate from the Jewish Theological Seminary in 1958 and the Mordecai M. Kaplan Medal in 1976.

STUART E. EIZENSTAT

b. January 15, 1943
Attorney; former presidential adviser

At the age of 33 Stuart Eizenstat was already a respected—and powerful—member of the White House staff of President Jimmy Carter during the late 1970s. As Carter's powerful domestic affairs adviser, Eizenstat brought with him several years of experience in administration on a state level in his native Georgia as well as a record of firm dedication to Democratic party ideals. In addition to his public service, Eizenstat has also devoted much time and energy to Jewish affairs wherever he has lived.

Stuart E. Eizenstat was born to Leo, who owned a wholesale shoe store, and Sylvia (Medintz) Eizenstat. Raised in Atlanta, he received his B.A. degree from the University of North Carolina in 1964 and a Bachelor of Laws degree from the law school at Harvard University in 1967. He was a speechwriter on domestic affairs for President Lyndon Johnson and joined the presidential campaign of then-Senator Hubert Humphrey in preparation for the election of 1968. A strong adherent of Johnson's Great Society reformist goals, he staked out an early reputation for expertise on domestic social issues in America.

When Humphrey was defeated by Richard Nixon, Eizenstat became a law clerk for Chief Judge Newell Edenfield in the U.S. District Court, Northern District of Georgia from 1969 to 1970. For the following seven years, he practiced law as a partner in an Atlanta firm. Throughout his private practice he remained active in Georgia politics, serving as advisor in the 1970 gubernatorial campaign of Jimmy Carter and as issues coordinator in both the successful Andrew Young-for-Congress campaign and Maynard Jackson for mayor of Atlanta. He was also a civil rights activist, and his many writings in this area included articles such as "Mental Competency to Stand Trial," in *Harvard Civil Rights-Civil Liberties Law Review* (1969) and "An Expanding Era of Civil Rights," *Mercer Law Review* (1971).

Always a close confidant of Jimmy Carter, Eizenstat joined the White House "inner circle" in 1977 as head of the Domestic Policy Staff. As President Carter's chief domestic policy adviser and an avowed liberal, Eizenstat's office developed policy proposals on welfare reform, national health insurance, a separate Department of Education and others. He is associated with losing efforts, such as the $50 tax rebate, real wage insurance and a consumer protection agency, but he also promoted deregulation of airlines, railroads and trucking. Respected for his total command of his own area and his dedication to social equality, he was often consulted on policy decisions concerning Israel and the Middle East as well. While not outspoken in public about his Jewishness, he nevertheless let his commitment to his ethnic heritage and belief be widely known. Although known to work long hours, Eizenstat always set aside time on Fridays to leave work early and observe Shabbat with his family.

A member of the Atlanta Bureau of Jewish Education from 1973 to 1976, and of the board of directors of the Atlanta Jewish Community Center from 1971 through 1976, Eizenstat remained active in Jewish affairs when he moved to Washington, where he joined the Tifereth Israel Synagogue. Since Carter's defeat in 1980, Eizenstat has been an occasional columnist for the *Jerusalem Post,* where he has continued to interpret President Reagan's social and domestic policies as harmful to all Americans in general and to Jews in particular.

DANIEL J. ELAZAR

b. August 25, 1934
Political scientist

Political scientist Daniel Elazar has dedicated his career to studying the impact of federalism on the lives of Americans and on Jewish communities in both Israel and in the Diaspora. Elazar maintains teaching positions in both countries: He is a professor at Israel's Bar-Ilan University and at Temple University in Philadelphia. He is also chairman of the Center of Jewish Community Studies, an international consortium of scholars of all aspects of Jewish life, based in Jerusalem and Philadelphia, and is the author of numerous books and articles concerning Jewish life and politics in Israel and elsewhere.

Daniel Judah Elazar was born in Minneapolis to Albert, an educator, and Nettie (Barzon) Elazar. He attended the Midrash College of Judaic Studies at Wayne State University in Detroit from 1950 to 1954 and received his master's degree and Ph.D. in political science in 1957 and 1959, respectively, from the University of Chicago. He demonstrated the beginnings of his interest in federalism in both his master's thesis, "Federal-State Relations in Minnesota: A Study of Railroad Construction in the Nineteenth Century," and his doctoral dissertation, "Intergovernmental Relations in Nineteenth Century American Federalism."

While pursuing his studies, Elazar worked as head librarian for United Hebrew Schools in Detroit from 1951 to 1959. Upon receiving his Ph.D., he became an assistant professor of government and public affairs at the University of Illinois, a position he held from 1959 to 1963. After teaching at the University of Minnesota from 1963 to 1964, he became a professor of political science at Temple University and since 1973 has been director of the Center for the Study of Federalism at Temple University and afterwards, a senior fellow.

In addition, since 1973 Elazar has spent half of his time in Israel as professor of political studies and head of the Institute of Local Government at Bar-Ilan University. He became chairman of the Jerusalem Institute for Federal Studies in 1976.

Elazar examines the relationship between federal and state realms in such books as *The American Partnership: Federal-State Relations in the Nineteenth Century* (Chicago, 1962), *American Federalism: A View from the States* (New York, 1966) and *Cities of the Prairie* (New York, 1970).

Elazar became chairman of the Center for Jewish Community Studies at its founding in 1970. As chairman, Elazar has written such articles as "Covenant as the Basis of the Jewish Political Tradition," (*Jewish Journal of Sociology*, June 1978) and "Toward a Renewed Zionist Vision" (*Forum*, 1977). In his writings he frequently scrutinizes three Zionist camps—the labor camp, the civic camp and the religious camp—and the relationship between Zionism and Jewish thought. He notes with irony that Diaspora thought has moved more rapidly from theology toward politics than Israeli thought has moved from politics toward theology. "It is always a mistake to underestimate the continuity of culture," he wrote in "Covenant as the Basis of Jewish Political Tradition." "Despite all the differences, the similarities and elements [among Jews] . . . have had an amazing persistence." He has asked, is a "covenantal basis" still valid, then? His answer is that despite the secularization of Jews throughout the world, many Jews—even those who reject religion—"seem to be striving" for

such ancient and traditional ties with God and their fellow Jews. Elazar's major work elaborating on these thoughts is *Community and Polity; The Organizational Dynamics of American Jewry* (Philadelphia, 1976). In another vein, he praised Zeev Jabotinsky, a Zionist Revisionist leader who died in the 1920s and has been a model for Menachem Begin: "Jabotinsky was indeed a giant in the Jewish national revival. . . . He flowered before his time and all of us are poorer because we could not keep pace with him." (*Sh'ma*, May 29, 1981). He has also written about the Palestinians from the Israeli view. Asserting that a consensus exists among virtually all Israeli groups, Elazar defines that agreement as consisting of "no separate Palestinian state west of Jordan, no recognition of the Palestine Liberation Organization as the spokesman for the Palestinians. . . . no Israeli withdrawal to the pre-1967 borders, no redivision of Jerusalem, and no substantial return of Arab refugees to Israeli territories."

Elazar is active in many Israeli organizations. He is a member of the Israel State Commission for Local Government Reform and the Israel Commission on Arts and Culture and is chairman of the Subcommittee on the Structure of Local Government. He is also a consultant to the U.S. Advisory Commission on Intergovernmental Relations, the Council of Jewish Federations and the Educational Commission of the United States.

He is a member of the Har Zion Temple in Philadelphia and former president of the B'nai B'rith Hillel Foundation at the University of Chicago. He is vice chairman of the educational commission of the Solomon Schechter Day School in Philadelphia. In addition, Elazar is a member of the American Political Science Association, the Israel Political Science Association and the World Union of Jewish Studies.

For further information:

Elazar, Daniel J., "Israeli Attitudes to the Palestinians," in Gruen, George E., ed. *The Palestinians in Perspective.* New York: 1982.

STANLEY ELKIN

b. May 11, 1930
Novelist, short story writer

Stanley Elkin is a comic master of both the novel and the short story. He has been described as a black humorist, and the critic Josh Greenfield has said that Elkin's humor is one of "expansive glib Jewish-American schizophrenia."

Elkin was born in Manhattan to Philip, a costume jewelry salesman, and Zelda (Feldman) Elkin. He attended the University of Illinois and received his B.A. degree in English in 1952. He completed his M.A. degree the following year at the same university. After serving in the United States Army from 1955 to 1957, he earned his Ph.D. from the University of Illinois in 1961. His doctoral dissertation was on religious themes found in the writings of William Faulkner.

That same year Elkin started teaching English at Washington University in St. Louis. In 1968 he was appointed professor of English at Washington University. In addition to teaching there, he has served between 1964 and 1965 as a visiting professor of English at Smith College, the University of California at Santa Barbara and Yale University.

Elkin has written four novels and three collections of short stories. Critics have said of his first novel, *Boswell* (New York, 1964), that like all art, this novel is "truth masquerading as deception." It is a comic chronicle of the post-World War II era as told by a marginal, hard-boiled and acidic observer.

As Elkin's work developed, critics began to identify some themes and patterns. He often uses the Jew and his dispersion in the world as an analogy for man's striving for absolute freedom. Furthermore, Elkin often tries to mask disintegration and deadening of inner life behind a kind of energy and eccentricity.

In the title story of *Criers and Kibitzers, Kibitzers and Criers* (New York, 1966), his first collection of short stories, Elkin evokes the hardened atmosphere of growing up Jewish in the late 1930s. As children stand in line to attend a movie, all the contradictory and complex ways in which they relate to each other are developed.

A very typical work of Elkin's is *The Dick Gibson Show* (New York, 1970). In this novel, Elkin's tendency to structure his longer works as a series of anecdotal episodes is given full rein. Through the book's radio talk show format, a full set of zany characters is created, each having only a peripheral relationship to the others. Some critics have remarked that *The Dick Gibson Show* suffers from an atmosphere of almost desperate improvisation. Elkins responds to this criticism by commenting that he has always been interested in the physics of personality rather than in schemes. In 1974 Elkin won an award for his work from the Institute of Arts and Letters.

Elkin's next novel, *The Franchiser* (New York, 1976; reissued in Boston, 1981), recounts the life of Ben Flesh, who literally collects franchises. He lives out of his Cadillac, eats fast food and sleeps in Howard John-son motels. He never settles down or marries, nor does he confront the emptiness of his life until he is diagnosed as having multiple sclerosis. The book twits sterile Americana with the irony of basic human vulnerability, and Elkin was described as an "inventive comic writer."

The Living End (New York, 1979) is a short (148-page) fantasy tracing the lives and afterlives of holdup victims in Minneapolis-St. Paul. The cast of characters includes Jesus, Joseph and Mary as well as other men and women who are living or dead. A critic describes Elkin's main characters—all losers— in *The Living End* as combining "the energy and appetites of the Middle West with the legendary qualities of Sholom Aleichem villagers." "The hero," says Elkin, "is not he who rises above it so much as he who can stand in it." Elkin himself has written of the predicament of being both a Jewish writer and a "regional" writer, since so few other active American authors are located in St. Louis.

RICHARD ELMAN

b. April 23, 1934
Poet; novelist; critic

For writer Richard Elman, there is no single theme to which his work is tied. He has written fiction and nonfiction on subjects as diverse as a Hungarian-Jewish family through World War II, the rock group Rolling Stones and public assistance as a way of life.

Richard Martin Elman was born in Brooklyn to Edward, a lawyer, and Pearl (Beckerman) Elman. He received a B.A. degree from Syracuse University in 1955 and an M.A. degree from Stanford in 1957. From 1961 to 1964 he was public affairs director of WBAI-FM, the listener-supported radio station in New York City associated with the Pacifica Foundation. He was a research associate at the Columbia University School of Social Work in 1965, and from 1966 through 1975 he taught English and writing at Hunter College, Bennington College and Columbia University.

His personal writing has always been his priority, and he contributed nonfiction, fiction and reviews to such magazines as *The Nation, New Republic, Commonweal, Paris Review, Present Tense, Evergreen Review, The New York Times Book Review* and *Book Week*. If there is any one way to describe Elman's approach to writing, it is one of continuous growth and change. An early concentration on social issues evolved into a focus on Jewish themes. But since 1972 he has looked beyond his own roots to explore a wider range of topics and ideas that have also intrigued him.

Elman's first novel, *A Coat for the Tsar* (Austin, Texas, 1959), dealt with a Jew who trades valuables to be spared a pogrom in Brest-Litovsk, returns home to confess what he has done and discovers that he is the only survivor. It was followed by *The Poorhouse State: The American Way of Life on Public Assistance* (New York, 1966), which examined conditions on New York's Lower East Side when the Department of Welfare becomes a "battleground" between the poor and society; *Ill-at-Ease in Compton* (New York, 1967), a study of urban decay in a California city; *Charles Booth's London* (New York, 1967); a trilogy about a Hungarian-Jewish family eventually destroyed by the Nazis: *The 28th Day of Elul* (New York, 1967); *Lilo's Diary* (New York, 1968); *The Reckoning* (New York, 1969); *An Education in Blood* (New York, 1971); and *Fredi & Shirl & the Kids* (New York, 1972).

The Jewish themes so prevalent in Elman's fiction ended with *Fredi & Shirl,* which was a quasi-autobiographical novel heavily based on his own childhood experiences in Brooklyn and his early married life. In a 1980 interview he said, "I didn't want to write about Jews anymore. I had written about them. A man is more than what he was when he grew up. He becomes what his experience has been. I wanted to write about my experiences and also about my fantasies. And I try not to repeat myself."

Since then, Elman's books are *Uptight with the Stones* (New York, 1973), an account of Elman's experiences accompanying the rock group Rolling Stones on a national tour; *Taxi Driver* (New York, 1975), a novelization of the movie directed by Martin Scorsese; and *The Breadfruit Lotteries* (New York, 1980), a spy parody.

Elman's book *Cocktails at Somoza's* (Cambridge, Mass., 1981) is a self-described "reporter's sketchbook of events in revolutionary Nicaragua," a harsh criticism of dictator Somoza and his allies plus doubts about whether the tyrant's successors can create a free country. Skeptical yet hopeful, he develops his theme in an aura of ambiguity.

Describing his approach to his work, Elman wrote, "All my life I have admired writers who have evinced a rage against personal injustice. Not that I believe writers must all exhibit the same dreary conscience. . . . In my case, I would not know how to write of a [nonfictional] subject if I were not deeply moved by it—through rage, or compassion, or, perhaps, amazement and a sense of wonder."

For further information:
Elman, Richard. *Homage to Fats Navarro.* St. Paul, Minnesota: 1980.

EDWARD JAY EPSTEIN

b. December 6, 1935
Writer

Edward Jay Epstein is a political scientist and media critic whose work has often provoked considerable controversy. He first attracted wide attention in 1966, when he published *Inquest: The Warren Commission and the Establishment of Truth* (New York), a highly critical account of the Warren Commission investigation into the assassination of President Kennedy.

The son of Louis J., a textile executive, and Betty (Opolinsky) Epstein, Edward Jay Epstein was born in New York City. He received his Bachelor of Arts degree from Cornell in 1957 and continued there to study for his M.A. degree, which he received in 1966. He has taught political science at the Massachusetts Institute of Technology and at Harvard, where he earned his Ph.D. in government.

Inquest was an expansion of his master's thesis. In it, he charged that the commission's inquiry had been superficial, and that discrepancies in the evidence were never resolved. These attacks were noteworthy because at the time few writers were ready to raise sensitive questions about something Americans wanted to resolve quickly and put behind them.

Several other works by Epstein have been related to the Kennedy assassination. In 1969 he wrote *Counterplot* (New York), which examined District Attorney Jim Garrison's charges in New Orleans that there had been a conspiracy to kill the president. And in 1978 he published *Legend: The Secret World of Lee Harvey Oswald* (New York), which traced Oswald's involvement with Soviet intelligence authorities and contended that Oswald, who had lived in the Soviet Union, was somehow connected to an intricate Soviet spy network.

As a reporter-at-large for *The New Yorker,* Epstein was encouraged to examine the media by his editor, William Shawn. In a notable 1971 article, he rebuked journalists for shoddy fact checking, demonstrating that Black Panthers' counsel Charles Garry had inflated the press reports of the number of Panther deaths due to police brutality.

Epstein's doctoral dissertation became *News from Nowhere: Television and the News* (New York, 1973), an analysis of news coverage on the three networks, which concluded that television news is primarily a product of the organization structure behind it and is superficial. His Panther article and essays on press treatment of other issues, including Watergate, the Pentagon Papers and Vietnam, were published as *Between Fact and Fiction: The Problem of Journalism* (New York, 1975).

Many critics have praised Epstein as a painstaking researcher with impressive academic credentials. Others though, have accused him of the same errors he has criticized others for: rushing into print, not reconciling loose ends and simplistic analysis. In *Agency of Fear: Opiates and Political Power in America* (New York, 1977), Epstein, for example, suggested that the Watergate affair was an outgrowth of the Nixon administration's approach to drug-related crime. He contends that Nixon deliberately expanded the power of law enforcement agencies under White House control to include secret police forces. Their ostensible motive, he says, was to oversee and halt illegal drug traffic, but they ultimately came to be involved in larger political operations. Although many critics were skeptical, they called the book "fascinating and depressing."

In 1979 Epstein published his first novel, *Cartel* (New York). He has also contributed to such periodicals as *Esquire, Commentary* and the *Columbia Journalism Review.*

For further information:

Epstein, Edward Jay. *The Rise & Fall of Diamonds.* New York: 1982.

JASON EPSTEIN

b. August 25, 1928
Editor; publisher

The publishing world is in continuous flux, but one constant since 1951 has been Jason Epstein, editorial director and a vice president of Random House in New York City, publisher of *The New York Review of Books* and a journalist in his own right. Since starting the first line of quality paperbacks at Doubleday when he was in his twenties, Epstein has shown an intuitive sense of what the public will read—and how it will read.

Jason Epstein was born in Cambridge, Massachusetts to Robert, a textiles businessman, and Gladys (Shapiro) Epstein. He attended Columbia University, receiving a B.A. degree in 1949 and an M.A. degree in 1950. In 1951 he joined the staff of Doubleday, soon started Anchor Books and developed the concept of more expensive, longer-lasting paperbacks. Epstein then joined Random House in 1958 and developed close working relationships with many major American literary personalities such as Susan Sontag, Norman Mailer and Robert Lowell.

In February 1963, Epstein used his Random House contacts to help co-found *The New York Review of Books* as a journal of literary (and later political) review, criticism and commentary during the 114-day newspaper strike that hit New York City that winter. By drawing on advertising revenues that were available because of the strike, Epstein was able to create a high-quality "temporary" publication whose first contributors included Nathan Glazer, Paul Goodman, Irving Howe, Alfred Kazin, Mailer and Sontag. Epstein's wife Barbara and *Harper's* editor Robert Silvers became co-editors, posts that they continue to hold.

The *Review* was so successful that by September 1963 it became an ongoing, permanent biweekly. Under Epstein's guidance, the *Review* became the flagship for American radical-liberal intellectuals and their opposition to the Vietnam War. It explored the Southeast Asian conflict in greater depth than most publications at the time. Reflecting Epstein's viewpoint, the *Review* sided with the supporters of community control during the controversial 1968 teachers strike in New York City. This move represented a major split among New York's intellectuals. (Epstein and former Columbia classmate Norman Podhoretz, colleagues until that time, began drifting apart. The split would soon become sharply defined, as Epstein remained on the left while Podhoretz became identified as a leader of the right-of-center neo-conservatives, thus exemplifying the growing national division between those who differed on the arms race, Israel's proper role in the Middle East, feminism, dissent and tolerance of the rights of homosexuals, among other topics.)

In 1969–70, Epstein covered the trial of the "Chicago 8"—eight men who were being prosecuted for their activities in the 1968 protests at the Democratic National Convention in Chicago. In 1970 Epstein's book *The Great Conspiracy Trial* (New York, 1970), a description of the trial and its implications for the American legal system, was published. Epstein has also coauthored a book, *Easthamptom: A History and Guide* (New York, 1975).

Under Epstein's tutelage, both Random House and especially *The New York Review of Books* continue to exert broad influence on support for individual freedom in all societies, left and right, communist and noncommunist—unlike the neo-conservatives, who are generally indifferent to violations of personal liberties in noncommunist nations. *The New York Review of Books,* for example, has criticized Communist Vietnam for its harsh treatment of its postwar populace. It has also published numerous articles supporting Israel's Peace Now movement and opposing Israeli settlements on the occupied West Bank and has repeatedly promoted arms control and a rein on the unrestricted growth and proliferation of nuclear weapons.

In addition to his posts at Random House and *The New York Review of Books,* Epstein is a consultant to the Children's Television Workshop in New York City, the director of Literary Classics, and a trustee of Bard College.

ERIK H. ERIKSON

b. June 15, 1902
Psychoanalyst; author

The term "identity crisis" is so ingrained in the American vocabulary (and psyche) that it seems to have always existed. In fact, it was coined by Erik Erikson, the psychoanalyst whose pioneering work in child development and critically acclaimed biographies of Mohandas Gandhi and Martin Luther have placed him on a par with Sigmund Freud and the great Swiss psychologist Jean Piaget. Erikson is now recognized as the most influential living psychologist/psychoanalyst today.

Erik H. Erikson was born in Frankfurt-am-Main, Germany to Danish parents. His mother's family was Jewish; an ancestor was chief rabbi of Stockholm. His father's family was Protestant. When Erikson was three years old, his then-divorced mother married Dr. Theodor Homburger, a Jewish pediatrician. Erikson—who grew up with the surname "Homburger" but adopted "Erikson" when he came to the United States—was raised Jewish and considered himself German despite his Danish roots.

In 1927 Erikson moved to Vienna, where he taught in an experimental school run by child analyst Peter Blos. At the same time Erikson was analyzed by Anna Freud and studied psychoanalysis, specializing in child analysis, at the Vienna Psychoanalytic Institute. He also became a Montessori teacher. When his analytic training was completed in 1933, Erikson began practicing. But later that year, with the rise of Hitler, he left Vienna via Denmark for the United States. He settled in Boston, where he became its first child analyst. He also became affiliated with Massachusetts General Hospital, the Harvard Pscyhological Clinic and the Judge Baker Guidance Center for emotionally disturbed youths. He taught at the Harvard Medical School from 1934 to 1935.

In 1936 Erikson went to Yale University, where he obtained a full-time research post at its Institute of Human Relations. While there, he and Yale anthropologist Scudder Mekeel studied how Sioux Indians in South Dakota trained their children. Erikson's aim was to find out how universal milestones in child development were handled by different cultures.

Erikson moved to San Francisco in 1939—the same year he was naturalized—where he set up a private practice and researched and taught at the University of California at Berkeley and San Francisco State until 1950. While there, he published "Hitler's Imagery and German Youth" on a government-sponsored grant to study Nazi propaganda. It appeared in *Psychiatry* in 1942.

After World War II Erikson worked with emotionally disturbed war veterans at Mt. Zion Hospital in San Francisco, but he left the University of California in 1950 rather than sign a loyalty oath. The following year he moved to Stockbridge, Massachusetts to work with severely disturbed children at the Austin Riggs Center, a private, upper-class institution. He also commuted regularly to Pittsburgh, counseling inner-city children. He published his first edition of *Childhood and Society* (New York, 1950), the now-classic analysis of how children of different cultures (including some of his work with Mekeel) passed through similar stages on the road to adulthood. (A second edition was published in 1963.)

Erikson left the Riggs Center in 1960 to return to Harvard as a professor of human development until 1970, when he retired. During this period, he published several additional important works. These include his two biographies, *Young Man Luther: A Study in Psychology and History* (New York, 1962) and *Gandhi's Truth: On the Origins of Militant Nonviolence* (New York, 1969), which earned Erikson the Pulitzer Prize and the National Book Award. The biographies explored the psychological motivations behind their subject's respective turns toward religion as an outlet for their personal beliefs. *Young Man Luther*—his first full-length psychohistory— represents an effort to explore how certain gifted individuals "find" themselves in the context of the era in which they live. Erikson examined Luther's childhood for clues to his "identity crisis" and ultimately to his role as a religious rebel and leader. *Gandhi* focuses on Gandhi's use of the fast as a leadership technique, particularly in the textile workers' strike in Ahmedabad in 1918. Combining Gandhi's personal history with the social and political history of India, Erikson showed how the two merged and how the Indian leader was able to direct a national movement of nonviolent civil disobedience. (Incidentally, Erikson dedicated the book to Martin Luther King Jr.)

Additional books published by Erikson while at Harvard and after his retirement continued to explore aspects of child development and problems of adulthood. They are *Insight and Responsibility: Lectures on the Ethical Implications of Psychoanalytic Insight* (New York, 1964); *Identity: Youth and Crisis* (New York, 1968); *In Search of*

Common Ground: Conversations with Erik H. Erikson and Huey Newton (New York, 1973); *Dimensions of a New Identity* (New York, 1974); *Life History and the Historical Moment* (New York, 1975); *Studies of Play* (New York, 1975), a reprint of articles spanning years of research, including some from as early as 1939; *Toys and Reasons: Stages in the Ritualization of Reality* (New York, 1977); and *Adulthood* (New York, 1978).

Books about Erikson include *Dialogue with Erik Erikson* by Richard Isadore Evans (New York, 1967) and Robert Coles' biography *Erik H. Erikson* (Boston, 1970), which first appeared in two installments in *The New Yorker* in 1970.

Erikson has been professor emeritus at Harvard since his retirement and received an honorary doctorate in 1978. He is a fellow at the Harvard Center for Advanced Study in the Behavioral Sciences. He is a fellow at the American Academy of Arts and Sciences, the National Academy of Education and the American Psychoanalytic Association. Erikson's many prizes include the Montessori Medal from the American Montessori Society (1973), the Aldrick award of the American Academy of Pediatrics (1971) and the McAlpin Research Award of the National Association for Mental Health (1974).

MILTON ESTEROW

b. July 28, 1928
Art publisher; writer

Milton Esterow, editor and publisher of *ARTnews* and *Antiques World* magazines, is one of the premier figures in the arcane world of art journalism. His current work with these award-winning publications came only after years of reporting and editorial experience with major newspapers and magazines.

Milton Esterow was born in New York City to Bernard, a grocer, and Yetta (Barash) Esterow. While a student at Brooklyn College, which he attended from 1946 to 1949, he joined *The New York Times* as a cultural reporter. From 1948 on he wrote news, feature and review articles on such topics as art, theater and film. Esterow was a writer for the motion picture and drama department for the bulk of his years with the *Times* and was promoted to the position of assistant to the cultural news director in 1963. Meanwhile, he was publishing articles in such periodicals as *The New York Times Magazine*, *Harper's* magazine and *The Atlantic Monthly*.

It was after those years of establishing the ever-important contacts that make a journalist a prominent figure in his field that Esterow, in 1972, branched out on his own and bought *ARTnews*, an established journal of the art world founded in 1902.

Under Esterow *ARTnews* has expanded its scope and prominence to become the most successful magazine of its kind. The Society of the Silurians presented *ARTnews* with an award for excellent journalism for the entire year of 1978, the first ever given to a publication by that group. When the Silurians, comprised of current and former journalists and editors, gave *ARTnews* the award, it was the only magazine to win that year. Specifically, the publication was cited for investigative reporting. Among the heralded articles fashioned by Esterow and his writers were a two-part series on "The Met's Sackler enclave: Public boon or private preserve?" and "The care and feeding of donors," the earliest examinations of the private arrangements between many museums and their major financial backers. *ARTnews* revealed that a special room had been established in the Metropolitan Museum of Art for the personal collection and staff of Met donor Arthur Sackler. Yet another article described how legal regulations made it very hard to print items detailing the problem of art authentication. The Mansoor Collection was investigated and Egyptologists who think the collection includes fakes, were interviewed, as were scientists who tended to think the collection valid. Another piece described the political and artistic conflicts surrounding "The FDR Memorial: A monument to politics, bureaucracy and the art of accommodation."

In 1975 Esterow began the first of a series of diversifications into new art-related publishing ventures, with the introduction of *The ARTnewsletter*, a biweekly focusing on the international art scene. ARTnews books was spawned in 1977, as the book publishing arm of the company. Esterow is editor and publisher of *The ARTnewsletter* and was also a co-editor and creator of *The American Art Journal* in 1969. *Antiques World*, published by Esterow and unveiled in November 1978, has proved to be a popular and respected periodical in its realm.

For his prowess in reporting, Esterow has received awards from the Newspaper Reporters Association of New York City, which in 1967 honored him for excellence in cultural news reporting. A frequent lecturer on the museum and university circuits, Esterow has spoken on such subjects as American art, international art and art forgeries, as well as on journalism and the American press. He is the author of *The Art Stealers* (New York, 1966), which explores the proliferation of art forgery throughout history.

ELI N. EVANS

b. July 28, 1936
Foundation executive

Eli N. Evans, a business executive who has been president of the Charles H. Revson Foundation since 1977, is author of the pioneering study *The Provincials: A Personal History of Jews in the South* (New York, 1973). In his book, Evans talks about the difference between Southern Jewish tradition and the more dynamic experience in the urban north.

Eli Evans was born to Emanuel J. and Sara (Nachamson) Evans. He grew up in the tobacco town of Durham, North Carolina, where his father ran the only Main Street store with an integrated lunch counter, and served as mayor during the bitter civil-rights struggle between 1950 and 1962. His maternal grandmother founded the first southern chapter of Hadassah, the women's Zionist organization, for which his mother worked and traveled.

His boyhood interests were simple: "My ambition was to marry a cheerleader and go into my father's business. I really knew no other Southern Jewish boys who didn't have the same ambition. Yet the story of the South is the story of fathers who built businesses to give to their sons who didn't want them," he writes in *The Provincials*. In that critically acclaimed book, Evans tries to resolve his feelings about his background. "I am not certain what it means to be both a Jew and a Southerner—to have inherited the Jewish longing for a homeland, while being raised with the Southerner's sense of home," he writes.

Evans received his B.A. degree in 1958 from the University of North Carolina and a law degree from Yale University in 1963. He spent a number of years working in government, first as a speechwriter for a North Carolina gubernatorial campaign in 1963–64 and then as a White House staff assistant from 1964 to 1965. He was program officer for the Carnegie Corporation of New York from 1967 to 1977, when he became head of the Revson Foundation. From 1977 to 1979 he was a member of the Carnegie Commission on the Future of Public Broadcasting.

Under Evans's leadership the Revson Foundation has focused on four program areas: urban affairs, with special emphasis on New York City; education; biomedical research policy; and Jewish philanthropy and education. The Foundation has awarded grants to study aliens in New York City; the impact of immigration on selected areas in the United States, including New York City; and the effectiveness of various types of cancer research. It has allocated money to the National Women's Education Fund to conduct workshops for women who want to run for public office and to the Women's Action Alliance to monitor state and federal action in areas of sex discrimination, abortion and the Equal Rights Amendment, thus devoting itself to placing more women in decision-making positions.

The foundation's program in Jewish philanthropy stresses Jewish education through the media. It provided substantial funding for "Civilization and the Jews," a 10-part public television series, produced by WNET in New York and narrated by Abba Eban. It documents the 4,000-year history of the Jewish people in a way, says Abba Eban, that shows "that not everything in Jewish history is tragic. There is also a mysterious talent for persistence—the stubborn resolve of a small people to survive in its own identity."

The foundation has also given a grant to the Jewish Theological Seminary of America and the Jewish Museum in New York to create the National Jewish Archives of Film and Broadcasting, which will ensure that programming on the Jewish experience recorded in the media will not be lost.

RICHARD ANDERSON FALK

b. November 13, 1930
Professor; author

Richard Anderson Falk, professor of international law at Princeton University, is a distinguished scholar and a radical political thinker. An activist against the Vietnam War, he has written many books suggesting an international world order of greater restraint and offering proposals for human survival in a nuclear world.

Richard Anderson Falk was born in New York City to Edwin Albert, a naval historian and attorney, and Helene (Pollak) Falk, a well-known tennis player. He graduated from the Fieldston School in New York in 1948 and received his B.S. degree in economics from the Wharton School at the University of Pennsylvania in 1952. He received his law degree from Yale University in 1955 and was admitted to the New York bar a year later. In 1962 he was awarded a Doctor of Juridical Science degree by Harvard. Falk taught law at Ohio State University from 1955 to 1961, the year he became associate professor of law at Princeton. He was made Albert G. Milbank Professor of International Law and Practice at Princeton in 1965.

A prolific writer, Falk often expresses his belief in the moral responsibility of citizens. In *Law, Morality and Man in the Contemporary World* (Princeton, New Jersey, 1963), he examines how nuclear war can be avoided through the exercise of military interventions, a willingness to mediate crises and conflicts, restraining military research and setting limits on the continued development of highly sophisticated weaponry.

Falk demonstrates his understanding of the expansion of international law in *The Status of Law in International Society* (Princeton, New Jersey, 1970). In it, he discusses the United Nations' relations with nonmember states, the use of outer space, and the difficult relationship between domestic and international law. In *This Endangered Planet: Prospects and Proposals for Human Survival* (New York, 1971), the author blames the ecological crisis on the war system, overpopulation, wastefulness of natural resources and abuse of the environment. He deals with a similar theme in *A Study of Future Worlds* (New York, 1975), in which he depicts the condition of the planet and its inhabitants in the year 2000.

As co-editor of *The Vietnam War and International Law* (four volumes, 1968, 1969, 1971, 1972), Falk brought together writings by international lawyers and political scientists on intervention in Vietnam, thereby helping readers make judgments on the legality of the United States effort there. He also edited a book entitled *Crimes of War* (New York, 1971), which portrayed how humans treat each other so cruelly, in order to help Americans evaluate their legal and moral obligations and responsibilities for American actions in Vietnam. He included in the book articles Noam Chomsky, Arthur Miller, Hannah Arendt and Jean-Paul Sartre, who stated that the United States was guilty of genocide in Vietnam.

In *Human Rights and State Sovereignty* (New York, 1981), Falk argues that with governments becoming more authoritarian, respect for human rights is decreasing throughout the world. He blames the growth of tyranny on a deteriorating world economy, poor results from trade and increasing energy costs.

Falk is a member of the advisory board of Amnesty International, the Institute for World Order and the Center for International Policy. He is on the editorial board of *Foreign Policy Magazine*, the *American Journal of International Law* and *The Nation*. He was a consultant to the United States Arms Control and Disarmament Agency from 1962 to 1963 and consultant to a member of the United States Senate Foreign Relations Committee in 1967.

He has also written numerous articles for magazines on arms limitation and international order and law.

HOWARD FAST

b. November 11, 1914
Writer

Howard Fast is best-known as a storyteller. In more than four decades he has written or edited more than 50 books that have been translated into 82 languages. Indeed, Fast may be one of the most widely read writers in the world today.

Howard Melvin Fast was born in New York City to Barney, a cable car gripperman, factory worker and pattern maker for women's dresses—and Ida (Miller) Fast. Young Fast wanted to become an artist but instead began writing soon after graduating from George Washington High School in 1932, when he sold a story to the *Ladies Home Journal*. In time he would publish novels, biographies, short stories, books for children and histories, and write for the theater, films and television.

In the beginning he began chronicling America's early years and major political leaders. The best-known include the novel *Conceived in Liberty* (New York, 1939), a sympathetic depiction of the sacrifices of Washington's men at Valley Forge; *The Last Frontier* (New York, 1942), which treated the Cheyenne Indians fairly; *Freedom Road* (New York, 1944), a passionate defense of the rights of blacks and their white supporters against slavery and post-Civil War reactionaries; *Patrick Henry and the Frigate's Keel* (New York, 1945), short stories about the new nation, and many others. He also wrote the biography *Citizen Tom Paine* (New York, 1945) and edited *Selected Works of Tom Paine* (New York, 1945).

In addition to his passionate interest in American themes, Fast also wrote about Jews, including *Haym Solomon, Son of Liberty* (New York, 1941); *My Glorious Brothers* (New York, 1948), about Judah Maccabeus; *Torquemada* (New York, 1966), about the Spanish Inquisition; and *The Jews* (New York, 1968), a history.

Many of Fast's themes have been political and reflect his belief in emphasizing the right of ordinary people to live in a society that accepts basic human rights as a natural right. His background and experiences drew him close to the American Communist Party, and sometime in the early 1940s, he joined. In 1942–43 he worked for the Office of War Information and in 1944 was assigned to an Army film project. By 1945 he was serving as a correspondent in Europe for *Esquire* and *Coronet*.

After the war he became a popular spokesman for the Communist Party, speaking and writing on social and political issues. As a result, and despite the fact that Communists were a legal political party, he was questioned and harassed by the House un-American Activities Committee. He refused to comply with its demand that he inform on friends and colleagues and answer a series of questions. For this, he was cited for contempt and forced to serve three months at Mill Point Prison in West Virginia during the summer of 1950.

In 1954 he ran for Congress on the American Labor Party ticket but lost. During these years he was black-listed by traditional publishers, fearful lest sales suffer for publishing a Communist author. To survive, he began writing under a pseudonym, E.V. Cunningham, and wrote a series of ephemeral novels—*Sylvia* (New York, 1960), *Helen* (New York, 1966), *Cynthia* (New York, 1968), etc.—because the American Legion and the Sons (and Daughters, too) of the American Revolution angrily demanded that his books be removed from public libraries. Abroad, the USSR published a number of his books and awarded him the Stalin International Peace Prize in 1953. At home, he self-published his novel, *Spartacus* (New York, 1951), the tale of a slave revolt in Rome, which became a best seller. Other books generated during that period of his life include *Peekskill, U.S.A.: A Personal Experience* (New York, 1951), an account of a physical attack on a Party meeting at an upstate New York city, and *The Passion of Sacco and Vanzetti* (New York, 1953).

In 1957 Fast renounced communism and described his experiences and reflections in *The Naked God: The Writer and the Communist Party* (New York, 1957). He wrote that Nikita Khrushchev's speech to the 20th Party Congress in 1956 denouncing Stalin's crimes "itemized a recorded barbarism and paranoic bloodlust." Although he insisted he had opposed the 1939 Nazi-Soviet Non-Aggression Pact, he remained in the Party until the mid-1950s, because he believed that the Communists were "the truest and most consistent fighters against the Nazis." Quitting, Fast told Harry Schwartz of *The New York Times* in February 1957 that communism was a "prison for man's best and boldest dreams" as well as a "sick God."

Eventually he turned to pacifism, and he joined the Jewish Peace Fellowship in the mid-1960s. He also continued to write books, especially the anti-war novel *The Hessian* (New York, 1972), a Revolutionary War book describing the dilemma of young men compelled against their conscience to fight in war.

In 1972 he moved to California, where he wrote screenplays. Eight years later he was back on the East Coast, where he produced his trilogy based on a fictional family: *The Immigrants* (Boston, 1977), *The Second Generation* (Boston, 1978) and *The Establishment* (Boston, 1979).

For further information:

Fast, Howard. *The American.* New York: 1946.
———. *The Crossing.* New York: 1971.
———. *The Proud and the Free.* Boston: 1950.
Meyer, Hershel D. *History and Conscience: The Case of Howard Fast.* New York: 1958.

JULES FEIFFER

b. January 26, 1929
Political cartoonist; writer

In his internationally syndicated cartoons, Jules Feiffer satirizes subjects as wide-ranging as atomic destruction, Richard Nixon and Ronald Reagan, marital discord and the rites of spring. Known primarily for his cartoons, which have appeared since 1956 in the New York weekly newspaper *The Village Voice*, Feiffer has also achieved success as a serious playwright, screenwriter and novelist.

Jules Feiffer was born in the Bronx to David and Rhoda (Davis) Feiffer. His father held a number of jobs, including salesman and dental technician, and his mother was a fashion designer. At the age of 5 Feiffer, who wanted to draw for as long as he can remember, won a drawing contest sponsored by Wanamaker's department store. After graduating from James Monroe High School in 1946, he enrolled that year at the Art Students League of New York, simultaneously attending drawing classes at Pratt Institute and working with several comic strip artists, including Will Eisner, creator of *The Spirit*. From 1949 to 1951, he drew a Sunday cartoon page feature dubbed "Clifford."

Feiffer was drafted into the United States Army in 1951, where he worked for two years in a cartoon animation unit. There he developed a character called "Munro"—a 4-year-old boy who is drafted by mistake into the Army. After leaving the service Feiffer worked at a series of jobs until *The Village Voice* agreed to publish his cartoons. They were an immediate hit and have appeared regularly in the paper ever since.

In his cartoons Feiffer is not merely amusing and clever but instead is making moral and political statements about the state of the world (the arms race, Nixon, male-female relationships, etc.). There is little action here; the reader is made privy to the private thoughts of his characters. In essence, he is the comic muse of the urban and urbane Jewish artist-intellectual, observing yet participating, and deeply committed to humane causes.

In the late 1960s Feiffer's plays *Little Murders* (1967), *God Bless* (1968) and *The White House Murder Case* (1969) and many of his cartoons were strongly political. *Little Murders,* which later became a film, portrayed the horrors of city life. *God Bless* dealt with the accommodation of American liberals to the status quo, and *The White House Murder Case* depicted a United States war in Brazil.

Feiffer says he was the first cartoonist to come out against the Vietnam War (in 1963). During that war he spoke at peace demonstrations in Washington and was a Eugene McCarthy delegate to the Democratic Convention in Chicago in 1968.

Feiffer's more recent work—his script for the 1971 movie *Carnal Knowledge* and his play *Knock Knock* (1976) —deal with more personal issues. *Carnal Knowledge* explores the conflicts of two men—friends since school days who are now reaching middle age—in the throes of mid-life crisis. *Knock Knock* presents two middle-aged Jewish men—one a skeptical realist, the other a romantic believer—who have been sharing a house for 20 years, when Joan of Arc knocks at their door and asks them to join her in a pilgrimage before the coming of the Holocaust. More philosophical in *Knock Knock* than in his other plays, Feiffer sought to reflect societal values in the work.

Feiffer's play *Grownups* (1981) explores the relationship between a successful Jewish newspaper reporter and his parents, wife and sister. What seems a happy life on the surface is revealed to be a superficial deception. In fact, as the play progresses, the reporter discovers deep-seated hostilities, resentments, bitterness and regrets around him.

Feiffer won the George Polk Memorial Award in 1962.

For further information:
Feiffer, Jules. *Ackroyd.* New York: 1977.
———. *Feiffer on Civil Rights.* New York: 1967.
———. *Feiffer on Nixon: The Cartoon Presidency.* New York: 1974.
———. *Passionella and Other Stories.* New York: 1959.
———. *Sick, Sick, Sick: A Guide to Non-Confident Living.* New York: 1958.
———. *Tantrum.* New York: 1979.

LEONARD FEIN

b. July 1, 1934
Writer; educator

Leonard Fein is in the forefront of political activism in Jewish American life. As writer, magazine editor or lecturer, he is well-known as an articulate and opinionated personality, more often than not criticizing what he believes to be excesses of the Menachem Begin government in Israel and stressing insted the alternatives offered by the prime minister's political opponents.

Leonard Fein was born in Brooklyn, New York to Isaac, a rabbi, and Clara (Wertheim) Fein. He earned his B.A. degree from the University of Chicago in 1955 and his M.A. degree at the same school three years later. In 1962, he received a Ph.D. from Michigan State University in political science. Almost immediately he began teaching the subject at the Massachusetts Institute of Technology, from 1962-70. He served as deputy director and director of research at the MIT-Harvard Joint Center for Urban Studies in 1968-70 and from 1970 to 1980 taught politics and social policy at Brandeis University. In 1974 he founded *Moment* magazine and continues as its editor.

In 1972 Fein and four colleagues (Robert Chin, Jack Dauber, Bernard Reisman and Herzl Spiro) issued a report for the Long Range Planning Committee of the Union of American Hebrew Congregations, *Reform Is A Verb* (New York). They concluded that American Reform Jews were very well educated in secular schools but sketchily educated in Judaism; that there was an "enormous variety in both behavior and in belief, both among temples and within temples"; that a serious generational gap existed in such areas as contributing to Jewish causes —older people thinking it vital and younger ones dismissing it as a requisite for being Jewish; and that there was disagreement between the generations on intermarriage. The report's central thesis was that "the future can be invented." Predicting vast changes ahead in American society, the report told Reform Judaism: The future "is something we shape, we create, we invent." Suggesting that the years to come would be more hospitable to experimentation and decentralization it urged Reform Judaism move toward "the intelligent and purposeful utilization of that freedom."

Writing on his own, in *Israel: Politics & People* (Boston, 1968), Fein tried to explain that complex nation before and after the 1967 Six Day War and made an effort to foresee the future in a turbulent region that more often than not defies predictions. In subsequent years, Fein has frequently opposed many of the policies of the government of Prime Minister Menachem Begin. (One of his magazine's leading writers is former Labor Party foreign minister Abba Eban, an ardent Begin critic.) He has also helped organize public statements—signed by well-known people in American Jewish life—opposing Begin's program of permitting more and more settlements on the occupied West Bank or in Judah and Samaria, as the Begin government prefers them to be known.

HENRY L. FEINGOLD

b. February 6, 1931
Historian

Historian Henry Feingold is one of America's major historical interpreters of the Holocaust and its impact on American history as well as of the forces that shaped United States policies toward Jewish refugees during the years of the Hitler regime in Germany.

Henry Feingold was born in Ludwigshaven, Germany to Marcus M., a merchant, and Frieda (Singer) Feingold. The Feingolds reached the United States in 1939. A graduate of Brooklyn College—he received a B.A. degree in 1953 and an M.A. degree in 1954—he taught in New York City secondary schools from 1953 to 1965, with time out for Army service between 1955 and 1957. He received a Ph.D. in American history from New York University the following year and in 1967 he became a lecturer at the City University of New York. In 1976 he became a full professor with responsibilities at the Graduate Center of the City University and at its Bernard Baruch College. He also taught at the University of Maryland from 1955 to 1956, Stern College for women from 1971 to 1973 and the Jewish Theological Seminary of America from 1973 to 1976.

Feingold's dissertation, which eventually became the subject of his first book, *Politics of Rescue: The Roosevelt Administration and the Holocaust 1938-1945* (New Brunswick, N.J., 1970), examined the reasons the Roosevelt administration had not saved European Jewry from Hitler. *Politics of Rescue* was a significant historial study, especially since he relied heavily on the Breckinridge Long papers, the Stephen Wise papers, the State Department archival documents and the War Refugee Board materials. Feingold sought to answer why the United States did not act forcefully enough to save Jews trapped in Nazi Europe. Absent a forthright commitment to save people (although there were "many individuals who wanted to do more") the Roosevelt Administration vacilated, and the anti-Jewish views of Breckinridge Long of the State Department tended to dominate American

policy. Even so, Long would not have been able to do so for so long a period of time had not other factors applied. For one thing, American Jewry—which was reluctant to take too public a stand—was constantly involved in internecine "bickering" over ideologies and tactics. "When one realizes how appallingly irrelevant the issues and personalities dividing them were, one can only shake one's head in disbelief," comments Feingold. Then, too, Jews unwisely expended much of their resources and energy trying to reconcile "expensive resettlement ventures [with] the pioneering effort in Palestine." Moreover, American public opinion was decidedly unsympathetic to the plight of European Jewry and everyone—Jew and especially non-Jew—believed that Hitler could not be dissuaded from his murderous scheme. He concluded that while the administration perceived itself as humanitarian with a view toward helping oppressed people in other lands, it ultimately lacked both the power and the commitment to rescue Jews. Upon publication the book was highly praised for its objectivity and meticulous research and won for Feingold the Leon Jolson Award of the Jewish Book Council for the best book on the Holocaust in 1972.

His next book, *Zion in America: The Jewish Experience from Colonial Times to the Present* (New York, 1975), dealt with the Jewish American experience. In it Feingold explores how the movement of Jewish immigrants to America differs from that of other ethnic and national groups. Specifically, he suggests that the Jews had an internalized system of being that made their reasons for immigrating and their value systems and goals distinct from those of other groups. For example, he has said that "Remarkable Jewish achievement stems from values inherent in Jewish culture" and adds that American Jews must acknowledge "how strongly rooted in Jewish tradition quality and achievement are, and move from an initial love of excellence to a still deeper attachment to the underlying Jewish culture."

In a wide-ranging essay, "The Condition of American Jewry in Historial Perspective: A Bicentennial Assessment," published in the *American Jewish Year Book* in 1976, Feingold discussed the question: "How does the condition of American Jewry appear from the historical point of view?" Looking backward and then into the present, he maintained an optimistic stance. Jews in the United States, he wrote, were free, have economic and social mobility and are to be found in all levels of government, as both elected and appointed officials. Rejecting the pessimistic conclusions of many observers about the future of the American Jewish community, Feingold observed that "The commitment [to preserve and enrich Jewish life] is still carried forward by the few. . . the many dance around the golden calf. [Still,] some return when summoned."

But time and again, Feingold returned to the Holocaust. In a paper he delivered in 1980 at a conference sponsored by the National Conference of Christians and Jews, he said, "We are left with a truth almost too difficult to accept because it flies in the face of everything we want to believe, at least about our time in history. It is more dangerous than ever to be powerless in the secular world because the modern nation state is not capable of making human responses, and the moral force . . . no longer exists." This ominous new fact, Feingold suggests, more than any other, bodes evil for future generations, Jew and non-Jew alike.

Feingold serves on the editorial boards of several leading Jewish history periodicals, including *Shoah* and *Reconstructionist,* and is the editor of *American Jewish History,* a publication of the American Jewish Historical Society. He is also on the board of the Executive Committee of the Jewish Historical Society of New York.

For further information:

Feingold, Henry L. "The Witness Role of American Jews: A Second Look," In *Human Resources to the Holocaust: Perpetrators and Victims, Bystanders and Resisters,* edited by Michael D. Ryan. New York: 1980.

———. "The Government Response." In *The Holocaust: Ideology, Bureaucracy, and Genocide,* edited by Henry Friedlander and Sybil Milton. Millwood, N.Y.: 1980.

DIANNE FEINSTEIN

b. June 22, 1933
Politician

Dianne Feinstein has been a public servant, liberal leader and active politician during her entire adult career in her native California. But her leadership ability shone through on November 27, 1978, when she became acting mayor of San Francisco following the assassinations of Mayor George Moscone and Harvey Milk, a member of the city's Board of Supervisors. She managed to steer San Francisco not only through the aftermath of the assassination tragedy but through the long and complex shock of the Jonestown massacre, whose victims had been members of a San Francisco-based cult. In November 1979 Feinstein was elected mayor of San Francisco and has remained popular for her astute ability to run a complicated and often troubled city.

Dianne Goldman was born in San Francisco to Leon, a professor of surgery at San Francisco's University of

California Medical Center, and Betty (Rosenburg) Goldman. Her mother, a former model, was a Russian-American Catholic, and her father a Jew, and she was educated in both religions. All the same, although she attended a Catholic high school in San Francisco, she considers herself Jewish, adopting it formally in 1953.

Feinstein received a B.S. degree in history in 1955 from Stanford University, where she was student body president a year earlier. After graduation she began what would become a long and committed career in government. Beginning as a public affairs intern with the prestigious San Francisco-based Coro Foundation in 1955–56, her subsequent positions included assistant to the California Industrial Welfare Committee in Los Angeles and San Francisco (1956–57); vice chairwoman, California Women's Board of Terms and Parole (1962–66), a job she received from Governor Edmund G. Brown after she sent him her Coro essay on criminal justice; chairwoman, San Francisco City and County Advisory Committee for Adult Detention (1967–69); and supervisor, City and County of San Francisco (1969–78). She was president of the Board of Supervisors in 1970–72, 1974–76 and 1978, when she assumed the mayoralty. Her performance as acting mayor was such that in 1979 she won a hotly contested race on her own merit.

In addition to these posts, Feinstein was a member of the Mayor's Committee on Crime (1967–69), the Board of Governors of the Bay Area Council (1972 to the present) and the Bay Conservation and Development Committee (1973–78). She was chairwoman of the Environmental Management Task Force of the Association of Bay Governments from 1976 to 1978 and of the Board of Regents of Lone Mountain College from 1972 to 1978. She belongs to many additional organizations concerned with conservation and San Francisco civic affairs.

A liberal, avoiding what she calls "volatile political rhetoric and personal politics," she challenged Democratic Mayor Joseph Alioto in the 1971 mayoralty election because cities were "where the salvation of America's problems lies. As the cities go, so goes the whole nation." She proceeded to denounce hard-core pornography prevalent in the city's North Beach district. She also opposed high-rise buildings, saying "San Francisco doesn't need the developers." Alone among all the candidates, she refused to oppose court-mandated busing for the goal of public school integration. She repeatedly told parents that court orders had to be obeyed. Her critics then publicized the fact that her own child was enrolled in a private school, and she finished third. She lost again in 1975.

Following her accession to the mayoralty in 1978, she sought to calm the city, known for its ethnic and racial diversity and widespread tolerance of all kinds of behavior. She chose to "reassure people . . . put the bricks back together and . . . do what's best, because sometimes what happens is violence begets violence." She promptly chose a homosexual, Harvey Britt, to replace the murdered Milk—who was also gay—but publicly asked the gay community to avoid embarrassing heterosexuals. But she strengthened law enforcement and has remained steadfastly middle-of-the-road on fiscal matters, too. Even so, she is customarily liberal on environmental and social questions, such as women's rights, including support for the Equal Rights Amendment. And when Wilson Riles, the first black ever to win a statewide election in California ran for reelection as state superintendent of public instruction in 1982, Feinstein supported him against his leading opponent, who was strongly opposed to busing to foster racial desegregation. Moreover, following the passage of California's Proposition 13, the law enacted by referendum in 1978 that reduced property taxes drastically and therefore badly denuded municipal treasuries and public services, Feinstein reduced some city agencies' budgets sharply to maintain the public services of the city as much as possible.

MOSHE FEINSTEIN

b. March 5, 1895
Rabbi

Rabbi Moshe Feinstein is generally acknowledged as one of the world's great authorities or *Poskin* (legal decisors) on Jewish religious law. His decisions concerning modern science and technology in light of *halakhah* are considered definitive by millions of his Orthodox followers.

Feinstein, the son of Rabbi David and Faya (Davidowitz) Feinstein, was born in Uzda, a small town near Minsk in Belorussia. He received his early education from his father, the spiritual leader of the community. In 1921 Moshe Feinstein became the rabbi of Luban, another small town near Minsk.

Feinstein came to America in 1937 and was appointed dean of Metivta Tifereth Jerusalem, an Orthodox yeshiva in Manhattan. Under his direction the yeshiva has achieved international stature and is widely regarded as one of the best in America. Feinstein also assumed the leadership of the U.S. section of Agudat Yisrael, a worldwide

organization of Orthodox Jews, which claims 5 million adherents. He is also one of their *gedolim,* or sages, who issues rulings based upon *halakhah.*

Agudat Yisrael was founded in 1912 by Russian, Polish and German Hasidim. Although it was initially hostile to Zionism—it once contended that only the Messiah could create a truly Jewish state—the organization has moderated its views. Agudat Yisrael maintains an international educational system, and Feinstein has been active in providing spiritual, educational and financial guidance for its many yeshivas.

Feinstein is highly admired for his dedication and selflessness. His seven volumes of commentary on the Talmud, *Dibrot Moshe*—the first appeared in 1946, published in New York—display his great erudition and scholarship. Beginning in 1959 seven collections of his responses to questions from rabbis around the world have been published by Agudat Yisrael. They are called *Igrot Moshe.* In addition to questions about science and technology, Feinstein has dealt with Jewish life under communist rule and in the United States.

"We must draw near to *Klal Israel* in general," he told the 58th Convention of Agudath in 1981, and "to feel close to the Torah community at large. This will facilitate a person's identifying with its needs and give fullest support to such vital communal institutions as our Yeshivas and day schools."

Feinstein has always emphasized the needs of right-wing Orthodoxy, what his followers call "Torah Judaism" in contrast to what they see as less observant practices among other Jews. When Prime Minister Menachem Begin sought to include three Israeli Orthodox parties in his government, the letter sought as a quid pro quo the right to further restrict the rights of non-Orthodox Jews in Israel. Advised Feinstein: "Do not let this opportunity pass you by," in a statement sent to Orthodox leaders. He urged the Israelis to make major efforts to keep Conservative and Reform groups "from making any inroads in Israel." Agudat Yisrael followed suit, and its American branch announced its unequivocal opposition to the notion of religious pluralism in the state of Israel.

From 1966 until 1976 Feinstein was the president of the Union of Orthodox Rabbis in America. Other examples of his legal rulings are one (in 1981) in which he said that a Jewish Theological Seminary professor (a religious Conservative) could not be asked to teach a course on Judaism in an Orthodox adult education class because presumably the professor held heretical opinions. In another decision that year Feinstein said that marriages performed by Reform rabbis may be nullified and no religious divorce need be obtained because Reform rabbis are "all evil and given to wanton Sabbath violation of all Torah commandments."

BERNARD T. FELD

b. December 21, 1919
Physicist; professor

Although—or perhaps because—he was involved with the development of the first nuclear chain reaction, which led to the creation of the atomic bomb, physicist Bernard T. Feld has since become one of the most outspoken scientists favoring nuclear arms control and civilian management of atomic energy resources.

Bernard T. Feld was born in Brooklyn to A. Louis, a dress cutter, and Helen (Taub) Feld. Both parents were Russian immigrants who raised their family in an atmosphere steeped in *Yiddishkeit* and in social democratic values.

Feld was educated at the City College of New York, where he received a B.S. degree in 1939. He pursued graduate studies in physics at Columbia University. While there, he became a teaching assistant to Enrico Fermi and Isador I. Rabi, two of the most eminent physicists of the time. They introduced him to another of Columbia's outstanding physicists, Leo Szilard, who recruited Feld to participate in a project designed to create the first nuclear chain reaction. From 1942 to 1944, while Feld temporarily dropped his studies at Columbia, he became group leader at the University of Chicago's metallurgy laboratory, where the chain reaction project was completed, and later went to Los Alamos, New Mexico, where the atomic bomb was perfected. The objective in developing the bomb had been to create an atomic deterrent to stop Hitler's continued incursions throughout Europe, and the plan had been to drop a "demonstration" bomb in a deserted region where no one would be hurt. However, the first bomb was subsequently dropped at Hiroshima. The devastation that followed affected Feld so profoundly that thereafter he became a dedicated pacifist.

After finally completing his Ph.D. at Columbia in 1945, Feld was appointed to the faculty of the Massachusetts Institute of Technology. However, he immediately took off six months to lobby in Washington, D.C. with other leading physicists for civilian control of the atom. The outcome of this effort was the passage by Congress of the MacMahon Act, which laid the groundwork for the creation of the Atomic Energy Commission. Feld began teaching at MIT in early 1946 as an instructor. He was appointed associate professor in 1952

and full professor in 1957. He spent the 1953–54 academic year in Rome and Padua as a Guggenheim Fellow and visiting professor, received a Ford Foundation Fellowship in 1960–61 as a visiting scientist at the European Center for Nuclear Research in Geneva, Switzerland, and from 1966 to 1967 was visiting professor at the Ecole Polytechnique in Paris and research associate at the Centre de Recherche Nucleaire in Saclay, France. His specialties include theoretical studies of atomic and molecular fine and hyperfine structures and theoretical investigations in low- and high-energy physics.

As part of Feld's role in arms control and disarmament since World War II, he has become one of the most active participants in the annual international Pugwash Conference on Science and World Affairs, which began in 1957. Held initially in the small Nova Scotia village of Pugwash, the conference, which moves to a different site each year, has evolved into one of the most prestigious meetings of scientists, more than 100 of whom discuss not only nuclear arms control but the general impact of advanced technology in safeguarding the world for peace and for political and ecological stability. Many of the arms control treaties that have been established throughout the world originated in behind-the-scenes discussions at Pugwash conferences. From 1973 to 1975 Feld was secretary-general of the Pugwash Conference, and in 1981 he was chair of the Executive Council.

Feld, who was visiting professor of theoretical physics at the Imperial College of Science and Technology in London from 1973 to 1975, has been head of the Division of Nuclear and High Energy Physics at MIT since 1975. He is a fellow of the American Association for the Advancement of Science and of the Council on Foreign Relations. His many awards include the Leo Szilard Award for Physics in the Public Interest, presented by the American Physical Society (1975), and the Public Service Award of the Federation of American Scientists (1975). Since 1975 he has been editor in chief of the *Bulletin of the Atomic Scientists,* a publication that has always pointed to the dangers of the nuclear arms race.

ELIOT FELD

b. July 5, 1942
Dancer; choreographer

Eliot Feld, who has been dancing professionally since he was 12 years old, is now considered among America's top young choreographers. Many of his innovative contributions to modern ballet repertory are now classics of their genre.

Eliot Feld, the son of Benjamin Noah, an attorney, and Alice (Posner) Feld, a travel agent, was born in the Boro Park section of Brooklyn. His interest in dancing as a career was cultivated early. He first studied at the School of American Ballet when he was 11 and the following year entered the High School of Performing Arts in New York City, a public but highly selective secondary school whose students combine a rigorous academic program with intensive performance training. By 1954 he played the child prince in the New York City Ballet production of *The Nutcracker*—his debut— and throughout his high school years and in his early twenties, he danced in many major Broadway productions, including *I Can Get It for You Wholesale, West Side Story* and *Fiddler on the Roof.* He also danced as a back-up on two of television's greatest variety shows, *The Ed Sullivan Show* and *The Garry Moore Show,* and from 1963 to 1969 he danced with the American Ballet Theater and performed with companies headed by Donald McKayle and Pearl Lang.

While with ABT Feld made his debut as a choreographer with *At Midnight,* a work that gave the 25-year-old dancer what *New York Times* critic Anna Kisselgoff described as "instant success." The piece, described by another critic as "an improbably assured first ballet with exceptional depth and emotion and controlled dance invention," set the tone for his future works. Indeed, while still in his twenties, Feld created several important dances that mixed neoclassic and romantic styles yet were very modern, profoundly personal, and often used contemporary American music and American themes. By the time he broke from ABT in 1969 to form the American Ballet Company, Feld had already developed a following. Even so, some critics questioned whether the young choreographer had achieved too much too soon and would be able to transcend his early successes.

In fact, Feld's company was plagued by financial problems, and two years later the American Ballet Company disbanded. For the following two years Feld freelanced in the United States and abroad, performing with such noted companies as the Royal Winnipeg Ballet, London Festival Ballet and the Joffrey Ballet.

Returning to the United States, he founded a new company in 1973, the Eliot Feld Ballet, which became the resident dance troupe at Joseph Papp's Newman Theater (part of the New York Shakespeare Festival). By this time Feld had created new ballets that established him firmly as an important new talent.

Feld's ballets are unique and combine playfulness and emotion. They are classical in form yet free of structural limitations imposed by classical ballet. And while they are abstract, their themes are often very clear. Feld—who has been influenced by such American-based giants of choreography as George Balanchine, Agnes DeMille and Jerome Robbins—believes that movement should be emotionally felt and therefore makes sure that his dancers project these feelings to the audience.

Among the 31 or more ballets Feld has created, 2 minor works reflect his Jewish background: *Tzaddick,* a theatrical piece about Judaic tradition and rituals using music by Aaron Copland, and *Sephardic Song,* which uses folk dance variations. His best-known dances, besides *At Midnight,* include *Intermezzo, Harbinger, Footsteps on Air* and *Variations on America.*

In recent years the Eliot Feld ballet has toured widely as Feld has fulfilled his promise and matured as a choreographer and artistic director. With federal funding, the Feld administration has been renovating the Elgin Theater, an old movie theater in the Chelsea section of Manhattan, as a permanent home for his company as well as a performance showcase for smaller, independent dance groups. He also teaches gifted young dancers from New York City public schools in a free professional program called the New Ballet School and occasionally uses some of these students in his ballets. In 1981 Feld choreographed the New York City Opera's production of *Song of Norway.*

Eliot Feld remains a major creative force in American dance.

LOUIS FINKELSTEIN

b. June 14, 1895
Rabbi, Seminary Chancellor

For more than 50 years, as scholar, teacher and administrator, Rabbi Louis Finkelstein helped shape the traditionalist Conservative mold of the Jewish Theological Seminary of America and to oversee its growth into a major institution of higher education in religion. But beside his lifetime dedication to Judaism, Finkelstein was one of the first Jewish leaders to promote the movement for interreligious learning and dialogue.

Louis Finkelstein was born in Cincinnati, Ohio, on June 14, 1895, to Simon, a rabbi, and Hannah (Brager) Finkelstein. His family moved to Brooklyn in 1902, when Finkelstein's father, a native of Lithuania, was appointed spiritual leader of the Orthodox congregation. Raised in the Brownsville section, Finkelstein received an intensive religious training from an early age, rising before 5:30 A.M. most mornings to pursue religious studies in addition to his regular schooling. He was an ardent believer in Jewish causes, and at the City College of New York, where he received an A.B. degree in 1915 and was elected to Phi Beta Kappa, he was president of the campus Zionist organization.

Finkelstein obtained a Ph.D. from Columbia University in 1918 and completed a Master of Hebrew Literature at the Jewish Theological Seminary in 1919, the same year he was ordained. From 1919 to 1931 he headed Congregation Kehillath Israel but kept his ties to the Seminary. In 1920 he joined the faculty as an instructor in Talmud and, from 1924 to 1930, was Solomon Schechter Lecturer in Theology.

During the early years of his career, Finkelstein distinguished himself as an insightful scholar of ancient Jewish history and as an important interpreter of modern Conservative Judaism. *Jewish Self-Government in the Middle Ages* (New York, 1924 and 1964) was the first of a prodigious output of histories and religious commentaries. His next published work was an expansion of his doctoral thesis, a study called *Kimchi's Commentaries on Isaiah,* (New York, 1926). Rabbi David ben Kimchi was a renowned 13th-century scholar who lived in southern France. Other publications by Finkelstein during the early part of his career include a two-volume edition of commentary on Deuteronomy (Philadelphia, 1936 and 1937), "Akiba—Scholar, Saint, Martyr" *(Harvard Theological Review,* 1936) and *The Pharisees, The Sociological Background of Their Faith* (Philadelphia, 1938).

At the Seminary, where Finkelstein was promoted to full professor in 1931, he also rose through the administrative ranks, serving as assistant to the president from 1934 to 1937, as provost from 1937 to 1940 and, upon the death of the Seminary's president Cyrus Adler, as president from 1940 to 1951. During this period, Finkelstein attained national renown, as he sought to bridge the communications gap among many different religious denominations in the U.S. In 1938, for example, he was co-founder and director of the Seminary's Institute in Interdenominational Studies (now the Institute for Religious Social Studies), which welcomes students of all faiths to study with theologians representing all religious backgrounds. Finkelstein also guest-lectured at Johns Hopkins University in 1937, Oberlin College in 1939, Harvard University from 1943 to 1944, and other educational institutions in the U.S. He also assumed Adler's role as advisor on Jewish Affairs to President Franklin D. Roosevelt between 1940-45. During this period he published several major theological works, including *Beliefs and Practices of Judaism* (New York,

1941), and co-authored *Faith For Today* (New York, 1941) and *Religions of Democracy* (New York, 1941). Several years later he edited a major three-volume study, *The Jews: Their History, Culture and Religion* (New York, 1949; 1960). This 1400-page project included chapters by 34 Jewish and Christian scholars.

As the Seminary expanded, so did Finkelstein's responsibilities. In 1951, he was elevated to the newly-created post of chancellor, a position which freed him from much of his administrative work so that he could return to scholarship and writing. In 1963 he was sent by President Kennedy as the American "ambassador" to the coronation of Pope Paul VI, and the following year he was honorary board chairperson for a poverty program to recruit young people for job training. He also preached in the Nixon White House.

Finkelstein is on the editorial board of the *Universal Jewish Encyclopedia* and, since 1942, has been co-editor of *Science, Philosophy and Religion Annual Yearbook.* He is a member of the Rabbinical Assembly of America and served as president of the group from 1938 to 1940. He is also a member of the American Academy of Jewish Research and the Jewish Academy of Arts and Sciences.

For further information

Finkelstein, Louis. *New Light from the Prophets.* New York: 1969.

———. *Social Responsibility in the Age of Revolution.* New York: 1971.

———. *Pharasaism in the Making; selected essays.* New York: 1972.

MURRAY HOWARD FINLEY

b. March 31, 1922
Labor union official

As president of the Amalgamated Clothing and Textile Workers Union of America since 1976, Murray Howard Finley has fought for racial equality and improvements in wages, pensions and working conditions; battled against foreign clothing imports; and worked to organize the unorganized in the apparel industry in the South and Southwest. He has helped establish an educational fund for the children of union members, day care centers, senior citizens' centers and housing projects.

Murray Howard Finley was born in Syracuse, New York. His first union affiliation was with the United Auto Workers in Saginaw, Michigan, where he worked as a machine operator from 1941 to 1942 while attending the University of Michigan. Finley served in the United

States Army from 1942 to 1945, after which he received a B.A. degree from the University of Michigan in 1946. He received his law degree from Northwestern University three years later.

Finley's earliest association with the Amalgamated Clothing Workers Union of America (ACWU) was in 1949 as its assistant regional attorney in Chicago, a position he held until 1955. From 1955 to 1961 he was assistant manager of the Detroit joint board for ACWU and then returned to Chicago as elected manager of the Chicago joint board in 1961. A year later he was elected international vice president of the union, a job he held until 1972 when he was made general president. In 1976 Finley was elected president. That same year ACWU merged with the Textile Workers Union of America (ACTWU). At the time of the merger, Finley explained that the joining of the two unions would create a stronger and more effective tool for collective bargaining and expanding organization activities.

As leader of more than 500,000 union members, Finley once told *The New York Times,* "The union is my whole life. . . . I believe in building a better world—not just a better house or more material things for myself— but to better people's lives. And I believe trade unions are necessary to preserve the American way of life."

Much of Finley's attention has centered on J.P. Stevens & Co., a huge corporation that has long refused to allow union representation in its plants. Since 1966 labor leaders have tried to organize Stevens' mills throughout the South. They organized a boycott of its products and compelled many of its board members to quit. Amalgamated also threatened to withdraw its pension funds from banks supporting Stevens. And the film industry helped the union's cause with the movie *Norma Rae,* which supported labor organizers in deep South mill towns. In 1978 the U.S. Supreme Court left standing a New York State Appeals Court ruling that found Stevens in contempt for violating three previous court orders concerning union organizing. And in 1980 Stevens and the ACTWU signed their initial contract, and the union was permitted to be bargaining agent at 10 of the firm's 70-odd mills plus any others in which the union won elections. Even so, in late 1981 Stevens employees at its denim mill in Rock Hill, South Carolina voted 433-299 to reject the union.

Finley is president of the Amalgamated Insurance Company, director of the Amalgamated Bank of New York and a member of the executive council of the AFL-CIO. He is a member of the Sloan Commission on Government and Higher Education, a trustee of the National Planning Association and on the board of directors of the African-American Labor Center.

MAX M. FISHER

b. July 15, 1908
Business executive; philanthropist

Although he has never held any political office, Detroit businessman Max Fisher may be the most influential and powerful Jewish American in the Republican Party. The friend and confidant of many prominent Republicans, the former board chairman of Aurora Gasoline Company and United Brands, the current director of many major corporations, an active civic leader in Detroit and the head of numerous Jewish organizations for which he is an extraordinarily successful fund raiser—Fisher represents the American Jewish dream come true.

Max Martin Fisher was born in Pittsburgh to William and Mollie (Brody) Fisher. His father, a Russian immigrant, started life in America as a peddler and eventually became a storekeeper and then part-owner of the small oil business that his son would later transform into a multimillion-dollar firm. The Fisher family settled in the small town of Salem, Ohio, where Max Fisher grew up and attended school. Although they were the only Jewish family in Salem and the nearest synagogue and Jewish community were far away, the Fishers observed traditional ritual as much as possible.

Fisher's initial venture away from Salem was to attend Ohio State University on a football scholarship. He received a B.S. degree in 1930. After graduation he joined his father's small oil firm in Detroit, where the Fishers had relocated. Through a series of astute maneuvers and mergers during the years that followed, Fisher turned the family firm into a hugely profitable company. He studied chemical engineering nights and entered into a partnership selling gas in tank-car amounts to service stations. Eventually, their firm—now called Marathon Oil—owned both sources of oil supplies and service stations and other companies needing oil. During and after World War II, his firm prospered and soon became the biggest independent oil firm in the Middle West. He also possesses vast holdings in real estate and United Brands and is a director of Michigan Bell Telephone, Freuhauf Corporation, the Manufacturer National Corporation and others.

As his wealth grew, so did his influence. A confirmed Republican, Fisher became an adviser to many Michigan Republican political leaders, including former Governor George Romney and President Gerald Ford. He was also close to President Nixon. During the latter's tenure in the White House, Fisher served as unofficial consultant on Jewish, urban and community affairs.

In addition, Fisher has been called by some "the best friend Israel has" in the United States. He has long been chairman of the Board of Governors of the Jewish Agency—the organization facilitating the settlement and absorption of immigrants in Israel—and is a staunch supporter of that country. During the Yom Kippur War in 1973, he was described by Nixon's aide Leonard Garment as omnipresent, always arguing Israel's cause. American Jews and non-Jews turned to him for counsel at that darkest of moments when it seemed as if Israel was in danger. "He was all over the place during the Yom Kippur crisis . . .," said Garment. "I know he talked to everyone, pressed every button, called every card." His message was elementary: Send Israel weapons, for a secure Israel was in America's interest. These sentiments were echoed in Yitzhak Rabin's second volume of the Hebrew-language version of his recollections, when the former Israeli prime minister wrote: "However, Israel is not alone. . . . I receive tremendous help from Max Fisher, one of America's top leaders, Republican, before whom the door of the White House is open. When necessary, Fisher prods his 'connections.' "

In Detroit Fisher has been board chairman both of Detroit Renaissance, an alliance of businessmen, and of New Detroit Inc. Both projects, created in the early 1970s following serious race riots, are dedicated to rebuilding the city as an industrial and residential center. In addition, Fisher has helped many minority-owned construction firms secure building contracts.

In the area of Jewish philanthropy, Fisher has few peers. According to *Detroit Monthly* (July 1980), he donates approximately half his annual nine-figure income to Jewish causes here and in Israel. He is a significant figure in the American Jewish Committee, the United Jewish Appeal, the Hebrew Immigrant Aid Society and the Jewish Welfare Foundation of Detroit. And he has few peers in raising money. In 1957, for example, while heading the JWF of Detroit, he helped raise $5,841,000, at the time the highest figure in the agency's history.

GEROLD FRANK

b. August 2, 1907
Author

Gerold Frank has won critical and popular acclaim for his biographies of such famous personalities as Dr. Martin Luther King Jr., Zsa Zsa Gabor, Sheila Graham and Judy Garland.

Gerold Frank was born in Cleveland, Ohio to Sam-uel, who owned several women's apparel shops, and Lillian (Frank) Lefkowitz. After receiving his B.A. degree from Ohio State University in 1929 and his M.A. degree from Case Western Reserve University in 1933, Frank worked for several years as a journalist. From 1933 to 1937 he was with *The Cleveland News*, and from 1937 to 1943 he was a free-lance writer and contributed to *The New Yorker, The Nation, Life, Saturday Evening Post* and other magazines. He was a foreign correspondent for the Overseas News Agency from 1943 to 1950 and was stationed in the Middle East and Europe. Following his return to the United States, he became a senior editor at *Coronet* magazine from 1952 to 1958.

Frank has written numerous nonfiction books exemplifying the painstaking research he brings to popular themes and personalities. *U.S.S. Seawolf* (New York, 1945) was a naval story about a U.S. submarine during World War II; *I'll Cry Tomorrow* (New York, 1954), a biography written with Lillian Roth and Mike Connolly, won the Christo award; *Beloved Infidel* (New York, 1958) was the life story of Sheila Graham and her romance with F. Scott Fitzgerald (New York, 1975); and *The Zsa Zsa Gabor Story* (New York, 1960) was the tale of a stormy and tempestuous life.

In *Judy* (New York, 1975), Frank's massive and definitive biography of actress-singer Judy Garland, the subject was depicted as thoroughly exploited by superiors, colleagues and friends in the film and entertainment business. Frank's compassion was boundless as he painstakingly detailed her rise to stardom as a child star and her ultimate descent into a drug-addicted existence and a profoundly troubled life.

Frank also dealt with political subjects. His book *The Deed* (New York, 1963) traced the history of Jewish terrorist and resistance organizations in Palestine by focusing on the 1944 murder of Lord Moyne, British minister of state in the Middle East, by two members of the Stern Gang just outside of Cairo. Frank probed the minds of all the characters, including the Arabs and the British. He took no sides in the inter-Jewish disputes, clarifying all but scorning none. The book won the Edgar Allan Poe Award, as did his *The Boston Strangler* (New York, 1966), which depicted the events surrounding a manhunt for a killer responsible for the deaths of ten strangled and sexually-molested women during an 18-month period in the Boston area. Frank did extensive research, delving into police records, letters, diaries and police reports, and conducted hundreds of hours of interviews to describe the victims and the many suspects.

In *An American Death: The True Story of the Assassination of Dr. Martin Luther King Jr.* (New York, 1972),

Frank told the story of the search for the murderer of the black leader and the subsequent conviction of James Earl Ray. He rejected the theory that King was killed (and Ray framed) by an FBI conspiracy. Ray was a psychotic loner who killed Dr. King alone, and there was no conspiracy, Frank concluded.

MAX FRANKEL

b. April 3, 1930
Journalist

As *New York Times* editorial page editor, Max Frankel is one of the most influential and powerful voices in the shaping of American political opinion. A journalist with the *Times* throughout his entire professional career, he won the Pulitzer Prize for international reporting in 1973.

Max Frankel, the son of Jacob, and Mary (Katz) Frankel, was born in Gera, Germany. The family was forced to leave Germany in 1938 because of Nazi anti-Semitism and migrated first to Poland and then to the United States in 1940. Frankel was naturalized eight years later. He attended the High School of Music and Art, a very selective public school, in New York until 1948 and then received his Bachelor of Arts degree in 1952 and an M.A. degree in political science the following year from Columbia University.

While still a student at Columbia, Frankel began to work for *The New York Times* as a part-time campus correspondent. He became a staff reporter immediately upon graduation and was soon awarded a prestigious foreign assignment. While posted in Moscow in 1956, he covered the Hungarian uprising against the Soviet-dominated Communist party. Three years later he wrote a series of articles from Siberia that were also printed—despite some critical charges made by Frankel in his reports—by the official newspaper of the Russian Communist party, *Izvestia*. Frankel also reported from Vienna, the United Nations and Havana, where he covered the 1961 invasion of the Bay of Pigs.

In 1961 Frankel was assigned to the *Times'* Washington bureau and in 1968 became its bureau chief. He covered President Nixon's summit meetings with Soviet leader Leonid Brezhnev and accompanied the president on his historic China trip in 1972. From China Frankel filed 35,000 words in eight days and won the Pulitzer Prize for his coverage. Later Frankel supervised the *Times'* early Watergate coverage.

But his most significant contribution while in Wash-

ington was to coordinate and defend the 1971 publication of the Vietnam Archive, better known as the Pentagon Papers, an extensive collection of classified documents recounting the history of American intervention in Indochina, including secret operations, which had been maintained by the State Department. When *Times* reporter Neil Sheehan contacted Frankel after being offered the papers by Daniel Ellsberg, Frankel made the decision—despite threats of litigation by the government—to print all the material. It was his feeling, and executive editor A.M. Rosenthal's too—and after some convincing, the *Times'*—that freedom of information and of the press were far more precious than "national security," especially when the secrets in question were kept, in Frankel's opinion, for hypocritical and self-serving reasons.

Frankel returned to New York in 1973, when he became the Sunday edition editor of the *Times* and assumed responsibility for the magazine section, book review section, the Week in Review, travel, and arts and leisure section. Since 1977 he has been editor of the *Times'* editorial page, where the newspaper generally takes a moderately liberal point of view, although it often criticized both the Carter and Reagan administration policies.

For further information:
Salisbury, Harrison. *Without Fear or Favor.* New York: 1980.

MONROE H. FREEDMAN

b. April 10, 1928
Attorney; professor; organization director

Although Monroe Freedman's work as director of the United States Holocaust Memorial Council focuses on commemorating the 6 million Jewish victims of Adolf Hitler, his career as attorney, professor and scholar has encompassed the defense of all oppressed people. Freedman's internationally recognized expertise in legal ethics, his activism in civil liberties and civil rights, and his dedication to legal education as law professor and law school dean have distinguished him as one of America's outstanding figures in his field.

Monroe Henry Freedman was born in Mount Vernon, New York and is the son of Chauncey, a retailer, and Dorothea (Kornblum) Freedman. He attended Harvard University, where he received an A.B. degree cum laude in 1951 and a law degree three years later. From 1954 to 1956 he was a faculty assistant at the Harvard

Law School and received a Master of Laws—a faculty fellowship—in his last year. For two years he practiced law in Philadelphia as an associate with Wolf, Block, Schorr and Solis-Cohen before moving to Washington, D.C., where he became a professor of law at George Washington University.

Throughout the 15 years he taught there, he was active in other areas of legal work. In 1959 he assumed the first of several consultancies with the federal government when he helped draft the Landrum-Griffin Act for Senator John L. McClellan. From 1960 to 1964 he was a consultant with the U.S. commission on Civil Rights, and from 1965 to 1966 he directed the Criminal Trial Institute. Freedman was also active in community law and neighborhood legal services programs, and from 1969 to 1973 he combined teaching with partnership in his own firm, Freedman and Temple.

That the training of lawyers has been paramount in Freedman's law career is evidenced by his active participation with the Society of American Law Teachers, for which he has served on the governing board since 1974, the executive committee since 1976 and as chair for the committee on professional responsibility since 1974. In 1973 he left George Washington University to become law school dean at Hofstra University in Hempstead, New York, and from 1977 until his appointment to the Holocaust Memorial Council, he was a professor of law.

As diverse as Freedman's law career are the areas of law that he practices and on which he writes. A member of the national board of the American Civil Liberties Union since 1971, he has been an ardent defender of the Equal Rights Amendment. In the late 1970s he spoke out forcefully to deplore the Cambodian "holocaust," in which nearly half the natives of that Southeast Asian nation died in a mass evacuation from the cities imposed by that nation's leader in 1975 and a subsequent famine. A prolific writer, Freedman is the author of three legal texts and of articles that have appeared in major American law journals covering virtually every area of law that touches on social and ethical issues, such as constitutional law, legal ethics, public interest law, psychological testing and torts.

Since joining the Holocaust Council, he has held an International Liberators Conference, featuring former American soldiers plus veterans from other countries, including the Soviet Union, who were present when the Nazi concentration camps were liberated in 1945. The point was that—unlike revisionists who deny the Holocaust—these men could attest to what had actually taken place. Freedman has long sought to reach an audience that knows little of the Holocaust.

BETTY FRIEDAN

b. February 4, 1921
Writer; feminist leader

Since the 1963 publication of her book *The Feminine Mystique* (New York), Betty Friedan has been the predominant spokeswoman of the feminist movement in America. Her contention that suburban married life represented a "bedroom (and sexual) ghetto" and her subsequent crusades on behalf of equal rights in employment, education and political power, plus freedom of choice in childbearing, child care and lifestyle for women signaled the beginning of a new era in American history.

Betty Naomi Goldstein was born in Peoria, Illinois to Harry, a Russian-immigrant jeweler, and Miriam (Horwitz) Goldstein. She attended Smith College and received a B.A. degree in psychology in 1942.

At Smith, Friedan became aware of anti-Semitism both among the non-Jews there and, in a subtle sense, even among those few Jews who failed to speak out in protest. She became editor of the Smith College newspaper as well as founder of a literary journal to which she submitted a short story entitled "The Scapegoat." Says Friedan, "It's about anti-Semitic Jews, about a girl that all the other Jewish girls turn against since everyone else was turning against her." As a result of her experiences, Friedan developed a strong sense of her Jewishness—although not religiously oriented—as part of her total identity. It never quite left her.

Following a brief period at the University of California at Berkeley on a fellowship, she married Carl Friedan in 1947. For the first 16 years of her marriage, she was principally engaged in raising her three children. But the conflicts of her situation had always troubled her, specifically the restlessness of being at home. "I kept vacillating between being a good wife and mother and playing Joan of Arc to the movement," she wrote. In 1963 *The Feminine Mystique* proved a shock to many, a sudden Declaration of Independence for millions of women across the United States and eventually throughout the Western world. It represented the bare beginnings of a women's movement, but it took a talented housewife to get it started.

By 1969 Friedan was divorced and living in New York City and spearheading NOW—the National Organization for Women. She was its president from 1966 to 1970. In 1978 she chaired the Emergency Project for Equal Rights and the following year the National Assembly on the Future of the Family. She has taught at the New School for Social Research (1971), Temple

University (1972), Yale University (1974) and Queens College (1975).

Although she would at times be accused of not being militant enough, Friedan's accomplishments in her writing and in her leadership with NOW represented huge strides in the evolution of women's roles and women's rights in America. She would say, correctly, that "younger . . . women as the result of the women's movement . . . take for granted that [they're] going to have serious professional work and . . . marry and have children. [They don't] see any conflict [and that is] the result of women's liberation." This thinking, said Friedan, applies especially to Jewish women, who are raised to achieve in school but then do little with what they've learned. "In the middle class at least, you were supposed to marry the doctor, not be one," she said. Partly due to Friedan's work, this attitude has changed.

In the 1980s Friedan has become one of America's "elder stateswomen" in the battle for equal rights between the sexes. An apparent retrenchment in women's rights by the Reagan administration forced her to become more vocal, and in a major *New York Times Magazine* article, "Feminism's Next Step" (July 5, 1981), Friedan outlined new directions for the women's movement. They include coming to terms with the ideas of feminism and raising a family as *not* being mutually exclusive and creating new social structures to allow young families to grow and be nourished while both parents, if they choose to, pursue careers. Such structures include greater sharing both at home and in the workplace so that people who want to can both work and contribute to rearing their children.

The article, an adaptation of Friedan's follow-up to *The Feminine Mystique* called *The Second Stage* (New York, 1981), is summed up in Friedan's words:

> I know that equality, the personhood we fought for, is truly necessary for women and opens new life for men. . . . But how do we surmount our own reaction, which shadows our feminism and our femininity (we blush even to use that word now)? How do we transcend the polarization between women and women and between women and men, to achieve the new human wholeness that is the promise of feminism and get on with solving the concrete, practical, everyday problems of living, working and loving as equal persons? This is the personal and political business of [what Friedan has dubbed] the second stage.

Through the years Friedan has moved closer to Jewishness. She denounced Arab anti-Semitism at a women's international rights meeting in Mexico City, serves on the board of the Jewish magazine *Present Tense* and was active in a monthly meeting of New York intellectuals exploring their lives as American Jews. She has also protested publicly the United Nations' cordial reception of gun-toting Yasir Arafat of the Palestine Liberation Organization: "When Arafat was received there, I started to get outraged and worried. I've never been a Zionist, but shortly after, I really began to feel there would be a new wave of anti-Semitism." At the same time, her children—Daniel, Jonathan and Emily—all became interested in examining their Jewish origins. "I figured it was some profound and strong and good response to reaffirm your Jewishness in the face of anti-Semites," she said.

Today she finds her opposition centered among right-wing women and Orthodox Jewish groups, who see women's liberation as a threat to their interpretations of family life and the role of the female in Judaism. Friedan's general response is aimed often at Orthodox males who still believe that women's primary role is to marry and bear children. "To suddenly again try to treat women as breeders is outrageous," she argues. "If you want Jewish women to have more children, you have to be strongly supportive of institutional changes so women don't have to choose between professional advancement and political participation and child-rearing."

MAURICE FRIEDBERG

b. December 3, 1929
Professor

In addition to being one of America's foremost scholars of Slavic literature, Professor Maurice Friedberg has also been active in exploring the cultural and intellectual life of Slavic peoples. He has also devoted much of his expertise to exploring the struggle of Russian Jews to live freely as they choose, either in the Soviet Union or abroad, and has written extensively on their role in Russian literature.

Maurice Friedberg was born in Rzeszow, Poland to Isaac, a building contractor in prewar Poland and a shipping clerk in the United States, and Ida (Jam) Friedberg. He came to the United States in 1948 and was naturalized in 1954. After receiving a B.S. degree from Brooklyn College in 1951, he pursued graduate studies in Slavic languages at Columbia University and its Russian Institute, where he completed an M.A. degree in 1953 and a Ph.D. in 1958. Much of his graduate study and subsequent research was funded with prestigious grants. Just a few he received are a Ford Foundation

Foreign Area Fellowship (1954–55), a travel grant from Oxford University (1962), a grant from the Munich-based Institute for the Study of the USSR (1963), a Senior Fulbright-Hays Fellowship (1964–65) and a Guggenheim Fellowship (1971).

Friedberg's first academic post was as associate professor of Russian and chairman of the Russian Division at Hunter College from 1955 to 1965. He taught at Hebrew University in Jerusalem from 1965 to 1966 and at Indiana University as full professor from 1966 to 1975. Since 1975 he has been professor of Russian literature and head of the department of Slavic Languages and Literature at the Urbana-Champaign campus of the University of Illinois.

While much of Friedberg's work has centered on the plight of Soviet Jews, he has also explored the struggle for freedom of the Soviet people as a whole, and especially their efforts to reach out to the West. For example, in "Foreign Authors and Soviet Readers" (*The Russian Review*, October 1954), he interviewed Soviet citizens who had been displaced during World War II and discovered that many of them actively sought to read as much American, English, German and French literature as they could obtain, either in the original language or in translation, even though it was often difficult to locate. He compared their deliberate reaching-out to what one emigre referred to as the "narrow-minded attitude of some Germans who feel content just knowing the works of Goethe and Schiller." In "Soviet School Reform" (*The New Leader*, September 29, 1958), he described the process by which the Khrushchev government attempted to modernize the school system, to expand the labor force through increased vocational training and to prevent unqualified students from attempting to get into the already-overcrowded university system. The reforms, which created distinct classes of students—an intelligentsia and a working class—were viewed negatively by Friedberg, who commented that the program would "result in fewer truly educated people."

Friedberg's first book, *Russian Books in Soviet Jackets* (New York, 1963), an extension of his doctoral thesis, explored the ways in which different Soviet regimes have used the literary classics for political ends. For example, at different times certain books were favored, while others were not; similarly, literary criticism also reflected the mood of the regime in power rather than the opinion of an individual writer. He has also edited *A Bilingual Collection of Russian Short Stories* (Volume 1, New York, 1964; Volume 2, New York, 1966) and has edited numerous pamphlets concerning Soviet Jews, including *The Jew in Post-Stalin Soviet Literature* (Washington, 1970) and *Why They Left: A Survey of Soviet Jewish Emigrants* (New York, 1972). In a 1973 essay in *Present Tense*, "Soviet Jews, Nationalism and Dissent," Friedberg predicted the following decade in Soviet Jewish life:

> A significant number of the country's Jews are eager to emigrate, and some succeed. Nevertheless, there can be little doubt that the majority will remain in the country of their birth, whether by reasoned choice, by inertia, or because they will not receive official permission to leave.

Other articles and studies on the subject have appeared in *Problems of Communism*, a publication of the United States Information Agency; in *Commentary and Midstream;* in the *American Jewish Yearbook* and *The Congressional Record;* and in such books as *The Jews in Soviet Russia Since 1917*, edited by Lionel Kochan (New York, 1970) and *Soviet Communism and the Socialist Vision*, edited by Julius Jacobson (New Brunswick, N.J., 1972).

Friedberg is on the editorial board of *Comparative Literature Studies* and on the editorial advisory board of *Present Tense* magazine and *Studies in Comparative Communism.*

For further information:

Friedberg, Maurice. *A Helsinki Record: The Availability of Soviet Russian Literature in the United States.* New York: 1980.

———. "The Homecoming of Yiddish Culture." *Present Tense* (Spring 1976).

———. *The Party and the Poet in the USSR.* (pamphlet). New York: 1963.

———. "A Play from the Soviet Underground." *The Jewish Digest.* Vol. 7 (September 1962).

———. "The Split in Israel's Communist Party." *Midstream* 12 (February 1966): .

———. "The State of Soviet Jewry." *Commentary*, January 1965.

WILLIAM FRIEDKIN

b. August 29, 1939
Film director

Film director William Friedkin became recognized in the early 1970s as a major talent with two of the biggest box office smash hits in movie history: *The French Connection* and *The Exorcist*. He has also frequently courted controversy, especially with two films with homosexual themes, *The Boys in the Band* and *Cruising.*

William Friedkin was born in Chicago to Louis, a salesman, and Rae (Green) Friedkin. He was a basketball player at Senn High School in Chicago and dreamed of becoming a professional athlete. Instead of going to college, Friedkin went to work in 1956 as a mail-room clerk at WGN, a local television station in Chicago. Within two years, after being promoted to floor manager and assistant director, he was directing. For the next eight years, Friedkin directed television movies over the ABC network, among them in *The Bold Man, Mayhem on a Sunday Afternoon* and *The Thin Blue Line.* His documentary *The People vs. Paul Crump* (1965) won the San Francisco Film Festival Award for documentary and caught the attention of producer David Wolper, who urged him to come to California.

Friedkin directed his first feature film in 1967, *Good Times,* a musical with Sonny and Cher. His second film *The Night They Raided Minsky's* about a burlesque theater and its performers, was received with mixed reviews. After directing *The Birthday Party,* a film adaptation of Harold Pinter's play, in 1968, Friedkin made *The Boys in the Band* (1970), a controversial film about a gathering of homosexuals who outwardly joke about their condition while inside they are torn by pain and ambiguity.

Although critics had been noting Friedkin's steadily developing artistry and versatility, they were not prepared for the impressive skills he demonstrated in the explosive, high-tension chase sequences of *The French Connection.* The 1971 film, which was based on an actual narcotics case in the files of the New York police department, won Friedkin an Academy Award as Best Director. A *New Republic* movie reviewer wrote: "Go see it—and take your viscera along. This thriller was made to grab your insides and it does." The following year Friedkin was named Best Motion Picture Director of the Year by the Directors Guild of America.

While *The French Connection* shocked audiences with its violence, *The Exorcist,* Friedkin's next film, startled people with its sexual explicitness. Produced in 1973, *The Exorcist* is an adaptation of Peter Blatty's novel about a 12-year-old girl possessed by the devil. It drew huge crowds worldwide.

Since *The Exorcist* Friedkin has made *The Sorcerer* (1977) and *The Brinks Job* (1978), adventure thrillers that won only moderate success. *Brinks Job* stripped away the romantic myths associated with a well-known robbery with acuteness and adept camera work. In *Cruising* (1980) Friedkin returned to the subject of homosexuality. The film starred Al Pacino as an undercover cop in search of a psychopathic killer who preys on customers of the heavy-leather homosexual bars in Greenwich Village.

In protest, homosexuals in both New York and San Francisco demonstrated against the film at its opening, charging that its portrayal of violence among homosexuals was slanted, biased and prejudiced. Whatever the intent, the film was vintage Friedkin, exploring subjects he is intensely interested in.

MILTON FRIEDMAN

b. July 31, 1912
Economist

Nobel Prize-winning economist Milton Friedman, whose theories have strongly swayed the economic policies of President Ronald Reagan, Prime Minister Margaret Thatcher of Great Britain and Prime Minister Menachem Begin of Israel, is best-known for his unwavering belief in free enterprise and opposition to state intervention in business and trade.

Milton Friedman was born in Brooklyn and reared in Rahway, New Jersey, by his Ruthenian (then part of Austria-Hungary) immigrant parents, Jeno Saul, a merchant, and Sarah Ethel (Landau) Friedman. As a high school student, he displayed a facility for mathematics and won a scholarship to Rutgers University, where he received a Bachelor of Arts degree in 1932. While there, he was forced to take a two-year ROTC course, and he has since said it gave him a permanent distaste for compulsory military service.

After receiving an M.A. degree in 1933 from the University of Chicago, Friedman held several research and teaching jobs before earning a Ph.D. from Columbia in 1946. From 1935 to 1937 he was associate economist with the National Resources Committee in Washington, and from 1937 to 1945 he was on the research staff of the National Bureau for Economic Research in New York. He was also director of research and statistics for the war research division at Columbia from 1943 to 1945 and was a visiting professor of economics at the University of Wisconsin in 1940 to 1941 and principal economist of the tax research division of the Department of Treasury from 1941 to 1943. Friedman had originally hoped to stay at Wisconsin, but there was already a token Jew in those days of quotas, and he could not get a regular post.

After teaching for one year at the University of Minnesota from 1945 to 1946, Friedman joined the faculty of the University of Chicago, and in 1962 he became Paul Snowden Russell Distinguished Service Professor of Economics, a position he held until 1977, when he joined the Hoover Institution at Stanford University as a research fellow.

When Menachem Begin was elected prime minister of Israel in May 1977, he invited Friedman, the recipient of the Nobel Prize in Economics in 1976, to visit Israel and suggest remedies for Israel's soaring inflationary spiral. The Begin government's respect for the University of Chicago advocate of the free market and his lifelong opposition to nearly all sorts of government intervention was matched by the Nobel judges when they honored him "for his achievements in the fields of consumption analysis, monetary history and theory and for his demonstration of the complexity of stabilization policy."

Dubbed a "pure intellectual" by admirers and critics, Friedman has also been described by his son David, also an economist, as a "libertarian anarchist," whose fundamental outlook is simple and uncluttered: Personal liberty is the supreme good—in business affairs, politics and social relations. Thus, he has condemned the New York Stock Exchange as a brokers' commission-fixing monopoly. He favors the school voucher plan; whereby parents can select any school for their child. He believes it will improve the chances of ghetto youngsters now trapped in inferior public schools. He also believes that the individual and not the government should decide if smoking is harmful. And he is against conscription and favors an all-volunteer military force because the draft is an unacceptable form of compulsion.

He is the author of a number of books and pamphlets, among them *Roofs of Ceilings,* co-authored with George Stigler (Chicago, 1946), which counsels against postwar rent controls and advances the idea that the free market would produce far more housing units than the federal government; *Capitalism and Freedom* (New York, 1962), which reflects the Friedman thesis—similar to 19th-century liberal philosophies—of free trade abroad and laissez-faire at home, with a minimum of federal involvement; *There is No Such Thing as a Free Lunch* (La Salle, Ill., 1975); and the best-selling *Free to Choose,* written with his wife Rose (New York, 1980) in which the authors contend that only when individuals are permitted to make their own economic decisions will other problems—economic, environmental, social and so on —be solved.

In 1980 his television program *Free to Choose,* a 10-part series produced for the Public Broadcasting System, proved to be extremely popular. A typical program was entitled "The Tyranny of Control." In it he argued in favor of a constitutional amendment prohibiting Congress from imposing any tax on imports or permitting subsidies for exports. The mid-19th-century British policy of free trade was—to him—ideal insofar as free trade and free markets flourished. By contrast, he says, protectionism has always resulted in stagnating economies and acted as a deterrent to the development of industrialization. Government subsidies, he says over and over again, are "always backward-looking, protecting the industries that already exist."

FRED FRIENDLY

b. October 30, 1915
Journalist

Like his hero and CBS colleague Edward R. Murrow, who stood for integrity and honesty in journalism, Fred Friendly has made ethics and sincerity the basis of his work in radio and television broadcasting in a career spanning 30 years. It might have lasted longer—Friendly left CBS in 1966—if his own strong belief in what broadcasting should be had not been compromised by CBS executives, who preferred *I Love Lucy* to examining the Vietnam War.

Frederick Wachenheim was born in Providence, Rhode Island to Samuel, a jewelry manufacturer, and Therese (Friendly) Wachenheim. He graduated from Hope High School in Providence and from Nichols Business College in Dudley, Massachusetts, in 1937.

Friendly—he adopted his mother's maiden name professionally—began his broadcast career on the local Providence radio station WEAN, writing, producing and narrating a series of dramatic biographies called *Footprints in the Sands of Time.* Those profiled included Thomas Edison, Marconi and other pioneers in the science of broadcasting.

He joined the Army in 1941, serving in the Pacific and in Europe, earning the Legion of Merit and four battle stars. But his greatest recognition came in 1945 after he had left the army and was in India for CBS, when his role in rescuing servicemen after a bunker exploded earned him a Soldier's Medal.

Back at CBS in New York, Friendly met Edward R. Murrow, and in 1948 their meeting evolved into a collaboration on an oral history of the period from 1932 to 1945 which became a radio series and a best-selling Columbia Record, *I Can Hear It Now,* which included the voices of Franklin Delano Roosevelt, Stalin, Hitler, Churchill, Will Rogers, and other figures who epitomized that period of history. Murrow and Friendly then worked on similar projects which covered the 1920s and the post-World War II period. From 1948 to 1949 Friendly also emceed a radio quiz show *Who Said That?* In 1951 he became joint producer with Murrow on a

CBS radio network series *Hear It Now* which became *See It Now* on television. He also worked on the project *Small World*. In *See It Now* Friendly took viewers around the world or into America's heartland to report on how individual people were making major contributions—for better or worse—to change the world. In one segment, he profiled an Israeli air pilot and zoomed in to show the man's tattoo from Buchenwald; in another in 1954, he reported on the red-baiting of the House Un-American Activities Committee and by Senator McCarthy, a critical look which reflected an uneasy coming-of-age for America. His work garnered literally dozens of Emmys and journalism prizes.

Friendly drew on the individualism and boldness of Murrow in his own work as a broadcaster, often challenging the timidity of broadcast executives with his own daring programming. From 1959 to 1964 he was executive producer of CBS, in which he featured a series of conversations conducted by Walter Lippmann, and from 1964 to 1966 he was president of CBS News, in which, among other large-scale projects, he supervised the production of a documentary "Vietnam Perspective."

As the war in Vietnam raged on, Friendly felt compelled to delve deeper into the motives and conflicts behind the struggle, both on the homefront, as the antiwar movement grew, and on the battlefield. But when his attempts to air Senate hearings on Vietnam in 1966 were thwarted by CBS executives because they were concerned about ratings and thought American audiences wouldn't watch the hearings, Friendly resigned from CBS in a fury. He didn't remain jobless for long, however; soon after he was appointed Edward R. Murrow professor of journalism at Columbia University and became an adviser on television to the Ford Foundation.

Friendly's run-in with CBS management also evolved into an emotional account of the events preceding his resignation entitled *Due To Circumstances Beyond Our Control* (New York, 1967). An "occupational memoir" of Friendly's years at CBS, the book was also a wholesale criticism of the institution of American broadcasting and, in a sense, of America as well. Historian Eric Goldman, who critiqued the book, commented that "no one can read it without a sharply heightened sense of the tragedy of American television," and the work propelled Friendly into a new role as spokesperson for a bygone era, when broadcasting had substance. As professor and consultant he wrote extensively about how he would have liked to see television improve its role as a dominant mass communicator in America.

In fact, as television began to take over the primary role of newscasting from newspapers, Friendly became concerned with freedom of speech issues over the air, a subject which was the focus of his book *The Good Guys, The Bad Guys and the First Amendment: Free Speech vs. Fairness in Broadcasting* (New York, 1976). In the work he explored the complex issue of unfettered freedom of speech in the face of broadcasters' supposed obligations that speech be "fair." Focusing on the landmark Supreme Court decision, *Red Lion Broadcasting vs. Federal Communications Commission* which originated the Fairness Doctrine, Friendly argued for both sides of the issue, showing how "fairness," depending on who exercised it, could be used to both promote religious or racial bigotry and political propaganda and to hamper investigative reporting. While some Fairness Doctrine opponents argued that its enactment violated the First Amendment, supporters said it fostered a balanced representation of controversial issues. Friendly's own conclusion was that if the networks took the initiative to present varying points of view and a wide range of newscasts and documentaries similar to the Op-Ed page or letters columns in newspapers, the need for FCC monitoring through the Fairness Doctrine would vanish. Instead, TV languished in mediocrity and the only doctrine broadcast executives seemed to advocate was profit-making.

In the early 1980s Friendly took up a new issue; the expansion of evening television newscasts—which had become the primary source of news information to American audiences—into hour-long, in-depth examinations of the news. Calling current news programs "punk news," Friendly lambasted the trend toward the sensational and the superficial and urged a rethinking by executives of their responsibility in airing information.

Friendly has received many awards throughout his career, including the 1982 Chet Huntley Award for Journalism from New York University.

ART GARFUNKEL

b. October 31, 1941
Singer; actor

Although Art Garfunkel was known as the quieter and "sweeter" half of the 1960s singing duo Simon and Garfunkel—whose songs came to represent an entire generation of young people growing up amid war, campus uprisings and the need to seriously question their life values and goals—he has since emerged as a songwriter, solo performer and screen actor of great sensitivity and sophistication. Nonetheless, his fame rests on his partnership with Paul Simon—and that may well always be so.

Arthur Garfunkel was born in Forest Hills, New

York. His father worked in the garment packaging and container business. In a sixth-grade play of *Alice in Wonderland* (in which he played the White Rabbit), he befriended another sixth-grader, Paul Simon, who played the Cheshire Cat. Garfunkel was also an accomplished singer who not only sang in the local synagogue but also served as cantor at his own bar mitzvah, and with Simon, who also liked music, he formed an amateur duo that sang at local parties and school events. Calling themselves "Tom and Jerry," the two gained the attention of a small record company, which gave them their first contract. In 1957 their song "Hey! Schoolgirl!" became a Top-100 hit, but the record company went bankrupt shortly afterward, and Simon and Garfunkel's recording career was prematurely aborted.

Garfunkel went on to study at Columbia College where, influenced by Ayn Rand's book *The Fountainhead,* he eventually transferred to the School of Architecture. He dropped out briefly, then returned, graduating with a B.A. degree in art history in 1965 and an M.A. degree in mathematics education two years later, at which point he began work on a doctorate, which he never completed.

Meanwhile, in the early 1960s, Garfunkel began singing again with Paul Simon, primarily in Washington Square Park and in small Greenwich Village clubs, where they adapted many of the folk styles and tunes then popular. After auditioning for Columbia Records, the pair completed their first album, *Wednesday Morning, 3 a.m.,* in 1964. The record combined original compositions with several songs by Bob Dylan and other writers. But in the wake of the Beatles' tide of popularity in the United States, the record was only a modest success—except for one song written by Simon, "The Sounds of Silence." Somehow, that tune caught on, and by November 1965 it had climbed to the top of the charts.

In early 1966 Simon and Garfunkel released their second album, *Sounds of Silence,* which included a new, electrified version of the title song and other pieces by Simon. Garfunkel arranged them and created the harmonies that other groups of the time would try—and fail—to duplicate. In each of their three subsequent albums—*Parsley, Sage, Rosemary and Thyme* (1966), *Bookends* (1968) and *Bridge over Troubled Water* (1970)—Simon and Garfunkel developed more sophisticated musical styles and lyrics, which reflected their own growing. From wondering about identity crises ("I Am a Rock" and "Homeward Bound") and the delights of a city night ("The 59th Street Bridge Song"), they wandered into mid-life crises ("Overs") and the emptiness of their lives ("America") and onward to more spiritual musings ("Bridge over Troubled Water") and reflection

("The Boxer," "Song for the Asking," "So Long, Frank Lloyd Wright"). Each new album had at least one major hit—"Mrs. Robinson" from *Bookends* had been commissioned for the 1968 film *The Graduate* with Dustin Hoffman and became a landmark of the era—and garnered numerous awards. *Bridge over Troubled Water* alone received six Grammys.

But in 1970 Simon and Garfunkel went their separate ways—Simon to further explore his musical identity, Garfunkel to strike out in other areas, particularly acting. Mike Nichols, who had directed *The Graduate,* cast Garfunkel in his next two films. In *Catch-22* (1970), Nichols' version of Joseph Heller's novel, Garfunkel played Capt. Nately, the upper-class bomber pilot. And in *Carnal Knowledge* (1971), with screenplay by Jules Feiffer, he played opposite Jack Nicholson as the latter's former college roommate. The two, now approaching their forties, are in the throes of mid-life crisis and try desperately to reclaim their youth. Garfunkel then set out to record solo albums, including *Angel Clare* (1973), *Breakaway* (1975), *Watermark* (1978) and *Fate for Breakfast (Doubt for Dessert)* (1979), which combined songs by other contemporary writers, some original works and traditional ballads. The albums did well, yet the magic wrought by the Simon and Garfunkel combination, absent here, prevented them from becoming genuine hits.

Garfunkel resurfaced in a new film role in 1980, playing an American pscyhoanalyst caught up in a mad love affair in Vienna in Nicholas Roeg's *Bad Timing—A Sensual Obsession.* As in his other films, his work was praised, yet not entirely realized.

Nonetheless—for better or for worse—and even as Garfunkel himself entered his forties, fans still clamored for the old melodies and the old sound. So in September 1981, as an experiment, he and Simon accepted an offer to sing at a free concert to benefit New York City's Central Park. The concert, which drew nearly half a million fans—many of them "graduates" themselves of the earlier Simon and Garfunkel era—was a remarkable success. Yet the implications for the future of Art Garfunkel, who has always seemed to want an identity completely his own, remain unclear.

LEONARD GARMENT

b. 1924
Lawyer; government official

Leonard Garment, special counsel to President Richard Nixon from 1969 to 1974, was an influential member of the White House staff, particularly in the areas of civil rights and government funding for the arts.

Leonard Garment was born in Brooklyn. He received his B.A. degree from Brooklyn College in 1945 and his law degree from Brooklyn Law School in 1949. During college and law school, Garment played the clarinet and tenor saxophone in several bands, including Woody Herman's. In 1949 Garment joined the New York City law firm of Mudge, Stern, Baldwin and Todd. Six years later he was made a partner. When Nixon joined the firm in 1963, Garment became friendly with the future president.

In 1968 Garment helped Nixon write and edit speeches for the presidential campaign. He was hired as special consultant to President Nixon several months after the inauguration. Under Nixon, Garment served as a strong patron of the arts and as the White House's chief liaison with civil rights groups. Garment defended the administration against criticism by blacks by pointing to Nixon's Philadelphia Plan to give construction jobs to blacks, a proposal to allocate $1.5 billion to assist in school desegregation and actual achievements in southern school desegregation.

Watergate, however, was by far the most difficult and touchy issue dealt with by Garment. Advised by University of Texas law professor Charles Alan Wright, a constitutional expert, Garment prepared the White House case, an overwhelmingly difficult job. "There are roughly 500 lawyers and investigators on the other side," he told a *Time* reporter in July 1973. "We're like a small country law firm. We're in the peculiar position of being isolated from the Justice Department and of not being able to develop information from the people involved in Watergate." Because Garment was not able to interview witnesses directly (for reasons of "propriety," he said), and because Nixon kept quiet and was unhelpful, Garment and other White House lawyers had to develop their defense from sworn civil depositions, testimony and newspaper reports.

In 1974 Garment was an assistant to President Gerald Ford, vice-chairman of the Administrative Conference on the United States from 1973 to 1974 and United States representative to the United Nations Commission on Human Rights from 1975 to 1976.

During his years in the White House, Garment was often described as different from other presidential aides. *Time* magazine characterized him as "more compassionate, more relaxed" than other presidential assistants. Having expressed what were often unpopular views at White House meetings, he was also referred to as "a liberal guest in a conservative house."

In 1975 Garment returned to New York and his old law firm, now called Mudge, Rose, Guthrie and Alexander. In 1980 he moved to Washington, D.C., where he is a partner at Dickstein, Shapiro and Morin.

DAVID GARTH

b. 1930
Media consultant

David Garth, media consultant for politicians, has a history of sometimes beating the odds. He has often crafted campaigns that have turned virtual unknowns into credible—usually successful—candidates and has become perhaps the most sought-after political image maker in the country. In recent years he has also ventured outside the United States to aid politicans in Israel and Venezuela.

David Goldberg was born in Hewlett, New York. He was the son of Leo, a Russian immigrant who was originally a tailor and became a lingerie manufacturer, and Beulah (Jagoda) Goldberg, a former national vice president of the American Jewish Congress. The family lived in Woodmere, Long Island, a comfortable, suburban community. Garth's interest in politics stems from his childhood, when the family dinner table topic was frequently Walter Lippmann's column in the *Herald-Tribune* and liberal politics. The tenacity with which he would eventually pursue his interests was shown in his youth: He survived a bout with rheumatic fever and rehabilitated himself to become a high school athlete.

Garth spent several months on a kibbutz just as Israel was achieving independence in 1948 and was impressed by the spirit of the kibbutzniks in the face of possible calamity. "I loved their passion and their intensity," he was quoted as saying in *New Times*. "They were living on the edge every day. It was all on the line, you know. Life and death, the whole shot."

Back in the United States, he completed college at Washington and Jefferson University in Virginia and spent three years with the ultra-secret U.S. Army Security Agency, where he learned communication techniques. He supposedly appropriated the name "Garth" when he was 22, after his father suggested he either change his name to the original "Nisinnyevich," which was the family name in Russia (immigration officials gave Leo Nisinnyevich the name "Goldberg"), or choose another. "Garth" came from the play *Winterset* by Maxwell Anderson.

In 1954 Garth began graduate studies in psychology at Columbia University, but he found the academic life too confining and in 1957 talked his way into a job producing high school sports for television. Three years later Garth was one of the promoters of a visible, albeit unsuccessful, effort to draft Adlai E. Stevenson as Democratic nominee for president. By 1965 he was chosen to be consultant for John V. Lindsay's first and successful New York mayoral campaign. Garth's reputation was firmly established when his commercials were credited by many as a major factor in the mayor's 1969 reelection.

Notable election long shots who profited from Garth's know-how included New York Governor Hugh Carey in 1974 and 1978 and Mayor Edward I. Koch in 1977. But Garth's clients could be found coast to coast and even abroad, including Los Angeles Mayor Tom Bradley; California Senator John Tunney; the late Connecticut Governor Ella Grasso; Venezuelan President Luis Herrera Campins; and Israeli's Likud bloc, whose leader was Menachem Begin. His clients have also included such losers as Adlai E. Stevenson; Bess Myerson, who ran for the Democratic senatorial nomination in New York in 1980; and independent presidential candidate John Anderson, who was defeated in 1980. In 1981 he was hired to advise Menachem Begin when the latter sought re-election.

In an era when television has made it possible for many candidates to break away from tight party discipline, Garth assumes many of the party's traditional functions and insists on virtually total control over a campaign, as he did during Anderson's unsuccessful candidacy. He chooses campaign staff members, arranges a schedule, conducts exhaustive research—even tells a candidate what to wear and how much to weigh. Unlike other media consultants, he retains the right to advise a client once elected. He also specializes frequently in clients who are unpopular incumbents. Garth's technique is for the candidate to become "honest," admitting his past errors and then running on his record, including his mistakes.

Legendary for the commitment he demands from his staff, Garth does not exempt himself and is available to clients 24 hours a day, 7 days a week. In fact, he was the model for the political consultant in the film *The Candidate*. "I love a fight," he said in *The New York Times*. "I love the science of campaigns, love to fight for what I believe in. There is nothing else in the world I'd rather do."

PETER GAY

b. June 20, 1923
Historian; educator

Peter Gay, Durfee Professor of History at Yale University since 1970, is one of America's foremost scholars on the Enlightenment and on prewar cultural life in Germany. A prolific writer, he has published more than 10 books and edited many collections of historical studies.

Peter Gay was born in Berlin to Morris Peter, who owned a small firm specializing in chinaware and crystal, and Helga (Kohnke) Gay. Although the family was almost completely assimilated within German culture, the rise of the Nazis made it necessary for them to leave. With the German quota of immigrants to the United States already filled when they left in April 1939, Gay and his family temporarily settled in Havana, Cuba. They received American entry papers in late 1940 and settled in Denver, Colorado in early 1941.

Shortly after his arrival in America and shortly before his scheduled graduation from high school in Denver, Gay had to drop out and work as a shipping clerk in a cap factory to help support his family. As he describes his early experiences in *American Scholar* (Winter 1976), he was "stupidly packing officers' caps and G.I.'s overseas caps, standing among wrapping materials in a dirty work shirt and leading a deeply private fantasy life." At nights he headed toward a local library "to read books with the kind of voraciousness that only one who has been starved can fully appreciate." An understanding teacher tutored Gay toward a high school diploma. He later attended the University of Denver, graduating with a B.A. degree in 1946. He was naturalized the same year.

In 1947 Gay received an M.A. degree from Columbia University and four years later his Ph.D. He was a faculty member at Columbia from 1947 through 1969. In 1962 he became a full professor of history and, during his last two years there, was William R. Shepherd Professor of History. While at Columbia he wrote *The Dilemma of Democratic Socialism: Eduard Bernstein's Challenge to Marx* (New York, 1952), an extension of his doctoral thesis that was essentially a history of revisionism through the biography of Eduard Bernstein, a German leader of revisionist socialism. In 1969 he became professor of comparative European intellectual history at Yale and the following year Durfee Professor at the school.

One of his major works since then is *Weimar Culture: The Outsider as Insider* (New York, 1968), an analysis of the cultural life of Germany from 1918 to 1933, when Berlin flourished as the artistic, architectural and literary capital of Europe. It was well-known as an international gathering place for "artists-in-exile," including many homosexuals. Gay's insights about Berlin are especially acute since, although it was his birthplace, as a Jew he was considered as much of an outsider as many of the foreigners who flocked there, and despite the many contributions of Jews to the culture of Berlin, they were eventually made to feel most unwelcome.

Gay received the Ralph Waldo Emerson Award of Phi Beta Kappa for *Weimar Culture* in 1969.

The two-volume *The Enlightenment: An Interpretation* (New York, 1966 and 1969) is the work for which Gay is best known. Volume one, *The Rise of Modern Paganism,* focuses on the philosophical struggles between traditional Christian thought and an approach to modern thinking, which is founded on classical pagan thought. The second volume, *The Science of Freedom,* is a social history of the 18th century in Europe, which examines the philosophers' environment, their view of politics, artistic developments, scientific achievements and a new social structure. After the first volume was published, he received the National Book Award and the Melcher Book Award, both in 1962.

Freud, Jews and Other Germans: Masters and Victims in Modernist Culture (New York, 1978) may be Gay's most personal work. A collection of essays analyzing German-Jewish cultural interactions, it appears, said one critic, to be an attempt by Gay to exorcise some of his own endemic hostilities toward German culture.

He is editor of *John Locke on Education* (New York, 1964); *Eighteenth Century Studies* (Hanover, N.H., 1972); and, with Gerald J. Cavanaugh, the four-volume *Historians at Work* (New York, 1972 through 1975). He coauthored with John Arthur Garraty *The Columbia History of the World* (New York, 1972). He is on the editorial board of the journal *American Scholar.*

Gay has been a fellow with the American Council of Learned Societies (1959–60), the Center for Advanced Study of Behavioral Sciences (1963–64), the Guggenheim Foundation (1967–68 and 1977–78), Churchill College at Cambridge University (1970–71) and the Rockefeller Foundation (1979–80). He is a member of the American Historians Society, the French Historians Society and Phi Beta Kappa.

For further information:
Gay, Peter. *Art and Act.* New York: 1976.
———. *The Bridge of Criticism: Dialogues on the Enlightenment.* New York: 1970.
———. *A Loss of Mastery: Puritan Historians in Colonial America.* Berkeley, Calif.: 1966.
———. *The Party of Humanity: Essays in the French Enlightenment.* New York: 1964.
———. *Style in History.* New York: 1974.
———. *Voltaire's Politics: The Poet as Realist.* New York: 1959 and 1965.
Gay, Peter and Webb, R.K. *Modern Europe.* New York: 1973.

WILLARD GAYLIN

b. February 23, 1925
Psychoanalyst; author; professor

Psychoanalyst Willard Gaylin is one of America's leading experts on the subject of bioethics as well as an acclaimed popular writer on a wide range of topics. He is also a professor, an eminent practitioner and a consultant. Co-founder and president of the Institute of Ethics and Life Sciences in Hastings-on-Hudson, New York (also known as the Hastings Center), he is in the forefront of the movement to assure that technological advances in medical care are not abused but are used exclusively in the best ethical and physical interests of all people.

Willard Gaylin was born in Cleveland, Ohio to Harry and Fay (Baumgard) Gaylin. He attended Cleveland public schools and, from the third grade to the ninth, was part of an experimental program for gifted children, which, he says, stimulated him to explore and learn with a passion that has become his trademark. He attended Harvard University, where he majored in comparative literature, the arts and creative writing, but interrupted his college education from 1943 to 1946 to serve in the U.S. Navy as a radar officer aboard an aircraft carrier. In 1947 he received his B.A. degree from Harvard and entered Western Reserve Medical School.

After obtaining his M.D. degree in 1951, Gaylin interned at the Cleveland City Hospital in 1952 and then did a two-year psychiatric residency from 1952 to 1954 at the Bronx Veterans Administration Hospital. He also trained from 1952 to 1956 in the Columbia Psychoanalysis School, where he is now a supervising analyst and clinical professor of psychiatry.

Gaylin has long been interested in the adaptations of psychoanalysis to social problems. "I have always felt that Freud's major contributions were not as a therapist, nor even as an illuminator of psychopathology, but as someone who made a massive contribution to understanding *normal* behavior," he once said. "What's exciting about Freud is not so much what he tells us about the sick, but what he tells us about healthy adaptation."

In 1969 Gaylin was offered an opportunity to apply his ideas about psychoanalytic theory and social issues after discussing the growing connection between ethics and biomedicine with his neighbor and colleague, Dr. Daniel Callahan, a philosopher who has since become director of the Hastings Center. As a result of their discussion, they invited 35 leading scientists and scholars to a meeting in New York City to help develop an interdisciplinary approach to evaluating moral and ethical problems arising from technological advances. The fruit of the meeting was the Hastings Center, which was established in 1969. Today it has an annual budget of over $1 million and is often consulted by the United Nations on such questions as how to deal with overpopulation. It is also consulted on health legislation issues and helps design medical school curricula. It has sponsored workshops on such subjects as test-tube fertilization, anti-aging drugs, recombinant DNA, cloning, the rights of the dying and the rights of the unborn.

Based on his experiences, Gaylin wrote *The Teaching of Medical Ethics* (Hastings-on-Hudson, N.Y., 1973). He edited *Operating on the Mind: The Psychosurgery Conflict* (New York, 1975), in which he insisted that surgical technology should not be prohibited but must remain subservient to "the transcending values of human worth and human dignity."

People's feelings—philosophically, psychologically and personally—are of major importance to Gaylin. In *Doing Good: The Limits of Benevolence* (New York, 1978), written with Steven Marcus, David Rothman and Ira Glasser, Gaylin explores the origins of human dependence, a theme he first investigated in a 1976 book called *Caring* (New York). *Caring* grew out of Gaylin's distress over the popular notion of humankind as hostile, aggressive and territorial—a view earlier voiced by sociologists Robert Ardrey and Desmond Morris. Gaylin asserts that the human impulse to love and nurture—to care—is biologically based. The human infant at birth is unequipped for either fight or flight and therefore, unlike other creatures, is "an obligate social animal."

After examining dependency and the needs of the human infant in *Caring*, Gaylin next published *Feelings: Our Vital Signs* (New York, 1979), which addresses the emotions of everyday life—boredom, anxiety, envy, pride and guilt. Dismissing what he calls the "emotions-are-bad" concept, Gaylin advocates giving serious attention to the small passions—our vital signs that serve as cautionary signals in our day-to-day lives.

Gaylin's other books include *In the Service of Their Country: War Resisters in Prison* (New York, 1970), a moving account of the background, ideas and ideals of conscientious objectors and war resisters jailed during the Vietnam War. The book, often written in the prisoners' own words, revealed aspects of the dehumanizing prison life that shook the youths' dedication to nonviolence and left them with doubts about the effectiveness of peaceful protest. In *Partial Justice: A Study of Bias in Sentencing* (New York, 1974), Gaylin illustrated the injustice in sentencing by investigating the procedures of the Federal Parole Board.

Gaylin has also written many articles on ethical issues. He has defended doing experiments on living fetuses before or after induced abortions, arguing that without such procedures it would be necessary to test new drugs or operative procedures on wanted fetuses or children. On the topic of recombinant DNA research, he has said that "the predictable benefits are worth the predictable risks." He thinks that to demystify genetic research and eliminate the public's fear of it, scientists should make greater efforts to make their work understandable to lay people.

In addition to working at the Hastings Center, teaching, writing and private practice, Gaylin serves on the executive board of the Committee for Public Justice and the board of directors of the Field Foundation. He has been named visiting professor at Harvard Medical School, Chubb Fellow at Yale University and Bloomfield lecturer at Case Western Reserve Medical School.

For further information:
Gaylin, Willard. *The Meaning of Despair.* New York: 1968.
———. *Psychoanalysis and Social Research.* New York: 1965.

ARTHUR GELB

b. February 3, 1924
Editor

As deputy managing editor of *The New York Times* since 1967, Arthur Gelb is responsible for coordinating the work of other journalists. But he has done a great deal of his own writing, on the theater and on municipal affairs in New York City, and has collaborated with his wife, journalist Barbara Gelb, and *New York Times* Executive Editor A.M. Rosenthal on several books.

Arthur Gelb was born in New York City to Daniel and Fanny Gelb. He joined *The New York Times* in 1944, while still attending New York University. He received a B.A. degree in 1946. As a young reporter he covered the New York City police, municipal health and hospital systems, and the United Nations. From this early experience came his first book, coauthored with Barbara Gelb and Dr. Salvatore Cutolo, *Bellevue Is My Home* (New York, 1956). Cutolo, deputy medical superintendent of Bellevue at the time, recounted his

26 years there, providing both a history of the hospital and a contemporary profile of the institution.

In 1954 Gelb became drama news reporter and reviewer for the *Times*. From 1958 to 1961 he was assistant drama critic, and from 1961 to 1963 he was chief cultural correspondent. His expertise in theater led to an additional collaboration with his wife on *O'Neill* (New York, 1962), a comprehensive exploration of the life and writings of playwright Eugene O'Neill.

In 1963 Gelb became assistant metropolitan editor and two years later assumed the post of metropolitan editor. In 1965 he collaborated with then-Assistant Managing Editor A.M. Rosenthal in the co-editing of two books. *The Pope's Journey to New York* (New York, 1965) was a description in words and pictures by *Times* journalists of Pope Paul's historic visit. *The Night the Lights Went Out* (New York, 1965) chronicled the massive blackout that darkened the East Coast on November 9, 1965. In 1967 Gelb and Rosenthal coauthored *One More Victim* (New York, 1967), an exploration of the life of Daniel Burros, a New York Ku Klux Klan leader who shot himself in 1965, after *The New York Times* broke the story that Burros had been born and raised a Jew.

Gelb became deputy managing editor in 1967, continuing his long-time close working relationship with executive editor Rosenthal. Among his achievements as editor are the introduction of women book reviewers to the daily newspaper and the revision of its Sunday travel section to make it "a literary as well as a service section," in which such writers as Muriel Spark (on Venice), Shirley Hazzard (on Naples) and Saul Bellow (on Chicago) have appeared.

He is also thought of as the force behind much of the circulation and advertising increases at the *Times*, because of the innovations he has introduced and developed for its new special sections, "Sports Monday," designed with a handsome typeface, and the weekly sections on science and "Living."

In addition to lecturing widely on theater, specifically on Eugene O'Neill, Gelb has written many magazine articles and has contributed to *Esquire, The Saturday Evening Post* and *Horizon*.

MURRAY GELL-MAN

b. September 15, 1929
Physicist

Murray Gell-man, a theoretical physicist, has often been described as a possible successor to Einstein. His seminal work in the classification of subatomic particles has won widespread acceptance in the scientific community. His discoveries and theories have been described as fundamental to the advancement of modern theoretical physics.

Murray Gell-man was born in New York City to Arthur, the proprietor of a language school and a learned man, versed in mathematics, physics and archeology, and Pauline (Reichstein) Gell-man. Both were immigrants from Austria. When Gell-man was 8 years old, he transferred to a school for gifted children. He entered Yale University at 15 and received a B.S. degree in physics in 1948, even though he still wasn't sure he wanted physics to be his life work. Gell-man decided to attend the Massachusetts Institute of Technology for graduate work, where his advisor was the noted Victor Weisskopf, the president of the American Physical Society. In 1951 Gell-man received his Ph.D. His thesis, an investigation into the intermediate coupling problem of subatomic particles, laid the groundwork for the research of Eugene Wigner, who won the Nobel Prize for physics in 1963.

After graduate school Gell-man spent the next year in residence at the Institute for Advanced Research at Princeton University, but he disliked the competitive attitude of many of the younger scientists there. After a summer at the University of Illinois in 1951, he became an instructor of physics at the University of Chicago in 1952. He spent two years at the Institute of Nuclear Studies in Chicago, which was directed by the eminent physicist Enrico Fermi.

After a year of teaching at Columbia University and some time as a faculty member at the Institute for Advanced Research, Gell-man joined the faculty of the California Institute of Technology. He began as an associate professor in 1955 and became a full professor in 1956. In 1967 Gell-man became the Robert Andrews Millikin Professor of Theoretical Physics at the California Institute of Technology, a position he still holds.

Gell-man's work deals with the understanding and classification of elementary particles, which have become the central problem of modern physics. His "strangeness theory" is designed to explain the odd behavior of some subatomic particles. Working coincidentally and in collaboration with Professor Yuval Ne'eman of Israel, his theory imposes—dubbed the Eight-fold way—a sense of coherence and predictability on particles in lieu of the complexity that had previously existed. This theory was confirmed by the discovery of the Omega particle, because—using his theory—he had foreseen the particle's existence before any concrete physical evidence had been found.

Gell-man is a fellow of the American Physical Society and a member of the National Academy of Science and the American Academy of Arts and Sciences.

CARL SAMUEL GERSHMAN

b. July 20, 1943
Author; government official

When Carl Gershman joined the Reagan administration as counselor to the United States representative to the United Nations in 1981, he brought with him a reputation as an outspoken anti-Communist, an ardent supporter of Israel and a harsh critic of "new liberalism" in American domestic policy. His articles in *Commentary* magazine have singled him out as one of the younger "stars" of neo-conservatism.

Carl Samuel Gershman was born in New York City to Joseph Saul, an attorney, and Josephine (Seitlin) Gershman. Educated at the Horace Mann Preparatory School, where he graduated in 1961, he went on to receive a B.A. degree magna cum laude from Yale University in 1965 and a Master of Education degree from the Harvard Graduate School of Education in 1968. Between Yale and Harvard he spent two years during the Vietnam War as a VISTA volunteer in Pittsburgh.

A prolific writer and lecturer on a wide range of domestic and foreign policy issues, Gershman spent 1968 as a research specialist at the Anti-Defamation League of B'nai B'rith and was research director at the A. Philip Randolph Institute from 1969 to 1971. He then directed the Youth Institute for Peace in the Middle East from 1971 to 1974 and from 1974 to 1980 was executive director of Social Democrats-USA. For one year he was resident scholar at Freedom House in New York prior to his appointment at the United Nations, from where he has reported "a relentless campaign of vilification and condemnation of the Jewish State." "I see an effort at the U.N. to galvanize international acceptance for a repetition of the Holocaust or something equivalent to it. They [the U.N. representatives] are creating the psychological and political climate for something like it to take place," he said in early 1982.

Gershman, who contributes frequently to *Commentary* magazine, gained further recognition in October 1980 for an article on race in America that appeared in *The New York Times Magazine*. Entitled "A Matter of Class," the article contended that race was no longer impeding individual advancement, but that the rigid class system in America was. Gershman argued that even blacks who had "made it" found it useful to use racism as an excuse for not being even more successful than they were. He described the widening rift between a seriously deprived black under class and the growing class of black professionals. Yet he contended that the latter group, sophisticated and liberal in orientation, still perpetuates some of the myths of racism to bolster its personal causes. In the same issue of the magazine, black psychologist Kenneth B. Clark praised Gershman's analysis but criticized his alleged lack of understanding of the true experiences of blacks, including those whose successes have failed to mute the genuine anguish they often feel in a society where white backlash, though subtle, is still a common response to black achievement.

A frequent lecturer, Gershman has also contributed articles and reviews on foreign policy issues to *The New Leader, The Wall Street Journal, The New Republic, The American Spectator* and *Midstream*, where he has been supportive of Israel and a hard-line foreign policy for this country. In 1981, following the election of Ronald Reagan, he was appointed to the staff of Jeane Kirkpatrick, U.S. ambassador to the United Nations. He is also on the board of directors of the International Rescue Committee.

For further information:
Gershman, Carl Samuel. "After the Dominoes Fell." *Commentary*, May 1978.
————. "The Andrew Young Affair." *Commentary*, November 1979.
————. "Blacks and Jews." *Midstream*, February 1976.
————. *The Foreign Policy of American Labor*, Sage Policy Paper 29. 1975.
————, co-editor. *Israel, the Arabs and the Middle East.* New York: 1972.

ALLEN GINSBERG

b. June 3, 1926
Poet

Allen Ginsberg, the popular, prolific, often outrageous poet and 1960s activist, changed the direction of American poetry. He was one of the first poets to use street language in his writing and to write spontaneous, free-flowing stanzas that resemble composition rather than poetry. In his language and in his lifestyle, Ginsberg has always been in the forefront of trends that would influence younger generations.

He was born in Newark, New Jersey to Louis, a

teacher and a poet, and Naomi (Levy) Ginsberg. He attended Grammar High School in Paterson, New Jersey, graduating in 1943. He received a B.A. degree in 1948 from Columbia College in New York, where he began his association with Jack Kerouac, Neil Cassady and other writers who later came to be known in the 1950s as the "Beat Generation." His early poems, including "Empty Mirror" were influenced by his acquaintance with poet William Carlos Williams, who lived nearby in Paterson. In a prose piece entitled "Some Metamorphoses of Personal Prosody," Ginsberg explains how Williams influenced his writing. It was Williams who first helped Ginsberg recognize that the mode best-suited for his own poetic expression was not coy verses, but rather eccentric modulations of long-line composition.

In the early 1950s Ginsberg traveled on various cargo ships to Mexico, Tangier, Africa, the Arctic and other destinations. In 1960 he spent six months in Chile, Bolivia and Peru; and in 1965 he spent a half year in Cuba, Russia and Czechoslovakia, climaxing in the May Day 1965 "election" of Ginsberg as King of May by 100,000 Prague citizens. He also began experimenting with the poetic effects of psychedelic drugs in 1952 and took part in Timothy Leary's experiments with LSD in 1961. Ginsberg has said that certain parts of "Howl" and "Wales Visitation" were written under the influence of peyote and LSD, respectively.

Ginsberg has been deeply swayed by oriental philosophies, and—as is usual with Ginsberg—his own intense involvement predated the 1960s popularization of eastern culture among young American radicals. He began studying Hare Krishna and Buddhist meditation in 1952 and has since attended mantra chantings and taught courses on "Meditation and Poetics." He has also been politically outspoken and was a vocal and consistent opponent of the Vietnam War. In 1967, for example, he was arrested with Dr. Benjamin Spock for blocking an Army medical examination entranceway for prospective draftees, but he was released immediately afterward.

All of Ginsberg's works demonstrate his belief that the relationship between poetry and society is sacred. His long poems "Howl" and "Kaddish" are probably the best-known works. In "Howl," which is considered an important early expression of the rage that characterized the 1960s, Ginsberg used obscene language that shocked many readers who had never known poetry to be anything other than pleasant and respectable. Ginsberg refers to this fact self-consciously in the poem, when he says that his generation dragged poetry out of

the university and into the streets. An avowed homosexual, Ginsberg has lived with poet Peter Orlovsky for more than 25 years and openly refers to his homosexuality in "Howl."

"Kaddish," which was made into a film by public television with Ginsberg as narrator, is a poem mourning the death of his mother. Ginsberg's mother came from Russia to America in 1905, learned English on the Lower East Side in Manhattan and became a Communist and bohemian in the 1920s and 1930s. She was active in the Paterson, New Jersey silk strikes of the 1920s, taught retarded children and wrote children's stories for radical publications. In her later years she became delusional and was hospitalized. In 1956 she died of a stroke. Ginsberg recorded the poem "Kaddish" in the rhythms of the Jewish prayer of mourning, from which the title is derived.

Since 1973 Ginsberg has taught at the Naropa Institute, a non-accredited Buddhist-owned university in Colorado. He is co-director there of the Jack Kerouac School of Disembodied Poetics, which is the poetry department.

Ginsberg has written many books of poetry and prose, has recorded his work on records, and has edited and contributed to various anthologies. His writing has been published in many magazines, including *Yugen, Kulcher, City Lights Journal, The New Yorker, Look* and *The New York Times.*

Ginsberg has also published his correspondence with Neil Cassady and William Burroughs, his journals from the early 1950s and 1960s, and his lectures on poetry.

For further information:
Ginsberg, Allen. *Airplane Dreams.* San Francisco: 1968.
———. *Angkor Wat.* London: 1968.
———. *Empty Mirror, Early Poems.* New York: 1961.
———. *The Fall of America, Poems of These States.* San Francisco: 1973.
———. *First Blues.* New York: 1975.
———. *The Gates of Wrath, Rhymed Poems 1948–1951.* San Francisco: 1972.
———. *Howl and Other Poems.* San Francisco: 1956.
———. *Iron Horse.* San Francisco: 1974.
———. *Kaddish and Other Poems.* San Francisco: 1961.
———. *Mind Breaths, Poems 1971–1976.* California: 1978.
———. *Planet News.* San Francisco: 1968.
———. *Poems All Over the Place, Mostly 70s.* New York: 1978.
———. *Reality Sandwiches.* San Francisco: 1963.

RUTH BADER GINSBURG

b. March 15, 1933
Lawyer; law professor; U.S. judge

Ruth Bader Ginsburg, U.S. Court of Appeals Justice for the District of Columbia and a recognized legal specialist in constitutional law and civil procedure, has long stressed her opposition to sex discrimination throughout her career as a lawyer and a professor at Columbia University Law School.

Ruth Bader was born in Brooklyn to Nathan, a manufacturer of fur coats, and Celia (Amster) Bader. Ruth Bader received an A.B. degree from Cornell University in 1954 and attended both Harvard Law School and Columbia Law School, where she received a Bachelor of Laws degree as well as a Doctor of Laws degree in 1959. At both law schools she was a member of the Law Review, and at Columbia she was a Kent Scholar.

Upon graduation Bader (who by now was Ruth Bader Ginsburg, married to Columbia University law professor Martin D. Ginsburg) discovered that women were not welcome in the city's major law firms, and she became instead a law clerk for Federal Judge Edmund L. Palmieri of the U.S. District Court, Southern District of New York, from 1959 to 1961. She was research associate (1961–62) and afterward associate director (1962–63) of the Columbia Law School's Project on International Procedure.

Ginsburg's most blatant personal experience with sex discrimination occurred in 1963, when she joined the faculty of Rutgers Law School as assistant professor and discovered that her salary was less than that of her male colleagues with similar background. Although she did not contest the issue then, the experience fueled her desire to become an activist in cases dealing with sex discrimination. She was promoted to associate professor in 1966 and full professor in 1969.

She became a tenured professor at Columbia University in 1972. The same year, she founded the American Civil Liberties Union Women's Rights Project and was a columnist on "Women's Rights" for *The Civil Liberties Review*. Among the cases she argued as an attorney was a Supreme Court case, *Struck* v. *Secretary of Defense* (1972), in which she successfully challenged the discharge of a pregnant officer in the Air Force. In *Weinberger* v. *Wiesenfeld* a New Jersey man who lost his wife in childbirth—their son survived—sought his wife's Social Security benefits to supplement his own income from part-time work so that he could support his son. At the time widowers could not receive Social Security

benefits, although widows could. Ginsburg's success in the widower's defense was a major breakthrough.

She was nominated by former President Jimmy Carter to the Federal Appellate Court in Washington, D.C. in late 1979 and seated in 1980. Ginsburg has been admitted to the bar in New York state, the District of Columbia, the U.S. Supreme Court, the U.S. Courts of Appeals and U.S. District Courts in New York and the District of Columbia. She is active in many bar associations and has written several books and many articles on legal procedure, with special emphasis on sex-discrimination issues and affirmative action. She is an active supporter of the Equal Rights Amendment.

For further information:
Ginsburg, Ruth Bader. "Judicial Authority to Repair Unconstitutional Legislation," 28 *Cleveland-Marshall Law Review* 301 (March 1980).
———. "Ratification of the Equal Rights Amendment: A Question of Time," 57 *Texas Law Review* 919 (1979)
———. "Sex Equality and the Constitution," 52 *Tulane Law Review,* 451 (1978) (George Abel Dreyfous Lecture)
———. "Some Thoughts on Benign Classification in the Context of Sex," 10 *Connecticut Law Review* 813 (Summer 1978)

ELI GINZBERG

B. April 30, 1911
Economist; manpower specialist

Eli Ginzberg, professor of economics at Columbia University, was described in 1966 by the *Atlanta Constitution* as "perhaps the nation's outstanding economist in the manpower field." Ginzberg, who has served as a manpower adviser to seven U.S. presidents, is widely considered to be the father of modern human resource studies and was the creator of the first course in the field at Columbia University in 1939.

Eli Ginzberg was born in New York City to Louis and Adele (Katzenstein) Ginzberg. His father was a well-known author and professor of Talmudic and rabbinical studies at the Jewish Theological Seminary. Ginzberg received the degrees of Bachelor of Arts (1931), Master of Arts (1932) and Ph.D. (1934) from Columbia. He also studied two semesters at the University of Heidelberg (Germany) and a summer session at the University of Grenoble (France). Before finishing his undergraduate education, Ginzberg completed his first book, *Studies of the Economies in the Bible* (Philadelphia, 1932). He joined the faculty of the Graduate School of

Business at Columbia in 1935 as an associate professor and has been director of the Conservation of Human Resources Project since its founding in 1941.

Ginzberg's long involvement in government service began during the administration of Franklin D. Roosevelt in 1942, when—as a member of the Committee on Wartime Requirements for Specialized and Scientific Personnel—he conducted a study on the use of military manpower. His analysis resulted in a major overhaul that called for the release of 250,000 civilians from the military payroll and the transfer of four divisions of soldiers from active duty. He acted as manpower adviser to General Brehon B. Somervell during the war, and from 1944 to 1946 was chief logistical adviser for the surgeon general of the Army. In this position he planned the creation of one of the most extensive military planning and predicting systems in history—beginning four months before D-Day (June 6, 1944), Ginzberg estimated the number of casualties and the amount of hospital assistance and evacuation that would be required for the invasion. Ginzberg was a representative to the Five Powers Conference on reparations for the non-repatriable refugees, held at Paris in 1946. He received the War Department's Gold Medal for exceptional civilian service.

Following the war Ginzberg was a consultant to numerous federal branches, including the departments of State; the Army; Labor; Defense; and Health, Education and Welfare. In 1963 he was appointed chairman of the National Manpower Advisory Committee, a governmental agency that advises the president and federal agencies about national manpower and the use of Congressional manpower appropriations. In addition, Ginzberg has studied overseas manpower problems for the U.S. government and nonprofit organizations, and with special emphasis on Israel and Venezuela.

The economics professor has been active in Jewish causes throughout his life. He served as director of the allotment committee of the United Jewish Appeal for the resettlement of refugees in 1941. For two terms he served on the board of governors of Hebrew University in Jerusalem. In 1960 and 1961 he was director of a hospital study for the Federation of Jewish Philanthropies in New York City.

Besides directing scores of studies under the auspices of the Conservation of Human Resources Project, Ginzberg has written or edited more than 35 books, primarily on human resources and manpower. His essential research probing was directed at marginal groups, among them "the uneducated, the emotionally disturbed, blacks, and ineffective soldiers," he wrote. "They demonstrated that being born into a low-income family

. . . being a member of a disadvantaged group, suffering the loss of a parent during childhood were so handicapping that only a relatively few growing up under such adverse conditions . . . [were] able to rise on the socioeconomic scale." His three-volume work *The Ineffective Soldier: Lessons for Management and the Nation* (New York, 1959) involved an eight-year study of 250,000 men who were rejected or prematurely discharged from the Army during World War II for mental or emotional disabilities.

Among his other books are *The Negro Potential* (New York, 1956), a study of the problems experienced by blacks in the job market, and *Life Styles of Educated Women* (New York, 1966). The latter's second volume, *Educated American Women* (New York, 1966), was later translated into Japanese and became a model reference work in the new women's movement in Japan. One of Ginzberg's more recent works, *Good Jobs, Bad Jobs, No Jobs* (Cambridge, Mass., 1980), is a comprehensive study on job and unemployment problems. He shows that all people are affected by economic and public policies, whether favorable or inimical to their needs and aspirations.

Ginzberg has always taken a humanistic approach to human resource research. The traditional commodity approach is too restricted, he has said, because it looks at human beings as though they were inert resources and "ignores the extent to which men, as individuals and particularly as members of groups, strive to alter the institutions they have inherited in order to make them more responsive to the goals they seek to realize."

MILTON GLASER

b. June 26, 1929
Designer; illustrator

If there is a visual iconography of the 1960s, it is epitomized in the work of the artists from Push Pin Studios, a New York-based organization of graphic designers founded in 1954 by Milton Glaser. Push Pin Studios developed bold, imaginative, colorful approaches to design in posters, record covers, book jackets and magazines that, by the mid-1970s, would make them comparable in impact to the Bauhaus/Swiss school of the 1920s and 1930s. Now president of his own company, Milton Glaser Inc., which he founded in 1974, Glaser continues to venture into new areas of design.

Milton Glaser was born in New York City to Eugene, a tailor, and Eleanor (Bergman) Glaser, immigrants from Hungary. He grew up in the Bronx and began drawing as a child. He attended the High School of Music and Art and graduated from Cooper Union with a Bachelor of Fine Arts degree in 1951. From 1951 to 1953 he studied at the Academy of Fine Arts in Bologna, Italy (the second of his two years as a Fulbright Scholar). Upon his return he joined artist Seymour Chwast in 1954 to create Push Pin Studios, of which Glaser became president.

At Push Pin, Glaser, Chwast and other artists developed new type styles and approaches to design that reflected the turbulence and color of the 1960s. His best-known poster is a multicolored profile of Bob Dylan, with the songwriter's face in silhouette, outlined in a rainbow of colors. A magazine, *Push Pin Graphic,* was begun in 1957 and eventually became a major design publication. The evolution of Push Pin into a studio with international influence culminated in two group shows in Europe, the "Push Pin Decorative Arts Show" at the Louvre in Paris in 1970, and "Push Pin Style" at the Castello Sforesco in Milan, Italy in 1971.

In 1968 Glaser became chairman of the board and design director of *New York* magazine, leaving in 1976 when it was purchased by Australian publisher Rupert Murdoch. He also designed *New West* magazine and redesigned four French magazines—*Paris Match, L'Express, L'Europe* and *Jardin des Modes*—as well as the New York weekly newspaper *The Village Voice,* for which he was design director and vice president from 1975 to 1977.

But Glaser's design work went beyond books and posters. In 1970 he was commissioned to design the Childcraft toy store in New York City, and in 1975 he designed the observation deck of the World Trade Center and two of its restaurants.

Glaser has illustrated children's books, including *If Apples Had Teeth,* written by his wife Shirley Glaser (New York, 1960); *Cats & Bats & Things with Wings,* with poet Conrad Aiken (New York, 1965); and *Fish in the Sky,* by George Mendoza (New York, 1971). He illustrated Isaac Asimov's *Don Juan* (New York, 1972) and has had two collections of his works published: *Graphic Design* (Woodstock, N.Y., 1973) and the *Milton Glaser Poster Book* (New York, 1977).

A close second to Glaser's love for art has been his love for gourmet food. With friend Jerome Snyder, Glaser wrote *The Underground Gourmet* (New York, 1970) and *The All New Underground Gourmet* (New York, 1977), a survey of unusual, lesser-known restaurants in New York City, and *The Underground Gourmet Cookbook* (New York, 1975).

Glaser had one-man shows in 1975 at the Museum of Modern Art in New York, the Royal Museum of Fine Arts in Brussels and the Portland Visual Arts Center in

Maine and in 1977 at the Pompidou Cultural Center in Paris.

Since 1961 he has taught at the School of Visual Arts in New York City and since 1977 at his alma mater, Cooper Union. He has won the Art Directors Club Gold Medal, the Society of Illustrators Gold Medal, the St. Gaudens Medal of Cooper Union and the American Institute of Graphic Arts Medallist Award and has received honorary degrees from the Philadelphia Museum School, Moore College of Art and the Minneapolis Institute of the Arts. He has been inducted into the Royal Society of Arts in London and the Art Directors Club Hall of Fame in New York.

IRA GLASSER

b. April 19, 1937
Civil liberties executive

When he became executive director of the American Civil Liberties Union in 1978, Ira Glasser was faced with an organization whose membership was divided, dwindling and deeply in debt. Under Glasser's leadership, however, the ACLU is thriving.

Ira Glasser was born in Brooklyn to Sidney, a construction worker, and Anne (Golstein) Glasser. He was the first in his family to graduate from college, receiving a B.S. degree in mathematics magna cum laude and Phi Beta Kappa from Queens College in 1959. The next year he received an M.A. degree from Ohio State University, and in 1961 he did graduate work in sociology and philosophy at The New School for Social Research in New York. In 1960 Glasser also began what would be a five-year teaching career, instructing mathematics at Queens College (1960–62) and mathematics and science at Sarah Lawrence College (1962–65). He also worked for one year (1964–65) as a research associate in the school science curriculum project at the University of Illinois Graduate School of Education.

Glasser's interest in civil liberties stems not from academic training, perhaps, but from earlier exposure to human problems. In 1954, when he was 17, and for nine years afterward, he worked at Vacation Camp for the Blind, a private social agency with programs for blind and deaf-blind adults. By the time he left, he was executive assistant to the executive director. He worked for *Current* magazine from 1962 to 1967 as associate editor and editor.

He joined the New York Civil Liberties Union in 1967 as associate director and became executive director in 1970 until 1978. He strongly defended the Ocean Hill-Brownsville school governing board against the

United Federation of Teachers during the bitter 1968 teachers' strike in New York City. Under his leadership, too, the NYCLU defended prisoners' rights and the rights of mental patients and opposed the death penalty.

In 1978 he succeeded Aryeh Neier as executive director of the ACLU. Under Glasser's direction the ACLU opposed draft registration after it was reinstituted in 1980, opposed the Supreme Court's 1981 ruling that a male-only draft was legal and took a leading role that same year in charging in *Wolman* v. *Rostker* that demanding Social Security numbers from draft registrants was a violation of the Privacy Act enacted by Congress. Under Glasser, the ACLU has continued its traditional support of the First Amendment as it did in 1978, when it defended the right of a neo-Nazi group to honor Hitler's birthday with a march in Skokie, Illinois—home of many Holocaust survivors. In its dedication to upholding the principles of free speech at all costs—even when the defendants are Nazi sympathizers—the nearly half-Jewish ACLU lost about 60,000 members, or about one-fourth of its enrollment at the time. In addition, the ACLU has opposed capital punishment, fought book censorship by local school boards and denounced the role of the Moral Majority in full-page advertisements.

A review of Glasser's writings underscores his commitment to civil liberties. Since 1970 he has contributed articles to a wide range of periodicals, including *Harper's, The New York Times, The Civil Liberties Review, Journal of Law and Education, Social Policy* and others. He wrote a chapter on "The Constitution and the Courts" in *What Nixon Is Doing to Us* (New York, 1973), wrote *Your Legal Rights: Making the Law Work for You* (New York, 1974) and coauthored (with Willard Gaylin, Steven Marcus and David Rothman) *Doing Good: The Limits of Benevolence* (New York, 1978).

For further information:

Glasser, Ira. "Civil Liberties in the Private Sector." *Social Policy,* March/April 1978.

———. "Cold Storage." *The New Republic,* March 8, 1980.

———. "Deinstitutionalization and Freedom: A Reply." *Columbia,* Summer 1978.

———. "Do Children Have Rights?" *Harper's,* March 1975.

———. "The Expanded Role of the Judiciary in Regulating the Political Process: The Curious Case of Campaign Financing Laws." American Enterprise Institute paper. *Proceedings of the American Enterprise Institute,* December 1978.

———. "Sexist Justice: A Review." *Social Policy,* March/April 1975.

———. "Viewpoint on Abscam: Are Sting Operations a Warrantless Search?" *Police Magazine,* May 1980.

———. "The Yellow Star and the Pink Triangle." *The New York Times,* September 9, 1975, Op-Ed page.

———. "Welfare Versus Liberty." *The Nation,* April 1, 1978.

Glasser, Ira; Gaylin, Willard; Marcus, Stephen; and Rothman, David. *Doing Good: The Limits of Benevolence.* New York: 1978.

NAHUM N. GLATZER

b. March 25, 1903
Professor; historian

The internationally respected Judaic scholar Nahum Glatzer is distinguished not only for the depth and scope of his expertise on Jewish history but for the dedication he brings to teaching younger generations of Jewish historians. Professor of Judaic studies and religion at Boston University since 1973, and at Brandeis University for more than 20 years before that, he is the author of dozens of books and articles and is as knowledgeable about ancient and medieval Jewish history as about the more recent accomplishments of contemporary Jewish philosophers and writers.

Nahum Norbert Glatzer was born in Lemberg, Austria to David, a businessman, and Rose (Gottlieb) Glatzer. Glatzer spent his formative years in the German-Jewish society that included Franz Kafka, Martin Buber and S.Y. Agnon. He attended Talmudic Academy in Frankfurt-am-Main from 1920 to 1922 and received his Ph.D. degree from the University of Frankfurt in 1931. As a student Glatzer was deeply influenced by one of his professors, the scholar and philosopher Franz Rosenzweig, who ultimately was responsible for Glatzer's having chosen to become a scholar rather than a rabbi. Glatzer later succeeded Martin Buber as a lecturer in Jewish religious history and ethics at the University of Frankfurt and held that position from 1932 to 1933, when he left Germany because of the Nazi threat.

From 1933 to 1938 he was an instructor in Hebrew literature at the Bet Sefer Reali in Haifa, Palestine. In 1938 Glatzer emigrated to America and taught at the College of Jewish Studies (now Spertus College) in Chicago until 1943. He was a professor at the Hebrew Teachers College (now just called Hebrew College) in Boston from 1943 to 1947 and a professor of history at Yeshiva University in New York for the next four years.

In 1951 Glatzer joined the Brandeis University faculty in Waltham, Massachusetts as associate professor of Jewish history. He became a full professor in 1956, a position that he held until 1973, when he became professor emeritus at Brandeis and joined the history department at Boston University.

Glatzer regards teaching as a sacred duty, and his devotion to it is legendary. The thousands of students he has taught over the years have responded in kind: On the occasion of his 70th birthday, he was presented with a tribute written by former students throughout the country. It was published in *Response* magazine two years later and included essays about the wide range of subjects within Jewish learning in which Glatzer had instructed his students as well as the inspiration and guidance he provided. In the introduction to the tribute, one student wrote:

> He sees his task not as converting them [his students] to his own point of view or using them for his own purposes but rather as being a guide and a friend who walks with them through the literature and shows them how to listen to the sources and how to respond . . . he has a great capacity for listening to his students, for helping them to grow in accordance with their own inner convictions and commitments and natures so that they can become what they are meant to be and not just imitators of himself.

Glatzer believes that all Jews live on the same continuum, whether they are German Jews who have attempted to merge their Jewishness with German culture or the first Russian Jews who have turned their backs on Europe and settled in Palestine, or whether they are Jews from cultures that vanished centuries ago or contemporary American Jews. He perceives all Jews as part of the same community, a community to which he himself is deeply committed. And the commitment extends beyond the academic world to which Glatzer is so tightly connected. He has been active in the suburban synagogue near his home in Watertown, Massachusetts and has edited many anthologies of Jewish sources and prepared curricula for high school classes and adult education programs. He has prepared and edited a Passover Haggadah and has contributed to the *Encyclopaedia Brittanica*, *Encyclopedia Judaica* and many other reference works and journals.

Glatzer, who received the B'nai B'rith Prize for Literary Excellence in 1973, is a fellow at the American Academy for Jewish Research and the American Academy of Arts and Sciences.

For further information:
Glatzer, Nahum N. *The Dimensions of Job.* New York: 1969.

———. *Faith and Knowledge: The Jew in the Medieval World.* Boston: 1963.

———. *Frank Rosenzweig: His Life and Thought.* New York: 1953.

———. *Hillel the Elder: The Emergence of Classical Judaism.* Washington, D.C.: 1956.

———. *The Judaic Tradition.* Boston: 1969.

Glatzer, Nahum N., ed. *The Essential Philo.* New York: 1971.

———. *Hammer on the Rock: A Short Midrash Reader.* New York: 1948, 1962.

———. *In Time and Eternity: A Jewish Reader.* New York: 1946, 1961, 1966.

———. *Maimonides Said: an Anthology.* New York: 1941.

———. *Parables and Paradoxes by Franz Kafka.* New York: 1961.

———. *The Way of Response: Martin Buber.* New York: 1967.

Fishbane, Michael A., and Flohr, Paul R., eds., *Texts and Responses,* Studies presented to Nahum N. Glatzer on the occasion of his seventieth birthday by his students. Leiden, The Netherlands: 1975.

NATHAN GLAZER

b. February 25, 1923
Sociologist

Two of Nathan Glazer's books, *The Lonely Crowd* and *Beyond the Melting Pot* (the latter coauthored with Daniel Patrick Moynihan), are considered classics in descriptive sociology. The eminent Harvard sociologist has spent the bulk of his career studying ethnicity in America, with special concentration on the American Jewish community.

Glazer was born in New York City, one of seven children of Louis, a sewing machine operator, and Tillie (Zacharevich) Glazer. He graduated from James Monroe High School in the Bronx in 1940 and enrolled at the City College of New York. CCNY was a radical hotbed at the time, and Glazer met other student activists such as Daniel Bell and Irving Kristol, with whom he would later participate in political affairs during the 1950s and 1960s. A self-described socialist during his student days, Glazer was also involved in student Zionist organization.

After receiving his Bachelor of Social Science degree in sociology in 1944, Glazer was awarded an M.A. degree the same year in an accelerated course in linguistics and anthropology at the University of Pennsylvania. The purpose of the program was to train linguists for the U.S. Army. Glazer completed his master's thesis on the Swahili language. He did not serve in the military, however, but instead joined *Commentary* magazine as assistant editor from 1944 to 1953. He also undertook graduate studies, receiving his Ph.D. in sociology from Columbia University in 1962.

Glazer took a leave of absence from the magazine in 1948 to collaborate with David Riesman and Reuel Denny on a mass communications project sponsored by the Yale University Committee on National Policy. The result of that project, *The Lonely Crowd* (New Haven, 1950), identified character types in society in accordance with their reactions to various sociopsychological pressures. In *The Lonely Crowd* the authors established relationships between socioeconomic eras and conditions and three types of personalities: tradition-directed, inner-directed and outer-directed. They also measured people's reactions to various sociopsychological pressures and categorized people as adjusted, anomic or autonomous. The book was an insightful, ground-breaking effort to understand the behavior, feelings and stress experienced by masses of contemporary Americans. A follow-up study, *Faces in the Crowd* (New Haven, 1952), gave an in-depth view of a few of the people who had participated in the original project.

From 1954 to 1957 Glazer was an editor with Anchor Books, the quality paperback book division of Doubleday. After departing, he continued as editorial adviser to editor in chief Jason Epstein from 1958 to 1962. Meanwhile, Glazer taught at the University of California at Berkeley (1957–58), Bennington College (1958–59) and Smith College (1959–60). He also taught at the Salzburg Seminar in American Studies in 1971 and in 1974.

After receiving a Guggenheim grant for 1966 to 1967, Glazer wrote *American Judaism* (Chicago, 1974). A survey of the American Jewish community, the book combined historical objectivity, sociological insight and religious sensitivity. Glazer's next book, *The Social Basis of American Communism* (New York, 1961), theorized that American workers who were attracted to communism were drawn more by material self-interest than by ideology. Glazer examined the condition of social and ethnic groups targeted by the American Communist party for recruitment, among them blacks and Jews. He concluded that Americans generally rejected or accepted communism for materialist reasons rather than for historical or sociological ideals.

Glazer worked as an urban sociologist with the Housing and Home Finance Agency in Washington, D.C. in 1962 and 1963. He helped create a number of programs that later served as the basis for President Lyndon Johnson's Great Society program. Then, under the sponsorship of the Harvard and MIT Joint Center for Urban Studies, Glazer collaborated with Daniel Patrick Moynihan on *Beyond the Melting Pot* (Boston, 1963). This book, a study of the various ethnic cultures of New York City, showed that the concept of America as a "melting pot" of many cultures was untrue and objected strongly to the heretofore prevailing mode of acculturation and assimilation among immigrant groups.

Twelve years after the revised second edition of *Beyond the Melting Pot* appeared, Glazer began modifying if not changing his view of ethnicity. Writing in *Commentary* in 1982 he observed that he foresaw much turbulence ahead. "The new [immigrant] groups, will, on the one hand, form more obvious targets for attack; on the other hand, they will find easier access to legal protection, and to legal rights that are unique in the experience of older Americans, and this will create resentment." Urging that a "fresh look" be taken, Glazer concluded that since assimilation served so many immigrants so well in the past, perhaps "it is not unreasonable to hope that the same processes can affect the new immigrants as well." There is a "virtue of forging a single society out of many stocks," he wrote, and assimilation may yet become a goal to be aimed at by those coming to the United States.

After teaching at the University of California at Berkeley from 1963 to 1969, Glazer became the first professor of education and sociology at Harvard University. The chair was one of five endowed by the Ford Foundation to allow for the study of urban values and change.

In 1970 Glazer wrote *Remembering the Answers* (New York), a series of essays in which he took a guarded, even critical, attitude toward the student uprisings of the late 1960s. Many students, he argued, unjustifiably impeded the academic functioning of the university. Despite the soundness of some student grievances, Glazer expressed serious reservations about some of the students' methods of protest. Five years later he published *Affirmative Discrimination* (New York, 1975), in which he objected to public policies that would establish quotas in college admissions and employment, suggesting that affirmative action might not be the best way to achieve racial balance and equality.

In 1982 he and Seymour Martin Lipset argued in *The New York Times* that the Israeli war in Lebanon was "ill-advised."

For further information:
Glazer, Nathan. "Ethnicity—North, South, West." *Commentary,* May 1982.
Glazer, Nathan, and Lipset, Seymour Martin. "Israel Isn't Threatened. The War's Ill-Advised." *The New York Times,* June 30, 1982.

BERTRAM H. GOLD

b. March 10, 1916
Jewish organizational executive

Executive vice president of the American Jewish Committee—this country's pioneer human rights organization, founded in 1906 and probably the most prestigious and influential non-Israeli Jewish organization in the world—Bertram Gold has moved the once-largely assimilationist and non-Zionist group toward Jewish identity and closer association with the State of Israel.

Bertram Haim Gold was born in Toronto, Canada, the son of Harry, who was a peddler and owner of a grocery and dress store, and Fanny (Rosnick) Gold, both Russian immigrants. He earned his B.A. degree in psychology from the University of Toronto in 1937 and then moved to the United States, where he matriculated at Western Reserve University and was awarded an M.A. degree in social science in 1939. Gold then became a lecturer at the University of Pittsburgh's School of Applied Sciences, teaching social work from 1939 to 1942. The next year he entered the United States Army and became an American citizen. He served until 1946 and was in the European theater of operations.

Following his discharge he was employed as an assistant professor at the University of Toronto, again teaching social work. Between 1947 and 1954 he was executive director of Jewish Community Centers in Essex County (Newark, New Jersey) and then, from 1954 to 1967, executive director of Los Angeles Jewish Centers Association and adjunct professor of organizational theory at the University of Southern California. In 1967 he was chosen executive vice president of the American Jewish Committee.

It is Gold's achievement that he reversed AJC's historic trend of non-Zionism and assimilationism, instead emphasizing a return to Jewish values and stressing Jewish identification. The threatened weakening of the Jewish family was high on his list of priorities, and in 1977 he began a nationwide study of the impact of intermarriage on families and their ties to the Jewish community. The study found among other things that the greater the degree of Jewish background and education of the Jewish spouse, the greater the' chances that children would be reared as Jews. He then launched the National Jewish Family Center to promote U.S. policies in support of family life. In other Jewish-related activities, he introduced *Present Tense,* a new magazine of world Jewish affairs, in 1973, and encouraged the founding of the Institute on Pluralism and Group Identity in 1969 (established under a different name), which stressed the importance of ethnic identification rather than the customary goal of assimilation and acculturation and the need to reduce tensions between white ethnics and blacks.

Abroad, Gold took the AJC into a closer relationship with Israel. Remaining steadfast in its desire to encourage diversity of opinion, Gold said in *New Realities in American Life* (New York, 1980):

> The plea for Jewish "unity" is heard most often in the attempt to discourage public criticism of Israeli policies. . . . It is one thing for an individual or a Jewish organization to refrain from public criticism of one or another Israeli policy, in the belief that it might be harmful to Israel. . . . It is quite another matter, however, to refrain from taking positions for the sake of so-called Jewish unity. A unity that cannot tolerate difference is a unity not worth maintaining.

Nevertheless, Gold directed the AJC toward powerful support for Israel, and the AJC was the first United States Jewish group to establish a full-time office in Jerusalem. His purpose was to interpret Israel's role as a friend and ally of democracy in the Middle East, and the AJC has successfully mobilized support nationally whenever Israel has been endangered.

Gold has also expressed his organization's views on the Palestinians, as a humanitarian issue and as a political problem. Declaring in 1982 that the United States should "pay attention" to their plight, he nonetheless added that "this is not the same, however, as permitting the agenda of U.S. policy vis-a-vis the Middle East to be dominated by Palestinian grievances." Such an approach, he declared, would be "simplistic" and would distort the "complex realities" of the area. Instead, he advised the United States to "weigh the many other matters that are at least as crucial, if not decisive, to American security and to peace in the Middle East."

HERBERT GOLD

b. March 9, 1924
Author

Herbert Gold, a prolific author of novels, short stories and critical essays, is often acclaimed for his vigorous, witty and insightful writing style. His themes revolve around the impact of modernity on the quality and character of American life. He is often brutally honest in his depictions of violence, racial discrimination, the dehumanized alienation of the urban metropolis and his strong convictions about right and wrong.

Herbert Gold was born in Cleveland, Ohio, the oldest of four sons of Samuel, a grocer and later real estate investor, and Frieda (Frankel) Gold. After graduating from Lakewood Ohio High School in 1942, he attended Columbia University, where he published in its literary and humor publications. From 1943 to early 1946 he was in the United States Army Intelligence and received his B.A. degree from Columbia in humanities in 1946. Gold continued his philosophy studies at the Sorbonne in Paris on a Fulbright Fellowship from 1946 to 1949. He spent 1950 in Haiti, writing and living on an Inter-American Cultural Relations grant, and taught philosophy and literature at Western Reserve University in Cleveland from 1951 to 1953.

His first novel, *Birth of a Hero* (New York, 1951), which depicts the questioning and development of a middle-class, educated man of 45, was praised for its artistic style, which, according to a *New York Times* critic, is "rich and rolling, with intoned rhythms and phrasing." His second novel, *The Prospect Before Us* (New York, 1954), which deals with racial discrimination, established Gold as an intelligent writer with a sensitivity for big-city sounds, sights and smells. Gold demonstrated his moral concerns in his third book, *The Man Who Was Not with It* (Boston, 1956), which is about a heroin addict who discovers that society's values— marriage, family, constructive work—are more desirable than being "with it."

About *Therefore Be Bold* (New York, 1961), which deals with adolescent love, a *New York Herald Tribune Book Review* critic wrote that Gold "has his own undeniable voice no matter what the idiom. If the voice is sometimes raw or wild, it is always rich and vigorous, genuine and almost never dull." In *Salt* (New York, 1963), the author describes the loneliness and alienation that exists in big cities; and in *Fathers* (New York, 1967), he writes, in the form of a memoir, about a boy's initiation into the adult world. He depicts the hip, trendy life of New York and Los Angeles in *Swiftie, the Magician* (New York, 1974) and the contrasting portrayals of a whorehouse madam who wants to unionize prostitution and a female mayoral candidate who is conducting a moral regeneration campaign in *Waiting for Cordelia* (New York, 1977). In a review of the latter, a *Saturday Review* critic wrote: "Gold is a skilled wordsmith, a master of the freak portrait gallery, an acute observer of not only the comedy but also the pathos of pretense."

In his collections of short stories, *Love and Like* (New York, 1960) and *The Magic Will: Stories and Essays of a Decade* (New York, 1971), Gold deals with the same issues—the violence, exploitation and human illnesses that he sees. He has also compiled a collection of essays on literature, love, marriage and work in *The Age of Happy Problems* (New York, 1962).

Gold has been a visiting professor at various universities, including Cornell University (1958), Harvard University (Summer 1965), the University of California at Berkeley (1963 and 1967) and at Davis (1973–80). He has been a Guggenheim fellow, a Ford Foundation grantee and a recipient of a 1975 award from the American Institute of Arts and Letters and a 1959 Longview award.

For further information:

Gold, Herbert. *A Walk on the West Side: California on the Brink.* New York: 1981.
Gold, Herbert, ed. *Fiction of the Fifties: A Decade of American Writing.* New York: 1960.
———. *First Person Singular: Essays for the Sixties.* New York: 1963.
———. *True Love.* New York: 1982.

ARTHUR GOLDBERG

b. August 8, 1908
Lawyer; judge

Whether in private practice or public service, former Supreme Court justice and United States representative to the United Nations Arthur Goldberg has devoted his long and outstanding career to defending the rights of all people—especially minorities—and to supporting causes that have led directly toward a more peaceful, just and humane world.

Arthur Joseph Goldberg was born in Chicago, the youngest of 11 children of Joseph, a peddler, and Rebecca (Perlstein) Goldberg. His parents were Russian immigrants. Goldberg worked his way through Northwestern University, earning a B.S.L. degree in 1929 and a Doctor of Law degree, summa cum laude, in 1930.

He set up a private practice in Chicago that year and became intensely involved in labor issues that emerged as a result of problems arising from the Depression and subsequent New Deal programs. He became active with the Franklin D. Roosevelt campaigns and became acquainted with most of Chicago's union leaders. In a short time he became their legal adviser. During World

War II Goldberg directed the labor division for the Office of Strategic Services and, in his capacity as legal specialist in labor, helped set up secret operations with anti-Fascist union chiefs in Nazi-held territories.

Goldberg became general counsel for two major unions in 1948—the Congress of Industrial Organizations (CIO) and the United Steelworkers (USW). Seven years later, in 1955, he was a primary negotiator in the merger between the CIO and the rival American Federation of Labor (AFL). He published his first book, *AFL-CIO: Labor United* (New York, 1956), about that merger and the history that preceded it, the following year.

From 1957 to 1958, during the McClellan Committee investigations of union corruption, Goldberg helped develop a code of ethics for the AFL-CIO. One major result of the hearings was the expulsion of some corrupt labor leaders as well as the entire Teamsters Union from the AFL-CIO.

Always in the forefront of liberal politics, Goldberg was an active supporter of John F. Kennedy's campaign for the presidency. Earlier, he had worked with the then-senator in writing labor reform laws that required public disclosure of union financing. When Kennedy was elected, Goldberg was appointed secretary of labor in 1961, over a slate of five union leaders whose names AFL-CIO head George Meany had submitted to the new president. Known as an activist official, Goldberg developed a program that included a hike in the minimum wage and in unemployment and Social Security benefits while diiscouraging excessive wage increases in the face of an inflationary economy that the Kennedy administration was then trying to control. Goldberg's efforts at union regulation created animosities with his former allies and contributed to a blowup between Kennedy and the steelworkers when the USW implemented substantial price hikes, which led to wage increases and created further inflation.

In 1962 Kennedy nominated Goldberg for the Supreme Court post—the "Jewish" seat—previously held by Felix Frankfurter, who had retired. Siding as always with liberal decisions, Goldberg voted regularly to reverse the convictions of civil rights sit-in demonstrators and in a major Florida case reversed the contempt conviction of an NAACP leader from Miami who had refused to provide membership rosters to state officials. He upheld the rights of naturalized American citizens and wrote the controversial *Escobedo* decision in 1964, which ruled that every prisoner had the constitutional right to legal counsel during police interrogation. He was instrumental in assuring legal services to poor people, and—to complete his total dedication to civil rights for

all people—expressed the opinion that the 14th Amendment supports access to public places for all citizens.

Goldberg resigned from the Court in 1965 at the recommendation of President Lyndon B. Johnson to become United States representative to the United Nations. During his tenure he became an active negotiator between Arab and Israeli factions during and after the 1967 Six Day War. Because he called for a cease-fire without stipulating that Israel withdraw from occupied territories, he incurred the anger of Arab representatives, who accused him of bending toward Jewish influences. Nonetheless, he continued to play an active role both in Middle East negotiations and in subsequent battles over the burgeoning war in Indochina. He resigned in 1968 over a disagreement with Johnson's policies in Vietnam, which led to an escalation of the fighting, and settled into private practice in New York. He was named United Nations ambassador at large in 1977–78.

Goldberg's foray into electoral politics as candidate for New York state governor in 1970 failed, and in 1971 he returned to private practice in the District of Columbia.

In addition to his early book on labor, Goldberg is the author of *The Defenses of Freedom* (New York, 1966), a collection of the major addresses and writings, including court decisions, of his career; and *Equal Justice: The Warren Court* (Evanston, Ill., 1971), a collection of lectures. He has taught law at Princeton (1968–69), Columbia (1969–70) and American University (1972–73) and has been distinguished professor at the Hastings College of Law in San Francisco since 1974. He was chairman of the Center for Law and Social Policy from 1968 to 1978 and since then has been its honorary chairman.

Goldberg is active in many Jewish causes. From 1963 to 1969 he was chairman of the Jewish Theological Seminary board of overseers and in 1968–69 was president of the American Jewish Committee, of which he is now honorary president. He has won many awards, including the prestigious Medal of Freedom in 1978 from President Jimmy Carter.

LEONARD GOLDENSON

b. December 7, 1905
Corporate executive

Leonard Goldenson, chairman and chief executive officer of the American Broadcasting Company, is one of the central figures in the development and evolution of the television industry. A boy wonder who began his career in the theater business, he is the man most responsible for building ABC into a billion-dollar corporation.

Leonard Harry Goldenson was born in Scottdale, Pennsylvania to Lee, a clothing store and local movie theater operator, and Esther (Broude) Goldenson. After completing high school in 1923, Goldenson went to Harvard University, where he obtained his B.S. degree in 1927 and his law degree in 1930. Upon graduation he began working as a law clerk for a railroad attorney. Then, in 1932 Goldenson was hired by a large law firm that had Paramount Pictures as its client.

Goldenson left his law firm in 1933 and joined Paramount Pictures to help reorganize its theaters in New England. Within a few years he was in charge of all of Paramount's 1,700 movie theaters throughout the country. In 1942 he was made vice president of Paramount Pictures and two years later was named president of Paramount Theaters Service Corporation. In 1946 he helped organize the American Theater Association, which provides a forum for the interchange of information on all aspects of theater, including production, acting and play writing, and draws membership from all facets of the theatrical field. Then in 1947 he assisted in organizing the Theater Owners of America, to which the owners, operators and executives of motion picture theaters belong.

Recognizing the large impact television was having on America's entertainment habits, Goldenson in 1951 announced the decision to merge Paramount Theaters with the American Broadcasting Company. Two years later, when the merger was approved by the FCC, Goldenson was named president of the new firm. From the beginning American Broadcasting-Paramount Theaters Inc., known as AB-PT, made almost as much money from radio and television as it did from all its movie theaters. To combat the big name stars that CBS and NBC had, Goldenson succeeded in signing up Walt Disney to turn out television programs. The move proved to be a shrewd one: *The Walt Disney Show,* which aired in 1954, and *The Mickey Mouse Club,* aired the following year, became hits immediately and remained so for years to come.

The Disney deal was a major coup for Goldenson and ABC. Disney had earlier approached CBS and NBC, but neither was interested. Goldenson then concluded an eight-year contract with Disney to film his productions and help finance Disneyland in Anaheim, California. Later, critics charged that one result was that New York City's TV industry thereby lost out to Hollywood, and ultimately, so did the development of quality television.

Whatever the truth, under Goldenson's leadership

ABC produced programs like *The Lawrence Welk Show, Kukla, Fran and Ollie* and *Nightbeat* with Mike Wallace. The company improved its news coverage, while its sports coverage was second to none, including the long-running *Wide World of Sports* and its remarkable reporting of the tragic Munich Olympics in 1972, when PLO terrorists murdered 11 Israeli athletes.

In order to diversify company activities, in 1955 Goldenson formed Am-Par Record Corporation, which makes phonograph records, and bought a 50 percent interest in Wind Tunnel Instrument Company Inc. in 1956.

By the early 1970s, however, ABC had slumped to third place among the three networks. Goldenson made a dramatic move that was to turn network programming on its ear. He lured away Fred Silverman, then the top programmer of the number-one network (CBS), to ABC. Under Silverman's leadership, ABC became the leading network by 1976, with innovative programs like *Soap*—a weekly (and then-controversial) parody of soap operas, with no holds barred on the subject matter it treated—and others. When Silverman left ABC to head NBC several years later, however, his masterful touch in programming seemed to have stayed behind at ABC, because he failed to move NBC out of the "cellar" while ABC remained on top. Goldenson became chief executive officer and chairman in 1972—a new post created for him as he continued to expand and diversify ABC. In 1978 he got rid of the last of the movie theaters owned by the company—which had turned out not to be a good business venture—and expanded into publishing, record production and distribution, and three recreational parks in Florida.

ABC has become what *Dun's Review* magazine called among the "five best managed companies." Goldenson built up each part of ABC one by one, using profits generated from one successful venture to finance a move into a new one. He is also responsible for pioneering in the production of Hollywood-produced television series and specials. Known for creating an atmosphere of innovation and experimentation, he urged ABC to expand its radio network services. Today, ABC has four separate radio network services with more than 1,700 affiliates.

ERIC GOLDMAN

b. June 17, 1915
Historian

As an unpaid special consultant to President Lyndon Johnson during the mid-1960s, historian and Princeton University professor Eric Goldman not only brought the insights of his academic background to the federal government but drew from his experience a unique, firsthand knowledge of how America's top policy makers think and work. His White House appointment was the result of Goldman's renown as one of the top scholars of American liberalism and reform during the 20th century.

Eric Frederick Goldman was born in Washington, D.C. to Harry E. and Bessie (Sauer) Goldman. His father ran a fruit and vegetable stand in Baltimore but turned to taxi driving when the Depression wiped out his business. Goldman, who worked as a youngster in a variety of odd jobs, was educated in Baltimore's public schools and graduated from Baltimore City College, a public high school, in 1931. He entered Johns Hopkins University on a scholarship and combined undergraduate and graduate studies in American history. He earned an M.A. degree in 1935—he never received a B.A. degree—and completed his Ph.D., also in American history, three years later. From 1935 to 1940 Goldman was an instructor at Johns Hopkins and from 1940 to 1942 was a national affairs writer at *Time* magazine.

In 1942 Goldman joined the faculty of Princeton as an instructor. Although he continued writing for *Time* for several years more, he focused on his academic career. He became an assistant professor in 1943 and in 1947 was named associate professor. He became a full professor in 1955 and was appointed Rollins Professor of History in 1962. Goldman was a popular teacher on campus, and his courses were always filled to capacity.

During the 1940s Goldman contributed regularly to *The New Republic,* a prominent liberal publication, and he completed several short books. The first was *Charles J. Bonaparte, Patrician Reformer: His Earlier Career* (Baltimore, 1943), a biography of the American activist; and the second, published the same year, was *John Bach McMaster, American Historian* (Philadelphia), an expansion of his master's degree thesis.

But Goldman's most significant contribution to American history was *Rendezvous with Destiny: A History of Modern American Reform* (New York, 1952), which received Columbia University's Bancroft Prize. A history of American reform from the Civil War to 1950, it traced two trends within the liberal movement. One trend concerned the rights of the individual against big business and big government, while the other focused on the role of government to assure the well-being of its people. A sequel to *Rendezvous,* entitled *The Crucial Decade: America 1945–55* (New York, 1956), explored the prospects for the continuation of the liberal tradition on both the domestic and international levels. It

became a best seller and was nominated for the National Book Award. In 1960 it was republished as *The Crucial Decade—and After* (New York).

Goldman's fame grew as a result of his writings, and he published articles in popular magazines like *Harper's, Life, National Geographic, Saturday Review* and *Holiday* as well as in scholarly journals. He also traveled to Eastern Europe in 1953 to 1954 and to India in 1957 as a State Department lecturer. In 1959 he became moderator of the NBC-TV program *The Open Mind,* one of the first discussion programs addressing intellectual issues to a sophisticated group of panelists and to knowledgeable viewers. The show, which Goldman moderated until 1967, won Emmy Awards in 1962 and 1966.

Goldman was named to Lyndon Johnson's staff in early 1964 on the recommendation of a former student who had become an influential aide in the administration. In his capacity as special consultant, Goldman assembled panels of experts in domestic and foreign affairs to advise and to help formulate policy. He was thus closely involved with many of the national social programs that President Johnson initiated. However, Goldman resigned in 1966, in growing opposition to Johnson's Vietnam policy, and in 1969 published a personal memoir and a history of the Johnson administration entitled *The Tragedy of Lyndon Johnson* (New York). In it he focused primarily on Johnson's positive achievements—the reforms he introduced during his first year in office—and later explored how the president was undone by his involvement in escalating the war in Vietnam. The book became a popular best seller and was described by Max Frankel in *The New York Times* as "one of the best journalistic accounts of L.B.J."

From 1975 to 1976 Goldman served as a commentator for CBS News and in 1976 was America's first representative in a newly created United States-Canada intellectual exchange program. In 1978 *Rendezvous with Destiny* was published in a 25th-anniversary edition. On that occasion *The New York Times* called the book "a modern classic."

MARSHALL I. GOLDMAN

b. July 26, 1930
Economist; professor

Wellesley College Professor Marshall Goldman's combined expertise in Russian area studies and in the economics of pollution has led to his becoming one of America's most distinguished scholars of the Russian economy and environment. In the fall of 1977 he was the first economist to be appointed Fulbright-Hayes lecturer at Moscow State University, and he has participated in many conferences between the United States and the USSR in an attempt to promote a positive exchange of information and better trade relations.

Marshall Irwin Goldman was born in Elgin, Illinois to Samuel, a wholesale liquor dealer, and Bella (Silvian) Goldman. He attended the Wharton School at the University of Pennsylvania, where he earned a B.S. degree in 1952, and Harvard University, where he received an M.A. degree in Russian studies in 1956 and a Ph.D. in economics in 1961. He has taught at Wellesley College since 1958, when he began as an instructor. He was assistant professor from 1961 to 1965, associate professor until 1968 and has been a full professor since then. He was chair of the Economics Department from 1971 to 1977.

Simultaneously, Goldman has been associate director of the Russian Research Center at Harvard since 1975 and since the early 1960s has had consultancies with several private corporations and foundations and with the U.S. departments of State and Commerce.

Goldman has traveled extensively in the Soviet Union and in Eastern Europe, studying Russia's marketing facilities, foreign and economic relations within the Soviet bloc and with neutralist countries, and problems of pollution resulting from expansion and industrialization. Some of his studies have compared how communist and capitalist systems produce different problems of environmental impact. While in Moscow in 1977, he delivered more than 40 lectures, including 20 to Soviet audiences and the remainder to foreign business executives and diplomats. He has attended international conferences on environmental disruption held in Tokyo in 1970, in Finland and France in 1971, and in the United States in 1972. In 1978 he was commissioned by the International Communications Agency of the U.S. government to lecture in Korea, Hong Kong and Japan; and in 1980 he visited the People's Republic of China to present a lecture series on the Soviet economy to the Chinese Academy of Social Sciences.

Goldman is the author of many books and articles about the Soviet economy and environment and has also written two studies on environmental control—*Controlling Pollution: The Economics of a Cleaner America* (Englewood Cliffs, N.J., 1967) and *Ecology and Economics: Controlling Pollution in the 70's* (Englewood Cliffs, N.J., 1972). In *Soviet Foreign Aid* (New York, 1967), he described trade programs by the Soviet government with Egypt, India, Afghanistan, the Middle East and Africa and illustrated how none of the aid recipients had accepted a communist regime. In *Detente and Dollars: Doing Business with the Soviets* (New York, 1975), Goldman looked at the possibilities of United States-Soviet trade. He concludes that "continued trade is dependent on mutually advantageous contractual arrangements rather than unilateral political and economic considerations." Again he returned to the Soviets' "most severe economic problems . . . the long-run prospects for fundamental improvement are very bleak" in an article in *The New York Times* (April 4, 1982). The article was titled "Let's Exploit Moscow's Weakness" and he continued to urge Washington policy-makers to recognize this development. "Given their problems, Soviet leaders may be prepared to cut back military expenditures and thus make some serious concessions," Goldman concluded. "We may lose a historic opportunity if we ignore this possible opening." *The Spoils of Progress: Environmental Pollution in the Soviet Union* (Cambridge, Mass., 1975) shows how rapid industrial growth and not the political system in the USSR has led to widespread environmental abuse.

In *The Enigma of Soviet Petroleum: Half Empty or Half Full?* (London and Winchester, Mass., 1980), Goldman analyzes a CIA report that includes data on Soviet energy resources and concludes that certain aspects of communist planning have resulted in inadequate petroleum exploration or in the improper monitoring of available resources. He notes that positive reforms, implemented in 1979 to enforce conservation, have helped stem waste. And he adds that although

> the Soviet Union has a long way to go . . . nonetheless, they have started to bestir themselves, and we in the United States should not be too patronizing. After all, our efforts at increased conservation, exploration, research and production leave much to be desired. Nor have we had the courage to adjust energy prices to world levels. Maybe someone can persuade the KGB to write a report about our energy problems.

For further information:
Goldman, Marshall I. *Comparative Economic Systems.* New York: 1964, 1971.
———. *Soviet Marketing: Distribution in a Controlled Economy.* New York: 1963.
———. *The Soviet Economy: Myth and Reality.* Englewood Cliffs, N.J.: 1968.

BENNY GOODMAN

b. May 30, 1909
Clarinetist; band leader

Benny Goodman, the most famous clarinetist and band leader of the 1930s and 1940s, became an idol to a generation of jitterbugging fans and is known throughout the world as the "King of Swing." As a result, his musical influence is still felt years after he stopped performing regularly.

Benjamin David Goodman was born in Chicago, the eighth of 11 children of David, a poor tailor from Warsaw, and Dora (Grisinsky) Goodman from Kovno in Lithuania. As a child, Goodman took music lessons at a local synagogue and at Hull House, the famous Chicago settlement house. Exhibiting an early musical talent, he began playing in Chicago clubs. By the age of 14, he left high school to perform full time. Playing in Chicago and, two years later, with Ben Pollack's band in Los Angeles, Goodman began to record solo and direct his own combos. By 1929 and for the five years following, he performed in a wide range of free-lance jobs, including a theatrical stint in New York City.

The turning point for Goodman came in 1933, when he met John Henry Hammond Jr., a well-known (and wealthy) jazz aficionado, impresario and critic who was responsible for introducing many new jazz talents to American audiences. Hammond arranged Goodman's first major recording and helped him form a band. During the 1934–35 season Goodman's band performed on a regular nationwide radio program, *Let's Dance,* as well as live before audiences, particularly on college campuses.

At this point Goodman's "swing" began to attract not only dancers, but listening audiences. He began giving concerts that sold out in major theaters across the United States, such as the March 10, 1937 performance at New York's Paramount Theater, where thousands danced in the aisle to Goodman, the "King of Swing." The greatest jazz soloists of the era joined his big band, and in a 1938 Carnegie Hall concert— memorialized since on broadcasts and recordings—he assembled trumpeter Harry James, drummer Gene Krupa, vibroharpist Lionel Hampton, pianist Teddy Wilson and others in a record-breaking (and record-selling) performance. The first significant white band leader to put black musicians on his bandstand was also responsible for making swing and jazz "respectable" and won fame for such songs as "Sing, Sing, Sing," "One O'Clock Jump," "Memories of You," "Stompin' at the Savoy" and "Don't Be That Way." In addition, he was among the first band leaders to integrate his musicians on a regular basis, among them Wilson, Hampton and singer Billie Holliday.

Since the end of World War II and despite the waning of enthusiasm for the big bands, Goodman's ensembles—large groups as well as trios and quartets— performed at the Brussels World's Fair in 1958, France, Southeast Asia, the Soviet Union and many other areas where his style of music had greatly influenced the local citizenry and musicians.

Goodman has also concentrated on his career as a classical clarinetist. In the early 1940s he performed in several concerts in New York City, and in 1949 he studied with Reginald Kell, a leading classical clarinetist who helped Goodman revamp his entire playing technique. Goodman has taught at the Juilliard School of Music and Boston University. He has played Mozart and Brahms with the Budapest String Quartet and commissioned a clarinet concerto from Aaron Copland. His influence as a swing clarinetist still remains enormous among the generation reared in the 1930s and 1940s and now among younger people who increasingly feel drawn to his style. In 1940 he abandoned his big band but since then has performed with smaller groups in Europe, Asia and the United States.

In 1955 Universal produced the film *The Benny Goodman Story,* with Steve Allen in the starring role. Goodman has had his own television show, *Swing into Spring,* in 1958 and 1959 and published his autobiography, *The Kingdom of Swing,* with Irving Kolodin (New York, 1939, 1961).

ELLEN GOODMAN

b. April 11, 1941
Journalist

Many journalists comment on what they see as observers on the sidelines. Ellen Goodman, who writes the syndicated newspaper column *At Large,* is very much a part of the world she writes about. Her subject is middle-class life and the changes that have occurred in it since the birth of the modern women's liberation movement. A popular and probing commentator who can laugh at herself as easily as at others, she has developed a huge national following through her column and her three books, many magazine articles and frequent appearances on radio and television.

Ellen Holtz was born in Newton, Massachusetts to Jackson Jacob Holtz, a lawyer, and Edith (Weinstein) Holtz. She graduated from Radcliffe College with a B.A. degree cum laude in 1963, married a young doctor and began a career as a researcher-reporter for *Newsweek* magazine. In 1965 she became a feature writer for the *Detroit Free Press* and in 1967 returned to her home base of Boston, where she began writing features for *The Boston Globe.*

Goodman's special ability to home in on the experiences of ordinary people—how their ideals conflict with the realities of their lives, and how they adjust to massive social change—soon surfaced in her writing, and by 1972 she began her own column. First appearing in the *Globe's* "Living" section (which in pre-feminist days was the "Women's Page"), the biweekly column was eventually switched to the editorial page when it became clear that it did not appeal exclusively to female readers. It was picked up for syndication in 1976 by the Washington Post Writers Group and now appears in more than 700 newspapers. Goodman has been a commentator on the CBS radio show *Spectrum* since 1978 and on the NBC television program *Today* since 1979.

In her writing, Goodman is never condescending, and one critic has gone so far as to call her "the thinking woman's Erma Bombeck." A divorcee herself and a single mother who relies on her family as an important source of support, Goodman has often focused on the changes in family structures, personal relationships and other social changes that have occurred in large part because of the women's movement. For example, in her book *Turning Points* (New York, 1978), she interviews 150 people whose lives have been altered either profoundly or indirectly because of the emergence of feminism. For example, a typically "macho" husband reveals how he has adjusted to his wife's working full-time, although he cannot entirely accept that she is now financially independent to a degree. And in her columns, which have been collected in two books, *Close to Home* (New York, 1979) and *At Large* (New York, 1981), she has even described her own foibles—her need, for example, for a regular schedule, to go to the office every morning and, before beginning work, to start out with coffee and a doughnut; "I get upset if my routines are changed," she writes.

Goodman is also a regular contributor to *McCall's* magazine and in a 1979 column, "Why Men Feel Like Failures and Women Don't," reflected that "while the women I know seem energized and even a touch manic, depression is running through the male half of the species like an Andromeda strain." Suggesting that men in the 1970s set impossibly high standards for themselves while women are pleased with the new level of their achievements, she added:

> I don't think this mass case of depression [among men] is part of a sexual see-saw—as women move up in the world, men feel relatively lower—though there may be some of that. Men are still suffering from expectations that were not only too high but too narrow. On the other hand, women at this moment in history have suddenly outreached their childhoods. But they have widened their definition of success, rather than transferring it. To the women in this transitional time, success is graded on a point system that counts personal as well as professional values.

In 1980 Goodman, who describes herself as part of the New Middle—the mass of people whose lifestyles would have been an anomaly 10 years ago, but which are now commonplace—received a Pulitzer Prize for her work.

NAOMI GOODMAN

b. August 26, 1920
Pacifist; feminist historian

Naomi Goodman has been described as an "active pacifist and feminist historian," an important figure in both movements. She has also been for many years the president of the Jewish Peace Fellowship, a 4,000-member havurah-type organization that believes that Jewish ideals and experience provide inspiration for a nonviolent way of life.

Naomi Ascher was born in New York City, the daughter of Moses, a businessman, and Helen (Meyerowitz) Ascher. She graduated from Wellesley with a B.A. degree in 1942 and subsequently studied at Columbia University from 1943–44 and at the Art Students League in 1945. She was originally drawn to interior design for religious institutions because of her marriage to the architect Percival Goodman in 1944. However, with the coming of the Vietnam War she turned increasingly to nonviolence as a way of resolving international conflict and as a method of breaking the interminable cycle of nations viewing war as merely an extension of politics. Between 1969–73 she worked as Secretary of the National Council to Repeal the Draft, a national coalition of groups from left to right wishing to end conscription—a result of the war in Vietnam and its constant demand for new draftees—and institute a volunteer army. During that period she also became a member of the national council of the Fellowship of Reconciliation, a religious group of pacifists first established in the United States in 1915 and in 1974 became a member of the executive committee of the International FOR. She was the first Jew to serve in this capacity, since IFOR was originated as a worldwide Protestant organization. She therefore represents Jews in an international religious peace movement.

Her most significant work as a pacifist has been with the Jewish Peace Fellowship, where she has served as president since 1972. Founded in 1941, the organization works mainly to establish and protect the right of young Jewish males to be recognized as conscientious objectors. Under Goodman's presidency, the JPF has continued its tradition of providing counseling for objectors, particularly concerning their beliefs in Judaism and against war. She has also expanded its activities, leading them to work on behalf of Soviet Jewry, for the rights of Falashas to be recognized as Jews and to be permitted to emigrate from Ethiopia to Israel and for a political and peaceful solution in the Middle East. In addition, she has been in the forefront of those Jews who wish to maintain a Jewish presence in the peace movement.

Goodman is equally a feminist writer. In *Eve, Child Bride of Adam,* edited by Marie Coleman Nelson and Jean Ikenberry (New York, 1979), she wrote of the impact of unrecognized incest in the Adam and Eve story in the debasement of the role of women and raises the question of why men in western society have had to deny their incestuous urges. She argues that Eve's birth from Adam's rib denigrated women and that her parthogenic birth from Adam's body made her his daughter. Thus, she concludes, the Judeo-Christian tradition is grounded on a form of father-daughter incest which goes unrecognized in male-dominated religious and psychological studies.

As a feminist historian, she is a member of the Institute for Research in History and of their work group in the study of women's history. In 1981 she presented a paper, "Images of Women in Judaism: Male Control of Women's Reproductive Functions as Documented in the Old Testament" at the Berkshire Conference in Women's History at Vassar College. In it she argued that the Hebrew scriptures assigned to women a main function, namely producing children. Even so, Eve and the celebrated four matriarchs are under reproductive control of one male God and can only give birth at his pleasure. Despite the fact that males praised their women, she insists that they were indeed powerless, since the males developed such controls to fortify their male-only religious system.

For further information:

Goodman, Naomi. "Flight of the Dove: The Story of Jeanette Rankin," *Fellowship.* December 1981.

———. "Liturgy for Survival," in *Human Security: Resources for Worship and Action.* New York: 1979.

———. "Pacifism, Not Passivism—Feminism Not Pseudo-Machismo," *Shalom,* Autumn 1977.

PERCIVAL GOODMAN

b. January 13, 1904
Architect

For more than 40 years Percival Goodman has been a major designer of synagogues and Jewish community centers across the United States. He is also a noted planner, with radical theories about the need to create environments that address the ecological and human limitations of the people who inhabit them. One of Goodman's most famous projects is his design for the Jewish Museum in New York City.

Percival Goodman was born in New York City to Barnet, an auctioneer, and Augusta (Goodman) Goodman. His father was never very successful, and shortly after the birth of Percival's younger brother Paul in 1911, he deserted the family, leaving Augusta Goodman alone to raise three children.

Goodman knew from the time he was very young that he wanted to be an architect, and at 13 he worked as an apprentice at an uncle's architectural firm. In 1925 he won the Prix de Paris, an award that enabled him to study fine arts and architecture at the Ecole des Beaux Arts from 1925 to 1929. Upon returning to the United States in 1930, he set up a private practice. He also taught architecture and planning, first as visiting critic at New York University in 1931, then at Columbia University as lecturer in city planning from 1944 to 1945. He joined the faculty of Columbia's School of Architecture and Design as professor in 1946. He became professor emeritus in 1972.

As an urban planner, Goodman has lectured widely and written extensively in addition to designing for cities. One of his best-known works is a book he wrote in collaboration with his brother Paul, who was a renowned social critic, entitled *Communitas* (Chicago, 1947). In the book they discussed on both concrete and theoretical levels how people interact with their environment and their potential to use it for good or for harm. Goodman's other major publication is *The Double E* (New York, 1977), based on a futuristic urban plan he had devised a year earlier. The two E's stand for "environment" and "ecology," and in the book Goodman lays out possibilities for the human community to cope with an increasingly large population with declining resources. Goodman is also widely known as one of the world's foremost designers of synagogues. He has, for example, designed houses of worship in Albany, New York (Temple Beth Emeth), Tulsa, Oklahoma (Temple Israel), Springfield, Massachusetts (Temple Beth El), Beechwood Village, Ohio (Fairmont Temple) and many more. *Architectural Forum* described his work in 1959 as "a genuine patron of the arts . . . who likes his art powerful, not fragile. Whether the subject is a painting, weaving or sculpture, his artistic appreciations are for large, simple shapes, strong hues. In a well-dressed, prim world he seems to be advocating the return of vigorous ancient ritualism." In 1979, Goodman amplified on his life's work, describing the synagogue of the future. He saw it as advancing a "Jewish" way of life within the general community. Here is a place where precept and practice merge, a place for those who believe; a good life is best achieved through mutual aid, compassion and meaningful work—since God created all, none may desecrate His handiwork—we strengthen our faith when we "sing unto the Lord a new song."

Goodman is also an accomplished graphic artist who has used this skill to illustrate some of his other futuristic urban plans. One of the best-known is entitled "City of Efficient Consumption," a 1938 proposal for a self-sufficient urban entity.

As a native New Yorker, Goodman has participated in a range of design projects as a member of the Mayor's Panel of Selected Architects and for the New York City Board of Education. He is a member of the American Institute of Architects and other planning organizations and is an honorary member of the Architects and Engineers of Israel.

WALTER GOODMAN

b. August 22, 1927
Author; editor

Walter Goodman is a writer and editor who received special acclaim from his extraordinary 1968 book *The Committee* (New York), a study of the House Un-American Activities Committee. The author of several other books on American historical topics, Goodman was an editor at *The New York Times* and between 1979-1982 was director of humanities programming at the public television station WNET/Thirteen in New York City.

Walter Goodman was born in New York City to Hyman, a coat manufacturer, and Sadie (Rybakof) Goodman. He received a B.A. degree, magna cum laude, from Syracuse University in 1949 and an M.A. degree from Reading University in England in 1953.

From 1954 to 1955 Goodman was a staff writer for *The New Republic* in Washington, D.C. and from 1957 to 1974 was a senior editor with *Redbook Magazine*. He was a contributing editor at *Playboy* from 1960 to 1961 and in 1974 joined the *Times* as assistant editor of its Sunday "Arts and Leisure" section. He became deputy editor of the *Sunday Magazine* in 1976 and in 1977 became a member of the *Times* editorial board. At WNET Goodman was executive editor of *City Edition*, a twice-weekly news show, and of *Skyline*, a weekly culture series hosted by Beverly Sills. He then became involved in one of the most ambitious programs to be produced by WNET/Thirteen, a series entitled *Civilization and*

the Jews, hosted by Abba Eban and filmed in sites around the world. *Civilization and the Jews* will be aired in 1983. In 1982 he joined *Newsweek* as a writer.

Goodman is a writer who has chosen as subjects aspects of American social and political history that he feels have been tainted by hypocrisy and compromise. His first book, *The Clowns of Commerce* (New York, 1957), took a critical view of the American advertising industry and its manipulation of consumers. It was followed in 1963 by *All Honorable Men* (Boston), a study of scandals that had racked American government and business during the previous 10 years.

With *The Committee* he established himself as both a fine historian and an astute analyst of human behavior. He traced the history of the House Un-American Activities Committee from its creation in the 1930s until 1967, interweaving psychological analyses of the men who ran it and the people who were called as witnesses to it with commentary about the actual accomplishments of the committee. According to historian Arthur Schlesinger Jr., Goodman has a "good understanding of the symbioses between the committee and witnesses," although he occasionally "sacrifices pathos to comedy." Although Schlesinger felt that Goodman did not do "full justice to the genuine wreckage which the committee made of people's lives," he nevertheless called it a "glorious piece of Americana" and a "first-rate historical study, exhaustive in research, cool in judgment."

The following year Goodman probed into another subject with *Black Bondage* (New York, 1969), a study geared to teen-age readers that explored the lives of plantation slaves in the American South during the second quarter of the 19th century. Using extensive documentation and first-person accounts, Goodman reconstructed the era, trying not only to explain slavery from the slave's point of view, but from the slaveowner as well. The book earned him a Christopher Award.

In *A Percentage of the Take* (New York, 1971), Goodman switched to a contemporary issue, the indictment and trial of a former New York City water commissioner who was jailed for bribe taking. In fact, the book was an exploration of the kind of corruption that in Goodman's view was a commonplace event in urban politics. Three years later Goodman co-wrote with Patsy Anthony Lepera *Memoirs of a Scam Man* (New York, 1974), an account of how Lepera used legitimate business and the banking industry to extort money for himself and for the Mafia through counterfeit scams, questionable loans, stock manipulation and other means.

Goodman, who was a Guggenheim Fellow in 1974, has lectured at the Bread Loaf Writers Conference in Middlebury, Vermont and at the Columbia School of

Journalism. A monthly columnist for *The New York Times Book Review* and a regular contributor to *The New Leader,* he has also written articles and reviews for *Life, Harper's* and other publications.

RICHARD N. GOODWIN

b. December 7, 1931
Author; attorney

Until the escalating war in Vietnam caused him to leave government service, Richard Goodwin was one of the closest confidants of President Lyndon B. Johnson and one of the architects of the president's liberal domestic programs. A brilliant young lawyer and a confirmed activist who had been a speechwriter with President John F. Kennedy, Goodwin distinguished himself as one of the most forceful and perceptive policy makers of the Great Society.

Richard Naradof Goodwin was born in Boston to Joseph C., an engineer, and Belle Fisher (Goodwin). Both his parents were immigrants, and the middle name "Naradof" was his father's family's surname prior to immigration to the United States.

Early on, Goodwin proved to be a gifted thinker and writer. At both Tufts University, where he received a B.A. degree summa cum laude in 1953, and at Harvard Law School, which he entered after serving two years in the U.S. Army (1953–55) and where he earned his Bachelor of Laws degree in 1958, he graduated first in his class. He was also president of the *Harvard Law Review.* From Harvard, Goodwin went to Washington, D.C., where he clerked for U.S. Supreme Court Justice Felix Frankfurter for one year from 1958 to 1959. Immediately thereafter he began his political career, first as assistant to then-Senator John F. Kennedy, and then, with long-time Kennedy aide Theodore Sorenson, as a speechwriter for the successful Kennedy campaign for the presidency in 1960.

After Kennedy's election Goodwin, only 30, was appointed assistant special counsel to the president. His first duties were as deputy assistant secretary of state for internal American affairs, and under this rubric he headed a small Peace Corps school. In 1963 he was named deputy assistant secretary of state and, with the expertise he had developed on Latin America, helped forge the Alliance for Progress.

Goodwin was nonetheless resented by some government officials, perhaps for his youth as well as for his quick accession to high position. Yet after Kennedy's assassination, he remained in the Johnson White House, became one of the new president's principal speechwriters and was named special assistant to the president in 1964. In his new post Goodwin drafted many of Johnson's poverty, civil rights and conservation programs and supervised the formation of task forces to oversee program development and execution. Goodwin was at the center of the Great Society—he is credited with coining the name—and wrote one of Johnson's most powerful speeches, in which the president sided with civil rights activists then staging massive demonstrations in the South.

Despite Goodwin's successes in Washington, he became increasingly disenchanted with the Johnson administration as it increased its contributions of money, military hardware and personnel to the fighting in Vietnam. He therefore quit the Johnson administration in the autumn of 1965 to become a fellow at Wesleyan University's Center for Advanced Studies, although he retained a close friendship with the president and wrote Johnson's 1966 State of the Union address.

In the meantime Goodwin was quite public about his own politics and in 1966 published *Triumph or Tragedy: Reflections on Vietnam* (New York), which provided a detailed and highly critical analysis of how the U.S. government had begun its incursion into Vietnam and how, through continual misjudgments, it had become involved. The book laid the groundwork for Goodwin's later attempt at a meeting of Americans for Democratic Action to form a national war resisters movement as well as to spearhead a "Dump Johnson" movement. In fact, under the pseudonym "Bailey Laird," he published an article in *The New Yorker* on September 16, 1967 documenting a strategy to push Johnson out of office.

Goodwin wanted to replace Johnson with Robert Kennedy, but before Kennedy would commit himself to run, Goodwin joined the camp of Senator Eugene McCarthy. He switched to Kennedy when the latter finally announced his candidacy but, following Kennedy's assassination, rejoined McCarthy in 1968 although he felt McCarthy could not win.

Goodwin left politics in 1968 to devote more time to teaching and writing. His next book, *The American Condition* (New York, 1974), purported to document the meaning of the American Dream during the 1960s and its slow erosion as materialism—represented by the constant push for increased productivity—began to sell out the Dream and individual freedom along with it. One critic referred to the book, written as a series of essays, as "an act of intellectual despair," while another called it the "confused reaction of a frustrated and depressed political activist."

For further information:
Goodwin, Richard N. *The Sower's Seed: A Tribute to Adlai Stevenson.* New York: 1965.

ROBERT GORDIS

b. February 6, 1908
Rabbi; professor

Robert Gordis, professor of biblical studies at the Jewish Theological Seminary of America, is a widely respected rabbinical scholar here and in Israel. Founder and editor of *Judaism* magazine, he is a prolific writer. He also founded the Beth-El (later renamed Robert Gordis) Day School in Belle Harbor, New York.

Robert Gordis was born in Brooklyn to Hyman, an insurance broker, and Lizzie (Engel) Gordis. He received his B.A. degree from the City College of New York in 1926 and his Ph.D. in Jewish studies from Dropsie College in Philadelphia in 1929. In 1932 he was ordained as a rabbi at the Jewish Theological Seminary of America.

Gordis taught at Hebrew Teachers Training School for Girls from 1926 to 1928, Yeshiva College from 1929 to 1930 and the Seminary College of Jewish Studies from 1931 to 1932. He lectured at the seminary from 1937 to 1940 and since 1940 has been professor of biblical studies at the Jewish Theological Seminary of America. He also has been a visiting professor at Temple University from 1967 to 1968 and at the Hebrew University in Jerusalem in 1970. From 1932 to 1969 Gordis was the congregational rabbi for the Rockaway Park (N.Y.) Hebrew Congregation.

Affiliated with the Conservative movement, Gordis has written many articles in which he expresses his belief that Halakhah must be influenced by the realities of contemporary Jewish life. Therefore, many of his books focus on the role of Judaism in modern society. For example, in *Judaism for the Modern Age* (New York, 1955), Gordis looks at Jews in the United States and explores their attitudes toward religion, their cultural traditions and Israel. In *A Faith for Moderns* (New York, 1960), he discusses the nature of religion, the concept of God and the relationship between God and humankind.

An eloquent spokesperson for organized religion, he examines how Judaism can be used to help find solutions to the world's major problems in *The Root and the Branch: Judaism and the Free Society* (Chicago, 1962). In this book Gordis discusses religious liberty in Judaism, the relationship between church and state, and the questions of religion in education and government aid to parochial schools, using the Bible, Talmud and Mishnah

to examine questions of race, democracy and nationalism, among others.

Other books by Gordis include *The Book of God and Man: A Study of Job* (Chicago, 1965), which considers the biblical book of Job as literature and its relevance to all people, and *Poets, Prophets and Sages: Essays in Biblical Translation* (Indiana, 1970), a collection of essays that deal with the origin and growth of the Bible, the structure of biblical poetry and individual Bible books such as the Song of Songs and Koheleth. In *Love and Sex—A Modern Jewish Perspective* (New York, 1978), he deals with divorce, birth control, homosexuality, and premarital and extramarital sex within the context of Jewish religious teachings.

A contributing editor to *Jewish Digest* and *Jewish Quarterly* and a contributing writer to many magazines, he accused President Jimmy Carter, in a 1979 article in *The Jewish Week-American Examiner,* of lacking the courage to expose to public view "the details of the campaign waged by the financial allies and henchmen of the Shah [of Iran]. Thus the United States has given asylum in America to one of the major tyrants and oppressors of the age."

Gordis founded *Judaism* magazine, which he has edited since 1969. He sees it as a medium of expression for all Judaic points of view—Orthodox, Conservative, Reform, secular, etc.—and as a forum to stimulate young people to think about the sociological as well as the religious aspect of Judaism.

Gordis has been on the executive committee of the Hillel Commission since 1960 and is currently on the national administrative council of the United Synagogue of America. He is past president of the Rabbinical Assembly and the Synagogue Council of America and is a member of the National Conference of Christians and Jews.

CYRUS H. GORDON

b. June 29, 1908
Historian and Semitic scholar

Cyrus H. Gordon is an eminent and prolific Semitic scholar and archaeologist whose studies of ancient cultures in the Near East have won him international recognition.

Cyrus Herzl Gordon was born in Philadelphia to Benjamin Gordon, a physician who was deeply interested in the history of medicine, and Dorothy (Cohen) Gordon. He was educated in the Philadelphia public schools and graduated from Gratz College, where he was certified as a teacher of Hebrew and Judaica in 1926. He earned his B.A. degree in 1927, his M.A. degree in 1928 and his Ph.D. in 1930, all from the University of Pennsylvania. His doctoral dissertation was entitled "Rabbinic Exegesism in the Vulgate of Proverbs" and was later published (Philadelphia, 1930).

His professional and academic work in Near Eastern history began immediately. Gordon was an instructor at the University of Pennsylvania from 1930 to 1931; an archeologist at the American School of Oriental Research in Baghdad, Iraq from 1931 to 1935; a teaching Fellow in Oriental Studies from 1935 to 1938 at Johns Hopkins University; a Lecturer at Smith College from 1938 to 1939 and 1940 to 1941; a member of the Institute for Advanced Study at Princeton, New Jersey from 1939 to 1940 and 1941 to 1942; a Professor of Assyriology and Egyptology at Dropsie College from 1946 to 1956; and the Joseph Foster Professor of Near Eastern Studies and Chairman of the Department of Mediterranean Studies at Brandeis University from 1956 until 1973. In that year he joined the faculty of New York University as Gottesman Professor of Hebraic Studies.

His scholarly studies, *Ugaritic Grammar* (New York, 1940) and *Ugaritic Text* (New York, 1949) altered the grammar of the language and proposed heretofore unknown transliterations. *In The Common Background of the Greek and Hebrew Civilizations* (New York, 1965— revised from *Before the Bible),* he compared Eastern and Western civilizations—"Helleno-Semitics" was his term —by studying early Greece and the Near East. His range of scholarship is broad and his reputation among his peers is extraordinarily high. Fellow scholars described *Ugaritic Grammar* and *Ugaritic Text* in their reviews as seminal. The latter book earned for Gordon a certificate of merit from the Academy for Liberal Judaism in 1956.

In 1962 he wrote that the ancient Cretan language of the Minoans was actually Semitic or Phoenician. Drawing on linguistic evidence and other proof, he also asserted that despite the traditional interpretation of generations of scholars, the Greeks and Hebrews were indeed parallel civilizations that grew from an identical Semitic base in the Near East.

In *Before Columbus: Links Between the Old World and Ancient America* (New York, 1971), Gordon claims that as far back as 5,000 years ago, European, African and Asian sailors had visited the Western Hemisphere and in some cases mixed with mesoAmerican cultures, producing the Incan, Mayan and Aztec peoples. Gordon illustrates this thesis by pointing out similarities in pottery, mythology, myths and religious rituals in the cultures under discussion. Not all scholars, however, accept his view.

The recipient of many awards and fellowships, Cyrus Gordon also won the UJA 40th Anniversary Award in 1979 for "distinguished record of service to the Jewish people and the very special qualities of leadership." He holds memberships in the American Historical Association, the American Oriental Society, the Society of Biblical Literature, the Archaeological Institute of America and the American Society for Study of Religion. He has written more than 20 books and hundreds of articles.

For further information:

Gordon, Cyrus H. *Adventures in the Nearest East.* New York: 1958.

———. *The Ancient Near East.* New York: 1965.

———. *Forgotten Scripts.* New York: 1968 and 1971.

———. *Hammurabi's Code.* New York: 1957.

———. *Loves and Wars of Baal and Anat, and Other Poems from Ugura.* New York: 1943.

———. *Smith College Tablets.* Northhampton, Mass.: 1952.

———. *Ugaritic Textbook,* fifth enlarged edition. Pontifical Biblical Institute: 1967.

Gordon, Cyrus H., editor and translator. *The Living Past.* New York: 1941.

VICTOR GOTBAUM

b. September 5, 1921
Labor leader

Victor Gotbaum, the powerful and influential labor leader of New York City's District Council 37, the largest union of public employees, is also a well-known liberal and reformer who has long fought for the economic rights of working people.

Victor Gotbaum was born in Brooklyn to Harry and Molly (Bernstein) Gotbaum. While working as a teenager in a factory managed by his father, he learned that blacks were earning less than whites. He threatened to "walk off the job" unless the blacks got equal pay, and he won. After his graduation from Samuel Tilden High School in 1939, he worked as a pressman—a "disaster," he said—until 1943, when he was drafted into the Army. In the military, away from the security of Brooklyn's Jewish community, Gotbaum encountered anti-Semitic epithets for the first time. But he won six battle stars and became a sergeant.

He was surprised by the warm reception concentration camp survivors of Buchenwald gave him when he came to the area as an education-information instructor. "My upbringing did not prepare me for Buchenwald. I took my Jewishness for granted," he told *The New York Times* years later. "The war and Buchenwald made me an emotional and cultural Jew. I call myself a fellow traveller of Israel now." In another, even later, interview, he said that his pride in Jewishness arose from its message of social justice.

When he returned to the United States, Gotbaum studied political science at Brooklyn College, receiving his B.A. degree in 1948. Two years later he was awarded his M.A. degree in international affairs by Columbia University.

Gotbaum taught school in Brooklyn in 1950–51, then joined the State Department as a foreign service officer. Several months later his career took another turn when he moved to the Department of Labor. He served as a labor education specialist in Turkey in 1954–55 until he was offered a job as an assistant education director for the Amalgamated Meat Cutters Union in Chicago.

Gotbaum found he preferred the trade union movement to government service. In late 1957 he became executive director of District Council 19, the Chicago area division of the American Federation of State, County and Municipal Employees (AFSCME). He made headlines by refusing to grant his union's routine and traditional support for the popular but demagogic Mayor Daley.

In 1965 Gotbaum moved to New York to head District Council 37, which grew to 122,000 members before the city's budget crisis forced layoffs. A political liberal, Gotbaum was noted for his ability to unify diverse groups of ethnic and professional members, whose jobs included, among others, stenography, physical therapy and computer programming.

His tenure at DC 37 has been marked by growth in services to the union's thoroughly integrated membership. For example, the union sponsors its own college at its headquarters in downtown Manhattan and extensive personal counseling services. Such concern for members' welfare has made Gotbaum a secure union leader and a powerful influence in municipal government. Gotbaum is frequently consulted by city and state officials in New York whenever major fiscal or labor-related changes are being planned.

LYNN GOTTLIEB

b. April 12, 1949
Rabbi

In every facet of her life as a Jewish woman, Lynn Gottlieb—Rabbi Gottlieb since 1981—has been a fighter, a pioneer and a leader. For many years she has

ministered in sign language to deaf congregations in the U.S.; she spearheaded the efforts of women to be ordained within the Conservative movement; and she has been a major force, through feminist theater and storytelling, in helping other women realize their Jewish heritage and their potential as modern Jews.

Lynn Gottlieb was born in Bethlehem, Pa., to David Abraham Gottlieb, a businessman, and Harriett (Coleman) Gottlieb, who was a puppeteer and the director and teacher of a theater school until her death in 1971. Raised in Allentown, Gottlieb attended public schools, graduating from William Allen High School in 1967. She also spent several months in 1966 as an exchange student at Leo Baeck High School in Haifa.

When it came time for further study, Gottlieb was determined to become a rabbi—a calling she says came to her when she was only four. But at the time, the route was closed to women, and she studied at several universities, including the State University of New York at Albany and Hebrew University in Jerusalem, completing a B.S. degree in 1972. Over the next nine years, she focused on preparation for the rabbinate, studying at Hebrew Union College in New York, at the Jewish Theological Seminary, and privately with different scholars and rabbis.

Meanwhile, because of her own difficulties in attaining recognition in her quest, and because of her personal beliefs, she became a vocal adherent of Jewish feminism, traveling throughout the U.S. to meet with women's groups and to perform what she calls "life cycle ceremonies."

Moreover, even without official ordination, Gottlieb served as rabbi for a deaf congregation, presiding since the mid-1970s at Temple Beth Or of the Deaf in Hollis, Queens, New York, and holding workshops on Jewish subjects at the Hebrew Association of the Deaf in New York City. She has also worked with the two other congregations for the deaf in the U.S., one in Skokie, Ill., the other in Van Nuys, California. She learned sign language from deaf members of her congregation, and with her background in theater and pantomime, was able to incorporate it in her subsequent religious preaching and storytelling.

Gottlieb's other major efforts involve activity in the peace movement and in alternative ways of celebrating Judaism. She is a board member of the Jewish Peace Fellowship and has been closely involved with New Jewish Agenda, a movement made up of mostly younger Jews seeking alternatives to the more conventional policies of organized American Jewry.

Gottlieb's involvement with New Jewish Agenda evolved naturally, after years of efforts to become ordained were thwarted by the Jewish "establishment." By 1980, even some Conservative Jewish leaders, most notably Rabbi Seymour Siegel, a professor of theology and ethics at the Jewish Theological Seminary, had become vocal in their support of ordination for women. For years, women had been enrolled at the Seminary as undergraduate and graduate students, but the rabbinate had been denied them, and as recently as December 1979, the seminary's faculty senate voted to table the recommendations of a faculty commission in favor of ordination. In 1981, Gottlieb finally turned for ordination to three rabbis prominent in "alternative" Judaism — Zalman Schachter, Everett Gendler and Shlomo Carlebach.

But Gottlieb is probably best-known for her work as a Jewish storyteller, work that has taken her to scores of synagogues, hospitals, college campuses and high schools, and other organizations across the United States, alone or with Bat Kol, a small troupe of feminist actors who portray Biblical women or other heroines of ancient and recent Jewish history. Often performing for women's groups, the troupe then has discussions with its audience about women, Judaism and other issues their work raises.

When in New York she participates as rabbi in a *havurah*, a small community of Jewish men and women who pray together in Mishkan-A-Shul, an informal synagogue that holds services in different sites in the city.

It is Gottlieb's work as a woman seeking full and equal recognition within the Judaic tradition that preoccupies her and affects her other activities. "God has a female presence," she once said, but noted, "the female presence is in exile. It is not until we redeem Her and bring Her home to rest in us that the entire world will be redeemed." Her nine-year quest for the rabbinate and her subsequent ordination privately by three teachers represented the beginning of the end of exile.

ROBERT GOTTLIEB

b. April 29, 1931
Publisher; editor

As chief editor and president of Alfred A. Knopf Inc., Robert Gottlieb has successfully balanced popular book publishing with a steady output of literature by some of America's finest authors. He was responsible for acquiring the novel *Catch-22* by the then-unknown Joseph Heller and has subsequently helped launch the careers of numerous young talents.

Robert Adams Gottlieb was born in New York City, the only son of Charles, an attorney, and Martha (Keen) Gottlieb, a schoolteacher. He graduated from Columbia University with a B.A. degree, Phi Beta Kappa, in

1952. Following two years of postgraduate study at Cambridge University, he returned to New York, where he became editorial assistant to Jack Goodman, then editor in chief of Simon and Schuster. When Goodman died two years later, Gottlieb assumed many of his responsibilities and became the editor for such authors as Meyer Levin, Walter Kerr and S.J. Perelman. He rose through the ranks at Simon and Schuster, eventually becoming editor in chief and a vice president.

According to Gottlieb, Joseph Heller, at the time an advertising copywriter, brought his manuscript for a whacky and bitter World War II satire, *Catch-18*, to Simon and Schuster and was convinced by the editor not only to make several major structural changes but to change the title, because best-selling author Leon Uris was about to publish a novel about the Warsaw ghetto called *Mila 18*. Needless to say, *Catch-22* (the number was suggested by Gottlieb) became a phenomenal best seller—and a hit movie some years later.

In 1968 Gottlieb was offered control of Alfred A. Knopf Inc., a division of Random House, where he became both editor in chief and executive vice president. He became president in 1973. There he has cultivated the fiction writing of such authors as John Updike, John Cheever, Doris Lessing, Toni Morrison and Chaim Potok, as well as the work of historian Barbara Tuchman and other writers. He has introduced the work of lesser-known writers Laurie Colwin and Scott Spencer and has produced best sellers for Knopf in the autobiographies of stage and screen stars Lauren Bacall, Sidney Poitier and Liv Ullman. He also acquired Jonathan Schell's *The Fate of the Earth,* the so-called "bible" of the nuclear freeze movement.

Gottlieb is not, like many editors, a writer as well but is a master craftsman who skillfully guides his authors toward the most cohesive organization of their material without infringing on their creativity. His subtle style is one reason authors stay with him and explains why Heller moved to Knopf to publish his second successful novel, *Something Happened.* "I can't see anything without wanting to fix it," Gottlieb said once, describing his approach to his work. "If I hadn't been an editor, I would have been an analyst, or a director, or a rabbi."

ALFRED GOTTSCHALK

b. March 7, 1930
Rabbi; professor

Alfred Gottschalk has combined the best traditions of Jewish scholarship and communal service to become one of Reform Judaism's major spokesmen. Named president of the Hebrew Union College—Jewish Institute of Religion (HUC-JIR) in Cincinnati, the flagship school for the training of Reform rabbis, he has been a member of the United States Holocaust Memorial Council since its creation in 1978.

Alfred Gottschalk was born in Oberwesel, Germany to Max, a businessman, and Erna (Grum-Gerson) Gottschalk. In 1939 his family fled the Nazis and settled in New York. From 1945 to 1948 Gottschalk, who was naturalized in 1945, attended Boys High School in Brooklyn. He then entered Brooklyn College, where he received a Bachelor of Arts degree in 1952. For the next five years he studied at HUC-JIR. He received a Bachelor of Hebrew Literature degree from its New York City campus in 1954 and completed an M.A. degree at its Cincinnati campus in 1956. He was ordained there the following year.

Gottschalk's role in Jewish higher education has been an influential one. From 1957 to 1958 he directed the California branch of HUC-JIR, which was then just forming, was its acting dean from 1958 to 1959 and from 1959 to 1971 was dean. During this period he completed a Ph.D. at the University of Southern California in 1965. At the same time he taught history and religion at the extension division and summer school of the University of California at Los Angeles in 1965, 1966, 1968, 1970 and 1971. He was active with the Southern California Historical Society and with several civic groups in Los Angeles, including the Mayor's Community Development Advisory Committee, the Governor's Poverty Support Corps Program and the Joint Committee on the Master Plan for Higher Education. He is past president of the Southern California Association of Liberal Rabbis.

In 1971 Gottschalk was named president of HUC-JIR and returned to Cincinnati. As in California, he has served in community organizations, such as the Cincinnati Council on World Affairs. He is a member of the American Civil Liberties Union.

Gottschalk's leadership is matched by his scholarship. Professor of Bible and Religious Thought since 1965, he has written extensively on Jewish history. Further, many of his works focus on Jewish service, such as *Your Future as a Rabbi: A Calling That Counts* (New York, 1967) and *The Future of Human Community* (Los Angeles, 1968). In 1979, in honor of Gottschalk's well-known dedication to community outreach, HUC-JIR established the Alfred Gottschalk Chair in Jewish Communal Service.

But perhaps Gottschalk's most significant contributions are as a pioneer in the evolution of Reform Judaism both in America and in Israel. He ordained the first woman rabbi in Jewish history and was responsible for opening graduate and rabbinical programs to larger numbers of women. In Jerusalem he supervised the ordination of Reform rabbis for congregations in Israel, beginning in 1980. This latter accomplishment is especially significant since Orthodox Jewish leaders have traditionally questioned the legitimacy of the Reform movement and have been notoriously hostile toward it.

Beyond his commitment to the Jewish community is Gottschalk's strong support of ecumenism, which stresses the importance of mutual understanding, collaboration and toleration among different religions while simultaneously appreciating and accepting the identities of each one. Gottschalk has similarly fought for such ecumenism with Jewish groups.

As a refugee from the Nazis, Gottschalk has been equally outspoken in his support for a permanent memorial to the Holocaust. As a member of the interdenominational Holocaust Council, he participated in recommending the creation of a Holocaust museum and memorial in Washington, D.C., an ongoing educational foundation to promote scholarly research on the Holocaust and the development of educational materials on the primary and secondary school levels. He also supports a day of remembrance of victims of the Holocaust.

For further information:

Gottschalk, Alfred. "Ahad Ha-Am as Biblical Critic—A Profile." *Studies in Jewish Bibliography, History, and Literature* in honor of I. Edward Kiev, edited by Charles Berlin. New York: 1971.

———. "Maimonides, Spinoza and Ahad Ha-Am." *Judaism*, 21 Summer 1972.

———. "Abraham Joshua Heschel, A Man of Dialogues," *Conservative Judaism*, 28 Fall, 1973.

———. "A Passion for Social Justice." (*Kivie Kaplan—A Legend in His Own Time*), edited by S. Norman Feingold and William B. Silverman, New York: 1976.

———. "Israel and Reform Judaism: A Zionist Perspective." *Forum*. Fall-Winter 1979.

ELLIOTT GOULD

b. August 29, 1938
Actor

Handsome and funny, Elliott Gould skyrocketed to fame in the late 1960s as a film star who represented the young and rebellious 1960s generation. Among his best-known movies are *M*A*S*H, Bob and Carol and Ted and Alice* and *Getting Straight*.

Elliott Goldstein was born in Brooklyn to Bernard, who worked in the garment industry, and Lucille (Raver)

Goldstein. He lived in the Bensonhurst neighborhood of Brooklyn until his teens when his family bought a home in West Orange, New Jersey. Encouarged by his mother, he studied speech, singing, dance and drama in Manhattan from the age of 8. By the age of 10, he had been on television shows including *The Colgate Comedy Hour.* (His mother renamed him "Gould" when he got his first television job; she believed it sounded nicer than Goldstein.)

After graduation from P.S. 247 and a neighborhood Brooklyn Hebrew school in 1951, Gould enrolled at the Professional Children's School in Manhattan. He sang and danced at Catskill resorts during summer holidays. Gould graduated from the Professional Children's School in 1955 and attended Columbia University for a brief period. It was during that time that he began looking for dance chorus work on Broadway. His first job was as a chorus boy in *Rumple,* an unsuccessful 1957 musical. During the next few years he held minor roles in Broadway and summer stock shows. In 1960 he succeeded Fred Gwynne as Polyte-le-Mou in *Irma La Douce.*

In 1962 Gould played the leading role in David Merrick's Broadway show *I Can Get It for You Wholesale.* Gould—who received mixed reviews as the amoral Harry Bogen, who lies until he reaches the best job in New York's garment center—married the play's star, Barbra Streisand, not long after the play closed. In 1963 Gould appeared in the London production of *On the Town* and the following year co-starred with Carol Burnett in a television presentation of *Once Upon a Mattress.*

Overshadowed by his wife's successes, Gould began studying with famed Lee Strasberg at the Actor's Studio, where, he says, he learned to act for the first time. This development was obvious when he acted in Jules Feiffer's *Little Murders* on Broadway in 1967. While critics generally liked his performance, they were offended by Feiffer's brand of humor. The play closed after only five days.

By portraying likable, irreverent, often irresponsible young men, Gould became increasingly popular. After appearing in the 1968 film *The Night They Raided Minsky's,* which was about a post-World War I burlesque theater in New York City, Gould signed with Columbia Pictures to appear in a film that became the hit of 1969. The film, *Bob and Carol and Ted and Alice,* directed by Paul Mazursky, portrayed the wife-swapping of two married couples who want to prove they can keep up with the new, swinging "with-it" style of life. Critics admired Gould's performance as the casual, ordinary Ted, who is thoroughly perplexed by his wife and friends and the inordinate requests they make on him. He won an Academy Award for the role.

In his next film, *M*A*S*H* (1970), Gould show-cased his comedic abilities as Trapper John, a sophisticated young surgeon determined to sabotage the Army's institutional rigidities. Gould again won much praise for *Getting Straight* (1970) as a graduate student caught between university bureaucracy and student revolutionaries. Gould has appeared in many subsequent films, including *Little Murders* (1971), *The Long Goodbye* (1973), *Spys* (1974) and *California Split* (1974). He remains a major film celebrity.

CHAIM GRADE

b. April 4, 1910
Poet; novelist

Chaim Grade, the Yiddish poet and novelist, is one of contemporary Jewry's finest interpreters of pre-World War II village life in Lithuania and Poland. A native of Vilna, he has been called the present-day Jewish national poet for the emotional and evocative lyrics of his verse, much of which is based on his experiences as a refugee and survivor of the Holocaust.

Chaim Grade was born in Vilna, Lithuania, the only child of Schlomo Motte, an impoverished teacher of Hebrew, and Vella (Blumenthal) Grade. After his father died while Grade was still young, his mother managed a fruit stand in order to assure her son a good education. He studied in some of the finest yeshivot in Vilna and was especially influenced by the renowned scholar and rabbi Hazon-Ish.

Vilna was a flourishing Jewish cultural community, and Grade was drawn to, and then became active in, the literary movement called Young Vilna. At that time efforts were being made to bring *Yiddishkeit* more in touch with the world literary community and to make it more accessible to less privileged Jewish homes. Grade moved with the trend and as a result began publishing his poetry in Yiddish journals throughout Europe and in America. During the early 1930s he abandoned his religious aspirations and attained prominence for his elegant lyrics, which at once reflected the traditions of an earlier age but also acknowledged the energy and progressiveness of the present. His first poems appeared in 1932 in the Vilna *Tog.* He published his first book, *Yo* (Vilna, 1936), and a major long poem, *Musernikes* in 1939. In both, the affirmation of faith and tradition combined with the need to make peace with the modern world were central themes. In the latter, Grade was the model for his figure Chaim Vilner, a young man struggling to reconcile the spirituality of his yeshiva background and his efforts to live a contemporary worldly life.

Grade ultimately turned to socialism, and in 1941,

as the invading German armies rolled across Poland and into Vilna, he fled eastward to the Soviet Union. For the next four years he survived by working on a collective farm and ultimately settled in Moscow. There he was befriended by Soviet Jewish writers, almost all of whom were executed by Stalin in the years following the end of the war.

In 1946 he returned to liberated Vilna and was horrified to learn of the death and destruction of his family—including his mother and his first wife—friends and city and departed for Paris with his second wife, whom he had met while living in Moscow. In Paris, Grade became active in the Yiddish literary movement among a community of survivors living there. But two years later he left again, this time for the United States, where he was a delegate to the Jewish Culture Congress. Settling in New York he began to write for the daily Yiddish newspaper *Jewish Morning Journal* while continuing to publish poems and novels.

Among the poems to emerge during that post-Holocaust period were "Dayres" ("Generations," 1945), which included a poem to his first wife called "Dayn Guf oyne Mayne Hent" ("With Your Body in My Hands"); Pleytim" ("Refugees," 1947); and "Shayn fun Farloshene Shtern" ("Light of Extinguished Stars," 1950).

Yiddish readers have honored Grade with nearly every award; indeed, he has been compared to Dickens because of his abiding interest in the problems of ordinary people as well as to Saul Bellow and William Faulkner. Yet until recently he might just as well have been writing in Urdu or in Finnish for all the literary world knew of him. Since 1967, however, his audience has begun to grow, as Rutgers University scholar Curt Leviant has translated many of his works into English. Despite the fact that much of Grade's writing contains religious references unknown to the layperson—which adds to the difficulty of translation—its almost-photographic imagery provides a unique insight into the recent Jewish past, which is nonetheless ancient history to many young readers.

Grade's novels were well received by literary critics. *The Agunah* (in Yiddish, New York, 1961; in English, 1974) related the story of a wife whose husband had been declared missing during World War I, yet she was not permitted to remarry because there were no witnesses to his death. His two-volume epic novel *The Yeshiva* (in Yiddish, New York, 1961; in English, New York, 1976)—its second volume was titled *Masters and Disciples* (New York, 1977)—is written on a broad canvas and tells the tale of yeshiva life. Elie Wiesel called Grade "probably the greatest living Yiddish writer. If he were writing in any other language, he would have been already recognized as the creator of masterpieces."

Many of Grade's poetic themes emanate from his experiences in the Soviet Union. He once recalled a conversation with the Soviet Jewish writer David Bergelson, who tried to persuade Grade to remain in the Soviet Union. Grade refused. "I am leaving," he told Bergelson, "because I am afraid it will be too easy for me to learn to write the way you want me to write." (On the evening of August 12, 1952, in the basement of Lubyanka prison in Moscow, Bergelson and 23 other Soviet Jewish writers were executed. Their murders have since obsessed Grade. Many years later, still anguishing over their deaths, he wrote a poem in their honor, "Elegy for the Soviet Yiddish Writers," which was translated into English by American writer Cynthia Ozick. "You left me your language, lifted with joy/ But, oh, I am bereft/ I wear your Yiddish like a drowned man's shirt/ wearing out the hurt."

He expressed his feelings as a writer to Morton Reichek after so many exiles and so many experiences:

> I have a complex. I don't know how to talk to non-Jewish readers. I want to talk to them, but I don't know how to. I will never understand American psychology. Therefore I don't write about America. . . . There is not enough time. I will never make it in your world.

Grade won the Jewish Heritage award for excellence in literature in 1976 and is a recipient of the B'nai B'rith award for excellence.

For further information:

Biletsky, I. *Essays on Yiddish Poetry and Prose Units.* New York: 1969.

Howe, Irving, and Greenberg, E., eds. *A Treasury of Yiddish Stories.* New York: 1954.

Leftwich, J., ed., *The Golden Peacock.* New York: 1961.

Whitman, R., ed. *Anthology of Modern Yiddish Poetry.* New York: 1966.

ADOLPH GREEN

b. December 2, 1915
Lyricist

With his writing collaborator, Betty Comden, lyricist Adolph Green has produced some of the most sophisticated musical entertainments of the American stage and screen. His songs include such classics as "The Party's Over," "Just in Time" and "Singing in the Rain." He has won Tony awards for *Wonderful Town* (1953), *Hallelujah Baby!* (1968) and *Applause* (1970).

Adolph Green was born in the Bronx to David and

Helen (Weiss) Green. He took a job as a Wall Street runner after he graduated from DeWitt Clinton High School in 1934. He was looking for acting work when he met Miss Comden. Their collaboration began when they, Judy Holliday and two other aspiring actors teamed up in 1939 to write and perform a cabaret act at the (Greenwich) Village Vanguard.

Green and Comden were only in their twenties when they wrote the book and lyrics for *On the Town*, their first of many Broadway musicals. The 1944 musical-comedy about three sailors on a 24-hour leave in Manhattan opened to rave reviews and made theater history because it was the first show in which its authors were also actors. It also helped secure the career of the musical's young composer, Leonard Bernstein.

All of Comden and Green's compositions have been written with a show or movie in mind. The collaborators meet every day in the living room of Comden's Upper East Side town house. Though at times they just sit and stare at each other with no inspiration, they believe that the continuity of working is important. They attribute the success of their partnership to the fact that they don't ever remember who thought up what line. They describe their work process as "mental radar."

In addition to their Tony award-winning shows, Comden and Green's other Broadway credits include *Say Darling* (1958), *Do Re Mi* (1960), *Bells Are Ringing* (1968), *On the Twentieth Century* (1977) and *A Party with Betty Comden and Adolph Green* (1958 and 1977). Among the films they have worked on are *Singin' in the Rain* (1952), *Band Wagon* (1953), *Auntie Mame* (1958) and *What a Way to Go* (1964).

GERALD GREEN

b. April 8, 1922
Writer; novelist

Gerald Green is well-known as the author of numerous commercially popular novels, including *The Last Angry Man* (New York, 1957). He won an Emmy Award for the screenplay of *Holocaust*, a television miniseries about the Nazi era that drew worldwide attention and acclaim.

Gerald Green was born in Brooklyn to Samuel, a doctor, and Anna Ruth (Matzkin) Greenberg. He obtained his B.A. degree in 1942 and his M.S. degree in journalism in 1947, both from Columbia University. He served in the United States Army from 1942 to 1946.

Green worked as editor for the International News Service from 1947 to 1950 and since 1950 has intermit-

tently been a producer and writer for NBC. Among the long-running programs he worked on are *The Today Show*, *Wide Wide World*, *Chet Huntley Reporting* and a number of documentaries.

Green's books resonate with a strong undercurrent of moral judgment. They not only entertain but deal with issues of major social concern. His most famous book, *The Last Angry Man*, depicts a Brooklyn doctor, like his father, who lives for 40 years in the slums of Brownsville in Brooklyn and is angry at the injustice he witnesses. The novel, written with integrity and compassion, received rave reviews. He has also published *The Lotus Eaters* (New York, 1959), a satiric novel set in Miami Beach that portrays corruption, vulgarity and sensuality; *The Heartless Light* (New York, 1961), a novel about a kidnapping that is a scathing indictment of American journalism; and *To Brooklyn With Love* (New York, 1968), a story about a boy's youth in Brooklyn during the Depression. About the latter, a *New York Times Book Review* critic wrote: "Mr. Green has the power to touch us where it hurts."

But it was his teleplay *Holocaust* (subsequently published as a book, *Holocaust: A Novel of Survival and Triumph*, (New York, 1978) that capped his career as it brought the unimaginable and unprecedented Nazi policy of genocide into homes around the world. While some Jews criticized it as a trivialization of a unique and cataclysmic event, many more defended it for its message and power. In 1979 Green was awarded the Prix International Dag Hammarskjold for the novel on which the television series was based.

Among his other works are *Faking It; or, The Wrong Hungarian* (New York, 1971), a suspense story that satirizes the American literary establishment and parodies the standard spy novel; *The Stones of Zion: A Novelist's Journal in Israel* (New York, 1971), a diary of observations written while visiting archeological sites in Israel; *An American Prophet* (New York, 1977), a novel about a retired literature professor who becomes active in promoting the preservation of nature; *The Hostage Heart* (New York, 1976) and *The Healers* (New York, 1979), both medical novels.

IRVING GREENBERG

b. May 16, 1933
Rabbi

Rabbi Irving Greenberg, director of the National Jewish Resource Center, is one of America's most important Orthodox rabbis, respected across denominational lines as a thinker, lecturer and Holocaust scholar who is trying to bridge the gap between religious and secular, tradition and the modern world.

Irving Greenberg was born in Brooklyn the son of Elias, a ritual slaughterer and rabbi of a small congregation of Orthodox immigrants, and Sonia (Szbinovitz) Greenberg. He received a B.A. degree summa cum laude from Brooklyn College (1953) and an M.A. degree (1954) and Ph.D. in American history (1960) from Harvard University. He was ordained at the Beth Joseph Rabbinical Seminary in 1953.

Greenberg believes that Jewish history has entered a period in which the covenant between God and the Jewish people is being renewed, a period of renewed revelation in the aftermath of the Holocaust and the rebirth of Israel. This "third era" of Jewish history (succeeding the biblical and rabbinic periods) requires a major infusion of new values into Jewish ways of life. All Jews, Greenberg believes, must be open to tradition, but even the Orthodox must incorporate new values into their daily rituals. Cross-fertilization is necessary as so-called secular Jewish organizations adopt religious values to deal wtih social and political concerns and religious groups adapt to the modern world.

Greenberg was director of the Hillel Foundation and lecturer in Judaic studies at Brandeis University (1957–58), rabbi of the Riverdale Jewish Center from 1965 to 1972. He was then chairman of the Jewish Studies Department at the City University of New York (1972–76) and professor of Jewish studies at CUNY (1972 to the present). He pursued research on the Holocaust in Jerusalem under a National Endowment for the Humanities grant in 1974–75.

Much of Greenberg's influence stems from the frequent lectures he gives to groups throughout the world as director of the National Jewish Resource Center, which he founded in 1974 with Elie Wiesel. Greenberg uses the National Jewish Resource Center as a base from which to pursue research on the Holocaust and to develop his theories of cross-ideological Jewish life, developing resource materials and sponsoring conferences that bring together branches of the Jewish community that rarely meet otherwise.

Greenberg co-edited *Confronting the Holocaust: The Impact of Elie Wiesel* with Alvin Rosenfeld (Bloomington, Indiana, 1978). Otherwise, much of his writing has been confined to articles in a variety of Jewish religious, educational and intellectual journals.

Greenberg helped found Yavneh, the national religious Jewish students organization as well as the Center for Russian Jewry, parent of the Student Struggle for Soviet Jewry, and serves on both of their advisory boards.

He is on the executive committee of the United States Holocaust Memorial Council, the board of trustees of the Joint Distribution Committee and the Federation of Jewish Philanthropies in New York, and the board of directors of the American Histadrut Cultural Exchange Committee. In 1970 he helped found the Association for Jewish Studies, the professional organization for Jewish studies in American universities.

For further information:

Greenberg, Irving. "Cloud of Smoke, Pillar of Fire: Judaism, Christianity and Modernity After the Holocaust," in Fleischner, Eva, ed., *Auschwitz: Beginning of a New Era?* New York: 1977.

———. "Judaism and Christianity After the Holocaust." *Journal of Ecumenical Studies,* Fall 1975.

———. "On The Third Era in Jewish History: Power and Politics." New York: National Jewish Resource Center, 1980.

———. "The End of Emancipation." *Conservative Judaism,* Summer 1976.

———. "New Revelation and New Patterns on the Relationship of Judaism and Christianity." *Journal of Ecumenical Studies,* Spring 1979.

JOANNE GREENBERG

b. September 24, 1932
Author

Joanne Greenberg is a highly acclaimed novelist whose books have often been devoted to describing the troubles that beset disabled people. Her best-selling *I Never Promised You a Rose Garden* (New York, 1964), written under a pseudonym, Hannah Green, and portraying a young, Jewish schizophrenic girl, was made into a successful film.

Joanne Goldenberg was born in Brooklyn to Julius Lester, a lawyer, and Rosalie (Bernstein) Goldenberg. She received her B.A. degree in 1955 from American University in Washington, D.C., where she majored in anthropology and English literature. Interested in the historical approach to language, Greenberg has taught at Ralston Elementary School in Colorado since 1963.

Encouraged by her husband, a vocational rehabilitation counselor for the state of Colorado, Greenberg published her first book, *The King's Persons* (New York) in 1963. The novel is an account of the York Massacre of 1190, centering on Jewish moneylenders and their relationship with the Christians among whom they lived. It was praised for re-creating a little-known aspect of English history with dialogue that echoes biblical cadences, simple Anglo-Saxon speech and the contrast between the warmth of Jewish communal life and the practice of usury.

The author established herself as a major talent with *I Never Promised You a Rose Garden,* a dramatic tale of an intelligent, psychotic girl and her agonizing fight to reenter the "normal" world. Critics were impressed by the novelist's ability to depict the internal world of a schizophrenic, stating that it seemed as though the author were writing from personal experience.

Through her husband's work with deaf clients, Greenberg became interested in communicating with the deaf and has assisted in setting up mental health programs for the deaf. She has also written about the plight of handicapped people. In *Monday Voices* (New York, 1965), the author focuses on a government agency for occupational rehabilitation, begging for society's support for the lame. In her novel *In This Sign* (New York, 1970), Greenberg focuses on a married deaf couple and their daughter who can hear. She vividly presents the isolation of the deaf couple and the burden felt by their daughter. She has published a collection of short stories in *Summering* (New York, 1966), which dealt with the plight of the stranger and society's pariah. One of the stories described a young Jewish girl whose marriage takes her back to the New York City ghetto that her grandfather fought to escape.

Greenberg is winner of the 1967 Fromm-Reichmann Award of the American Academy of Psychoanalysis.

In *A Season of Delight* (New York, 1981), Greenberg relates with warmth and compassion a tale of children who have abandoned the Jewish tradition for cults and modern fads and fashions. As a volunteer for a local fire and emergency rescue squad, the heroine meets a young man—born a Jew but untutored in Judaism—and rediscovers passion and friendship. Her major theme, the rejection of parents' values by their children's generation, is probed incisively. In a complex metaphor she likens Jews to someone hemorrhaging and in shock and doomed unless there is an immediate blood transfusion.

ALAN GREENSPAN

b. March 6, 1926
Economist

Alan Greenspan, a leading business economist, has long been the confidant of Republican presidents. A firm supporter of traditional Republican economic poli-

cies such as fiscal restraint and the need for a balanced budget, he served as the chairperson of the Council of Economic Advisors for presidents Nixon and Ford.

Born in New York City to Herman Herbert, a stockbroker, and Rose (Goldsmith) Greenspan, Alan Greenspan attended George Washington High School, where he was two grades behind Henry Kissinger, and graduated in 1943. He then studied music at the Juilliard School and toured the United States in 1944 as a clarinetist. Deciding against a career in music, Greenspan entered New York University and received his B.S. degree summa cum laude in economics in 1948. Two years later he received his M.A. degree, also in economics, from Columbia University, where he studied under Arthur F. Burns, who later became the chairperson of the Federal Reserve Board.

In 1948 Greenspan joined the Conference Board, a nonprofit research group for business, serving as an economist. Four years later he formed an investment counseling company. After the death of his partner, William Townsend, in 1958, Greenspan became the president of Townsend-Greenspan and Co., which caters to a small but select clientele, including most of the 100 largest financial and industrial concerns in America as well as the top 10 banks. Greenspan's firm provides its clients with research, forecasts and other economic consulting services.

From 1953 until 1955 Greenspan taught economics at New York University. His economic philosophy has been heavily influenced, he says, by Ayn Rand's concept of "rational selfishness." In fact, Greenspan met Rand in 1952 and remained her friend and disciple for 20 years. Therefore, Greenspan is hostile to the concept of the "welfare state" and is a firm believer in the free market.

Greenspan was a top economic aide to Richard Nixon in 1967 and served as Nixon's director of domestic policy research in the 1968 presidential campaign. He served in the transition period between the Nixon and Lyndon Johnson administrations, but he declined a full-time role in the Nixon White House. However, during Nixon's first term in 1969, Greenspan did serve on the Task Force on Economic Growth, the Commission on Financial Structure and the Commission on an All-Volunteer Army, in which he favored an end to military conscription.

Greenspan campaigned for Nixon again in 1972, and he assumed the chairmanship of the Council of Economic Advisors in 1974. Under Nixon he argued for less governmental regulation, a reduction of tariff rates and opposition to wage and price controls. When Gerald Ford became president that same year, Greenspan was retained in that key economic position and soon became one of Ford's closest aides. During his tenure with the Council of Economic Advisors, Greenspan pushed for a strong program against inflation, calling for budgetary restraint and a tough monetary policy. And during the Reagan administration, he has been a strong backer of the president's efforts to pare the budget for domestic programs severely.

Greenspan completed his Ph.D. in economics at N.Y.U. in 1977, the same year he left government to resume the presidency of Townsend-Greenspan and Co. He is a director of General Foods Corp., J.P. Morgan Co., Morgan Guaranty Trust Co., Mobil Co. and Alcoa. Greenspan is also a member of the board of economists of *Time* magazine and an adjunct professor at the Graduate School of Business at New York University. He is a member of the board of overseers of the Hoover Institute of War, Revolution and Peace at Stanford University.

JOEL GREY

b. April 11, 1932
Actor; singer; dancer

In 1966, after years of playing the "warm-up" act in nightclubs and small roles in minor films, Joel Grey catapulted to fame as the macabre master of ceremonies at the Kit-Kat Club in the hit Broadway musical about the pre-Hitler Weimar Republic era, *Cabaret*. His critically acclaimed performance won him a 1967 Tony award and in 1973 an Academy Award as Best Supporting Actor for the film version. The diminutive, 5'5" actor also won the Variety Critics Award as Best Actor and a Tony nomination for his title role in the 1969 Broadway musical *George M*.

Joel Katz was born in Cleveland, Ohio to a theatrical family descended from Russian Jews. His parents, Mickey and Grace Katz, performed in a Yiddish vaudeville troupe directed by his father, and it was here that Joel Katz first learned to sing and dance. His formal dramatic career began at age 10, when he played the role of Pud in *On Borrowed Time* at the Cleveland Playhouse. During his teen-age years he performed in his father's show *The Borscht Capades*. After completing high school—by which time the Katz family had been living in Los Angeles for several years—Katz dropped plans to attend college, and changing his name from "Katz" to "Kaye" and finally to "Grey," he headed toward a solo nightclub career. After being spotted by Eddie Cantor in a Miami performance, he was booked on Cantor's television show and then performed in some of the best-known clubs in the United States, including the Chez Paree in Chicago and New York's Copacabana.

However, the nightclub circuit did not suit Grey's talents or personality, and during the mid-1950s he left club work and began studying acting at the Neighborhood Playhouse in New York, where his teachers included Wynn Handman and Sanford Meisner. During the years before his big break in *Cabaret*, he acted in what he calls a series of "Grade Z" films, including the forgettable *About Face, Calypso Heat Wave*, and *Come September*. He starred as Jack in a 1956 NBC-TV "Producers Showcase" production of "Jack and the Beanstalk," which received mixed reviews, and appeared in a Phoenix Theater production of *The Littlest Review* the same year.

His Broadway debut occurred in 1961, when he replaced Warren Berlinger in Neil Simon's *Come Blow Your Horn*. His next Broadway roles were also the result of understudying for stars: In 1963 he took over Anthony Newley's role in *Stop the World, I Want to Get Off*, and two years later replaced Tommy Steele in *Half a Sixpence*.

But *Cabaret* signaled a turnaround for Grey. No longer a career understudy, he initially received second billing in the show. But when his rave performance became the drawing card, he demanded and got first billing with his co-star. Roles were now virtually his for the asking. In 1969 he was acclaimed by critics for his sensitive portrayal of George M. Cohan in the 1969 Broadway musical and the 1970 television adaptation of *George M*. His next two Broadway shows were less successful, however. *Goodtime Charley*, the 1975 musical in which he starred as the dauphin who became King Charles VII of France, was an instant failure; and *The Grand Tour*, the 1979 musical adaptation of a play by S.N. Behrman in which Grey played Jacobowsky, a Polish Jew escaping from the Nazis, had a limited run. But the role Grey played was personally meaningful to him. As he told *New York Times* reporter Robert Berkvist: "I've never played a Jewish person before. I've played Nazis and Irishmen and WASPs—but never a Jew. It feels good."

And, to that end, Grey was an activist outside the theater, serving in 1974 as West Coast chairperson of the Committee to Free the Panovs. Valery Panov, a Jew, and his wife, Galina, who were acclaimed ballet dancers in Russia, had been denied visas to emigrate to Israel but meanwhile had been forbidden to perform. Pressure from western countries finally forced the Soviet government to let the Panovs leave, and in 1974 Grey received the Israel Cultural Award in San Francisco for his efforts.

Grey has also appeared in the films *Man on a Swing* (1974), *The Seven Per Cent Solution* (1976) and Robert Altman's *Buffalo Bill and the Indians* (1977). Also in 1977 he appeared off-Broadway in John Guare's play

Marco Polo Sings a Solo; and in 1980 he made his opera debut as Officer Olim, a character who shoots a man for stealing a pineapple and later regrets it, in a revival of Kurt Weill's opera *Silverlake* for the New York City Opera.

But the cabaret experiences Grey knew as a child remain integral to his career. A vibrant performer who exudes energy from the stage, whether singing or dancing, Grey continues to perform at clubs in New York and other cities singing many of the songs he grew up with. He has also made one recording, *Songs My Father Taught Me,* which includes nostalgic Yiddish ballads and lullabies, Israeli songs and other romantic melodies.

CHAIM GROSS

b. March 17, 1904
Sculptor, graphic artist

Chaim Gross has made a highly individual and distinctive contribution to sculpture in America. At a time when many artists are reaching for new materials and methods, Gross has rediscovered an ancient medium, wood, and ancient methods of shaping it.

Chaim Gross was born in Wolowa in the Carpathian Mountains of East Austria, the 10th child of Moses and Leah (Sperber) Gross. His father, a Hassid, was a lumber merchant. At the beginning of World War I, Gross's town was pillaged by warring Russian and Austrian troops. He fled to Hungary but was deported from that country in 1919. In 1921 he joined his brother Naftali in New York City.

Gross found work as a delivery boy and began to study art at the Educational Alliance on the Lower East Side. The school had a polyglot environment, with immigrant students from all over the world, and they nurtured each other's artistic development. In 1925 Gross studied under Elie Nadelman at the Beaux Arts Institute, and in 1927 he studied for a short period of time at the Art Students League, where he learned the fundamentals of wood carving from Robert Laurent.

Gross held his first one-man show at The Gallery on West 13th Street in New York City in 1932. With the coming of the Depression, he joined the WPA's Federal Art Project. He won a commission to do a direct carving called *Alaskan Mail Carrier,* which stands in the office of the Postmaster-General in Washington, D.C. He also did a figure of the dancer Helen Tamiris for the James Monroe High School in the Bronx and a stone lintel piece for the Federal Trade Commission building in Washington, D.C. In 1937 Gross won the national sculpture prize of the Art Program of the U.S. Treasury, which had replaced the Federal Art Project. He also won the silver medal at the Paris Exposition that same year.

Jewish themes were not among Gross's subjects in his early work. However, after a visit to Israel in the 1950s, he began to reexamine his Jewish roots, and from then on a Jewish consciousness dominated both his sculpture and his graphic art. Traditional Judaic ritual and Hassidic lifestyles now became common inspirations for Gross, who thereafter received many commissions from synagogues, hospitals, universities and other institutions with Jewish, as well as non-Jewish, affiliations. He did *Six Days of Creation,* a series of six plaques, for Temple Shaaray Tefila in New York City, and *The Ten Commandments* for the International Synagogue at Kennedy Airport in New York. Gross's sculpture *Birds of Peace* stands on the campus of the Hebrew University in Jerusalem. His sculpture *Mother Playing,* a design of a mother happily at play with her child, which stands in front of a large pavilion at Jerusalem's Hadassah Medical Center, is typical of the exuberance and sensitivity of Gross's work.

Gross, who can be described as an expressionist artist, has won prizes from the Pennsylvania Academy of Fine Arts, the National Institute of Arts and Letters, and the American Academy of Arts and Letters and received an honorary degree from Yeshiva University in 1978. He has had many one-man shows. The major ones include an exhibit at the Whitney Museum of American Art (1959) and two shows at the Jewish Museum (1953 and 1977)—the latter show was a major retrospective. His work is featured in the permanent collections of museums all over the world, including the Tel Aviv Museum and the Metropolitan Museum of Art in New York City.

For further information:
Gross, Chaim. *Chaim Gross: Sculpture and Drawing.* Washington, D.C.: 1974.
Gross, Chaim, with text by Getlein, Frank. *Chaim Gross.* New York: 1974.
Gross, Chaim, with text by Werner, Alfred. *Chaim Gross: Watercolors and Drawings.* New York: 1980.

HENRY ANATOLE GRUNWALD

b. December 3, 1922
Editor

As editor in chief of Time Inc., Henry Grunwald is one of the most powerful editors in the world. Under his leadership, *Time* magazine promoted its points of view, created task forces from several editorial departments to deal with major trends, expanded its use of color photography and completely redid its typographical format.

Henry Grunwald was born in Vienna, the son of Alfred, a playwright, and Mila (Lowenstein) Grunwald. He came to America in 1940 and was naturalized eight years later. Grunwald received his B.A. degree in philosophy from New York University in 1944.

While still in college Grunwald began to work part-time at night for *Time* in 1944 as a copyboy. He left briefly to be a reporter for a labor newspaper but returned to *Time* in 1945. At the end of his first year at the magazine, Grunwald was assigned to the foreign news department. In the six years that followed, he wrote 30 cover stories ranging in subject from Pope Pius to the American sexual revolution.

In 1951 Grunwald became the youngest man ever to be named a senior editor at *Time*. Since then Grunwald has been an editor in most of the departments of the magazine, and he was the first editor of the "Essay" section, which offers a subjective and personal view of events. In 1966 Grunwald was appointed assistant managing editor, and two years later he became the managing editor.

During Grunwald's tenure as managing editor, the magazine introduced several new departments, including sections on the environment, behavior and the sexes, and energy. At the same time, under Grunwald's tutelage, *Time* has maintained its centrist political perspective. It has done special issues on the transition from President Nixon to President Ford, on blacks in America, Jewish leadership in America and two Bicentennial issues that were written as if *Time* had existed during the era of the American Revolution. An article in *New Republic* in 1981 accused *Time* of being consistently anti-Israel. In September 1981, during the Reagan administration's efforts to sell AWACS and other arms to Saudia Arabia, *Time* suggested that sanctions be applied against Israel if necessary. Critics insist that under Grunwald's aegis, the magazine showed repeated biases— e.g., pro-nuclear power, attacks on various politicians and its generally lukewarm approach to any serious criticism of big business. Whatever the truth, it remains extraordinarily powerful and is read throughout the non-Soviet world.

In 1977 Grunwald was appointed corporate editor of Time Inc., and two years later he became editor in chief of all Time Inc. publications. In 1979 he was elected to the board of directors of Time-Life Books Inc., Time Inc. and the *Washington Star*.

Grunwald still occasionally writes for *Time* and has contributed essays on the contemporary challenges of patriotism, the conflict over the First Amendment (freedom of the press) and South Africa. He contributed a long biographical essay about Winston Churchill to a collection of articles published as *Churchill: The Life Triumphant* (New York, 1965). Grunwald also edited *Salinger: A Critical and Personal Portrait* (New York, 1962), which explores the life and writings of author J.D. Salinger. In both books he combined a critical if sympathetic perspective with his own knowledge of each man.

For further information:

Grunwald, Henry A. *The Age of Elegance*. New York: 1966.

————. *Sex in America*. New York: 1964.

HERBERT GUTMAN

b. March 18, 1928
Historian

Herbert Gutman is one of the most prominent American historians specializing in social history and Afro-American history. His studies of black American families from Colonial days to the 20th century, especially *The Black Family in Slavery and Freedom, 1750-1925* (New York, 1976), are landmarks of the genre.

Herbert Gutman was born in New York City to Joseph and Anna (Zaentz) Gutman. He earned his B.A. degree from Queens College in 1949, his M.A. degree in American history from Columbia University in 1950 and his Ph.D. in American history from the University of Wisconsin in 1959. Gutman has taught at Fairleigh Dickinson University (1956-1963), the State University of New York at Buffalo (1963-1966) and the University of Rochester (1966-1972). He returned to New York in 1972 to accept the chairmanship of the History Department of the City College of New York. Gutman is currently professor of history at the Graduate School of the City University of New York.

Among his many honors Gutman has served as Harrison Distinguished Visiting Professor of History at the College of William and Mary (1976–77) and as Neilson Visiting Research Professor of American Studies at Smith College (1977–78). He has held fellowships and research grants from the National Endowment for the Humanities (1975–76), the Ford Foundation (1978–79) and the Rockefeller Foundation (1977–79).

Herbert Gutman's books have opened up new areas of exploration in American social history and challenged many prevailing views. After researching black history for 10 years, Gutman wrote *Slavery and the Numbers Game: A Critique of Time on the Cross* (Urbana, Illinois, 1975), in which he challenged the conclusions reached by a number of economists that slavery was a benign institution and not as cruel as it was portrayed to be. In *The Black Family in Slavery and Freedom, 1750-1925,* Gutman demonstrated the strength and vitality of the black family as it confronted slavery and freedom and examined the changes forced upon it by urbanization, industrialization and new forms of racism. The research was prodigious and the book was hailed by many historians as seminal and long overdue, challenging the view expressed by other scholars that the black family was disintegrating. Gutman tried to show—with plantation birth and death records and other primary evidence, almost always overlooked by earlier investigators—that slavery and poverty did not destroy the family among black people and that through "powerful familial and kin associations" they supported the evolving Afro-American culture.

Along with his studies of black history, Gutman has been interested in American immigration history and especially the conflicts working class immigrants faced in trying to preserve their own culture yet having to survive in the American workplace. In *Work, Culture and Society in Industrializing America, 1815-1920* (New York, 1976), Gutman examines these tensions in a collection of essays which previously appeared in scholarly journals. A common theme is the impact of industrialization on workers who grew up in a pre-industrialized America.

In addition to writing and teaching at CUNY, Gutman is the director of the History and Humanities Program at the Graduate Center of the City University of New York.

HESKEL HADDAD

b. September 26, 1928
Physician; Sephardic leader

Heskel Haddad has combined a career as a researcher and practitioner in pediatric ophthalmology with leading the movement to raise international consciousness regarding the plight of Jews still living in Arab lands. A native of Iraq, he experienced firsthand many of the degrading conditions to which these Jews have been subjected.

Heskel M. Haddad was born in Baghdad to Moshe,

a plumbing contractor, and Mesuda (Cohen) Haddad. Raised in an affluent family but nonetheless in Baghdad's Jewish ghetto, Haddad had early contact with anti-Semitism. In one instance, when he was 10 years old, he was so threatened by three Moslem children that, he has said, "if adults hadn't intervened, I think they would have killed me." In 1941 a Haddad cousin was one of nearly 900 Iraqi Jews killed in a pogrom spearheaded by Arab rebels sympathetic with the Nazis. These experiences fueled his drive to learn more about his Jewishness, and in 1945, after graduating from the Shamash Secondary School, he enrolled in the Baghdad Yeshiva. However, he soon switched to medical studies and entered the Royal College of Medicine in Baghdad. He quickly distinguished himself there, and in 1946 he won the Boswell Prize for Biology. With the founding of Israel in 1948, renewed anti-Semitism in Iraq resulted in Haddad's expulsion from the school. He managed, however, to take final exams—he scored highest in his class —and completed his studies in 1950. Soon after, he emigrated with his parents and five siblings to Israel. In March 1953 he received his M.D. from the Hebrew University Hadassah School of Medicine and emigrated that same year to the United States. He was naturalized in 1962.

Settling first in Boston, Haddad became a pediatric resident at the Children's Medical Center. From 1956 to 1958 he was a fellow in pediatric endocrinology at Johns Hopkins Hospital in Baltimore and from 1958 to 1960 was both a research fellow and clinician at the National Institute of Health in Bethesda, Maryland. From 1959 to 1960 he also taught at the Howard University School of Medicine in its department of pediatrics.

Turning to a specialty in ophthalmology, Haddad moved in 1960 to the Washington University School of Medicine in St. Louis, where he was a resident and a U.S. Public Health Special Fellow until 1964. However, he took a leave of absence from mid-1962 to mid-1963 to do ophthalmic research in Paris and then spent one month in 1964 as an ophthalmic practitioner in Algeria—his first return visit to an Arab country since he left Iraq. From the remainder of 1964 to 1967, Haddad was both an ophthalmic surgeon and a professor of ophthalmology at Mt. Sinai Hospital and Medical School in New York. From 1967 to 1971 he continued teaching at Mt. Sinai and also directed the Ophthalmology Department at Beth Israel Medical Center in New York. Since 1971 he has been clinical professor of ophthalmology at New York Medical College. He is also affiliated with several hospitals in the New York metropolitan area as a consultant or attendant in ophthalmology, and since 1975 he has been editor in chief of *Metabolic and Pediatric Ophthalmology*. He has published more than 100 articles on pediatrics and ophthalmology since 1953.

Haddad has never abandoned his Jewish consciousness and his particular awareness of the plight of the more than 1 million Jews who were forced to flee from Arab lands. In Baghdad alone, for example, there had once been a thriving community of 150,000 Jews. By the early 1970s that number had dwindled to 2,500, and when Haddad settled in New York, he was just one of an estimated 30,000 Iraqi Jewish refugees to do so. Those Jews who remained in Arab lands were subject to frequent discrimination in employment and education and often had all their property confiscated. Thus, in 1968 Haddad founded and became president of the American Committee for Rescue and Resettlement of Iraqi Jews Inc. and from 1971 to 1976 was a member of American Professors for Peace in the Middle East. In 1975 he joined the executive board of the World Organization of Jews from Arab Countries and since 1978 has been its U.S. president.

In the latter capacity, Haddad has been instrumental in striking up dialogues with Arab leaders and between Jewish and Arab professionals. For example, in 1978 he initiated a meeting with Egypt's President Sadat in Ismailia to discuss the property claims of Jewish refugees and other matters relating to the problems faced by those 30,000 Jews still residing in Arab countries. As an Arabic speaker, Haddad had a special advantage in being able to communicate with Sadat.

Although Sadat appeared skeptical and mistrustful, he was nonetheless attentive to Haddad, and the dialogue led less than two years later to the organization of the Cairo Symposium on Metabolic Eye Disease. Directed by Haddad, the symposium was also attended by 40 Israeli ophthalmologists. A follow-up conference in Jerusalem enabled the ophthalmologists from both countries to continue their discussions. Despite the Egyptians' difficulties in accepting the Israelis—during the first symposium the Egyptian press hardly mentioned their presence, and printed programs distributed there did not list their names, although other doctors present were listed—the very existence of the conference signaled the beginning of a positive exchange of information and personnel between the two countries.

While in Egypt for the symposium, Haddad also visited Cairo's Jewish quarter and talked with Egyptian officials about upgrading the security and maintenance of the few remaining synagogues. Receiving assurances, Haddad thus asserted his role as one of the world's preeminent Sephardic leaders.

DAVID HALBERSTAM

b. April 10, 1934
Journalist; author

Since 1963, when he angered American officials for his frank reporting of U.S. government blunders in South Vietnam, David Halberstam has been recognized as one of the most perceptive, bold and independent members of the so-called fourth estate. Formerly a reporter for *The New York Times,* he has since gained national renown as the writer of two major books—*The Best and the Brightest* (New York, 1972), a critical and powerful study of the leaders who brought America into Vietnam; and *The Powers That Be* (New York, 1979), an intensive and analytical study of the impact of the media in shaping American politics.

David Halberstam was born in New York City to Charles, a surgeon, and Blanche (Levy) Halberstam, a schoolteacher. As a youth, he lived in several cities as his father was assigned to different posts. His interest in journalism blossomed early; as a student, he wrote for the Roosevelt High School paper in Yonkers. Upon graduation in 1951 he entered Harvard College—a momentous event for his family as well as for himself. In an interview, he commented how "in a Jewish home, you can never underestimate the lure of Harvard. It stood for everything." But he did not have a distinguished academic career there and says he was "in the bottom third of my class. In another age I would have been a dropout." Nevertheless, Halberstam did become managing editor of the Harvard *Crimson* and worked as a stringer—a part-time reporter—for *The Boston Globe.* When he received his B.A. degree in 1955, he pursued a professional career as a journalist.

Halberstam's first job was for *The Daily Times Leader* in West Point, Mississippi, where—in the wake of the momentous 1954 *Brown* v. *Board of Education* Supreme Court decision, which mandated the integration of southern public schools—civil rights was the most pressing and emotional issue of the time. A year later, in 1956, he moved to *The Tennessean* in Nashville, where for four years he continued to cover civil rights issues as well as politics and free-lanced for *The Reporter* and other magazines. He also wrote his first novel *The Noblest Roman* (Boston, 1961), which chronicled life and politics in a southern community.

In 1960 Halberstam was hired by *The New York Times* and was assigned to its Washington bureau, where he covered the inauguration and first year in office of President John F. Kennedy. In late 1961 he was sent to cover guerilla warfare in the Congo, an experience that he claimed was even more dangerous and frightening than Vietnam. His reporting earned him a 1962 Page One Award from the Newspaper Guild of New York and an assignment to South Vietnam, where from the start Halberstam noted glaring inconsistencies between official U.S. government statements, which claimed growing American strength, and the realities of what he saw—disintegration and chaos in the pro-American Diem regime. Along with other journalists, Halberstam filed candid, graphic reports about the disorder in Vietnam. His own increasingly angry and critical accounts especially raised the ire of American Pentagon officials and even President Kennedy. However, when Kennedy suggested to *Times* publisher Arthur "Punch" Sulzberger that perhaps Halberstam should be reassigned, Sulzberger refused. In 1963 Halberstam received the George Polk Memorial Award for his reporting and the following year shared the Pulitzer Prize with Associated Press reporter Malcolm Browne, who was in Vietnam at the same time.

Halberstam returned to New York in 1964 to cover the metropolitan bureau. Soon after, the anti-war movement began to develop, and in 1965 Halberstam published his first book about Vietnam, *The Making of a Quagmire* (New York), in which he chronicled his experiences in Southeast Asia and also in the Congo and commented on the blunders of American policy in both places. In January 1965 he was sent by the *Times* to Warsaw and by the end of the year had so infuriated the Polish government for his controversial reporting of anti-Semitism and oppressive practices of the communist regime that he was ordered to leave.

After spending some time in Paris for the *Times,* Halberstam returned to New York. He resigned in 1967, however, feeling he needed a change, and became a contributing editor for *Harper's* magazine. For that publication he wrote a number of major articles, including a pessimistic "Return to Vietnam" (1967); profiles of Bobby Kennedy, Richard Daley, McGeorge Bundy and Robert McNamara; and a series of political commentaries. He also published *The Unfinished Odyssey of Robert Kennedy* (New York, 1969) and *Ho* (New York, 1971), a biographical study of Vietnamese leader Ho Chi Minh. When a management shake-up at *Harper's* resulted in the departure of its editor, Willie Morris, Halberstam also resigned, and he turned toward extensive free-lancing for *Esquire, Atlantic Monthly* and other publications.

But this change also gave Halberstam the opportunity to direct his energy toward larger projects. His experiences as a Vietnam reporter and his close association with many of the highest government officials dur-

ing the Kennedy and Johnson administrations led him to try to explain in some way how the Vietnam situation came to pass. This Halberstam did in a series of biographical studies about those in power who helped set the policy for war in Indochina, including both presidents, as well as Dean Rusk, Walt Rostow, generals Maxwell Taylor and William Westmoreland, and several others. Halberstam's research included more than 500 interviews as well as thorough background reading. The book, *The Best and the Brightest,* became a national best seller.

Riding on the crest of that success, Halberstam continued to free-lance and then in 1974 embarked on his next project, which took five years to complete. In *The Powers That Be,* he set out to explore how the media— and specifically the people who control it—manipulate the political process in the United States and even influence elections. He focused on CBS, *The Washington Post, Time* magazine and *The Los Angeles Times* and their respective ruling groups, William Paley—for whom he reserved the most biting criticism—the Grahams, the Luces and the Chandlers. He conducted nearly 1,000 interviews as part of his research and produced a searing indictment of the media's domineering impact in the molding of public images. As he wrote, "print defines, television amplifies" in their coverage and choice of news. *The Powers That Be,* though sometimes criticized for being overlong and occasionally rhetorical, was hailed as a major contribution to popular understanding of how the media function behind the scenes.

For further information:
Halberstam, David. *The Breaks of the Game.* New York: 1981.
———. *One Very Hot Day,* novel. Boston: 1968.

BEN HALPERN

b. April 10, 1912
Scholar

Scholar, activist, non-Marxian socialist and influential Socialist-Zionist, Ben Halpern has been in the vanguard of Zionist activities and intellectualism for more than four decades.

Ben Halpern was born in Boston, Massachusetts, the son of Zalman, a farmer, peddler and owner of a small tailor's trimmings store and Fannie (Epstein) Halpern. He studied simultaneously at the Hebrew Teachers College where he earned his Bachelor of Jewish Education degree and at Harvard University, receiving a Bachelor of Arts degree—both in 1932. The next year he earned an M.A. degree from Harvard. There he worked with the legendary Professor Harry Wolfson on his doctoral dissertation, which dealt with Jewish life in Europe before the 19th century. He was awarded his Ph.D. in 1936.

Already a convinced Zionist, he went to work as national secretary of the Hechalutz Organization of America, a group that trained Jewish young people for farm labor in Palestine. He wrote their literature and passionately publicized the cause of Zionism to an as yet largely unresponsive American Jewish population. He also freelanced as a writer and taught in Hebrew schools to augment his income and save for his trip to Palestine.

In 1939 he and his wife arrived in Haifa and promptly settled in a kibbutz. He developed tuberculosis and the couple moved to Jerusalem where he was employed by the Jewish National Fund. Still sick, they moved back to the United States in 1940. His first attempt to settle in Palestine had failed.

Back in New York, he worked briefly for the American Jewish Committee and then as an editor for the Institute of Jewish Affairs of the World Jewish Congress from 1941–45. Beginning in 1943 he was managing editor of *The Jewish Frontier,* the magazine of the Labor Zionist Farband. Passionately Zionist, a utopian and moral socialist who eschewed dogma and recognized the failures and promises of socialism, he worked closely with editor Hayim Greenberg. In 1949 he went to work as director of education and information at the Jewish Agency for Palestine, staying until 1956. Soon he began writing scholarly and reflective books. *The American Jew* (New York, 1956) looked closely at the condition of American Jewry. A "Zionist analysis," it scrutinized the dilemma of those who were Zionists in America but could not bring themselves to believe they were in exile. Nor would they settle in the new state of Israel. The health of the American community, he suggested, depended in large part on its definition of "exile": the term conjured up visions of "a disordered condition of the Universe as a whole, which is epitomized in the fact and symbol that the Jewish people live outside their own proper place, the land of Israel. . . ." Yet he still lived in the United States, although he and his wife tried once more—and failed—to move to Israel. When their youngest son became sick, they again departed for the United States.

Still, he continued to contend that the heart of Zionism is the rejection—not the denial—of exile and the acceptance of the notion of Jewish sovereignty. In *The Idea of a Jewish State* (Cambridge, Massachusetts, 1969)

he writes that Zionism and Israel persistently deferred the concept of sovereignty for one reason or the other during the 20th century. But when Israel finally achieved its independence in 1948, the world was hardly enthusiastic, despite the fact that the post-World War II world welcomed the birth of other new national states.

About Arab-Jewish relations, Edward S. Goldstein's "A Tentative Intellectual Profile" in *Essays in Modern History: A Tribute to Ben Halpern,* edited by Frances Malino and Phyllis Cohen Albert (New York, 1982), Halpern's words written in 1967 in a Hebrew publication in Israel:

> As for the Arabs, we feel a measure of our guilt towards them. We all know and understand out of what necessity we came to it . . . how much justice validates that which we did. . . . Yet we must aspire to proper neighborly relations built upon the feeling of mutual guilt between ourselves and the Arab peoples. Let us, then, first of all do what is incumbent upon us to do.

What he was urging was—in Goldstein's phrase—to "open relations between Arabs and Israelis." His attitude towards the territories acquired since the Six Day War is that slow annexation may cause more problems for Israel then a Palestinian nation on the West Bank and that except for crucial areas such as Jerusalem and several other salients, all else could be traded for genuine peace and security.

"As I think of Ben's career," wrote Marie Syrkin in 1982 in a warm and sympathetic memoir (see *Essays in Modern History*), "I find pleasure in the reflection that not only the noisy are heard, that true achievement finds recognition in the academic and literary marketplace, and that the pure in heart, in addition to more ethereal rewards, also get Guggenheims and even *Festschriften.*"

Halpern taught for many years, from 1961 until 1982, at Brandeis University, where he was ultimately appointed Richard Koret Professor of Near Eastern and Judaic Studies.

For further information:

Halpern, Ben. "The Americanization of Zionism: 1880-1930," *American Jewish History.* September 1979.

———. "Exile and Redemption: A Secular Zionist View". *Judaism.* Spring 1980.

———. *Jews and Blacks: The Classic American Minorities.* New York: 1971.

———. "Marie Syrkin: Observations and Arguments," *The Jewish Frontier.* August-September 1980.

Halpern, Ben, and Wurm, Shaloms. eds. *The Responsible Attitude: Life and Opinions of Giora Josephtal.* New York: 1966.

MARVIN HAMLISCH

b. June 2, 1944
Composer

By the time he was 35, Marvin Hamlisch had accomplished as much in his career as a composer for Hollywood and Broadway as others have done in a lifetime. The recipient of three Oscars, four Grammys, a Tony Award and a Pulitzer Prize, Hamlisch has a unique and intuitive sense of romance, soaring melody and rhythm and is best-known for his landmark work in the long-running Broadway hit *A Chorus Line* and for the music in such films as *The Way We Were* and *The Sting.*

Marvin Frederick Hamlisch was born on the West Side of Manhattan to Max, who played accordion in his own band, and Lilly (Schachter) Hamlisch. His natural musical talents were recognized early, and he began studying piano when he was 6. His progress was so great that the following year he was admitted to the Juilliard School—at that time its youngest student—where he studied until 1964. According to one anecdote, even as a young child Hamlisch could transpose pieces into different keys on demand. He was educated, meanwhile, at the Professional Children's School in Manhattan and completed a B.A. degree in music at Queens College of the City University of New York in 1967.

While at Juilliard, Hamlisch met Liza Minnelli, who introduced him to vocal arranger Buster Davis. He became Davis's assistant on two shows in 1964, *Funny Girl* and *Fade Out-Fade In.* The following year he composed his first hit song, "Sunshine, Lollipops and Rainbows," which was popularized by teen-age singer Lesley Gore. But his career did not really begin in earnest until he graduated from college, at which point he wrote the music for two Broadway shows in 1967, *Golden Rainbow* and *Henry, Sweet Henry.* Hamlisch had his first major break in 1968, when he was invited to Hollywood to write the score for the film *The Swimmer.* Numerous commissions followed, and Hamlisch scored such films as Woody Allen's *Take the Money and Run* (1969) and *Bananas* (1971); *Save the Tiger* (1973); *The Way We Were,* with Barbra Streisand and Robert Redford (1974), for which Hamlisch received his Oscars; *The Sting,* with Redford and Paul Newman (1974); *Same Time, Next Year* (1979); *Ice Castles* (1979); and *Chapter Two* (1979).

Meanwhile, while spending the 1974–75 season on tour as straight man to Groucho Marx, Hamlisch also composed the score for a musical play by a young choreographer named Michael Bennett titled *A Chorus Line.* The story of the struggles of young dancers in a mythical chorus line to break out and "make it" on Broadway, the show debuted in Joseph Papp's Public Theater as a low-budget showcase. It turned into a surprise hit and moved to Broadway, earning for Hamlisch the 1975 Pulitzer Prize and Tony Award. His other Broadway effort includes scoring the Neil Simon comedy *They're Playing Our Song* (1979), a not-well-camouflaged retelling of Hamlisch's own (since-ended) romance with lyricist Carole Bayer Sager. With Sager, Hamlisch coauthored the hit song "Nobody Does It Better," which has been performed by many well-known vocalists. In fact, 1975 was Hamlisch's banner year: In addition to his Pulitzer and Tony, he won four Grammys for his work on *The Sting,* in which he arranged the Scott Joplin rag "The Entertainer," which became a popular hit, and on *The Way We Were.*

Needless to say, Hamlisch's work has also been featured on television, where he composed the theme music for the ABC news show *Good Morning, America,* the short-lived series *Hot l Baltimore* and the CBS dramatic series *Beacon Hill.*

ARMAND HAMMER

b. May 21, 1898
Industrialist; art collector

In addition to being a leading industrialist and president of Occidental Petroleum, the world's largest independent oil firm, and playing a crucial role in opening up trade between the United States and the Soviet Union in the early 1970s, Armand Hammer is a world-renowned art collector.

Hammer was born in New York City. His father, Julius Hammer, a physician and businessman, emigrated to America from Russia in 1875 after losing a fortune in the shipbuilding industry. His mother was Rose (Robinson) Hammer. While a student at Columbia University Medical School in 1918, Hammer joined his father's business, a chain of drug stores, which then verged on bankruptcy. He proceeded to make more than $1 million by buying medicine wholesale at depressed prices at the end of World War I and reselling when the prices rose afterward.

Although Hammer went to Columbia Medical School on a part-time basis, he graduated third in his class in 1921 and won an internship at Bellevue Hospital. In the six months between the end of Columbia's term and the beginning of the internship, Hammer went to the Soviet Union to help set up a medical clinic. The Russian health-care system was in complete disarray at the time in the wake of the Russian Revolution. While in Russia, Hammer arranged a business deal in which the

Soviet Union would buy wheat from the United States for furs and caviar.

Lenin himself asked Hammer to stay in Russia to arrange other business deals. He awarded Hammer a mining concession in Western Siberia, and Hammer, in turn, arranged for Ford, U.S. Rubber, Allis Chalmers and other American corporations to do business in the Soviet Union.

In 1922 Hammer's brother Victor, who had majored in art at Princeton University, joined him in Moscow. Together, they started to purchase Russian art treasures that the new leadership in Russia was selling in an effort to raise badly needed cash. In 1925 the Russian government decided to handle its own foreign trading concessions, and in return for Hammer's trading contacts, it gave Hammer the exclusive concession to manufacture wooden pencils in Russia. In the first year of this concession, Hammer earned more than $1 million.

In 1930 Hammer left the Soviet Union, bringing with him most of the art collection of the Romanovs, Russia's former royal family. When he encountered difficulties selling the art in the United States during the Depression, he devised a plan that revolutionized art dealing. He sold his collection through big department stores, including Macy's and Gimbels. He wrote a book about his adventures collecting art in Russia called *The Quest for the Romanoff Treasure* (New York, 1936).

In the 1940s Hammer made millions of dollars buying and selling distilleries, and in 1956 he retired in California. He soon grew bored with retirement, however, and when a business associate offered to sell him a controlling interest in the Occidental Petroleum Company, he accepted. At the time Occidental was on the verge of bankruptcy but held three leases for exploratory oil wells. Unexpectedly, all three wells struck oil. Within 10 years the company was worth more than $300 million.

When trade restrictions between the United States and the Soviet Union were eased during the early 1970s, Hammer was instrumental in closing the first large-scale business deal between an American company and the Soviet government. He negotiated an $8 billion, 20-year chemical fertilizer deal. This venture helped open the market between the Soviet Union and other American companies. Today he is extraordinarily influential, maintaining—as an article in *The New York Times Magazine* noted—a large coterie of friends and allies in Washington, "almost all of whom formerly served as Government officials."

Hammer has remained interested in buying and selling art work. In 1981 he bought the last privately held handwritten notebook of Leonardo da Vinci at a London auction for $5.2 million. And he has continued to expand his economic power, buying Iowa Beef Company and Inland Creek Coal, a major coal producer. Since 1968 he has also owned Hooker Chemical Co., the firm that dumped toxic wastes into the Love Canal near Niagara, New York. He has contributed pieces by the great masters to the Los Angeles County Art Museum, the National Gallery of Art and The Hermitage. Cancer research is another personal concern, and he has contributed heavily to the Eleanor Roosevelt Cancer Foundation and the Salk Institute in San Diego.

For further information:
Epstein, Edward Jay. "The Riddle of Armand Hammer." *The New York Times Magazine*, November 29, 1981.

OSCAR HANDLIN

b. September 29, 1915
Historian

The Pulitzer Prize-winning historian Oscar Handlin has devoted the bulk of his career to exploring the emotional and social impact of immigration among specific ethnic groups in America. While his focus has been broad enough to include an overview of the many immigrant groups who have settled in the United States, he has also taken a particular look at the unique aspects of Jewish immigration movements during the last 300 years.

Oscar Handlin was born in Brooklyn, the son of Joseph, who was a merchant, grocer and real estate salesman and Ida (Yanowitz) Handlin. He graduated from Brooklyn's New Utrecht High School in 1931 and completed his Bachelor of Arts degree three years later at Brooklyn College. He received a Master of Arts degree from Harvard University in 1935 and went to Europe the following year on a Sheldon Traveling grant for research. From 1936 to 1938 he was a history instructor at Brooklyn College. In 1939, while studying with such prominent historians as Arthur Schlesinger Sr. and Samuel Eliot Morison, he was appointed instructor of history at Harvard. The following year he earned his Ph.D. there.

In 1944 Handlin was named assistant professor and four years later became associate professor of history at Harvard. He became a full professor in 1954 and thereafter, in recognition of his prodigious talents—he was producing important books even while teaching—he received endowed professorships. From 1962 until 1965 he held the Winthrop chair in history at the university and then was appointed Charles Warren Professor of American History and director of the Center for the

Study of American History in 1965. Since 1972 he has been Carl H. Pforzheimer University Professor.

Handlin's books often concern some aspect of the immigrant experience. His first work (based on his dissertation), *Boston's Immigrants* (Cambridge, Mass., 1942), traced the commercial development of Boston through the industrialization of the city and its environs in the 1830s and 1840s. That process led to a large influx of immigrants and turned Boston into a bitterly divided community. Handlin outlined the slow integration of the Irish newcomers, aided in part by Irish support for the Union side in the Civil War. By 1865 the Irish, according to Handlin, had successfully developed a separate, distinct community with its own leadership, coexisting with the older Boston residents.

The Uprooted: The Epic Story of the Great Migrations that Made the American People (Boston, 1951; second edition, 1972), which earned Handlin the 1952 Pulitzer Prize for history, explored the question of what it meant for an Irish or Italian peasant to tear himself from his farm or small village to start life anew in America. Handlin considered the physical and spiritual challenges placed before such immigrants and expressed concern both for the mechanics of the event itself and the effect of the event on the lives of the people involved. Handlin was intrigued by the problems encountered by the masses of foreigners coming to America's shores to start over and wrote in *The Uprooted,* "Once I thought to write a history of the immigrants in America. Then I discovered that the immigrants *were* American history."

Handlin next set his sights on the American Jewish community. In *Adventure in Freedom: Three Hundred Years of Jewish Life in America* (New York, 1954), he traced the major trends in the American Jewish groups. He looked first at Jewish migration to America as only one of many national groups to contribute to the overall growth of the United States. He then examined the specific ramifications of the American experience and the opportunities it offered to generations of Jews seeking refuge from oppression. In this book Handlin took the conventional point of view that legal acceptance of Jews preceded their social acceptance.

In his biography of the failed presidential candidate, *Al Smith and His America,* (Boston, 1958), Handlin contended that Smith lost the 1928 election because he was the son of an immigrant and Catholic. Even so, Smith's greatest achievement, according to Handlin, was breaking the barriers for the immigrant communities to enter full political life in America.

Increasingly traditional in his views, Handlin engaged in a bitter dispute in the 1970s with younger, more radical historians over research methods and the direc-

tion the profession was taking. In *Truth in History* (New York, 1979), Handlin wrote that changes in methods of scholarship, the intrusion of economists and political scientists into the field and the occasional acceptance of less-than-accurate research were contributing to decay within the profession and to an erosion of professional standards. However, many of the targets of Handlin's criticism—some younger historians, including many of his former students—claim that the same sense of experiment that permitted Handlin to develop his own novel theses about immigration was precisely what the eminent historian disdained among his successors.

The Distortion of America (Boston, 1981) is a series of essays in which Handlin expands on the theories set forth in *Truth in History* and expresses his personal dismay at the alleged corruption of values and the lower moral standards of life in America. Criticized by those who feel Handlin was predisposed to take a jaundiced and emotional view toward the recent past—especially in view of his growing conservatism—the book was nonetheless praised for its vigilance and concern about the future path of America. The following year he and his wife, Lilian, published *A Restless People: Americans in Rebellion, 1770-1787* (New York, 1982), a history of the pre-Revolutionary "style of life" and how it led to the forging of an American "national" character.

A contributor to many journals, Handlin is a member of several history-oriented organizations, including the American Jewish Historical Society.

For further information:

Handlin, Oscar. *Newcomers: Negroes and Puerto Ricans in a Changing Metropolis.* Cambridge, Mass.: 1959.

Handlin, Oscar and Burchard, John. *The Historian and The City.* Cambridge, Mass.: 1966.

Handlin, Oscar, and Handlin, Mary F. *Commonwealth: A Study of the Role of Government in the American Economy.* Cambridge, Mass.: 1969.

———. *Dimensions of Liberty.* Cambridge, Mass.: 1961.

LOUIS HARRIS

b. January 6, 1921
Pollster

Louis Harris, president of the public opinion polling firm Louis Harris and Associates Inc., is one of the best-known pollsters in America. His polling results have been used by government leaders to evaluate public opinion on political issues, by corporate executives to analyze consumer response to products, and by newspapers and magazines to delineate changing moods and trends.

Louis Harris was born in New Haven, Connecticut to Harry, who worked in real estate, and Frances (Smith) Harris. After graduating from New Haven High School in 1938, where he was on the newspaper and literary magazine, he attended the University of North Carolina and obtained a B.A. degree in economics in 1942. Harris served in the United States Navy from 1942 to 1946 and upon his discharge joined the American Veterans Committee, a liberal rival to the conservative American Legion and Veterans of Foreign Wars, as national program and research director. The job introduced him to the study of public opinion. In 1947 he was hired by Elmo Roper, another well-known public opinion analyst, to ghost Roper's newspaper columns and radio scripts. In 1951, he became a Roper partner but left in 1956 to form his own company.

Harris attributes the success of his firm to the development of interviewing methods. Rather than being concerned with percentages alone, he tries to understand the reasons behind the responses by shaping questions so that they cannot be answered by just yes or no. His interviewees, who represent a cross-section of the community being polled, are encouraged to volunteer their views to well-trained interviewers whom Harris hires to canvass pre-selected neighborhoods. After answers are coded and fed into a computer, Harris analyzes the percentages and interprets their meaning.

Originally, Harris was mainly involved in market research for corporations like Johnson and Johnson, American Airlines and Standard Oil of New Jersey. However, after using his expertise to help John F. Kennedy win the presidential election in 1960 by conducting polls and determining from them how Kennedy should project himself to the public, Harris soon became known as an election strategist. Since then, his company has done research on more than 200 campaigns, although its corporate accounts have continued to grow.

From 1962 to 1968 Harris conducted opinion polls for CBS News, and since 1964 he has used the Voter Profile Analysis, a method he developed, to determine the voting patterns of Americans by assuming that most people vote according to the ethnic, religious and economic group to which they belong.

Harris was a columnist for the *Washington Post* and *Newsweek* magazine from 1963 to 1968 and for the *Chicago Tribune-New York Daily News* syndicate and *Time* magazine since 1969, reporting on the implications of his firm's research.

He has published several books presenting the results of his research. In *Is There a Republican Majority?* writ-

ten with William Brink (New York, 1954), Harris looked at political trends and analyzed the differences of voting patterns among various social, ethnic and religious groups. He based his second book, *The Negro Revolution in America,* also written with William Brink (New York, 1964), on a national survey sponsored by *Newsweek* seeking to define what black Americans hoped for from the civil rights movement. In *Black and White: A Study of Racial Attitudes Today* (New York, 1967), he examined racial conflict since 1965 by interpreting the results of questionnaires distributed through another *Newsweek* survey. He depicted the changes taking place in America since 1960 in *The Anguish of Change* (New York, 1973). His firm also conducted two surveys of the Ocean Hill-Brownsville (Brooklyn) school district in 1969 and 1970 to determine public attitudes among nonwhite residents toward the district's Governing Board, its schools and teachers, and the 1968 teachers' strike that received national and international attention. The poll discovered that the people were far more interested in the schooling of their children than in the labor and political struggles.

Harris also taught political science at Columbia University from 1953 to 1964 and since 1964 has been an adjunct professor at the University of North Carolina.

MARK HARRIS

b. November 19, 1922
Author

Mark Harris is a prolific writer of both fiction and nonfiction, whose range of interests reaches from baseball to Richard Nixon, with assorted stops in between. In addition to books, he has written for television, the theater and the movies.

Mark Finklestein was born in Mount Vernon, New York, the son of Carlyle, an attorney, and Ruth (Klausner) Finkelstein. He graduated from A.B. Davis High School in Mount Vernon in 1940 and in 1943 joined the U.S. Army, serving until 1944. That year he became a reporter for the Port Chester (N.Y.) *Daily Item.* After a year there he worked on the New York City newspaper *PM* for three months and then at the St. Louis bureau of the International News Service for a year.

In 1946 Harris returned to the South, where he had been stationed in the military, and wrote *Trumpet to the World* (New York, 1946), a novel about a young black man who marries a white woman. At that time Harris attended Clemson Agricultural College in South Carolina. He subsequently transferred to the University of

New Mexico and then to the University of Denver, where he received his B.A. degree in 1950 and his M.A. degree in 1951.

The Southpaw (New York, 1953) was the first of a series of books Harris wrote about the fictional baseball pitcher Henry Wiggen. Thus far, Harris has completed two books about the star pitcher of the New York Mammoths. The second, *Bang the Drum Slowly* (New York, 1956), about a catcher dying of an incurable ailment, was made into a major motion picture, starring Robert DeNiro, in 1973.

Harris joined the faculty of San Francisco State College in 1954. Though he remained a member of the faculty there until 1968, he also received his Ph.D. from the University of Minnesota in 1956 and the following year was the Fulbright Professor at the University of Hiroshima. He was a visiting professor at Brandeis University in 1963. In 1967 Harris moved to Purdue University, where he taught English. He stayed until 1970, when he joined the faculty at the California Institute of Arts. After three years there he moved again, this time to Immaculate Heart College in Los Angeles and then to the University of Southern California. In 1975 he was appointed professor of English at the University of Pittsburgh.

Over the more than twenty years that Harris has been a nationally recognized writer, his work has often drifted away from fiction toward the personal and autobiographical, focusing on his *angst* as a writer struggling to evaluate his accomplishments. He sums it up in *The Best Father in the World: The Autobiography of Mark Harris* (New York, 1976), in which he describes his entree into journalism as a runner for a well-known newsman, his army experiences, his success with *Bang the Drum Slowly* through the ensuing years. His books since 1964 share the same tendency toward first-person reportage. In *Mark the Glove Boy; or, The Last Days of Richard Nixon* (New York, 1964), he describes the California state gubernatorial campaign of Nixon in 1962 from his vantage point as a reporter on assignment for *Life* magazine. In *Twentyone Twice: A Journal* (Boston, 1966), he gives an account of his role as a special investigator for the Peace Corps in Africa and his encounter with the FBI as he underwent clearance for the post. In *The Goy* (New York, 1970), Harris reverted to fiction in telling the story of a Dr. Westrum, a middle-aged historian who is the one non-Jew among Jews in a New York City university. Married to a Jew, he turns toward Jewishness for warmth and human contact, yet retains the reserve and inwardness of his Gentile upbringing. *Saul Bellow: Drumlin Woodchuck* (Athens, Ga., 1980) is more an account of Harris's efforts to get

close to and understand the sometimes enigmatic Bellow than a true biography.

Harris adapted the Mark Twain story "The Man That Corrupted Hadleyburg" for Public Television in 1980. He has also written a play, *Friedman & Son* (1963) which was produced by the Actors Workshop.

RITA E. HAUSER

b. July 12, 1934
Lawyer; diplomat

International lawyer; U.S. representative to the United Nations; adviser on education, journalism, politics and other vital matters; involved in Jewish affairs—Rita Hauser is influential in Republican Party circles and in groups concerned with foreign policy.

Rita Abrams was born to Nathan, who was in the real estate business, and Frieda (Litt) Abrams, a buyer of women's shoes, both of whom had emigrated from Russia. Twenty years later, she graduated from Hunter College in New York City with a B.A. degree, magna cum laude, and took a Ph.D. in political economy at the University of Strasbourg, France, again magna cum laude, in 1955. Then, alternating between this country and France, she attended Harvard University Law School and New York University Law School, receiving a Bachelor of Laws in 1958. That year she also gained a *licence en droit* (French Bachelor of Laws) at the University of Paris, magna cum laude.

She began to practice law in New York City in 1959, specializing in corporate law and serving mainly an international clientele. Today she is a partner in the old and respected law firm of Stroock & Stroock & Lavan, specializing in private and public international law. She is a member of the District of Columbia bar as well as the New York bar. Her corporate legal work frequently takes her to France, especially to Paris, where she conducts her business in fluent French.

A prolific writer and frequent lecturer, Hauser has for many years served in a variety of organizations. She is active in top levels of the Republican party, where she played a key role behind the scenes in the election campaigns of presidents Richard Nixon and Ronald Reagan and Senator Jacob K. Javits and Governor Nelson A. Rockefeller in New York state. Presidents—both Democratic and Republican—have appointed her to various posts. In 1976 she was co-chairperson of the presidential debates between Jimmy Carter and Gerald Ford, sponsored by the League of Women Voters. She was a member in 1976 of the organizing group of the Committee on the Present Danger, which aims to "expose Soviet expansionism" and to promote expanded U.S. military power.

In 1978 Hauser announced her candidacy for the Republican nomination for attorney general of New York state but dropped this plan shortly afterward, in the wake of an inter-party dispute. In 1975 and 1981, under Republican administrations, she was reported under consideration for appointment to the U.S. Supreme Court.

On the international level Hauser served as this country's delegate to the United Nations Commission on Human Rights from 1969 to 1972 and as a member of the U.S. delegation to the 24th U.N. General Assembly in 1969. From 1974 to 1977 she was a member of the Advisory Panel on International Law of the Department of State. She represented the United States on the delegation to the World Conference of the International Women's Year in Mexico City in 1975.

She has been (and still is) active in legal organizations such as the American Society of International Law, the American Bar Association, the Association of the Bar of the City of New York, the Lawyers Committee for Civil Rights Under Law, the Legal Aid Society of New York and the American Foreign Law Association. She serves on the board of the Center for Strategic and International Studies at Georgetown University; is a trustee of the Institute for International Education, the Center for Inter-American Relations and Freedom House; and is on the board of advisers of the National News Council.

Her particular interest in Israel, the Middle East and Jewish problems is exercised at the American Jewish Committee, where she is a member of the board of governors and chairperson of its Foreign Affairs Commission. She is also on the board of the Synagogue Council of America's Institute for Jewish Policy Planning and Research. In 1975 she was a member of the Middle East Study Group at the Brookings Institution, which produced a report on issues in the area that was widely studied by Israeli and Arab leaders and served as the basis for President Carter's policy after his election in 1976. In September 1981 her letter to *Time* appeared, commenting on that magazine's very hostile essay "What to Do About Israel." She wrote: *"Time* does grave injury to a strong and solid alliance by its clarion call for such a debate between the United States and Israel."

Among the places where Hauser has lectured are the U.S. Army War College (on international law in 1971) and—under the aegis of the U.S. Information Agency—in Egypt, India, Australia and New Zealand (on constitutional law in 1970, 1971 and 1973). Her views on

major issues have appeared in such newspapers as *The New York Times, The Washington Post* and *The Wall Street Journal.* In her articles she has mainly discussed and analyzed such questions as a negotiated settlement between Israel and the Arab countries, the role and significance (or lack of it) of the Palestine Liberation Organization, the need for the United States to express its concern about human rights in Eastern Europe to the Soviet Union and the right of Soviet Jews to emigrate.

Asked if she considers herself a feminist, Hauser replied, "In the sense of being totally independent in views and profession." In 1978, discussing women and careers with a *New York Times* reporter, she said that men try "to discourage women by arguing that a woman has to be tough, bitchy and hardshelled. I want to show that this is not so. A woman can be natural, feminine, pretty—and tough when she must be, too." In her career, where she has encountered many misogynists, she has put forth her defense of human rights throughout the world and other key issues in just that fashion.

FRED MICHAEL HECHINGER

b. July 7, 1920
Newspaper editor and executive

Fred Michael Hechinger, president of The New York Times Company Foundation, has been a journalist, specializing in education, for over three decades. He is the recipient of two George Polk Memorial Awards, four Education Writers Association Awards, the British Empire Medal and the Fairbanks Award.

Fred Hechinger was born in Nuremberg, Germany to Dr. Julius and Lily (Niedermaier) Hechinger. He emigrated to the United States in 1937 and became a naturalized citizen in 1943. Hechinger attended New York University and City College of New York, from which he was graduated with a B.A. degree, Phi Beta Kappa in 1943. From 1944 to 1946 he served with the Office of Military Attache at the American Embassy in London and the British War Office. While in England, Hechinger did graduate work at the University of London and did some writing for the educational supplement of the *London Times.*

From 1946 to 1950 Hechinger worked as education editor as well as foreign correspondent for *The Bridgeport* (Conn.) *Herald,* education columnist for *The Washington Post* and foreign correspondent for the Overseas News Agency. He was education editor of *The New York Herald-Tribune* from 1950 to 1956 and associate publisher and executive editor of *The Bridgeport Sunday Herald* from 1956 to 1959.

In 1959 he joined *The New York Times*, where for 10 years he was education editor. In 1969 he became a member of the editorial board, and in 1977 he became president of The New York Times Company Foundation. Since 1978 he has written an occasional column about education in the *Times*.

Hechinger has been teaching at Hunter and Queens College as an adjunct professor and at the New School for Social Research as a special lecturer since 1973. He was appointed to the President's Commission on Foreign Language and International Studies in 1978 and is a Carnegie fellow as well as a special adviser to the Aspen Institute.

He has co-written with his wife, Grace, numerous books on education, including *Teen-Age Tyranny* (New York, 1963), in which they blame the irresponsible behavior of teen-agers on the lenience of parents and the low standards they set; *The New York Times Guide to New York City Private Schools* (New York, 1968); and *Growing Up in America* (New York, 1975), in which they trace the relationship between society and education throughout American history. The latter book explores the conceptualization of American schools from early Colonial days through the present and considers the impact of new immigrant groups, the development of progressive schools, the education of American blacks, the influence of industrialization and the reality of modern schools as compared to the American myth. Hechinger is also the editor of *Pre-School Education Today* (New York, 1966), a book that offers new approaches to teaching youngsters aged 3 to 5.

Many of Hechinger's writings on education have dealt with two sets of obstacles—those within the social structure and those within the individual school—that need to be overcome to achieve quality schooling. Thus, he has written on such matters as pedagogy and efforts at school reform, on racism and sexism, and on teaching evolution and religion in public and private schools. During the 1970s he strongly favored measured and cautious reform in school systems.

Hechinger is a contributing editor to *Saturday Review*, *Harper's* and other magazines and is task force chairman for the Modern Language Association.

JASCHA HEIFETZ

b. February 2, 1901
Violinist

For more than 60 years the name Jascha Heifetz has been synonymous with violin virtuosity and musical mastery. His legendary performances have set the standards of excellence that other violinists often strive for.

Jascha Heifetz was born in Vilna, Lithuania, the son of Ruvin, a first violinist with the Vilna Orchestra, and Anna Heifetz. When he was 3 years old, his father started training him on a $5 violin. The boy's talent was such that the next year he began studying at Vilna's Royal Music School, which had only reluctantly granted him an audition. Three years later, when Jascha was 7 years old, he performed a Mendelssohn concerto before a packed audience in Kovno.

By the time he was 9, Heifetz was ready for study at the prestigious Russian Imperial Conservatory of St. Petersburg under the tutelage of the eminent teacher Leopold Auer. Heifetz was Auer's youngest pupil, and since the only Jews permitted to reside in St. Petersburg were conservatory students, Ruvin Heifetz was allowed to enroll as a student in order to be with his son. Under Auer's instruction the younger Heifetz perfected the technique to which many critics attribute his virtuosity. The young musician made his debut with the Berlin Philharmonic when he was 12 and not only impressed the public but the great violinists of the day. One of them, Fritz Kreisler, is said to have told his colleagues after hearing Heifetz perform at a dinner party that they might as well break their instruments.

Shortly after immigrating to the United States with his family in 1917, Heifetz made his Carnegie Hall debut. The October 27 concert was a historic event. The publicity that had preceded his arrival was further underscored by the raves bestowed on him by virtually every critic. As one wrote, "For once, yesterday, the star of Enrico Caruso was overshadowed, if not eclipsed, in the musical firmament, and strangely enough, by a mere stripling." What surprised critics most of all was that, despite Heifetz's age, he displayed an extraordinary maturity in his approach to the music he performed. Unlike many young prodigies, whose mastery of technique was their greatest attribute, Heifetz was an equally adept interpreter of the music he performed.

Thereafter, Heifetz combined extensive concertizing with recording commitments. The growing record industry helped spread his fame, and a legends about the youthful virtuoso soon developed around him as he performed across the country with such conductors as Koussevitsky, Stokowski and Toscanini. But Heifetz transcended the legends, and while many youthful prodigies faded into obscurity upon reaching adulthood, Heifetz grew into a thoughtful and intelligent performer.

From the 1920s through the 1960s Heifetz toured frequently throughout the United States and abroad. He often voiced his opinion that despite the spread of "popular," nonclassical music on the radio, the American public was first and foremost wedded to the tradition of fine, classical music, as proved by the fact that his concerts sold out immediately, even in large stadiums and auditoriums. To add to his popularity, he performed in two films—*They Shall Have Music* (1939), a Sam Goldwyn production, and *Carnegie Hall* (1949)—and he appeared often for free in fund-raising benefits. During the 1960s he toured in a series of highly acclaimed recitals with cellist Gregor Piatigorsky.

Heifetz's instrumental technique is unexcelled, and his vast repertoire includes the greatest baroque and romantic works written for the violin as well as many of his own transcripts of compositions for other instruments. While critics have long marvelled at the purity of his tone, some have complained that he has less success as a musical interpreter and that his playing is "cold." Others have commented that the violinist's austere manner—he became known as the "Great Stone Face" because he never smiled during a performance—contributed to that impression. He has also drawn criticism for playing and recording such "fluff" pieces as "White Christmas." But the criticism pales in the face of Heifetz's extraordinary achievements since he first learned to play at the age of 3.

Heifetz has performed in Israel with the Israel Philharmonic Orchestra several times. In 1953 he was attacked by an angry youth there after he played music by Nazi sympathizer Richard Strauss. A controversy ensued in which Heifetz argued that music should take precedence over politics, but the specific problems in Israel at the time deemed otherwise.

Since a 1975 shoulder operation, Heifetz has not performed in public. But he has been a member of the faculty at the University of Southern California since 1962 and since 1974 has occupied a special teaching chair established in his honor. The renowned young violinist Eugene Fodor is one of Heifetz's former students, but he has been criticized as being too restrictive and domineering as a teacher, preventing the natural development of those who choose to study with him. Nonetheless, teaching has a great meaning to Heifetz, who once said: "Violin playing is a great but perishable art. It must be passed on as a personal skill—otherwise, it is lost."

ROBERT LOUIS HEILBRONER

b. March 24, 1919
Economist; author

Robert Heilbroner, professor of economics at the New School for Social Research in New York City, is possibly the best-selling economics author of all time. In his books he makes the study of economics lively and

challenging by placing economic principles in a social and political framework rather than restricting the discussion to economics.

Robert Heilbroner was born on New York City's upper West Side to Louis, a businessman, who helped establish Weber & Heilbroner, Inc., a group of men's clothing shops, and Helen (Weiller) Heilbroner. He was educated in private schools and Harvard University, from which he was graduated summa cum laude in 1940 with a B.A. degree in economics history and government. Following graduation he went to work for the federal Office of Price Administration and afterward as a store clerk in one of his father's stores. He was drafted into the Army during World War II and was an interrogator of Japanese prisoners of war until 1946 in the Pacific theater of war.

In 1948, upon his discharge, Heilbroner worked as an economist with a commodity trading firm and started writing magazine articles, specializing in economics. When he sold several articles to *Harper's* magazine, he left the nine-to-five business world never to return. Meanwhile, as he free-lanced, Heilbroner took occasional graduate courses at the New School for Social Research, beginning in 1946.

Heilbroner published his first book in 1953, *The Worldly Philosophers* (New York), a very readable portrayal of the lives and thoughts of such major economists as Adam Smith, Karl Marx, J.M. Keynes, David Ricardo, Thomas Malthus and others written in lively and engaging prose. The book, which received predominantly favorable reviews, was adopted as a text at colleges throughout the country and was hailed for making economic theory accessible to the lay reader.

His subsequent works established his reputation as an important social critic. In *Quest for Wealth: A Study of Acquisitive Man* (New York, 1956), he explores the historical origins of the widespread acquisitive drive. And in *The Future as History: The Historic Currents of Our Time and the Direction in Which They Are Taking America* (New York, 1960), he writes of the growth of science and technology, economic and spiritual hopes in the Third World, and the drive for bureaucratic control in capitalist democracies. In this work Heilbroner takes a critical and pessimistic view toward the future of America based on current trends of the time. Critics praised Heilbroner's analysis, and one said the book should be a sign for Americans to "wake up."

Heilbroner received his Ph.D. degree from the New School for Social Research in 1963. His dissertation, a historical exploration of economics from ancient Rome to the contemporary era was published in 1962 as *The Making of Economic Society* (New York).

Among Heilbroner's other works are *The Great Ascent:*

The Struggle for Economic Development in Our Time (New York, 1963), a study of economic evolution in developing nations; and *A Primer of Government Spending* (New York, 1963), an examination of deficit financing and its consequences.

Heilbroner's judgments are often tinged with a strong streak of pessimism about the future of the human race and its enormously complex problems. *An Inquiry into the Human Prospect* (New York, 1974) is a chilling view of the dangers of a nuclear war, enormous population growth and exhaustion of the world's resources. *Business Civilization in Decline* (New York, 1976) discusses the limitations and inevitable decline of American capitalism as it exists today and projects the evolution of a society in which individualism is discouraged and a kind of collective religion evolves. Heilbroner's personal conclusions are ambivalent; while not altogether unhappy about the death of capitalism, he is nonetheless not sure that the alternatives are any better.

Heilbroner, who calls himself a "radical conservative," once commented in *Business Week:*

> I'm a radical in that I see capitalism in its historical context, in the process of flux, and I support many changes toward equality that are called socialism. But I'm conservative in that I no longer believe institutional change will make the problems go away.

For further information:

Heilbroner, Robert L. *Between Capitalism and Socialism: Essays in Political Economics.* New York. 1971.
———. *The Economic Problem.* Englewood Cliffs, N.J.: 1968.
———. *The Limits of Capitalism.* New York: 1966.
———. *Understanding Macroeconomics.* Englewood Cliffs, N.J.: 1965.
———. *Understanding Microeconomics.* Englewood Cliffs, J.J.: 1968.
Heilbroner, Robert L, and Thurow, Lester. *Five Economic Challenges.* Englewood Cliffs, N.J.: 1981.

JOSEPH HELLER

b. May 1, 1923
Novelist

Joseph Heller has said that his writing can be fairly described as "sour sarcasm or ugly satire." In his three novels, *Catch-22, Something Happened* and *Good as Gold,* he has directed his cutting wit at war, big business and government, respectively. The books are among the most sardonic and humorous attacks on those institutions in contemporary fiction.

Heller was born in the Coney Island section of Brooklyn to Isaac and Lena Heller. His father drove a delivery truck for a bakery and died when he was 5 years old. He graduated from Lincoln High School in 1941 and in October 1942 enlisted in the U.S. Army Air Force just a few months before he was to be drafted. He was ordered to gunnery school, but after hearing that the life expectancy of a gunner was relatively brief, he requested a transfer to air cadet training. In 1944 he was sent into combat in Italy, where he flew 60 missions and returned to the United States with the rank of lieutenant.

After the war Heller continued his education and received his B.A. degree from New York University in 1948 and his M.A. degree from Columbia University in 1949. The following year he spent at Oxford on a Fulbright scholarship. After returning home he taught freshman English at Pennsylvania State University, then left academia to take a job as an ad writer for *Time* magazine. He continued in advertising for the next 10 years. Meanwhile, he began publishing short stories in *Esquire* and *Atlantic Monthly.*

In 1961 *Catch-22* was published in New York. The novel, heavily influenced in structure by Kafka and Celine, is a satirical parody of the military and a brilliant indictment of the senselessness of war. Yossarian, the story's hero, is confronted with the moral question of how a sane man ought to act in a world gone mad. Heller answers the question by writing "his last loyalty must be . . . to himself."

Catch-22 received mixed critical reviews when it was released, and initial sales were slow. But as the Vietnam War grew in intensity, the book struck a responsive nerve in American readers. By 1969 more than 8 million copies had been sold. A generation of American anti-war activists were nurtured on its razor-sharp humor and incisive dissection of the blind obedience demanded by the military.

During the 1960s Heller taught fiction and dramatic writing at the University of Pennsylvania and Yale University. In 1967 his play *We Bombed in New Haven,* written in revulsion at the Vietnam War, opened at the Yale School of Drama Repertory Theater. In it illusion becomes reality as real and recognizable characters commit ghastly and horrendous acts. The play later moved to Broadway, where it received reviews that reflected its extreme and controversial nature.

Since 1971 Heller has been the Distinguished Visiting Writer at the City College of the City University of New York. In 1974 his second novel was published. *Something Happened* (New York), was intended to do to the business world what *Catch-22* did to the military.

Heller's novel *Good as Gold* (New York, 1979) aims his wit at government, the family and ambition. Some critics have called *Good as Gold* Heller's bleakest, blackest outpouring. Yet the author insists it is supposed to be a funny book. The problem, he claims, is that he just can't write a funny book without being serious, and he can't write a serious book without being funny. It is also a "Jewish" novel, in which Heller uses an epigraph from Bernard Malamud: "If you ever forget you're a Jew, a gentile will remind you." Wrote critic Irving Malin: "Despite the outwardly sarcastic, crazy tone of the novel, it is a warm testament . . . [suggesting] that Jewishness however differently it is interpreted [or misinterpreted], is heartfelt and golden."

LILLIAN HELLMAN

b. June 20, 1907
Playwright; author

Lillian Hellman, one of America's celebrated playwrights, has also dedicated herself to political causes. An outspoken anti-Fascist, she has written several highly acclaimed and controversial memoirs that include accounts of her public denunciation of the Franco regime in Spain and her refusal to name Communist party members when called to testify before the House Un-American Activities Committee during the McCarthy era.

Lillian Hellman was born in New Orleans to Max Bernard, a businessman, and Julia (Newhouse) Hellman. She grew up and attended public schools in New York and studied at New York University from 1922 to 1924 but did not get a degree.

After leaving college she worked in 1924 as a manuscript reader for the book publishing firm of Horace Liveright. One year later she married playwright Arthur Kober and decided to become a writer. In 1925 she reviewed books for the *New York Herald-Tribune* and read plays for Broadway producers until 1930, when she moved to Hollywood with her husband and read filmscripts for Metro-Goldwyn-Mayer. Two years later, divorced, she returned to New York and began working on a play of her own.

Hellman's first work, *The Children's Hour,* based on a historic Scottish trial in which two schoolteachers were tried for being homosexual on an unfounded accusation by a student, opened in 1934 to mixed reviews. But years later it received wide praise when it was made into a popular film with Audrey Hepburn and Shirley MacLaine in the lead roles.

Her second play, *Days to Come,* a study of a labor strike in the United States and its impact on a small town, opened in New York in 1936 and closed within one week. (In 1979 it was shown again in an off-Broadway theater, again to negative reviews.)

She then visited Russia, Paris and Spain in 1936, where for a month she was caught up in the Spanish civil war. She returned to America in 1937 to actively support the cause of loyalist Spain, the first of her many political stands.

Hellman's next effort was *The Little Foxes,* which was produced in 1939 and starred Tallulah Bankhead. A harsh portrayal of avarice and affectation in a southern family around 1900, it was highly praised and became a successful film in 1941 featuring Bette Davis. The power and durability of the play were reaffirmed in a triumphant 1981 Broadway revival with Elizabeth Taylor —who made her Broadway debut in the play—and Maureen Stapleton in the lead roles.

Hellman's most famous play, *Watch on the Rhine,* opened in 1941 to rave reviews. Based on the playwright's strong anti-Fascist beliefs, it depicts a German who risks everything to resist Hitler's new regime. It won the New York Drama Critics Circle Award for the 1940–41 Broadway season.

Other plays by Hellman include *Another Part of the Forest* (1946), which features the same characters as *The Little Foxes; The Autumn Garden* (1951), which focuses on growing older and the need to prepare for one's later years; and *Toys in the Attic* (1960), a portrayal of self-absorption and immorality in a Louisiana family. In addition to her plays, Hellman has worked on many filmscripts, including *Dark Angel* (1935), *Dead End* (1937), *The North Star* (1941) and *The Searching Wind* (1946). She also wrote the book for the Broadway production *Candide* (1956), with music by Leonard Bernstein.

Because of her romantic relationship with writer Dashiell Hammett—a Communist party member since 1938 with whom she lived from the early 1930s until his death in 1961—Hellman was asked to testify before the House Un-American Activities Committee in 1952. Disclaiming membership in the Communist party, she refused to answer questions about the political activities of her friends and acquaintances.

Her memoirs, *An Unfinished Woman* (New York, 1969) and *Pentimento* (New York, 1973), recall various stages of her life in New Orleans, New York and abroad. Particularly noteworthy was her poignant portrait of "Julia" in *Pentimento* (later made into a film starring Jane Fonda and Vanessa Redgrave), about a woman who sacrifices her life in the anti-Nazi underground in Germany. In *Scoundrel Time* (New York, 1976), her third volume of reminiscences, Hellman recounts her experiences during the McCarthy period and those of Hammett, who went to jail for refusing to name donors to a fund set up to support Communist causes. She has since been praised by those who saw her actions as courageous and criticized by those who insisted that she had been too uncritical of Stalinist Russia.

Hellman is also the editor of *The Letters of Anton Chekhov* (New York, 1955) and a member of the Dramatists Guild.

NAT HENTOFF

b. June 10, 1925
Journalist; commentator

To some, Nat Hentoff is known as a jazz expert. To others, he is an outspoken critic of public education in America. And to others still, he is a controversial defender of constitutional rights in America, espousing political viewpoints that alienate almost everyone some of the time. For more than 25 years, Hentoff has been a prolific author of books and articles in most major publications, sparking debate at almost every turn. An angry advocate, journalism is his soapbox—and audiences respond in kind.

Nathan Irving Hentoff was born in Boston to Simon, a traveling salesman, and Lena (Katzenberg) Hentoff. He graduated from Northeastern University in Boston in 1945, did postgraduate work at Harvard in 1946 and studied at the Sorbonne in Paris as a Fulbright fellow in 1950.

As a jazz aficionado, he wrote, produced and announced for the Boston radio station WMEX from 1944 to 1953. He was music adviser for CBS-TV's *The Sound of Jazz* and *The Sound of Miles Davis* and was associate editor for *Down Beat* magazine from 1953 to 1957. He co-founded and co-edited *The Jazz Review* from 1958 to 1960.

Hentoff believes that jazz is more than just a musical form but reflects a lifestyle—one that is peculiarly American and particularly black—and that to understand jazz one must also understand its social and historical roots and the contemporary problems (drug use among musicians, for example) that go with it. His many writings therefore go beyond a mere look at the music to explore the men and women who make the music. Some of his views were controversial at first, especially those that focus on jazz as an indigenous black art form, but are now widely accepted and respected. His books on jazz are *Hear Me Talkin' to Ya* and *The Jazz Makers,* both co-edited with Nat Shapiro (New York, 1955 and 1957, respectively); *Jazz: New Perspectives*

on the History of Jazz, co-edited with Albert McCarthy (New York, 1961); *Jazz Country* (New York, 1965); *Journey into Jazz* (New York, 1968); and *Jazz Is* (New York, 1976). He is the jazz reviewer for *The Nation, Progressive* and *Cosmopolitan* and has written liner notes for many jazz albums.

Hentoff's educational and political commentary has centered on the allegedly inferior quality of American big-city schooling plus an added measure of repeated sharp attacks on teachers and administrators as responsible for the inability of nonwhite students to perform as well as whites. During the 1968 teachers' strike in New York City, he bitterly attacked the teachers' union and defended the largely black Ocean Hill-Brownsville Governing Board. And when New York City appointed its first school chancellor in 1970, Hentoff continued attacking the teachers and their unions.

But he has also been quick to praise a few teachers and administrators he judged to be effective. In *Our Children Are Dying* (New York, 1966), he singled out the principal and staff of a Harlem elementary school whose work he deemed to represent extraordinary dedication, especially in the face of overwhelming odds working in a depressed community. Other books on education include *This School Is Driving Me Crazy* (New York, 1975), a juvenile novel about an adolescent in private school—his children attended nonpublic schools—and *Does Anybody Give a Damn? Nat Hentoff on Education* (New York, 1977). On a different subject, he wrote *A Doctor Among the Addicts* (New York, 1968), in praise of a psychiatrist, Dr. Marie Nyswanger, who developed new treatments for heroin addicts and pioneered the use of methadone.

Hentoff's writing is published regularly in the New York City weekly newspaper *The Village Voice,* where he has been a columnist since 1957. In this arena he writes about a wide range of issues, focusing especially on civil liberties. For example, he wrote a series of articles about book censorship in a West Virginia town and the young librarian who tried to resist it; the efforts of two Orthodox Jewish high school students in Virginia to change their public high school graduation date from a Saturday to a Sunday so they could attend; the jailing without trial of a black woman suspected of drug dealing; and the existence in several American cities of police "Red Squads," which conduct illegal surveillance of left-wing groups.

Hentoff's uncompromising and absolutist view of the First Amendment, his espousal of community control by the Ocean Hill-Brownsville Governing Board during the bitter 1968 teachers' strike in New York City and his sympathy for pacifism and for Israel's Peace

Now movement have aroused harsh opposition as well as cheers. In *State Secrets: Police Surveillance in America,* which he coauthored (New York, 1973), he showed how files taken from a government office in Media, Pennsylvania proved that the FBI and CIA had repeatedly violated the constitutional rights of many citizens during the Vietnam War era. But his *The First Freedom: The Tumultuous History of Free Speech in America* (New York, 1980), a summary of highlights from 15th-century England to the contemporary period, was superficial.

He is a member of the American Civil Liberties Union and a director of the New York Civil Liberties Union. He also belongs to the Reporters Committee for Freedom of the Press.

For further information:

Hentoff, Nat. *Black Anti-Semitism and Jewish Racism.* New York: 1969.
———. *The Collected Essays of A.J. Muste.* New York: 1963.
———. *Peace Agitator: The Story of A.J. Muste.* New York: 1963.
———. *A Political Life: The Education of John V. Lindsay.* New York: 1969.

SEYMOUR HERSH

b. April 4, 1937
Journalist

Seymour Hersh, an award-winning journalist, has been likened to Lincoln Steffens and other muckrakers. Through his probing, persevering and endless legwork, he has broken some of the most important news stories of the past 15 years.

Seymour Hersh was born in Chicago, the son of Isadore and Dorothy (Margolis) Hersh. After he received his B.A. degree in history from the University of Chicago in 1958, he went to work as a police reporter for the City News Bureau in Chicago. He stayed with the City News Bureau for only one year and left because he was frustrated over the bureau's lack of crime coverage in the Chicago ghetto.

After an attempt to launch his own journal failed, Hersh joined United Press International as its correspondent in Pierre, South Dakota in 1962. Once again Hersh quickly grew tired of the limitations placed on him by the assignment, and in 1963 he joined the Associated Press. After a first assignment in Chicago, Hersh was transferred to Washington, D.C. and soon

was assigned to cover the Pentagon. There, he established a reputation as a persistent investigator who, once onto an important breakthrough, would not stop until he had covered all bases several times over and collected every piece of information he needed. Often, if he felt that a government spokesperson was telling less than the truth or if a statement was unimportant, he would walk out in the middle of an official briefing, behavior unheard of at the time.

In 1967 Hersh left AP and worked as a free-lance reporter. He served as Senator Eugene McCarthy's press agent in the New Hampshire presidential primary in 1968, but he determined he was not cut out to be a press secretary and soon left the campaign. Later that year he published his first book, *Chemical and Biological Warfare: America's Hidden Capacity* (New York, 1968).

In 1967 and 1968 Hersh heard persistent rumors of alleged massacres conducted by U.S. troops in Vietnam. These rumors had been denied by the Defense Department and ignored by the rest of the Pentagon press corps. Hersh—through tireless research and detective work—ultimately heard of the then semi-secret trial of Lt. William Calley at Fort Benning, Georgia. At his own expense he traveled to Georgia and interviewed Calley. He also contacted a high-ranking U.S. general who had served in Vietnam and wanted to clear the record about the events surrounding the alleged massacres. Slowly, Hersh pieced together the story of the atrocity that occured at My Lai.

But even when the story was complete and irrefutable, Hersh could not find a publisher. Finally, he contacted the Dispatch News Service, a small organization run by a friend of Hersh's that provided feature articles to various newspapers. The Dispatch News Service could not place the story, however, until another friend, a lawyer, promised to defend, free of charge, any publication carrying the story against libel charges. Only then did the news of the My Lai atrocities reach the American public.

Hersh won the Pulitzer Prize for international reporting in 1970, the same year that he published *My Lai 4: A Report on the Massacre and Its Aftermath* (New York), summarizing his findings about the affair. After the publication of *Cover-Up: The Army's Secret Investigation of the Massacre of My Lai 4* (New York, 1972), Hersh joined the staff of *The New York Times* as a special-assignment investigative reporter.

Using Washington D.C. as a base from 1972 until 1975, Hersh won the George Polk Memorial Award for his stories about secret B-52 bombings in Cambodia conducted by the Nixon administration. In 1974 he won the Sidney Hillman Award for exposing the domestic spying operations of the CIA. The following year he won the Drew Pearson Prize for his articles about the CIA's involvement in Chile. In 1981 the *New York Times Magazine* published a two-part article he wrote detailing how former CIA agents were selling sophisticated weaponry and electronic equipment to foreign governments, including Libya.

Hersh's investigative writing often reads like a mystery or spy novel. In the *Atlantic Monthly* (May 1982), he charged that Kissinger "lied about his role in the [Watergate] wiretapping and his knowledge of the Plumbers was widely assumed in the Washington press corps, and even inside the Watergate Special Prosecution Force, but Kissinger was permitted to slide by with his half-truths and misstatements. . . . Kissinger [concluded Hersh] was involved."

For further information:

Hersh, Seymour, "Kissinger and Nixon in the White House," *The Atlantic Monthly,* May 1982.

ARTHUR HERTZBERG

b. June 9, 1921
Rabbi

By most standards, Rabbi Arthur Hertzberg may be American Jewry's most articulate and provocative and perhaps most brilliant representative speaking and writing on public issues of serious Jewish concern.

Arthur Hertzberg was born in Lucbaczow, Poland, the son of Zvi Elimelech, a distinguished rabbinical scholar, and Nehamah (Alstadt) Hertzberg. He was brought to the United States five years later, and the family ultimately settled in Baltimore. Hertzberg is descended from a long line of Hassidic scholars, and the males traditionally prepared for the rabbinate (his two brothers are also rabbis.) Until he was well into his teens, he was, in fact, a "little Belze Hassid," wearing long sideburns and black *kipote,* or coat, and was a devout Talmud student. But as a newly transplanted American, he found himself torn between his Judaic background and modern American life. He made the ultimate compromise: He became a modern American rabbi with many radical ideas but with a foundation based on traditional values.

Hertzberg entered Johns Hopkins University in 1937 and graduated with a B.A. degree Phi Beta Kappa in 1940. That year he began studies at New York's Jewish Theological Seminary and three years later received a Master of Hebrew Literature degree and his ordination

as a Conservative rabbi. His activism began at this time: In the wake of the Holocaust and the destruction of his birthplace as a Jewish community, he turned his focus toward Israel and became an ardent Zionist.

Upon ordination in 1943 Hertzberg directed the Hillel Foundation chapter at Amherst College and the University of Massachusetts. The following year he headed his first congregation, Ahavath Israel of Oak Lane in Philadelphia. In 1947 he became rabbi of Nashville, Tennessee's West End Synagogue, and then from 1951 to 1953 he volunteered to serve as chaplain in the Air Force during the Korean War. "Knowing from the very beginning that I was going to plow my own furrow," he said, "I was not going to give anyone the handle which said, 'he ducked.' I don't duck, I do not duck." These words summarize his approach to controversial issues in subsequent years.

Following his Air Force service, Hertzberg returned briefly to Nashville and shortly after was appointed spiritual leader of Temple Emanu-El in Englewood, New Jersey, where he developed his reputation as an eloquent and, when necessary, sardonic speaker. For example, as early as 1963 during a Yom Kippur sermon, he warned his congregation of the perils of American intervention in Indochina, long before opposition to the Vietnam War had developed into a national movement. And in a 1966 article in *Midstream,* he critiqued the American rabbinical establishment, describing its members as "institutional executives" who had evolved into "entertainers." Indeed, he wrote, the American rabbinate was a ghost of its former self and an institution in the process of atrophying and dying. Yet nine years later he admitted to an audience at a rabbinical convention that he had erred. In his final sentence there, he summed up his own feelings: "We are rabbis who have nothing going for us except our own passion, our own conviction, our own lives and what we are willing to put them on the line for." Another time, in a sermon, Hertzberg addressed the need for a greater role of Jewish values in the daily life of synagogue members, referring to the majority of Jews who attend services only on the High Holy Days as the "silent two thirds."

Hertzberg's work has often taken him beyond the confines of his congregation. From 1972 until 1978 he was president of the World Jewish Congress, and he has also served as president of the American Jewish Congress, as a member of the Conference of Presidents of Major Jewish Organizations and is on the Board of Governors of the Jewish Agency for Israel and the Executive of the World Zionist Organization. Presently he is vice-president of the World Jewish Congress.

In addition, Hertzberg is a scholar and historian.

An adjunct professor of history at Columbia University since 1961, he received a Ph.D. there in 1966 and wrote his dissertation on "The Jews in France Before the Revolution: Prelude to Emancipation," which later became a book, *The French Enlightenment and the Jews* (New York, 1968). Hertzberg has also taught at Rutgers University (1966–68), Princeton (1968–69) and the Hebrew University in Jerusalem (1970–71). His book *The Zionist Idea* (New York, 1968), is considered essential reading for an educated citizen.

He also writes regularly in a variety of publications such as the Israeli dailies *Ma'ariv* and *Ha'aretz* and *The New York Times, The Nation* and many others on a variety of polemical and contemporary subjects. A number of these articles were brought together in one volume under the title *Being Jewish in America* (New York, 1979), in which he wrote in the *Introduction:*

> A generation which began in the 1930s believing in its own capacity to succeed is less confident now, more aware of problems than hopeful of their solutions. . . . The prevailing mood today is not thus going forward boldly to new adventure. It is rather one of defending a heritage which we weakened in the boldness of the ardor of many of my contemporaries for grand solutions.

His public arguments with the Jewish Agency, the Jewish Telegraphic Agency and various Israeli prime ministers began when, as a newcomer to the Jewish Agency in 1969, he openly objected to Golda Meir's telegram to President Richard M. Nixon supporting the war in Vietnam. Two years later he bitterly criticized Israel's treatment of its "Black Panthers"—the poor, slum-dwelling children of North African and Southwestern Asian immigrants. He is opposed to Israel's policy of settlements in the West Bank and has written extensively against the widely backed American Jewish position favoring "merit" in employment and college admissions over "affirmative action." "Arthur and Nahum Goldmann [the former head of the World Jewish Congress]," says Rabbi Wolfe Kelman, head of the Rabbinical Assembly, "are the only two people I know who were members of the Jewish Agency and who attacked the official Zionist line." In February 1982 Hertzberg wrote a much-discussed essay in *The New York Review of Books* in opposition to the policies of Prime Minister Begin, declaring that most American Jews were embarrassed by Begin's actions.

As part of his leadership work in the American Zionist movement, Hertzberg has spoken often of the need for Jews in Israel and the Diaspora "together to become Zionist again." In "Mass Aliya for the Moderates" (*Jewish Chronicle,* August 29, 1980), he writes, "The tragic truth is that the very element in Jewish life which created Zionism and for whom it was intended, those who really need a Jewish country in which to live out their contemporary selves without fear of evaporating, have chosen to do everything for Israel except go there." He urges Jewish leaders as well to consider returning to Israel and adds, "We cannot wait for Israel to be more pleasant and less full of problems." In fact, as Jews acknowledge that Diaspora life is tantamount to an exile from true Jewish values, says Hertzberg, *aliya* will become inevitable. And meanwhile, "the world might look upon us with some positive amazement and say: here indeed is a strange people, consciously trying to move itself from its ease and even glory in the West for the sake of its spiritual authenticity."

For further information:
Estelle Gilson, "Arthur Hertzberg: Writer, Scholar, Polemicist, Rabbi," *Present Tense,* Summer, 1980.

LEON HESS

b. 1914
Oil company executive

Leon Hess is a self-made entrepreneur who built the Amerada Hess Corporation, the giant oil company of which he is now chairman. Long known as one of the most efficient marketers and producers of refined products, he is a significant figure in big business, who insists on running his huge operation as a one-man show.

Leon Hess was born in Asbury Park, New Jersey. At 18 he started driving a fuel delivery truck with his immigrant father. Shortly before World War II, Hess began to expand his father's fuel oil business by displaying daring and innovative tactics. He increased the business's storage capacity for oil, which protected it from problems affecting the oil import market. During World War II he served as a petroleum supply officer with General George Patton's troops in Europe.

In 1945 Hess returned to the family business and started sending tank trucks from Perth Amboy, New Jersey to as far away as Binghamton, New York to sell to new markets. In the process he gradually built a network of oil storage "terminals." While other terminal operators rented tanker vessels, Hess bought them. In 1958 he built his first refinery near Perth Amboy, and five years later the Hess Oil and Chemical Corporation became publicly owned. From 1962 to 1965 Hess was president of the corporation, and from 1965 to 1969 he was chairman of its board and chief executive officer. Since 1969, when Hess took over the Amerada Petroleum Corporation, a leading independent crude producer, he has been chairman and chief executive officer of the Amerada Hess Corporation.

While Hess's enterprise has grown from a small family business to a multibillion-dollar corporation, he has insisted on avoiding the complex bureaucracy that characterizes most major oil companies. He controls 21 percent of Amerada Hess's stock and fills positions in the company with family members. His son is director of the company, his father-in-law sits on the board and his nephew is senior vice president for international exploration and production.

Hess, who operates the world's largest refinery—in St. Croix, Virgin Islands—and one other in Purvis, Mississippi, detests publicity. He rarely talks to the press, almost never allows himself to be photographed and avoids Wall Street analysts. An outsider of the close-knit oil "fraternity," his corporation is probably the largest public firm that functions without a public relations or investor-relations department. He once told a *Business Week* reporter: "I have always shunned publicity. I've been brought up all my life to stay out of the limelight, and I'm never going to change."

Nonetheless, when necessary, Hess has made some very public moves. For example, when oil shipments were being cut off from Iran after the Shah's overthrow, Hess flew to Iran to negotiate personally with the new regime for a resumption of supplies. He has been more successful in getting oil from Iran than any other company.

Hess's major interest outside of oil is the New York Jets professional football team. In the early 1960s he bought a 25 percent interest in the team for $250,000 in order to help a friend attain control of what was then a financially troubled franchise. The oil tycoon has since increased his interest to 50 percent and has become the club's chairman.

STEPHEN HESS

b. April 20, 1933
Political scientist; government official

White House staff member under two presidents, author of numerous books on American politics and senior fellow at the Brookings Institute in Washington,

Stephen Hess is considered an expert on American governmental affairs and the modern presidency.

Stephen Hess was born in New York City to Charles, who owned an Oldsmobile dealership, and Florence (Morse) Hess. He studied at the University of Chicago from 1950 to 1952 and received his B.A. degree from Johns Hopkins University in 1953. Hess taught political science at Johns Hopkins from 1953 to 1955 and served in the United States Army from 1956 to 1958. He was a ghost-writer for President Dwight D. Eisenhower from 1959 to 1961 and assistant to the Republican Party leader in the Senate in 1961.

Hess was an associate fellow at the Institute for Policy Studies from 1964 to 1965 and a fellow at the Institute of Politics at the John F. Kennedy School of Government at Harvard University from 1967 to 1968. He was appointed deputy assistant to President Richard Nixon for urban affairs in 1969. He served as national chairman of the White House Conference on Children and Youth from 1969 to 1971 and has been a senior fellow at the Brookings Institution since 1972.

Hess has also been active in many political and governmental organizations. He was a member of the Washington regional selection panel for the President's Commission on White House Fellows in 1973 and has been an associate of the Academy for Contemporary Problems since 1973. He was a member of the Washington, D.C. Board of Higher Education from 1973 to 1976, a member of the U.S. National Commission for UNESCO from 1975 to 1977, a consultant to the U.S. Office on Management and Budget in 1977 and a member of the Twentieth Century Fund task force in 1975 and 1978.

Hess's experience in politics has helped make him a successful political writer. In his first book, *Hats in the Ring: The Making of Presidential Candidates,* written in collaboration with Malcolm Moos, (New York, 1960), Hess writes about what makes a political convention tick. He offers a history of the development of the American system of nominating presidents and explains the intricacies of national committees, convention delegates, candidate managers and choice of running mates. In his second book, *America's Political Dynasties: From Adams to Kennedy,* again written with Moos, (New York, 1966), the author traces the influence and pattern of political inheritance in America. His third book, *The Republican Establishment: The Present and the Future of the G.O.P.,* written with David S. Broder (New York, 1968), is an assessment of the condition of the Republican Party.

In *The Ungentlemanly Art: A History of American Polit-*

ical Cartoons, written with Milton Kaplan, (New York, 1968), Hess surveys the work of caricaturists throughout American history and examines what issues most inflamed the passions of the people. He provides a close look at Richard Nixon's checkered career—at the time still unblemished by Watergate—in *Nixon: A Political Portrait,* written with Earl Mazo (New York, 1968). In *Organizing the Presidency* (Washington, D.C., 1976), Hess proposes a drastic redefinition of the president's innumerable tasks and calls for the restoration of power to the Cabinet.

Perhaps his most significant work to date is *The Washington Reporters* (Washington, D.C., 1981), a study of journalists who cover the Washington beat for daily newspapers. It is based upon empirical evidence, including interviews and questionnaires mailed to 1,200 men and women who are employed to follow the activities of the federal government. He found that the most influential media were those with the best access to sources—the three TV networks, the Associated Press and United Press International; *Time, Newsweek* and *U.S. News and World Report;* and four dailies; *The New York Times, Wall Street Journal, Washington Post* and *Washington Star.* Just behind them were seven newspapers (including the *Los Angeles Times, Christian Science Monitor* and *New York Daily News)* and two chains, Knight-Ridder and Cox. Hess also concluded that the terms "liberal" and "conservative" when applied to reporters were essentially meaningless. "Few reporters have strongly held political beliefs," a reporter told Hess. "Many do not vote." An odd finding, but Hess believes reporters are largely apolitical, though irresistibly drawn to celebrities and strong, articulate politicans and wielders of influence.

HOWARD H. HIATT

b. July 22, 1925
Physician

Howard H. Hiatt, who is dean of the Harvard School of Public Health, is one of America's foremost supporters of reform in health care delivery and in medical education. Since 1980, when he participated in a Boston forum that explored the impact of nuclear war on the medical community, he has become leading spokesman for his colleagues in medicine on the subject of arms control.

Howard Haym Hiatt was born in Patchogue, New York to Alexander, a shoe manufacturer, and Dorothy (Askinas) Hiatt. He was educated at Harvard College but left before completing a degree so that he could begin studies at the Harvard Medical School. He received his M.D., cum laude, in 1948.

From 1948 to 1950 Hiatt was an intern and resident at Beth Israel Hospital in Boston. Over the nine years that followed, he received a series of research and teaching appointments that took him to New York Hospital, the Cornell University Medical Center, the University of Chicago Hospital, the National Institute of Health, the Harvard Medical School and back to Beth Israel. From 1958 to 1959 he was American Cancer Society Scholar in cancer research at Harvard and has since received many additional grants for special research projects.

Hiatt's affiliation with Beth Israel, which has close ties with Harvard, grew into a permanent one; from 1959 to 1963 he was assistant visiting physician and from 1963 to 1972 he was physician-in-chief. Since 1972 he has been on Beth Israel's consultation board in medicine. At the same time Hiatt became a faculty member at the Harvard Medical School. From 1959 to 1963 he was assistant professor of medicine and from 1963 to 1972 was named Herrman L. Blumgart Professor at Harvard Medical School. Since 1972 he has been dean of the School of Public Health and professor of medicine.

Hiatt became a public figure after he presented the opening speech at a Boston forum sponsored by medical students at Tufts and Harvard. In the speech, which he has since presented to the American Medical Association and other bodies, he described graphically the effects of a nuclear attack on a typical urban center. According to his research, a very high percentage of doctors and nurses would be killed since so many hospitals are located in central cities. In addition to the immediate devastation— one-fourth of the city's inhabitants would be killed, and an even larger portion would be seriously injured— most of the medical resources that could possibly help the survivors would be destroyed. By refusing to over-dramatize the scenario and instead presenting it as straightforwardly as he could, Hiatt made an even stronger case for a nuclear freeze and nuclear disarmament. He was eventually invited to testify before U.S. Senate subcommittees on the subject.

Hiatt belongs to many organizations, including the New World Foundation, of which he is on the board of directors; the National Academy of Sciences; and the National Health Insurance panel to the Subcommittee on Health of the Senate Committee on Ways and Means. In the past he has been closely involved with the National

Cancer Institute, the Congressional Office of Technology Assessment and the Brookings Foreign Assistance Study.

MILTON HIMMELFARB

b. October 21, 1918
Writer; researcher

As director of information and research for the American Jewish Committee since 1955 and as editor of the *American Jewish Yearbook* since 1959, Milton Himmelfarb has become one of the major voices for the safeguarding of Jewish traditional life within the modern American mainstream as well as a leading conservative. He has also been a contributing editor to *Commentary* magazine since 1960 and as such has been one of the more forceful influences in neo-conservatism.

Milton Himmelfarb was born in Brooklyn to Max' and Bertha (Lerner) Himmelfarb. He attended the City College of New York, where he received a B.A. degree in 1938 and an M.S. degree in 1939. He simultaneously attended the Jewish Theological Seminary of America, where he received a B.H.L. in 1939, and that same year he also earned his diplome from the University of Paris.

In the 1940s Himmelfarb joined the American Jewish Committee and since 1955 has directed its information and research department. Moreover, as coeditor of the *American Jewish Yearbook,* published by the AJC, he oversees its annual compilation of articles surveying the major trends in Jewish life not only in America but around the world. Each volume begins with a major essay exploring the most pressing issue of the past year (feminism, Jewish philanthropy and the future of civil liberties are examples of some of the themes covered) and then follows with shorter articles by Jewish scholars and commentators discussing Jewish life, Jewish influence in American politics, social issues and so on. Although Himmelfarb is strictly an editor—he rarely contributes an article to the *Yearbook*—his concerns are strongly reflected in the book's contents.

Himmelfarb has often written or spoken about the need to preserve and expand, if possible, the Jewish population. He is alarmed about increased intermarriage and a low birthrate among Jewish couples. He thus advocates large Jewish families and promoted the proselytization of non-Jews in a presentation before a conference of rabbis in 1977.

Himmelfarb is the author of one book and co-editor of another. *The Jews of Modernity* (New York, 1973) is a collection of essays that appeared originally in *Commentary* and whose unifying theme is the conflict faced by Jews trying to preserve the history and traditions of Jewish life while successfully meeting the demands of modern American life. These demands, Himmelfarb contends, make it very tempting for Jews to discard their past. Throughout, Himmelfarb favors "traditionalism," and he reveals a strong distaste for Jewish "universalists," whom he described as "those who make their livings in business or the professions and live on Park Avenue or in the prosperous suburbs" and "the writers, editors, publishers, and professors" who are addicted to modernism and fundamentally uninterested in Jewish issues per se. Incidents of anti-Semitism leave these groups unconcerned, he argued, for they are too universal in their interests to care about ordinary Jews. As a result he has often urged fellow Jews to vote for Republicans in national elections, as he did in supporting the candidacies of Richard Nixon and Ronald Reagan for the presidency.

Notwithstanding his political articles, however, Himmelfarb's reputation in Judaic thought is one of a thoughtful and writer and philosopher. In "The 1967 War," which appeared in *Commentary* in October 1967, he concluded: "In the last third of the twentieth century we may be beginning to believe again that the history of the Jews points to some kind of providential order, which—for reasons having to do not with our merits, but at most with the merits of the Fathers—has a special place for it." In deed, one writer once attempted to write a piece about Himmelfarb's many essays and entitled it "The Achievement of Milton Himmelfarb."

In 1978 he co-edited with Victor Baras *Zero Population Growth: For Whom?* (Westport, Conn.). The essays in the book, originally presented at an American Jewish Committee conference in 1975, were prompted by the concern among many Jewish leaders that the "small family syndrome" and other sociological and demographic factors would surely contribute to the demise of Jews in America. It proposes that although population control is a pressing worldwide issue, minority groups in danger of extinction might take exception to it.

As a regular contributor to *Commentary,* he is a frequent writer on the role of Jews in politics. In "Are Jews Becoming Repubican?" (August 1981), he wrote that "what was old about the 1980 [election] is that Jews as a group are still unassimilated politically. . . . And they still worry about Israel. What was new was very new: fewer than one-half voted for the Democrats [because of] the desire for a strong resolute America and a secure Israel."

Himmelfarb has been a visiting professor at the Jewish Theological Seminary (1967–68 and 1971–72) and at the Reconstructionist Rabbinical College (1972–73) and in 1971 was a visiting lecturer at Yale University.

For further information:
Bauman, Steven. "An Interview with Milton Himmelfarb." *Jewish Spectator,* Spring 1978.

ART HODES

b. 1904 or 1906
Blues pianist

Blues pianist Art Hodes, whose performing career has spanned more than 50 years, has excelled in a field long dominated by southern blacks, so much so that *New Yorker* magazine critic Whitney Balliett describes Hodes' slow blues as "[surpassing] those of any other blues pianist." Hodes has also been a major jazz archivist, whose magazine of the 1940s, *The Jazz Record,* was the first of its kind to consciously collect oral interviews as a means of preserving jazz history.

Arthur William Hodes was born in Nikolayev, Russia to William, a tinsmith, and Dorothy Hodes. His exact date of birth is uncertain because, he explained once, his family left Russia with too little time to take family papers with them. The family settled in Chicago, where Hodes was educated in its public schools and studied music at the music school of the famous Hull House, a settlement house. Although Hodes' father was an opera fan who listened to Caruso and Chaliapin at home, and Hodes' training at Hull House was classically oriented, he tended naturally toward the jazz styles popular in the 1920s.

Hodes' mother had pushed her son to become a concert pianist, but was to be disappointed. After Hodes graduated from high school, he supported himself by day with a series of odd jobs and then worked nights as an accompanist in local dance halls, where he perfected his swing and then gravitated toward the Chicago jazz community. His earliest influences came from listening to recordings of Bessie Smith, Louis Armstrong and Bix Beiderbecke. By the mid-1920s Hodes had begun to pick up blues piano and was soon playing with some of the performers he had once admired at a distance. His first jam session, while he was still quite young, was with Benny Goodman.

Hodes continued playing in Chicago through the 1930s—and also raised a family with six children. But by 1938 the Chicago jazz community had become extinct, and Hodes followed the route taken by his predecessors and moved to New York. Once there, he ultimately settled in Greenwich Village, where he soloed at such clubs as the Pirate's Den, the Village Vanguard and the Stuyvesant Casino. Working constantly, he also became involved in broadcasting and writing about jazz. In the early 1940s he had a daily radio show on WNYC, which combined old jazz recordings, live performances, interviews and narrative background about jazz.

Before the year was up Hodes co-founded *The Jazz Record* with another jazz aficionado, Dale Curran. Unlike other jazz periodicals, which were targeted for record collectors, the *Record* not only discussed current jazz trends but balanced its focus equally between black and white musicians—a novelty at the time. Among those profiled were Louis Armstrong, Pee Wee Russell, Kaiser Marshall and many more, and the writers for the *Record* included the arts patron and photographer Carl Van Vechten and playwright Robert Alan Aurthur. The magazine folded in 1947.

Hodes, who performed in Carnegie Hall in 1946 and 1947, returned to Chicago in 1950 and has remained there ever since, although he tours Europe twice a year and continues to play throughout the United States and in Canada. He has performed in 12 specials for educational television and participated in a five-hour interview for the jazz archives at the Smithsonian Institution in Washington. One of his TV programs, "Plain Ol' Blues," won an Emmy award, and in 1977 he co-edited with Chadwick Hansen a collection of interviews, *Selections from the Gutter: Portraits from The Jazz Record* (Berkeley, Calif.).

The appeal of the blues is difficult to define, but in an interview with Balliett, Hodes explained: "The blues is an emotion that is happening inside you, and you're expressing it. . . . The blues heal you. Playing the blues becomes like talking trouble out. You work the blues out of you."

ABBIE HOFFMAN

b. November 30, 1936
Political activist; writer

With a seething energy, a raucous sense of humor, a refusal to bow to convention and a generous dose of chutzpah, former Yippie Abbie Hoffman has weathered changing political winds in America (and seven years "underground" as a political fugitive) to emerge again as an always anti-establishment leader of the anti-war, anti-nuclear- pro-civil rights and pro-human rights left. The author of seven published books and the survivor of many arrests, he epitomizes the "non-Jewish Jew" who rejects institutionalized movements.

Abbott Hoffman was born in Worcester, Massachusetts to John, a pharmacist who later became a wholesaler of medical supplies, and Florence (Schanberg) Hoffman. Although Hoffman's upbringing was typically middle-class, the teen-age rebellion that eventually led to his expulsion from a public high school turned out to be more than a passing phase. After graduating from Brandeis University with a B.A. degree in psychology in 1959, Hoffman went on to the University of California at Berkeley, where he received an M.A. degree in psychology in 1960 and was initiated into full-fledged political activism.

Despite the fact that he spent the next three years in Worcester as a pharmaceuticals salesman, he devoted the bulk of his energy and time to the burgeoning civil rights movement. In 1964, participating in Freedom Summer in Mississippi, he was arrested for the first time. He seemed to revel in challenging the law when he felt he had to, and getting arrested—combined with Hoffman's astute ability to attract media attention—became instrumental in his becoming one of the primary movers in the anti-war movement and in the growth of the 1960s counterculture.

In 1966 Hoffman settled in New York City, but his civil rights work came with him, as he founded a crafts store called Liberty House, which sold goods made by blacks and poor people from the South. But when Hoffman and other white civil rights activists were edged out of the movement by the increased militancy of some black leaders and by polarization among blacks themselves, he refocused his direction toward the growing anti-war movement. He found a niche among other middle-class refugees who had opted for an "alternative" lifestyle and set off on a path of prankishness, which earned him some celebrity while spurring the alienation between the older and younger generations. In 1967 he and some friends threw dollar bills onto the floor of the New York Stock Exchange, nearly causing a riot among traders. He was the organizer of "happenings" and "be-ins" during the late 1960s, which catalyzed the politicization of the youth movement.

In 1968 he was a founder of the Youth International Party, the Yippies, who allegedly subscribed to utter anarchy and urged adherents not to trust anyone over 30, although by this time Hoffman should have been among those not to be trusted. Under the pseudonym "Free," he also published his first book, *Revolution for the Hell of It* (New York, 1968), a collection of anecdotes, photographs and drawings ostensibly intended as a Yippie bible.

But it wasn't until the summer of 1968 that the movement Hoffman had helped inspire flowered into a fully political effort with more than superficial undertones. He helped spearhead demonstrations against the Democratic National Convention in Chicago, which ended in a series of violent clashes with the police. The following year Hoffman and six cohorts—they were dubbed the Chicago Seven—were tried for conspiracy, and in the ensuing proceedings, went on to make a mockery of the judicial system. In one instance, Hoffman and Jerry Rubin, co-founder of the Yippies, came to the courtroom wearing judicial robes. Because the Vietnam War, and not the actions of the Chicago Seven, had become the underlying issue of the trial, the defense, headed by attorney William Kunstler, took the opportunity to call well-known political and artistic personalities to testify. The seven were sentenced by Judge Julius Hoffman, but the convictions were eventually overturned on appeal, and none of the defendants served time in jail.

The experience did little to quiet Hoffman; if anything, in fact, it only made him more vociferous, turning him into a spokesperson for the counterculture. His second book, *Woodstock Nation: A Talk-Rock Album* (New York, 1969), became the movement manifesto, and during the early 1970s he traveled cross-country as a full-time organizer, knowing full well (and apparently relishing it) that the FBI was on his trail. In 1971 he published *Steal This Book* (New York), a how-to on "cheating" the system. Forced to publish it independently when his regular publisher refused to, Hoffman arranged with Grove Press to distribute it. Bookstores then refused to sell it until a favorable review in *The New York Times* gave the book respectability, if not acceptability. He campaigned for Democratic presidential candidate George McGovern in 1972 and that year coauthored, with Jerry Rubin and Ed Sanders, *Vote!* (New York), an account of the Republican and Democratic conventions held in Miami.

Hoffman's life changed dramatically in 1973, however, when he was arrested for his role in the sale of cocaine. He was imprisoned for six weeks, but after being released on bail, he fled underground several months later rather than face the prospect of a long jail sentence. During this period he apparently traveled a great deal, had plastic surgery to alter his looks and erratically published interviews in alternative publications as well as a book of letters, written with Anita Hoffman, entitled *To america with Love: Letters from the Underground* (New York, 1976), an account of life on the run as shown in the correspondence between Hoffman and his wife.

But running away was inimical to Hoffman—especially when faced by political causes. Having settled in upstate

New York under the alias "Larry Freed," and working as a free-lance writer, he became active as an environmentalist fighting attempts by the U.S. Army Corps of Engineers to dredge the St. Lawrence River. At one point he even testified before the U.S. Senate. When the ensuing victory turned "Freed" into a local celebrity, he decided to shed his mask and in late 1980 appeared on a national television interview with Barbara Walters. The following day he turned himself in to New York authorities and in early 1981 was permitted to plead guilty on reduced drug charges. He also published his autobiography, *Soon to Be a Major Motion Picture* (New York, 1980), a reflection on his life and political work. Hoffman was permitted to serve his sentence as a drug counselor in a work-release program and soon resumed his former activist stance.

Outspoken as ever, though less deliberately ridiculous, he spoke out against American involvement in El Salvador and was highly critical of the Begin administration in Israel, whose policies he described as "based on hysteria and disgrace." He added that American Jews should come into greater contact with Israel's peace movement. "We have to be in touch with them," he said. "We have to keep the bridges open to the Palestinians. We have to keep talking away, explaining and using the right language so it's not so easily said that you're anti-Semitic. We have to point out that the other policy isn't working."

In 1982 Hoffman's seventh book, *Square-Dancing in the Ice Age* (New York), was published. A collection of Hoffman's writings while underground, it was originally to be dedicated to Anne Frank, another underground diarist whom Hoffman said he admired a great deal, especially during his own years in hiding. "But I didn't think my book serious enough to link her name with it," although, he said, she had served to inspire him at critical points in his life.

As with everything else in his life, Hoffman spurns belonging to any established Jewish organization, although his Jewishness has been an essential part of his makeup, and his heroes are three Jews who chose to make it on their own—"to go for broke," in Hoffman's words: Spinoza, Marx and Freud.

DUSTIN HOFFMAN

b. August 8, 1937
Actor

Dustin Hoffman is one of America's finest young character actors. His remarkable ability to absorb entirely new personae in each film is a tribute not only to his versatility but to his total dedication to his art. And true to his profession, he cannot be typecast: Hoffman—who rose to prominence as the awkward post-adolescent in *The Graduate,* and whose roles have since included a down-and-out would-be pimp, a suicidal jet-set songwriter, the comic Lenny Bruce, one of the journalists who uncovered the Watergate scandals and a newly divorced father—is the actor's actor.

Dustin Hoffman was born in Los Angeles, where his father, Harry, was a furniture designer and former prop man at Columbia Studios. Always the shortest in his class—Hoffman is still shorter than average—he made his stage debut as "Tiny Tim" in a junior high school production of *A Christmas Carol.* From then on Hoffman determined to become an actor, and after quitting Santa Monica City College, he attended the Pasadena Playhouse, where he completed a two-year course in 1958. He then moved to New York, where for six years he acted sporadically and supported himself with a variety of odd jobs and help from home. In retrospect he has commented that these difficult years actually helped his career; he has often drawn on some of his early job experiences to formulate his characters.

Hoffman landed his first significant role in 1964, when he appeared in the off-Broadway play *Harry, Noon and Night* at the American Place Theater. As a result of his impressive debut, he was scheduled to replace Martin Sheen as the son in Frank Gilroy's play *The Subject Was Roses* in 1965 during its Broadway run. Unfortunately, however, he was sidelined by injuries. But the following year provided Hoffman a break—a role in Ronald Ribman's *The Journey of the Fifth Horse,* again at the American Place (and later televised), in which his portrayal of a Russian clerk earned him an Obie as best off-Broadway actor. During the 1966–67 season, Hoffman next garnered attention for his performance in *Eh?* in which he played a purposely inept assembly line worker. His performance was compared to silent film clowns Keaton and Chaplin. This time he won not only a Drama Desk Award for off-Broadway achievement but his first movie offer.

The Graduate premiered one year later. Directed by Mike Nichols and starring Hoffman and Anne Bancroft, it chronicled the messy (but hilarious) seduction of a confused young college graduate by the mother of his girlfriend. Set to the music of Simon and Garfunkel, *The Graduate* was a box office smash. It became one of the great period pieces of the late 1960s and propelled Hoffman to an Oscar nomination and instant stardom. His portrayal of Benjamin Braddock, a young man in his early 20s, was so convincing that at the time few people believed he was already 31.

In contrast to the $20,000 Hoffman earned for *The Graduate,* he was able to command slightly more— $430,000—for his next film. In John Schlesinger's *Midnight Cowboy* (1969), he played the greasy pimp to Jon Voight's male prostitute. Although fants went to see Hoffman-the-Graduate, they saw Ratso Rizzo—a transformation indicative of the actor's range and that earned him his second Academy Award nomination. Subsequent roles— the "swinging single" in *John and Mary* (1969); the grizzled ancient veteran of the American Indian wars who was present at Custer's Last Stand in Arthur Penn's *Little Big Man* (1971); the convict in *Papillon* (1973); the intense, intellectual graduate student caught up in Nazi intrigue and a complicated love affair in *The Marathon Man* (1976)—are only some examples of the characterizations he has adapted. To achieve his portrayals, Hoffman immerses himself totally in his characters, trying in advance to absorb as much as possible their environment and experiences. For example, when he prepared for his role as *Washington Post* reporter Carl Bernstein in *All the President's Men* (1975), he spent several months on the job with a reporter whose beat was similar to Bernstein's, and later he visited a prison several times incognito to familiarize himself with the jail environment and the personality dynamics it fostered for his role as a small-time ex-con in *Straight Time* (1978).

But perhaps Hoffman's peak achievement to date was his performance as the ambitious young advertising executive in Robert Benton's *Kramer vs. Kramer* (1980) who is left alone with his 6-year-old son when his wife, played by Meryl Streep, leaves him. For the first time since his son's birth, Ted Kramer must confront the responsibilities of fatherhood head-on as well as his own motives in work, in play, in life in general. In a subsequent bitter court battle, he fights for—and wins— custody of his son. The role, for which Hoffman won his first Oscar, ironically coincided with his own divorce —so that this time the actor was able to draw on his own experiences to realize the intensity and anguish of Kramer.

STANLEY HOFFMANN

b. November 27, 1928
Political scientist

Stanley Hoffmann is a noted political scientist and writer in international affairs and foreign relations. He is chairman of the Western European studies department at Harvard University and a member of the Center of International Relations at Harvard.

Stanley Hoffmann was born in Vienna. He was mainly educated in Paris and was helped and protected as a child by French non-Jews during the Nazi occupation. He received a diploma from L'Institut D'Etudes Politiques in 1948. In 1952 he earned an M.A. degree from Harvard University and in 1953 was awarded a doctorate degree from the University of Paris Law School.

Hoffmann entered the French army in 1953. After his military service ended two years later, he came to the United States to stay and joined the faculty of Harvard University. He was an instructor at Harvard from 1955 to 1957, an assistant professor from 1957 to 1959 and an associate professor from 1959 to 1963. In 1963 he became a full professor. Hoffmann, who was naturalized in 1960, was appointed the chairman of the Western European studies department at Harvard in 1969, and in 1971 he joined its Center for International Relations, where he is presently Douglas Dillon Professor of the Civilization of France and chairman of the Center for European Studies.

Since 1954 Hoffmann has written or edited books on foreign affairs and international relations. His first book, *Organisations Internationales et Pouvoir Politiques des Etats* (France, 1954), won a Carnegie award. His works since then include *In Search of France* (Cambridge, Mass., 1963), *The State of War* (New York, 1965), *Gulliver's Travels: Or the Setting of American Foreign Policy* (New York, 1968) and *Decline or Renewal?* (New York, 1974). He has also edited three volumes on international law and foreign affairs, including *Contemporary Theories in International Relations* (New York, 1960), *Conditions of World Order* (New York, 1970) and *The Relevance of International Law* (New York, 1971).

Hoffmann's main thesis in international relations is that the concepts that have defined international relations in the Cold War era are no longer adequate. A new set of parameters, which account for the shifting balances of power, must be established. In *Foreign Policy* (Winter 1976–77), he wrote that "the world we face today is neither the world in black and white of the cold war, nor one in which we can indulge our economic preferences. . . . Today [we] oscillate . . . between exaggerated anxieties about America's present strength and a rather lackadaisical attitude about the perils of the future."

He has also written extensively about the Middle East and Jewish affairs. In another article in *Foreign Policy* (Winter 1977–78), he commented that "Sooner or later, the United States must confront the issue of the PLO and enlist the help of the Soviet Union. . . . the tactical problem is that of timing, of selecting the right angle of attack." And following the bombing of a

Paris synagogue in October 1980 by right-wing extremists and an ensuing spate of articles in the press condemning French anti-Semitism and linking French government policy supporting a Palestinian homeland to such violent outbursts, Hoffmann demurred in a letter to *The New York Times* (October 23, 1980) denying the existence of a "wave of anti-Semitism in France" and then concluding: "But to suggest that any departure [by the French government] from the orthodoxy of Israel's foreign policy stands is a license for anti-Semitism is obnoxious."

In acknowledgement of Hoffmann's academic and scholarly achievement, he has been made a member of many distinguished organizations. He is a member of the American Academy of Arts and Sciences, the American Political Science Association, the American Society of International Law and the Council on Foreign Relations.

For further information:

Hoffmann, Stanley. *Duties Beyond Borders: On the Limits and Possibilities of Ethical International Politics.* Syracuse, New York: 1981.

————. *Primacy or World Order: American Foreign Policy Since The Cold War.* New York: 1978.

———— and Andrews, William G. eds. *The Fifth Republic at 20.* Albany, New York: 1980.

ROBERT HOFSTADTER

b. February 5, 1915
Physicist

Dr. Robert Hofstadter, professor of physics at Stanford University, won the Nobel Prize in Physics in 1961 for designing a device that enabled the development of the first exact measurements of the size and shape of protons and neutrons, which make up the atomic nucleus.

Robert Hofstadter was born in New York City to Louis, a salesman, and Henrietta (Koenigsberg) Hofstadter. It was at City College in New York that Hofstadter decided to major in the physical sciences. In 1935 he graduated with a B.S. degree. He was also awarded a prize for meritorious work in physics.

After graduating with an M.A. and Ph.D. degree from Princeton University in 1938, Hofstadter spent one year studying photoconductivity in crystals at Princeton from 1938 to 1939 and then did research at the University of Pennsylvania, where he also taught physics from 1940 to 1941. He was an instructor in physics at City College from 1941 to 1942.

Hofstadter worked as a physicist from 1942 to 1943 at the National Bureau of Standards in Washington, D.C., where he helped invent the proximity fuse, a major antiaircraft weapon that explodes a shell when it senses something approaching by radar. Hofstadter then worked as assistant chief physicist at Norden Laboratories Corporation in New York from 1943 to 1946, when he returned to teaching as an assistant professor of physics at Princeton University. In 1950 he joined the faculty of Stanford University as associate professor and in 1954 was promoted to a full professorship. He has taught there ever since.

Soon after Hofstadter arrived at Stanford he began to study the composition of the atomic nucleus. He and his colleagues invented a "scattering machine," the most powerful microscopic instrument to date, that enabled him to perceive the different positions of nuclear particles. In 1961 he described the appearance of the neutron and proton. Both particles, he stated, are comprised of a thick, pointed core of mesons (even smaller nuclear particles) and two penetrating tiers of meson clouds surrounding the core. He was presented with the Nobel Prize for providing the first "reasonably consistent" portrait of the atomic nuclear structure.

Hofstadter, who has received many awards besides the Nobel Prize, has written dozens of papers on molecular structure, solid state physics and nuclear physics. He wrote, with Robert Herman, *High-Energy Electron Scattering* (Stanford, 1960) and *Electron Scattering and Nuclear Structure* (Stanford, 1963). He has been editor of many publications, including *Investigations in Physics, Reviews of Modern Physics, Physical Review* and *Review of Scientific Instruments.*

ELIZABETH HOLTZMAN

b. August 11, 1941
Lawyer; politician

The election of Elizabeth Holtzman to the House of Representatives in 1972 marked the beginning of a distinguished career as an articulate progressive on a national level. In her eight years in Congress, she marked herself as an outspoken defender of the rights of minorities, women, the elderly and the poor. She gained nationwide attention as a sharp interrogator during the 1973 and 1974 Watergate hearings. Since leaving the Congress in 1981, the Harvard-trained attorney has remained an eloquent spokeswoman and active worker for a wide range of humanitarian causes. And in 1981 she became the first woman ever elected to be district attorney of Brooklyn (Kings County).

Elizabeth Holtzman was born in Brooklyn, the daughter of Sidney, a criminal lawyer, and Filia (Ravitz) Holtzman, former chairperson of the Russian Department at Hunter College in New York City. Even as a youngster she was an over-achiever: she and her twin brother, Robert, now a neurosurgeon, ran for and won the positions of vice president and president, respectively, of the student body at Abraham Lincoln High School in Coney Island, from which both graduated in 1958.

Holtzman entered Radcliffe College, graduating with a B.A. degree magna cum laude in 1962. She then entered Harvard Law School, earning her Doctor of Law degree in 1965. While there, she helped form the Law Students' Civil Rights Research Council, a national student group. This signaled the beginning of her abiding interest in civil rights; even as a law student, Holtzman worked on civil rights cases in Georgia.

Once out of law school, she joined the New York City law firm of Wachtell, Lipton, Rosen, Katz and Kern but left in 1968 to become liaison to the Department of Parks, Recreation and Cultural Affairs in the administration of Mayor John Lindsay. She resigned in 1970 to resume private practice with Paul, Weiss, Rifkind, Wharton and Garrison, where she remained until 1972, but at the same time became more involved in electoral politics.

That year she was elected Democratic state committeewoman from Flatbush in Brooklyn by a 2-1 margin— and she left the law to enter the campaign for Rep. Emanuel Celler's seat in Congress. In a Democratic primary campaign in 1972—in which Holtzman aggressively canvassed neighborhoods, leafleted at subway stations and spoke at many local organizations, while the confident Celler remained relatively aloof—Holtzman emerged the winner, defeating Celler, who had held his seat for 50 years, by only a few hundred votes. But in the election that November, in which Celler ran on the Liberal ticket in the overwhelmingly Democratic district, Holtzman won the post by a large plurality, and at age 32 was the youngest woman ever elected to the House of Representatives.

Although a freshman in Congress, Holtzman began immediately to push for those programs that she supported and to display her talents as a legislative designer and analyst. In the Congress she was a member of the Judiciary Committee and its subcommittees on immigration, criminal justice and crime. In this post she was actively involved in deliberations on the impeachment of then-President Nixon. She also took part in the interrogation of President Gerald Ford about the pardon of Nixon in the first appearance by an American president before a congressional committee.

The list of Holtzman's accomplishments in her eight years in Congress reflects a formidable commitment to human rights, in the United States and abroad. For example, she introduced an amendment, passed by the House in 1976, to prevent the State Department from negotiating or disseminating information about contracts that discriminate against Americans on the basis of religion, race, sex or national origin. An opponent of the Vietnam War, she consistently opposed massive increases in the military budget and favored an end to conscription.

She collaborated with Peter W. Rodino Jr. (D., N.J.), chairman of the House Judiciary Committee, on the introduction of legislation designed to thwart the attempt by Arabs to boycott American businesses owned by or employing Jews or that have dealings with Israel. Introduced in the 94th and 95th congresses, the Holtzman-Rodino bill calls for stiff criminal penalties for those corporations that comply with boycotts based on racial, religious, sexual or national grounds.

Holtzman has been active in publicizing the violation of the rights of Jews in the Soviet Union. In 1973 and 1976 she sponsored two congressional vigils to underscore support for Russian Jews. The 1973 vigil was especially significant in its backing of the Jackson amendment, which penalizes nations that restrict the freedom of movement of their citizens. The second vigil dramatized the separation of Soviet Jewish families, where some members had been allowed to emigrate while others had not. She also visited the Soviet Union in 1975 to learn firsthand about the plight of Soviet Jews.

Holtzman has also been a persistent attacker of the Immigration Service's so-called "half-hearted, dilatory investigation" of alleged Nazi war criminals residing in the United States. In a detailed memorandum, she documented the neglect of the Immigration Service over many years to follow up numerous leads and other information regarding Nazis in America. As a result, the Immigration Service stepped up deportation and denaturalization proceedings against nine such criminals, and in addition the State Department renewed efforts in 1976 to obtain more information about Nazis in America from sources in Israel and countries in Eastern Europe.

In areas of social legislation, Holtzman obtained increased benefits for poverty-stricken aged and disabled individuals in New York and four other states. She became very involved in services for the elderly, and while she helped provide food programs for those in her community, she also exposed waste and fraud in a Brooklyn food program in 1976.

Holtzman has been especially active in all areas of legislation concerning women. These include a sex discrimination amendment in federally funded employment programs, which was passed in 1976, as well as expanding Medicare coverage to include breast cancer detection tests and introducing legislation to safeguard the privacy of a rape victim when being interrogated. Throughout her tenure, Holtzman was vocal in her support of the Equal Rights Amendment.

In 1980 Elizabeth Holtzman ran for the New York senate seat then held by Republican Jacob Javits. She won a close and hotly contested primary race, whose candidates included Bess Meyerson, but was narrowly defeated the following November in the conservative sweep that adversely affected so many liberal and centrist Democrats. In a three-way race—which featured Alphonse D'Amato as a Conservative and Republican, Jacob Javits as a Liberal and Holtzman as a Democrat—D'Amato won, Holtzman was second, while Javits ran a poor third. Holtzman claimed that Javits' candidacy had spoiled her chances.

Since leaving Congress, Holtzman has resumed private practice. In addition she joined the faculty of the New York University Graduate School of Public Administration in 1981 to teach "Congressional Oversight of Presidential Policy-Making and Administration" and "Financing Political Campaigns." She has remained very active as a public figure, especially in support of extending the deadline for enactment of the Equal Rights Amendment and in safeguarding individual civil liberties. In 1981 she ran for district attorney of Kings County and was elected.

IRVING LOUIS HOROWITZ

b. September 25, 1929
Sociologist

The German poet Walter Hollerer has described sociologist Irving Louis Horowitz as "a kind of poet, with a poet's sense of rhyme, metaphor, gesture and, at times, a poet's amiable capacity for presenting his wishes as accomplished facts." A prolific writer, Horowitz's work has covered the sociology of knowledge, war and revolution; development in the Third World with a focus on Latin America; and the relationship of the Jewish people to Israel.

Irving Louis Horowitz was born in Harlem, the son of Louis, a union organizer and later a "fixer" of "locks and windows" who "made everything from shoe lasts to kitchens," and Esther (Tepper) Horowitz. He received a Bachelor of Social Science degree in sociology from the City College of New York in 1951 and the following year an M.A. degree from Columbia University. In 1955 he was appointed assistant professor of social theory at Buenos Aires University in Buenos Aires, Argentina. He completed his Ph.D. at that university in 1957 and did a year of postdoctoral study at Brandeis University in 1958. Horowitz's first book, *The Idea of War and Peace in Contemporary Social and Philosophical Theory* (New York, 1957), won a special citation from the Carnegie Endowment for International Peace in 1958.

After a year as an assistant professor of sociology at Bard College in 1959, Horowitz became chairman of the Department of Sociology at Hobart and William Smith College in Geneva, New York until 1963. That year he moved to Washington University in St. Louis, Missouri, first as an associate professor and after 1965 as a professor of sociology.

He stayed at Washington University until 1969, when he founded *Transaction* magazine (later renamed *Society*) and then joined the graduate faculty of Rutgers University in New Brunswick, New Jersey as a professor of sociology and political science. That year he was also the founding chairman of the Department of Sociology at Livingston College, an experimental undergraduate division of Rutgers University. He also moved *Transaction/Society,* which had begun to publish books on the social sciences, to Rutgers. He remained at Livingston College until 1973, when he returned to the graduate faculty. In 1977 Horowitz was appointed distinguished professor of sociology and political science at Rutgers University and the following year was awarded its Hannah Arendt Chair of Sociology and Political Science.

Horowitz has also been a visiting professor at 19 different universities throughout the world. In South America he has taught in Mexico, Argentina, Brazil and Venezuela. He was a visiting lecturer at the London School of Economics in 1962 and 1969 and the distinguished visiting professor of American civilization at the Hebrew University in Jerusalem. He has held similar appointments in Japan and India as well as in many of the most respected institutes of higher learning in the United States, including Stanford University and the University of Wisconsin.

In many of his writings on the interaction between social scientists and public policy makers, Horowitz argues that the United States is directed by a bureaucratic sector that is responsive but not always responsible to older social classes. In many ways that sector is isolated from the masses of people, and the challenge it faces is to find a course of action that satisfies the needs and interests of many, often antagonistic groups. *Israeli Ecstasies/Jewish Agonies* (New York, 1974) is a collection of Horowitz's essays concerning the disintegration of

Israel's position in the world following the June 1967 war as well as the Jewish position in the political structures of the United States and Latin America. He argued that the Jews' best hope for survival still lies in liberal political ideologies.

Since 1957 Horowitz has written 18 books as well as numerous magazine articles and scientific studies. His most common topics are the role of ideology in modern society, militarism in the Third World and the United States, and the interaction of the social sciences and public policy.

Horowitz has long held a deep interest in Jewish affairs. From 1973 until 1975 he was the principal investigator for a study of Latin American nationalism and its bearing on Jewish ethnicity in South America. It was sponsored by the Memorial Foundation for Jewish Culture. From 1976 until 1980 he was the associate editor of *Contemporary Jewry* magazine and is a contributing editor of *Present Tense* magazine, sponsored by the American Jewish Committee.

Among the many organizations to which Horowitz belongs are Amnesty International; the Council on Foreign Relations; the American Association for the Abolition of Involuntary Mental Hospitalization, of which he was a founding member in 1970; and the Center for Inter-American Relations. In 1970 Horowitz was named Man of the Year in the behavioral sciences by *Time* magazine.

For further information:

Horowitz, Irving Louis. *Beyond Empire and Revolution. Militarization and Consolidation in the Third World.* New York: 1982.

———. *Genocide, State Power and Mass Murder.* New Brunswick, N.J.: 1976; republished in an expanded and revised edition as *Taking Lives: Genocide and State Power.* New Brunswick, N.J.: 1981.

———. *Revolution in Brazil: Politics and Society in a Developing Nation.* New York: 1964.

———. *The Struggle Is the Message: The Organization and Ideology of the Anti-War Movement.* Berkeley, Calif.: 1970.

———. *The War Game: Studies of the Civilian Militarists.* New York: 1963.

LEVI ISAAC HOROWITZ

b. July 3, 1921
Rabbi

Since 1944 Levi Isaac Horowitz has been the spiritual leader—the Rebbe—of the Bostoner Hasidim, one of Boston's three Hasidic sects. As the first American-born Rebbe, he is uniquely familiar with the mores and problems of contemporary American youth and has developed a distinct style of leadership that combines traditional Hassidic observance with a liberal, flexible approach toward his followers, many of whom are newcomers to the Hassidic way of life.

Levi Isaac Horowitz was born in Boston to Pinchos David and Sorah Sosha (Brandwein) Horowitz. His father, the first Bostoner Rebbe, traced his ancestry to the Baal Shem Tov through Rabbi Moshe of Lelov and through four generations of Jerusalem-based Hasidic rabbis. He arrived in Boston in 1914 from Jerusalem by way of Poland, where he had been stranded during the outbreak of World War I. Once there, he was appointed leader by the small community of Hasidim who had arrived before him. Their own varying backgrounds—a contrast to most other Hasidic sects, whose members are originally from the same Eastern European villages—set the groundwork for a new form of Hasidism, the Bostoner branch, which tolerates differences among its followers. This open-minded approach to leadership was passed on to the son.

Levi Isaac Horowitz was educated in New York and Jerusalem and was in fact a student when his father died in 1942. Two years later he returned to Boston to assume his father's position as head of the New England Hassidic Center and of Congregation Beth Pincus. However, most of his followers were elderly (one account says the average age then was 80 and that it is now 26), and in order to keep the movement vibrant and growing, he developed an outreach program in the early 1950s to attract new members. He appealed primarily to second- and third-generation American Jews in the New England area who had since become assimilated by showing that his movement represented a living link to their past. He founded the New England Torah Institute in Boston, which offered an ongoing series of adult education classes for college students and adults and opened his home as a retreat for young Jews seeking some form of identification with their heritage.

In 1962 Horowitz moved both his synaogogue and his Hassidic Center to the Boston suburb of Brookline, where many of his followers had already moved. By conducting regular *shabbatons*—weekend retreats designed to explore the essence of Hasidism in the context of modern American life—he opened the way for Jewish college students in Boston to ask questions and familiarize themselves with Hasidic customs. New members of the Bostoner community are referred to as *ba'alai t'shuva*—"the people returning."

The Bostoner sect—which numbers about 3,000 members around the world, including a small group in New York City headed by Horowitz's older brother

Moshe and another in Jerusalem—has nearly 300 families among its followers in Boston. Included among these members are several scientists who find in Horowitz's leadership an ability to bind contemporary technology with ancient spirituality. A computer scientist and *baal t'shiva* ("one who has chosen to return to traditional Judaism") thus refers to the Bible as "the instruction manual of creation"; and a physicist, explaining his acceptance of a *shiduch* ("agreement to marry") with a woman he scarcely knew, used his professional experience as a comparison. "In the laboratory, there are many processes you don't understand," he said, "but they work anyway." And Horowitz's brand of Hasidism seems to work as well. His members need not wear traditional clothing nor abandon modern-type careers, as long as they integrate the spiritual meaning of Hasidism into their lives.

His blend of traditional and Western customs, including a service providing medical and other diagnostic counsel, has sparked some controversy and derision from other Hasidic sects, who express skepticism toward Horowitz's open acceptance of "inauthentic" members. But to the Bostoner Rebbe, pride in Jewish identity reigns above all, and he feels a strong responsibility to reclaim many young Jews who have lost their roots. Thus, in the article "Understanding Ourselves Through Others" (*Jewish Observer*, May–June 1980), he writes:

> We are faced with a generation of young people who lack knowledge and understanding of what living a Jewish life means, and we must declare ourselves partners in their guilt. Today's youth have not rejected Judaism after studying and understanding it; they have ignored it because of misconceptions, a lack of interest, and their own struggle for identity and meaning in life. The young person who says, "I am proud to be a Jew," should indeed be proud. It is our responsibility to give him that spirit and pride in being a Jew.

VLADIMIR HOROWITZ

b. October 1, 1904
Pianist

Eccentric and brilliant, Vladimir Horowitz is hailed by many as the world's greatest living pianist.

Born in Kiev, Russia, the youngest of three children of Simeon, an electrical engineer, and Sophia (Bodik) Horowitz, he acquired an enduring love for music from his mother, an amateur pianist. He began his lessons when he was 6 and attended the Kiev Conservatory, where he studied under Felix Blumenthal, a pupil of the pianist Anton Rubinstein. His early ambition was

to become a composer, but after the Russian Revolution in 1917, he turned to concertizing to earn money to help his family. The audience response led to a tour of Russia in 1923–24. In 1925 Horowitz left Russia on a study permit and never returned. During the next two years he performed throughout Europe. He was by now being compared with great pianists of an earlier generation, including Busoni and Paderewski.

Horowitz made his American debut at Carnegie Hall with the New York Philharmonic on January 12, 1928. The young Russian pianist, playing the Tchaikovsky Concerto in B-flat Minor, was hailed as "sensational" and drew standing ovations. He continued to perform at a frantic pace. Following his 1935 season, seven years after he first came to America, Horowitz went into seclusion, living in France and Switzerland. This was the first of many periodic absences from the concert stage, reportedly due to fatigue. In 1938 he resumed performing, and in 1944 he became an American citizen.

In 1953 Horowitz gave a recital in Carnegie Hall to celebrate the 25th anniversary of his American debut. He played the Tchaikovsky concerto he had played in 1928. Horowitz was described by critics as having matured into a performer of greater sophistication and depth rather than a pure technician. Yet after the concert he once again left the stage, not to be seen for 12 years. Rumors of nervous exhaustion added to the Horowitz mystique. Yet he continued to record and, in addition, studied the work of composers with whom he had not been familiar in order to broaden his repertoire.

On May 9, 1965, with much advance fanfare and publicity, Horowitz returned triumphant to Carnegie Hall. Playing selections by Chopin, Scriabin, Bach and Schumann, he received thunderous ovations as a performer whose virtuosity, intensity and artistry were undiminished.

Horowitz is one of the most extraordinary piano technicians of this or any century. This gift can be seen clearly in his playing of pieces like Chopin's *Etudes*, which are designed to show off various facets of the pianist's technique. His tonal palette is varied; he can produce massive metallic sonorities, play the most delicate passagework and is also capable of producing a beautiful singing cantalena. To play a singing line, difficult on a percussion instrument like the piano, he recommends that pianists listen to great singers as part of their studies. His use of the pedal is often spare but canny, especially when building large sonorities. He often brings out hidden inner voices and his use of pianistic color makes his playing sound orchestral in conception.

The winner of 15 Grammy awards, Horowitz has

since continued to perform and record at a less frantic pace than he did as a youth but remains a living legend. He has also been a highly successful teacher. Among his students were Byron Janis, Gary Graffman, Alexander Fiorillo, Coleman Blumfield and Ivan Davis. All his pupils acknowledge his pianistic talents, particularly his way of orchestrating chords and independent voices, and his mastery of extreme ranges of colors and dynamics, yet some now question him on interpretation.

Horowitz has been married to conductor Arturo Toscanini's daughter Wanda since December 21, 1933.

For further information:
Hamilton, David. *The Listener's Guide to Great Instrumentalists.* New York, 1982.

IRVING HOWE

b. June 11, 1920
Editor; critic; writer

The distinguished writer, critic and scholar Irving Howe is probably best-known to the reading public as the author of the award-winning book *World of Our Fathers* (New York, 1976), a lively chronicle of the voyage of Eastern European Jews to a new and thriving cultural and religious life in New York's teeming Lower East Side. But his activities include far more: he is the versatile editor of the magazine *Dissent,* a social-democratic journal of political and social issues, and of many books and articles on Yiddish and other literature and many other subjects. And in deed as well as in writing, he is an outspoken and articulate commentator on a wide range of problems affecting contemporary Jews and anyone else to whom the concepts of democratic socialism—which Howe actively supports—are important.

Irving Howe was born in the Bronx, the only child of Bessarabian immigrants David and Nettie (Goldman) Howe. His father eked out a marginal existence, first as a grocer and then as a "customer peddler" of linens and cloth products. Yiddish was his primary language until he attended high school. In 1940 he graduated from the City College of New York, where he had joined a Trotskyite group, the Young People's Socialist League, at the urging of his fellow student, Irving Kristol, whom Howe describes now as a "conservative ideologue."

Howe served in the United States Army in Alaska from 1942 until 1945. After his discharge he worked for *Labor Action,* a socialist newspaper, then for the historian-philosopher Hannah Arendt and for a time

as book editor of Schocken Books. His first book of importance was a revised edition of Rabbi Leo Baeck's *The Essence of Judaism* (New York, 1948). It was soon followed by *The United Automobile Workers and Walter Reuther* (New York, 1949), *Sherwood Anderson* (New York, 1951) and *William Faulkner* (New York, 1952).

In the early 1950s, during the peak of intellectual fear and political hysteria induced by Senator Joseph McCarthy and his sympathizers and emulators, Howe and Lewis Coser, a German-born Jewish sociologist, founded the journal *Dissent.* Now in its third decade of publication, its pages have always expressed the essence of Howe's central beliefs: democratic socialism, reverence for freedom, opposition to neo-conservatism and its genuflection before business and military interests, and skepticism of all extremist panaceas.

Rather than excoriate communism as a political and emotional exercise, Howe turned to a careful examination of the party and its authoritarian nature. With Coser, he wrote *The American Communist Party: A Critical History* (New York, 1958), a tempered and judicious study in which the authors praise the non-authoritarian socialist Eugene Debs as a moral prophet. In a later work, *Essays in the Politics of Democratic Radicalism* (New York, 1967), he identified "with the 'revisionists,' those political marranos who, forced to employ Communist jargon, [yet] spoke out for a socialism democratic in character."

In the 1970s he turned to scrutinizing the immigrant world of his family and childhood. *World of Our Fathers* received the National Book Award for exploring "the journey of the East European Jews to America and the life they found and made." For many years before and after, he and the Yiddish poet Eliezer Greenberg had been editing and translating works of Yiddish literature and publishing them at intervals: *A Treasury of Yiddish Stories* (New York, 1954), *A Treasury of Yiddish Poetry* (New York, 1969), *Voices from the Yiddish: Essays, Memoirs, Diaries* (Ann Arbor, Mich., 1972) and *Ashes out of Hope: Fiction by Soviet-Yiddish Writers* (New York, 1977). After the death of Greenberg, Howe initiated a collaboration with Ruth R. Wisse, and they edited *The Best of Sholom Aleichem* (Washington, D.C., 1979).

Howe also turned to American Jewish political life in the 1970s during the brouhaha over whether an American Jewish group named Breira (in Hebrew, "alternative") had the right to question Israeli policies in public. Breira was bitterly attacked by Israel and American Jewish organizations such as the Anti-Defamation League and the American Jewish Congress, which distributed harsh criticism of the group, charging it with being anti-Israel. Howe was never a member of Breira, but he very quickly became its major public defender, writing and speaking on its behalf. Afterward, he said he was outraged by "the very nasty sort of witch-hunting campaign against them in the Jewish world" and that it was essential that Breira "people should be able to speak freely without assault inside the Jewish world." He also ventured a judgment on Israel's policy of introducing settlements in the West Bank, declaring it "politically and morally deplorable and dangerous for Israel to try to rule over 800,000 Arabs and try to adopt an imperial stance."

In recent years Howe has been an outspoken supporter of American Friends of Peace Now. Formed in 1978 by 350 Israeli combat soldiers and reserve officers, Peace Now/Shalom Achshav advocates direct negotiation with Palestinians—and their right of self-determination—and calls for the end of Israeli domination in the Gaza and the West Bank. As Diaspora Jews, Howe acknowledged that the American Friends group, which include many prominent citizens, cannot determine policy. However, they can influence Israel's interaction with its neighbors simply by expressing their concern that Israel could not be torn apart by internal divisiveness if free expression —especially dissent—is repressed. As Howe said in a conference in Washington, D.C. on June 23, 1980, "You know, the only way to avoid divisions of opinion is to destroy democracy. And I believe that's too high a price for Israel or anywhere else. I don't believe divisions of opinion are signs of weakness. I believe this is a sign of the great strength of Israel."

Howe, a distinguished professor of English at the Graduate Center of the City University of New York, is also the director of the school's Center for Jewish Studies.

JACOB C. HUREWITZ

b. November 11, 1914
Political scientist

Jacob C. Hurewitz is one of this country's eminent specialists on the Middle East. In his writings and lectures, as a consultant to the United States government, as a leader in curriculum design and in numerous other ways, he has analyzed and explained the myriad problems in that turbulent region as fairly and as objectively as possible.

Jacob Coleman Hurewitz was born in Hartford, Connecticut, to Isaac and Ida (Aronson) Hurewitz. After receiving his B.A. degree from Trinity College in Con-

necticut in 1936, he earned an M.A. degree the following year from Columbia University. From 1937 until 1940 he studied at the Hebrew University in Jerusalem.

Hurewitz worked as a Middle East expert for the U.S. Army and the U.S. government. From 1943 to 1945, while serving as a first lieutenant in the Army, Hurewitz was assigned to the Near East department of the Office of Strategic Services, the forerunner of the CIA. After World War II ended he moved to the Near East section of the State Department and finally became an adviser on Middle Eastern affairs for President Harry S. Truman. He remained at the White House until 1949, when he was appointed a political affairs officer for the newly formed United Nations Security Council. At the same time, he lectured on Middle Eastern political history at Dropsie College in Philadelphia.

After receiving his Ph.D. degree from Columbia University in 1950, Hurewitz joined its graduate faculty in political science. He also became a staff member at the Near and Middle East Institute at Columbia University, assuming its directorship in 1971.

Throughout his career, Hurewitz has attempted to elucidate as objectively as possible the historic and international roots of many of the Middle East's problems rather than focusing exclusively on the Arab-Israeli dispute. In his first book, *The Struggle for Palestine* (New York, 1950), he analyzed the unfolding Jewish and Arab politics in Palestine from 1936 through the disintegration of the British mandate. This was followed by *Middle East Dilemmas* (New York, 1953), which investigated the origins of U.S. interests and responsibilities in the Middle East. Hurewitz weighed the increasing U.S. involvement in the region against the evolving pattern of European diplomatic rivalry in the area from the beginning of the 20th century through the early 1950s.

Hurewitz has also invested much time in collecting and translating documents relevant to the region's political evolution. In *Diplomacy in the Near and Middle East* (New York, 1956), a two-volume work, he assembled documents that illuminated the external politics of the major European and Middle Eastern powers from the 16th century and onward. The volumes also include the author's introduction to each document and an analysis. Then, under the auspices of the Council on Foreign Relations, Hurewitz wrote *Middle East Politics: The Military Dimension* (New York, 1969), a full-length study of the interplay of domestic, regional and international military politics in the Middle East.

Hurewitz is currently engaged in a major effort to revise and enlarge his earlier work, *Diplomacy in the Near and Middle East.* Two volumes of a projected three-volume work called *The Middle East and North Africa in World Politics* (New York, 1975 and 1978) have been completed. These volumes include basic documents about the region spanning from Pakistan to Morocco, covering a time period from the 16th century to the mid-20th century.

Hurewitz has also contributed many scholarly articles to journals assessing the instability of the Persian Gulf area and the vulnerability of Western oil routes.

DAVID IGNATOW

b. February 7, 1914
Poet

David Ignatow is a poet whose work often draws on themes of New York City life or on his Jewish roots. Described by one reviewer as "mainly a poet of urban life and of that New York City whose mayor is not John Lindsay but Franz Kafka," he is respected as a master of poetic form, but his often gloomy and despairing verse has restricted his following.

Born in Brooklyn, David Ignatow is the son of Max, a businessman, and Yetta (Reinbach) Ignatow. Although he never received a college diploma, Ignatow studied at Brooklyn Evening College in 1934 and the New School for Social Research in 1942. From 1933 until 1939 he worked for the Federal Writers Project and edited *The American Scene* magazine. This was followed by a long period of free-lance writing.

When the War of Independence broke out in Israel in 1948, Ignatow became active in Zionist affairs. He was assistant to the editor of *The Labor Zionist* from 1948 until 1950 and the chairman of the education committee of the Labor Zionist Organization of America during the same two years. In 1950 Ignatow joined the United Jewish Appeal as a publicity writer, remaining until 1953.

Although Ignatow's first collection of poetry, *Poems* (Prairie City, Ill., 1949), was not especially well received, shortly after its publication he was appointed editor of the *Beloit Poetry Journal.* He remained as editor of the journal for the next 10 years.

His next volume of poems, *The Gentle Weightlifter* (New York, 1955), showed tremendous growth. The poems combined surrealistic images and the bleak vision of urban life that would typify so much of his work—and perhaps his personal life as well. In 1955 Ignatow was

hired as treasurer of the Enterprise Bookbinding Company, one of many nonliterary jobs he took over the years just to survive.

After the publication of his next two books as part of the prestigious Wesleyan University Poets series, *Say Pardon* (Middletow, Conn., 1961) and *Figures of the Human* (Middletown, Conn., 1964), which delved deeply into the techniques and themes developed in his second work, Ignatow was appointed instructor at the New School of Social Research. From then on, his reputation secure, he began receiving grants and teaching positions, which gave him greater freedom to write. In 1965 he was a visiting lecturer at the University of Kentucky, and the following year he held a similar position at the University of Kansas. In 1967 he taught for one year at Vassar College and then was appointed in 1969 poet-in-residence at York College, a division of the City University of New York, and adjunct professor at Columbia University in 1965.

Ignatow struck out in a new direction with the publication of *Rescue the Dead* (Middletown, Conn., 1968). He abandoned the surreal urban landscapes of his earlier work, and his poems became more introspective, filled with fantasy and self-analysis. Themes of his own life dominate Ignatow's later work, including *Facing the Tree* (Boston, 1975) and *Tread the Dark* (Boston, 1977). In these works Ignatow examines his own failures, his marriage, becoming middle-aged and preparing for death.

Of himself, Ignatow has written, "My avocation is to stay alive; my vocation is to write about it; my motivation embraces both my intentions and my viewpoint is gained from a study and activity in both ambitions." Of Ignatow, poet James Dickey wrote that he "employs a deceptively simple language to reveal the dreams and agonies of the city-dweller," adding that "Ignatow is one of those rare writers who begin somewhat out of step and end up decades later sounding unquestionably contemporary."

And in an *American Poetry Review* article called "David Ignatow: The Meshugenah Lover" (May/June 1973), Harvey Swados wrote, "He comes to exist for us as one of Bellow's people comes to exist for us, in Chicago or on the Upper West Side, uniquely and centrally American in the way that urban Jews have come to be taken as representative Americans," in the way that he portrays the unhappiness and frustration of people, their cultural and moral starvation and purposeless jobs.

Ignatow has published in many respected magazines, including *The Nation* and America's most important poetry journals. One example of his most recent work is "Kaddish," a poem in memory of his mother. He writes:

I love you. Whisper to the rock,
I found you. Whisper to the earth,
Mother, I have found my mother and I am safe
and always have been.

Another poem, "1905," evokes images of his father's
impoverished youth in Russia:

. . . My father
was not heard from, he was the silent one
walking through the streets where the hot arguments
went on about guilt and poverty. He walked,
his work bundle under arm, from cellar
to monastery to bind holy books and volumes
of the Russian classics, and when they had enough
of classics and needed blood, he fled,
for this was real to them; only he
worked and starved.

For further information:
Ignatow, David. *Lie Close to the Ground.* Boston: 1981.
————. *The Notebooks of David Ignatow.* Chicago: 1973.

RAEL JEAN ISAAC

b. June 17, 1933
Writer

Rael Jean Isaac is an iconoclastic journalist and writer
whose articles on Breira, Reform rabbis, liberal Protestants and the Institute for Policy Studies, among others, have caused widespread argument and comment.
Arguing from her strongly held conservative ideology,
she has become a controversial and provocative scourge
of those she believes to be anti-Israel.

Rael Jean Isaacs was born in New York City to
Judah M., an insurance broker, and Fannie (Shapiro)
Isaacs. She received a Bachelor of Arts degree from
Barnard College in 1954 and a M.A. in English literature from Johns Hopkins in 1957. From the City College of New York she received a Ph.D. in Sociology in
1972. After holding two brief teaching positions at
Briarcliff and Brooklyn Colleges, she turned to freelance
writing.

In 1976 and 1977 the Breira organization was born.
Breira, which means "alternative" in Hebrew, consisted
of Jewish Americans who felt that certain Israeli policies merited public disapproval. In 1977, she and her
husband, Erich Isaac, professor at City College of New
York, published "The Rabbis of Breira" in *Midstream*
(April), in which she flayed the group and its supporters as enemies of Israel. Her attack was probably the

first to bring Breira to the attention of the general
public and as a result of the harsh criticism it received,
Breira soon disintegrated.

Taking up the mantle of the defense of Israel as she
perceived it, her article "The Seduction of the Quakers," *(Midstream,* November 1979) dubbed the group
pro-PLO and the American Friends Service Committee
as "prepared to deny Israel's right to exist and ready to
condone terror on the ground that it is injustice that
drives people to terror and it is only the elimination of
injustice that can end violence." In the June/July 1980
issue of *Midstream* she bitterly attacked the Washington-
based Institute for Policy Studies, coming close to describing it as a subversive group. "IPS has had a major
impact in the weakening of United States intelligence
capabilities," she charged. In the same magazine in
October 1981 she attacked the "Liberal Protestants Against
Israel," alleging that their "hostility" toward Israel has
been something liberal Jews have found difficult to
accept. As a result they have largely ignored it.

Her book, *Israel Divided: Ideological Politics in the
Jewish State* (Baltimore, 1976), is far more detached and
scholarly. In it she scrutinizes the Land of Israel Movement, which approves of settlements throughout the
West Bank area captured during the Six Day War in
1967, and the Israel Peace Movement, both of which
have helped break up the traditional political consensus
of the elite in Israel. She sees the two movements as
having a significant impact on Israel's future. They
will, she concludes, frame the issues in the years ahead
and spell out the alternatives that will confront that
embattled nation.

For further information:
Isaac, Rael Jean. *Party and Politics: Three Visions of a Jewish
State.* New York: 1981.
————. *Breira: Counsel for Judaism.* New York: 1977.
————. " 'Time' Against Israel." *The New Republic,*
October 18, 1980.

CHARLOTTE JACOBSON

b. April 27, 1914
Organization executive

Charlotte Jacobson, chairperson of the American
Section of the World Zionist Organization since 1972,
is one of America's leading Zionists. She has been active
in Hadassah for more than 40 years and has held prominent positions in many major Jewish organizations.

Charlotte Stone was born in New York City to Jonas, a manufacturer of men's hats, and Lena (Alexander) Stone. She was educated in the New York City public schools. In 1932 she attended New York University but left before graduating.

Jacobson joined Hadassah in 1939 and was Hadassah's national vice president and national treasurer prior to her election as president in 1964, a position she held until 1968. In 1966 she led a special Hadassah mission to the Soviet Union to study the condition of Jews there, which she found to be lamentable. She led another Hadassah trip in 1969 to South American Jewish communities. From 1968 to 1972 she was national chairwoman of the Hadassah Medical Organization, a position that put her in charge of the rebuilding of the Hadassah Hospital on Mt. Scopus in Jerusalem.

She was elected to the executive board of the Jewish Agency in 1968 at the 27th World Zionist Congress and served on the Committee for the Reorganization of the Jewish Agency. She was co-chairwoman of a committee that resulted in the founding in 1970 of the New American Zionist Federation, a movement dedicated to revitalizing Zionism in the United States.

Jacobson has been a close friend of many of the leading Israelis and a lifelong defender of their country. She was a delegate to the last six sessions of the World Zionist Congress and is vice president of the National Conference on Soviet Jewry, a member of the presidium of the Brussels Conference on Soviet Jewry and a board member of the United Israel Appeal, the Hebrew University, the Keren Kayemeth, the Jewish National Fund and the Jewish Telegraphic Agency.

Among her consistent public positions was that of sharply criticizing American Jewish groups such as United Hebrew Immigration Aid Society who were aiding Soviet Jewish emigres who refused to move to Israel and chose instead to go to Western nations, especially to the United States. Jacobson spoke in Canada and the United States against subsidizing those who rejected Israel as a homeland. Her critics there charged that American Jews could not turn their backs on the emigres and that since American Zionists refused to immigrate to Israel, why place the burden on the new refugees? Even so, she continued to insist that since Israel desperately needed immigrants, American Jewish money should not help them settle anywhere but in Israel at the beginning. "HIAS is doing so much work for the Russian Jews," she said in 1981, "that they are looked upon as competing with Israel."

She received three awards in 1980: the Solidarity Award of the National Conference on Soviet Jewry, the Philip W. Lown Medal of the Hebrew Teachers College of Boston and the Henrietta Szold Award of the Association of Americans and Canadians in Israel.

For further information:
Bole, William. "The Jewish Agency vs. HIAS: What's Best for Soviet Jewry?" *Long Island Jewish World,* October 2–8, 1981.

ROMAN JAKOBSON

b. October 11, 1896
Linguist; professor

Since the early 1920s, Roman Jakobson has been one of the most influential and independent formulators of modern linguistic theory. His most important contribution was probably the development of the concept of "distinctive features" in speech forms, which states that single speech sounds are not "atomic entities" with no relation to other sounds but are components of a larger set of universal phonetic systems.

Roman Jakobson was born in Moscow on October 11, 1896 to Osip and Anna (Volpert) Jakobson. He began studying linguistics at the Lazarev Institute of Oriental Languages in Moscow, where he received a Silver Medal for his work upon completion of an A.B. degree in 1914. He continued linguistic study at Moscow University, earning the Busalaev Prize in 1916 and a Master of Arts degree in 1918. He remained at the university for two additional years as a research associate.

Jakobson's intuitive understanding of linguistics and his independent thinking led him to stray from the formalist school which typified the field among Moscow scholars. His first published papers suggested that poetics and metrics had a linguistic structural foundation beyond their literary origin. In 1920 he left Moscow for Prague, where he studied at Prague University. He began publishing in 1921 and he was instrumental in the formation in 1926 of the so-called "Linguistic Circle of Prague." The scholars in that circle enlarged the scope of linguistic study into a structured set of laws based on the premise that phonological theory (phonology is the study of sound changes in language) should lead to the development of structured phonological systems which would make it possible to discover how and why language evolved across time and place. Jakobson completed his Ph.D. at Prague University in 1930.

Remaining in Prague during the 1930s, Jakobson developed his theories about "distinctive features." He taught Russian philology at Masaryk University in Brno, Czechoslovakia, from 1933 to 1939, and continued to publish steadily. One of his most important works was a paper, "Observations sur le classement phonologique des consonnes," which appeared in *Proceedings of the Third International Congress of Phonetic Sciences* (Ghent, 1938), which summarized his conclusions that distinctive features were the "linguistic primes" and that so-called "binary distinctive feature opposition" was the foundation of the phonological system.

Like many of his peers on the university level, Jakobson was forced to flee Prague in 1939 when Hitler invaded Austria and Czechoslovakia. For the next two years he lived in Denmark, where he taught at the University of Copenhagen; Norway, where he taught in Oslo; and Sweden, where he taught at Uppsala University. Despite the constant moving around, he continued to publish, and some of his most important work on the structure of phonemes emerged during this unsteady period. His seminal research into the development of speech in children and his exploration of aphasia, a neurological speech disability whose victims are unable to translate their thoughts into verbal language, was published in Uppsala in 1941. It appeared in English as *Child Language, Aphasia and Phonological Universals* (The Hague, 1968).

Jakobson came to the U.S. in 1941, settling first in New York City. From 1942 until 1946 he taught general linguistics at the Ecole Libre des Hautes Etudes and in 1943 joined the faculty of linguistics at Columbia University as visiting Professor. From 1946 to 1949 he was Masaryk professor of Czechoslovak Studies at Columbia. During the 1940s he expanded his study of distinctive features in language to focus on the evolution of Slavic languages and how the different cultures and historical traditions of Slavic peoples affected the development of their languages in different countries. Among his studies was an exploration of the culture and language of Jewish communities in Slavic countries. During this time he also conducted a lengthy study of a medieval Russian epic poem whose origin had been questioned by scholars. Through intensive linguistic analysis, Jakobson was able to prove the poem's authenticity.

In 1949 Jakobson joined the Slavic languages and literature faculty of Harvard University as full professor—he became professor emeritus at retirement in 1967—and was also Institute professor of linguistics at the Massachusetts Institute of Technology from 1957 to 1967 where his work on phonological theory and the development of generative phonology influenced the younger linguistics scholar Noam Chomsky. During the 1950s he published major works on the study of linguistics, including *Preliminaries to Speech Analysis* (Cambridge, Mass., 1952) and *Fundamentals of Language* (The Hague,

1956), complex works which have had an impact upon most modern linguistic schools of thought. His influence is evident in *Studies Presented to Professor Roman Jakobson By His Students* (Cambridge, Mass., 1968) and in several scholarly studies about Jakobson and his work such as *Roman Jakobson's Science of Language* by Linda Waugh (Lisse, Holland, 1976), *Roman Jakobson's Approach to Language* by Elmar Holenstein (Bloomington, Ind., 1976) and *The Acquisition of Distinctive Features* by Stephen Blache (Baltimore, 1978). A massive six-volume collection of *Selected Writings to Honor Roman Jackobson* (The Hague, 1967) contains the list of 374 books and articles he wrote (or co-wrote) from 1921 until publication date as well as about 100 newspaper articles, reviews and book introductions.

Jakobson was visiting professor at Yale in 1967 and 1971, at Princeton University in 1968, at Brown University in 1969 and elsewhere. Although in retirement since 1967, he has continued writing and lecturing.

For further information:
Jakobson, Roman *Main Trends in the Science of Language.* New York: 1974.
———. *Russian Fairy Tales.* New York: 1945.
———. *Studies on Child Language and Aphasia.* The Hague: 1971.

MORRIS JANOWITZ

b. October 22, 1919
Sociologist

A sociologist at the University of Chicago, Janowitz, a dedicated student of American Society, has spent more than 30 years analyzing the evolution of technological change in society and its impact on individuals and groups.

Morris Janowitz was born in Paterson, New Jersey to Samuel, a silk weaver and manufacturer, and Rose (Meyers) Janowitz. He was educated at New York University, where he received a Bachelor of Arts degree in economics, cum laude, in 1941, and at the University of Chicago, where he completed his Ph.D. in 1948. He served in the U.S. Army from 1943 to 1945 in the Psychological Warfare branch and earned a Bronze Star and Purple Heart.

Janowitz taught at the University of Chicago from 1948 to 1951, joined the faculty of sociology at the University of Michigan, where he rose to full professor in 1957, and returned to Chicago in 1962. He was department chairperson from 1967 to 1972 and has held endowed professorships in 1973 and 1977. Since 1980 he has been Distinguished Service Professor of Sociology.

Janowitz's specialty has been the examination of modern social institutions, with particular focus on the military. His first book, coauthored with psychologist Bruno Bettelheim, *The Dynamics of Prejudice* (New York, 1950), surveyed the attitudes of army veterans, concentrating on how their residual anxieties turned them against minority groups, especially blacks and Jews. His next book—his first solo effort—was *The Community Press in an Urban Setting* (Chicago, 1952; Chicago, 1967; 1980), which examined how English-language weekly newspapers published in Chicago communities influenced citizen action. *The Professional Soldier* (Glencoe, Illinois and New York, 1971) is a detailed study of the military establishment in America during the last 50 years, including the political role of the military, the impact of technology and new weapons systems, and changing ideologies.

Janowitz has also explored nonmilitary, unique qualities of American society, such as its own brand of the welfare state that has evolved. He contends, for example, that contrary to the myth that dependence on welfare belongs to the lower classes, America's middle classes also rely on welfare aid in the form of Social Security benefits, subsidies at state and city universities, unemployment insurance and other forms of support, which he describes in *Social Control of the Welfare State* (Chicago, 1977).

Janowitz has written articles for many professional journals and for inclusion in books. He has also edited several sociological texts, including *Psychological Warfare: A Case Book* (Baltimore, 1958) and *On Military Intervention* and *On the Military Profession* (Rotterdam, 1971) and others. He has been a consultant to the U.S. State Department, the U.S. Public Health Service, the U.S. Arms Control and Disarmament Agency and many other government departments and committees. He has also been active in local community groups.

For further information:

Janowitz, Morris. *Campaign Pressures and Democratic Consent: An Interpretation of the 1952 Election.* New York: 1964.

———. *A Comparative Study of Juvenile Correctional Institutions: A Research Report.* Ann Arbor: 1961.

———. *The Last Half Century: Societal Change and Politics in America.* Chicago: 1978.

———. *The Military in the Political Development of New Nations.* Chicago: 1964.

Janowitz, Morris, and Bettelheim, Bruno. *Social Change and Prejudice.* New York: 1964 and 1975.

Janowitz, Morris, and Blackwell, James. *Black Sociologists: Historical and Contemporary Perspectives.* Chicago: 1974.

———. *Judaism of the Next Generation.* Miami, n.d.

JACOB JAVITS

b. May 18, 1904
Lawyer; politician

Throughout his 24 years in the United States Senate, Jacob Javits was regarded by members of both parties as one of the most valuable people in that body. He was the author of much important legislation, an activist in civil rights and social issues, and one of Israel's most ardent supporters in the Congress.

Jacob Javits was born in New York City, the son of Morris and Ida (Littman) Javits. His father, a former rabbinical student in Austria, worked as a janitor. His mother came to the United States by way of Palestine and sold dry goods from a pushcart on the Lower East Side.

After graduating from George Washington High School in Manhattan in 1920, Javits worked his way through New York University. He received his Bachelor of Laws degree from NYU in 1926, and the following year he was admitted to the New York bar. He entered a partnership with his brother and quickly established his reputation around New York as a vigorous and dynamic lawyer, specializing at the beginning in bankruptcy law.

Javits first became involved with organized politics as an aide to Fiorello La Guardia, the popular mayor of New York. In 1941 Javits ran the Citizens' Committee for La Guardia during La Guardia's election bid for the mayoralty. Shortly before the bombing of Pearl Harbor in December 1941, and after La Guardia's November victory that year, Javits was appointed special assistant to the chief of the Chemical Warfare Service in Washington, D.C. When the United States entered World War II, he enlisted as a major in the Army. He served with the Chemical Warfare Service in Europe and the Pacific, attaining the rank of lieutenant colonel.

After his military service Javits resumed his political career, once again in the La Guardia camp. He was the director of research for the mayor's "fusion" ticket in 1945. The following year he was nominated by the Republicans to run for Congress from New York's 21st congressional district, which included Washington

Heights, Harlem and Morningside Heights. Garnering bipartisan support in an otherwise Democratic area, Javits held the seat in the House of Representatives from 1946 until 1954. That year he was the only Republican to win a statewide race in New York, against Franklin Roosevelt Jr. for the office of attorney general.

Two years later Javits returned to Washington to stay, when he defeated Robert Wagner Jr. for the U.S. Senate seat vacated by Herbert Lehman. He held that position until 1980, when, slowed by a debilitating disease, he was upset in the Republican primary by the conservative Alphonse D'Amato. It was the first electoral loss he had ever experienced in 32 years of public service.

Throughout his career, Javits was one of the Senate's most liberal Republicans. He was a ranking member of the Senate's Labor and Human Resources Committee, and he used his position to speak on behalf of working people and to create extensive social service legislation.

Known as a workaholic, Javits devoted much of his energy to creating programs to feed the poor, including the food stamp program. He was the central figure in the passage of the Civil Rights Act of 1964. Summer jobs for youth and job-training ventures such as the Comprehensive Employment and Training Act (CETA) also bore the Javits imprimatur. He spearheaded the successful drive to protect the pensions of workers employed by private firms.

In foreign affairs Javits argued for a balanced defense policy. His major accomplishment was the War Powers Act, which he developed and co-sponsored and which curbs the power of the president to go to war without asking Congress for its approval, as was not done in Korea and Vietnam. He staunchly supported the nuclear non-proliferation treaty and opposed the development of the antiballistic missile system urged by President Nixon. Javits originally supported the Vietnam war, but in time became a major Senatorial opponent. He remained a supporter of political rather than military solutions. He was a firm supporter of SALT II.

Javits has always strongly backed Israel in its many international crises. He was also a national vice chairman of the Anti-Defamation League of the B'nai B'rith, the honorary chairman of the Jewish War Veterans and a trustee of the Federation of Jewish Philanthropies. In addition, he is a member of the Zionist Organization of America, American ORT and the American Jewish Committee.

After his electoral defeat in 1980, Javits returned to New York City to practice law and to lecture at Columbia University on urban and national affairs. His autobiography, *Javits*, with Rafael Steinberg (New York,

1981), provides a vivid account of his ascent from Lower East Side poverty to a prominent national career as an activist politician. He has had, wrote *New York Times* book reviewer Martin Tolchin, "an illustrious career."

ERICA JONG

b. March 26, 1942
Writer; poet

Erica Jong—writer, poet and feminist—became a sudden success with her initial novel, *Fear of Flying* (New York, 1973). The work presented, with humor and sympathy, the plight of contemporary American women. It was all the more dramatic in its overnight acceptance inasmuch as the larger women's movement had not yet gained full recognition.

Erica Mann was born in Manhattan to Seymour, an importer of gift items, and Edith (Mirsky) Mann, a designer of ceramics. She grew up on Manhattan's West Side neighborhood, where, she says, "We were smothered with opportunity—piano lessons, skating lessons, summer camp, art school." Upon graduation from New York City's prestigious High School of Music and Art in 1959, she entered Barnard College, where she began to write poetry for the college's literary magazine. She obtained her B.A. degree in 1963. Then she taught English at the City College of New York while simultaneously pursuing a master's degree in 18th-century literature at Columbia University. She received her M.A. degree in 1965.

From 1966 until 1969 she lived in Heidelberg, Germany, where her husband (now her ex-husband) was serving in the U.S. Army. In Germany she ran a child guidance clinic for the children of military personnel and also taught part-time at the University of Maryland's Overseas Division in Heidelberg. She also continued to write poetry, which gradually moved from verse about "unicorns, Venetian paintings, Roman fountains and the graves of English poets" to free expression about her own violent feelings, many of which revolved about the anger she felt relating to a male-dominated world.

Two years after returning home, she published her first collection of poetry, *Fruits and Vegetables* (New York, 1971). The title poem includes images of copulating fruits, onions without hearts and other images of desire and passion. Other poems explored the situation more and more women were finding themselves in as artists and females.

Jong's second collection of poetry, *Half-Lives* (New

York, 1973), contained works that had previously appeared in *American Poetry Review, Ms., Poetry, The Nation* and other magazines. Some of the poems dealt with double-binds and Laingian knots, revealing her experiences in psychoanalysis. Others looked at feminist concerns; for example "Seventeen Warnings in Search of a Feminist Poem" included angry lines like: "Beware of the man who wants to protect you; he will protect you from everything but himself" and "Beware of the man who denounces his mother; he is a son of a bitch." A *New York Times* critic noted: "Inside her rigid frames of syntax, a playful metaphorical mind is at work, busy in plentiful invention of little fables."

During all this time Jong was writing fiction yet never showing it to anyone else. She began *Fear of Flying* in September 1971. "I never *dreamed* it would find a wide audience," she said in a lecture given at Hofstra University. "It seemed to me the book I *had* to write whether it was ever published or not. . . . For the first time I was writing as if my life depended on it, and to some extent it did."

In *Fear of Flying* the heroine, Isadora Wing, conveyed much of the spirit of Jong's own youth and early adulthood—her intellectual and well-to-do left-wing Jewish upbringing, a childhood enmeshed in culture and art. Its focus was on the attempt of Isadora, in her early 30s and confused about her marriage to a Chinese-American psychoanalyst, to "find herself" by running off with a nutty British psychiatrist in Europe. (It also included a sensitive chapter on her Jewish heritage, as she wandered the streets of Germany, so soon after the defeat of the Nazis.) The critical response to *Fear of Flying* was mixed. While many were shocked and enraged by its sexual outspokenness, others claimed it would make literary history. In any event, it spawned greater opportunity for women writers to publish novels that explore their experiences with a new frankness.

Jong's popularity as a novelist was reinforced with the success of her next two novels, *How To Save Your Own Life* (New York, 1977), a sequel to *Fear of Flying* that looked at Isadora Wing's experience with divorce and learning to trust again, and *Fanny: Being the True History of the Adventures of Fanny Hackabout-Jones* (New York, 1980). Set in 18th-century England, *Fanny* answered the question "What if Tom Jones had been a woman?" The novel, which demonstrated Jong's serious, academic side, with allusions to Fielding and Thackeray, as well as her lusty appetite for bawdy sex scenes and good laughs, was hailed by critics. By undertaking the writing of a full-length novel in 18th-century English, Jong established herself firmly as one of America's major talents.

Jong is winner of the Alice Faye di Castagnolia Award of the Poetry Society of America and a CAPS (Creative Artists Program Service) award. She has published two additional volumes of poetry, *Loveroot* (New York, 1975) and *At the Edge of the Body* (New York, 1979).

LEO JUNG

b. June 20, 1892
Rabbi; educator; author

With the publication of his autobiography in 1981, *The Path of a Pioneer* (London), Rabbi Leo Jung celebrated a long career as an eminent leader in the modern neo-Orthodox movement in America. Called "one of the most venerable living sages of the Jewish people" by Herman Wouk, he taught ethics at Yeshiva University for nearly 40 years and was spiritual leader of The Jewish Center in New York City for more than 50 years.

Leo Jung was born in Ung Brod, Moravia to Dr. Meir Z., who became chief rabbi of the Federation of Synagogues in London, and Ernestine (Silbermann) Jung. He studied at Vienna University from 1910 to 1911 and at the University of Berlin from 1911 to 1914. He received a B.A. degree from the University of London in 1919 and a Ph.D. from there in 1921. In 1920 he was ordained a rabbi at the Hildesheimer Rabbinical Seminary and in 1924 was awarded an M.A. degree from Cambridge University.

Jung came to the United States in 1922 and that year became head of the Jewish Center, an Orthodox congregation on Manhattan's Upper West Side. He joined the faculty of Yeshiva University in 1931 and also taught ethics at Yeshiva's Stern College for Women, beginning in 1956. When Jung retired in 1968, he was named professor emeritus.

In addition to his teaching and rabbinical duties, Jung has been a prolific writer and editor. In all he has written or edited 31 books and was the only American contributor to the Soncino translation of the Talmud, working on Tractates Yoma and Arakhim in 1937 and 1949. He has been editor of The Jewish Library since 1928 and has written many guides to Jewish living. One of them, *Love and Life* (New York, 1979), explores the Jewish concept of family life, including the particular roles of men and women as spouses and friends and as parents and teachers to their children. The book is geared toward a general audience seeking a broad definition of Jewish family life, especially "the mutual relations of love" and its implications for the shaping of children's personalities.

Among his other teachings, Jung is known for his

studies of ethics. In one significant article published in 1951, he looked at "Ethics of Business According to Jewish Law" and called for *Tsedakism,* by which he meant acting with "righteousness, fair play and human compassion. The same *Tsedek* insists on scrupulous avoidance of any looseness in connection with commercial affairs." All Jews, he insisted, are obliged to "do everything [to] enhance reverence for G-d . . . and to avoid any actions" that may reflect badly "on the Divine Lawgiver." He has also spoken out against intermarriage, noting that it was in the best interests neither of the Jewish people, the non-Jews or the institution of marriage itself. In 1964 he declared that intermarriage had become "a grave problem."

Years earlier, in 1943, widely respected, he had been called on to chair a committee mandated by the Synagogue Council of America to study "Textbooks in Jewish Religious Schools." The final report urged that books eliminate remarks "counter to the teachings of our faith," declaring, that in many regions, and especially in the United States, church persecution of Jews was "a matter of the past," that "pious, kindly non-Jews are beloved by God" and that "Judaism in a hundred ways has taught us the greatest human art, that of forgiving iniquity and of not returning anger."

Jung was chairman of the Cultural-Religious Commission from 1941 to 1980; in 1981 he was named honorary chairman. From 1950 to 1981 he was president of the Jewish Academy of Arts and Sciences; at age 89 he was named honorary president. Jung became an honorary trustee of Yeshiva University in 1941 and from 1935 to 1965 was chairman of the New York State Advisory Board for Kosher Law enforcement. His other posts include world president, Beth Jacob Movement for Religious Education of Jewish Girls from Cracow to Jerusalem; and honorary national president of the American Committee for Shaare Zedek Medical Center of Jerusalem.

Since 1968 he has been emeritus professor of ethics at Yeshiva University and since 1976 rabbi emeritus of The Jewish Center.

For further information:
Jung, Leo. *Crumbs and Character.* : 1940.
———. *Essentials of Judaism.* 12th ed. 1964.
———. *Fallen Angels.* : 1926.
———. *Harvest.* : 1958.
———. *Heirloom. : 1961.*
———. *Living Judaism.* : 1927.
———. *Mistranslations as Sources of Lore.* :1934.
———. *The Path of a Pioneer: The Autobiography of Leo Jung.* London: 1981.
-———. *Rhythm of Life.* :1950.

PAULINE KAEL

b. June 19, 1919
Film critic

As movie reviewer for *The New Yorker* magazine since 1968, Pauline Kael has established herself as one of the country's leading film critics. Sharp, humorous and quite irreverent, she is as likely to berate an avant-garde or moralistic picture as she is to ridicule a vulgar film.

Pauline Kael was born in Petaluma, north of San Francisco, to Isaac Paul, a Polish immigrant farmer, and Judith (Friedman) Kael. During her youth she was an avid reader and moviegoer. After graduating from Girls High School in San Francisco in 1936, she majored in philosophy at the University of California at Berkeley from 1936 until 1940. Following her graduation in 1940, Kael spent time in San Francisco and New York City, experimenting with filmmaking and play writing.

She published her first film review in 1953 in *City Lights,* a San Francisco magazine. Then shortly after, she began to publish reviews in *Partisan Review, Kulchur, Film Culture, Moviegoer* and on a contributing basis in *Film Quarterly.* She also broadcast reviews on Pacifica radio network.

From 1955 until the early 1960s, Kael ran the Berkeley (California) Cinema Guild Theaters, twin movie theaters known for revivals of films by W.C. Fields, Mae West and Busby Berkeley. During this time she was also contributing essays to several film anthologies and lecturing on film at various colleges and universities in California.

But it was with the publication of her first collection of reviews, *I Lost It at the Movies* (Boston, 1965), that Kael established herself as one of the country's preeminent film critics. She praised some of her old favorite films—like *La Grande Illusion, Shoeshine* and *Forbidden Games*—and criticized many of her fellow critics for their exaggerated appreciation of pompous art films. Richard Schickel of the *New York Times Book Review* wrote that the book confirms "what those of us who have encountered them [her reviews] separately over the last few years . . . have suspected—that she is the sanest, saltiest, most resourceful and least attitudinizing movie critic currently in practice in the United States."

An intellectual with expertise in many areas, Kael never just talks about the movie she is reviewing but brings in references to an endless array of international films, literary works, artistic, cultural, historical and political topics and ideas that have some bearing on her subject. She has written several anthologies of her reviews, all of which confirm her position as an irreverent scrutinizer of films who is as interested in the psychology and sociology of watching and responding to movies as in the movies themselves.

Following publication of her first book, Kael moved to New York City and wrote for such magazines as *Life*, *Holiday* and *Mademoiselle*. She worked for several months at *McCall's* but was fired, allegedly for criticizing *The Sound of Music*.

Kael was hired by *The New Yorker* in 1968, the same year she published her second book, *Kiss Kiss Bang Bang* (Boston). The book's title is, according to Kael, "perhaps the briefest statement imaginable of the basic appeal of movies." In *Kiss Kiss Bang Bang*, Kael demonstrated her interest in evaluating movies in the context of their audience. Eliot Fremont-Smith of *The New York Times* praised Kael for relating "movies to other experience, to ideas and attitudes, to ambition, books, money, other movies, to politics and the evolving culture, to moods of the audience, to our sense of ourselves."

Kael published her first collection of *New Yorker* reviews in *Going Steady* (Boston, 1970). Since then she has published several more collections of her *New Yorker* reviews, including *Deeper into Movies* (Boston, 1973), which won the National Book Award; *Reeling* (Boston, 1976); and *When the Lights Go Down* (Boston, 1980) which discussed films from September 1975 to March 1979, including *The Deer Hunter* and *Saturday Night Fever*. It also drew a sharp, critical portrait of directors and producers who rely on violence as a stock-in-trade. She also wrote *The Citizen Kane Book* (Boston, 1971) and charged Orson Welles with assuming all credit for the film when coauthor Herman J. Mankiewicz had really conceived the film and worked on it.

She is the winner of the 1970 George Polk Memorial Award for criticism and a member and past chairwoman of the National Society of Film Critics.

MEIR KAHANE

b. August 1, 1932
Rabbi; JDL leader

Meir Kahane, the controversial leader of the militant Jewish Defense League, readily acknowledges his belief that violence is a viable means to achieve his goals. Since founding the JDL in the early 1960s, Kahane has regularly aroused furor from Jewish and non-Jewish groups alike for his unabashed offensive tactics against whomever he deems are his enemies. As a result of his

work, he was described by *New York Post* editor James Wechsler as "a political rightist with an apocalyptic vision of international confrontation" and by Mayor Edward Koch as a terrorist.

Martin David Kahane was born in the Flatbush section of Brooklyn. His father, Rabbi Charles Kahane, had emigrated with his wife, Sonia (Trainin) Kahane, from Safed, Palestine and was spiritual leader at Congregation Shaarei Tefiloth in Brooklyn's Bensonhurst neighborhood. Kahane's mother was born in Dvinsk, Latvia, but she fled to Palestine with her family in 1918 to escape the Bolsheviks.

With the immediate tradition of oppression as part of his background, the younger Kahane became passionately interested in biblical stories—especially those of historic biblical conquests—while a student at the Orthodox Yeshiva Mirer. At the same time, while a teen-ager, he spent summers in the Catskills at a Betar camp. Betar, an organization allied to Herut, the Israeli right-wing nationalist party, stressed military and ideological training. By the late 1940s Kahane was helping to load and pack guns for shipment to the Irgun, Israel's underground army, from docks in Hoboken and Bayonne, New Jersey.

He also acquired a police record when he was arrested in Manhattan in 1947 for stoning the anti-Zionist British Foreign Minister Ernest Bevin's motorcade as it proceeded to the United Nations. Since then he has been arrested and jailed on numerous occasions as his JDL instigated bombings of Soviet and Arab offices in New York City, harassed Soviet diplomatic families and, in one infamous assault in 1972, bombed the offices of impresario Sol Hurok, a major promoter of Soviet musical talent, killing a young Jewish secretary. Afterward, Kahane confessed to writer Robert Friedman that it was the work of his JDL. Rationalizing, he explained: "I once asked Begin how he felt when he learned that 30 or 40 Jews were killed in the bombing of the King David Hotel [during the British Palestine Mandate years]. Begin told me he felt horrible. That's exactly how I felt after the Hurok bombing."

Kahane studied evenings at Brooklyn College, where he received a B.A. degree, and two years later he received a law degree from New York University. At the same time he studied for the rabbinate and in 1956 he was ordained—at which time "Martin David" Kahane became "Meir" Kahane—and also was awarded an M.A. degree in international relations from NYU. By now he was married, and in 1958 he became the rabbi of the Howard Beach Synagogue in Queens. However, he was dismissed because, he says, the Conservative congregants disagreed with many of his Orthodox ideas, such as his overriding belief that Diaspora Jews live inauthentic Jewish lives and tend to adopt Christian values instead.

At this point Kahane's record turns murky. He has told interviewers that he went to work as an undercover agent for the FBI, infiltrating the John Birch Society. "It was a very dangerous job," he says. Later, he and a friend from Betar organized a pro-Vietnam War Fourth of July Movement to promote support for the war among college students. As part of this effort, he coauthored with Joseph Churba, (using the pseudonym "Michael King"), *The Jewish Stake in Vietnam* (Nashville, 1967), which argued that if the United States reneged on commitments to South Vietnam, it would do the same to Israel and that therefore American Jews must support the war.

While working for the Orthodox *Jewish Press,* a Brooklyn weekly, and at the Traditional Synagogue of Rochdale Village in Queens, Kahane created the JDL, garnering much of its support from working-class Orthodox youths. As the JDL strengthened, Kahane left the synagogue and was ousted from the *Press* because the publisher charged he was using the JDL as a "personal political club." Amid reports of growing incidents of anti-Semitism throughout the New York area, especially in neighborhoods undergoing racial transitions, and following the bitterness of the 1968 New York City teachers' strike, Kahane introduced the slogan "Never Again," an allusion to the slaughter of Jews during the Holocaust. By "Never Again"—which became the title of Kahane's life story (New York, 1971)—he meant that Jews would do battle with anyone they perceived to be their enemy or were thought to be anti-Semitic. Under this rubric, Jewish groups as well as Arab and Soviet officials were attacked or annoyed.

In time, though, the JDL fell apart, largely because less extremist and more responsible Jewish organizations condemned Kahane's tactics as reprehensible and because these organizations accomplished in fact what the JDL only claimed in theory to have done. Thus, while the JDL asserted that it had been the prime mover in liberating 250,000 Soviet Jews, the fact is that the National Conference on Soviet Jewry, a moderate coalition group, was far more active in obtaining permission for Jews to depart the USSR.

Kahane grew increasingly bitter at the Jewish establishment, which he called "tyrannical and feudal baronies." In 1975 he attempted to form a new JDL front, "Democracy in Jewish Life," urging "direct and open elections" of an American Jewish representative group that would "truly speak for American Jews." (Jewish Telegraphic Agency, October 15, 1975).

Another reason for the JDL's disintegration was Kahane's 1975 imprisonment for violating a no-weapons provision of a 1971 conspiracy conviction for planning to manufacture fire bombs. He spent four months in a New York City prison and eight months in the federal penitentiary in Allenwood, Pennsylvania.

He moved to Israel in 1971, although he continues to commute regularly to the United States. His premise remains constant—namely, that non-Jewish societies create assimilated Jews who live by gentile values, and only in Israel can one live a genuine Jewish life. In Israel he has lost several contests for a seat in the Knesset (Parliament). His book *Letters from Prison* (Jerusalem, 1974) charged that the Israeli government had purposefully silenced Soviet Jewish dissenters and deliberately sought to prevent public protests in the USSR, an allegation promptly dismissed by the Israelis. However, his Kach party, founded in 1976, has sought to transplant the old JDL strategy to Israel, and its essential thrust is to try to oust the Arabs from Israel. "I'm not a racist," Kahane asserts. "A racist is a Jew who says Arabs can be equal citizens in a Jewish state." The Israeli Arabs are "a time bomb" that should be removed, he argued in *They Must Go* (New York, 1981).

Kahane has repeatedly been accused of fomenting acts of violence against Arabs in Israel, and the Israeli government has moved, as a result, to limit his activities. On May 12, 1980, for instance, in an unprecedented action, then-Defense Minister Ezer Weizmann ordered him held without charges on suspicion of having planned to bomb Al Aqsa Mosque in Jerusalem. He was the first Jew ever detained in Israel under the 1945 Emergency Powers Act enacted by the British Mandate.

Kahane and his wife have dual U.S. and Israeli citizenship and live in Jerusalem.

For further information:
Kahane, Meir. *Why Be Jewish?* Briarcliff Manor, N.Y.: 1981.

HERMAN KAHN

b. February 15, 1922
Futurist

Herman Kahn, director of the Hudson Institute "think tank," has been called the Von Clausewitz of the nuclear age. He is a leading theorist about nuclear deterrence and alternative strategies if deterrence should fail and a nuclear war occur.

Born in Bayonne, New Jersey, Herman Kahn, the son of Abraham and Yetta Kahn, spent his early childhood in New York City. When he was a teen-ager, his family moved to Los Angeles, and he graduated from Fairfax High School in 1940. Although he initially matriculated at the University of Southern California, he transferred in his first year to the University of California at Los Angeles, where he stayed until he was drafted into the military in 1943. After two years in the service, he returned to UCLA, where he received his B.A. degree in mathematics in 1945.

Upon graduation, Kahn went to work in the southern California aircraft industry. He joined Douglas Aircraft in 1945, and two years later he moved to the Northrup Aviation Corp. After a short stint at Northrup in 1947, he returned to Douglas as a lab analyst on a project for the Rand Corporation, a nonprofit research firm working on Air Force contracts. After Kahn received his M.A. degree from the California Institute of Technology in 1948, he was appointed senior physicist at Rand.

An intense interest in economics, public affairs and physics eventually led Kahn into work on nuclear military strategy. He became a leading proponent of "games theory," with its multiple strategies and alternate rewards, as it applied to military thinking. A series of lectures he delivered at Princeton University in 1959 led to the publication of On Thermonuclear War (Princeton, N.J., 1960). In that book Kahn expressed a lack of faith in nuclear deterrence, which has been based on the concept that if both sides involved in a nuclear attack were certain to be destroyed themselves, neither side would initiate an attack. Kahn argued that defense strategies based on this concept of "mutually assured destruction" were unsound because "degrees of awfulness" short of total annihilation were possible in a nuclear war. He then suggested that the proper defense strategy would be directed toward making life as normal as possible for the survivors of a nuclear attack. Until the book appeared, said Kahn, "Nobody had stopped to figure out that everybody didn't have to be killed, and that life could be saved."

His iconoclastic point of view elicited a flurry of critical reaction. Some people praised Kahn for dealing with thermonuclear war in all its possibilities and probabilities, while others condemned his views as a rationalization for mass murder. As a direct result of the book, an anonymous benefactor made a donation of a large enough sum of money to establish the Hudson Institute in Croton-on-Hudson, New York, with Kahn as its director. The institute's stated goals were to study problems of national security and international order. It has received numerous contracts from multi-national corporations and the military.

Alternate scenarios of life after a nuclear attack continued to fascinate Kahn. He wrote Thinking About the Unthinkable (New York, 1962), in which he speculated about the aftermath of a nuclear attack and argued that the facts of life after such an attack should be faced. These same themes were elaborated on in On Escalation Metaphors and Scenarios (New York, 1965).

Since 1965 speculating about the future has increasingly occupied Kahn's time. In three books—The Year 2000 (New York, 1967), Things to Come (New York, 1972) and The Next 200 Years (New York, 1976)—he attempted to establish a reasonable framework for understanding the development of trends and their impact on the future of the planet.

Kahn has written two additional books, The Emerging Japanese Superstate (New York, 1971) and The Japanese Challenge (New York, 1979), about the Japanese economic miracle and its economic and social ramifications both in America and in that country. Indeed he predicted in 1962 that Japan would have the largest gross national product in the world by the year 2000. In his 1971 book he asserted that his prediction was coming true and before long Japan would become a major world power.

For further information:
Kahn, Herman. The Coming Boom. New York: 1982.
———. The Future of the Corporation. New York: 1974.
———. Win in Vietnam. New York: 1968.

ROGER KAHN

b. October 31, 1927
Writer

Roger Kahn is one of the most highly regarded sportswriters in this country, but his talents go beyond sports. His The Boys of Summer (New York, 1972) a book containing childhood reminiscences plus a close scrutiny of the Brooklyn Dodgers baseball team over a period of more than 30 years, as well as his books on such topics as Jews in America and the Columbia University strike in 1968 led a critic to describe him as a "sportswriter in the same sense Leonard Bernstein is a pianist."

Roger Kahn was born in Brooklyn, the son of Gordon Jacques, a teacher and editor, and Olga (Rockow) Kahn, a high school teacher of English. Kahn was educated in private schools in Brooklyn and at the University College at New York University, class of 1948, but left without earning a degree.

Kahn recounted his love affair with baseball in the best-selling *The Boys of Summer,* a remarkably poignant portrayal of his early years as a *New York Herald-Tribune* reporter covering the fabled Brooklyn Dodgers of the 1950s. His book also dealt with ex-Dodgers Jackie Robinson, Carl Erskine, Preacher Roe, Clem Labine, Billy Cox and others in the years following their retirement from baseball. The book was widely hailed and resulted in a three-part television series.

In addition to free-lance writing for such publications as *Esquire, Time* and *The New York Times,* Kahn served as sports editor of *Newsweek* and editor at large for the *Saturday Evening Post.* "My work," he once said, "seems to have appeared in all magazines, living and dead." He often specialized in profiles, describing Robert Frost, Jascha Heifetz, Willie Mays, Walter O'Malley and Leo Durocher.

Kahn is an acute political and social analyst whose talents are not restricted to sports. His book *The Battle for Morningside Heights* (New York, 1970) was a dramatically written and essentially sympathetic account of student unrest at Columbia University during the turbulence of the Vietnam War era. Another book, *The Passionate People* (New York, 1968), dealt with the larger question of what it meant to be a Jew in contemporary America. In it he depicts keenly the bewildering variety of Jewish life centered about character sketches of people throughout the country. "It was," said Kahn, "the first good book I wrote." The book also offered a serious account of the extent of anti-Semitism. Another book, *But Not to Keep* (New York, 1979), was autobiographical and tried to sum up his life, marriages and children.

Kahn was awarded the E.P. Dutton Prize for best sports magazine pieces three times. In addition, he has lectured occasionally at Yale University and the Smithsonian Institution, supervised nonfiction writing at the University of Rochester and taught writing at Colorado College.

For further information:
Bailey Willard. "The Writer's Digest Interview." *Writer's Digest:* March 1976.
Kahn, Roger. *How the Weather Was.* New York: 1973.
———. *Inside Big League Baseball.* New York: 1962.
———. *A Season in the Sun.* New York: 1977.
———. *The World of John Lardner.* New York: 1961.
Kahn, Roger, and Wismer, Harry. *The 1955 Mutual Baseball Almanac.* New York: 1955.
———. *The 1956 Illustrated Mutual Baseball Yearbook.* New York: 1956.

BERNARD KALB

b. 1922
News correspondent; author

When Bernard Kalb was named State Department correspondent for NBC News in August 1980, he brought with him an almost unparalleled background in coverage of international crises and American diplomatic affairs, which included coverage of the Vietnam War, travels with Henry Kissinger during his historic shuttle diplomacy and participation in the precedent-setting trip of Richard Nixon to mainland China.

Kalb was born in New York City, the son of East European immigrants Max and Bella (Portnoy) Kalb. Graduated from the City College of New York, he served in the U.S. Army during World War II. Based on the Aleutian Islands, he wrote for an Army magazine edited by Dashiell Hammett.

Kalb began his journalistic career as a reporter for *The New York Times* in 1946, beginning as a general assignment reporter and then moving on to the United Nations. In 1955 he began traveling for the *Times.* One year later he settled in Indonesia as the newspaper's Southeast Asia correspondent. In 1961 he returned to the United States on a one-year fellowship awarded by the Council on Foreign Relations. He joined CBS News the following year.

Initially based in New York, Kalb was later named Southeast Asia bureau chief based in Hong Kong. In 1965 he became Paris bureau chief for a year and a half but returned to Hong Kong in late 1966, from which base he covered the Vietnam War until 1970. In 1968 he received an Overseas Press Club Award for a documentary he produced about the Viet Cong.

In 1970 Kalb was named Washington anchor for the *CBS Morning News,* and two years later he began covering foreign affairs and U.S. diplomacy. A "Kissinger-watcher" for many years, Kalb joined the secretary of state's 1975 travels in the Middle East, where he reported on Kissinger's treaty negotiations between Israel and Egypt. His first trip to China with President Nixon in 1972 was followed by a second trip with President Ford in 1975. His coverage has frequently included the most sensitive strategic negotiations between the United States and other major powers, including the SALT talks with Moscow. He has also regularly accompanied state department secretaries Cyrus Vance, Edmund Muskie and Alexander Haig on trips abroad.

With his brother Marvin, a news correspondent who also left CBS News for NBC News, he wrote two books —a biography, *Kissinger* (New York, 1974), and a novel,

The Last Ambassadors (New York, 1981), a fictionalized account of the last days of Vietnam. *Kissinger* received much praise together with the general criticism that it was only mildly critical toward the flamboyant diplomat.

Kalb, whose collection of Oriental porcelain is almost as renowned as his accomplishments as a journalist, is a regular contributor to *The Saturday Review* and other periodicals.

MARVIN KALB

b. June 9, 1930
Television journalist; author

In mid-1980, when the Iranian Revolution following the ouster of the Shah was still a mystery for many Americans, Marvin Kalb was in its midst, ·reporting from Teheran. It was he who quoted Iran's then-foreign minister Sadegh Ghotbzadeh as describing the Ayatollah Khomeini as out of touch with reality, a move that resulted in the CBS News bureau's being forced out. His similar daring in other situations—Kalb was responsible, for example, for introducing the writings of Russian dissident novelist Alexander Solzhenitsyn to American audiences in 1963—has made him one of America's most respected and principled television journalists.

Marvin Leonard Kalb was born in New York City to Max and Bella (Portnoy) Kalb. A graduate of the City College of New York, where he received a Bachelor of Social Science degree in 1951, he pursued graduate studies at Harvard, Columbia and Middlebury College. In 1953 he earned an M.A. degree from Harvard in Russian and Chinese and, after serving two years in the Army, returned to Harvard, where in 1956 he taught Russian history and completed his course work toward a doctorate.

The following year Kalb worked as State Department press attache in Moscow. And in 1957—after traveling throughout Asia, where his brother, journalist Bernard Kalb, was then based for *The New York Times*—he wrote a series for the *Times* magazine. The same year he joined CBS News as a New York-based reporter/writer and staff researcher on the series *Where We Stand*. Again using his expertise in Russian, he accompanied Vice President Richard M. Nixon to Moscow covering the latter's "kitchen debate" with Primier Nikita Khruschev. Following completion of a CBS fellowship at Columbia University, Kalb was named Mos-

cow correspondent for CBS News in 1960, a critical year that included the Soviet Union's breaks with China and Albania, its first manned space flight and the Francis Gary Powers spy case. In 1961 he covered the building of the Berlin Wall and the following year, still from Moscow, the Cuban missile crisis. His Moscow coverage earned him his first Emmy Award.

In 1963 Kalb was named CBS's first Washington-based diplomatic correspondent. That year he wrote the introduction to a short novel, *One Day in the Life of Ivan Denisovich* (New York). It was the first English-language edition of the works of Alexander Solzhenitsyn and represented a significant turnaround in the awareness of Americans about the existence and extent of the Russian dissident community. Solzhenitsyn's other novels and those of other suppressed Russian writers would eventually appear.

Meanwhile, Kalb also wrote several books of his own, including three nonfiction accounts of life and politics in Eastern Europe: *Eastern Exposure* (New York, 1958), *Dragon in the Kremlin* (New York, 1961) and *The Volga: A Political Journey Through Russia* (New York, 1967). With journalist Elie Abel he coauthored *Roots of Involvement: The United States in Asia 1784-1971* (New York, 1971), a history focusing on American involvement and historic failures in Indochina, and he coauthored two novels: *In the National Interest* (New York, 1977), with television journalist Ted Koppel, and *The Last Ambassador* (New York, 1981), with his brother Bernard. He and Bernard also wrote *Kissinger* (New York, 1974), a generally admiring but not uncritical book. The coauthors deeply respect Kissinger's search for stability *sans* "utopian illusions" but criticize him for the India-Pakistani crisis and for ignoring Japan while courting China. At the same time, they believe Kissinger when the latter stated that it was he, not others, who forced the Pentagon to resume arms shipments to Israel during the 1973 Yom Kippur War.

Kalb left CBS News to join NBC News in July 1980 as its chief diplomatic correspondent in Washington. In addition to regular appearances on *NBC Nightly News* and *Meet the Press* where he is a permanent panelist, Kalb reports on NBC News documentaries and in "instant specials." His first NBC documentary, which was aired in September 1980, was "The Castro Connection," a 90-minute white paper exploring the extent of Cuban leader Fidel Castro's influence in Central America. In August 1981 he was principal reporter on "NBC Reports: Why Poland Makes Moscow Shudder."

A regular contributor of articles to *The Saturday Review* and *The New York Times,* Kalb has won nine Overseas Press Club Awards for his foreign affairs reporting.

MAX KAMPELMAN

b. November 7, 1920
Attorney; government official

Like many Democrats of his generation, Max Kampelman grew up with very liberal leanings and shifted to the right following the social and political turmoil of the late 1960s and early 1970s. A close associate of Senator Hubert Humphrey for many years, the outspoken Kampelman served as ambassador and co-chairman for the U.S. delegation to the conference on Security and Cooperation in Europe, held in Madrid in 1980 and 1982. Originally appointed to the post by Democratic President Carter, he was reappointed and promoted to chairperson by Republican President Ronald Reagan.

Max M. Kampelman was born in New York City to Joseph, a retailer, and Eva (Gottlieb) Kampelman. He received a Bachelor of Arts degree from New York University in 1940 and spent the next year as a researcher with the International Ladies Garment Workers Union. From 1941 to 1943 he clerked with the law firm of Phillips, Nizer, Benjamin and Krim. While attending law school at NYU, where he received a J.D. in 1945, he also worked in civilian public service with the American Friends Service Committee, having earned a designation as a conscientious objector. (He later had second thoughts about serving in the armed forces, because from 1956 to 1962 he served in the Marine Corps' Inactive Reserve.)

In 1946 Kampelman received an M.A. degree in political science from the University of Minnesota. Still at Minnesota, where he first met Hubert Humphrey, he studied for a doctorate, which he completed in 1951. His thesis explored the struggles between the Communist Party and the CIO. It was later published as a book, *The Communist Party vs. The C.I.O.: A Study in Power Politics* (New York, 1957).

After lecturing at the University of Minnesota from 1946 to 1948 and at Bennington College in Vermont from 1948 to 1950, Kampelman moved to Washington, D.C., where he became legislative counsel to Senator Humphrey, serving from 1949 to 1955. He taught political science at Howard University from 1954 to 1956 and then entered private law practice as a partner in Fried, Frank, Harris, Shriver and Kampelman. But he remained a prominent public figure on the Washington scene, both in the community and on Capitol Hill. He also joined several Jewish organizations and was, for example, chairperson of the Martin Luther King Jr. Memorial Forest Committee in Israel and served several terms as chairperson of American Friends of Hebrew University. He is a lay executive with the Anti-Defamation League of B'nai B'rith, is on the Board of Governors of Hebrew University and is vice president of the Jewish Publication Society of America. From 1967 to 1970 Kampelman was the first moderator of *Washington Week in Review*, a panel discussion program that has been one of the longest-running and most successful programs on public television.

Kampelman's rightward drift reflects the sentiments of those Democrats who favor a strong defense posture by the United States. Along with other prominent neoconservatives, Kampelman belongs to the Committee on the Present Danger, a hard-line group formed in 1976, and is vice chairperson of the centrist Coalition for a Democratic Majority. In 1981 he joined the Board of Trustees of Freedom House in New York City.

He has written many articles on foreign policy, domestic issues and Jewish affairs for a range of law journals and other publications. In 1978 a long critical piece he wrote on "The Power of the Press: A Problem for Democracy" created a stir of controversy when it appeared in *Policy Review*, the magazine of the right-wing think-tank the Heritage Foundation.

As a result of his widely heralded actions in Madrid, Kampelman often cites the plight of Soviet Jews as evidence of the need for a realistic and, if need be, strong approach to the Russians. He believes it has been a significant factor in forcing the Kremlin to permit larger numbers of Russian Jews to emigrate. During negotiation sessions in Madrid, Kampelman frequently angered and embarrassed Soviet delegates by "undiplomatically" naming names of many Soviet Jews who had applied for exit visas and were subsequently stripped of jobs and even imprisoned although they were not permitted to leave.

Despite Kampelman's overall support of the foreign policy of the Reagan administration, he was vocal in his protest and outrage when the administration pushed to sell the sophisticated AWACS planes and other weapons to the Saudi government in late 1981.

JOHANNA KAPLAN

b. December 29, 1942
Author; teacher

Although she has written only two books—a collection of short stories and one novel—Johanna Kaplan has emerged as one of the most talented younger Jewish writers of the 1980s.

Johanna Kaplan was born in New York City to Max and Ruth (Dukes) Kaplan. Her father was a teacher and her mother a social worker. Kaplan followed in their footsteps, and after graduating from New York University with a B.A. degree in 1964 and from Columbia University with an M.A. degree two years later, she became a teacher of emotionally disturbed children in the New York City school system and at Mt. Sinai Hospital.

She meanwhile cultivated an interest in writing and in 1973 received grants from the National Endowment for the Arts and the New York State Council for the Arts. Two years later her collection of stories *Other People's Lives* (New York) appeared. Kaplan proved to be masterful at character development, as she depicted in the title story the plight of a disturbed young woman who had been abandoned and hospitalized for many years by her refugee parents and is taken to live in a "normal" household in Manhattan. In another story Kaplan's main character is an eccentric retired schoolteacher whose early years had been devoted to the support of left-wing causes and who disdains the materialism of the 1970s. By the time Kaplan's book was published, one critic remarked that "it doesn't seem possible that any literary vitality can be squeezed out of Jewish life in the Bronx—or in any borough." Yet, the critic concluded, Kaplan's stories "prove that the chicken soup has not yet turned into water." In another review writer Dorothy Rabinowitz agreed that Kaplan has an "impeccable ear" for dialogue and an extraordinary sensitivity for the nuances of her characters. *Other People's Lives* was nominated for a National Book Award in 1975.

Kaplan's first novel, *O My America!* (New York, 1980), represented a maturity of her storytelling powers, especially her ability to develop characters who are not only symbolic of the time and culture Kaplan is describing but who are individually unique and believable. The main character, Ezra Slavin, has just died as the book begins, and his story is told in flashback by his daughter Merry, one of his six children and the second from the first of four matings (not all involving marriage —an institution he came to disdain). Slavin's story starts in poverty on the Lower East Side, moves through Upper West Side intelligentsia and on to campus culthood and a rejection of his roots. Throughout, the attempt to forge a new identity for himself is thwarted by the undeniability of his essential Jewishness; the conflict results in a character steeped in self-hate who has difficulty being nice to anyone around him. The novel, in addition to being the story of one man, was also the chronicle of several generations of Jewish life as it evolved

in America. The book received wide praise, as much for its style as for its ability to focus on elements in American Jewish life that have been difficult for many authors to deal with. It also won the Kenneth B. Smilen/*Present Tense* Literary Award for the best novel with a Jewish theme published in 1980.

In addition to her own writing, Kaplan regularly reviews books for *The New York Times* and other periodicals.

JUSTIN KAPLAN

b. September 5, 1925
Biographer

As the biographer of some of America's most important literary and political figures, Justin Kaplan has set out not only to demystify their lives but to explain their influence on American history and culture. A specialist on the life and works of Mark Twain, he received the Pulitzer Prize and National Book Award for biography for *Mr. Clemens and Mark Twain* (New York) in 1966.

Justin Kaplan was born in New York City to Tobias D., a manufacturer, and Anna (Rudman) Kaplan. By the time he was 13, both parents had died—a fact, he said in an interview, that contributed to his interest in biography, because he wanted to find out "how people make their lives over." He studied at Harvard University, where he received a B.S. degree in 1945, and the following year began free-lancing for several New York publishers. From 1954 to 1959 he was an editor with Simon and Schuster and since his departure has been a full-time writer.

Kaplan's first major literary ventures were editorial. In 1950 he edited a Pocket Book version of *Dialogues of Plato* (New York) and in 1958 edited *The Pocket Aristotle* (New York).

In 1959 Kaplan began his research into the life of Mark Twain, using documents from the author's life that had never been published and had only recently become available. *Mark Twain, The Gilded Age* (New York, 1964) was the first project he completed as a biographer. But it was with *Mr. Clemens and Mark Twain* that Kaplan became the acknowledged Twain expert who had penetrated the personality and the myth of the author of so many American classics. Beginning with Twain at age 31, Kaplan examined in great detail how the free-spirited midwesterner had been transformed— inhibited—by the New England life into which he eventually settled. The portrait Kaplan painted was of a complex, frustrated man whose life was tinged by tragedy. He was praised for having incorporated a plethora of details into Twain's story without drowning his subject in them and became established as a Twain expert, partly because of the new information about Twain that he had acquired. In 1967 Kaplan both edited *Great Short Stories of Mark Twain* (New York) and published *Mark Twain: A Profile* (New York).

Kaplan's next major project took six years to complete. But when *Lincoln Steffens: A Biography* was published (New York, 1974), it was hailed as a masterpiece. Steffens was a journalist and editor who grew up in California and made his way to New York at the turn of the century when Greenwich Village was at its most creative and turbulent—or, as critic Peter Schrag wrote, "when Freudians and Marxists drank from the same bottles." Steffens was credited with being one of the first "muckrakers," so-called by Teddy Roosevelt when he and other writers exposed corruption in American cities. He later joined other Americans in "exile" in Paris and in 1931 published a now-famous autobiography. But even the autobiography, according to critics, failed to give as true a picture of Steffens as Kaplan's book did.

Kaplan tackled yet another complex and controversial subject in 1980, when he completed *Walt Whitman: A Life* (New York). Like his previous works, meticulously researched, it was also constructed to be read equally well by the lay reader as by the scholar. Kaplan probed the psychological characteristics of Whitman the man and poet, the alleged homosexual, the guru to other writers and artists of the time, the martyr who selflessly nursed victims of Civil War battles, a person of continuous self-doubt who finally, later in life, came to some sort of terms with the conflicts that had racked him for decades.

To tell Whitman's story, Kaplan began at the end of the poet's life and moved back and forth in time trying to uncover his personality and identity. His technique worked. Critic John Domini called Kaplan's biography a "gem," writing that "Everything glimmers, every detail or line of quotation sets off those around it. . . . Practically every line of 'Song of Myself' [one of Whitman's greatest poetic works] now resonates specially."

In addition to his biographies, Kaplan has also written articles and taught. He has lectured at Harvard University periodically since 1969 and was prose writer-in-residence at Emerson College in the 1977–78 academic year. His articles have appeared in *Atlantic Monthly*, *American Scholar*, *The New York Times*, *Harper's* and other publications.

For further information:
Kaplan, Justin. *Mark Twain and His World.* New York: 1974.
Kaplan, Justin, ed. *With Malice Towards Women.* New York: 1956.

MORDECAI KAPLAN

b. June 11, 1881
Rabbi; founder of Reconstructionism

As formulator and founder of the iconoclastic Reconstructionist movement in 1922 as an alternative to more traditional modes of Jewish life and observance, Mordecai Kaplan synthesized elements of Conservative Judaism, American pluralism and the concept of an "evolving religious civilization" which adjusts to changes in the social environment while retaining a strong sense of Jewish nationhood. Before other movements even thought of it, Reconstructionism welcomed an active and egalitarian role for women in all areas of Jewish life, and although membership has always been small, the movement has been influential in provoking new ideas among Jewish thinkers and in effecting changes within Conservative and Reform Judaism.

Mordecai Menahem Kaplan was born on June 11, 1881, in Svencionys, Lithuania. The year of his birth coincided with a series of pogroms that swept through southern Russia and the Ukraine which were followed the next year by the imposition of the May Laws. These laws dictated a vicious and official policy of anti-Semitism which would force most Soviet Jews to either emigrate, assimilate or be killed. The Kaplans chose migration, and in 1890 settled in New York, where Mordecai Kaplan was educated initially under Orthodox auspices. As he grew up, however, he found himself drawn to a broader, more heterodox approach to religious life and study. He then attended City College of New York, earning a B.A. degree and Columbia University, receiving a M.A. degree. He was also ordained by the Jewish Theological Seminary and became rabbi of Kehillath Jeshurun, an Orthodox congregation in New York City.

In 1909 Kaplan was named by Solomon Schechter to be dean of the just founded Teachers Institute of the Jewish Theological Seminary. Shortly, he also began teaching homiletics, Midrash and philosophy of religion in the Seminary's rabbinical school.

But soon Kaplan branched out on his own, becoming active within the Jewish community. He was a founder of the New York Kehillah and in 1917 helped form the

Jewish Center, a synagogue which doubled as a communal setting for Jewish activities. For the next five years he was the center's rabbi, but in 1922, a turning-point in his career, Kaplan founded the Society for the Advancement of Judaism, a congregation which served explicitly to follow the Reconstructionist theories he had developed.

Kaplan was a maverick, willing to experiment and explore. The same year his Reconstructionist congregation was formed, the first Bat Mitzvah in history took place. He felt it was vital for the community to feel free to modify rituals, as necessary, and still adhere to Jewish commandments and traditions, but within the framework of contemporary American society. Reconstructionists looked to Israel as a Jewish homeland, yet supported the viability of a rich Jewish life in the Diaspora. His critics lambasted Kaplan's apparent repudiation of certain theological "givens," such as the importance of historical revelation and the conception of God as a unique, transcendent being. (Kaplan interpreted God as a more abstract concept—a universal and perhaps impersonal power by which human beings shaped their destiny.) Nonetheless, they observed how Kaplan's development of community among his followers had forged a close-knit, progressive congregation—a model others followed.

Kaplan's philosophy of Reconstructionism appeared in book form in 1934, with the publication of his classic, *Judaism as a Civilization* (New York). It explained his beliefs in Jewish creativity as a source for growth, of the need to incorporate the capacity for change within standard Jewish ritual and observance, the importance of collective worship and study and other new values which came to symbolize the movement.

The following year Kaplan began publishing *The Reconstructionist* magazine and by 1940 the movement had grown large enough to necessitate the creation of the Jewish Reconstructionist Foundation as a national focal point for the movement. Indeed, the movement sprouted; in 1942 the Foundation published *The New Haggadah*, in 1944 *The Sabbath Prayerbook*, in 1947 *The High Holiday Prayerbook* and in 1958 a *Festival Prayerbook*. It also published more than 50 other books of Jewish works relevant to Reconstructionism.

The emphasis on community led the Foundation in 1954 to form the Federation of Reconstructionist Congregations and *Havurot* or religious fellowships, which sought to create communities of Jews to share in study, prayer and collective action; by Kaplan's centennial in 1981 there were more than 40 such congregations.

Meanwhile, Kaplan remained a devoted educator, teaching at the Jewish Theological Seminary for 50 years, often challenging his Conservative students with new approaches to traditional ways of thinking. He published several important monographs, including an edited translation of *Messillat Yesharim* by Moses Hayyim Luzzatto, an 18th-century Italian Kabbalist and dramatist (New York, 1937 and 1966); *The Meaning and Purpose of Jewish Existence* (New York, 1964), a study of the philosophy of Hermann Cohen; and an exploration of modern Jewish thinking entitled *The Greater Judaism* (New York, 1960).

But perhaps the most important step Kaplan took with the Reconstructionist Foundation was the creation in 1968 of the Reconstructionist Rabbinical College in Philadelphia, which, from the beginning, counted women among its students. In fact, the first woman to become a senior rabbi with her own congregation in America was a Reconstructionist.

Essential to Reconstructionism is the concept of constant renewal—that in every crisis, Jews can affirm their identity and their strength and rebuild, growing and changing like any living organism—but at the core remaining essentially the same.

In 1981, with the observance of Kaplan's 100th birthday, the Reconstructionist Foundation reaffirmed its commitment to growth and evolution with a campaign to expand the college endowment fund, to create regional centers and to prepare an updated Jewish prayerbook. Indeed, as a statement from the Foundation noted, "memories are not enough: Judaism will survive for the next generation only if we give meaning to our experience of it today"—a summary of Mordecai Kaplan's theory of Reconstructionism.

For further information:

Kaplan, Mordecai M. *Basic Values in Jewish Religion.* New York: 1957.
———. *The Future of the American Jew.* New York: 1948.
———. *Judaism in Transition.* New York: 1936.
———. *Judaism without Supernaturalism.* New York: 1958.
———. *The Meaning of God in Modern Jewish Religion.* New York: 1937.
———. *The Purpose and Meaning of Jewish Existence.* Philadelphia: 1964.
———. *A New Zionism.* New York: 1959.
———. *Questions Jews Ask.* New York: 1956.
———. *The Religion of Ethical Nationhood.* New York: 1970.
Eisenstein, Ira and Kohn, Eugene, eds. "Mordecai M. Kaplan: An Evaluation," *Judaism.* Winter 1981.
Liebman, Charles. "Reconstructionism in American Life," *American Jewish Yearbook.* New York: 1970.

RHODA KARPATKIN

b. June 7, 1930
Consumer affairs executive; lawyer

Rhoda Hendrick Karpatkin, an attorney and civil rights advocate, became the first female executive director of the Consumers Union of the United States in January 1974. In this role Karpatkin has worked to enlighten and educate consumers about their rights and has supervised the testing of products for value and performance.

Rhoda Hendrick was born to Charles and Augusta (Arkin) Hendrick in New York and graduated from Brooklyn College with a Bachelor of Arts degree in 1951. The same year she married Marvin Karpatkin, a lawyer, now deceased, who became well-known as a defender of civil rights and civil liberties. She obtained her Bachelor of Laws degree from Yale University Law School in 1953 and was admitted to the New York State Bar Association in 1954. With her husband in 1958 she founded the law firm of Karpatkin and Karpatkin, which in 1961 became Karpatkin, Ohrenstein, Karpatkin.

During her years in private practice until 1974, when she was named director of the Consumers Union, Karpatkin was active on her local public school board. From 1967 to 1969 she was chairman of school board number three in central Harlem, and from 1966 to 1970 she was a member of school board number five on the West Side of Manhattan, taking the side of those parents who wished to support decentralized control of schools. From 1970 to 1971 she was special counsel for decentralization of the New York City Board of Education.

As executive director of the Consumers Union, Karpatkin has instituted a weekday radio show, *A Report to Consumers*, which is broadcast by 60 stations; a newspaper column, *From Consumer Reports*, which is picked up by 300 national newspapers; and a new national consumer magazine for children, *Penny Power*, for which she writes a column, *A Memo to Members*. Under her leadership, circulation of the union's magazine, *Consumer Reports*, has grown to 2.8 million. Even before assuming her position as director, Karpatkin represented the Consumers Union for 16 years as a New York lawyer in private practice and gained a reputation as a civil rights advocate.

At the time she took over, the organization was divided between those, like Ralph Nader, who thought it should channel money and energy into activism on behalf of customers, and those who felt its objective testing program was its most effective weapon to help consumers. Karpatkin has proved that the Consumers Union can function well in both areas without losing its reputation for accuracy and impartiality.

Karpatkin has also been involved in other consumer organizations. Since 1973 she has been a member of the New York City Consumer Advisory Council, and from 1975 to 1978 she was commissioner of the National Commission on New Technological Uses of Copyrighted Works. In 1976 she became a member of the board of directors of the National Resource Center for Consumers of Legal Services.

She is on the board of advisers of the School of Law at Columbia University, was a member of the Commission on Law and the Economy of the American Bar Association from 1976 to 1979 and is a trustee of the Public Education Association. She was an adjunct professor in the Department of Urban Studies at Queens College from 1972 to 1974.

ABRAHAM I. KATSH

b. August 10, 1908
Scholar; educator

Among Jewish educators and scholars, Abraham I. Katsh is one of the most dedicated and prolific. He not only pioneered the teaching of Hebrew on the college level but was responsible for meticulously piecing together and interpreting some of the rarest and most significant Talmudic manuscript fragments in existence.

Abraham I. Katsh was born in Amdur, Poland to Reuben, the chief rabbi of Petah Tikva and a member of the Chief Rabbinate of Israel, and Rachel (Maskileison) Katsh, a descendant of a noted family tracing its origin to King David. He came to the United States in 1925 and attended New York University, where he received a B.S. degree in 1931, an M.A. degree from its School of Education in 1932 and a Doctor of Law in 1936. During the summer of 1941 he was a graduate student at Princeton University's Islamic Institute. In 1944 he received a Ph.D. from Dropsie College for Hebrew and Cognate Learning (since renamed Dropsie University).

But his list of academic degrees only barely reveals the scope and influence of Katsh's career as educator and scholar. In 1933, as an instructor at NYU, he instituted the first college-level Hebrew course in America and later, as founder and first president of the National Association of Professors of Hebrew, coordinated the introduction of Hebrew language programs in more than 200 universities across the country. In 1937 he founded the Jewish Culture Foundation at NYU and five years later established the NYU Library of Judaica and Hebraica, which contains 45,000 rare books, manuscripts and microfilms. He was responsible for the first Hebrew courses to be taught on radio and was director from 1949 through 1967 of the America-Israel Student and Professional Workshop in Israel, a summer program sponsored by NYU and run in conjunction with the U.S. State Department and Office of Education. So extensive is Katsh's influence and achievement that a 1953 private audience between him and Pope Pius XII resulted in an official papal acknowledgment of "modern Hebrew as an important language for the study of Scripture" in Catholic universities.

Named full professor, Katsch was honored by the NYU board of trustees in 1957 with the creation of The Abraham I. Katsch Professorship of Hebrew Culture and Education. In 1965 a Hebrew Studies Fellowship at NYU was established in Katsh's honor. He left NYU in 1967 to become president of Dropsie University in Philadelphia, where he remained until his retirement in 1976.

Although Katsh has written, edited and translated many books about the Hebrew language, ancient and modern Jewish history and Jewish scholarship, the work for which he is probably best-known around the world is his three-volume interpretation of the Talmud based on a 17-year period of research and writing beginning in 1956. The first Western scholar to gain access to the Antonin Geniza collection of manuscripts in the Saltykov-Shchedrin Library in Leningrad, he was also the only scholar permitted to photostat copies of thousands of manuscript fragments dating from the 7th to the 10th centuries. Based on this work and on subsequent visits to libraries in Poland and Hungary as well as return visits to the Soviet Union through 1976, Katsh pieced many of the fragments together and was able to uncover startling new phrases and meanings to many old *mishnayot* —the legal codification of fundamental Jewish law. His original research material, now housed at Dropsie University, was published as *Ginze Mishna* (Jerusalem, 1971), *Ginze Talmud Babli, Volume I* (Jerusalem, 1976) and *Ginze Talmud Babli, Volume II* (Jerusalem, 1979).

Katsh has also dealt with the role of Judaic tradition in American history, including its impact on the Pilgrims and the writers of the Declaration of Independence, in two books, *Hebraic Foundations of American Democracy* (New York, 1951) and *Biblical Foundations of American Democracy* (New York, 1977), and with the Jewish influence on the Moslem religion and culture in *Judaism in Islam* (New York, 1954 and 1980) and *Judaism and the Koran* (New York, 1962). Besides extensively cata-

loging Hebrew manuscripts in the Soviet Union in *Catalogue of Hebrew Manuscripts in the U.S.S.R.* (part I, New York, 1957; part 2, 1958) and *The Antonin Geniza Collection in Leningrad* (New York, 1963), he has also translated into Hebrew several 13th-century Judeo-Arabic manuscripts and edited *Yiggal Hazon,* 50 unpublished Hebrew poems written during the Golden Age in Spain (1964).

His 1965 translation from Hebrew into English of *Scroll of Agony—The Chaim Kaplan Diary of the Warsaw Ghetto* (New York) has also appeared in French, German, Swiss, Japanese and Braille and was republished in English in 1973 and with updated material in 1980. The diary, an eyewitness account of the Nazi takeover of Warsaw, records the initial occupation, the quartering of the city and the building of the ghetto walls, and the ensuing deterioration of life for the Jews as well as their struggle to retain their dignity and humanity. Begun in 1939, it was smuggled out by a friend of Kaplan's in 1942 and rediscovered in a kerosene can on a farm near Warsaw 20 years later.

Katsh has contributed articles to *The Hebrew Encyclopedia, Encyclopaedia Brittanica, The New International Encyclopedia, The Encyclopedia Judaica* and *The Encyclopedia of Religion.* He has been on the editorial board of many professional journals, including *Jewish Quarterly Review* and *Jewish Apochryphal Literature,* and belongs to many scholarly organizations, including the Jewish Academy of Arts and Sciences, the Society for Biblical Literature and the Middle East Studies Association of North America. Just a few of his many prizes are the Mayor's Citation of the City of New York (1965), the Municipality of Haifa Prize (1979) and the Avodah Award from the Jewish Teachers Association in New York (1980).

IRVING KAUFMAN

b. June 24, 1910
Judge; writer

The achievements of Judge Irving Kaufman throughout his formidable legal career touch on virtually every aspect of constitutional law, with an emphasis in recent years on human rights for the American underclass and for torture victims abroad. Yet he will be remembered most for one case only: his controversial handling of the espionage trial of Ethel and Julius Rosenberg, convicted spies who were handed a death sentence by Kaufman in 1951 and electrocuted two years later.

Irving Robert Kaufman was born in New York City to Herman, a manufacturer of tobacco-related goods, and Rose (Spielberg) Kaufman. A gifted student, he entered Fordham University after graduating from De-Witt Clinton High School in 1926. When he received his Bachelor of Laws degree in 1931, he was a dean's list student and the youngest in his class.

From 1932 to 1935 Kaufman worked in the law office of Louis Rosenberg, who became his father-in-law the next year. In 1935 he was appointed assistant U.S. district attorney in the Southern District of the state of New York and handled a number of highly publicized cases, for which he was dubbed "boy prosecutor." (He was only 25.) The following year Kaufman received a permanent appointment as assistant U.S. attorney and continued to distinguish himself as he supervised the breakup of a major insurance scam in which a ring of swindlers was defrauding several insurance companies of millions of dollars.

Kaufman returned to private practice in 1940 but seven years later was recruited by Attorney General Tom Clark to become his assistant on "special legal matters." These "matters" turned out to be a major investigation of lobbying groups in Washington that, unregulated in Congress, had come to wield significant influence over the legislative process. Under Clark's aegis, Kaufman supervised the registration of federal lobbyists and prosecuted those who failed to do so. Kaufman received his first judicial appointment in 1949, when President Harry Truman named him to the federal bench as U.S. district court judge of the Southern District of New York. The youngest such judge named, he immediately became involved in a series of espionage cases, reflecting the fervor to prosecute alleged Communists at the time. Thus in 1951 he was selected to handle the Rosenberg case.

Julius and Ethel Rosenberg and two others were charged with conspiring to reveal information about American atomic prowess to the Russians in the mid-1940s. When one of the other defendants, David Greenglass (Ethel Rosenberg's brother), became a government witness and affirmed the charges alleged against the four, a jury found them all guilty of wartime espionage. On that basis, Kaufman sentenced the Rosenbergs to death, while handing a 15-year jail sentence to Greenglass and a 30-year sentence to the fourth defendant, Morton Sobell (whose sentence was later reduced). For the two years following, the Rosenbergs' case was appealed in the state and federal appellate courts and the Supreme Court. Requests for executive clemency from Presidents Truman and Eisenhower were also turned down, and the Rosenbergs were executed in 1953. Rosenberg supporters claimed both then and later that material pertaining to the case was being suppressed and that Kaufman in particular was involved in behind-the-scenes negotiations with the Justice Department and especially with J. Edgar Hoover, the FBI head, in the determination of final sentencing. In 1976 the Rosenbergs' sons, Robert and Michael Meeropol, secured more than 30,000 pages of documents regarding their parents' trial under the Freedom of Information Act. They contended that the papers "prove" that Kaufman and other principals in the case had violated the judicial code of ethics and have attempted since then to reopen the case.

In the meantime Kaufman went on to different cases. Named in 1961 to the Federal Court of Appeals, he ruled in an important segregation case, in which he determined that the New Rochelle, New York school board had used neighborhood schools as a means to perpetuate segregation, and he ordered an alternate plan to end it. He also ruled in favor of voting rights for minorities, spoke out for prison reform and supported the constitutional rights of conscientious objectors during the Vietnam War. In 1971 he ruled favorably for *The New York Times* in its effort to avoid federal prosecution for having published the Pentagon Papers. In 1979 Kaufman ruled in Kodak's favor in a highly publicized case in which the photographic firm was accused of maintaining a monopoly in the film processing industry. He strongly defended the First Amendment in 1982 when he ruled that the Communist Party did not have to comply with an election law compelling the disclosure of the names of campaign contributors. "Privacy is an essential element of the right to express dissent effectively," he wrote. On behalf of a unanimous court, Kaufman observed that "anonymity has long been essential to uninhibited political activity in a democratic society" and that insisting on disclosures by the Communist Party was reprehensible "in the face of the clear chilling effect this activity will inevitably have."

Despite his role in the Rosenberg case—and his alleged behind-the-scenes actions may remain forever murky—he has remained a consistent defender of the American legal system and of the values it represents. He felt the death sentence was appropriate for the Rosenbergs during the Cold War fever that dominated the early 1950s, and there appears to be little doubt that he would not do otherwise if faced with that decision today.

STANLEY JULES KAUFFMANN

b. April 24, 1916
Theater and film critic

Stanley Jules Kauffmann, film critic for *The New Republic* magazine, theater critic for *Saturday Review* magazine and former *New York Times* theater reviewer, is one of America's respected writers in the arts world. His thoughtful and provocative pieces have been anthologized in several books, one of which, *A World on Film: Criticism and Comment* (New York, 1966), has become a standard in the field.

Stanley Kauffmann was born in New York City to Joseph, a dentist, and Jeannette (Steiner) Kauffmann. Kauffmann, who graduated from New York University in 1935 with a Bachelor of Fine Arts degree, was a member of the Washington Square Players from 1931 to 1941. He left the acting field to become a writer and published his first novel, *The Hidden Hero* (New York), in 1949. The book, a thriller set in Mexico and Connecticut, was praised for its tension and suspense.

In 1949, the same year that he published his first work, Kauffmann entered the publishing field. For the next decade he led a dual life as a writer and an editor. From 1949 to 1952 he was associate editor at Bantam Books, from 1952 to 1956 he was editor in chief of Ballantine Books, and from 1959 to 1960 he was editor at Alfred A. Knopf.

During that time, Kauffmann wrote several other novels, including *A Change of Climate* (New York, 1954), in which a young college professor decides to leave teaching to become a businessman, and *Man of the World* (New York, 1956), which portrays a 35-year-old married man who runs off with a younger, more inexperienced woman. In his novels Kauffmann is interested in stripping his characters to their basic emotions and examining their thoughts about life.

In 1958 Kauffmann became the film critic for *The New Republic*, a position he held until 1965. He also worked at *The New Republic* as associate literary editor from 1966 to 1967 and as theater critic from 1969 to 1979. He has been the theater critic for *The Saturday Review* since 1979 and was drama critic for *The New York Times* in 1966. He also conducted the television program *The Art of Film* on Channel 13 from 1963 to 1967.

In his now-classic text, *A World on Film: Criticism and Comment*, Kauffmann presents film reviews he wrote from early 1958 to 1965. They reveal his broad knowledge of film history and a smooth literary style. They also examine domestic and foreign films as an evolving art and filmmakers as developing artists. The book was praised for the author's appreciation of good acting, his knowledge of the literary and theatrical backgrounds of film adaptations, and his insightful perceptions and intellectual contributions to the cinema world.

Kauffmann examined symbolism in film in his second book about movies, *Figures of Light: Film Criticism and Comment* (New York, 1972), a collection of the author's reviews from 1966 to 1970. Kauffmann's insistence upon the importance of the meaning below the surface motivated book reviewers to cite Kauffmann as one of America's most valuable film critics.

Kauffmann was a visiting professor of drama at Yale University from 1967 to 1968, from 1969 to 1973 and since 1977. He was also a distinguished professor at City College of New York from 1973 to 1976 and has been a visiting professor of drama at the City University of New York Graduate Center since 1977. He was the recipient of the George Jean Nathan award for dramatic criticism for 1972–73 and was a Guggenheim fellow in 1979–80.

DANNY KAYE

b. January 18, 1913
Entertainer

Danny Kaye, one of the world's most popular entertainers, has attained extraordinary success on stage, television, film and in concert halls. With his mobile face, agile movements and double-talk ditties, he has long been famous as a comic actor with a talent for relating to youngsters. As permanent ambassador for UNICEF (The United Nations International Children's Emergency Fund), he has toured the world performing to audiences of children and raising extraordinary amounts of money for them.

Daniel David Kominski was born in Brooklyn to Jacob, a tailor, and Clara (Nemerovsky) Kominski, both Russian immigrants. From the time he was a child, he loved entertaining. "People always laughed at my craziness and I loved that," he said in 1970. Kaye made his debut in a minstrel show in elementary school but pursued athletics rather than acting at Thomas Jefferson High School in Brooklyn. He dropped out of high school after 3½ years and worked at odd jobs—as an unhappy soda jerk and an insurance clerk.

His career in business proved abortive, and between 1929 and 1933, in the summers, he was a *toomler*—Yiddish for "noisemaker"—to entertaining the largely Jewish guests in the Catskill Mountains' Borscht Belt of New York State. During the rest of the year he tried unsuccessfully to interest Broadway producers in his talents. In 1933 he joined two dancers and, changing his name to "Kaye," formed a team called "The Three Terpsichoreans," which played the vaudeville circuit. When the team reached Detroit, a producer signed them to a five-month tour of the United States and a tour of the Orient, which lasted two years. It was in the Far

East, where he was confronted with non-English-speaking audiences, that Kaye developed his face-making and pantomime techniques.

Kaye returned to America in 1936 and—after time spent looking for jobs, performing nightclub engagements and working at another camp— he was invited, in 1939, to Camp Tamiment, a summer spot for young professionals in Pennsylvania. Assisting Kaye in producing the camp's weekly revues was a young songwriter, Sylvia Fine. The sophisticated humor of Miss Fine's satire was well fitted to Kaye's technique and, at camp, they experimented with a few of Kaye's popular songs, including "Anatole of Paris," "Stanislavsky" and "Pavlova." For the season's finale the best tunes were incorporated into one show—*The Straw Hat Revue*, which opened on Broadway in September 1939 with Imogene Coca. Kaye was an instant hit.

He married Miss Fine on January 3, 1940. She has continued to write his sketches and serve as personal director, coach, critic and occasional accompanist.

After his marriage, Kaye was offered a booking at the New York nightclub La Martinique. After playwright Moss Hart saw Kaye's act, he wrote a part for him in 1940 for *Lady in the Dark,* a show starring Gertrude Lawrence. Again the critics loved him. In 1941 Kaye left *Lady in the Dark* for the featured lead in *Let's Face It,* a Broadway hit.

Rejected by the U.S. Army during World War II because of a back problem, Kaye directed his efforts to performing at Army camps and hospitals. In later years he performed the same role during the Korean War and the 1973 Yom Kippur War, when he visited hospitals throughout Israel.

In 1944 Kaye appeared in his first motion picture, *Up in Arms,* where he perfected the double-talk that made him so admired on the stage. During the 1940s and 1950s, Kaye appeared in numerous additional films, including *Kid from Brooklyn* (1945), *Secret Life of Walter Mitty* (1946), *A Song Is Born* (1947), *Inspector General* (1948), *Hans Christian Andersen* (1952), *Knock on Wood* (1954), *Me and the Colonel* (1958) and many others. In the early 1960s, he had his own television program, *The Danny Kaye Show,* which ran four years and won a 1963 Emmy Award and a George Foster Peabody Award.

Kaye's services to UNICEF began in 1955. In the years since he has devoted a large part of every year to traveling around the world performing and raising money for children. Kaye himself admits that his charm is attributable to the fact that he's still a kid at heart.

Kaye also conducts benefit concerts regularly for musicians' pension funds. According to a *Playbill* reporter, "The baton work of this maestro must be seen to be disbelieved. He dances, writhes, skips, jumps, out-Bernsteins Bernstein, lies down and conducts with his feet, faces the audience, jokes with the concertmaster" and, in general, just acts like the typically crazy Danny Kaye.

Always energetic, Kaye starred as Noah in Richard Rodgers' 1970 Broadway hit musical *Two by Two* after an almost 30-year hiatus from the stage. He also won an Emmy Award for Best Children's Special in 1975. In 1981 he was the star of "Skokie," a television drama in which he portrayed a concentration camp survivor intent on preventing neo-Nazis from parading in his hometown. "I have done it all," says Kaye.

ALFRED KAZIN

b. June 5, 1915
Literary critic

The prolific critic and memoirist Alfred Kazin has been a distinguished writer of major interest and importance since the appearrance in 1942 of his first collection, *On Native Ground*. In critical studies and memoirs that have since followed, Kazin has emerged as one of America's chief chroniclers of literary history in the 20th century.

Alfred Kazin was born and raised in the impoverished Brownsville section of Brooklyn to immigrant parents. His father, Charles, was a house painter; his mother, Gita (Fagelman) Kazin, worked as a dressmaker. Commuting to the City College of New York during the day, returning to Brownsville at night, Kazin soon became swept up in the crosscurrents of contemporary radical politics. He viewed himself, however, as a literary radical, indifferent to economics, suspicious of organizations, more concerned with art and ideas. He received his Bachelor of Social Science degree from City College in 1935 and his M.A. degree in English from Columbia University in 1938. From 1937 until 1942 he was a tutor in English at CCNY.

Kazin became established in literary Manhattan with the publication of his first book, *On Native Grounds* (New York, 1942). An analytic and pioneering social history tracing the development of American literature starting in 1890, *On Native Ground* was hailed as a work of high moral seriousness and fastidious discernment. In keeping with historic trends, as he explored the works of such writers as William Dean Howells, William Faulkner and Thomas Wolfe, Kazin divided the book into three parts. The first, "The Search for Reality," covered 1890 to 1917. Part two was called "The Great Liberation," covering 1918 to 1929. The third section was "The Literature of Crisis" (1930 to 1940).

His reputation secure, Kazin worked for a year as the literary editor of *The New Republic* (1942–43) and in 1944 served briefly as associate editor of *Fortune* magazine.

His second book, *A Walker in the City* (New York, 1951), added a new dimension to Kazin's writing. In one of the most moving accounts of first-generation life ever written, Kazin focused on his youth in Brownsville and his slow awakening to life beyond the confines of his neighborhood and family. The book is sensitive and intense yet remarkably free of cant and sentimentalism.

Kazin then began to lecture at many of America's universities. He served as visiting professor at Harvard (1952), Smith (1953–54), Amherst (1955–58), University of Puerto Rico (1959), New York University (1960), Princeton (1961) and the University of California at Berkeley (1962). In 1963 he was appointed professor of English at the State University of New York at Stony Brook. Since 1973 he has been distinguished professor of English at Hunter College and the Graduate Center of the City University of New York.

After the publication of a collection of essays called *The Inmost Leaf* (New York, 1955), Kazin completed *Contemporaries* (New York, 1962). The more than 70 essays in this collection reveal Kazin's wide range of interests from Israel, the Holocaust and Yiddish literature to J.D. Salinger, travel in Soviet Russia, the Kennedy administration and early American writers. The essays, most of which appeared originally as book reviews, are distinguished by their attempt to place literature into its social and cultural contexts.

Kazin continued his memoirs with *Starting Out in the Thirties* (New York, 1965), in which he describes his own development as an important critic and writer in the literary hotbed of Manhattan. At that time—a period of depression, experimentation and the ominous clouds of war and fascism in Europe and Asia—many writers felt themselves to be movers of history as well as observers. His book details his disillusionment with radicalism and the further development of his critical sensibilities.

Kazin's final memoir, *New York Jew* (New York, 1978), created much interest when first published. Chronicling his life and world events from 1938 through the present, Kazin explores his Jewish roots and connections to the Holocaust; his marital problems (he has been married two times); the emergence and anguish of McCarthyism in the 1950s and radical uprising during the 1960s; and his attempts to come to grips with himself. Some of the authors he discusses include Edmund Wilson, Lionel Trilling and Saul Bellow and the poets Ezra Pound, Robert Frost and T.S. Eliot.

In addition to his own work, Kazin has edited volumes of critical studies of several writers and poets, including *F. Scott Fitzgerald* (New York, 1951), *William Blake* (New York, 1956), *Theodore Dreiser* (Bloomington, 1956) and *Ralph Waldo Emerson* (New York, 1958). He wrote the introduction to Shalom Aleichem's *Selected Short Stories* (New York, 1956) and, with his wife Ann Birstein Kazin, *Collected Works of Anne Frank* (New York, 1959).

WOLFE KELMAN

b. November 27, 1923
Rabbi; administrator

Rabbi Wolfe Kelman, executive vice president of the Rabbinical Assembly (Conservative rabbinate), is a significant American organizational, educational and Conservative Jewish leader and former director of the United Synagogue of America.

Wolfe Kelman was born in Vienna to Hersh Leib, a rabbi, and Mirl (Fish) Kelman. When he was still very young, he moved with his family to Toronto, Canada, where he attended elementary and high school. Following service in the Royal Canadian Air Force between 1943 and 1945, he returned to school. He received his B.A. degree from the University of Toronto in 1946 and Master of Hebrew Literature degree and rabbinical ordination from the Jewish Theological Seminary of America in 1950.

Since 1951 he has served as executive vice president of the Rabbinical Assembly, a professional association of 1,200 Conservative rabbis, and from 1951 to 1966 was director of the United Synagogue and the seminary. He has been a member of the governing council of the World Jewish Congress since 1968, a member of the board of directors of the Hebrew Immigrant Aid Society since 1974 and president of the Committee of Neighbors Concerned with the Elderly, Their Rights and Needs. He is also a former president of the Hebrew Arts Foundation, a former chairman of the cultural commission of the World Jewish Congress and a member of numerous civic and community organizations.

Kelman, who became a naturalized United States citizen in 1962, has been a rabbi of various congregations, including the West London Synagogue of British Jews in London from 1957 to 1958. He has also taught Jewish homiletics and history at the seminary since 1967 and has been chairman of the academic board of the Melton Research Center from 1969 to 1971.

Essentially an optimist, Kelman has written and

spoken consistently on American Judaism. In his article "Religion" *(American Jewish Yearbook,* 1961), he cites as "witnesses" to God's existence "the harassed and financially embarrassed parent who makes a great sacrifice to send his child to a Jewish school, [who] maintains the Jewish tradition in his home and in his heart; the disciples of R. Israel Ba'al Shem Tov, who serve their people with love and understanding and compassion, and the underpaid teachers and social workers who serve the community and those most in need. They are indeed witnesses." This led him to his sense of hopefulness concerning the viability of Jewish religious life, what he called "The dawn of a genuine renaissance."

It was a theme he repeated over and over again. In 1971, in "The American Synagogue: Present and Prospects" *(Conservative Judaism,* Fall 1971), he listed the causes of his endemic optimism: "The explosion in the numbers of chairs and departments of Jewish studies"; the seminary and yeshiva graduates turning to teaching; the decline of "social activism"; and the improvements he saw in Jewish education. Other than intermarriage and the fact that none but the Orthodox accepted halakah, "there never has been a better time in American Jewish history than the present."

THEODORE WOODROW KHEEL

b. May 9, 1914
Labor mediator

Theodore Kheel is a lawyer by profession but best-known as one of the nation's prominent labor mediators. He has helped settle bitter disputes in both the private and public sectors, on both the local and federal levels.

Theodore Woodrow Kheel was born in Brooklyn to Samuel, owner of a real estate firm, and Kate (Herzenstein) Kheel. Theodore Kheel graduated from DeWitt Clinton High School in 1931 and then went to Cornell University. He received his B.A. degree in 1935 and stayed on to get his Bachelor of Laws degree in 1937. He then returned to New York and entered private law practice.

The next year Kheel joined the staff of the National Labor Relations Board. In 1942 he became a staff member of the War Labor Board, which ruled in wartime labor disputes. He was regional director of the New York area until 1944, when he became executive director of the national board. When New York City established the Mayor's Division of Labor Relations in 1946, Mayor William O'Dwyer asked Kheel to serve as its

deputy director. The following year he became director. In 1948 Kheel resumed private law practice in the firm now known as Battle, Fowler, Jaffin, Pierce and Kheel.

In addition to his private practice, Kheel has been the mediator in many public labor disputes. In 1949 Mayor O'Dwyer had asked him to help settle disputes between the city's private bus lines and the Transport Workers Union. His success in that role led to his appointment in 1956 as impartial arbitrator between the New York City Transit Authority and the TWU. Both union and city officials have praised his objectivity until 1982, when Mayor Edward Koch, a long time political opponent, recommended to transit officials that Kheel be fired. Kheel replied that the Mayor's action constituted "tampering with a quasi-judicial process"—a charge Koch rejected—but decided not to seek reappointment.

In recognition of his role in helping to end the 114-day strike that deprived New Yorkers of newspapers in 1962–63, Kheel was honored by the Columbia University Graduate School of Journalism for his "enlightenment and good sense." In the following years he mediated New York City's first transit strike (1966), the garbage strike (1968), college and professional sports disputes, and struggles between teachers and boards of education.

On a national level President Lyndon B. Johnson asked Kheel to join the mediation team to settle the railroad industry's work rules dispute. The workers received a pay increase, but the railroads won more control over employee assignments.

In the 1970s Kheel remained close to the newspaper scene, helping newspaper management and unions devise a plan for phasing in more computer operations, a controversial subject among labor unions because they saw it as a way of eliminating human employees and replacing them with machines.

His style of labor negotiations and mediation is based on distinguishing between "factual issues" in the dispute and "difficult decisional issues," such as determining maximum and minimum amounts of money acceptable to both sides and whether a strike is acceptable to one or both. "Face is very important," he says, and "Nothing happens at meetings. It happens away from meetings." And, "The doctrine of me-tooism pervades everything," meaning that every union in the same industry wants to receive what another allied union wins. "You really have to persuade people who are looking at the dispute from their own interest, who may have blind spots, who are emotionally upset . . . what the dynamics of the situation indicate," he told *The New York Times* after the settlement of another newspaper strike in 1965.

Kheel has served on many corporate boards. He has devoted much of his spare time to civil rights, serving as president of the National Urban League from 1956 to 1960.

"When I die," he told *The New York Times*, "I want it engraved on my tombstone, 'He believed in collective bargaining.' "

For further information:

Kheel, Theodore W. *Guide to Fair Employment Practices.* 1964.

———. *How Race Relations Affect Your Business.* 1963.

———. *Kheel on Labor Law.* 1974.

———. *Pros and Cons of Compulsory Arbitration.* 1961.

———. *Transit and Arbitration.* 1960.

MICHAEL KIDD

b. August 11, 1917

Dancer; choreographer

Michael Kidd has reaped tremendous success as a choreographer, winning Tony Awards for five Broadway musicals, *Finian's Rainbow, Guys and Dolls, Destry Rides Again, L'il Abner* and *Can-Can.* Since his debut as a choreographer with the American Ballet Theater in 1945, Kidd has displayed an ability to take typical American themes and create dance styles that combine the best of American folk traditions with ballet and jazz forms.

Michael Greenwald was born in Brooklyn to immigrant parents, a barber, and Lillian Greenwald. His early upbringing had nothing to do with dance; in fact, as a student in New Utrecht High School, where he graduated in 1935, he excelled in math and science and was on the track team. And at City College of New York, he studied chemical engineering for three years, working nights as a copyboy at the *New York Daily Mirror* to help finance his studies. He also worked as a photographer and has pursued the craft studiously but as a sideline throughout his life.

However, it was Kidd's exposure to a modern dance class while in high school that first whetted his appetite for the art, and he continued to study modern dance in college. The turning point occurred when he realized engineering did not offer the kind of future life he aspired to. He wrote:

> I didn't think I could seriously devote my life to engineering with the amount of concentration required to become successful at it. It seemed too devoid of any relationship to human emotions to satisfy me. The break

was precipitated when a fellow student in the organic chemistry lab asked me to demonstrate a pirouette. I did so but smashed an elaborate setup and caused several people to be burned by flying acid.

At the recommendation of a professor, who consulted Kidd's parents, he left CCNY and in 1937 joined the School of American Ballet and Lincoln Kirstein's Ballet Caravan, the touring branch of the school. He toured the United States for the next three years when he joined the Dance Players as assistant director.

In 1942 he joined Ballet Theater, where he danced lead roles and had the opportunity in 1945 to direct and perform in his original ballet *On Stage,* which was based on the tale of a backstage handyman who befriends a shy dancer. The ballet demonstrated Kidd's gift for using dancing as fun and entertainment instead of as a vehicle for poetic expression. It used a great deal of pantomime and was described by one critic as "more like a silent film comedy than like a dance." Yet overall, *On Stage*—a first of its kind for Ballet Theater and the beginning of a new dance genre—was acclaimed by critics and became part of Ballet Theater's repertoire. Within a year and a half after the performance of *On Stage,* Kidd accepted a job as choreographer of *Finian's Rainbow,* his first of many Broadway productions.

Kidd's career from then on was a string of successes on Broadway and in Hollywood. From the 1950s through the 1970s, he choreographed, and in some cases directed, many hit shows, for which his animated and seemingly easygoing style was suited. In 1956 he made his Broadway debut as director, choreographer and producer, as well as dancer, in *L'il Abner.* Although some critics questioned whether a comic strip could be made into real theater, most agreed on the high quality of Kidd's work. Previously he had performed on Broadway in *Can Can* (1954) and later choreographed *Destry Rides Again* (1959), based on a Max Brand western story; *Ben Franklin in Paris* (1964); *The Rothschilds* (1970); a revival of *Candide* (1971); the short-lived *Cyrano* (1973); and a revival of *The Music Man* (1980).

Kidd's screen debut as a choreographer came with *It's Always Fair Weather* and also included *Subways Are for Sleeping* (1961), *Seven Brides for Seven Brothers* (1953), *Finian's Rainbow* (1949) and *Hello, Dolly!* (1970) with Barbra Streisand.

He remained in California and has done work in regional theater there in recent years, including a 1978 staging of *The Sound of Music* with Florence Henderson by the Los Angeles Civic Light Opera.

Kidd's contributions to American theatrical dance were recognized in 1981, when he was elected to the

Theater Hall of Fame, whose nominees' careers must span at least 25 years on Broadway and include five major credits.

ALAN KING

b. December 26, 1927
Comedian

Alan King, one of America's leading comedians, has made millions of people laugh by parodying and mocking the suburban lifestyle in this country. He attributes his great love of comedy to his Jewish heritage, for as he once told the *New York Post,* "It is the syndrome of the Jews. If you don't laugh, you die."

Irwin Alan Kniberg was born in New York City, King was the son of Bernard, a ladies' hat cutter, and Minnie (Solomon) Kniberg. The family lived in New York's Lower East Side and Williamsburg, then largely Jewish sections in Manhattan and Brooklyn, respectively.

As for many young comedians, the road to success for King led through burlesque theaters and the borscht belt hotels in the Catskill Mountains. He never finished high school, and at the age of 17, in 1944, he was a regular performer at Leon and Eddie's, a new talent showcase in New York. He free-lanced for five more years, until in 1949 he was signed by Paramount and appeared as a comic on a publicity tour with singers Lena Horne and Patti Page.

His big break, however, came in 1956, when he appeared with Judy Garland at the Paramount Theater in New York. By then he had begun mastering his style, using a staccato delivery of brief jokes, a technique made famous by George Burns, Jack Benny, Bob Hope and Milton Berle. The Paramount performance led to a concert tour of the United States and Europe with Garland and later to guest appearances on the televised Ed Sullivan, Garry Moore and Perry Como shows. King then settled into a comfortable niche playing the top nightclubs in New York and Las Vegas.

Early in his career, King concentrated his wit at the rapidly developing American suburban environment. This was the topic of his first book, *Anyone Who Owns a House Deserves It* (New York, 1962). His second book, *I Am a Prisoner in a Chinese Bakery,* coauthored by Jack Shurman, (New York, 1964), is a madcap, helter-skelter romp directed at a myriad of different comic targets. Though during the 1960s King became more political in his approach, he resisted the biting satire of a Lenny Bruce or a Mort Sahl.

King's stage career blossomed after the publication of his second book. In 1965 he played Nathan Detroit in the New York revival of *Guys and Dolls,* and the following year he portrayed a psychiatrist who can't understand his own daughter in *The Impossible Years* (1966). He had a role of a rabbi in the 1968 satire about New York Jewish intellectuals, *Bye Bye Braverman.*

In recent years King has continued to play at the top night spots in America. His act has gotten more political and he spares no sacred cows. In 1980 he hosted a post-election special on network television, called "Alan King and Friends." Dressed in a tuxedo and smoking a huge cigar, unruffled and with a gleam in his eye, a man with perfect timing, King continues to lampoon—gently, if irreverently, as he always does—everything, including Hollywood, the media and himself.

CAROLE KING

b. February 9, 1941
Singer; songwriter

Although singer-songwriter Carole King was identified as one of the "fresh new faces" to arrive on the pop music scene in the early 1970s, in fact she was already a seasoned veteran whose songs—performed by other singers—had been hits for well over a decade. The "soft-rock" music she popularized proved to be a welcome antidote to the "acid-rock" music of the late 1960s, and her second solo album, *Tapestry,* released in 1971, sold more than 10 million copies, garnering for her one of the four Grammy awards she received that year.

Carole Klein was born in Brooklyn. Her father was an insurance salesman, and her mother a schoolteacher. Raised in a middle-class neighborhood, she attended James Madison High School, where she befriended Neil Sedaka, a classmate who would become a successful popular singer in his own right and who was a major influence on King's own musical development. Sedaka had already formed a successful singing group, The Tokens, and King followed with one of her own, the Cosines. Copying 1950s ensemble pop music, she showed an early talent for harmony, musical arrangement and catchy melody that would overlap into her professional career.

After high school graduation in 1959, King entered Queens College but dropped out to marry Gerry Goffin, a chemistry student. The partnership was as much professional as marital; they were soon writing songs together—Goffin the lyrics, King the music. They soon followed the route taken by many young aspiring songwriters, renting work space in the Brill Building in Manhattan and then trying to vend their pieces to one of the many music producers also located there.

But unlike many novice songwriters who floundered for a while and then abandoned their hopes, King and Goffin had an early succession of hit songs, beginning in 1960 with "Will You Love Me Tomorrow?". Produced by the promoter Don Kirschner and recorded by a black women's quartet, The Shirelles, the song became a Top-100 hit and reached the top of the charts in January 1961. Other hits to follow included "Go Away, Little Girl," sung by Steve Lawrence in 1962; "Up on the Roof," performed by the Drifters; and "The Locomotion," which was recorded by Goffin and King's babysitter, who called herself "Little Eva."

King made her own singing debut in 1962, when she cut a demonstration record with her song "It Might as Well Rain Until September." Also a best seller, it established her potential as a performer, but her efforts were temporarily stilled by the sudden popularity of the Beatles and other British rock ensembles, who introduced an entirely new musical style, which overwhelmed the pop music scene for some years. King did not have another hit until her song "Natural Woman" was recorded by the gospel and soul singer Aretha Franklin in the late 1960s. Now on the verge of a comeback as the popularity of hard-rock music began to wane, King ended both her marriage and work/partnership with Goffin and set out to establish a separate identity as a writer and performer.

Moving to the West Coast, King recorded her first album, *Writer: Carole King,* which was released in 1970. Although it contained some Goffin-King collaborations, it also included new pieces of her own. Her subtle, unmenacing (some have described them as "schlock") lyrics had a broad appeal, and a King following developed. The next year all her past efforts were combined to create *Tapestry,* the album that signaled not only King's arrival after a long apprenticeship but her permanent role in popular music. With songs like "You've Got a Friend" and "It's Too Late," which would become popular hits by other performers as well, King became the top recording figure of the early 1970s. She thus won a Grammy award not only for Best Album but also for Best Song ("You've Got a Friend"), Best Single Record ("It's Too Late") and Best Female Performer in the Pop Field.

King has completed several albums since *Tapestry,* but none has had the same success. Most critics agree that her style has simply not changed over the years, so

that where *Tapestry* was special, her subsequent records have been bland and undistinguished. Nonetheless, in a Central Park concert during the summer of 1977, King drew a record crowd, and she seems to remain popular because she has never succumbed to the superficial glitter common to performers in her field.

HENRY ALFRED KISSINGER

b. May 23, 1923
Government official

In its editorial noting the departure of Henry Kissinger from public service in Washington in 1977, *The New York Times* noted, "Henry Kissinger has not been President of the United States for the past eight years; it only seemed that way." Indeed, the former secretary of state, 1973 Nobel Peace Prize winner and originator of the concept of shuttle diplomacy played such a major and controversial role in the determination and execution of American foreign policy, that it was often he—and not presidents Nixon or Ford—whom foreign leaders sought for guidance and advice or blamed for policy failures. His roles in negotiating the Middle East peace treaty; tragically expanding and then ultimately ending the war in Vietnam; instituting detente with Russia; establishing relations with mainland China and overthrowing the democratic Allende regime in Chile are only a few of his accomplishments and failures. The sum total of his legacy, however, will probably not be known for years to come, since out of office he retains a significant, almost mystical influence on policy making.

Heinz Alfred Kissinger, the second son of Louis and Paula (Stern) Kissinger, was born in the Bavarian city of Furth. The elder Kissinger was a teacher of geography and history in a girls' school, and after Hitler was elected head of the German government and anti-Semitic harassments began, the family departed in 1938 for London and then to Washington Heights in northern Manhattan, a neighborhood dubbed the "Fourth Reich" because of the large number of Austrian and German Jews who had taken refuge there. His father worked as a clerk and bookkeeper and his mother as a cook in the homes of wealthy families downtown, while he attended George Washington High School at night and worked days in a shaving brush factory. In 1941 Kissinger began studying accounting nights at the City College of New York until he was drafted into the Army in 1943.

He served with the 84th Infantry Division and with the 970th Counterintelligence Corps as a German interpreter for his commanding general as well as an interrogator. After Germany's surrender in May 1945, Kissinger was given the task of reorganizing the town government of Krefeld. Later he became a district administrator with the United States military government.

Discharged, he enrolled in Harvard University, where he earned his B.A. degree summa cum laude in 1950. By 1954 he completed an M.A. degree and received his Ph.D. His doctoral dissertation was about Prince Metternich's efforts to restore the status quo ante in post-Napoleonic Europe. He reworked the study into his first book, *A World Restored: Castlereagh, Metternich and the Problems of Peace* (Boston, 1957). In it he viewed history as a struggle between revolutionary and conservative forces.

In the ensuing years, while teaching at Harvard, where he was named a professor in 1962, he associated himself with New York Governor Nelson Rockefeller and the Council on Foreign Relations, chairing several of its study groups exploring non-nuclear methods of countering the Soviet Union. This effort resulted in his major book *Nuclear Weapons and Foreign Policy* (New York, 1957), in which he took issue with Secretary of State John Foster Dulles's doctrine of "massive retaliation." Instead, Kissinger enunciated the doctrine of "flexible response," arguing that American survival and victory depended "not only on our strength, but also on our ability to recognize [and fight] aggression in all its forms. In the nuclear age, by the time a threat has become unambiguous, it may be too late to resist it." The book helped establish Kissinger's reputation among political leaders and strongly influenced Richard M. Nixon.

Thus, when Nixon was elected president in 1969, Kissinger was chosen assistant for national security affairs and later, secretary of state, emerging as the most powerful man in the two Nixon administrations. When he left office in January 1977, following the defeat of Gerald Ford by Jimmy Carter, he sought to rationalize his role in memoirs, the first of which, *White House Years* (New York, 1979), won the 1979 American Book Association award for best work of history. In it he deals with the Middle East, possibly his single outstanding feat inasmuch as he restored American-Arab friendship and began to construct a tentative "step-by-step" series of disengagements between Egypt and Israel. "If there was no chance of success, I saw no reason for us to involve ourselves," he wrote in *White House Years*. But he had good reason to believe he would succeed, for he understood more than most that whatever successes he achieved came from wooing moderate Arabs rather than

putting pressures on Israel. His trip to China, veiled in secrecy—a Kissinger trademark—was the high point of the Nixon administration's foreign policy triumphs.

Detente, another of his policies, was worthwhile in its muting of the Cold War, although some critics contend that he oversold it and helped create the delusion that it would lead to an end to conflict and "the achievement of a lasting peace"—one of his and Nixon's pet phrases. It may also be argued that the Strategic Arms Limitation Talks (SALT I) were also a diplomatic triumph concluded in the best interests of the two nuclear powers.

All the same, he has serious critics, including those who believed his errors led to the invasion of Cyprus and hurt the United States badly in Greece and Turkey. His African policy has also been denounced for its support of the Portuguese colonists and, when that was no longer possible, for his resorting to covert warfare and his favoring of the white majority in Rhodesia. He was a central figure in the CIA's attempts to influence the Chilean elections of 1970 and the subsequent overthrow of the legally elected Salvador Allende and the installation of a murderous dictatorship.

But Kissinger may be most remembered for his role in Indochina, where even an admirer such as Max Lerner believes "his miscalculations were grave. . . . He could have ended it [the war] earlier and saved thousands of lives without producing the backlash in American opinion which he feared." To the historian Barbara Tuchman, "Kissinger lacked the imagination and, doubtless the influence" to withdraw from Vietnam after Nixon was elected in 1968. "In the end, Christmas bombing and all, after four years' talk at a cost of 19,000 more American lives and destruction in Vietnam, the terms obtained were no better than might have been obtained at the start. The four years of additional death and devastation were a waste." Yet, for his efforts in bringing the different parties together to negotiate a "long-lasting peace," Kissinger was awarded the Nobel Peace Prize in 1973, which he shared with North Vietnamese peace negotiator Le Duc Tho.

On the sidelines during the Carter administration, Kissinger was nevertheless courted extensively by both sides in 1979 during the aborted SALT-II debate and remained as candid as ever about foreign policy issues. For example, he spoke out against the human rights policies favored by Carter, referring to them as "a permanent intervention in the internal affairs of other countries," which in the long run, he claimed, were more detrimental than beneficial. And when the ex-Shah of Iran was unexpectedly admitted into the United States in 1979 despite warnings of dire consequences from several American diplomatic officials, former under-Secretary of State George W. Ball attributed the move to excessive pressure on the White House from Kissinger and colleague David Rockefeller.

Kissinger denied any direct role, saying, "I strongly supported the decision. It just so happened I did not bring it about." But his glib and offhand response reflected once again the power and mystique of the contradictory man whom *New York Times* columnist Anthony Lewis described bitterly as America's "P.T. Barnum," for whom showmanship often outweighed the actual effect of his actions. For example, although Kissinger claims close ties to Israel because of his Jewish roots—he lost many relatives in the Holocaust—some Jewish leaders regard him as an ambivalent Jew who has tailored his views according to political expediencies.

Kissinger will remain one of America's most intriguing and puzzling personalities. His impact in and out of office has been so great that columnist Max Lerner wrote that "historians may look back at the period from 1969 to 1977 as the Kissinger years rather than the Nixon-Ford years."

His second volume of memoirs, *Years of Upheaval* (Boston, 1982), recalls Richard M. Nixon's abbreviated second term as President. During that period—from 1972-1974—Watergate and the Middle East were the primary events. Still, as national security advisor and Secretary of State, Kissinger was also intimately concerned with ending the war in Vietnam, the Cambodian conflict, the fall of President Salvador Allende Gossens of Chile, the onset of the oil boycott, and a harsh domestic battle concerning United States-Soviet Union relations. The central theme in the book is Watergate, which in Kissinger's view, destroyed the promise of the Nixon Administration. "Liberals," wrote *The New York Times* critic Christopher Lehmann-Haupt, "will, as usual, be repelled by his *machtpolitik*. . . . Conservatives will scoff at his case for detente. . . . Yet, here is towering drama and amusing detail. . . . brilliantly argued, skillfully paced, sensitively proportioned, consistently charming, altogether masterly and by far the most consequential memoir to come out of the Nixon Administration."

Perhaps the best view of Kissinger comes from Kissinger, who wrote in his first book about the Congress of Vienna, "Men become myths, not by what they know, or even by what they achieve, but by the tasks they set for themselves." In evaluating the career of Henry Kissinger, future historians will have to measure whether the myth of the man translates into the best he could have done.

GILBERT KLAPERMAN

b. February 25, 1921
Rabbi

A prominent Jewish leader, Rabbi Gilbert Klaperman of Congregation Beth Shalom in Lawrence, New York is chairman of the board of the Emet World Academy in Jerusalem, chairman of the Rabbinic Committee of American ORT and vice president of the Rabbinical Council of America.

Gilbert Klaperman was born in New York City to Louis, a merchant, and Frieda (Rubinstein) Klaperman. He obtained a B.A. degree in 1940 from Yeshiva University and the following year was ordained a rabbi by the Rabbi Isaac Elchanan Theological Seminary of Yeshiva University in New York. During the next few years he held several different positions. He served as chaplain in the Canadian army during World War II.

From 1942 to 1943 he was director of the B'nai B'rith Hillel at Queens University in Kingston, Ontario; from 1943 to 1945 he was professor and director of the Hillel at the State University in Iowa. He obtained his M.A. degree in philosophy from the University of Iowa in 1946. From 1945 to 1947 he was head of a congregation in West New York, New Jersey, and from 1947 to 1950 he was head of Congregation Brith Sholom and director of the Hillel Foundation at Clemson College in Charleston, South Carolina. Since 1950 he has been rabbi of the congregation of Beth Shalom in Lawrence, New York. He received a Doctor of Hebrew Literature degree in 1955, and a Doctor of Divinity degree in 1971 from Yeshiva University and a Doctor of Law degree from Hofstra University in 1978.

Rabbi Klaperman taught sociology at Yeshiva University from 1954 to 1967 and was professor of Judaic studies at Lehman College from 1973 to 1975. Since 1979 he has taught sociology at Stern College. A strong Zionist and ardent supporter of Israel and the Jewish people, Klaperman was a member of a five-man Rabbinical Council of America delegation that conducted a seven-week fact-finding trip to Eastern Europe and the USSR in 1956 to study the condition of Jews. He was vice president of the American Zionist Rabbinical Council of America in 1958, chairman of the board of the Emet World Academy in Jerusalem since 1960, president of the Jewish Book Council of America from 1962 to 1966, president of the New York Board of Rabbis from 1968 to 1970 and chairman of the Greater New York Conference on Soviet Jewry from 1970 to 1972. He is currently a special professor of law at Hofstra University and president of the Alumni of Rabbi Isaac Elchanan Theological Seminary, an affiliate of Yeshiva University.

The life of the congregational rabbi has also fascinated him. In "Exploring the Rabbi's Inner Security," in *Papers Presented at the Annual Rabbi Harold Gordon Conference* (New York, 1981), he dealt with the dilemmas of the modern American rabbi: living "in a glass bowl," working "all hours of the day and night as well" and, with sadness—"there are many rabbis who are unsuited. They are simply not spiritually endowed for their profession." Concluding, he wrote: "The intensity of his faith must be the major factor . . . [he] must always believe as if he had no doubts . . . [he] must be Torah scholar, not a secular scholar . . . the essence of the rabbi's message emanates from his rabbinical knowledge."

For further information:

Klaperman, Gilbert. *How and Why of the Old Testament.* New York: 1964.

———. *The Story of Yeshiva University.* New York: 1969.

Klaperman, Gilbert, and Klaperman, Libby. *The Story of the Jewish People.* New York: 1961.

LAWRENCE R. KLEIN

b. September 14, 1920
Economist

Upon receiving the Nobel Prize for economics in 1980, Professor Lawrence Klein joined the ranks of such eminent theoreticians as Paul Samuelson, Kenneth J. Arrow and Milton Friedman. Klein had been selected by the Nobel Committee for his development of econometrics, a revolutionary system of models that uses mathematics and statistics to analyze economic policies and to forecast trends.

Lawrence Robert Klein was born in Omaha, Nebraska to Leo Byron and Blanche (Monheit) Klein, both clerical workers in a wholesale grocery. Much influenced by the effects of the Depression on his family and his community as he grew up, he chose to study economics in college. He received a B.A. degree from the University of California at Berkeley in 1942 and a Ph.D. from the Massachusetts Institute of Technology in 1944. Within two years he had already begun developing the concept of econometrics and was gaining distinction within the economic community.

He taught at the University of Chicago from 1944 to 1947 and from 1948 to 1950 was a research associate with the National Bureau of Economic Research. From 1949 to 1954 he combined teaching at the University of Michigan with research at the Survey Research Center. For the four years that followed, Klein carried on research at the Oxford Institute of Statistics and in 1958 joined the faculty of the University of Pennsylvania as a full professor. He was appointed university professor in 1964 and Benjamin Franklin Professor in 1968. Klein has also been a visiting professor at several institutions in the United States and abroad, including Hebrew University in 1964. (He visits Israel annually, he said in an interview.) He has also been a consultant to private industry and government organizations, including the state of New York in 1969 and the Congressional Budget Office since 1977.

In an interview in late 1980, shortly after receiving the Nobel Prize and after the election of Ronald Reagan to the presidency, Klein cited some economic measures the U.S. government might take to solve its financial woes and noted that both Japan and West Germany had successfully solved similar problems. For example, he supported larger expenditures on research and development as well as substantially larger tax cuts for business than for individuals. In concert with business breaks, he added that energy efficiency had to be emphasized, perhaps with special incentives. Klein felt that the tax legislation proposed by the Reagan-dominated Congress in 1981 was too general and did not address specific economic problems. He supported tax breaks for individuals that would encourage them to save their money rather than to spend it.

Critical of traditional government approaches to the economy, which he said were composed of "people reaching to every problem of the day" instead of taking a "long view and [planning] accordingly," Klein recommended a steady, "gutsy" government policy with a definite long-term goal. But because policy makers are politicians concerned with reelection, Klein is skeptical that such changes could come to pass.

For further information:

Klein, Lawrence R. *An Introduction to Econometrics.* Westport, Ct.: 1977.

——— and Goldberger. *Econometric Model of the U.S. 1929-1952.* New York: 1964.

——— and Burmeister, Edwin, eds. *Econometric Model Performance: Comparative Simulation Studies of the U.S. Economy.* Philadelphia: 1976.

——— and Young, Richard M. eds. *An Introduction to Econometric Forecasting and Forecasting Models.* Lexington, Mass.: 1980.

NATHAN S. KLINE

b. March 22, 1916
Psychiatrist

Dr. Nathan S. Kline, the eminent and often controversial research psychiatrist, is responsible for innovations in modern psychiatric practice that have transformed the nature of treatment of mental illness in the United States. He introduced modern tranquilizers in the early 1950s and later was the first to test anti-depressant drugs on mental patients.

Nathan Kline was born in Philadelphia to Ignatz and Florence (Schellenberg) Kline. His father owned a chain of department stores. An older brother, Dr. Benjamin Kline, developed the Kline cure for syphilis. Nathan Kline was brought up in Atlantic City, New Jersey and attended Swarthmore College, where he received his bachelor's degree in 1938. His combined interests in philosophy and the natural sciences led to a profound curiosity about the relationship between mind and body.

After completing graduate work in psychology at Harvard in 1938–39, Kline entered New York University College of Medicine, receiving his M.D. in 1943. He was analyzed by and has worked with Karen Horney and Harry Stack Sullivan. He served his internship and residency at St. Elizabeth's Hospital in Washington, D.C. and then joined the Public Health Service in 1944, where he worked as an assistant surgeon in the Navy for two years. There, Kline had the opportunity to observe emotionally disturbed men managing to control their disturbances and perform their duties despite their disabilities. He credits this experience with granting him greater tolerance for people's ability to function outside of the hospital environment.

Kline undertook further graduate studies at Princeton and received an M.A. from Clark University. After a short period as director of research at Worcester State Hospital in Massachusetts, he joined the staff of the Rockland State Hospital in Orangeburg, New York, becoming director in 1952. Under his leadership, Rockland State has become a major research institute.

At Rockland State, Kline performed his renowned experimentation upon violent psychotic patients. Despite widespread professional skepticism about the effectiveness of drug treatment, Kline proceeded with his experiments. He discovered that the Indian snakeroot derivative reserpine enabled schizophrenics to carry on conscious interaction with their environment. In later years he tested anti-depressants, or psychic energizers, on severely depressed patients, with favorable results.

Kline's research earned him the prestigious Albert Lasker Clinical Research awards in 1957 and 1964, the latter of which became the subject of a hotly contested lawsuit in the 1970s, in which a colleague claimed he was entitled to a portion of the award since the idea had originated with him and not with Kline. A court ruled Kline had to share the proceeds from his Lasker prize.

Kline has researched treatments for alcoholism and narcotics addiction. Because of his successes over the years in treating mental patients with drugs, he urged that increased funds for research into pharmacotherapy be made available.

Kline is clinical professor of psychiatry at Columbia University and permanent visiting professor at the University of California at San Diego. He is an attending physician at Lenox Hill Hospital in New York and director of psychiatric services at Bergen Pines County Hospital in New Jersey. Kline has maintained a private and consultative practice in New York City for over 25 years.

According to a 1981 interview, Kline treats 1,500 patients a year, or 80 a day, many of whom have been referred by other doctors because their cases were too difficult. Although some experts claim that Kline's emphasis on drug therapy over psychotherapy is counterproductive, he argues that there are simply not enough psychotherapists to care for patients in need.

Kline has traveled extensively investigating the state of psychiatry worldwide and has received awards and decorations in Mexico, Colombia, England, Indonesia, Japan, Liberia and Haiti. He is affiliated with dozens of national and international professional societies, among them the American Psychiatric Association, the American Medical Association, the Royal College of Psychiatrists Foundation (England) fellow, the World Federation for Mental Health, the International Committee Against Mental Illness (president), New York Academy of Sciences (fellow), New York Academy of Medicine (fellow) and Sigma XI. In the course of his extraordinary career, Dr. Kline has published more than 450 scientific papers and served on the editorial boards of numerous publications, including the *International Journal of Social Psychiatry, Excerpta Medica,* and *Psychopharmacologia.*

PHILIP M. KLUTZNICK

b. July 9, 1907
Businessman; communal leader

Philip M. Klutznick, millionaire businessman, U.S. diplomat and Jewish communal leader, served as secretary of commerce in the administration of President

Jimmy Carter. Credited with building many of the suburbs of Chicago and the Israeli port town of Ashdod, Klutznick has served every U.S. president from Franklin Roosevelt to Carter, with the exception of Richard Nixon. He also succeeded Nahum Goldmann as president of the World Jewish Congress.

Philip Klutznick was born in Kansas City, Missouri, the son of Morris, a small merchant, and Minnie (Spindler) Klutznick. Klutznick attended the University of Kansas from 1924 until 1925 and then transferred to the University of Nebraska, where he graduated in 1926 with a B.A. degree. He continued his education at Creighton University in Lincoln, Nebraska and received his Bachelor of Laws degree in 1929. The following year he was admitted to the bar and began to practice law.

In 1944 Klutznick entered public life, serving until 1946 as the United States commissioner of the Federal Public Housing Authority. He was the United States delegate to the United Nations in 1957, 1961 and 1962. From 1961 until 1963 he was the United States representative to UNESCO, holding an ambassadorial title. His governmental career was capped with his 1979 appointment to the Carter cabinet.

In private life Klutznick developed a far-flung business empire headquartered in Chicago, which includes vast real estate holdings. He is a member of Salomon Brothers, the New York investment banking house, and is chairman of the board of directors of a number of large financial organizations and institutions, including the Swiss-Israel Trade Bank and the now-defunct American Bank and Trust Company. He directs the Urban Investment and Development Company and sits on the boards of directors of many other companies.

Klutznick has long been deeply involved with the Jewish community. One indication of his impact on and service to the Jewish community is the number of honorary degrees he has received from Jewish universities in America. He has been awarded an honorary Doctorate in Hebrew Letters from Dropsie College in 1954 and has been similarly honored by the Hebrew Union College in 1954, the College of Jewish Studies in 1968 and Brandeis University in 1974.

Klutznick publicly lashed out against Soviet anti-Semitism and the repression of Jews in Eastern Europe as early as 1966, when it was not yet fashionable to do so. In 1978 he created a minor flap by agreeing to meet with Egyptian President Anwar Sadat after other Jewish communal leaders had refused to do so. He steadfastly defended Jimmy Carter during the Camp David peace negotiations that year, whenever Carter was attacked by Jewish leaders.

Klutznick himself holds a political position that often runs counter to prevailing established Jewish opinion. In a report to the WJC Plenary in Jerusalem in 1981, for instance, he spoke of the need to support human rights for all peoples and of his opposition to "the continuing escalation of armaments" throughout the world. He urged continuing support for Israel. The latter, he went on, is "alone . . . finally responsible for its policies," while Diaspora Jewry remains "a creative part of contemporary Zionism . . . fully legitimate and enduring." Tensions between the two "will remain," but "what must go are Israeli condescension and American Jewish self-consciousness." Each one needs the other, he concluded.

Klutznick also touched on the crucial issue of the Palestinians, "a subject we all-too-often avoid." He asked:

> Should not we Jews have the courage to say to the Arabs, including those who are called Palestinians, that we wish only to protect the independence of Israel, not to deprive you of yours . . . only to speak with your leaders ready to coexist with and understand us; that we seek not to oppress and dominate, but rather to advance the cause of Israel and her neighbors sharing and living together in brotherhood and peace.

In October 1981 he was the sole Jew who took part in the Seven Springs Center mission to the Middle East. The final report, "The Path To Peace: Arab-Israeli Peace and the United States," by Joseph N. Greene, Jr., Philip M. Klutznick, Harold H. Saunders and Merle Thorpe, Jr. (Mount Kisco, New York, 1981) explores ways to peace in that embattled region. Among its most controversial suggestions for future American policy was the need to deal with the Palestine Liberation Organization. As a result, Klutznick, whose Jewish credentials in this country and in Israel are unchallenged, was savagely attacked as all but a traitor. "Naive," and "intellectually weak" were some of the kinder terms used. Moshe Decter, editor of *Near East Report,* an Israeli-supported newsletter published in Washington, D.C., described the report as "a sinister canard whose unequivocal intent is to vilify Israel by equating the fate of Palestinian Arabs with that of the Jews at the hands of the Nazis."

To all this, Klutznick had replied, "If I have a deep interest in Israel, and I want it to live, why shouldn't I express my views?" And to the *Baltimore Jewish Times,* he said: "I'm reminded of that PLO fellow I met in Cairo who said we can't have real peace until the present generation is gone. But he's wrong to wait. You've got to raise the next generation with the notion that the pieces are in place to bring about a peace. We've got to get to the idea of directing a machinery whereby you learn to trust, and we have to maintain security during that process."

For further information:

Solender, Elsa A. "Why Philip Klutznick Says The PLO Must Be Reckoned With," *Baltimore Jewish Times,* February 5, 1982.

ALFRED A. KNOPF

b. September 12, 1892
Publisher

Throughout his career as a publisher of books, Alfred A. Knopf has earned the well-nigh universal accolade as the most distinguished publisher this country has ever produced.

Alfred A. Knopf was born in New York City to Samuel, who was in advertising and later a businessman, and Ida (Japhe) Knopf. Knopf attended De Witt Clinton High School and then Mackenzie Preparatory School, graduating in 1908. That year he matriculated at Columbia College, earning his B.A. degree in 1912. It was at Columbia, in its classrooms and especially on its publications, that Knopf was smitten by the love for literature and business.

In 1913, following graduation, he went to work for Doubleday in its accounting department and then in its manufacturing and advertising divisions where he helped publicize the books of the novelist Joseph Conrad. Before he left in 1914, he had also worked in its editorial department.

In 1914 he joined the avant garde publisher Mitchell Kennerly but his entrepreneurial urge was too great to resist. In 1915 he started Alfred A. Knopf, book publishers, together with his new wife Blanche and his father, who served as a business consultant. With $5,000 and a Borzoi—the Russian wolfhound he and Blanche loved all their lives—as the firm's logo, Knopf began publishing the sort of books he would always be identified with: continental and cosmopolitan writers, still-obscure, many of them to become extraordinarily famous. In his first publishing season he published *Taras Bulba,* by the Russian writer Gogol; Guy de Maupassant's short stories and G.F. Hudson's *Green Mansions.*

His books all bore the marks of quality—both editorially and in their production. Each volume indicated the typeface used and its history. When a buyer purchased a Knopf book he knew that he was getting his money's worth. Knopf, in John Hersey's words, "was

not the publisher of books, but of authors." Among the many writers he did publish were Thomas Mann, E.M. Forster, Jean-Paul Sartre, Albert Camus, Simone de Beauvoir, Ezra Pound, T.S. Eliot, H.L. Mencken, Willa Cather, Dashiell Hammett, John Cheever, John Updike, Sigmund Freud, Franz Kafka, and the Russians Ilya Ehrenburg and Mikhail Sholokhov. It was he who published John Hersey's stunning fictional account of the Warsaw Ghetto in 1950, *The Wall.* In addition, he was co-founder, with H.L. Mencken and George Jean Nathan, of the acerbic and pungent and sardonic magazine, *American Mercury.*

In 1982, Knopf was presented the Award for Distinguished Service to the Arts by the prestigious American Academy and Institute of Arts and Letters. Ninety years old, wan and frail, he received the only standing ovation of the evening as he walked slowly to the podium. He told the audience: "I was born at the right time. The kind of publishing we did, where a young man with little capital could start his own company, won't be around again."

EDWARD I. KOCH

b. December 12, 1924
Politician

Edward I. Koch, who rose to greater national prominence as mayor of New York City than when he was a congressman in Washington, is one of America's most popular—if controversial—politicians. Best-known, perhaps, for always asking his constituents "How'm I doing?" (and often providing his own answer—he thinks he's doing just fine), he has been as much New York City's greatest public relations representative as its top administrator.

Edward Irving Koch was born in the Bronx, the son of Louis, a furrier, and Joyce (Silpe) Koch, who had come to the United States from Poland. During the Depression, the family moved to Newark, New Jersey and shared an apartment with Louis Koch's brother. In the 10 years he lived in Newark, Edward Koch helped his family with a succession of odd jobs—the delicatessen counter in a grocery, the hat-check concession in his uncle's catering hall, and a babysitters' cooperative he organized.

After Koch graduated from Southside High School in 1941, the Koch family then moved to Brooklyn, and Koch attended City College while working at night as a shoe salesman. In 1943 he entered the Army and was a combat infantryman, winning two battle stars and serving as a de-Nazification technician in Bavaria after the surrender of Germany. Discharged as a sergeant in 1946, he returned home and attended New York University Law School, where he received his Bachelor of Laws degree in 1948.

Koch campaigned for Adlai E. Stevenson in 1952, but his own political career took shape when he moved to Greenwich Village in 1956 and became one of the charter members of a local liberal and reformist political club, the Village Independent Democrats. In 1962 he ran for the State Assembly and lost, but the following year he defeated the Democratic county leader, Carmine DeSapio, by 39 votes to become the neighborhood's Democratic leader. In 1964 and again in 1965, he repeated his victory, each time by larger margins. Meanwhile, in 1963 he also helped form a law firm—Koch, Lankenau, Schwartz, and Korner—and became a senior partner.

In 1966 Koch was elected as a Democrat-Liberal to the New York City Council, where he served until he went to Congress in 1968. Strongly pro-Senator Eugene McCarthy and anti-Vietnam War, Koch swept the primary and general election in Manhattan's 17th Congressional District, which runs from Greenwich Village to the posh upper East Side (the so-called silk stocking district) to Spanish Harlem. He was reelected easily on four occasions and was the generally accepted leader of New York City's congressional delegation. A liberal and a dove, he supported mass transportation, public housing, tax reform, home care for the aged and federal payments for abortion and opposed a federal loan to the Lockheed Aircraft Corporation. He also was one of the earliest congressional supporters of amnesty for Vietnam draft resisters. In foreign policy matters, he was also a strong backer of assistance to Israel and Soviet Jewry. He voted against the sale of weapons to the Chilean junta and against the B-1 bomber and opposed U.S. intervention in Angola in 1975. In 1976 he received a 100 percent rating from the Americans for Democratic Action (ADA) and the AFL-CIO's Committee on Political Education (COPE).

When he was elected mayor in 1977, Koch was only the second Jew, after his immediate predecessor Abraham Beame, to hold that post. But with the help of a media blitz and David Garth's advice and TV commercials, Koch coasted to a general election victory after a two-step primary that included besting Mario Cuomo, the incumbent Beame and another well-known Jew, Bella Abzug.

As mayor, Koch presided over a city floundering in debt. In the face of enormous cuts in city services, Koch's ability to sustain his popularity among the electorate—he was regarded as the most popular mayor

since Fiorello LaGuardia—evoked the admiration of his fellow politicians. During the 1980 subway-bus strike, he appeared daily on the Brooklyn Bridge to greet citizens who were forced to walk or bicycle to work. He denounced municipal unions, waste and crime, although incidents of crime continued to rise during his administration. Like LaGuardia, Koch aspired to three terms in office. He stressed that he had no plans to use the mayoralty as a stepping-stone to higher office. "I will never run for any other office than re-election as mayor," he vowed on a local television interview in 1980. "It's the only position that interests me."

The ebullient mayor was dubbed a "cheerleader" for his vocal efforts to keep New Yorkers' spirits up. He openly criticized officials who he felt failed to act in New York City's interests. He also played a significant role in forcing the city and state to recognize and act upon the city's precarious finances. His "recovery plan" predicted a balanced budget by July 1983. Always sensitive to the mood of his constituents, he has favored the death penalty and rent control and refused to heal the growing alienation between him and the black community.

Just as outspoken on matters of foreign policy, Mayor Koch caused many headlines by denouncing American policies and officials he viewed as harmful to Israel.

As a politician Koch has used his Jewish heritage astutely, tossing about Yiddish phrases in his remarks to Jewish groups. "He has all the street smarts of a New York politician coupled with the sense of humor and timing of a Borscht Belt comic," observed *Newsday* writer Thomas Collins (November 26, 1980).

But during his mayoralty, despite his liberal record in Congress, Koch displayed a growing conservatism and was criticized for breaking promises his critics charged he had never intended to keep in the first place. Although as a candidate he had vowed never to support the construction of Westway, a major federally backed but highly controversial highway along the Lower West Side, after his election he reneged on his vow and ultimately backed the project. He has also been accused of being uncommitted to preserving mass transit and, for that matter, a viable way of life for lower- and middle-class families in New York City, since he is allegedly receiving major backing from real estate concerns. In the late 1970s and early 1980s, for example, both apartment and commercial rentals soared in price. And in 1980 Koch was at the center of the stormy decision to close Sydenham Hospital in Harlem, which left residents of that neighborhood with only one already overburdened health facility. Nonetheless, following noisy demonstrations and sit-ins, Koch ultimately negotiated with community leaders and, as a result, Sydenham retained outpatient clinical services.

In one of his most controversial moves, Koch accepted the endorsement of New York City's Republican Party to run on its line in the 1981 mayoral primary. Perceiving himself as a representative of all the people, and perhaps riding on the conservative swing sweeping the United States with the election to the White House of Ronald Reagan, Koch aimed to run on a fusion ticket in the 1981 election, which he won easily. Still, his critics claimed that by doing so—and with all the automatic publicity he already receives—he was effectively quashing the possibility for a healthy opposition. Soon after his election as mayor—and following repeated denials that he sought higher office—he ran for governor on the Democratic ticket.

Koch is known to be as abrasive as he feels is necessary toward his closest allies as well as his opponents. A loner, he has often stated that he favors no one group over any other. He has, however, encouraged a hiring policy in New York that requires that new employees be city residents, and a report in mid-1981 revealed that about half of those most recently employed belonged to Hispanic and black minorities. Also during his administration, a number of New York City neighborhoods have undergone a successful renaissance of residential and commercial activity, including Manhattan's Upper West Side, although critics claim this has occurred at the expense of long-time lower-class residents who have been forced out, including many small neighborhood shops.

Koch loves publicity, served as narrator in a production of *Peter and the Wolf* at the Greenwich House Music School in 1980 and in 1981 had his first book published, *How'm I Doing?: The Wit and Wisdom of Ed Koch* (New York), a collection of sayings and photographs.

KENNETH KOCH

b. February 27, 1925
Poet; playwright; teacher

Kenneth Koch is twice gifted; not only has he been recognized as one of America's leading poets, whose free-flowing, often humorous verse brought him fame when he was still in his 30s, but he has turned his talent toward making poetry accessible to others through a unique approach to teaching. His technique has helped bring out the poet in young children and in the elderly, and Koch has received perhaps as much acclaim for the

anthologies he has edited as for his own substantial body of work.

Kenneth Jay Koch, who began writing as a child, was born in Cincinnati, Ohio to Stuart J. and Lilian Amy (Toth) Koch. He recounts having become a serious writer at age 17 after reading the works of John Dos Passos and being encouraged by a sympathetic high school teacher to keep writing the "angry outbursts" that characterized his teen-age work. After high school Koch served in the Army in the Pacific and then entered Harvard College—from which he graduated in 1948 with a B.A. degree—and where he studied writing with Delmore Schwartz and was drawn to the modernist school of poetry then developing. He also befriended another Harvard undergraduate, John Ashbery, who would later, with Koch, be one of the core poets of the so-called New York School of the 1950s. Koch was also strongly influenced by the work of Wallace Stevens and William Butler Yeats.

Moving to New York he began graduate studies at Columbia University in 1949 and became involved in the Beat Movement of jazz musicians, visual artists and writers centered in Greenwich Village. Along with Ashbery and Frank O'Hara, Koch formed a triumvirate of writers who did for poetry what the abstract expressionists did for art, creating a free-form verse that was often improvisational, deliberately incoherent and satirical of poetic traditions. After interrupting his sojourn in New York for one year to study in Paris (1950–51) as a Fulbright fellow, Koch completed his M.A. degree at Columbia in 1953 and his doctorate at the same school in 1959. At the same time, during the mid-1950s he taught at Rutgers University and for one year (1958–59) at Brooklyn College.

The Beat period not only produced the New York School of poets but fostered a unique interaction of artists. In Koch's case there was a long-lasting friendship and collaboration with a jazz musician-turned-artist named Larry Rivers. In 1960 the fruit of their friendship became a book-with-paintings, *Poems 1950–1960* and another collection, *Post Cards*. Koch also wrote a number of short absurdist plays, which were produced off-Broadway and off-off-Broadway, including *George Washington Crosses the Delaware* (1962), a childlike parody of American history. Also in 1960 Koch was an editor of one of the most significant literary journals of the period, *Locus Solus*.

During the 1960s Koch's reputation as poet and teacher grew. He had several collections of poetry published and became a popular teacher at Columbia, whose faculty he joined upon completing his doctorate. In 1962 he became an assistant professor of English and comparative literature, was appointed associate professor in 1966 and five years later was named full professor. His poetry, meanwhile, evolved from the satirical and incoherent to a more fluid, still often satirical, but more mature and insightful writing. For example, one of his earlier published works, *Ko* (New York, 1960), was a 115-page slapstick epic poem—presumably auto- (or pseudo-) biographical—taking place in Cincinnati, Tucson, Paris, Tahiti, Tibet, etc., which one critic described as "a lesser Catskill among epics; good comedy." But nearly 10 years later his collection *The Pleasures of Peace and Other Poems* (New York, 1969) would reflect more directly on his anguish about the war in Vietnam, whose pressures he felt acutely among the students on the Columbia campus.

Koch's directions also changed in the late 1960s, when he turned from the frivolous "artiness" of his earlier work to working with children and old people and using his poetry as a tool of communication. He began by teaching poetry writing to children at a New York City elementary school in the Lower East Side, sharing with them the writing of Shakespeare, Blake, Donne and other early poets and evoking in the children the same spirit. The result of his work was *Wishes, Lies and Dreams* (New York, 1971), in which he described his teaching technique and included many children's poems. It was followed two years later by an anthology of more poems by children and text by Koch, *Rose, Where Did You Get That Red?* (New York). Koch subsequently taught poetry at a nursing home in New York City, where he hoped that the life experiences of the residents would enable them to express in poetry what by now was perhaps too painful to verbalize directly. His instincts were correct, and in 1977 he published the highly praised *I Never Told Anybody: Teaching Poetry Writing in a Nursing Home* (New York).

For further information:
Koch, Kenneth. *Days and Nights.* New York: 1982.
Myers, J.R., ed. *The Poets of the New York School.* New York: 1970.

HERBERT KOHL

b. August 22, 1937
Educator; author

Since becoming a schoolteacher in the early 1960s, Herbert Kohl has been one of the most outspoken critics of the traditional American system of education and one of its most creative reformers. His highly praised book *36 Children* (New York, 1967) is considered, along with Jonathan Kozol's *Death at an Early Age* and John Holt's *How Children Fail,* to be one of the classic iconoclastic studies of how and why American schools have failed their students.

Herbert Kohl was born in the Bronx to Samuel, a building contractor, and Marion (Jacobs) Kohl. After graduating from Harvard University in 1958 (where he and Kozol were classmates) with a Bachelor of Arts degree magna cum laude, Kohl studied for one year (1958–59) at University College in Oxford, England and then returned to New York, where he completed an M.A. degree at Columbia University Teachers College in 1962.

For the next four years Kohl taught sixth grade in a New York City elementary school in East Harlem—a frankly unconventional career for a Harvard graduate at the time. But as he said in a 1973 interview, he had always wanted to teach—and from that experience he produced the book that would mark his emergence as a major spokesperson for progressive, nontraditional education. In *36 Children* Kohl describes how his own initial racism and fear about teaching black and Puerto Rican children—and their skepticism about him— grew into a warm relationship of mutual trust. Kohl adjusted his teaching techniques to allow more flexibility in his classroom and more freedom for the students. But within that structure he set high standards that enabled the students to begin to learn and to create. Moreover, the students developed a sense of self-esteem rather than of defeat, which had been drummed into them in the past. Kohl concluded—and this was hardly a new theory, but his account made it that much more devastating—that ghetto children often fail because the system they are in preordains them to. He set out to change it.

From 1966 to 1967 Kohl became a research fellow at the Horace Mann-Lincoln Institute of Teachers College and the director of the Teachers and Writers Collaborative in New York City, which set up special writing programs for children in the New York City schools. He became increasingly involved in developing reading programs for children considered "unteachable" (he published an essay, "Teaching the Unteachable," in the *New York Review of Books* in 1967) and moved to California in 1967, where he became visiting associate professor of English at the University of California at Berkeley for one year.

In 1968 he founded an alternative school in Berkeley, Other Ways, in which he attempted to practice the educational theories he espoused, particularly the open classroom. He then published his next major book, *The Open Classroom: A Practical Guide to a New Way of Teach-*

ing (New York, 1969), which was more an overview of the theories of the open classroom than of the day-to-day mechanics of employing the method. Although the open classroom was highly touted at the time and remained in vogue through the early and mid-1970s, one critic wondered if Kohl's wholesale rejection of traditional teaching was not misguided and whether his contention that a child could not "discover himself" in a "controlled" environment was valid.

After Other Ways folded in 1971, Kohl became a consultant on alternative education within the Berkeley school system. Since 1972 he has been co-director of the Center for Open Learning and Teaching at Berkeley, and he has consulted for other school systems and universities in the United States.

Kohl's other major books include *Half the House* (New York, 1974), a chronicle of his experiences— positive and negative—with Other Ways; *On Teaching* (New York, 1976), an analysis of the craft and politics of teaching, teacher-student and teacher-parent relationships, and the positive uses of confrontation to repudiate the restrictiveness of traditional schools; and *Growing with Your Children* (Boston, 1978), a personal look at raising children through his own experiences as the father of three as well as an educator.

Kohl believes that the struggles involved with educational reform are due not to the problems of schoolchildren but to the refusal of adults to bend to the true needs of their students—especially when the children come from different ethnic groups than their teachers. And he believes that students whose early school years have been marked by failure can learn, as long as they are placed in a nurturing, supportive atmosphere where even small successes are richly rewarded.

For further information:
Kohl, Herbert. *A Book of Puzzlements: Play and Invention with Language.* New York: 1981.

MILTON R. KONVITZ

b. March 12, 1908
Professor; author

Milton R. Konvitz, professor emeritus at Cornell Law School, is a leading expert on constitutional law, whose books have been cited in many United States Supreme Court opinions. He has written books on philosophy, political theory, intellectual history and religious thought.

Milton Konvitz was born in Sefad, Palestine to Rabbi Joseph and Welia (Ridvas-Wilosky) Konvitz. He moved with his family to America in 1915 and became a naturalized citizen in 1926. In 1928 Konvitz was graduated from New York University with a B.S. degree. Two years later he received his law degree and in 1933 his Ph.D. in philosophy, both from Cornell University.

Admitted to the New Jersey Bar Association in 1932, Konvitz practiced law in Jersey City and Newark from 1933 to 1946. During that time he was appointed general counsel for the Newark Housing Authority from 1938 to 1943 and for the New Jersey Housing Authority from 1943 to 1945. From 1943 to 1946 he was also assistant general counsel for the NAACP Legal Defense & Education Fund, and from 1938 to 1946 he lectured on law and public administration at New York University.

In 1946 Konvitz joined the faculty at the New York State School of Industrial and Labor Relations at Cornell University as one of its original professors. He served there until 1973. From 1956 to 1973 Konvitz was a professor at Cornell Law School as well.

From 1952 to 1980 Konvitz directed a project that prepared laws for the Republic of Liberia and edited the opinions of its Supreme Court. The project resulted in the publication of over 30 volumes of statutes and cases, all of them published by Cornell University Press. For this work, the government of Liberia has given Konvitz two awards, including the highest award Liberia can give to a foreigner.

Among the many books Konvitz has written are *On the Nature of Value: Philosophy of Samuel Alexander* (New York, 1946), a summary and evaluation of the theory of the late Samuel Alexander, a British philosopher who lived from 1859 to 1938, and *The Alien and the Asiatic in American Law* (Ithaca, N.Y., 1946), which examines how the United States Supreme Court has reacted to the problems of the alien and Americans of Asiatic descent. The latter is the first of many works Konvitz has written in which he expresses a critical attitude toward the American immigration process, usually siding with the alien.

In *The Constitution and Civil Rights* (New York, 1947), he analyzes the principal Supreme Court cases on civil rights, the federal and state laws prohibiting discrimination and those allowing discrimination. In *Civil Rights in Immigration* (Ithaca, N.Y., 1953), a critical study of American immigration and naturalization policy, he argues for more liberal treatment of the newcomer. *Bill of Rights Reader: Leading Constitutional Cases* (Ithaca, N.Y., 1954) is a compilation of judicial opinions from

108 cases dealing with First Amendment and equal protection laws, prefaced by the author's own comments.

He has also written extensively about the political process. *Expanding Liberties: Freedom's Gain in Postwar America* (New York, 1966) traces the emergence of a "new freedom" by discussing religious liberty, congressional efforts to deal with communism, and the problems of obscenity and civil rights. *Judaism and the American Idea* (Ithaca, N.Y., 1978) is a collection of eight essays that highlight the Jewish-American way of life. In it Konvitz asserts that the nation's pioneering and revolutionary past allows Jews to live in America without the ambiguities of identity and loyalty they find elsewhere.

Konvitz is co-founder of the magazine *Judaism;* is on the editorial board of the *Encyclopedia Judaica, Philosophy Forum, New Leader* and *Employee Relations Law Journal;* is chairman of the editorial board of *Midstream;* and has written articles for the *Encyclopaedia Britanica, The International Encyclopaedia of Social Sciences* and the *Dictionary of the History of Ideas.*

Konvitz is actively involved in Jewish life and has often spoken out on the importance of Jewish education. In a speech delivered in 1964 at Harvard University, he said: ". . . it is not necessary for the Jew to drift with the mainstream in the world of opportunism, and to become rootless, trivial and alienated; . . . it is still possible for the Jew to assert himself in his Jewishness through an autonomous decision and a free act." He is an ardent supporter of the Hillel Foundations and has publicly stated:

> We must give increased support to the Hillel Foundations so that they may attract and be able to serve the spiritual and cultural interests of the nearly 300,000 Jewish students and the thousands of faculty members of our colleges and universities; and the organized American Jewish community must act as a Johnny Appleseed, and go up and down the land to plant the seeds of Jewish learning.

Konvitz is chairman of the Hebrew Culture Foundation, fellow of the American Association for Jewish Education, a director of the Conference on Jewish Social Studies and a director of the American Zionist Federation. He was one of the first two American scholars to have been awarded the Kaplan International Prize by the Hebrew University in Jerusalem.

For further information:

Konvitz, Milton R. *Judaism and Human Rights.* Ithaca, N.Y.: 1972.

———. *Religious Liberty and Conscience.* Ithaca, N.Y.: 1968.

WILLIAM KOREY

b. June 16, 1922
Scholar

William Korey has matched scholarship with activism to become one of the American Jewish community's leading experts on Soviet Jewry and related human rights issues. For nearly 30 years he has been an executive with the Anti-Defamation League (ADL) of B'nai B'rith and is the author of many articles and a major book about anti-Semitism in the USSR.

William Korey was born in Chicago to Russian-immigrant parents, Louis, a storekeeper, and Rose (Berman) Korey. After attending Hebrew elementary and high schools for 10 years, Korey studied at the University of Chicago and the College of Jewish Studies (since renamed Spertus College) in Chicago from 1940 to 1943. After serving in the U.S. Army from 1943 to 1946, he received a B.A. degree in history from the University of Chicago in 1946 and an M.A. degree two years later in East European history from Columbia University's Russian Institute.

From 1948 to 1954 Korey taught at Long Island University and at the City College of New York, while beginning work on a doctorate in Russian history at Columbia. He joined the staff of the ADL in 1954, serving for two years as director of the Illinois-Missouri regional office, then moving to Washington, D.C., where he headed the District of Columbia-Maryland regional office until 1960—the same year he completed his Ph.D.

Korey has been based in New York since 1960. Through 1976 he directed B'nai B'rith's United Nations office, during which period he also taught courses in Russian history at Columbia, Brooklyn College, Yeshiva University and YIVO. From 1976 to 1978 Korey headed B'nai B'rith's International Council, and in 1978 he assumed his current post as director of policy research for the International Council, in which capacity he was a lobbyist during the 1980 Madrid Conference of the Helsinki Final Act signatories.

Korey's writings have appeared in such scholarly journals as *Foreign Affairs, Slavic Review* and *Problems of Communism,* among others, and such popular publications as *Commentary, The New Republic, The Progressive, Commonweal, Present Tense, Midstream, The New York Times, The Wall Street Journal, The Washington Post* and *Newsday.* While specializing in Soviet issues, Korey has also honed his focus on politics within the United Nations.

His book *The Soviet Cage: Anti-Semitism in Russia* (New York, 1973) traces official anti-Semitism from the beginning of the Bolshevik regime to the present and is a comprehensive examination of the complex problems of the treatment of those Jews who have sought to leave the Soviet Union—a minority of the total Jewish population—and of the vast majority of Jews who stay. Much of Korey's research continues to be directed at Soviet anti-Semitism. In a *Midstream* article in 1978, he noted the coincidence between the notorious *Protocols of the Elders of Zion* and Moscow's portrait of Zionism: endowed with "cosmic power, diabolical evil, and the urge to dominate." In the *Israel Yearbook on Human Rights* (Tel Aviv, 1979), Korey wondered whether the increasing anti-Semitism of the Soviet Academy of Science ("vulgar hate peddling," he called it) would not one day become a "Warrant for Genocide" if and when "seized upon and exploited by a ruthless and unrestrained leadership."

And in that same year in *Foreign Affairs,* he expressed pessimism about the "future of Soviet Jewry." In spite of the fact that many Soviet Jews still wished to maintain their heritage, "reality cannot be blacked out. The trends scarcely generate a sanguine perspective about the preservation of Jewish identity. . . ." Konstantin Pobedonostsev's prognostication at the turn of the century —he was the Jew-hating procurator of the Holy Synod and Czar Alexander III's main adviser—that one-third of Russian Jews would die, one-third assimilate and one-third emigrate seems to be coming true, concludes Korey.

For further information:

Korey, William. "Babi Yar." In *The Unredeemed: Anti-Semitism in the Soviet Union,* edited by R. Rubin. New York: 1969.
———. "The Future of Soviet Jewry: Emigration and Assimilation."
———. "Human Rights at the UN: Illusion and Reality." In *Of Law and Man,* edited by S. Shoham. Tel Aviv: 1971.
———. "International Law and the Right to Study Hebrew in the USSR." *Soviet Jewish Affairs* [London] 11 (February 1981):
———. "The Kremlin's Anti-Semites." *Midstream,* October 1978.
———. "The Legal Position of the Soviet Jewish Community." In *Ethnic Minorities in the Soviet Union,* edited by E. Goldhagen. New York: 1968.
———. "The Legal Position of Soviet Jewry: A Historical Enquiry." In *The Jews in Soviet Russia Since 1917,* edited by L. Kochan. New York: 1970.
———. "Legitimizing Anti-Semitism: The Role of the Soviet Academy of Sciences." *Israel Yearbook on Human Rights* [Tel Aviv] 9 (1979).
———. "Zinoviev on the German Revolution of October, 1923." In *Essays in Russian and Soviet History,* edited by J.S. Curtiss. New York: 1963.

JERZY NIKODEM KOSINSKI

b. June 14, 1933
Author

Polish-born Jerzy Kosinski rocketed to fame in 1965 with his grotesque, brilliant, best-selling novel *The Painted Bird* (Boston), about a young Polish boy wandering in Nazi-occupied eastern Poland—a story similar to his own. All of his novels since have depicted the manipulation of human freedom in a corrupt and increasingly programmed world.

Jerzy Kosinski was born in Lodz, Poland, the only child of Mieczyslaw, a manufacturer who had fled Russia during the Bolshevik Revolution, and Elzbieta (Binieka) Kosinski, a pianist who never performed in public. When World War II erupted in 1939, the Kosinskis sent their son eastward into the Polish rural countryside for safety. Though he escaped the brunt of Nazi brutality, he did not escape the primitive and superstitious rural Poles. In the autobiographical *The Painted Bird,* he describes this experience. The dark, swarthy boy, like Kosinski, is victimized by fairer-skinned, lighter-haired peasants, and he in turn is horrified by their brutal and often bestial natures.

After the war Kosinski rejoined his parents. He studied at the University of Lodz, where he received a B.A. degree in 1953 and M.A. degrees in history and political science in 1955. His dissertations dealt with 19th century Tsarist Russia, a subject he pursued further at the Polish Academy of Sciences, Lomonosov University in Russia and the Soviet Academy of Sciences.

In 1957 Kosinski arrived in the United States after obtaining a passport on the ground that he had been offered a study grant for the following year. In 1958, with a study grant from the Ford Foundation, he began work on a doctorate in political sociology at Columbia University. He received his Ph.D. in 1965, the same year he became a naturalized American citizen.

Published under the pseudonym "Joseph Novak," Kosinski's first two books—both nonfiction—dealt with Soviet society. In *The Future Is Ours, Comrade: Conversations with the Russians* (New York, 1960), he gave an account of lengthy discussions he had with Soviet citizens. In it ordinary people spoke with extraordinary frankness about the strengths and weaknesses of their country. In *No Third Path* (New York, 1962), he tried to create a collective picture of how the Soviet mind works by personal observations of meetings with Russians and their attitudes toward war, peace, communism and other major issues.

But his nonfiction efforts were ephemeral in contrast to his fiction. Critics were unanimous in their praise of *The Painted Bird,* calling it "dazzling," "unforgettable," "a blow on the mind." The symbol of "the painted bird"—used to represent nonconformity and human survival—is one that can be used to describe the author himself. *The Painted Bird* was awarded the Prix du Meilleur Livre Etranger in France and symbolized the themes of 20th century bestiality and evil that would recur in his later works.

Steps (New York, 1968), which recounts acts of violence and perversion, was praised for its experimental and sophisticated structure and won the 1969 National Book Award. Lack of self-identity, one of the central themes of *Steps,* was explored more gently in his next book, *Being There* (New York, 1971), whose protagonist is an illiterate gardener named Chance, whose only contact with the outside world is a television set. Chance, whose identity shifts with the channels, is eventually elevated to national leadership. Arthur Curley of *Library Journal* commented, "[Kosinski] writes with the cool assurance of one who possesses some deep secret knowledge about all of us." *Being There* was later made into a critically acclaimed film of the same title in 1979, directed by Hal Ashby and starring Peter Sellers and Shirley MacLaine.

In *The Devil Tree* (New York, 1973), he depicts an orphaned heir to an American industrial fortune whose quest for self-identity grows more frantic, until he eventually realizes that he exists only in the eyes of others—according to Kosinski, a horrible fate. *Cockpit* (Boston, 1975) is, again, a grim tale—this time of an ex-spy who continues to live an elusive, self-sufficient life of a secret agent and devises frightful stunts to punish his enemies. Kosinski's novel *Blind Date* (Boston, 1977), painting a coolly detached man in search of pleasure, according to a *Saturday Review* critic, shows that man "chooses survival and cheap thrills over the historical accidents of ideology."

His novel *Passion Play* (New York, 1979) tells the story of a poverty-stricken polo player who looks for rich players willing to pay him for the special challenge he can offer them—a one-on-one game in which each man fights to maim the other. *Passion Play* ended the

seven-novel cycle that began with *The Painted Bird.* In describing this *ouevre,* Kosinski wrote:

> While at one end of my fiction stands the simple and innocent Chauncy Gardiner of *Being There,* at the other stands Fabian, the morally complex and sexually obsessed hero of *Passion Play* . . . its essence is the development and survival of one's self-hood.

In 1981 Kosinski tried something entirely new. He acted in Warren Beatty's panoramic film *Reds,* the story of the Communist John Reed and the coming of the Bolshevik Revolution and civil war. Kosinski played Zinoviev, one of the more important early Bolsheviks.

Kosinski has taught English at Princeton University in 1969 to 1970 and was professor of English prose and criticism at Yale University from 1970 to 1973. He received the B'rith Shalom Humanitarian Freedom Award in 1974.

For further information:
Kosinski, Jerry. *Pinball.* New York: 1982.
Gelb, Barbara. "Being Jerzy Kosinski," *The New York Times Magazine,* February 21, 1982.

ROBERT KOTLOWITZ

b. November 21, 1924
Author; broadcasting executive

Although since 1971 Robert Kotlowitz has been a prominent programming executive in public television, he is also a writer, whose two novels, *Somewhere Else* (New York, 1972) and *The Boardwalk* (New York, 1977), are recollections of Jewish experiences in Europe and America.

Robert Kotlowitz was born in Paterson, New Jersey to Max, a cantor at Beth Tfilah Synagogue in Baltimore, and Debra (Kaplan) Kotlowitz. He studied at the Peabody Conservatory of Music, where he received a preparatory diploma in 1941, and pursued college studies at Johns Hopkins University, where he earned a B.A. degree in 1947, after serving in the military from 1943 to 1946.

Prior to entering broadcasting Kotlowitz was a writer and editor for several magazines and publishing companies. From 1950 to 1955 he was associate editor of Pocket Books, which included editing its "Discovery" series (from 1952 to 1955), in which little-known poets and prose writers had their work published in what became a series of prestigious paperback collections. From 1955 to 1960 Kotlowitz was manager of press and information for RCA Records, and from 1960 to

1964 he was senior editor of *Show,* a sophisticated, large-format arts magazine. Before joining WNET/Thirteen in 1971, Kotlowitz was senior editor and then managing editor at *Harper's* magazine from 1967–71. In his public television post as vice president of programming, he oversees the production of WNET's extensive range of dance, opera, music, drama and news offerings, many of which have won Emmy awards for the station.

Kotlowitz's novel *Somewhere Else* tells of the journey of Mendel, a young Polish rabbi's son, from a small provincial town first to Warsaw and then to London, where he works in an uncle's diamond shop. Once in London, he becomes involved with emergent Zionist and socialist political movements and meets women whose lifestyles differ drastically from those of the more conventional women back home. The novel is essentially a story of Mendel's homelessness—he becomes the proverbial "wandering Jew"—and of the conflict between what he left behind (and cannot return to) and life in London, which is equally alienating to him. Kotlowitz's novel was favorably compared to the works of Isaac Bashevis Singer, and he was praised for his ability to evoke the atmosphere of the *shtetl* [the Jewish small town in Eastern Europe] and Diaspora life without sentimentalizing or overdramatizing either.

In *The Boardwalk* Kotlowitz contrasts one summer in the life of a sensitive 14-year-old Jewish boy, Teddy Levin, with the events of the world around him. The place is Atlantic City, and the year is 1939. It is a year of momentous change for Teddy and a year of tremendous change for the world; by summer's end the Germans have marched into Poland. As with Kotlowitz's previous novel, critics praised the author's skill in conjuring up another era and the memories and sentiments that accompanied it.

"SANDY" KOUFAX

b. December 30, 1935
Baseball player

"Sandy" Koufax, once called the "man with the golden arm," began and ended his exceptional 11-year baseball career as a Dodger pitcher. One of the great pitchers of all time, he set one record after another in strikeouts and victories, until arthritis forced him to retire permanently from baseball.

Sanford Koufax was born in Brooklyn to Jack and Evelyn Braun. His mother was divorced from his father when Koufax was very young and remarried Irving Koufax, an attorney. They lived for a while in Rockville Centre on Long Island and later moved back to Brooklyn.

His step-father, he says, was a great influence in his life. He used to take "Sandy" and his step-sister Edith to the Yiddish theater in New York City. In addition, he was extremely supportive of Koufax's endeavors at Lafayette High School, where young Koufax played baseball and basketball, graduating in 1952.

He attended the University of Cincinnati for a year on a basketball scholarship in 1953. In fact, he had never pitched in a baseball game until, at 15, he pitched with an organization in Brooklyn called the Ice Cream League. Still, he played basketball night and day at the Jewish Community House in Brooklyn. However, one day while pitching in a baseball game, he was spotted by a Pittsburgh Pirates scout. Later, Brooklyn and Milwaukee sent their scouts, and finally, in 1954, he signed with the Dodgers.

Inconsistent and uncoordinated was the way baseball people and writers described him in his first three seasons with Brooklyn. Koufax's fast ball was very fast, indeed, but he could not control his speed. He would often walk three or four batters in a row before getting anyone out. While the Dodgers were slowly losing faith in him, however, manager Walter Alston sensed greatness in the young pitcher, even though Koufax floundered through the 1960 season. Koufax cites two meetings that turned his career around. First, he asked General Manager Buzzie Bavasi to let him pitch regularly. Too many rest days were not good for his arm, he argued. Second, in 1961 Norm Sherry, a Jewish catcher with the team, along with pitching coach Joe Becker taught him to throw more curve balls and changeups. That season he won 18 games and broke a league record for striking out 269 batters.

In 1962 Koufax almost ended his career when a blood clot developed in his hand. His index finger was nearly amputated. Yet he came back in 1963 and beat the Yankees twice in the World Series.

In the 1965 World Series, one of the games fell on Yom Kippur. The club indicated its respect for Koufax by acceding to his request to stay away from the ballpark on this most sacred day and thereby skip his place in the pitching rotation. Because the team lost that day, he received a lot of criticism in the southern California press, but Koufax insisted that his personal beliefs took priority over business. And the Dodgers did go on to win the series, anyway.

"Pitching is an art in the sense that the driving force . . . is the pride you have in yourself," said Koufax in his autobiography *Koufax,* written with Ed Linn (New York, 1966). With that philosophy, the two-time recipient of the Cy Young Award—the highest honor accorded annually to pitchers—was elected to the Baseball Hall of Fame in 1972.

Koufax's overall record is impressive. Voted the Dodger's Most Valuable Player in 1963, he was the National League leader for his win-loss record in 1964 (19-5) and 1965 (26-8). He was league leader for his 1962 earned run average (ERA) of 2.54, and in strikeouts he was league leader in 1961, with 269 strikeouts in a 154-game season, and in 1963, with 306 strikeouts in a 162-game season. His astonishing 1965 record of 382 strikeouts in a 162-game season was second only to Nolan Ryan's first-place record. Overall, he pitched three no-hit games and on September 9, 1965 hurled a perfect game against the Chicago Cubs. His lifetime ERA was 2.76 (it went as low as 1.88, 1.74 and 1.73 in 1963, 1964, and 1966), and he won 165 and lost 87 games during his remarkable career.

Koufax, a broadcaster and real estate agent, lives quietly on the West Coast. He once wrote, "I only want to be successful and make my family proud of me."

In the spring of 1979 he returned to the Los Angeles Dodgers training camp as a guest pitching coach. It was the first time since his retirement in 1966 that he put on his old number 32 jersey.

JONATHAN KOZOL

b. September 5, 1936
Educator; author

Jonathan Kozol—educational writer, critic and iconoclast, innovator and participant-observer of what happens in the classrooms of America's have-not neighborhoods—was awarded the National Book Award in 1968 for *Death at an Early Age* (Boston, 1967). He is one of the country's most influential educational voices.

Jonathan Kozol was born in Boston, the son of Harry Leo, a physician, and Ruth (Massell) Kozol. He received his B.A. degree summa cum laude from Harvard University in 1958 and won a Rhodes scholarship, which allowed him to spend the following year at Magdelan College, a part of Oxford University.

His initial goal was to write fiction, and to that end, he went to live in Paris after he completed his studies at Oxford in 1959. In 1962 he won an Olympia Award for a short story he had written. The $1,000 grant that went with it enabled him to lengthen his stay in Europe. Two years later he was appointed Sexton fellow in creative writing by the publishing house of Harper and Row.

That same year Kozol became a teacher in the Boston public school system. After three years he published his observations of the system and his recommendations for its improvement. *Death at an Early Age* was based on his experience as a fourth- and fifth-grade teacher in the Boston public school system between 1964 and 1968. He was fired for reading a poem by Langston Hughes to his predominantly black students because the work was not part of the standard curriculum. The impact of *Death at an Early Age* was felt throughout the educational community. In it the former schoolteacher examined the failure of the Boston public schools to help enough students master basic skills. Kozol was particularly outspoken about the failure to reach black pupils. He argued for increased use of the open classroom method of teaching and more freedom and flexibility of students so that they might help fashion their own learning environment.

In the school system Kozol saw the extensive use of corporal punishment. His own classroom was in an auditorium that was used simultaneously by the glee club and a sewing class. No effort was made to provide remedial work to compensate students with disadvantaged backgrounds. Indeed, as Kozol saw it, total obedience was the compulsive concern of the system. *Death at An Early Age* received immediate national acclaim and won the National Book Award the next year. Many critics believed it should be required reading for anybody entering the field of education.

In 1968 Kozol left the public schools to try to implement some of his free school and open classroom ideas, which became popular among progressive educators in the 1960s. The open classroom attempts to provide a better learning environment by establishing a number of different activity centers within an area. Students and teachers move freely from center to center, combining personalized instruction with independent study. From 1968 until 1971 he worked at the Store Front Learning Center in Boston, in which he taught ghetto children and their parents. He tried to show them the necessary skills to survive in a complex and demanding society. He believed that free schools directed toward basic skills plus parent involvement could help overcome cultural disadvantages. *Free Schools* (Boston, 1972), in addition to explaining the pedagogic philosophy of his school, is a manual on how to establish and run a free (independent of established school bureaucracy) school. While acknowledging some difficulties inherent in his educational strategy, Kozol defended this new and somewhat radical approach to education in his book.

Kozol has lectured about education in universities throughout the country and has published essays in America's most prestigious magazines and newspapers, including *The New York Times, Atlantic Monthly, Saturday Review of Literature, The Washington Post, The Boston Globe* and others. He also wrote *The Night Is Dark and I*

Am Far from Home (Boston, 1975), about his stay at the Documentation and Research Center at Cuernavaca, Mexico. This was followed by a study of "analfabetismo" in Cuba called *Children of the Revolution* (New York, 1978), which examines how the Castro government moved to eradicate illiteracy among its large peasant population by temporarily closing schools for one year and sending students into the countryside to teach the "campesinos" to read and write.

His book *Prisoners of Silence* (New York, 1980) discusses the problems of illiterate adults in America and proposes methods to reach out to them and teach them effectively, such as a strategy "to launch an all-out national attack on adult illiteracy, giving it the same priority as plague, pestilence or war." He urges the recruitment of "five million literacy teachers," most living in the areas in which they would teach. "Literacy centers" would be established, a modest stipend paid by the federal government, and in a space of 60 days to seven months, he hopes that the success in eradicating illiteracy would emulate the achievements of Brazil, Cuba and Israel. Above all, Kozol insists students are not uninterested, and many would gladly give up six months on so worthy and vital a cause and serve as teachers.

JOSEPH KRAFT

b. September 4, 1924
Journalist

Joseph Kraft, writer for the *Washington Post* and a widely syndicated columnist, is one of the country's most respected journalists. A specialist in foreign affairs who has also written extensively about the executive branch of American government, Kraft has published several major books dealing with world politics.

Joseph Kraft was born in South Orange, New Jersey to David Harry, an affluent textile manufacturer, and Sophie (Surasky) Kraft. A graduate of the Fieldston School, he served as a Japanese language officer from 1943-46 and then obtained his B.A. degree from Columbia University in 1947, where he was valedictorian. He did postgraduate work in history at Princeton University from 1948 to 1949 and at the Institute for Advanced Study from 1950 to 1951.

Kraft started his journalism career as an editorial writer in 1951 at the *Washington Post,* where he worked for one year. He then became a staff writer for the "Week-in-Review" section of *The New York Times* from 1953 to 1957. In 1957 he began free-lancing and the following year received an Overseas Press Club award

for best magazine reporting for his coverage of the Algerian civil war. During the 1960 presidential campaign he served as a speechwriter for John F. Kennedy.

Kraft's reportage on the national and international level earned him much renown and praise. Theodore H. White, author of *The Making of the President 1960* and himself a journalist of long experience, called Kraft "one of the two ablest writers in America." After serving three years as the Washington-based correspondent for *Harper's* magazine, Kraft started his regular column for the *Washington Post,* in which he focused on national issues and demonstrated an unusual insight into the operations of government and the people who run it. Over the years Kraft came to be much admired by such colleagues in journalism as *New York Times* columnist Anthony Lewis and writer David Halberstam, who in his book *The Best and the Brightest,* called Kraft one of the best political writers in America and the successor to Walter Lippmann for his acute analytical abilities. For example, Kraft was one of the first columnists to assert that the war in Vietnam could not be won; he perceived before most people the weaknesses of President Lyndon B. Johnson's Great Society social programs; and he insisted long before anyone else that Richard Nixon had to be intimately connected with the Watergate scandals, despite the then-president's denials.

Nonetheless, Kraft has been criticized by the Washington-based writer James Fallows as often missing the human dimension in his articles and as being too elitist. For example, Kraft was highly skeptical about the validity of the Pentagon Papers because Daniel Ellsberg, the person responsible for their publication, led what Kraft considered an unconventional lifestyle in Malibu and consulted a psychiatrist. He was also loath to listen to anything poet Allen Ginsberg had to say about America because Ginsberg lived in a manner so far outside the traditional American mainstream.

Kraft's best work is probably that which appears from time to time in *The New Yorker.* (He also writes occasional essays for *Atlantic.*) Here he presents long, detailed, deliberate essays based on trips abroad, often in "letter" format, with frequent visits to the Middle East, where his thoughts on the Arab-Israeli conflicts have helped unravel their intrinsic complexity for readers. Even his comments on American life are considered important source material for American readers, and it is Kraft who is credited with coining the term "middle America."

Kraft has published several books in which he elaborated upon international situations with a depth that is not possible in short news columns. In *The Struggle for Algeria* (New York, 1961), Kraft described the international conflict centering in Algeria when settlers aligned themselves with the extreme right in French politics. He detailed the political, economic and historic background of Algeria and the philosophies of the Algerian adversaries. Kraft's attitude was described by critics as "pro-rebel."

In Kraft's book *The Chinese Difference* (New York, 1973), he looked at the differences between the new Chinese society and the West. The book was based on Kraft's observations when he remained in China for one year after President Nixon's visit. In the book Kraft sympathetically described Chinese steel factories, rural peasants on communes and Communist officials and quoted from interviews with foreign diplomats. In 1979, as a result of Kraft's Chinese experiences, he was the only journalist chosen to travel with Henry Kissinger on a private visit to China.

In his syndicated newspaper columns, Kraft is generally thought to be a liberal. Yet in September 1978 he said that Iran—then still ruled by the Shah—was viewed by the USSR as "a rotten piece of fruit" ready to be taken over. "In these conditions," wrote Kraft, "the United States does not have the luxury of sniffing at corruption in Iran, or playing missionary on human rights, not to mention being a super-sleuth on weapon sales." But in contrast to this column, his "Letter from Iran" in the December 18, 1978 *New Yorker* was quite different in tone, portraying instead a widespread grass-roots insurrection emerging against the Shah. This disparity, concluded one Kraft-watcher, Michael Massing, executive editor of the *Columbia Journalism Review* (in *The Nation,* May 23, 1981), was "the most marked contrast between Kraft the harried columnist and Kraft the deliberate analytic writer." As if in response, Kraft wrote, "I have, almost from the start, been, in a classical way, Great Power oriented. I've always been more concerned about geopolitics than about human rights."

Following the Iranian taking of American hostages in 1979 and the Soviet invasion of Afghanistan that same year, he began calling for military action to save the Persian Gulf for United States interests. He has also, since the late 1970s, called for restoration of military conscription and the development of a harder line toward the Third World and the Soviet Union.

In 1981, with the advent of the Reagan administration in Washington, Kraft seemed increasingly partial to a theoretical conservatism while remaining critical of the actual achievements of the new leadership. Commenting on the tendency of Reagan and his colleagues in Congress to favor the wealthy, Kraft wrote:

> True conservative doctrine favors a just social order, and questions chiefly government's ability to achieve that ideal. It does not license giving advantages to the rich and the powerful at the expense of the poor and the humble. So to baffle its nemesis, what the administration mainly needs is the will to cleanse itself of the commercial greed that has so often in the past besmirched conservatism in America.

For further information:

Kraft, Joseph. "The Imperial Media." *Commentary,* May 1981.
———. *Profiles in Power.* New York: 1966.

STANLEY KRAMER

b. September 29, 1913
Film producer

Stanley Kramer is known as one Hollywood film producer and director who uses brains instead of huge budgets to create original, and sometimes controversial films. Kramer has striven for depth and meaning in most of his work, and the product often reflects provocative political stands.

Born in New York City, Kramer, whose family was involved in film distribution, graduated from DeWitt Clinton High School in 1929. He went to New York University, where he received his Bachelor of Social Science degree in 1933. Although he wanted to be a professional baseball player, he went to Hollywood instead. On the strength of work he had done for the NYU campus humor magazine, he found a job as a junior writer at Fox studios.

Kramer remained in Hollywood for 15 years before he had his first success. He was virtually ignored at Fox and instead worked as a stagehand for a short time. This experience would help him understand the fundamentals of making movies when he became a producer many years later. He then went to MGM, where he worked in the research and film-cutting departments. After selling a script he had written to Columbia Pictures, he moved to that studio as a writer. He also sold radio scripts for stars like Rudy Vallee and Edward G. Robinson.

Still, he had a long road ahead of him. During World War II Kramer served in the U.S. Army, where he made training and orientation films for the Army Signal Corps. He was discharged with the rank of lieutenant in 1946 and the following year formed his own film production company.

His first production was *So This Is New York* (1949), based on a short story by Ring Lardner. Made on a shoestring, the film turned a small profit and attracted the attention of the studios. After Kramer made *The*

Champion (1949), starring Kirk Douglas as an ambitious and cruel boxer, (and *Home of the Brave,*) (1949), his reputation was established as an effective and responsible operator, who could stick to budget and still make a fine film.

From that point Kramer's career simply took off. He was named producer of the year in 1950 by *Look* magazine. Two years later his cowboy drama *High Noon* (1951) won four Academy Awards. This was followed by *The Caine Mutiny* (1953), another smash hit based upon Herman Wouk's book and starring Humphrey Bogart, Van Johnson and Fred MacMurray.

Since that time Kramer has produced or directed 17 feature films, including *The Defiant Ones* (1958), for which he won the New York Critics Circle award for best director. Kramer quickly won the reputation of making realistic and nonconforming films about very controversial subjects. *The Defiant Ones* and *Guess Who's Coming to Dinner* dealt with racial conflict, the former a serious examination of racism and the latter a lighter film in which the daughter of a well-to-do couple chooses to marry a black. *The Men* (1950) was unlike most films seen on American screens. It dealt with paraplegic veterans of World War II — ex-servicemen and their families. The film starred a young Marlon Brando and a cast of disabled veterans with no previous acting experience.

On the Beach predated the several anti-nuclear bomb movements and stressed the theme that there is "no place to hide," as the last survivors of a nuclear war huddle in Australia while the deadly fallout approaches. *Inherit the Wind* was the dramatic rendering of the anti-evolution Scopes "monkey" trial in Dayton, Tennessee in the early 1920s, in which Spencer Tracy as Clarence Darrow and Frederic March as the fundamentalist William Jennings Bryan take center stage in their courtroom confrontations. In *Judgment at Nuremberg* (1961), Kramer scrutinized the post-World War II trials of Nazi war criminals. And his *Ship of Fools* (1965) was a chilling look at a small corner of pre-World War II society. These films, probing people's most desperate moments, will provide the basis for Kramer's future reputation.

ARTHUR B. KRIM

b. April 14, 1910
Corporate executive

Arthur B. Krim has had a distinguished career in business, law and politics. He was president of United Artists, the film production company for 18 years, and the chairman of the board of the Transam Corporation.

Arthur Krim was born in New York City to Morris and Rose (Ocko) Krim. He attended Columbia University and received his B.A. degree in 1930 and his law degree in 1932. In 1933 he was admitted into the New York bar. He also joined the prestigious law firm of Phillips, Nizer, Benjamin, Krim and Ballon as an associate partner.

During World War II he joined the Army as a lieutenant and rose rapidly through the ranks to become a lieutenant colonel. He served in Europe and was decorated with medals of honor by the French and Italian governments for general valor.

After the end of the war and demobilization, Krim turned to the world of films. From 1946 to 1949 he headed Eagle Lion Films, a distributing company. Then, in 1951, together with longtime partner Robert Benjamin, he purchased Charlie Chaplin and Mary Pickford's United Artists. UA, located in Manhattan, had no studios but was instead a financier and distributor for creative filmmakers looking for an honest accounting from distributors. UA's producers and stars were generally opposed to the traditional big studio's tightly controlled Hollywood system. Krim attracted Woody Allen, Francis Ford Coppola and Joseph Levine, among many others. In 1977, UA distributed such box office smashes as *Rocky* and *One Flew Over the Cuckoo's Nest* and earned nearly $470 million from films, television, records and music publishers. Even so, that year Krim and Benjamin quit UA, which had been merged with Transamerica in 1967, claiming that UA had become an "invisible" firm, and even its listing on the stock exchange was no longer permitted by the parent company. The following year (1978), Transamerica successes included Krim's *Hair, Apocalypse Now* and Woody Allen's remarkably successful *Annie Hall*.

Along with his career in the law and in films, Krim has taken an active role in Democratic Party politics. He served as chairman of the President's Club, a group of wealthy business leaders engaged in fund-raising for presidents John F. Kennedy and Lyndon B. Johnson. He was chairman of the finance committee of the Democratic National Committee from 1966 to 1968 and in 1968 served as a special consultant to President Johnson, advising him on a wide range of party and national policy.

Krim serves on the board of directors of many organizations. He is on the board of directors of the Weizmann Institute of Science in Rehovot, Israel, as well as the African-American Institute and Lincoln University. He is a trustee of the John F. Kennedy Library in Cambridge, Massachusetts and Columbia University and received an honorary doctorate from the latter institution in 1982.

IRVING KRISTOL

b. January 22, 1920
Writer; editor

Irving Kristol has been called the quintessential neo-conservative and indeed is generally credited with being the intellectual father of that movement. His vigorous defense of capitalist theory and ideology is respected even by his sharpest critics. "Kristol's power is not in his visibility; it is in his ability to guide ideas," wrote Geoffrey Norman in *Esquire.*

Irving Kristol was born in New York City, the son of Joseph, a clothing subcontractor, and Bessie (Mailman) Kristol. He graduated from Boys High School in 1936 and attended the City College of New York, where he majored in history and befriended such future influential figures as Irving Howe and Seymour Martin Lipset. He was also involved with the Young People's Socialist League, an anti-Communist leftist organization at the college, and the Trotskyites. He graduated cum laude in 1940 with a Bachelor of Social Science degree.

After graduation Kristol became a machinist's apprentice at the Brooklyn Navy Yard and later a freight handler in Chicago. He was drafted into the U.S. Army in 1944 and saw combat in France and Germany as an infantryman in the 12th Armored Division. He was discharged in 1946 as a staff sergeant.

Kristol and his wife, Gertrude Himmelfarb, the historian, then went to England, where she had won a scholarship to Cambridge University. There, he began to write for the American Jewish Committee's *Commentary* magazine, and in 1947 he returned to New York as the publication's managing editor. In his most famous article, " 'Civil Liberties,' 1952—A Study in Confusion," Kristol concluded: "For there is one thing that the American people know about Senator McCarthy; he like them, is unequivocally anti-Communist. About the spokesmen for American liberalism, they feel they know no such thing."

Five years later he returned to England to co-edit, with Stephen Spender, a British-American intellectual journal, *Encounter.* In the late 1960s it was revealed that *Encounter* had received secret money from the CIA. Kristol denied all knowledge of such funding but acknowledged that he was aware of the allegations and had investigated them while he was the editor of *Encounter.*

In 1958 Kristol left to become editor of *Reporter* magazine, a liberal anti-Communist journal in New York. Two years later he became executive vice president and senior editor of Basic Books, a small but prestigious New York publishing house specializing in the social sciences. In 1965, with Daniel Bell, he founded

Public Interest magazine, which they hoped would promote rational dialogue about social issues and policy making. (Bell eventually resigned.)

While Kristol was a research associate at the Russell Sage Institute in 1968 and 1969, he wrote a series of articles on urbanization, education and utopianism. These articles were later collected into a book called *On the Democratic Idea in America* (New York, 1972). The articles focused on what he believed to be the breakdown of the democratic idea in America and the dangers posed by the emergence of the New Left. He argued that although the American system needed to be reformed, the reforms must be moderate and implemented by moderate people. In other platforms, he began to formulate ideas on domestic and foreign policies that signified his movement to the right. He also supported the war in Vietnam.

Kristol co-edited *Encounters* (New York, 1963), a collection of articles that had appeared in *Encounter* magazine, and *Capitalism Today* (New York, 1971), a reprint of a special issue of *Public Interest.* He collaborated with Daniel Bell in writing *Confrontation: The Student Rebellion and the University* (New York, 1969), a highly critical treatment of student unrest in the 1960s.

Since 1969 Kristol has been Henry R. Luce Professor of Urban Values at New York University. He is a member of the American Academy of Arts and Sciences, the National Council on the Humanities, the American Political Science Association and the Council on Foreign Relations and is a senior fellow of the conservative American Enterprise Institute.

His book *Two Cheers for Capitalism* (New York, 1978) condemns environmentalists, government regulations and egalitarian reformers and is a spirited defense of the free enterprise system while acknowledging its cultural shortcomings. He censures the "new class" of liberal intellectuals for its hostility toward corporations and the commercial ethic. "It is the ethos of capitalism that is in gross disrepair, not the economics of capitalism—which is, indeed, its saving grace," he argued in *The Third Century,* edited by Seymour Martin Lipset (Stanford, Calif., 1979).

Seeking to defend the Reagan administration's "prudent policy on human rights," Kristol denounced Jacobo Timerman's book, *Prisoner Without a Name, Cell Without a Number* (New York, 1981). Timerman was an Argentine newspaper publisher-editor who had been arrested, tortured, seen his newspaper *La Opinion* expropriated by the ultra-right-wing Argentine government and been deported to Israel. Kristol sought to associate Timerman with a missing Jewish bank swindler who had allegedly supported left-wing terrorists, and he excoriated Timerman's supporters in the United

States, who he claimed had ignored communist violations of human rights. In 1981, in the *Wall Street Journal,* Kristol concluded: "The military regime in Argentina, for all its ugly aspects, is authoritarian, not totalitarian."

Kristol, a regular contributor to the *Wall Street Journal,* has also appeared frequently in *Atlantic Monthly, Harper's, Foreign Affairs, Fortune* and *The New York Times Magazine.* He has also become closely associated with Representative Jack Kemp (R., N.Y.) and the Arthur Laffer "supply side" school of economics and is prominent in Republican Party and conservative circles.

For further information:
Kristol, Irving. *The American Revolution As a Successful Revolution.* Washington: 1973.
———— and Bauer, Peter T. *Two European Essays on Income Distribution and The Open Society.* Ottawa, Illinois: 1977.
———— and Glazer, Nathan. *The American Commonwealth.* New York: 1976.
———— Goodman, Walter. "Irving Kristol: Patron Saint of the New Right," *The New York Times Magazine,* December 6, 1981.

STANLEY KUBRICK

b. July 26, 1928
Film director

Stanley Kubrick is one of the great innovative directors currently working in cinema. With films like *2001: A Space Odyssey, Barry Lyndon* and *The Shining,* Kubrick has shown time and again an ability to mold entirely new cinematic genres, which often become the definitive work in that area.

Stanley Kubrick was born in Manhattan, the son of Dr. Jacques L. and Gertrude (Perveler) Kubrick. He graduated from William Howard Taft High School in 1946 and briefly enrolled at the City College of New York. In 1946 he joined *Look* magazine as a staff photographer, but his true interests were not in still photography. At the age of 21, in 1949, he made a film called *Day of the Fight,* a 15-minute documentary about a fighter about to enter the ring. His success with this movie led to a chance to make a short film for RKO called *Flying Padre.*

In 1952, at the age of 24, Kubrick made his first feature film, a low-budget drama called *Fear and Desire.* He continued in the same mode with a movie called *Killer's Kiss* in 1954 and *The Killing* in 1956, the latter based on the novel *Clean Break* by Lionel White.

In 1956 Kubrick began to receive national attention with the anti-war classic *Paths to Glory,* starring Kirk Douglas. This was followed by *Spartacus* in 1960, also starring Kirk Douglas, in an adaptation of Howard Fast's novel about a Roman slave who led an uprising against the Roman Empire. The award-winning film firmly established Kubrick as one of America's leading young directors.

After completing *Lolita,* a film adapted from the Nabokov novel in 1962, Kubrick directed *Dr. Strangelove: Or How I Learned to Love the Bomb* in 1964. *Strangelove* was a savage satire on the narrowness of the military mentality and the passion of its leaders for nuclear weapons. Starring George C. Scott and Peter Sellers, who played Strangelove, a mad nuclear scientist, the film has since become a cult classic and is periodically rereleased. It won a New York Critics award in 1964.

With *2001: A Space Odyssey* (1969), Kubrick moved in an entirely different direction. This dazzling science fiction film, a futuristic thriller that pits a temperamental computer against human space explorers, set new frontiers in the use of visual and sound effects in the movies. Its use of Richard Strauss's tone poem "Thus Spake Zarathustra" and 19th-century waltz music against an eerie cosmic backdrop placed *Space Odyssey* in a category apart from the usual science fiction film. It won an Academy Award for Special Effects in 1969 and set the stage for a new wave of science fiction films with an ominous message for the future.

Not resting on his laurels, Kubrick directed a quite different film, *A Clockwork Orange,* in 1971. Based on the novel by Anthony Burgess and starring Malcolm Macdowell, it is a stark vision of the world in the future, where violent juvenile delinquents roam the streets terrorizing the inhabitants of a modern, ultrascientific society. Here Kubrick created an ironic contrast by using music of Beethoven to create an eerie atmosphere.

In 1975 Kubrick's next film, *Barry Lyndon,* was released. Based on the 19th-century novel of Thackeray and set in the 18th century, it was a three-hour-long love story noted for its visual beauty and a minimum of dialogue. For this film Kubrick experimented with specially made lenses that allowed him to photograph scenes with minimal light, creating a very subtle, romantic, otherworldly aura. A dramatic departure from Kubrick's earlier work, *Barry Lyndon* was received with mixed reviews by critics, who increasingly perceived Kubrick as an eccentric, almost reclusive, genius.

And yet his next film, *The Shining,* released five years later, signaled another total change. A horror film, *The Shining* was only one of many such films to be made in the late 1970s and early 1980s. But Kubrick's was different in that his story was a highly developed tale with a strong psychological base. The tale of a failed writer—played by Jack Nicholson—who has moved with his family to an old and isolated western hotel, where he hopes to get on with his writing, *The Shining* becomes a battleground for the anxieties of deviant personalities dealing with their aloneness. Kubrick has made the characters "normal" enough to evoke audience identification but strange enough to create an out-of-the-ordinary situation. Some critics have called *The Shining* one of the best horror films ever made.

Now living in England, Kubrick is known as a slow and meticulous artist with an exceptional visual sense and an ability to create dramatic new film styles.

For further information:
Ciment, Michel. *Kubrick*. New York: 1982.

MAXINE KUMIN

b. June 6, 1925
Poet; author

Maxine Kumin is a Pulitzer-Prize winning poet and a prolific, popular writer of children's books and adult novels who is best-known for her ability to sort out and describe the minute and intimate details of both human nature and the natural world as symbols of experiences on a grander scale. Her writing is often highly emotional, and she has often been compared to the 19th-century American transcendentalists.

Maxine Winokur was born in Philadelphia to Peter and Doll (Simon) Winokur. She received her Bachelor of Arts degree from Radcliffe College in 1946 and two years later her master's degree in English literature, also from Radcliffe. After free-lancing for several years and contributing poems to magazines, she became an English instructor at Tufts University from 1958 to 1961. From 1961 to 1963 she was a scholar at the Radcliffe Institute for Independent Study. In 1965 she resumed teaching at Tufts, and she has been visiting professor at Columbia, Brandeis, Princeton and other major universities. She has also taught for many summers at the famous Bread Loaf Writers Conference in Middlebury, Vermont.

In 1960 Kumin published her first children's book, *Sebastian and the Dragon* (New York), a story about a boy who searches for a dragon. The following year she published her second children's book, *Spring Things* (New York), about a boy's springtime discoveries. Among

her many other children's books are *Follow the Fall* (New York, 1961), a science story about the marvels of autumn, and *The Beach Before Breakfast* (New York, 1964), which recounts a walk along the beach.

But it is as a poet that Kumin is most recognized. Praised by many critics for her "clipped nervous line," she has—in the words of a *Choice* reviewer in 1976—been able to create an authentic contemporary sonnet. In her poetry Kumin offers detailed observations of phenomena injecting these tangible images with deep feeling.

The poet John Ciardi wrote that "she teaches me, by example, to use my own eyes. When she looks at something I have seen, she makes me see it better. When she looks at something I do not know, I therefore trust her."

In 1961 Kumin published her first poetry collection, *Halfway* (New York). In the 40 short poems anthologized, Kumin wrote, among other subjects, about the complexities of her relationships—with her daughter, as a Jew to Christians and others. In *The Nightmare Factory* (New York, 1970), the poet dealt with the disillusionment of human love, pain, illness and death. She won the Pulitzer Prize in 1973 for *Up Country: Poems for New England* (New York, 1973), which in verse and prose brought the tastes, sounds, textures, smells and sights of New England to life. Kumin herself has commented that the poet should be "terribly specific about naming things . . . bringing them back to the world's attention [and] dealing with things that are small and overlooked." Her other collections of poetry include *The Privilege* (New York, 1965) and *House, Bridge, Fountain, Gate* (New York, 1975).

Kumin has published several novels, but they have not fared as well as her poetry. The themes generally focus on complex relationships in families or situations in which the main character must cope with a combination of ongoing personal crises. *Through Dooms of Love* (New York, 1965) explores the relationship between a pawnbroker and his daughter, a Radcliffe student whose education and background have aggravated a rift between the two. In *Designated Heir* (New York, 1974), Kumin focuses on a 23-year-old girl in a troubled family who inherits a million dollars from an eccentric grandmother but chooses not to keep the money. In *Abduction* (New York, 1979), a Jewish woman who is trying to get over a traumatic divorce and the death of her daughter becomes involved in an educational program in a Washington ghetto and falls in love with the project chairman, whose affections for her turn out to be superficial.

From January 1981 until May 1982 Kumin was a consultant in poetry at the Library of Congress.

For further information:
Kumin, Maxine. *Our Ground Time Here Will Be Brief:
New and Selected Poems.* New York: 1982.
————. *Why Can't We Live Together Like Civilized Human
Beings?,* a novel. New York: 1982.

STANLEY KUNITZ

b. July 29, 1905
Poet, educator

Pulitzer-Prize-winning poet Stanley Kunitz has been
active in poetry education for the past half century. He
has been called America's senior statesman of poetry,
and through his writings—both poems and critical
essays—he has delineated the individualistic style of
this generation and its quest for selfhood.

Stanley Jasspon Kunitz was born in Worcester, Massachusetts. His father, Solomon, a dress manufacturer,'
committed suicide shortly before his birth, which poet
Stanley Moss, in an article about Kunitz, calls "the
primordial curse" and seminal influence on his life and
work. His mother, Yetta Helen Jasspon, who had emigrated from Russia, operated a dry goods store to support the family.

Kunitz went on to become valedictorian of his class
at Classical High School, from which he graduated in
1922. He then received a scholarship to attend Harvard
University and graduated summa cum laude with an
A.B. degree in 1926 and received a Master of Arts
degree from Harvard the following year. It was during
his university days that he began to write poetry.

After working briefly as a Sunday feature writer for
the *Worcester Telegram,* Kunitz began to work as an
editor for the H. W. Wilson publishing house in New
York, remaining until 1942. There, using the pseudonym "Dilly Tante," and later under his own name, he
was responsible for editing and co-editing with Howard
Haycraft a series of biographical reference books, including *Living Authors: A Book of Biographies* (1931) and
similar references for adults and younger readers that
have since become the most popular and important books
of their genre.

In 1930 Kunitz's first volume of poetry, *Intellectual
Things,* was published in New York. The poems in that
volume, which had appeared in *The Dial, The Nation,
New Republic* and other periodicals, dealt with the inner
workings of the self and were compared by the critic
from *The New York Times* to the poetry of William
Blake. Overall reception to Kunitz's debut was positive, and his career as a published poet was launched,
although 14 years would pass before the publication of
his next collection.

In 1943 Kunitz entered the United States Army as a
private and was discharged as a staff sergeant in the Air
Transport Command two years later. While in the Army
he edited a weekly Army news magazine called *Ten
Minute Break.* Also while still in uniform, he published
his second collection of poetry, *Passport to War* (New
York, 1944).

After the war Kunitz became actively involved in
teaching creative writing. From 1946 to 1948 he taught
English at Bennington College, where he organized a
literary workshop. For one year he was a visiting professor of English at the New York State Teachers College
at Potsdam, and then he became director of the poetry
workshop at the New School for Social Research in New
York City from 1950 to 1958. He also became director
of the Poetry Center at the Young Men's and Young
Women's Hebrew Association at 92nd Street in New
York from 1958 to 1962. The Poetry Center served as
one of the major showcases for established and new
poets to read and share their work.

In addition to these positions, Kunitz has organized
numerous summer workshops in creative writing and
has served as a visiting professor at the University of
Washington (1955–56), Queens College (1956–57) and
Brandeis University (1958–59). In 1967 he read his
poetry in the USSR and Poland under a cultural exchange agreement. He says of his teaching: "Essentially what I am trying to do is help each person rediscover the poet within himself. I say 'rediscover' because
I am convinced that it is a universal human attribute to
want to play with words, to beat out rhythms, to fashion images, to tell a story, to construct forms."

In Kunitz's more mature work he exhibited a more
open style than before, reminding some critics of Whitman, as he explored both the guilty and joyful recesses
of the human personality, his own nature and the world
he lives in. He moved from drawing dark, morbid interiors to clean, well-lighted places, where personalities
were integrated through love and art.

In 1958 his *Collected Poems* (New York) won the
Pulitzer Prize for poetry. In 1979 his *Selected Poems
1928–1978* (New York) was very warmly received by
critics and readers, who noted Kunitz's growth into a
highly sophisticated lyric poet. Two years later he was
awarded the Lenore Marshall poetry prize for *The Poems
of Stanley Kunitz 1928–1978* (Boston, 1980). The
$5,000 award is given to the writer of the best book of
poems in the United States.

His work has appeared in dozens of anthologies,
including *War Poets: An Anthology of the War Poetry of the*

20th Century (New York, 1945); *How Does a Poem Mean?*, edited by John Ciardi (Boston, 1959); *American Lyric Poems: From Colonial Times to the Present* (New York, 1964); and the anti-war *Where Is Vietnam?: American Poets Respond* (New York, 1967).

In addition to his own poetry, Kunitz has translated from the Russian the poems of Anna Akhmatova, Andrei Voznesensky and Yevgeny Yevtushenko. He is a member of the National Institute of Arts and Letters and the Academy of American Letters.

WILLIAM KUNSTLER

b. July 7, 1919
Attorney

William Kunstler likes to call himself the "people's lawyer," and the title is fitting. Since the 1950s he has been perhaps the most controversial and passionate defender of civil liberties and civil rights cases in the United States, the attorney for the New Left, black defendants and others prosecuted during the 1960s and 1970s.

William Moses Kunstler was born in New York City to Moses Bradford, a physician, and Frances (Mandelbaum) Kunstler. He grew up in a cultured middle-class environment; attended DeWitt Clinton High School, from which he graduated in 1937; and then went to Yale University, where he received a B.A. degree in French magna cum laude and Phi Beta Kappa in 1941.

Kunstler had always wanted to be a writer, and at Yale he and a fellow student privately published a collection of poems called *Our Pleasant Vices*. But after Army service in the Pacific from 1941 to 1946, he entered Columbia University Law School instead, opting for the prestige and secure income a law career would provide. Upon receiving his Bachelor of Laws in 1948, he joined his brother Michael in founding Kunstler and Kunstler, a firm that dealt primarily with marriage, estate and business law but took on civil liberties cases from time to time, many of which in those days focused on racial issues. In the late 1950s he defended a black reporter, William Worthy, whose passport had been revoked after he had illegally visited mainland China. Kunstler lost the case, but the experience whetted his appetite to handle more like it.

Thus, as the civil rights and student movements evolved during the early 1960s, he became increasingly involved in defending black activists and freedom riders in the South. He successfully appealed the convictions of demonstrators who had defied the policies of segregated seating on buses and became special counsel to the Southern Christian Leadership Conference headed by Martin Luther King, Jr. He specifically defended Stokely Carmichael, the young leader of the Student Non-Violent Coordinating Committee, for his role in demonstrations in Selma, Alabama and then broadened his defense to challenge the constitutionality of jury selection that had traditionally resulted in blacks being excluded from juries. He also successfully defended Harlem Representative Adam Clayton Powell, whose threatened expulsion from Congress would, in Kunstler's opinion, have deprived Powell's constituents of their right to be represented by a person of their choosing.

But Kunstler, flamboyance notwithstanding, did not become a public figure until 1969 when he defended the Chicago Seven—a group of seven political radicals, including Yippie leaders Abbie Hoffman and Jerry Rubin, accused of conspiracy and inciting to riot during the 1968 Democratic National Convention. The ensuing trial, which lasted into 1970, pitted Kunstler and partner Leonard Weinglass against Judge Julius Hoffman, who proved to be stubborn, theatrical and often arbitrary in managing his courtroom. By the end of the trial, Kunstler accused Hoffman of "legal lynching" when he refused to permit former Attorney General Ramsey Clark and black leader Ralph Abernathy to testify for the defense; Kunstler was charged with 24 counts of contempt and given a four-year and 13-day jail sentence. (Half the counts were dropped in appeals, and the sentence was suspended.) Meanwhile, the jury acquitted the Chicago Seven, although it found five guilty of inciting to riot. An appeals court later found the trial judge to be biased and the trial record filled with errors, and the case was dropped.

The experience transformed Kunstler into a radical social activist and afterward he defended such clients as the Black Panthers; the activist priest Rev. Philip Berrigan, who was charged with and acquitted of a kidnap plot; students at Kent State University (Ohio) involved in anti-war demonstrations, which turned violent and resulted in the murder of four students by National Guardsmen; American Indians trying to reclaim territories they said were theirs; and others. At the time Kunstler worked for $100 a week for the Center for Constitutional Rights and supplemented this salary with an active calendar of speaking engagements. He also worked with Ramsey Clark in the defense of two inmates at the Attica, New York state prison who had been accused of killing a prison guard during a now-notorious uprising in 1971. As a result of the lawyers' work, the two convicts had their sentences commuted by New York Governor Carey in 1976.

Despite having abandoned a professional writing career for law, Kunstler never, in fact, gave up writing. He has published numerous books and many articles about his personal experiences and about legal history. In *Beyond a Reasonable Doubt* (New York, 1961), Kunstler is coauthor with convict Caryl Chessman in documenting Chessman's 1948 trial for attempted rape, kidnap and robbery. Although Kunstler's critics often accuse him of over-emotion, this book is notably devoid of judgment and provides an incisive look into the mechanics of the court system. *First Degree* (Dobbs Ferry, N.Y., 1961) summarizes 18 murder cases spanning from 1849 to 1954 and explores their impact on American law, especially in the way that the "ordinary" people in each case caused major changes to be made. In *The Case for Courage* (New York, 1962), Kunstler profiles 10 American lawyers from 1735 through the 1950s, including Alexander Hamilton, Clarence Darrow and Harold Medina, who risked their careers by undertaking unpopular causes and in the end were vindicated through their victories. But his most personal book is *Deep in My Heart* (New York, 1966), Kunstler's account of his work in the civil rights movement, in which he declares that—contrary to accepted thought about proper behavior for lawyers—it is important to become emotionally involved in one's work.

SIMON S. KUZNETS

b. April 30, 1901
Economist

Simon S. Kuznets, professor emeritus at Harvard University, won the Nobel Prize in Economic Science in 1971 for developing a method to measure the nation's economic growth. His theory, now called the gross national product, is considered by economist John Kenneth Galbraith to be "one of the greatest discoveries of all time."

Simon Kuznets was born in Kharkov, Russia to Abraham, a fur dealer, and Pauline (Friedman) Kuznets. In 1907, when Simon was 6 years old, his father emigrated to America. Simon remained in Russia with the rest of his family until 1922, unable to leave because of the outbreak of World War I followed by the Russian Revolution, the Russian civil war and foreign intervention. During these years he attended the Gymnasium, the equivalent of an American post-high school education, where he first studied economics. Even then, he says, he was certain that most social problems stemmed from economics.

In 1922 he joined his father in New York City and enrolled at Columbia University as an economics student with advanced standing. A year later he received a B.A. degree and in 1924 an M.A. degree. In 1926 Kuznets received his Ph.D. degree from Columbia University, where he studied with the well-known economist Wesley Clair Mitchell.

In 1927 Kuznets was invited by Mitchell to become a member of the prestigious National Bureau of Economic Research. He accepted the offer and initiated a program for calculating and analyzing the United States national income. Kuznets was hired as an assistant professor of economic statistics at the University of Pennsylvania in 1930. With the Depression the federal government started to recognize that it had little data on the financial structure of the country and no reliable statistics on national earnings and income levels. The United States Senate thus assigned the National Bureau of Economic Research to collect official income estimates.

Having long believed that economics could be transformed from mere theory to a science by careful measurement and quantitative analysis, Kuznets used national accounts to study wealth, depression and growth potential. On January 4, 1934 the nation's first income statistics were issued in an official Senate publication, revealing a tremendous drop in national income from $89 billion in 1929 to $49 billion in 1932. Kuznets defined the gross national product, which included payments on consumer goods and services, and the country's income, which is the total of wages, interest, rents and profits gained in creating the national product. Today, all countries use his gross national product (GNP) to forecast their economic potential.

Much of his talent lies in his ability to amass data and apply them to theories already established. He has published numerous books dealing with national incomes accounting; domestic trends; and the changing roles of capital, labor and productivity. His books, all highly statistical, include *National Income and Its Composition 1919–1938* (Washington, 1941), *National Income: A Summary of Findings* (Washington, 1946) and *National Product Since 1869* (Washington, 1946).

After World War II, in order to establish guidelines for the successful economic growth of developing countries, Kuznets did a comparative study to determine why some nations are prosperous and others decline. In his study of the postwar period, he found that a decrease in the growth of national income correlated with a decrease in the growth of the labor supply.

In 1954 Kuznets was appointed professor of economics at Johns Hopkins University and in 1960 was made a professor of economics at Harvard, where he taught until 1971. He remained a staff member of the National Bureau of Economic Research, the nonprofit agency that supported his major studies, until 1961.

The economist's studies show that since the 1870s America's national product per capita has increased about 20 percent in each decade. Kuznets, however, has long cautioned that economic growth has disadvantages as well as advantages and that national expenditures must be examined very carefully.

He is a fellow of the Royal Statistical Society of England and the American Statistical Association and is a member of the American Economics Association and the American Philosophy Society.

SEYMOUR P. LACHMAN

b. December 12, 1933
Educator

Seymour Lachman's reputation as an innovating educational administrator and policy maker began with his membership on and later presidency of the New York City Board of Education during an especially stormy period. It has continued on the university level over the last decade and in a somewhat different guise in his role as an organizer and activist in Jewish causes.

Seymour P. Lachman was born in the Bronx to Louis, a candy store owner and presser, and Sarah (Koniarsky) Lachman. When he was a child his family moved to Brooklyn. He earned his B.A. degree from Brooklyn College in 1955 and his M.A. in education from the same school three years later. In 1963 he was awarded a Ph.D. in education by New York University. Following several years of teaching high school studies (1956–62), he became dean and professor of history at Kingsborough Community College from 1963 to 1969, a member and president of the New York City Board of Education from 1969 to 1974 and director of the Foreign Affairs Department of the American Jewish Committee in 1972–74. In 1974 he was appointed professor of educational administration at Baruch College and the Graduate School of the City University of New York and university dean in 1980.

When Lachman assumed a position on the New York City Board of Education in 1969, it was after the State Legislature had dismissed the previous board members and created a decentralized school system. For a number of years various issues such as decentralization, desegregration, the rights of teachers, the curriculum and parents' rights created many problems in New York

public schools. In April 1969 the schools underwent a series of violent and nonviolent disturbances, the first revelation that the confusion emanating from a fragmented America engaged in an unpopular war had reached the high schools. Personally committed to civil liberties as well as to reconciling the warring factions, Lachman moved to introduce the first student "bill of rights and responsibilities" in the country. It restated previously granted rights, permitted freedom of the student press, and as he wrote in 1970, it "formalized what is viable and constructive behavior. . . . We have to earn the right to administer by responding to the felt needs of our constituency. Students are a part of that constituency." In addition, he introduced due process into previously arbitrary procedures for suspension of students and supported the development of alternative schools for those who chose to be educated in somewhat different surroundings than the formal school. Thus, a city-as-school was established with his impetus, where students studied in the mornings and then departed for employment throughout the city. In 1973 he was named president of the Board of Education.

His experiences at the helm of the Board of Education were amplified in *Black, White, Green and Red: The Politics of Ethnic America*, written with David Bresnick and Murray Polner (New York, 1978). Lachman entered the schools as a reformer and departed a bit chastened, although still dedicated to the possibility of serious improvements and changes in public schools. "Shouldn't a board of education be concerned with upgrading education?" he asked. Such improvements in the classroom depended much less on decentralization, community control or any political form, he answered, than they did on the classroom teachers and their organizations and other organizations with national impact. "Boards of education," he concluded, "will have little more effect on educational technique than they have had in the past. Like it or not, education will continue to be more a badge of social status than a lever for equalizing opportunity in the social system. . . ." For while the educational system is "unusually sensitive to the demands of emergent ethnic groups, [it is] still a captive of the power realities of the larger society."

In 1980 he was named university dean for community development at the City University of New York. Much of his work involved him in serving as liaison with community groups as well as within the vast university. To that end, he chaired the Conference of Public and Non-Public Schools, the only such group in the nation involving the leaders of public, parochial and nonpublic schools in regular discussions on matters of mutual concern. One of the results was that New York state overhauled the quality and delivery of health services to pupils in all its schools.

A past president of the American Professors for Peace in the Middle East (1971–72), he organized and became chairman of the National Committee for Middle East Studies in 1975, which grew into a nationwide organization of academics and administrators promoting teaching about the Middle East. As head of the Greater New York Conference on Soviet Jewry from 1980 to 1982, he led an umbrella group of 85 organizations with a membership of 2 million in defense of Soviet Jewry. In 1981, for example, he chaired Solidarity Sunday for Soviet Jewry in New York City, at which 150,000 people gathered at the United Nations, perhaps the single largest demonstration for human rights ever held in the United States. He has also headed the Task Force on Cults and Missionary Activity since 1978, in which he warns fellow Jews of efforts to convert children and young people.

For further information:

Lachman, Seymour P. "The American Jewish Community and the Bicentennial." *Jewish Education,* Summer 1976.

———. "Report from Moscow: Pictures from an Exhibition." *Present Tense,* Autumn 1979.

———. "Students' Rights and Responsibilities: The New York Experience." *The P.T.A. Magazine,* May 1971.

Lachman, Seymour P., ed. *Proceedings of the Fifth Annual Conference of Public and Non-Public Schools: Education Faces the 80s and Beyond.* New York: 1980.

Lachman, Seymour, and Polner, Murray. "How Much Freedom for High School Students?" *New York University Quarterly,* Summer 1970.

NORMAN LAMM

b. December 19, 1927
Rabbi

Norman Lamm, who has served since 1976 as the third president of Yeshiva University, America's oldest Orthodox university, is an ordained rabbi, philosopher and writer and the first American-born person to head Yeshiva University. With the growth of Orthodoxy in this country and elsewhere, Lamm's influence seems certain to spread.

Born in the Williamsburg neighborhood of Brooklyn to Samuel, a civil servant, and Pearl (Baumol) Lamm,

Norman Lamm was educated at the Yeshiva Torah Vadaath in Brooklyn and then spent almost a year studying the Torah with his grandfather, a distinguished biblical scholar.

Lamm received a B.A. degree summa cum laude in chemistry from Yeshiva University in 1949, where he was class valedictorian. It is said that while still a student in 1948 he worked on a clandestine arms research project in upstate New York on behalf of Israel, then engaged in its 1948 War of Independence. The director of the project and Lamm's superior was Dr. Ernest D. Bergmann, who eventually became director of Israel's Atomic Energy Commission. While pursuing graduate studies in chemistry at Brooklyn Polytechnic Institute, he talked with his *rebbe*—or spiritual leader—Dr. Samuel Belkin, and decided to change his direction, turning instead toward rabbinic studies at Yeshiva's Rabbi Isaac Elchanan Theological Seminary, receiving ordination in 1950.

Once a rabbi, he assumed congregational posts, first as an assistant rabbi at the Congregation Kehilath Jeshurun in Manhattan in 1951 and three years later as a rabbi of Congregation Kodimah in Springfield, Massachusetts. Simultaneously he was associate editor of *Hadarom,* a journal dedicated to *halakah,* or Jewish law. In 1957 he organized *Tradition,* a quarterly of Orthodox life and thought. By now he had become so well-known in Orthodox circles that he was invited in 1958 to become rabbi of the Jewish Center on Manhattan's West Side, one of Orthodoxy's most distinguished synagogues.

In 1966 he was awarded a Yeshiva University doctorate. His dissertation was entitled "The Concept of Torah Lishmah in the Works of R. Hayyim of Volozhin." Soon after, he started teaching part-time at the school and was also a visiting professor of Judaic studies at Brooklyn College.

Congregational activities and writing filled his life in those years and his literary output was prolific. His most significant work to date is *Torah Lishmah* ("Torah for Its Own Sake") (Jerusalem, 1972), which examined the religious practices of the Hasidim in 18th- and 19th-century Eastern Europe. Even so, his interests embrace far more than one topic. In *Hedge of Roses* (New York, 1966), he discussed Judaism and the marital and sex relationship, writing:

> The Jewish family . . . the bedrock of the home [was] as solid and reliable as the ancient and sacred traditions from which the character of our people is hewn. Squeamishness never allowed the sexual nature of this marital love to be overlooked or minimized; modesty never permitted it to be vulgarized and dishonored.

In *The Royal Reach* (New York, 1970), he criticized "doing your own thing" and commented: "Peace—personal, domestic, and communal peace—is considered in the Jewish tradition the greatest of all blessings." He also wrote *Faith and Doubt: Studies in Traditional Jewish Thought* (New York, 1971), in which he incisively probed the meaning of religious skepticism and concluded that "God makes Himself available to His creatures wherever they are." He edited a collection, *The Good Society: Jewish Ethics in Action,* in 1974 (New York). In addition, he has written and spoken on American constitutional and Jewish law, violence, space exploration and the family.

On the future of the Jewish community in America, he said: "Thirty years ago people said that Judaism had no future in America. Well, today more than one-fourth of all religious school students attend yeshivas. And look at the yarmulke-wearing young men in the streets of New York. We have a future. We will make a future."

When he assumed the presidency of Yeshiva University, he concluded his inaugural speech by saying:

> While there has been erosion on the peripheries of the Jewish community as a result of intermarriage and assimilation, there has also been an intensification on the part of the committed. This core group will enable us to halt the erosion on the periphery, and can aid in providing the educational resources to make the community aware of the rich intellectual and spiritual resources of our people.

In 1980 Lamm was appointed by President Jimmy Carter to serve on the United States Holocaust Memorial Council.

He has led the fight to invigorate the Orthodox rabbinate. Speaking to the Rabbinical Council of America in 1981, he declared that the "synagogue is weakening" from too many Jewish competitors such as yeshivas and federations and urged rabbis "to assert their power and influence" by obtaining power in the Jewish community, finding allies, developing knowledge not only in religion but in the "learning and culture [of] the secular world. There is a new generation that looks for learning . . . without learning we are nothing. Without it we are just masters of ceremony."

Lamm is also the principal leader of a "centrist," or more moderate, Orthodoxy, eschewing the extreme positions of some Orthodox groups. For example, in late 1981 he told Richard Yaffe, an interviewer, that he regretted the furor caused in the Jewish world by the insistence of Agudath Israel—an ultra-Orthodox bloc—changing the law of return (whereby any Jew may become a citizen of Israel if he or she chooses to live there) because it pitted each of the different branches of Judaism against the others. What Agudath Israel wants to do is have Israel enact a law asserting that conversions to Judaism are only valid if made "according to halacha"—that is, only if made by an Orthodox rabbi. This would render Reform and Conservative conversions invalid, as the Orthodox rabbinical establishment in Israel does not recognize these branches as Jewish. Said Lamm:

> I think it's a mistake to base everything upon which rabbis we do or do not recognize, because it then develops into a kind of *ad hominem* . . . argument. That's divisive and disruptive and not conducive to the communal peace that we desperately need at this critical juncture of history.

PEARL LANG

b. May 29, 1922
Dancer; choreographer

One could say that dancer and choreographer **Pearl Lang** is a deeply religious woman. Although not an observant Jew, she nevertheless is thoroughly absorbed in Jewish culture and tradition, which has surfaced in her greatest work. Perhaps best identified with her full-length dance *The Possessed,* based on Solomon Ansky's play *The Dybbuk,* Lang has often drawn on Hasidic and other Jewish themes as source material for her work.

Pearl Lack was born in Chicago to Russian immigrant parents, Jacob, a tailor, and Frieda (Feder) Lack, a dress designer. Although poor, the family was, as Lang describes it, "culture-hungry," and as a child she was taken to poetry readings and lectures. Her father died when Lang was young, so without the benefit of a babysitter, her mother took Lang everywhere. Exposed to dance at an early age, Lang knew that would be her profession and began studies in folk, ballet and modern dance when she was 11. Then for seven years she studied on scholarship at the Francis Allis Studio in Chicago.

When she was 18 Lang went to New York, where she studied with Martha Graham and at the American School of Ballet. A featured soloist with the Graham troupe since 1941, Lang also appeared on Broadway in *One Touch of Venus* (1944), *Carousel* (1945), *Finian's Rainbow* (1947) and *Touch and Go* (1949). Then, in 1949 Lang formed her own company, teaching, choreographing and performing ever since.

Although her style was obviously very close to Graham's—very fluid, emotional and expressive—Lang developed a style of her own, often drawing on mythical themes and Jewish subjects for her work. She was also strongly influenced by Israeli music and themes. *Shirah* draws on Hasidic spirituality and joy as its basis, although its composer, the American contemporary Alan Hovhaness, has been identified with Oriental themes. *Cantigas Ladino* uses Sephardic rhythms and melodies in a dance combining Spanish and Jewish movements. In a program of short dances choreographed for a Holocaust memorial at the 92nd Street Y in New York City in 1977, Lang presented three pieces: "I Never Saw Another Butterfly," based on poems written by children in a concentration camp; "Kaddish," a prayer for the departed; and "Lamentations of Jeremiah."

Not all of Lang's work is based on Judaic material, however. Like her counterparts in modern dance, Lang has drawn on themes of mythology and on contemporary pressures in life for her works. *Piece for Brass* uses a factorylike set to depict the alienation of young workers caught up in the mechanistic modern world, and *Rites* (1955) uses three string quartets by Bartok to set off the portrayal of the passage of life from birth to death.

In 1968 Lang became a principal choreographer for the Batsheva Troupe, a modern dance company in Tel Aviv, and for many years she has been a prominent teacher at dance festivals in the United States and abroad. She choreographed the 1958 Israel Bonds Chanukah Festival at Madison Square Garden to celebrate Israel's 10th anniversary and in 1977 performed *The Possessed* with her company at the opening of the Entermedia Theater in New York City at Second Avenue and 12th Street. This dance was especially significant because, in its first incarnation in 1926, the Entermedia Theater was the Yiddish Art Theater headed by the great actor Maurice Schwartz.

And what has the dance meant to her? Quoting Martin Buber, she has often remarked: "He whom the divine storm of the Spirit inspires not with his instrument of speech alone but with his whole being and life is speaker of the hidden voice."

JOSEPH P. LASH

b. December 2, 1909
Biographer; journalist

The life and career of Joseph Lash are in many ways as colorful as the subjects he has written about. The biographer of Eleanor Roosevelt, Dag Hammarskjold and Helen Keller was also a prominent student activist

in the 1930s political movements very much in the style associated with the 1960s. An accomplished journalist, Lash received the Pulitzer Prize, the National Book Award and the prestigious Francis Parkman Prize for his 1971 biography *Eleanor and Franklin,* about the Roosevelts.

Joseph P. Lash was born in New York City to Samuel, a grocer, and Mary (Avchin) Lash, both Russian immigrants. He graduated from DeWitt Clinton High School in the Bronx in 1927 and received a B.A. degree from the College of the City of New York in 1931 and an M.A. degree in English literature from Columbia University the following year.

Unable to find work in the Depression years, Lash joined the Association of Unemployed College Alumni and Professional People and later became its chairman—and so began an active career in politics. He had already devoted much time to the Socialist Party and in 1935 was one of the first organizers of the American Student Union, a coalition of Socialist and Communist youth organizations. Lash became national secretary of the ASU, remaining until 1939. During that period he coauthored his first book, a history of both student and peace movements, called *War, Our Heritage* (New York, 1936). His co-writer was James A. Wechsler, the director of publications for the ASU, who would later become an editor for the *New York Post.*

But in 1939 the Nazi-Soviet pact disillusioned Lash and many other young socialists who also flirted with communism. That year, sent to Washington to participate in a congressional panel on Communist infiltration in political youth groups, Lash met Eleanor Roosevelt, who would become both a professional colleague and an intimate friend. They began working together to promote liberal causes. Lash later worked full-time in Franklin Delano Roosevelt's 1940 presidential campaign and, after working with the International Student Service, an aid program for foreign students, he entered the Army in 1942, serving until 1945.

Upon returning, Lash joined the newly formed liberal and anti-Communist Union for Democratic Action. In 1946, with Eleanor Roosevelt and others, he helped organize Americans for Democratic Action, an influential liberal organization, remaining until 1948, when he stopped to edit two volumes of the letters of Franklin Delano Roosevelt, which were published in 1950.

Lash became a correspondent for the *New York Post* in 1950 and for 10 years was its United Nations correspondent. He was its editorial writer in 1961 and from 1964 to 1966 worked closely with James Wechsler on its editorial page.

In 1961 Lash published his first biography, *Dag Hammarskjold: Custodian of the Brushfire Peace* (New

York), which concentrates sympathetically on the United Nations secretary general's career. Following Hammarskjold's death that year, Lash added an epilogue to update the book. It was well received by critics, and a new career as biographer began.

Following Eleanor Roosevelt's death in 1962, Lash began work on a memoir of her life. *Eleanor Roosevelt: A Friend's Memoir* (New York) appeared two years later. He was then assigned by her executors to write her definitive biography. With access to papers and letters previously denied to others, Lash began work in 1966. *Eleanor and Franklin* (New York, 1971) was published five years later and was acclaimed as an outstanding if predictably sympathetic analysis of the complex woman who had been raised in a stifling and racist upper-class environment but who became one of the world's greatest humanitarians. A sequel, *Eleanor: The Years Alone* (New York), was published in 1972, with additional analyses of letters and other accounts of Mrs. Roosevelt's often-troubled life. Lash received overall praise for his tact and subtlety in discussing some of the more personal aspects of both Roosevelts' lives plus her clashes over public policies with John F. Kennedy and Cardinal Francis Spellman.

Lash's other books are also biographical works and include his editing of *From the Diaries of Felix Frankfurter* (New York, 1976), a look at the writings of the former Supreme Court justice; *Roosevelt and Churchill* (New York, 1976); and *Helen and Teacher* (New York, 1980). The last book was written to commemorate the centennial of Helen Keller's birth. An in-depth analysis of the life of the famous deaf-blind woman and her companions throughout her life, particularly Annie Sullivan, the book attempted not to glorify Keller's accomplishments but to create a realistic portrayal of who she really was, what her achievements really meant, who was responsible for them and how personal dependencies—Helen on her various helpers and vice-versa—evolved.

FRANK LAUTENBERG

b. January 23, 1924
Philanthropist; businessman

As former general chairman, president and chairman of the board of the United Jewish Appeal, Frank Lautenberg has been a major leader in Jewish philanthropic efforts. While actively serving as the chief executive officer of the largest data processing company in the world, he has also found time to campaign tirelessly for funds, consult with top American and Israeli leaders, and participate in the work of the Jewish Agency as well as guide the UJA.

Frank Lautenberg was born in Paterson, New Jersey, the son of Samuel and Mollie (Bergen) Lautenberg. His father was a businessman. After serving in the U.S. Army during World War II, Lautenberg attended Columbia University, where he received his B.S. degree in 1949.

Four years after completing his degree, Lautenberg and Henry Taub founded Automatic Data Processing Inc., which grew to be the largest data processing firm in the world, owing to hard work, keen interest in computer technology and business acumen. Lautenberg's career grew along with the company. He was executive vice president in charge of administration from 1961 until 1969, president since 1969, and chairman of the board and chief executive officer since 1975.

Self-described as a man who found his Jewish identity comparatively late in life, Lautenberg has compressed a lifetime's worth of Jewish communal responsibility into a decade and a half. He led the record-setting fund-raising efforts by the UJA in New Jersey following the Yom Kippur War in 1973. He was then appointed general chairman of the UJA, and in 1976 he became president. He has also served as president of American Friends of Hebrew University and established the Lautenberg Center at the Hebrew University School of Medicine. In 1982 he ran for the U.S. Senate as a Democrat in New Jersey.

Frank Lautenberg describes his work on behalf of the Jewish people as an act of affirmation, which, for him, is the very essence of Jewish life. He believes that Jews are bound together by memory, tradition, faith and the refusal to succumb to indifference. He sees his own work as bearing witness to the eternity of the Jewish people.

In addition to his work in the Jewish community, Lautenberg serves the rest of his community as well. He is a commissioner of the Port Authority of New York and New Jersey, a member of the finance committee of the Democratic National Committee and the board of overseers of the New Jersey Symphony Orchestra.

Lautenberg has received many awards for his distinguished record of public service. In 1975 he received, along with Isaac Stern and Hubert Humphery, the Scopus Award from the American Friends of Hebrew University. Three years earlier that same group had given him the Torch of Learning Award. Lautenberg received honorary degrees from the Hebrew Union College in 1977 and the Hebrew University in 1978.

In 1980 Lautenberg was one of 60 prominent American Jews appointed by President Jimmy Carter to participate in the United States Holocaust Memorial Council.

NORMAN MILTON LEAR

b. July 27, 1922
Producer; writer; director

Norman Milton Lear, television's most successful independent producer, flouted the taboos of broadcasting and changed television programming when he created the socially relevant situation comedy *All in the Family* in 1971. With such subsequent television shows as *Maude, Mary Hartman, Mary Hartman, Soap* and *The Jeffersons,* Lear has brought some of the vexing issues of the real world—bigotry, homosexuality, rape, impotency—into the living rooms of Americans, offering them popular entertainment combined with social concerns.

Norman Lear was born in New Haven, Connecticut to Herman, a salesman, and Jeanette (Seicol) Lear. He studied at Emerson College in 1940 and was in the U.S. Air Force from 1941 to 1945. He worked in public relations from 1945 to 1949. From 1950 to 1954 Lear was a comedy writer for such television programs as *The Colgate Comedy Hour* and *The Martha Raye Show.* In 1955 he began writing and producing movies. Among them were *Come Blow Your Horn* (1963), *Divorce American Style* (1967), *The Night They Raided Minsky's* (1968) and *Cold Turkey* (1971). During that period he also produced such television specials as "Henry Fonda and the Family" (1963), "Robert Young and the Family" (1970) and several Andy Williams specials.

In 1971, when Lear and Bud Yorkin created *All in the Family,* the ground-breaking comedy that brought ethnic humor into the open, it was considered unusual for television executives to treat the network audience as intelligent adults. In the initial program, the now-famous character Archie Bunker returns from church to find a romantic Gloria and Mike—his daughter and her husband—ready to retire to their bedroom and says, incredulously, "Eleven o'clock on a Sunday morning?"

The reception was mixed but Lear refused to concede. "I don't think there is any danger in overestimating the intelligence of TV audiences—the real danger lies in underestimating it," Lear said. By making Archie Bunker a lovable bigot, Lear hoped that "Many people [would] see a little bit of Archie in themselves and understand."

Three of Lear's other top-rated shows—*Maude* (1972), *The Jeffersons* (1975) and *Good Times* (1974)—grew from characters developed in *All in the Family.* In *Maude* the title character is the embodiment of a suburban-liberal-feminist, and examines women's liberation issues; *The Jeffersons* and *Good Times* deal with black family life from the points of view of rich and poor blacks. Among the touchy issues Lear examined were menopause, abortion, cancer, rape, adultery, venereal disease and mental retardation.

Despite the controversies Lear's shows raised because of the themes he depicted, his programs dealt primarily with contemporary family life. The essential core of every Lear comedy—including *Sanford and Son* (1972), about a black father and his grown son; *Mary Hartman, Mary Hartman* (1976), an ongoing serial takeoff on soap operas and middle-American values; and *Soap* (1977), a satire of soap operas—is the inevitable bickering and loving between husband, wife, children and in-laws. Despite their daring nature Lear's television shows also have an important element of nostalgia—exemplified by the title and opening theme song of *All in the Family,* "Those Were the Days"—and reveal a longing for the past and its allegedly simpler times and less complex choices.

Lear supervises every aspect of his shows—from the business negotiations to script revisions to direction to casting to promotion. He won Emmy awards in 1970, 1971, 1972 and 1973 for *All in the Family.* Despite a few TV flops, such as *Hot l Baltimore* (1975) and *All That Glitters* (1977), Lear is considered the major influence on television in the 1970s. One example of his efforts to probe sensitive issues is his collaboration with Alex Haley, author of *Roots,* on a short-lived television series, *Palmerstown, U.S.A.* (1980), about two little boys, one black and one white, growing up in a segregated southern town in the 1930s.

Since 1979 Lear has stopped producing shows for prime-time television. Instead, he is involved in nearly every other aspect of the video world. He has created a pilot for a show aimed at the cable market, based on average people talking intimately about their lives; he is part-owner of a company that owns subscription television services around the country and is working on a series for children entitled *No Adults Allowed.*

Most of Lear's time, however, is spent working for an organization he founded in 1980 called People for the American Way, a national group formed in response to the growing power of the Rev. Jerry Falwell's Moral Majority. The organization developed when Lear was researching the phenomenon of the evangelicals for a satirical movie he was working on. "I spent a year researching it, but by last July, I realized the whole thing had taken a more serious turn," he told a *New York Times* reporter in April 1981. Lear asserts that the "Christian New Right" is threatening the freedom of expression of others through a rapidly growing network of television and radio stations that are "blanketing the country, espousing the same far right, fundamentalist points of view while attacking the integrity and the character of anyone who does not stand with them."

In 1981 Lear won the fifth annual William O. Douglas First Amendment Award for his leadership in opposing attempts to censor television programming. The award is sponsored by Public Counsel, a public interest law office established by the Los Angeles County and Beverly Hills bar associations. "I love being associated with the First Amendment," he said in 1980. "Terrific words. Precise, impeccable."

JOSHUA LEDERBERG

b. May 23, 1925
Scientist; university president

Joshua Lederberg—who received a Nobel Prize when he was 33 and has been president of Rockefeller University, the prestigious research institute in New York City since 1978—is one of America's most eminent geneticists.

He was born in Montclair, New Jersey, the son of Zwi Hirsch, an Orthodox rabbi and Esther (Goldenbaum) Lederberg. He attended the highly selective, science-oriented Stuyvesant High School in New York City and in 1944 received a Bachelor of Arts degree from Columbia College. Following two years at Columbia's College of Physicians and Surgeons, he went on leave to conduct research for the late Edward L. Tatum at Yale University. His work there signaled the end of his aspirations toward medical practice and the beginning of a distinguished career in research. At Yale he was awarded a Ph.D. in microbiology and genetics in 1947. While there, he discovered the mechanism of genetic recombination in bacteria and demonstrated for the first time that a type of sexual reproduction occurs in these microorganisms.

In 1947 Lederberg joined the genetics faculty at the University of Wisconsin, where he remained until 1959, serving the last two years there as department chairperson. While there, in 1958 he was co-recipient of the Nobel Prize in physiology of medicine for continued productivity in the field. (One of the other winners was his former mentor from Yale, Dr. Tatum.) He then went to the medical school of Stanford University in 1959, where he was named professor of genetics, biology and computer science, remaining until he was appointed president of Rockefeller University in 1978. He has also been a visiting professor of bacteriology at the University of California at Berkeley (1950) and Fulbright Visiting Professor of Bacteriology at the University of Melbourne, Australia (1957).

Lederberg's interest in bettering understanding between scientists, the general reader and government led him to write a syndicated *Washington Post* column, *Science and Man,* between 1966 and 1971. He wrote extensively about genetics, chemistry and evolution of unicellular organisms and of humans; computer models of scientific reasoning; the origin of life; and applications of scientific understanding to public health policy. The articles also took note of his serious interest in disarmament.

In addition to his personal research, writing and teaching responsibilities, Lederberg has been active in a wide range of national and foreign programs related to science and the public good. He served on President John F. Kennedy's Panel on Mental Retardation (1961–62) and played an active role in the Mariner and Viking missions to Mars from 1960 to 1977, sponsored by the National Aeronautics and Space Administration. Between 1970 and 1973 he served as a consultant to the U.S. Arms Control and Disarmament Agency—because of his keen interest in limiting the spread of nuclear weaponry—and contributed to its successful negotiation of the treaty on biological weapons disarmament. He is presently a director of the Center for Advanced Study in the Behavioral Sciences at Stanford University in California and of the Institute for Scientific Information in Philadelphia. He is also a member of the board of governors of the Weizmann Institute in Rehovoth, Israel; a trustee of the Sackler Medical School at Tel Aviv University, Israel; and on the advisory board of the Technion Medical School in Haifa, Israel.

An unusually gifted scientist of world stature, Lederberg was cited in a public announcement on January 19, 1978 by the board chairperson of Rockefeller University for having shown a "deep concern for the strengthening communications between science and the society it serves."

SAMUEL J. LEFRAK

b. February 12, 1918
Housing and building developer

Samuel J. Lefrak is one of the world's most successful apartment house developers. The builder of hundreds of modestly priced housing developments in the greater New York area, Lefrak is regarded as the hero of the middle class, a brilliant real estate executive and a philanthropist.

Samuel J. Lefrak was born in Manhattan to Harry, a glazier and carpenter from Palestine, and Sarah (Schwartz) Lefrak. He attended Erasmus High School. In 1936 he enrolled in a pre-dental program at the University of Maryland but soon switched to economics and engineering. He graduated with a B.A. degree in 1940.

After graduation Lefrak made a $5,000 investment in the family construction firm with money saved from spare jobs during college and graduation gifts. In 1948 he was elected president of the Lefrak Organization, which chiefly built apartment houses in Brooklyn, some of which it also managed. The company was only fairly successful until 1951, when Lefrak convinced his father to take a gamble. They then bought 29 parcels at auction, took out a loan and started building housing on each site. Within six years Lefrak put up 2,000 new apartments, most in Brooklyn and Queens. By 1960 he had constructed major developments costing nearly $50 million.

In 1955, when the Mitchell-Lama Law, which subsidized middle-income housing, was passed by the New York State Legislature, the Lefrak Organization became the first private construction firm to become legally involved with the plan. Through cooperation with city housing authorities, Lefrak built even more apartment houses. The major consequence was an $8 million cooperative development—King's Bay Houses—in the Sheepshead Bay area of Brooklyn, one of the pioneering urban housing developments in the country privately built with city financing.

Lefrak was one of the first to merge luxury apartments with office space when he built the Parc Vendome in 1959 in Queens, which contains the Municipal Court of the City of New York. In 1956 he suggested utilizing the "air rights" over the city's new underpass-approach to the George Washington Bridge, though the four high-rise apartment buildings that were built on the site were constructed by another developer.

Lefrak City, a 40-acre, $150 million housing development made up of twenty 18-story buildings near the Long Island Expressway in Forest Hills-Elmhurst in Queens was his most massive operation. Housing 25,000 people, it is one of the largest privately financed apartment developments in the world.

Lefrak's success is due to his obsessive control of his costs. He minimizes costs by buying early and warehousing his building materials until needed. He produces bricks in his own plants and keeps large amounts of cash in reserve and is therefore able to borrow at lower rates of interest.

Lefrak believes that people care very much for extra facilities. Consequently, under what he calls the "Lefrak concept of total living," he provides adjoining shopping areas, beauty parlors, dance studios, restaurants, movie theaters, specialty shops, swimming pools, tennis courts, and other facilities. Nor does he restrict tenants from owning pets, as do most municipal housing authorities.

Landlord to about half a million people in New York, Lefrak has long divided his time between business and civic affairs. In 1957 he was a member of the board of directors of the Citizens Housing and Planning Council and from 1965 to 1968 was commissioner of the Landmarks Preservation Commission of New York City. Because of his knowledge of housing and finance, in 1963 he served on the Committee on World Housing of the United Nations and has been a consultant for urban affairs to the State Department.

A generous contributor to Jewish organizations, Lefrak is a trustee of the Jewish Hospital in Denver, a founder of the Albert Einstein College of Medicine, chairman of the national board of Histadrut and trustee of Beth-El Hospital. He has been given awards by the Jewish National Fund, the B'nai B'rith and the Religious Zionists of America.

ERICH LEINSDORF

b. February 4, 1912
Conductor

As one of the world's greatest conductors, Erich Leinsdorf has earned international respect for his solid perfectionism and the versatility of his repertoire. The former music director and principal conductor of the Boston Symphony Orchestra—Leinsdorf retired in 1969 and has been free-lancing since then—he is considered one of the outstanding interpreters of Wagnerian opera and of the symphonies of Mozart.

Erich Landauer was born in Vienna to Ludwig Julius and Charlotte (Loebl) Landauer. His father, who was a shoe salesman, died when Leinsdorf was 3, and he was raised by his mother and an aunt. He began studying piano when he was 8 but early on was drawn to orchestral music. Thus, although both his mother and his teachers pushed him to become a concert pianist, Leinsdorf turned toward conducting instead. Vienna was a perfect place to cultivate this interest, for such conductors as Wilhelm Furtwangler, Otto Klemperer and Bruno Walter appeared frequently there. In 1930, when Leinsdorf completed his formal academic schooling, he enrolled at Vienna University as a music major. But the school's focus on the academic side of music frustrated him, and after three months he switched to the State Academy of Music, where he was able to study conducting. At graduation three years later, he made his formal conducting debut with a student orchestra performing the Concerto in A by Liszt and the first movement of Brahms' violin concerto.

As the Nazi influence grew in Vienna, Leinsdorf had to abandon hopes for a conducting position. He spent the next few years as an opera coach and rehearsal accompanist. But summers he spent at the Salzburg Festival, where he met the great conductor Arturo Toscanini. For the following three summers he returned to Salzburg as Toscanini's protege—he even earned the nickname "Little Toscanini"—and trained as an assistant conductor. However, Leinsdorf finally felt he had to leave Vienna, and with recommendations from Toscanini and the other major conductor at Salzburg, Bruno Walter, he secured a post in 1937 as assistant conductor to Artur Bodanzky at the Metropolitan Opera.

Once there, Leinsdorf was able to specialize in German opera, particularly the grand works of Wagner. In 1938 he made his American debut conducting Wagner's *Die Walkure* to much critical praise—especially in view of his age; he was only 26. That year he conducted 10 operas and the following season, 36. Then in late 1939, just as the new season began, Bodanzky fell ill and died shortly thereafter, and Leinsdorf became his replacement. It was a formidable challenge for such a young man—many of the Met's singers resented him, and the tenor Lauritz Melchior at one point refused to perform for him—but Leinsdorf ultimately completed a successful season and remained at the Met for two more years.

In 1943 he accepted the post of music director of the Cleveland Symphony Orchestra. However, the job lasted one month. Leinsdorf, who had been naturalized the year before, was drafted into the Army, and when he was discharged several months later, the Cleveland job was no longer available. He free-lanced for several years more, then joined the Rochester Philharmonic Orchestra as music director, remaining from 1947 to 1956. A short stint with the New York City Opera in 1956—its consistently avant-garde repertory and its near-bankruptcy made the job precarious and uncomfortable—was followed by a return to the Met, where Leinsdorf conducted until 1962. In the meantime he had established an international reputation for his recordings with some of the great symphony orchestras in America and Europe and with the Israel Philharmonic as well as for his performances abroad.

But the peak of Leinsdorf's career was his appointment to direct the Boston Symphony Orchestra, one of the oldest and finest in America. From 1962 to 1969 he maintained a rigorous schedule of performances and recordings with the orchestra, which included summers at the Berkshire Music Festival—Leinsdorf's happiest times during his tenure there—and frequent guest appearances with other orchestras. In his autobiography, *Cadenza* (Boston, 1976), Leinsdorf writes that his Boston years "gave me altogether a clearer idea of what the whole complex interpretation of music meant." Having succeeded two eminent but very different men, Serge Koussevitzky and Charles Munch, he was able to balance their own approaches toward music and the impact it left on the orchestra with his own. It gave him an opportunity to explore the nuances of emotion, different traditions toward classical music and new trends in avant-garde music as he continuously developed a more sophisticated and personal style. But in 1969 Leinsdorf resigned, abandoning the tension of being an administrator as well as a conductor so that he could relax his schedule, travel and also write (articles, not music), including his autobiography.

In his book on composers and conducting, *The Composer's Advocate: A Radical Orthodoxy for Musicians* (New York, 1981), he insists that while a conductor's authority is necessary to direct a symphonic orchestra, it need not reflect the authoritarianism he encountered when he first arrived in the United States in 1937. And as for conducting, he declares his doubts about the so-called baton method of conducting: "I have always refused to teach conducting, supporting my refusal with the argument that the motions are of no consequence."

In *Cadenza* Leinsdorf makes passing references to his upbringing as a Jew and his travels to Israel. Although he describes himself as a "conscious Jew," he rejects the claims of some Jews who feel that the music of Wagner or Richard Strauss, or even Bach's *St. John's Passion*, should not be played because in the first two cases the composers were notoriously anti-Semitic, and in the third the text of the music seems to be. Leinsdorf has always placed higher value on the music itself than on the politics surrounding it, writing that "an immortal composition [has] its own laws and [can] not be judged by the yardstick of a political tract." In this regard he is like violinist Jascha Heifetz, who was physically attacked after he performed works by Strauss in Israel, and conductor Zubin Mehta, who has introduced some of Wagner's repertoire to the Israel Philharmonic and been bitterly attacked by some Israelis.

ROBERT LEKACHMAN

b. May 12, 1920
Economist

Economist, teacher, public speaker, writer, consultant, adviser—in all these roles, Robert Lekachman consistently advances the liberal, compassionate point of view. An unorthodox thinker who writes extensively and speaks widely, he describes himself as a democratic socialist, at times a radical. Throughout his career he has fought vigorously for economic and social justice.

Robert Lekachman was born in New York City to Samuel, a commercial printer, and Jenny (Kominsky) Lekachman, both of whom came to the United States from Galicia, Poland early in the century.

Aside from military service in World War II, Lekachman has always been in the academic world. He gained his B.A. degree and a Phi Beta Kappa key at Columbia University in 1942 and his Ph.D. in economics at that university in 1954. From 1942 to 1945 he served with the United States Army as an infantryman in the Pacific. After working as a teaching assistant at Columbia's School of Business for a year in 1947, he went to Barnard College and stayed until 1965, teaching economics and reaching the rank of professor. During the Barnard period he also directed the Contemporary Civilization Program at Columbia College from 1962 to 1963.

In 1965 Lekachman became professor of economics at the State University of New York (SUNY) at Stony Brook, where he remained until 1973. Since then he has been distinguished professor of economics at the City University of New York's Lehman College in the Bronx, teaching also at the institution's Graduate Center in Manhattan.

During the 1960s Lekachman held three distinguished fellowships—a Rockefeller, for research in economics in 1960-61; a Guggenheim in 1965-66, for research in the history of economic ideas, which he put to use in writing an early book, *The Age of Keynes* (New York, 1966); and a Liberal Arts Fellowship in Law and Economics at Harvard University Law School in 1968-69.

The Keynes book, which was translated into several languages and published in three paperback editions, discusses John Maynard Keynes' basic theory of employment, interest and money and analyzes its application to American economic life from Franklin D. Roosevelt's New Deal in the 1930s to Lyndon Johnson's Great Society three decades later. Reviewers described this work as "vigorous," "incisive" and "lucid," words used frequently to describe subsequent Lekachman books.

An enthusiastic and convincing speaker, Lekachman has addressed groups in universities across the country and abroad as well as political, labor, research and religious organizations in many places on such subjects as the state of the American economy, the future of capitalism, welfare reform, prices, taxes and free trade. In his talks and discussions, he expressed liberal—some dubbed them "leftist"—views, pointing out weaknesses in much current economic theory and methods and in the capitalist system.

He has also given testimony to legislative bodies, including the New York State Legislature and the U.S.

House of Representatives on such problems as the measurement of unemployment, the New York City economic crisis in the 1970s and the New York state budget. Appearing on a variety of radio and television programs, he has discussed and cast light on issues of concern to business and government and the average family.

A prolific writer, Lekachman's output ranges across the economic front. Among his books published in the last decade are *Inflation* (New York, 1974), *Economists at Bay* (New York, 1976) and *Capitalism for Beginners* (New York, 1982). In *Inflation* he outlines the inflationary process and its causes, describes various public and private efforts to combat it and appraises those strategies. *Economists at Bay* tackles the ideas and methods of present-day economists, documenting Lekachman's view that economics has become a branch of applied mathematics and must return to the tradition of social analysis to be useful again. *Capitalism for Beginners*, a profusely illustrated handbook, sketches the history of capitalism from Adam Smith and Karl Marx to the latest financial page headline, explaining such major elements of the system as economic boom periods, the impact of the energy crisis, monetarism and the business cycle and ending with the statement that "The self-interest of those who live by their labor requires replacement of capitalism by democratic socialism."

In one of his major works, *Greed Is Not Enough* (New York, 1982), Lekachman attacked the Reagan administration's economic programs and accused them of improving the well-being of the rich at the expense of the working poor, the labor unions and the nonwhites. He suggested that their economic failures would be so great that the future might bring in their wake classic authoritarianism or "friendly fascism" or an attempt to utilize corporate planning, at once highly centralized and undemocratic.

Lekachman has also edited and written introductions to numerous books by well-known economists and has contributed to a healthy list of other works. His name frequently appears over articles written with authority and wit in many newspapers and magazines, including *The New York Times, The Washington Post, Christianity and Crisis, The Nation, Present Tense, The New Republic, Social Policy, Harper's, Civil Liberties Review* and *Partisan Review,* and he has contributed reviews to scholarly journals and articles in several encyclopedias. He serves on almost a dozen editorial boards, including *Dissent, Social Policy* and *Christianity and Crisis.*

A key aspect of Lekachman's thinking appeared in an article titled "Social Justice in Hard Times" in the magazine *Adherent,* late in 1980. He wrote:

American capitalism, luckily planted in a bountiful environment of lavish natural resources, blessed with the cheap labor of successive waves of energetic immigrants, and furnished with a huge, growing domestic market for its artifacts, has always operated as wastefully of its natural environment as of its employees.

Defining economics today, he says: "In good hands, it is an intelligently practiced art, in poor ones a fake science." He expects to spend a good part of his time in the future as in the past—about half of his working hours, he estimates—in writing books, articles and other works. His current advice to his students, most of whom are New Yorkers and members of minority groups, is "Leave town!"—the job market being so tight in the city that he suggests they move on to the Sun Belt or the mountain states.

MAX LERNER

b. December 20, 1902
Journalist

Max Lerner has been an "America-watcher" since his early days as a writer for *The Nation* and the newspaper *PM* in the 1940s. The author of many books since then, he has continued to watch, write, teach and comment, but he has noticeably departed from his left-liberal views.

Max Lerner was born in Minsk, Russia to Benjamin, a shopkeeper and petty tradesman, and Bessie (Podel) Lerner. The family came to New York in 1907. Lerner attended Yale University, graduating with a B.A. degree in 1923. He earned an M.A. degree from Washington University in St. Louis, Missouri in 1925 and a Ph.D. from the Robert Brookings Graduate School of Economics and Government in Washington, D.C. in 1927.

Lerner's professional career has been devoted to writing about, researching or teaching American history, politics and sociology. In 1927 he began work as assistant editor, then managing editor, of the *Encyclopedia of Social Sciences* in New York City. After five years there he joined the faculty of Sarah Lawrence College in Bronxville, New York, where he taught in the Social Sciences Department. His other academic posts have taken him to Harvard University as a lecturer on government (1935–36); Williams College (1938–43) and Brandeis University (1949–73). At Brandeis, Lerner was professor of American civilization, and since leaving he has been named professor emeritus. Since 1974 Lerner has been a distinguished professor at the Gradu-

ate School of Human Behavior at U.S. International University in San Diego, California.

But Lerner is best-known to the American public as a journalist. From 1936 to 1938 he was editor of *The Nation,* one of America's oldest and best-known liberal publications. From 1943 through 1948 he was editorial director at *PM,* a leftist newspaper. Lerner was a columnist at the *New York Star* for one year after leaving *PM,* and then in 1949 he joined the staff of *The New York Post,* where his syndicated columns originate and now appear throughout the United States.

As a younger journalist Lerner was part of an active group of Jewish intellectuals who adhered to basically socialist and reformist ideals and who advocated a wide range of social programs for America's deprived classes and moderation in foreign policy. In the late 1960s and throughout the 1970s, Lerner gradually changed his point of view, along with many of his peers, to take a harder line both on foreign policy planning and in domestic program support. Much of this was in reaction to the burgeoning anti-Vietnam War movement, which firmly established, then widened, the rift between older Democrats (many of whom are now newly Republican) and younger, more liberal Democrats. Denouncing left-liberals, he wrote in 1981:

> The concept of freedom had been turned into anarchy, and equality had become a quota system. "The social issues" this [new] class reacted to—affirmative action, pornography, abortion—were not part of the liberal agenda. Further: national defense was not part of the liberal mentality either. Appeasement was . . . self-hatred . . . a paralyzing fear of nuclear weapons and power. . . .

Lerner has written many books that variously examine aspects of American and world history and facets of contemporary life. Some are collections of his previously published essays, while others are original in book form. His major books include: *Actions and Passions: Notes on the Multiple Revolution of Our Time* (New York, 1949), a collection of Lerner's early work for *PM* that examined his opinions about ethics, culture and the economy in postwar America; *America as Civilization: Life and Thought in the U.S. Today* (New York, 1957), an analysis of the "American experience" in the mid-1950s, an essentially middle-of-the-road position, noncommittal other than to celebrate his adopted country; and *The Age of Overkill* (New York, 1963), a discussion of the implications of nuclear weapons, the emergence of Asia and Africa as major new powers to contend with, the rise of the United Nations and new political warfare between the Communists and the western world.

Lerner's drift toward the center is evident as he analyzes the impact of nuclear weaponry on traditional
systems of politics and war. For example, in his March
25, 1981 column for *The New York Post* he celebrates
the emergence of neo-conservatism in the Age of Reagan.
Referring to the "liberal intellectual class" as a "destructive force" that had been "spawned by the liberal
welfare state since Franklin Roosevelt," Lerner heartily
endorses the administration's hard line toward the Soviet Union and its other policies.

Apparently relishing the role of elder statesman, Lerner remains an active critic of American values, teaching and writing with the same fervor that typified his
years as a journalist four decades earlier.

For further information:

Lerner, Max. *Education and a Radical Humanism: Notes
    Towards A Theory of the Educational Crisis.* Columbus,
    Ohio: 1962.
———. *The Essential Works of John Stuart Mill.* New
    York: 1961.
———. *Ideas Are Weapons.* New York: 1939.
———. *It Is Later Than You Think.* New York: 1943.
———. *The Mind and Faith of Justice Holmes.* Bos-
    ton: 1943.
———. *The Portable Veblen.* New York: 1948.
———. *Public Journal.* New York: 1945.
———. *Ted and the Kennedy Legend.* New York: 1980.
———. *Toqueville and American Civilization.* New York:
    1966.
———. *The Unfinished Country.* New York: 1959.
———. *Values in Education: Notes Toward a Values Phi-
    losophy.* Bloomington, Ind.: 1976.

EDWARD H. LEVI

b. June 26, 1911
Professor of law; U.S. attorney general

Edward H. Levi served as a widely praised United
States attorney general from 1975 to 1977 under President Gerald Ford. Prior to his government service, Levi
was president of the University of Chicago from 1968
to 1975. He was one of the first Jewish scholars ever
chosen to head a major American university.

Edward Hirsch Levi was born in Chicago to Gerson,
a rabbi, and Elsa (Hirsch) Levi. His grandfather, Rabbi
Emil G. Hirsch, was on the University of Chicago's
first faculty and presided over Hyde Park's Sinai Temple; his congregation included many of Chicago's leading German-Jewish families. His brother Julian H. Levi

is a professor of urban studies at the university. Levi
grew up in the Hyde Park neighborhood near the university and attended one of its experimental children's
schools. After graduating from high school in 1928, he
attended the University of Chicago, where he received
his B.A. degree in 1932 and his Bachelor-of-Law degree
in 1935.

In 1936 Levi became an assistant professor of law at
the University of Chicago, a position he kept for four
years. From 1940 to 1945 he served as special assistant
to the attorney general. Levi rejoined the University of
Chicago Law School faculty in 1945 as a full professor,
gaining an excellent reputation for scholarship and teaching ability. An expert in the antitrust field, Levi published his first book in 1949, *An Introduction to Legal
Reasoning* (Chicago).

In the 1940s Levi served as adviser to Chicago physicists who conducted atomic energy research during and
after the war. Interested in keeping laws up-to-date
with developments in nuclear research, he played a major
role as attorney for the Federation of Atomic Scientists
in writing the United States Atomic Energy Act of
1946, which formed the basis for the Atomic Energy
Commission.

From 1950 to 1962 Levi was appointed dean of
Chicago's Law School. Believing that a future lawyer
should develop a point of view about civil liberties and
the theory of economics and politics, he helped reexamine and redo the law school's curriculum. He stressed an
interdisciplinary approach, combining legal studies and
the social sciences by adding an economist and a sociologist to the law school teaching staff. He helped establish the law school's *Journal of Law and Economics* in
1958 and sponsored the development of a continuing
assessment of the antitrust laws and the impact they
had on the economy. In 1962 Levi was appointed provost at the university. Under his leadership the number
of faculty members rose to an all-time high of more
than 1,000 with faculty salaries among the highest in
the nation.

Levi was the first graduate to become president in
the University of Chicago's history. During his presidency from 1968 to 1975, Levi concentrated on reorganizing the undergraduate program so that the college
was divided into five academic units—biology, humanities, physical sciences, social sciences and general
studies—each one making up a small community. He
also placed much emphasis on improving the relationship between the university and the Chicago neighborhood in which it was situated.

As U.S. attorney general (1975–77), Levi stood
somewhere between a conservative and a liberal. He

overruled the FBI, commanding that papers from the Julius and Ethel Rosenberg case be released to their sons, yet asked Congress not to give raw FBI files to either the General Accounting Office or Senator Frank Church's subcommittee—both of whom were then investigating actions of the FBI during the Vietnam War era. He also criticized J. Edgar Hoover's practice of keeping files on political personalities and requested that the Justice Department look into the FBI's questionable COINTELPRO (counterintelligence program, aimed at domestic surveillance).

Levi is a fellow of the American Bar Foundation and a member of the American Law Institute. He has been a member of the advisory board of the *Antitrust Bulletin* and an associate editor of the *Natural Law Forum*. He published lectures he gave between 1963 and 1969 as president of the University of Chicago in *Point of View: Talks on Education* (Chicago, 1969). In his book Levi deals with the question of what a university is and is not, what are the purposes of undergraduate education and graduate research, the relationship between a university and its surroundings, and the reasons for student unrest. Levi does not believe that universities should be activist centers, but rather "social and political resources" whose chief functions are research and teaching. After serving as Attorney General he returned to the University of Chicago where he is Glen A. Lloyd Distinguished Service Professor.

CARL LEVIN

b. June 28, 1934
United States Senator

Carl Levin, United States Democratic senator from Michigan, represents a major wing in American political life—the outspoken and consistent liberal who is as much at home promoting domestic civil rights and the causes of peace and reconciliation abroad as he is in backing the moral ties between this country and Israel and diverse humane causes.

Carl Levin was born in Detroit to Saul, an attorney, and Bess (Levinson) Levin. After graduating from Detroit's Central High School in 1952, he attended Swarthmore College, where he received a B.A. degree in 1956, and Harvard Law School, where he completed his Doctor of Laws degree in 1959. Returning to Detroit, he practiced law for five years with the firm of Grossman, Human and Grossman. But the pull of public service was great— Levin's father's legal specialty was prison reform; his

brother, also a lawyer, had been a state senator; an uncle was a Michigan federal judge; and other relatives held important elected or appointed positions. Thus, in 1964 he secured an appointment as attorney general and special counsel for the Michigan Civil Rights Commission. Four years later he became special assistant attorney general of Michigan and the chief appellate attorney for the public defender's office in Detroit. The following year he ran successfully for the City Council.

In the wake of race riots that racked Detroit in 1967, Levin's leadership ability was put to a strong test. It bore fruit; in 1973 he was reelected to the City Council with a higher plurality than any other City Council member, thus becoming Detroit City Council president.

Levin's success was such that when his term expired in 1977 and he ran for the U.S. Senate, he not only defeated five other primary candidates but upset the Republican incumbent, Robert Griffin, in the November general election. Levin was the first Jewish senator ever elected from Michigan and the only progressive Democrat to defeat an incumbent Republican conservative in 1978 or 1980.

Throughout his tenure in office, Levin has been an ardent social reformer and a firm supporter of scrupulous budget control in government. He wrote legislation that supports the adoption of hard-to-place children and sets up a nationwide clearinghouse to facilitate the voluntary reunification of adopted children with their natural parents. He strongly opposes the death penalty for certain federal crimes and is an active partisan of the human rights movement, whether in countries dominated by the left or the right. He played a major role in obtaining the release of a Roman Catholic priest held as a political prisoner for five years in the Philippines and was also an active supporter of the move to free political prisoners in the Soviet Union and of their right to emigrate.

Levin believes strongly in the need to streamline government and to assure that funds are spent prudently. To that end, he advocates reforming the regulatory process and supports the legislative veto, sunset legislation, regulatory negotiation and competitive bidding. He headed an important investigation into abusive tactics by the Internal Revenue Service against small businessmen. In addition, Levin has fought for changes in Defense Department purchasing practices that would promote competitive bidding. He has sponsored many amendments to tighten wasteful military management practices that also weaken the fighting capability of American forces. He opposed the draft registration as unnecessary and was a leader in 1981 in the Senate's successful fight against the Reagan administration's attempt to sell AWACS to Saudi Arabia.

One example of his strong support for Israel was his remarks at a 1979 annual dinner of the Jewish Reconstructionist Foundation, in which he asserted critically, even sardonically:

> Oil and idealism do not mix. If idealism stands between Governor Connally's America [Connally, then a candidate for the 1980 Republican presidential nomination, had delivered a speech condemning the so-called Jewish lobby] and a secure oil supply—then IDEALISM [sic] must go. And if Israel—the one democratic state in the Middle East, the one stable, friendly government that exists in the Middle East—if Israel stands between Governor Connally's America and a secure oil supply—then Israel must go.

For his home state Levin headed the successful battle in Congress that prevented the bankruptcy of the Chrysler Corporation, thus preserving the jobs of 140,000 workers. He was also instrumental in bringing a Volkswagen of America auto plant to Michigan.

Levin is a member of the Armed Services Committee, the Governmental Affairs Committee and the Small Business Committee. He is active on the Democratic Senatorial Campaign Committee and the Environmental Study Conference, and he chairs Members of Congress for Peace Through Law.

In 1980 Levin's efforts on behalf of human rights earned him the first Alexander Solzhenitsyn Award presented by the Christian Solidarity International and the first Herbert H. Lehman Ethics Medal from the Jewish Theological Seminary of America.

Levin has regularly supported human rights everywhere, in Latin America and among rightist dictatorships, along with the rights of those trapped in Soviet-dominated societies. In early 1981 he, together with 50 senatorial co-sponsors, introduced a bill to make two Soviet families—both Pentecostalist Christians—living as refugees in the American Embassy in Moscow since June 27, 1978, eligible for U.S. citizenship. The next month he delivered the prestigious Raoul Wallenberg Lecture of the University of Michigan College of Architecture and Urban Planning, honoring the Swedish diplomat, a 1935 Michigan architecture graduate, who saved the lives of 100,000 Hungarian Jews destined for Nazi gas chambers and who then vanished into Soviet prisons, never to be heard from again. Levin said:

> We can learn from him that the moral dimensions of action demand our attention and that the ethical issues of conduct require our continued concern. That is, after all, the task we ultimately must accept when we realize that while a truly human life may be neither simple nor easy, it is both possible and desirable.

IRA LEVIN

b. August 27, 1929
Playwright and author

Ira Levin, popular writer and playwright, is perhaps most widely known for his fanciful novel, *Rosemary's Baby* (New York, 1967) and his highly-successful, witty Broadway whodunit, *Deathtrap*. Both these works reflect his wizardry at telling original stories and his talent for doing so with literary style and taste.

Ira Levin was born in New York City to Charles, a toy importer, and Beatrice (Schlansky) Levin. He studied at Drake University, the University of Iowa at Des Moines and then at New York University, where he was graduated in 1950 with a B.A. degree. He promptly set out to become a writer, which, save for a two year stint in the Army (from 1953-55), he has succeeded in doing.

His initial work of fiction, *Kiss Before Dying* (New York, 1953), was a book with expert characterization—a mark of his work—psychological probing, sharp evocation of place, stunning and unexpected developments, and a fine sense of writing. *Kiss* was a thriller, as so many of his books are, yet it also portrayed an avaricious and amoral social climber. It was later made into a film. Not until *Rosemary's Baby* did he achieve international recognition. The book tells a tale about wizardry and devils and the power of these strange beings. The story is about a young couple living on New York's fashionable West Side who fall in with a warm and friendly older couple—their neighbors—who succeed in bringing Rosemary's baby and Rosemary herself into their unearthly scheme. It became an enormously successful film.

Much the same blurring between the real and the make-believe is to be found in his other works, such as *The Boys From Brazil* (New York, 1976)—also made into a film. Here Levin composes a novel about ex-Nazis living in Brazil who hatch a plot to create clones of Adolph Hitler so as to recreate the Nazi Reich and its Fuhrer. It is an eerie, keen work of fantasy, riveting to the reader. And it could just possibly be true, or so his millions of readers might reason.

Very popular as a novelist, Levin is also a successful playwright. *No Time for Sergeants* (1955), a comedy adapted from a book by Mac Hyman, starred Andy Griffith as a rural Southern semi-literate draftee and showed how his innocence brought to heel the more sophisticated and realistic non-commissioned officers forced to cope with him. His first original play, *Interlock* (1958) was a psychological drama which closed after four performances. All the same, several subsequent plays were hits, including the comedy *Critic's Choice* (1960) which was directed by Otto Preminger and starred Henry Fonda, and *Deathtrap* (1978), in which a playwright, whose works have begun to be panned by the critics, plots to steal a wonderful drama, *Deathtrap*, written by a fledgling writer. The play is typically Levin: very funny, very creative, very entertaining and very popular with theater audiences.

For further information:
Levin, Ira. *The Stepford Wives.* New York: 1972.
————. *This Perfect Day.* New York: 1970.

DAVID LEVINE

b. December 20, 1926
Caricaturist; painter

David Levine is one of this country's most incisive and popular caricaturists of the powerful and well-known. His work appears regularly in the *New York Review of Books, Washington Post,* the *London Sunday Times* and on the covers of major news weeklies.

David Levine was born in Brooklyn, to Harry, a garment worker, and Lena (Isaacman) Levine. While still in grade school, Levine studied art at Pratt Institute in Brooklyn and the Brooklyn Museum Art School. In 1943 he graduated from Erasmus High School and began studying at the Stella Elkins Tyler School of Fine Arts in Philadelphia but left when he was drafted into the United States Army. Later he returned to Tyler and graduated with a Bachelor of Fine Arts degree in 1949, after which he returned to New York City to study with Hans Hofman, a leading abstract expressionist artist.

Levine had his first solo show in 1953 at the Davis Gallery in New York City and seven more shows there over the next 10 years. He drew garment workers at work, recalling his childhood visits with his father to Manhattan's garment district sweatshops, and people spending their summers at the beach. With his emphasis on mood and light, Levine's works called to mind the art of such 19th-century masters as James Whistler.

During all this time that Levine was involved with serious painting, he continued to draw satirical pictures, an avocation since his youth. In the late 1950s he tried to make money by designing Christmas cards in the elaborate style of 19th-century cartoonists. The venture failed. But soon after, Levine fashioned a catalog to accompany a show at the Davis Gallery. His art caught the eye of Clay Felker, then *Esquire* editor, who asked Levine to do small drawings for the magazine's cultural pages. It was then he began drawing caricatures of the famous.

In 1963, when the *New York Review of Books* was established, Levine found his most important platform. His drawings, which inspired people who felt the need to question the status quo, appear there regularly. With his singular gift of insight and precision, Levine not only draws attention to his subjects' physical appearance but also to their political and moral views. His subjects have included such popular figures as Philip Roth, Evelyn Waugh, Pope John XXIII, Charles de Gaulle, Sigmund Freud, Gore Vidal, John Updike and hundreds of others. He has also done caricatures of countless political figures. President Lyndon B. Johnson was drawn displaying a stomach scar in the shape of Vietnam. Levine drew former Vice President Spiro T. Agnew as a balloon. Levine has said that he looked for contradictory features, like the pained look in Lyndon Johnson's eyes as he smiled. While the artist's paintings are based on live models, his caricatures are drawn from photographs—yet they all have substance, feeling and depth.

In 1966 Levine held his first exhibition of caricature drawings at the Forum Gallery in New York City. He has since shown them at the Hirshhorn Museum in Washington, D.C., the Museum of Modern Art, the Whitney Museum of American Art and many others. He has published several books of his work, including *The Man from M.A.L.I.C.E.* (New York, 1966), *Pens and Needles: Literary Caricatures* (Boston, 1969), *No Known Survivors: David Levine's Political Plank* (Boston, 1970) and *The Art of David Levine* (New York, 1978). He has also illustrated several children's books, including *The Fables of Aesop* (Boston, 1975).

In addition to being a popular caricaturist, Levine's paintings are on exhibit in museums and galleries throughout the country. He tends to favor watercolors, relying on traditional methods, a dramatic sense of design and color. In *The Watercolors of David Levine: The Phillips Collection* (Seattle, Wash., 1981), his work reveals, too, his particular emphasis on human beings and the situations in which they find themselves. His subjects are commonplace people involved in mundane affairs, "enhanced and ennobled," said one catalog description aptly, "by a tragic element which is the vision of David Levine."

Levine has also taught at the Brooklyn Museum Art School and the School of Visual Arts in New York City. In 1965 he received both a Polk Award and a Guggenheim Fellowship.

IRVING M. LEVINE

b. December 7, 1929
Organization executive; social worker

Urban affairs specialist Irving Levine was one of the first American social activists to focus on the problems and dynamics of American ethnic groups. The founder in 1968 of the National Project on Ethnic America, which evolved in 1974 into the Institute of Pluralism and Group Identity at the American Jewish Committee, Levine has forged coalitions and dialogues among religious, ethnic, racial and social groups across the United States. His work has been instrumental in promoting a greater appreciation of diversity in America.

Irving M. Levine was born in the Brownsville section of Brooklyn to Meyer, a Lithuanian immigrant who made pockets in the garment district and Rebecca (Mansky) Levine, who was from Poland. Levine's leadership ability emerged while he was still a teen-ager. At age 17 he helped organize and then became president of the Brownsville Boys Club, whose membership ultimately numbered 2,000.

Levine did his undergraduate study at New York University, where he earned a B.S. degree in 1953. He then attended the NYU Center of Human Relations in 1954, where he studied social work, and completed a master's degree at the School of Social Work at the University of Wisconsin in 1956.

Levine's natural involvement in community relations kept him in Milwaukee for a while, to do community center work and to serve on the Wisconsin Governor's Advisory Commission. In the late 1950s, as the civil rights movement was in its earliest stirrings, Levine returned to Brooklyn, where he specialized in Jewish community relations work for the American Jewish Congress and became a consultant to the New York City Commission on Human Rights. He returned to the Midwest in 1959 to become director of the Indiana Jewish Community Relations Council and of the Ohio office of the American Jewish Committee. At the same time, he became involved in civil rights activities in

both states and played a leading role in the formation of the Indiana Civil Rights Commission and in the enactment of new civil rights legislation in Indiana and Ohio. These experiences made Levine a perfect candidate to become director of urban affairs for the American Jewish Committee's New York headquarters, a post he assumed in 1964. That year, in light of the many contributions he had already made in the human relations field, Levine received the Pope John XXIII Award from the Ohio Conference for Interracial Justice.

Sponsoring conferences and publishing papers in various aspects of ethnicity in the United States, Levine organized the National Consultation on Ethnic America, which was funded by the Ford Foundation and held at Fordham University in 1968. This was the year of some of the most violent racial clashes in America, and locally it was the year of the Ocean Hill-Brownsville teachers' strike in New York City, which led to the decentralization of New York City's public schools and to a polarization between Jews and New York City's blacks that has never quite been resolved. Levine used his role to develop new strategies of communication among ethnic group leaders that would result in a coming together to ventilate their feelings and an effort to try to understand each other.

Levine's major emphasis on a national scale was on what has often been called the "forgotten American"— America's white ethnics, whose particular problems, he feels, have often been overlooked in the process of addressing the problems of America's racial minorities. Urging a better understand of the "white ethnics" rather than rejecting them, Levine said: "Once you've dramatized people as racists, you throw them on the junk pile. It's not enough. You have to see their real grievances."

He is credited with devising a "white ethnic strategy," which was endorsed by a black American newspaper, *The Michigan Chronicle*, in a 1972 editorial. Levine's response to the editorial was to write:

> It is important for both blacks and whites that black opinion begins to take the realistic view that lower middle class whites have legitimate grievances that blacks as well as the establishment must respond to. Racism may be part of the problem, but an anti-white racist strategy may not be enough to win long overdue change.

With the formation of the Institute of Pluralism and Group Identity in 1974, Levine put into practice the American Jewish Committee's guiding principle that the protection of pluralism was always in the best interests of Jews and other ethnic groups. Within the Institute, four centers focus on group identity and mental health, women's issues, pluralistic education, and pluralism and the media. His programs include developing strategies among community leaders to depolarize racial and religious tensions; training and sensitizing professionals to special problems in their community or workplace; addressing special employment problems of working-class women and other minorities; and employing the media to promote a better image of America's ethnic groups, including blue-collar whites as well as blacks, Hispanics and others.

Levine has also been involved in immigration issues and is a board member of the American Immigration and Citizenship Conference. In that role he heads a special committee on Immigration and Human Rights. He has been an urban affairs consultant with government and private groups and served the New York City Mayor's Office as an adviser on "neighborhood government."

Levine has written many articles about the new pluralism and its effect on white Americans, urban Jews and minorities. He hosted a weekly radio show entitled *New York Tomorrow* and in 1976 narrated a one-hour documentary for NBC called "The Ethnic Factor." He has also lectured in universities across the United States.

In 1982, along with like-minded fellow Jews, he helped organize opposition to the nuclear arms race and nuclear proliferation, a movement designed to increase Jewish resistance to those promoting reckless armament policies.

For further information:

Lahart, Kevin. "Ethnics '71. What Happens When the Melting-Pot Fire Goes Out." *Newsday*, June 5, 1971.

Levine, Irving M. "The Urban Crisis and the Jewish Community." *Union Seminary Quarterly Review*, Spring 1968.

Levine, Irving M., and Herman, Judith M. "The New Pluralism." In *Overcoming Middle Class Rage*, edited by Murray Friedman. Philadelphia: 1971.

JAMES LEVINE

b. June 23, 1943
Conductor

James Levine, appointed principal conductor and music director of the Metropolitan Opera in 1972, had been conducting professionally since his teens and had made his professional piano debut at age 10 with the Cincinnati Symphony Orchestra. He came from a family steeped in theater and music, so his affinity for opera was natural.

James Levine was born to Lawrence and Helen (Gold-stein) Levine in Cincinnati, Ohio. His father, an executive with a dress manufacturing company, played the violin and during the 1930s led a dance band under the name of "Larry Lee." Levine's mother was an actress on Broadway playing ingenue roles prior to her marriage. Levine was picking out melodies on the piano at about age 3, sang before he talked and began piano lessons at age 4. He began conducting amateur groups as a child in addition to performing on the piano regularly. In his teens he conducted orchestras in the Cincinnati area.

Levine studied piano with Rudolf Serkin at Marlboro, Vermont in 1956. In 1961 he enrolled at Juilliard, where he studied with Rosina Lhevinne. But conducting was his strength, and from 1964 to 1970 he was apprentice, then assistant to conductor George Szell of the Cleveland Orchestra before coming to the Metropolitan Opera in New York.

The "kid who conquered the mighty Met," as he was dubbed, was appointed principal conductor in 1972 and musical director in 1975 and has been called "possibly the most significant operatic conductor/administrator since Toscanini." Noted particularly for his skill with Italian opera, Levine told Speight Jenkins that he "will not conduct the music of a composer whose life he has not sufficiently immersed himself in to gain an 'artistically valid' relationship" (*New York Post*, October 11, 1979).

Levine's tenure at the Met has combined financial success with controversy. Critic Irving Kolodin once wondered in the *Saturday Review* (June 1980) if Levine was "wrecking the Met" because of the supposed way he had alienated some stars and what Kolodin charged were poor artistic choices. Yet the Met continues to thrive, and two 1981 productions, the Stravinsky triple bill designed by David Hockney and the Franco Zeffirelli staging of *La Bohème*, played to capacity audiences and received laudatory reviews. Attendance at all performances is higher than ever. In addition, he has commissioned two American operas from John Corigliano and Jacob Druckman, which will be performed in 1985. He also hopes to found a "Piccolo Met" in New York City—a smaller theater appropriate for more intimate operas and ballet.

Levine still plays the piano occasionally, to much praise. He also guest-conducts the Chicago Symphony at the Ravinia Festival for a month each year and does two operas yearly at the Salzburg Festival. Also, he regularly conducts the spring tour of the Philadelphia Orchestra and, when in Europe, frequently leads the Berlin and Vienna Philharmonic orchestras. In 1982 he conducted Wagner's *Parsifal* at Bayreuth, to commemorate the opera's centennial.

NAOMI LEVINE

b. April 15, 1923
University official; attorney

Long before it was commonplace for women to combine demanding, full-time careers with raising a family, Naomi Bronheim Levine was doing both. A lawyer, a former professor, and the first woman to hold the post of national executive director of the American Jewish Congress, Levine is also an outspoken supporter of Jewish family life within the context of changing lifestyles and needs of family members.

Naomi Bronheim was born in New York City on April 15, 1923, to Nathan and Malvena (Mermelstein) Bronheim. She graduated from Hunter College with a Bachelor of Arts degree in 1944 and from the Columbia University Law School, where she was an editor on the *Law Review,* with an LL.B. in 1946 and a J.D. in 1963.

Levine practiced law privately with two New York City firms, Scandrett, Tuttle and Chalier and Charles Gottlieb and Associates, and was for many years assistant professor in race relations at the John Jay College of Criminal Justice, a branch of the City University of New York. In concert with her teaching, she also wrote extensively about the problems of integration in public schools. She is the author of a study guide entitled *Crisis in the Classroom,* published in 1960, which sympathetically explores academic freedom, and *From Color Blind to Color Conscious,* (New York, 1964), a book strongly in favor of civil rights. *Schools in Crisis: Ocean-Hill Brownsville Case Study* (New York, 1969), written with Richard Cohen while Levine was director of the Commission on Urban Affairs at the American Jewish Congress, was critical of decentralization in New York City public schools and examined the bitter fights that divided blacks and union teachers during the 1968 teachers' strike in New York City.

Levine has also written and spoken about specific Jewish social problems. Her book of readings, *The Jewish Poor: An American Awakening* (edited with Martin Hochbaum) (New York, 1972), examined one of the most sensitive, and until then for the most part, ignored problems in the Jewish community: There were literally hundreds of thousands of Jewish men and women living in poverty, hidden from the government, the media and most fellow Jews.

At the American Jewish Congress, Levine helped develop a more specifically Jewish agenda reflecting more closely the concerns of its membership. The AJC

supported the Union Federation of Teachers in the school strike and was a "friend of the court" on behalf of Baake, who sued the University of California at Davis Medical School for discriminating against him because he was white. At the same time, the AJC continued to adhere to its traditional loyalties to liberalism and civil liberties.

Levine is now vice-president for external affairs at New York University. But she has maintained active participation in Jewish communal affairs, speaking frequently to Jewish groups. In a 1981 talk at a Federation of Jewish Philanthropies Sunday Seminar, she shared many of her concerns about the changing textures of Jewish life with her audience. "Unfortunately, many of us, including myself, have substituted Jewish politics for Jewish culture and literacy," she said. "We have made fighting anti-Semitism our religion, or fighting for Russian Jews or Israel, our religion. And if by chance anti-Semitism were no more, and the Russian Jews were finally free to emigrate, and peace finally came to the Middle East—how in the world would we identify as Jews?" On the subject of changing roles of women, she added, "Women's liberation will not go away. More and more, your daughters will have careers. Federation should support institutions which help a woman to have a career, and, at the same time, a family life if that is her wish. More attention must be given, too, to the single parent."

PHILIP LEVINE

b. January 10, 1928
Poet; teacher

One might call Philip Levine an "applied poet," for he believes that poetry can be a political tool and that it should reach out to audiences whom poets seldom address. He thus not only writes poetry that often deals with themes of working-class life but is an active and popular poetry teacher.

Philip Levine was born in Detroit, Michigan to Harry, a businessman, and Esther Gertrude (Priscol) Levine. Levine studied at Wayne State University in Detroit, where he received a B.A. degree in 1950 and a Master of Arts degree four years later, While a graduate student, he also worked in a variety of odd jobs, one of which included an assembly line at a Ford automobile plant. These experiences helped significantly to fuel his direction as a poet, as did studies with poet John Berryman. He left Detroit in 1955 both to teach and to pursue additional graduate studies at the University of Iowa. After earning a Master of Fine Arts degree there two years later, he headed west and in 1958 became an instructor at the Fresno campus of California State University. In 1969 he was named a professor of creative writing.

But academic credentials do not appeal to Levine as do the experiences of the "real world," a world of ordinary pople and commonplace objects. In a 1981 interview for *Life* magazine, Levine explained: "My aim has been to write for the people for whom there are no poems. It's also partly a reaction against the extraordinary elitism of poets I read, like Pound and Eliot."

To that end, Levine often uses harsh language, simple words and a vernacular vocabulary in his poems, which might thus seem deceptively simple but are in fact quite complex. Poet Hayden Carruth comments that "to distinguish exactly the quality of Philip Levine's poems is not easy. He falls outside categories." Yet the consensus is that, according to critic Richard Schramm, his "poetry is nearly relentless in its excellence. Open any Levine volume and the first thing you encounter is a vibrant, concentrated realness caught through a matrix of details and precisely placed acts. . . ."

Levine published his first collection, *On the Edge* (New York), in 1963 and has followed with new volumes on the average of every other year. He has been a Guggenheim fellow (1973-74) and a National Endowment for the Arts grantee and has lectured widely. During the Vietnam War, Levine was prominent in the anti-war movement and is generally recognized as one of the outstanding American poets to emerge in the 1960s and 1970s. In 1979 he won a National Book Award and in 1980 he was among the select group of poets invited to the Carter White House for an afternoon of reading. "Philip Levine is the great American poet of proletarian revolution in our time," said a *Village Voice* critic in 1982. Indeed, *One For The Rose* (New York, 1982) is dedicated to Buenaventura Durruti, a Spanish anarchist who shot the Catholic archbishop of Saragossa and who was himself killed during the Spanish Civil War.

For further information:
Levine, Philip. *Ashes: Poems New & Old.* New York: 1979.
————. *Don't Ask.* Ann Arbor, Mich: 1981.
————. *One For The Rose.* New York: 1982.
————. *The Names of The Lost.* New York: 1976.
————. *Nineteen Thirty-Three.* New York: 1974.

ANTHONY JOSEPH LEWIS

b. March 27, 1927
Journalist

Pulitzer Prize-winning Anthony Lewis is one of America's most respected and influential journalists. A former United States Supreme Court reporter for *The New York Times* and author of the highly acclaimed *Gideon's Trumpet* (New York, 1964), a book based on a historic Court decision, Lewis is probably best-known for the liberal positions he assumes as twice-weekly editorial columnist for *The New York Times*.

Anthony Lewis was born in New York City to Kassel, a textile executive and Sylvia (Surut) Lewis, who worked at the Young Men and Women's Hebrew Association in Manhattan for many years. Lewis demonstrated an interest in writing from his youth. After graduating from New York's Horace Mann School in 1944, where he was president of the student organization and editor of the school's weekly paper, he matriculated at Harvard College, where English was his major. At the school he joined the Signet Society, a literary club, and worked on the *Harvard Crimson,* the undergraduate daily, as executive editor and then managing editor.

Upon graduation with a Bachelor of Arts degree from Harvard in 1948, Lewis was hired to write for the "Week in Review" section of the *Sunday New York Times*. He left in August 1952, when Sunday editor Lester Markel suggested he get some reporting experience. After several months working for the Democratic National Committee, Lewis became a general assignment reporter for the Washington *Daily News* in December 1952.

It did not take long for Lewis to gain distinction as a reporter. He covered stories on the Pentagon, presidential press conferences, interviews with politicians, as well as Senate subcommittee hearings led by Senator Joseph McCarthy in 1953. During the McCarthy era Lewis was assigned to compare the number of persons dismissed by the government as security risks with the number that was publicized, a job that led to Lewis's winning the 1955 Pulitzer Prize for national reporting. The award was received for his series of articles in 1954 on the case of Abraham Chasanow, a civilian employee of the U.S. Navy who had been discharged as a "security risk." Lewis proved that the charges were groundless, Chasanow was reinstated and the articles later became the basis for a film, *Three Brave Men*. The American Newspaper Guild gave Lewis its annual Heywood Broun Award in 1955 for his Chasanow articles.

Lewis's defense of justice was further demonstrated when he worked as Supreme Court and Department of Justice correspondent for the Washington bureau of *The New York Times* from 1955 to 1964. Considered by many to be one of the finest analytical journalists to cover the Supreme Court, Lewis displayed his legal expertise in *Gideon's Trumpet*. The book is an illuminating account of Clarence Earl Gideon, who was sentenced to a five-year prison term for breaking into a Florida poolroom. From his jail cell the semiliterate Gideon wrote a petition to the Supreme Court asking it to review his conviction on the ground that he had not been given a lawyer to assist in his defense. The Court unanimously reversed the conviction in 1963, and at a new trial, with legal counsel, Gideon was acquitted.

Lewis, who won an award for *Gideon's Trumpet* as the best factual crime book from the Mystery Writers of America, has also published *Portrait of a Decade: The Second American Revolution* (New York, 1965), which deals with the struggle to achieve civil rights for blacks; and *The Supreme Court and How It Works* (New York, 1967), a text for young high school readers that explains the institution.

From 1964 to 1972 Lewis was chief of the *Times'* London bureau; since then he has been a regular columnist. Through those years he has maintained a consistently liberal stance and written many impassioned pieces on the major issues of the day. During the Watergate era he was one of the first to question the veracity of Nixon. An early opponent of the Vietnam War, he has also challenged American assumptions about El Salvador and Central America, harshly criticized the Reagan administration's favorable attitude toward Argentina and strongly supported the Polish Solidarity union against the Polish and Soviet Communist parties.

Above all a universalist who rejects the dichotomy articulated by neo-conservatives and others on the right between "good" authoritarians and "bad" totalitarians, he wrote a front-page *Times* review in 1981—*Prisoner Without a Name, Cell Without a Number*—extolling Jacobo Timerman's biographical account of torture by Argentines and damning his opponents. When, for example, Secretary of State Alexander Haig was asked in 1981 by Rep. Gerry Studds (D., Mass.) what values the United States shared with Argentina's military other than anti-communism, Haig answered, "A belief in God." To which Lewis retorted, "Could he have meant the God of Torquemada? Of the Cossacks who terrorized the Jews? Of Julius Streicher?" And when U.S. Ambassador to the United Nations Jeane Kirkpatrick attended a dinner at the Argentine Embassy in Washington after the Argentines had occupied the Falkland Islands in 1982, Lewis was extremely critical of her action.

Much of Lewis's criticisms have also been aimed at Menachem Begin's government in Israel, particularly his Greater Israel policies and the treatment accorded Palestinians on the West Bank and in Gaza. Very often Lewis's columns on the subject are greeted with intense counter-criticism in the *Times'* letters column as well as in occasional Anglo-Jewish newspapers. In mid-1981, following the Israeli bombing of Beirut, which left hundreds of civilians dead and injured, and the Palestinian rocketing of northern Israeli towns, Lewis wrote that "only American leadership can rescue Israel from the dead end where a policy of force without diplomacy, without politics, has brought it." And when in 1982 some Palestinians were killed by Israeli troops, he repeated his condemnation.

He is outspoken on other human rights issues as well, including the plight of Soviet Jews, political prisoners abroad and America's minorities. For example, in several columns he described the persecution of Soviet physicist Vladimir Kislik and Argentine physicist Elena Sevilla. Both were arrested and imprisoned by their governments: Kislik after he applied for a visa to go to Israel; Sevilla with no ostensible explanation—but five days after giving birth. Public pressure led to Kislik's release, but he was soon rearrested and jailed and was eventually sentenced to three years' hard labor on unfounded accusations of "hooliganism." After serving some time in prison, Sevilla was finally allowed to immigrate to the United States. Lewis wrote that their "stories . . . make a simple and fundamental point: the indivisibility of concern for humanity . . . . If we close our eyes to official brutality here or there—in the Soviet Union, in Uganda or Cambodia—we risk our own civilization."

When President Reagan threatened to end federal funding to a legal aid program for the poor, Lewis attacked him, writing:

> the lawyers who represent the poor in civil matters are doing conservative work in the most fundamental sense. They are building respect for the law among people who tend to be disconnected from society and give them the sense that they have a stake in the system.

And later, in a column about the efforts of the Moral Majority to impose their personal stands against abortion and the Equal Rights Amendment and for prayer in public schools, Lewis commented, "Another irony is that some of the same men who talk about translating the word of God into American legislation show little concern for the godless cruelties in other governments."

FLORA LEWIS

d.o.b. not available (app. 1919 or 1920)
Journalist

In the days when women seeking journalism careers usually found themselves assigned to the society column or the women's page, *New York Times* columnist Flora Lewis was busy reporting hard news. Her ability to describe and analyze the most intricate political processes and events has since taken her to nearly every corner of the globe, reporting for a major wire service and for the most prestigious newspapers in the United States. She has received many press awards for her distinguished and perceptive writing which includes coverage of the Vietnam War, the Six-Day War in Israel and the 1968 political conventions in Chicago and Miami, as well as an in-depth examination of Islam in 1980 for *The New York Times,* for which she has written since 1972.

Flora Lewis was born to Benjamin and Pauline (Kallin) Lewis. She received a B.A. degree from the University of California at Los Angeles in 1941 and an M.S. degree in journalism from Columbia University in 1942.

Her first newspaper job was with the *Los Angeles Times* during her senior year at UCLA, where she was campus reporter. For the next four years she reported for the Associated Press from New York; from Washington, where she covered the Navy and State Department; and from London, where she arrived on assignment two days before V-J Day. She then free-lanced from 1946 to 1954, writing for *Time, The New York Times Sunday Magazine, The Economist* of London, *The London Observer* and *France-Soir* of Paris. (Lewis also found time in 1945 to marry Sydney Gruson, now vice chairman of *The New York Times* Company, and raise three children. They were divorced in 1972.)

In 1956 Lewis joined the *Washington Post* as its correspondent in Warsaw and Prague. Two years later she was transferred to Bonn, West Germany, where she remained for four years. During this period she covered the 1961 division of Berlin into a walled city. She went to London for the *Post* in 1962, and in 1965 she returned to the United States to open the *Post's* New York bureau.

From 1967 to 1972 Lewis wrote a syndicated column published throughout the United States under the auspices of *Newsday.* She joined *The New York Times* in 1972 as its Paris bureau chief and became European diplomatic correspondent in 1976. In March 1980 Lewis was named *New York Times* foreign affairs correspond-

ent. Several months later a twice-weekly column by Lewis became a regular feature on the *Times'* op-ed page.

Lewis had used the column to discuss events from the world's major capitals and from its more obscure locales. She does not merely report but analyzes her subjects in depth and detail, and if at times her work seems to be straight reportage, in fact she often takes strong stands, based on her years of experience and her innate sense of justice. For example, in a column entitled "Hot and Cold Terrorists," she describes the impact of various terrorist movements in West Germany, Italy, Spain and elsewhere on their respective populations and then moves into a discussion about the proposed nomination by President Reagan of Ernest W. Lefever to be his human rights administrator, writing: "Distinctions between 'friendly authoritarians' and 'hostile totalitarians,' as would be made by Ernest Lefever, the nominee to run the State Department's human rights program, can do more damage to the cause of freedom than murderous gangs." She said of Northern Ireland that "[it] is a disgrace to the whole European community and the whole western world" and then wrote:

> It's hard to feel sympathy for any faction in this struggle of blind hatred which can bring no solution. But it's becoming intolerable to watch the agonies and flames on TV screens in a world which considers the noble compromise of democracy and respect for liberty as its mark of superiority.

And she has been consistently critical of Prime Minister Menachem Begin's foreign policies.

During the French elections in 1981, Lewis wrote several columns describing French sentiment for the "old guard" of then-President Giscard and new leanings toward the Socialist candidate Francois Mitterand. Although she felt the elections would be close—as indeed they were—just before the election she predicted correctly that Mitterand would win and indirectly indicated her support for the change in government.

A visit to Ghana proved emotional as she toured several buildings, now museums, that once housed slaves en route to the Americas. Viewing the progress that has been made in modern Africa, she commented that Africans do not look back into their past—they cannot.

Throughout her years as newspaper correspondent, Lewis has published articles in most major American magazines, including *The New York Times Magazine, The New Yorker, Atlantic, Saturday Review* and *Life.* She has also written three books. *Case History of Hope* (New York, 1959) covers events in post-Stalin Poland from 1953 to 1957. The focus is on the evolution in Poland from an atmosphere of total despair to one of hope for a better life ahead. *Red Pawn* (New York, 1964), Lewis's second book, explores the 1949 disappearance of an American named Noel Field and members of his family while living in Prague and Warsaw, although their alleged involvement in spy cases and purges was never confirmed. *One of Our H-Bombs is Missing* (New York, 1967) is the story of a mid-air accident near Palomares, Spain, during which a B-52 bomber carrying four H-bombs literally lost one of them. The book traces the events leading up to and following the accident.

Lewis received the first of three awards from the Overseas Press Club, for magazine reporting, in 1956. The other two, for foreign reporting, were awarded in 1962 and 1978. She also won the Columbia Journalism School's 50th Anniversary Honor Award in 1963, the Aspen Institute's Award for Journalistic Excellence in 1977 and the Award for Distinguished Diplomatic Reporting from Georgetown University's School of Foreign Affairs in 1978. Her most recent award is the cross of Chevalier of the Legion of Honor from the French government in early 1981.

JERRY LEWIS

b. March 16, 1926
Comedian; actor; film director

Like the lost boys in *Peter Pan,* Jerry Lewis is an actor who, by most standards, just "won't grow up." The eternal child, whose movie audiences are primarily children but whose gutsier live performances have greater adult appeal, Lewis is in fact a skilled comedian whose slapstick style and originality have made him a popular figure in Europe, often compared to the screen clowns Buster Keaton and Charlie Chaplin.

Joseph Levich was born in Newark, New Jersey, the son of vaudeville performers Danny and Mona Levich, who themselves took the professional stage name "Lewis." Danny Lewis was a songwriter and performer, while Mona Lewis played piano on the radio and accompanied her husband on tour. Jerry Lewis began his career at age 5, when he sang "Brother, Can You Spare a Dime?" at a Borscht Belt hotel in the Catskills. Even then he cultivated a reputation as a comic "nut." By the time he entered high school in Irvington, New Jersey, he was nicknamed "Id" for "idiot." He dropped out of high school in the 10th grade and began performing in some of the hotels where his parents had been earlier, specializing in an act in which he mouthed the lyrics to records. This routine, combined with the frenetic antics he had perfected on stage, earned him early success, and

before he was 20 he was working regularly and earning a comfortable income.

In 1946 Lewis formed a partnership with Dean Martin—the suave, Italian-American singer, straight man and perfect foil to Lewis's seeming lunacy. Beginning with a nightclub act in Atlantic City in which they exchanged insults and injected slapstick into their routines, the pair became one of the most popular comic duos of the time. For the next 10 years, as their weekly salaries soared from $350 to several thousand dollars, they also appeared together in 16 films produced by Paramount Pictures, including *My Friend Irma* (1950), *At War with the Army* (1951), *The Caddy* (1953), *Pardners* (1956) and others. For the most part, their cinema following in the United States was juvenile—but very lucrative.

But in 1956 the partnership dissolved, and Lewis went out on his own, performing in nightclubs and starring in many films. His nightclub act was then, and has remained, a successful and distinctive component of his career. Beginning in 1956, when he replaced Judy Garland in Las Vegas, and to the present, Lewis has been outstanding in pantomime, slapstick and satire and has a particular skill in engaging his audiences directly into his skits—and ridiculing them, but without malice.

His film career, though prolific and financially successful at the outset, has been more erratic. From 1956 to 1969 he starred in many films, most of them directed by Frank Tashlin, whose previous work as a cartoonist marked his style as a film director. Tashlin's films with Lewis, including *Rock-a-Bye Baby* (1958), *Cinderfella* (1960), *The Disorderly Orderly* (1964) and others, were superficial, kooky and especially popular with children. In the early 1960s Lewis began directing his own films, starring himself, including *The Bellboy* (1960), *The Nutty Professor* (1963), *One More Time* (1969) and others, all marked by the same chaotic humor. By the late 1960s, however, Lewis's popularity was on the wane, as audiences seemed fed up with the comic's role of perpetual adolescent and fumbling failure.

In the United States Lewis dropped out of sight as a comic performer, except for occasional nightclub performances and his annual stint as organizer and host of a Labor Day television "telethon" to raise money for muscular dystrophy. Begun in 1953 as a two-hour show broadcast from Los Angeles, the telethon has grown into a production more than 20 hours long, which invariably generates millions of dollars. Although some of Lewis's critics have questioned whether personal aggrandizement is the primary motive in his fund-raising efforts, most agree that the telethon is one of the most genuine and successful of its kind.

In 1981 Lewis appeared in a film he directed called *Hardly Working,* about an unemployed clown trying to make a comeback. His first movie in nearly 12 years, it was roundly panned, as Lewis's style had not changed. Nonetheless, 1981 signaled an important turn in his career, when Lewis appeared in his first dramatic role as television personality Jerry Langford in Martin Scorsese's *The King of Comedy.*

Although Jerry Lewis fans rarely see the serious side of the comedian, in fact, he is a dedicated and committed artist whose best work has not been seen. In the mid-1960s, for example, he made a film that was never released called *The Day the Clown Cried,* in which a clown entertaining children at Auschwitz later followed them into the gas chamber.

For further information:
Lewis, Jerry. *The Total Film-Maker.* New York: 1971.
Marx, Arthur. *Everybody Loves Somebody Sometime (Especially Himself).* New York: 1974.

ROBERT JAY LIFTON

b. May 16, 1926
Psychiatrist; author

Robert Jay Lifton, psychoanalyst, psychohistorian and prolific writer, has been extensively involved in the study of the major traumas of our time—the atomic destruction of Hiroshima, the Holocaust and the Vietnam War. He is especially concerned with the relationship between individual personality and historical change.

Born in New York City to Harold, a businessman, and Ceil (Roth) Lifton, Robert Jay Lifton attended Cornell University between 1942 and 1944 and was awarded his medical degree from New York Medical College in 1948. He interned at the Jewish Hospital of Brooklyn in 1948–49 and conducted his psychiatric residency training at the Downstate Medical Center in Brooklyn in 1951–53. Then, for two years he served as an Air Force psychiatrist in Japan and Korea. Following his discharge, he was a faculty member of the Washington School of Psychiatry in 1954–55, and afterward, from 1956 to 1961 he was named Research Associate in Psychiatry at Harvard, where he was affiliated with the University's Center for East Asian Studies. In 1961 he joined the faculty of Yale University, where he holds the Foundations' Fund for Research of Psychiatry professorship.

Much of the thrust of his work revolves around the impact of war and barbarism on human beings. His book *Death in Life: Survivors of Hiroshima* (New York, 1968) received the National Book Award in the Sciences and the Van Wyck Brooks Award for nonfiction in 1969. It was a study of the psychological impact of the atomic bombing of Hiroshima on its survivors. In it he argued that the nuclear destruction of Hiroshima had much to do with what he has termed the "boundarylessness of human destruction. That is why I called my book about Hiroshima *Death in Life.* The death that survivors carried on in their continuing lives was not the ordinary structured death of individuals; it was grotesque, absurd, collective, unacceptable, unabsorbable death. That's what the politicians don't talk about."

His other books include *Home from the War: Vietnam Veterans—Neither Victims nor Executioners* (New York, 1974), which dealt with anti-war veterans and how they were harmed by the military experiences in a war they learned to hate (it was nominated for the National Book Award in 1974); *Six Lives/Six Deaths: Portraits from Modern Japan,* with Shuichi Kato and Michael R. Reich (New Haven, 1979); and *The Broken Connection: Death and the Continuity of Life* (New York, 1979), in which he argues that the thread between life and death has to be understood in order to reduce anger, anxiety, depression, guilt and violence. His most recent work, titled *From Healer to Killer—The Doctors of Auschwitz* (New York, 1981) deals specifically with medical behavior in Auschwitz and with Nazi physicians in general. In an interview published in *American Medical News* (June 13, 1980), Lifton admitted that 27 interviews with Nazi doctors often left him pained and unsettled. But he has long been committed to "studying the extreme historical situations in our era and to developing a suitable psychological approach to them." After his interviews with the Nazi doctors, he said, "Doctors were crucial to everything that furthered Nazi racial policies, including mass killings."

For relaxation, Lifton is a caricaturist, and he has published his drawings in two collections, *Birds* (New York, 1969) and *PsychoBirds* (Taitsville, Vermont, 1978). In one sketch two birds are speaking to each other. "Do your studies demonstrate that American society can recover from a nuclear attack?" asks the first. "Yes!" answers the second, "all except the people." His humor is deadly serious, reflecting his very real concerns about the extreme historical situations of our times.

Lifton is a member of Physicians for Social Responsibility. He delivered a major address at its February 1980 symposium on the Medical Consequences of Nuclear Weapons and Nuclear War, taking issue, among other things, with those "like Edward Teller . . . in his extraordinarily misleading book, *The Legacy of Hiroshima* [who] believe that 'rational behavior' means having the 'courage' to use nuclear weapons when tactically necessary and to be 'prepared to survive an all-out nuclear attack.'" Said Lifton, "My response is that this rational behavior is the logic of madness, and deadly madness at that." And in an interview in the *Sunday Cape Cod Times* (August 17, 1980), he underlined the theme of the serious risks of a limited nuclear exchange: "[Military strategists] project scenarios. They don't imagine or picture human beings being burned, destroyed, annihilated in the most grotesque way."

For further information:

Lifton, Robert Jay. *America and the Asian Revolutions.* Chicago: 1970.
———. *Boundaries: Psychological Man in Revolution.* New York: 1970.
———. *History and Human Survival.* New York: 1968.
———. *Revolutionary Immortality: Mao Tse-tung and the Chinese Cultural Revolution.* New York: 1968.
———. *Thought Reform and the Psychology of Totalism: A Study of "Brainwashing" in China.* New York: 1961.
Lifton, Robert Jay; Falk, Richard A.; and Kolko, Gabriel. *Crimes of War.* New York: 1971.
Lifton, Robert Jay and Olson, Eric. *Living and Dying.* New York: 1974.
Lifton, Robert Jay, and Olson, Eric, eds. *Explorations in Psychohistory: The Wellfleet Papers.* New York: 1975.

SOL M. LINOWITZ

b. December 7, 1913
Corporate executive; attorney; diplomat

Sol Linowitz, who helped build the Xerox Corporation into one of the major world firms dealing with high technology, has also been a presidential troubleshooter and diplomat in such unstable regions as Central America and the Middle East.

Sol Myron Linowitz was born in Trenton, New Jersey to Joseph, a fruit importer, and Rose (Oglenskye) Linowitz, both of whom had emigrated from Austria. When the Depression arrived, his family was hurt economically. As a result, he worked his way through Hamilton College in Clinton, New York waiting on tables and playing the violin in dance bands. In 1935 he was awarded his B.A. degree and elected to Phi Beta

Kappa. Three years later he earned his Doctor of Laws degree from Cornell University Law School, having served as editor in chief of the *Cornell Law Quarterly.*

Linowitz then went to work for a small law firm in Rochester, New York. Following a stint in the Office of Price Administration from 1942 until 1944, he joined the Naval Reserve as a Lieutenant, serving from 1944 until 1946. Discharged, he returned to Rochester to resume the practice of law and to start, with Joseph C. Wilson, the Haloid Company, a smallish manufacturer of photographic equipment that was eventually transformed into the multi-national Xerox, for which he ultimately became general counsel, chairman of the executive committee and chairman of the board (1955-66). During his tenure, Xerox integrated its work force and also began advertising quality television programs, such as William Shirer's "Rise and Fall of the Third Reich" and Arthur Miller's drama "The Death of a Salesman."

Linowitz left Rochester and Xerox in 1966 and became a partner in the Washington, D.C. law firm of Coudert Brothers, specializing in international law. It was there that he became known for his quiet and conciliatory manner, a quality that stood him in good stead as a diplomat. Between 1966 and 1969 he was United States representative to the Alliance for Progress and, simultaneously, United States Ambassador to the Organization of American States. In 1977 he was named co-negotiator (with Ellsworth Bunker) to develop the Panama Canal treaties (which were ratified by the United States and Panama) and given the rank of ambassador once again. Soon after, he was named President Jimmy Carter's emissary in the arduous peace deliberations between Egypt and Israel. Linowitz became well-known as an extremely patient and very deliberate negotiator and diplomat and almost always earned the respect of all parties because of these characteristics and because of his fair-mindedness even in the most emotional disputes.

When Linowitz served as President Carter's representative on Middle East peace negotiations from 1979-1981, he recognized the fact that there were no easy solutions to the impasse between Egypt and Israel. "It was the genius of the negotiators at Camp David that they understood that too many past efforts" had not succeeded "because the parties had grasped for too much too soon." Linowitz quickly realized that he could only hope to succeed in his mission if he took into consideration the historic mistrust between Egypt and Israel, their profound emotional anger, and the enormous stakes involved. "The Palestinian problem is among the most inflammable," he said in 1982, reflecting on his experience as a diplomat. "It will not go away."

Devoted to the concept of public service, Linowitz has been chairman of the National Urban Coalition and chairman of the American Jewish Committee's National Executive Council. In addition, he has served on the boards of the Center for Inter-American Relations, the Salk Institute, the Council of Foreign Relations and the National Humanities Center.

SEYMOUR MARTIN LIPSET

b. March 18, 1922
Sociologist

Political scientist and sociologist Seymour Martin Lipset employs neither a conservative nor a liberal approach to his studies of sociology, history and society. Instead, he stresses the role of ideas as the prime movers of history. In the nearly 40 books that he has written or edited—covering such topics as socialism, trade unions, the student rebellion and the effects of the industrial revolution—Lipset argues frequently that a key motivating idea in American history was not so much freedom or individualism as equality and achievement.

Lipset was born in Manhattan, the son of Max, a printer, and Lena (Lippman) Lipset. After he received his B.S.S. degree from the City College of New York in 1943, he studied at Columbia University until 1945 and then lectured in sociology at the University of Toronto from 1946 until 1948. He received his Ph.D. in sociology from Columbia University in 1949, while he was an assistant professor at the University of California at Berkeley.

Much of Lipset's earlier work involved socialism and trade unionism in America. His first book, *Agrarian Socialism* (Berkeley, 1950), studied the socialist government of Saskatchewan, Canada in the 1940s. At the time the proletariat constituted only 5 percent of the population in the province. Lipset investigated the economic and cultural factors that produced socialism in Saskatchewan and compared them to agrarian radicalism in America in the 1870s and 1880s, suggesting along the way that reform groups become conservative when they assume power, since they soon become upholders of position and status.

Lipset left the University of California at Berkeley in 1950 and spent the next six years as a professor of sociology at Columbia University. He returned to Berkeley in 1956 and spent the next decade there. In 1966 he joined the faculty of Harvard University.

Lipset soon began to explore the wider dimensions of political dynamics in America. *The First New Nation: The United States in Historical and Comparative Perspective* (New York, 1963) treats the American national experience as a potential model for the emerging countries of the world, comparing it to other established democracies. *The Politics of Unreason,* co-authored with Earl Raab (New York, 1970), is an examination of right-wing extremist movements in America from 1790 to 1970. Focusing on extremist movements before and after the Civil War, during the "bigoted twenties" and the Depression, Lipset examines such organizations and individuals as the Ku Klux Klan, Senator Joseph McCarthy, the John Birch Society and George Wallace. He describes right-wing extremism as a politics of backlash and despair that arises when a traditional ruling class feels threatened by outsiders who have been traditionally excluded from government or society. The book won the first Gunnar Myrdal Prize in 1971 as a major contribution to the study of humankind and the environment.

Along with many of his academic contemporaries, Lipset was startled and challenged by the student rebellions of the 1960s and 1970s. He wrote and edited *The Berkeley Student Revolt* (New York, 1965) and *Rebellion in the University* (Boston, 1972), in which he studied the dynamics of the student revolt on American campuses and joined with distinguished sociologists from France, Israel and South America to compare and contrast student politics around the world. Lipset has also written extensively on the unionization of university professors in *Professors, Unions and American Higher Education* (Berkeley, 1973), and he edited *The Third Century: America as a Post-Industrial Society* (Stanford, 1979), in which such writers as Peter Berger, Andrew Greeley, Nathan Glazer, Daniel Elazar, Aaron Wildavsky, Orlando Patterson, Robert Nisbet, Irving Kristol and Stanley Rothman discuss respectively religion, Catholics, Jews, federalism, the presidency, blacks, universities, intellectuals and the mass media. While all suggest future trends and prescribe possible solutions to the problems raised, Lipset himself comments on the inability of the social sciences to predict the future, and he notes his "refusal to engage in long-range futurology." Instead, he writes that his book concentrates on the examination of the recent past "and suggests scenarios for the immediate future."

In 1975 Lipset became professor of political science and government at Stanford University and a senior research fellow at the Hoover Institute of War, Revolution and Peace. In 1981 he was a visiting professor at

Columbia University. From 1975 until 1979 he was national chairman of the B'nai B'rith Hillel Foundation and since 1977 has been the national president of American Professors for Peace in the Middle East. Since 1978 Lipset has been co-editor of *Public Opinion,* the magazine published by the conservative American Enterprise Institute. He has been a member of or consultant to numerous Jewish organizations, including the American Jewish Committee and United Jewish Appeal.

For further information:

Lipset, Seymour Martin. *Group Life in America.* New York: 1972.

———. *Labor and Trade Unionism.* New York: 1960.

———. *Revolution and Counterrevolution.* New York: 1968.

———. *Union Democracy.* New York: 1956.

Lipset, Seymour Martin, and Glazer, Nathan. "Israel Isn't Threatened. The War's Ill-Advised." *The New York Times,* June 30, 1982.

Lipset, Seymour Martin, and Horowitz, Irving Louis. *Dialogues on American Politics.* New York: 1978.

STANLEY H. LOWELL

b. April 13, 1919
Attorney; community leader

Stanley H. Lowell is best known as an activist in the Jewish community and in the human rights movement. He is a member of the Presidium of the World Conference on Soviet Jewry and a past Chairman of the National Conference on Soviet Jewry. He helped found the New York City Commission on Human Rights in 1955 and aided in the establishment of the country's initial fair busing law in 1958.

Stanley Lowenbraun was born in New York City to Isidore and Mildred (Cohen) Lowenbraun. He was educated in the New York City public schools, received his Bachelor of Social Science degree from City College in New York in 1939 and graduated from Harvard Law School in 1942, the same year he was admitted to the New York bar.

From 1942 to 1943, Lowell was an Associate with the law firm of Root, Clark, Buckner & Ballantine. He was an attorney with the Department of Justice from 1943 to 1947, at which time he wrote briefs for the American Civil Liberties Union in two landmark cases argued in the U.S. Supreme Court. The first helped end the "white primary" in Texas and in the second the Court decided

that "separate but equal" was not equal for segregated black citizens.

From 1947 to 1958, Lowell was a partner at Corcoran, Kostelanetz, Gladstone & Lowell. He is currently a partner at Fink, Weinberg, Fredman, Berman & Lowell. He is also a former member of the Admissions Committee of the New York Bar Association and a former trustee of the Harvard Law School Association of New York.

Lowell was instrumental in the passage of the first Fair Housing Law (1958) by any government agency in New York City and was co-founder of the Mid-Manhattan Chapter of the National Association for the Advancement of Colored People. He was a member of the White House Conference on Civil Rights and served on the Board of the Urban League of Greater New York.

He has been active politically as a liberal Democrat for many years. In 1947 he helped reorganize the New York Young Democratic Club and was campaign executive for Franklin D. Roosevelt Jr. for Congress, Robert F. Wagner for Borough President of Manhattan and Herbert Lehman for the U.S. Senate. He served as assistant to Borough President Robert Wagner from 1950 to 1953, executive assistant to Wagner from 1954 to 1958 and as deputy mayor to Wagner in 1958. For many years, Lowell was State Chairman and a National Board member of Americans for Democratic Action and he was a member of the Executive Committee of the Democratic State Committee in New York from 1962 to 1968. He was a delegate to the Democratic National Convention in 1960, 1964 and 1968. He was appointed a United States Delegate to the Madrid Conference on the Helsinki Final Act in November 1980, another reaffirmation of his dedication to human rights.

In addition to his successful law practice and government service, Lowell stands out as a strong, concerned Jewish leader. Well-known and respected in the Jewish community, Lowell has served as senior vice president of the American Jewish Congress and on the advisory council of the New York Board of Rabbis. As chairman of the Greater New York Conference on Soviet Jewry, a coordinating body for 72 organizations in the New York area, from 1972 to 1974, Lowell was in charge of the very successful "Solidarity Sunday" parade on behalf of Soviet Jews. During his years of government service at City Hall, he was Chairman of the American Jewish Tercentenary Celebration of New York City and was Co-Chairman of the Israel Day Parade, which celebrated the 30th anniversary of the founding of Israel. Lowell is as well a member of the board of governors of the United Jewish Appeal and served as chairman of the Lawyer's Division of the UJA and the Federation of Jewish Philanthropies.

J. ANTHONY LUKAS

b. April 25, 1933
Journalist

With an eye for detail and an ear for nuance that separates the mere observer from the professional journalist, J. Anthony Lukas has become one of the most perceptive recorders of both American and foreign affairs with a particular focus on personalities. A Pulitzer Prize winner and former *New York Times* reporter, he is the author of three books and many articles whose subjects often reflect a common concern with an internal malaise in the American psyche.

Jay Lukas was born in New York City to Edwin Jay, an attorney and employee of the American Jewish Committee, and Elizabeth (Schamberg) Lukas, an actress. A 1951 graduate of the private Putney School in Vermont, he received a B.A. degree magna cum laude from Harvard University in 1955 and spent the following year doing postgraduate study at the Free University of Berlin. From 1956 to 1958 Lukas served in the U.S. Army as a news commentator and propaganda writer. On his return to civilian life, he began his career as a reporter.

His first post was as City Hall reporter for the *Baltimore Sun* from 1958 to 1962. Lukas then joined the *Times*, serving overseas for five years—three in the Congo, two more in India. He then covered the New York metropolitan area and Washington, D.C. for two years, spent an additional year at Harvard as a Nieman fellow in journalism (1968-69) and was assigned to be roving national correspondent based in Chicago until 1970. During this time he covered the 1968 Democratic National Convention in Chicago and its violent aftermath, when anti-war demonstrators clashed with Chicago police. His reportage of these events and the ensuing prosecution of the leaders of the protesters earned him his Pulitzer Prize and several other prestigious press awards and was the source material for his first book, *The Barnyard Epithet and Other Obscenities: Notes on the Chicago Conspiracy Trial* (New York, 1970). In the book Lukas assembled a series of vignettes that collectively described the dynamics of what took place between the defendants in the trial, protesters accused of conspiracy and inciting to riot; their attorney, William Kunstler; and the trial judge, Julius Hoffman. Through anecdotes and pure reportage—and deliberately very little personal

observation—Lukas succeeded in providing a clear and coherent account of what to many observers was pure chaos.

From 1970 to 1972 Lukas was a staff writer for the *Times* magazine. His second book once again illustrated his ability to explain a complex trend in American life through the atomized experiences of individual people. *Don't Shoot—We Are Your Children* (New York, 1971) consisted of profiles of 10 young people trying to bridge the generation gap with their elders. The outgrowth of Lukas's obsession with the murder of a wealthy Connecticut girl in Greenwich Village, *Don't Shoot* was ultimately a study of how the 1960s created a new generation of young people whose experiences were vastly different from those of any previous generation.

Lukas has traditionally espoused liberal causes, and when he left the *Times* in 1972, he went on to become senior editor of the *{More} Journalism Review*, an alternative journal of the press, and contributing editor of *New Times* magazine from 1973 until 1975. *More* became defunct in 1978; *New Times* even sooner. At the same time he free-lanced regularly for the *Times* and for other periodicals and in 1976 published his third book, *Nightmare: The Underside of the Nixon Years* (New York). Like his two earlier books, *Nightmare* is a masterpiece of research and reportage. Again avoiding having to insert his personal opinions, Lukas scoured material from Nixon transcripts and tapes of testimony before congressional committees to illustrate in minute detail the extent of the ex-president's abuse of power. Although some critics accused Lukas of being excessively hostile in his portrayal of Henry Kissinger, most praised him for his thoroughness and objectivity.

Since 1977 Lukas has continued to free-lance and has taught journalism at Boston University's School of Public Communications (1977-78) and at the Kennedy School of Government at Harvard since 1979. In 1978 he was a Guggenheim fellow. He has been a consultant to the Hastings Center and is a member of the Committee on Public Justice. His concerns have remained sharply focused on the social issues that threaten individual freedom. Thus, his 1979 *New York Times* magazine article "The ACLU Against Itself" closely scrutinized the directions being taken by the American Civil Liberties Union in the wake of its defense of the American Nazi Party when party members sought to march in Skokie, Illinois, a city inhabited by many Holocaust survivors. The ACLU had subsequently suffered a crisis in leadership and a significant loss of contributions and membership, which symbolized the general confusion of the liberal community.

Lukas also contributes to *The New Republic, Esquire, Harper's, Atlantic, The Nation* and other periodicals.

ALISON LURIE

b. September 3, 1926
Author; professor

With an uncanny ear for the physical and verbal nuances of upper-middle-class couples trying to be what other people "expect them to be" and for their children (if adolescent, awkward, pimpled and troubled)—and a sardonic wit to boot—Alison Lurie has in recent years gained renown as one of America's most biting and brilliant novelists. She is best-known for her novel *The War Between the Tates* (New York, 1974), but since then has also ventured into children's literature and non-fiction, choosing to focus on how traditional depictions of women have molded later perceptions of them.

Alison Lurie was born in Chicago, Illinois, to Harry L. Lurie, who was director of the Council of Jewish Federations and Welfare Funds, and Bernice (Stewart) Lurie. In a 1982 article entitled "No One Asked Me to Write a Novel," Lurie described how her career evolved. During much of her childhood and teenage years, she constantly wrote fantasy stories, retreating from what she perceived as an ungainliness in herself to create an elaborate other-world into which she could comfortably escape. A loner through much of her youth, she entered Radcliffe College in 1943 and graduated with an A.B. degree *magna cum laude* in 1947. Unlike her early fantasy of herself as an "old maid," Lurie in fact married and had two children, and for a while abandoned writing altogether to be wife and mother. But unsatisfied trying to fulfill a role she never truly felt comfortable with, she returned to writing in 1959, privately publishing a memoir of a close friend who had died suddenly. Reception of the memoir was heartening—another friend arranged to have 300 copies printed, including one that was shown to an editor at Macmillan—and Lurie set out to write further.

Her first novel, *Love and Friendship* (New York, 1962), had many of the themes that would surface in her later works. It told the story of Emmy Turner, a young faculty wife at a New England college whose affair with a musician tempts her—but only temporarily—to leave her loveless marriage. Lurie's debut was received with mostly good reviews, and *Atlantic Monthly's* critic compared her wit to Jane Austen's, describing it as "wicked and delicious." Now plunged into a literary career, Lurie received grants to write at

Yaddo, a New York state artists' colony, in 1963, 1964 and 1966, as well as a Guggenheim fellowship in 1966 and a Rockefeller Foundation grant in 1968. In her second novel, *The Nowhere City* (New York, 1965), the wife of a young Harvard historian follows her husband to California where, while he relishes life and work on the West Coast, she resists it—until she falls in love with a slightly batty analyst. Lurie used this book to spoof the looniness of California life in the mid-1960s, as many of the adults she portrayed were overaged flower children.

She became more introspective—yet with tongue always in cheek—in *Real People* (New York, 1969), in which a middle-aged would-be short story writer, spending time at a New England writer's colony realizes she's been repressing her true artistic instincts in order to conform to the demands of suburban life. Written in the form of a journal, the book focuses on the main character's realization that the unconventional lives of many of her artist-friends are far more real, satisfying and "connected" than hers.

As Lurie's own artistic instincts flowered, she soon joined the academic life which she had previously only been observing. In 1969 she became a lecturer in English at Cornell University and in 1973 was named adjunct associate professor. From 1976 to 1979 she was associate professor and in 1979 was appointed to full professor.

Meanwhile, she used the themes of her early novels and her own growth to triumph with *The War Between the Tates,* a novel whose story apparently hit so hard in so many American households that it was later filmed for television. Set on an idyllic college campus in New York State, its focus was the deteriorating relationship between Brian and Erica Tate—he a political scientist, she a faculty wife—and the coming-of-age of their two teenaged children. But the backdrop was as much the era of the late 1960s as the college campus. Antiwar protests, women's liberation, the disintegration of the nuclear family, campus unrest, mysticism and drugs, hard rock music and midlife crisis are large themes in the book. It made for a riveting portrayal of an era seen through the tensions in the Tate family, and as Lurie used satire instead of deadpan seriousness to spice up her story, she captured the idiosyncrasies of thought and speech of the time, using what *New York Times* critic John Leonard called "Lurie's faultless prose."

Lurie's novel *Only Children* (New York, 1979) expanded on some of her familiar early themes—conflict in love and marriage and in child-rearing—as it chronicled a long Fourth of July weekend as seen through the eyes of two little girls, schoolmates whose parents spend the holiday together in an upstate New York retreat in which arguing alternates with romping around.

Her childhood preoccupation with fantasy led Lurie in another direction with her next books. *Heavenly Zoo: Legends and Tales of the Stars* (New York, 1979) and *Clever Gretchen and Other Forgotten Folk Tales* (New York, 1980) were both collections of children's stories retold by Lurie. In *Heavenly Zoo* she selected 16 myths about how the constellations were named, drawing on sources from ancient Greece, Rome, Babylon, the Bible, Norway, the Balkans, Indonesia and Native-American traditions. In *Clever Gretchen* she chose 15 stories of European origin and stressed how the women portrayed in them were as strong, intelligent and forceful as the men.

Lurie's illustrated book, *The Language of Clothes* (New York, 1981), which departs altogether from her previous work, is a non-fiction series of essays which combine wit and meticulous history to analyze how styles of dress resemble a language. Some of the essays describe the special and often humorous vocabulary and grammar of clothing—how a person's clothes "speak" for his or her occupation, origin, tastes or sexual desires, for example. Others explore the historical role of clothing like the floor-length robes of men in Greece and Rome, or the literary use of clothes, which Lurie points out occurs frequently in the novels of Henry James.

Lurie's many articles and reviews have appeared in such publications as *Ms.*, *The New York Review of Books*, *The New Republic*, *Psychology Today*, *The Times Literary Supplement*, *Children's Literature* and others. She is co-editor of The Garland Library of Children's Classics, a facsimile edition of 117 titles in 73 volumes with scholarly introductions and bibliography. Since 1977 Lurie has been a member of the New York State Arts Council (CAPS) Literature Panel, and in 1978 received the American Academy of Arts and Letters Award in Literature.

For further information:
Lurie, Alison. *Imaginary Friends*. New York: 1967.

EDWARD LUTTWAK

b. November 4, 1942
Military writer

Edward Luttwak is a writer and consultant whose specialty is war and weaponry. By his mid-20s he had already distinguished himself as an astute military ana-

lyst, and he has since become one of the most prominent writers in the area of military strategy.

Edward Nicholae Luttwak was born in Arad (Transylvania), Rumania to Joseph, a businessman, and Clara (Baruch) Luttwak. From 1949 to 1955 he attended schools in Palermo and Milan, Italy, and in 1964 he received a Bachelor of Science degree from the London School of Economics. The following year Luttwak worked for CBS-TV in Eastern Europe, and from 1965 to 1967 he was a lecturer at the University of Bath in Bath, England. He spent the following year as an oil consultant for Walter J. Levy in London.

During the late 1960s Luttwak began publishing articles on aspects of weaponry and military history and strategy. In 1969 he became a strategic consultant in Washington, D.C., and from 1970 to 1972 he was deputy director of the Middle East Study Group in Jerusalem. His book *A Dictionary of Modern War* (New York) appeared to much fanfare in 1972. Literally a dictionary with illustrations, it described contemporary weaponry, the concepts behind it and its implementation.

Luttwak returned to the United States in 1972 to join the Washington Center of Foreign Policy Research prior to assuming his post at Georgetown's Center for Strategic and International Studies. The books he has published since then include *The Israeli Army*, with Dan Horowitz (New York, 1975), which traces the army from its inception with the Haganah in 1948 through the development of more sophisticated forces under Moshe Dayan after 1953 and on to its uses of advanced technologies and strategies in its subsequent wars; *The Grand Strategy of the Roman Empire from the First Century A.D. to the Third* (Baltimore, 1976), in which Luttwak maps out and describes Roman military tactics based on historical accounts; and *Coup d'Etat: A Practical Handbook* (Cambridge, Mass., 1979), an exploration of the techniques used by outside groups to infiltrate and topple governments. His essays have been collected in *Strategy and Politics: Collected Essays* (New Brunswick, N.J., 1980).

Luttwak, many of whose articles appear in *Commentary*, is a hard-line proponent of extremely high levels of military expenditures and is hawkish in foreign affairs. In 1977, for example, he wrote that Soviet military power was growing ever stronger, signifying "an expansionist intent." He blamed U.S. military weakness on the "disarray" brought on by the Vietnam War and urged the United States to accept the fact that the USSR "understands very little except for the uses of power, which they understand all too well." In late 1979 he warned that "the pieces are on the chessboard;

the operation [directed at the Persian Gulf oilfields] could unfold at any time." Directing sharp criticism at the Carter administration, he concluded:

> What has been revealed as empty of strategic significance is not the Soviet brigade in Cuba, but rather the obsessive pursuit of the cumbersome legalisms of SALT at a time when our chief adversary is ceaselessly maneuvering to prevail. While our best minds use their energies to explain away all Moscow tries to do, in Moscow a machine of imperial ambition is at work, whose goal is to exploit all our points of weakness around the world.

In 1982 he sought to explain why he believed the Reagan administration was correct in spending vast amounts of money on the U.S. military. Critics of the Reagan rearmament budget, he charged, "remain blessedly ignorant of the full dimension of the Soviet military upsurge and of our weakness." Calling the budget expenditures "greatly overdue," he urged his readers to "resist those politicians" who failed to recognize the emergency. And following the introduction of popular initiatives to freeze United States and Soviet nuclear arsenals, Luttwak told *Newsweek* in an April 1982 symposium that he considered it a "colossally insane proposal . . . born out of impatience and fear . . . the politics of unilateral surrender." Instead, he proposed a "Supreme Nuclear Council" to deal with the control of nuclear weapons.

For further information:
Luttwak, Edward. "Cubans in Arabia?" *Commentary*, December 1979.
————. "Defense Reconsidered." Ibid., March 1977.
————. *The Political Uses of Sea Power.* Baltimore: 1974.
————. "Why We Need More 'Waste, Fraud and Mismanagement' in the Pentagon." *Commentary*, February 1982.

NORMAN MAILER

b. January 31, 1923
Writer

Since the publication of *The Naked and the Dead* (New York, 1948), a novel about World War II, Norman Mailer has been the *enfant terrible* of American letters. In addition to his prolific literary output, which includes both fiction and nonfiction and covers many diverse elements of American society, the gifted and often brilliant Mailer has been a prominent and controversial personality on the American cultural and political scene.

Norman Mailer was born in Long Beach, New Jersey to Isaac Barnett, an accountant, who had immigrated from England by way of South Africa, and Fanny (Schneider) Mailer. When Norman was 4, his family moved to Brooklyn, where he attended P.S. 161 and Boys High School, graduating in 1939. His earliest ambition was to be an aeronautical engineer. As a 16-year-old freshman at Harvard University, he became interested in writing, and one of the many short stories he wrote while in college won a contest sponsored by the famous *Story Magazine* in 1941.

Mailer graduated from Harvard in 1943 with a degree in engineering and was inducted into the United States Army, serving as an infantryman in the Philippines and with the American occupation forces in Japan. Mailer was discharged in 1946 and began working on a novel based on his war experience. He wrote *The Naked and the Dead* in 15 months, and it became an immediate best seller. It also received much critical acclaim and, according to critic Brock Bower, made the American G.I.'s language into a "new vulgate in American letters."

Mailer's second novel, *Barbary Shore* (New York, 1951), reflected Mailer's growing political doubts. It showed both a rejection of Stalinism and a deepening sadness with authoritarian tendencies within the United States. It was written while Mailer was spending a short and unhappy stint as a scriptwriter in Hollywood.

In 1951 Mailer returned to New York, where he helped found the alternative newspaper the *Village Voice*. For two years he wrote columns in which he developed his "hip" philosophy of American existentialism. The definitive exposition of this outlook appeared in an essay entitled "The White Negro" in 1953. In it he defined his personal outlook. Confronted with the prospects of instant annihilation by nuclear catastrophe, a less rapid annihilation through the repression of the state or slow annihilation through social conformity, Mailer wrote that one must accept the terms of life, live with the prospect of death and exist without roots, if necessary divorce oneself from society.

Mailer spent four years writing and rewriting his next novel, *The Deer Park* (New York, 1955). Although the book initially did not receive good reviews, many now see it as Mailer's most sensitive and insightful novel. *The Deer Park* is about sex and drugs in Hollywood. The main character, Eitel, is a "hip" movie director driven to psychopathic sexual and political extremes. Many critics recognized large portions of Mailer's personal life in the book.

Meanwhile, Mailer began to lead a celebrated "private" life that became notoriously public. Friends have said that in this period he began to manipulate real people like fictional characters. It reached a dramatic denouement when he stabbed his second wife at a party, seriously injuring her. He received a suspended sentence and emerged from this experience a changed man.

Advertisements for Myself (New York, 1959) and *The Presidential Papers* (New York, 1963) were collections of columns Mailer had written for *Esquire* magazine. In *Advertisements* the individual pieces were strung together with confessional commentary by Mailer. Professing to want to live by Hemingway's dictum that it is more important to be a man than to be a good writer, Mailer said he would never be a good writer if he lost his nerve. Many of the pieces in *The Presidential Papers* were open letters to John F. Kennedy, criticizing him for not fulfilling his great promise. Perhaps the most discerning of them was "Superman Comes to the Supermarket," a column about the 1960 Democratic convention in which Mailer compared Kennedy to the comic book character who is changed from an "average man" to a super-hero in phone booths. As a result of these two collections, Mailer established himself as one of the foremost essayists in America. This reputation was enhanced by his perceptive, highly personalized reportage of the presidential nominating conventions in wartime 1968, called *Miami and the Siege of Chicago* (New York, 1968).

Mailer was one of the central leaders of the anti-Vietnam War movement, and his literary reputation was solidified by his account of an anti-war demonstration in Washington, D.C. in which he participated in 1967. Called *The Armies of the Night* (New York, 1968), the book won the 1969 Pulitzer Prize for nonfiction as well as a National Book Award. *Why Are We in Vietnam?* (New York, 1967), which he described as the story of "reasonable people going absolutely apeshit up in Alaska," served as a metaphor for America's traumatic Vietnam adventure.

Mailer also made a brief foray into politics when, along with journalist Jimmy Breslin, he ran in the 1968 New York City mayoralty primary on a secessionist ticket calling for New York City to leave New York state and form the 51st state.

Continuing in the nonfiction mode, Mailer has written, among other things, the story of the landing of the first man on the moon, *A Fire on the Moon* (New York, 1970); *The Prisoner of Sex* (New York, 1971), an attack on the women's liberation movement; and *Marilyn* (New York, 1973), a biography of film star Marilyn Monroe.

His dazzling work *The Executioner's Song* (New York, 1979) blurred the distinctions between fiction and nonfiction. Although it was basically a factual account of the life and death of condemned Utah murderer Gary

Gilmore, Mailer insisted that the work was fiction. It won the Pulitzer Prize for fiction in 1979.

In 1981 Mailer made his formal acting debut as Stanford White in the film version of E. L. Doctorow's novel *Ragtime* directed by Milos Forman. During the late 1960s he had made three documentary-style films of his own in which he starred, but the *Ragtime* role fulfilled a desire to perform on a large stage.

Mailer was involved in a tragedy when Jack Henry Abbott, a long-time prison inmate, began sending him samples of his writings. Detecting a budding literary talent, Mailer urged that Abbott be paroled and used his influence to have Abbott's book, *In the Belly of the Beast* (New York, 1981) published. However, after being paroled, Abbott murdered a young unemployed actor working as a waiter in a restaurant in New York City in 1981. Abbott was tried and convicted, and Mailer was then confronted by a good deal of harsh criticism for his role.

For further information:
Mailer, Norman. *An American Dream.* New York: 1965.
———. *Cannibals and Christians.* New York: 1966.
———. *The Fight.* New York: 1975.
———. *Of Women and Their Elegance.* New York: 1981.
———. *Pieces.* New York: 1982.
———. *Pontifications.* New York: 1982.
———. *St. George and the Godfather.* New York: 1972.

BERNARD MALAMUD

b. April 26, 1914
Novelist

Winner of two National Book Awards and the Pulitzer Prize, Bernard Malamud combines the influences of the 19th-century Russian masters, Kafka and traditional Jewish storytellers. In novels and short stories, he writes that human salvation can come only from an adherence to a strict code of personal morality in the face of life's overwhelming despair and oppression.

Bernard Malamud was born in Brooklyn, the elder of two boys, to Max and Bertha (Fidelman) Malamud, poor Russian Jewish immigrants who owned a small and barely profitable grocery store. They worked 16-hour days and maintained a Jewish though nonreligious environment, although there were no books, music, photographs or cultural interests in his home, Malamud has said. Both English and Yiddish were spoken, and some of his mother's family actually performed on the Yiddish stage. When he was 15, his mother died.

He attended Erasmus Hall High School, where he was an editor of the school magazine. He received his B.A. degree from City College of New York in 1936, and after working for a number of years in the family store, in various factories and at the Census Bureau, he received his M.A. degree from Columbia University in 1942.

After graduation he taught English at night between 1940 and 1942 at Erasmus Hall and then years afterward at Harlem Evening High School in 1949, but always writing in his spare time. He said that the rise of Nazism and Stalinism, World War II and the tragedy of the Jews in Europe helped him determine what he wanted to say as a writer and how he interpreted his Jewishness. He began reading Jewish history and literature. As he once said: "The suffering of the Jews is a distinct thing for me. I for one believe that not enough has been made of the destruction of six million Jews. Somebody has to cry—even if it's a writer, 20 years later."

Although his first book, *The Natural* (New York, 1952), which symbolically chronicled the rise and fall of a baseball player, did not have any Jewish influences, his remaining work did. The publication of Malamud's second novel, *The Assistant* (New York, 1957), symbolized his emergence as a major American Jewish writer, as he drew in part on the immigrant past of his mother and father for source material. The book revolves around Frank Alpine, an Italian-American who helps rob a poor, elderly Jewish grocer. After the theft Alpine is engulfed by guilt and remorse for his act. He takes pity on the old man and, in an attempt at atonement, without revealing his identity, begins to help the grocer around the store for almost no money. Later, when his past is discovered, the old man forgives Alpine, and after the grocer's death his "assistant" secretly converts to Judaism.

Malamud then published a collection of short stories, *The Magic Barrel* (New York, 1958). The tales illustrate Malamud's ability to fuse fantasy and realism, as well as his complete mastery of idiom. Malamud won his first National Book Award in 1958 for *The Magic Barrel*.

Perhaps Malamud's best-known work is *The Fixer* (New York, 1966). In it a poor Russian-Jewish handyman, Yakov Bok, the fixer of the title, is falsely accused by anti-Semitic Czarist officials of committing a ritual murder. He is then thrown into the Kafkaesque labyrinth of the Czarist Russian penal system and is subjected to two and a half years of degradation and defilement. Incredibly, he survives and emerges with his human integrity not only intact but enhanced. It is a story of the domination of humanity and personal honor over the bestiality and cruelty of the world. At the end of the book, Bok, the fixer, concludes that there is "no such thing as an unpolitical man, especially a Jew."

The Fixer raised a storm of critical controversy. Some reviewers felt that the book represented a retreat into historical realism for Malamud, while others saw the accused Jew as a true hero, a rare creation in contemporary literature. In 1967 Malamud was awarded the National Book Award and a Pulitzer Prize for *The Fixer*. In 1968 the book was turned into a movie by MGM with British actor Alan Bates in the title role.

In all, Malamud has spent more than 40 years teaching narrative fiction. From 1949 until 1961 he taught English at Oregon State College. Since 1961 he has taught at Bennington College in Vermont. He was elected to the National Institute of Arts and Letters in 1964 and to the American Academy of Arts and Sciences in 1967.

Currently Malamud teaches a quarter schedule at Bennington and spends the rest of his time in New York City, where he writes and serves as the president of the American Center of PEN, the international writers association, protesting the suppression of writers in the Soviet Union, South Africa and all other countries that seek to limit literary freedom. His literary output consists of seven novels and three collections of short stories. His latest work is the complex, realistic novel *Dubin's Lives* (New York, 1979), a tale of a middle-aged biographer working to escape the limitations of his consciousness.

For further information:
Malamud, Bernard. *Idiots First*. New York: 1963.
————. *A Malamud Reader*. New York: 1967.
————. *Picture of Fidelman*. New York: 1969.
————. *The Tenants*. New York: 1971.
————. *Rembrandt's Hat*. New York: 1973.

JEROME R. MALINO

b. June 7, 1911
Rabbi

Rabbi Jerome Malino has been in the forefront of the Reform Jewish movement for nearly 50 years and is a major supporter of the acceptance of women into the rabbinate, of Jewish conscientious objectors, of nonviolence and of other modifications in Jewish traditions that satisfy changing social attitudes and lifestyles without diluting the essence of Judaism.

Jerome R. Malino was born in New York City to Wolff, a businessman, and Henrietta (Rosenbaum) Malino. He attended the City College of New York, where he received a B.A. degree in 1931, and the Jewish Institute of Religion, where he was ordained in 1935 and received a Master of Hebrew Literature degree.

Upon ordination Malino became spiritual leader of the United Jewish Center in Danbury, Connecticut, a position he has held ever since. Working with one congregation for nearly five decades has given Malino a unique perspective in observing Jewish community development, which he described in a 1980 president's message before the Central Conference of American Rabbis:

> Perhaps the most rewarding aspect is the opportunity for abiding personal relationships. I am able, without hesitation . . . to utter the same prayer of gratitude I spoke after twelve years in my pulpit when I said the Rabbi "will feel himself a partner with God in creating souls." As he confirms those he knew as infants, marries those he has confirmed, as he sees his handiwork in happier and better integrated lives, as he grows with his labors and earns the love of those he served, he will say, "the reward was worth the effort."

In the same speech Malino described how Jewish community life is significantly different in a small city like Danbury, where religious rather than ethnic qualities are the distinguishing features. "One does not determine the merit of a work of art by taking its dimensions," he said when discussing the problems of rabbis who are never able to move to a larger congregation from a small one. "Some miniaturists and illuminators of manuscripts have poured more intensity of color and feeling into their modestly proportioned exercises than have graced large murals." In the same vein Malino's long-time service in Danbury has enabled him to contribute to other civic activities, including 20 years on the local Board of Education (he was president for nine terms), and participation on the Human Relations Commission, the Danbury Concert and the Danbury Music Center. He has been chaplain at the Federal Correctional Institute in Danbury for more than 40 years.

Malino served as president of the Central Conference of American Rabbis (Reform) from 1979 to 1981. But in or out of office, he has always been outspoken on many liberal issues, including opposition in 1980 to mandatory draft registration—a position at odds with, for example, that of the Anti-Defamation League; support for Jewish peace movements in Israel; and stressing

a more tolerant attitude on the part of Jewish leaders in the Begin government toward non-Orthodox Jews. Similarly, he urges greater recognition of the needs of Israel's Arab residents while maintaining a firm commitment to the sovereignty and stability of Israel. He has participated in the World Union for Progressive Judaism, an organization designed to stem the tide of secularism among Jews, and the Jewish Peace Fellowship, which, as the name implies, seeks nonviolent solutions to world problems. During World War II he was the rabbi of young Jews who, because of their moral or religious objections, refused to be drafted into the armed services and were imprisoned at the Danbury Federal Penitentiary. Again in the Vietnam War era, he actively supported those young men who could not in good conscience serve in the military.

As a member of the Task Forces on Women of the Central Conference of American Rabbis, Malino has been intimately involved with the integration of women into the rabbinate and has encouraged women to become otherwise involved in Jewish leadership. His aim, he has said, "is to press the importance of Torah and not sex in establishing the Rabbi's worth or status. . . . Every one of us is diminished when our female colleagues fail to receive the respect and the opportunity which we would aspire to for ourselves."

DAVID MAMET

b. November 30, 1947
Playwright

It is rare enough for a playwright to have a work on Broadway when he is 29. To have two is unheard-of. But in 1977 two plays by David Mamet, *American Buffalo* and *The Water Engine,* opened separately on Broadway, and acclaim for the young dramatist since then—two or three new plays of his premier each year— has been nonstop.

David Alan Mamet was born in Chicago to Bernard Morris, an attorney, and Lenore June (Silver) Mamet. His interest in theater jelled while he was in high school; he did volunteer work at a neighborhood playhouse and worked briefly as a busboy for the Second City Theater cabaret, a well-known improvisational troupe in Chicago.

At Goddard College in Plainfield, Vermont, Mamet wrote his first play and studied acting. After receiving a B.A. degree in 1969, he briefly acted, realized he was better at writing and, after a spell of short jobs, turned permanently to play writing. He taught briefly at Marlboro College in 1970 and later returned to Goddard as an artist-in-residence from 1971 to 1973. Shortly thereafter, he and three friends co-founded the St. Nicholas Theater Company in Chicago, which became a vehicle for many of his earlier works.

In Chicago, Mamet established a substantial reputation, and over the subsequent years, most of his plays were "exported" to New York, where they became known to wider audiences. In 1976 two plays, *Duck Variations* (written in 1971) and *Sexual Perversity in Chicago* (written in 1973), appeared together off-Broadway. *Duck Variations* is a two-character play: Two elderly Jewish men discuss, among many other things, the habits of ducks. (Mamet says the idea "came from listening to a lot of old Jewish men all my life, particularly my grandfather.") *Sexual Perversity in Chicago* is about the uncertain relationship between two "swinging singles," and how the interference of their friends eventually destroys it. It won the Joseph Jefferson Award for best play in Chicago (1974) and a *Village Voice* Obie in 1976.

The plays that "made" Mamet in New York are, like his others, spare in plot and cast, and often shorter than an average full-length production, yet rich in dialogue. *American Buffalo,* which takes place in a cluttered junk shop, is about three small-time "con men" hoping to "make it big" through a meticulously planned burglary, which they eventually talk themselves out of. It includes the use of four-letter words and other "select" dialogue, not so much to create shock value as to lend an extra intensity to the characters' frustration and claustrophobia. It won a *Village Voice* Obie (1976) as well as the New York Drama Critics Circle Award (1977) and was revived in 1981 to critical raves, with Al Pacino in the starring role. *The Water Engine,* which began as a radio play for National Public Radio, is a fable about an inventor from the Depression who claims to have designed an automobile engine fueled by water, only to see his idea stolen and abused.

The "kid playwright" (a description often foisted upon Mamet, and one that he despises) also wrote *A Life in the Theater* (1976), which depicts the relationship between two actors, one a veteran of the stage, the other just beginning, each assuming different roles as one fulfills the needs of the other; *Reunion* (1977), which is about a father and daughter who meet again after a 20-year separation following the parents' divorce—the daughter is now 25 and married; *The Woods* (1977), which traces a day in the life of a young couple as they hash out aspects of their relationship during a brief retreat in the country.

Mamet's use of dialogue at the expense of other elements of drama has been both praised and criticized. But it is his strength, and it is what makes his plays work. *New York Times* critic Richard Eder wrote: "To congratulate David Mamet upon his ear for words is to miss the main thing about him. His is no ear, but a stethoscope." And Mamet adds: "What I write about is what I think is missing from our society. And that's communication on a basic level."

Some of Mamet's other plays are: *Marranos* (depicting life in Lisbon during the Inquisition), *Squirrels* (1974), *Lone Canoe* (1978), *Prairie de Chien* (1978), *The Postman Always Rings Twice* (a screenplay, 1979) and *The Poet and the Rent* (a vaudeville play for children and adults, 1979). He directed *Twelfth Night* in 1982.

Mamet received the Outer Critics Circle Award for contribution to American Theater in 1978. He was a CBS Creative Writing Fellow at the Yale School of Drama in 1976-77 and a Rockefeller grantee in 1977. In addition, he was artistic director of the Goodman Theater in Chicago and guest-lectured at the University of Chicago in 1975 and 1979.

David Mamet now lives in New York City. In 1977 he married actress Lindsay Crouse (daughter of playwright Russel Crouse), who has appeared in several of his plays.

BARRY MANILOW

b. June 17, 1946
Recording artist; musical arranger; composer

Barry Manilow was a star before anyone had heard of him, and he may remain one long after his popularity as a performing artist fades. For Manilow is perhaps one of the most successful composers and arrangers of commercial jingles for products that have long since replaced mom's apple pie in American households across the country.

Barry Manilow was born in Brooklyn to Harold Pincus and Edna Manilow. Deserted by his father when he was only 2, Manilow was raised by his mother and grandmother in the working-class neighborhood of Williamsburg. His introduction to music came by way of accordian lessons when he was 7, followed by piano lessons when he was 13. Manilow had an evident gift for music, and while in high school he became an accomplished performer of Broadway and classical tunes and worked as an accompanist. When he graduated from Eastern District High School in 1964, he received the school's best musician award.

Meanwhile, in the late 1950s Manilow's mother remarried. Her new husband, a truck driver named Willie Murphy, was a jazz aficionado who shared his love for music with his stepson and was an important overall influence on Manilow's development. As he said once: "I got Willie Murphy as a step-father for my Bar Mitzvah. He tipped me off to serious music, taking me to my first jazz concert: Gerry Mulligan at Town Hall."

After high school Manilow briefly enrolled in the advertising program at the City College of New York but switched to the Juiliard School of music at night while working days at the CBS mail room. (He often cites his earlier music studies to describe his serious music background to the many skeptics who question his training.) From the CBS mail room Manilow went on to become a film editor for the local affiliate. His talent as a music arranger became known, and he arranged the well-known theme "Syncopated Clock" for the series *The Late Show*. He also expanded his free-lance accompanying and arranging to help off-Broadway singers, even touring for several months with one of them. In the late 1960s he returned to New York and became music director of *Callback*, a CBS weekly afternoon program that offered television exposure to young performers. Manilow's ability to improvise virtually anything the *Callback* performers wanted won him his first Emmy, and his reputation grew.

During the early 1970s he began to do some informal club performing, but he really made his mark as a writer of commercial songs that became American institutions. Melodies such as McDonald's "You Deserve a Break Today"—now an American song classic—and jingles for Dr. Pepper, Pepsi, Maxwell House and many more were Manilow's making. He wrote and arranged them.

Perhaps the most fortuitous event in his career, however, occurred in 1972, when he became the substitute accompanist for an offbeat singer named Bette Midler during a performance she gave to her primarily homosexual audience of men at the Continental Baths. Although initially they disliked each other, Manilow eventually became Midler's music director and was instrumental in producing two of her albums. As her show progressed on tour, Manilow eventually began to perform warm-up numbers. The response was positive, and in 1974 he recorded his first single and solo album and soon became a top-10 recording star.

Clearly, then, although Manilow seemed to have achieved overnight success, in fact he had put in a long apprenticeship. During the mid-1970s every album he recorded sold over one million records—four of his six albums earned Double Platinum records (indicating sales of more than 2 million)—and at one time Manilow had five simultaneous hit albums, a record matched only by Frank Sinatra and Johnny Mathis.

The appeal of Manilow's music comes, perhaps, from its schmaltzy romance, its breezy melodies, its simple lyrics and an ingenious combination of sentimental ballads, soft rock and the 1940s styles, which are easy to listen to and unthreatening—so much so that some critics have labeled him "Mr. Middle-of-the-Road" and called his music "bubblegum." He calls it "permanent wave" because "I think a good love song will never go out of style." Yet even his severest critics have to admit that Manilow is doing something right—his crosscountry tours have been hits; his two-week Broadway run in 1976 was sold out (and Manilow won a Tony); and his two television specials in 1977 and 1978 were among the highest-rated programs of their respective seasons, and both won Emmys. His best-known hits—"Mandy" and "Weekend in New England," sung in his always rich pop baritone—remain consistently popular. *New York Times* critic John O'Connor, while describing Manilow as "super-vanilla," nonetheless acknowledged that his talent was a true phenomenon on the popular music scene.

FRANK MANKIEWICZ

b. May 16, 1924
Journalist; broadcasting executive

When Frank Mankiewicz became president of National Public Radio in 1977, he brought with him a lifetime of experience in journalism, an idealism forged by work in the Peace Corps and as one of Robert Kennedy's closest friends, and a healthy cynicism bred from personal experience in politics and dealings with Richard M. Nixon. As a result of his broad background and a seemingly endless font of energy, he has turned public radio into a vibrant and competitive medium offering such a wide and sophisticated range of drama, news and music programming that when asked what radio cannot do, his only response was "ballet."

Frank Fabian Mankiewicz was born in New York City to Herman, a journalist and screenwriter, and Sara (Aaronson) Mankiewicz. The elder Mankiewicz was drama critic for *The New Yorker* until he decided in the 1930s to try film writing in Hollywood. The experience was disillusioning, and only two substantial screenplays emerged from that period, "Citizen Kane" and "Pride of the Yankees." Frank Mankiewicz inherited a dislike for Hollywood and headed toward his father's first career —journalism. After beginning college at the University of California at Los Angeles in 1941 and serving in the army from 1943 to 1946, he received a Bachelor of Arts degree from the University in 1947 and headed east, where he completed an M.S. degree in journalism from Columbia Univeristy in 1948. He then free-lanced briefly and returned to California in 1950 to run, unsuccessfully, for the California State Legislature on the Democratic ticket headed by Helen Gahagan Douglas. It was during this campaign that Mankiewicz met Douglas's opponent, Richard Nixon, a man for whom he developed an enduring distaste.

Following the election he returned to free-lancing and then entered law school at the University of California at Berkeley, completing his degree in 1955. For six years Mankiewicz was a "Hollywood lawyer"—but an unhappy one—and as a change he joined the Peace Corps in 1962, as regional director in Lima, Peru for two years and from 1964 to 1966 as Latin American regional director based in Washington. During this period Mankiewicz befriended Robert Kennedy and became his press secretary. He was with Kennedy throughout the latter's presidential campaign in primaries across the country, and it was Mankiewicz who had to announce that Kennedy had died after being shot in a Los Angeles hotel in 1968.

Mankiewicz returned to journalism after Kennedy's death, coauthoring a liberal syndicated column with Tom Braden. He also spent part of 1969 on a Ford Foundation grant exploring the progress of the Peace Corps in Latin America and served on the board of directors for the Center for Community Change, an organization that monitored and supported self-help groups in depressed communities around the country. (Mankiewicz explained that although he could have taken the safe route and become a millionaire attorney, he had felt far greater satisfaction from his Peace Corps involvement, and that this latter experience in turn fueled his further involvement in social causes.)

In 1971 and 1972 Mankiewicz worked for the unsuccessful presidential campaign of Democratic Senator George McGovern, and until becoming president of National Public Radio, he continued writing columns and wrote several books, two of which focused on one of his favorite subjects—Richard Nixon. *Perfectly Clear: Nixon from Whittier to Watergate* (New York, 1973) traces patterns in the ex-president's behavior from the 1940s onward to prove that the person who emerged from Watergate had been decades in the making. One year later Mankiewicz published *The U.S. v. Richard M. Nixon* (New York), a study of the judicial process that led ultimately to Nixon's resignation. In the book Mankiewicz set out to prove that it was indeed the judiciary,

and not the press, that had lawfully forced Nixon out of office. (However, Mankiewicz did say upon hearing of Nixon's resignation that he was "delighted. I think we should celebrate August 9th as a national day of liberation every year.") *Remote Control: Television and the Manipulation of Life* (New York, 1977) is Mankiewicz's indictment of the television industry and its negative impact on American society, especially in propagating myths and artificial realities for viewers and in the way ethnic and racial minorities and women are (or are not) portrayed either in television programming or in commercials.

At National Public Radio, Mankiewicz aggressively sought (and received) extra funds from Congress to expand its services. Under his aegis NPR—which has a network of 264 stations in the United States and Puerto Rico—introduced *Earplay*, an innovative drama series featuring the work of such playwrights as David Mamet and Archibald MacLeish, a series called *Jazz Alive!*, a one-of-its-kind reading of the "Jonestown" tapes and a wide range of folk, classical and contemporary music. Children's programming also gets significant attention, including storytelling and related shows, as do senior citizens' audiences, for whom NPR produces *Senior Edition*. Its news coverage has won numerous awards, especially *All Things Considered*, a daily afternoon program, and its morning counterpart, *Morning Edition*. Since Mankiewicz's arrival, the audience for NPR has increased nearly 100 percent.

Nonetheless, he has said that of all the periods in his life, the most satisfying was when he worked with Bobby Kennedy.

HERBIE MANN

b. April 16, 1930
Jazz flutist

Herbie Mann, who in the late 1950s became the first musician to use the flute as a solo jazz instrument, has since become renowned for his mastery of a wide range of musical forms and rhythms in which the flute remains central. He has recorded dozens of records, formed numerous ensembles, played in concerts around the world and has played alongside the world's greatest jazz performers.

Herbert Solomon was born in New York City to Harry and Ruth (Brecher) Solomon. He began his musical training at the age of 6 when he studied piano. At 9 he began playing clarinet after hearing Benny Goodman and at Abraham Lincoln High School switched to the tenor saxophone. While in high school Mann first became interested in flute.

After serving in the United States Army from 1948 to 1952, Mann studied at the Manhattan School of Music until 1954, then joined the Mat Matthews Quintet for a year and afterward toured Scandinavia, France and Holland. When he returned to the United States in 1957, he played with a few groups and eventually formed his Afro Jazz Sextet in New York. Mann soon developed a following of fans who loved his Latin flute sound and intense rhythms. By 1960 he was a national figure and was chosen by the U.S. State Department to tour 15 African countries with his ensemble. In 1961–62 he was U.S. "musical ambassador" to Brazil; in 1964 he toured Japan; and in 1971 he visited Scandinavia, Cyprus and Turkey in the same capacity.

Nicknamed the "Traveling Mann," the flutist has visited many American cities and foreign countries, where he has attempted to learn and absorb new musical forms within his own repertory. "What I've always done," he once explained, "is to go to cities that have rhythm sections which are indigenous to the area, rhythm sections which have a slightly different feel from those in other cities." Even in New York City, he was exposed to a multitude of musical influences, including the Caribbean "salsa" and rhythm and blues. His music has also included the Brazilian bossa nova; African rhythms, a transcription of the French composer Erik Satie's piano pieces "Gymnopedies," Japanese *gagaku* music and even a Middle Eastern treatment of "Fiddler on the Roof." When criticized because he is not a "pure" jazz musician, Mann has retorted by saying of his mixture of forms, "mutts are a lot more fun than pure breeds."

Nevertheless, over the years, Mann has performed with such jazz greats as Bill Evans and Herbie Hancock on piano, Ron Carter on bass, Billy Cobham on drums and many other musicians who have been soloists or led their own bands. Among his best-known recordings are *Push Push* (1970), *The Evolution of Mann* (1972), *Hold on, I'm Comin'* (1973) and *Reggae* (1974).

A popular performer at many jazz festivals, Mann has a command of the flute that prompted one critic to describe it as "a sparrow in the treetop, lightly flitting and chirping above a heavy, sensuous beat laid down by the rhythm section. On alto flute the mood is more softly introspective, evoking languid afternoons by the sea." He is also open to experimentation, not only with different forms, but different formats. Throughout his career Mann has played with small jazz ensembles, Latin groups, large orchestras, once in a duet with a bagpipe and in another instance with an audience playing whistles.

When he signed a new contract with Atlantic records in 1973 after 13 years with the company, Mann referred to that milestone as his "bar mitzvah." And it was indeed a turning point: Mann was by now a top-billed performer able to sell out concerts, and on its part Atlantic agreed to give Mann the kind of publicity reserved only for its best-selling artists.

In recent years, when asked to describe his music, Mann sometimes labels it "Afro-Yiddish" because of its blend of indigenous American forms and his new interest in Middle Eastern and Hebraic themes. (Indeed, he toured Israel in 1982.) At other times he describes his blending of Brazilian songs and Middle Eastern music as "a bouillabaisse of rhythmic music."

JACOB RADER MARCUS

b. March 5, 1896
Historian and archivist

Jacob Rader Marcus, founder and director of the American Jewish Archives in Cincinnati, is the pioneering historian of American Jewish life. Author of numerous books on American Jewish history, Marcus has taught at the Hebrew Union College-Jewish Institute of Religion in Cincinnati since 1926 and is a former president of the Central Conference of American Rabbis.

Jacob Marcus was born in Connellsville, Pennsylvania to Aaron, a Lithuanian immigrant peddler and shopkeeper, and Jennie (Rader) Marcus. Raised in Homestead and Pittsburgh, Pennsylvania and Wheeling, West Virginia, Marcus attended public school and *cheder* ("Jewish religious school") in both states. At 15 he moved to Cincinnati, where he attended high school in the morning and classes at Hebrew Union College in the afternoon. After graduation from high school in 1913, he enrolled at the University of Cincinnati, where he received his A.B. degree in European history in 1917. In April 1917 Marcus volunteered for the army and, after fighting for 10 months in France with the Allied Expeditionary Force, was discharged in 1919 as a second lieutenant.

In 1920 Marcus was ordained as a rabbi by the Hebrew Union College, where he began teaching Bible studies. In 1922 Marcus went to the University of Berlin, where he received his Ph.D. degree in history in 1925. After doing more postgraduate work at Ecole Rabbinique in Paris in 1925 and at the University of Jerusalem in 1926, Marcus returned to Hebrew Union College in 1926 as assistant professor of Jewish history. Three years later he became associate professor, and in 1934 he became a full professor. From 1946 to 1965 he was Adolph S. Ochs Professor of American Jewish History, and since 1965 he has been Milton and Hattie Kutz Distinguished Service Professor of American Jewish History.

His first important study, *Israel Jacobson* (New York, 1928), was a look at the founder of the German Reform movement. His next book, *The Rise and Destiny of the German Jew* (New York, 1934), though strong on facts, was less than accurate in its prediction that the massacre or expulsion of the Jews of Germany "seem[s] rather remote." In *The Jew in the Medieval World: A Source Book 1315-1791* (New York, 1938), Marcus presented an edited reference source for a history of the Jews.

Despite his training in European Jewish history, Marcus had been fascinated by American Jewish history almost from the start of his professional life. He lent increasing stress in his classes to American Jewry and granted awards for dissertations in that discipline. In 1934 he joined the American Jewish Historical Society, and he traveled to libraries and historical societies throughout the country tracking down source materials on American Jewish history.

Marcus brought together an extraordinary collection of American Jewish materials at the Hebrew Union College in the early 1940s. By 1947 he witnessed his dream come true when the American Jewish Archives was established on the campus of the college and he was taken on as its director. Since then it has become a major research center, housing vast collections, including unpublished recollections of American Jews, minutes of synagogue congregations and various societies and institutions, and letters and papers of rabbis and others.

He has also been described by many as the "father" of serious American Jewish history. Before he began producing estimable and scholarly works, the field was dominated by self-congratulators or by insecure writers seeking to prove that American Jews were no different from their non-Jewish counterparts. Few if any historians ever tapped—as he did—the rich source material that was to be found; instead, much American Jewish historiography before Marcus was based largely on derivative materials.

Marcus has also edited the semi-annual journal *American Jewish Archives* since its founding in 1948. Based on the premise that valid history can be written grounded in fact and without apology, the journal regularly features autobiographical accounts of Jews, both obscure and well-known, as well as scholarly historical essays that examine the American Jewish experience.

His published books of Americana include a two-volume study, *Early American Jewry* (Philadelphia, 1951 and 1953); *Memoirs of American Jews, 1775-1865* (Philadelphia, 1955-56), a three-volume collection of autobiographical materials. In it he criticized—among other things—the low level of intellectualism and creativity found among those Sephardic Jews who arrived here in the 17th and 18th centuries. He prepared the handbook *How to Write the History of an American Jewish Community* (Cincinnati, 1953) to help novices in his field.

Marcus is a former president of the American Jewish Historical Society, a former vice president of the Jewish Publication Society and a member of the executive committee of the American Academy for Jewish Research. He belongs to the Jewish Academy of Arts and the B'nai B'rith.

For further information:

Marcus, Jacob R. *American Jewry: Documents; Eighteenth Century*. Cincinnati: 1958.
———. *The American Jewish Woman, 1654-1980*. New York: 1981.
———. *The American Jewish Woman: A Documentary History*. New York: 1981.

STANLEY MARCUS

b. April 20, 1905
Department store executive

Stanley Marcus, chairman emeritus of the Dallas, Texas-based Neiman-Marcus Company, one of the most innovative and high-quality department stores in the United States, with branches throughout the country, has strongly influenced the fashion world with his talent for marketing, design and promotion of fashion.

Stanley Marcus was born in Dallas to Herbert, co-founder and president of the Neiman-Marcus Company, and Minnie (Lichtenstein) Marcus. While he attended high school, Marcus worked summer vacations in the family store, a training that was considered by his family to be as serious as his academic preparation. After receiving his B.A. degree in 1925 and his master's degree in business administration in 1926, both from Harvard University, Marcus returned to Dallas and began his career as a salesman. During his first year he started the first of the later famous weekly department store fashion shows. He also initiated the idea of advertising store merchandise in national publications.

Marcus was promoted to secretary, treasurer and

director of the company in 1928; merchandise manager in 1929; and executive vice president in 1935. In 1938 he established the Neiman-Marcus Awards, considered the "Oscars" of fashion, which have since been presented to designers and others "for distinguished service in the field of fashion." Marcus was also among the first to combine fashion and culture, wedding exhibitions of clothes with exhibitious of paintings, for example.

Marcus, who was decorated by the French government in 1949 for his role in aiding the economic recovery of that country by stimulating the sale of French fashions in America after World War II, was president of Neiman-Marcus from 1950 to 1972, chairman of the board from 1972 to 1975, chairman of the executive committee from 1975 to 1977 and chairman emeritus since 1977. He has overseen the evolution of Neiman into the highest quality store, often offering the most expensive and frequently outrageous items to its super-rich clientele. The Neiman-Marcus catalogs themselves are often collectors' items.

The Texas executive has compiled some of his fashion and retailing expertise in books he has written. In *Minding the Store: A Memoir* (Boston, 1974), he presents remembrances of his life and family business as well as a chapter on how the Texas economy has affected Neiman-Marcus trade over the years. In *Quest for the Best* (New York, 1979), he reveals his retailing principles and emphasizes the way to discern the qualities of taste and elegance. He offers a list of surviving quality, which includes Levi's, Galanos dresses, Sara Lee pound cake, Crane's stationery and London cabs.

Known for his progressive business ideas, Marcus is a member and former chairman of the American Retail Federation, an organization that he has tried to make a "powerful force to protect consumer interests." He is honorary director of Carter Hawley Hale Stores Inc. in Los Angeles, which owns the Neiman-Marcus chain, and is former co-chairman of the Interracial Council for Business Opportunity.

An art collector and patron of the arts, Marcus is a founding member of the Dallas branch of the Business Commission for the Arts, a past president of the Dallas Symphony Society, past member of the Texas Fine Arts Commission, past president of the Dallas Art Association and a member of the executive committee of the National Council on the Arts and Education. He is also a noted bibliophile and is a member of the executive committee of the Center for the Book and the Library of Congress.

Active in the civic life of his city, Marcus is a former board member of the Dallas Council on World Affairs, former director of the Texas Law Enforcement Foundation, and past president of the Dallas Citizens Council. He is also a former regional vice president of the National Jewish Hospital.

STEVEN MARCUS

b. December 13, 1928
Professor; author

Since the 1965 publication of his study *Dickens from Pickwick to Dombey* (New York), Steven Marcus has been recognized as one of America's most eminent scholars of 19th-century English literature and society. He has been on the faculty of Columbia University since 1956.

Steven Marcus was born in New York City to Nathan, an accountant, and Adeline Muriel (Gordon) Marcus. He received a Bachelor of Arts degree from Columbia University in 1948 and an M.A. degree there the following year. From 1949 to 1950 he was a teaching fellow at the University of Indiana at Bloomington and spent the next two years as a lecturer at the City College of New York. From 1952 to 1954 Marcus was a Fulbright fellow at Cambridge University. After serving in the U.S. Army from 1954 to 1956, he returned to Columbia to pursue his doctorate, which he completed in 1961. At the same time, he began teaching in Columbia's English Department. He was an instructor from 1956 to 1961, an assistant professor from 1961 to 1963 and an associate professor from 1963 to 1967, before becoming a full professor. During the 1967–68 academic year, he was a Guggenheim fellow.

In addition to his teaching, Marcus is the author of several books and has contributed many articles and reviews to professional journals and popular periodicals. He often specializes in probing psychological and political factors that motivate—often unconsciously—the writings of the authors he is studying. For example, in *Dickens from Pickwick to Dombey*, Marcus explored the psychological patterns during the first half of Dickens' life by analyzing the seven novels that appeared during that time, both for their intrinsic content and in the context of the era during which they were written. Marcus's attention to detail in his analyses and his meticulous research were applauded by critics, although the relevance of his strict Freudian approach—a characteristic of some of his other works—was occasionally questioned.

In his next book he expanded on some of the themes broached in *Dickens. The Other Victorians: A Study of*

Sexuality and Pornography in Mid-Nineteenth Century England (New York, 1966) was a comprehensive survey of the pornographic literature of the era, with detailed research into some of the more prominent, as well as several lesser-known, writers of the time. Marcus was commissioned to write the book by the Institute of Sex Research, whose library and archives had never been fully investigated. With Marcus's past experience, he was able to pull the materials together and draw comparisons between sexual attitudes of the Victorian age and those of the present.

Engels, Manchester and the Working Class (New York, 1974) reflects Marcus's political orientation. In it he examines Friedrich Engels' experiences in Manchester, England, where he was sent in the mid-1840s by his wealthy father, a textile manufacturer, to finish his business education. After spending time in Manchester's textile mills, Engels wrote *The Conditions of the Working Class in England,* which was published in 1844. Engels' sojourn coincided with the major changes in Western society wrought by the Industrial Revolution, with Manchester as its hub. In his study Marcus explores how Engels' own thinking was revolutionized as a result of the social upheavals he observed from the vantage point of a privileged citizen (or noncitizen in this case) and as a German in England.

A collection of essays by Marcus covering 20 years of study and growth appeared in *Representations: Essays on Literature and Society* (New York, 1976). He also contributed a long essay to *Doing Good: The Limits of Benevolence* (New York, 1978), which explored the impact of the so-called helping professions and of a welfare-oriented society on its poorest and neediest people. In the book's four essays—the other three were written by psychoanalyst Willard Gaylin; social historian David Rothman; and Ira Glasser, who was then chair of the New York Civil Liberties Union—the basic contention is that different forms of social service have inadvertently created generations of totally dependent, helpless people and that nothing tangible is done to wean these people from their dependence on outside help. Marcus's focus was 19th-century England as Dickens knew it—a miserable and oppressive time for the British poor.

Marcus's articles have appeared in *Commentary, Daedalus, Salmagundi, The New York Review of Books, The New York Times Book Review* and other periodicals. He has been associate editor of the *Partisan Review* since 1965.

For further information:
Marcus, Steven. *Art, Politics and Will.* New York: 1977.
Marcus, Steven, ed. *The World of Modern Fiction,* 2 vols. New York: 1967.

Marcus, Steven, and Trilling, Lionel, eds. *Ernest Jones: The Life and Work of Sigmund Freud.* New York: 1961.

WALTER MATTHAU

b. October 1, 1920
Actor

Walter Matthau, one of Hollywood's most popular actors, catapulted to fame in 1965 with his Oscar-winning comic performance in Billy Wilder's film *The Fortune Cookie* and the Broadway show, *The Odd Couple.* Since then he has appeared in dozens of films, most often as the older leading man who has a lovable irascibility and roguish warmth. His performance in the film *The Sunshine Boys* won him an Oscar nomination.

Walter Matthau was born in New York City to Milton, a clothing peddler from Kiev, Russia, and Rose (Berolsky) Matthau, a Lithuanian immigrant. He once told an interviewer in jest that his father had been a Catholic priest in Russia whose name was Melas Matuschanskayasky and who had had to emigrate because of his role in a theft. Without questioning the story, the interviewer included it in a biography of Matthau, thus helping the actor create his own legend. Actually Matthau lived in tenements on the Lower East Side of Manhattan. He first acted at the age of 4 in a holiday play at his Jewish nursery, where his mother placed him while she worked in a garment center shop. His interest in acting grew when, as a boy, he began peddling ice cream and soda in the Yiddish theaters on Second Avenue. Ultimately, he began to play small parts in Yiddish musical comedies.

After graduating from Seward Park High School in 1939, where he spent much of his time reading and reciting Shakespeare, Matthau worked in a series of odd jobs, including floor scrubber, file clerk and boxing instructor, until 1942, when he enlisted in the United States Army Air Force. Upon his discharge Matthau returned to New York to study acting at the New School for Social Research Dramatic Workshop, where he studied with German director Erwin Piscator. He began appearing in summer stock and local productions and had his first chance to act in a Broadway play in late 1948, when he played a candle bearer in Maxwell Anderson's *Anne of the Thousand Days.*

During the next decade and a half, Matthau appeared in dozens of Broadway plays, mostly in supporting roles. Among his Broadway credits are *The Liar* (1949), *A Season in the Sun* (1950), *Fancy Meeting You Again*

(1951), *One Bright Day* (1951), *The Grey-Eyed People* (1952), *The Ladies of the Corridor* (1953), *Will Success Spoil Rock Hunter?* (1955) and a 1955 revival of the musical *Guys and Dolls*. Matthau won a 1959 New York Drama Critics Award for his comic portrayal in *Once More, with Feeling* and a 1962 Tony Award as best supporting actor in the Broadway hit *A Shot in the Dark*.

In addition to the theater, Matthau played numerous supporting roles in Hollywood films. His film debut as a nasty character in the 1955 motion picture *The Kentuckian* was followed by *A Face in the Crowd* (1957), *King Creole* (1958), *Ride a Crooked Trail* (1958) and *Charade* (1964). He won a Film Daily Award for his portrayal in 1962 of a sheriff chasing an anarchistic highly individualistic cowboy in *Lonely Are the Brave* and critical acclaim for his part in *Fail Safe* (1964).

Yet, despite all of his acting experience, it wasn't until 1965, when he appeared in the Broadway comedy *The Odd Couple* (for which he was nominated for another Tony Award) and the movie *The Fortune Cookie* whose co-star, Jack Lemmon, became his closest friend, that he had his long-awaited success. Since then Matthau has appeared only in films, among them *Cactus Flower* (1969), *Hello Dolly* (1969), *The Bad News Bears* (1976), *House Calls* (1979), *Casey's Shadow* (1978) and *Little Miss Marker* (1981), to name a few.

Once called by playwright Neil Simon "the greatest instinctive actor," Matthau considers acting "the hardest job known to mankind." Matthau, who speaks with a benign snarl and often assumes a slouching posture, looks and acts like the neighborhood shopkeeper. Though he is most often associated with his role as Oscar, the lovable slob in *The Odd Couple*, Matthau is a versatile actor who can ease himself into any sort of role: smooth thief, shyster lawyer, sensitive cop, bumbling fool, comic genius.

In recent years he has teamed up with British actress Glenda Jackson in several romantic film comedies, including *Housecalls* and *Hopscotch* (1980). Their performances together have been compared by some critics to such early screen partnerships as Katherine Hepburn's with Spencer Tracy.

ELAINE MAY

b. April 21, 1932
Actress; playwright; director

Actress Elaine May, best known for the cynical and nutty humor that characterized her comedy partnership with Mike Nichols during the early 1960s, has since distinguished herself as a serious actress, playwright and director.

She was born Elaine Berlin in Philadelphia, to Jack and Ida Berlin. Her father was an actor on the Yiddish stage, and as a child, she often appeared with him. In 1946 the family settled in Los Angeles, and shortly thereafter Elaine Berlin dropped out of high school. She married Marvin May at 16, had a child two years later and then, divorced, moved to Chicago, where she studied the Stanislavsky method of acting and in 1952 began auditing classes at the University of Chicago.

At the university she met Mike Nichols, then an undergraduate involved in student drama productions, and later (after Nichols had graduated) joined with him and four other young actors to form an improvisational group based in a Chicago club called The Compass. Using audience suggestions, the troupe created spontaneous skits—a technique since copied by subsequent groups over the years. When the "six-some" disbanded after several years together, Nichols and May remained a professional pair and in 1957 moved to New York City, where they secured an agent and began performing.

After hit engagements at the Village Vanguard and the East Side club The Blue Angel, Nichols and May began performing throughout New York and other American cities and on television, including *The Steve Allen Show*, *The Jack Paar Show* and *Omnibus*. Their method of devising and presenting topical, often self-mocking satire eventually drew praise form *New York Times* critic John S. Wilson after their 1959 performance at New York's Town Hall. He wrote that "they create an atmosphere [more like] a concert performance than vaudeville." In late 1960 Nichols and May reached Broadway, where *An Evening with Nichols and May* was hailed for the ability of the two young performers to home in on the idiosyncrasies of relationships between lovers, parents and children, or complete strangers, in both pre-written skits and impromptu dialogue. The following year they made a best-selling recording, but shortly afterward the duo disbanded.

Seeking new avenues for her dramatic skills, May became involved in numerous off-Broadway productions as playwright and director, writing short plays that often used the same topical satirical themes that typified her work with Nichols, but with even more bite. Her play *Not Enough Hope* appeared in 1962, and she made her debut as a director in 1964 with *The Third Ear*. Neither work was a major success. But her short 1969 play *Adaptation*, which used humor to explore uneasy mother-child relationships, artificially liberal attitudes toward blacks and couples whose marriages were held together by the slenderest of threads, was highly praised by *New York Times* theater critic Walter Kerr, who noted May's keen ability to make fun of and offend virtually everyone—yet in a healthy and instructive way.

She also appeared in many films, including Carl Reiner's *Enter Laughing* and Murray Schisgal's *Luv*, both in 1967, and acted in and directed *A New Leaf* in 1971. She wrote the screenplay for the widely hailed Lois Gould novel *Such Good Friends* and directed *The Heartbreak Kid* (1972), which featured her daughter Jeannie Berlin, and *Mikey and Nicky* (1975), which examined the long-term friendship between two middle-aged men.

In general May's work takes a witty and lightly sarcastic view of contemporary lifestyles, focusing in particular on human foibles in forming relationships. But in 1980 May demonstrated the depth of her ability as a dramatic actress when she rejoined Mike Nichols—to critical acclaim—to act in a revival of Edward Albee's difficult and highly emotional play *Who's Afraid of Virginia Woolf?* at the prestigious Long Wharf Theater in New Haven, Connecticut.

EGON MAYER

b. December 23, 1944
Sociologist

Sociologist Egon Mayer has conducted some of the most important studies of Jewish family life in America, with particular focus on the impact of intermarriage and the role of Jewish education in American-born Jewish youth. The author of a major book, several monographs and many articles, he is one of America's foremost younger scholars in his field.

Egon Mayer was born in Switzerland to Eugene, a sales purchasing manager in a plastics firm, and Hedwig (Tauszky) Mayer and raised in Budapest, Hungary. Mayer emigrated to the United States with his family during the Revolution of 1956 and settled in the Borough Park section of Brooklyn, where he attended local yeshivas. He then entered Brooklyn College, graduating with a B.A. degree in 1967, and received his master's degree in sociology from the New School for Social Research two years later and a Ph.D. in sociology from Rutgers University in 1975.

While he pursued his graduate studies, Mayer taught in the New York City public school system from 1967 to 1970. Since 1970 he has taught in the Sociology Department at Brooklyn College, first as an instructor, then as an assistant professor and, since 1978, as an associate professor. He has also held adjunct positions at the New School for Social Research, Adelphi University and Manhattanville College.

Mayer is the author of *From Suburb to Shtetl* (Philadelphia, 1979), a book that analyzes how European-born Orthodox Jews who settled in the Borough Park neighborhood in Brooklyn where he grew up transformed the area into a veritable urban *shtetl* (or East European Jewish village) modeled closely on the communities from which they came. He has also written extensively on Jewish Orthodoxy in America for such periodicals as *The Jewish Journal of Sociology, The Journal of Jewish Communal Service, Jewish Social Studies* and *Jewish Spectator*. His two monographs are *Jewish Intermarriage: Patterns of Intermarriage Among American Jews* (1978) and *Intermarriage and the Jewish Future* (1979), both published by the American Jewish Committee. In these studies Mayer insisted that the traditional ways of deterring intermarriage are irrelevant, that the real question is not one of percentages who marry out, but cures, and that organized Jewry must develop novel responses grounded in reality rather than merely indulge in condemnations of those who do intermarry. Mayer's view is that there is a need to stress the positive aspects of Judaism to the young.

Mayer, who has spoken at many conferences on Jewish issues, believes that, contrary to popular predictions, there will not be a decline in the American Jewish population in the next 10 years but either a modest increase or at least a stabilization of the current figure of just under 6 million. However, he says, the composition of that population will differ significantly from that of 1980. By 1990 more than three-fourths will be college-educated, and many more will be professionals than entrepreneurs. In addition, the under-30 group will decline, while age groups of 30 and over will be substantially larger. Moreover, their lifestyles as Jews will reflect some of the social changes that have affected other aspects of their lives. For example, women, who are no longer primarily "typical housewives" but are frequently highly educated, professional and independent, will play a new and different role in the fabric of Jewish communal life.

Mayer is a consultant to the Council of Jewish Federations, the Rabbinical Council of America, the Jewish Board of Family and Children's Services, and the National Jewish Resource Center. He was a participant in the 1977 Conference on Religious Life Among America's Jews, sponsored by the Synagogue Council of America, and a trustee of the Jewish Association for College Youth from 1976 to 1978.

He is a member of the Association for Jewish Studies, the Association for the Sociological Study of Jewry and the Society for the Scientific Study of Religion.

MARTIN MAYER

b. January 14, 1928
Writer; critic

Martin Mayer is one of America's most prolific and versatile writers, whose studies of the American school system and the American economy are highly regarded among both lay readers and experts in the areas. His reputation for thorough and provocative reporting and his ability to write about virtually any topic make him unusual in a field where specialization is the norm.

Martin Prager Mayer was born in New York City to Henry and Ruby (Prager) Mayer, both trade union lawyers. An excellent student, he attended public elementary schools and the private McBurney High School. When he completed Harvard University as an economics major with a Bachelor of Arts degree in 1947, he was only 19.

Mayer had always aimed for a writing career and, once out of college, headed straight toward reporting and editorial work. From 1947 to 1948 he reported for the *Journal of Commerce* and the following year was assistant editor for *Labor and Nation*. From 1949 to 1951 he was an editor with Hillman Periodicals and from 1951 to 1954 an associate editor for *Esquire*. After 1954 he was able to begin free-lancing and divided his abundant energy among a variety of interests, including fiction and nonfiction book writing, active participation in a wide range of specific projects and pursuit of hobbies that he would also write about frequently, including opera and the recording industry.

Mayer's first books focused on the world of finance. His novel *The Experts* (New York, 1955) concerned a group of up-and-coming young bankers and stockbrokers. Like his two subsequent novels, it was not well received, for although Mayer was praised for his mastery of the subject, his ability to fictionalize it fell flat. But his other books—*Wall Street, Men and Money* (New York, 1955 and 1962); *Madison Avenue, USA* (New York, 1958); *New Breed on Wall Street,* with photographs by Cornell Capa (New York, 1969); and later books about banking, finance and the economy, including *The Bankers* (New York, 1974), *The Builders* (New York, 1978) and *The Fate of the Dollar* (New York, 1980)—have been praised, particularly for their lucid approach to otherwise complex subjects. Mayer has the ability to

synthesize huge areas of discussion, break them down into sections and at the same time provide a comprehensive —and comprehensible—overview of his topic.

He is recognized as an astute critic of the American school system, and in addition to his extensive writing about it, he has also served professionally with several organizations. From 1965 to 1966, for example, he was research director of a study of international secondary education at the Twentieth Century Fund; for five years (1961 to 1966), he served on the President's Panel on Educational Research and Development; and from 1962 to 1967 he was chairperson of a local school board in New York City. His books on education began with *The Schools* (New York, 1961), a study for which he spoke to more than 1,500 people and visited more than 100 classrooms in five countries. His other book-length critiques on public schools include *Where, When & Why: Social Studies in American Schools* (New York, 1963) and *The Teachers Strike* (New York, 1969).

In recent years Mayer has targeted the media as a new area for study and criticism. His book *About Television* (New York, 1972) explores the history of the medium, network politics, the role of the government through the Federal Communications Commission, the development of public broadcasting, the structure of news programming and new inroads to be made by cable. Mayer also writes frequent articles about television.

Mayer's stunning output (he was 27 when his first book was published and has written more than 20 in all—combined with years of magazine writing and active community participation) is perhaps attributable to a compulsion over which he has little control. He works very late at night, he told an interviewer, and has always lived to write. He recalled, "I literally cannot remember a time when I was not writing essentially for my own satisfaction but also with confidence of the grace that others were going to read it."

For further information:
Mayer, Martin. *All You Know is Facts.* New York: 1969.
———. *Bricks, Mortar and the Performing Arts.* New York: 1970.
———. *Conflicts of Interest: Broker-Dealer Firms.* New York: 1975.
———. *Diploma.* New York: 1968.
———. *Emory Buckner,* biography. New York: 1968.
———. *The Lawyers.* New York: 1967.
———. *Today and Tomorrow in America.* New York: 1976.
———. *Trigger Points,* novel. New York: 1969.
———. *A Voice that Fills the House,* novel. New York: 1959.

PAUL MAZURSKY

b. April 25, 1930
Motion picture director; actor; screenwriter

There is a bumbling humanity in the characters populating Paul Mazursky's films that makes them identifiable and almost automatically likable to audiences. Mazursky's special ability as screenwriter and director, particularly in his most successful films, *Blume in Love, Next Stop Greenwich Village, An Unmarried Woman, Harry and Tonto,* has been to draw people—self-doubters with the foibles most of us share—who only sometimes get what they're after.

Irwin Mazursky was born in Brooklyn to David, a laborer, and Jean (Gerson) Mazursky. He was raised in the working-class neighborhood of Brownsville and, while still quite young, set his sights on an acting career. Mazursky graduated from Thomas Jefferson High School in 1947 and entered Brooklyn College, where he changed his name to "Paul" during his senior year. In 1951, shortly before he would have graduated, he took a leave of absence to star in his first film, *Fear and Desire.* It was directed by another first-timer named Stanley Kubrick.

Fear and Desire turned out to be inauspicious for both star and director, since no major film studio wanted to distribute it. When an independent distributor finally did arrange for a screening in 1953, it was panned. Mazursky thus began to study acting seriously, and in late 1953, under the tutelage of Lee Strasberg, Paul Mann and other eminent acting teachers, he starred in summer stock productions of *Death of a Salesman, The Seagull* and *Major Barbara.*

In 1954 Mazursky was offered the role of a juvenile delinquent in the MGM film *The Blackboard Jungle.* Opening to good reviews the following year, the film enabled Mazursky to go on to better roles. He appeared in live television drama and in a series of off-Broadway plays during the late 1950s and filled his spare time with odd jobs. With comedian Herb Hartig he formed a comedy duo that performed with great success in Manhattan nightclubs. The contacts Mazursky formed as a result enabled him to move to Los Angeles in 1959, where he continued to perform stand-up comedy and became a writer for *The Danny Kaye Show.* Mazursky was also one of the writers for the pilot of the briefly popular television series *The Monkees.*

At the same time, he continued dramatic acting by appearing with the repertory company of UCLA and by taking a role in a film version of Jean Genet's play *Deathwatch.* He also studied filmmaking at the University of Southern California and discovered he had a greater penchant for film production than for acting.

Mazursky's first effort in that direction was the script for *I Love You, Alice B. Toklas,* a collaboration with a long-time friend from stand-up comedy days in New York, Larry Tucker. The story of a straight-laced Los Angeles lawyer played by Peter Sellers, and his courtship of a kookie "flower child" whose favorite pastime was baking marijuana brownies, it was the success Mazursky had been waiting for. With it came offers for more work—and more freedom—from major studios.

In 1969 Mazursky and Tucker collaborated on *Bob and Carol and Ted and Alice,* (1969), an ironic comedy whose target was the New Morality and wife-swapping and its effect on two middle-class couples in California. Produced by Columbia and directed by Mazursky, it featured Elliott Gould, Dyan Cannon, Robert Culp and Natalie Wood. It not only signaled Mazursky's debut as a director but underscored his particular talent as a satirist of modern mores. *Bob and Carol* opened the prestigious New York Film Festival in 1969.

The next Mazursky-Tucker effort, *Alex in Wonderland* (1970), the story of an egotistical and hung-up would-be filmmaker, starring Donald Sutherland and featuring Mazursky in a cameo role, was a major flop. It set Mazursky back in his standing with the studios, but he proceeded the following year to write the screenplay for another comedy-drama, which explored the particular social dilemmas faced by upwardly mobile people on the verge of middle age. *Blume in Love* (1972), in which Mazursky had a supporting role in addition to being director and producer, elicited good reviews for its story of a confused Los Angeles attorney, played by George Segal, obsessed with reclaiming his ex-wife, played by Susan Anspach, whom he rapes at one point as a display of his "love."

In a departure from his focus on "modern problems," Mazursky next went on to make *Harry and Tonto* (1974), the story of the travels and (mis) adventures of an elderly man (Art Carney) and his cat. As Harry, Carney balanced the character's eccentricities with great dignity and won an Academy Award. *Next Stop, Greenwich Village* (1976) was Mazursky's most autobiographical work. Set in the 1950s, it told of a young man from Brooklyn who settles into the Bohemian life of Greenwich Village in pursuit of a serious acting career. A popular comedy, which featured Shelly Winters as the overbearing Jewish mother, *Next Stop* became a minor cult film.

But Mazursky's greatest accomplishment to date has been his 1978 film *An Unmarried Woman* which featured Jill Clayburgh as Erica, the well-to-do, attractive, Upper

East Side wife and mother whose life falls apart when her husband abruptly announces that he wants a divorce because he has fallen in love with someone else. Suddenly alone, Erica must pick up the pieces of an entirely different identity, an unnerving new experience. Because the film mirrored many changes in modern American life and especially reflected the experiences of many middle-aged women, it became a critical and popular success and received two Oscar nominations. But because Erica was not really alone for long—she meets an artist (Alan Bates), whom she eventually moves in with—some critics called the happy ending an unrealistic, easy "out." Erica never really deals with independence.

Mazursky made another go at pseudo-fantasy with his latest film, *Willie and Phil* (1980). In an apparent imitation of François Truffaut's classic *Jules and Jim,* Mazursky recounted the intertwining friendship between a Jewish schoolteacher, whose real ambition is to become a successful jazz pianist, and an up-and-coming commercial photographer of Italian background named Phil and their competition in love for Jeanette, who in the fashion of the 1970s, has a baby by one and lives with both. Like *Alex in Wonderland,* which some critics compared to a Fellini film, Mazursky's spin-off of Truffaut was received lukewarmly, at best. As one critic wrote: "[Mazursky's] best films—*Blume in Love, Bob and Carol and Ted and Alice, Next Stop Greenwich Village*—work because their compassion and satirical wit balance each other; together they create the aura of passion . . . in *Willie and Phil,* Mazursky's characteristic balance topples. Compassion overturns satire and the result is the most lifeless movie he has ever made." Although Mazursky features such symbols of the 1970s as "est" therapy, hot tubs and LSD, he fails to evoke the heart of the era he is attempting to portray, and *Willie and Phil* is not a convincing film.

SEYMOUR MELMAN

b. December 30, 1917
Author; industrial engineer

Seymour Melman, professor of industrial engineering at Columbia Univeristy, is widely known as a scholar and peace activist. Author of numerous books and co-chairman of SANE: A Citizens' Organization for a Sane World, he has long argued that America should switch from a military to a civilian economy in order to finance understaffed educational and health resources and create a healthier economy.

Seymour Melman was born in New York City to Abraham, a pharmacist, and Pauline (Kazdan) Melman. He was educated in New York City public schools and received his B.S. degree in 1939 from the College of the City of New York. He earned his Ph.D. in engineering from Columbia University in 1949.

Melman was a member of the research staff of the National Industrial Conference Board from 1944 to 1945. In 1948 he joined the faculty at Columbia University as an instructor and has taught there ever since. He was made a full professor in 1963.

Ignoring customary academic boundaries, Melman has used economics, engineering and public policy to study the uses of technology for serving human needs. His research has focused upon industrial productivity, the impact of economics on technology and problems of conversion from a military to a civilian economy.

He has written books, including *Our Depleted Society* (New York, 1965), in which he asserts that America is experiencing a decline in the areas of industry, technology and social services because of its concentration of technical talent and money on military production—what he calls the cold war economy. He states that because of military extravagance, American research programs for civilian purposes are severely understaffed and that the depletion in American society can be repaired only by focusing on other areas, such as health and education, rather than the military.

In *Pentagon Capitalism: The Political Economy of War* (New York, 1970), Melman contends that the American government not only regulates business but in fact *is* business. He points to the control that the Pentagon has over industry, Congress and universities, claiming that the military-industrial complex is a formalized system—perhaps the single most important management in the United States. He analyzes the over-$1,000 billion expenditure for defense between 1946 and 1969 and compares that with the deficiencies in housing, food, education and medical care.

He continued restating this theme in *Profits Without Production* (New York, 1981), arguing that the ever-growing American military budget transfers to the economy of war preparation "machinery, tools, engineers, energy, raw materials, skilled labor and managers, harms the renewal of declining American industries and damages vital aspects of the non-military economy."

He has played an important role in pro-peace politics in the United States by doing research in the area of nuclear weaponry and the economic consequences of military policies. Since 1969 he has been co-chairperson of SANE, an organization devoted to bringing about major cuts in arms spending, a nuclear freeze, the conversion of defense industries, shipyards, and military bases to non-military production as they are no longer needed for defense, and advance planning and preparation to assure defense workers economic security during the changeover.

For further information:
Melman, Seymour. *The Permanent War Economy.* New York: 1974.

YEHUDI MENUHIN

b. April 22, 1916
Violinist

Through his music, Yehudi Menuhin has become known as "America's Best Ambassador" because of the innovative role he has played in fostering cultural exchanges with other countries. He has sustained a remarkable resilience as a musician, having first made headlines as a child prodigy on the violin, and remaining throughout his career an internationally respected virtuoso in technique and in musical interpretation.

Yehudi Menuhin was born in New York City to Moshe, a Hebrew teacher who later became superintendent of the Jewish Education Society, and Martha (Sher) Menuhin. Both parents were of Russian origin, although Moshe Menuhin was raised in Palestine. In early 1917 the Menuhin family moved to San Francisco, where Menuhin grew up.

According to one account, Menuhin was brought to concerts as an infant because his parents, who loved music, couldn't afford a baby-sitter. He was given a toy violin at age 3 and soon after received a real violin. His talents became clear by the time he was 5, and Menuhin began studying with Sigmund Anker, who specialized in working with young children. Two years later he switched to Louis Persinger, concert master of the San Francisco Symphony Orchestra, who sponsored Menuhin's first public solo appearances in 1923, a performance of the *Symphony Espagnole* of Lalo. As Menuhin became deeply engrossed in learning violin, the remainder of his education was taken over by his parents and later by private tutors, who taught him and his siblings Hebrew, German, French, Italian, Spanish, mathematics and history.

In 1924 a San Francisco attorney and philanthropist, Sidney Ehrman, became a sponsor of Menuhin's further studies and subsequent travels. Following Menuhin's New York debut in 1926 at the Manhattan Opera House, Ehrman financed a trip to Europe for the entire Menuhin family. In Paris, Menuhin studied with the Rumanian violinist and composer Georges Enesco and with Adolph Busch, a German violinist, and performed to great critical acclaim in 1927. Later that year, upon returning to the United States, Menuhin performed two historic concerts in New York. Prior publicity attracted mobs to hear him play the Beethoven concerto with the New York Symphony Orchestra, which was soon followed by a solo recital at Carnegie Hall. Despite the usual cynicism of critics toward child prodigies, Olin Downes of *The New York Times* was spurred to write: "It seems ridiculous to say that he showed a mature conception of Beethoven's concerto, but that is the fact. . . . A boy of 11 proved conclusively his right to be ranked, irrespective of his years, with outstanding interpreters of this music." And according to another account, following a performance in Berlin in 1928, Menuhin was embraced by Albert Einstein, who was alleged to have said, "Now I know there is a God in heaven!"

With these early triumphs, Menuhin signed with an agent and embarked on an international career. His parents restricted his schedule to 20 concerts a year, and only in top halls. His sister Hepzibah, a pianist, became his frequent accompanist. In 1934 Menuhin took his first around-the-world tour, performing in 110 concerts in 13 countries.

But in 1935 he withdrew from concertizing for a two-year retirement—a needed period of reflection as he made the transition into adulthood. He used this break to study violin technique, something he had not done so thoroughly as a child. When he returned to the concert stage in 1937, he had successfully conquered the onus of having been a prodigy and developed into one of the world's most respected violinists.

In the years to come, Menuhin soloed with the world's top orchestras and conductors, including Toscanini, Stokowski, Beecham, Monteux, Koussevitsky and others. During World War II he toured extensively, playing for American and Allied armed forces and in camps and newly liberated European cities. He was the first American musician to perform in the Soviet Union after the war and later toured Eastern Europe and the Soviet Union as well as Japan, India, South America, Australia, South Africa and elsewhere. He also performed in postwar Germany and supported the right of Wilhelm Furtwaengler, a known Nazi sympathizer, to resume conducting, a stand for which Menuhin was severely criticized.

In the early 1950s Menuhin made several appearances in India and during a 1952 tour raised $74,000 for a famine fund. He subsequently became immersed in Indian philosophy and yoga and switched to vegetarianism, subjects that he discussed in a 1963 BBC-TV presentation, "Yehudi Menuhin and His Guru." His increasing work for humanitarian goals earned him the Jawaharlal Nehru Award for International Understanding in 1968. Menuhin made a historic musical tie with India when he began performing with the Indian sitar virtuoso, Ravi Shankar.

Menuhin settled in England, where in 1959 he became head of the Bath Festival, which was primarily a chamber orchestra. In 1969 the festival moved to Windsor and was renamed the Menuhin Festival Orchestra. Six years earlier Menuhin had added to his credits the founding of the Yehudi Menuhin School in Surrey, which specialized in teaching gifted young musicians; he taught master classes. And in line with his propensity for innovation, he emphasized the revival of works by generally neglected composers, including his mentor Enesco, as well as Bloch, Walton and Bartok, who has since risen far above his past obscurity.

Menuhin has performed numerous times in Israel but is an outspoken critic of Zionism, which he has defined as a "parochial nationalism." He has appeared in two films, *Stage Door Canteen* (1943) and *The Magic Bow* (1973), and is the subject of a 1971 French-made documentary, *Yehudi Menuhin—Chemin de Lumiere.* He has also made six educational films for the BBC, entitled *Menuhin Teaches.*

Menuhin's involvement in the internationalist movement was further promoted by his participation in a 1971 UNESCO conference in Moscow in which, as president of the International Music Council, he condemned political nationalism, which he claimed limited opportunities to fully develop creative abilities.

Menuhin is the author of four books: *Theme and Variations* (New York, 1972), a collection of personal essays: *The Violin and Viola* (New York, 1976); *Unfinished Journey,* an autobiography (New York, 1977); and *The Music of Man,* which he wrote with Curtis W. Davis (New York, 1979).

DAVID MERRICK

b. November 27, 1912
Theatrical producer

David Merrick is invariably described in hyperboles: He is Broadway's most innovative, controversial, flamboyant and possibly most successful producer. With 84

shows to his credit by the time his updated version of *42nd Street* opened in 1980, he is also the most prolific.

David Margulies was born in St. Louis, Missouri to Samuel, a merchant, and Celia Margulies. Little about Merrick's childhood has been documented because he has always been notoriously vague about his personal life, but according to some accounts, after he reached his early teens, his parents were divorced, and he was raised by a sister much older than he. He attended Washington University in St. Louis, where he received a B.A. degree, probably in 1934, and then studied law at St. Louis University, where he completed a Bachelor of Laws in 1937.

Since his early youth, Merrick had been interested in theater and even as a private practice attorney in St. Louis began to invest in plays in New York. By around 1950 he decided to move to New York—and to adopt a new name—and make the gradual transition to producing full-time. His first effort, *Clutterbuck,* was only barely a financial success, but his next production, *Fanny* (1954), turned a profit for its investors and turned Merrick permanently away from law and into theater. He aggressively sought new projects and managed to produce such blockbusters as *Look Back in Anger* (1957), *Gypsy* (1958) and *Carnival* (1961)—to name only 3—and a fair number of clinkers. He often had several shows running simultaneously and during this period grossed $60 million in tickets—a record-breaking amount at the time. In 1960, for example, he opened 11 shows in one season, including 3 in one week—*Irma La Douce, A Taste of Honey* and *Becket*. In ensuing years hit play followed hit play. *I Can Get It for You Wholesale* (1962), *Stop the World—I Want to Get Off* (1962), *Luther* (1963), *Marat/Sade* (1966), *Rosencrantz and Guildenstern Are Dead* (1967), *Promises, Promises* (1969), *Travesties* (1975) and many others were produced with dazzling regularity.

With the making of his name came an ample share of notoriety. Merrick immersed himself in theater producing with a passion unusual in a job that was supposed to be all business. He often threw his personal savings into a play just to keep it alive, and he frequently became involved in (or, according to some observers, "interfered with") the creative process of assembling a production. He devised unconventional advertising gimmicks that elicited the attention he wanted for his shows but, as often as not, also aroused the animosity of his competitors as well as of his colleagues and co-workers. He was quoted as being contemptuous of actors, whom he described as childlike—a statement not exactly geared toward winning friends.

Probably Merrick's best-known publicity stunt was the full-page newspaper ad he designed for *Subways Are for Sleeping,* which opened in 1961 to poor reviews. He located about a half dozen New Yorkers with the same names as the major Broadway drama critics and invited them to a free performance of the play. He then used quotes (only positive ones, of course) which they gave about the show, with their names—and tiny photographs of the speakers—to plug it. Although Merrick's prank did not turn *Subways* into a hit, it certainly introduced more theater-goers to David Merrick. Another gimmick, used to plug *The Matchmaker,* was to put on the streets in the theater district a British taxicab which was ostensibly driven by a monkey, and with the sign, "I am driving my master to see 'The Matchmaker.' "

Merrick's methods of inducing more people to attend theater went beyond mere gimmickry. He innovated the use of advertising in subways and trains and on billboards and was a pioneer in selling tickets by mail order and telephone, methods that have since become standard. When Merrick's show *Sugar* opened in 1972, he offered free parking to his prospective audience.

Merrick's highly publicized feuds with actors, the press, unions and other producers eventually earned him the nickname "the abominable showman." In 1966, after a play of his received poor reviews by television drama critics, he petitioned the Federal Communications Commission for equal time to respond. The FCC denied his request, however, since the equal-time doctrine applied only to "controversial issues of public importance." Although Merrick might have contested the FCC decision, he moved, instead, to drop several critics from his first-night list.

Despite the consistently critical reviews of Merrick's own behavior—his personal life as well as his professional conduct earned him poor marks in the press—he has also made major contributions to theater producing that are less well known. In 1965 he organized and accompanied a theater ensemble featuring Mary Martin that traveled through Vietnam by helicopter to perform for American troops. And he was responsible for encouraging the hiring of minorities both onstage and backstage. According to one account, as of 1968 Merrick alone accounted for about 95 percent of all blacks employed on Broadway. It was his idea, for example, to mount the highly successful all-black production of *Hello, Dolly!,* starring Pearl Bailey.

But Merrick's "good deeds" have been outweighed by his reputation for inspiring feuds with almost everyone. For example, a long-running fight with producer Joseph Papp grew so bitter that when the two men appeared in a panel together, they completely ignored each other. In 1970, after Merrick became a dominant shareholder at 20th Century-Fox, he was sued by the company and forced after four years of often nasty proceedings to sell back his stock. Merrick's foray into cinema, besides his attempted take-over of the studio, includes the 1975 production of *The Great Gatsby,* which flopped. His frequent tampering with casting and his publicized feuds with personnel involved with the film were held responsible for the fiasco it became. Such is the feeling about Merrick that journalist Dick Schaap, in an article about the producer, wrote "To hear his detractors, Merrick combines the delicacy of the Marquis de Sade, the humanity of Attila the Hun, the generosity of Ebenezer Scrooge and the sophisticated taste of Yogi Berra."

Merrick fueled Schaap's commentary when he turned the opening date of his 1980 show *42nd Street* into one of the greatest secrets in America, second only, perhaps, to Zsa Zsa Gabor's real age. The show, in the planning for months and known to be one of the most expensive and largest-cast productions in Broadway history, suddenly became classified material. Merrick kept rescheduling opening dates, closed the box office and did not advertise. When opening night arrived at last—at the highest prices in Broadway ticket history and to rave reviews—Merrick committed what some critics still think was a huge gaffe while others think it was a well-timed, well-contrived and ironic piece of drama. Unbeknownst to the public and to some of the show's cast, *42nd Street*'s director, Gower Champion, had been dying of a blood disease, and Merrick's manipulation of opening night was meant to keep Champion's illness secret. He died hours before the show opened, and as audiences cheered at the final curtain, Merrick went on stage to announce Champion's death. His move was a testimonial to Champion, but some critics described it as in poor taste and badly timed. In any case, *42nd Street* proved to be enormously successful.

ROBERT MERRILL

b. June 4, 1919
Opera singer

Robert Merrill, the world-renowned operatic baritone whose first performances were at synagogues, bar mitzvahs and weddings, became an overnight star when he made his debut with the Metropolitan Opera in December 1945.

Moishe—later Morris—Miller was born in Williamsburg, Brooklyn to Abraham, a tailor and Lillian (Balaban) Miller. His immigrant mother, who had had a singing and concert career in Poland and sang on a local radio station in Brooklyn, tutored her son in the early years of his musical training. However, it was not until he was 18 and saw a Metropolitan Opera rehearsal of *La Traviata* that he decided upon a musical career. Arrangements were made for him to take singing lessons from the eminent teacher Samuel Margolis, who later arranged for Merrill to attend his first opera performance at the Met of *Il Trovatore*.

To pay for Margolis, Merrill—who had graduated in 1935 from New Utrecht High School, where he played baseball—worked winters in his father's store and summers singing at hotels in the Catskills and the Adirondacks. He also sang on the cruise ship *Rotterdam* and in Yiddish theaters on Manhattan's Second Avenue. Working hotels, he once remarked, "has the advantage of teaching the young performer to face audiences."

When Merrill was signed by an agent scouting Grossinger's, a wider world opened for him with radio shows, a nine-week contract at Radio City Music Hall and a concert tour. He developed a "crooning" style similar to Bing Crosby's and began singing on radio. It was then that he changed his name.

That year—1944—he made his professional debut in *La Traviata* with the Detroit Opera Company as well as his first recording, with popular singer Jeanette MacDonald. The following year he sang for and won first prize in the Metropolitan Opera Auditions of the Air. In 1945 Merrill made his stage debut at the Met as the elder Germont in *Traviata;* he was then the youngest performer to sing what would become his most famous role. Among his many parts in the Met repertoire for which he has since earned his reputation are Figaro in *The Barber of Seville,* Count di Luna in *Il Trovatore,* Sir Henry Ashton in *Lucia di Lammermoor* and the High Priest in *Samson et Dalila.*

Merrill quickly became a popular figure beyond the world of opera. In July 1946 he was the only singer to perform in a memorial to President Roosevelt held by both houses of Congress, and he has sung at birthday parties for presidents Eisenhower, Kennedy and Johnson. He also performed in 1950 on the television program *Your Show of Shows.*

Ambitious for publicity and fame, Merrill broke his contract with the Met in 1951 to perform in a Hollywood picture, *Aaron Slick from Punkin Creek.* A flop, the film nearly ruined Merrill's career, especially when Met director Sir Rudolf Bing refused to allow him back. He toured briefly with the USO in Austria and Germany and in 1952, after making a public apology to Bing, was reinstated. He remained with the Met until 1976, when he resigned, complaining that he was no longer being given choice roles.

Merrill, who has also performed as Tevye in *Fiddler on the Roof,* is as successful in Las Vegas as he is on the opera stage. He has recorded dozens of albums, ranging from popular songs to folk melodies to operatic selections. He is winner of many awards, including the Handel Medallion, City of New York (1970); the Harriet Cohen International Music Award (1961); and Best Record Awards for 1946, 1962 and 1964.

The bel canto baritone is best-known for his extraordinary technical command. He produces a dramatic baritone without any apparent effort, and his booming voice can be heard throughout the hall. Merrill's voice is as familiar to New York Yankee baseball fans as to opera lovers, for his singing of the national anthem is frequently heard before baseball games.

He is the author of two autobiographies, *Once More from the Beginning* with S. Dody (New York, 1965), and *Between Acts: An Irreverent Look at Opera and Other Madness,* with R. Saffron (New York, 1965).

HOWARD (MORTON) METZENBAUM

b. June 4, 1917
United States senator

Howard (Morton) Metzenbaum, the liberal Democratic senator from Ohio, has been involved in politics for over three decades. During his election campaigns, Metzenbaum, a wealthy businessman, has stressed his support for measures to help people in need and has enjoyed strong backing from organized labor. As a member of the Senate Energy Committee, he has strongly opposed policies backed by oil companies and is in favor of strict regulation of oil and gas prices. He is a firm supporter of Israel and has been active in forcing the federal administration to investigate and prosecute alleged Nazi war criminals.

Howard Metzenbaum was born in Cleveland, Ohio to Charles, who owned a dry goods store, and Anna (Klafter) Metzenbaum. He received his bachelor's degree in 1939 and a law degree in 1941, both from Ohio State University. He became a member of the Ohio House of Representatives in 1943, the youngest person elected to that office, and a member of the Ohio Senate in 1947, remaining until 1950. He introduced and had enacted the Metzenbaum Act, which was among the first measures in the United States to provide consumers with protection in credit matters, and it became a model for federal truth-in-lending legislation. He also tried to have enacted legislation prohibiting racial, religious and ethnic discrimination in employment. Although Metzenbaum's effort was unsuccessful, it pre-dated later federal measures that became law.

During the 1950s and 1960s, Metzenbaum also es-tablished himself as a successful businessman. He co-founded the Airport Parking Company of America (APCOA) in 1949 and was chairman of its board from 1958 to 1966. In that same time Metzenbaum contin-ued his activity in politics by working as campaign manager for Senator Stephen M. Young in 1958 and 1964, elections that the candidate won. When APCOA merged in 1966 with International Telephone and Telegraph, Metzenbaum became a multimillionaire and was also named chairman of the board of the ITT Con-sumer Services Corporation from 1966 to 1968. From 1969 to 1974 he held the same position with ComCorp, a weekly newspaper corporation. He distinguished him-self as an innovator in business and was also a selective investor in newspapers and banks throughout Ohio.

Metzenbaum first ran for the Senate seat from Ohio in 1970, losing in the general election to the Republi-can son of a well-known Ohio senator, Robert Taft. He then served for 11 months in 1973 as an appointed senator after Senator William Saxbe departed the Senate to become U.S. Attorney General under President Nixon. He lost the Democratic nomination to former astronaut John Glenn in 1974. In the primary Glenn blasted Metzenbaum for a dispute with the IRS over tax shelters.

Since 1976, when he was elected senator, defeating Taft, Metzenbaum has won a reputation as a hard-working and well-prepared politician with a profound interest in helping people. Besides participating on en-ergy committees—he is an ardent conservationist—Metzenbaum also serves on subcommittees related to health and science research; employment; poverty and migratory labor; alcoholism and drug abuse; and anti-trust, monopoly and business rights. He is a fighter of big oil companies, utilities and corporations and advo-cates the cutting of the defense budget. He also backs the creation of a new consumer protection agency and passage of national health insurance. He favors public job bills, horizontal divestiture for oil companies and opposes deregulation of natural gas. He has long-time ties to labor organizations throughout Ohio. In 1978 he won a 100 percent rating from Americans for Demo-cratic Action, a liberal organization that regularly rates the voting records and achievements of legislators. He is against draft registration and conscription.

In 1981 Metzenbaum opposed the planned U.S. sale of advanced military equipment to Saudi Arabia, claim-ing that "providing AWACs to Saudi Arabia would be a true catastrophe for Israel [and] would amount to a reversal by the United States of our commitments to the

security of a loyal and courageous Democratic ally." He also co-sponsored a bill aimed at making Raoul Wallen-berg—a former Swedish diplomat who saved thousands of Hungarian Jews during World War II and who was arrested by the Soviet army in 1945 and never heard from again—an honorary American citizen, a move that would permit the United States to make official inquir-ies. He has also experienced an anti-Semitic remark on the floor of the United States Senate. In 1981, during floor debate on voluntary prayer in public schools, Sen-ator Ernest F. Hollings (Democrat-South Carolina) called Metzenbaum "the Senator from B'nai B'rith." Hollings lamely explained, "I said it only in fun," but Metzen-baum's Jewish colleague, Senator Arlen Spector (Repub-lican-Pennsylvania) excoriated Hollings, calling his re-mark "inappropriate and offensive."

Metzenbaum is vice chairman of fellows at Brandeis University and a former trustee and treasurer of Mt. Sinai Hospital. He is on the board of directors of the Council on Human Relations and United Cerebral Palsy.

LEONARD MICHAELS

b. February 2, 1933
Author; professor

With the publication in 1981 of his novel *The Men's Club* (New York), Leonard Michaels emerged as the counterbalance to the many women novelists of the era who depicted their struggles in fiction and fact in a complex and not-always-brave new world of personal relationships, sex and an endless and often elusive search for something called self. Michaels did the same for men as he documented a dark and incisive yet satirical plunge through the lives of seven middle-aged males anxiously sharing their frustrations and secrets. The book, incubated after years of short story writing and life in academia, was a critical success.

Leonard Michaels was born in New York City to immigrant parents, Leon, a barber, and Anna (Czeskies) Michaels. He attended New York University, where he received a B.A. degree in 1953, and the University of Michigan, where he earned his M.A. degree in 1956 and his Ph.D. in 1967. He taught English at Paterson (New Jersey) State College from 1961 to 1962 and at the University of California, first at the Davis campus (1966 to 1968) and since 1969 in Berkeley. He also began writing and publishing short stories, which were later collected in two books—*Going Places* (New York, 1969), which was nominated for a National Book Award and *I Would Have Saved Them If I Could* (New York, 1975).

The sardonic and kooky humor that would characterize *The Men's Club* was already evident in the earlier stories. In *I Would Have Saved Them If I Could*, for example, Michaels created the character of Phillip Liebowitz, who appeared in several stories and both embodied and acted out many of Michaels' own perceptions as one who had come of age during the 1950s. Liebowitz—compared often to Philip Roth's Alexander Portnoy—haggles with his own confused adolescent sexuality as well as the compromises of his adult yearnings to become successful on his own. But when the occasion presents itself, he is not above having sex with someone he thinks can help him. With equal ambivalence he both succumbs to and resists the pressures from his mother to be the nice Jewish professional she raised.

But with the publication of *The Men's Club*, Michaels' storytelling abilities and his personal insights merged with full force. Originally a short story, which appeared in *Esquire* magazine in 1978, *The Men's Club* documents the meeting of seven men in the Berkeley, California home of one of them. Middle-class and middle-aged, they have achieved a level of success in their lives—at least on the surface. Underneath, their self-doubt and unhappiness lurk like demons, awaiting release. Without knowing it, the "club" the men form will become an escape valve, not merely for their frustrations but for a violent acting-out and revenge, which they will take against themselves and against the women they feel have destroyed their lives. For if anything threatens each man more, it is, Michaels implies, the struggle of women they have known for autonomy from the men, for their independence first and then for the opportunity to make decisions about their lives on their own terms. In the book Michaels writes:

> I thought again about the women. Anger, identity, politics, rights, wrongs. I envied them. It seemed attractive to be deprived in our society. Deprivation gives you something to fight for, it makes you morally superior, it makes you serious. What was left for men these days? They already had everything. Did they need clubs? The mere sight of two men together suggests a club. Consider Damon and Pythias, Huck and Jim, Hamlet and Horatio. The list is familiar. Even the Lone Ranger wasn't lonely. He had Tonto.

Told primarily in dialogue as the conversations of the seven men bounce back and forth, and with an unnamed first-person narrator (presumably Michaels), *The Men's Club* was in fact based on a true experience of the author, who, when first invited, agreed to attend with great reluctance but later found himself deeply affected by the experience. "I went very cynically, ready for all kinds of silliness," he said in an interview, but "meeting after meeting, I found myself profoundly concerned about the unhappiness of a man whom I hardly knew." And he continued to attend. "There's something about the fact that it's a group of men talking which makes for a kind of happiness, even if the stories are downers." So he took his own positive experience of the club, despite its mishmash of emotions, including his own, wrote the story and then expanded it into a novel.

Although Michaels' fiction shares some common qualities with such writers he admires as Isaac Babel, Franz Kafka, Flannery O'Connor and Jorge Luis Borges, he avoids reading their work when he writes because:

> It's so contagious, you don't even know it's happening sometimes. You pick up the peculiar rhythm of another writer, or you find yourself playing with attitudes you discover in some other novelist that are not yours at all. I don't want to be subjected to that kind of temptation when I write.

For further information:
Michaels, Leonard. "My Father's Life: Leonard Michaels on Leon Michaels," *Esquire*, October 1981.

ARTHUR MILLER

b. October 17, 1915
Playwright

Arthur Miller's *Death of a Salesman* may well be the greatest American play written in the last 35 years and Arthur Miller the finest American playwright. The play applied the same concepts as classic Greek tragedies in its consideration of the plight of the common man, elevating him to heroic dimensions. *Death of a Salesman* is imbued with great pathos as Willie Loman, the salesman, barters his soul away for the capitalist dream of wealth and success and then watches helplessly as that dream turns sour.

Arthur Miller was born in Harlem to Isidore, an immigrant from Austria-Hungary who manufactured ladies' coats, and Augusta (Barnett) Miller, a public school teacher. Miller, the middle of three children, says that as a child he was barely conscious of Judaism. He attended P.S. 29 and, following the family's move to Brooklyn in 1928, James Madison and Abraham Lincoln high schools, graduating in 1932. During high school he was more interested in sports than literature, but his literary interests grew after reading Dostoevski's *The Brothers Karamazov*.

Following high school graduation, Miller worked for two years to earn money for a college education. On his second attempt he was accepted by the University of Michigan and studied playwriting there. During his college years he wrote a number of award-winning plays that went unproduced, including *They Too Arise* (1936), in which a Jewish clothing manufacturer opposes using scabs to end a strike. "I can't see that it's the way for Jewish men to act," Abe Simon, the manufacturer, says. He received his B.A. degree in English in 1938.

After college Miller began to work for the Federal Writers Project, but the project ended before any of his work was produced. His first publication was a collection of war reportage about Army camps in 1944. The book was called *Situation Normal* (New York, 1944). Also in 1944 Miller's first play, *The Man Who Had All the Luck,* was produced on Broadway. It concerned a man frustrated by the role blind fate played in his life and whether life was predetermined or shaped by free will. It was not well received and closed after four showings.

After the publication of a novel, *Focus* (New York, 1945), which dealt with anti-Semitism directed at a non-Jew thought to be a Jew, *All My Sons,* Miller's second play, opened on Broadway in 1947. The story of a man who supplied the government with faulty materials during the war and then foisted the blame on his hapless business partner, the play established Miller as a serious playwright. *All My Sons* won a New York Drama Critics Circle Award in 1947.

Death of a Salesman opened on Broadway in 1949. It won a Pulitzer Prize and a New York Drama Critics Circle Award and made Miller famous, earning him comparisons to Ibsen and the Greeks.

Miller's next play was *The Crucible* (1953). Set during the Salem witch trials of the 1600s, it focused on one man's refusal to become involved with an inquisitorial system. Despite the historical backdrop, most viewers understood *The Crucible* to be a thinly disguised attack on McCarthyism, which was then rampant in the country. Miller received a Tony Award for this work.

After *A View from the Bridge* (1955), a drama of a working-class family, which was turned into a movie in 1962, Miller was cited for contempt by the House Un-American Activities Committee for refusing to name former political associates. He was sentenced to prison for contempt of Congress, but this judgment was reversed by an appellate court.

After the Fall, produced in 1964, is the story of a man who feels he must go through a period of atonement and absolution before he can marry for a third time. The critics felt the play was heavily autobiographical and reflected Miller's second marriage, to Marilyn Monroe. They found the play exploitative and embarrassing.

In 1965 Miller was elected to the presidency of PEN, the international writers' organization. In that same year, as a protest against the Vietnam War, he refused to go to Washington, D.C. for the signing of the Arts and Humanities Act.

Miller next published a book detailing a journey in Russia. Called *In Russia* (New York, 1969), it was richly illustrated with photographs by his wife Inge Morath. He and his wife also collaborated on *Chinese Encounters* (New York, 1979), a chronicle of a visit to China. His next play was the surrealist *In the Creation of the World and Other Things* (1972), about the remaking of the Book of Genesis. A more recent but unsuccessful effort was *American Clock* (1980), in which he returns to some of his older themes about upper middle-class Jewish family life and financial loss in the Great Depression of the 1930s.

In a 1966 interview in the *Paris Review,* Miller said: "There is tragedy in the world but the world must continue. The Jews can't afford to revel too much in the tragic because it might overwhelm them. I have, so to speak, a psychic investment in the continuity of life."

In 1980 his play *Playing for Time*—described by the Jewish Telegraphic Agency as a flawed, but "powerful story of a handful of women prisoners struggling for survival at Auschwitz"—was performed on CBS-TV to the accompaniment of protests from many Jews because Vanessa Redgrave, an outspoken supporter of the Palestinian Liberation Organization, was cast as Fania Fenelon, a half-Jewish musician and author of the book on which the script was based. Miller rejected the complaints, arguing that "Turning her down because of her ideas was unacceptable to me; after all, I suffered the blacklist myself." The artist, he told the House Un-American Activities Committee in 1956, has "a peculiar mandate, a mandate not only in his literature but in the way he behaves and the way he lives—in short, that art comes before politics.

Miller's writings are filled with Jewish themes. *Focus* and *Incident at Vichy,* which dealt with French anti-Semitism during World War II, mirrored his Jewish sentiments. In the early 1950s Joseph Buloff played the role of Willy Loman in *Toyt fun a Salesman,* the Yiddish version, and a critic wrote that it was "as if Miller was thinking in Yiddish and unconsciously translating into English."

For further information:
———. *Arthur Miller's Collected Plays,* vols. 1 and 2. New York: 1979 and 1980.
———. *The Portable Arthur Miller.* New York: 1972.

MARVIN MILLER

b. April 14, 1917
Labor official

Marvin Miller has single-handedly transformed baseball from being merely an American pastime to a big business. As executive director of the Major League Baseball Players Association, he has created a legitimate labor movement among athletes, garnering huge salary deals for the top players and healthy minimums for the greenest rookies. In 1972 and again in 1981 he spearheaded the almost unheard-of: a baseball players strike.

Marvin Julian Miller was born in New York City to Alexander, who was a salesman in a women's clothing store and an organizer for the Retail, Wholesale and Department Store Employees Union, and Gertrude (Wild) Miller, a former schoolteacher. Raised in Brooklyn, he graduated from James Madison High School in 1933 and attended Miami University in Ohio for three years. He transferred to New York University and received a B.A. degree in economics in 1938. After a brief stint at the Department of the Treasury in Washington, Miller returned to New York to work for the Welfare Department in 1940. His first labor-related position began when he became a disputes hearing officer with the Wage Stabilization Division of the War Labor Board during World War II.

Using this experience, Miller went on staff with the U.S. Conciliation Service as a personnel trainer. He got his first union post in 1947, when he worked for the International Association of Machinists. From 1950 to 1966 he was on staff with the United Steelworkers, first as associate research director, then in 1960 as assistant to the president. During this period Miller emerged as a major spokesperson for union causes and as an effective negotiator. In 1959 he was instrumental in designing a contract for the workers at Kaiser Steel that not only made them the best-paid steelworkers in the United States but also permitted them to participate in the growth of their plant as shareholders.

Innovative in other ways that resulted in greater job security and benefits for workers, Miller was appointed by President Kennedy to a national labor-management panel in 1963 and was reappointed by President Johnson in 1964 for a three-year term.

Miller became executive director of the Major League Baseball Players Association in 1966, when association members decided to appoint a full-time administrator. His reputation at Kaiser made him a target of hostility among team owners, but Miller established rapport with them at the same time that he began to design stricter—and fatter—contracts for players than they had ever had

previously. In 1968, for example, minimum player salary rose to $10,000 from $6,000—the first such increase in 20 years—and by 1972 it was $13,500. Other changes in players' contracts concerned travel conditions and pension benefits.

As an advocate of collective bargaining, Miller attempted to strike compromises between owners and players, but when the owners were too obstinate for his tastes, he led a strike in the spring of 1972—the first in baseball history. When it ended after 13 days, the players had a pension fund $1 million richer than when it began, and Miller became widely known as the "Ralph Nader of professional sports."

Miller did not appear in the limelight again for another nine years, but when he did, it was with terrific impact on baseball management. This time the players were not demanding new pay increases—as of 1981 the minimum player salary was $32,500, average was $175,000, and the top players were raking in more than a million a year—but major changes in the contracts management negotiated with team members. Miller played the "tough guy" and threatened to strike. Indeed, he followed through, and when the strike ended in August 1981 after two months, the baseball season was nearly destroyed—and many fans had turned into cynics.

But Miller is a staunch defender of labor movements. When team owners intimated that Miller was a labor "boss," he replied: "They talked about racketeers' swallowing up baseball. But it's not difficult to make major strides in an industry 100 years behind in labor relations."

NATHAN MILSTEIN

b. December 31, 1904
Violinist

Though neither as eccentric as Jasha Heifetz nor as eclectic as Yehudi Menuhin, Nathan Milstein has nevertheless attained top ranking as one of the world's greatest violinists. Since his start as an "accidental" child prodigy, he has proceeded nonstop to forge a flourishing international career as a top interpreter of Bach, a great master teacher, and a composer-arranger for violin.

Nathan Milstein was born in Odessa in the Ukraine to Myron Milstein, an importer of Scottish and English woolens and tweeds, and Maria (Bluestein) Milstein. He began playing violin as a child, not because he was attracted to music, but because, as several biographies recount, Milstein's mother wanted to keep her mischievous son out of trouble and the violin seemed to be the way to do it. However, Milstein seemed to have a natural rapport with the instrument, and he was soon accepted as a student by the well-known Odessa-based violinist Peter Stoliarsky. By the time he was nine, Milstein had already developed a considerable repertory of performance-quality pieces.

In 1914, however, it became clear that Milstein had a substantial career in the making. During a concert to honor the composer Alexander Glazunov, who was visiting Odessa, the scheduled soloist fell ill and the ten-year-old Milstein was called in to replace him at the last minute. Milstein had by then learned Glazunov's difficult Violin Concerto, and when he performed it, he displayed not only a remarkable technical command of the violin, but sensitivity to the music unusual in such a small boy. Word of his talent spread and in 1915 Leopold Auer, Russia's greatest violin teacher and head of the violin department at the St. Petersburg Conservatory, arranged to hear him. At Auer's urging, Milstein set off to study with him in St. Petersburg. His mother came with him, but she had to get a special permit to reside in the city, normally off-limits to Jews.

Milstein flourished at the Conservatory and completed his studies in 1917—the last formal period of violin instruction he had. When his father's business was badly affected by the Russian Revolution, Milstein began to concertize as much as he could to provide additional income for the family, his sister frequently accompanying him on the piano. He became known throughout Odessa and then in Kiev, where he was heard by Vladimir Horowitz, another young musician—a pianist—who was already developing a name as a brilliant performer. The two paired up musically, and for the next three years—sometimes joined by cellist Gregor Piatigorsky—they played together and Milstein, in his turn, became known throughout Russia.

But life in Russia had become difficult, and in 1925 Milstein took advantage of a two-year permit given him by the government to concertize in Europe. The Russian government apparently thought it was good propaganda —proof that the country could produce good musicians. Milstein saw it as a way out; he never returned.

Stopping first in Berlin, he then travelled to Brussels, where he remained for eight months to perform for and study with Eugene Ysaye. He then set off for Paris and performed throughout Europe and Latin America, establishing himself as a musician of international stature. By 1929 he was ready for his American debut. It took place in October that year, when he performed the piece that first "made" him—the Glazunov concerto— with the Philadelphia Orchestra under the baton of Leopold Stokowski. The triumphant performance was followed by an American tour and by Milstein's decision to remain in America; in 1942 he became a citizen.

Over the years his reputation continued to grow, as did the breadth of Milstein's repertoire. He performed with the world's top conductors, including Toscanini, Koussevitsky, Munch and Monteux, and with the best orchestras. He taught master classes at Juilliard in New York and at the Foundation for International Master Classes in Zurich. He recorded widely, specializing in the violin compositions of Bach, Beethoven, Mozart, Lalo, Mendelssohn, Tchaikovsky and Bruch. In 1976, he won a Grammy for a new recording of the complete unaccompanied sonatas and partitas of Bach. In addition, Milstein has arranged music by Lizst, Chopin, Mussorgsky and other composers, transcribed music composed for other instruments into versions for violin and he has composed original music, among them the "Paganiniana," a complex set of variations of Paganini's twenty-fourth caprice and other themes.

In 1979 Milstein capped his career in America by observing the 50th anniversary of his debut with a performance of the Beethoven Concerto for violin with the Philadelphia Orchestra at Carnegie Hall.

NEWTON MINOW

b. January 17, 1926
Lawyer

While chairman of the Federal Communications Commission from 1961 until 1963, Newton Minow strove to improve the quality of television broadcasting, which he then characterized as a "vast wasteland," a phrase immortalized ever since. Following his departure from the FCC, he has continued to write provocatively about the role of media in society and the challenges facing television programmers.

Newton Minow was born in New York City to Jay, an owner of a chain of laundries, and Doris (Stein) Minow. After Minow graduated from George Washington High School in Manhattan in 1944, he enlisted in a special program conducted by the U.S. Army Corps of Engineers at the University of Michigan. Upon completion of this program, he served for two years in the China-Burma-India theater of war with the U.S. Army Signal Corps. He was discharged in 1946 as a sergeant.

Like many returning G.I.s, Minow resumed his education. He studied at Northwestern University, where he received his B.S. degree in speech and political science in 1949. The following year he completed his

Bachelor of Laws degree at the Northwestern University School of Law, where he was the top student in his class and editor of the law review.

Minow was quickly identified by his superiors as a promising young attorney. After a year at a Chicago law firm, he became a clerk for Justice Fred Vinson, Chief Justice of the United States in 1952. When his clerkship ended, he was hired as an administrative assistant to Governor Adlai Stevenson of Illinois. He remained closely allied with Stevenson for many years. In 1955 Minow joined Stevenson's Chicago law firm, and six years later he was made a partner in the firm, the youngest man ever awarded the honor. Even so, that same year he resigned from the firm when John F. Kennedy appointed him chairman of the FCC.

From that powerful position, Minow attempted to make commercial television broadcasting more responsive to the public's needs and interests. He honored the maxim that radio and television broadcasters held a public trust and could therefore be held responsible to the will of the people. He outlined his views on broadcast regulation and recounted his experiences in the FCC in his book *Equal Time: The Private Broadcaster and the Public Interest* (New York, 1964), which came out the year after Minow resigned from office.

After Minow left government employment, he became the vice president and general counsel of the Encyclopaedia Britannica and joined the law firm of Sidley and Austin in Chicago. He also lectured about television at the Medill School of Journalism at Northwestern University.

In recognition of Minow's long relationship with Adlai Stevenson, he was appointed a director of the Adlai E. Stevenson Institute for International Peace. In 1966 Minow wrote a fond and personal remembrance about Stevenson, *As We Knew Adlai* (New York).

Minow has written two other books. In *Presidential Television* (New York, 1973), he analyzed the way the broadcast medium is manipulated by the president and, in turn, the power television has in forming the public's perception of the chief executive. In *Tomorrow's America— Electronics and the Future* (New York, 1977), Minow examined the rapid technological advances in communications and tried to unravel some of the implications of those advances.

Although no longer in the public eye, Minow is still active in media policy decisions in Chicago—he is former chairperson of Chicago Educational Television Association and is now director of the Chicago-based Prime Time School Television, an organization that devises and disseminates curricula materials—and his opinions are held in high esteem. Thus it was significant when

Minow spoke out in 1980 to voice his opposition to and general dismay about the presidential selection process and the impact of media on it. It has "degenerated to the point where there is serious question whether it can produce outstanding candidates," he said. "With the growing number of state primaries, plus the constant concern in the media with who wins and loses every Tuesday, we have almost eliminated thoughtful discussion from the political scene."

Minow is on the board of trustees of the Rand Corporation, Notre Dame University—he is its first Jewish trustee—and the Mayo Clinic. From 1974 until 1977 he was the chairman of the board of overseers of the Jewish Theological Seminary of America.

HERBERT MITGANG

b. January 20, 1920
Journalist; author; playwright

Noted journalist Herbert Mitgang has spent all but three years of his professional career at *The New York Times,* as a weekly columnist, former member of the editorial board and from 1976 through 1981 as publishing correspondent. He is now its cultural correspondent. An author and playwright in his own right, he has also written numerous books of history, biography and fiction, with a special focus on the life and accomplishments of Abraham Lincoln.

Herbert Mitgang was born in New York City to Benjamin, a dress contractor and cutter, and Florence (Altman) Mitgang. He worked as a stringer on the *Brooklyn Eagle's* sports desk while attending St. John's University, from which he graduated with a bachelor's and a law degree in 1941. From 1942 to 1943 he served in the counter-intelligence branch of the United States Army Air Force, and from 1943 to 1945 he worked as Army correspondent and then managing editor of *The Stars and Stripes,* the United States Army newspaper, while stationed in Algiers and later Sicily.

In 1945 Mitgang joined the staff of *The New York Times,* where he worked as an editor-writer until 1964, when he became executive editor and assistant to the president of CBS News. In 1967 he rejoined the *Times* as an editorial board member and founding editor of the Op-Ed page. Mitgang's informed book reviews and literary articles for the *Times* reveal intelligence, broad knowledge and an effort to understand and explain the publishing business with emphasis on authors.

He told *Publishers Weekly* in 1976 that he chose to become publishing correspondent for the *Times* rather than to cover other cultural areas—he could have been arts correspondent—because "writing books remains one of the last individual acts in the arts in this country." Mitgang disdains the emphasis on books as commercial products and particularly the media attention given to six-figure paperback sales. He thus often focuses on small, independent publishers who do not have publicity departments and are not merely one component of a large conglomerate. Mitgang singles out Farrar, Straus & Giroux, the New York publishing house that has bucked trends in the field to remain autonomous and preserve its integrity while other houses have been bought out by corporations.

Until he left the post in 1981, Mitgang wrote not only about books but on the general field of communications, including such subjects as censorship, satellite communications and copyright laws. He continues to do much the same and covers the subject of culture. His interviews with authors are regular features of *The New York Times Book Review*.

In his articles and reviews, Mitgang has often voiced strong liberal political opinions. For example, he accused Richard Nixon in 1976 of being the prime cause of cynicism and disbelief in our government and mocked former Vice President Agnew's sponsorship of a democratic organization, which, wrote Mitgang, makes a kind of "demonic sense." He called attention to the "fat fee" former Lt. William Calley—who ordered civilians to be killed at My Lai in Vietnam—earned on publicity tours around the country and in lectures on the perils of war. And he condemned President Gerald Ford for pardoning Nixon and permitting the country to remain "under a cloud of deception."

A lifelong admirer of Abraham Lincoln, Mitgang is the author of several books about him as well as a 1980 Broadway play. The two-act *Mr. Lincoln*—which appeared as a book (Carbondale, Ill., 1982) was chosen to be the first *Hallmark Hall of Fame* television play on PBS. In his works Mitgang emphasizes Lincoln's lifelong opposition to slavery and his independent mind. The Lincoln he portrays is both vulnerable and awesome, a genuine American hero in contrast to the plasticity of media-created contemporary personalities.

Mitgang's books on Lincoln include two biographies —*Lincoln as They Saw Him* (New York, 1956) and *The Fiery Trial: A Life of Lincoln* (New York, 1974)—and he is editor of *Lincoln's Long Shadow* (New York, 1972), *Washington in Lincoln's Time* (New York, 1958) and *The Letters of Carl Sandburg* (New York, 1968). He has also published *Working for the Reader* (New York, 1970), an anthology of his book reviews, and *America at Random*

(New York, 1969), a collection of outstanding journalistic essays that appeared in the *Times*. In addition, he has written four novels including *The Return* (New York, 1959), a suspense and love story set in Sicily, and *Get These Men Out of the Hot Sun* (New York, 1972), a satiric political novel about a United States president.

Among the many documentary films Mitgang has written are *Lincoln's Prairie Years* (1961), *Ben Gurion on the Bible* (1967), *Henry Moore: Man of Form* (1965) and *D-Day Plus Twenty Years* (1964).

For editorials, magazine writing and biography, he has received four Gavel Awards from the American Bar Association. And from 1971 to 1975 Mitgang was president of the Authors Guild.

For further information:
Mitgang, Herbert. *Kings in the Counting House*. New York: 1983.
———. *The Montauk Fault*. New York: 1981.

BESS MYERSON

b. July 16, 1924
Columnist; consumer consultant; television personality

Bess Myerson rose from lower middle-class obscurity in the Bronx to become the first Jewish Miss America and·a nationally admired consumer activist and television personality. Although she has never held elective office, she is widely regarded as an important and influential ally among New York City leaders.

Bess Myerson was born in New York City to Russian immigrant parents, Louis, a house painter, and Bella Myerson. She grew up in the Sholem Aleichem housing project in the Bronx and attended the High School of Music and Art, where she was a piano student. In 1945 she graduated from Hunter College with a B.A. degree, and the same year she entered and won the Miss America competition. The apparent awkwardness of pageant sponsors at Myerson's triumph was reflected in their recommendation that she change her name to Meredith or Merrick. But Myerson she remained.

In 1946 she made her concert debut at Carnegie Recital Hall, and in 1947 she began what would become a long career as a television announcer and commentator, first with WOR-TV and then, from 1951 to 1957 as emcee for *The Big Payoff* on CBS-TV. She hosted NBC's *Philco Playhouse* during the 1954–55 season and was commentator for the Tournament of Roses annual parade and football game from 1960 to 1968 and the Miss America Pageant from 1964 to 1968. But Myerson was probably best-known on television as a regular panelist for CBS-TV's long-running and popular program *I've Got a Secret.*

Myerson has few peers in knowing how to exploit the media. Having become a national public figure through television, she parlayed her visibility into a job in 1969 as commissioner of consumer affairs during the administration of New York Mayor John V. Linsday. Although many observers were skeptical of Myerson's ability, she proved to be an aggressive and hard-working commissioner and expanded what had been a small and limited office into an effective and important agency that fought hard to protect the "little person." Under her leadership, New York City passed the Consumer Protection Act, the most comprehensive legislation of its kind in the United States, and the concept of consumer protection changed as a result. Again using the press, she made the rounds, according to one anecdote, of restaurants claiming to serve 100 percent beef hamburgers that were not what they were advertised to be. Such ploys were most successful, and when Myerson left Consumer Affairs in 1973, she went on to write consumer columns for the *Daily News* and to broadcast consumer advice on the radio. She also wrote *The Complete Consumer Book* (New York, 1979).

Myerson has had her share of controversy. From 1973 to 1980, in addition to many other posts and responsibilities, she served as chairperson of the Consumer Credit Counseling Service, a nonprofit private organization that ostensibly helped individual consumers with credit problems. Some critics questioned Myerson's role, but in the end her reputation remained unsullied, her integrity intact. To New Yorkers she was—as *Life* once described her—like "a well-scrubbed New York housewife" who had led the fight to protect consumers and advise them of their rights. The same year she made her first bid for political office, running unsuccessfully in the Democratic primary for U.S. senator from New York. Among her opponents was her former employer, John Lindsay. She lost the primary to Representative Elizabeth Holtzman, who, however, lost the November election.

In 1982 Myerson published the *I Love NY Diet Book,* with Bill Adler (New York).

For further information:
"A consumer champion lays down the law," *Life,* July 16, 1971.

ERNEST NAGEL

b. November 16, 1901
Philosophy professor

Philosopher Ernest Nagel, a member of the Columbia University faculty since 1931, is one of America's foremost scholars of the 20th century. In 1980 he won the Nicholas Murray Butler medal in gold from Columbia University, an honor that places him in the company of Bertrand Russell, George Santayana and John Dewey. A philosopher of science, Nagel has succeeded in bridging the gap between the physical and social sciences and philosophy.

Ernest Nagel was born to Isidor, a dry goods merchant, and Frida (Weisz) Nagel in Nove Mesto, Slovakia, then a part of Hungary and now a part of Czechoslovakia. During his youth, Nagel learned several languages, including Slovakian, Hungarian, German and Hebrew. His father's family was "extremely orthodox" and refused to take even tea in his home, which was less religious. Nagel's father went bankrupt and left for America. Later he sent for his family, and they arrived in 1911. Nagel was naturalized eight years later.

Upon graduating from City College of New York with a B.S. degree in social studies in 1923, Nagel started teaching in the New York City school system while studying part-time at Columbia University for a master's degree in mathematics. Nagel obtained the degree in 1925, thus adhering to Bertrand Russell's advice that in order to be a philosopher, one should know mathematics. Nagel taught at Walton High School in the Bronx between 1925 and 1930 while studying part-time for his doctorate in philosophy at Columbia. With the support of a privately sponsored fellowship arranged by his City College mentor, Morris Raphael Cohen, Nagel published his dissertation, *On the Logic of Measurement* (New York), in 1930 and received both his Ph.D. and an offer, which he took, to teach at Columbia the following year. Nagel was appointed full professor in 1946. He was honored as John Dewey Professor of Philosophy in 1955, became university professor in 1967 and has been professor emeritus since 1970.

He is known as a logical empiricist and a rationalist—one who prefers the knowledge of life and nature to illusion. Through his teaching, lecturing and writing, he fights the current trend against rationalism, which prefers pscyhological or sociological interpretations to conclusions made on a logical basis.

Nagel is famous for his application of reason and order to unresolved problems in history, sociology and biology. In his major work, *The Structure of Science* (Indianapolis, Ind., 1961), he examines problems of methodology, explanation and inquiry in biology, the social sciences and history. He studies the nature of scientific explanations, their logical structures and their devices for systematizing knowledge.

Godel's Proof, written with James R. Newman (New York, 1958), explains the theorum of Godel, a mathematician who set out to prove Russell and Whitehead's theory of logical classes—that the whole is greater than the sum of its parts. Nagel's book, which deals with what is regarded as an important theorum for social scientists—logical typing, a theory that clarifies how things can be categorized—is considered a classic by philosophers and scientists.

Among Nagel's other works, which deal with similar issues concerning the systematization of knowledge, are *The Principle of The Theory of Probability* (Chicago, 1939); *Teleology Revisited and Other Essays in the Philosophy and History of Science* (New York, 1934); and *An Introduction to Logic and Scientific Method* (New York, 1934), which he wrote with the late Morris Raphael Cohen, with whom he studied at City College in his undergraduate days.

He is a former president of the American Philosophy Association (eastern division), the Association for Symbolic Logic and the Philosophy of Science Association.

VICTOR NAVASKY

b. July 5, 1932
Editor; journalist

As editor of *The Nation* since 1977, Victor Navasky has carried on the liberal tradition of one of America's oldest continuous and independent publications. An author in his own right, Navasky has dedicated his career to supporting freedom of expression in the United States and abroad.

Victor Saul Navasky was born in Manhattan to Macy, a clothing manufacturer, and Esther (Goldberg) Navasky. He attended the progressive, private Elizabeth Irwin High School and graduated magna cum laude with a B.A. degree from Swarthmore College in 1954. He then served for two years as a medic in the United States Army. After his discharge in 1956, he went to Yale Law School and received his Bachelor of Laws in 1959.

Following graduation, Navasky, who had always been interested in politics, became a speechwriter and special assistant to G. Mennen Williams, then governor of Michigan, in his aborted bid for the presidency. In

1960 he embarked on a free-lance writing career and made his first entree into publishing. In 1961, along with former Yale classmates Christopher Lehmann-Haupt, Calvin Trillin and others who would eventually become renowned journalists, Navasky founded a New York-based quarterly humor magazine called *Monocle*. He thus once phoned the U.S. Department of Agriculture posing as a subsidy farmer who, instead of not planting wheat, wanted permission not to plant potatoes. Another time, following a sharp increase in the price of steel, Navasky ordered one ton of steel from the U.S. Steel Company and asked that it be delivered to his home. Navasky published and edited *Monocle* until 1970, during which period he also coauthored his first book. Under the joint pseudonym of "William Randolph Hirsch," Navasky, Marvin Kitman and Richard Lingeman (now a scholar and critic and *Nation* editor, too) wrote *The Red Chinese Air Force Exercise, Diet and Sex Book* (New York, 1967), a parody of physical fitness books then in vogue.

In 1970 Navasky joined *The New York Times*, first as an editor for the Sunday magazine section and one year later as a regular columnist for the Book Review section. In the latter post, he wrote a weekly column about the publishing world called *In Cold Print*, a candid and often critical analysis of the sociology of book publishing. Under John Leonard's direction, Navasky was allowed free rein in his writing, despite frequent protests from publishers. However, he left after a year to return to political work in 1974, aiding former U.S. Attorney General Ramsey Clark in his losing bid for the U.S. Senate seat from New York.

Meanwhile, Navasky published his first serious book, a detailed analysis of Robert Kennedy's tenure as attorney general called *Kennedy Justice* (New York, 1971). In it he focuses particularly on Kennedy's dealings with then-FBI Director J. Edgar Hoover, who had long been given virtual carte blanche to secretly monitor domestic left-wing and right-wing political groups.

During the Clark campaign in 1974, Navasky met Hamilton Fish III, a New Yorker from one of America's wealthiest families. In 1977 Fish bought *The Nation*, a liberal-leftist journal founded in 1865, and invited Navasky to become editor. Navasky agreed, having come to admire *The Nation* during research for his next book, *Naming Names* (New York, 1980). Under Navasky's leadership, *The Nation* continues to be an authoritative voice of traditional liberalism, evoking admiration and criticism, as happened when Susan Sontag said that the *Readers Digest* through the past decades had been a more accurate forecaster of Soviet intentions than *The Nation*. *Naming Names* is a study of the ex-Communists who informed on Communists, fellow travelers, acquaintances and innocent bystanders during the 1947 investigation of Hollywood conducted by the House Un-American Activities Committee. Navasky reflects on the pscyhology and morality of informing, and although his sympathies clearly lie with those who refused to name names, he does not prejudge those who did. The result is a remarkable, fair and moving study.

Navasky is a frequent contributor to publications such as *The Los Angeles Times* and major periodicals and participates on panels whose subject matter is often freedom of the press. In an article published in *Newsday* (February 16, 1981), for example, he expressed his concern that the proposed creation of a subcommittee on security and terrorism in the U.S. Senate during the Reagan administration might signal a return to the McCarthy witch-hunts of old. Although he says that present conditions are different enough from those in the 1950s to preclude the same kinds of blacklisting that then existed, he warns readers to beware of the atmosphere of fear and the threat to civil liberties that can develop. "The subcommittee's very existence is bound to contribute to the anti-democratic mood," he writes, "and be a source of inspiration to state and local Red Squads and vigilante groups such as the Ku Klux Klan." And he adds: "The danger represented by the new security and terrorism boys is that they will move, with the support of the administration, to legitimize the illegitimate, to make respectable that which was previously done only undercover and because it was fundamentally shameful."

ARYEH NEIER

b. April 22, 1937
Civil libertarian; writer; professor

As a former executive director of both the New York Civil Liberties Union and the American Civil Liberties Union, Aryeh Neier distinguished himself as one of the most ardent supporters of First Amendment freedoms due all Americans, no matter how extreme or abhorrent their point of view. Although at times he has had to take unpopular and controversial stands—including defending the American Nazi Party in 1978 when it sought to march in heavily Jewish Skokie, Illinois—he has never wavered in his firm commitment to the right of and the need for free and open expression of opinions.

Aryeh Neier was born in Berlin to Wolf, a teacher, and Gitla (Bendzinska) Neier. According to one account, his mother purposely delayed Neier's birth so it would

not coincide with the April 20 birthday of Adolf Hitler. The immediate family escaped to London in 1939, but Neier lost many relatives in the Holocaust, including three grandparents. He was brought to the United States in 1947, where his family settled first in the Bronx, then in Brooklyn, and he became a citizen in 1955.

Graduating from Cornell University (where he worked with the United Mine Workers while still a student) with a B.S. degree in industrial relations in 1958, Neier went to work for the League for Industrial Democracy, a lobbying group that promoted the concept of production for the general welfare of all people rather than profit for a select few. Before his first year was up, the executive director resigned, and Neier took his job. In 1960 he became an associate editor at *Current* magazine, a public affairs monthly. He joined the ACLU as a field development officer in 1963. At the time the ACLU was directing its energies primarily to the civil rights movement in the South. Neier was there, participating in voting drives. In the legislative forum, he was successfully fighting laws that prohibited interracial marriage and laws that perpetuated segregated schools and housing as well as deliberate job discrimination.

But the civil liberties movement extended further. Under Neier's administration when he became executive director of the NYCLU in 1965, some of the causes it fought against included school prayer, state support to parochial schools and the harassment of anti-war protesters. And in 1966, although the organization had also targeted itself as a fighter against police abuse, it defended the rights of police officers to join organizations of their choice—in that case, the John Birch Society. In 1968 the NYCLU took the side of local communities in support of efforts to decentralize the New York City public school system.

Neier became executive director of the ACLU in 1970, spearheading some of its most highly publicized actions. Inheriting the job just as the ACLU was expanding into the international arena with denunciations of an American presence in Indochina and the defense of anti-war protestor Dr. Benjamin Spock, Neier pushed the ACLU into an even more activist stand in helping to initiate impeachment proceedings against President Nixon. Soon after, the organization lobbied successfully for the Freedom of Information Act, which required that the public be given access to government files on demand. As the ACLU continued from one victory to another—it worked for the rights of mental patients, prisoners, the disabled community and retarded persons and fought for such causes as free choice in abortion, affirmative action and an end to the death penalty—it thrived, with its membership by 1975 nearly double what it had been in 1970.

But by 1978 the tide began to turn. With the ACLU's defense of the American Nazi Party in its effort to march in Skokie, it suffered a crisis in membership and financial support. Yet Neier—closer to the Holocaust than many of his critics—was passionate and outspoken in supporting the American Nazis' right to speak. "Freedom has its risks," he later wrote in a book about the experience, *Defending My Enemy* (New York, 1979). "Suppression of freedom, I believe, is a pure prescription for disaster. . . . [The Nazis] must be free to speak because Jews must be free to speak and because I must be free to speak."

Several months following the Skokie incident— despite all the uproar, or perhaps because of it, the Nazis decided not to march there, after all—Neier received an appointment to the New York University Institute of the Humanities and left the ACLU. And he taught at the New York University School of Law as an adjunct professor. Also in 1979 he directed a study of litigation and social change for the Twentieth Century Fund.

Neier, who is on the editorial board of *The Nation* and frequently publishes articles there, has written several books and many magazine articles. His first book, *Dossier: The Secret Files They Keep on You* (New York, 1975), originated as a magazine article and evolved into a detailed exploration of how records are used—and abused—to violate individual rights in such areas as employment and housing. His second book was *Crime and Punishment: A Radical Solution* (New York, 1976), in which Neier describes how contemporary views of crime, law enforcement and correction should be remolded to deemphasize victimless crimes. During his tenure at the ACLU, he coauthored with ACLU Board Chairman Norman Dorsen a series of handbooks on the rights of Americans, which were published by Avon.

HOWARD NEMEROV

b. March 1, 1920
Poet; professor

When Howard Nemerov received both the Pulitzer Prize and the National Book Award in 1978 for the publication of his *Collected Poems* (Chicago, 1977), he was honored as much for his prodigious output over three decades as an introspective and humanistic poet as for his discriminating essays, his novels and his contributions to the education of younger generations of poets.

Described by poet James Dickey as "one of the wittiest and funniest poets we have," he has used humor to frame an ironic and often pessimistic attitude toward the human condition.

Howard Nemerov was born in New York City to David and Gertrude (Russek) Nemerov. His father was president and chairman of the board of Russeks Department Store in New York and a prominent philanthropist. Many of Nemerov's early influences were derived from his family's strong cultural orientation, which included art collecting. Educated at the Fieldston School, from which he graduated in 1937, Nemerov received a Bachelor of Arts degree from Harvard University in 1941. Even then he had begun to distinguish himself as a writer, having won the first of what were to be many awards throughout his life, the Bowdoin Prize in 1940.

After wartime military service in the Royal Canadian Air Force from 1942 to 1944 and the U.S. Air Force for an additional year, Nemerov became an instructor at Hamilton College in Clinton, New York. That year he also became associate editor of the periodical *Furioso,* a post he held until 1951. His first book of poetry, *The Image and the Law* (New York), published in 1947, displayed the duality that would typify his later work and that would be the source of praise and criticism from other poets and scholars. In this case, one scholar pointed out Nemerov's "two ways of looking at the world," which he described as "poetry of the eye" and "poetry of the mind." Too obviously influenced by such then-active poets as Auden, Yeats, Eliot and Wallace Stevens, Nemerov was nonetheless considered a leading young poet. For a first book—Nemerov was only 27— *Image* received a great deal of attention, and even the qualified praise was significant.

Nemerov joined the literature faculty of Bennington College in Vermont the following year, and during his tenure there—he taught at Bennington until 1966, with a one-year break to teach at the University of Minnesota (1958–59) and another as a poet-in-residence at Hollins College (1962–63)—he produced five more volumes of verse, three novels, one short story collection and two books of essays. In 1963 he served a one-year term as poetry consultant to the Library of Congress, succeeding Louis Untermeyer.

His second book of poems, *Guide to the Ruins* (New York, 1950), like *Image,* was criticized as relying too heavily on the influence of other poets, and reviewer I.L. Salomon pointed out the "dichotomy of personality" in Nemerov's work, which he described on the one hand as Nemerov's "instinct for perfection" and on the other as his "carelessness in expression." Yet others saw what Peter Meinke called Nemerov's modern awareness of contemporary man's alienation and fragmentation," one of the qualities that set Nemerov apart from—and perhaps above—other working poets.

Over the years, as the poet found his own voice, Nemerov's breadth of perceptions expanded to include a more precise and philosophical view of the world as he knew it, and his influences were no longer other poets but his own experiences. Thus in "Redeployment," a poem from *The Salt Garden* (Boston, 1955), he would begin:

> They say the war is over. But water still
> Comes bloody from the taps, and my pet cat
> In his disorder vomits worms which crawl
> Swiftly away . . . .

> The end of the war. I took it quietly
> Enough. I tried to wash the dirt out of
> My hair and from under my fingernails,
> I dressed in clean white clothes and went to bed.
> I heard the dust falling between the walls.

* * *

From this period on, Nemerov began regularly to receive recognition for his poetry. While his fiction was received kindly by critics, however, it was never considered on a par with his verse.

He left Bennington in 1966 to become professor of English at Brandeis University for two years, and in 1969 Nemerov went to Washington University in St. Louis, Missouri as a visiting professor of English. The "visit" turned into an appointment the following year as professor of English, and since 1976 Nemerov has been the Edward Mallingckrodt Distinguished University Professor of English.

Although poets frequently convey their thoughts most accurately through their verse, Nemerov has proven himself an adept essayist capable of explaining himself through analytic prose. His book *Figures of Thought: Speculations on the Meaning of Poetry and Other Essays* (Boston, 1978)—a collection of 19 essays, reviews and lectures—was acclaimed by Benjamin DeMott, who said the book "communicates throughout a vivid sense of the possibility of a richer kind of knowing in all areas than we're in process of settling for." Novelist Joyce Carol Oates, after calling the book "rewarding . . . for what it tells us about poetry in general, and the poetry of Yeats, Williams, Shakespeare, Randall Jarrell and others," concludes that "Nemerov is, quite simply, a brilliant mind."

Nemerov's special skill is his ability to see symbols in the most simple objects of everyday life. An acorn is not just an acorn; it represents the autumn and changes

in nature—and life changes—and provides the basis for a 1979 poem (excerpted here), "Acorn, Yom Kippur":

> Look at this little fallen thing, it's got
> Its yarmulka still on, and a jaunty sprig
> Of twig, a feather in its cap, and in its head
> There is a single-minded thought: *White Oak.*

> Language and thought have changed since I was young
> And we used to say it had an oak inside,
> The way some tribes believe that every man
> Has a homunculus inside his head;
> Already, though, matter was going out
> And energy coming in; though energy
> Wasn't the last word either, the last word
> Is information, or more tersely, The Word . . .

For further information:

Nemerov, Howard. *The Blue Swallows,* poems. Chicago: 1967.
———. *A Commodity of Dreams, and Other Stories.* New York: 1959.
———. *Federigo; or the Power of Love,* fiction. Boston: 1954.
———. *Gnomes and Occasions,* poems. Chicago: 1973.
———. *The Homecoming Game,* fiction. New York: 1957.
———. *Journal of the Fictive Life.* New Brunswick, N.J.: 1965; Chicago: 1981, with a new preface.
———. *The Melodramatists,* fiction. New York: 1949.
———. *Mirrors and Windows,* poems. Chicago: 1958.
———. *New and Selected Poems.* Chicago: 1960.
———. *The Next Room of the Dream,* poems. Chicago: 1962.
———. *Poetry and Fiction: Essays.* New Brunswick, N.J.: 1963.
———. *Reflections on Poetry and Poetics.* New Brunswick, N.J.: 1972.
———. *Stories, Fables and Other Diversions.* Boston: 1971.
———. *The Western Approaches, Poems 1973–75.* Chicago: 1975.
Nemerov, Howard, ed. *Poets on Poetry.* New York: 1965.

JAY NEUGEBOREN

b. May 30, 1938
Author

By age 24 Jay Neugeboren had written 7 unpublished books and 12 stories and had collected 576 rejection slips. Then his luck fared better, and he has since published 5 novels and an autobiography, all of which reflect to some extent his Brooklyn roots and his Jewish heritage.

Jay Neugeboren was born in Brooklyn to David, a printing salesman, and Anne (Nassofer) Neugeboren, a registered nurse. He graduated from Columbia College with a B.A. degree in 1959 and from Indiana University with an M.A. degree in 1963. From 1963 to 1966 he was a doctoral student at Columbia but did not complete the Ph.D. From 1961 to 1962 he taught at the Saddle River Country Day School and from 1962 to 1971 held a variety of university-level teaching positions, including a yearlong stint at Stanford University in 1966–67, during which he became active in the anti-Vietnam War movement. Neugeboren joined the faculty of the University of Massachusetts in Amherst in 1971 as professor and resident writer and received tenure in 1975.

Neugeboren's first novel, *Big Man* (New York, 1966), told of Mack Davis, a former college basketball star whose career is wiped out when he is implicated in a point-fixing scheme. Now out of school—and out of luck—he ruefully watches his younger brother strive toward success as a music student in one of New York City's special high schools. The fact that Mack is black and from a poor Brooklyn neighborhood adds pathos to the tale, in which Mack develops a friendship with an elderly Jewish sportswriter named Ben Rosen. Rosen's attempt to expose sports corruption provides Mack with a new insight into what has happened to him in the process of aborting a promising future. *Big Man* was well received as a first novel.

Neugeboren next wrote *Listen Ruben Fontanez* (New York, 1968), which features an elderly Jewish man trying to cope with being alone after his wife's death. For the first time—in a published novel, at least—Neugeboren tried to create a three-dimensional Jewish character, but the book was considered less successful than *Big Man*. He followed with a novella, a collection of short stories entitled *Corky's Brother* (New York, 1969) and *Parentheses: An Autobiographical Journey* (New York, 1970). In 1974 he completed his third novel, *Sam's Legacy* (New York). A story-within-a-story—a gimmick Neugeboren would use in subsequent novels—*Sam's Legacy* tells of a former player in the Negro Baseball Leagues named Mason Tidewater who is the black janitor in the Brooklyn apartment building of Sam Berman. Juxtaposing the stories of two men who are at the same time very different and yet very much alike—have-beens still living on dreams—Neugeboren embellishes their tale with Tidewater's stories about his old baseball days, stories that with the telling become more and more unbelievable.

Further development of character and increased plot complexity marked *The Orphan's Tale* (New York, 1976), the story of 13-year-old Danny Ginsberg, who lives in the Maimonides Home for Jewish Boys in Brooklyn. Obsessed with his uniqueness as an orphan, Danny seeks out an "alumnus" of the home, Charlie Sapistein, who has gone on to become a success in the "outside" world. He locates Charlie, who temporarily "adopts" Danny and becomes the mentor Danny had been looking for. Both discover a deep need for the other, having passed through life so alone.

The Stolen Jew (New York, 1981) is Neugeboren's most complex novel. Interweaving stories-within-stories, it focuses on 64-year-old Nathan Malkin, who gave up a promising writing career in his youth to become a successful businessman. After having settled in Israel, he returns to Brooklyn to tend to family affairs following the suicide of his brother Nachman. The visit evokes both pleasant and painful memories of his childhood in Brooklyn—an era long gone—contrasted with the repetitions of mistakes he made as a youth, which are now being committed by his son and his nephew. He decides to join Nachman's son Michael, an idealistic psychiatrist, in a trip to the Soviet Union to make contacts with the Jewish community there and in so doing looks even further into his past—the roots of his parents—to a Jewish life that had been the subject of his own youthful dreams as an incipient novelist.

Neugeboren has not yet attained the renown of such Jewish writers as Saul Bellow, Philip Roth or Bernard Malamud, and critics of his work have tended to be qualified in their praise. Still, *The Stolen Jew* received the best reviews of all—and has been optioned by a film producer. In a positive review of *The Stolen Jew*, *New York Times* critic John Leonard commented on what he described as a "landscape of angry beginnings." And it was awarded the Kenneth B. Smilen/*Present Tense* Literary Award for 1981's finest novel with a Jewish theme.

JACOB NEUSNER

b. July 28, 1932
Professor; scholar

Jacob Neusner is one of America's most eminent and prolific Jewish scholars, whose particular expertise is ancient Jewish history and the translation and analysis of ancient Jewish texts.

Jacob Neusner was born in Hartford, Connecticut to Samuel, the publisher of the *Connecticut Jewish Ledger* until his death in 1960, and Lee (Green) Neusner. He was an outstanding student throughout his academic career, and from the beginning of his studies at Harvard College, where he received a Bachelor of Arts degree magna cum laude in 1953 to the completion of his Ph.D. at Columbia University in 1960, he was awarded fellowships and scholarships. A member of Phi Beta Kappa since 1952, he spent the academic year 1953–54 as a Henry fellow at Oxford University in England. He began formal graduate study in religion at the Jewish Theological Seminary of America in 1954. As a Fulbright scholar, he continued these studies at Hebrew University in Jerusalem from 1957 to 1958. From 1958 to 1960 Neusner studied both at the JTS and in a program in religion jointly sponsored by Columbia University and the Union Theological Seminary. In addition to earning his doctorate at Columbia, he also received an M.H.L. degree from the JTS in 1960.

Neusner's career can be divided into sections. On one hand, he is a dedicated educator. For one year he was an instructor in religion at Columbia before moving to the University of Wisconsin as an assistant professor of Hebrew from 1961 to 1962. He was a research associate at Brandeis University from 1962 to 1964 and then taught religion at Dartmouth College, first as an assistant professor from 1964 to 1966, then as an associate professor from 1966 to 1968. Since 1968 Neusner has been on the faculty of Brown University as a professor of religious studies. In 1975 he was named university professor of religious studies and the Ungerleider Distinguished Scholar of Judaic Studies. Since 1968 he has also lectured extensively throughout the United States and in Sweden, Denmark, Germany, Austria, the Netherlands, Great Britain, South Africa and Israel.

But Neusner is also a prodigious writer. Since the early 1960s he has produced a formidable list of scholarly books devoted to Jewish history. Beginning with *A Life of Yohanan ben Zakkai* (Leiden, Holland, 1962), which won the Abraham Berliner Prize in Jewish History from the Jewish Theological Seminary, he has gone on to publish a five-volume *History of the Jews in Babylonia* (Leiden, Holland, 1965–70), the three volume *Rabbinic Traditions About the Pharisees before 70* (Leiden, Holland, 1971), five volumes of translation from the Hebrew of *The Tosefta* (New York, 1977–80) as well as various other studies, including *Aphrahat and Judaism: The Christian-Jewish Argument in Fourth Century Iran* (Leiden, Holland, 1971), *Eliezer ben Hyrcanus: The Tradition and the Man* (Leiden, Holland, 1973), *The Idea of Purity in Ancient Judaism* (Leiden, Holland, 1973) and *The Glory of God as Intelligence* (Provo, Utah, 1979).

But the masterwork of Neusner's scholarly career has been his studies of the Mishnah, the book of codes

providing many of the foundations for contemporary Judaism. From 1974 to 1977 he published 22 volumes covering *The History of the Mishnaic Law of Purities* (Leiden, Holland), including commentaries and explorations of literary and historical problems of divisions of Mishnaic law. *A History of the Mishnaic Law of Holy Things* (Leiden, Holland) appeared in six volumes, all in 1979. In 1979 and 1980 five volumes explaining *A History of the Mishnaic Law of Women* (Leiden, Holland) appeared, and in 1981 he completed five volumes of *A History of the Mishnaic Law of Appointed Times* (Leiden, Holland). Five volumes of *A History of the Mishnaic Law of Damages* (Leiden, Holland) appeared in 1982. He has also published *Judaism: The Evidence of the Mishnah* (Chicago, 1981), which is the first of a series of books on Jewish history to be published by the University of Chicago Press, and two volumes of an ongoing project of translation and explanation of *The Palestinian Talmud* (Chicago, 1981). With 35 volumes planned in all, Neusner will supervise the publication of approximately two volumes a year.

He is also the author of many Jewish textbooks that explore modern Judaism as well as the Talmudic era and has written many essays that probe the Jewish experience in America as well as in the ancient past. They are collected in such books as *Fellowship in Judaism: The First Century and Today* (London, 1963), *Judaism in the Secular Age: Essays on Fellowship, Community and Freedom* (London, 1970; New York, 1970), *Stranger at Home, Essays on Zionism, the "Holocaust," and American Judaism* (Chicago, 1980) and others. In the last-named book, Neusner discusses the "false consciousness" that pervades non-Orthodox contemporary Jewish life in America, which he feels is both spiritually and ideologically empty. The Holocaust, he says, takes on mythical proportions in the lives of American Jews, who are divorced from what real Jewish life is about. It gives them something to identify with because, he says, they have little else. (One critic, disagreeing with Neusner, claims that for assimilated Jews, learning about the Holocaust provides an important entree to further study of Jewish history and tradition.) Neusner also claims that for American Jews belief in Zionism without fulfilling *aliyah* (or moving to Israel) is a weak substitute for making a commitment to Jewish life and consciousness. Yet he also acknowledges the vitality of Diaspora life, which he sees as complementing the religious and cultural life of Jews in Israel. In one essay he writes:

Zionism . . . cannot be made the whole, because Jews are more than people who need either a place to live or a place on which to focus fantasies. The profound existential necessities of Jews—both those they share with everyone and those they have to themselves—are not met by Zionism . . . alone. Zionism provides much of the vigor and excitement of contemporary Jewish affairs, but insofar as Jews live and suffer, are born and die, reflect and doubt, raise children and worry over them, live and work—insofar as Jews are human, they require Judaism.

LOUISE NEVELSON

b. September 23, 1899
Sculptor

Many of Louise Nevelson's huge abstract sculptures now adorn plazas in New York and other cities and are in museums around the world. But it took the artist nearly 40 years of hard work before she could make a living from art, and another 10 to gain the renown she has today. But for Nevelson there was never any choice about her work—for art was not merely work, but life. As she once said: "Work in the sense of labor is not what I do. My work is a feast for myself."

Louise Berliawsky was born in Kiev, Russia to Isaac, a landowner in Russia who became a successful builder, lumberyard owner and realtor in the United States, and Minna Sadie (Smolerank) Berliawsky. The Berliawsky family emigrated to the United States in 1905 and settled in Rockland, Maine, a small town with few Jews. From her youth, Louise Berliawsky was "different." She knew she wanted to be an artist and looked forward to pursuing art full time. (She would later recall that the combination of being a Jew and an artist in Rockland was a double stigma as she grew up, and she always felt like an outsider.)

In 1918, the year she graduated from high school, she met Charles Nevelson, a New Yorker who had been visiting Maine, and married him two years later. She settled with him in New York and for the next few years studied drawing and painting as well as dramatics and dance. From 1928 to 1930 Nevelson studied at the Art Students League. By now the mother of a young son (who has since become a renowned sculptor in his own right), Nevelson separated from her husband—the conventional domestic life expected of her was more than she could fulfill—and in 1931, after leaving her son with her parents in Maine, went to Europe for one year to study with painter Hans Hofmann in Munich. After the year was up, she returned to New York and assisted the Mexican muralist Diego Rivera, who was then in the city, and continued her personal work. She also

taught in 1937 at the Educational Alliance Art School on the Lower East Side as part of a WPA-funded program.

Nevelson first exhibited in 1933, and two years later some of her work was featured in a group show at the Brooklyn Museum. She was just beginning to do sculpture and was always looking outward for new influences to inspire her work. At the time she was much drawn to the cubism of Picasso, the forms of pre-Columbian Central American art and African design. Working in wood, plaster, terra cotta, stone, aluminum and bronze, Nevelson created pieces whose titles often seemed removed from the piece until some further exploration was undertaken. In some cases one "piece" consisted of several sculptures together as part of an ensemble, such as *Black Majesty* (1956) and *The Forest* (1958).

Nevelson survived her long, difficult years by selling her work to artist-friends and by accepting family help. But during the mid-1950s she began selling sculpture to the Whitney Museum. By now she had exhibited widely and had cultivated a following. She even had one-woman shows at the Sidney Janis, Pace and other galleries. Her works grew larger. Some were free-standing sculptures, while others—her trademark—were monochromatic (often all-black or all-white) "sculptured murals"—that is, large relief works meant to be hung on a wall. "Found objects"—hats, trees, wheels, furniture legs and a variety of odds and ends—have often been the main components of her work.

But the turning point in Nevelson's career occurred when the Whitney Museum sponsored her first one-woman retrospective in 1967. The show, a huge critical success, established at last Nevelson's international reputation. But the retrospective in no way marked an end to Nevelson's productivity. Continuing energetically through the 1970s and 1980s, Nevelson also used her art to make significant political statements. As early as 1964 she created *Homage to 6,000,000*, a memorial piece to the Jews killed in the Holocaust, which was purchased by the Israel Museum. And in 1977 she withdrew a work worth $125,000 that she had been planning to donate to the Centre Beauborg in Paris when the French government released a Palestinian terrorist, calling its action similar to "the Hitler era, because it gives to the world another symbol of one person who can get away with terrorist actions." She then joined a boycott of artists, including Roy Lichtenstein, George Segal, James Rosenquist, Saul Steinberg and many others, as well as many eminent critics and dealers, to protest the opening of the French cultural center that year.

In 1979 a Nevelson sculpture was erected in lower

Manhattan near the World Trade Center, and the area was renamed Louise Nevelson Plaza.

JACK NEWFIELD

b. February 18, 1939
Journalist

As an investigative reporter for the often-controversial New York-based weekly *The Village Voice* for nearly 20 years, Jack Newfield has devoted the bulk of his energies to exposing greed and corruption in New York City. Focusing for the most part on landlords, judges and political power brokers, Newfield combines thorough research and astute analysis with personal outrage as he strives to use his journalistic powers to make New York City a better place to live.

Jack Newfield was born in New York City to Philip and Ethel (Tuckman) Newfield and was raised in the Bedford-Stuyvesant section of Brooklyn, then as now a working-class neighborhood. His father died when he was 4 years old, and his mother had to work to support her family. He attended the predominantly black Boys High School in Bedford-Stuyvesant and then graduated with a B.A. degree from Hunter College in 1961, in the days—now long gone—when the City University of New York was tuition-free. (He comments in *The Abuse of Power*, which he coauthored with Paul DuBrul, that he might not otherwise have attended.)

In the 1960s Newfield became an early and articulate voice in the peace and civil rights movements as both commentator and journalist. He was a member of the Southern Christian Leadership Conference and distinguished himself as a political writer. His first book *A Prophetic Minority* (New York, 1966), describes the rise of the New Left and the various organizations and personalities involved. He deeply sympathized with the Students for a Democratic Society. His subsequent books are *Robert Kennedy: A Memoir* (New York, 1969), a very favorable treatment focusing on Kennedy's changes in style and thought after the assassination of his brother; *Cruel and Unusual Justice* (New York, 1974), an expose of "ordinary" events in New York City courts and prisons —incompetent judges, favoritism, Mafiosi, political patronage, the wretched juvenile institutions, police corruption; and *The Abuse of Power: The Permanent Government and the Fall of New York* (New York, 1977), another expose of New York City governmental malfeasance and its relationship with business, unions and the banks.

Newfield is probably best-known, however, as a writer for and senior editor of *The Village Voice*. In 1981 he was honored by admirers as "the conscience of New York." In his speech he described his technique of investigative reporting:

> When I wanted to understand the nursing-home rackets, I talked to the nurses' aides who bandaged the infected bedsores of [Rabbi Bernard] Bergman's patients. When I wanted to identify the bigoted, malingering and unfit judges, I went to cops and Legal Aid attorneys. When I wanted to understand how [politicians] rigged the bus-shelter bid, I talked to a civil service auditor. And when I wanted to understand the plague of lead poisoning, I went to the South Bronx and interviewed a woman whose 22-month-old daughter had just died of lead poisoning because of the landlord's callous neglect.

In the *Voice*, Newfield annually publishes scathing articles evaluating New York's "Ten Worst" judges, landlords, politicians, etc. His pioneering investigation details the corruption in the political machinery of New York and has served as the starting point for formal investigations by the city as well as the adoption of his causes by the mainstream news media. He also helped reveal maltreatment of patients—many of them Jewish— in New York nursing homes, often owned and operated by wealthy Jewish investors. In 1974 and 1975 he helped expose the corruption of Rabbi Bernard Bergman, a nursing-home operator, and others, leading to the appointment of a special prosecutor by Governor Carey to clean up the nursing home business and the subsequent jailing and fining of Bergman.

In recent years Newfield has begun to write increasingly about his Jewishness. "Anti-Semitism and the Crime of Silence," the cover article in *The Voice* (June 17–23, 1981), is a bitter and incisive examination of what he perceives to be growing anti-Semitism within the United States and abroad, with a focus on the cynicism and hypocrisy of those liberals who defend every minority cause except that of Jews and on the neoconservatives who support repressive and brutal governments everywhere.

In addition to *The Village Voice*, Newfield has contributed to *Playboy, The Nation, Partisan Review, Evergreen Review* and *The New York Times Book Review*.

ARNOLD NEWMAN

b. March 3, 1918
Photographer

When the British Museum commissioned a photographer to take portraits of important British government and royal officials, they hired an American, Arnold

Newman. Newman's special skill is environmental portraiture—that is, photographing his subjects in surroundings that match their work and their personalities—and he has not limited himself to Americans. He has been the official photographer of several U.S. presidents, and his photographs of artists, musicians, scientists and other people of accomplishment around the world are internationally known.

Arnold Newman was born in New York City to Isidore and Freda (Perell) Newman. He was raised in Atlantic City, New Jersey and Miami Beach, Florida because his father, a clothing manufacturer and dry goods businessman until the 1929 economic crash, then leased and operated resort hotels. In 1934 he moved with his family to Miami Beach. Newman's early artistic talent was encouraged by his parents, and he studied from 1936 to 1938 at the University of Miami; financial problems forced him to leave college without a degree, but this turned out to be a blessing for Newman. In 1938 he became apprenticed to a studio photographer in Philadelphia, a friend of his parents. Although the work he did there was strictly according to formula, he learned the fundamentals of the photographic process, which he could later apply in the development of a personal style. In fact, he began doing his first experiments with portraiture even while shooting 49-cent snapshots in a commercial studio.

In 1941 Newman moved to New York for the first time and made many of his most important contacts with—and first portraits of—photographers and artists. After a return to Florida during the war, where he opened a studio, he settled in New York in 1946 and had his first one-man show, called "Artists Look Like This," at the Philadelphia Museum of Art. Working for the famous art director Alexey Brodovitch, Newman perfected his personal style. That year he was assigned to photograph Eugene O'Neill for *Life* magazine and got his first jobs for *Harper's Bazaar* and *Fortune*. Assignments for other magazines, including *Holiday, Horizon, Look, Travel & Leisure* and *Town & Country*, soon followed, and Newman became well-known.

One of his most famous photographs, taken in 1946, is of Igor Stravinsky, in which the great composer's head and arm are seen in the lower left-hand corner by the keyboard leaning on a grand piano. The top of the piano is raised, creating a dramatic angle in the picture. Stravinsky and the piano are in harmony in this portrait: They are one.

The Stravinsky photograph embodies Newman's ability to capture precisely his subjects' spirit and personality and is only one example of the many portraits of musicians, artists, politicians and celebrities in science, architecture and other areas that he has been photographing since 1941, people such as Grosz, Mondrian, Pollock, the Soyers, Levine, Guston and others. In each one he creates an environment that integrates the person into his or her particular world. Mondrian fits in with the squares of his paintings. J. Robert Oppenheimer is surrounded by copious scientific notes in an otherwise bare and somber office. Golda Meir sits informally in an office full of books and photographs, the eternal cigarette in hand. The use of light is scrupulously controlled in all the portraits. Newman intuitively knows how to frame his subjects.

Even as he became an established professional, Newman did not allow his photographic style to become standardized, and he remained constantly aware of the individual qualities of his sitters, often experimenting until he arrived at the final photograph. He has cut out or even torn photos to conform to his image of a person (Joan Miro, the abstract artist), glued two or three together or superimposed them (Andy Warhol), or he will crop a photo—select only a portion of it for the final print—so that the end result might be a very horizontal or vertical rectangle (his portrait of Dr. Leo Szilard, the physicist). Newman experiments and surprises: The viewer always finds something new and dramatic in Newman's images.

Since the late 1940s Newman's career has included a string of editorial assignments and commissions to do portraits (he has done official portraits of presidents Eisenhower, Kennedy and Johnson) as well as exhibitions around the world, teaching assignments and many publications. His work is owned by the Metropolitan Museum of Art, the Museum of Modern Art in New York, the Art Institute of Chicago, the National Portrait Gallery in London, the Israel Museum in Jerusalem and the Moderna Museet in Stockholm. In 1972 he signed with the Light Gallery in New York and exhibits there regularly. Since 1968 he has been a visiting professor of advanced photography at Cooper Union in New York and was named acting curator and adviser to the photography department of the Israel Museum in 1965. Newman's major collection of photography is *One Mind's Eye* (Boston, 1974). He has also published *Faces U.S.A.* (Garden City, N.Y., 1978) and *The Great British* (Boston, 1979).

Newman has received several awards, including the Newhouse Citation from Syracuse University in 1961, a gold medal from the Fourth Biennale Internazionale Della Fotografia in Venice in 1963, and a Life Achievement award from the American Society of Magazine

Photographers. He was the subject of a film produced by Nebraska Educational Television called "The Image Makers—The Environments of Arnold Newman."

Newman lives in New York City with his Israeli-born wife, the former Augusta Rubenstein, a onetime member of *Hagana,* the pre-State of Israel underground army.

EDWIN NEWMAN

b. January 25, 1919
Journalist; author

Unlike many younger television journalists, Edwin Newman began his career in print before turning to broadcasting. As a result, he has brought to his television commentary as an NBC News reporter a literary richness that probes beyond the superficial aspects of what he is describing and an intrinsic respect for the role of language as his original medium.

Edwin Harold Newman was born in New York City to Myron, a credit manager in a men's clothing store and later a self-employed businessman, and Rose (Parker) Newman. He attended public schools in New York, graduating from George Washington High School in 1936, and received a B.A. degree from the University of Wisconsin in 1940. A brief stint at Louisiana State University on a Fulbright Fellowship with the Department of Government was followed in early 1941 by a civil service position with the Department of Agriculture in Washington.

Finding neither academia nor government work appealing, Newman turned toward journalism, an old love that he first cultivated working on school papers in New York and Wisconsin. His first job was as "dictation boy" with the Washington bureau of the International News Service in 1941, followed by a post with United Press in 1941–42. Newman spent the war years in the U.S. Navy as a communications officer in Trinidad and in the Brooklyn Navy Yard. He returned to United Press in 1945 and in late 1946 joined the liberal New York daily *PM,* reporting from Washington. He then worked briefly as a Washington stringer for several newspapers in New Jersey and Michigan and in 1947 got his first break into broadcasting when he was hired as Eric Sevareid's assistant in the Washington bureau for CBS from 1947 to 1949.

From 1949 to 1952 Newman free-lanced from London as a magazine writer and as a broadcaster for NBC

and the BBC. During 1951 to 1952 he also worked for the Marshall Plan, visiting countries throughout Europe that were undergoing rebuilding and reporting back to the United States on progress in each one. He began to work full-time for NBC News in London in late 1952 and became NBC News bureau chief there in 1956. In 1957 he was transferred to Rome and the following year to Paris. Although Newman headed the news bureaus in both capitals, he also traveled extensively and developed a reputation as a top diplomatic reporter. After returning to the United States to cover the political conventions of the major parties in 1960, he went back to Paris and in 1961 received the Overseas Press Club Award for his reportage. He returned to the United States once more, this time permanently, to report for NBC from New York. He appeared regularly on the *Today* show and on other news programs and specials, including the periodic "JFK Reports," an attempt to provide television audiences with insights into the presidency.

Newman also hosted NBC documentary specials covering a wide range of subjects. One included a study of lifestyles in California; another took viewers from Paris to Istanbul on the Orient Express; a third, aired in 1962, discussed the growing role of American military advisers in Southeast Asia; while still another explored the treatment of the mentally ill. He also hosted a 1964 special on the New York World's Fair.

In 1965 Newman became NBC News drama critic in addition to appearing as a regular news commentator on early evening and late night news broadcasts. His astute criticism—he was one of the first broadcasters to perfect the "60-second review"—earned him an Emmy in 1966. The same year he received a Peabody Award for his radio news commentary. He also continued writing magazine articles, which were published in such periodicals as *Progressive, Esquire, Atlantic Monthly, The New York Times Magazine* and others.

Newman aroused controversy in 1971 when, as *Today* host, he cut short an interview with George Jessel, who had been making continuous references to *The New York Times* and *The Washington Post* as "Pravda," implying that both newspapers were organs of Communist propaganda. Newman's personal respect for freedom of the press was too great to tolerate Jessel's ravings, although ironically he cut off Jessel's own free speech in the process.

Newman is the author of two books of commentary, *Strictly Speaking* (New York, 1974), which became a best seller on the subject of language, and a sequel, *A Civil Tongue* (New York, 1976).

MIKE NICHOLS

b. November 6, 1931
Actor; director; producer

Calling Mike Nichols a "Renaissance Man" of the American theater is no careless exaggeration. Beginning with early success as one half of the improvisational comedy duo "Nichols and May" when he was in his 20s, he has since received high critical acclaim for directing some of America's most significant films and plays and has shown remarkable intuitive skill as a producer. He remains a formidable and versatile actor as well.

Michael Igor Peshkowsky was born in Berlin to Paul, a Russian-Jewish physician, and Brigitte (Landauer) Peshkowsky, who came from a prominent and politically active German-Jewish family. Forced to flee Germany, the family settled in New York, where Paul Peshkowsky established a medical practice and took the name "Nichols." After attending private schools in New York and Connecticut, Mike Nichols proceeded to the University of Chicago in 1950 as a premedical student. But his undergraduate extracurricular activities in drama soon became his primary interest, and he left in 1953 to study acting in New York with Lee Strasberg.

He returned to Chicago and joined an improvisational troupe whose other five members included Elaine May, a young actress he had met earlier. She began working with Nichols as a duo, and after the larger ensemble disbanded following a successful stint in a Chicago club called The Compass, the two traveled to New York in 1957. There, with the help of an agent, they received engagements at the Village Vanguard and the Blue Angel, two prestigious clubs. Their improvisational comedy—the two would perform skits devised on the spot based on audience suggestions—was a hit, and they performed in other cities in the United States, on major television variety shows, in a Town Hall "recital" in 1959—a rarity, since Town Hall was usually reserved for musical performances—and on Broadway in 1960. By now Nichols and May, who made a best-selling record together in 1961, were nationally famous, and their brand of comedy would often be copied. But shortly afterward, ready to pursue other areas of performance, they split up, and Nichols began directing plays and then films.

Although best-known for his comedic skills, he proved an astute interpreter of contemporary drama as well as comedy. His range included such Neil Simon plays as *The Odd Couple* (1965), *Plaza Suite* (1968) and *The Prisoner of Second Avenue* (1971), all directed for Broadway, and serious works like a revival of Lillian Hellman's *The Little Foxes* (1967), Chekhov's *Uncle Vanya* (1973) and David Rabe's anti-war drama *Streamers* (1976). In film Nichols showed the same remarkable versatility by directing the drama *Who's Afraid of Virginia Woolf?* with Elizabeth Taylor and Richard Burton (1966), which he followed with the award-winning *The Graduate* (1967), which featured Dustin Hoffman in his first major role. He then directed the complex, satirical, yet profoundly serious anti-war film *Catch-22* (1970), based on Joseph Heller's novel, and Jules Feiffer's incisive look into sexual mores and mid-life crisis with *Carnal Knowledge* (1971). Some other films include *The Day of the Dolphin* (1973) and *The Fortune* (1975).

Whether Nichols' knack for success as performer and director was based on pure skill, good luck or a combination of both, it followed him when he made his debut as Broadway producer of *Annie,* the phenomenal musical-comedy surprise hit of 1978.

Although the Nichols and May partnership was formally dissolved in the early 1960s, many people still considered them a classic comedy duo. In 1980 they reunited, but this time as dramatic performers in Edward Albee's *Who's Afraid of Virginia Woolf?* at the New Haven, Connecticut Long Wharf Theater. In their new roles they proved as successful in parrying the intense dialogue of Albee's bitter and unhappily married couple as they were in tossing about their improvisational merriment.

HUGH NISSENSON

b. March 10, 1933
Author

While many Americans readily identify Philip Roth, Bernard Malamud and Saul Bellow as the great interpreters of Jewish life in American fiction, it is Hugh Nissenson who perhaps comes closest to capturing the definitive American-Jewish experience in his work. The author of two collections of short stories, one novel and an autobiographical chronicle of experiences in Israel before and after the Six Day War, Nissenson has brought an acute awareness of the "Jewish condition" to his writing, on both a personal and a general level.

Hugh Nissenson was born in New York City to Charles Arthur, a manufacturer, and Harriette (Dolch) Nissenson. He received a B.A. degree from Swarthmore College in 1955. Since 1958 Nissenson has been a freelance writer. Although based in New York, he spent one year at Stanford University as Wallace Stegner Literary Fellow in 1961–62 and has traveled widely in Israel, the setting for many of his stories.

Nissenson's first published story collection was *A Pile of Stones* (New York, 1965). Of the seven stories, two were set in Poland during the pogroms of the early 1900s; two were in Israel during the 1950s; and the remaining three were in contemporary America. Despite the different locations, there was a common theme in which Nissenson attempted to explore the relationship of modern man to God and to the surrounding society.

Nissenson's next book, *Notes from the Frontier* (New York, 1968), is a record of his experiences in Israel during visits to a kibbutz in the Galilee in 1965 and just after the Six Day War in 1967. Nissenson reflects on the impact of war on life in the kibbutz as a whole and on certain individuals.

In the Reign of Peace (New York, 1972) is Nissenson's second short-story collection. While the eight stories have different locations, and in one case the subjects are not Jewish, but Quaker, they all concern the dilemma reached when one has lost faith but has nothing to replace it with.

In 1976 Nissenson published his first novel, *My Own Ground* (New York). Told first-person by 68-year-old Jake Brody, the story goes back to Brody's youth in the tough Jewish ghetto of the Lower East Side just before the First World War. Brody explores a series of sordid relationships between people he knew and grew up with, trying to find a Jewish connection—a resolution of sorts—within them. In the story Jake believes that Jews cannot survive in the United States because they have abandoned so much of their religious faith. Yet Nissenson's message is ultimately positive as his characters attempt to find a way that transcends a dangerous world.

In a critique of Nissenson's early work, Robert Alter wrote:

> Nissenson is . . . the only genuinely religious writer in the whole American Jewish group. His fiction represents an attempt to follow the twisting, sometimes treacherous ways between God and man; his stories reach out for Jewish experiences in Eastern Europe, in Israel and in America, in an effort to discover what Jews do with their faith in a God who so often seems conspicuous by his absence.

In subsequent years, while Nissenson's work has matured, his essential themes have remained the same.

In addition to his books, Nissenson has written stories, articles and criticism for a wide range of magazines, including *The New Yorker*, *Harper's*, *Present Tense*, *Commentary*, *Holiday*, *Esquire* and *Playboy*.

LOUIS NIZER

b. February 6, 1902
Attorney

Louis Nizer, who has been one of New York's most prominent attorneys for more than 50 years, is also the author of two best-selling books about his courtroom experiences. Through his work and his writings—there are nine books in all—the famous trial lawyer has helped bring the mechanics and drama of the legal world to life for the general public.

Louis Nizer was born in London to Joseph, who worked in real estate, and Bella (Bialestock) Nizer. His family came to the United States in 1905. Nizer received his B.A. degree in 1922 from Columbia College and a law degree from Columbia University in 1924 and began practicing law that year. In 1928 he helped form the firm Phillips, Nizer, Benjamin, Krim and Ballon, where he is now senior partner and general counsel for the Motion Picture Association of America.

As an attorney Nizer is known to be a meticulous researcher who brings a sense of authority to the courtroom. Among his major legal triumphs have been the libel suit brought by journalist Quentin Reynolds against columnist Westbrook Pegler and the suit instituted by broadcaster John Henry Faulk, who was blacklisted by a group of right-wing extremists during the McCarthy era in the 1950s. Nizer once battled successfully to prevent movie mogul Louis B. Mayer from winning control over Metro-Goldwyn-Mayer. In another case involving divorce, he received a $288,000 fee from his grateful liquor executive client.

Many of his cases have been described in his books. In his most famous book, *My Life in Court* (New York, 1962), Nizer details the *Reynolds* v. *Pegler* trial, the *Eleanor Holm* v. *Billy Rose* and the John Astor divorces, and Konrad Bercovici's suit against Charlie Chaplin. The book, which was praised for its vivid and dramatic descriptions of legal procedures and interactions, became a best seller. Most critics praised it highly, although one referred to Nizer as "an ego with a law degree." His sequel, also a best seller, *The Jury Returns* (New York, 1966), told of other dramatic trials in which he served as lawyer.

Nizer has also dealt with other social and political events in books. An early work, *What to Do with Germany* (New York, 1944), reflected the then-popular get-tough-with-defeated-Germany school, in which he sought to prove that Nazism was not a unique strain in German history but rather one that grew from an "inherent characteristic of the German people." Some critics objected, however; *New Republic* damned it for its "legalistic pettifoggery" and oversimplifications. Years later Nizer added the controversial book, *The Implosion Conspiracy* (New York, 1972), in which he argued that, based on the trial record, accused spies Ethel and Julius Rosenberg were guilty. "One cannot help wondering," wrote a reviewer in the *Library Journal*, "whether that verdict would have been rendered if a lawyer of Nizer's caliber had volunteered his services to the Rosenbergs at the time."

But lawyers also lose major cases as he did in 1982 when he defended the California resort La Costa's libel suit against *Penthouse* magazine because the magazine had allegedly defamed two of the resort's founders and had suggested that La Costa was connected to organized crime. (The case was later ordered retried.)

Nizer is also a serious painter, and his work has been shown at the Hammer Gallery and at the Permanent Art Gallery of the American Bank and Trust Company in New York City.

For further information:
Nizer, Louis. *Between You and Me.* New York: 1948; 1963.
———. *Commentary and Analysis of the Official Warren Commission Report.* New York: 1964.
———. *Legal Essays.* New York: 1939.
———. *New Courts of History.* New York: 1933, 1972.
———. *Thinking on Your Feet: Adventures in Speaking.* New York: 1940, 1963.

IVAN J. NOVICK

b. April 5, 1927
Jewish organization president; businessman

With his election as president of the Zionist Organization of America in 1978, Ivan Novick capped a long career in Jewish service, on both the national and international level. He is a staunch supporter of the hardline policies of the government of Menachem Begin and of a strong defense buildup by the United States.

Ivan J. Novick was born in Butler, Pennsylvania to Harry, a businessman, and Sadye (Breman) Novick. Raised in Butler and in Pittsburgh, he attended Johns Hopkins University and the Virginia Polytechnic Institute and graduated from the University of Pittsburgh with a B.A. degree in 1949. He made Pittsburgh his home after completing military service as a United States Air Force lieutenant and became a real estate broker handling commercial and residential sales and leases.

In 1957 he became president of the San Toy Mining

Company, which he merged with two other companies the following year, leaving him with major corporate responsibilities as executive vice president of what was renamed Apollo Industries. He has since returned to real estate development as a principal in West Penn Realty Co. in Pittsburgh, which builds shopping centers across the United States, and with N-N-B Corp., based in Florida.

While Novick's business accomplishments are impressive, his contributions in energy and time to Jewish causes since 1959 have placed him in the top ranks of the Jewish establishment. In clout, he has been called the "next Max Fisher," referring to the Detroit industrialist who has had easy access to presidents Nixon and Reagan and many other political leaders.

To list all of Novick's positions and the dates he held them would be unwieldy. In brief, Novick has been deeply involved with the United Jewish Federation on all levels, has been president of his congregation and has served in executive positions with Israel Bonds, United Jewish Appeal, Jewish Family and Children's Service, and with major Jewish groups in Pittsburgh. He has been on the board of directors of the American Jewish Committee and of the Jewish Home and Hospital for the Aged and has been prominent in Zionist activities since the early 1960s. He has also been vice president of the American section of the World Jewish Congress.

In his post as ZOA president—he was elected to a second two-year term in 1980—Novick met with Egypt's President Sadat during a visit to the United States that year and supported the presidential candidacy of Ronald Reagan in 1980. He has been sharply critical of past policies of some American delegates to the United Nations, especially Andrew Young and Donald McHenry, who seemed to him to bend toward acceptance of the PLO, and was relieved when the anti-PLO Jeane Kirkpatrick was named to succeed McHenry. Novick also strongly favors retaining Jerusalem as Israel's capital. In early 1981 Novick spoke out in support of Israel's bombing of an Iraqi nuclear reactor as a defensive act. Later that year he harshly criticized the move by the Reagan administration to sell AWACS and other sophisticated weapons systems to the government of Saudi Arabia.

ROBERT NOZICK

b. November 16, 1938
Philosopher

Robert Nozick, professor of philosophy at Harvard University, is best-known as perhaps the strongest and clearest new voice of classical libertarian principles today.

Robert Nozick was born in Brooklyn to Max, a manufacturer, and Sophie (Cohen) Nozick. He received his B.A. degree from Columbia University in 1959, an M.A. degree in 1961 and a Ph.D. in philosophy in 1963, both from Princeton University. From 1962 to 1963, while pursuing his doctoral studies, Nozick was an instructor in philosophy at Princeton. Upon finishing his degree, he was appointed an assistant professor there and remained until 1965. From 1965 to 1967 he was an assistant professor at Harvard University and from 1967 to 1969 was an associate professor at Rockefeller University in New York. Since 1969 Nozick has been professor of philosophy at Harvard.

Essentially, Nozick believes in the argument, grounded in the natural rights position of the 17th and 18th centuries, that the minimal state is best, or as it was put in early American history, "that government is best which governs least." His book *Anarchy, State and Utopia* (New York, 1974) received the National Book Award in 1975. In it Nozick limits state functions to the barest minimum: defense, enforcement of contracts, controlling crime and the like. Other governmental actions, he argues, are an intrusion and therefore morally illegitimate. His response predates the position of many who in later years questioned the role of central government. The implications of Nozick's arguments are that intervention on behalf of social justice or righting wrongs—real or imagined—is unjustified. Commenting in *The New York Review of Books* in 1975 on Nozick's far-reaching arguments, the Australian philosopher Peter Singer wrote that *Anarchy, State and Utopia* was "a major event in contemporary political philosophy. [Until the book appeared] there has, in recent years, been no sustained and competently argued challenge to the prevailing concepts of social justice and the role of the state."

In a subsequent book, *Philosophical Explanations* (Cambridge, Mass., 1981), he identifies the individual—always crucial to his way of thinking—as one capable of selecting his or her own body of ethical and moral behavior. One critic wrote: "One cannot fail to admire Nozick's refusal to bully; for it is a melancholy fact that many philosophers are bullies. . . . His method is the method of charming. . . . He simply wants to suggest explanations. . . ."

Nozick has also expressed much interest in Israel. In an article published in *Moment,* for example, titled 'Orthodox Coercion in Israel," he argued on behalf of the Orthodox Jews in that country who refuse to permit autopsies. "The advancement of medical knowledge and medical treatment does not justify any and every imposition upon people." As always, he focused on people first.

TILLIE OLSEN

b. January 14, 1913
Author

Although Tillie Olsen was nearly 50 when her first book was published in 1962, and her literary output since then has been limited, her stature as a prose writer has mounted steadily, and she is now regarded by many as one of America's finest living authors. A self-taught writer with no formal higher education, she specializes in writing about the struggles of working people—problems she has known intimately—with a focus on women trying to cope with the many roles they have traditionally been expected to play.

Tillie Lerner was born in Omaha, Nebraska to Samuel, a farmer, worker, house painter and paper hanger, and Ida (Beber) Lerner, Russian immigrants. As a young girl she developed a passion for writing, especially after reading a 19th-century account of factory workers called *Life in the Iron Mills* by an obscure woman writer named Rebecca Harding Davis. However, she was equally passionate about the plight of workers during the Depression of the 1930s, and she became involved in a variety of political and trade union movements. After quitting high school, she was briefly jailed in Kansas City for trying to organize packing house workers. She worked full-time in various union headquarters and wrote for left-wing journals, eventually following the movement to California.

In 1945 she met and married Jack Olsen, a printer and a committed unionist, and thereafter she devoted herself to managing a household—Olsen raised four daughters—and supplementing the family income with menial jobs, including one (ironically) as a typist-transcriber. A novel that she began in the early 1930s was left incomplete while family demands took precedence; she finished it 40 years later.

Olsen's first published book was *Tell Me a Riddle* (Philadelphia, 1962), a collection of four short stories—all she had written to date—each of which explored the breakdown of human relationships, although the surface themes were entirely different. The title story, for which Olsen received the O. Henry Award when it was published separately in 1961, focuses on an elderly woman—modeled, one critic has suggested, on Olsen's mother—who is terminally ill and wants to spend her last months visiting her grown children and resolving conflicts between her and her husband that have plagued their marriage since the beginning. She is a fiercely independent woman whose married life has been one of denial rather than affirmation, and she would like to end her life on terms of her own making. Irving Howe called the story a "tour de force," a reaction generally shared by critics. Another story in the collection, "I Stand Here Ironing," perhaps the closest to Olsen's experiences, depicts a mother watching her teen-age daughter grow and musing at her own lost opportunities and the distances between the two.

As a result of Olsen's new visibility, she began receiving writing fellowships, including grants from the National Endowment for the Arts, and was a guest professor at Amherst College (1969–70), Stanford University (1971), Massachusetts Institute of Technology (1973), the University of Massachusetts (1974) and the University of California (1978). The recognition that gave Olsen time to write now allowed her to return to her long-unfinished project, and in 1974 the novel *Yonnondio: From the Thirties* (New York) appeared to critical raves. The story of a midwestern family, struggling to cope with the Depression as they fail first at mining in Wyoming and then at tenant farming in South Dakota and end up scrounging their meager way through life in Chicago, *Yonnondio* was called by one reviewer "the best novel to come out of the so-called proletarian movement of the '30s" and reflected once again Olsen's commitment to documenting the plight of people in trouble.

Olsen has also written nonfiction, including a biographical social and literary commentary about her "mentor," Rebecca Harding Davis, and a collection of essays and speeches called *Silences* (New York, 1978). In this book the title essay, which received much attention when it was published, explores the dilemma of women like Olsen who must set aside and even repress their desires to realize personal goals if they are also to raise a family. But if the alternative is total isolation, Olsen does not quite know the way out of the problem.

Although Olsen's reputation was first established through word of mouth and by women's organizations, she is no longer considered exclusively a "woman writer." Her manuscripts belong to the Berg Collection of the New York Public Library, several of her stories have been dramatized or recorded, and in 1980 a film version of *Tell Me a Riddle*, starring Melvyn Douglas, was a moderate commercial success.

RICHARD LAWRENCE OTTINGER

b. January 27, 1929
U.S. Congressman

Richard L. Ottinger, Democratic Congressman from Westchester County in New York since 1975, has long been a major supporter of liberal and Jewish concerns. He has sponsored legislation opposing the Soviet Union's

treatment of Jews, supporting America's recognition of Jerusalem as the capital of Israel and advocating the establishment of a permanent U.S. Holocaust Memorial Council. He was an early and articulate opponent of United States involvement in the Vietnam War and in El Salvador and voted against draft registration in 1980. He has also voted against increased military spending, supported a nuclear freeze and is in the forefront of the defense of consumers.

Richard Lawrence Ottinger was born in New York City to Lawrence, the founder of U.S. Plywood Co., and Louise (Loewenstein) Ottinger. He received his B.A. degree from Cornell University in 1950, a law degree from Harvard in 1953 and did graduate work in international law at Georgetown University from 1960 to 1961. He was in the U.S. Air Force from 1953 to 1955 and from 1955 to 1960 worked for several law firms.

From 1961 to 1964 he was director of programs in South America for the Peace Corps and from 1965 to 1971 was a congressman for the 25th district in New York, composed of western Westchester and Putnam counties. From 1971 to 1974 he organized and directed Grassroots Action, Inc., a non-profit corporation established to assist citizen action groups to organize and act effectively, primarily in consumer and environmental matters. In 1975 he was elected Congressman of the 24th district with a 58 per cent majority vote.

From the beginning Ottinger was one of the most committed environmentalists in Congress. Since he belonged to the Energy Subcommittee of the House Commerce Committee, Ottinger took a prominent role in challenging legislation designed to aid the major oil companies at the expense of the consumer. He founded the House Environmental Study Conference and has also been involved with many of the more significant national and regional preservationist groups including the Friends of the Hudson, designed to prevent the Hudson River from becoming irreversibly polluted.

Ottinger has also taken a strong political stand in defense of human rights. He has sponsored legislation urging Rumania to restore religious freedom and the Soviet Union to end its policies of discrimination against Jews. He has protested on behalf of Soviet dissidents Andrei Sakharov, Anatoly Sharansky, Ida Nudel and others who are punished for their activities. In 1980 he expressed his alarm to Soviet President Leonid Brezhnev about a drastic drop in Soviet Jewish emigration. He also sponsored a resolution condemning the systematic interruption of mail sent to people in the Soviet Union.

The Congressman's commitment to Israel is equally strong. He condemned Ambassador Andrew Young's assertion in 1979 that the United States needs an "effective relationship" with the Palestine Liberation Organization (PLO) and in 1980, attacked the French government for endorsing PLO participation in any Middle East peace talks. He applauded the Israeli-Egypt Peace Treaty signed in 1979 and backed an amendment in 1980, which stated that the PLO should not be given membership in the International Monetary Fund.

Ottinger's record shows that support for domestic liberal programs, opposition to military interventions abroad, backing for Israel and the shaping of an international policy that does not embrace tyrants of the left or right is a practical policy.

CYNTHIA OZICK

b. April 17, 1928
Author

Describing Cynthia Ozick's brilliant collection of stories, *The Pagan Rabbi* (New York, 1971), Arthur A. Cohen says that the author "comes forward . . . not as a Jewish writer, but as a Jewish visionary." Indeed, Ozick's fiction—for she is primarily a novelist and short story writer—and her nonfiction magazine articles explore Jewish life not so much as a matter of economics, sociology or politics but as a deep spiritual, historical and often-troubling experience. One critic has even gone so far as to say that although Ozick writes in English, her work has more in common with that of Hebrew and Yiddish writers.

Cynthia Ozick was born in New York City to Russian immigrant parents, William, a pharmacist, and Celia (Regelson) Ozick. Her passion for writing flowered early, as did her talent, and she graduated from New York University with a B.A. degree in 1949 cum laude with honors in English. She received an M.A. degree from Ohio State University the following year. Ozick then married and raised a daughter and published short essays, criticism and reviews in a variety of periodicals. From 1964 to 1965 she was an English instructor at New York University, and except for other occasional short-term teaching positions, she has been writing full-time since 1965.

Ozick's first novel, *Trust* (New York, 1966), was an intellectual, political and social exploration of the rich in Europe, spanning the 1930s to the present. Told from the point of view of a young woman, it signified the debut of a writer of deep sophistication of language but without the direction her later work would take. Her next book reflected Ozick's arrival as an important Jewish writer, as *The Pagan Rabbi* received wide critical acclaim. And yet, although each of the seven stories in

the book had at least one Jewish character, the transcendent tone of the writing goes beyond Jewishness into more universal and spiritual themes. In the title story, for example, a brilliant young talmudic scholar discovers an all-consuming love for nature (something very contrary to what he has learned) and to resolve his seemingly impossible conflict, he hangs himself—and returns to nature. *The New York Times* critic reviewing *The Pagan Rabbi* described Ozick as a "narrative hypnotist," and the book received the 1972 National Book Award and the Jewish Heritage Award. By now Ozick had developed a solid following of readers.

They would have to wait five more years for her next book, however. *Bloodshed and Three Novellas* (New York, 1976) contained four more stories that weaved in the Ozick magic. Again, as in her earlier works, the stories dealt not with surface aspects of Jewish life but with deeper, mystical themes. Or, as one reviewer wrote: "Unlike many Jewish writers, Ozick is less concerned with modern Jews fending for themselves in Western culture than with their coming to terms with ancient Judaism, a primal force buried deep in their being."

Despite the complexity of Ozick's fiction, which has appeared in most major magazines, she has also written many nonfiction pieces. Among her most important is an essay that occupied the entire issue of *The New Leader* magazine on June 30, 1980, entitled "Carter and the Jews." In the essay Ozick pieced together events and trends, both subtle and blatant, that indicated, in her view, the erosion of concern for American Jews and Jews abroad during the Carter presidency. Nonetheless, she wondered if there were anyone else among the candidates who could offer a healthier and more promising alternative for Jewish voters. The article sparked much controversy as several subsequent issues of *The New Leader* contained critiques of Ozick's article as well as her own reply.

Levitation: Five Fictions (New York, 1982) was her first book since *Bloodshed*. Her tales brilliantly examine the odd lives of nonconforming men and women who seek refuge in the worlds of fantasy, obsession and illusion. In one novella her protagonist—a woman attorney—passes delusion and creates a *golem* from potting soil. In the tale that bears the title of the book the Jews levitate at a New York literary cocktail party. Ozick's imagination and writing "shimmers," as a reviewer wrote, "with intelligence."

For further information:

Ozick, Cynthia. "The Laughter of Akiva." *The New Yorker,* November 10, 1980.

Cole, Diane. "I want to do Jewish dreaming: Profile of Cynthia Ozick," *Present Tense,* Summer 1982.

GRACE PALEY

b. December 11, 1922
Author; peace activist

Grace Paley, author and peace activist, may be known equally well for her prose and her protest. Her first book of short stories, *The Little Disturbances of Man* (New York, 1959), received wide acclaim after its publication. Her writing about ethnic urban life in New York City is honest and ironical, sympathetic but unsentimental. Long active in the peace movement, she has on numerous occasions appeared in vigils, sit-ins and demonstrations on behalf of peace and civil rights. More recently she has become a leading spokesperson against nuclear power and nuclear weapons.

Grace Goodside was born in the Bronx, the daughter of Isaac and Manya (Ridnik) Goodside. Her father was a doctor, though she remembers him as an "artist and storyteller." Paley attended Hunter College from the fall of 1938 to the spring of 1939 but dropped out and supported herself as a typist. She married Jess Paley, with whom she had two children.

Paley's volume *Enormous Changes at the Last Minute* (New York, 1974), containing 15 stories, established her as a powerful and original voice in modern fiction. She writes about what she knows—life on the streets of New York, relationships between lovers and among families—using Jewish colloquialisms in a thoroughly unselfconscious and believable style. E.L. Doctorow said that she expresses "a whole life in one line." Her writing has been praised for its truth, its beauty and its simplicity and has been favorably compared to Chekhov.

Grace Paley was among 11 protesters who stepped out onto the White House lawn on Labor Day 1978, carrying a banner that read, "No Nuclear Weapons! No Nuclear Power! US or USSR." While a simultaneous demonstration in Moscow by fellow members of the War Resisters League led to a mere reprimand from the Soviet authorities, Ms. Paley and her Washington colleagues were charged with unlawful entry and found guilty after a seven-day trial in federal court. PEN, the international writers' group, came out in strong support of her, condemning the arrest and prosecution on the grounds that it violated her right to free and open expression.

Paley's protest and prose grow out of an inner commitment to speak the truth about social conditions. She says:

> I was raised by secular Jews who had a strong Jewish identification, though they weren't religious. My par-

ents believed in an ethical, idealistic way of life. I always assumed that that's what Jews were all about. That and storytelling—we have a tradition of great Jewish storytellers. Look at the Bible!

She has also taught writing courses "on and off" at Columbia University and Sarah Lawrence College since 1966. Her stories have appeared in the *New Yorker, New American Review, Esquire,* the *Atlantic Monthly* and elsewhere.

Paley received the Brandeis University Creative Arts Award Citation in Fiction in 1978. She was elected to the American Academy and Institute of Arts and Letters in 1980.

WILLIAM PALEY

b. September 28, 1901
Broadcasting executive

No one has experienced the broadcast revolution quite like William Paley, who single-handedly built a huge communications empire from a small network of radio stations. The founder of CBS Inc., he was a pioneer in using radio as a news medium.

William Samuel Paley was born in Chicago to Samuel, a Russian immigrant who became a successful cigar manufacturer, and Goldie (Drell) Paley. He studied at the University of Chicago from 1918 to 1919 and at the University of Pennsylvania, where he completed a B.S. degree at the Wharton School of Finance in 1922. Upon graduation, Paley joined the Philadelphia-based family business, which was called the Congress Cigar Company, and by 1925 had been named company secretary and vice president.

The bold pioneering that characterized Paley's later ventures into the new medium of television surfaced during his early career. While Paley's father and uncle, who was a business partner, went to Europe, Paley initiated an advertising campaign for the family company on a new local radio station. Although the deal angered Paley's father, it whetted the younger man's appetite for broadcasting. In 1928 he purchased a broadcasting chain that then owned a dozen stations in the Northeast. By the time Paley renamed the chain the Columbia Broadcasting System Inc., its reach extended to the West Coast. By 1930 there were 70 stations in all.

Paley proved to be an innovative programmer. In 1930, in conjunction with the U.S. Office of Education, he broadcast *Columbia School of the Air* and later that year added live broadcasts of the New York Philharmonic Symphony Society concerts. The station soon began airing newscasts as well, and such print journalists as Edward R. Murrow and William Shirer joined the news staff. Live drama, presented by Norman Corwin and titled *The Columbia Workshop*, made its debut in 1936. CBS also ventured outside radio to develop the CBS Concert Corporation and to control Columbia Records.

In the late 1930s CBS branched into shortwave broadcasting, and in 1938, under Paley's aegis, the station broadcast the famous abdication speech of King Edward VIII. Later, the station was responsible for transmitting historic on-the-spot news of Nazi invasions throughout Europe.

During World War II Paley took a leave of absence from CBS to help organize radio activities for the Office of War Information in Europe. He had been promoted to colonel by the time he returned to civilian life in 1946 and received medals for his service from the U.S. government as well as the French and Italian governments.

Paley became CBS board chairman in 1946 and, in the next few years, helped usher in the transition of CBS to the television medium. He helped introduce into television many of the radio programs that had placed CBS ahead of the other networks. Especially memorable was the *CBS Was There* series, which took full advantage of the visual and audio potential of the television medium, and which later became known as *You Are There*, hosted by Edward R. Murrow.

Paley's imprint remained especially strong in CBS news coverage. But as television expanded and diversified and Paley grew older, some conflicts began to emerge among top management at the network. Although CBS had a mandatory policy of retirement at 65, Paley made himself the sole exception to the rule, and he was criticized for making frequent changes among his so-called hand-picked successors, giving rise to the belief that he trusted no one. Still, in the 1980s, as the push toward cable television and new technologies increased, CBS continued to dominate the airways and many of its shows—from *60 Minutes* to the most inane—led the ratings race.

Paley has been active for many years in charitable and cultural organizations and has had a long affiliation with Jewish organizations. He is a life trustee of the Federation of Jewish Philanthropies and has been a fund raiser for the United Jewish Appeal. His efforts in the area of broadcast news earned him the First Amendment Award from the Anti-Defamation League.

In 1979 Paley wrote *As It Happened: A Memoir* (New York), his version of a remarkable career.

JOSEPH PAPP

b. June 22, 1921
Producer; director

Joseph Papp, founder and director of the New York Shakespeare Festival for more than 25 years and often called the most productive, ubiquitous and powerful man in the American theater, has brought a new generation of playwrights into the American theater and has made a major contribution to the visibility of minority theater in this country. Though by no means the first or only producer with a commitment to bringing theater free or at low cost to the public, Papp has had the greatest success in doing so.

Joseph Papirofsky was born in the Williamsburg section of Brooklyn. His father, Shmuel, a Polish immigrant, was a trunk maker. His mother, Yetta (Morris) Papirofsky, was born in Lithuania and worked as a seamstress. The immigrant community in which he was raised valued literary and musical culture, especially the classics. Papp attributes his desire to bring free theater to the people to the influence of his early schoolteachers of English and the social climate of the 1930s. At Eastern District High School, Papp studied drama and worked for the school newspaper before graduating in 1938. At the same time, he worked nights in a laundry.

From 1942 to 1946 Papp served in the Navy. After World War II and until 1948 he studied acting and directing at the Actors Laboratory Theater in Hollywood under the GI Bill. In 1950 he toured with the National Company production of Arthur Miller's *Death of a Salesman* as assistant stage manager and understudy for the two sons of the main character, Willy Loman. He returned to New York City, where he worked as a stage manager for CBS-TV (at which time he changed his named to "Papp") for such shows as *Studio One* and the long-running *I've Got a Secret*. He made his directing debut in 1951 with the One-Act Play Company at Lake Arrowhead, New York and the following year directed the Equity Library Theater production of *Deep Are the Roots*. In his time off from the CBS job, he worked on scenes from Shakespeare with a group of actors in a Lower East Side Sunday school basement and in 1954 founded the New York Shakespeare Festival on a shoestring budget.

Papp's earliest Shakespeare productions were staged at the East River Amphitheater, at Belvedere Lake in Central Park and the Heckscher Theater in the late 1950s. Under his leadership the Shakespeare Festival began to grow, and with it came the firm tradition of free performances and continuous experimentation. Despite protests against the free admission policy by then-Parks Commissioner Robert Moses, Papp stood firm and found backers to subsidize his park performances.

Meanwhile, in 1958 Papp was dismissed from CBS for refusing to talk to the House Un-American Activities Committee. However, he was later reinstated, only to resign because his activities with the Shakespeare Festival took more of his time. It moved to the newly constructed Delacorte Theater, an outdoor amphitheater in Central Park, in 1962 and performed three plays (later reduced to two) each summer season to thousands of New Yorkers at no charge. Several of these early productions were televised by CBS. In 1964 the Mobile Stage brought *A Midsummer Night's Dream* to 39 playgrounds and parks throughout the city. The Mobile Theater continues to tour the city, bringing theater to neighborhoods whose residents do not normally attend Broadway or off-Broadway shows.

In 1966 Papp expanded the Shakespeare Festival into the old Astor Library in New York's East Village. Now called the Public Theater, it houses six theaters and sponsors experimental workshops, poetry readings and a jazz cabaret. During the 1960s Papp made a commitment to produce socially relevant plays by young American playwrights. His show *Hair* (1967), a musical that combined popular anti-war sentiment of the era with an outpouring of song about youthful liberation and the "Age of Aquarius," was his first major production. It later went to Broadway and has been produced all over the world. Papp produced plays about the Vietnam War and its veterans, prison life, race relations and other timely subjects by such new writers as David Rabe (*Sticks and Bones,* 1970), Miguel Pinero (*Short Eyes,* 1974), Jason Miller (*That Championship Season,* 1972) and Ntozake Shange (*For Colored Girls,* 1976). Other playwrights who became well-known through Papp include David Mamet, Thomas Babe, Dennis Reardon, Charles Gordone, Sam Shepard, John Ford Noonan, Elizabeth Swados and David Rudkin.

Papp also adapted a number of Shakespearean plays to make them interesting to New York's black, Puerto Rican and white working-class audiences. He wanted Shakespeare to be topical, to relate to the turbulence of urban life. Most notable is *Two Gentlemen of Verona* (1971), which cast Raul Julia, a Puerto Rican actor, in the role of Proteus, a black actress as Sylvia, and flaunted a lively rock music score. In the late 1970s Papp created a Shakespeare repertory company at the Public Theater comprised exclusively of black and Hispanic actors, which was received with mixed reviews from critics and the public.

Lincoln Center's ill-fated theater division was turned over to Papp in 1973, in the hope that his innovative approach and flair for fund raising could establish a viable repertory theater in the Vivian Beaumont and Forum theaters. Four years later Papp withdrew from the directorship, decrying the lack of government support for nonprofit theater and all the arts.

In 1981 he visited Israel for the first time. "I was always afraid to go," he told Jane Perlez of *The New York Times.* "I felt I couldn't take it emotionally." This was echoed by the playwright David Rabe. "When I first met him, no one knew what his background was." And a friend, Bernard Gersten, recalled that Papp "concealed his Jewishness for the first 18 years of our friendship." But that has ended, and he is busily engaged in public acknowledgment of his background, personally and, naturally, professionally, at the Public Theater. In 1977 two of the season's plays included an updated revival of *The Dybbuk* by S. Ansky and *Tales of the Hasidim.* In 1980 Elizabeth Swados wrote and directed a multiracial musical play, *The Passover Haggadah,* which combined Hebraic traditional melodies with gospel music to tell the story of the Jews'—and by example all oppressed people's—struggles for freedom. That year the theater also sponsored a sold-out reading of Yiddish poetry.

Papp's productions have garnered three Pulitzer Prizes and numerous Drama Critics Awards and Tony Awards. Through his willingness to experiment and take risks, he has enabled such playwrights as the black writers Charles Gordone (the first black to win a Pulitzer Prize, incidentally) and Ed Bullins, and the Puerto Rican ex-convict Miguel Pinero to mount their plays—and subsequently win national recognition. The long-running Broadway musical *A Chorus Line* (1975) also originated at the Public Theater and is one of the major sources of revenue for its less popular—but often equally significant—presentations.

In 1978 Papp, who has taught at the Yale School of Drama (1966–67) and Columbia University (1967–69), made his performance debut as a singer at a small New York cabaret, The Ballroom. There he honed some of the skills learned as a teen-ager singing in synagogue when he presented a medley of tunes including Yiddish songs and Depression ballads.

RAPHAEL PATAI

b. November 22, 1910
Anthropologist

Raphael Patai was the first anthropologist to study the folklore and customs of Oriental Jewish communities in Palestine and throughout the Middle East and to promote the use of anthropology in understanding Jewish civilization and culture.

Raphael Patai was born in Budapest, Hungary to Josef, who was a prominent writer and Zionist leader, and Edith (Ehrenfeld) Patai. He attended the University of Budapest and that city's Rabbinical Seminary and received a Ph.D. in 1933 and a rabbinical diploma in 1936. After he completed his doctorate in Semitic languages and literature, which included complete mastery of Arabic, he went to the Hebrew University of Jerusalem, which had been founded only eight years earlier, to focus on the study of biblical and Jewish folklore. In 1936 he received his second doctorate—the first granted by Hebrew University. His dissertation, which won the Bialik Prize of the municipality of Tel Aviv, was entitled "Water: A Study in Palestinology and Palestinian Folklore in the Biblical and Mishnaic Periods."

Remaining in Jerusalem, where he taught Hebrew at the university, and spending 1942 to 1943 as a research fellow in Haifa, Patai continued to explore biblical folklore. He contributed articles to Israeli newspapers and magazines. He began to focus especially on Oriental Jewish folk customs associated with birth, marriage, death and other aspects related to daily life. By 1944, as the Ashkenazic Jewish presence began to dominate in Palestine, Patai founded the Palestine Institute of Folklore and Ethnology, a scholarly research center. In 1945 he started *Edoth,* a quarterly Hebrew-language journal devoted to the study of folklore and ethnology. His own focus began to expand beyond the study of historical folk traditions into examinations of contemporary lifestyles and the forces that help shape them.

In 1947, with the aid of a Viking Fund fellowship, Patai went to New York to study, with the intention of returning the following year. But with the partition of Palestine and the outbreak of the War for Independence in 1948, Hebrew University was temporarily closed, the institute he had founded ceased operations and *Edoth* folded. Patai thus remained in the United States and accepted an appointment to teach anthropology at Dropsie College in Philadelphia, where he taught until 1957, and became visiting professor at the University of Pennsylvania and Columbia University and later at New York University, the New School for Social Research in New York, Princeton University and Ohio State University. Continuing his earlier studies, he published a sociological work, *Israel Between East and West* (Philadelphia, 1953), and in 1957 was commissioned to edit a series of monographs about Syria, Lebanon and Jordan, which were published by the Human Relations Area Files in New Haven.

From 1956 to 1971 Patai was research director of the Herzl Institute in New York and editor of the Herzl Press. In this capacity he edited seven volumes of the *Herzl Yearbook,* five volumes of *The Complete Diaries of Theodore Herzl* (New York, 1960) and the two-volume *Encyclopedia of Zionism and Israel* (New York, 1971). He also continued his personal studies of Middle Eastern folklore and in 1962 published *Golden River to Golden Road: Society, Culture and Change in the Middle East* (Philadelphia), a collection of his major writings. A third, enlarged edition appeared in 1969.

While with the Herzl Press, Patai also joined the faculty of Fairleigh Dickinson University as professor of anthropology in 1966, where he taught for 10 years, and was visiting professor of anthropology at Brooklyn College from 1971 to 1972.

In the 1960s Patai directed his focus toward the study of the feminine element in Jewish folklore and religion, which became the theme for *The Hebrew Goddess* (New York, 1967 and 1978). With *Myth and Modern Man* (New York, 1972), he explored the role of modern thought processes in the incorporation of mythical traditions into contemporary life. In a related vein he published *The Arab Mind* (New York, 1973), an analysis of Arab mental characteristics; *The Myth of the Jewish Race* (New York, 1975), coauthored with his daughter, geneticist Jennifer Patai Wing, which concluded that Jews are not a single race but have genetic traits similar to their host peoples; and *The Jewish Mind* (New York, 1978), a massive three-part study that investigates the concept of the "Jewish mind," its evolution from encounters with the ancient Canaanites through the European Enlightenment and assimilation, and the development of the modern Jewish mind— its psychology, values, personality and distinguishing traits.

Since completing *The Jewish Mind,* Patai has returned to studies of biblical mythology. His books *The Messiah Texts* (Detroit, 1979) and *Gates to the Old City: A Book of Jewish Legends* (New York, 1980) contain collections of legends from a wide range of sources spanning biblical and later times. In each volume Patai has meticulously annotated his source material, which he has translated from Hebrew, Aramaic, Arabic, Greek, Yiddish, Ladino, German and Hungarian. A collection of his essays, *Folklore Studies—Biblical, Jewish, Comparative* (Detroit), was published in 1982.

Although Patai never returned to Israel to live, his close ties with it and his devotion to education were influential in the founding of Tel Aviv University. From 1956, just after it opened, through 1968, Patai was the first president of the American Friends of Tel-Aviv University. He received the Jewish Book Award in 1975 and 1976.

JAN PEERCE

b. June 3, 1904
Opera singer

The synagogue has probably been the greatest influence in Jan Peerce's life. He began singing there as a child, and long past formal retirement from the opera stage, he is known to return to synagogue to perform at services. At the peak of his career, he sang top roles with the Metropolitan Opera. He has since continued an active career on the recital circuit, much to the amazement of critics, who never thought the richness of his tenor would survive for so long.

Jacob Pincus Perelmuth was born in New York City to Russian immigrant parents, both Orthodox Jews. His father was a caterer. He attended New York City public schools and graduated from DeWitt Clinton High School.

As a child Peerce studied the violin and also sang in a synagogue choir. Music soon became a serious pursuit for him, and by age 14 he formed a trio with a drummer and a pianist. The following year he joined the Musician's Union Local 802. Through the union he acquired local jobs and a steady summer spot at a Catskill Mountains resort. Although most people think of Peerce exclusively as a singer, in fact violin dominated his career until he was in his late 20s, and he performed at the Catskills for 14 years following his debut there. In New York during the off-season, he appeared in cabarets, theaters, with orchestras and at private parties.

Peerce had begun some singing in his early 20s, but to satisfy family demands he also briefly undertook medical school studies. Whenever he could, however, he also sought singing jobs with orchestras. By 1932 his voice became his premier instrument, and a performance at the Astor Hotel proved to be an important turning point in his career. The performance was heard by a well-known impresario, S.L. Rothafel—also known as "Roxy"—who offered Peerce the opportunity to sing at Radio City. Following "Roxy" 's cue, Jacob Pincus Perelmuth anglicized his name and devoted himself exclusively to singing.

Peerce remained at Radio City for eight years as one of the theater's major attractions, and he was featured regularly in a popular Sunday morning radio show entitled *Music Hall of the Air*. His renown as a singer of both popular music and opera spread, and he eventually had a show of his own, *Great Moments of Music*.

In the mid-1930s Peerce began to study voice seriously, and in early 1938, with the help of NBC music director Samuel Chotzinoff, he auditioned for Arturo Toscanini. Toscanini was impressed, and shortly afterward Peerce performed in a New York Philharmonic concert of Beethoven's Ninth Symphony, with the great maestro conducting. His formal operatic debut followed soon after, when he performed as the Duke in *Rigoletto* with the Columbia Opera Company in Philadelphia. Peerce's New York recital debut occurred in late 1939, to great acclaim. Engagements for the tenor with other opera companies, including the San Francisco Opera, were soon forthcoming, and the most coveted opportunity —a role with the Met—was offered in 1941.

For the next 26 years, Peerce was a fixture at the Met, specializing in French and Italian repertory. He also guest-appeared regularly with companies throughout the United States and in Europe and with symphony orchestras in live concerts, on radio and on television. He made history during his 1956 tour of the Soviet Union, when he became the first American singer to perform at the Bolshoi Opera and the first ever in Russia since the Second World War. He also appeared in several films, including a 1946 version of Verdi's *Hymn of Nations,* which was conducted by Toscanini; *Carnegie Hall* (1947), which featured the top musical performers of the day; *Something in the Wind* (1947); and *Of Men and Music* (1951).

Following his 1967 retirement, Peerce continued performing in recitals and in occasional guest appearances with opera companies. He claims his voice retained its richness at an age when many singers have long since passed their peak. He visited Europe and Israel in 1968 and played Tevye in a 1971 touring company of *Fiddler on the Roof.* He also played that role briefly during the first Broadway run.

An Orthodox Jew, Peerce has performed Jewish ceremonial music widely and has continued his childhood tradition of occasionally singing in the synagogue of which he is a member.

Peerce's memoirs, *The Bluebird of Happiness,* written with Alan Levy (New York), appeared in 1977.

ARTHUR PENN

b. September 27, 1922
Director

Critics of Arthur Penn, who directed such films as *Bonnie and Clyde* and *The Miracle Worker,* complain that his work focuses too heavily on themes of alienation. Penn considers isolation not only a creative force in his plays and films but one of the features that gives them unity and strength. Alone for much of his life when he was growing up, Penn draws on his own firsthand knowledge of estrangement in his directing and often refers to it as the greatest influence in his personal life and his art.

Arthur Hiller Penn was born in Philadelphia to Harry, a watchmaker, and Sonia (Greenberg) Penn, a nurse. His parents were divorced when he was barely 3, and he lived with his mother until he was 14 in New Jersey and then in New York, on the Lower East Side, the Bronx and Brooklyn. Penn has stated that his own lonely and unsettled youth has been the motivating theme of his work.

In 1936 he returned to Philadelphia to live with his father. He attended Olney High School there, where he was first drawn to technical backstage work in school plays, and later worked at an amateur local theater.

Drafted into the Army in 1943—the year his father died—Penn met Fred Coe, a television and stage producer who became his mentor. In the service Penn stage-managed Army performances overseas. Discharged, he then studied performing arts and theater at the experimental Black Mountain College in North Carolina from 1947 to 1950. He also studied briefly in Italy and in Hollywood. Returning to New York, Penn got a job with NBC-TV as a floor manager, which entailed general production assisting. After working up to a post as assistant director at NBC studios in Los Angeles, he was invited back East by Coe in 1953 to direct six live dramas in a summer series called *First Person*. His success led to a regular staff job directing for *Philco Television Playhouse* and *Playhouse 90*. His good fortune, of course, was to arrive on the scene during this truly Golden Age of television. It provided a rare proving ground for the young director to work in serious drama, and there has been no similar opportunity since.

By the late 1950s Penn had begun to receive offers, through Coe, to direct for Broadway. His first play was William Gibson's *Two for the Seesaw* (1957–58), with Anne Bancroft and Henry Fonda, the story of a failed love affair between a bohemian New Yorker and a midwestern salesman. His banner season, 1959–60, included the direction of Lillian Hellman's *Toys in the Attic;* William Gibson's play about the blind and deaf little girl Helen Keller and her teacher, Annie Sullivan, *The Miracle Worker;* and the musical *Fiorello!* All three plays won awards and brought Penn substantial fame. The following season he directed the Pulitzer Prize-winning *All the Way Home* by Tad Mosel, based on James Agee's novel *A Death in the Family,* and *An Evening with Nichols and May,* a revue that introduced the young comedians Mike Nichols and Elaine May to an adoring public.

Penn began directing films in 1958, but it was not until the United Artists release of *The Miracle Worker* in 1962 that he gained recognition in that arena. He complained that his earlier films, which were critical failures, had been butchered by editors once they left his hands. He thereafter combined theater and film directing but became better known to American audiences for his films. *Bonnie and Clyde* (1967), his first big hit, told of an offbeat, renegade, nonconformist couple in the 1930s living closer to the standards of the counterculture 1960s, when Penn shot the film. Introducing Warren Beatty and Faye Dunaway as a dynamic and unconventionally romantic pair, it has since become a cult classic. *Alice's Restaurant* followed two years later. Like *Bonnie and Clyde* it dealt with a community of outsiders, in this case of war-resisting "flower children" (including some not-so-young children), who elected not to live according to the dictates of society's mainstream. Based on the satirical folk-rock ballad by Arlo Guthrie, son of 1930s folk singer Woody Guthrie, it recounted—among other kooky events—the younger Guthrie's arrest for littering and its subsequent role in his being rejected by the Army. On a larger scale, which was the film's reason for being, it addressed the irrationality of the military draft, of the war in Vietnam and of bureaucracies that participated in it and that sent young men to die in it. The following year Dustin Hoffman starred in Penn's film *Little Big Man* as the cynical, elderly white man who had spent much of his youth among American Indians and who was consequently alienated from his own "kin."

In the mid-1970s Penn had less success in films, which included *Night Moves* in 1975 and *The Missouri Breaks* in 1976. He always had many projects in development, and returned to off-Broadway theater with a highly praised production of *The Wild Duck,* presented at the Brooklyn Academy of Music in 1980. He resumed film work with *Four Friends* in 1981. In the latter Penn used Steve Tesich's screenplay to portray the conflicts of a young man, Danilo, born in Czechoslovakia but raised in America, who feels the kind of pride in his accomplishments and in the possibilities offered by America that was more common a generation or two earlier. His friends, already first- and second-generation Americans, regard him skeptically. As always in Penn's work, a grim separateness of one or more individuals is a pivotal theme.

Arthur Penn is the brother of Irving Penn, the renowned fashion photographer for *Vogue* magazine whose unusual, stark portraits of California hippies, African tribesmen, Cretan peasants, New Guinea bushmen and other so-called exotica, collected in his book *Worlds in a*

Small Room (1974), reflect his shared understanding of Arthur Penn's preoccupation with being and feeling different.

IRVING PENN

b. June 16, 1917
Photographer

Irving Penn's biography is his photography. As one of the world's foremost photographers, he has worked regularly for *Vogue* magazine, where he has been a major contributor since 1943; and as a portraitist, Penn has a style that cannot be imitated.

Born in Plainfield, New Jersey to Harry, a watchmaker, and Sonia (Greenberg) Penn, a nurse, Irving Penn studied painting with the intention of becoming an artist. In the early 1940s he lived and studied in Mexico and realized he would never be the accomplished painter he had hoped to become. He returned to New York and was an art director at Saks Fifth Avenue for two years before becoming a staff photographer for *Vogue*. He soon developed a highly formalized studio style that stayed with him throughout his career. He evokes a penetrating quality in his subjects that is distinctively Penn, whether they be Indian children in Cuzco, Peru—the first, and now famous, photograph in his book *Worlds in a Small Room* (New York, 1974); a high-fashion model; or the writer Colette—one of many well-known people featured in his book *Moments Preserved* (New York, 1960). Articles about Penn rarely talk about the man. Known to be shy, he speaks through his camera.

Penn sees himself as a designer and not a photojournalist or interpreter of people. Thus in a brief essay in *Worlds in a Small Room,* he describes how over a period of more than 20 years he was not interested in photographing people in their own environment. Wherever he went, he set up a studio—often a large tent—and created his own environment where he could control the lighting. The results are remarkable: His subjects—ranging from New Guinea claymen to African tribespeople, a "hippie" couple in Haight-Ashbury, a Gypsy family in Spain, or a plumber in New York—project a similar directness. Penn's first book, *Moments Preserved* is a collection of more than 300 portraits. His other two books are *Inventive Paris Clothes 1909–39* (New York, 1977) and *Flowers* (New York, 1980).

Penn is a meticulous artist who is not above controversy and bucking the establishment. At his 1975 Museum of Modern Art show he astonished viewers with a few huge platinum prints whose subjects included large cigarette butts and old gloves. The platinum process involves a difficult recreation of old photographic techniques to produce a paper that will print a wider range of tones than is possible on commercially available silver papers. With his use of old (and expensive) techniques and his peculiar choice of subject matter, Penn aroused critics to such an extent that many have never quite "forgiven" him for "glorifying garbage."

Penn's work is included in the permanent collections of the Museum of Modern Art and the Smithsonian Institution. There and elsewhere his photos are often compared to paintings because of their deliberately structured composition. He is very sensitive to minute detail and color balance. Even in his black-and-white photos, there is a sense of knowing exactly how much black and white and intermediate tones there should be. His portraits tend to be stark and straightforward—there is little overt manipulation and certainly no sham or contrivance in them.

MURRAY PERAHIA

b. April 19, 1947
Pianist; conductor

With a natural gift for lyricism that makes it seem as though he could sculpt poetry from music, the young pianist Murray Perahia has in a short time developed a reputation as one of the finest interpretative musicians currently on the concert circuit. A specialist in the music of Chopin, Schumann and Mendelssohn, he has been accorded the highest accolades by the world's top critics. As a *New York Times* reviewer wrote, "Perahia . . . has fingers that he can command to do anything he wants; his sheer, understated virtuosity is continually remarkable."

Murray Perahia was born in New York City to David, who worked in the cloak and suit business, and Flora (Pipano) Perahia, a secretary. His parents, Sephardic Jews, were immigrants from Greece, and Perahia grew up speaking Ladino, a language combining 15th-century Spanish with Jewish linguistic forms. He only learned English when he entered school. Perahia's musical talents were recognized when he was only 3½ and, according to some accounts, he was able to identify a tune he heard on the radio at home one day as the same piece he had heard at a concert he attended with his father the day before. His parents soon had him studying piano, and he received most of his early training from Jeanette Haien.

He attended the High School of Performing Arts, graduating in 1963, and then enrolled at the Mannes College of Music in New York City, where he majored in orchestral conducting and graduated with a B.S. degree in 1969.

Even before Perahia graduated, the signs of a major career were evident. In 1965 he won the first contest he ever entered, the Chopin Prize from the Kosciusko Foundation. The same year he passed auditions with Young Concert Artists, a prestigious firm that has cultivated many of the music world's top new talents. Through the firm, he made his solo debut at Carnegie Recital Hall in 1966 and the following year participated in the Marlboro Music Festival in Vermont. He eventually became part of the Marlboro Festival's "inner circle," which included Alexander Schneider, Rudolf Serkin and many other great musicians.

Perahia's ascent into national recognition began as he appeared in more solo and orchestral performances. His Carnegie Hall debut was held in 1968, with Schneider conducting, and although Perahia took a teaching post at Mannes after graduation, he also began touring nationally with the Budapest, Guarneri and Calimar String Quartets and other great soloists and ensembles. In 1972 he made his debut with the New York Philharmonic.

The turning point in Perahia's career—the difference between mere renown and international stardom—was his reluctant entry into the triennial Leeds International Pianoforte Competition in England in late 1972. Winning first prize, he was besieged with offers to perform throughout England and on the European continent. Andrew Porter in The New Yorker wrote that "the judges have awarded first prize not to a hard hitter, or to a conventionally 'big' pianist, but to a poet." Perahia recalled the experience with deep ambivalence. "Rather than it being the happiest moment of my life, it was one of the saddest," he said. "It was kind of crazy. All I could do was cry, and I did. It meant life was ahead of me, and I didn't know if I was ready for it."

But he soon embarked on a busy touring career, which took him throughout the United States, Europe, Israel and Japan, and made many solo and ensemble recordings, the latter primarily with the English Chamber Orchestra, which he conducts. He also took regular sabbaticals from touring to rest, study and learn the work of more composers. In addition to mastering the romantic composers as well as Mozart and Beethoven, Perahia has studied Handel, Haydn and others. He has shied away from contemporary music, with the sole exception of the work of Bela Bartok.

In 1975 Perahia shared with cellist Lynn Harrell the first Avery Fisher Prize, which was awarded not through competition but on recommendation. As with his appearance at Leeds, Perahia was swamped with concert offers and received almost without exception rave reviews, such as the one in The Montreal Gazette that described a performance he gave as "one of the most exhilarating piano recitals I have ever attended. Not since the last time Rubinstein or Ashkenazy was here have I found myself so completely captivated by a performer."

Perahia is known to be shy and introspective, and as Donal Henahan wrote in a New York Times review in 1976, "his appearance [summons] up romantic images of Dinu Lupatti or Chopin himself. Motherly types yearn to brush his hair out of his eyes and to fatten him up on chicken soup."

With or without chicken soup, Perahia has maintained a strong identity with his Sephardic Jewish roots and attributes his playing style to his background. "The Sephardic Jews were the designers of the Alhambra, and the Latin influence survives," he said in a 1981 interview. "Maybe that's what makes me like melody more and abstract things less."

MARTIN PERETZ

b. July 30, 1939
Editor; college teacher

As editor and publisher since 1974 of The New Republic, Martin Peretz has taken this traditionally liberal weekly journal of arts and literature down a slow and often unpredictable road to eclecticism, with a passionately pro-Israel stance as a major component of the magazine.

Martin Peretz was born in New York City to Julius, a businessman, and Ellen (Weberman) Peretz. After graduating from the Bronx High School of Science in 1955, he received his B.A. degree in history from Brandeis University in 1959 and his M.A. and Ph.D. degrees, both in political science, in 1965 and 1966, respectively, from Harvard University. He has taught political science at Harvard since 1965, first as an instructor until 1968, and then as an assistant professor until 1972 when he assumed a position as lecturer at Harvard.

In 1974 he bought The New Republic and became its board chairman. Though Peretz had been actively involved with liberal causes for many years prior to his association with The New Republic, when he became the magazine's editor in 1975, he found a perfect vehicle to air his personal political beliefs, which are neither traditionally left nor right. Under Peretz the magazine adopted his strong views supporting Israel. "The security of Israel is for me as much a moral issue as Indochina was a decade ago," he told a *New York Times* reporter, recalling his opposition to the Vietnam War. "The Palestinians have a right to decide their own life, but not Israel's life."

"I was raised with the redemptive vision of Zion," he told the Jewish Student Press Service in 1982. "It is important to me in my personal life, in the life of my family and in the values that I have. I would not be a full-thinking, working person if I did not express these things in the magazine." He went on to clarify his present day opinions. "People whose view of the world has not been affected by the coalition between the oil powers and the communist bloc, in reference to the State of Israel, are the ones who have not seen the important changes in the world. If you ask whether my new appreciation of the role of American power has anything to do with the precariousness of Israel's situation . . . the answer is yes. It made me think about the predicament of where freedom would be in the world without American power."

Despite his support of Israel, Peretz has signed public statements condemning Israeli settlements on the West Bank as "unrelated to Israel's security." One such letter in *The New York Times* in 1979 stated that the new Israeli West Bank settlement Elon Moreh "is a nationalist extravaganza which Israel can ill afford." "I think Zionism is an ally of democratic values, however that Zionism may be distorted, perverted and tainted by the incumbent (Begin) government in Israel." Even so, he supported Israel's invasion of Lebanon in 1982.

Some long-time liberals claim that Peretz has shifted *The New Republic* somewhat to the right, citing, for example, its criticism in 1978 of former President Carter's trip to mainland China as a "betrayal, not so much of the government of Taiwan as of its people," a move that provoked complaints and subscription cancellations. Peretz himself admitted in a letter published by *The New York Times* that the magazine's "writers and editors are no longer quite so up on limitless liberalism," and the managing editor he later hired, Michael Kinsley, added in an interview that "The liberal consensus has broken up. We're not moderating our views to cope with realities, we're changing them." While in earlier years Peretz embraced the views of Students for a Democratic Society, he is now allied with more centrist views, though his thoughtful publication continues to publish frequent harsh criticisms of neo-conservatives

and the radical right as well as the left and liberals. It is more diverse than ideological on most subjects, save that of Israel, upon which Peretz is unyielding.

The magazine has published articles like those by Marxist economist Paul Sweezey, Marxist historian Eugene Genovese, democratic socialists Irving Howe and Michael Harrington, and such liberals as Ronald Steel and Fred Kaplan, both of whom are extremely critical of the "Rearm America" program fostered by hardliners. But at the same time it has condemned the work of the American Friends Service Committee for allegedly displaying hostility to Israel and supported El Salvador's President Duarte, a renewed draft and the downing of Libyan jets in August 1981. Peretz, a significant force in the reshaping of liberalism, says that his influence on the magazine has been to "reevaluate the possible strategies for liberalism" and to make it "more unpredictable." In doing so, Peretz and *The New Republic* have become a vital factor in the shaping of public opinion.

ITZHAK PERLMAN

b. August 31, 1945
Violinist

Itzhak Perlman, the virtuoso violinist who attained international recognition when he won the coveted Leventritt Prize in 1964 at age 19, has been called the world's best younger violinist performing today. He has used his fame, coupled with the fact that he has been handicapped by polio since childhood, to fight for the rights of disabled people.

Itzhak Perlman was born in Tel Aviv to Chaim, a barber, and Shoshanna Perlman. His parents, both natives of Poland, met and married in Palestine, where they had settled in the mid-1930s. Perlman, who says he remembers always wanting to play the violin, first practiced on a toy fiddle and then on a second-hand violin his parents bought for $6.

Perlman was stricken with polio when he was 4 years old. Left permanently disabled, he still walks with leg braces and crutches and is the only violin soloist who plays sitting down. Studying under Rivka Goldgart on scholarship from the America-Israel Cultural Foundation, he gave his first solo recital when he was 10.

Perlman was chosen to come to the United States in 1958 to participate in the "Ed Sullivan Caravan of Stars," a group picked to represent Israel on the televised *Ed Sullivan Show* and then to tour America. He and his mother traveled with the tour for two months. They then decided to stay in New York, where he studied violin with Dorothy DeLay and Ivan Galamian, two violin teachers at the Juilliard School and considered the greatest teachers of the time. "What set Itzhak apart from the beginning," DeLay once recalled, "was his sheer talent and enormous imagination."

Perlman made his Carnegie Hall debut on March 5, 1963 and drew the attention of violinists Isaac Stern, Yehudi Menuhin and Zino Francescatti. After winning the $1,000 Levenritt Memorial Award, he performed in 1964 and 1965 with the New York Philharmonic and other major symphony orchestras. He also played Tchaikovsky's Violin Concerto in October 1964 at Carnegie Hall with the Israel National Youth Symphony.

Isaac Stern has often remarked that Perlman's warm, generous, expansive personality shines through in his music. His music is an expression of his love for life. "One is astonished at the delicacy of Perlman's huge hands and fingers one moment, and their dramatic power the next," a *Newsweek* critic wrote in 1980. "The music seems not so much played as *felt,* spilled out in great rushes of warm, lyrical sound." In his music Perlman communicates only what great artists—like Rubinstein, Segovia and Horowitz have—a love of playing music and an enthusiasm that is contagious. In one memorable performance in September 1980, he appeared with Isaac Stern and Pinchas Zukerman on a PBS show, "Live from Lincoln Center," while Zubin Mehta conducted the New York Philharmonic.

Perlman, who now plays on a Stradivarius violin worth several hundred thousand dollars, has performed all over the world. He has appeared on many solo recordings and with pianist Vladimir Ashkenazy, violinist Pinchas Zukerman and his mentor, Isaac Stern.

In recent years Perlman has ventured into chamber music and is playing new compositions, such as the Earl Kim Concerto, which he performed in 1980 with Mehta and the New York Philharmonic. Then, too, he is becoming known for his versatility outside of classical music: He recorded a group of Scott Joplin rags with James Levine at the piano for RCA. For Angel Records he did *A Different Kind of Blues,* with Andre Previn at the piano, Jim Hall on guitar, Red Mitchell on bass and Shelly Mann on the drums.

Perlman has since the mid-1960s campaigned with Rehabilitation International U.S.A. to make airplanes more accessible to the disabled and is on the board of two rehabilitation hospitals, Blythedale Children's Hospital in Valhalla, New York and the ALYN Hospital in Jerusalem. He has appeared at special education classes in New York City public schools to perform and to discuss the meaning of disability, and he is known to arrange for rehearsals to be open free of charge to disabled audiences who otherwise could not attend such concerts.

For further information:

Kupferberg, Herbert. "Itzhak Perlman: The Year of His Big Breakthrough." *Ovation,* February 1981.

NATHAN PERLMUTTER

b. March 2, 1923
Jewish organizational executive

As national director of the Anti-Defamation League of B'nai B'rith (ADL), Nathan Perlmutter has become one of America's most prominent spokespersons defending the civil rights of Jews in education, employment and housing in the United States and speaking out against anti-Semitism on national and international levels. Since its founding, the ADL has been one of the most influential agencies of its kind. Under Perlmutter's aegis, it has evolved into a more militant organization, focusing more on Jewish interests than on universal concerns.

Nathan Perlmutter was born in New York City to Hyman, a tailor, and Bella (Finkelstein) Perlmutter. He attended Georgetown University from 1942 to 1943 and Villanova College (now University) from 1943 to 1944, when he received his undergraduate degree. He served in the United States Marine Corps from 1944 to 1946 and obtained a law degree from New York University in 1949.

Perlmutter began working as civil rights director with the ADL in 1949 in Denver, Colorado. In 1952 he moved to ADL's Detroit office, where he stayed a year. From 1953 to 1956 he worked for ADL as assistant director of community services in New York and from 1956 to 1964 in Miami. Perlmutter was associate national director of the American Jewish Committee in New York from 1964 to 1969, the year he became vice president of Brandeis University. In 1973 Perlmutter became assistant national director of ADL, a position he held until 1979, when he became national director.

As head of ADL, he has attacked affirmative action as discriminatory, too much like the quota system—anathema to most Jews. ADL also monitors the activities of extremist groups such as the Ku Klux Klan, although some critics charge it tends to exaggerate the strength and therefore the anti-Semitic potential of such fringe elements. ADL was also the only national Jewish organization to endorse draft registration following President Jimmy Carter's recommendation in January 1980. Many of these policies reflect Perlmutter's positions, as he now stresses opposition to all those groups and individuals who question Israel's policies, especially in the United Nations. In one magazine article published in 1981 Perlmutter concluded: "The Common Market nations sell arms to Israel's sworn enemies. Swelling Soviet and Arab choruses sing the virtues of the PLO. These policies—in the former instance, free of classical anti-Semitism; in the latter barely skirting it—are megatons more dangerous to Jewish interests than are neo-Nazis."

In recent years, under Perlmutter's leadership, the ADL has taken a turn toward self-interest. While the ADL had been the first Jewish organization to support affirmative action in the 1960s, a decade later it took a strong stand in opposition to reverse discrimination. The ADL has also abandoned its previous position supporting detente and now advocates a stronger military stance in the arms race.

Perlmutter has contributed numerous articles to magazines, including *The Nation, New Leader, National Review, Commentary, National Jewish Monthly* and *Midstream.* He has also written two books: *How to Win Money at the Races* (New York, 1964) and *A Bias of Reflections: Confessions of an Incipient Old Jew* (New Rochelle, N.Y., 1972), an autobiographical work about being Jewish and middle-aged and the personal and political changes in his life.

Perlmutter has also made extensive efforts to improve Jewish-Catholic relations. The ADL maintains a consultant in Rome who meets frequently with Vatican officials. In the United States the ADL has established a special Department of Jewish-Catholic Relations.

The ADL was outspoken in its endorsement of the television mini-series *Holocaust,* aired in 1979, and in its protest against the planned—but later aborted—Nazi march in Skokie, Illinois in 1979.

ROBERTA PETERS

b. May 4, 1930
Operatic singer

Perhaps the most durable of the vigorous breed of musical performers who appear in American opera is the soprano. Among them, few match the record of Roberta Peters, who—in 1980, when she was 50 years old—celebrated her 30th year with the Metropolitan Opera, the longest such career of any coloratura in the Met's history.

Roberta Peterman was born to Solomon, a shoe salesman, and Ruth (Hirsch) Peterman, a milliner. She was "discovered" by the renowned tenor Jan Peerce when she was 13 and began voice lessons at once. Her parents managed to find the funds for tutoring in languages, ballet, piano and other tools of the trade. Six years later Sol Hurok, the famous impresario, heard her sing at her teacher's studio. Deeply impressed, he signed her on with his agency and arranged an audition at the Met. There she was immediately offered a contract, and her debut was set.

Here her story takes another familiar turn. She was to sing the difficult role of the Queen of the Night in Mozart's *The Magic Flute,* but fate intervened. Before her opening night, another soprano became ill and—on a few hours' notice and with practically no rehearsal—she sang Zerlina in Mozart's *Don Giovanni.* Acclaimed by critics and public, she quickly became a familiar name. Her even and warm tone and her ability to sing the hardest roles, as in the sterling 1954 production of *The Barber of Seville* at the Metropolitan Opera, received unanimous kudos from critics. By then Peters was a household name among opera fans.

Since then, in addition to key coloratura parts at the Met, she has sung in recitals throughout the United States, Europe and Israel; has had works dedicated to her by leading contemporary composers, such as Roy Harris and Aram Khachaturian; and has appeared in light operetta on tour and in summer theater (e.g., *The King and I* and *The Merry Widow.*) She is often associated with the major heroines of opera, particularly those calling for virtuoso coloratura talent, such as the title role in Donizetti's *Lucia de Lammermoor* and Rosina in *The Barber of Seville.* She has also been hailed for her performances in Puccini's *La Boheme* and Verdi's *La Traviata. Debut at the Met* (New York, 1967), written with Louis Biancolli, is her version of her life on the operatic stage.

LEO PFEFFER

b. December 25, 1910
Attorney

Leo Pfeffer is one of America's most outspoken supporters of separation of church and state. A constitutional lawyer long affiliated with the American Jewish Congress and a professor of law, he is regarded as one of the nation's top authorities on the subject.

Leo Pfeffer was born in Hungary to Alter Saul, an Orthodox Rabbi, and Hani (Yager) Pfeffer. He was brought to the United States in 1912 and naturalized in

1917. Educated at the City College of New York, where he received a Bachelor of Social Science degree in 1930, Pfeffer attended New York University Law School, where he completed a Doctor of Laws degree in 1933, the same year he was admitted to the New York State bar.

Beginning private practice in 1933, Pfeffer also taught law at New York University from 1933 to 1945, lectured at the New School from 1954 to 1958 and at Mt. Holyoke College from 1958 to 1960 and was professor of constitutional law at Yeshiva University from 1962 to 1963.

Pfeffer's association with the American Jewish Congress began in 1945, when he left private practice to join the legal staff of the Commission of Law and Social Action, a branch of the Congress. Two years later he became the commission's assistant director and in 1957 its director. He became special counsel of the Congress in 1964 and that year joined the political science faculty of Long Island University as a professor of constitutional law.

For much of his career Pfeffer has been involved on the national level with legislation regarding separation between religion and government. In 1948, for example, he participated in a Supreme Court case in which the use of public schools by religious groups was ruled illegal. His stands are often controversial, as much among Jews as among non-Jews. He believes that churches and synagogues in the United States should pay taxes—an unpopular view, especially among directors of parochial schools—and that they should not get such entitlements as free busing, lunches and textbooks. Despite his views, he is often invited to Catholic universities to speak in an attempt by the church to bridge dissenting viewpoints.

Although he has written several books about religious freedom and church-state relations, Pfeffer is best known for his massive study *Church, State and Freedom* (Boston, 1954; second edition, 1977). In the book, he explores historical movements for religious freedom and the dilemmas faced in the present. His updated version was extended to include Asian religious movements; the effect of legislation such as Sunday closing laws; biblical oaths taken by elected public officials; and Bible reading and the singing of Christmas carols in public schools. It also explored the impact of religion on the Peace Corps and such new American movements as the Black Muslims.

In his book *Creeds in Competition* (Westport, Conn., 1978), Pfeffer described his perception of the future of American Judaism in the face of social and political changes during the preceding century and subsequent contact with other religions and traditions. He wrote:

Judaism . . . has experienced much change in outlook and way of life as a consequence of cultural competition. Of all the groups it has adjusted itself most completely and most happily to the values of secular humanism. When one compares the Judaism of mid-twentieth-century America with the Judaism of mid-nineteenth-century Eastern Europe, one can see the radical changes effected by the alliance [with other religious experiences].

Pfeffer has received awards from many Jewish and Christian organizations. He is a member of the American Civil Liberties Union and has been on the editorial board of *Church and State* since 1958 and of *Judaism* since 1964.

For further information:
Pfeffer, Leo. *God, Caesar and the Constitution*. Boston: 1975.
———. *The Liberties of an American*. Boston: 1956.
———. *Religious Freedom*. Skokie, Ill.: 1977.
———. *This Honorable Court*. Boston: 1963.
Pfeffer, Leo, and Stokes, Anson Phelps. *Church and State in the United States*. Westport, Conn.: 1975.

MOLLY PICON

b. June 1, 1898
Actress

Molly Picon is one actress who hasn't suffered the long periods of unemployment so typical of the profession. Working almost without interruption since she was 6 years old, the multi-talented (and multi-lingual) Picon has performed regularly in Yiddish plays, in English-language vaudeville, in movies, in Broadway drama, on radio and on television ever since. To aficionados of the form, Picon is the "First Lady of the Yiddish Theater."

Molly Picon was born in New York City to Lewis, a rabbinical student in his native Warsaw who worked in the garment industry after immigrating to the United States, and Clara (Ostrow) Picon, a dressmaker, originally from Kiev. It was through her mother's trade that Picon began acting as a child. Clara Picon became a seamstress for a Yiddish theater troupe in Philadelphia, where the family had moved, and at the age of 5, Molly Picon performed in a children's amateur night at the local Bijou Theater, which was normally a burlesque house. Her success was such that she was invited to join a Yiddish company, and in 1904, at the age of 6, Picon made her professional stage debut. For the next three years, she appeared in Yiddish versions of *Uncle Tom's Cabin, Shulamite, Gabriel, Sappho* and other productions. In her teens she continued performing and singing, and in 1915 she joined an English-language stock company, the Chestnut Street Theater. Her formal education ended after three years at William Penn High School.

While appearing in a Boston vaudeville act during the 1918–19 season, Picon suddenly found herself unemployed and broke when an outbreak of influenza forced Boston theaters to close. She sought help through the local Yiddish troupe, which had not closed, and it was through that contact that Picon returned to Yiddish theater. In late 1919 she married the theater manager, Joseph Kalich, who also became her mentor and wrote many plays for her. In 1921 they toured Europe, where Picon performed in operettas, including one Kalich had written just for her, entitled *Yankele*. A success in Europe, it opened in the Second Avenue Theater in the heart of the Yiddish theater district in New York City in 1923 and was a smash hit. Picon remained on Second Avenue for the next seven years, appearing in a string of plays, including *Zipke* and *Ichmendrile* (1924), *Mamele* and *Gypsy Girl* (1925), *Molly Dolly* and *Rabbi's Melody* (1926), *Little Czar* (1927), *Hello, Molly!* (1928) and many others.

She also performed "uptown" in vaudeville and in singing tours. Her output was so prolific and her renown so great that she became known as the "Sweetheart of Second Avenue." She also became a radio personality, featured on *Maxwell House Coffee Time* on WEVD from 1932 to 1951. Tours to Europe, Palestine, South Africa and Latin America followed in the 1930s. In 1936 Picon went to Warsaw to act in a film entitled *Yiddle with His Fiddle* for a Polish-Yiddish film company.

Her first serious attempt at an English-language role came in 1940, when she played a Jewish immigrant mother in the Broadway play *Morning Star*. Although the play got only fair reviews, her performance was praised. Over the next few years she balanced her career between English-language vaudeville and drama and Yiddish musicals and plays.

The years after World War II were emotional for Picon, who traveled with her husband throughout Europe to perform for Jews who had survived the Holocaust. According to one account, they brought with them several hundred packages of cosmetics, jewelry and candy for the people they met in displaced persons camps, hospitals and orphanages.

Returning to the United States, Picon appeared on Broadway in the comedy *For Heaven's Sake, Mother* in 1948. And in 1949 she returned to Second Avenue to star in *Abi Gezunt*, her first Yiddish play in some years. Popular as ever, she continued to play for sold-out audiences. During the Korean War, she toured for the USO and in the early 1950s also toured Israel in performances of Yiddish shows. During the latter half of the 1950s, she was featured in such plays as *Farblonjet Honeymoon* and *The Kosher Woman*. In the early 1960s, she was featured in the role of Clara Weiss in the Broadway version and U.S. tour of *Milk and Honey*.

As Yiddish theater waned, Picon turned to summer stock, regional theater and to Jewish-type roles on Broadway and in films. She appeared in a 1967 off-off-Broadway revue of *How to Be a Jewish Mother* and in 1971 appeared as Dolly Gallagher Levi in *Hello, Dolly!* in a touring company. Picon's film roles in the 1960s and 1970s include parts in *Come Blow Your Horn* (1963), *Fiddler on the Roof* (1970), *For Pete's Sake* (1974) and others. She also had occasional small roles on television shows and has been a guest on many talk shows.

Picon's family biography—quite dated because she has accomplished so much since it was published—is *So Laugh a Little* (New York, 1962).

HARRIET PILPEL

b. December 2, 1911
Attorney

Attorney Harriet Pilpel is one of America's most consistent and distinguished civil libertarians. In a career spanning more than four decades, she has litigated successfully in many areas of constitutional and civil rights. She is an eloquent speaker and a prolific writer who has laid the groundwork for generations of activist lawyers.

Harriet Fleischl was born in New York City to Julius, a businessman, and Ethel (Loewy) Fleischl. She attended Vassar College, where she received a B.A. degree in 1932, and Columbia University, where she earned an M.A. degree in international relations and public law in 1933. In 1936 she completed a Bachelor of Law degree at Columbia's Law School, where she was a Kent scholar.

Admitted to the New York bar that year, she entered private practice at Greenbaum, Wolff and Ernst, a firm whose co-founder, Morris Ernst, was a renowned writer and leader in the civil liberties field and a great influence on Pilpel. Remaining with that firm throughout her career, Pilpel was instrumental in effecting major reforms in constitutional rights to privacy, reproductive freedom and birth control; women's rights; family law; and communications issues related to censorship, copyright, defamation and obscenity. One of the most famous cases in which she was a successful litigator was *New York Times* v. *Sullivan* (1964), in which the scope of protection for the press against libel suits was significantly enlarged.

Despite being a private practice attorney, Pilpel has been an active public educator. She has written several books, including *Your Marriage and the Law* (New York, 1952) and *Rights and Writers: Handbook of Literature and Entertainment Law* (New York, 1960). Co-written with attorney Theodora Zavin, both books use extensive case histories to explain to the layperson his or her rights in marriage or as a professional writer. From 1955 to 1959 Pilpel and Zavin co-wrote a regular column for *Publishers Weekly, But Can You Do That?* Her other books are *A Copyright Guide*, with Morton David Goldberg (New York, 1960) and *Know Your Rights*, with Minna Post Peyser (Washington, D.C., 1965).

Pilpel is general counsel for Planned Parenthood of New York City and for National and International Planned Parenthood. She is also a general counsel of the American Civil Liberties Union and for 17 years was a member of its national board. She is co-chairperson of the Commission on Law and Social Action of the American Jewish Congress and is active in many organizations related to reproductive rights, the arts, media and civil liberties.

Pilpel has won many awards, including the Margaret Sanger Award in 1964; the Louise Waterman Wise Award of the American Jewish Congress in 1978, in which she was cited for her "abiding personal commitment to social justice and human dignity"; the Earl Warren Civil Liberties Award in 1978; and the Annual Columbia Law School Alumni Medal for excellence in 1980.

RICHARD PIPES

b. July 11, 1923
Professor; government adviser

As the senior staff member and Russian expert on the National Security Council during the Reagan administration, Harvard historian Richard Pipes brought with him a reputation as a solid hard-liner who favored a massive conventional and nuclear build-up. His controversial and provocative statements regarding the USSR and war and peace earned him the nickname "Reagan's Dr. Strangelove," but he is also acknowledged to be an outstanding scholar and analyst of early Russian history.

Richard Edgar Pipes was born in Cieszyn, Poland to Mark, a businessman, and Sara Sofia (Haskelberg) Pipes. He was educated at the Gimnazyum A. Kreczmara, a secondary school in Poland, before fleeing to the United States with his family in 1940 to seek refuge from the Nazis. From 1940 to 1943, the year he was naturalized, Pipes attended Muskingum College in Ohio. He joined the U.S. Air Force in 1943 and at the same time continued his college studies at Cornell University. He received a B.A. degree from Cornell in 1945. He left military service in 1946. From 1946 to 1950 Pipes pursued graduate work in history at Harvard University, where he completed an M.A. degree and a Ph.D. by 1950. He joined the Harvard faculty as an instructor that year and was appointed associate professor in 1958 and full professor in 1963. From 1962 to 1965 he was associate director of Harvard's Russian Research Center and served as director from 1968 to 1973. In 1956 he was a visiting professor of history at the University of California at Berkeley.

Pipes' involvement in government predates the presidency of Ronald Reagan. From 1973 to 1978 he was a senior research consultant at the Strategic Studies Center of the Stanford Research Institute in Washington, and in 1978 he was a consultant with the Advanced International Studies Institute there. He reviewed national intelligence estimates for the government in 1976 and is a member of the Council on Foreign Relations and is on the board of directors of the National Committee on American Foreign Policy Inc. Pipes also belongs to the Committee on the Present Danger, an organization comprised of such neo-conservatives as Norman Podhoretz, Midge Decter and Irving Kristol to publicize what they perceive to be a growing Soviet threat against the non-Communist world and to respond accordingly. It was Pipes, too, who wrote articles in *Commentary* challenging what he considered to be too moderate an evaluation by the CIA of Soviet military developments and plans. As a result, "Team B" was organized by President Ford, which included Pipes and it declared that the Soviet Union was a far greater danger than previously believed.

In March 1981 Pipes provoked controversy in Washington when he was quoted in an interview as having said that the Soviet Union could either follow the trends and ideals of the West or "go to war. There is no alternative, and it could go either way." His unexpected remark frightened many and was instantly repudiated by White House officials. Critics of Pipes included *New York Times* columnist Flora Lewis, who referred in one column to his "reputation for primitive anti-Bolshevism," and journalist Jonathan Alter, who profiled Pipes in *The Washington Monthly* in mid-1981, noting that the scholar's field of expertise, for which he has justifiably earned high praise, is Russia of the 19th and early 20th century, and not the modern-day Soviet Union, about which he is expected to make expert judgments in his current role. His supporters, however, praised him for his hard-headed realism.

Whatever the truth, Pipes' reputation as a first-rate scholar of Russian history is well-established. In *Russia Under the Old Regime* (New York, 1974) he attempts to show that the origin of totalitarian Russia lies in its past and not in Western ideas. He covers the geographical milieu which shaped Czarist Russia, the different classes and the clash between government and the intelligentsia. *The New York Review of Books* called it "unusually interesting" and the *Library Journal* described it as "a very fine book from a major historian of Russia." Similarly, an earlier important work, *Formation of the Soviet Union: Communism and Nationalism, 1917-23* (Cambridge, Mass.: 1954 and New York: 1968) dealt with the minority peoples of the border regions and led the *Political Science Quarterly* to describe it as "balanced, mature." The book earned him the George Louis Beer Prize of the American Historical Association for 1955.

For further information:

Pipes, Richard. *Karamzin's Memoir on Ancient and Modern Russia.* New York: 1979.
———. *Revolutionary Russia.* Cambridge, Mass.: 1968.
———. *Russian Intelligentsia.* New York: 1961.
———. *Social Democracy and the St. Petersburg Labor Movement.* Cambridge, Mass.: 1963.
———. *Struve: Liberal on the Left, 1870-1905.* Cambridge, Mass.: 1970.
———. *Struve: Liberal on the Right, 1905-1944.* Cambridge, Mass.: 1980.

FRANCES FOX PIVEN

b. October 10, 1932
Social scientist

Frances Fox Piven is both a social activist and a social theorist with a strong commitment to civil rights, welfare rights and civil liberties. She has combined an academic career in urban planning and social work with participation in community organizing on a local and national level.

Frances Fox was born in Calgary, Alberta, Canada to Albert, a storekeeper, and Rachel (Paperny) Fox. She was brought to the United States in 1933 and became a U.S. citizen in 1953. She attended the University of Chicago, where she received a B.A. degree in 1953, an M.A. degree in urban planning in 1956 and a Ph.D. in social science in 1962.

From 1963 to 1966 she was a research associate with Mobilization for Youth, a program created during the administration of President Lyndon Johnson to develop job and educational opportunities for young people. She taught at the School of Social Work at Columbia University from 1966 to 1972 as an associate professor. While there, she published a book, coauthored with Richard A. Cloward, a Columbia colleague, entitled *Regulating the Poor: The Functions of Public Welfare* (New York, 1971). In it the authors contended that American social programs as they then existed were in fact designed to control the behavior of poor people and were usually initiated during periods of massive social discontent and major economic shifts. Instead of the welfare program that existed at the time and that prevented recipients from working, the authors proposed an alternative relief program enabling those involved to learn skills so that they could ultimately become self-supporting. The book also examined the historical and political precedents for the civil unrest of the late 1960s, which served as the background to the book.

Concurrent with Piven's period at Columbia, she was a member of the National Welfare Rights Organization (1966–72), the Mayor's Task Force on Housing (1966) and the U.S. Civil Rights Commission (1967).

Piven taught political science at Boston University from 1972 to 1974 and was a Guggenheim fellow during the second of those two years. Her second book, also written with Cloward, was a collection of articles that had appeared in *The Nation, The New Republic* and *Social Policy.* The book, *The Politics of Turmoil: Essays in Poverty, Race and the Urban Crisis* (New York, 1974), evaluated many Great Society programs and compared them to similar social efforts of previous presidential administrations. It argued in favor of black separatism as a means of community organizing and explored the increasing difficulty of urban black poor people to become integrated into the political mainstream.

In 1974 Piven joined the political science faculty of Brooklyn College of the City University of New York but the following year returned to Boston University, where she has remained. She became involved in several

Boston-based community organizations, including Massachusetts Fair Share and Boston Hospital Workers as well as the Movement for Economic Justice. She and Cloward published their third book, *Poor People's Movements: Why They Succeed and Why They Fail* (New York), in 1977. An extension of their earlier collaborations, it contends that the strength of civil rights and protest movements derives from efforts to mobilize people at the grass-roots level to fight for themselves rather than to allow a select "elite" to fight for them, and that collective action and occasional disruption can be important strategic tools. Although some critics claimed that the authors' thesis could result in backlash from "the powers that be," they praised the thorough analyses that explained how mass movements are formed and why they are (or are not) effective. And in a major article published in *The Nation,* ("Reagan Sows The Wind: The New Age of Protest," April 17, 1982) she and Cloward wrote: "Large-scale protest in the United States now seems certain." With so many without jobs and with the added strains of Reagan's economic policies affecting more and more people, they see "the simultaneous defection of different constituencies" amid the fact that "it is capitalism rather than democracy that has become ungovernable, for it is capitalism that has responded to economic contraction and instability with chaotic disinvestment and speculation."

Piven has been active in academic and other organizations as well as in community movements. From 1973 to 1976 and from 1977 to 1980, she was on the board of directors of the American Civil Liberties Union. She was on the council of the American Political Science Association from 1974 to 1976 and served as program co-chairperson during her last year there. She was elected vice president of the Society for the Study of Social Problems in 1976--77 and served as its president in 1979–80. Piven has served on advisory committees on poverty and related problems at Princeton University and the University of Wisconsin and for several federal programs, including the National Institute of Mental Health, the Institute for Labor Education and the National Academy of Public Administration project on Metropolitan Reorganization. She has been similarly involved in urban planning programs in Europe and was visiting professor at the Institute for Advanced Studies in Vienna in 1978.

Piven has been working on a fourth book, to be titled *The Structuring of Deviant Behavior,* and has written articles for such popular periodicals as *Saturday Review, The Nation* and *The New Republic* and for professional journals, including *Politics and Society, Journal of the American Institute of Planners* and *Social Work.*

NORMAN PODHORETZ

b. January 16, 1930
Editor

Throughout his tenure as editor of *Commentary* magazine since 1960, Norman Podhoretz has been a controversial and influential figure whose views on American life and international policies have stirred furious criticism and wide praise from all parts of the American political spectrum. His role as spokesman for the rightist neo-conservative movement of the 1970s and 1980s has made him the center of much debate. Under Podhoretz's leadership, *Commentary*—the magazine he inherited from previous editors, sponsored by the American Jewish Committee—has become one of America's foremost political journals.

Norman Podhoretz was born in Brooklyn to Julius, a milkman, and Helen (Woliner) Podhoretz, who were immigrants from Eastern Europe and lived in the Brooklyn neighborhood of Brownsville. Podhoretz began his Jewish education at age 8 in a local synagogue. He graduated from Hebrew High School when he was 15. Podhoretz achieved an outstanding record at Boys High School, where he edited the school newspaper. In 1946, at the age of 16, he entered Columbia University as a Pulitzer scholar and graduated with a B.A. degree in English in 1950. The same year he received a bachelor's degree in Hebrew literature from the Jewish Theological Seminary of America.

Podhoretz then went to study at Cambridge University in England on a Kellett Fellowship and a Fulbright Scholarship. He received an M.A. degree from Cambridge in 1952, winning first class honors. During his stay at Cambridge he published his first piece, an homage to the critic Lionel Trilling. Soon he discovered his heart was no longer in literary scholarship. By his own admission he was more interested in seeing his name in print and winning the attention of "the family," a coterie of New York—mainly Jewish—intellectuals. In 1952 he began to write book reviews for *Commentary*. His highly critical review of *The Adventures of Augie March* by Saul Bellow won him praise and attention.

After a two-year stint in the United States Army (1953–55), during which he continued to write occasional reviews, Podhoretz became the assitant editor of *Commentary* in 1955. The following year he was made associate editor of the magazine. During this period he published reviews in *Harper's, Esquire, The New Republic, The New York Times Book Review* and the *New Yorker*. With his attack on Nelson Algren's *Take a Walk on the Wild Side,* he became a minor literary celebrity.

He left *Commentary* in 1958, dissatisfied with the magazine's editors, and worked at Doubleday in the Anchor Books division and at Random House with its Looking Glass Library. But in 1960, following the death of founding *Commentary* editor Elliot Cohen, Podhoretz returned to the magazine as editor. He immediately redesigned the magazine, intent on using far more general articles and far fewer Jewish-oriented articles. Irving Howe, Hannah Arendt, Trilling and others began to contribute more regularly. His new liberal-left image became fully apparent when Podhoretz serialized Paul Goodman's *Growing Up Absurd,* after it had been repeatedly rejected by publishers. It was the peak of his attraction to liberalism. In 1962, for example, he published Hans Morgenthau's warning that Vietnam was a deadly trap should this nation ever choose to intervene militarily.

Podhoretz's first *Commentary* article in his own voice, not within the context of a review, was called "My Negro Problem—and Ours." Published in 1963, the article candidly recounts some of his early experiences with blacks as he was growing up in Brownsville, some favorable and some unfavorable. The reaction to the article alternated between damnation for alleged racism and applause for his supposed honesty in dealing with so sensitive a topic.

In 1968 *Making It,* a biographical work, was published in New York. Podhoretz dealt with his lust for success in life. Many critics found his candor and integrity refreshing, while others felt it was written with embarrassing frankness and utter vulgarity. Podhoretz was so taken aback by the many harsh and negative reviews that he charged it had received the "most disgraceful and incomprehending press of any book in years."

During the late 1960s Podhoretz's left-liberal political sympathies began to change as—along with such peers as his wife Midge Decter and Irving Kristol—he reacted with shock to student rebellion at universities across the United States—particularly his alma mater Columbia—and to racial outbreaks in many American cities, including the furor of the teachers' strike in 1968 in New York City, which he perceived as a sharp attack on Jewish teachers. In addition, he saw the burgeoning anti-war movement as a sign of America's weakness in the face of the allegedly growing power and influence of Soviet communism in the world. He began a gradual shift to the right, which manifested itself in a strong anti-communism and support for a United States military buildup, opposition to SALT II and several attacks on Senator Edward Kennedy. He published an article

by a Soviet emigré in 1982 severely criticizing European anti-nuclear arms movements. "Your recent mass demonstrations were disastrous," wrote Vladimir Bukovsky, who spent twelve years in Soviet prisons, labor camps and psychiatric hospitals, because in them you identified yourselves, willingly or unwillingly, with the rulers of the Eastern countries." He opposed busing to promote integration as well as the feminist push toward sexual parity and the struggle of homosexuals to end discrimination against them. Articles in *Commentary* included attacks on left-liberal ideas, the peace movement in Israel, which opposed settlements on the West Bank and took a dim view of American social programs. One article in 1977 called for a consideration of a United States occupation of Arab oil fields. Another (in 1982) called for a restoration of the military draft.

More outspoken as an author than as an editor in recent years, Podhoretz also wrote *Breaking Ranks* (New York, 1979), another biographical work, which censures liberal ideas that he contends have held sway in America in the past few decades. Viewing them as destructive, he attacks liberalism and radicalism as he chronicles his own journey toward conservatism.

In *The Present Danger* (New York, 1980) and elsewhere, he argues that America has "lost its nerve" with the Soviet Union, that SALT II was a menace to American security and that the United States suffers from an inability to exert its military might because of its defeat in the Vietnam War. Anti-communism is the overarching imperative in United States foreign policy and, he argued, the only way to halt the global tide of communism, which he saw as dominant and ever-menacing. In 1982 Podhoretz also began criticizing President Reagan for not being hostile enough to communism and the USSR. Writing in *The New York Times Magazine,* the onetime Reagan supporter complained that the President was reverting to the customary pro-détente policy of the Nixon, Ford and Carter administrations. Continuing in this vein in his book *Why We Were in Vietnam* (New York, 1982), he concluded that while the United States intervention was politically reckless, it was also politically idealistic in its goal of saving South Vietnam from communism. Predictably, it set off another furious argument. His defenders, among them *The Wall Street Journal,* argued in April 1982 that he was again "visiting an epidemic of apoplexy upon Manhattan's literary salons" and was "the starting gun for a new debate," while such critics as Theodore Draper in *The New Republic* in March 1982 asserted that not only could the book not "be taken seriously . . . as history" but that "it opens the door to a viciously dangerous stab-in-the-back legend by inferentially blaming the horrors of the war on those who opposed it rather than those who waged it."

Earlier, in another article in *Commentary*, Podhoretz defined his view on Jewish life:

> Looking back on the 1950's and the early 1960's we can now see that being absolved of the need to worry about and press for the Jewish interest—the need to face the world with the humiliating question, *Is it good for the Jews?* perpetually on one's nagging lips—was itself one of the more luxurious perquisites of what may some day come to be considered the Golden Age of Jewish security in America. The Golden Age, as golden ages must, now seems to be reaching an end, and nothing is to be gained by Jews or anyone else from denying the signs in the air. In the brassier age aborning, Jews will either ask, Is it good for the Jews? and act on the answers, or else they may wake up one day to find themselves diminished, degraded, discriminated against, and alone.

In 1974, after the Yom Kippur War between Egypt and Israel, Podhoretz published an article in *The New York Times Magazine* entitled "Now, Instant Zionism," in which he expressed the view that Soviet-backed Arabs "placed Israel in mortal danger—in danger that is, not merely of losing its independence but of losing its life. It is this very danger that has turned almost every Jew in America into a Zionist."

Described by the *Christian Science Monitor* as "the most unpredictable intellectual of today," to his admirers Podhoretz has come to symbolize independence in the highest editorial tradition. By acting as a provocateur and polemicist, often supporting unpopular views, he has, they believe, caused many people to reconsider seriously their commitment to certain beliefs. Even so, he is ever the lightning rod for his many critics.

For further information:

Podhoretz, Norman. "The Neo-Conservative Anguish Over Reagan's Foreign Policy," *The New York Times Magazine*, May 2, 1982.

Avishai, Bernard. "Breaking Faith: Commentary and the American Jews." *Dissent*, Spring 1981.

Bartley, Robert L. "A Most Improbable 'Conservative'." *Wall Street Journal*, November 19, 1970.

Grubisich, Thomas. "Norman Podhoretz." *The Washington Post*, April 11, 1971.

Hills, Rust. "The Dirty Little Secret of Norman Podhoretz." *Esquire*, April 1968.

LETTY COTTIN POGREBIN

b. June 9, 1939
Magazine editor; feminist leader

As founding editor of *Ms.* magazine, a writer of *The Working Woman* column in the *Ladies Home Journal* and author of three books relating to women in business and non-sexist child rearing, Letty Cottin Pogrebin is one of America's leading feminist journalists.

Loretta Cottin was born in New York City to Jacob, an attorney, and Cyral (Halpern) Cottin, a designer. After graduating cum laude from Brandeis University in 1959 with a B.A. degree in English and American literature, she worked for one year as an editorial assistant in the book publishing firm of Coward-McCann. After a short stint as an advertising copywriter for another company, in 1960 she joined another publishing company, Bernard Geis Associates. During the next 10 years she worked at Geis as director of publicity, advertising and subsidiary rights and by 1970 was made a vice president of the company. That same year she published her first book, *How to Make It in a Man's World* (New York), which was a practical and humorous guide on how to succeed in the male-dominated world of business. Chapter titles included: "How to Succeed in Business Without Really Typing," "Executive Sweets" and "If You Can't Stand the Heat, Get Back to the Kitchen."

In 1971 Pogrebin helped found *Ms.* magazine, the pioneering magazine of feminism. Since then she has been editor of *Ms.* and has been author of a monthly column, *The Working Woman*, in the *Ladies Home Journal*. Pogrebin's emphasis in her column and in articles she contributes frequently to *Good Housekeeping* and other publications is on feminism, women and employment, the psychology and sociology of child rearing, politics and women's status in family life.

Pogrebin has published two other books. In *Getting Yours: How to Make the System Work for the Working Woman* (New York, 1975), she discusses how women can secure the greatest benefit from union membership, the need to fight for child care centers and maternity rights, the Equal Rights Amendment, sexism in religious groups and other feminist issues. In *Growing Up Free: Raising Your Child in the 80's* (New York, 1980), she presents a strong case for non-sexist child rearing. She explains her purpose as "to question everything we do with, to, for and around children—our speaking habits, living styles, adult relationships, household chores, academic standards and way of dealing with punishment, privilege, religion, television, sex, money and love." Cynthia Ozick wrote, "Just as 'Dr. Spock' long ago became a synonym for popular common sense in baby health, so will 'Letty Pogrebin' enter the language as an emblem of common sense in prizing children and other human beings."

In 1971, Pogrebin helped found the National Women's Political Caucus. She has worked with actress Marlo Thomas on *Free to Be You and Me*, a record, book and television special of non-sexist songs and stories, and is on the board of directors of Action for Children's Television, which monitors television programming. She is also a director with the Ms. Foundation for Women. She has lectured throughout the nation on women's issues.

Pogrebin has been outspoken about the extent of anti-Semitism she has encountered in the feminist movement. In an article in *Ms.*, in June 1982, "Anti-Semitism in the Women's Movement," she said that Jewish women have two battles to fight: against sexism and against anti-Jewish beliefs. "Must we identify as Jews within feminism with as much discomfort as we identify as feminists within Judaism?"

ALLEN POLLACK

b. May 19, 1938
Professor; Zionist executive

Allen Pollack, a professor of Russian history, has inherited from Marie Syrkin and Judah Shapiro the mantle of being the leading Labor Zionist in America. He has been active in Labor Zionism since his youth, when he was the national president of Habonim Labor Zionist Youth.

Allen Pollack was born in New York City, the son of Jacob, who owned a dry goods store, and Rae (Liebhaber) Pollack. He attended Columbia University, where he received his B.A. degree in history in 1955. He received his M.A. degree from the University of Stockholm in 1961, studied in the USSR the following year and in 1965 was awarded a Ph.D. from Princeton University.

Pollack's area of academic specialization is the history of the Communist Party in the Soviet Union and the role of the Jews in the revolutionary movements in Czarist Russia. Under a Ford Foundation grant, he was a visiting fellow at the Marx-Engels-Lenin Institute at the University of Leningrad. Pollack has taught Russian history at Brooklyn College, the University of Pittsburgh and Yeshiva University, where he is currently on the faculty.

Pollack's greatest area of activity, however, has been in Jewish communal affairs. He is a member of the executive board of the World Zionist Organization and the board of governors of the Jewish Agency. He is also a director of the United Israel Appeal and a trustee of the United Jewish Appeal.

A past president of Friends of Labor Israel, Pollack was elected president of the Labor Zionist Alliance in 1978. He is a former chairman of the Young Leadership Cabinet of the United Jewish Appeal, and he serves as the treasurer of the American Zionist Youth Foundation. Pollack is on the board of directors of the North American Jewish Student Appeal and the New York Association for New Americans (NYANA), which works closely with new Russian-Jewish immigrants in the New York metropolitan area. He is also on the executive committee of the American Zionist Federation and the board of governors of Tel Aviv University.

The American Professors for Peace in the Middle East was created to a large extent through the initiative of Pollack, who has served as its national chairperson. The organization includes 18,000 academics on 600 campuses throughout North America. The governments of Israel, Jordan, Syria and Egypt have invited members of APPME to conduct study missions in their respective countries, and Pollack has participated in many of them.

Pollack has had a long and close relationship with many of the leaders of Israel's Labor Party. He took a leading position in the American Jewish community against the West Bank settlement policies of Menachem Begin's Likud government and has long articulated a moderately dovish stance in regard to the Arab-Israeli conflict, often taking the lead in organizing letters of protest and advertisements against the policies of the Begin government. In the United States he has argued for increased funding for youth education and a revitalization and crystallization of the social values underlying Jewish communal values. When asked what sets him apart from other Jewish leaders, he responds, "Everything."

ABRAHAM POLONSKY

b. December 5, 1910
Film director; screenwriter; novelist

There is a 17-year gap in the rich and active life of Abraham Polonsky, whose promising career as film director and screenwriter was abruptly aborted in the early 1950s by the Hollywood blacklist. His writing and film work, which peaked in the late 1940s, had always had an upsetting moral tone to it—Polonsky was deeply concerned that men could so easily compromise their values—and during his "exile" (which Polonsky spent in New York City), he was not silenced. Instead he continued to work on projects pseudonymously, and when he returned to film directing, he resumed with his old vigor the same themes he had broached before the blacklist.

Abraham Lincoln Polonsky was born to Henry, a pharmacist, and Rebecca (Rosoff) Polonsky. Raised in the Bronx, he received a B.A. degree from City College of New York in 1932 and a law degree from Columbia University in 1935. A childhood passion for the works of Charles Dickens, which his father introduced to him, turned Polonsky into a voracious reader and led him to a writing career. Despite earning the law degree, Polonsky never practiced; instead, he taught English at CCNY from 1932 to 1942 and began writing short stories, essays and novels.

His first book, *The Goose Is Cooked* (New York, 1940), an adventure described as "quasi Sherlock Holmesian" was coauthored with Mitchell A. Wilson and published under the pseudonym "Emmett Hogarth." It was not exactly an auspicious beginning for Polonsky, whose hero, Marty Cohen, never resurfaced in his other books.

Polonsky's first solo novel published under his own name was *The Enemy Sea* (New York, 1943), also an adventure tale. It chronicles the love triangle between a female reporter, an ex-lover and her current beau, a photographer, during a voyage by tanker from Galveston to New York.

Polonsky's flair for adventure writing and character development transferred into his new vocation, screenwriting, to which a friend had introduced him. His first effort was an early version of *Golden Earrings*, a 1947 film with Marlene Dietrich. Although Polonsky is credited on the film, he claims his original work was so adulterated in rewrites that he disavowed any involvement in it. The film was not well received.

But Polonsky's next endeavor, over which he had substantial control, received the critical praise and commentary that would mark his subsequent work. *Body and Soul,* a 1947 film directed by Robert Rossen and starring John Garfield, told of Charlie Davis, a young boxer from the Lower East Side slums seeking to fight his way to stardom and wealth. En route, however, he was manipulated and later "owned" by gamblers and promoters who claimed to "help" him. Ultimately, he was corrupted and later abandoned and left destitute. Although social dramas like *Body and Soul* had become a cliche by the late 1940s, Polonsky managed to transcend the banality and, in concert with Garfield, created a real cinematic thriller. For his screenwriting, Polonsky was nominated for an Academy Award.

His next screenwriting effort would also represent his directorial debut. Paired again with Garfield, Polonsky created another masterpiece, *Force of Evil* (1948), based on Ira Wolfert's novel *Tucker's People*. In this film Garfield played a corrupt lawyer who had long ago abandoned any pretense at ethics and now dealt largely with organized crime. A bleak story to begin with, it only proceeded deeper and ended in death and desperation. *Force of Evil* was a critical success. Of Polonsky's work, Bosley Crowther wrote in *The New York Times,* "new to the business of directing, Mr. Polonsky here establishes himself as a man of imagination and unquestioned craftsmanship."

As the threat of the House Un-American Activities Committee loomed over Hollywood, Polonsky squeezed in one final screenwriting job, an adaptation in 1951 of Jerome Weidman's play *I Can Get It for You Wholesale.* It was not one of his better works and did not fare well.

That year, Polonsky published his novel *The World Above* (New York). It traced the life of Carl Myers, a young and idealistic psychiatrist, as he grew from medical researcher to chief doctor of a V.A. hospital and confronted the bleak reality of masses of suffering veterans. (Polonsky served in the Office of Strategic Services during World War II.) Also that year Polonsky was interrogated by the HUAC, "accused" of Communist activities and blacklisted. Unable to work in Hollywood, he moved to New York.

For the next 17 years Polonsky continued to be a prolific writer, but his credits appeared nowhere. As with many writers in his situation, he "loaned" his work to a "front," a non-blacklisted writer who could act in his stead. In this fashion Polonsky managed to write more than one-third of the scripts for Edward R. Murrow's series *You Are There* for CBS-TV.

In 1968 a changed atmosphere made it possible for Polonsky to "go public" again, and he was invited back to Hollywood to work on *Madigan*, a detective thriller for which he wrote the screenplay. Free to work, finally, he began preparing his next film, *Tell Them Willie Boy Is Here* (1969), which he wrote and directed.

Apparently the 20-year gap between directing jobs had not affected Polonsky's skill. *Willie Boy,* which featured Robert Redford and Katherine Ross, was enthusiastically received—even more so in Europe than in the United States. The story of a rebellious Native American who ends up being shot when he will not "behave" according to white American standards, *Willie Boy* represented the kind of "moral tale—the struggle for acceptance"—that Polonsky's own life had become. Calling Polonsky's screen absence "perhaps the most wasteful injustice of the late 1940s Hollywood blacklisting," critic Roger Greenspun also cited *Willie Boy* as "one of the best American movies."

In 1970 Polonsky completed his third film, *Romance of a Horsethief*, with Eli Wallach, Yul Brynner and Lainie Kazan. Based on a Yiddish story, which the actor David Opatashu adapted for the screen, it was set in 1904 and told of poor Jews in a Russian-controlled border town in Poland struggling with Cossacks for control of a horse-dealing ring.

Although Polonsky was now officially in the Hollywood mainstream again and had many projects in development after *Romance,* he did not direct another film. However, he did publish a new novel, *Zenia's Way* (New York, 1980), about a young boy's relationship with his aunt, from his Bronx childhood through to adulthood, when they meet again in Israel and elsewhere. He has also prepared numerous film projects for future production, including adaptations of Thomas Mann's story "Mario and the Magician" and Arthur Clarke's science fiction novel *Childhood's End.* He also wrote the screenplay for *Bless me, Godfather, for I Have Sinned* (1982), directed by Frank Perry and starring Christopher Reeve.

Polonsky's short stories have appeared in *American Mercury, Colliers, American Magazine* and other publications. He has also been interviewed in several film magazines, including *Sight and Sound, Film Quarterly* and the French *Cahiers du Cinema;* and in books, such as Andrew Sarris's *American Cinema* (New York, 1968) and Eric Sherman's *The Director's Event* (New York, 1970). He also wrote the Introduction to *Films of John Garfield* (New York, 1975) and is included in *The Hollywood Social Problem Films* (Indiana University Press, 1981).

For further information:
Polonsky, Abraham. *Season of Fear.* New York: 1956.

SYLVIA PORTER

b. June 18, 1913
Financial writer

For nearly 50 years, Sylvia Porter has been one of the most successful financial columnists in America. Her ability to translate the complex vocabulary of economic "bafflegab" (her term) into clear and lucid English has made her columns and books as popular with lay audiences —one of her syndicated columns once received 150,000 letters—as with specialists in all areas of banking, investment and business.

Sylvia Feldman was born in Patchogue, New York to Louis, a physician, and Rose (Maisel) Feldman. The family moved to Brooklyn, where Sylvia Feldman grew up and attended James Madison High School, from which she was graduated in 1929. In the interim her father died, and her mother, who changed the family name to Field, had built up a successful millinery business. She entered the all-women Hunter College in 1929 as an English major with plans for a writing career. But when the stock market crashed that year and her mother lost $30,000—a fortune in those days—she switched to economics because of her fascination with the processes that led to the Depression. Upon graduation with a B.A. degree magna cum laude in 1932, she became assistant to one of the principal investment counselors in a Wall Street firm.

As her knowledge of the stock market grew, which she supplemented with graduate courses in business administration at New York University, Porter began writing a weekly column on U.S. government securities for *The American Banker.* In 1935 she was hired by *The New York Post,* which assigned her to cover Wall Street. She became the newspaper's financial editor in 1938 and published her first book, *How to Make Money in Government Bonds* (New York), in 1939. Her second book—as practical a discussion as any of her future columns and books would be—was *If War Comes to the American Home* (New York, 1941), a discussion of the probable impact of a war economy on American daily life.

But it wasn't until 1942 that Porter's readers learned she was a woman. Her previous by-line was S.F. Porter, and *Post* editors only now felt that her readers could accept a woman as their financial guide. She took full advantage of her uniqueness—she was virtually alone in an all-male field—and began lecturing and writing for mass media magazines. In 1944 she was co-founder of a weekly newsletter for the banking and securities community, *Reporting on Governments,* and in 1947 her column was syndicated nationally. She retained her *Post* job until 1978, when she moved to the *New York Daily News* and continued writing five columns a week.

As her public image grew, Porter became identified as an expert in comprehensive money management. She could provide advice on how and when to take vacations for less, how to finance superior medical care without going bankrupt, structuring a budget for a growing family, decorating a house or an apartment and so on. Beginning with *How To Live Within Your Income* (New York, 1948) and onward with *Money and You* (New York, 1949), *Managing Your Money* (New York, 1953 and 1963) and, since 1960, her annual tax guides, Porter also became identified as America's foremost consumer advocate. She topped all her previous work in the public interest in 1975 with *Sylvia Porter's Money Book: How to Earn It, Spend It, Save It, Invest It, Borrow It and Use It to Better Your Life* (New York). An updated edition, *Sylvia Porter's New Money Book for the 80s* (New York, 1979), though expensive at $24.95, became a best seller.

More women have crowded the field of business and financial journalism since Porter's debut nearly 50 years ago, and the field continues to grow as the world of business and finance becomes more central to more people's lives. But Porter, who appears occasionally on WABC-TV's *Good Morning, America,* is not only recognized as the pioneer in the area but is still acknowledged to be the best.

CHAIM POTOK

b. February 17, 1929
Author

For many people, the life of Orthodox Hasidic Jews might seem quaint or mysterious. But in his four novels, Chaim Potok has translated the parochial life of the Hasidim into an idiom of universal meaning and importance. He has opened the door to a whole segment of Jewish culture.

Chaim Potok was born to Benjamin, a jeweller, and Mollie (Friedman) Potok in New York City and reared as a Hasidic Jew. He graduated summa cum laude from Yeshiva University in 1950 with a B.A. degree in English literature and then left Orthodoxy. In 1954 he was ordained as a rabbi by the Jewish Theological Seminary, the institution of higher learning of the Conservative branch of Judaism. He also received a master's degree in Hebrew literature from the seminary that same year. In 1965 Potok completed his Ph.D. in philosophy at the University of Pennsylvania.

In 1954 and 1955 Potok was the national director of the Leadership Training Fellowship, sponsored by Conservative Judaism. The following year he served as a chaplain in the United States Army and was stationed with a combat engineer battalion in Korea. When he returned home, he spent three years as the director of Camp Ramah in Los Angeles, sponsored by the Conservative Judaism movement's program for youth. While he worked for Camp Ramah, he was also an instructor at the University of Judaism in Los Angeles.

Har Zion Temple in Philadelphia appointed Potok scholar-in-residence in 1959, and he remained in that position until 1963, when he became a member of the Teachers' Institute of the Jewish Theological Seminary. In 1964 Potok became the managing editor of *Conservative Judaism* magazine and the following year was editor at the Jewish Publication Society. In 1974 Potok was made the special projects editor for the Jewish Publication Society.

Potok's first book, *The Chosen* (New York, 1967), sensitively portrays the growing pains of two Hasidic Jewish boys as they grapple with their own process of maturing and coming to terms with their personal beliefs and goals and with the world around them. Potok paid exquisite attention to detail, creating a vivid and unique world, but one readily understandable and even poignant to an unknowledgeable reader. He displayed a deft touch in handling the clash of cultures and generations dealt with in *The Chosen*. In fact, it became a central motif of his writings—that is, the tension created by the interaction of Judaism with the secularism of the host society.

The Promise (New York, 1969) follows the same characters created in *The Chosen* through later life. In *My Name Is Asher Lev* (New York, 1972), Potok studied the conflicts an artistic Orthodox Jewish boy suffers as he tries to come to terms with his talent and the demands placed on him by an environment that looks down on the arts. Once again, Potok elevates the story above its parochial setting in creating a powerful tale.

In *Wandering—Chaim Potok's History of the Jews* (New York, 1978), a personalized interpretation of the past, he writes with a passion more common to fiction than to history. Potok shows how Jews changed as they came into contact with the cultures of others yet managed to maintain their own identity. "I am an American writer writing about a particular situation," he said. "In fact, my first novels are not even about Jews." All the same, his concern lies with religious conflicts within a worldly milieu. His characters blend into the larger community or else resist assimilation.

For further information:
Potok, Chaim. *The Book of Lights,* novel. New York: 1981.

GABRIEL PREIL

b. August 21, 1911
Poet

In a Bronx neighborhood whose Jewish flavor is nearly gone except for a dreary, run-down *shul* and a kosher deli and bakery, Gabriel Preil remains an oddity, writing Hebrew poetry for an audience an ocean away. Little-known in America, Preil has been writing modernistic poetry for more than 50 years and has been an influential figure among younger generations of Israeli poets.

Gabriel Joshua Preil was born in Dorpat, Estonia to Elias Faivel, a pharmacist who wrote occasionally for Hebrew-language magazines, and Chaya (Matzkel) Preil. His parents were Lithuanian but moved to Estonia for Preil's birth in the university hospital. The family returned to Lithuania, where Preil grew up near Kovno and attended Tarbut schools and Hebrew secular schools. He thus grew up speaking Yiddish at home but acquired fluency in Hebrew at school.

In 1922 Preil emigrated to the United States with his mother—his father had died shortly before their departure—and settled in the Williamsburg section of Brooklyn. He spent 1923 to 1926 at the Rabbi Isaac Elchanan Theological Seminary, the precursor to Yeshiva University, but Preil describes himself as primarily self-educated. Having begun writing at age 9, he eventually supported himself through a range of odd jobs that included manual labor as well as free-lance writing, editing and translation of Hebrew, Yiddish and English prose and poetry.

Not until 1935 did Preil begin to have his work published, when a Yiddish poem appeared in a weekly publication, *New Yorker Wochenblatt*. His Hebrew debut came the following year, when a poem appeared in another weekly, *Hadoar*. Subsequently, his poems were included in most Yiddish and Hebrew-language magazines in Israel and the United States, including *Mozhaim, Molad, Achshav, Knesset, Zukunft* and many others.

Early in his career, as later, Preil was very much a loner as a poet of Hebrew, since his work was considered too modernistic and experimental, although he was using the imagistic forms then popular in English-language poetry. But he began to have a mark on the writing of younger Israeli poets, including Yehuda Amichai and Nathan Zach. In the 1930s and 1940s, he became involved in the Hebrew cultural community in New York, including the organization Histadrut HaNoar HaIvri, which published an arts magazine entitled *Niv* ("Expression"), co-edited by Preil. But his reputation grew most quickly in Israel, and in 1953 he was invited by the city of Haifa to become a resident for life. Preil, however, chose to remain in America, and as the always-small community of Hebrew writers dwindled, he described himself as the "Last Mohican" among them.

Preil sees little hope for continuity among writers of Hebrew in the United States. In a 1982 interview he mentioned that, except for himself, most older Hebrew writers had either died or emigrated to Israel and that

there was no younger generation of writers to take their place. He said:

> There is very little secular Hebrew education provided here . . . . The Hebrew education that does exist involves Bible and prayer but hardly any modern literature. It's not a question of blame, though, but simply a recognition of the realities of the situation. The dominant culture is very strong in the United States, in contrast to Lithuania, for instance, so that it is difficult for a small culture to survive.

Preil is the author of seven collections of Hebrew poetry, among them *Landscape of Sun and Frost* (New York, 1944), *Candle Against Stars* (Jerusalem, 1954), *Map of Evening* (Tel Aviv, 1961), *Fire and Silence* (Tel Aviv, 1968) and *Courteous to Myself* (Tel Aviv, 1980). A collection of his Yiddish poetry entitled *Lider* ("Poems") was published in New York in 1966, and a bilingual collection of Preil's work was in preparation by the Jewish Publication Society of America as part of its series on 20th-century Jewish poets. In 1980 two books of Preil's poetry appeared in English translation: *Autumn Music* (St. Louis) and *Gabriel Preil—Selected Poems* (London). Preil has also translated into Hebrew the poetry of Robert Frost, Carl Sandburg and Robinson Jeffers.

His work has also appeared in many periodicals in the United States, England and Israel. In 1977 several of his poems were featured in the journal *Triquarterly*, which devoted an entire issue to contemporary Israeli literature. The following poem was among them:

"From a late diary"

Gabriel turned at last into old Mr. Preil.
Overnight began the pamperings
that go with taking off a coat
and opening a door.
Suspicions and hypotheses
sprouted in him like weeds.

And he tried to ignore
the marginal things
the fortuity of time—
not wanting to give up
the young wininess in him,
the flow of his young streams.

As for the obtuse, they do not realize
that the self-same Gabriel
shares his time with them,
that no change threatens him.
It would also seem the coffee is hotter now,
and longer now the lightning-play of jets,
and longer lasting the bird-trees in full bloom.

Preil has won many awards throughout his career,

including the Louis LaMed Award for Hebrew Literature (1943), the Jewish Book Council of America Prize for Hebrew Poetry (1955 and 1962), the Bitzaron Award for Hebrew Poetry (1960), the Lise and Willy Groot Award of the Congress for Jewish Culture and Yiddish PEN Club (1965), the Newmann Award for Lifetime Achievement in Hebrew Literature from New York University (1974) and the Friedman Prize for Hebrew Culture (1980).

From 1955 until 1975 Preil was contributing editor on Hebrew literature to the *Encyclopaedia Britannica Book of the Year.*

For further information:

Carmi, T., ed. *The Penguin Book of Hebrew Verse.* New York: 1981.

Garber, Jeremy Simcha. "A Conversation with Gabriel Preil," *Present Tense,* Winter 1982.

Rudolf, Anthony and Schwartz, Howard, eds. *Voices Within the Ark: The Modern Jewish Poets.* New York: 1980.

Silberschlag, Eisig, ed. *From Renaissance to Renaissance: Hebrew Literature.* New York: 1972.

Waxman, Meyer, ed. *A History of Jewish Literature.* Cranbury, N.J.: 1960.

SALLY JANE PRIESAND

b. June 27, 1946
Rabbi

Sally Priesand was ordained by the Hebrew Union College-Jewish Institute of Religion in Cincinnati in 1972, thus becoming the first female rabbi in the United States. She is also the first woman to become head rabbi of a congregation. The Reform movement, which first agreed in 1922 that the ordination of women was acceptable to Jewish law, "has taken the first step," Priesand once commented. "There's no turning back. A basic principle of our movement is complete equality for women."

Sally Priesand was born in Cleveland, Ohio to Irving Theodore, a construction engineer, and Rosetta Elizabeth (Welch) Priesand. Her ambition, while growing up, was to become a teacher. By the time she was 16, she realized the subject she wanted to teach was Judaism. She served as a visiting student rabbi—it was required of rabbinical students at HUC-JIR—at a number of temples during her college years at both the University of Cincinnati, where she majored in English and received a B.A. degree in 1968, and Hebrew Union College, where she earned a Bachelor of Hebrew Litera-

ture degree in 1971 and a Master of Hebrew Literature the following year. She was student rabbi in Hattiesburg, Mississippi from 1969 to 1970 and in Jackson, Michigan from 1970 to 1971. The following year she was a rabbinic intern in Cincinnati. "Undoubtedly, many believed that I was studying at HUC-JIR to become a *rebbetzin* [the wife of a rabbi] rather than a rabbi," she wrote. "Four years passed before people began to realize that I was serious about entering the rabbinate."

After her ordination in 1972, Priesand was offered the position of assistant rabbi at the Stephen Wise Free Synagogue in New York City, where her duties included conducting worship services, giving a sermon every Shabbat, teaching in the adult institute, supervising the youth program, lecturing the Golden Age Club and attending all committee meetings.

In August 1979 she took the pulpit at Congregation Beth El in Elizabeth, New Jersey. Her experience in finding a congregation of her own was a stormy one, she told *The New York Times* because, she said, of an inability of the Reform movement to accept the role of women in the rabbinate. She applied to 12 synagogues, 9 of which rejected her application without granting her an interview, before she was accepted by Beth El as an assistant. "Words must be supplemented by deeds," she said. "If the Reform Jewish community is unable to install women in roles of leadership, as examples to others, then what we're doing is giving a double message to our congregations . . . disproportionately few women are represented in the upper echelons of the Reform movement." In 1981 she became full-time rabbi of the Monmouth, New Jersey, Reform Temple, again the first time a woman had held such a post.

Priesand, who has written articles published in numerous periodicals and authored a book, *Judaism and the New Woman* (New York, 1975), wrote in one of her articles:

> we tread on dangerous ground when we separate the contributions that women can make from those that men can make. . . . When congregations hire women rabbis, they ought to be asking, "What does she as an individual have to offer?" rather than, "What does she as a woman have to offer?"

Some of Priesand's many Jewish organizational affiliations include Hadassah, B'nai B'rith Women and the Jewish Peace Fellowship. She is also politically active with the American Civil Liberties Union, Common Cause, the National Organization for Women—she avidly supported the Equal Rights Amendment—and Religious Leaders for a Free Choice. Along with other clergy members, she opposes the spread of nuclear power plants.

HAROLD PRINCE

b. January 30, 1928
Producer; director

Rarely has a Broadway producer made the daring step into directing and been as consistently successful in both roles as has Harold Prince. Widely regarded as one of the most original directors currently working on Broadway, he has been responsible for bringing to theatergoers *Fiddler on the Roof, Evita, Sweeney Todd* and a host of shows that might never have made it without his astute eye and creative daring.

Harold Smith Prince was born in New York City to Milton A., a stockbroker, and Blanche (Stern) Prince, who was active in the theatrical and artistic communities of the city. Both parents attended theater frequently with their son, so the stage became a familiar place for him when he was still very young. After graduating from the Franklin School in 1944 and from the University of Pennsylvania with a B.A. degree in English in 1948, Prince plunged immediately into theatrical work, starting in the office of producer-director George Abbott doing a variety of odd jobs. Abbott became his mentor, and after being drafted into the Army and serving in Germany from 1950 to 1952, Prince returned to Abbott's office and began stage managing for him. He later admitted that this experience was critical to his development as a director as well as a producer, for he had the unique opportunity to observe firsthand the evolution of a show from script to finished production

In 1954 Prince got his first taste of producing when he co-produced *The Pajama Game* with Robert E. Griffith. The show, which was a hit, ran for two years and earned for Prince his first Tony Award. He then proceeded to collaborate with Griffith on four more hits: *Damn Yankees* (1955–57), which made Gwen Verdon a star; *New Girl in Town* (1957–58); *West Side Story* (1957–59); and *Fiorello!* (1959–61), which won a Tony Award and a Pulitzer Prize. Although during the same period Prince and Griffith also produced two shows that flopped, *Tenderloin* and *A Call on Kuprin*, Prince, the younger of the two, had already developed a reputation on Broadway as a "wunderkind." After Griffith's death in 1961, Prince went on to produce independently and presented such hits as *Take Her, She's Mine* (1961–62), *A Funny Thing Happened on the Way to the Forum* (1962–64), *Fiddler on the Roof* (1964–72) and other musicals.

Prince proved to have a remarkable instinct for good theater and for business—his profit rate as of 1974, after he had produced or co-produced a total of 20 shows, reached 85 percent, a stunning figure in the precarious world of theatrical producing. *Fiddler,* for example, premiered during a major newspaper strike in New York City and received a mediocre review from the theater weekly *Variety.* Yet it became one of Broadway's longest-running and top-grossing musicals and Prince's greatest success to date because it had such unexpectedly wide appeal.

Prince made his transition to directing in 1963, when he both produced and directed the musical *She Loves Me.* Successful at it, he continued to both produce and direct, and his credits added up to a formidable list of successful shows and only a few failures. Among the hits, besides *Fiddler,* were *Cabaret* (1966–69), *Company* (1970–72), *A Little Night Music* (1973–74), *Evita* (London, 1978; Broadway, 1979–   ) and *Sweeney Todd* (1979–81). He has had his share of failures, of course, but even they often represented noble experiments at unconventional theater. Most of all, Prince has been recognized for his ability to see the theatrical possibilities in a concept—he in fact coined the term "concept musical"—which no one else could grasp. Often a project would evolve from concept to final production in close collaboration with lyricist Stephen Sondheim or choreographer Jerome Robbins, two giants of Broadway in their own right.

Prince's skills have overlapped into other areas of performance. He has directed two films, *Something for Everyone* (1976) and *A Little Night Music* (1978), which as a Broadway show was a spin-off from a 1956 film by Ingmar Bergman, *Smiles of a Summer Night.*

But his most daring venture has been into opera, which he has directed on several occasions since 1976. Prince claims, however, that directing opera is not so different from directing musical theater since "the elements . . . are interchangeable." His first effort was a production of *Ashmedai,* an Israeli opera based on a Talmudic legend about a community at peace for hundreds of years that is suddenly disrupted by a visit from the devil. It was commissioned for the New York City Opera in 1976 but played only three scheduled performances. In 1978 he directed *The Girl of the Golden West,* an opera set in the California wilderness of the 1840s, for the Chicago Lyric Opera. He also staged *Silver Lake,* an anti-Nazi opera by Kurt Weill, for the New York City Opera in 1980 and directed *Willie Stark* for the Houston Grand Opera in 1981. Based loosely on Robert Penn Warren's book *All the King's Men, Willie Stark* was aired on Public Television.

But Prince has been continuously involved in Broadway theater, often carrying on several projects simultaneously. In 1981 his teamwork with Sondheim in *Merrily We Roll Along* turned out to be one of his few real disasters. Plagued with problems from the outset, the show closed almost immediately. But Prince has always been bold about taking risks and began working on a new project, *A Doll's Life,* which was envisioned as a sequel to Ibsen's play *A Doll's House.*

Prince has also been outspoken about the need for government support of the arts, and in 1982 when the Reagan administration threatened to slash its subsidies to arts organizations, Prince testified in the U.S. Congress against the proposed cuts.

For further information:
Prince, Harold. *Contradictions: Notes on Twenty-Six Years in the Theater, An Autobiography.* New York: 1975.

JAY PRITZKER

b. August 26, 1922
Attorney; industrialist

In Chicago and elsewhere in America's financial community, the name Pritzker is usually stated in the plural. The Chicago-based family, one of America's wealthiest and the owners of the Hyatt International Corp., the luxury domestic and international hotel chain, generally acts as a unit. But since the early 1960s, Jay Pritzker has been the best-known in the clan as its dominant spokesperson.

Jay Arthur Pritzker was born in Chicago, the eldest of three sons of Abraham Nicholas, an attorney, and Fanny (Doppelt) Pritzker. The Pritzker presence in Chicago began with the arrival of Nicholas J. Pritzker from Kiev before the turn of the century. He began his life in America as a pharmacist but later studied law and opened a general practice in 1902. The firm he founded evolved into Pritzker & Pritzker. Since the early 1960s it has been concerned exclusively with family business.

Jay Pritzker attended Northwestern University, where he received a Bachelor of Science degree in 1941. Following military service in the Navy during World War II, he returned to Northwestern and, in the family tradition, received a law degree in 1947. The next year he joined the family firm.

The Pritzker family keeps a low profile and is identified in two areas only: its generous tradition of philanthropy and its extensive business transactions. In the former, the Pritzkers are, according to one report, "annual six-figure contributors to Jewish charities" *(New York Times,* October 14, 1973). In 1968 they donated $12 million to the University of Chicago medical school, which bears their name. In the latter, they are the owners of the Marmon Group, of which Jay Pritzker is chairman, and of the Hyatt Corporation, the only one of their holdings that is public and of which Jay is senior executive officer.

Through the private Marmon Group, the Pritzkers have developed a diverse industrial empire, including auto-parts and truck equipment manufacturers, real estate, publishing and many other ventures. They specialize in purchasing and reorganizing troubled firms to make them profitable again. Sometimes they retain the companies within the Marmon enterprise, or else they resell them at a substantial profit.

Extremely reluctant to parade their deals and enterprises before the public, the Pritzker family operation is nonetheless quite familiar to the financial community. In 1961, for example, Jay Pritzker became a director of Continental Airlines. The family also bought *McCall's* magazine and firms producing auto parts and construction equipment. Through the years they have been tied to deals with the Ford Motor Company (abroad, Hyatt obtains a lease-management contract from firms like Ford on condition that Hyatt will find the money to operate the hotel; Hyatt borrows from banks at just a little more than prime rate and is repaid for the interest from the owner of the hotel). In addition, the family has extensive land holdings northwest of Chicago and in Florida. In 1959 they bought property in Rosemont, not far from Chicago, for almost 75¢ a square foot; since then its value has increased nearly 10 times. They owned the land for 10 years before building the pink Regency Hyatt O'Hare Hotel on it.

Jay Pritzker has been chairman of the Marmon Group Inc., a privately owned family corporation. In 1953 the family bought the assets of the Colson Company, a caster maker. The president of Colson wanted to retire and was seeking a buyer. The family then sold Colson's losing bicycle plant and used the improving caster division as a means of finding other businesses to buy. Soon the company acquired a store-fixtures firm, purchased from an estate, and another firm bought from an aging racing car maker. They then sold its unprofitable military vehicle division and enlarged its coal mining equipment operation. Next they altered the corporate name to the Marmon Group Inc. and proceeded with acquiring and "straightening out" companies in deep financial trouble, such as American Steel and Pump Company and Fenestra Inc.

Also in the 1950s Jay Pritzker purchased a debt-ridden chocolate company, Rockwood, located in Brooklyn. Since he could not make it profitable, he gave up and sold its candy division to Tootsie Roll but retained the Rockwood name, which included among its assets cocoa beans listed on the books at a minute proportion of current market prices. This bookkeeping technique—perfectly legal—allowed Rockwood to buy its initial Hyatt Hotel. "We buy where we can improve management and reduce the amount of assets necessary to run the business," Jay Pritzker told *The New York Times* in 1973, explaining their technique. "The financial maneuvering is prologue. The management is everything. . . . The whole thing is a game. If you're not having fun, you shouldn't play. We're competitive type guys, though, and we're out to win."

Ownership of the Hyatt chain began in 1956, when Jay Pritzker bought the Hyatt House in Los Angeles. As the corporation expanded, hotels were built at major American airports, in urban centers and overseas. In addition, already existing hotels, including the well-known Regency in Atlanta—whose architect, John Portman, has become renowned for his innovative design—were absorbed into the Hyatt wing. (It is now the Regency Hyatt.) Tragically, two crowded skywalks collapsed at the Hyatt Regency Hotel in Kansas City in July 1981, killing 113 persons on a crowded dance floor and injuring nearly 200 more.

The Pritzkers introduced the annual Pritzker Architecture Award, supported by the Hyatt Foundation, to recognize the achievements of major American architects, especially in the area of hotel design.

ISIDOR RABI

b. July 29, 1898
Physicist

Isidor Rabi, distinguished winner of the Nobel Prize, was one of a very small group of scientists who enabled the United States to become the first country to develop the atomic bomb. Later, this eminent physicist devoted much of his time and effort to the development of peaceful applications of atomic energy.

Isidor Isaac Rabi was born in Rymanow, Austria. His parents, David, who was in the grocery business, and Scheindl (Teig) Rabi, brought him to the United States in 1900. He received a B.S. degree in chemistry from Cornell University in 1919 and from 1924 to 1927 tutored physics at the City College of New York while pursuing graduate studies at Columbia University. He received his Ph.D. in physics from Columbia University in 1927. His thesis was on the magnetic properties of crystals.

In 1928 Rabi won a Rockefeller Fellowship and went to Europe to study with the great physical scientists working there, spending time in Munich, Leipzig, Zurich and then Copenhagen, where Neils Bohr, the discoverer of quantum mechanics, had his laboratory. Rabi returned to the United States in 1929 and was appointed lecturer in theoretical physics at Columbia.

The following year he began a series of experiments on the magnetic properties of atomic nuclei. His efforts were directed toward determining the exact nature of the forces that held the protons of an atom in the nucleus. This information, he theorized, would reveal the magnetic and electrical properties of the atom. This work dominated Rabi's attention for the next 15 years.

In the meantime he rose through the ranks of academia and in 1937 was appointed a professor of physics at Columbia. In 1938–39 he also became a member of the Institute for Advanced Study in Princeton, New Jersey. And in 1940, while still on the Columbia faculty, Rabi moved to the Radiation Laboratory at the Massachusetts Institute of Technology. There, he continued his work on the nature of bonds in the atom and participated in projects concerning the development of radar and the atomic bomb.

Otto Stern, who had conducted research similar to that of Rabi, won the Nobel Prize in physics in 1943 for his discovery of the molecular beam that held the various parts of a molecule together. Rabi then determined the spectrum of the wavelengths of those beams, a process 100,000 times more sensitive than determining the light spectrum. For his discovery, Rabi was awarded the Nobel Prize in 1944 for his resonance method of recording the magnetic properties of atomic nuclei.

In 1945 Rabi was appointed chairman of the Physics Department at Columbia University. He also began work at the Brookhaven Laboratory in Suffolk County in New York. The laboratory explores peaceful applications of atomic energy. Rabi was a fierce opponent of a plan presented shortly after World War II that would have placed control of atomic energy in the United States in the hands of the military. In 1950 Rabi became Columbia's Higgins Professor of physics.

From 1946 until 1972 he was a member of the General Advisory Committee of the Atomic Energy Commission. He is also a member of the National Research Advisory Committee and was a member of the general advisory committee of the Arms Control and Disarmament Agency from 1962 to 1969.

In recognition of his substantial contributions in physics, Rabi has been awarded the United States Medal for Merit (1948); the King's Medal (Britain, 1948); the Commander, Order of the Southern Cross (Brazil, 1952); the Henrietta Szold Award (1956); the Earl Warren Medal (1961); and was named university professor from

1964 to 1967, the first ever appointed by Columbia University. Since 1967 he has been Columbia University professor emeritus.

For further information:
Rabi, Isidor. *My Life and Times as a Physicist.* New York: 1960.
———. *Science: The Center of Culture.* New York: 1970.

EMANUEL RACKMAN

b. June 24, 1910
Rabbi; college president

When Emanuel Rackman became president of Bar-Ilan University in Tel Aviv in 1977, he fulfilled the Zionist ideal he had preached as a rabbi, legal expert and professor in New York City for more than four decades. He is an outspoken advocate of religious education as a means of preserving Jewish traditions, and also speaks, teaches and writes about the necessity of resisting intermarriage and assimilation.

Emanuel Rackman was born in Albany, New York to David, a rabbi and merchant, and Anna (Mannescovitch) Rackman. He was educated at Yeshiva University, where he was ordained as a rabbi in 1931 and at Columbia College, where he received a B.A. degree the same year and was a member of Phi Beta Kappa. In 1933 he received a Bachelor of Laws from the law school of Columbia University and in 1953 completed a Ph.D. in the Department of Public Law at Columbia.

Rackman is descended from a line of rabbis, but like his father, who was a businessman, following a family tradition, he combined his religious calling with a non-religious profession. He practiced law and later served as spiritual leader in two different congregations in New York.

Rackman was a member of a thriving law firm in New York until World War II, but in 1943 he became an Army chaplain and a trainer of chaplains, serving first in Texas and later in Germany. He remained in Germany after the war to help in the resettlement of survivors and as military aide to the special adviser on Jewish affairs. He also became involved with the Haganah-organized group Bricha, which helped Jews escape to Palestine through a network of underground routes.

Rackman returned to the United States in 1946 to become rabbi at Shaaray Tefilah Congregation in Far Rockaway. At the same time, he taught political philosophy and jurisprudence at Yeshiva University, remain-

ing for 21 years before moving on to the City University of New York to teach Jewish studies. While there, he instituted a popular series of weekly lectures in Judaic issues at the CUNY Graduate Center. In addition, he wrote essays and articles for many Jewish publications and since 1972 has been a regular columnist for *Jewish Week.* Rackman left Shaaray Tefilah in 1967 to become head of the Fifth Avenue Synagogue, a post he held until he was invited to become president of Bar-Ilan.

Rackman's appointment to Bar-Ilan posed an ironic dilemma for him. For although he was a lifelong supporter of Israel, he had also become deeply involved in communal Jewish life in America. But Bar-Ilan offered him an unusual and irresistible opportunity. Rackman's concern about worldwide Jewish assimilation also included Israel, whose younger generations, he felt, were forgetting their Jewish heritage. At Bar-Ilan, which combines a secular curriculum with Jewish studies, he has been able to foster a progressive educational atmosphere while instilling a strong Jewish consciousness in the teaching. Thus, Bar-Ilan can boast that it has strong science and humanities departments and yet be confident that its students have not sacrificed their Jewish roots in the learning process.

Although Rackman left New York in 1977 with an optimistic view of what he could accomplish at Bar-Ilan, in the early 1980s he began increasingly to express his fear of a new "spiritual Holocaust" caused by the assimilation of Jews in their native countries around the world. In one *Jewish Week* column (October 19, 1980), he not only decried the decline of Jewish life in the Diaspora but stated with alarm that Israel is experiencing the same problem. He wrote:

> The extent to which Israeli Jews feel that they are Israelis rather than Jewish is worrying many Jewish leaders, religionists and secularists alike. . . . Intermarriages between Israelis and non-Jews who come to tour Israel are frequent. And Israelis who go abroad to work or study have a notoriously high rate of intermarriage with non-Jews wherever they go. The rate may even exceed that of the native Jewish population.

But in the same column Rackman counters this pessimistic commentary by describing the unique qualities that have supported Jewish survival in the worst of times:

> There is a dimension in Jewish history which even Abba Eban—a secularist—describes as mystical. The laws of universal history simply do not apply to the Jews. And for that reason the optimists can reassure us. Israel exists not because humanity ever wanted her—rather despite the express wishes of the major world powers.

Israel also expanded not because the free world hoped to bring the good life to more people but rather because Israel demonstrated a military capacity no one dreamed she had. . . . Israel's cities continue to be safer than those of the rest of the world despite acts of terror; and in Israel no one wants for food. . . . In brief, Israel and her history are simply one big bag of surprises. And every crisis yields only something good.

Rackman contends that even though some Western leaders seem to tend toward acceptance of the Palestine Liberation Organization and the Arab powers, ultimately they will have to realize their need to support Israel as the only true democracy in the Middle East. And the new rise of anti-Semitism that accompanied the economic disarray of the early 1980s will, Rackman feels, infuse new strength into Jews around the world and into Israelis seeking pride in their ethnic identity. "I am sure that there is hardly a Jew who would not have preferred the growth of Israel for reasons positive rather than negative," he writes, but he foresees a new migration of Jews to Israel in the coming years.

Rackman is a founding member of the International Conference for PEACE (Preventing the Emergence of Another Arab Country) in Judea, Samaria and Gaza, a group opposed to a Palestinian state on the West Bank.

TONY RANDALL

b. February 26, 1920
Actor

Although in his acting persona Tony Randall often projects the image of a frustrated bumbler and a lonely "schlemiel" who can't quite pull himself together, in real life he is a versatile and accomplished comedian and dramatic actor who in more than 40 years in show business has made his mark in radio, film, television and stage.

Leonard Rosenberg was born in Tulsa, Oklahoma, on February 26, 1920, to Philip, an art and antiques dealer, and Julia (Finston) Rosenberg. An early interest in a dramatic career led him to study speech and theater at Northwestern University from 1937 to 1938. But after that year he moved to New York to concentrate on acting at the Neighborhood Playhouse School of the theater, where he studied with Sanford Meisner and dancer Martha Graham, who coached him in movement.

Randall's initial acting jobs were in small, semi-professional theater groups outside of New York City in 1939 and 1940. He also tried his hand at directing at the Sussex County (N.J.) Playhouse. In 1941 he began performing in New York City, making his debut in the

role of Chang Ling in *The Circle of Chalk* at The New School for Social Research. For the next year, before entering the U.S. Army, Randall performed as Marchbanks in a summer stock production of George Bernard Shaw's play *Candida* and as a miner in *The Corn is Green*, starring Ethel Barrymore, with the so-called New York City Subway Circuit, which performed in New York's outer boroughs and in nearby suburbs. During his four years in the army, from 1942-1946, Randall tried to maintain sporadic involvement in the theater, but it took a return to full-time civilian life in 1946 for him to fully develop his career.

Radio was a key to Randall's recognition as a character actor, and as early as 1941 he was a radio announcer for WTAG in Worcester, Massachusetts. From 1946 to 1955 he was a featured actor in many popular radio serials similar in format to present-day soap operas, including *I Love a Mystery*, *When a Girl Marries*, and *Life's True Story*.

Randall also began performing on stage, although he rarely played a major role. His Broadway debut was in the role of Scarus in *Antony and Cleopatra* in 1947. His most noteworthy subsequent appearances included the role of a drunken movie star, which he assumed as a replacement for actor Gig Young in *Oh, Men! Oh, Women!*, (1954), a spoof on psychoanalysis, and the part of E.K. Hornbeck, the Mencken-like character in the drama *Inherit the Wind* (1955). In 1958, Randall displayed his singing and dancing talents in a less-than-memorable musical comedy production entitled *Oh, Captain!*

But the role which brought Randall national exposure and renown was as the twitty high school teacher in the NBC-TV weekly comedy series *Mr. Peepers*, which aired from 1952 to 1955. This role established Randall as the guy who constantly trips over himself, either literally or figuratively. Randall continued playing similar characters in film, stage and TV in years to come, usually in comedies, but one rare exception was when he was featured in the 1957 drama *No Down Payment* (20th-Century Fox) and portrayed an alcoholic used-car salesman whose life and marriage in a post-World War II suburban development was steadily disintegrating. During the late 1950s and early 1960s, Randall performed in television dramatic specials, such as *Philco Playhouse*, *Sunday Showcase*, *Playhouse 90* and *Alcoa House*, appeared in a 1957 film version of *Oh, Men! Oh, Women!* (20th-Century Fox) and in other films, including *Pillow Talk* (Universal, 1959), *Adventures of Huckleberry Finn* (MGM, 1960), *Let's Make Love* (20th Century Fox, 1960), *Boy's Night Out*, (MGM, 1962), *The Seven Faces of Dr. Lao* (MGM, 1964), and other comedies, including Woody Allen's *Everything You've Always Wanted to Know About Sex But Were Afraid to Ask* (United Artists, 1972).

While his part in *Mr. Peepers* was responsible for Randall's national recognition—he subsequently was called on to substitute several times for Steve Allen to host the *Tonight* show and to fill in for a two-week stint on *The Arthur Godfrey Show*—the role which secured Randall a place in television annals was that of Felix Unger in the series based on Neil Simon's play *The Odd Couple*. Although Randall was not in the original Broadway cast, he performed the play in tours in Las Vegas and Chicago in the early 1970s and was then cast to play in the ABC-TV series based on the play, sharing top billing with Jack Klugman. As one half of a cantankerous "couple" of divorced middle-aged men sharing an apartment, Randall excelled as the fussy, irritable foil to Klugman. The show lasted five seasons and in 1975 earned an Emmy for Randall.

Randall has since had his own program, *The Tony Randall Show* for one season (1975-76) and in 1981 starred in a short-lived series, *Love, Sidney,* in which he played an aging bachelor who befriends a young woman and her daughter, both of whom eventually move in to his large apartment. When the show began, Sidney Shorr was supposed to be a homosexual, but the story was later modified and Randall's character was merely a repressed and lonely eccentric of questionable (if any) sexuality.

Randall is an avid opera buff and over the years he has appeared on a radio program "Opera Quiz", aired during intermissions of live Metropolitan Opera broadcasts.

In 1981 and 1982, as a representative of Actors Equity, Randall led the movement to preserve several Broadway theaters threatened with demolition to make way for a luxury hotel. Although Randall and his many followers lost their hard-fought battle and two theaters, the Helen Hayes and the Morosco, were torn down, the planned construction of the hotel was later thrown into doubt.

Randall has made two record albums, a 1967 collection of nostalgia songs entitled *Vo, Vo, De, Oh, Do,* and a 1973 record with Klugman, *The Odd Couple Sings.* He has also been especially active in the movement to free Soviet Jewry and has lent his presence to many public rallies in their behalf.

BERNARD RAPOPORT

b. July 17, 1917
Businessman

Bernard Rapoport has the distinction of being one of the few leaders in American business to claim a radical upbringing and a commitment to liberal causes and yet to espouse pure capitalism as the foundation of a free society. He is active in national Democratic Party politics, in the Texas political and cultural scene, and in the Jewish community on the national and international level.

Bernard Rapoport was born in San Antonio, Texas to David, a Russian-immigrant peddler who later became an insurance salesman, and Riva (Feldman) Rapoport. He attended Thomas Jefferson High School in San Antonio and the University of Texas in Austin, where he received a B.A. degree in 1939. For five years he worked for Zale Jewelry and then opened his own jewelry shop in Waco.

Rapoport inherited his political zeal from his father, who was once imprisoned in Siberia for his political activities and who became a member of the Socialist Party of America. Like his father, Bernard Rapoport was not afraid to take risks; in 1946 he not only actively raised money to support a liberal candidate for the Texas governorship but contributed many of his own assets to the campaign. When his candidate lost, Rapoport was forced to sell his store. He turned to insurance sales work to support himself.

In 1951, with the help of a relative, Rapoport founded his own company, American Income Life Insurance. Although its initial specialty was hospitalization and disability insurance, the company became successful primarily for developing policies oriented to labor union members. Rapoport opened his own company to the Office and Professional Employees International Union in 1966, and his subsequent unabashed commitment to the labor movement, plus the fact that few insurance companies in America reach out to unions as he does, contributed to American Income Life's rapid growth and to Rapoport's personal clout. By 1980 the self-made millionaire was cited by *Texas Business* magazine as one of the state's 20 most powerful individuals, based on wealth, independence, influence and ability to organize.

During the 1980 national campaign, Rapoport, who has been a member of the Democratic National Finance Committee since 1976, supported the senatorial candidacies of George McGovern and Frank Church and the presidential primary fund of Edward Kennedy as well as other Democratic candidates. He has also held positions with the San Francisco-based Mexican-American Legal Defense and Educational Fund; the Scientists' Institute for Public Information; the Center for the Study of Democratic Institutions; the United Negro College Fund; the American Federation of State, County and Municipal Employees Advisory Board; and the National Council on Crime and Delinquency.

He is a member of the American Israel Public Affairs Committee, the Jerusalem Foundation, the Wise Circle of the Hebrew Union College in Cincinnati and the board of delegates of the Union of American Hebrew Congregations, the flagship organization of the Reform Jewish community in America. In 1981 Rapoport was a donor to a fund created by the union to draw non-Jews to Reform Judaism.

Rapoport is also a contributor to civic and cultural organizations in Texas, including the Texas Consumer Foundation in Houston, the University Cancer Foundation in Houston, and Paul Quinn College and the Baylor Opera, both in Waco.

He has received many prizes, including an award for services to B'nai B'rith Youth Programs (1971), an award for his service to the A. Philip Randolph Institute (1979) and a Century Club Award from the State of Israel Bonds.

Public service advertisements reflecting Rapoport's views appear regularly in the liberal newspaper *The Texas Observer*. One, entitled "Philosophy of a Company Which Rejects the 'Plantation Theory' " (July 27, 1979), discussed his staunch advocacy of organized labor in the United States. Rapoport wrote:

> America's employers should thank their lucky stars for the labor movement that has evolved in this nation. . . . That movement stands as a bulwark against statism from both right and left. The day American labor is rendered impotent, free capitalism as we know it will be on its deathbed.

Thus Rapoport combines his socialist background with an ardent social consciousness, a commitment to liberal causes and a firm faith in capitalism that grants any individual the right to achieve his or her optimum potential. Despite his support of labor unions, he acknowledges that some are corrupt and unproductive. "Perfection is a noble but unattainable goal," he said in an August 1980 interview in *Texas Business*. "Corruption is an alternative to giving some element in a system absolute power, as in a dictatorship. You can ferret out corruption, even in the presidency, but you can't overcome unlimited power. Not having a labor movement would be worse than putting up with its flaws." In economics, he says, "I am a true conservative. I want a free, competitive marketplace that is free of monopolism."

A.H. RASKIN

b. April 26, 1911
Journalist

In *The Kingdom and the Power* (New York, 1969), a profile of *The New York Times*, author Gay Talese described how in the mid-1930s the management of the *Times* was reluctant to give its young, feisty labor reporter, A.H. Raskin, a by-line with his complete name so as not to give an impression that the paper was "too" Jewish. Had Raskin been on staff a long time by then, he might have offered his acerbic commentary on that event. Instead, he spent the next four decades as the *Times'* most important labor reporter.

Abraham Henry Raskin was born on April 26, 1911, in Edmonton, Alberta, Canada, to Henry Raskin, a fur trader, and Mary (Slatkin) Raskin. In 1913 the family moved to Seattle, Washington, and in 1920 they were all naturalized. For a brief period in 1924, the Raskins lived in Germany while Henry Raskin was trading in Russia. Upon their return to the United States, they settled in New York City, where Abe Raskin attended Townsend Harris High School, a public high school for gifted boys, and graduated in 1927. He then entered the City College of New York, where his flair for writing led him to edit the college newspaper, yearbook and literary magazine. He graduated from CCNY with a B.A. degree in 1931, Phi Beta Kappa.

With almost no hope of employment during the Depression, Raskin remained at City College as a graduate student, but began writing part-time for *The New York Times* as a campus stringer. He seized that opportunity to cover the trauma of unemployment and subsequent work-relief programs that were instituted following the election of Franklin Roosevelt. In 1934, Raskin was hired full-time by the *Times*. Early on, he developed a reputation as a tireless, meticulous reporter and soon mastered the labor field. In the process, he managed to antagonize some of the more staid *Times* staffers and although dozens of his pieces were published, he didn't get a byline until 1936.

Raskin's understanding of labor included not only an overview of how events evolved, but insights into the movement's underside, including the infighting and corruption that went on among many—but not all—labor leaders (and management). His nose for news meant that Raskin almost always managed to be on top of an important breaking story. In 1940, for example, he exposed a long-standing struggle among labor leaders at a New Orleans convention over self-policing of racketeering within the American Federation of Labor. At the time, David Dubinsky, then president of the International Ladies Garment Workers Union had proposed a resolution to eliminate racketeering from the inside, but was opposed by Union of Operating Engineers' head Joseph Fay. Fay elected to show his disapproval by having a fist fight with Dubinsky—with Raskin caught in the middle. His account made page one of the *Times*.

During World War II Raskin was drafted into the army, where he headed the industrial services division in the Pentagon. His labor-related work there led to his subsequent appointment to a series of government consultancies. He returned to the *Times* in 1946, when he was named national labor correspondent. In his new slot, Raskin had the freedom to cover labor from a myriad of viewpoints, from the poorest, least-skilled laborer to top-level management across the United States —and he did. Many of his pieces were investigative articles which not only mirrored the state of American labor as a whole, but also the state of America and, in several instances, his reporting helped shape federal legislation. For example, a 1956 series describing the failure of northern blacks to make headway in the workplace although the national economy was flourishing, eventually led to the enactment of fair employment laws and the creation of job training programs for minorities. Raskin also was one of the first journalists to note the growing crisis in America of a class of chronically unemployed people—individuals who in some cases were victims of automation and who never gained new skills. '

Raskin was marked by a crusty independence and integrity. Despite his basic advocacy of labor, he was not always well-loved by labor leaders, who occasionally resented his probing into their affairs. Among his top enemies were teamster president Jimmy Hoffa and transit workers union head Mike Quill, whose allegedly corrupt activities Raskin exposed.

In 1961, he was named to the editorial board, but continued to report on labor news. In April 1963, Raskin wrote a lengthy, detailed story describing the newspaper strike that had paralyzed New York City for the previous four months. Raskin's account included the commentary that newspaper publishers were like big businessmen anywhere—almost inaccessible when it came to trying to sort out information. Nonetheless, he succeeded in putting together the complex pieces behind the strike and later that year earned many major press awards. In 1964 Raskin was appointed assistant editor for the *Times* editorial page. Even then, he remained as independent and occasionally provocative as before; at one point he wrote a highly critical editorial of American conduct in Vietnam—with no words minced— which publisher "Punch" Sulzberger nearly killed. Only the intervention of editorial page editor John Oakes saved the editorial—somewhat rewritten (and toned down) by Oakes.

Raskin retired from the *Times* in 1976, but continued writing, not only for the paper but for other publications. They included *The New Yorker, Commentary, Saturday Review* and *The New York Times Magazine*. With age, Raskin can hardly be said to have mellowed. In a long analytical article in *The New Yorker* on September 7, 1981, Raskin lamented on the deterioration of the American labor movement, which he attributed as much to labor leadership as to the contempt in which labor was held by the Reagan Administration. (In a 1982 business journalism conference, he described Reagan as an "economic idiot.") Yet he concluded his article on a hopeful note, focusing on the enthusiasm of a young organizer with the National Consumer Cooperative Bank who had worked in a variety of union-sponsored projects for the bank in Louisiana, Arizona, Texas and the District of Columbia, and whose energy and idealism surprised—and heartened—Raskin. Asked by the veteran labor reporter why he continued to work in labor even when its own management was rife with corruption, the young man, perhaps summing up Raskin's own reasons for covering labor, replied,

> "It bothers me very much that there should be any of that, but I know that, of the hundreds of people I have worked with, 99 per cent are totally honest. Our big need is more education of the membership and of the millions who ought to be members. The thirties were a long time ago. The sitdowns were a long time ago. Today's workers don't remember. We have to show them that our labor movement has a great track record. Our social stability is built on it. It is the heart of America."

Raskin has written one book, *David Dubinsky: A Life with Labor* (New York, 1977). Since early 1978 he has been Associate Director of The National News Council, an independent, non-profit, voluntary organization whose purpose is to expand the freedom and responsibility of American news organizations. He was adjunct professor at the Graduate School of Business at Columbia University in 1976 and at Pace University in 1977. In 1979-80 he taught labor reporting at Columbia's Graduate School of Journalism.

Raskin's recent awards include prizes in 1977 from the Labor Press Council of Metropolitan New York and in 1978 from the Institute of Collective Bargaining and Group Relations.

JUDITH RASKIN

b. June 21, 1928
Opera singer; recitalist

As a child, Judith Raskin studied violin and piano because her parents thought her singing voice was too weak. But she doggedly persisted with voice lessons and eventually became a soloist with New York City's two leading opera companies and earned recognition as one of the greatest American interpreters of German lieder.

Judith Raskin was born in New York City, the only child of Harry, a high school teacher of music, and Lillian (Mendelson) Raskin, a grade school teacher. Raised in Yonkers, she went to Smith College on a singing scholarship, the Harriet Day Barnum award. She received her B.A. degree in 1949 and continued studying in New York City with Anna Hamlin, a well-known voice teacher with whom she had begun lessons while at Smith.

For the next years, Raskin sang sporadically with the Symphony of the Air and the New York Oratorio Society, and in the summer of 1957 she performed in Central Park with the City Symphony of New York. Later that year she auditioned for Samuel Chotzinoff, music director of NBC. The audition provided her first professional "break." She was then "discovered" by George Schick at NBC Opera—Schick would remain Raskin's accompanist in solo recitals for many years to come—and received free voice lessons prior to singing with NBC-TV Opera.

Raskin toured with NBC Opera in Mozart's *Marriage of Figaro* and in December 1957 performed in the NBC-TV telecast of Poulenc's *Les Dialogues des Carmelites*. These early performances led to engagements in 1958 with the Santa Fe Opera Company (in *Cosi Fan Tutti* and *La Boheme*) and with the American Opera Society in New York (*The Marriage of Figaro* and Cherubini's *Medea*).

In 1959 Raskin joined the New York City Opera. For the next four years she specialized in Mozart, receiving critical acclaim for her performances and becoming preeminent among singers.

Raskin's Metropolitan Opera debut took place on February 23, 1962, when she performed as Susanna in *The Marriage of Figaro*. "There was the repertory I enjoyed doing," she told *The New York Times*, "the Mozart soubrettes, Nanetta in 'Falstaff,' Sophie in 'Rosenkavalier.' The mainstay of my operatic career was the young 'inna' and 'etta' ladies." Her singing and acting received rave reviews. "But I knew that my repertory in opera would be limited, as everybody's is by the range of voice and its quality. In my heart of hearts, I've always been a recitalist." While at the Met, she was compared with an earlier Met star, Elizabeth Schumann, for her interpretations of Mozart (one critic raved about her "perfect artistry"), Strauss and Verdi. She made her European debut at the Glyndenbourne Festival in England the following year, where her extraordinary acting skill plus her vigorous and remarkably lucid style were once again noticed and widely commented on.

But her true vocation as a singer surfaced in 1964, when Raskin made her debut as a singer of German lieder and other classical vocal music in a recital at the Metropolitan Museum of Art as the winner of a Ford Foundation grant. During the next few years, she concentrated on solo recitals, often singing music rarely heard otherwise. In 1965 she sang in a recital of lieder at New York's Town Hall—a historic event remembered years later by a *New York Times* critic who called Raskin "one of the few important lieder singers this country has produced" (*New York Times*, October 1, 1974). She also performed in the 1962–63 Chanukah Festival for Israel at Madison Square Garden in New York.

During the early 1970s she was ill and hardly performed. But by 1973, Raskin was artist-in-residence at the new Davis Center for the Performing Arts at City College of New York. She is a voice instructor at the Manhattan School of Music and the Mannes College of Music, both in New York City. In 1979 she taught master classes at the 92nd Street YM-YWHA, where she also sang the role of Pearl, the rabbi's wife in the new opera *The Golem* in 1981. She participates in music advisory boards for such organizations as Young Concert Artists, the National Opera Institute and the National Endowment for the Arts. She has recorded for Columbia, London, Decca, RCA Victor and CRI records.

MARCUS RASKIN

b. April 30, 1934
Political scientist

Since 1963, when he co-founded the Institute for Policy Studies (IPS), a left-liberal research center in Washington, D.C., Marcus Raskin has come to be acknowledged as one of the most astute thinkers of the left. Through his writing and lectures, he has had significant influence on national and international policy formulation. He was one of the earliest—and most incisive—critics of U.S. involvement in Vietnam and since then has been an outspoken and often controversial advocate of alternative modes of government and of social structures.

Marcus Goodman Raskin was born in Milwaukee, Wisconsin to Benjamin Sam, who was a self-employed plumbing and heating contractor, and Anna (Goodman) Raskin. He attended the University of Chicago, where he received a B.A. degree in 1954 and a Doctor of Laws in 1957. From 1958 to 1960 he served as legislative counsel to 12 Democratic congressmen and congresswomen and concurrently was staff editor of a congressional publication, *Liberal Papers*. From 1961 to 1963 he worked on the Special Staff of the National Security Council. In 1962 he was a member of the U.S. Disarmament Delegation to the Geneva Conference. He also consulted on the President's Panel on Educational Research and was closely involved with drafting the Elementary and Secondary Education Act.

Raskin left government employ in 1963 to co-found the IPS with Richard J. Barnet, who shared Raskin's disillusionment with the unfulfilled ideals of the Kennedy administration. He did, however, continue to do government consulting and from 1963 to 1965 was an educational consultant in the White House Office of Science and Technology and participated on the Presidential Panel on Educational Research and Development.

The Institute for Policy Studies, which was started with private funding, was designed from the outset as a center for the promotion of scholarship, an exchange of alternate ideas and the support of activism (almost exclusively with a left-leaning orientation) through publications and conferences. One of its first efforts was a critique of U.S. government policy in Indochina. With the late journalist Bernard Fall, Raskin wrote *The Vietnam Reader* (New York, 1965), which became a bible of sorts for university "teach-ins," signalling the beginning of the anti-war protest movement. Two years later he coauthored with IPS fellow Arthur Waskow a document entitled "Call to Resist," which became a rallying point for growing ranks of draft resisters. In 1971 he collaborated with Barnet and with Ralph Stavins in writing *Washington Plans an Aggressive War* (New York), which described the Americans in charge of making and implementing U.S. policy in Vietnam as "war criminals."

But protest against involvement in Vietnam was only one IPS activity. The institute also established the Washington School, a lecture and seminar center open to the public. Some of its offerings have included "Organizing on the Left" and "Human Rights and Economic Development in Latin America." The latter course was team-taught and included among its staff Patricia Derian (a former State Department official in the Carter administration who had been vocal in her outrage over the repressive treatment by many Latin American regimes of political dissidents and in some cases of religious minorities). In 1974 a European branch of IPS, the Transnational Institute, was created in Amsterdam, with a notably Marxist orientation among its principals. IPS also publishes a socialist weekly, *In These Times* (based in Chicago), and two quarterly journals, *Race and Class* (co-published with the Institute of Race Relations in London) and *The Transnational Information and Exchange Bulletin* (co-published with the World Council of Churches). The institute also produced a highly-acclaimed anti-nuclear documentary, "Paul Jacobs and the Nuclear Gang," which won a 1979 Emmy. The film chronicled the efforts of Jacobs, a radical journalist, to uncover abuses by the military during the 1950s in conducting atomic bomb experiments near residential areas in Nevada and Utah by interviewing residents of the area 20 years later.

In concert with the aims of IPS to promote social action through the development of dialogue and theory, Raskin has been an activist in his own right. In 1968 he was one of the "Boston Five," defendants prosecuted by the pro-war Johnson administration in a draft resistance case. Raskin and all his co-defendants were ultimately acquitted.

For his part, Raskin remains committed to the struggle for political, social and economic equality by oppressed peoples around the world. In "End of a Faustian Bargain," a paper he wrote following the election of Ronald Reagan to the American presidency, he described his personal goals within the framework of that struggle:

> At the Institute for Policy Studies, I have been concerned with questions similar to those of sociology of knowledge in the hopes of developing a path of inquiry which is action-oriented and which seeks to make concrete a set of propositions around the principle of liberation . . . .
>
> I have called this the knowledge of reconstruction and its purpose social reconstruction. . . . I see reconstructive knowledge as an epistemological and conversational path that uses all we know and perceive relating them together in such a way as to help humankind become subject actors of history conscious of their dignity, liberation and non-dominating purpose toward one another.

In *Being and Doing* (New York, 1971) Raskin clarified his outlook. He contended that American society was still in the clutches of colonialism, and analyzed the present condition of the nation-state and proposes alternatives. He suggested four elements of America as he saw it: the "Violence Colony" in which the citizens become hostages forced to fight wars they don't believe in; the "Plantation Colony" in which jobs are distributed by corporations beyond the reach of democratic control: the "Channeling Colony" which prepares children *for* organized life before they can find out what options might be available to them; and the "Dream Colony" in which the mass media feed people with images of an America they would like to experience but can do so only vicariously. Raskin foresaw an evolution toward a non-Marxist "re-construction" to replace authoritarianism and the status quo in which a populist vision and redefined social ethic would rule. Although he described his approach as "existential pragmatism," at least one critic saw it as a mixture of anarchism, Gestalt psychology, Jeffersonian democracy, Deweyan pragmatism and some Marxist influences.

Raskin, who was a contributing editor to *Ramparts* magazine from 1965 to 1968, is on the editorial board of *The Nation, Working Papers* and *Southern Exposure*. His articles have appeared in *The New York Times,* the *Yale Law Journal, The New York Review of Books* and many other publications.

In 1978 Raskin relinquished his post as co-director of IPS and was named Distinguished Fellow.

For further information:

Raskin, Marcus. *An American Manifesto.* New York: 1970.
———. *The Common Good.* New York.
———. *The Federal Budget and Social Reconstruction.* New Brunswick, N.J.: 1978.
———. *The Limits of Defense.* New York: 1962.
———. *Notes on the Old System: To Transform American Politics.* New York: 1978.
———. *The Problem of the Federal Budget.* Washington, D.C.: 1977.
Raskin, Marcus, and Barnet, Richard. *After Twenty Years: Alternatives to the Cold War in Europe.* New York: 1965.

JOSEPH L. RAUH JR.

b. January 3, 1911
Attorney

For decades Joseph L. Rauh's name has been synonomous with the lawyer whose professional and personal life has been devoted to the defense and expansion of civil rights and civil liberties.

Joseph Louis Rauh was born in Cincinnati, Ohio to Joseph Louis, a manufacturer, and Sara (Weiler) Rauh. His father had come to Cincinnati from Germany in 1891 and in 1912 had begun a shirt manufacturing firm. Following completion of high school in 1928, Rauh entered Harvard, where he received his B.S. degree in economics in 1932. Three years later he earned his law degree from Harvard Law School, where he received the Fay Diploma for being first in his graduating class.

At Harvard Law School he studied administrative law with Felix Frankfurter. Through Frankfurter's influence he became a law clerk for Supreme Court Justice Benjamin Cardozo in 1935. The position took him to Washington, D.C., where he has worked ever since.

While employed by Cardozo, he also served as enforcement attorney for the U.S. Wage and Hour Administration

and afterward helped with the Federal Communications Commission's investigation into monopoly practices in the radio broadcast industry. It was the heyday of the Roosevelt New Deal, and after Cardozo died in 1938 and Frankfurter was named to the Supreme Court (he clerked for him, too, from 1938 to 1939), Rauh began counseling regulatory agencies (1939–42), among them the Lend-Lease Administration.

He enlisted in the Army and served from 1942 to 1945, first assigned to General Douglas MacArthur's staff, and then, from 1943 to 1945, working in the civil affairs department of the U.S. Pacific Command. Once the war ended Rauh returned to Washington and in 1946 was general deputy housing expediter of the Veterans' Emergency Housing Program. That year he also helped found the liberal, anti-Communist Americans for Democratic Action. It was designed to counter the Progressive Party (backed by the Communist Party) presidential candidate Henry A. Wallace and the conservative Republican candidate Thomas E. Dewey. He served as the chairman of ADA's executive committee from 1947 to 1952. In 1948 he was a delegate to the Democratic National Convention and was a prime mover in placing a civil rights plank in the party's platform.

Since 1947 Rauh has been a senior partner in the Washington firm Rauh & Levy. Opposed to the Smith Act and the McCarran Internal Security Act—which on the one hand made membership in the Communist Party illegal, yet on the other hand made it compulsory to report membership in that party—Rauh defended many clients charged with Communist affiliation at loyalty hearings and in passport refusal cases. In 1957 he successfully represented Arthur Miller, who was on trial for contempt of Congress because of his refusal, at a hearing of the House Un-American Activities Committee the previous year, to name fellow writers he believed to be Communists.

As attorney for the United Auto Workers, Rauh won a spectacular victory in 1957, when a federal court jury found the UAW not guilty of violating the Corrupt Practices Act in 1954 when it presented nine Democratic candidates on its weekly television program in Detroit.

Rauh's lobbying for the civil rights bills of 1957 and 1964 have made him famous in Washington. At the 1964 Democratic National Convention, at which he was a delegate, he fought for the seating of the black delegates of the Mississippi Freedom party at the risk of alienating the rest of the South. In his acceptance of the Florence Lasker Award from the New York Civil Liberties Union in 1965, Rauh charged J. Edgar Hoover, director of the Federal Bureau of Investigation, with showing a "lack of determination" regarding the enforcement of civil rights laws.

Almost from the start of United States intervention in Southeast Asia, Rauh was in the ranks of the opposition. As early as 1965, following the commitment of massive numbers of American troops to an Asian land war, Rauh helped form Negotiations Now, one of the first anti-war groups. Three years later he backed anti-war Senator Eugene McCarthy's bid for the Democratic presidential nomination, opposing the Democratic incumbent President Lyndon B. Johnson.

From 1968 on he was also extremely active as the lawyer for civil rights plaintiffs, suing the United States Department of Justice and the Department of Health, Education and Welfare for not acting swiftly enough to desegregate public schools. He actively and successfully opposed President Nixon's nomination of a southerner he considered a segregationist to the Supreme Court. And in 1971 he declared against Nixon's choice of William Rehnquist for the Supreme Court because of his lack of enthusiasm for school desegregation in Phoenix, Arizona and his membership in the John Birch Society. He also served as a counsel for the defense (the school) in the Bakke case in 1978, in which a white medical student at the University of California at Davis Medical School sued because he believed he was a victim of "reverse" discrimination. The student, Bakke, was admitted when the Supreme Court struck down the quota scheme and held that race may only be one factor among many, in the interests of diversity, for admission into Davis's medical school.

In late 1981 *The New York Times* published an article stating that younger lawyers no longer had the wish to "do good deeds and reform society." Rauh bristled at the statement and denied its validity. Calling himself a "public interest lawyer," he wrote a letter to *The New York Times* complaining of "the Reagan Administration's budget cuts for legal services for the poor. . . ." He bemoaned the lack of public interest jobs for young and idealistic attorneys. Many younger lawyers do indeed want to "practice their idealism," he wrote, just as he has done for nearly four decades.

DIANE RAVITCH

b. July 1, 1938
Educational historian

Diane Ravitch's long and steady career as an educational historian has made her one of America's experts on the phenomenon of the American school. Two books

and dozens of articles and speeches attest to her commitment. Her membership on many panels and task forces only underscores the fact that hers is more than a purely academic perspective.

Diane Silvers was born in Houston, Texas to Walter and Ann (Katz) Silvers. Her parents operated a small liquor store. She received a B.A. degree from Wellesley College in 1960 and a Ph.D. in the history of education from Columbia University Graduate School of Arts and Sciences in 1975.

In the late 1960s and early 1970s, she published her first reviews on education. They mainly examined experimental programs and the quandaries experienced in troubled urban schools. Her articles and reviews appeared in *The New York Times, Commentary, The New Leader, Change* and major educational journals.

Ravitch's first book, *The Great School Wars: New York City, 1805-1973—A History of the Public Schools as Battlefield of Social Change* (New York, 1974), received wide critical acclaim. More than a history, it also examined political influences on the educational system, racial and religious issues within the schools and early experiments with progressive approaches in the late 1960s and early 1970s. It stressed the limits of school reform, given the limits in the larger society.

Her second book, *The Revisionists Revised* (New York, 1978), is a series of essays analyzing 10 major works on progressive education and scrutinizing their effectiveness, often critically, because they attacked the liberalism that, she writes, helped shape American history and social reform. The book sought to illustrate that current problems are a replay of earlier problems—schools have always contended with large numbers of poor immigrant children, she argues, and decentralization and community control have been tried before, with little success.

Ravitch worked directly with the Carnegie Corporation in 1968 to evaluate two New York City school districts that got funding from the Ford Foundation—P.S. 201 in East Harlem and Ocean-Hill Brownsville—and she observed closely and critically the process and effect of decentralization in these districts, which led directly to the New York City teachers' strike in the fall of that year.

In general, her educational views coincide with the philosophies of those critics who questioned what she perceives as the "anything goes" attitudes of the 1960s and 1970s. She believes that the "upward mobility" that education made possible for her own generation still exists today without extensive supplementary "enrichment" programs.

Ravitch is presently adjunct associate professor of history and education at Teachers College, Columbia

University. Her participation in educational and civic associations includes trusteeships at the Museum of American Folk Art, the Field Foundation and the New York Public Library; directorship of the Institute of Educational Affairs; and memberships in the American Historical Association, the History of Education Society, the National Academy of Education Panel on the Value Assumptions Underlying Educational Policies and Practices, and the Cleveland Conference. She is also on the board of editors of *Character.*

Ravitch, whose husband, Richard Ravitch, is a prominent civic leader and builder, lives in New York City.

RICHARD RAVITCH

b. July 7, 1933
Builder; civic leader

One of the most prominent "movers and shakers" in New York City has been Richard Ravitch. Although a successful private businessman, he has participated actively in the operations of several New York city and state agencies as well as many Jewish and civil rights organizations. His most recent challenge is as the unpaid chairman of the Metropolitan Transportation Authority (MTA). In this role, which he assumed in October 1979, he supervises the operations of commuter lines carrying millions of passengers throughout the New York metropolitan area and within New York City and is trying to unravel and effectively manage a system fraught with very serious and enormously complex problems.

Richard Ravitch was born in New York City to Saul and Sylvia (Lerner) Ravitch. His grandfather, Joseph Ravitch, immigrated to the United States from Russia as a young boy in 1888. Starting out as a laborer, he was later the founder of HRH Construction Company, a huge firm that was responsible for building many important and beautiful apartment and office complexes, including the San Remo Apartments and the Beresford on Central Park West. Both of Ravitch's parents were college graduates—a rarity at the time—and he grew up steeped in political idealism: He admired Franklin Delano Roosevelt and Adlai Stevenson.

Ravitch graduated from Columbia College with a B.A. degree in 1955 and from Yale Law School in 1958. He served briefly as counsel to the military operations subcommittee of the government operations committee in the House of Representatives. In 1960 he joined the family business.

Although he remained with HRH and is currently president and chairman of the City Development Corporation, Ravitch is widely known for his public service. In the past he has been chairman of the New York State Urban Development Corporation and the New York City Economic Development Board; president of the Citizens Housing and Planning Council of New York; director of the Citizens Union of the City of New York, the New York City Municipal Assistance Corporation and the National Committee Against Discrimination in Housing; and a member of the National Commission on Urban Problems and the New York Urban Design Council.

Ravitch's past Jewish affiliations are as president of the Jewish Community Relations Council of New York and as vice president of both the American Jewish Congress and the Federation of Jewish Philanthropies.

When he came to the MTA, Ravitch inherited a system that was terribly outdated and in poor condition. Its unions were continually pushing for higher salaries, the quality of its management was less than satisfactory and at the same time rampant vandalism and crime were adding to the deterioration of the system, decreased ridership and higher maintenance costs. To keep the system running, Ravitch was forced to seek new means of raising revenues, which included fare increases and new taxes, difficult moves that he claimed were necessary. He considered other strategies, such as closing some subway stations and possibly curbing hours of operation. He also demanded greater productivity from transit workers but met stiff resistance from union leaders. Ravitch insists that fare increases can only maintain the system as it is and that the trend of the Reagan administration toward withholding subsidies to mass transit is adding to the burden of the MTA. He adds that mass transit systems in many large cities are suffering the same problems.

At present, in addition to his chairmanship of the MTA, Ravitch is a trustee of Teachers College of Columbia University, WNET/Thirteen and the Central Synagogue; director of the A. Philip Randolph Institute and of the Recruitment and Training Program Inc. These two latter organizations, both New York City-based, help to bring racial minorities into the construction industry. Ravitch also lectures at the Columbia University School of Law.

Ravitch has received many awards and citations. These include the Distinguished Service Citation from the City of New York (1973); a Special Award from the Citizens Housing and Planning Council of New York (1975); Man of the Year from the Jewish Guild for the

Blind, the New York University Urban Leadership Award and the Fiorello H. LaGuardia Award (all in 1976); and many others.

Ravitch's wife, Diane, is a noted educational historian.

LEWIS REGENSTEIN

b. February 23, 1943
Conservationist

Lewis Regenstein, the highest professional officer of the Fund for Animals, a major national organization that works to preserve wildlife and save endangered species, is also extremely active in efforts to avert the chemical destruction of the environment.

Lewis Graham Regenstein was born in Atlanta, Georgia to Louis Jr., an attorney, and Helen Lucile (Moses) Regenstein. He graduated from Westminster High School in 1961 and went on to earn his B.A. degree in political science at the University of Pennsylvania in 1965 and his M.A. degree in political science at Emory University in 1975.

Following receipt of his undergraduate degree, Regenstein worked from 1966 to 1971 as an intelligence officer and analyst at the Central Intelligence Agency in Washington, D.C. There he was involved in collecting, analyzing and reporting foreign intelligence data to the intelligence community, concentrating largely on China. He also worked on resettling defectors and other foreign nationals brought to the United States for national security purposes. In three and a half years at the CIA, he was promoted five times.

When he left the CIA, he began writing articles on the environment in leading newspapers, such as *The New York Times, Washington Post, Los Angeles Times* and *Philadelphia Inquirer*, beginning in 1971. In 1973, acting perhaps on the Judaic mandate of *tsa'ar ba'alei chayim*, in which individuals must show compassion to all animals, he became wildlife editor of the now-defunct *Environmental Quality* magazine. Almost simultaneously, from 1972 on, he has been vice president of the Fund for Animals and between 1979 and 1981 served as president of The Monitor Consortium, a coalition of 35 national conservation, environmental and animal protection groups that attempt to lobby Congress and the executive branch.

Much of Regenstein's work is political, performed among the politicians and their staffs in Washington, D.C. He is also a strong believer in using the media to bring to the attention of millions of readers and viewers the many wildlife problems. Thus, he was extremely active in 1971-72 in lobbying and writing on behalf of the Marine Mammal Act, a landmark bill, and the Endangered Species Act. Considering that until Regenstein and others opened Washington offices and took up the struggle for voiceless animals no effective federal laws existed to protect wildlife and that today the situation is quite reversed, there have indeed been many success stories. Typical of his approach, for example, was the struggle to preserve the bowhead whale in 1979 and to have the International Whaling Commission ban or severely limit the kills permitted. Through Regenstein's writing in the *Washington Post*, appearing on Capitol Hill and joining with The Monitor Consortium, the bowhead whale was saved from extinction.

In *The Politics of Extinction: The Shocking Story of the World's Endangered Wildlife* (New York, 1975), Regenstein outlines his philosophy:

> Unfortunately, protecting animals seems to be a matter of politics; situations are decided not on their merits, but on the amount of power each side can bring to bear on the decision makers. The campaign to save the ocean mammals shows that informed public pressure, if steady and strong enough, can overcome commercial and other vested-interest groups, which normally work quietly behind the scenes to kill or cripple efforts of this sort.

His book, which details how the Marine Mammal Protection Act of 1972 was enacted, is also an expose, and it tells about those inside and outside the government who are eliminating wildlife and why.

Continuing in this vein, Regenstein wrote *America the Poisoned: How Deadly Chemicals Are Destroying Our Environment, Our Wildlife—And Ourselves* (Washington, D.C., 1982), in which he continues to press his grim thesis that special interests—such as industry and its political allies—plus poorly fashioned laws, conflicts-of-interest and lax enforcement make governmental regulation next to impossible and are continually threatening our wolves, grizzly bears, prairie dogs, wild horses, cougars and other animals. "The world," he has written, "need not, and cannot afford to, lose any more species. Yet, the present situation is more critical than at any other period in recorded history; we are on the verge of losing forever most if not all of our wildlife." Then, too, his book discusses such examples of environmental menaces as Love Canal; dangerous, carcinogenic pesticides; ground water contamination; and the like.

CARL REINER

b. March 20, 1922
Actor; author; producer; director

Being a "career second banana" has not been a problem for Carl Reiner. In fact, it has been the key to his success. As a comedy writer for television and as an actor, director and producer, he has often had to yield center stage for someone else to read the lines Reiner wrote.

Carl Reiner was born to Irving, a watchmaker, and Bessie (Mathias) Reiner in the Bronx. Following graduation from Evander Childs High School in 1938 and a brief stint as a shipping clerk, he entered the Army in 1942, where he performed in various G.I. comedy revues. These led directly to a number of postwar acting jobs. The first one, in 1946, was in the road company of *Call Me Mister*, a variety revue like the shows of his Army days. Next he appeared on Broadway in *Inside U.S.A.* (1948), a potpourri of songs and skits based on John Gunther's book about America. He got his first television role in 1948—just as television was starting out—as a fashion photographer in the ABC series *Fashion Story*. His next Broadway role was in 1950 in another revue called *Alive and Kicking*. Through its producer-director, Max Liebman, Reiner was invited to work with Sid Caesar on NBC's *Your Show of Shows*, which was to become a milestone in Reiner's career. He joined Sid Caesar in 1950 and moved to Hollywood with the show in 1952. He has been part of the Hollywood comedy community ever since. Starting as a writer and performer on *Your Show of Shows*, Reiner has gone on to become a writer, director and producer in his own right of major feature film comedies.

Reiner's association with Caesar lasted eight years—until 1954 as writer-performer on *Your Show of Shows* and on a slightly revised *Caesar's Hour* from 1954 to 1958. He was emcee for a short-lived quiz show, *Keep Talking* (1958–59), and a writer for *The Dinah Shore Show* in 1960.

Reiner truly came into his own, however, as the producer-writer for *The Dick Van Dyke Show* on CBS and a later version, *The New Dick Van Dyke Show*. Here, using his own life as a model, he designed a program about a suburban family where the father commutes to New York City to write comedy while the wife and child experience the ups, downs and assorted tribulations and growing pains of the typical family of the era. Although Reiner originally hoped to star (the original title was "Head of the Family"), the role of Rob Petrie was assumed by Dick Van Dyke; Mary Tyler Moore got her first big break as Rob's wife, Laura. The show, which first aired in 1960, was a phenomenal success and ran through 1973, when Reiner quit in protest because CBS refused to air an episode it considered controversial. In question was a scene in which the Petrie's son stumbled into his parents' bedroom while they were making love. Although the subject was treated with sensitivity, the mores of the early 1970s made it taboo for TV.

Throughout his career Reiner often strayed from television. As a member of a transplanted community of comedy writers in Hollywood, mostly Jews from New York, he turned to his youth and his early associations for material. He published the autobiographical novel *Enter Laughing* (New York, 1958), which told the story of a Jewish adolescent working as a shipping clerk; he really wants to be an actor, and, despite the discouragement of everyone around him, eventually follows his "muse" and becomes one. It was adapted as a play by Joseph Stein and opened on Broadway in March 1963 with the young actor Alan Arkin in the starring role. It became a film in 1967 (which Reiner directed) and starred Elaine May, with Reni Santoni in the Arkin part.

In the early 1960s Reiner formed a comic duo with Mel Brooks. Reiner was the straight man—the "second banana" again—while Brooks became the 2000-year-old man, a fellow with an accent remarkably Yiddish, who had miraculously survived hundreds of marriages, thousands of children and dozens of catastrophes en route. Together, they made three records: *The 2000-Year-Old Man* (1960), *The 2001-Year-Old Man* (1961) and *The 2013-Year-Old Man* (1973).

In recent years Reiner has concentrated on directing films and plays and occasionally acting. His most notable role was in *The Russians Are Coming, The Russians Are Coming* (1966) as a resident in a quiet New England town invaded by a troop of lost Russian sailors. He also appeared in *The End* (1978), which starred Burt Reynolds. In 1967 he wrote a play, *Something Different*, which opened on Broadway to lackluster reviews. It dealt with a once-successful playwright and his writer's block. To overcome the handicap, the protagonist recreates his mother's slum tenement kitchen—complete with cockroaches—in the den of his affluent, Tudor-style home. His endeavors in film directing have been more successful. They include *The Comic* (1969), with Dick Van Dyke; *Where's Poppa?* (1971), starring Ruth Gordon and George Segal; *Oh, God!* (1977), with George Burns in the title role; *The One and Only* (1978), featuring Henry Winkler; and *The Jerk* (1979), a farce with comedian Steve Martin starring as the son of southern black sharecroppers. In 1980 he directed a Broadway play, *The Roast,* a satire on the tradition among comedians of parodying each other from time to time at special ceremonial dinners. Unfortunately, the play, co-written by television writers Jerry Belson and Garry Marshall, was not well received by Broadway critics and closed after a short run.

Reiner, the father of actor Rob Reiner, has received many Emmys for his work in television.

ABRAHAM ALEXANDER RIBICOFF

b. April 9, 1910
Politician; attorney

A long-time power in Connecticut and United States politics, liberal in outlook, state legislator, congressman, governor, senator and cabinet member—Abraham A. Ribicoff remains a model for progressive and pragmatic politicians.

Abraham Alexander Ribicoff was born in New Britain, Connecticut to Samuel, a poverty-stricken Orthodox immigrant bread peddler and factory worker, and Rose (Sable) Ribicoff. He worked his way through school as a newspaper boy, milkman's aide, gasoline station filling attendant, construction laborer and then in 1927 went to work in the zipper factory of G.E. Prentice in New Britain. In 1928 he enrolled at New York University but left the following year to become head of Prentice's Chicago office, at the same time taking night classes at the University of Chicago. Although he never received a bachelor's degree, Chicago permitted him to attend its law school and he earned his Bachelor of Laws degree in 1933.

In 1938, after several years of practicing law in Hartford, Connecticut, he moved into local politics at the behest of Connecticut Democratic Party leader John Bailey, who saw in Ribicoff a potentially successful challenger to Republicans in the State Legislature. Within a few years the *Hartford Courant* described him as the state's "most able legislator." Afterward, he became a Hartford Police Court judge and then Connecticut's fair employment practices commissioner. In 1948, with Bailey's strong support, he was elected for the first of two terms as Hartford's congressman. Running for the Senate in 1952, he was defeated, but he outpolled Democratic presidential candidate Adlai E. Stevenson by nearly 100,000 votes. Two years later he was elected governor —the first Jewish governor in New England—by a margin of only 3,000 votes. During that campaign he was faced with growing objections to his Jewishness throughout the state. An adept performer before televi-

sion cameras, Ribicoff confronted his challengers. "Any boy regardless of race, creed or color, has the right to aspire to public office," he declared. "Abe Ribicoff is not here to repudiate the American dream. Abe Ribicoff believes in that American dream, and I know that the American dream can come true." It did for him; in 1958 he ran for reelection and won by 250,000 votes.

In 1960 Ribicoff interrupted his governorship when he was named secretary of Health, Education and Welfare by President John F. Kennedy, with whom he had developed a close friendship while in Congress and whom he later supported very early on in his race for the Democratic presidential nomination. Ribicoff spent just a year at HEW—it was the only job he admits having regretted taking because of what he describes as "politically unpopular" decisions he had to make. In one case Ribicoff drafted the original Medicare plan, which was defeated after intense lobbying by the American Medical Association. In 1962 he ran successfully for the U.S. Senate.

Backed by Hartford's Jewish community, Ribicoff has always been a practical liberal, supporting the death penalty and L. Patrick Gray's ill-fated leadership of the Federal Bureau of Investigation. But he wrote the Clean Air Act of 1963, conducted the Senate's earliest automobile safety hearings, and favored Medicare and mental health laws for the young. He fought for jobs for black residents of America's forgotten ghetto neighborhoods yet lent support to the so-called Rap Brown Anti-Riot Act. The novelist Norman Mailer once described Ribicoff and others like him as people who practice a "kind of calculation which does not take large chances," a characterization that infuriated Ribicoff. In 1968, at the embattled Democratic Party Convention in Chicago, where pro- and anti-Vietnam War delegates and demonstrators fought one another in the convention hall and in the streets, Ribicoff nominated Senator George McGovern for the presidency and then, leaning over the rostrum and peering directly at Chicago Mayor Richard Daley, whose police had attacked anti-war protesters, said: "With George McGovern as president of the United States we wouldn't need police using Gestapo tactics in the streets of Chicago. With George McGovern, we wouldn't need the National Guard." That November, Ribicoff was reelected to the Senate.

In the Senate he never departed from his pro-Israel stance. He backed arms sales to Israel; opposed efforts to force it to return captured Arab territories; co-sponsored the Jackson Amendment, which refused most favored nation status to the Soviet Union unless it relaxed its ban against Jews seeking to depart for Israel; and lent his name to anti-Arab boycott legislation.

In 1971 Ribicoff had a now-famous standoff with the only other Jewish senator, Jacob Javits, when he supported extending school desegregation legislation to the North and charged Javits with "hypocrisy," saying, "I don't think you have the guts to face your liberal constituents who have moved to the suburbs to avoid sending their children to school with blacks." Ribicoff's willingness to provoke this controversy reflects his consistent liberalism as well as his astute ability to form unlikely alliances; his partnership with southern Senator John Stennis at the time enabled him to secure a much-sought-after post on the Senate Finance Committee.

In January 1981 Ribicoff retired from the Senate after 40 years in public life and joined the New York law firm of Kaye, Scholer, Fierman, Hays & Handler, where he specializes in international trade and transportation.

HYMAN RICKOVER

b. January 27, 1900
Naval officer

Until his forced retirement in 1982, Admiral Hyman Rickover *was* the U.S. Navy and was responsible for bringing it into the nuclear age. He supervised the development of the first atomic submarine and for many years strove to upgrade the educational training programs of naval scientists and technicians. In later years he became a fixture in the Navy and yet grew increasingly estranged from its leadership.

Hyman George Rickover was born in Russia to Abraham, a tailor, and Rachel (Unger) Rickover. His family emigrated to the United States when Rickover was quite young and settled in Chicago. After graduating from John Marshall High School, Rickover was appointed to the U.S. Naval Academy in 1918—where he was often victimized by anti-Semitism—and in 1922 was commissioned an ensign.

After serving on the U.S.S. *Lavallette* and the U.S.S. *Nevada* for five years, Rickover returned to Annapolis to do graduate work in electrical engineering. Continuing at Columbia University, he received an M.S. degree in 1929. He then studied submarine science in 1930 at the submarine base in New London, Connecticut. Several land assignments were followed by a return to sea duty in 1935, and two years later Rickover received his first command post, aboard the U.S.S. *Finch* in the Philippines. In 1939 he returned to the United States to the Bureau of Ships in Washington and headed the Electrical Section during World War II.

Rickover gradually rose through the Navy ranks, in position and in influence. By mid-1945, after serving briefly on the commanding staff of the U.S. Pacific Fleet, he became industrial manager at Okinawa and was named commanding officer of the Naval Repair Base there. Later that year he became inspector general of the San Francisco-based 19th Fleet and, shortly after, received an assignment through the Atomic Energy Commission to work on the Manhattan Project at Oak Ridge, Tennessee, in which he participated in the development of the atomic bomb. His experience there fueled his belief that a nuclear-powered submarine could be built, and he prepared designs for one.

Despite resistance from his superiors, Rickover convinced officials at the AEC of the viability of an atomic sub and, by finagling an assignment to the AEC as head of its Naval Reactors Branch, was able to begin the project anyway. He recruited a staff that included civilians from university and industry and set up a three-year course at the Massachusetts Institute of Technology devoted to atomic submarine technology. Rickover's success at pushing through what was justifiably considered to be a risky, hugely expensive and unwieldy project, reflected an insuperable will, which some government officials found intolerable.

Rickover's plans for the nuclear sub, to be named *Nautilus,* called for expenditures of more than $40 million. To save time, the reactor was built separately in Idaho while the submarine construction took place at the Electric Boat Company in Groton, Connecticut. When the Nautilus was well under way, Rickover began designing a second nuclear sub as well as a nuclear aircraft carrier and a related project. But these never got off the drawing board, as controversy concerning his naval status created an uproar in Congress.

Rickover had been passed over for promotion to admiral, and naval codes required retirement if this occurred twice. Congressional leaders suspected that Rickover's superiors had deliberately failed to promote him, and after an investigation into the matter, he was named rear admiral in 1953.

As a permanent fixture in the Navy, Rickover became an outspoken critic of the institution and of other aspects of American life, most notably its educational system. Comparing American schools unfavorably with British schools, he wrote a blistering attack on American education and offered proposals for reform in *Education and Freedom* (1959). In 1962 he was consulted by an appropriations committee in Congress for his ideas on how educational expenditures should be made. During the administration of President Johnson, Rickover spoke out strongly against tying the military with big business, since he felt that business involvement would inevitably compromise the quality of military development. His critique of the military-industrial complex, later shared by many liberal politicians (some of Rickover's enemies intimated that the admiral might secretly be a Communist), carried over with increasing fervor into subsequent presidential administrations.

Rickover is frequently credited with having been the mentor of President Jimmy Carter, who was a graduate of Annapolis with training in nuclear engineering. When President Reagan was elected, Rickover wasted no time in lambasting what he regarded as the administration's huge and wasteful defense budget. In 1982 he was forced into ungracious retirement, although he retained a lifelong reputation for being cantankerous and testy.

At his departure he had the last word on his views on nuclear power. He admitted his regrets for the role he had played in nuclear proliferation and called for an international agreement outlawing nuclear weapons and reactors because of the radiation hazards they pose. But Rickover is not optimistic about the prospects for peace and foresees that humankind "will probably destroy itself and be replaced by a wiser species."

For further information:

Polmar, Norman, and Allen, Thomas B. *Rickover*. New York: 1982.

SIMON H. RIFKIND

b. June 5, 1901
Attorney; jurist

Simon H. Rifkind is an attorney and jurist who has had a long and distinguished career devoted to public service and civil liberties as well as to a wide range of Jewish causes.

Simon H. Rifkind was born in Meretz, Russia, the son of Jacob, a merchant, and Cecelia (Bluestone) Rifkind. He came to the United States with his family in 1910 and was naturalized in 1924. He earned his B.S. degree from City College of New York in 1922 and his Bachelor of Laws from Columbia University in 1925.

Rifkind's varied career began when he served as Senator Robert F. Wagner's legislative secretary from 1927 to 1933. In 1930 he began practicing law as a partner with the firm of Wagner, Quillinan and Rifkind until 1941, when he was appointed United States district judge of the Southern District of New York by President Roosevelt. In 1950 he resigned to return to private practice as a partner with the prestigious firm of Paul,

Weiss, Rifkind, Wharton and Garrison, whose members have included Theodore Sorenson and Morris Abram. Concurrently he was a partner in the Chicago firm of Stevenson, Rifkind and Wirtz from 1957 to 1961. He was admitted to the New York bar in 1926 and to the Illinois bar in 1961.

His pamphlet *Reflections on Civil Liberties* (New York, 1954), issued in the midst of "subversive"-hunting congressional committees' running amok, stressed instead that congressional committees were not designed to enact laws or to serve as courts of law.

A lifelong Democrat, Rifkind has had an extensive public service record. He acted from 1955 to 1961 as special master for the United States Supreme Court in a case involving the Colorado River. He has also been involved in work on administrative commissions and on quasi-judicial fact-finding bodies. He was on the New York City Board of Higher Education from 1954 to 1966 and the New York Commission on City Government Operations from 1959 to 1961. Rifkind was appointed chairperson in 1961–62 of the Presidential Railroad Commission by President John F. Kennedy, participated in the 1963 New York teachers' strike talks, served as counsel to New York state Democrats in reapportionment litigation in 1965–66 and sat on the Cox Commission that investigated the 1968 Columbia University student strike.

Rifkind's professional involvement with Jewish concerns began in 1945–46, when he was temporary special adviser on Jewish affairs to General Dwight D. Eisenhower to explore and analyze the problems of the disrupted European Jewish community. In 1946 he testified before the Anglo-American Commission of Inquiry on Palestine, stating his strong conviction that the only solution to the problem of Jewish displaced persons would be to open Palestine as a safe place of settlement.

Since 1975 Rifkind has been chairperson of the Revson Foundation, which, under the leadership of Eli Evans, embarked on studies of the relations of Jews and other ethnic groups with the black community and other aspects of the immigrant-ethnic experience in America. In 1982 it financed a PBS-TV series on *Jewish Civilization*, with Abba Eban as narrator.

He has also been involved with other Jewish organizations. He joined the board of directors of the Jewish Theological Seminary in 1947 and has since been chairman of the board (1963–67) and is now honorary chairman. He has served as administrative board chairman (1953–56) and executive board chairman (1956–59) of the American Jewish Committee and since 1972 has been on the board of directors of New York City's Beth Israel Medical Center.

Rifkind's many awards and honorary degrees include a U.S. Medal of Freedom (1945) and the Louis Dembitz Brandeis Medal for Distinguished Legal Services from Brandeis University in 1980.

DAVID RIESMAN

b. September 9, 1909
Sociologist; lawyer

With the publication of his 1950 masterwork and popular best seller *The Lonely Crowd* (New York), sociologist David Riesman established himself as one of the most important interpreters of the American character and of the motivating forces that have shaped it. Now a professor emeritus at Harvard University, Riesman has since become highly regarded for his studies of the role of higher education in America, including changing academic values and proposals for school reform.

David Riesman Jr. was born in Philadelphia to David, a physician, and Eleanor (Fleisher) Riesman. His father had emigrated to the United States from Germany and in 1892 received his M.D. from the University of Pennsylvania, where he subsequently practiced medicine and taught. Riesman attended the William Penn Charter School in Philadelphia, graduating in 1926, and Harvard University, where he majored in biochemistry and was assistant managing editor of the *Harvard Crimson.* Graduating in 1931 with a Bachelor of Arts degree Phi Beta Kappa, Riesman entered the Harvard Law School and received his Bachelor of Laws in 1934. He remained at Harvard for an additional year on fellowship and then from 1935 to 1936 was clerk to Associate U.S. Supreme Court Justice Louis Brandeis. He returned to Boston and practiced law privately for about a year.

From 1937 to 1941 Riesman was professor of law at the University of Buffalo. Concurrently he was executive secretary of the American Committee for the Guidance of Professional Personnel, an organization formed to assist war refugees in the professions upon their arrival in the United States. Riesman spent 1941 at the Columbia University Law School as a visiting research fellow and from 1942 to 1943 was deputy assistant district attorney for New York County. From 1943 to 1946, during World War II, he did legal work for the Sperry Gyroscope Corporation in Lake Success, New York. In 1946 he joined the faculty of the University of Chicago as visiting associate professor of social sciences. He became a full professor in 1949.

In 1948 Riesman took a leave of absence from Chicago to direct a research project for the Yale University Committee on National Policy. Its purpose was to explore the evolving nature of the American persona in the wake of the war and in view of social changes that affected the role of individuals within their families and their communities. Collaborating with scholars Reuel Denny and Nathan Glazer, Riesman was the principal author of the book resulting from the study, *The Lonely Crowd: A Study of the Changing American Character.* The book identified three periods in the evolution of a society and the qualities of the people living during them. Periods of high population growth potential characterized areas that were not yet industrialized and were populated by what Riesman called "tradition-directed" people, whose lifestyles were based on long-lasting and little-changed standards and styles. People growing up in periods of transitional population growth (Riesman's example was the Renaissance-Reformation period) were labeled "inner-directed," which means that they strove to fulfill goals decided early in their lives by their elders. Although there was more individuality in the inner-directed person than in the tradition-directed person, the goals he or she chose still originated from the immediate environment. The third period was characterized by incipient population decline—contemporary industrialized areas—and the people were what Riesman called "other-directed" because they drew on outside peer groups for direction.

But Riesman's study was far more complex than the above description, for it attempted to place into perspective the role of history, technology, economy and other factors in shaping the American character. Since nothing of this scope had ever been attempted before, it laid the groundwork for further close examination of the American people. The book itself became a permanent campus classic.

In 1952 Riesman followed up with *Faces in the Crowd* (New Haven), a series of interviews with a wide range of American "types," including housewives, students and others, to give some credence to his theories of two years earlier.

Riesman joined the Harvard faculty in 1958 as Henry Ford II Professor of Social Sciences and specialized in studying the impact of higher education in America. He sympathized with student struggles in the 1960s for more openness on campus and more self-determination in their course of studies. But he was upset by the violent evolution of some of the student movements of the late 1960s and began to espouse a return to more traditional values. By 1981 Riesman favored a return to the military draft.

Riesman is nonetheless firmly committed to the women's movements—the plural is deliberate—which he called in a 1980 interview "the most important of my time." Although he opposed the Equal Rights Amendment, which he called self-defeating from his standpoint as a constitutional lawyer, he contends nevertheless that he has seen an "enormous widening of career opportunities for women" and has always supported their branching into fields once almost exclusively male-dominated, such as the sciences and engineering. To that end, Riesman has been a firm supporter of single-sex higher education because he feels women in such schools receive more encouragement to pursue nontraditional specialties without male competition or discouragement.

In 1980 Riesman received the de Tocqueville Literary Prize from the French Academy. Only the second recipient of the annual prize, Riesman was selected because his work represents the highest traditions of the 19th-century French statesman and philosopher after whom the prize is named.

For further information:

Riesman, David. *Abundance for What? and Other Essays.* 1963.

———. *Academic Values and Mass Education: The Early Years of Oakland and Monteith.* 1970.

———. *Constraint and Variety in American Education.* 1956.

———. *Individualism Reconsidered and Other Essays.* 1954.

———. *On Competence: A Critical Analysis of Competence-Based Reforms in Higher Education.* 1979.

———. *The Perpetual Dream: Experiment and Reform in the American College.* 1978.

———. *Thorstein Veblen.* 1953.

Riesman, David, and Jenks, Christopher. *The Academic Revolution.* 1968.

Riesman, David, and Lipset, Seymour M. *Education and Politics at Harvard.* 1975.

Riesman, David, and Riesman, Evelyn Thompson. *Conversations in Japan: Modernization, Politics and Culture.* 1967.

Riesman, David and Stadtman, Verne, eds. *Academic Transformation.* 1973.

SHLOMO RISKIN

b. May 28, 1940
Rabbi

Beginning in the early 1960s, a young rabbi single-handedly turned a small, once-a-year Conservative New York City congregation into the thriving Orthodox Lincoln Square Synagogue. The rabbi, Shlomo Riskin, has since become one of America's leaders in religious education for young people and in the return to active participation in observant Jewish life of hundreds of individuals and families.

Steven Riskin was born in the Bedford-Stuyvesant section of Brooklyn. His parents, Harry and Rose (Walter) Riskin, like many of the congregants he would later work with, were nominally observant, and as a youth Riskin had little contact with Jewish life. But, influenced by his devout grandparents, he began to attend services regularly and became a student at a yeshiva, where his first ideas on a contemporary Orthodoxy began to form. By age 12 he was completely observant. By 16 he dedicated an entire summer to reading the transcripts of the Nuremberg Trials. He was also fascinated by the philosopher Martin Buber while still very young, although not uncritically. "Buber gave us a theology, but not a life style," he said.

In 1960 Riskin graduated from Yeshiva University with a B.A. degree summa cum laude in classics and English literature. He was class valedictorian and had been an active debater as well as editor of the Yeshiva student newspaper. He then studied for the rabbinate at Rabbi Isaac Elchanan Theological Seminary of Yeshiva and was ordained in 1963. In 1970 he earned an M.A. degree from the Bernard Revel Graduate School of Yeshiva University and soon after became chairman of the governing board of the Center for Russian Jewry in the Student Struggle for Soviet Jewry.

The year of Riskin's ordination was pivotal to his career. In 1963 Yeshiva was approached by a small congregation on Manhattan's Upper West Side seeking a spiritual leader. Until then its members had met annually in a rented space for the High Holy Days. Riskin was recommended, and at age 23 he agreed to take on the job only if he could conduct weekly services and a class in Jewish law and offer extensive adult education classes to the congregation, and if he would not be required to pray with them since men and women sat together. In addition, the group was asked to drop "Conservative" from its name. Hence was born the Lincoln Square Synagogue.

Riskin's presence spelled the beginning of a new revival of faith in the congregation. His thorough scholarship and his total dedication to Jewish teaching, combined with a personal charisma, resulted in the growth of Lincoln Square from a dozen or so families and individuals to several thousand. In 1966 a synagogue building was dedicated, and in the years that followed, Riskin spearheaded the establishment of two Hebrew high schools in Riverdale, New York, one for boys (1974) and one for girls (1976); the creation of a comprehensive offering of adult education courses—the Joseph Shapiro Institute was opened in 1966—which are known to be packed with people of all ages; an outreach program to attract curious but non-observant Jews to the synagogue; and a variety of other programs concerned with *aliyah*—immigration to Israel—(he has helped found a settlement, named Efrat, in 1980 in the Gush Etzion belt south of Jerusalem); interpretation of Jewish law in family life and political involvement in issues relating to the defense of Israel, freedom for Soviet Jews and related causes.

Controversial at times—many women active in progressive Jewish movements are disturbed by what they call Riskin's evasive and traditionalist approach to the role of women in and out of the synagogue—he has nevertheless remained one of the foremost advocates of the preservation and growth of Jewish family life in America and abroad.

Riskin sees as his mission the bridging of the gap between Orthodox Judaism and the modern world. "There are two types of Jews," he says, "the religious and the not-yet-réligious." And in fact he sees his function in terms of attracting people to religion and not in counseling them, once they have become religious, to remain so. All his methods are geared merely toward giving them the first taste.

He stresses the importance of law for the sustenance of a world of love by quoting the rabbinic tale of the doves who complained to God about the weight of their wings until they learned that it was their wings that permitted them to fly. Yet, though inherently traditional and committed to Jewish law, Riskin understands the moderating function of Conservatism and Reform within Judaism: "If things continue as they are now the only Jewish movement left will be Right-wing Orthodoxy. Implicit in its message is writing off 90 percent of Jewry." In Israel, too, he is of the opinion that healthy competition from Conservative and Reform elements will destroy the more complacent aspects of Orthodoxy. Ultimately, although responsible for a limited renaissance among secular Jews in America, Riskin despairs for the future on this continent. Even the religion of the religious he mistrusts: "America has spawned inverted Marranos: Jews who act out the rituals but have the inner responses of the secularists." He sees the hope for world Jewry as coming from Israel and spends two months every summer with his family in a religious Israeli kibbutz, Ein Tsurim.

He visits the hospital every week and is deeply affected by death. "It's very important to me for people to like me," he says. Concern, not intellectual relevance, remains the ultimate key to his appeal. "The ministry must create a community of people whom the rabbi cares about and who care about each other," he says, and yet, when one speaks to him privately, he sees his most important role as that of the teacher.

For further information:
Kanfer, Neal, and Shanken, Zev. "An Interview with Shlomo Riskin." *Response,* Spring 1976.

MARTIN RITT

b. March 2, 1920
Film director; producer; actor

If there is a unifying theme that inspires the work of movie director Martin Ritt, it is, perhaps, the social dilemma of the outsider, the little man or woman who cannot quite conform, caught up in a basic struggle to survive against larger forces often working to keep him or her down. This struggle was clear in his first film about an interracial friendship, *Edge of the City* (1956), and it characterized the Oscar award-winning *Norma Rae* (1979), which saluted the courage of a southern mill worker in risking her job and possibly her family to organize a union. It typified the early roles Ritt played as an actor in the 1930s and 1940s, and it marked his personal struggle in the early 1950s when he was blacklisted for his political beliefs and surrendered a promising career in television.

Martin Ritt was born in New York City to Morris and Rose Ritt, immigrants who settled in the Lower East Side. According to a 1957 article in the *New York Daily Mirror,* Ritt's father, who called himself Abe Lewis, was a gypsy dancer who performed in the Palace Theater. But Ritt grew up with no particular interest in the arts and became instead an avid athlete. As a football star at DeWitt Clinton High School, he was able to get a scholarship to Elon College in North Carolina. But while there, he developed a fascination with law and returned to New York to study at St. John's University in Brooklyn. But his law career was unexpectedly cut short when he met actor-director Elia Kazan and joined the Group Theater, the innovative theater company founded by Lee Strasberg whose primary focus was the production of naturalistic social drama.

Ritt's first role as an actor was a part in Clifford Odets' *Waiting for Lefty* (1937), in which he had exactly two lines. He had trained star Luther Adler in some of the essentials of boxing and later understudied for John Garfield. He performed with the Group Theater in several other productions before joining the U.S. Air Force during World War II, where he continued to act and began to direct.

Returning to New York after the war, he resumed

theater work, but primarily as a director, and was also one of the first to direct live television theater during the medium's "golden age." From 1948 to 1951 Ritt acted in more than 150 teleplays and directed over 100. But his career, like that of many other creative artists at the time, was cut short when his youthful involvements with the Communist Party became the excuse for television moguls to blacklist him in the heat of the 1950s "Red scare." Ritt lost the starring role in Paddy Chayefsky's play *Marty*, a part that had been written expressly for him.

Ritt spent 1951 to 1955 teaching at the Actor's Studio, performing occasionally, doing some directing and working at odd jobs when necessary. Among his students were Paul Newman and Joanne Woodward, who later acted in many of his films. He made the transition to film when, after directing Robert Alan Aurthur's play *A Very Special Baby*, he was hired by David Susskind—the first studio executive willing to give Ritt a job—to direct Aurthur's film adaptation of his own teleplay *Edge of the City*. Produced by MGM in 1956, it told of a misfit Army deserter, played by John Cassavetes, and his comradeship with a black dock worker, portrayed by Sidney Poitier.

Edge of the City not only signaled a permanent film career for Ritt but marked his entry into serious social commitment through the medium. Many of his subsequent films touched on similar themes, although Ritt's original aims as a director were often diluted by studio heads who had difficulty dealing with some of his films' serious subjects. Thus, productions of William Faulkner's *The Sound and the Fury* (20th Century-Fox, 1957) and *The Long Hot Summer* (20th Century-Fox, 1958) were praised for their dramatic power yet criticized for their implausible happy endings—a touch far removed from Ritt's original direction. His next few movies were mediocre, but with *Hud* (Paramount, 1963), Ritt was permitted to tell the story of a young man battling to decide which family role model to follow—an unprincipled but attractive uncle or an honest but vulnerable grandfather. The unusual non-Hollywood-type ending— the young man winds up totally alone when his grandfather dies—marked a victory for Ritt in the effort to direct realistic, confrontational, often bitter drama.

Similar themes of struggle over adversity marked Ritt's best work. In *Sounder* (20th Century-Fox, 1972), for example, he told of a southern black sharecropper family trying to make ends meet during the Depression after the father has been imprisoned for stealing a ham so that he can feed his family. And in *Conrack* (20th Century-Fox, 1974), he filmed a fictional version of a true story about an idealistic, young white man who becomes a teacher in a very poor, southern black community. A very personal story colored Ritt's drama, *The Front* (Columbia, 1976), which had a screenplay by Walter Bernstein—also a blacklist victim—and starred Woody Allen. In an unusual dramatic role, Allen starred as a mediocre young writer in New York City who sells the work of blacklisted television writers under his own name as a "front" until he is called for interrogation by HUAC.

Ritt's best-known work to date is probably *Norma Rae* (20th Century-Fox). With Sally Field starring in a role based on the story of a southern worker who raised her own consciousness through her efforts to unionize her colleagues, the film became a popular hit and a landmark in Ritt's career.

In January 1980 the Museum of Modern Art saluted Ritt with a day-long retrospective of his finest films.

ELLIS RIVKIN

b. September 7, 1918
Historian; professor

Ellis Rivkin is a scholar whose specialty is early Jewish history and especially the development and impact of Pharisaic Judaism. He has taught Jewish history at the Hebrew Union College-Jewish Institute of Religion in Cincinnati since 1949.

Ellis Rivkin was born in Baltimore to Moses I., who was a traveling salesman, and Beatrice (Leibowitz) Rivkin. He studied at Johns Hopkins University, where he received a B.A. degree in 1941 and a Ph.D. in 1946, and at Baltimore Hebrew College, where he was granted a Bachelor of Hebrew Literature degree in 1944.

From 1946 to 1949 Rivkin taught history at Gratz College and at Dropsie College, both in Philadelphia, and was Cyrus Adler Post-Doctoral Research Fellow. He then joined the faculty of Hebrew Union College and in 1965 was named its Adolph S. Ochs Professor of Jewish History. He has also been visiting professor or lecturer at Antioch College (1963), University of Utah (1967 and 1973), Dropsie University (1971) and Southern Methodist University (1977). He studied in Europe in 1962 as a Gregg Fellow.

Rivkin has contributed articles to many Jewish academic journals, including *Judaism, Jewish Heritage, The Jewish Quarterly Review, The Jewish Teacher* and others, and to *The New International Encyclopedia*, the *Encyclopaedia Britannica* and the *Interpreters Dictionary of the Bible*. His writings have also appeared in *The New York Herald-Tribune, Saturday Review of Literature* and the *Journal of Modern History*.

In the mid-1960s Rivkin began to focus on the

Pharisees, a faction of Jews who lived during the Hellenic period. "Pharisee" literally means "separatist," and the goals of the Pharisees were to resist assimilation into Greek society and to preserve the idealistic philosophies of the Jewish prophets who preached social justice under a system of monotheism. Rivkin's book about the Pharisees is *A Hidden Revolution: The Pharisees' Search for the Kingdom Within* (Nashville, 1978). His related articles are "Pharisaism and the Crisis of the Individual in the Greco-Roman World" *(The Jewish Quarterly Review,* New Series, vol. 61); "The Pharisaic Revolution" *(Perspectives in Jewish Learning.* 1966); "Defining the Pharisees: The Tannaitic Sources" *(HUC Annual,* vols. 40–41, 1969–70); and "The Scribes, Pharisees, Lawyers, Hypocrites: A Study in Synonymity" *(HUC Annual,* vol. 49, 1978).

Rivkin has also written about alternative ways to view the evolution of Judaism and the Jewish people. *The Shaping of Jewish History* (New York, 1971) was a challenging look at Jewish history, from earliest times to the recent past. Generally, Jews were permitted some measure of freedom only where the economy was growing; where the reverse was true, pogroms often resulted. Delving more deeply into the interrelationship with the prevailing economy, Rivkin elaborated on the beneficial aspects of capitalism and religious toleration, especially where Jews were concerned. Jews only became emancipated, concluded Rivkin, where there was a healthy and vibrant community of private ownership and where official religion therefore lost its authority. Where the reverse proved true, as in Nazi Germany, Jews became easy marks for demagogues.

For further information:

Rivkin, Ellis. *The Dynamics of Jewish History.* Sarasota, Fla.: 1970.

———. *Leon da Modena and the Kol Sahkhal.* Cincinnati: 1952.

JEROME ROBBINS

b. October 11, 1918
Dancer; choreographer

Jerome Robbins has won acclaim as a dancer, outstanding and imaginative choreographer and director for his work on the stage, in television and in motion pictures. He is perhaps best-known for his work on two of Broadway's greatest musicals, *West Side Story* and *Fiddler on the Roof.*

Jerome Rabinowitz was born in New York City. His parents, Harry and Lena (Rips) Rabinowitz, had emigrated from Russia and Robbins was raised in Weehawken, New Jersey. Although he briefly studied dance as a youngster, he realized in college that he would pursue dance professionally, and after his freshman year at New York University in 1936, he left to study ballet, modern dance and Spanish and oriental dance full-time. He also did chorus work in Broadway shows. His career moved quickly. He joined the American Ballet Theatre in 1940 and two years later had his first solo in *Petrouchka.* Sometime after he changed his name.

Robbins made his debut as a choreographer on April 18, 1944, when *Fancy Free,* with music by Leonard Bernstein, opened at the Ballet Theater—and received 20 curtain calls. In *Ballet in America,* George Amberg called *Fancy Free* "the first substantial ballet entirely created in the contemporary American idiom." It evolved into the Broadway musical hit *On the Town* (1945), with Betty Comden and Adolph Green, and signalled the start of an international career in ballet and musical comedy for Robbins.

He went on to choreograph many Broadway shows, including *High Button Shoes* (1947), *Call Me Madam* (1950), *The King and I* (1951) and *The Pajama Game* (1952). *New York Times* critic Clive Barnes commented that Robbins "revolutionized the American musical—he gave it style."

Robbins has been the recipient of many awards, including a Tony for *West Side Story* in 1957. He also won Oscars for his choreography and direction of the movie version four years later. He was honored with both a Drama Critics Award and Tonys for choreography and direction in *Fiddler on the Roof* (1965), a show based on stories of Shalom Aleichem that hardly reflected Robbins' Jewish background which he once described as a "very emancipated, assimilated upbringing."

Robbins maintained an active ballet career side-by-side with his work on Broadway. After he stopped dancing in the 1950s, he became associate artistic director of the New York City Ballet under George Balanchine. He has choreographed dozens of ballets for the NYCB and for companies around the world, including the Sephardic Inbal Dance Company in Israel, with whom he worked in the 1950s.

In 1969 Robbins became ballet master of the NYCB when he choreographed his first work for the company after a 13-year hiatus. At that time he had become disenchanted with the enormous sums of money needed to produce Broadway shows and was eager to contribute to the ballet, which he saw was attracting increasing public interest.

Nonetheless, he returned again to the musical theater to **stage** revivals of *Peter Pan* (1979), *West Side Story* (1980) on Broadway and *Fiddler on the Roof* (1981) at Lincoln Center. The new *Fiddler* received rave reviews and Robbins was praised for his ability to capture perfectly the spirit and sensibility of the Shalom Aleichem tales of the *shtetl*.

For television Robbins has directed and staged famous productions of *Peter Pan* with Mary Martin in 1955, 1956 and 1960; "Salute to Israel" in 1978, featuring Mikhail Baryshnikov; and a 1980 NBC telecast "Live from Studio 8H: An Evening with Jerome Robbins and members of the New York City Ballet."

FELIX ROHATYN

b. May 29, 1928
Financial consultant

Financial whiz, corporate merger specialist, part-savior of New York City during its fiscal crisis of the mid-1970s and economic writer, Felix Rohatyn is a dominant figure in New York's financial community.

Felix George Rohatyn was born in Vienna and arrived in the United States with his mother and stepfather in 1941. His Polish father, Alexander Rohatyn, was a beer-brewer. The family name was of Tartar origin, and there is a small town in Poland called Rohatyn. Felix Rohatyn is the great-grandson of a grand rabbi of Poland. His Austrian mother was born Edith Knoll and divorced Rohatyn's father in the late 1930s and remarried shortly thereafter. The family survived the Nazi occupation of France on false papers and came to the United States via Oran, Casablanca, Lisbon and Rio de Janeiro.

In New York City Rohatyn lived on East 74th Street and attended the McBurney School and then Middlebury College in Vermont, from which he graduated with a Bachelor of Arts degree in 1948. At the college he was accepted by a non-Jewish fraternity, Alpha Sigma Psi, which, he recounts, was "expelled because of me."

He was drafted into the Army in 1951 and served until 1953, mainly in Germany. Discharged, he joined the investment banking firm Lazard Freres and came under the powerful influence of its head, Andre Meyer, whom he described as "one of the two or three most brilliant men I've ever worked for." The others included Harold Geneen of ITT and Charles Revson.

When New York City was on the verge of financial collapse in the mid-1970s, no one in the financial community did more to rescue it from bankruptcy than Rohatyn. As chairman of MAC, the Municipal Assistance Corporation—a position he still holds—Rohatyn played the crucial role. He was able to apply the expertise used as the reorganizer of many major American corporations in the reorganization of New York City's fiscal structures, and he helped raise money through the issuance of municipal bonds. This public exposure has led to a greater participation on Rohatyn's part in urban affairs and politics, and he was once even rumored to be considering a run for mayor.

In 1980 independent presidential candidate John Anderson brought in Rohatyn as an economic adviser, and he preached his doctrine of national economic planning, protectionism, wage and price controls, and gasoline rationing.

In late 1979 and early 1980, he wrote two major articles in the *New York Review of Books*—"The Coming Crisis and What to Do About It" and "The Disaster Facing the East." In the former he outlined his views on the economy; in the latter he looked at the economically weakening northeastern states and their shrinking political clout. In still another article, "What This Old Town Needs Is a Taxurb," which appeared in the *New York Daily News* (April 7, 1981), Rohatyn proposed the consolidation of urban centers and their suburban surroundings in the creation of a broader tax base, stating that suburban dwellers should contribute more to the central cities where they work and frequently spend so much leisure time, thus utilizing many city services.

And in yet another delineation of the enormously complicated and unresolved problems facing the country today, Rohatyn told the graduating class at Middlebury College in May 1982 that these difficulties include the swift development of a permanent black and Hispanic underclass, with little or no hope of rectifying their condition; the division between the South and northern and middle western states, in which the latter will suffer serious economic losses; the deterioration of the auto, glass, rubber and steel industries which will lead to even more joblessness; nuclear proliferation and the necessity of controlling and reducing the level of weaponry while remaining realistic about Soviet military might; the weakening of the written press and the rising authority of television in politics; an economy which is caught between inflation and recession and is unable to stabilize. All these warnings, plus his suggestions for their resolutions, make Rohatyn highly sought after by politicians and opinion-makers.

CHARLES ROSEN

b. May 5, 1927
Pianist; critic

Charles Rosen has said: "I was doing nothing but playing the piano until I was 40. Then I wrote a book. It became, if you like, a sort of hobby." The book, *The Classical Style* (New York, 1971), won a National Book Award in the arts and letters category in 1972 and distinguished Rosen, a concert pianist and professor of music at the State University of New York at Stony Brook, as one of America's leading music critics, whose special ability is to explain clearly the intricacies of music so that even the lay reader can understand.

Charles Rosen was born in New York City, the son of Irwin and Anita (Gerber) Rosen. He graduated summa cum laude from Princeton University in 1947, receiving a B.A. degree in French literature. He went on to complete his Ph.D. at Princeton in 1951, also in French literature. His degree led most critics to assume that Rosen was an expert in French music, but Rosen claims that he studied French only because the man he admired the most at Princeton, Ira Wade, was the head of the French department there.

While a Fulbright fellow from 1951 until 1953, Rosen, who had also studied with teachers trained in the Viennese school of music, made his New York City concert debut at Town Hall. He also recorded all the Debussy etudes, the first pianist ever to do so. He has maintained a vigorous recording and concert schedule, appearing at Orchestra Hall in London 10 times and has recorded, among other works, the last six sonatas of Beethoven and Bach's *Art of Fugue*.

In 1953 Rosen joined the modern literature department at the Massachusetts Institute of Technology, teaching French literature for two years, and at the same time he continued to concertize and record. In 1971 Rosen was appointed professor of music at Stony Brook, where he teaches music history and performance. Rosen has also lectured at Cornell University and the University of California at Berkeley. In 1980 he was appointed the Charles Eliot Norton Professor of Poetry at Harvard University to lecture on the aesthetics of romanticism.

Following *The Classical Style,* which explored the music of Haydn, Mozart and Beethoven, Rosen delved into the work of Arnold Schoenberg in *Schoenberg* (New York, 1975). His thesis was that classical music is best understood and appreciated by examining the concerti and string quartets of Mozart, the symphonies and string quartets of Haydn, and Beethoven's piano compositions. Rosen's book *Sonata Forms* (New York, 1980) includes an elaborate classification of binary, minuet and slow-movement forms as well as insightful treatments of Mozart's *Prague* Symphony and Schumann's F-sharp Minor Sonata. The book is extensively researched and scholarly but as accessible to the lay reader as to the music expert. In a review *New York Times* critic Edward Rothstein praised Rosen as one of the "few musicologists who can not only articulate the effects of a work, but can explain how it attains that effect and establish its meaning."

In late December 1981 Rosen explained his role as a critic.

> Journalistic criticism is essential to the economy of music. Public concerts take place in order to permit musicians to make a living at what they love best. The fact that the public wants to hear music is really a secondary matter. The public, in fact, has to be persuaded to go to concerts—that is why criticism exists.

Rosen, who has contributed articles to the *New York Review of Books,* has also been singled out by scholar William Youngren, who, in reviewing *Sonata Forms,* wrote that "[the public] should . . . be grateful that so learned, perceptive and eloquent a writer as Rosen is around to battle the old myths that still inhibit and confuse our best efforts to understand our greatest music."

For further information:
Rosen, Charles. "The Real Business of the Critic." (London) *Times Literary Supplement,* December 25, 1981.

A.M. ROSENTHAL

b. May 2, 1922
Newspaper editor; journalist

The way to the top of *The New York Times* for executive editor A.M. Rosenthal took more than 30 years of dedicated reporting, an eye for innovation and a willingness to support younger journalists in the breaking and development of major, and often controversial, stories.

Abraham Michael Rosenthal was born to Harry and Sarah (Dickstein) Rosenthal in Sault Ste. Marie, Ontario, Canada. His parents were Russian Jewish immigrants; his father, a fur trader, was born Harry Shipiatsky in Byelorussia and was a pioneering socialist farmer in the Canadian wilderness. Rosenthal came to the United States with his family in 1926 (he was naturalized in 1951) and was raised in the Bronx. He received no Jewish education and had no Bar Mitzvah and was reared in the socialist Bronx Amalgamated housing project. Rosenthal was himself a Young Socialist, supposedly swayed by an older sister who joined the Young Communists. The turning point that made him a staunch anti-Communist was the 1939 Hitler-Stalin Pact—the same year he graduated from DeWitt Clinton High School—and his experiences since then, especially as a correspondent in Warsaw in 1958, only solidified his anti-communism. He received a B.S.S. degree from City

College of New York in 1944 and immediately joined the staff of *The New York Times*.

From 1946 to 1954 Rosenthal was United Nations correspondent. For the next nine years he reported for the *Times* from India (1957–58); Warsaw (1958–59); Geneva and also Vienna, the Congo and Central Africa (1960–61); and Tokyo (1961–63). Returning to New York, he became metropolitan editor (1963–66), assistant managing editor (1968–69) and managing editor (1969–77) before becoming executive editor in 1977.

Certainly his major achievement as executive editor was the extraordinary publication of the equally extraordinary Pentagon Papers. The Papers were commissioned by United States Secretary of Defense Robert McNamara in what one writer called a "spirit of self-criticism" or as a way of assessing the thought processes and activities of the foreign policy-making elite. Fundamentally the Papers confirmed what critics had been saying all along, though without total accuracy or knowledge. The Pentagon Papers did not prove any warmakers' "conspiracy" or portray Vietnam as an act of "imperialism." Rather, they indicated that the intervention in Southeast Asia was a continuation of the conventional American policy of unceasing hostility to Soviet power—real and imagined—since the first United States intervention in Russia in 1918. The Papers also showed that the so-called elite had no more special insights or sagacity than the intelligent reader of any good newspaper. It also indicated that major blunders had been made.

Various anti-war United States senators had refrained from publicly revealing its contents—they had been classified "secret"—until Daniel Ellsberg gave them to the *Times*. By all accounts, Rosenthal's decision to print the Pentagon Papers was decisive, inasmuch as various *Times* officials and counselors urged the publisher to refrain from doing so. The Papers were published by him as a journalistic obligation, and after Nixon halted publication and sought to impose the doctrine of prior restraint—never done in the United States—the *Times* went to the Supreme Court, which ruled against suppression. Then the *Times* resumed publishing the Papers. The First Amendment was vindicated, thanks to Rosenthal.

Since assuming his present position in 1977, Rosenthal has been responsible for making America's most prestigious newspaper its trendiest. By dividing the daily paper into four sections, with special excursions into sports on Monday, science on Tuesday, "living" on Wednesday, the "home" on Thursday and the New York City weekend on Friday, Rosenthal created a new style for daily newspapers that others would soon copy. His leadership has earned him the title "Mr. New York Times."

His assignments abroad garnered much attention and many awards. The Overseas Press Club cited his work on three occasions: in 1956 for his reporting in India; in 1959 for both India and Poland; and in 1966 for two major magazine articles. Expelled by the Polish Communist government in 1959 for "probing too deeply" into Poland's affairs, he received the Pulitzer Prize for reporting in 1960. Additional awards include the George Polk Memorial award in 1960 and 1965, and the Page One award of the Newspaper Guild of New York in 1966.

Rosenthal has written one book and coauthored a second. *Thirty-Eight Witnesses* (New York, 1964) is an account of the highly publicized and particularly brutal murder in Queens of a young woman, Kitty Genovese. There had been 38 witnesses who heard her screams and may have seen the murder, but no one came forward to help her. *The Night the Lights Went Out* (New York, 1965) is a *New York Times* publication describing the blackout that hit a major portion of the East Coast on November 9, 1965. Rosenthal co-edited the book with deputy managing editor Arthur Gelb and wrote one chapter. Also with Gelb, Rosenthal coauthored *One More Victim* (New York, 1967), a biography of Daniel Burros, a prominent Ku Klux Klan leader who shot himself in 1965 when *The New York Times* revealed he was Jewish.

In 1968 he covered the student uprising at Columbia University, and as an ex-Socialist turned hard-line anti-New Left, he repeatedly condemned the students for their disruptive roles. Rosenthal was sharply criticized by many for this view and was later criticized for ignoring most students' essentially peaceful roles, the violence by the police after they were called to the campus by the university, and an inept school administration.

He has also written magazine articles for *Saturday Evening Post, Colliers, Foreign Affairs* and *The New York Times Magazine*, including a major exploratory two-part series, "Memoirs of a New China Hand," for which he also took photographs (July 19 and 26, 1981). In the latter he wrote: "How does a new China hand make any attempt to separate the empathy he feels for China after just a few weeks from the decades of distaste he has felt for authoritarianism or totalitarianism, take your pick? China doesn't care, but the new China hand does."

In Harrison E. Salisbury's *Without Fear or Favor* (New York, 1980), a book detailing America's most powerful newspaper, Salisbury wrote that Rosenthal "always considered himself Jewish because he was perceived as Jewish." Salisbury reports that Rosenthal once claimed his by-line was removed by higher-ups from a series of articles about Palestine in the late 1940s. Yet Salisbury was uneasy about the explanation. "It was always 'they' who did these things . . . who 'they' were Abe [Rosenthal] could never quite understand."

Ironically, the *Times* has also been criticized regularly by the New York-based *Jewish Week* and others as allegedly anti-Israel in its news columns and editorials. Even so, under Rosenthal's tutelage, the newspaper remains the most influential in the world today and its coverage of Israel extensive.

BENJAMIN ROSENTHAL

b. June 8, 1923
U.S. congressman

In more than 20 years in Congress, Representative Benjamin Rosenthal has espoused a consistently liberal viewpoint, which has been reflected especially in his strong anti-war stands and in his role in designing programs to aid less privileged Americans. He is also a firm supporter of Israel.

Benjamin Stanley Rosenthal was born in New York City to Joseph, an optical manufacturer, and Ceil (Fisher) Rosenthal. Educated at Long Island University and at the City College of New York, he received a Bachelor of Law from Brooklyn Law School in 1949, the year he was admitted to the New York state bar, and a Master of Law from New York University in 1952. He served in the U.S. Army from 1943 to 1946.

A Democrat-Liberal, Rosenthal first entered Congress after winning a special election in February 1962. During the mid-1960s he became closely allied with President Lyndon B. Johnson in the drafting of Great Society social programs. He participated on a task force that changed the function of food stamps so that instead of being a means to distribute surplus foodstuffs, the stamps would supplement the food needs of lower-income families. He fought a fruitless battle to create a federal-level consumer agency, though he remained an ardent consumer advocate, and was instrumental in the creation of inspector generals to monitor federal departments of government. (In a 1982 interview he reflected that the lack of this kind of monitoring of social programs was probably the reason their budgets ballooned out of control and that the Reagan administration received so much cooperation from Congress in cutting back or eliminating these programs.)

Rosenthal was also one of the earliest and most vocal critics of American military involvement in Vietnam, a stance that alienated him from his former close ally

President Johnson. In 1969 he was responsible for keeping the House of Representatives open all night in a move of sympathy with anti-war demonstrators in Washington. Thirteen years later he demonstrated the same fervent opposition to American military presence abroad when he introduced a resolution to end American military involvement in El Salvador.

As chairperson of the Subcommittee on Commerce, Consumer and Monetary Affairs, Rosenthal has been involved in investigations of manipulations of the silver market, the involvement of the Kuwaiti government in American defense investments, and in abuses of securities and banking laws by corporations or prominent officials. Because of his role in exposing alleged bank fraud by former Carter administration official Bert Lance and in investigating the conduct of the American Invsco Corporation, whose principals included the wife of New York Governor Hugh Carey, Rosenthal proved himself unswerving in his nonpartisan willingness to check all abuses.

Rosenthal, who was a strong opponent of sales by the Reagan administration of AWACS planes to Saudi Arabia, took issue with the contention of some government officials in 1981 that Jews should not as a group take political stands on foreign policy issues. If Jews and other groups were not to speak out, said Rosenthal, foreign policy would be left in the hands of banks, the oil industry and the defense industry, which "would be a disaster for this country and the democratic institutions we all believe in." Indeed, Rosenthal added that much of the corporate maneuvering that went into the AWACS deal, such as the role of Mobil as the purchasing agent for the Saudis, was withheld from the American public.

Rosenthal is a member of the Subcommittee on Europe and the Middle East and of the Subcommittee on Inter-American Affairs. During the 95th and 96th Congresses, he was one of three deputy whips in the House and was a member of the Democratic Steering and Policy Committee.

M.L. ROSENTHAL

b. March 14, 1917
Poet; critic; educator

Poets seldom live on poetry alone. But M.L. Rosenthal has, by writing extensively about poetry, teaching it and editing it, as well as by publishing four collections of his own work. Emile Capouya called him "a poet who is glorious with some regularity . . . and, it seems . . . little appreciated as a poet." Yet he is recognized as one of America's outstanding poetry critics and has developed a devoted following.

Macha Louis Rosenthal was born in Washington, D.C. to Jacob, a house painter and later a liquor salesman, and Ethel (Brown) Rosenthal. He studied at the University of Chicago, receiving a B.A. degree in 1937 and an M.A. in 1938. From 1939 to 1945 he was an English instructor at Michigan State University, and in 1946 he began teaching at New York University, where he received a Ph.D. in 1949. He was a visiting professor at the University of New Mexico in 1956. He became a full professor at NYU in 1961. Rosenthal was poetry editor for *The Nation* from 1956 to 1961, *The Humanist* from 1970 to 1978, and since 1973 he has been poetry editor of *Present Tense*.

Rosenthal was a Guggenheim fellow in 1960–61 and 1964–65. He is a member of the Modern Language Association, the American Association of University Professors, the American Society for Aesthetics and the National Book Critics Circle.

He has participated in United States Cultural Exchange Programs in Germany (1961), Pakistan (1965) and Poland, Rumania and Bulgaria (1966). In 1974 Rosenthal was visiting poet in Israel.

Rosenthal's specialty is contemporary American and British poetry. He has introduced modern works to a larger audience than most poets, emphasizing poetry that can be understood by anyone. *In Sailing into the Unknown: Yeats, Pound and Eliot* (New York, 1978), he explores the life of their poetry, relating it to his own experiences.

His personal work, published in many magazines, has been brought together in four collections, *Blue Boy on Skates* (New York, 1964), *Beyond Power* (New York, 1969), *The View From the Peacock's Tail* (New York, 1972) and *She* (Brockport, N.Y., 1972). *Blue Boy* was his first volume of poetry, and he wrote in 1976 of his surprise that so many of the poems in that collection were "explicitly Jewish." One dealt with his father's funeral, another with juvenile anti-Semites who once attacked him ("Shylock," he wrote, "would probably have approved one pair of lines along the way: When the Christian martyrs were burned/ we agreed, Anonymous Jews were used for kindling.") A third poem in the book associated the danger of nuclear war with the recollections of suffering by East European Jews. Referring in part to his mother, he wrote:

I was thinking how the hunters will come to the shelters;
They'll have war-heroes' hands, smelling of raw meat.
They'll brain the babies and take the canned salmon.
Then I remembered the smell of strawberries in Jonava.

Whatever the subject—and Rosenthal's poems vary widely in length and subject—a sampling of their imagery is evident in the short poem "Albatross" from *She:*

Near the Wailing Wall
An old woman in the sun
    head hanging.

For further information:
Rosenthal, M.L. *The Modern Poets: A Critical Introduction.* New York: 1960.
———. *Poems 1964-80.* New York: 1981.
———. *Poetry of the Common Life.* New York: 1974.
———. *A Primer of Ezra Pound.* New York: 1966.
———. *The Nation,* October 1 and 22, 1977 and January 21, 1978.
Rosenthal, M.L. "On Being a Jewish Poet." *Present Tense,* Winter 1976.

LEO ROSTEN

b. April 11, 1908
Author; political scientist

A unique and prolific writer who has blended a love of language with immersion in Yiddishkeit, the training of a political scientist with the ability to capture amazing detail in his reportage, and a broad sense of humor combined with an insatiable curiosity, Leo Rosten has become a monument to the American appetite to learn as much as possible about virtually everything. As the creator of Hyman Kaplan, the immigrant tripping over English in night school classes, Rosten has contributed an enduring folk hero to American literature. Although Kaplan is a Polish Jew, his hilarious experiences and observations have mirrored those of the millions of "greenhorns" from all over the world who have ever arrived on America's shores, wide-eyed and hopeful of the opportunity to "make it" in the Golden Land—as Rosten himself has done.

Leo Calvin Rosten was born in Lodz, Poland to Samuel C., a textile manufacturer, and Ida (Freundlich) Rosten. He arrived in the United States two years later and was raised in Chicago, where he eventually attended the University of Chicago and was awarded a Bachelor of Philosophy degree in 1930. Upon graduation, and with work difficult to find during the Depression, Rosten took a variety of odd jobs, including teaching English in night school, before returning to the University of Chicago to pursue advanced study in political science. He lectured in literature and psychology from 1932 to 1934 and was a faculty research assistant from 1934 to

1935. The next year he moved to Washington, D.C. on a two-year fellowship from the Social Science Research Council to study the effect of the press on public perception of federal government. He completed his Ph.D. in 1937 and that year published *The Washington Correspondents* (New York), an outgrowth of his doctoral dissertation research.

Rosten has always had the remarkable gift of being able to work on several projects at once. As "Leo Rosten, Ph.D.," he embarked upon a career as a highly respected political scientist. But under the pseudonym Leonard Q. Ross, he also began writing humor, and in the mid-1930s, his short stories about English-language classes at night—no doubt based on his own experience—were featured regularly in *The New Yorker*. In 1937, the year his dissertation was published, his first humor collection, *The Education of H*Y*M*A*N K*A*P*L*A*N* (New York) also appeared and American readers were regaled with such new versions of American history, courtesy of Hyman Kaplan, as the following account of George Washington:

> "Hau Kay! So foist abot Jawdge Vashington. He vas a fine man. Ectually Fodder fromm His Contry, like dey say. Ve hoid awreddy, fromm planty students, all abot his movvellous didds. How, by beink even a leetle boy, he chopped don de cherries so he could answer, 'I cannot tell lies, Papa. I did it mit mine leetle hatchik!' But ve shouldn't forgat dat Vashington vas a beeg ravolutionist! He vas fightink for Friddom, against de Kink Ingland, Kink Jawdge Number Tree, dat tarrible autocrap . . ."

From then on Rosten produced a steady stream of political science, humor and commentary. He dabbled in popular fiction with *Dateline: Europe* (New York, 1939, under the Ross pseudonym), an adventure story about the Parisian exploits of an American foreign correspondent and two young women he met and *Adventure in Washington* (New York, 1940), an intrigue featuring a young Washington reporter. But with grants from the Carnegie Corporation and the Rockefeller Foundation in 1939 and 1940, he embarked on the first comprehensive study of Hollywood, and completed *Hollywood: The Movie Colony; The Movie Makers* (New York, 1941). A two-part work, *Hollywood* combined a fact-filled, meticulously researched sociological exploration of the film industry with personal observations and anecdotes.

Rosten served in World War II as deputy director of the Office of War Information in Washington from 1942 to 1944, and in 1945 went to France, Germany and England as special consultant to the Secretary of War to study morale problems in the American armed forces. After the war he joined the Rand Corporation as senior staff researcher in 1947 but left in 1949 to become editorial adviser at *Look* magazine, a slot which enabled him to write a regular column for many years, "The World of Leo Rosten."

In the meantime, Rosten continued writing, lecturing at several American universities, including Stanford, New York University, Yale and others, and working in occasional consultancies on social science topics. Because he had an instant "soap-box" through his *Look* column, Rosten had the unusual opportunity to write about virtually anything, and his columns and essays—collected in several books including *The Many Worlds of L*E*O R*O*S*T*E*N* (New York, 1964), *The Look Book* (New York, 1975) and *Passions and Prejudices* (New York, 1978)—enabled him to write travel pieces, literary critiques, and social or political commentary.

Hyman Kaplan, who never seemed quite to master the English language, was revived in *The Return of H*Y*M*A*N K*A*P*L*A*N* (New York, 1959) and *O K*A*P*L*A*N! MY K*A*P*L*A*N* (New York, 1976) and provided the inspiration for an unmemorable Broadway musical adaptation in 1968. But Rosten scored a big hit of his own with his best-selling *The Joys of Yiddish* (New York, 1968), a work which, he stated, was not about Yiddish but about how English had been influenced by it. The alphabetical format—covering more than 500 pages—provided historical and anecdotal, often humorous, explanations of how Yiddish had been adapted by English-speakers. "Bagels," Rosten suggested, are "doughnuts with a college education—and the college is probably Yeshiva." Rosten expanded on the Yiddish/Jewish theme with *Leo Rosten's Treasury of Jewish Quotations* (New York, 1972).

From 1942 to 1952 Rosten combined his literary career with screenwriting using the pseudonym Leonard Ross. He coauthored his first original screen story *All Through the Night* with Leonard Spigelgass in 1942 for Warner Brothers and also collaborated with Spigelgass on *They Got Me Covered* for RKO the same year. Some of his other screen efforts include the screenplay for an Independent Artists' 1948 production *Velvet Touch* and the original story of *Double Dynamite,* made by RKO in 1950. Rosten's novel *Dateline: Europe* was filmed by 20th-Century Fox in 1946, and his 1962 novel, *Captain Newman, M.D.* (New York), a black comedy set in the psychiatric ward of an army hospital, was filmed by Universal the following year.

In 1955 Rosten edited *A Guide to the Religions of America* (New York), which was republished in 1967 and 1975.

For further information:

Rosten, Leo. *The Dark Corner.* New York: 1945.

———. *Hurray for Yiddish: A Book about English.* New York: 1982.

———. *A Most Private Intrigue.* New York: 1967.

———. *People I Have Loved, Known or Admired.* New York: 1970.

———. *The Story Behind the Painting.* New York: 1961.

———. *The 3:10 to Anywhere.* New York: 1976.

———. *A Trumpet for Reason.* New York: 1970.

EUGENE VICTOR ROSTOW

b. August 25, 1913
Legal scholar; government official

Eugene Victor Rostow is widely recognized for the contributions he has made as a legal scholar and for the crucial roles he played in various presidential administrations.

Eugene Rostow was born in Brooklyn to Victor Aaron, a metallurgical engineer, and Lillian (Helman) Rostow. His father was a Russian immigrant active with the Social Democrats, and he named his son after his hero, Eugene V. Debs. Rostow graduated from Yale with a Bachelor of Arts in 1933 and a law degree in 1937. The following year he joined Yale's law faculty, where he would develop renown as a liberal legal scholar.

His first government affiliation was during 1942 to 1944, when he was legal adviser to Assistant Secretary of State Dean Acheson for the duration of World War II. Returning to Yale, he wrote an article for the *Yale Law Journal* in June 1945 expressing outrage at what had happened to the Japanese in this country. It was probably influential in forcing the federal government to restore citizenship and return property to Japanese-Americans unjustly incarcerated during World War II.

Rostow's first book was a *National Policy for the Oil Industry* (New Haven, 1949). Perhaps anticipating the controversies to come a generation later, the book outlined how the federal government should reorganize and regulate oil companies. Rostow became dean of the Yale Law School in 1955 and, in that position over the succeeding 10 years, developed what he hoped would be a "humane and broadly-based" curriculum. During that period he published *Planning for Freedom: The Public Law of American Capitalism* (New Haven, 1959) and *The Sovereign Prerogative* (New Haven, 1962).

While still at Yale, Rostow became a member of the Peace Corps Advisory Panel in 1961 and later a consultant to the State Department. He also became a strong advocate of the Johnson administration military interventions in Vietnam and the Dominican Republic in 1965. He joined that administration as undersecretary of state for political affairs from October 1966 through January 1969. Rostow's publications during that period were *Perspectives on the Court,* coauthored with Max Freedman (Evanston, Ill., 1967) and *Law, Power and the Pursuit of Peace* (Lincoln, Nebraska, 1968).

Since returning to Yale, Rostow has continued to publish and lecture widely. He edited a series of lectures by scholars, including Hannah Arendt, Michael Harrington and others, called *Is Law Dead?* (New York, 1971). He has also written *Peace in the Balance: The Future of American Foreign Policy* (New York, 1972), in which he argues that the United Nations is necessary. America's role and strength in the world will not come from sterile anti-communism or aggressiveness, he wrote, but rather from a confident assertion growing from a free and harmonious society. Essentially a political centrist, Rostow insists that the American concept of freedom is a powerful model for the other world nations and their peoples.

His concerns for world affairs are also reflected in *The Middle East* (Boulder, Colo., 1976) and *The Palestine Question in American History,* coauthored with former Secretary of State Clark Clifford (New York, 1978). His vital concerns about the quality of life for Americans as perceived through its legal system are discussed in *Law and Ethics: The Case of the American Negro,* a four-track stereo tape produced in the early 1970s, and *The Ideal in Law* (Chicago, 1978), a series of essays examining how laws evolved to reflect the ideas and customs of different societies, minority groups and economic structures.

In addition, he is a firm supporter of Israel's legal right to settle the occupied West Bank. He has also insisted that campaigns to expel Israel from the United Nations violate the U.N. charter. "Western nations should stand firmly on the binding 1973 Security Council Resolution which commands Israel's neighbors to make peace, and block every other initiative on the subject until they do," he stated in 1980. In addition, he has written regularly of his belief that the Middle East is "not an Arab-Israel conflict or a conflict among different tendencies in Arab politics. It is a NATO crisis, an attempt to drive the United States out of Europe, to dismantle NATO and thus to bring the resources and energies of Western Europe under effective Soviet control." In "American Foreign Policy and the Middle East" in *World Politics and the Jewish Condition*, edited by Louis Henkin (New York, 1972), he restated support for "the line of [foreign] policy . . . followed since 1947" plus "nothing less than acceptance of the UN Charter, and therefore abandonment of the idea of international support for revolution. He urged the U.S. and its allies "to stand fast" in the hope that the USSR and China "will accept the logic of genuinely peaceful coexistence."

In 1981 Rostow was appointed director of the Arms Control and Disarmament Agency by President Ronald Reagan.

For further information:

Rostow, Eugene Victor. "American Foreign Policy in the Middle East." In *World Politics and the Jewish Condition*, edited by Louis Henkin. New York: 1972.

———. *Peace in the Balance: The Future of Foreign Policy.* New York: 1972.

WALT WHITMAN ROSTOW

b. November 7, 1916
Economist; presidential adviser

Although he is a world-renowned historian with expertise on the development of the British economy and has analyzed how it served as a model for subsequent societies in the throes of industrialization, Walt Rostow is known primarily for his close relationship with President Lyndon Johnson. He is particularly remembered for his hawkish position on the American role in Vietnam, which included recommendations to increase military involvement there.

Walt Whitman Rostow was born to a Russian immigrant family in Brooklyn. His parents were Victor Aaron, a metallurgical engineer, and Lillian (Helman) Rostow. Like his brother Eugene, three years older than he, Walt Rostow attended Yale University, receiving a Bachelor of Arts degree in 1936 and a Ph.D. in 1940. He was a Rhodes Scholar from 1936 to 1938, attending Balliol College at Oxford.

During World War II Rostow was a major with the Office of Strategic Services in London and actively participated in the development of air strategies against the Germans. He was secretary of the "Jockey Club," an officers' organization that selected targets for American and British bombers. His experience there is considered the basis for some of his later strategic choices for Vietnam.

Rostow's first government service was from 1947 to 1949 with the State Department as assistant to the executive secretary of the Economic Commission for Europe. In 1950 he joined the faculty of the Massachusetts Institute of Technology, where he taught economics. From 1951 to 1960 he was affiliated with the Center for International Studies—an entity at MIT supposedly receiving aid from the CIA. During this early period in Rostow's career, he published *The American Diplomatic Revolution* (New York, 1947); *The British Economy of the Nineteenth Century,* essays (New York, 1948); *The Process of Economic Growth* (New York, 1952); and, in conjunction with other faculty members at MIT, *The Prospects for Communist China* (Cambridge, Mass., 1954). He also published *The Stages of Economic Growth: A Non-Communist Manifesto* (Cambridge, England, 1960 and 1971), which offered alternatives to Marxist theories of economic development. In it he saw a pattern in technologically advanced countries and believed it to be replicable in poorer countries. Marxist critics charged that Third and Fourth World poverty was not merely a lag—as Rostow wrote— but was a result of the policies of richer nations.

During the latter part of the 1950s Rostow became a policy analyst for Senator John F. Kennedy in Washington and became active in the Kennedy presidential campaign. The slogans "The New Frontier" and "Let's Get the Country Moving Again" are attributed to Rostow. After the election he was named deputy special assistant to Kennedy, working closely with McGeorge Bundy.

The developing conflict in Indochina and Rostow's firm stance on stopping what he viewed as a monolithic Communist enemy through bombing and intervention made him an important presence in Washington during the Johnson administration. In May 1964 he became the U.S. representative to the Inter-American Committee on the Alliance for Progress, and in April 1966 he succeeded McGeorge Bundy as LBJ's special assistant for national security affairs. Called a "key architect of LBJ's Vietnam policy" by the *London Times,* he became one of Johnson's staunchest defenders and closest friends. In fact, many believe he was Johnson's principal theoretician in the step-by-step escalation of American military intervention. Rostow believed that the U.S. national interests were involved in Southeast Asia and that American "nerve" or "will and character" were most important. His critics charged, however, that it was American "judgment" and "wisdom" that was tested, as was common sense, and not national prestige.

Rostow's premise in urging American intervention was that in the end it might be the best way to stave off communism. Almost from the start he urged a policy of escalation. Three days before the Bay of Pigs fiasco in 1961, Rostow suggested to Vice President Lyndon B. Johnson that he travel to Saigon and that, in the meantime, the number of U.S. MAAG advisers be raised from 685 to 785. This, he said, "involves some diplomacy," because it violated the Geneva limit on foreign military personnel. President John F. Kennedy approved the request but chose to keep it a secret. For the balance of the war, Rostow continued urging the steady bombing of North Vietnam to cripple its economy. (Soon the CIA would demur, suggesting instead that such actions as operation Rolling Thunder —the steady bombing of North Vietnam—would only make the war grow in intensity, that the North would counter every escalation with more escalation and instead fight on. Rather, the CIA argued that North Vietnam would eventually be defeated by a "slow squeeze.")

By the summer of 1965 and after, Rostow was known internationally as a super-hawk on the war. He urged that ground troops be dispatched into Laos "across the Ho Chi Minh Trail" and into North Vietnam to deter a "long uncertain attritional struggle," which would erode American public opinion. Rostow believed the war was an act of aggression and not a civil war. Accordingly, he continually suggested to the president that he up the ante: more bombs, more soldiers. He accompanied LBJ to the Glasboro, New Jersey summit meeting with Russian Premier Aleksei Kosygin in June 1967 and was said to have advised the president during the Israeli-Arab Six-Day War in 1967. That same year he returned again to the war in Southeast Asia in the *Department of State Bulletin*, writing that "if we have the common will to hold together and get on with the job" then Vietnam could well become "the last great confrontation of the postwar era."

In 1969, when LBJ was about to leave office, he presented Rostow with the presidential Medal of Freedom. Both the ex-president and Rostow moved to Texas —LBJ into retirement, where he worked on the presidential papers and the establishment of the Lyndon Baines Johnson Library at the University of Texas in Austin, and Rostow to an academic position there as Rex G. Baker Jr. Professor of Political Economy. He later helped organize the Lyndon B. Johnson School for Public Affairs.

Rostow was once referred to as a "fanatic in sheep's clothing" (*London Times Higher Education Supplement*, November 10, 1978). After Johnson left office and the Vietnam conflict ended, Rostow stood firm by his original policies. Whether these views will overshadow Rostow's many other accomplishments will be left for later generations to determine.

It has been rumored that Rostow sought to return to one of several East Coast Ivy League universities but

that his record on Vietnam made him an "undesirable" appointee. Nevertheless, he has continued to publish distinguished books on economics and history, including *Politics and the Stages of Growth* (Cambridge, England, 1971), a discussion of security, welfare and constitutional order in eight different countries; *The Diffusion of Power—An Essay in Recent History* (New York, 1972); *How It All Began: Origins of the Modern Economy* (New York, 1974), an analysis of British expansion during the Industrial Revolution; *Getting from Here to There* (New York 1978), an examination of national and regional planning to cope with energy shortages; and *The World Economy: History and Prospect* (Austin, Texas, 1979), a look at trends and cycles in economic growth since the 18th century, focusing on the problems of supply and demand and the availability of food and raw materials.

For further information:
Rostow, Walt. "Power and Economics." *Society*, May/June 1981.
———. *Pre-Invasion Bombing Strategy: General Eisenhower's Decision of March 25, 1944*. Austin, Texas: 1981.

PHILIP ROTH

b. March 19, 1933
Novelist

Philip Roth, gifted novelist, is one of the giant literary figures of the second half of the 20th century and perhaps one of the most controversial.

Philip Milton Roth was born in Newark, New Jersey to Herman, an insurance salesman, and Bess (Finkel) Roth. Even as a youngster, he was known as a storyteller and jokester in his Jewish neighborhood in Newark. In college he began writing seriously. He attended Rutgers University in Newark for one year and transferred to Bucknell University in Pennsylvania, where he received a B.A. degree in 1954, graduating magna cum laude and Phi Beta Kappa. He received an M.A. degree in English literature from the University of Chicago in 1955.

Roth entered a Ph.D. program at Chicago but never finished. Instead, he wrote prolifically and began publishing stories in *The Chicago Review, Paris Review, Commentary, Esquire* and *The New Yorker. Goodbye, Columbus* (New York, 1959), which earned Roth the National Book Award, propelled him to fame. The story that did it—the title story, actually a novella—told of a summer romance between a young male librarian from Newark and a wealthy Radcliffe undergraduate from suburban

Short Hills, New Jersey. Many angry Jewish critics charged that Roth's characterizations were those of a Jew-hating Jew. Four of the five other stories also dealt with Jewish characters. In addition to the National Book Award, Roth received the Daroff Award from the Jewish Book Council in 1960, and in 1969 a film version starring Richard Benjamin and Ali McGraw was produced by Paramount Pictures.

Roth received a Guggenheim fellowship for 1959–60, which he used to write. His next novel, *Letting Go* (New York, 1961), told of Gabe Wallach, an English instructor who moves from the University of Chicago to New York, and the academic crowd—primarily a Jewish one—he circulates in. *When She Was Good* (New York, 1967) was Roth's first novel-length venture into American WASP-dom. His main character, Lucy Nelson, considers herself above everyone around her and consequently becomes alienated from her surroundings. Less successful than Roth's previous works, *When She Was Good* was praised nevertheless for its characterizations.

Philip Roth's early promise as an interpreter of the Jewish experience using humor as his vehicle (or, to some critics, his weapon) has been borne out over the many years he has published stories, novels and articles, including the controversial *Portnoy's Complaint* (New York, 1969), which explored the tribulations of Jewish malehood. Although Roth has written about non-Jewish themes, he is perceived as a primarily Jewish writer, and it is his books on Jewish subjects—many of those subjects being quasi-autobiographical—that are his most successful.

Much hoopla preceded the publication of *Portnoy's Complaint,* portions of which had appeared in *Playboy.* Alexander Portnoy, a successful young lawyer in Mayor John V. Lindsay's New York City administration, details his fantasy life—which consists primarily of the sexual conquest of non-Jewish women as revenge on his overbearing Jewish mother—to a mostly silent psychoanalyst. The response to *Portnoy's Complaint* was as remarkable as the book—the Jewish son comes of age, sheds his guilt (or thinks he does) and fights back. The book was a best seller.

Roth proceeded further into satirizing American lifestyles with *Our Gang* (New York, 1971) and *The Great American Novel* (New York, 1973), which parody politics and baseball, respectively. *Our Gang* tells of such sleazy characters as President Trick E. Dixon and his White House cronies, as well as the late Charisma brothers, John F. and Robert F., New York Mayor John Lancelot and other American politicians. *The Great American Novel,* narrated by 87-year-old sportswriter "Word" Smith, chronicles the history of a fictional baseball team.

Fantasy, sex, Jewish maleness and the influence of Kafka played major roles in the formation of *The Breast* (New York, 1972), *My Life As a Man* (New York, 1974) and *The Professor of Desire* (New York, 1977). David Kepesh is the protagonist of *The Breast* and *The Professor of Desire.* The latter book, which precedes *The Breast* chronologically, describes the sexual (mis)adventures of Kepesh, an English professor, his subsequent marriage and his later flight from marriage. In *The Breast,* a novella, Kepesh awakens in a hospital to discover himself mysteriously transformed into a huge female breast. *My Life As a Man* consists of three stories: The first two are written by the subject of the third, Peter Tarnopol, a blocked writer, whose problems ring familiar—women.

In 1979 Roth's book *The Ghost Writer* (New York, 1979), first serialized in *The New Yorker,* appeared. In it he went back to an earlier time. His youthful narrator, Nathan Zuckerman, has an infatuation not for a young non-Jewish woman, but for an older Jewish writer—male—whom Zuckerman considers his mentor. Staying briefly at the home of the writer, E.I. Lonoff—it is the early 1950s—Zuckerman meets Lonoff's young and mysterious assistant, one Amy Bellette, a European woman who later hints that she is really Anne Frank, who, unbeknownst to the world, never died after all. Roth was given the Kenneth B. Smilen/*Present Tense* Literary Award for the novel. In his acceptance speech, he declared in 1979:

> I hope you know what you're doing. However much it pleases me to accept this award, I must remind you that not only have you repudiated the long-standing judgment of many wise men and women, but what is even more disturbing, you have confirmed the exasperated assessment of the Jews made by none other than the late Nikita Khrushchev. "They are all individualists," complained Khrushchev, "and all intellectuals. They want to talk about everything, they want to discuss everything, they want to debate everything—and they come to totally different conclusions!"

During the 1970s Roth explored the nature of writing, both his own and the work of other writers. *Reading Myself and Others* (New York, 1975) is a collection of 23 essays, articles and interviews previously published in *The New York Times, The New York Review of Books* and the *American Poetry Review.* Roth particularly spoke out in support of Czech writer Milan Kundera, whose work is banned in his native land but has become popular in the United States.

In 1981 Roth published *Zuckerman Unbound* (New York), which, like many of his novels, was suspected of being autobiographical. Nathan Zuckerman, who earlier appeared as an aspiring young novelist in Roth's Pulitzer Prize-winning *The Ghost Writer*, reappears as the successful middle-aged writer of a recent best seller (possibly modeled on *Portnoy's Complaint*). Stalked by fans, he is frequently mistaken for Carnovsky, the novel's main character, whose sexual exploits have apparently rocked—and titillated—the reading public. Many critics felt that this book was Roth's attempt to apologize for *Portnoy's Complaint* and for his apparent decline in popularity since then, and to explain how fame had affected him—negatively, for the most part—as a result. His writing craft was widely praised, but many critics urged Roth to move on to new territories rather than dwell on the past.

In addition to his writing, Roth has taught English at the University of Chicago (1956–58) and the University of Iowa (1960–62). He was writer-in-residence at Princeton (1962–63) and visiting writer at the State University of New York at Stony Brook in 1966–67 and the University of Pennsylvania from 1967 to 1977. He received a Ford Foundation grant to write in 1965 and was a Rockefeller fellow in 1966.

DAVID ROTHENBERG

b. August 19, 1933
Prison reformer

As founder and executive director of the Fortune Society in New York, David Rothenberg is one of the pioneers in the self-help movement for former offenders and one of the most ardent supporters of massive prison reform in America. Ironically, Rothenberg's activism originated from his previous career as a theatrical press agent, when his exposure to prisons through a play he publicized and produced completely changed his life.

David Paul Rothenberg was born in Hackensack, New Jersey to Leon, a real estate agent, and Leanore (Weinberg) Rothenberg. After graduation from Teaneck (New Jersey) High School in 1951, he entered the University of Denver, where he received a B.A. degree in 1955 with a combined major in English literature and social sciences. In 1956, after a brief experience as an "extra" in a Chicago road company of *Inherit the Wind*, he was drafted into the U.S. Army. He served for two years as a public information officer and in 1958 returned to New York, where he held a series of odd jobs in advertising and in a theatrical agency. He soon became directly involved in theatrical promotion. From 1959 to 1961 he served as an apprentice and associate press representative for a range of plays and musicals, the most notable of which was *A Shot in the Dark*. By 1962 he advanced to general press representative, publicizing drama, comedy and dance, including the play *School for Scandal*, the British comedy revue *Beyond the Fringe* and the Israeli Karmon dancers. In 1964 he was the major publicist for Richard Burton's tour in *Hamlet.*

Rothenberg had become a successful and respected agent in the mid-1960s and began using his influence to promote overtly political theater groups that he believed in even if the commercial rewards were limited. Among these were the Free Southern Theater, a drama troupe that toured rural Mississippi, and the Yale Drama School's production of an anti-war play, *Viet Rock*. In 1966 he received a script of a play by a Canadian ex-convict named John Herbert. Entitled *Fortune and Men's Eyes*—based on a phrase from a Shakespearean sonnet—the play recounted a first-time offender's exposure to the brutalities of prison life, not the least of which included a gang rape. Overwhelmed by the play's power, Rothenberg went on to produce it as well as publicize it. It opened off-Broadway in early 1967.

The play was a turning point in Rothenberg's life. As part of the production process, he and the cast visited Riker's Island to gain firsthand knowledge of the prison experience. Through his contacts, and as a result of the play's impact—despite mixed reviews, it ran for a year, and one of its actors received a Drama Critics Circle Award nomination—Rothenberg became more interested in prison life. The same year the play opened, he founded the Fortune Society.

Initially a one-man operation, the society was designed as a self-help group for ex-offenders to aid in their reentry into the social mainstream. On a minimal budget—much of it his own money plus whatever he could raise on the outside—Rothenberg soon expanded the organization to encompass a comprehensive range of support services, including legal advice, general counseling and tutoring, and an emphasis on education as a priority goal in enabling the ex-offender to be able to fend for himself or herself once out. Within 10 years the society occupied two floors of an office building in Manhattan and had a full-time staff of 28 supplemented with many volunteers.

Needless to say, Rothenberg utilized his press agent expertise to publicize his organization. He became active in a number of civic organizations and task forces related not only to prison reform but to all human rights. In 1973 he was appointed to the Governor's Commission on Education and Vocational Training in Prisons in New Jersey and in 1976 participated in the Governor's Special Task Force on Juvenile Violence in the State of New York. Among his other appointments are the American Bar Association Commission on Correctional Facilities and Services (1977); the Mayor's Task Force on Child Abuse in New York City (1979); and New York City's Commissioner of Human Rights, New York City (1979). He is on the board of directors of a number of organizations, including the National Council on Crime and Delinquency and the New York Legal Aid Society.

Outspoken in his beliefs, Rothenberg campaigned vigorously against the passage of the New York state bond issue proposed in 1981 to expand prison facilities because he does not see the construction of more jails as being a practical solution to crime.

Rothenberg has also been vocal in the area of gay rights. Since 1974 he has been an articulate supporter of the rights of homosexuals and he has participated in various gay rights rallies and task forces.

· Rothenberg edits the *Fortune News*, a monthly newsletter whose motto is a Dostoevsky quote: "The degree of civilization in a society can be judged by entering its prisons." He has written articles on criminal justice and other subjects related to prison reform for *The New York Times*, *The Village Voice*, and many other publications. He has taught criminology at Columbia University Teachers College, the New School for Social Research and Montclair (New Jersey) State College. He has also taught a special course to prisoners at the Rahway (New Jersey) State College.

RICHARD L. RUBENSTEIN

b. January 8, 1924
Rabbi; professor; author

Richard Rubenstein's obsession with understanding humankind's periodic tendency toward genocide has resulted in his becoming one of Judaism's foremost thinkers, writers and teachers on the Holocaust and related themes.

Richard Lowell Rubenstein was born in New York City to Jesse George, an industrial engineer, and Sara (Fine) Rubenstein. Raised in New York, he attended Townsend Harris High School, a highly selective public high school, from 1937 to 1940, and then spent two years at the City College of New York. In 1942 he transferred to the University of Cincinnati, where he studied from 1942 to 1946 and received a Bachelor of Arts degree. He also undertook religious studies at the Hebrew Union College in Cincinnati from 1942 to 1945. Rubenstein continued his religious training at the Jewish Theological Seminary of America in New York in 1948 and upon completion in 1952 received both his

Master of Hebrew Literature degree and ordination. Feeling that his religious education was unbalanced without an adequate knowledge of Christianity, he then entered the Harvard Divinity School, where he received a master of theology degree in 1955.

From 1956 to 1958 Rubenstein accepted an interim appointment as chaplain to Jewish students at Harvard, Radcliffe and Wellesley Colleges. He also pursued doctoral studies in the psychology of religion at Harvard and completed a Ph.D. in 1960. His thesis was an essay in applied psychoanalysis. It focused on the role of ancient rabbis following the destruction of Jewish communities by the Romans in 70 C.E. and 135 C.E. Referring to this era as the Holocaust of ancient times, he compared it to modern-day Holocausts. A revised version of the thesis became Rubenstein's book *The Religious Imagination* (Indianapolis, 1968). He was chaplain to Jewish students at the University of Pittsburgh from 1958 to 1970 and from 1966 to 1970 lectured in French literature and the humanities there. He joined the faculty of Florida State University as professor in 1970 and was named distinguished professor of religion in 1977. Since 1973 Rubenstein has been director of the university's Center for the Study of Southern Culture and Religion, an interdisciplinary research institute.

Since the 1960s Rubenstein has complemented his academic work in the United States with extensive periods of study and teaching in Spain, Holland, France, Italy and West Germany. As part of his lifelong quest to understand the historical implications of Holocausts—and Rubenstein considers the Armenian massacres of the early 20th century and the murders of millions of Cambodians in the mid-1970s as part of his studies—he has worked closely with Protestant and Catholic scholars in Europe. In 1965 he was the first Jewish theologian to lecture at the Catholic University in Lublin, Poland and while there visited Auschwitz. Rubenstein's first book, *After Auschwitz: Radical Theology and Contemporary Judaism* (Indianapolis), was published the following year. The book was an attempt to understand how Judaism had evolved and been transformed in the aftermath of the systematic murder of 6 million Jews and in relation to the Protestant establishment. It was perhaps the first book to explore in depth the implications of the Holocaust and, according to Rubenstein, signaled the beginning of debates on the subject in theological circles.

His third book was *Morality and Ethos* (New York, 1970), an exploration of how human values develop according to ethical norms that do not consider religious foundations for their source. Rubenstein's next book, *My Brother Paul* (New York, 1972), was a psychoanalytic study of St. Paul. In it he raised the possibility that New Testament literature contained much of the source materials that directly contributed to later anti-Semitism and the Holocaust. Rubenstein took an autobiographical turn in the book that followed, *Power Struggle: An Autobiographical Confession* (New York, 1974), in which he explored the effect of the Holocaust on his life and achievements. He says, however, that despite the personal approach of the book, it is, in fact, "an essay in contemporary religious thought." It was followed by *The Cunning of History: Mass Death and the American Future* (New York, 1975), a study of the Holocaust from a political and social perspective rather than a theological one. *The Cunning of History* inspired author William Styron, who referred to it in his best-selling novel *Sophie's Choice,* and led Rubenstein to pursue a sequel tentatively entitled *The Age of Triage.*

Rubenstein's books reflect an ongoing concern with how various civilizations and cultures cope with advanced technology and what he refers to as "surplus people." By the late 1970s and early 1980s, he expanded his vision from the Holocaust and the Jews to embrace a more universal view including other cultures and eras. He visited the Far East and met with scholars and officials from Japan, Malaysia, Taiwan, Singapore and South Korea and lectured at conferences and universities. He also visited Mexico City, where overpopulation and new technologies have created monumental problems in the polyglot region.

Rubenstein has been instrumental in designing course curricula for Holocaust studies on the university level. He has guest-lectured throughout the United States and in Israel as well as in Europe and East Asia and has received fellowships from the Rockefeller Foundation, the National Humanities Institute at Yale University, the National Endowment for the Humanities and the Charles E. Merrill Educational Charitable Trust.

ARTHUR RUBINSTEIN

b. January 28, 1887
Pianist

For nearly nine decades, until the onset of blindness impaired his ability to perform in the mid-1970s, pianist Arthur Rubinstein stunned the world with his brilliant and ebullient performances of works by Mozart, Chopin, Liszt, Beethoven, Schubert, Debussy and other baroque and romantic composers. His music always had a special flair, for it mirrored the charmed life and the *joie de vivre* for which the musician had become renowned

and loved. Indeed, this legend among pianists has written: "I was born with music, it was my sixth sense. . . . It was always in me."

Arthur Rubinstein was the youngest of seven children born to Ignace and Felicia (Heyman) Rubinstein in Lodz, Poland. His father, who owned a hand-loom factory, recognized his son's musical talent and bought him a violin when he was 4. But piano proved to be his forte—he could sound out pieces with facility—and he began serious training in Warsaw and later in Berlin. There he came under the tutelage of the great German violinist Joseph Joachim, through whom Rubinstein's debut playing a Mozart concerto with the Berlin Symphony Orchestra when he was 11 was arranged. In 1902 he performed with the Warsaw Symphony and thereafter began touring the major cities of Europe, where his fame grew, at the same time that he befriended such major musical figures as Paderewski in Switzerland, Saint-Saens in Paris and others.

Rubinstein made his American debut on January 8, 1906, playing with the Philadelphia Orchestra in Carnegie Hall in New York, and then embarked on a tour of other American cities. But even as he arrived, Rubinstein made quite an impression on his growing following. According to news reports, during a stormy period on the ship *La Touraine,* the 18-year-old played from 9 to 12 hours nonstop in an effort to soothe the frightened passengers. By then he was earning $300 a concert—a high sum in those days.

Over the years Rubinstein became an inveterate and energetic traveler, who was known to perform in a short period of time a series of 10 concerts with 10 completely different programs and with a virtuosity and emotion few musicians had then equaled. His repertory, while focusing on many of the German and French romantic composers, was, however, much broader. After a 1916 concert in Spain, for example, he received national acclaim for his performances of works by Manuel de Falla and Isaac Albeniz and has been a favorite among Spanish and Latin American audiences ever since.

Settling in Paris, Rubinstein became known as much for being a womanizer as a pianist. Stories about him abounded, many of which he finally verified in his memoirs *My Young Years* (New York, 1973), which carried him through 1917, when he was 30. Fifteen years later, Rubinstein married Aniela Mlynarski, the daughter of the conductor Emil Mlynarski, for whom he had originally performed in Warsaw in 1902, before his wife-to-be was even born. The marriage was a turning point for Rubinstein in many ways. The younger pianist Vladimir Horowitz had begun to make a mark in international circles, and Rubinstein, who until then had been frequently criticized for lazy technique, now focused much more intensely on his playing. In fact, Rubinstein credits Horowitz for the improvements that resulted. He performed without rules, guided often only by his inspiration. The result was, as one critic put it, a "volcanic technique." He became a master virtuoso who later turned increasingly lyrical and a musician who strove constantly for perfection. His recordings became extraordinarily popular—Rachmaninoff's Second Concerto and Tchaikowsky's Concerto No. 1, in particular—but always the critics and the public associated Rubinstein with the music of Chopin. Certainly he was and is the greatest interpreter of Chopin.

Rubinstein toured the United States in 1932 and in 1936 began an association with the concert impresario Sol Hurok that would last until Hurok's death. In 1941 he moved to the United States permanently, settling in Los Angeles, and was naturalized five years later. The Second World War had a profound effect on Rubinstein: Virtually all his family that remained in Europe was wiped out. He refused to perform in Germany and Austria and only returned to play in Warsaw in 1958 after an absence from Poland of 20 years. The weeping audience received him with a standing ovation—a rare occurrence in Poland—and the following year he was made an honorary citizen. In 1975 Rubinstein returned to Lodz, his home town, where he received a standing ovation even before he played. The experience was a wrenching and traumatic one for the pianist, who described how the Germans "had killed off all my family. We were 70, 80, an enormous clan. They desecrated the synagogue. They desecrated my father's grave. I was frightfully bitter after the war and never wanted to come back here. I was afraid I would break down."

As early as 1935 Rubinstein, who often expressed his pride at being a Jew, turned his sights toward Israel, where he has often performed—and for free. Sol Hurok commented in 1961 that even when Rubinstein could command $24,000 a concert—he was the highest-paid performer in the world—he would not accept payment in Israel. And in a 1969 documentary, "Arthur Rubinstein: Love of Life," which covers Rubinstein's travels in Paris, New York, Iran and Tel Aviv, one of the most emotional moments occurs when Rubinstein is seen with one of his two daughters at the Western Wall in Jerusalem. He recalls his large family in Poland, which had been destroyed in pogroms. According to Hurok, Rubinstein "wept and said he wished only that his father could be alive to see this."

As an American, Rubinstein continued the same extraordinarily active life he had led in Europe, performing almost constantly, once playing the Second

Concerto of Rachmaninoff as background for the Hollywood film *I've Always Loved You* (for which he received $85,000), and he appeared in the 1949 film *Carnegie Hall*, which featured many other great musicians.

By his 70s and 80s, when Rubinstein should have been slowing down, he continued his unremitting and frenetic pace. In 1961, after hearing a recital that included etudes and waltzes by Chopin, the *Mephisto Waltz* and a sonata by Liszt, and the Schumann *Fantasiestuecke*, an amazed critic wrote: "It is no secret that Mr. Rubinstein is a man in his seventies. To choose a program like this is sheer defiance. To carry it off the way he did was a miracle. Not only a pianistic miracle but a biological one."

In 1980 Rubinstein published his second volume of memoirs, *My Many Years* (New York), a follow-up to *My Young Years*. He was the founder and president of the Frederic Chopin Fund, which has sponsored concerts to aid needy young concert artists in postwar Europe. He also sponsored the Arthur Rubinstein International Competition in Jerusalem for young master pianists. He has received numerous awards, including the Medal of Freedom from the White House in 1976.

A. JAMES RUDIN

b. October 7, 1934
Rabbi

As assistant national director of interreligious affairs of the American Jewish Committee, Rabbi A. James Rudin has been a leader in promoting greater communication within Jewish groups and among groups of all religious denominations, races and creeds. In recent years he has specialized in exploring the growth of religious cults and their particular attractiveness to certain Jewish youth.

Arnold James Rudin was born in Pittsburgh to Philip, a dentist, and Beatrice (Rosenbloom) Rudin. Raised in Alexandria, Virginia, he attended Wesleyan University and George Washington University, where he received a B.A. degree in 1955 and distinguished himself in student government and sports activities. In 1960 he received both his M.A. degree and rabbinical ordination from the Hebrew Union College-Jewish Institute of Religion in New York City. As in his undergraduate years, he excelled academically and wrote a thesis on "Some Aspects of the Transmission of the Isaiah Dead Sea Scroll." He did further graduate study in Jewish history at the University of Illinois.

Following service as an Air Force chaplain in Japan

and Korea from 1960 to 1962, Rudin became assistant rabbi of Congregation B'nai Jehudah in Kansas City, Missouri. Then, from 1964 to 1968 he served as Rabbi of Sinai Temple in Champaign, Illinois. During that time he became active in the American civil rights movement, helping out in the drive for voting rights in Hattiesburg, Mississippi in 1964. In 1968—the year he came to the American Jewish Committee—Rudin became national coordinator of the American Jewish Emergency Effort for Biafran Relief.

In the AJC post Rudin has lectured nationwide and on radio and television and has published articles in a wide range of religious and secular publications, including *Present Tense, Midstream, The New Republic, Christian Century, Christianity Today* and *The Ecumenist*. From 1970 to 1973 he was a regular panelist on a weekly radio program on WMCA (New York City) radio, *Religion on the Line*. He has also coordinated numerous conferences across America to promote dialogue among religious and other organizations. These include the Black-Jewish National Consultation in Nashville, Tennessee; a series of Lutheran-Jewish meetings; the Catholic-Jewish-Protestant Convocation at Seton Hall University; and many others.

His international work includes serving in 1974 as co-leader of the first group of interdenominational religious leaders to visit Israel, Jordan and Lebanon. In 1977 he led a task force to the Belgrade Conference on European Security and then went to the Vatican to speak out for civil rights and freedom of religion for Soviet Jews and other peoples victimized by repressive governments. In 1980, he led an interreligious delegation to the Madrid Conference on European Security in which he again pressed for human rights and religious liberty in the Soviet Union.

But perhaps the most provocative work Rudin has done is his in-depth exploration of the religious cult groups that have mushroomed in the United States in recent years. With his wife, Marcia Kaplan Rudin, he is the author of *Prison or Paradise? The New Religious Cults* (Philadelphia, 1980), an examination of why people are drawn to cults and why so many young Jews seem to be involved, far out of proportion to the general population. In response, the Rudins suggest that cults conduct many of their recruitment drives in college communities where Jewish students live and that they offer a supposedly secure and supportive environment that idealistic, impressionable and perhaps isolated young people may find appealing. However, what new recruits fail to realize, write the Rudins, is that the enticements used to draw them in are often deceptive and that some cults frequently discourage rational thought, are anti-woman and anti-family, and occasionally use brainwash-

ing techniques. The Rudins offer basic guidelines to parents of children in cults in order to encourage their return home and suggest that the best way to thwart the spread of cults is to prevent people from joining in the first place:

> People must be made aware of the rich variety of life styles and religious options that exist within contemporary Judaism and Christianity which can be accomplished by more effective intensified religious education. If one seeks more structure, regulation and authority in life, one need not join one of the new religious cults.

Rudin has also co-edited with Marc Tanenbaum and Marvin Wilson, *Evangelists and Jews in Conversation* (Grand Rapids, Michigan, 1978).

For further information:
Rudin, A. James. *Israel for Christians*. Philadelphia: 1982.

ALBERT B. SABIN

b. August 26, 1905
Scientist

World famous because of his development of an oral vaccine against polio, Albert Sabin has been honored repeatedly for his extraordinary achievement, which has led to the drastic decline of the dreaded disease, once a major crippler of children and young people.

Albert Sabin was born in Bialystock, Poland, one of four children of Jacob, a silk and textile manufacturer, and Tillie (Krugman) Sabin. The family emigrated to the United States in 1921 and settled in Paterson, New Jersey, where Sabin graduated from high school in 1923 and was a member of the debating society and worked on the literary magazine.

After performing odd jobs to earn money for his undergraduate and medical studies, Sabin graduated from New York University in 1928 with a Bachelor of Science degree and received his M.D. degree in 1931 from the same university. While still an intern at Bellevue Hospital in New York in 1932–33, he isolated virus B, a virus that was inherent in monkeys and fatal to human beings. He decided to devote his life to medical research.

After a year of postgraduate studies at the Lister Institute of Preventive Medicine in London (1934), Sabin joined the staff of the Rockefeller Institute for Medical Research for four years (1935–39). Early in his career he became interested in the childhood crippler polio and reported some of his initial findings about that disease as early as 1941.

During World War II, Sabin joined the U.S. Army Medical Corps. In that time he developed a vaccine against dengue fever, an acute and epidemic tropical disease. He was responsible for the successful inoculation against Japanese encephalitis of 65,000 American servicemen in Okinawa. He was also sent on special missions to Panama, Japan, Korea, China and Germany after the war.

Between 1946 and 1960 he was professor of research pediatrics at the University of Cincinnati College of Medicine and the Children's Hospital Research Foundation. From 1960 to 1971 he was named distinguished service professor of research pediatrics at the University of Cincinnati. During these years he devoted much of his time and energy to the fight against polio. He began testing his polio vaccine on animals in 1953 and on humans in 1955. It began to be used on a wide scale in the early 1960s. The live polio vaccine he developed is considered superior to the Salk vaccine by many because it provides for a longer period of immunization and can be stored indefinitely. Moreover, the Sabin vaccine, taken orally, is considered simpler to administer to patients.

Sabin has published hundreds of scientific articles detailing his extensive research. He is a member of the American Academy of Arts and Sciences, the National Academy of Science and the American Academy for the Advancement of Science. He has also been granted innumerable honorary degrees by many institutions, including Hebrew University, Hebrew Union College, Tel Aviv University, Hahneman Medical College, The Albert Einstein College of Medicine, Ohio State University and Temple University. He is also a recipient of the U.S. Medal of Science. In recent years he has continued his biomedical studies at the Weizmann Institute of Science in Rehovot, Israel; the University of South Carolina; and as consultant to the World Health Organization.

ABRAM SACHAR

b. February 15, 1899
University chancellor; historian

Abram Sachar has been a pioneer in Jewish higher education. He presided over the expansion of the Hillel Foundation into a national movement and was the first president of Brandeis University, the first and only college-level institution in America created by Jews as a secular institution. Founded in 1948, Brandeis offers a wide range of Jewish studies on the undergraduate and grad-

uate level as well as superior offerings in other non-Jewish fields.

Abram Leon Sachar was born in New York City. His father, Samuel, was a Lithuanian immigrant who came to the United States in the 1880s and eventually became a successful realtor in St. Louis. His mother, Sarah (Abramowitz) Sachar, was born in Jerusalem and settled in the United States as a teen-ager. Sachar began his college studies at Washington University in St. Louis in 1916 and then spent one academic year at Harvard University in 1918. Returning to Washington University, he received both a B.A. degree and an M.A. degree in 1920. He completed doctoral studies in history at Cambridge University in 1923.

From 1923 to 1929 Sachar was a history instructor at the University of Illinois, and from 1929 to 1933 he directed the university's Hillel Foundation. Rising into the executive ranks of the Hillel Foundation, Sachar became national director of the B'nai B'rith Hillel Foundation from 1933 through 1948 and then became chairperson of the National Hillel Foundation Committee, a post he held until 1955. Upon retirement from active participation in Hillel in 1955, Sachar became honorary chairperson.

Brandeis University first came into being in 1948 with Sachar at the helm. A remarkable academic fund raiser, he was the driving force behind Brandeis' rise to excellence. John C. Roche, who once taught there, described Sachar as "a strange mixture of scholar, dreamer and impresario." One of Sachar's major innovations in sustaining Brandeis was the creation of "foster alumni." As a private yet new institution, it had no endowment, so by inducing established philanthropists to become committed on an ongoing basis, he was able to add graduate degree programs in 1954; by 1959 there were 15 graduate departments. Sachar retired from the presidency in 1968 and was named chancellor.

From 1967 to 1972 he was a member of the U.S. Advisory Committee on International Education and Cultural Affairs. And in keeping with his past involvements, he is an officer of the American Organization for Rehabilitation Through Training Federation, a member of the American Jewish Historical Society, on the board of governors of Hebrew University and is active in many other Jewish organizations.

Sachar is also the author of several books. His first, *A History of the Jews* (New York), was originally published in 1929 and has been updated several times, most recently in 1965. It is a popular account, aimed at general readers. Other books include *Sufferance Is the Badge* (New York, 1939), a survey of the plight of Jews around the world from the Versailles Treaty through

1939, and *The Course of Our Times* (New York, 1972), a collection of commentary written by Sachar to accompany a 1968 public television series that described 20th-century events and personalities.

For further information:
Sachar, Abram. *The Course of Our Times.* New York: 1969.
———. *Factors in Jewish History.* New York: 1927.
———. *A History of the Jews.* New York: 1967.
———. *A Host at Last.* Boston: 1976.
———. *The Jew in the Contemporary World.* New York: 1939.
Rothchild, Sylvia. "Brandeis University: The Making of a First-Class Institution," *Present Tense,* Autumn 1979.

WILLIAM SAFIRE

b. December 17, 1929
Columnist

When former Nixon and Agnew speechwriter William Safire was hired as a columnist for *The New York Times* in 1974, readers of the newspaper were astonished that so conservative a journalist was being brought on board. He has since proved to be not only a brilliant political analyst—when necessary attacking members of his own party as well as his opponents—but an excellent balance for the *Times'* other, more liberal writers. In addition, his column *On Language,* an often-humorous weekly discussion of idiosyncrasies in written and spoken English, has become one of the *Times'* most popular features.

William Safire was born in New York City to Oliver, a thread manufacturer, and Ida (Panish) Safire. He attended Syracuse University for two years, but financial considerations forced him to drop out in 1949. He then found a job that year as a researcher for Tex McCrary, who then wrote a gossip column called *New York Close-up* for the *New York Herald-Tribune.* He began a meteoric rise in public relations and journalism. After serving briefly as a roving correspondent in Europe and the Middle East for WNBC radio and WNBC-TV in 1951, the following year he joined the U.S. Army, where he worked for the Armed Forces Radio Network. He was discharged two years later.

After the service Safire embarked on a career in public relations. He was made a junior partner in McCrary's and Jerry Finklestein's public relations firm. He became the producer for Tex McCrary's syndicated radio show and vice-president of Tex McCrary, Inc. in 1955–56.

In 1959 he founded his own firm. Safire traveled to the American National Exhibition in Moscow on behalf of All-State Properties. There he met Richard Nixon and helped set up the famous "kitchen debate" between the vice president and Soviet Premier Nikita Khrushchev, in which both men argued the merits of their respective countries.

Safire had long been interested in Republican Party politics, and in 1960 he became the chief of special projects for the Nixon-Lodge campaign. He handled much of the public relations aspect of the campaign and wrote promotional material to be distributed by campaign volunteers. In 1961 Safire founded Safire Public Relations Inc., which became profitable by Safire's use of unconventional gimmicks to promote his clients. In subsequent years he worked on campaigns for Nelson Rockefeller, Jacob Javits and John Lindsay. He also wrote *The Relations Explosion* (New York, 1963), in which he analyzed the problems of public relations firms as they then operated and proposed that they expand the services they offer. In his second book, *Plunging into Politics* (New York, 1964), Safire outlined methods of running political campaigns without resorting to party bosses.

Safire began to work for Richard Nixon's drive for the presidency in 1965 as an unpaid speechwriter, and he also ghostwrote Nixon's syndicated newspaper column. In 1968 he wrote Nixon's election victory speech and was appointed a special assistant to the president. That year *The New Language of Politics* (New York, 1968) was published. In it Safire took a close look at political rhetoric and how politicians manipulate language to blur meaning.

In the White House, Safire wrote major speeches for Nixon defending the Vietnam War and the administration's economic policies and led an in-house attempt to define Nixon's position on a wide range of subjects. In 1972, while on loan to the Spiro Agnew campaign, Safire coined the memorable phrases "nattering nabobs of negativism" and "hopeless hysterical hypochondriacs of history," which assured Agnew a place in American linguistic history. That year he also wrote a series of signed articles that appeared in *The New York Times* and *The Washington Post* alongside articles written by high-ranking officials in the McGovern campaign. The articles led to an offer by the *Times* for Safire to become a columnist, which he accepted.

After Safire left the White House, he wrote his memoirs. Called *Before the Fall* (New York, 1975), the book paints a positive picture of the pre-Watergate Nixon. Dismayed that the book did not sell as well as those written by aides implicated in the Watergate scandals, Safire wrote his first novel, a political thriller called *Full Disclosure* (New York, 1977). The plot concerns the efforts of White House aides to maintain in office a president who has been blinded in a helicopter accident. *Full Disclosure* was a best seller.

Safire proved himself an apt investigative reporter as well as a columnist while at the *Times*. In 1977 he began a probe into the financial affairs of Bert Lance, a former special assistant to President Jimmy Carter, and uncovered many conflicts of interest and irregularities in Lance's personal and professional dealings. The op-ed page columns led to an investigation and eventually to Lance's resignation under protest. The work earned Safire a Pulitzer Prize in 1978 as well as the comment by Republican Senator Howard Baker that "Safire may be to the Carter peanut warehouse what Woodward and Bernstein were to Watergate."

But he has not limited his attacks to Democrats. In 1980 Safire questioned President-elect Reagan's appointment of William French Smith as attorney general, noting Smith's dealings with Frank Sinatra, who had allegedly made some deals in Las Vegas in violation of federal antitrust laws. His expressions of doubts about Smith's integrity reflect Safire's own strong feelings about the need for absolute integrity among American political leaders. He is also a self-described "hawk" in foreign affairs and repeatedly calls for military responses abroad. Safire, in addition, is very strongly supportive of Israel and especially of Menachem Begin's government. "I think of Israel as a strategic asset and I'm for treating it as such," he told *Esquire* in January 1982. "Middle East policy really isn't a Democrat-Republican or liberal-conservative issue. It's a hard-line, soft-line. I'm a hard-liner. I was a hawk on Vietnam. I think abandoning Taiwan is an indication of a willingness to abandon Israel."

After the publication of *Safire's Political Dictionary* (New York, 1978), an updated version of his earlier book about the use of language in politics, Safire published two collections of his columns, *On Language* (New York, 1980) and *Safire's Washington* (New York, 1980). In the former he defends the proper use of language and objects to worn-out phrases, misuse of words and sugar-coated sentences that obscure meaning. When *Publishers Weekly* asked him, "How do you come by your keen memory for the odd phrase or anecdote," he answered, "I'm in my anecdotage."

For further information:

Navasky, Victor. "Safire Appraised." *Esquire*, January 1982.

"William Safire," *Publishers Weekly*, April 30, 1982.

MORT SAHL

b. May 11, 1927
Satirist

Although the career of satirist Mort Sahl peaked in the early 1960s and never fully recovered its early glamour, as a stand-up performer of topical humor he laid the groundwork for a generation of younger "intellectual" comics, including Woody Allen, David Frye and Dick Cavett. His no-holds-barred approach to his subjects, from Eisenhower to Kennedy to Reagan, and his unremitting iconoclasm—at every show he invariably asks, "Are there any groups I haven't offended?" and if any hands are raised, he proceeds to devastate them—have marked Sahl as difficult to tolerate yet important to listen to. As a *Daily News* reviewer once remarked, "What Sahl does is very simple and therefore very difficult: he merely mentions the events of the day and points out their bizarre implications."

Morton Lyon Sahl was born in Montreal, Canada to Harry Sahl, a tobacco shop proprietor. His father, an American citizen, eventually became a U.S. government clerk in the Department of Justice and after moving the family around to several cities, he finally settled in Los Angeles in 1934. Sahl attended high school there but lied about his age in 1940 to enlist in the Army. After only two weeks, however, his mother located him and fetched him home. After he completed high school, he reenlisted and was stationed in Anchorage, Alaska, where he edited the local Army post newspaper.

Returning to California, Sahl attended Compton Junior College from 1947 to 1949 and the University of Southern California, where he received a B.S. degree in city management and engineering in 1950. However, rather than begin a career in that field, he opted to pursue his interest in theater. From 1950 to 1953 he performed in experimental theater ensembles, wrote for literary magazines and supported himself with odd jobs.

In 1953, having developed a topical stage show, he was hired for a short run at the Hungry i (the *i* was for "intellectual"), a San Francisco nightclub. As he would do in subsequent acts, he walked on stage in a collegiate-style outfit—a V-neck sweater was his trademark—and read from the daily newspaper. The comments that followed were what captivated the audience—gibes at politicians, barbs at the social mores of everyday people —and they soon led to engagements in other clubs, including the Copacabana, the Blue Angel and The Village Vanguard, all in New York City.

By the mid-1950s, not yet 30, Sahl was already a national media figure and one of the highest-paid comedians. One of his favorite targets of the era was Richard Nixon, whom Sahl never liked. Describing his first meeting with Nixon in 1956, he recounted how Nixon stretched his hand to him and said, "I'm from California," to which Sahl replied, "Well, there's not an awful lot you can dispute there, but you have given me something to think about." He became especially good at taunting Republicans. In 1958 he had a movie role in a 20th Century-Fox film, *In Love and War*. The reviews were mediocre. The same year, Sahl also appeared in a Broadway revue, *The Next President*, but that, too, was a failure and ran only 13 performances. Apparently Sahl's stand-up solo nightclub style was not transferable to another medium, and his appeal was very specific; if you didn't like him, you hated him. Or, as *Journal-American* critic Jack O'Brien wrote in a 1960 review of a Sahl television appearance, "Mort Sahl, on TV at least, is consistent; he gets worse each time he goes on."

By the late 1950s Sahl had befriended Senator John Kennedy and even wrote some speeches for him. When Kennedy was elected president, Sahl maintained a close friendship and often told an anecdote about a chat Kennedy had with his father when the younger man was still a senator: "His father says to him, 'Jack, what do you want as a career?' Jack answers, 'I want to be president.' 'I know about that,' says his father, 'but I mean when you grow up.' " Sahl also made his first recordings during the Kennedy administration—*The New Frontier, Look Forward in Anger* and *The Future Lies Ahead*.

After Kennedy was assassinated, Sahl became obsessive about a possible conspiracy theory and temporarily joined New Orleans District Attorney Jim Garrison in an independent investigation. Much of his act at that time concerned his obsession. He would walk on stage and read excerpts from the Warren Commission report, adding his own acid comment. Audiences were turned off, and his career began to slump. By the mid-1960s he developed a reputation for erratic behavior. Scheduled television appearances were abruptly canceled as was a planned appearance in a Broadway drama in 1964, *The Sign in Sidney Brustein's Window*. Although he continued appearing in Las Vegas hotels, in nightclubs around the country and on college campuses, for the most part Sahl had lost his early appeal.

But with Vietnam and Watergate, he had new targets for his acid wit. Of Vietnam, he commented, "You know why the liberals say we should get out of Vietnam, why it's a 'senseless war'? Because we're losing." And in 1973 he released a new record, *Sing a Song of Watergate—Apochryphal of Lie*. He also found new topics to pick over, including women's liberation ("It's that Women's Lib thing—they want to be men. Why should

women want to be second class men when they can be first class women?") and Israel, which he described as "the only privately endowed country in the world."

For several months in 1978, Sahl hosted a call-in radio show in Washington, D.C., but that folded after seven months. He made a successful comeback in 1981, however, when he opened in a New York City nightclub and found in Ronald Reagan a new butt for his bite. "Reagan? We're good friends," he said. "Basically, however, you have to be careful of a guy who classifies ketchup as a vegetable."

For further information:
Sahl, Mort. *Heartland,* an autobiography. New York: 1976.

JONAS EDWARD SALK

b. October 28, 1914
Scientist

In 1954 Jonas Salk made medical history when, after years of research, he developed the first effective polio vaccine. By 1955 conquest of the disease that had ravaged the lives of countless young people in the United States and around the world was within easy reach. The New York-born physician has since carried on his mission to conquer other crippling diseases, with special emphasis in recent years on the nerve-degenerating ailment multiple sclerosis.

Jonas Edward Salk was born in Manhattan to Daniel, a manufacturer of ladies' scarves and blouses, and Dora (Press) Salk. After graduating from Townsend Harris High School, a highly competitive high school for gifted boys on the City College campus, he attended City College of New York, where he received a B.S. degree in 1934. Then, from 1935 to 1937 he attended New York University as a chemistry fellow and by 1939 had earned his M.D. He worked one more year at New York University in bacteriology—his forte as a researcher had become clear early in his medical studies—interned at Mt. Sinai Hospital from 1940 to 1942 and then went to the University of Michigan, where for the next five years he was a researcher and professor in epidemiology at its School of Public Health.

In 1947 Salk moved to the University of Pittsburgh, where his work in bacteriology blossomed. As an associate research professor at the medical school and director of its virus research laboratory, a position he held until 1963, Salk initiated and supervised experiments with a form of killed virus-type vaccine that ultimately proved effective in the prevention of polio. After successful testing on nearly 2 million school children across the United States, as well as on Salk's wife, his three sons and himself, Salk's vaccine was recognized internationally as one of the great advances in immunology. And although an oral polio vaccine developed some years later by Dr. Albert Sabin ultimately supplanted Salk's four-shot method in many countries, his accomplishment nevertheless represented one of the great leaps forward in the conquest of disease.

In 1955 Salk was named commonwealth professor of preventive medicine at Pittsburgh and two years later was named commonwealth professor of experimental medicine. He left in 1963 to found the Salk Institute of Biological Studies in La Jolla, California and in 1965 was honored for his work by a joint resolution of Congress.

Salk won many awards for his polio research, including the Albert Lasker Award in 1956, and has received many honorary degrees. However, rather than dwell on past achievements, he is most excited about his current research work on multiple sclerosis, a progressive degenerative disease of the nervous system, which attacks its victims in their late 20s or early 30s. As of 1980 he was developing a myelin basic protein, which he theorized would divert the antibodies from attacking the myelin sheaths that protect the nerve cells in M.S. victims.

He has written two books, both extensive explorations of human development from scientific and philosophical points of view intended for general readers. *Man Unfolding* (New York, 1972) discusses the biological processes that led to the evolution of humankind and compares these processes to theories about the evolution of the universe. In *The Survival of the Wisest* (New York, 1973), Salk continues his speculations on whether the human species can co-exist with nature and its evolutionary processes cooperatively rather than destructively. Above all, he writes, a human must learn to "respect wisdom and to behave as if he were wise."

PAUL SAMUELSON

b. May 15, 1915
Economist

Paul Samuelson may well be the most influential economist in America, although his espousal of some Keynesian theories (for instance, the theory that the cycles of boom and depression in capitalist economies are inevitable without some controls) have not endeared him to recent presidential administrations. Awarded a Nobel Prize in economics in 1970, Samuelson was a

close adviser to presidents Kennedy and Johnson and supported spending programs to aid the unemployed and the needy.

Paul Anthony Samuelson was born in Gary, Indiana to Frank, a pharmacist, and Ella (Lipton) Samuelson. He graduated from Hyde Park High School in Chicago in 1932 and received a B.A. degree from the University of Chicago in 1935. He then went on to Harvard University, where he completed an M.A. degree in 1936 and a Ph.D. in 1941. His career at MIT began the year before, when he was appointed assistant professor of economics. He became associate professor in 1944, full professor in 1947 and institute professor in 1966.

Samuelson's abilities to formulate economic ideas and apply them to current problems were recognized early in his career, and in 1941 he served for two years as consultant to the National Resources Planning Board. He was often called upon to serve as a consultant to government or private industry and has testified at many congressional hearings on the economy. Since 1948 he has consulted for the Rand Corporation, and he served presidents Eisenhower, Kennedy and Johnson in an advisory capacity.

As a major shaper of economic policy during the Kennedy years, Samuelson devised what was named "Operation Twist," a program designed to stimulate foreign investment by keeping short-term interest rates high and to promote domestic development of plants and equipment by keeping long-term interest rates low. He advocated more housing and education programs, especially in depressed areas, and was a supply-sider to the extent that he supported lowering taxes to fuel the economy in periods of economic stagnation. He urged deficit spending in times when social needs were greatest and surpluses otherwise. Although Kennedy rejected a tax cut proposed by Samuelson, President Johnson had one passed in 1964. But when the economy began to show signs of "demand-pull" inflation, Samuelson urged institution of a tax increase. When LBJ refused, Samuelson was vocal in stating that anti-poverty programs should not become the casualties of budget cuts. In 1968 Congress passed a 10 percent increase.

Samuelson, long considered a "mainstream liberal," dropped out of government favor when Richard Nixon was elected to the presidency, although his stature as an economist continued to grow. He attacked Nixon's proposals to build the Supersonic Transports—the SST's—and Nixon's policies of tight credit. Although Nixon later accepted some tenets of Keynesian economics, he placed Samuelson on his infamous "enemies list."

When he received the Nobel Prize, Samuelson was only the second economist to win it. His response to it, however, was to give credit to the influential teachers with whom he studied in Chicago and at Harvard and to the collaborators with whom he shared extensive hours of study and writing.

Samuelson's clear style of writing and thinking formed the basis for a now-historic textbook entitled *Economics* (New York), which he completed in 1948. Updated many times since then, more than 3 million copies have been printed, and the book has been translated into 20 foreign languages. Samuelson has been a Guggenheim fellow (1948–49), has edited and published widely in professional journals, and is a regular columnist for *Newsweek*.

For further information:

Samuelson, Paul. *The Collected Scientific Papers of Paul A. Samuelson.* 4 vols. Cambridge, Mass.: 1966, 1972, 1978.

———. *Foundations of Economic Analysis.* Cambridge, Mass.: 1947.

Samuelson, Paul. ed. *Readings in Economics.* New York: 1955, 1958, 1961, 1964, 1967, 1970, 1973.

Samuelson, Paul; Dorfman, R.; and Solow, R.M. *Linear Programming and Economic Analysis.* New York: 1958.

NAHUM MATTATHIAS SARNA

b. March 27, 1923
Scholar

Nahum Sarna is one of America's foremost scholars of Biblical history and has been instrumental in translating many ancient Biblical texts as well as contemporary Hebrew learning on Biblical themes. By devoting his life to study and to teaching—he began teaching in 1946 and since 1965 has been affiliated with Brandeis University—he has prepared dozens of younger students to carry on the task of Bible study, especially interpreting and updating familiar texts and exploring and studying obscure manuscripts from other regions of the world and from other eras.

Nahum Mattathias Sarna was born in London, England to Jacob, a bookseller of Jewish goods, and Milly (Horoznick) Sarna. He was educated at the University of London, where he received a B.A. degree with first class honors in 1944, and an M.A. degree in 1946. In 1947 he received a Ministers diploma from Jews College in London. He came to the United States in 1951 and in 1955 completed a Ph.D. in Biblical Studies and Semitic Languages at Dropsie College in Philadelphia. Sarna was naturalized in 1959.

His teaching career began at Hebrew University College in London, where he was an assistant lecturer from 1946 to 1949. After arriving in the United States, he became a lecturer at Gratz College in Philadelphia from 1951 to 1957. During that time he formulated some of his ideas about the teaching of Bible and Jewish studies and published *A Syllabus of Biblical History* (Philadelphia, 1953). He moved to New York in 1957 to join the Bible faculty at the Jewish Theological Seminary of America. From 1957 to 1963 he was librarian and assistant professor of Bible, and from 1963 to 1965 associate professor of Bible. While at the Seminary, Sarna published several essays exploring the Book of Job, including one for the *Journal of Biblical Literature*, which examined the mythical interpretations of chapter 18. This kind of intensive study is an example of Sarna's approach to Bible—picking apart texts verse by verse or chapter by chapter in order to reach a clearer understanding of the deeper meaning not apparent to the untrained reader.

Since 1965 Sarna has taught Biblical studies at Brandeis, for two years as associate professor, and since 1967 as Dora Golding Professor of Biblical studies. From 1967 to 1975 he chaired the department of Near Eastern and Judaic Studies. He has also held visiting professorships at Columbia University (1964-65), Andover-Newton Theological School in Newton, Mass. (1966-67) and Dropsie College (1967-68).

The work for which he is best known is *Understanding Genesis* (New York, 1966), which earned him the 1967 Jewish Book Council Award for the Best Book on Jewish Thought. *Understanding Genesis* symbolizes Sarna's lifetime effort to make Biblical writing accessible to the general reader and it was the first result of a Translation Committee of the Jewish Publication Society of America, on which he played a key role from 1965 to 1982. In 1982 he was co-translator (with Moshe Greenberg and Jonas C. Greenfield of the Hebrew University) of *The Writings*—Kethubim in Hebrew. The translation was more than a quarter century in the making. It relies on the language of the day, utilizing the findings of modern archaeology and Biblical scholarship to transmit the original Hebrew text into modern literary English. For example, the first line of Ecclesiastes—"Vanity of vanities . . . all is vanity" from the Revised Standard Version of 1952 (official Bible of the National Council of Churches)—is now translated as "Utter futility . . . all is futility," a less literal but more valid rendering of the writer's intention, according to Sarna. Furthermore, the 23rd Psalm's "valley of the shadow of death" is now translated as "valley of deepest darkness." The contents of *The Writings* include the books of Psalms, Proverbs, Job, Ezra, Nehemiah, the First and Second Chronicles, etc.

Sarna has also worked on other projects of similarly

vast scope. He has served as department editor of the Bible Division of the *Encyclopedia Judaica* and authored thirty entries. He was on the editorial board of the *Journal of Biblical Literature* from 1973 to 1975 and is currently on the board of *Biblical Archaeology*. His writings also appear in such authoritative works as *Encyclopedia International* (1963); *Encyclopedia Hebraica* (1972); *Encyclopedia Migraith* (Jerusalem, 1971 and 1976); *Encyclopedia Britannica* (1973); and *Encyclopedia Ivrith* (1978).

Sarna was a senior fellow at the American Council of Learned Societies in 1971 to 1972 and became a fellow of the American Academy for Jewish Research in 1974. He joined the Council of the World Union of Jewish Studies in 1981 and in 1982 received a one-year fellowship from Hebrew University to attend its Institute for Advanced Studies.

For further information:
Sarna, Nahum Mattathias. "The Bible and Judaic Studies," in *The Teaching of Judaica in American Universities*, ed., Leon A. Jick. New York: 1970.
———. *The Heritage of Biblical Literature*. New York: 1964.
———. "A Psalm for the Sabbath Day—Psalm 92," *Journal of Biblical Literature*, LXXXI 1962.
———. *The Teaching of the Bible*. Cleveland: 1965.
Sarna, Nahum Mattathias, Greenberg, Moshe, Greenfield, Jonas C. *The Book of Job: A New Translation According to the Traditional Hebrew Text with Introductions*. Philadelphia, 1980.
———. *A New Translation of the Book of Psalms*. Philadelphia, 1973.

ROBERT W. SARNOFF

b. July 2, 1918
Radio and television executive

Robert W. Sarnoff, former president of the Radio Corporation of America (RCA) and current chairman of the RCA board of directors, is one of America's most successful corporate executives.

Robert William Sarnoff was born in New York City to Russian immigrant David, founder of RCA, and Lizette (Hermant) Sarnoff, who was born in France. He was educated at private schools in New York and graduated from Phillips Academy in Andover, Massachusetts in 1935. He earned his B.A. degree in government from Harvard in 1939. Upon graduation Sarnoff spent a year at Columbia Law School but left to enter the federal government employ in Washington, D.C. in August 1941.

There he worked in the broadcasting department of

the office of the coordinator of information until March 1942, when he was commissioned an ensign in the United States Navy. His job was to supervise the creation of direct radio circuits to the United States from important Pacific islands. Back in the United States by the end of 1944, Sarnoff became the liaison between the Navy and the radio networks in Southern California until late 1945, when he was discharged.

Sarnoff had a brief career in the newspaper and magazine field before joining NBC, a subsidiary of RCA, as an account executive in 1948. He was quickly promoted to aide to the national programs director, television production manager and program sales manager. Named as director of unit productions in 1951, Sarnoff oversaw the production of such television shows as *The Kate Smith Hour, Your Show of Shows, All Star Revue* and *The Colgate Comedy Hour*. After being made NBC vice president in 1951, he was, a year later, put in charge of its infant film division and before long began urging the development of color programming.

After his election to the presidency of NBC on December 7, 1955, Sarnoff demonstrated his commitment to color television. He dedicated the world's first "all color" television station, WNBQ-TV Chicago, an NBC-owned station, on April 15, 1956.

That year he also took a strong stand against government regulation of networks and testified before a 1956 congressional antitrust subcommittee on the television industry that he favored more competition in television utilizing more fully the UHF (ultra high frequency) and VHF (very high frequency) television channels.

Sarnoff was president of NBC until 1958, when he became chairman of the board, a position he held until 1966. During those years, television became *the* major mass medium in this country. He was president of RCA from 1966 to 1975, at which time he was forced to resign because the board was dissatisfied with his performance on account of lagging profits. He is still chairman of the RCA board, a position he has held since 1970.

ZALMAN SCHACHTER

b. August 28, 1924
Rabbi

Carrying on a tradition whose roots began with the ancient master Rabbi Akiva, Rabbi Zalman Schachter has brought Jewish mysticism to the modern age. As founder of B'nai Or (Children of Light), he has invited Jews of all ages and persuasions to join him in a quest for spiritual and mystical knowledge. As one of his goals, he attempts to use Jewish study and being "to create a stoned or peaked experience without using drugs."

Zalman Meshullam Schachter-Shalomi was born in Zolkiew, Poland to Salomon, a merchant, and Eugenia (Yagid) Schachter. Until 1938 he attended a Hebrew high school, the Chajas Gymnasium, in Vienna. But when the political ambience became too threatening for his family as the Nazis grasped for power, he moved to Belgium, where he continued to study in yeshivas. From 1940 to 1941, when the Vichy government controlled France, Schachter was interned at Montlucon and Remoulins. Finally released, he left for the United States in 1941 and settled in Brooklyn, where he attended yeshivas under the sponsorship of the Lubavitcher Hasidim. He was ordained in 1947, and in 1949 Schachter received his American citizenship.

With ordination came the beginning of Schachter's teaching career. From 1947 to 1948 he taught at Yeshiva Achei Timimim in Rochester, New York and from 1948 to 1952 was rabbi and Hebrew school principal for Congregation Ahavath Achim in Falls River, Massachusetts. He served the same duties at Congregation Agudath Achim in New Bedford, Massachusetts.

Over the years Schachter developed a reputation as an outstanding teacher. But he remained a serious student as well, seeking to broaden his own perspectives on his life as a Jew and on the world around him. To that end, he studied psychology and in 1954 completed clinical training and was awarded a diploma from the Boston Jewish Chaplaincy Committee. In 1956 he received an M.A. degree in the psychology of religion from Boston University.

During this period, Schachter began to open himself to experiences beyond what he perceived as the limitations of Hasidism. Moving to the University of Manitoba in Canada in 1956, where he headed the Department of Judaic Studies, he began to explore Eastern religions and to experiment with zen and yoga. Eventually he drew a connection between the practice of *davening* [praying] and Eastern meditation. In the mid-1960s, he founded B'nai Or, a movement devoted to the practice and study of Jewish mysticism as a form of life enrichment.

All along, Schachter had been working on a doctorate, and in 1968 he received his Doctor of Hebrew Literature from Hebrew Union College in Cincinnati. His dissertation was titled "The Encounter: A Study of Counselling in Hasidism."

During the 1968–69 academic year, Schachter took a leave of absence from Manitoba to study ancient Near Eastern languages at Brandeis University and to teach in the Boston area. There he not only continued his mystical pursuits but joined in the formation of the Havurah movement among young Jews seeking a richer, alternative Jewish lifestyle. He returned to Manitoba in 1969, and in 1970 the Department of Judaic Studies was expanded and renamed the Department of Near Eastern and Judaic Studies. Several times throughout his career at the university, Schachter was cited for his excellence in teaching.

He became involved in many of the new mystical movements springing up throughout the United States, contributing at different times to Esalen, the Lama Foundation, the Naropa Institute and to the mystical commune called The House of Love and Prayer, founded by Schachter's California counterpart, the "hippie rabbi" Schlomo Carlebach.

In 1975 Schachter was named professor of religion in Jewish mysticism at Temple University in Philadelphia. Once settled, he established national headquarters for B'nai Or, and he attracted followers from all over the United States. Although actual membership is small, participants in B'nai Or number in the thousands. Schachter continually studies other religions, including Catholicism, Buddhism, Sufism and Native American religions as well as studying and teaching Kabbalah. He sees in B'nai Or an answer to the spiritual quest of young, often alienated, Jews, some of whom have opted to leave Judaism altogether and to follow alternative cults. In B'nai Or young Jews can find a crossroads where mainstream and disaffected Jews can share growth experiences.

Since the 1950s Schachter has published several books about his work and many scholarly monographs and articles. He has contributed a chapter on the study of Jewish mysticism to *The Jewish Catalogue,* published by the Jewish Publication Society of America. His most recent books include *Fragments of a Future Scroll: Hasidism for the Aquarian Age* and *The First Step: A Jewish Spiritual Handbook* (New York, 1982). He has also provided production research and assistance to drama production of *Fiddler on the Roof, The Dybbuk* and other plays.

Schachter, who founded the Aquarian Minyan during a stay in Berkeley, California, is on the editorial board of *Menorah,* a publication of the Washington, D.C.-based Center for Jewish Renewal.

SUSAN FROMBERG SCHAEFFER

b. March 25, 1941
Novelist; poet

With four novels and numerous critically acclaimed collections of poetry to her credit, Susan Fromberg Schaeffer has established herself as an important contemporary American-Jewish writer.

Susan Fromberg was born in Brooklyn to Irving, a clothing manufacturer, and Edith (Levine) Fromberg. After graduating with a B.A. degree in 1961, an M.A. degree in 1963 and a Ph.D. in 1966, all in English from the University of Chicago, she began a teaching career as instructor in English at Wright Junior College in Chicago, where she worked from 1963 to 1964. From 1964 to 1966 she was assistant professor of English at the Illinois Institute of Technology in Chicago. Since 1966 she has taught at Brooklyn College.

Schaeffer published her first book of poetry, *The Witch and the Weather Report* (New York), in 1972. She has since published *Granite Lady* (New York, 1974), *The Rhymes and Runes of the Toad* (New York, 1976), *Red White and Blue Poems* (St. Paul, Minn., 1977), *Time of the King and Queen* (Cambridge, Mass., 1979), *The Blue Man* (Birmingham, Ala., 1979), *The Queen of Egypt* (New York, 1980) and *Bibles of the Beasts of the Little Field* (New York, 1980).

Schaeffer's poems often deal with death, loneliness and isolation and blur the boundaries between the real and the surreal. *Granite Lady,* Schaeffer's most acclaimed volume of poetry—for which she was nominated for the National Book Award—was praised by a *Poetry* magazine reviewer for its "intelligence heightened and transmitted through vivid imagination, brilliant imagery and remarkable formal integrity. How she can sustain such power, poem after poem, makes one marvel at her craft."

Schaeffer's first novel, *Falling* (New York, 1973), which focuses on a Jewish female graduate student whose life seems to be falling apart, was praised as a convincing and funny work. All the same, it is with *Anya* (New York, 1974), a Holocaust-based novel about an upper-class Polish-Jewish woman whose childhood is destroyed by the Gestapo and who ultimately emigrates to America, that Schaeffer became recognized as a major talent. A *New York Times* critic wrote that it "represents a new stride toward maturity in Jewish-American writing." And author Cynthia Ozick said: "*Anya* makes experience —no, gives it, as if uninvented, or as if, turning around in your own room, you see, for the first time, what has happened, who you are, and what is there, and why."

She departed from her usual Jewish themes in her next book, *Time in Its Flight* (New York, 1978), a family saga set in 19th-century Vermont. The book was panned by critics as a dull historical novel, poorly organized and without purpose. In her most recent book, *Love* (New York, 1981), the author returns to the theme of *Anya*—how personal destiny is often abruptly disrupted by history and circumstance—and to Jewishness.

In *Love,* Schaeffer focuses on the life of Esheal Luria,

a Russian boy abandoned by his widowed mother when she remarries, who makes his way to America and becomes an affluent pharmacist in Brooklyn during the 1930s. In the novel Schaeffer portrays Luria's maturity and the youthful memories of his mother's desertion and of a mystical "witch" that haunts him through adulthood. Praised by writer Margaret Atwood as Schaeffer's "finest novel to date," it underscored Schaeffer's strength as a chronicler of the Jewish experience.

SYDNEY SCHANBERG

b. January 17, 1934
Journalist

In 1975 *New York Times* readers were exposed to a series of chilling and often unbelievable firsthand reports of the forced evacuation of millions of Cambodians from cities to the countryside and the subsequent mass starvation, which wiped out nearly half that country's population. The author of these remarkable (and award-winning) articles, Sydney Schanberg, has since emerged as one of the more important humanistic journalists to write for the *Times*—or any other publication.

Sydney Hillel Schanberg was born in Clinton, Massachusetts to Louis, a grocer, and Freda (Feinberg) Schanberg. Educated at Harvard University, where he received a B.A. degree in 1955, he joined the *Times* as a copyboy in 1959 after serving in the U.S. Army. The following year he became a reporter and in 1967 became the *Times'* bureau chief in Albany. Schanberg became a foreign correspondent in 1969, when he was sent to New Delhi, India. Transferred to Singapore in 1973, where he became the *Times'* Southeast Asian correspondent, he traveled through the subcontinent reporting on and photographing the turmoil following the pullout of American troops from Vietnam and its effect in surrounding areas.

Schanberg next traveled to Cambodia, where, with the aid of a native interpreter named Dith Pran, he reported on the effects of American bombing raids and on the take-over of the government by a Cambodian guerilla leader, Pol Pot. As conditions became dangerous for foreigners—as well as for native Cambodians—Schanberg's editors ordered him to leave. But he refused and at great risk continued to file stories from Phnom Penh. Meanwhile, Dith Pran was arrested and only by cloaking his identity as a writer and masquerading as a laborer was able to survive several years of deprivation under the new regime. As a known journalist, he would probably have been killed. His family had escaped Cambodia separately, settling in California with the help of Schanberg, who returned to the United States and became metropolitan editor of the *Times* in 1977. Schanberg's stories on the Cambodian atrocities earned him the 1976 Pulitzer Prize for international reporting "at great risk" and many other journalism prizes as well. In the meantime, in his new post, he significantly expanded the *Times'* coverage of New York City's outer boroughs and those smaller, lesser-known communities and neighborhoods that tended to get lost in the shuffle as Manhattan stories seemed to take greater priority.

In 1979, after a four-year search, Schanberg and Dith Pran were reunited when the Cambodian was able to flee the country after an arduous journey on foot. With aid from the *Times*, he rejoined his family in California. His story became the subject of a long, highly personal and emotional article by Schanberg in the *New York Times Magazine* on January 20, 1980, entitled "The Life and Death of Dith Pran."

Schanberg began writing regular columns for the *Times* op-ed page in early 1981. They are typified by a strong awareness of the "ordinary" people and of the so-called lesser incidents in life that in fact are most consequential. His sensitivity is such that when he wrote an article critical of the quality of life in the South Bronx, he subsequently devoted an entire column to the responses to his article by South Bronx high school students who criticized his failure to see the good in their community. In another column following Yom Kippur 1981, he expressed sympathy and support for his rabbi's sermon expressing deep chagrin at those Jews who no longer seem interested in showing "compassion" for the poor and helpless in American society and have discarded the universalism of Judaism for a more parochial and particularistic manner of expressing their Judaism. In addition, he has written many columns on the displacement of the elderly and the poor from New York's Upper West Side's apartment houses by avaricious landlords.

MEYER SCHAPIRO

b. September 23, 1904
Art historian

Meyer Schapiro, the dean of American art historians, is a scholar who has made important contributions to the understanding of medieval and modern art. A highly respected educator and a popular lecturer, he is the author of several acclaimed books on art and professor emeritus at Columbia University.

Meyer Schapiro was born in Shavly, Lithuania to Nathan, a businessman, and Fanny (Adelman) Schapiro. He was brought to the United States by his parents in 1904 and became a naturalized citizen in 1914. Schapiro obtained a B.A. degree in 1924 and a Ph.D. in art in 1931, both from Columbia University. He was a lecturer in Columbia's Department of Fine Arts from 1928 to 1936, was made an assistant professor in 1936, an associate professor in 1946 and a full professor of art history six years later. From 1965 to 1973 he was university professor and since 1973 has been professor emeritus. He has also taught as a visiting professor at Harvard University from 1966 to 1967 and at Oxford University from 1968 to 1969.

Since his retirement to professor emeritus, Schapiro has found an even wider audience. In 1977 he published *Romanesque Art* (New York). It traced the genesis and history of the art of the Middle Ages—which was characterized by round arches, decorative use of arcades and profuse ornamentation—as it developed in Italy and Western Europe after 1000 C.E.

Schapiro's second volume, *Modern Art* (New York, 1978), demonstrated his expertise in the field of 19th- and 20th-century European and American art. The collection of essays, ranging from the broadly philosophical to detailed analyses of specific paintings, won the 1978 National Book Critics Circle award. Among the artists Schapiro discusses in the book are Cezanne, Courbet, Van Gogh, Seurat, Picasso, Chagall and Gorky.

Schapiro's areas of specialty are extremely broad and extend to several eras and art styles. In *Modern Art* he examines the still-life painting *The Apples* by Cezanne from a psychological as well as an aesthetic view. He analyzes Picasso's *Woman with a Fan* as a transformation and development from an earlier drawing, and he traces and explores the imagery, and in particular the Biblical themes, so prevalent in Chagall's paintings.

In his third volume of his series of selected papers, *Late Antique, Early Christian and Mediaeval Art* (New York, 1981), Schapiro sets himself apart from the medievalists of his generation by concerning himself with more than strictly Christian religious subject matter. His understanding and interpretation of secular aspects of the Middle Ages is as significant as his knowledge of the Semitic religions and their art. Schapiro's ability to combine discussions of the relationship between secular and religious art, literary sources of the era and stylistic and iconographic detail of the period distinguishes him as not only a brilliant art historian but also as a social historian.

Unlike most art historians, Schapiro rarely addresses himself only to the specialists in his field. Rather, he explores his subjects not only in the context of their own time but in terms of the present. In his essays and lectures he reveals a commitment to the living artists and to using achievements of the past to help illuminate the present. Schapiro's collections of papers will conclude with an expected fourth volume, *The Theory and Philosophy of Art*.

Schapiro has won numerous awards, including a creative art award for notable achievement from Brandeis University in 1966, an award for excellence in art history from the Art Dealers Association in 1973 and an award for distinguished scholarship in the humanities from the American Council of Learned Societies in 1960.

He is a fellow of the American Academy of Arts and Sciences, the American Philosophy Society, the Medieval Academy of America and the National Institute of Arts and Letters. He is also a member of the board of editors of *The History of Ideas*.

MORRIS URMAN SCHAPPES

b. May 3, 1907
Editor; historian

As educator, historian and editor, Morris Urman Schappes has been an avid commentator on the Jewish experience in America as well as an impassioned debater on the role Jews have played in the United States and in the Soviet Union. He has also been active in fostering an interchange of opinions and support with other American minorities, most notably with American blacks. For this, Schappes was once investigated, blacklisted and briefly imprisoned. But ultimately, he has been vindicated and much honored.

Morris Urman Schappes was born in Kamenets-Podolsk, the Ukraine to Hyman, a wood-turner, and Sonia (Urman) Shapshilevich. Schappes' father had served in the Russian army for 25 years—the common fate of many drafted Jewish boys at the time. The family moved briefly to Sao Paulo, Brazil to escape the oppression of government-sanctioned pogroms against the Jews but with the intention of returning home some day. A detour to visit relatives in New York in 1914 became permanent. Settling in New York City, Schappes' parents took the name "Shapiro," which other relatives had already adopted, but the son, who was born Moise ben Haim Shapshilevich, kept the name "Schappes" given to him in Brazil.

He received a B.A. degree in 1928 from City College of New York and an M.A. degree in 1930 from Columbia University. He did four additional years of graduate work at Columbia but did not receive a degree.

From 1930 to 1941 Schappes taught English at his alma mater, CCNY. Always politically active (he describes himself in *Contemporary Authors* as "Radical"), he became the center of statewide investigations when two New York state senators, Frederic Rapp and Rene Coudert, headed up a commission formed to identify and suspend educators allegedly belonging to the Communist Party. (The work of the Rapp-Coudert Investigating Committee eventually expanded to include suspected Fascists and Nazis.) Although Schappes denied party membership, he was convicted on several counts of perjury and sent to prison. An active defense committee assisted Schappes, and he wrote *Letters from the Tombs* (New York, 1941), which included an introduction by the black American writer Richard Wright. Schappes was paroled after a brief internment, and shortly afterward the Rapp-Coudert Committee—witch-hunters, Schappes now calls them—was disbanded.

As a result of these experiences, Schappes was blacklisted in the academic world. But in 1948 he resumed teaching, first as instructor of Jewish studies at the Marxist-oriented Jefferson School of Social Studies in New York until 1957, then at the School of Jewish Knowledge in New York from 1958 to 1969. Since 1972 Schappes has been an adjunct professor of American Jewish history at Queens College of the City University of New York.

In October 1981 the City University of New York belatedly apologized to Schappes and other college employees who had been unjustly dismissed for their political opinions during the "Red scare" periods that frequently overtake American political life. Addressing the CUNY board of trustees on behalf of himself and his colleagues, Schappes emphasized the special significance of "a courageous, honest official action in these times of growing intolerance and growing repression."

In early 1982 he was honored when the authoritative *The Jewish Book Annual*, published by the National Jewish Welfare Board, selected his birth date as one of the five anniversaries of living American Jewish literary figures to be commemorated in 1982.

Throughout the period including and since his blacklisting, Schappes has been editing, researching and writing about American Jewish history. In 1944 he edited *Selections of Prose and Poetry of Emma Lazarus* (New York, 1944), which was followed six years later by *The Letters of Emma Lazarus* (New York, 1950). His major work, however, which has been revised and updated twice, is *A Documentary History of the Jews in the U.S.A.: 1654–*

1875 (New York, 1950, 1971). He has also compiled *The Jews in the United States, 1654–1954: A Pictorial History* (New York; 1958, 1965).

Schappes joined the editorial board of *Jewish Currents*, a left-leaning monthly devoted to Jewish affairs, in 1946. As editor in chief of the magazine since 1958, Schappes has created a forum for dialogue among Jews and non-Jews representing a wide spectrum of opinions on the left. The magazine defends detente and world Jewry and is sharply critical of Soviet anti-Semitism and Soviet and American military interventions. It also opposes the Greater Israel movement in Israel and argues for Palestinian-Israeli reconciliation and mutual recognition of the right of each to exist in peace.

In addition, he has contributed articles to many magazines, including *Saturday Review, Poetry, Journal of Ethnic Studies, Negro History Bulletin* and others. Although well into his 70s, Schappes is active in many organizations, including the American Historical Association, American Jewish Historical Society, Immigration History Society, Association for the Study of Afro-American Life and History, and the Yiddisher Kultur Farband.

Among Schappes' many awards are the Tercentenary award from the Emma Lazarus Federation of Jewish Women's Clubs in 1954 and the Zhitlovsky Award from the Zhitlovsky Foundation for Jewish Culture in 1969.

ALVIN SCHIFF

b. August 8, 1926
Educator

Perhaps no individual has shown as thorough and devoted a commitment to the survival of Jewish education in America as Alvin Schiff. In word and in deed—he is the author of a major book on the subject and many articles and since 1970 has been executive vice president of the Board of Jewish Education of Greater New York, the world's largest central agency for Jewish education—Schiff has been a major force in the resurgence of Jewish day schools and after-school education programs throughout the United States as well as in the education of teachers of Jewish studies.

Alvin Irwin Schiff was born in Boston, Massachusetts to Jacob, a scholar who had studied in yeshivas in Lithuania, and Miriam (Schriebman) Schiff. He received a B.A. degree in psychology from Yeshiva University in New York in 1947; an M.A. degree in educational

psychology from Columbia University in 1950 and a Ph.D. in educational administration from Yeshiva in 1959.

Schiff's interest in Jewish education is lifelong. Even before he completed college, he was active as a counselor and youth leader in summer camps and Zionist youth groups. Immediately after graduating from Yeshiva, he began teaching, first at the Passaic Park (New Jersey) Jewish Center in 1947, then at Yeshiva University High School the following year, where he remained until 1951. While teaching at the high school, Schiff also assumed the first of many college-level positions, lecturing at Yeshiva's Teachers Institute for Men. Schiff's subsequent posts have included directing educational programs at congregations in Lawrence, New York (1951–56) and Far Rockaway, New York (1952–54); supervising student teachers at Yeshiva's Teachers Institute for Women (1952–61); and teaching education at the Ferkauf Graduate School of Humanities and Social Sciences at Yeshiva University. Schiff joined Ferkauf in 1961 as an assistant professor and was a full professor by 1969. Since 1970 he has been an adjunct professor of education while assuming his responsibilities at the Jewish Board of Education. He has also held positions at Queens College of the City University of New York (visiting honors professor of social science research, 1968–70) and Antioch College in Yellow Springs, Ohio (adjunct professor of research, 1970–72), and he has lectured at New York University, Brandeis University, City College of New York, Spertus College in Chicago and other institutions of higher learning.

In addition to teaching and administration, Schiff has written *The Jewish Day School in America* (New York, 1966), which historically and sympathetically delineates its development, and has participated in many committees and organizations related to Jewish education, almost always as chairperson or president. Among his current assignments are honorary president, Educator's Council of America (1977–); co-chairperson, Social Service Division, UJA-Federation Campaign (1979–); and chairperson, Children's Forest Project, Jewish National Fund (1977–).

Schiff is a member of many boards and councils connected with Jewish education. He is on the board of trustees of the New York Committee for State of Israel Bonds; the American Zionist Youth Foundation and the Rabbi Isaac Elchanan Theological Seminary of Yeshiva University. He has contributed actively to a wide range of educational organizations within New York City and throughout New York State.

For his many contributions to leadership in Jewish

education, Schiff has been amply honored. Under Schiff's leadership, the Board of Jewish Education has developed a wide variety of new programs and activities for the 210 Jewish day schools in the metropolitan area it serves. Among other innovations, Schiff helped create four regional teacher centers, began English-as-a-second-language program and developed materials for Russian immigrant pupils, introduced new nutritional education programs, founded a department of special education, with special attention to the disabled and retarded, many of whom live in foster homes and started training programs for teachers of gifted children in association with Teachers College of Columbia University. His major awards include the Bernard Revel Memorial Award for Outstanding Achievement in Education and Religion from the Yeshiva College Alumni Association (1968), the Israel Bonds Masada Award (1974) and the Alexander M. Dushkin Prize of the International Cultural Center for Youth in Jerusalem (1976; Schiff was the first recipient of this honor). In 1977 Schiff received an honorary doctorate from Yeshiva University.

But it has not been enough for Alvin Schiff merely to direct programs. He is also an innovator, who has initiated a wide range of projects in early childhood education, curriculum planning and the use of media in instruction. Under his direction the Board of Jewish Education has also conducted major advertising campaigns in secular and Jewish publications aimed at arousing popular interest in Jewish schooling for young children. In addition, he founded the National Commission of Torah Education in 1969 and the Educators Council of America in 1970; he developed seminars in Israel for teachers and principals and for high school students; and he created *Contact,* a magazine for Jewish adolescents co-published with the *Jerusalem Post.*

As editor since 1970 of the quarterly *Jewish Education,* published by the National Council for Jewish Education, Schiff has published many articles and editorials on the subject he holds dearest. But he summed up his career of nearly 40 years best in one sentence in a Spring 1978 article in *Jewish Education,* when he wrote: "There is no nobler vocation in Jewish life than the Jewish education profession."

For further information:
Schiff, Alvin I. "Funding Jewish Education—Whose Responsibility?" *Jewish Education.* Summer 1973.
———. "Jewish Continuity Through Jewish Education: A Human Resource Imperative." *Jewish Education.* Summer 1980.
———. "Jewish Education in Light of Peace," *Jewish Education.* Fall 1979.

———. "The Synagogue and the Jewish Supplementary School," *Jewish Education.* Spring 1978.

ALEXANDER M. SCHINDLER

b. October 4, 1925
Rabbi; administrator

Rabbi Alexander M. Schindler—president of the Union of American Hebrew Congregations, the congregational arm of Reform Judaism, and former chairman of the Conference of Presidents of Major American Jewish Organizations, a very influential coalition group that purports to speak on behalf of millions of American Jews—has also long been a powerful defender of religious toleration and diversity and political liberalism.

Alexander Moshe Schindler was born in Munich, Germany, the son of Eliezer and Sali (Hoyda) Schindler. His father was a poet and an early opponent of the Nazis. Following emigration to the United States in the 1930s, he served in the United States Army's 10th Mountain Division ski troops and received a Purple Heart and Bronze Star. After his discharge he received a degree from the College of the City of New York and was later ordained by the Hebrew Union College-Jewish Institute of Religion in 1953.

For six years, from 1953 to 1959, he was assistant rabbi and later associate rabbi at Temple Emmanuel in Worcester, Massachusetts. He also simultaneously led the Hillel Foundation at nearby Clark University and Worcester Polytechnic Institute. In 1959 he left the pulpit and became an administrator with the Union of American Hebrew Congregations' Federation of Reform Temples in the six-state New England region, serving until 1963. Then he became director of education for the UAHC and the Central Conference of American Rabbis from 1963 to 1967. Then, until 1973 he was vice president of the UAHC.

Schindler became one of the major Jewish leaders of the efforts to expand Reform Judaism's role in the United States and Israel. Behind the drive to increase the number of adherents lay the recognition that intermarriage rates were soaring; more children resulting from these unions were being born; and secularism, materialism and acculturation were making serious inroads among their followers. Then too, in Israel, Orthodoxy had grown increasingly intolerant of Reform's activities. All this led Schindler to declare in late 1979 that Reform's strategy would reflect its refusal to "be read out of the Jewish people."

Under his administration, the UAHC advanced several crucial positions. First, Schindler called upon the Reform movement to define a child as Jewish if the father was Jewish. In traditional law a child is considered Jewish only if the mother is Jewish; the father's faith has no bearing on the child. "I want the genealogical factors to be paternal as well as maternal," said Schindler. "Surely the father counts for something when we affix his child's religious identity." The assumption behind his reasoning was explained by Dr. Eugene Mihaly, a dean at Hebrew Union College in Cincinnati:

> According to biblical tradition, the lineage followed the father. If your father was of the priestly group, you were too. But that began to change 2,000 years ago when rabbis were concerned with reducing illegitimacy. To adhere to that ruling now would be absolutist, fundamentalist, and not biblical at all.

In another departure from tradition, Rabbi Schindler argued that given the rising rate of intermarriage, and with the "preponderant majority" of such unions involving Jewish men and non-Jewish women, "the right of these men to determine the religious character of their children must be secured. Here is still another way to make certain that our grandchildren will be Jews, that they will remain a part of our community and share the destiny of this people Israel."

Earlier, in 1978, he proposed that Reform become the "champions of Judaism" and seek converts among the millions of "unchurched" American non-Jews. As with his proposal to allow fathers to transmit their Jewishness, the result was intense criticism from Orthodox and Conservative rabbis.

Within Israel, Reform is trying to assert its rights to establish rabbinic privileges. Its power rests on American Jewish and Diaspora public opinion, and Reform leaders do not hesitate to use it. Under Schindler's leadership, they have organized a legal challenge to present restrictions on Reform rabbis in that Orthodox-dominated nation. Reform Jews, he warned, "refuse to be beggars at Jerusalem's gates." Today, Israeli religious authorities do not allow Reform rabbis "to marry or bury their congregants or to teach or accept converts." Said Schindler: "We regret this unconscionable and unjust and unholy conception of our status in the Land." And when Prime Minister Begin put together, in 1981, a coalition including three Orthodox religious parties that might sharply curtail the rights of non-Orthodox Jews in Israel, he issued a public protest, declaring that any such compact "threatens to become a serious rupture of the unity of the Jewish people."

In 1976 he was chosen chairman of the Conference of Presidents of Major American Jewish Organizations and served until June 1978. As leader of this pro-Israel coalition of 32 groups, he was the "Jewish voice" in this country and in Israel. Shortly after his term of office ended, he was honored with the Solomon Bublick Prize at the Hebrew University in Jerusalem—the award having been granted only 13 times previously (to Harry Truman, David Ben Gurion and Herbert H. Lehman, among others). The prize described Schindler as a man "who, during the two years preceding the award has made the most significant contribution to the progress and development of Eretz Yisrael."

Schindler has also been active in efforts to curb the nuclear arms race. In May 1982 he joined other clergymen—Christian and Jewish—in a Washington, D.C. press conference to air their hopes that a nuclear arms weapons freeze could be instituted as quickly as possible.

MENAHEM MENDEL SCHNEERSON

b. April 18, 1902
Rabbi; spiritual leader of Lubavitch Hasidim

The preservation of traditional Jewish values and style of life is the uppermost priority of Menahem Mendel Schneerson, who as the rebbe of the worldwide Hasidic Lubavitcher movement, oversees an active recruitment campaign to return "lost" Jews to the "fold." From his base in the Crown Heights section of Brooklyn, the octogenarian Schneerson, who is the seventh Lubavitcher rebbe, carries on a generations-long tradition that began in 18th-century Russia to study Torah and carry the message of the Lubavitch to all Jews.

Menahem Mendel Schneerson was born in Nikolaev, Russia and is descended from the *tzaddik* (the Righteous One) Schneur Zalman of Lyady who founded the Chabad Hasidim. His great-grandfather was the third grand rebbe, and he is the son of Rabbi Levi Yitzhak, a noted talmudic scholar and kabbalist, and Chana Schneerson. A child prodigy, he received private instruction in Talmud because he was too quick for *cheder* (elementary school for instruction in Judaism) and by the time of his bar mitzvah, he was considered an *ilui,* or Torah genius. In 1929 he married Haya Mushkah Schneerson, daughter of the then-Rebbe Yosef Yitzhak Schneerson, in Warsaw and then began studying engineering at the University of Berlin and at the Sorbonne in Paris, where he received a degree—the first rebbe in history to do so. (He is also fluent in 10 languages.) Many past rebbes had spent some time in jail for challenging Czarist bans on Jewish education. Schneerson, too, was nearly arrested in 1940 for sending religious materials to Jews in occupied France.

In 1941 Schneerson moved to the United States, where his father-in-law, newly freed from prison in Russia, had settled. There he contributed to the growing Lubavitch community by supervising educational programs and writing extensive treatises on Hasidic and talmudic texts and *responsa*—literature amassed down through the centuries from the questions and answers to religious law. Nine years later, when Yosef Yitzhak died, Menahem Mendel inherited the "throne." Since then, from quarters on Eastern Parkway in Brooklyn, Menahem Mendel Schneerson has been spiritual leader in the phenomenal spread of the religious activist movement of *Habad*—a Hebrew acronym for wisdom, understanding and knowledge—in college campuses across the United States and in cities with large Jewish communities around the world.

Without leaving the United States—or rarely even leaving his Crown Heights quarters—Schneerson has attained a nearly mystical significance, as younger Lubavitchers, including many who have joined in their teens and 20s, some from middle-class, assimilated backgrounds, participate in an aggressive campaign to draw in non-observant Jews or those who otherwise live observant lives but do not subscribe to Hasidic traditions. Pictures of the rebbe adorn the "mitzvah tanks"—Lubavitch vans that travel to neighborhoods in large cities on recruitment drives—and they are featured in the Lubavitch literature, which is frequently distributed in busy New York City neighborhoods. The movement has also been known to seek out newly-arrived Jewish immigrants from the Soviet Union, Iran and North Africa for whom its programs offer a sense of community, safety and freedom that these people have rarely known. There is even a *Kfar Habad* near Lod in Israel. In the center of the movement, the rebbe acts as the spiritual and energizing force, answering letters from followers around the world and meeting with people seeking guidance in all areas of Jewish life. When he speaks, the crowds that come to hear him are invariably overflowing, even if, as is his wont, he goes on for hours.

Adhering to the pious and joyous lifestyle advocated by Schneerson also means, according to some critics, reverting to a rigid structure that limits individual freedom of expression. Women are educated separately, with an ultimate goal of following traditional roles of mothering and tending home. Couples are urged to have large families. Nonetheless, many well-known secular Jews, including U.S. Senator Rudy Boschwitz (R., Minn.) and several notable Jewish philanthropists who feel that *Habad* is helping keep Jewish values alive, have contributed to the movement.

Oddly, the rebbe has never visited Israel, despite the depth of feeling for the country exhibited by the Lubavitcher. No one is quite certain why he has never gone. The Israeli right-wing politician and journalist Geula Cohen once posed the question in *Ma'ariv*, an Israeli daily newspaper: "Why won't you come and give the order (for his followers to emigrate to Israel)?" Answered the Rebbe:

> My place is where my words are likely to be obeyed. Here I am listened to, but in the Land of Israel I won't be heard. There, our youth will follow only somebody who has sprung up from its own ranks and speaks its own language. The Messiah will be a man of flesh and blood, visible and tangible, a man whom others will follow. And he will come.

ALEXANDER SCHNEIDER

b. October 21, 1908
Violinist; conductor

A master violinist and conductor, Alexander Schneider has come to symbolize the chamber music player *par excellence*. He played for nearly a quarter of a century with the Budapest String Quartet, founded various ensembles of his own, recorded 50 of Haydn's 83 quartets and established a number of concert series in New York.

Alexander Schneider was born to Isak and Chasia (Dainowski) Schneider in Vilna, a center of Jewish culture. He began studying the violin at an early age from the same teacher who taught Jascha Heifetz and, at 16, went to Germany to study at the Frankfurt Conservatory and in Berlin. He supported himself by playing with the Frankfurt Symphony Orchestra, where he was soon promoted to concertmaster.

In the early 1930s he joined the Budapest String Quartet as a second violinist and toured with it through Europe and the United States. He immigrated to the United States and became an American citizen before World War II. In 1944, after leaving the Budapest ensemble, Schneider founded the Albeneri Trio, with which he performed chamber music concerts in the United States and Canada. In 1945 he played with harpsichord virtuoso Ralph Kirkpatrick in sonata performances that earned warm praise for both artists.

An indefatigible organizer of concerts, in 1950 Schneider convinced cellist Pablo Casals to come out of exile and begin performing again. Schneider is now in charge of the annual Casals festival in Puerto Rico. Determined to make good chamber music available to young people at popular prices, he has created a series of outdoor summer concerts in Washington Square Park in New York's Greenwich Village, Christmas Eve Bach and baroque concerts at Carnegie Hall, and a concert series at the New School for Social Research in New York. In 1960 he organized a chamber music festival for Israel in which Pablo Casals, Isaac Stern and Rudolf Serkin appeared. He has also been the guiding force for the Lincoln Center Mostly Mozart Festival.

Schneider has taught at the University of Washington; the State University of New York at Buffalo; Mills College; and the Royal Conservatory in Toronto, Canada. He conducts the annual, week-long Christmas String Seminar in New York, in which adolescent musicians are taught by him in master classes and later perform at Carnegie Hall with Schneider as their conductor.

He has also conducted the Brandenburg Ensemble, the Los Angeles Philharmonic, the St. Louis Symphony, the English Chamber Orchestra, the Israel Philharmonic and others.

Schneider, who plays a 1723 Guarneri violin, wrote in *Who's Who in America:* "For me, my purpose is to get young people to learn how to make music. When you make music, it has to come from your heart, from your soul, or it has no meaning."

DAVID SCHOENBRUN

b. March 15, 1915
Television correspondent

Television correspondent David Schoenbrun is perhaps best-known for his 15 years as CBS reporter in France following the Second World War. A gifted interpreter and analyst of personalities, politics and social conditions, Schoenbrun has also covered events in Vietnam and Israel for American audiences.

David Schoenbrun was born in Manhattan, the son of Max, a jeweler, and Lucy (Cassirer) Schoenbrun. After graduating from Townsend Harris High School in 1930, he received his B.A. degree in French from the City College of New York in 1934 and began to teach French in high schools in the New York City area. In 1936 he became a labor relations adjuster and editor of a trade magazine for the Dress Manufacturers of America. Four years later he became a free-lance writer.

A series of articles he wrote about psychological warfare that appeared in *PM* and the Chicago *Sun* led to his appointment to the propaganda analysis division of the U.S. Office of War Information, Western European

desk. In 1943 he joined the U.S. Army and was assigned to military intelligence. He was posted in Algiers, where he directed the Mediterranean theater news desk, the Allied Forces newsroom and broadcast a weekly commentary in French and English into territories held by Nazi Germany.

His work as an Army newsman soon brought him to the front lines. In August 1944 he went to France as the combat correspondent of the 7th Army and military intelligence liaison with the French army. He reported from every major battlefront and was one of the first American soldiers to reach the Rhine.

After his discharge from the service in 1945, he stayed in Paris as a correspondent for the Overseas News Agency. There he met Edward R. Murrow, who immediately hired him to be CBS correspondent in Paris. From that vantage point, Schoenbrun reported on the tribulations of the Fourth Republic, the triumphant return of Charles de Gaulle, the Indochina war, and the indigenous independence movements in Tunisia and Algeria. He won the Overseas Press Club award for distinguished reporting in 1951, 1953 and 1956. In 1958 he won an Emmy award and the following year a Dupont award for his distinguished broadcast journalism.

Schoenbrun synthesized his great knowledge and love of France in *As France Goes* (New York, 1957). He described France as a once-great empire in its last gasp, dying because "no people are so learned in history and so willfully defiant of its lessons." Yet the book goes beyond a simple balancing of the political ledgers and presents a witty and insightful analysis of the French psyche.

Schoenbrun returned to the United States in 1960 and was made CBS chief correspondent and bureau chief in Washington, D.C. He held that position for three years, when he left CBS to become the chief correspondent for Metromedia News in New York.

France continued to fascinate him, however, and his next book was a biography of his friend Charles de Gaulle. In *The Three Lives of Charles de Gaulle* (New York, 1965), Schoenbrun tells about de Gaulle in his three roles in modern France—soldier, savior of the country after the war and statesman. The book conveys a sense of the man, whom Schoenbrun clearly admired.

Based on his knowledge of the French involvement in Indochina, Schoenbrun actively opposed American intervention in Vietnam. In *Vietnam: How We Got In, How to Get Out* (New York, 1968), Schoenbrun argued that there was no such thing as monolithic Asian communism and the Geneva conference in 1954 never envisioned the creation of two separate states in Vietnam.

The book was long considered a useful primer for anti-war activists.

Schoenbrun always had a deep love of Israel and a highly developed Jewish consciousness. In 1973 he collaborated with his daughter Lucy Szekely and son-in-law Robert Szekely to write *The New Israelis* (New York, 1973), a book about the first generation born in an independent Jewish state. He found that although a generation gap did exist in Israel, it was not marked by the same estrangement that characterized prevailing relationships in America.

Schoenbrun returned to Paris for material for his next two books. *Triumph in Paris: The Exploits of Benjamin Franklin* (New York, 1976) is a portrait of—in Schoenbrun's words—"the greatest American of his day." The book is his account of Franklin's diplomatic, scientific and patriotic talents.

Soldiers of the Night: The Story of the French Resistance (New York, 1980) is a romantic and anecdotal account of the anti-German underground in occupied and Vichy France. People from all walks of life, Schoenbrun wrote, spontaneously came together to resist the Nazis. He meticulously details, in the words of critic John Leonard, that "terrible moral beauty," and the book, like all his books, sums up his penchant for honest reportage and clear and thoughtful contemporary and historical analysis.

In June 1981, during the historic reunion of Holocaust survivors and their families in Jerusalem on the 36th anniversary of their liberation, Schoenbrun was the principal correspondent covering the event for the Public Broadcasting Service.

DANIEL SCHORR

b. August 31, 1916
Journalist

Daniel Schorr, the independent and distinguished radio and television correspondent, has proved that aggressive reportage can yield large benefits. He has been covering the news for wire services, newspapers and electronic broadcasting for nearly 50 years, and his ability to investigate and analyze some of the most complex issues in American and international politics has earned him an outstanding reputation among his colleagues in journalism.

Daniel Schorr was born to Louis and Tillie (Godiner) Schorr in New York City. His father died when Schorr was 12, and his mother supported the family by working as a seamstress. Schorr graduated with a B.S.S.

degree from the City College of New York in 1939 and worked for the Jewish Telegraphic Agency from 1934 to 1941.

He became the New York news editor for ANETA, the Netherland News Agency, between 1941 and 1943, served in the army until 1945 and then free-lanced for the *Christian Science Monitor* and *The New York Times*. His work so impressed CBS's Edward R. Murrow that Schorr was invited to join the radio network's news staff in 1953 and cover Europe and Latin America. In 1955 Schorr became CBS's Moscow correspondent but was expelled during the Cold War in 1957 for being "anti-Soviet" and a "provocateur." He then worked as a roving diplomatic correspondent and as head of CBS's news bureaus in Central Europe until 1966, when he was assigned to Washington, D.C.

During the early Nixon years, Schorr's aggressive investigations frequently embarrassed the administration. In a 1970 report he criticized the Nixon administration for failing to develop a national health insurance program, and in 1971 he published an expansion of his report in *Don't Get Sick in America!* (New York). Schorr also uncovered evidence in the same year that Nixon's chief science adviser, Dr. James C. Fletcher, had personally questioned the need for a Safeguard Missile System. As a result of his probings into the Nixon White House, the FBI conducted a security check on Schorr. When Schorr and the *Washington Post* disclosed this investigation, the embarrassed Nixon administration claimed—untruthfully—that the president had planned to appoint Schorr to an environmental position.

Following the Watergate break-in, CBS assigned Schorr to cover the investigation and any possible cover-up. Schorr's reports complemented the disclosures of Robert Woodward and Carl Bernstein of the *Washington Post* and Seymour Hersh of *The New York Times*.

Schorr's tough dispatches drew frequent protests from some CBS affiliates, but they also garnered praise from his peers. In 1972, 1973 and again in 1974 he received Emmy awards for his Watergate coverage, but his criticism of what he considered CBS's conciliatory approach to the Nixon administration alienated him from some CBS News executives.

When Richard M. Nixon resigned from the presidency in 1974, CBS shifted Schorr to the growing congressional controversy over the illegal role of the CIA within the United States. When Schorr gave a copy of the transcript of House of Representatives and Senate hearings to the New York weekly newspaper *The Village Voice* because the House had decided to keep the contents classified "secret," CBS forced his resignation in 1976. For his deed, however, he received an American

Civil Liberties Union award. In his book *Clearing the Air* (New York, 1977), Schorr recounts his experiences covering the Watergate and CIA stories.

In 1982 Schorr and his family visited Israel and in an interview with *The Jerusalem Post* he commented upon charges that Israel is discriminated against by the foreign press. Schorr said that Israelis tend to believe those allegations because "they're very sensitive." Still, he concluded, no one is conspiring against Israel. Nor have petro-dollars in the United States lured the press and the television networks into supporting Arabs at the expense of Israel.

Schorr is now a Washington-based correspondent for the Cable News Network and National Public Radio.

PETER SCHRAG

b. July 24, 1931
Writer

Peter Schrag is a critic of contemporary American culture and its educational system. He was one of the first to diagnose the ailments of the post-World War II urban public school system.

Peter Schrag was born in Karlsruhe, Germany, the son of Otto, a businessman, and Judith (Haas) Schrag. He received his B.A. degree from Amherst College in 1953 and, following his graduation, worked for two years as a reporter for the El Paso *Herald Post*. In 1955 he returned to Amherst as assistant to the Secretary of the college and began graduate work at the nearby University of Massachusetts. He was an instructor in American Studies at Amherst from 1960 through 1964.

Schrag's first book concerned public education, an interest to which he would return time and again throughout his career. *Voices in the Classroom—Public Schools and Public Attitudes* (Boston, 1965) was based on an extended tour he conducted, observing the spectrum of public schooling offered in America. He visited schools in decaying urban areas, bright new suburbs and seemingly static rural communities. He saw overcrowded and underutilized schools and traditional and nontraditional curricula. Based on this evidence, he developed his prognosis for the survival of public education, which he claimed could come only if teachers and administrators could free themselves from the rigid stereotypes that at the time threatened to destroy the educational system and take America's students with it.

He narrowed his focus in *Village School Downtown* (Boston, 1967), a study of the Boston public school system published while he was associate education editor of the *Saturday Review*, a position he held from 1966

until 1968. In this book Schrag started from the assertion that a good society cannot exist without good public education and argued that American society was shortchanging public schools. He said that many people who have greatly benefited from free public education have since turned their backs on it. Public schools, Schrag contended, used outdated teaching methods and were becoming repositories for the culturally deprived, while being run by the establishment, whose aim was to maintain the status quo.

After the publication of the book, Schrag became the executive editor of the *Saturday Review* for one year, 1968. The next year he was appointed editor of *Change* magazine, and in 1970 he became a contributing editor to *Saturday Review*.

During this period Schrag began to critique American society in general. *Decline of the WASP* (New York, 1972) stimulated a healthy debate over ethnic pride, as Schrag argued that the prototype American—the white Anglo-Saxon Protestant—who supposedly built American institutions in his image, had lost his vitality. The myth of cultural hegemony of the WASP had receded in the face of cultural pluralism, Schrag claimed. The following year Schrag published *The End of the American Future* (New York, 1973), a Cassandra-like book based on extensive interviewing throughout the country. Everywhere, Schrag wrote, he found the American spirit sapped, people apprehensive about the future.

After a sympathetic book about the trial of Daniel Ellsberg, called *Test of Loyalty* (New York, 1974), Schrag turned toward the use of psychiatry in society. *The Myth of the Hyperactive Child*, coauthored with his wife, Diane Divoky (New York, 1975) exposed the coercive power of the public schools in administering dangerous, mood-affecting drugs to more than 1 million children diagnosed as hyperactive. Using incisive polemical writing, Schrag contended that a child could be diagnosed as having a minimal brain dysfunction based solely on erratic behavior in school with no medical corroboration and yet be subjected to a medical treatment for the problem.

He expanded his thesis to society at large in *Mind Control* (New York, 1978), in which he argued that psychiatry has blurred the boundaries between welfare, education, criminal justice, mental health and oddball behavior. Any form of atypical behavior can be labeled and given over to medical treatment, Schrag asserted, ignoring even minimal, sound scientific procedures. He further contended that the power elite in America had no interest in the social and economic origins of abnormal behavior and would prefer psychological means to keep the masses under control.

In 1978 Schrag was named editorial page editor of the Sacramento *Bee*. Following his years with *Saturday Review*, Schrag was on the editorial advisory boards of *The Columbia Forum* (1972–75) and *Social Policy* (1971 to the present). He was also a contributing editor to the influential but now defunct journalism magazine *More* and has taught at the University of Massachusetts (1970–72), Stanford University (1973–74) and since 1974 at the University of California at Berkeley.

BUDD SCHULBERG

b. March 27, 1914
Screenwriter; novelist

At the age of 27, Budd Schulberg published a first novel that was remarkable not only for its author's youth but for the insights it provided. *What Makes Sammy Run?* (New York, 1941) told an insider's story of Hollywood so full of ugliness and cynicism but so accurate that even Schulberg's critics had to concur that he was utterly on the mark. And if *Sammy* signaled Schulberg's own declaration of independence from the magnetism of the Hollywood fairy tale, it also signaled his emergence as a major American writer.

Budd Wilson Schulberg was born in New York City to Benjamin P. and Adeline (Jaffe) Schulberg. His father was originally a reporter for *The New York Evening Mail* but moved to Los Angeles in 1919 to become one of the movie industry's first major producers. Known as "B.P." and the head of Paramount Studios until 1932, he was credited with discovering Clara Bow and a host of other talents. Adeline Schulberg, known to everyone as "Ad," became a prominent agent. Thus, Budd Schulberg grew up thoroughly immersed in Hollywood glitter and in turn was expected by his parents to become a great writer when he first showed an interest in the craft. Schulberg himself, as part of the elite circle of Hollywood insiders, felt a deep ambivalence about his surroundings; his father's career peaked and plummeted periodically, and his friends were often only as reliable as his business standing. Thus, when the opportunity arose to go to college, Budd Schulberg went to the faraway New England town of Hanover, New Hampshire, where he studied at Dartmouth College.

After receiving a Bachelor of Arts degree from Dartmouth in 1936, Schulberg headed back to the West Coast and for three years worked for such Hollywood producers as David Selznick, Samuel Goldwyn and Walter Wanger, first as a $25-a-week play reader and later as a screenwriter. At the same time, he wrote short stories and articles that he began publishing. He also

became active in the Communist Party, but two sets of circumstances caused him to resign in 1939. First, he was revolted and disillusioned by the signing of the Hitler-Stalin Pact that year. Second, the Party was trying to influence the direction of the novel he was then working on, a situation he found intolerable. The book was *What Makes Sammy Run?* A chronicle of the life of one Sammy Glick, a former newspaper office boy who becomes an important movie magnate, the novel was as frank about the sordid behind-the-scenes maneuverings of the movie industry's "comers" as it was factual about the up-front dealings that only a Hollywood intimate could describe in detail. According to one critic, the novel was a "squalid story, relieved by an ironic humor which illuminates with a lurid intensity the incredibilities of that existence which in the Cloud Cuckoo Land of Hollywood passes for life."

Schulberg served in the United States Navy from 1943 to 1946, including one year in the OSS gathering photographic evidence of war crimes for the Nuremburg trials.

Nonetheless, Schulberg remained part of the film industry before and after his Navy years as an independent writer and later as president of Schulberg Productions, became an influential presence in Hollywood. Among his film credits were the screenplays for *Little Orphan Annie* (1938); *Winter Carnival*, a collaboration with F. Scott Fitzgerald (1939); *On the Waterfront* (1954), which earned him an Academy Award; *A Face in the Crowd*, based on his short story "Your Arkansas Traveler" (1957); and *Wind Across the Everglades* (1958).

He also wrote a number of plays for Broadway and television, the most prominent including *The Disenchanted*, based on his 1950 novel of the same name (New York), which opened on Broadway in 1958, and adaptations of *What Makes Sammy Run?*, one for NBC-TV in 1959, the second for Broadway in 1964.

But a writer and reporter above all, Schulberg continued writing stories and novels even while producing movies. His second novel, *The Harder They Fall* (New York, 1947), was an expose of the boxing world—Schulberg was an avid boxing fan and for a while was boxing editor for *Sports Illustrated*. It was praised by former boxing champion Gene Tunney as "far more accurate than most modern writers have been in their numerous works on the subject." *The Disenchanted* (New York, 1950) was the story of a celebrated novelist-turned-Hollywood screenwriter who is commissioned to write about a college theater production. Focusing more on the personality of the main character, the novel was a poorly camouflaged biography of F. Scott Fitzgerald. *Waterfront* (New York, 1955) was a novelization of

Schulberg's 1954 screenplay *On the Waterfront* and dramatized the brutal life of dock workers as well as the personal struggle of one to pull himself out of it.

During the 1960s Schulberg turned from socially conscious writing to direct social action. In 1965, in the aftermath of serious race riots in the Watts section of Los Angeles, a depressed black neighborhood, he established the Watts Writers Workshop, a training program for young writers that evolved into a hugely successful program. From it Schulberg edited *From the Voices of Watts* (New York, 1967), a collection of work from workshop participants. In 1979 he was a founder of the Frederick Douglass Creative Arts Center in Harlem, New York City's counterpart to Watts.

In the meantime Schulberg continued to explore the roots of writing and in his collection of essays *Four Seasons of Success* (New York, 1972) he profiled and analyzed the lives of six American writers: Sinclair Lewis, Nathanael West, F. Scott Fitzgerald, John Steinbeck, Thomas Heggen and William Saroyan. He carried on his obsession with boxing in *Loser and Still Champion: Muhammad Ali* (New York, 1972), an analysis of the complex personality of a young boxer named Cassius Clay, who, as Muhammad Ali, became one of the most potent and controversial figures in sports history.

He also published his memoirs, *Moving Pictures: Memories of a Hollywood Prince* (New York, 1981). In it he celebrated "Home Sweet Hollywood," as he called it, but also revealed some of the bitterness of growing up in the compromised atmosphere of the Hollywood community, the son of a powerful man who was often absent when most needed. The book excels, however, in its anecdotes and recollections of such stars as Cary Grant, Marlene Dietrich, Gary Cooper, Mary Pickford and Mae West as well as such moguls as Louis B. Mayer, Jack Warner and Harry Cohn, whose aging and immigrant fathers, strangers to their sons, banded together to co-found Hollywood's first synagogue.

For further information:
Schulberg, Budd. *Everything that Moves,* New York: 1980.
————. *Sanctuary V.* New York: 1969.
————. *Some Faces in the Crowd.* New York: 1953.

HAROLD SCHULWEIS

b. April 14, 1925
Rabbi

At a time of great change, ferment, dissent and unease among Jewish leaders in America, theologian and spiritual leader Harold M. Schulweis has been one of the few voices calling for unity and reconciliation within the American Jewish community. Although he is a Conservative rabbi and adheres to certain strong Conservative traditions, Schulweis openly embraces a "multi-dimensional" character of Judaism which offers followers different—and correct—responses and theologies for different conditions and needs.

Harold Maurice Schulweis was born in New York City to Maurice and Helen (Rezak) Schulweis. He studied at Yeshiva University, where he received a B.A. degree in 1945 and at New York University, where he completed an M.A. degree in philosophy in 1948. Pursuing rabbinic studies at the Jewish Theological Seminary of America, he earned an M.H.L. and was ordained in 1950.

Schulweis spent the next 20 years as a congregational leader, heading Temple Emanuel in Parkchester, New York, from 1950 to 1952, and Temple Beth Abraham in Oakland, California, from 1952 to 1970. He arrived at his current pulpit at Valley Beth Shalom, a synagogue in Encino, California, in 1970 and the same year began teaching at the University of Judaism in Los Angeles, the West Coast branch of the Jewish Theological Seminary, as adjunct professor of contemporary civilization. In 1971 he joined the faculty of Hebrew Union College as lecturer in theology.

Although social action had always been part of Schulweis' rabbinical work—he in fact received the 1969 Social Actions Award from United Synagogues of America—his most innovative work began at Valley Beth Shalom. Schulweis added to his usual work a commitment to his congregation which transcended the standard expectations of a rabbi's role. For example, he added an active counseling center and a senior citizen center to the synagogue. He did this, he said, because he felt the synagogue had more to offer its members than merely an occasional prayer sanctuary. "The synagogue became an empty shell," he said in a Spring 1982 article in *Present Tense.* "The sanctuary was not filled with the concerns of people. People would say, 'The last place I would come to is the synagogue when I'm in trouble.' It should be the first; it should respond to needs which are real but which are often dismissed as selfish."

Moreover, he encouraged regular study by congregants who, under his instruction, formed as many as 60 small learning groups, or "havurot," and he trained a group of members for several years to become "para-rabbinics," who learned Jewish theology and ritual and sometimes served as assistant rabbis for families in the congregation observing Jewish ceremonies.

As part of his teaching, either with the havurot or para-rabbinics, Schulweis introduced his students to the teachings of scholars who influenced his own personal development, especially Reconstructionist leader Mordecai Kaplan. Kaplan, Schulweis has said, was responsible for teaching him the value of "religious humanism, pluralism and volunteerism as well as a respect for the contemporary, which many movements don't have. They are either tied to the past or too futuristic." In keeping with this philosophy, Schulweis has tried to mold a Judaic way of thinking that could counteract "secular religions" such as est and Scientology, which have often proved attractive to some American Jews. He was also much influenced by the teachings of Abraham Joshua Heschel, who Schulweis claimed stressed the need to cultivate a strong individual inner life.

Perhaps one reason Schulweis has garnered so much respect is for the honesty and forthrightness with which he has shared his personal views and struggles with his congregation. "I feel most fulfilled in and through my relationship to the community," he explained in the *Present Tense* article. "The rabbinate is really far from an occupation or profession in the sense that medicine or law is a profession. Every talk I give is autobiographical. My struggles are expressed in lectures, sermons, comments. I have never withheld from the congregation my wrestlings with the nature of God, prayer, the chosen people. They are quite aware that these are things I have difficulty with."

By sharing his struggles, Schulweis has allowed his congregation, in turn, to reach out to him. "I've opened up people's mouths," he said, "people who were muted, who were afraid to express their feelings because they were afraid they had to be formal or thought only the rabbi was qualified. These formerly paralyzed, immobile people are starting to move."

Schulweis has written *Approaches to the Philosophy of Religion* (1952) and has been on the editorial board of *Reconstructionist* since 1970 and of *Moment* and *Sh'ma* since 1974. In 1961 he was a founder of the Institute for the Righteous Arts at the Judah Magnes Museum in Berkeley, California.

GEORGE SEGAL

b. February 13, 1934
Actor

Actor George Segal, whose career has included dozens of Hollywood films, several Broadway plays and appearances on television shows, can play with equal skill a serious role of great intensity or a comic romantic lead. Compared at times to Cary Grant for his perform-

ance in *A Touch of Class* (1973), he has also been called the "Jewish Jack Lemmon, the lovable *schlemiel* always getting hit in the face by life's little slices of Danish."

George Segal Jr. was born in New York City to George Sr., a beer dealer, and Fanny (Bodkin) Segal. Raised in Great Neck, New York, he attended high school in Great Neck and finished at a Quaker-run private school in Pennsylvania called the George School, where, as a student, he formed a musical ensemble and played the banjo. Upon graduation he entered Haverford College, then transferred to Columbia University, where he received a B.A. degree in 1955.

Segal had known since his teen years that he wanted to be an actor. However, his entree to the theater was literally through the back door, where he performed a series of menial jobs, including janitor, ticket taker, soft drink salesman and usher at New York's Circle in the Square Theater. He made his professional acting debut in a one-day revival of *Don Juan* at the New York Downtown Theater. The following year he landed a small role in a revival of Eugene O'Neill's *The Iceman Cometh*, which starred Jason Robards Jr. and Peter Falk. Following service in the Army from 1956 to 1957, Segal performed with the New York Shakespeare Festival in *Antony and Cleopatra*. It took five years for him to make headway on Broadway, however, and it was only in 1962, when he played the role of Tammy Grimes' brother in *Rattle of a Simple Man*, that he first garnered attention as a serious actor.

Meanwhile, in 1961, Segal ventured to the West Coast, where he performed in a variety of undistinguished films, including his first one that year, *The Young Doctors*. His emergence as a major star occurred four years later with his performance in *King Rat*, the movie version of the James Clavell novel about small-time rackets run by British and American prisoners in a Japanese prisoner-of-war camp during World War II.

Segal quickly followed up his success with a featured role in the film version of Edward Albee's play *Who's Afraid of Virginia Woolf* (1966). In the film, which starred Richard Burton and Elizabeth Taylor, Segal played the male foil to Burton. He received an Academy Award nomination for best supporting actor as a result.

Segal's best-known films include *Ship of Fools* (1965); *A Touch of Class*, in which he co-starred with British actress Glenda Jackson; and *Fun with Dick and Jane* (1976), with Jane Fonda. In *Bye, Bye Braverman*—based on Wallace Markfield's comic novel of New York Jewish intellectuals—he played the lead role. In all, Segal has made more than 25 films since his inauspicious debut in 1961.

He has also done some notable work in television,

including a brilliant performance as Biff, Willy Loman's son in *Death of a Salesman* (1966), which was presented on CBS-Television. He also starred in *Of Mice and Men* (1968).

Segal brings wit, intelligence and savoir faire to his roles. He is refined without being stuffy, a bit of a dilettante without being pompous. Despite the tendency for Segal to be cast as a youthful male lead, he has the capacity to perform roles of great emotional complexity and, in fact, considers himself more a serious dramatic actor than a comedian.

GEORGE SEGAL

b. November 26, 1924
Sculptor

George Segal went from being a New Jersey chicken farmer to becoming one of America's most successful sculptors, whose works are internationally famous and command high prices. Nonetheless, he continues to live on the chicken farm where he started out, and his sculptures—life-size representations of people in a wide range of activities—are deceptively simple, like the man who created them.

George Segal was born in the Bronx to Russian immigrant parents, Jacob, a kosher butcher, and Sophie (Gerstenfeld) Segal. When Jacob Segal's shop failed, the family moved to New Jersey, where they set up the chicken farm that George Segal would later take over. Meanwhile, Segal developed a passion for art, which his parents nurtured, and he studied painting at several of New York's major art schools, including Cooper Union and Pratt Institute, and privately with Hans Hoffmann. He earned a B.A. degree in art education from New York University in 1950 and, 13 years later, a Master of Fine Arts degree from Rutgers University.

As an unknown painter, Segal was initially forced to support himself by teaching art and running the chicken farm. (He would later say that the experience was worthwhile; shoveling up after the several hundred chickens gave him the stamina to work with heavy sculptured pieces.) At the time, the abstract expressionist movement was in full flower, and Segal was swept along by the energy of American artists who strove, he said, to "surpass the school of Paris . . . Picasso, Matisse, Cezanne, Van Gogh and company—staggering achievement, the world's measure of great art. And these New York upstarts were insisting that here was a new rhythm, movements, it could be abstract. . . ." He joined the movement by exhibiting periodically at the Hansa Gal-

lery in New York City from 1956 to 1959. But in 1959 he turned to sculpture, and as his personal style evolved, he moved from abstract expressionism toward neo-realism, where he would spearhead a return to more realistic—sometimes super-realistic—images.

In the beginning Segal's sculptures were white plaster-like forms (he worked in a medium called hydrostone) made by casting on to people he knew in a variety of prearranged poses. (These would be done in three stages: head, torso and legs.) The finished works, once assembled, would then be placed in settings he built, often from found objects, which would therefore become set ensemble pieces of one or more white figures within realistic settings. The result was eerie, especially when Segal had a show with several pieces scattered on one floor. Meanwhile, although some critics were initially skeptical of what they called Segal's "gimmick," they soon acknowledged him as one of the leading proponents of neo-realism, the next significant movement in modern art to emerge, along with neo-realism's satirical counterpart, pop art.

Moreover, his work started to improve as he experimented with painting his figures and with casting them from the inside—that is, casting his reliefs directly from people, then casting new reliefs from inside the newly formed casts. The end result contained far greater texture, detail and rhythm.

Soon Segal was being given one-man shows in museums and galleries across the country, including a major retrospective at New York's Whitney Museum in 1979. *New York Times* critic John Canaday compared him to Degas, writing that "both [artists] are uncanny masters in their own way of selecting a pose, in adjusting the angle of a hand, of showing how a body sags into rest or the way it moves into action. . . . The power of Mr. Segal's sculpture is that it evokes another life so vividly that that life impinges on our own." And in a 1964 review he added that he "continues to create the most haunting presence in sculpture today, managing to create effects of maximum isolation with the most direct physical images of people."

Perhaps because Segal's works are so direct, and so simple and complex at the same time, they have become sources of fascination and admiration —and of controversy —both within and beyond the art world. In 1978, for example, he was commissioned by a private Ohio-based foundation to design and execute a memorial to the four Kent State University students killed in an anti-war march in 1971. The resulting work, designed as an updated version of Abraham preparing to sacrifice his son, was ultimately rejected by the university as "inappropriate." And in 1981 a design called "Gay Liberation," which depicted one male and one female homosexual couple near a park bench, was proposed for placement in a New York City Greenwich Village Park but aroused widespread argument and was never placed.

As for Segal, the controversy is merely part of the artistic process of challenging one's psyche in the process of creating. "Like everybody's work, my own work is about my mental state," he once said. "And that's a mix between a lot of levels of feeling and a lot of thinking. It's very hard work to be able to put a fraction of your experience into the work."

MAURICE SENDAK

b. June 10, 1928
Illustrator

Although we all share childhood in common, most of us also grow out of it, forget it and then look upon it as a beguiling, foreign and mysterious state of being. Not so illustrator Maurice Sendak, whose brilliant drawings for dozens of books, and more recently for the stage, have perfectly captured the essences of childhood —its fears, boredom, fantasies, nightmares and triumphs. The poetic power of his work is often compared with that of Durer and Blake.

Maurice Bernard Sendak was born in Brooklyn to Philip, a dressmaker, and Sadie (Schindler) Sendak. Both parents were immigrants from Poland who settled in New York before World War I. A sickly, isolated child, he acted out his fantasies through drawing. One could easily speculate—and many have—that Sendak's uncanny ability to tap the fantasies of contemporary children derives from his own prolonged solitude, which was, he has said, reinforced by his father's dismal outlook on life. He contributed illustrations to the Lafayette High School newspaper, but his artistic talent would not flower until after he left home.

Following high school graduation in 1946, Sendak moved to Manhattan, where he worked as a window display dresser and designer and took night courses at the Art Students League. He then collaborated with his brother Jack, who became an engineer, in designing miniature toy models for the windows of the F.A.O. Schwarz toy store. Through a book buyer at the store to whom Sendak had shown a portfolio of illustrations, he met a publisher who gave him his first commission in 1951. The book Sendak was to illustrate was Marcel Aymé's children's story *The Wonderful Farm* (New York). His simple pen-and-ink drawings became the spring-

board for further work, and before the decade was over, he had not only illustrated many books for other writers, including the now-classic *A Hole Is to Dig* (New York, 1952), but began writing books of his own, including *Kenny's Window* (New York, 1956) and *Very Far Away* (New York, 1957), whose title signaled, perhaps, Sendak's instinctive ability to know what, how and why children think.

As Sendak's reputation grew, so did his artistic daring. Much influenced by 18th-century illustrators, he allowed their styles to creep into his work, which filled the allotted space with intricate and cluttered detail and with expressions on his characters, whether human or animal, reflecting super-realistic qualities. For example, in his widely praised drawings for the two-volume set *The Juniper Tree and Other Tales from Grimm* (New York, 1973), he recreated 18th-century settings for the stories that captured much of the dreamy—or sometimes nightmarish—characteristics of the original tales. Even psychologist Bruno Bettelheim, who has criticized the sterility of modern children's literature, which eliminates adverse possibilities, noted Sendak's utter faithfulness not only in his depiction of the bleakness of the Grimm tales but in his portrayal in his other books of the negative experiences and feelings children often have.

Bettelheim was referring to Sendak's own highly successful creations, *Where the Wild Things Are* (New York, 1964), *In the Night Kitchen* (New York, 1970) and *Outside Over There* (New York, 1981). As though he had unleashed long-repressed memories of the five-year-old's psyche, Sendak conjured in illustration, and with minimal—or sometimes no—text, the interior world of a child. *Where the Wild Things Are* transforms a child's bedroom into an endless, mystical jungle populated by the creatures of his imagination—huge animals with enormous, round, furry faces, funny ears and contorted smiles. Are they friend or enemy? Who knows? Likewise, Sendak's other books propel the reader—child and grown-up—into a world quite unlike anything that has proceeded it.

By the mid-1960s Sendak's talent had become widely recognized, and in 1964 he had his first solo show at the School of Visual Arts Gallery in New York City. The same year he also received the prestigious Caldecott medal for *Where the Wild Things Are,* awarded for accomplishment in children's literature. In 1970 he became the first American to win the Hans Christian Andersen illustrators award.

In 1975 Sendak temporarily left book illustration for an experience on a far larger scale: He wrote the lyrics and did the illustrations for an animated television film, *Really Rosie,* whose music was written by a fellow Brooklyn native, the popular singer-composer Carole King. The story of a middle-class little girl growing up in a Brooklyn neighborhood, *Really Rosie* became a modestly successful off-Broadway show in 1980. But the experience expanded into other areas for Sendak. A long-time opera fan with a passion for Mozart, he designed sets for a Houston Opera Company production of *The Magic Flute* in 1980 and for a contemporary opera, *The Cunning Little Vixen* by Leos Janacek, for the New York City Opera in 1981. His work on both projects was widely hailed, and in 1981 Sendak was honored with an exhibition of drawings and watercolors at the Pierpont Morgan Library in New York City. Paired with exhibitions of musical manuscripts by Mozart and drawings by William Blake—two of the artist's major influences—Sendak's retrospective was unique in that few living artists ever have their works on display at the Morgan.

For further information:

Coburn, Randy Sue. "The Wizard of 'Wild Things,' " *Smithsonian Magazine,* February 1982.

Lahr, John. "The Playful Art of Maurice Sendak." *The New York Times Magazine,* October 12, 1980.

Sendak, Maurice; text by Selma Lanes. *The Art of Maurice Sendak.* New York: 1981.

GERALD SEROTTA

b. July 6, 1946
Rabbi

Since the late 1960s Rabbi Gerald Serotta has been in the vanguard of progressive Jewish movements that seek to draw disaffected, unaffiliated, primarily younger Jews into a Judaism that is forward-looking and more accepting of changed values and styles of life. He is steering committee chairperson of the New Jewish Agenda, an organization founded in 1979 to develop a new, unified approach to Jewish issues that runs counter to the right-leaning trend of the Jewish establishment.

Gerald Serotta was born in Miami, Florida to Maurice, a dentist, and Dorothy (Levin) Serotta. He was educated at Harvard College, where he received a Bachelor of Arts degree in social relations in 1968, and at Hebrew Union College-Jewish Institute of Religion, where he completed a Master of Hebrew Literature degree in 1974. He did additional graduate work at the New York Theological Seminary, where he received a master's degree in pastoral counseling in 1977, and the Postgraduate Center for Mental Health, which certified him as a pastoral counselor the same year.

Serotta's involvement in communal Jewish life began when he co-founded the New York Havurah in 1969, a group of young Jews who in some cases lived together but for the most part formed a fellowship that prayed together and shared other experiences relating to Jewishness.

In Israel in 1971 to 1972, Serotta worked on the Action Committee for a Beautiful Jerusalem and was Israel bureau editor of the Jewish Student Press Service. He became Hillel Counselor at Vassar College in 1973 and the following year became director of the City College of New York Hillel. From 1976 to 1977 he was Hillel director for Adelphi University and since 1977 has been associate director of the Hillel Foundation at Rutgers University. Since 1976 Serotta has also been involved with National Hillel, including two summer experiments in a Jewish Living Community in 1976 and 1978, and in the International Association of Hillel Directors, of which he has been second vice president since 1979.

Serotta participated in Breira, a group wishing to develop alternatives to some Israeli policies, in 1973; *Mazon,* the Jewish Committee on World Hunger, in 1975; and the Rutgers Committee on black-Jewish relations in 1979. He has also worked with elderly Jews in a program known as *Dorot* [Generations], headquartered in New York City's Upper West Side.

Serotta's activities culminated in the creation of the New Jewish Agenda. It began when a nucleus of 50 young activists assembled in 1979 to form a coalition of Reform, Conservative, Reconstructionist and Orthodox Jews, Zionists and non-Zionists, and those who use no label but identify strongly as Jews, to support a wide range of issues that they felt were not being appropriately addressed by America's Jewish leaders.

These issues included such global concerns as the uncontrolled spread of nuclear technology and of military buildups around the world; personal questions, such as the reproductive rights of women and the tolerance of individual lifestyles; and Jewish topics, such as anti-Semitism in the workplace and elsewhere. The New Jewish Agenda also reaches out to other minority groups in supporting civil rights and liberties, social justice and economic egalitarianism. In relation to Israel, it seeks to unite with Israeli doves—those Israelis who strive for a more peaceful and positive resolution to traditional problems with Arabs in Israel and in neighboring lands. In addition, it aims to create networks with Jewish communities around the world, including oppressed communities in the Soviet Union, Arab countries, Ethiopia and Latin America.

ALBERT SHANKER

b. September 14, 1928
Labor union official

In the 1960s Albert Shanker single-handedly spearheaded the movement to unionize teachers. Beginning in New York City, where he won major contract victories for his members, he rose to national prominence as the leader of the bitter New York City teachers' strike in 1968. As president of the American Federation of Teachers since 1972, Shanker has become one of America's most influential union leaders.

Albert Shanker was born of working-class parents, Morris and Mamie (Burko) Shanker, on the Lower East Side. Soon after, he moved with his family to non-Jewish, heavily industrialized Long Island City in Queens. His father, a former rabbinical student, delivered newspapers; and his mother, a seamstress, was active in both the Amalgamated Clothing Workers Union and the International Ladies Garment Workers Union. The neighborhood where he was reared was Irish-Italian, and Shanker, whose family heroes included Norman Thomas and Franklin Delano Roosevelt, spoke only Yiddish until his 8th birthday. He recalled that a group of thugs once encircled him, hung a rope around his neck, damned him as a Christ-killer and left him barely conscious and tied to a tree.

In his teens he attended the then all-boys Stuyvesant High School in Manhattan, whose prestigious and competitive academic program focused on mathematics and science. He then went to the University of Illinois, planning to major in philosophy. Drawn emotionally to socialism, he was chairman of the Socialist Study Club on campus. He also became a pacifist and planned to become a conscientious objector during the Korean War, but a collapsed lung barred him from serving in the military forces.

After graduating from the University of Illinois with a B.A. degree in 1949, he worked as a substitute mathematics teacher from 1952 to 1964, first in an East Harlem junior high school and later in Long Island City. Stung by the abysmally low pay and authoritarian milieu many teachers were forced to work in, in 1959 he went to work as an organizer for the New York Teachers Guild. One year later the Guild became known

as the United Federation of Teachers, while Shanker rose through the ranks to become its second president by 1964. The union had by now won full recognition from the AFL-CIO, which it joined that year, and in 1972 Shanker merged the UFT with the American Federation of Teachers, whose president he then became.

Much of Shanker's national reputation originates from his leadership in the 1968 teachers' strike against the largely black Ocean Hill-Brownsville Governing Board in Brooklyn, which had chosen to dismiss union faculty in order to hire teachers allegedly more representative of the local population. The result was a national furor, and Shanker became a major personality. The strike became a watershed in black-Jewish relations in the city.

Shanker was instrumental in expanding the UFT into an influential power base in New York City. From a small office in a midtown walk-up, the union eventually moved into its own building and became one of the most effective voices in New York City electoral politics; candidates endorsed by the UFT stood an excellent chance of being elected, since the organization would invariably mount an active campaign by telephone and direct mail. In addition, under Shanker's leadership, teacher salaries and benefits increased dramatically, and para-professionals hired by the Board of Education—classroom assistants drawn mostly from the predominantly black and Hispanic neighborhoods in which they worked—were also organized and given generous benefits, including financial incentives to continue their education. "Al Shanker delivers" became a frequently heard remark.

As Shanker's personal power base grew—by 1973 he was a vice president with the AFL-CIO—he became more vocal in national politics. Despite his early days as a pacifist, he was hawkish on Vietnam. He is also firmly against hiring quotas and, during the declaration of martial law in Poland in late 1981, was a major backer of that country's Solidarity union.

Shanker calls himself a pragmatist, one who has often had to make difficult decisions and strike compromises for the overall good of the union. Thus, he and his union were prominent supporters of the massive AFL-CIO Solidarity Day in September 1981 in Washington, D.C. to protest President Reagan's economic programs. His overriding concern, he says, is to reshape the image in society of teachers, whom he considers vastly underrated. And that he has done. When asked by journalist Lawrence Spivak on NBC's *Meet the Press* in 1975 to state the goal of the teacher union movement, Shanker replied, "To see to it that teachers in America have the economic advantages [of other citizens], that they have an organization which fights for them."

In recent years, however, the shrinking of financial support by the federal government and the coming of recession has fostered a climate of fiscal crises. In 1982 Shanker told a Great Neck, New York audience: "We will live through a decade or two of financial crises unknown until now." The reasons? $90 billion sent out of the country for foreign oil, sufficient to purchase the entire industrial capacity of a nation. Steel and auto industries suffering badly. Profits used for everything but reconstructing industrial plants and supporting research and development. Half the infrastructure of the country—bridges, roads, railroads and the like—will have to be rebuilt in a decade. "We'll be living on less and less and we'll be getting meaner and meaner," declares Shanker. In education, therefore, the pro-school forces are diminishing in political power and influence as everyone fights for a piece of the shrinking pie. The result is that fewer people are positive about public education. Still, the nation desperately requires a healthy public school system. Else it will break up into special-interest, ethnically-based private academies. Such an event, he believes, will prove to be a blow to unity in America and increase the divisions between classes, races and religions.

HARVEY SHAPIRO

b. January 27, 1924
Poet; editor

Jewish themes pervade much of the poetry of Harvey Shapiro, who is probably better-known as the editor of *The New York Times Book Review*, a position he has held since 1975. Shapiro's work has been published in seven volumes and in many of America's finest popular magazines and poetry journals.

Harvey Shapiro was born in Chicago to Jacob, a businessman, and Dorothy (Cohen) Shapiro. After serving in the U.S. Army from 1943 to 1945, he attended Yale University, where he received a B.S. degree in 1947, and Columbia University, where he completed an M.A. degree the following year. From 1949 to 1950 and from 1951 to 1952, Shapiro was an English instructor at Cornell University. In the intervening year, he was a creative writing fellow at Bard College. His first volume of poetry, *The Eye* (Chicago), was published in 1953, his second, *The Book and Other Poems* (Omaha, Nebraska), in 1955.

Shapiro settled in New York City, where he worked

as assistant editor of *Commentary* magazine from 1955 to 1956 and as fiction editor at *The New Yorker* for part of 1957. That year he joined *The New York Times Magazine* and became its assistant editor in 1964 before joining the *Book Review* staff. He became its editor and under his aegis the *Times Book Review* has become the most influential in the United States. In addition to reviews, Shapiro has injected thoughtful essays, profiles of writers and shorter reviews in fiction, nonfiction and science fiction, the better to comment on as many books as possible.

In 1966 two volumes of Shapiro's poetry were published, *Mountain, Fire, Thornbush* (Chicago) and *Battle Report* (Middletown, Conn.). Part of Wesleyan University's prestigious series of poetry books, *Battle Report* received considerable critical attention. While there is no unifying theme to the book, many of its poems, which had appeared in *The Nation, Midstream, Beloit Poetry Journal* and elsewhere, draw on religious sources ("The Prophet Announces," based on an 18th-century Haggadah illustration; "The Talker," from a *midrash;* "Feast of the Ram's Horn"; "Spirit of Rabbi Nachman"), while others draw on Jewish secular origins based, perhaps, on the poet's life.

One example is the following selection from his poem "Death of a Grandmother":

> My grandmother drank tea, and wailed
> As if the Wailing Wall kissed her head
> Beside the kitchen window;
> While the flaking, green-boxed radio
> Retailed in Yiddish song
> And heartache all day long.
>
> * * *
>
> To what sweet kingdom do the old Jews go?
> Now mourned by her radio and bed,
> She wishes me health and children,
> Who am her inheritor.

For further information:
Shapiro, Harvey. *The Eye.* New York: 1977.
———. *Lauds and Nightsounds.* New York: 1978.
———. *This World.* Middletown, Conn.: 1971.
Carruth, Hayden, ed. *The Voice that Is Great Within Us.* New York: 1970.

IRVING SAUL SHAPIRO

b. July 15, 1916
Industrialist; lawyer

When Irving S. Shapiro was named head of E.I. du Pont de Nemours & Company in 1974, not only was it the first time a Jew had directed the fortunes of the world's largest chemical manufacturer and 23rd largest industrial concern, but it was also the first time a Jew was asked to lead a major American business.

Irving Saul Shapiro was born in Minneapolis, Minnesota, one of three sons of Lithuanian immigrants Samuel I. and Frieda (Lane) Shapiro. The family was poor and earned a marginal living with a dry cleaning shop. Still, Shapiro graduated from the University of Minnesota in 1939 and then graduated from its law school in 1941, serving as editor of the *Minnesota Law Review* as well.

During World War II he was classified 4-F because of asthma. In 1943 he joined the Department of Justice and, wrote Peter Vanderwicken in *Fortune,* "quickly gained a reputation at Justice as a superb writer of briefs, with an ability to grasp the critical issue, classify it, and argue convincingly in support of the government's position." In 1948 he was named one of a team of United States prosecutors in the trial of 11 American Communists. Three years later he departed government employment and joined the law division of E.I. du Pont de Nemours & Company. His decision to leave the government was partly due to the fact that promotion to higher ranks at the Justice Department was largely dependent on strong political backing.

In a short time he became the corporation's principal lawyer and then the family's adviser. His government experience was invaluable. "Having spent 10 years in Washington as a young man, I have a feel for how the system operates," he told *The New York Times* in 1980. In 1974 he was appointed Du Pont's chairman of the board and chief executive officer.

Under Shapiro, Du Pont tightened management controls, discarded some older and unprofitable products and shut several factories. Shapiro introduced much more centralization and the demands for strict accountability at Du Pont, originally a family-dominated business separated into various quasi-independent fiefdoms. This transformation was forced by necessity, inasmuch as the demand for synthetic fibers sagged badly between 1974 and 1977, and the rising price of oil caused earnings to fall. A new management team was formed—smaller and extremely knowledgeable. Where, for example, senior vice presidents traditionally met with the corporate executive committee annually, Shapiro now required them to appear once weekly.

The key has been innovation of products, more competitive salesmanship and the cutting of costs. He also accelerated the search for newer or improved products. He has since described his technique of management at Du Pont at "lean and tough," stressing profit making

and lowering overhead and not diversification. And in a speech delivered to the New York Board of Trade in 1976, he spoke of the need for social progress, better and safer consumer goods and improved business ethics. He also became, as the *Philadelphia Inquirer* noted, "the closest thing there is to a spokesman for American private enterprise." He was consulted by presidents Nixon and Carter and leads the Business Roundtable, a group of 170 important corporate executives.

IRWIN SHAW

b. February 27, 1913
Novelist; short story writer

A writer who receives critical acclaim at age 23 and then produces consistent best sellers on a regular—and frequent—basis for nearly 50 years is bound to change and perhaps be criticized. That, in fact, has been the fate of Irwin Shaw, the prolific playwright, short story writer and novelist, whose earlier works were highly praised for their moral content and firm commitment to political justice.

Irwin Shaw was born in the Bronx and raised in the Brighton Beach section of Brooklyn. His parents were William, a hat trimming salesman, and Rose (Tompkins) Shaw. As a youth Shaw was a prolific reader and was particularly influenced by the works of Hemingway, Dos Passos, F. Scott Fitzgerald and Alexandre Dumas, whose novels of adventure and passion especially inspired Shaw's writing. Despite his mother's skepticism about the merits of being a professional writer, Shaw pursued his craft. After graduating from Brooklyn College in 1934 with a B.A. degree, he began immediately to support himself as a writer of scripts for radio serials while he continued his personal work.

Within two years Shaw's short stories were being published in *The New Yorker,* and he had a Broadway hit. *Bury the Dead* (1963), a one-act play that had begun off-Broadway but was brought to the Barrymore Theater for a long run, told of six dead soldiers who refused to remain buried and ultimately return to the battlefield. A confirmed pacifist and anti-Fascist, Shaw continued writing plays and stories in the same vein and received regular acclaim. He was perhaps most expert at portraying ordinary people—New York City cabdrivers, college students, street people, frustrated wives. And when possible, as in *Troubled Air* (New York, 1951), he inserted his strong political and ethical sentiments. In the novel a radio program director is told to fire five actors suspected of Communist Party sympathies, and he must decide how—and if—he will confront them. Meanwhile, Shaw's first novel (he had already published many short story collections), *The Young Lions* (New York, 1948), was a landmark work as it traced the fate of three men whose lives interlock—in one case fatally—during the Second World War.

When Shaw turned from political themes to earthier works and included sex and glamor in his novels as though he were writing according to formula, critics turned against him, and despite the consensus that Shaw is one of the great masters of the short story form and an outstanding writer of plot and dialogue, his reputation has nevertheless been on a steady decline.

By 1956 Shaw, who had moved to Europe 5 years earlier and who rarely mixed with literary "crowds," had published nearly a dozen books of short stories, plays and fiction. He then ventured into a new form of fiction. *Lucy Crown* (New York, 1956) depicts the unexpected summer love affair between a married woman and a younger man. Reviewers were especially disappointed because the otherwise skilled craftsman Shaw had faltered dramatically in his plot structure and technique. Shaw fans bought the book anyway, and over the next 20 years he continued to produce similar best sellers of complicated family intrigues, the paramours of alcoholic ex-Hollywood film directors, of has-beens trying to recapture their youth and so forth. Television producers loved his novels—*Rich Man, Poor Man* (New York, 1970), a chronicle of three generations in one family, became a blockbuster mini-series—and serious writers who once admired Shaw wondered what had happened. About *Rich Man*, one reviewer commented on Shaw's unflagging command of technique, saying "It's a book you can't put down. Once you do, it won't occur to you to pick it up again."

Yet in 1981, 45 years after premiering as a young playwright, Shaw's latest novel, *Bread upon the Waters* (New York), seemed to signal a return to the old style. An ordinary man—a middle-aged high school English teacher with three children who lives on New York City's Upper West Side—sees his life change radically when his teen-aged daughter helps rescue a mugging victim who turns out to be a millionaire. The man then becomes the family's benefactor. The fantasy element, present in many of Shaw's earlier works, is in full force here and provides the setting for a new moral tale, much like his works of old. It was critically well received, and although writer Bruce Jay Friedman compared Shaw to Isaac Bashevis Singer and John Cheever for the quantity of high-quality stories he has produced, it is hard to say which Shaw will one day be remembered by literary historians.

For further information:
Shaw, Irwin. Act of Faith, (stories). New York: 1946.
———. *Acceptable Losses,* (novel). New York: 1982.
———. *Beggarman, Thief,* (novel). New York: 1977.
———. *Evening in Byzantium,* (novel). New York: 1973.
———. *The Gentle People: A Brooklyn Fable,* (stories). New York: 1939.
———. *God Was Here but He Left Early,* (stories). New York: 1973.
———. *In the Company of Dolphins,* (novel). New York: 1964.
———. *Love on a Dark Street,* (stories). New York: 1965.
———. *Mixed Company,* (stories). New York: 1950.
———. *Report on Israel.* New York: 1950. With photographs by Robert Capa.
———. *Sailor off the Bremen and Other Stories.* New York: 1939.
———. *Short Stories: Five Decades.* New York: 1978.
———. *Tip on a Dead Jockey,* (stories). New York: 1957.
———. *Two Weeks in Another Town,* (novel). New York: 1960.
———. *Voices on a Summer Day,* (novel). New York: 1965.

WILLIAM SHAWN

b. August 31, 1907
Editor

Under William Shawn's aegis as editor, *The New Yorker* has evolved from being a humor magazine somewhat isolated from "real life" to one of the great magazines of the world, which combines an astute political consciousness in its editorial stances and choices of work with high wit and an unparalleled respect for perfection in language.

William Chon was born in Chicago to Benjamin and Anne (Bransky) Chon. He attended the University of Michigan between 1925 and 1927 but never graduated, dropping out and working briefly as a newspaper reporter in New Mexico before joining *The New Yorker* in 1932. Starting as a reporter for the magazine's "Talk of the Town" section, Shawn became an editor two years later—he was only 28—managing editor from 1939 to 1952 and from then on editor in chief, succeeding Harold Ross. Shawn is only the second editor in chief since *The New Yorker's* founding in 1925.

Despite his long career at *The New Yorker,* Shawn has attached his by-line to only one piece. It is a short story, "Catastrophe," written in 1936, which describes how the five boroughs of New York City are struck by a meteorite, casuing the city to disappear from view—and from consciousness. Aside from "Catastrophe," Shawn remains virtually anonymous about himself, letting *The New Yorker* be his mouthpiece through the works of its many authors, poets, critics and cartoonists, as well as through pieces he prefers to leave unsigned.

During his tenure at the magazine, he has had a major role in the publication of John Hersey's *Hiroshima* in the pages of *The New Yorker* in 1946 prior to the book's publication and in the later publication in the magazine of James Baldwin's *The Fire Next Time* (1962), Rachel Carson's *The Silent Spring* (1962), Hannah Arendt's *Eichmann in Jerusalem* (1963), Barry Commoner's *The Closing Circle* (1971), Charles Reich's *The Greening of America* (1972) and Saul Bellow's *To Jerusalem and Back* (1976). He has also published regularly the short stories of Isaac Bashevis Singer along with the works of such writers as John Updike, Hugh Nissenson, Cynthia Ozick and John Cheever and the brilliant nonfiction of Roger Angell on baseball, Whitney Balliett on jazz, Pauline Kael on films, George Steiner and Naomi Bliven on literature, and John McPhee on Alaska, the New Jersey Pine Barrens and other subjects. The cartoon art of Saul Steinberg, William Steig, Ronald Searle and other great artists has graced the covers and inside pages of *The New Yorker.*

In 1981 *The New Yorker* devoted most of an entire issue to a large portion of journalist Jacobo Timerman's searing book about his own jailing and torture and about anti-Semitism in Argentina, *Prisoner Without a Name, Cell Without a Number* (New York, 1981). That same year it serialized in four issues Jervis Anderson's history of Harlem and Susan Sheehan's account of a schizophrenic patient and a state mental institution. And in 1982 it published Jonathan Schell's noteworthy report on the nuclear arms race.

To know Shawn is more or less to know *The New Yorker.* One of the best sources for Shawn stories is therefore Brendan Gill's *Here At The New Yorker* (New York, 1975). Through anecdotes describing Shawn's dealings with his writers, his own tribulations at learning to drive a car ("It seems to me,' he says, 'that if one is disengaging the gears, one ought to have to let the clutch *out,* instead of pushing it *in.* To me, "in" represents engagement and "out" represents disengagement.' 'Aw, come on now, Mr. Shawn-baby,' the instructor says. 'Let's get the show on the road, awright?' ") or his dislike of speeding cabs, especially when he is in one of them ("I'll tip you just as much," he said, "if you'll

drive me just half as fast"), it is possible to assemble a composite picture of the man.

STANLEY K. SHEINBAUM

b. June 12, 1920
Economist; businessman; political activist

Although Stanley Sheinbaum is hardly a household name, his activity on behalf of local, national and international civil liberties causes has helped make many of the organizations he supports household names. An ardent fund-raiser with a background in economics, the California-based Sheinbaum has been a leader in liberal Democratic Party politics, in legal defense committees on behalf of liberal causes and in organizations designed to stem human rights violations in the United States and abroad.

Stanely K. Sheinbaum was born in New York City to Herman H., a manufacturer of leather goods, and Selma (Klimberg) Sheinbaum. After his father's business collapsed during the Depression, Sheinbaum worked at a series of odd jobs. At one point he learned to operate a sewing machine in his father's newly reopened plant and sewed dresses. During World War II he served in the Army and then in 1945 entered Stanford University, where he majored in Far East history. He graduated with a Bachelor of Arts degree in 1949 Phi Beta Kappa. From 1949 to 1956 he pursued doctoral studies in economics at Stanford. From 1950 to 1953 he also taught there, and from 1953 to 1955 he studied in Paris as a Fulbright economics fellow.

During this latter period he developed expertise in foreign exchange markets and balance of payments—a knowledge that the U.S. government would put to use some years later as it began making inroads into Indochina. On his return to the United States, Sheinbaum spent a short period as a staff fellow in the Program on Overseas Development at Stanford's Hoover Institute.

Up to this point Sheinbaum seemed well on the way to becoming entrenched within the academic establishment. But an experience during the next few years represented a turning point. While on the economics faculty at Michigan State University, where he taught from 1955 to 1960, he learned that a project he had been assigned to by the university in 1957, which involved fiscal policy planning for the South Vietnamese government, was, in fact, a cover for CIA covert operations. Appalled by the deceit of the government—he had also helped a covert government operation to gain the release from jail of Greek activist Andreas Papandreou (who was elected Greece's first socialist prime minister in 1981) and only later realized that the American government was actually supporting a repressive military junta—he became one of its loudest critics and directed his energies toward working for civil liberties causes, focusing on freedom of expression as the foundation for his work.

Describing his transition to activist, Sheinbaum said in an interview that after learning of his own indirect involvement in secret government work in Vietnam,

> I realized then the real threat was not in Vietnam but right here at home, where we were gradually being involved in a war that appeared to be a tragic blunder. I turned my attention to domestic policies, especially to civil liberties, to the challenge of keeping society open and informed, because our government seemed to be trying to shut up everyone who objected to the war in Vietnam.

From 1960 to 1970 Sheinbaum worked as an economics fellow at the Center for the Study of Democratic Institutions in Santa Barbara, California and became politically active in local and national Democratic Party politics. In 1966 and 1968 he ran unsuccessfully for Congress from Santa Barbara; in 1968 he was a McCarthy delegate to the Democratic National Convention in Chicago and in 1972 a McGovern delegate at the Miami convention.

From 1965 to 1973 Sheinbaum was a consulting editor with *Ramparts* magazine, one of the best-known radical political publications to emerge from the free speech movement of the 1960s, and it was in these pages that he wrote an expose of CIA operations in Vietnam through his own unwilling involvement during the Michigan years. Previously, other publications had rejected his offers to write about it.

Sheinbaum grew to be especially critical of President Kennedy for sending troops to Vietnam without congressional authorization and of President Johnson for his all-out escalation of the war. And he felt that President Carter hedged when he sent out a mixed message of commitment to civil rights groups during his four years in Washington.

He also expanded his involvement in a variety of public interest causes, which ranged from his role from 1961 to 1962 as executive director of the Committee to Improve Teacher Education (CITE), a citizen's lobby, to his active participation in legal defense programs and causes. In 1970, for example, he was a founder of the Legal Defense Center of Santa Barbara: from 1971 to 1973 he played a critical role as a fund raiser to organize and coordinate the defense team in the Pentagon Papers trials.

He has also been on the board of directors of several civil liberties organizations, most notably as the board chairman of the American Civil Liberties Union of Southern California since 1973 and as a member of the ACLU National Advisory Council since 1974. In 1974 he also helped found the People's College of Law in Los Angeles. He was one of the ACLU's most vocal supporters during the critical period in 1978 when the organization defended the American Nazi Party's right to demonstrate in Skokie, Illinois, although the scheduled event (which, in the end, did not take place) nearly cost the ACLU much of its Jewish support and ultimately its existence. Since 1976 Sheinbaum has been on the board of the Center for Law in the Public Interest in Los Angeles and has been a board member of the Los Angeles chapter of the American Jewish Committee.

Concurrent with his political and civic involvements, Sheinbaum has also been active since the mid-1960s as a businessman and real estate developer.

In the 1980s Sheinbaum continued to focus his energies on large-scale civil liberties projects, especially in the wake of the election of Ronald Reagan, who appeared to be curbing some of the gains made in that area. He is, for example, a director of People for the American Way, a nationwide lobbying organization founded in 1980 by Norman Lear to counter the Moral Majority. And in 1981 he joined the board of Helsinki Watch and Americas Watch, organizations that monitor human rights violations in Latin America, the Caribbean and elsewhere. He is also a board member of *democracy* magazine.

MORRIS SHERER

b. June 18, 1921
Rabbi; communal leader

Rabbi Morris Sherer is president of Agudath Israel of America, a broad-based and politically active Orthodox Jewish coalition in North America. An advocate for Jewish rights in Washington, he is regarded as one of America's major spokesmen for Orthodox Jewry, with strong links to Agudath Israel in the State of Israel.

Morris Sherer was born in New York City to Chaim, a businessman, and Basya (Moruchnik) Sherer, Russian immigrants. He was ordained as a rabbi by the Mesifta Torah Vodaath Rabbinical Seminary in Brooklyn and graduated from Ner Israel Rabbinical College in Baltimore in 1943. His public career began that same year, when he became the executive director of the Agudath

Israel Youth Council of America. In 1951 he became executive vice president of the organization and in 1963 was elected national president.

Rabbi Sherer made headlines in 1961 as the first Jewish leader to publicly support federal aid to parochial schools. Testifying before the House Education and Labor Subcommittee, he condemned the "double taxation of American Orthodox Jews" for public education and private tuition. He and Agudath Israel have formed a close alliance with Catholic educators who advocate greater government spending for parochial schools. He has also cultivated politicians, many of whom now argue for increased federal aid for parochial schools.

Under Rabbi Sherer's leadership, Agudath Israel has addressed a wide range of concerns, including senior citizens, children's welfare, immigrant absorption, international affairs, career training and social services. Agudath Israel's government-funded job-training program has served many Soviet Jewish emigres. He is also responsible for developing policies that assure that Jewish hospital patients will receive kosher food on request, that employment rights of religious Jews in the civil service are protected and that sporadic threats against kosher slaughtering practices are beaten down. "Orthodox Jews have unique concerns," he has said, "and they, rather than Jewish secularists or those who believe that being Jewish is as easy as chewing gum, should represent their cases before governmental bodies."

In his lectures and articles, often in the *Jewish Observer*, Rabbi Sherer has demonstrated his belief that *halakah* (Torah law) should be used as the basis for Jewish policy decisions in the United States and in Israel, too, where his organization has very close ties with the Agudath political party, a member of Prime Minister Begin's governing coalition. He has testified before United States congressional committees on behalf of aid for yeshiva education, job protection for Jewish civil service sabbath observers, safeguarding of *shechita* (religious slaughter of animals) and other laws affecting Jews and Judaism. In 1980 an article in *New York* magazine described him as one of the 10 "most powerful" rabbis in both commitment and organization.

He is a member of the executive committee of the National Jewish Commission on Law and Public Affairs, a director of New York state's Welfare Research Inc. and the Association of Advanced Rabbinic and Talmudic Schools. In 1980 he was elected chairman of the Agudath Israel World Organization, which is devoted to promoting stronger links between Orthodox Jewish communities throughout the world.

JEROME SHESTACK

b. February 11, 1925
Attorney; human rights activist

Although Jerome Shestack could have lived his life exclusively as a successful corporate attorney, he has opted to contribute much of his time to civil liberties and civil rights issues and to Jewish affairs. He has been especially prominent in the international human rights area, fighting for the rights of individuals to travel freely to and from their homelands.

Jerome Joseph Shestack was born in Atlantic City, New Jersey to Isidore, a clothing manufacturer, and Olga (Shankman) Shestack. He attended the University of Pennsylvania, where he received his Bachelor of Arts degree in economics in 1943. Following service in the U.S. Navy as a lieutenant j.g. from 1943 to 1946, he entered Harvard Law School, where he served as president of the Harvard Law School Record and completed his Bachelor of Laws in 1949.

Before entering public service, Shestack taught law at Northwestern University and at Louisiana State University from 1949 to 1952. In 1953 he became first deputy solicitor of Philadelphia for the reform administration of Mayor Joseph Clark. During his two years in that post, he helped supervise a staff of 50 attorneys. At the same time he became involved in civil rights work, serving as the first counsel to the Philadelphia Commission on Human Relations from 1952 to 1955. This effort included desegregating municipal amusement parks and Girard College.

In 1956 Shestack became a partner in the Philadelphia law firm of Schnader, Harrison, Segal and Lewis, specializing in a wide range of trial and business issues for such clients as NBC, Hertz, Bell Telephone and other large corporations. But along with private practice, he remained active in public life and was a consistent and outspoken advocate of the need for lawyers to donate some of their time to popular, if not lucrative, causes. In 1963 he was one of the founders of the Lawyers Committee for Civil Rights Under Law. In that post he helped create a Mississippi Office that trained lawyers to handle civil rights cases. From 1965 to 1972 he was on the steering committee that helped found the Legal Services Corporation of the Office of Economic Opportunity. When the Reagan administration threatened to abolish the Legal Services Corporation, Shestack headed the move within the American Bar Association to save it.

During the same period he was also involved in

programs to support mass transit—another example of Shestack's reaching out to issues of public importance—as a member of the Southeastern Pennsylvania Transit Authority, which helped create a mass transit system. In 1982 he continued his record of municipal involvement when he was appointed by Philadelphia Mayor William Green to the Mayor's Task Force on Minority Employment in the Police Force.

As early as 1970 he initiated the push for law firms to do *pro bono publico* work, a cause he has championed ever since. He headed the ABA's first Commission on the Mentally Disabled, for which he obtained funding of $1 million to found pilot projects to assist the mentally ill across the United States, from 1973 to 1976.

In 1972 Shestack became president of the International League for Human Rights, an organization with 35 affiliates that has consultative status at the United Nations. He served until 1979, when he was appointed by President Jimmy Carter to be U.S. Representative to the United Nations Commission on Human Rights, then became president again in 1981. As part of his effort with the league, Shestack was founder and co-chair of the Lawyers Committee for International Human Rights, which has more than 100 volunteer lawyers handling cases.

Liberal political activism is an essential part of Shestack's life, and he has been involved with the Democratic National Committee since 1975. He has written speeches for presidential candidates Adlai E. Stevenson, Hubert Humphrey and Edmund Muskie and has been an active campaigner for national and local Democratic candidates.

During the heated public debate following the publication of Jacobo Timerman's book, which strongly condemned his Argentine jailers as neo-Nazis and anti-Semitic and Argentine Jewish organizations as timid and silent, Shestack defended Timerman publicly and condemned as spurious Reagan administration and right-wing efforts to defend Argentina by distinguishing between "authoritarian" and "totalitarian" regimes. He also deplored "the divisiveness and confusion in the Jewish community promoted by Kristol and some other neo-conservatives."

Shestack has also been active in Jewish organizations since 1955, when he became a trustee of the Jewish Publication Society of America, based in Philadelphia. Since then he has served as the society's president from 1973 to 1976, has been on the board of directors of the Federation of Jewish Agencies since 1962 and has been on the board of overseers of the Jewish Theological Seminary since 1968. He has been active

with the American Jewish Committee as past chair of its Foreign Affairs Commission and is on the board of governors of both Hebrew University and Tel Aviv University.

For further information:

Shestack, Jerome. "Jacobo Timerman: The Perils of Silence." *Congress Monthly*, September/October 1981.

MARSHALL D. SHULMAN

b. April 8, 1916
Academician; government official

Marshall D. Shulman, who served in the administration of President Jimmy Carter as special adviser on Soviet affairs to the secretary of state, is one of America's authorities on international politics, Soviet foreign policy and arms limitation.

Marshall Darrow Shulman was born to Harry Max, an engineer, and Bessie (Waldman) Shulman in Jersey City, New Jersey. He received a B.A. degree in 1937 from the University of Michigan and then studied at the University of Chicago from 1938 to 1939 and at Harvard University the following year. He worked for the *Detroit News* from 1937 to 1939 and for six months in 1940. During World War II he served with the Army Air Corps. Following his discharge he entered the Russian Institute of Columbia University, where he earned a certificate and an M.A. degree in 1948.

In 1949 he was information officer at the United Nations. Between 1950 and 1953 he worked as a special assistant to Secretary of State Dean Acheson and then returned to Columbia to earn his Ph.D. in 1959. During this time he also served at Harvard's Russian Research Center as associate director from 1954 to 1962 and then as research associate from 1962 to 1967. From 1962 to 1967 he was also a professor of international politics at the Fletcher School of Law and Diplomacy at Tufts University.

On a visit to the USSR in 1966, he was expelled. The reasons offered were vague, but one Soviet allegation was that he had tried to "infiltrate" their academic community. After his return he was named director of the Russian Institute at Columbia University and Adlai E. Stevenson Professor of International Relations.

Shulman's initiatives to help stem nuclear war through careful negotiation helped establish him as a major influence on foreign policy decisions. "Those who think nuclear war is inconceivable place too much reliance on an assumed rationality in the decision-making process," he said in 1971. "Decisions are more often than not the result of interplay of pressures, and the outcome does not always—perhaps not even often—correspond to what anyone would decide as a rational choice." This philosophy would follow Shulman to Washington, but its moderation would ultimately prove unpopular to an uneasy administration trying to prove its strength.

Shulman's firm belief in the need for arms limitation, and specifically his support of SALT II, were among the reasons for his 1977 appointment to the State Department by Secretary of State Cyrus Vance. During this period, however, Shulman observed the worsening of relations between the United States and the Soviet Union, especially when the Carter administration ceased negotiations of any kind with the Russians after their invasion of Afghanistan in 1979. Disagreeing with Carter's tactics, he described the United States-Russia relationship from that time on as "a terminal case of myopia" and expressed pessimism about the major powers' ability to prevent nuclear war if they continued on their current track.

Then, not long after his arrival in Washington, Shulman was compelled to take a secondary role in decision making to National Security Council adviser and Columbia University Professor Zbigniew Brzezinski, whose more aggressive policies were favored by Carter. And when his mentor, Secretary of State Vance, resigned because of policy differences with Brzezinski, Shulman followed, aware that his more moderate and conciliatory views had been subordinated to Brzezinski's more confrontational approach. "Sometimes I get the feeling I'm sitting on a hilltop watching two trains racing toward each other on the same track," he observed in July 1980, only weeks before he announced his decision to resign. "I don't think either of us [the Americans and the Russians] has been acting very sensibly. This period of tension promises to continue for a long time."

Shortly before his departure from Washington, Shulman was honored with the Foreign Affairs Award for Public Service from the Department of State, which was presented to him by Vance's successor, Edmund Muskie. Shulman then returned to his post as director of the Russian Institute at Columbia University.

For further information:
Shulman, Marshall D. *Beyond the Cold War.* New Haven: 1966.
———. *Stalin's Foreign Policy Reappraised.* Cambridge: 1963.

SEYMOUR SIEGEL

b. September 12, 1927
Rabbi

Rabbi Seymour Siegel, professor of ethics and theology at the Jewish Theological Seminary and chair of the Committee on Jewish Law of the Rabbinical Assembly, has also played a crucial role in urging American Jews to move politically to the right while at the same time nudging conservative Judaism to become more liberal and open the ranks of the rabbinate to women.

Seymour Siegel was born in Chicago to David, a lawyer, and Jeanette (Morris) Siegel. After earning his B.A. degree from the University of Chicago in 1947, he received his Master of Hebrew Literature degree from the Jewish Theological Seminary of America in 1951, the same year he was ordained as a rabbi. He received his Doctor of Hebrew Literature degree from the seminary in 1958 and has taught at the seminary since 1959. He has also been a visiting professor at the Seminario Rabinico in Buenos Aires from 1962 to 1964 and an adjunct professor in Jewish studies at City College from 1971 to 1973.

Siegel, who had been supportive of liberal Democratic Party policies since his youth in Chicago, became politically disillusioned in the late 1960s. Though he had backed civil rights, he drew back when black politicians began to urge racial quotas; students protested at Columbia University, across the street from his office; and Democrats started taking what he calls an "accommodationist philosophy" toward radical and left-wing governments. "Jewish self-interest demanded a more conservative politics," he told a *New York* magazine reporter.

Along the way he became a supporter of the Vietnam War. In addition, he has been an adviser in the election campaigns of conservatives James Buckley, Richard Nixon, Gerald Ford and Perry Duryea and has emerged as the earliest and most visible Jewish communal leader to support the Republican right. In 1980 he helped found the American Jewish Forum, an organization designed to support conservative stances in foreign and domestic policies, oppose quotas and favor Israel. And following the publication in 1981 of Jacobo Timerman's book *Prisoner Without a Name, Cell Without a Number,* he criticized the exiled Buenos Aires newspaper publisher for exaggerating the extent of Argentine anti-Semitism in an appearance on Bill Moyers' PBS-TV show.

While Siegel has become increasingly conservative

in his politics, he has become more liberal in defining religious practices. He strongly advocates allowing women to be included in a minyan (quorum) in the Conservative movement and ardently supports the ordination of women as rabbis. "The reasons for excluding women in the past are no longer valid today," he insisted. "It's *only* fair that they be included as members of the praying community."

He is on the board of directors of the Jewish Museum and a fellow at the Institute of Religious and Social Studies; the Society for Religion in Higher Education; and the Conference on Science, Philosophy and Religion. He is also a member of the editorial board of the Jewish Publication Society, the *Encyclopedia Judaica* and the *Encyclopedia of Bio-Medical Ethics*.

For further information:

Siegel, Seymour. *Conservative Judaism and Jewish Law.* New York: 1976.

―――. *The Jewish Dietary Laws: Contemporary Issues in Jewish Ethics.* New York: 1977.

CHARLES ELIOT SILBERMAN

b. January 31, 1925
Writer; journalist

In his controversial books investigative journalist and social analyst Charles Silberman has confronted three problems that affect every American: education, racism and crime. They have motivated specialists and laymen to reconsider their thinking, and in so doing, Silberman has made major contributions to American society. His newest project, a study of Jewish life in America, promises to have similar impact.

Charles Eliot Silberman was born to Seppy Israel, a salesman, and Cel (Levy) Silberman, a camp director, in Des Moines, Iowa. Raised in New York, he got an early start in journalism as editor of the DeWitt Clinton High School newspaper, graduating in 1941. Between 1943 and 1946 he was in the U.S. Naval Reserve, rising from the lowest rank to lieutenant j.g. He graduated from Columbia University with a B.A. degree in 1946. Following three years of postgraduate study in economics, he taught briefly as an instructor at Columbia.

In 1953 Silberman became an editor at *Fortune* magazine, concentrating on economics and remaining until 1971. While there he published a major article, "The City and the Negro," in March 1962 that formed the foundation for his first major book, *Crisis in Black and White* (New York, 1964). Whites, he concluded, have to bear "the shame" of both slavery and present unsatisfactory conditions for blacks. "Political self-interest" demanded that radical remedies be sought. He also blamed blacks' "behavior" that "helps perpetuate white prejudice." They had, he wrote, fewer ambitions, revealed greater sexual laxity and were less family-oriented than whites. Their crime rate was staggering, and black students did far worse than whites on I.Q. tests. They also had an abysmal record of achievement in business and the professions—miserable statistics he blamed on "350 years of white oppression" and "a system designed to destroy ambition, prevent independence and erode intelligence." He observed "Only the Blacks had to be beaten into submission before they made the crossing [to North America] and they've never forgotten it. Violence has thus been an intrinsic part of the 'Black American Experience.' " He urged that decision-making authority be given to blacks in areas that affected them and that their children be permitted to attend school at earlier ages—a precursor of the Head Start Program.

The book, funded by a Ford Foundation grant for Silberman to use in conjunction with Columbia University, analyzed myths and facts behind the growing racial crisis in America, which, he insisted, was "the most urgent piece of public business facing the United States" as well as "the most difficult." As a result of his probing and passionate work, Silberman received the Four Freedoms Literary Award and the National Conference of Christians and Jews Superior Merit award.

His next major project had mammoth impact on another critical area of American life: its system of education. *Crisis in the Classroom: The Remaking of American Education* (New York, 1970) took 3½ years to research and write. Silberman directed this project with a $300,000 grant from the Carnegie Corporation and interviewed educators across the country. He concluded that the current system was stagnant and repressive—"joyless" and "mindless" were words he used—and was too often based on rote learning marked by the lack of critical thinking. Silberman advocated the exploration of progressive systems similar to those practiced in certain European countries, such as the "open classroom" technique, which granted the public and teachers greater creative possibilities. In addition to being a best seller, the book received six national awards, including the John Dewey Award from the United Federation of Teachers (1971) and the National Council for the Advancement of Education writing award. As an adjunct to

Crisis in the Classroom, Silberman edited *The Open Class-room Reader* (New York, 1973), to delineate ways in which this method of instruction could be utilized.

Silberman left *Fortune* in 1971 to write and lecture full-time. In 1972 he was asked by the Ford Foundation to head a study of law and justice. With a $537,000 grant he developed a massive research project that evolved into *Criminal Violence, Criminal Justice* (New York, 1978). He concluded that most of the prevailing beliefs about how the criminal justice system operates in the United States today are either false or simply not understood. Again, Silberman took on a difficult problem and apparently relished the challenge and his role as provocateur. Violence is "as American as Jesse James," and criminal arts are "endemic in every sector of American society," he wrote. Young black men commit a disproportionate number of crimes—a fact Silberman blamed on their disastrous and chaotic slum existence and their peculiar history in the United States. Nor would more police, strict legal codes or prisons reduce crime. He did praise the court system in part, though he criticized its often shabby and inefficient operation and inexplicable unevenness in meting out justice. He proposed the organization of community-controlled innovations and self-help programs but insisted the long-range answer lay in the reduction of poverty, inequality and racial bias.

Silberman has been active in Jewish affairs in America for many years. He is on the board of directors of the United Synagogue of America, the Synagogue Council of America and the Institute for Jewish Policy Planning and Research. In addition, he is a member of the Union of American Hebrew Congregations, the National Program Commission of the Anti-Defamation League, the Commission on Social Action of the United Synagogue, the Editorial Board of *Reconstructionist* magazine and the Commission on Jewish Life of the American Jewish Congress.

For further information:
Silberman, Charles Eliot, ed. *The Myths of Automation.* New York: 1960.

LEONARD SILK

b. May 15, 1918
Economist; journalist

Leonard Silk, economics editor and columnist for *The New York Times,* has had a prestigious career in the fields of economics and journalism that has led him through such noteworthy doors as the *Times, Business*

Week, professorships at major universities and appointments to numerous presidential commissions and has resulted in a string of honors and awards.

Leonard Solomon Silk was born in Philadelphia, the son of Harry Lewis, a clothing merchant, and Ida (Ender) Silk. His early college years found him at the University of Wisconsin, where he received his Bachelor of Arts degree in economics in 1940, and then at Duke University, for a doctorate in economics in 1947.

Silk's professional career began at his alma mater, Duke, where he was an economics instructor during his years as a graduate student. He has maintained affiliations with major universities throughout his career, including professorships at the University of Maine (1947–48); New York University (1955–56); Columbia University (1962–63); Carnegie Institute of Technology (1965–66); the Brookings Institution (1969–70); Yale University (1974–75); and Pace University (1980–), where he is a visiting distinguished professor of economics.

Professional journalistic activities for Silk began in 1954 with *Business Week,* where he served as the magazine's economics editor for 10 years and as senior editor through 1966, reporting and commenting on domestic and international economic developments. In 1966 he was named vice chairman and economist, and in 1967 he was promoted to the chairmanship of the magazine's editorial board. Silk left *Business Week* in 1969, joining *The New York Times* as an editorial board member (1970–76) and later as economics columnist. In one typical column, "Political Unrest and Violence," in the April 16, 1982 *Times,* Silk asked "Is the common cause of the political troubles world economic disorder, with military adventuring the common but dangerous solution?" To Silk the connection between "economic decay and war" seemed "fundamentally mistaken," despite Marxists and other economic determinists who believe in such a connection. Citing the flagging equity and bond markets—despite various wars in recent years—as well as the disastrous inflation kicked off by the Vietnam War and the Arab oil embargo triggered by the 1973 Yom Kippur War, Silk suggests wars and rearmament campaigns are "more likely to be bearish than bullish for national economies," a fact recognized by Western Europeans and the Japanese as they refuse to spend more money for weapons "to the chagrin of the Reagan Administration and the Carter Administration before it."

Silk has edited or authored more than a dozen books on various aspects of economics. One of his earlier books, *The Research Revolution* (New York, 1961) explores the need for the American government to invest more time and money in basic and applied research. During the late 1950s and early 1960s, Russia's growth rate was twice that of the United States, and Silk feared that without more research, the gap would become still greater. *Nixonomics* (New York, 1972) is a collection of Silk's essays that analyzed Nixon's continuous policy changes in managing the American economy. At one point, claims Silk, Nixon openly borrowed the policies of his Democratic adversaries at the same time that he denounced them, and eventually the Republican president's credibility began to suffer. Silk edited and wrote the first half of *Capitalism: The Moving Target* (New York, 1974), an overview of capitalism from a very conservative to a Marxist point of view. Besides Silk's own long essay in the book, other contributions were made by writers as diverse as John Kenneth Galbraith, the poet Gilbert Sorrentino, Paul Samuelson, Wassily Leontief and others. Many of the essays had previously appeared as op-ed page articles in *The New York Times,* which published the book.

The American Establishment (New York, 1980), written by Silk and the oldest of his three sons, Mark, traces the beginnings and development of the meaning behind the commonly accepted, peculiarly American, notion of an unchartered club of powerful businessmen, businesses, government offices, officials and universities that constitute "the establishment." Silk and his son follow the power structure as developed in such places as Harvard, where the younger Silk is a teaching fellow, the Brookings Institution, *The New York Times* and other upper echelons of the corporate and governmental world, with which the elder Silk is intimately familiar.

Silk's accomplishments in journalism and economics have been noted by his peers and the government, and he has been the recipient of numerous honorary degrees in economics and law, awards from major journalistic organizations (including five Loeb awards for Distinguished Business and Financial Journalism) and appointments to government commissions. He was a member of and consultant to the President's Advisory Committee on Labor-Management Policy (1961–62), the President's Commission on Budget Concepts (1967) and the Research Advisory Board of the Committee for Economic Development.

For further information:

Silk, Leonard. *Contemporary Economics: Principles and Issues.* New York: 1970.
————. *Economics in Plain English.* New York: 1978.
————. *The Education of Businessmen.* New York: 1960.
————. *Forecasting Business Trends.* New York: 1956.
————. *Sweden Plans for Better Housing.* New York: 1948.
————. *Veblen: A Play in Three Acts.* New York: 1966.
Silk, Leonard, and Curley, Louise M. *A Primer on Business Forecasting.* New York: 1970.
Silk, Leonard, and Silk, Mark. *The Economists.* New York: 1976.
Silk, Leonard, and Silk, Mark, eds. *The Evolution of Capitalism.* New York: 1972.
Silk, Leonard, and Vogel, David. *Ethics and Profits.* New York: 1976.

BEVERLY SILLS

b. May 25, 1929
Opera singer; opera company director

In her autobiography, *Bubbles: A Self-Portrait* (New York, 1977), Beverly Sills, the brilliant opera singer and director of the New York City Opera, describes a scene in which her father objected to her stage aspirations. To which her mother replied, "No, Morris. The two boys [her brothers] will go to college and be smart. This one will be an opera singer."

Belle Miriam Silverman was born to Morris, an insurance broker, and Shirley (Bahn) Silverman. As if by design, she won a beautiful-baby contest in 1932 and that same year made her radio debut as Bubbles Silverman on *Uncle Bob's Rainbow House.* Five years later she was a regular performer on the Major Bowes radio *Amateur Hour* and afterward sang on such radio soap operas as *Our Gal Sunday* and in Rinso White commercials. By the time she was 16, she was touring in Gilbert and Sullivan operettas.

By 1955 the coloratura soprano was a member of the New York City Opera and began appearing with other world-famous companies. She soared to overnight success when she sang Cleopatra in Handel's *Julius Caesar* in 1966. But she reached her apogee at the Metropolitan Opera, where she was so warm and vibrant one New York night as she sang *Manon,* that one admirer was moved to say, "Her audience practically wept with her." Her fame in both New York opera companies, plus her triumphant appearances at La Scala and San Carlo, led the *New Yorker's* former music critic Winthrop Sargeant to call her "a superstar . . . one who sings certain roles superlatively well (better than anyone else) . . . and . . . is in the difficult position of having to reach a new peak every season, attaining new heights of skill and personal charm or dramatic force."

Somehow, Sills was always able to top what seemed to be her greatest achievements, and into the 1970s she remained one of America's best-known and best-loved singers. She was the exception to the stereotype of the opera star as temperamental and difficult and also proved that a singer trained exclusively in the United States could perform as brilliantly as one who had trained abroad. Sills also appeared at the White House, the United Nations and on television, even singing once in 1979 on *The Muppet Show,* and performed regularly in benefits. By 1980, however, she determined that it was time to retire while her voice was still in good form, and in October she sang in a lavish farewell concert at Lincoln Center's Avery Fisher Hall, which doubled as a benefit for the City Opera. There, Sills shared the stage with such old friends from the non-opera world as Carol Burnett, Mary Martin, Bobby Short, Ethel Merman and Dinah Shore, as well as opera colleagues Sherrill Milnes, Placido Domingo, Leontyne Price and others.

One year earlier Sills had already begun her transition from performer when she replaced Julius Rudel, who was retiring after 20 years at the helm of the New York City Opera. Under her tutelage, the company has pursued an aggressive program of experimentation and diversification. Light opera, operas in English, rarely-performed works and "multimedia" operas have become a staple with the City Opera. Such non-opera figures as Broadway actor Joel Grey and modern dance choreographer Eliot Feld have been involved in the revival of Kurt Weill's *Silbersee* (Grey made his opera debut in 1980) and *Song of Norway* (1981), for which Feld did the choreography. Through Sills' leadership, opera has become far more accessible and available to wider audiences.

Sills has also used her fame to publicize causes unrelated to opera. Because she has a daughter who is totally deaf and a son who is retarded, Sills has frequently appeared on television programs or in films to discuss these disabilities. For example, she narrated the 1978 film *The Silent Dancers,* which described a special program of the Joffrey Ballet in New York City to teach dance to profoundly deaf students. It is a tribute to Sills' professional career—and perhaps one of the reasons she had reached the pinnacle so long ago and remained on top—that the seeming tragedies of her personal life have been converted into examples of deep love.

JOAN MICKLIN SILVER

b. May 24, 1935
Director; producer

Joan Micklin Silver is a relative rarity, a female film director and producer, who began her career by raising enough money—together with her husband, Raphael Silver—to produce the memorable film *Hester Street*

(1975), which was based on Abraham Cahan's story about a young Russian-Jewish immigrant couple on New York's Lower East Side. The film, which cost only $370,000 to make and grossed more than $5 million, launched her career.

Joan Micklin was born in Omaha, Nebraska to Maurice David, a lumber merchant, and Doris (Shoshone) Micklin. She received a B.A. degree from Sarah Lawrence College in 1956. After marriage to Raphael Silver that same year, she lived in Cleveland, where she taught music and wrote plays that were produced at the Cleveland playhouse.

The Silvers moved to New York City, where she wrote and directed short films for the educational division of Columbia Pictures. Her attempts to develop feature projects were thwarted by major studios, so she and her husband created an independent film company, Midwest Productions. Raphael Silver helped finance the productions by recruiting investors among his clients in his large real estate business.

Hester Street, produced on a minimal budget and shot in only 34 days—very little for a feature—earned an Academy Award nomination for its star, Carol Kane. Silver's next project was the film *Bernice Bobs Her Hair* (1976), based on an F. Scott Fitzgerald short story, for the Public Broadcasting System. Her third film, *Between the Lines* (1977), sympathetically portrayed a Boston "underground" newspaper and how it was destroyed by outside entrepreneurs and the commercial spirit. The film helped introduce several young actors, including Lindsay Crouse, Jill Eikenberry and Jeff Goldblum, to large audiences. In a role-switch, Raphael Silver then directed a film his wife produced, *On the Yard* (1979) based on Malcom Braly's 1967 novel of the same name. Braly, an ex-prisoner, wrote the novel to portray prison life realistically and to illustrate many of the same social structures that develop "inside" as outside the walls.

In 1979 Silver finally received the support of a major studio, United Artists, in the last stage of financing and in the distribution of her $2.5 million film *Head Over Heels,* based on Ann Beattie's 1976 novel *Chilly Scenes of Winter,* in which a young civil servant tries to rekindle an old love affair with a woman who has since married. The film was well received by critics.

In 1980 Silver proved her versatility by directing a widely praised off-Broadway comedy, *Album* by David Rimmer. *Album* traces four 1960s teen-agers from early adolescence to their "coming of age."

Silver's style of directing is to allow her actors to try to create their own characters within the context of the script. It allows for extensive improvisation and change, so that the actors can feel comfortable with the roles they are portraying.

Joan Micklin Silver has successfully combined motherhood (she has three daughters) with a blossoming career in a field normally limited to men. She is an active member and original founder of New York's Women in Film, which promotes unity among women in media and offers support to individuals seeking assistance in completing projects.

IRA SILVERMAN

b. January 20, 1945
College president; Jewish communal leader

A trip to Israel at age 16 was the turning point for Ira Silverman, who until then had a nebulous sense of his Jewishness and no particular commitment to it. Appointed president of the Rabbinical Reconstructionist College in 1981, he is one of the leaders in a generation of younger, American-born Jews dedicated to perpetuating Jewish values and traditions within a progressive framework.

Ira Silverman was born in Rockville Centre, New York to Irving, an accountant who has also been a corporate director, and Ruth (Kover) Silverman. Following his tour of Israel while still a teen-ager, he decided to pursue Jewish studies and to commit himself to a career in some way related to Judaism. He studied Hebrew at Harvard College, where he received a B.A. degree in 1966. Two years later he completed a master of public affairs degree at Princeton University.

He taught at Princeton's Woodrow Wilson School before moving to Washington, D.C. in 1971 to work for the Federation of American Universities. At the same time he wrote part-time for *The Jerusalem Post* and *Yediot Achronot*, a Hebrew-language daily. He became more absorbed in the latter work and eventually left the federation to become director of the Institute for Jewish Policy Planning and Research. The institute, a "think-tank" modeled on larger organizations like the Rand Corporation and the consumer-oriented Center for the Study of Responsive Law, was founded in 1972 by the Synagogue Council of America, whose membership is represented by Orthodox, Conservative and Reform Jewish leaders. During Silverman's tenure there its projects ranged from commissioned studies from the federal government for research on Soviet Jewish emigration to studies of marriage patterns among American Jews, electoral trends in Israel and other subjects. It also published yearbooks and a periodical called *Analysis,* which focused on one topic per issue.

Silverman left the institute in 1977 to become director of special programs at the American Jewish Committee. In that role he coordinated all national program activities of the AJC and was closely involved with monitoring Arab influence in the United States for that organization.

In November 1981 Silverman was installed as president of the Rabbinical Reconstructionist College in Philadelphia, succeeding Rabbi Ira Eisenstein, who had held the post since the college was founded in 1968. Although not brought up as a Reconstructionist, Silverman was considered especially suited to lead the college because of his expertise in Jewish community relations and public affairs and because of his personal stance on contemporary Judaism. For example, he supports the increased inclusion of women in leadership roles in Jewish movements and is intent on melding the best Jewish traditions with changes in social structure that require a constant reexamination of traditional lifestyles and attitudes. In addition, his leadership encompasses the unique "bi-cultural" qualities and conflicts of American Jewry—a heritage that, as he described at his installation ceremony, combines "the legacies of both Jefferson and Maimonides, of both Martin Luther King and Theodore Herzl, too."

In committing himself to the physical and spiritual growth of the Reconstructionist Rabbinical College, Silverman explained the compelling need to remain in constant contact with the world at large. "We are not satisfied that a broad range of secular knowledge, in history, philosophy, theology, linguistics, psychology, is really applied to our Jewish studies," he noted in his first speech as college president, adding:

> And we are not satisfied that our Jewish studies are connected to more worldly political or social issues of our day. We . . . must reject insularity, for the good of our people and our country. At the College, we will work toward an ever more successful integration of our cultures, for the good of our future leaders.

ROBERT B. SILVERS

b. December 31, 1929
Editor

The winter of 1962–63 brought New Yorkers a 114-day newspaper strike and a new, important periodical, *The New York Review of Books.* Originally designed as a temporary substitute for Sunday newspaper literary supplements, the *Review* was so well received that by the autumn of 1963 it became a permanent fixture. One of its founders and co-editors, Robert Silvers, is largely responsible for its survival, growth and widespread influence.

Born in Mineola, New York to James J., a businessman, and Rose (Roden) Silvers, Robert B. Silvers received an A.B. degree from the University of Chicago in 1947. He was not yet 18, but had entered the university in his mid-teens, arranged to have certain courses waived and completed his degree in two and a half years. He then went to Yale Law School, class of 1951, but dropped out. In 1950 he worked as press secretary to Connecticut's Governor Chester Bowles.

From 1953 to 1958 Silvers lived in Paris, studying and editing. He received a baccalaureate degree from l'Ecole des Sciences Politiques in 1956 and for a while shared a barge on the Seine with musician Peter Duchin. He became a member of the editorial board of the *Paris Review* in 1954 through his acquaintance with George Plimpton. (He still edits it.) In 1958 he met an editor at *Harper's* while in Paris. Hired as that magazine's literary editor, he came to New York where he met many of the writers and critics he would later recruit for *The New York Review*. He also developed a supplement for *Harper's* called "Writing in America."

Silvers was brought on to help found and edit *The New York Review of Books* by several prominent New Yorkers including Random House president, Jason Epstein, whose wife Barbara became Silvers' co-editor at the *NYRB*. The first issue, which appeared in Feburary 1963, enlisted such writers as Mary McCarthy, Robert Jay Lifton and Susan Sontag along with poets Adrienne Rich and John Berryman, all of whom contributed their work for no payment. The subsequent success of the periodical permitted Silvers to quit *Harper's* and pay his writers.

Since its debut *NYRB* has become a forum for many American—and European, especially British—writers and thinkers, including Sir Kenneth Clark, J. Bronowski, Josef Brodsky and the late Hannah Arendt. Not only a literary publication, it also represents the left-liberal spectrum politically and its pages have become a forum for such issues as the Vietnam war, the boat people, the postwar events in Cambodia, the struggle of intellectuals to remain free in dictatorial nations and the Israel-Arab conflicts. The magazine was, for example, a major and consistently articulate opponent of American military intervention in Southeast Asia and many of its articles featured devastating accounts of My Lai and other atrocities, the terrible destruction inflicted by the American air war and other commentaries on American culpability. *NYRB* has also been highly critical of postwar developments in Communist-controlled Vietnam, without however ignoring the horrors of American involvement in that war.

In addition, Silvers has stressed the Middle East. It has published essays by Leon Wieseltier, I.F. Stone and Bernard Avishai among others, taking a generally dovish, anti-Begin position favoring the peace forces in Israel. It has also published much on Jewish life in America, most notably Alfred Kazin's excerpt from his book, *New York Jew*. Finally, *NYRB's* letters columns rival its articles and reviews in length and contentiousness. Especially noteworthy are its appeals in defense of human rights in *all* nations. Under Silvers the publication also initiated extensive "personal" ads in which intellectuals, or people pretending to intellectual interests, solicit other readers for love and companionship.

Silvers dislikes being interviewed—he doesn't see the point—but is described as a workaholic who spends long hours and often weekends at this office. Quoted in an article by Philip Nobile in *Esquire* (April 1972), Alfred Kazin called Silvers "the best literary editor I've ever known." In the same article, Robert Heilbroner called the *NYRB* "the closest thing to intellectual skywriting we have in the United States." *Newsweek* (October 29, 1973) cites a 1971 poll by the *Public Opinion Quarterly* calling it "the most influential publication read by the nation's intelligentsia."

ISAAC BASHEVIS SINGER

b. July 14, 1904
Writer

Isaac Bashevis Singer, Yiddish writer and storyteller, internationally heralded for his prodigious outpouring of books, was awarded a Nobel Prize for Literature in 1978. His writings—many of them as yet untranslated—include works from autobiographies to stories to books written for juveniles.

Isaac Bashevis Singer was born in Radzymin, a village near Warsaw, the son of Pinchas Menachem, a rabbi, and Bathsheba—from which the name "Bashevis" is derived—(Zylberman) Singer. From 1920 to 1927 he was a student at a yeshiva and a rabbinical seminary in Warsaw. Then he began to write and to translate for the Yiddish press. In 1935 he followed his elder brother, I.J. Singer, a well-known novelist in his own right (*Brothers Ashkenazi, East of Eden* and *Yoshe Kalb,* among others), to the United States. Reminiscing, he said, "For seven or eight years, I wanted to earn $15 a week—$4 for a furnished room. I was always grateful to the United States and I still am."

When Singer left Poland, he had a wife and small son, who later went to the Soviet Union. ("[My wife] was a Communist. But after two years they kicked her out, and she went with the child to Israel. My son's name is Israel Zamir. Zamir is like 'Singer' in Hebrew, it means nightingale," he said.) In 1940 he married Alma Haimann, a native of Munich, Germany.

His brother—in Singer's words, his "master and teacher"—introduced him to the *Jewish Daily Forward*, where nearly all of his novels were serialized in Yiddish before their appearance in English translation. The publication of his first book, *Satan in Goray*, (New York, 1935) was followed by years of struggle. In 1953, after the appearance of "Gimpel the Fool," a story translated by Saul Bellow in *Partisan Review*, he was finally recognized as a preeminent writer.

Singer's book *In My Father's House* (New York, 1966) ends:

> I was exalted; everything seemed good. There was no difference between heaven and earth, the most distant star, and my red hair. My tangled thoughts were divine. . . . The laws of nature were divine; the true sciences of God were mathematics, physics, and chemistry. My desire to learn intensified.

The book, published in English, is a memoir of Singer's childhood in Warsaw, where his father served as a rabbi in an impoverished neighborhood. The housewives, shopkeepers, beggars and others who came to 10 Krochmalna Street for help and guidance are reflected in this and many of Singer's other works.

Singer's prodigious literary output deals with the real, the make-believe and above all the supernatural. His pages are filled with people broken by the Holocaust, the devil in various guises, agonizing rabbis, brutish peasants, fumbling lovers and failed writers, set against the backdrop of the lost world of Eastern European Jewish life, and in their varied exiles in such places as Canada, Argentina and especially the United States. In one of his memorable stories, a haunted woman sits in an Upper West Side cafeteria in New York and whispers that a man at an adjoining table is really Hitler in disguise. In *Crown of Feathers* (New York, 1973), a rabbi's daughter finds herself in league with the devil. As a child, he once wrote, "I suffered deep crises, was subject to hallucinations. My dreams were filled with demons, ghosts, devils, corpses. Sometimes before falling asleep I saw shapes. They danced around my bed, hovered in the air." His work reflects this world.

Then, at the age of 49, he became famous, lionized by readers and literary critics, in constant demand on the lecture circuit, besieged by interviewers here and abroad. He received a National Book Award twice (in 1970 and 1974) and a Nobel Prize in 1978. Part of his acceptance speech captures his feelings about writing:

> I am not ashamed to admit that I belong to those who fantasize that literature is capable of bringing new horizons and new perspectives—philosophical, religious, esthetical and even social. In the history of old Jewish literature there was never any basic difference between the poet and the prophet. Our ancient poetry often became law and a way of life.

Rebecca West called him "the greatest writer of today." Edmund Wilson nominated him for the Nobel Prize. His stories appear regularly in *The New Yorker* and other magazines, his books are translated into dozens of languages, and his stories and his books for youngsters ("Why shouldn't I write children's literature? Children are the most independent readers. They are not influenced by authorities. You can't tell a child that a book got a great review.") are extraordinarily popular. A play, *Yentl* (from his short story "Yentl the Yeshiva Bocher"), about a young woman whose passion for Talmud study leads her into an outrageous violation of Orthodox Judaism, had a successful run on Broadway in 1975–76 and toured the United States.

Among Singer's other interests are animal welfare and vegetarianism. "For animals every day is Treblinka," he wrote in *Enemies* (New York, 1972), an allusion to the suffering of Jews and others in a Nazi concentration camp. "I one day decided [in 1962] no meat, no fish. I just think it's the wrong thing to kill animals."

For further information:

Kresh, Paul. *Isaac Bashevis Singer: The Magician of West 86th Street.* New York: 1979.

Singer, Isaac Bashevis. *The Estate.* New York: 1969.

———. *The Family Moskat.* New York: 1950.

———. *Gimpel the Fool.* New York: 1957.

———. *The Magician of Lublin.* New York: 1960.

———. *The Manor.* New York: 1967.

———. *Old Love.* New York: 1979.

———. *Passions.* New York: 1976.

———. *The Power of Light,* children's book. New York: 1980.

———. *Satan in Goray.* New York: 1935.

———. *The Seance.* New York: 1958.

———. *Short Friday.* New York: 1964.

———. *The Slave.* New York: 1962.

———. *The Spinoza of Market Street.* New York: 1961.

———. *Zlateh the Goat,* children's book. New York: 1966.

Singer, Isaac Bashevis, and Moskowitz, Ira. *A Little Boy in Search of God: Mysticism in a Personal Light.* New York: 1976.

MARSHALL SKLARE

b. October 21, 1921
Sociologist

There are many scholarly commentators on the nature of the Jewish community in America, but few have scrutinized it more closely than sociologist Marshall Sklare. The author and editor of many books and journals, Sklare also lectures widely and since 1970 has been a professor at Brandeis University.

Marshall Sklare was born in Chicago to Irving, a businessman, and Bee (Lippman) Sklare. He studied at Northwestern University from 1938 to 1939 and from 1940 to 1943 and received a diploma from the College of Jewish Studies in Chicago in 1943. In 1948 he earned a master's degree in sociology from the University of Chicago and in 1953 a Ph.D. from Columbia University.

Sklare's first academic position was at the City College of New York in 1952–53, where he lectured in sociology and anthropology. From 1953 to 1966 he was study director to the director of the Division of Scientific Research at the American Jewish Committee in New York City. He lectured at Yeshiva University's Wurzweiler School of Social Work from 1960 to 1966 and at its Stern College for Women from 1963 to 1964. He became a professor of sociology at Wurzweiler and at Yeshiva University's Ferkauf Graduate School of Humanities and the Social Sciences from 1966 through 1970. In 1965 Sklare was a Fulbright lecturer at Hebrew University in Jerusalem for one year, and in 1968–69 he was a visiting lecturer at Princeton Theological Seminary. Prior to coming to Brandeis full-time, Sklare taught there as a visiting professor of American Jewish sociology.

Sklare's many books have made major contributions to an enhanced awareness of the nature and complexity of the Jewish community in America. *Conservative Judaism: An American Religious Movement* (Glencoe, Ill., 1955; New York, 1972), a revision of his doctoral dissertation, represented the first significant extended and thoroughgoing sociological study of the history, ideology and practices of the movement. *America's Jews* (New York, 1971) focused on the desire of Jewry to participate fully in American society yet retain its Jewishness. In it Sklare examines family structures and intermarriage, the private and public faces of Jewish identity and the conflicts among Jews of different national origins.

Sklare also coauthored numerous books, including *Jewish Identity on the Suburban Frontier: A Study of Group Survival in the Open Society,* with Joseph Greenblum (New York, 1968; Chicago, 1979), a study of the patterns and attitudes of a midwestern suburban Jewish community. *The Riverton Study: How Jews Look at Themselves and Their Neighbors,* with M. Vosk (New York, 1957), was a pioneering effort aimed at understanding the post-World War II younger generation. He discovered that they held no common religious beliefs nor practiced rituals but chose instead to believe that Judaism meant mainly leading "an ethical and moral life." Indeed, only 24 percent thought it essential to go to a synagogue.

Some of the organizations Sklare belongs to are Synagogue Council of America (academic advisory board), Tay-Sachs Foundation, National Foundation for Jewish Culture, American Jewish Historical Society, the Association for Jewish Studies and many others. Sklare is a consultant to the Max Weinreich Center for Advanced Jewish Studies at the YIVO Institute for Jewish Research in New York.

For further information:

Sklare, Marshall. *Not Quite at Home: How an American Jewish Community Lives with Itself and Its Neighbors.* New York: 1969.
Sklare, Marshall, ed. *The Jewish Community in America.* New York: 1974.
————. *The Jews: Social Patterns of an American Group.* New York: 1977.

STEPHEN SOLARZ

b. September 12, 1940
Politician

Since his election to the U.S. Congress in 1974, liberal Democrat Stephen Solarz has become known as Israel's most outspoken supporter and one of Congress's most consistent human rights activists. One of his greatest diplomatic feats was to secure the release from Syria of several young Jewish women to come to live in the United States with other Syrian-Jewish expatriates. On domestic issues, Solarz has supported a bill requiring the teaching of Holocaust history in all public schools.

Stephen Joshua Solarz was born in New York City to Sanford and Ruth (Fertig) Solarz. He attended Brooklyn public schools and is a graduate of Midwood High School. He received a B.A. degree from Brandeis University in 1962 and completed a master's degree in public law and administration at Columbia University in 1967.

Solarz's first political experience was as manager for the campaign of an anti-Vietnam War candidate in 1966. From 1967 to 1968 and periodically since 1969, he has taught political science at Brooklyn College. He also taught at New York City Community College from 1968 to 1969. Solarz's other jobs prior to entering political life full-time were as Max Lerner's assistant at The *New York Post*, as national news editor of the now-defunct monthly *Newsfront* and as associate editor of *Greater Philadelphia*.

Solarz was elected to the New York State Assembly in 1968 and served for three consecutive terms. His commitment to his constituency was evidenced in a regular television show he hosted entitled *Spotlight on Albany*, which was designed to inform viewers of legislative accomplishments.

But his election in 1974 to Congress—he defeated an incumbent as he had six years earlier in his run for the State Assembly—signaled the flowering of Solarz's career. Unabashed in his vigor for reform, he exerted influence in all areas of Jewish concern and in many general areas as well.

In the human rights arena, in addition to bringing several Syrian-Jewish women to settle in Brooklyn's Syrian-Jewish enclave, Solarz helped obtain freedom for 1,500 dual nationals in Cuba, who had been separated from their families in the United States for many years. He also sponsored an administration decision to aid thousands of Cambodian refugees. He has also consistently opposed violations of human rights everywhere and not selectively, as the Reagan administration chose to do. A member of the President's Commission on the Holocaust, Solarz has conducted many study missions to the Middle East and has been co-chairperson of the International Conference on Arab and North African Jews, an organization whose aim is to explore the plight of the few Jews remaining in Arab countries.

Consistent in efforts to obtain help for New York City, Solarz earned the "Highly Qualified and Preferred Rating" of the Citizen's Union and has received awards and citations from Jewish and non-Jewish groups, including the American Jewish Congress, Hadassah, the American Federation of Government Employees and the Postal Workers Union, for whom he waged a successful battle to assure more equitable treatment.

A member of the Foreign Affairs Committee in Congress, Solarz fought unsuccessfully to stop the sale of AWACS and other sophisticated military equipment to the Saudi government in 1981 but pushed through a $600 million increase in foreign aid to Israel. Overall, there are few more consistent backers of Israel in the Congress than Solarz.

Solarz remains consistently liberal and deeply opposed to much of the Reagan administration's policies in, for example, Central America and in the civil war between Morocco (armed by the United States) and the Polisario rebels.

BARBARA PROBST SOLOMON

b. December 3, 1929
Author; critic; translator

Writer Barbara Probst Solomon is one of America's experts on contemporary Spain, who has helped many Spanish writers get their work published in Spanish and in translation. The author of a memorable memoir of her participation in the Spanish resistance during the late 1940s and early 1950s, she is also a novelist and critic, whose articles have appeared in America's most prestigious periodicals.

Barbara Probst was born in New York City to J. Anthony, an attorney, and Frances (Kurke) Probst. She attended the Dalton School, graduating in 1946. While most of her high school friends attended Ivy League colleges, Probst opted to go to Europe to work and study. She attended the Sorbonne in Paris from 1947 to 1950, and it was then that she first became involved with the Spanish expatriate community. She befriended a group of young Spaniards in exile—eventually falling in love with one and living with him in Paris for a few years—and became involved in anti-Fascist activities with them. The romance, temperament and ideals of these Spaniards was something Probst had wanted very much in her youth; raised in what she describes as a sterile, upper-class, East Side Jewish family, she spent most of her youth rebelling against her upbringing. The adventure and danger of her Spanish experiences (she helped the exiles "spring" some of their comrades from a Spanish prison, and she met many of their families while in Spain) permanently bound her spiritually to Spain.

Probst spent most of the 1950s in New York—she married Harold Solomon, a law professor who died in 1969, and raised two daughters—and after a long delay, completed university studies. She received a B.S. degree from Columbia University in 1960.

Solomon's first novel was *The Beat of Life* (New York, 1960). It described two young lovers trying to cope with a tentative relationship within the tensions of life in New York City. Her next book was her memoir, *Arriving Where We Started* (New York, 1969), in which she documented her love affair with Spain and vividly recreated her romantic life and political dealings during her student years. It includes an account of a follow-up visit 20 years later to renew some friendships, reflect on the changes that had occurred and to find out about those she had known who had since died. She also wrote extensively about Spanish literature based on her contacts with several Spanish writers and filmmakers. For *Arriving Where We Started*, she won the Pablo de Olivide Prize in Barcelona, the only American to have been so honored. Solomon's second novel was *Night* (New York, 1981), about Europe and America in the late 1970s. Solomon has also translated the works of Juan Benet, Juan Goytisolo and other authors. Her many articles have appeared in *Harper's*, *The Nation*, *The New York Review of Books*, *The New York Times* and other publications.

Solomon ventured into filmmaking with *The Anatomy of Cindy Fink*, a 40-minute spoof on the pop art movement of the 1960s. Made on a budget of $5,000, the film received an award at the Venice Film Festival and is shown occasionally at the Museum of Modern Art and alternative film festivals. Her second film venture was as co-producer and writer of *One Morning for Pleasure*, directed by Jose Luis Borau and filmed in 1981. It is the first feature film that is a Spanish-American co-production.

She has been writer-in-residence at Yale University and the State University of New York in Buffalo and has taught film at the New School in New York and fiction writing at Boston University.

JOSEPH DOV SOLOVEITCHIK

b. 1903
Rabbi

Rabbi Joseph Dov Soloveitchik has carried on the mission of Orthodox Jewry to bring enlightened Jewish thought to the modern Orthodox movement. A scholar in the highest sense, and one of the world's greatest and most respected living Jewish philosophers, he is known around the world as the rav—the rabbi's rabbi.

Joseph Dov Soloveitchik was born in Pruzhan, Poland into a family distinguished for centuries for scholarship. His paternal grandfather, Haim Soloveitchik, was rabbi of Brest-Litovsk and was responsible for revolutionizing talmudic scholarship. His maternal grandfather was Rabbi Elijah Feinstein, who presided in Pruzhan. Soloveitchik is the son of Rabbi Moses Soloveitchik, who served in Haslovitz, Belorussia, where he grew up, while his mother introduced him to the works of Ibsen, Bialik and Pushkin. In 1925 he entered the University of Berlin to study mathematics, philosophy and physics. In 1931 he received a doctorate and then married Tanya Levitt, who had received her doctorate in education from the

University of Jena. In 1932 they and their first child departed for the United States and settled in Boston.

American religious life appalled him, and the synagogues he attended seemed cold and unresponsive places for alienated and acculturated people. Prayer—which he called "a mirror of human behavior rather than a hollow decorum"—and not elegant services appealed to him. Then, too, the failure of American Jewry to do more to rescue Jews trapped in Nazi Europe also proved a bitter experience for him.

In 1941 he succeeded his father as professor of Talmud at Yeshiva University in New York City. From this vantage point he was able to exert an extraordinary influence on generations of Orthodox students. In fact, many contemporary rabbis and scholars who first encountered him during their student days view him as their supreme religious authority.

Even so, he has published comparatively few books and in fact confesses an aversion to publication, although he has hundreds of manuscripts in his personal files, and describes himself as "a perfectionist. I'm never sure something is the best I can do." However, when he lectures, the audience is inevitably filled at least to capacity, and according to some reports, his lectures are widely recorded. The pirated tapes are then often published and distributed. In one of his books, *The Lonely Man of Faith*, Soloveitchik pictured himself as "a stranger in a modern society that is technical-minded, self-centered, self-loving." He asked: "What can I say to a functional, utilitarian society?"

Elsewhere, homelessness and loneliness are among his paramount themes. In 1974 Yeshiva University issued his *A Conspectus of the Public Lectures of Rabbi Joseph Dov Soloveitchik*. Three other essays he published separately revealed his compelling interest in people as divided beings, active and passive. Contradictory and paradoxical as people are, he argued, torn as they are by stress and conflict, lured and repelled by divinity, he nonetheless concluded that every human being was capable of childlike innocence and faith no matter how cynical he or she had become.

Soloveitchik is especially interested in nourishing an Orthodoxy that can thrive in a modern, constantly changing society and rejects that Orthodox wing that, he says, would cut itself off from contemporary lifestyles. "We are committed to God and to observing his laws," he once said, "but God also wills us to be committed to mankind in general and to the society in whose midst we live in particular. To find fulfillment, one must partake of the human endeavor."

Today he speaks warmly of Israel but refuses to encourage his followers to go on *aliyah* (move to Israel). His explanation is that Orthodoxy can thrive in the United States. He once turned down an offer to become Israel's chief Ashkenazic rabbi because, he explained, "I was afraid to be an officer of the state. A rabbinate linked up with the state cannot be completely free." In a 1972 lecture at Congregation Kehilath Jeshurun in Manhattan, he alluded to the offer and his declination by saying that the notion of exile is the "essence of the Jewish people." Always, his theme is the stress on the balance between *"halakah* [Jewish law] and spontaneity, between reason and emotion," wrote Chana Heilbrun.

For further information:

Besdin, Abraham R. *Reflections of the Rav: Lessons in Jewish Thought,* adapted from lectures of Rabbi Joseph D. Soloveitchik. Jerusalem: 1981.

Peli, Pinchas, ed. *On Repentance in the Thought and Oral Discourses of Rabbi Joseph Soloveitchik,* Jerusalem: 1980.

HELMUT SONNENFELDT

b. September 13, 1926
State Department official

During the administration of Richard Nixon, Helmut Sonnenfeldt was one of the most influential, least-known government officials in Washington, D.C. A senior aide to Henry Kissinger, Sonnenfeldt was a chief planner of Nixon and Kissinger's detente policy between the United States and the Soviet Union.

Helmut Sonnenfeldt was born in Berlin, the son of Walter H. and Gertrude (Liebenthal) Sonnenfeldt, both physicians. The family fled Nazi Germany in 1938 and arrived in the United States by way of England in 1944. After a semester at Johns Hopkins University, he joined the U.S. Army in 1945, serving in the Counter-Intelligence Corps. When the war ended, Sonnenfeldt was posted in the American occupation zone in Germany, where, in 1946, he met Sgt. Henry Kissinger.

Upon discharge Sonnenfeldt resumed his studies, earning a B.A. degree from Johns Hopkins University in 1950 and an M.A. degree in political science from the same institution the following year. He then joined the State Department in 1952 as a specialist in Soviet affairs in the Office of Research and Analysis. Respect for his abilities as a Soviet specialist continued to grow. In 1966 he became the director of Soviet and Eastern European research at the State Department. Three years later Henry Kissinger appointed him to the National Security Council.

Rising in the foreign policy echelon, he was counselor of the State Department from 1974 until 1977 and senior adviser to Kissinger on European and East-West relationships. As counselor he was a member of a group managing the daily activities of a number of the State Department bureaus. Sonnenfeldt worked with Kissinger to design detente, the relaxation of tension between the United States and the Soviet Union, and was intimately involved with much of Kissinger's ground-breaking diplomacy. Unlike his superior, Sonnenfeldt had a professional penchant for secrecy. He studiously avoided the limelight. However, the key role he played as a Kissinger staffer has been widely acknowledged. In 1974 he became the undersecretary of the Treasury responsible for the supervision of the growing Soviet-American trade and giving Treasury officials political advice and a link to the national security apparatus.

Between 1969 and 1977 he was a part of all summit-level meetings between presidents Johnson, Nixon and Ford; their secretaries of state; and European leaders. He played a major part in preparing for the Washington Energy Conference in 1974, the Rambouillet economic summit in 1975, the Paris conference on worldwide economic cooperation in 1975 and the Puerto Rican summit in 1976. In 1977 Sonnenfeldt retired from the foreign service with the rank of career minister.

Sonnenfeldt has also written articles in *Foreign Affairs, Washington Quarterly,* the *NATO Review* and other publications. An *Adelphi Paper,* "Soviet Perspectives on Security," written with William G. Hyland, appeared in 1979.

Since 1978 Sonnenfeldt has been a guest scholar at the Brookings Institution, conducting research into Soviet-American affairs.

SUSAN SONTAG

b. January 16, 1933
Writer; critic; filmmaker

Susan Sontag, critic, writer and filmmaker, has always been one step ahead of most people in her awareness of new artistic, social and political trends. Often controversial—she is not afraid to challenge society's sacred cows—Sontag rejects what she deems to be superficial in American life and always probes deeper in her search for substance. Her work, which is sophisticated and complex, nevertheless has attracted a wide following, and Sontag is considered among the more brilliant critics and writers in America today.

Susan Sontag was born in New York City to Nathan

and Mildred (Jacobsen) Sontag. Her father was a traveling salesman, and the family eventually moved to Tucson, Arizona and Canoga Park, California, outside Los Angeles, where Sontag spent most of her youth. Always a prodigious reader, she graduated from North Hollywood High School in 1948. After a year at the University of California at Berkeley, she transferred to the University of Chicago, where she received a B.A. degree in 1951. She pursued graduate studies at Harvard University, receiving first an M.A. degree in English in 1954, then another M.A. degree in philosophy in 1955. She was a Ph.D. candidate in philosophy at Harvard— she also studied for one year at St. Anne's College at Oxford—but never completed the degree.

From 1953 to 1965 Sontag held a variety of academic posts. She was instructor at the University of Connecticut from 1953 to 1954, lecturer in philosophy at City College of New York and Sarah Lawrence College from 1959 to 1960, an instructor in religion at Columbia University from 1960 to 1964 and writer-in-residence at Rutgers University from 1964 to 1965.

But Sontag is best-known for her essays and her novels, which are steeped in symbolic and surrealistic themes. Her first novel, *The Benefactor* (New York, 1963), is the story of the rootless Hippolyte, a man in his mid-60s who cannot distinguish his dreams from his waking life. *Death Kit* (New York, 1967) is equally enigmatic. The main character, Diddy, takes a train trip and thinks he has seen a murder; he may even have committed it. A blind woman whom he meets claims to have "sensed" what happened.

Against Interpretation (New York, 1966) was Sontag's first collection of essays, most of which had been published from 1961 to 1966 in magazines such as *The Partisan Review, The New York Review of Books, Book Week, Evergreen Review* and *The Nation.* It contained the controversial "Notes on Camp," which placed Sontag in the ranks of America's most prominent literary and art critics. "Notes on Camp" distinguished Sontag because she dared to define something that until then had defied definition. It reflected her ability to perceive trends at a very early stage in their development and somehow to legitimize them. She touched on topics still very controversial for the time (homosexuality was not yet so public) and made casual references to Jewish liberalism and a variety of American institutions (films like *The Maltese Falcon,* operas like *Il Trovatore,* actress Greta Garbo) as relating to some of the values of Camp taste. Her next collection of essays, *Styles of Radical Will* (New York, 1969), contained longer essays on film and philosophy and included her "Trip to Hanoi," an account of a visit to North Vietnam in early 1968. (Sontag was one of the earliest opponents of the war in Vietnam.)

Sontag wrote and directed two fiction films in Sweden, *Duet for Cannibals* (1969) and *Brother Carl* (1971), and a documentary, *Promised Lands* (1974), about Israel in the wake of the 1973 Yom Kippur War. Although she was raised nominally Jewish, she explained in an interview: "I identify as a Jew but I'm not religious at all. I come from an assimilated family that's been here for several generations. My identification is within the context of secular America."

In 1977 Sontag published *On Photography* (New York). Her essays in the book, previously published in *The New York Review of Books,* explored aspects of photography —its validity (if any) and its true social impact (again, if any)—that aroused the anger and admiration of critics. The book created a great stir because Sontag seriously challenged the value of visual images as honest records of history. She implied, in fact, the photographs trivialized history and human values—in a way, she said, like television, photographs steal from the depth of an object, a person, an idea. Yet she admitted the power of photography over her own youth and maturity. At least Sontag did not exclude herself from the same criticism she directed at those who love photography.

Sontag's own bout with cancer was the compelling force for her next book, *Illness as Metaphor* (New York, 1978), a discussion of the 19th- and 20th-century "roles" of tuberculosis and cancer in society. That same year a collection of stories, *I, Etcetera* (New York, 1978), appeared, blending the European symbolism of Kafka, Robbe-Grillet, Sartre and other writers so influential to Sontag.

Under the Sign of Saturn (New York, 1980) is Sontag's most recent collection of essays, previously published in *The New York Review of Books* and elsewhere. Her work was capped in 1981 with the publication of *The Susan Sontag Reader* (New York). She has also edited the works of the French theorists Antonin Artaud and Roland Barthes.

In November 1979 she directed her first play, Pirandello's *As You Desire Me,* in Turin, Italy. In early 1982 Sontag spoke at a rally in support of Poland's Solidarity labor movement. She declared that "Communism is fascism . . . [It is] the most successful variant of fascism. Fascism with a human face." Her remarks stirred up a public argument, from those who felt she had given "aid and comfort" to the reactionary right. There were those who resented her inclusion of Chile and Argentina as fascist states. Sontag reflected the view that one should maintain a single standard where freedom was concerned. Supporting her opinions, James Wechsler wrote in the *New York Post:* "It is not the mission of free men to grope for congenial distinctions among totalitarians [authoritarianism versus totalitarianism]. It is not to sell the sanctity of free enterprise. It is to affirm the universality of the Bill of Rights. That is what matters in the storm over Sontag."

Sontag has received many awards, ranging from a 1957 fellowship from the American Association of University Women to Rockefeller Foundation grants in 1966 and 1974 and Guggenheim Foundation fellowships in 1966 and 1975. She received the George Polk Memorial Award in 1966 for contributions toward a better appreciation of theater, motion pictures and television and many honors and prizes for her achievements in literature and the creative arts. In 1979 she was elected to the American Academy and Institute of Arts and Letters as a member of the department of literature.

MICHAEL I. SOVERN

b. December 1, 1931
University president

When Michael Sovern became Columbia University's 17th president in 1980, it represented another record in the eminent law professor's career. First in his class at Columbia Law School in 1955, he was the youngest full professor appointed in the university's history five years later. And when he assumed the presidency, he was the first Columbia College alumnus, the first Jew in the post and the first to admit women as college undergraduates.

Michael Ira Sovern was born in the Bronx. His father, Julius, was a dress salesman, and his mother, Lillian (Arnstein) Sovern, was a bookkeeper. Sovern's father died in 1943, and his mother supported the family. He graduated from the Bronx High School of Science in 1948 and then attended Columbia College, graduating with a B.A. degree in 1952, and Columbia Law School, where he received his Bachelor of Law three years later. He went on to teach at the University of Minnesota for two years and then returned to Columbia to teach at the law school. He became a full professor in 1960, law school dean in 1970, and university provost and vice president for academic affairs in 1979.

Despite his extensive academic commitments, Sovern has long been active as a specialist in civil rights and labor law in both mediation and administration. He has participated in a wide range of race bias and labor disputes on a local and national level as well as other highly complex legal issues of a different sort. He has written extensively on racial discrimination in employment and from 1962 until 1965 was research director for the Twentieth Century Fund's Project on Racial Discrimination in Employment. The following year he published *Legal Restraints on Racial Discrimination in Employment* for the fund, an analysis of how attempts to enforce anti-discriminatory legislation were being thwarted by insufficient personnel or budgets to review complaints.

On the federal level Sovern worked on researching past civil rights court rulings with the NAACP to oppose (successfully) Richard Nixon's nominations in 1970 of both Clement F. Haynsworth Jr. and G. Harold Carswell for seats on the Supreme Court. He has also been chairman of the committee on labor and industry for the American Civil Liberties Union and a founding director of the Mobilization for Youth Legal Services. He was a director of the Mexican-American Legal Defense Fund and the Puerto Rican Legal Defense Fund from their founding until 1975.

Sovern has also been active in New York City municipal negotiations between the employers and unions of the police, fire fighters, teachers, transit workers and other employee groups. He was involved in the city's transit negotiations in 1971, 1974 and 1976; the fire department negotiations in 1973 and the negotiations between the city and the police department in 1976. His ability to create a "package deal" quickly that is acceptable to both sides in a dispute is his special talent, and one that was especially useful on his home turf, Columbia.

In the wake of the 1968 student uprisings, he was involved in negotiating with student protesters and in the creation of a university senate made up of students, faculty, administrators, alumni and staff designed to formulate and enforce university policy. Sovern has remained in the senate since its inception.

The decision to accept women as freshmen into Columbia College beginning in September 1983 was made by Sovern and Barnard President Ellen V. Futter in early 1982. The negotiations between the two institutions had dragged on for years as Columbia College remained the last all-male school in the Ivy League. Until, that is, Sovern and Futter reached agreement.

Sovern's reputation for roundedness—and a sense of humor—was epitomized in his inaugural speech in September 1980, when he quoted such eminent figures as Alexander Solzhenitsyn, Lionel Trilling, C.P. Snow and Woody Allen. As far as being Jewish is concerned, Sovern has never felt it to pose a problem, saying:

> I think I've been terribly lucky to be just young enough to have missed the barriers. Though I was the first Jewish dean of Columbia I was not the first Jewish dean of a major law school by a long shot. And I'm not the first Jewish president of an Ivy League university. The idea that I've had to overcome something extra to get here is an attractive one; I think it's probably not true.

For further information:
Sovern, Michael I. "The Case for Keeping U.S. Aid to Colleges," *The New York Times Magazine,* February 7, 1982.

STEVEN SPIELBERG

b. December 18, 1947
Film director; producer

A childhood fascination for electronics and fantasy helped make Steven Spielberg one of the most successful American directors in cinema history. *Jaws* (1975), completed when Spielberg was only 27, was one of the most profitable films ever made, and *Close Encounters of the Third Kind* (1977), Spielberg's second endeavor, helped set off a new wave of sophisticated science fiction films during the late 1970s. Spielberg remains in the forefront of a new generation of young Hollywood filmmakers weaned on television and real-life space walks.

Steven Spielberg was born in Cincinnati, Ohio to Arnold, an electrical engineer, and Leah (Posner) Spielberg. He later lived with his family in New Jersey and Scottsdale, Arizona. He recalled Saturday afternoon matinees at the Kiva Theater in Scottsdale, where he watched newsreels, coming attractions, a plethora of cartoons, a double feature and weekly serials. Always fascinated with machinery and electronics, he became his family's "official" photographer and toyed with filmmaking as an adolescent. A 40-minute war movie, *Escape to Nowhere,* won a film award for Spielberg when he was 13. He made his next film, *Firelight,* when he was 16, after his family moved to Southern California.

Unable to gain admission to the prestigious West Coast film schools, Spielberg attended California State College at Long Beach, where he received a B.A. degree in 1969, majoring in English. He attended movies constantly and also managed to observe the production of television shows firsthand by walking onto studio lots—normally off-limits to the public—wearing a suit and carrying a briefcase, looking as though he absolutely belonged. No one questioned him.

A short film, *Amblin',* about two hitchhikers, which Spielberg made in 1970, earned him wide recognition and a seven-year directing contract with Universal. *Amblin',* 22 minutes long, recounted the trip of a young couple from the Mojave Desert to the Pacific Ocean. It was distributed as a short to accompany *Love Story.*

At Universal, Spielberg directed episodes in 1970–71 of *Marcus Welby, M.D., Colombo* and other television series segments. He also directed several made-for-television films, including *Duel* (1971), a thriller with Dennis Weaver, and *Something Evil* (1972), with Sandy Dennis and Darren McGavin. *Duel,* which was never distributed in the United States, grossed more than $5 million in Europe and Japan and won several awards.

Spielberg's first full-length feature was *Sugarland Express* (1974), a comedy-drama based on a true story about a young couple's attempt to retrieve their child from a foster home in Sugarland, Texas. The film, which starred Goldie Hawn, has a chase scene that distinguished Spielberg as a master of action scenes and timing, the same qualities that had made *Duel* so popular.

But *Jaws* was Spielberg's making, in more ways than one. He made it—and it made him. With Richard Dreyfuss, Robert Shaw and Roy Scheider heading the cast, *Jaws* became the surprise hit of 1975. Based on the Peter Benchley novel about a shark terrorizing people in a summer beach community, it appealed perfectly to the American need for escapism in the wake of Watergate, Vietnam and the resignation of Richard Nixon. *Jaws,* completed in 1975, grossed more than $60 million in its first *month* of domestic release and eventually earned its distributor, United Artists, more than $400 million. Ironically, when Spielberg went over budget with *Jaws* (the film cost more than twice its originally planned $3.5 million), he almost lost the project. Nobody at United Artists recalled that later—or seemed to care. *Jaws* won many Academy Awards and was followed by a sequel, *Jaws 2* (not directed by Spielberg).

In 1977 Spielberg entered the world of science fiction and fantasy with *Close Encounters of the Third Kind,* a tale about UFOs and an ordinary man. Using some of the most sophisticated special effects available and a skilled crew and cast (which included Richard Dreyfuss and French director Francois Truffaut as a scientist), Spielberg garnered praise from the critics and tremendous enthusiasm from audiences.

Spielberg's next film, *1941,* opened in 1979. A comedy about war panic in Los Angeles following the attack on Pearl Harbor, *1941* was a $26.5 million flop. Critics agreed that it was more chaotic than comic.

In addition to directing, Spielberg produced the 1978 film *I Wanna Hold Your Hand,* written by two of his protegees. The film, which recounts the exploits of a group of New Jersey teen-agers in 1963 en route to New York to see the Beatles, was received unenthusiastically.

Spielberg's career has been erratic. Phenomenal successes are sandwiched between near misses and clear misses. *Raiders of the Lost Ark* (1981), which he directed, was a smash hit, critically and at the box office. It depicted an American archeologist vying with the Nazis in 1936 to find a sacred relic with cosmic powers. But he has established himself firmly as one of the new and influential voices of the Hollywood film community. "If we [young directors] don't take chances, who will?" he asked in 1981. "Without some degree of failure—you can't move ahead."

MARK SPITZ

b. February 10, 1950
Athlete

Jewish athletes are comparatively rare in America, so when one comes along as extraordinary as superstar swimmer Mark Spitz was in the 1972 Munich Olympics, everyone takes note. Since childhood, he had been breaking swimming records with phenomenal regularity. And in Munich he only continued what by then seemed to come naturally; He garnered an unequalled seven gold medals.

Mark Andrew Spitz was born in Modesto, California to Arnold, a scrap-steel dealer, and Lenore Spitz. He began training as a swimmer at the Sacramento YMCA when he was 8 and was soon swimming every day, with double lessons on Saturdays. Even then, a professional athletic career appeared to be in the works. Arnold Spitz would occasionally cut his son's Hebrew lessons short for a swimming class, and according to a news story, he offered the rabbi the explanation that "Even God likes a winner."

Three years later the family moved to Santa Clara, where Spitz began working with coach George Haines, the first major influence on his professional career. By 14, under Haines's tutelage, Spitz was competing on the national level. In 1965 he entered international competition when he swam in the Maccabiah Games in Israel and won five gold medals.

By 17 Spitz was considered a top-ranked world swimmer who was continuously setting new records. The following year he swam in the 1968 Mexico City Olympics but did not turn out to be as successful as he had predicted. He "only" won one silver and one bronze medal in individual races and several golds on relay teams. Afterward, it was revealed that Spitz had encountered significant anti-Semitic sentiment from some of his teammates—a brutal new experience for him. Apparently he internalized it, because he never confided in his coach or made an issue of it. But Spitz's subsequent coach, Sherm Chavoor, says that the incidents definitely interfered with his swimming. Chavoor explained:

After the [1968] Olympic trials the swimmers went to train at Colorado Springs. Mark ran into a lot of anti-Semitism from his teammates. . . . Some of the older guys really gave it to him. They tried to run him right off the team. It was "Jew-boy" this and "Jew-boy" that. It wasn't a kidding type of thing, either. I heard it with my own ears.

He didn't know how to handle it. He tried to get ready for a race and he'd get so wound up he'd come up with all sorts of imaginary sicknesses: sore throat, headache, like that. He was psyched.

In 1968 Spitz graduated from Santa Clara High School and entered Indiana University. He continued training and in 1969 won six gold medals at the Maccabiah Games in Israel. When he arrived in Munich for the 1972 Olympics, journalists and fans were curious about more than just having the world's best swimmer in Germany. What they really wanted to know was how the world's best swimmer—a Jew—felt in Munich. Spitz claimed to have had no qualms because his own immediate family had never been involved with Hitler Germany. However, he later admitted that "you never know. I could be standing on the grave of a relative right now."

In Munich Spitz went to victory after stunning victory, collecting four gold medals for individual events and three for relays. Shortly afterward, however, his triumph palled temporarily when Munich became the scene for a modern Jewish massacre after Palestinian terrorists murdered 11 Israeli athletes.

After the Olympics, Spitz terminated his athletic career and then briefly entered show business—which did not work out. He completed college and now works in real estate in California. Although Spitz is no longer active in sports, his triumph at Munich in 1972 stands out as a tribute to his extraordinary achievements.

HOWARD SQUADRON

b. September 5, 1926
Organization president; attorney

As president of the American Jewish Congress since 1978 and with over two decades of service to that organization, Howard Squadron has been committed to furthering the struggle of American Jewry against anti-Semitism and other forms of racism and in support of Israel. In July 1980 he was elected to a one-year term as chairman of the Conference of Presidents of Major Jewish Organizations, an umbrella group of 32 national Jewish groups.

Howard Maurice Squadron was born in New York

City to Jack and Sarah (Shereshevsky) Squadron. In 1947 he received both a Bachelor of Arts degree in history from the City College of New York and a Bachelor of Laws degree from Columbia University, where he was an editor of the *Columbia Law Review*. From 1947 to 1954 Squadron divided his time between further law study and teaching at the University of Chicago, private practice and serving for two years as staff counsel to the American Jewish Congress. He returned to private practice in 1954, when he formed the partnership of Squadron, Ellenoff, Plesent and Lehrer in New York City, a firm specializing in corporate law.

From 1961 to 1964 Squadron chaired the New York Metropolitan Council for the American Jewish Congress, in which capacity he lobbied successfully for the passage of a fair sabbath law, which exempted sabbath observers from state laws requiring Sunday closings. He also spearheaded the founding of a volunteer lawyers' panel to handle civil rights cases and organized a demonstration to protest an anti-Semitic mural at the Jordanian pavilion at the 1964 New York World's Fair.

Squadron continued to wage a fight for civil rights and civil liberties when he was appointed chairman of the American Jewish Congress National Committee on Law and Social Action. He was elected co-chairperson of the governing council of the American Jewish Congress in 1968 and chairperson in 1972. He was elected senior vice president two years later. Squadron is on the governing board of the World Jewish Congress and is a trustee of the Society for the Advancement of Judaism. As an active Reconstructionist, he has brought a non-traditional religious perspective to the American Jewish Congress.

RONALD STEEL

b. March 25, 1931
Author

Without becoming a politician, statesman or other type of public official, Ronald Steel has nonetheless exerted substantial influence on the thinking of American leaders and scholars with the several books and many articles he has published on domestic affairs and foreign policy. His most recent work, the award-winning *Walter Lippmann and the American Century* (Boston, 1980), was hailed as the most thorough and lucid study of the complex political thinker and journalist who was a major behind-the-scenes power in American government for 50 years.

Ronald Steel was born in Morris, Illinois, to Abraham, a merchant, and Beatrice (Mink) Steel. He received a B.A. degree from Northwestern University in 1953 and spent the following year at the Sorbonne in Paris. In 1955 Steel completed an M.A. degree at Harvard University. He spent 1954 to 1956 as a French interpreter for the commanding general of the U.S. Army in eastern France and was a Foreign Service officer in Washington and Cyprus from 1957 to 1958. From 1959 to 1962, Steel was an editor with Scholastic magazines in New York.

His first book was published two years later. *The End of Alliance* (New York, 1964) analyzed American foreign policy in Europe and called for widespread changes. NATO had outlived its function, Steel concluded, and the United States should withdraw its armed forces from European bases. His next work, *Pax Americana* (New York, 1967), further probed the dilemmas posed by American foreign policy decisions during the cold war. But in this work Steel was even more adamant in his opposition to American interventionism since the end of World War II and to the "American empire" which had resulted.

Even as he worked on his book projects, Steel also developed renown as a perceptive, though often cynical, commentator. In 1965 he joined *The New York Review of Books* as a contributing editor, a post which gave him a regular outlet to present his views. A first collection of these essays was published in 1971 as *Imperialists and Other Heroes* (New York).

In 1972 Steel went to Yale University, where he became visiting lecturer in political science. He subsequently returned to Yale in 1973, 1975 and 1977 and also taught at the University of Texas at Austin in 1977, 1979 and 1980; Wellesley College (1978); Rutgers University (1980); and at the University of California at Irvine and at Los Angeles, both in 1981. He has also worked as an editor on several projects of varying size. In one, *New Light on Juvenile Delinquency* (New York, 1967), he compiled articles by writers as diverse as Federal Judge David Bazelon, playwright Arthur Miller, psychiatrist Robert Coles, journalist Joseph Lelyveld and many others. He coauthored an illustrated work, *Tropical Africa Today* (with George H.T. Kimble, St. Louis, 1967), for junior high school students, and he was general editor of a 42-volume series entitled *The United States in World Affairs* (New York, 1972). He also contributed an essay "The Atlantic Mirage" to *Atlantis Lost*, a 1976 study published by The Council on Foreign Relations and was adviser to the 1979–80 six-part television series *Inside Europe*, produced by Granada TV in London.

Yet the consensus is that Steel's biography of Lippmann is his crowning achievement. The biography was an incisive portrait of a fascinating man and his times, and critics were nearly unanimous in hailing Steel's accomplishment. In his review of Steel's book in *New York* magazine, Murray Kemptom called the biography "a marvelous rummage through the attic of a house whose owner was continually changing his furniture, casting off his costumes, and storing away objects left behind by guests he had ceased to invite." In the work Steel managed to portray a complex personality no other biographer had been able to master. Lippmann's ambivalence towards his Jewishness—an especially delicate subject because of its impact on how Lippmann advised the federal government to react to the rise of Nazism—was treated with tactful directness, as was Lippmann's relationships with women. (Lippmann had had an affair with —and later married—the wife of his best friend.) The book earned Steel the 1980 Bancroft Prize in American History, the 1980 National Book Critics Circle Award and prizes from the *Los Angeles Times* and the *Washington Monthly*.

Steel, whose articles have appeared in *The New York Times, The Washington Post, Commentary, Newsday, Harpers,* the *London Observer* and many other publications, is also a contributing editor to *The New Republic,* where he publishes frequent commentary and criticism. A no-holds-barred writer, he was outspoken in his response to the human rights policy intentions announced by supporters of then president-elect Ronald Reagan in December 1980. "A concern for human rights is not a sentimental self-indulgence for a country like the United States," Steel wrote in one column. "Rather it is a direct expression of its basic values and a realization of where its true interests lie. Those who claim to speak for president-elect Reagan are doing him, and the nation, no service by promoting rightist dictatorships and viewing with amused indifference flagrant abuses of human rights by allied regimes. Politics makes strange bedfellows, and we cannot, it is true, always choose our friends. But we can choose some of them, and we can help them avoid mistakes likely to be disastrous to them, and to our own interests as well."

Steel has also challenged many writers of the hardline right who he charges have exaggerated the Soviet military threat in order to manipulate the massive rearming of the United States. In 1981 Steel joined the Carnegie Endowment for International Peace.

For further information:
Steel, Ronald. "The Absent Danger," *The New Republic,* August 16, 1980.

HERBERT STEIN

b. August 27, 1916
Economist

Conservative economist Herbert Stein is best-known for his role as a prominent policy maker during the Nixon administration. A firm advocate of the free market and a staunch opponent of wage and price controls, he chaired the Council of Economic Advisers during the latter half of Nixon's presidency and received some of the blame for the devastating recession that befell the United States in 1974.

Herbert Stein was born in Detroit to David, a Polish Jew who immigrated to the United States as a boy and worked as a machinist with the Ford Motor Company, and Jessie (Segal) Stein. He received a Bachelor of Arts degree from Williams College in 1935 and a Ph.D. from the University of Chicago in 1938. From 1938 until 1945 he worked in various branches of government, including the Federal Deposit Insurance Company, the Wages and Prices Board and the Office for War Mobility and Reconversion.

He first gained distinction in 1944, when he won a prestigious $25,000 prize in a national competition sponsored by the Pabst Brewing Company for an essay he wrote describing how the United States could return to full employment following the war. Having won the prize, he was able to enter into full-time economic research and after the war was recruited by the Committee for Economic Development, a private organization sponsored by a group of business executives. In that job he wrote and edited many influential analytical papers and developed expertise in government fiscal problems and policy. In 1956 he was named research director of the CED and in 1966 left to join the Brookings Institute as a research economist.

Always politically conservative, Stein was adviser to Barry Goldwater when the Arizona senator ran for president in 1964. Four years later he was recruited by President Nixon to direct economic policy in anticipation of a supposed wind-down of the Vietnam War.

Stein was planning for Nixon when the American economy plunged into a two-year recession, beginning in 1969. He blamed the problems on the excessive spending for social programs of Lyndon Johnson and attempted to put tight constraints on credit and on the money supply. Unemployment rose, as Stein had predicted, but so did inflation, which he did not expect. A production slowdown followed and had dire effects on the economy. During this period the United States experienced what was then dubbed "stagflation"—a word soon adopted into the American vocabulary. But in 1969 a recession combined with inflation was a new and frightening phenomenon, and Nixon turned to Federal Reserve Board chairperson Arthur Burns for advice and policy adjustments.

Although Stein was briefly in the shadows during much of 1971, late that year he was brought back to head up the Council of Economic Advisers. During the next 2½ years, Stein tried to help shape a healthy post-Vietnam economy. But he finally quit the CEA in mid-1974, shortly before Nixon's resignation, and not long before a recession even more severe than the one that began in 1969 set in.

Stein returned to private life as professor of economics at the University of Virginia, senior fellow at the American Enterprise Institute and member of President Reagan's Economic Advisory Board. He also writes occasional columns for The Wall Street Journal, where he is a member of the advisory board. In one such column he asked, "Do We Know What Reagan Economics Is?" (March 11, 1982) and concluded that "on the whole the administration has been moving away from that detour [exaggerations and simplifications] and by now is back on the main line of conservative economics." Describing the Reagan administration's approach, Stein wrote that "it seems to be unusually attracted to off-beat ideas in economics . . . but for the present the best evidence is that Reagan economics is, and will increasingly be, main-line conservative."

Stein continues to be much respected among such main-liners and will surely play a prominent part of any future conservative national administration.

SAUL STEINBERG

b. June 15, 1914
Artist

"Saul Steinberg," said the late art critic Harold Rosenberg in his monograph Saul Steinberg (New York, 1978), "is a frontiersman of genres, an artist who cannot be confined to a category." Describing himself, Steinberg, whose unique drawing style has made him internationally famous, has said, "The tradition of the artist is to become someone else."

Saul Steinberg was born in Ramnicul-Sarat, Rumania. His parents were Moritz, a manufacturer, and Rosa (Iacobson) Steinberg, who made cakes with elaborate icings. He studied philosophy at the University of Buch-

arest and in 1933 entered the Facolta di Architettura in Milan, Italy, where he received a doctorate in architecture in 1940. He became a cartoonist for an Italian magazine, Bertoldo, while practicing architecture. At the outbreak of World War II, Steinberg tried to enter the United States, only to be diverted to Santo Domingo because he did not have an American sponsor. He finally got one—The New Yorker—and made his way into the United States through Miami in 1942. He was both drafted into the U.S. Navy and naturalized in 1943.

His career as a free-lance artist and with The New Yorker and the newspaper PM began almost immediately in 1942. His first one-man show was at the Museum of Modern Art in 1946, and he has since had one-man shows at the Galerie Mai and the Galerie Maeght (Paris), the Institute of Contemporary Art (London), the Kunstmuseum (Basel, Switzerland), Galerie Blanche (Stockholm), the Stedelijk Museum (Amsterdam), Museu de Arte (Sao Paulo, Brazil), the Betty Parsons and Sidney Janis galleries (New York City), and others.

In 1967 Steinberg was artist-in-residence at the Smithsonian Institution in Washington, and in 1974 he received a Gold Medal from the American Academy of Arts and Letters.

He has had major exhibitions in galleries and museums around the world, and his work is also in many permanent museum collections. His drawings appear regularly within The New Yorker magazine and have graced many of its covers. Perhaps his most famous, which appeared on the March 29, 1976 New Yorker cover, is a map of the world as New Yorkers see it. It is an aerial view, perhaps from one of the upper-floor offices in the midtown building where The New Yorker is located, looking westward. From Ninth Avenue to the West Side Highway and the Hudson River, the city is shown full of activity on the streets below, surrounded by tall buildings and industrial lofts. The Hudson River is a light blue strip separating New York (reality) from the rest of the world (an abstraction). A green trapezoid beyond the Hudson neatly takes in Washington, D.C.; Kansas City; Utah; Las Vegas; and Los Angeles. Another light blue strip is the Pacific Ocean, and beyond it three cloudlike shapes are labeled China, Japan and Russia. Steinberg's uncanny sense of how people perceive the world and his ability to translate it into ironic humor led John Gruen to say of Steinberg in Art News (May 1978), "One doesn't quite know whether one is in the presence of Groucho Marx or James Joyce."

As his original training was in architecture, Steinberg frequently uses his drafting skills to create bizarre perspectives and improbable scenes. Mathematical formulae and animals are sometimes the main characters of his pictures. Using line drawings in ink, Rosenberg noted:

> [Steinberg] is a writer of pictures, an architect of speech and sounds, a draftsman of philosophical reflections. . . . Steinberg's compositions cross the borders between art and caricature, illustration, children's art, *art brut*, satire, while conveying reminiscences of styles from Greek and Oriental to Cubist and Constructivist.

Steinberg is the author of eleven books: *All in Line* (New York, 1945); *The Art of Living* (New York, 1949); *The Passport* (New York, 1949); *Steinberg's Umgang mit Menschen* (Hamburg, 1954); *Dessins* (Paris, 1956); *The Labyrinth* (New York, 1960); *The Catalogue* (Cleveland, 1962); *Steinberg's Paperback* (Hamburg, 1964); *The New World* (New York, 1965); *Le Masque*, with texts by Michel Butor and Harold Rosenberg and photographs by Inge Morath (Paris, 1966); and *The Inspector* (New York, 1973). Harold Rosenberg's monograph, published in conjunction with a major retrospective of Steinberg's work at the Whitney Museum in New York during the spring of 1978, contains a comprehensive chronology of Steinberg's life plus an extensive bibliography of books and articles with further descriptions of Steinberg's contributions to modern art.

GEORGE STEINER

b. April 23, 1929
Critic; educator

George Steiner's ability to synthesize his direct knowledge of the several languages and the four cultures to which he was exposed (Jewish, Austrian, French and American) has earned him recognition as one of the world's brilliant philosophical essayists and critics on the role of language and culture in Western society. Steiner's particular focus, reflected in his vast body of writing, is an ongoing exploration of how so-called humanistic civilization could have permitted the development in modern times of the political barbarism called nazism.

Francis George Steiner was born in Paris to Frederick George, a physician, and Elsie (Frazos) Steiner. His Viennese parents had settled in Paris in 1924 and moved to New York in 1940. Steiner became a naturalized American citizen in 1944.

Although raised in the United States, Steiner returned to Europe to study and received a Bachelier es Lettres from the Sorbonne in 1947. Back in the United States,

he received a B.A. degree from the University of Chicago in 1948—he was barely 19—and an M.A. degree in English from Harvard University in 1950. At Harvard, Steiner displayed the thorough and insightful scholarship that would distinguish him in his later career, and he was awarded the Bell Prize in American literature. He then received a Rhodes Scholarship, which he used at Oxford University toward the completion of a Ph.D. degree in 1955. While studying in England, Steiner was a member of the editorial staff of *The Economist* from 1952 to 1956.

Upon completing his doctorate, Steiner joined the world of academia. From 1956 through 1960 he taught and wrote at Princeton University, first as a fellow at the Institute for Advanced Studies, then as a Fulbright Professor and finally as Gauss Lecturer. In 1961 Steiner became a fellow at Churchill College of Cambridge University in England.

Steiner has written and edited many books of criticism that explore the role of language in past and present cultures and analyze how linguistic differences have influenced the social, political and cultural development of entire societies and of individuals. His first work, *Tolstoy or Dostoevsky* (New York, 1958), published when Steiner was only 29, is therefore not only an analysis of the contrasts between the Russian literary giants of the title but a comparison of the larger aspects of Russian political and cultural life that each represents.

Steiner's next major work, *The Death of Tragedy* (New York, 1961), explores how, in the author's view, tragic drama has declined since it flourished among the ancient Greeks. In this work he compares the themes and styles of the Greek masters—including Aeschylus, Sophocles, Euripides and others—with Shakespeare and Racine and with later playwrights, such as Strindberg and Ibsen, and tries to show how the so-called moderns have been unable to realize the same depth of understanding of the human condition as did the ancients. Steiner even includes an analysis of Wagnerian operas within the scheme of the book.

Language and Silence (New York, 1967), Steiner's next book, is a collection of essays that explore how language can be manipulated through media, political propaganda (Nazi double-think) and other means to influence people. Further discussions of the impact of language and of its evolution (or lack of it) on society appear in *Extraterritorial: Literature and the Language Revolution* (New York, 1971), *In Bluebeard's Castle: Notes Towards the Redefinition of Culture* (New Haven, 1971) and *After Babel: Aspects of Language and Translation* (New York, 1975).

Steiner has also published short stories and poetry, but these have been decidedly less successful than his criticism. *Anno Domini* (New York, 1964), a collection of three stories, was described in *Bookweek* (November 8, 1964) as "a catastrophe of overwriting."

Despite his American upbringing, Steiner claims to feel closer to the European environment that produced Marx, Freud and Einstein. Since his parents left Austria for a better life in Paris and came to the United States as refugees from anti-Jewish oppression, Steiner has become obsessed with trying to unravel the mysteries language holds to explain its influence on people's actions. In 1968, for his work in *Language and Silence* and for previous contributions, he received the Jewish Chronicle Book Award. Three years later he won a Guggenheim fellowship to continue his writing and research.

Steiner's novel, *The Portage to San Cristobal of A.H.* (New York, 1982) is the story of a group of four Nazi-hunting Jews who capture a ninety-year-old Adolf Hitler and spirit him to the Amazon where they await an Israeli plane to fly their captive to Israel for trial. All the great powers are opposed to their action, fearful that Israel will stage an even more publicized version of the Eichmann trial and that Hitler will arouse passions they would prefer remain buried. In the final chapter of this provocative book, Steiner allows Hitler to defend himself. Hitler says, "I was not the worst." He proceeds to blast Christianity, Communism, and of course, Jews. "In this tour de force," commented *The Wall Street Journal* critic Edmund Fuller, "Mr. Steiner makes his readers re-examine, to whatever conclusions each may choose, a history from which we would prefer to avert our eyes."

Steiner continues to write and teach at Cambridge University and is a regular contributor to *The New Yorker* and other publications.

ISAAC STERN

b. July 21, 1920
Violinist

Isaac Stern—once described as "more than a violinist, less than a head of state"—is America's greatest musical ambassador. Besides being one of the top virtuosos of his generation, he has taken a leadership role in sponsoring and cultivating young musicians around the world, was in the forefront of the movement to save Carnegie Hall in 1960, when developers wanted to raze it (he is now Carnegie Hall's president), and has been especially active in the music world in Israel.

Isaac Stern was born in Kreminiesz, Russia to Solomon and Clara (Jaffe) Stern. As an infant he was brought with his family to San Francisco, where he was raised, and began studying violin when he was 8. His talent was evident even then; he soon left grade school to pursue music full-time in a small conservatory. At age 12 he began studying with Naoum Blinder, concertmaster of the San Francisco Symphony, and three years later made his debut with that orchestra in a concert conducted by Pierre Monteux. In 1937 he gave a recital at New York's Town Hall. But another six years of cross-country touring would elapse before a triumphant 1943 concert at Carnegie Hall finally put Stern's name on the musical map. (Today he says, only half-joking, that his struggles were greater because "I didn't have Isaac Stern blocking for me"—a reference to many young violinists whom he has since introduced to the concert stage.)

He became a prominent soloist with orchestras across the United States and abroad and performed in chamber ensembles with other great musicians of the day. For many years he has been one third of the Istomin-Stern-Rose Trio, and in 1970 they performed a cycle of Beethoven chamber works for piano. Stern was also one of the most active performers in the Casals Festival in Puerto Rico for many years.

But when one thinks of Isaac Stern, one thinks not only of a performer but of an eloquent spokesperson for a wide range of musical causes, some of which have accompanying political themes. Since the State of Israel was founded, Stern has played a leading role in the music world there, as performer, teacher and impresario. Stern was the primary force in recognizing two young musicians who have since become international stars; it was he who arranged for Itzhak Perlman and Pinchas Zukerman to travel to, study and perform in the United States. He is founder and president of the America-Israel Cultural Foundation, which sponsors an active musical exchange program. And he appeared in a documentary with Leonard Bernstein, *Journey to Jerusalem*. Stern's prestige in Israel is such that he has been called "half-Israeli, half-American," and his opinions on Israeli matters are highly regarded, even (or especially) when they are bound to be controversial.

For example, on October 7, 1979, at a reception given by Tel Aviv's Mayor Shlomo Lehat to celebrate the opening of the Israel Philharmonic Symphony's fall season, the virtuoso violinist openly criticized the country he loved:

As a Jew I am always happy to come to Israel, but if the present Begin government continues with its policies and if it continues to project the image of Israel that it has projected abroad and among Jews of the Diaspora, I do not know how long it will take until Jews like myself would not wish to come to Israel any more. . . . I believe to this day that there is more talent and ability and intelligence in Israel than in most countries with the same demographic breakdown. Properly developed it could be the Greece, the Athens. . . . [But] it is a country that seems built on fratricide, driving itself to suicide as if the devil were pushing it. Does this country really need a war in order to pull itself together? . . . Israel cannot live alone in the world. . . . It needs its friends and it is endangering that friendship. That is what concerns me and this is what hurts me.

For uttering these words, Stern was condemned by some Jews in the United States on the grounds that no foreign Jew had the right to criticize Israel. Yet ironically many Israelis praised him for his courage. The novelist Hanoch Bartov wrote in *Ma'ariv*, the Tel Aviv daily newspaper: "But the true facts are that you need not be Isaac Stern and you need not be a guest to see what Stern saw and said."

In 1980, commemorating his 60th birthday and 45th year of performing, Stern announced that from May 15 until the close of November, he would play in Paris and Israel; open the New York Philharmonic season with Zubin Mehta conducting; perform with the National Symphony in Washington, D.C.; travel to San Francisco to play in the San Francisco Symphony's new home, Davies Symphony Hall; and then return to his beloved Carnegie Hall for a series of concerts. It was hectic and frenetic but typical of the energetic Stern, who won't stop playing or saying what he believes is right.

Indeed, perhaps Stern's greatest strength is as a communicator through music, words and acts. But his gift somehow transcends verbal expression. At the invitation of the Chinese government in 1979, he held master classes in violin at the conservatory in Beijing, where, despite language barriers, he was able to transmit his love for music and evoke superior sounds and feeling from his pupils. Stern's Chinese experiences were turned into a highly praised documentary film, *From Mao to Mozart: Isaac Stern in China* (1981). In *The Boston Globe* Richard Dyer described the film and Stern this way: "*From Mao to Mozart* is a wonderful movie because Isaac Stern is a wonderful man, a famous violinist, a great human spirit, and a face that cameras love."

For further information:
Rubin, Stephen E. "Isaac Stern: The Power and the Glory." *The New York Times Magazine,* October 14, 1979.

I.F. STONE

b. December 24, 1907
Journalist

I.F. Stone, perhaps the most important investigative journalist of our era, has served as the prototype and mentor for a generation of younger reporters. He has been called the Thomas Paine of his age for his celebration of the rights of humankind. He has also been called the Benedict Arnold of his era by those who disagree with his bold and independent stances in confronting injustice and militarism throughout his career.

Isidor Feinstein was born in Philadelphia to Bernard and Katherine (Novack) Feinstein. He grew up in Haddonfield, New Jersey, where his parents, both Russian immigrants, owned a dry goods store. Stone began his career as a journalist when he was still a 14-year-old sophomore in high school. He and a friend published a newspaper called *The Progressive,* in which Stone attacked the newspaper publisher William Randolph Hearst and supported Mohandas Gandhi and the League of Nations. The venture lasted three months before the paper ceased publishing. However, while still in high school, Stone began to work for the *Haddonfield Press* and as a part-time correspondent for the *Camden Courier-Post.*

In 1924 Stone enrolled at the University of Pennsylvania as a philosophy major while working nights as a copyeditor and rewriter for the *Philadelphia Inquirer.* When Stone left the university in 1927 without a degree, he returned to the *Camden Courier-Post.* He joined the Socialist Party in 1927 and during the 1928 presidential election did public relations for Norman Thomas, the Socialist candidate for president. However, after that campaign Stone left the party because he felt that political affiliation might compromise him as a journalist.

During the 1930s and the 1940s, Stone worked as an editorial writer, reporter and columnist for The *New York Post* and the *Philadelphia Record* and as the Washington correspondent and columnist for the liberal daily newspaper *PM.* The paper, published in New York and owned by Marshall Field, carried no advertising. During the same period, Stone was the Washington editor of *The Nation,* the highly respected liberal weekly magazine. Following the collapse of *PM* in 1948, he worked for the liberal daily *New York Star* until its demise in 1950 and also reported for the short-lived, left-leaning *New York Daily Compass* under editor Ted O. Thackeray in 1952.

Throughout his years as a reporter, Stone also published several books. His first, *The Court Disposes* (New

York, 1937), is about the workings of the Supreme Court. This was followed by *Business as Usual* (New York, 1941), an attack on waste and inefficiency in the Defense Department prior to World War II. In 1945 Stone, who speaks fluent Hebrew, went to Palestine to report on the survivors of the concentration camps in their epic secret trek from Eastern Europe, through the British blockade, to Palestine. He was deeply impressed by what he saw, and his experiences and observations were captured in a book called *Underground to Palestine* (New York, 1946).

In 1948 Stone wrote an openly pro-Zionist work called *This Is Israel* (New York), in which he recounted the overpowering effect of visiting the new Jewish state founded by Holocaust survivors and earlier Jewish pioneers. He had attended a Passover seder in an English detention camp on Cyprus with homeless Jewish survivors. Later, in his newsletter on February 6, 1956, he recalled the event:

> I had the privilege of seeing my people in some of the greatest moments of their long history—as they emerged from the hells of Auschwitz and Buchenwald—packed into the old freighters which served as the Mayflowers on the Mediterranean, fighting against odds which seemed overwhelming to establish a Jewish nation. . . . The Jews had no recourse [in 1948] but to fight for their lives, and the war was stopped only when the [British] Foreign Office and the State Department suddenly realized that the Arabs were losing.

Stone's next book was the controversial *The Hidden History of the Korean War* (New York, 1952), in which he charged—but never proved—that the Korean War had been plotted by the South Koreans in collusion with the United States government. The popular belief at the time was that the North Koreans had been the aggressors.

After the *Daily Compass* closed, Stone, unable to find work, started his own paper, *I.F. Stone's Weekly*, in 1953. In the iconoclastic four-page newsletter, for which he initially did all the research, reporting, writing, editing and proofreading—with the long-time assistance of his wife—Stone regularly attacked the Defense Department and the enormous waste and corruption of its bloated budget and military procurement practices and the Vietnam War, to which Stone was adamantly opposed. As a result he became a hero to huge numbers in the anti-war movement, especially the young. He was particularly admired for his reputation for thoroughly and meticulously researching his subjects using primary government publications as source material.

Stone has published three collections of his columns from 1953 to 1970; *The Haunted Fifties* (New York, 1963), *Polemics and Prophecies* (New York, 1970) and *The I.F. Stone Weekly Reader* (New York, 1973). He also wrote *The Killings at Kent State—How Murder Went Unpunished* (New York, 1971), in which he condemned the murder of four students as unwarranted and as an unjustifiable expression of authority. The book included the full text of the Justice Department's secret summary of the FBI findings about the Kent State tragedy, which Stone claimed had been whitewashed.

Shortly after the 1967 Six-Day War, Stone began expressing compassion for the rights of Palestinians as well as Israelis. "How," he asked, "can Israel talk of the Jewish right to a homeland and deny one to the Palestinians? How can there be peace without some measure of justice?"

In 1978 *Underground to Palestine* was reissued by Pantheon Books (New York) with a new concluding section in which Stone clarifies his positions on Zionism, Israel and *Yiddishkeit*. He divides his last chapter into "Confessions of a Jewish Dissident" and "The Other Zionism," writing that it is "only rarely that we dissidents on the Middle East can enjoy a fleeting voice in the American press. Finding an American publishing house willing to publish a book that departs from the standard Israeli line is about as easy as selling a thoughtful exposition on atheism to the *Osservatore Romano* [the Vatican newspaper]." He adds that if American journalists "dare express one word of sympathy for the Palestinian Arab refugees, they are flooded with Jewish hate mail accusing them of anti-Semitism" and also that such Jewish critics are labeled "self-hating Jews." "We are asked why we cannot be narrow ethnics, suspicious of any breed but our own. Isaiah is out of fashion." And he concludes that Gentile critics are too often unfairly regarded as anti-Semites.

Stone closed down his newsletter in 1975 because of the heavy work burdens it created and joined *The New York Review of Books* as a contributing editor. He was also appointed distinguished scholar-in-residence at American University in Washington, D.C.

Although less active than in the past, Stone in recent years has remained an outspoken writer and commentator. His column appears occasionally in the New York weekly newspaper *The Village Voice* and in *Newsday,* and he has been a forceful presence on television programs in the 1980s speaking out against the new foreign policies of the Reagan administration, which he claims are regressive. In his retirement he has also undertaken studies in the Greek classics—a resumption, he said in a *New York Times* article in 1978, of the university studies he never completed.

A one-hour film, *I.F. Stone's Weekly*, was made in the early 1970s by filmmaker Gerry Brock Jr. for the Public Broadcasting Service.

For further information:
Stone, I. F. *The Best of I. F. Stone's Weekly.* New York: 1973.
———. *In a Time of Torment.* New York: 1967.
———. *The Truman Era.* New York: 1953.

IRVING STONE

b. July 14, 1903
Author

The prolific author Irving Stone is best known for his ability to make the lives of major historical figures become human and identifiable in the many award-winning biographical novels he has written. The chronicler of such personalities as Michelangelo, Vincent Van Gogh, Charles Darwin, Eugene Debs and many others, Stone blends meticulous research with masterful and animated writing, so that the dialogue and scenes he creates are as authentic as if his subjects had conveyed them to him directly.

Irving Tennenbaum was born in San Francisco, the son of Charles, who worked for the Hercules Power Plant, and Pauline (Rosenberg) Tennenbaum. Both his parents were the children of immigrant shopkeepers. When Stone was 7 years old, his parents separated, and the boy went to live with his maternal grandmother. After his mother remarried, Stone returned to live with her and assumed his stepfather's last name, "Stone."

He graduated from Manual Arts High School in Los Angeles in 1920, and following one semester at the University of Southern California, he transferred to the University of California at Berkeley. He majored in political science and received a B.A. degree in 1923. While in college, he won a one-act-play-writing contest sponsored by the university. Stone returned to the University of Southern California for graduate studies and received his M.A. degree in economics in 1924. He spent two more years pursuing a Ph.D. but never completed the program.

In 1928 Stone went to Europe, where he encountered the work of the then relatively unknown Dutch painter Vincent Van Gogh. He became obsessed with the artist and endeavored to discover all he could about

his life. After six months in Europe, Stone returned to New York and began to support himself by writing detective and murder stories for pulp magazines. He still considered himself primarily a playwright, and his show *The Dark Mirror* was produced off-Broadway in 1929.

Two years later Stone finished his manuscript about the life of Van Gogh. It was turned down by 17 publishers. In 1933, however, he did publish a novel called *Pageant of Youth* (New York), about campus life at the University of Southern California. At a cocktail party following the book's publication, Stone met Maxwell Aley, a noted New York publisher, who agreed to publish *Lust for Life* (New York, 1934), Stone's biographical novel about Vincent Van Gogh. Within two weeks of publication, the book was a national best seller and years later was made into an Academy Award-winning film in 1956, with Kirk Douglas in the starring role.

Stone made one last effort to establish a reputation as a playwright, but his play *Truly Valiant* closed after only one performance in 1935. Since that time he has devoted his efforts to writing books and has maintained a special interest in the biographical novel. Between 1934 and 1956 he wrote 12 books, including extraordinarily well-researched and well-written biographical novels about, among others, Mary Todd Lincoln; Clarence Darrow; Jack London; Sigmund Freud; and Jessie B. Fremont, the wife of the explorer and failed 19th-century presidential candidate John Fremont.

"My books are based 98 percent on documentary evidence," he said. "I spend several years trying to get inside the brain and heart of my subjects, listening to the interior monologues in their letters, and when I have to bridge the chasms between the factual evidence, I try to make an intuitive leap through the eyes and motivation of the person I'm writing about." In preparing for his book about Van Gogh, he spent a half year visiting places where the painter had once lived. In *The Origin* (New York, 1980), a book about Charles Darwin, Stone and his wife lived in Darwin's house and worked in his library using the scientist's papers.

In 1956 Stone began research on a project that was to consume 4½ years of his life. He and his wife spent more than two years in Italy gathering background and details for the work. The result was *The Agony and the Ecstasy* (New York, 1961), the story of the life of the brilliant Italian sculptor and painter Michelangelo. This book received the same rave reviews and instant acclaim that had greeted *Lust for Life*.

Stone went on to write three more books about Michelangelo: *I Michelangelo, Sculptor* (New York, 1962), a fictional autobiography; *The Story of Michelangelo's Pieta*

(New York, 1963), which was released to coincide with the exhibition of the *Pieta* at the New York World's Fair in 1964; and *The Great Adventure of Michelangelo* (New York, 1965).

For further information:
Stone, Irving. *Adversary in the House* (Eugene Debs). New York: 1947.
———. *Clarence Darrow for the Defense*. New York: 1941.
———. *Immortal Wife* (Jessie Fremont). New York: 1944.
———. *Lincoln: A Contemporary Portrait*. New York: 1962.
———. *Love is Eternal* (Abraham and Mary Todd Lincoln). New York: 1954.
———. *Passions of the Mind* (Sigmund Freud). New York: 1971.
———. *The President's Lady* (Andrew and Rachel Jackson). New York: 1951.
———. *Sailor on Horseback* (Jack London). Boston: 1938.
———. *Those Who Love* (Abigail Adams). New York: 1965.

MICHAEL STRASSFELD

b. February 8, 1950
Writer

The Baby Boom generation has produced a number of young leaders who offer a hopeful future for Jewish life in America, among them Michael Strassfeld. Active in the Havurah movement since its formation in the early 1970s, he has also edited and written several important books that address the questions and needs of young people whose values reflect new roles for women in Jewish life and generally different attitudes toward being Jewish and being Americans.

Michael Strassfeld was born in Saratoga Springs, New York to Rabbi Meyer Jehiel and Ruth E. (Goldstein) Strassfeld, a medical researcher. Raised in Dorchester, Massachusetts, he attended the Maimonides Hebrew Day School in Brookline. In 1967 he entered Yeshiva University and Rabbi Isaac Elchanan Theological Seminary in New York but remained for only one year. In 1968 he transferred to Brandeis University and in 1971 received a B.A. degree magna cum laude in Near Eastern and Judaic studies. He completed an M.A. degree at Brandeis the following year. Strassfeld continued graduate studies toward a doctorate in Jewish history but did not complete it.

Throughout his student years Michael Strassfeld was also active in many Jewish groups, including the Student Struggle for Soviet Jewry, as well as the burgeon-ing Havurah movement. In 1970 he married Sharon Nulman, with whom he later collaborated on book projects and in organization leadership. From 1971 to 1974 he was a member of Boston's Havurat Shalom Community and participated in several other Boston Jewish student groups. He moved to New York in 1974, continuing his involvement in Havurah. He also began publishing what he called "Jewish Catalogues." *The First Jewish Catalogue*, co-edited with Sharon Strassfeld and Richard Siegel (Philadelphia, 1973), was a vast compendium of information concerning many aspects of Jewish life. A physically large book and profusely illustrated, it provided readers with many "how-to's" as well as addresses of organizations they could contact or of places to purchase Jewish books or other materials. Second and third *Catalogues*, edited only by the Strassfelds and published by the Jewish Publication Society, followed in 1976 and 1980. The Strassfelds were joined by Jewish genealogist Arthur Kurzweil in co-editing *Behold a Great Image* (Philadelphia, 1978), a collection of several hundred photographs documenting Jewish life and experiences throughout the world.

Michael Strassfeld has also collaborated with Richard Siegel in the production of an annual *Jewish Calendar* (New York) since 1975. On his own he edited *A Passover Haggadah* (New York) in 1979. His most recent work is *The Jewish Holiday Book* (New York, 1982), a comprehensive history and explanation of Jewish holiday traditions.

Strassfeld has also attempted to cope with the by now familiar question often directed at many American Jews: "Why do I live in America rather than in Israel? Don't I accept the religious *mitzvah* (obligation) of *aliyah* (immigration)? Have I forgotten Jerusalem for the flesh-pots of New York?" In an essay in *Response* in the summer of 1980, he confesses that he resides in the United States "for both ideological and pragmatic reasons." Rejecting those who argue that Israel should be a country just like every other country (since it would erase the uniqueness of Judaism), he discusses the differences between Zionism and Judaism. Are they "irreconcilably opposed?" he asks, and answers, "Of course not," adding, however, that the differences between the two are real. Thus, he finds it difficult to move to Israel because becoming an immigrant is a trying experience, because Jerusalem and Tel Aviv are too parochial, so different from New York City's cosmopolitanism. Then he writes of other problems: "Israel's objectionable foreign policy, the role of women in her society and Orthodox domination of official religious life." Most upsetting to him is the stark choice in Israel for would-be emigrants: Orthodoxy or secularism. All the same, he finds himself irresistibly attracted to Israel and confesses ". . . it is so easy to be a Jew in Israel, so hard in *galut* [exile] . . . How do I reconcile living here . . . I am still grappling with these questions. . . . I remain torn—*libi be-mizrah*—at times my heart lies in the East, but right now my life is here in the galut."

In 1979 Strassfeld was a founding member of Minyan Mi'at, an informal prayer group, and of Lishmah, an adult study institute. He has also been active in Havurah on a national level.

For further information:
Strassfeld, Michael. *A Shabbat Haggadah: For Celebration and Study.* New York: 1982.

SHARON STRASSFELD

b. March 10, 1950
Writer

Since the early 1970s Sharon Strassfeld has been a leader in the revitalization of Jewish life among younger Americans. Her traditional background combined with contemporary values have resulted in a conception of Jewish life in which men and women share responsibilities equally in every phase of life, including religious observance, and in which Jewish values are incorporated to provide an important and necessary spiritual dimension.

Sharon Nulman was born in Providence, Rhode Island to Saul, owner of a catering business, and Ruth (Finkelstein) Nulman, a Polish immigrant who was a schoolteacher. She received a traditional Europeanlike upbringing and attended religious day schools in Providence. After graduating from Classical High School in 1967, she spent two years at Stern College for Women in New York City. She then transferred to the University of Massachusetts in Boston and received a B.A. degree with honors in English in 1971.

In 1970 Nulman married Michael Strassfeld, with whom she later collaborated on numerous Jewish communal projects and books. From 1971 to 1974 she was a member of the Havurat Shalom in Massachusetts. Settling in New York City, she became similarly involved in the Havurah movement and was a founder of Minyan Mi'at and the West Side Minyan. She was also a founding member of the National Havurah Summer Institute.

In 1973 the Strassfelds joined Richard Siegel in compiling *The First Jewish Catalogue* (Philadelphia, 1973), an informal yet comprehensive collection of crafts, history, traditions and general information relevant to the contemporary Jewish experience. In addition to the data contained within the book, addresses indicating where other resources could be obtained were also listed. Second and third *Catalogues*, edited only by the Strassfelds, followed in 1976 and 1980. They also co-edited, with Arthur Kurzweil, *Behold a Great Image* (Philadelphia, 1978), an album of several hundred photographs documenting modern Jewish life in America and around the world.

Independently, Sharon Strassfeld, who is also a real estate investor, has become deeply involved in exploring how Jewish families have changed in line with the vast social changes that occurred in America following the turmoil of the late 1960s and the important emergence of the women's movement. To that end, she co-authored with Kathy Green *The Jewish Family Book* (New York, 1981), which provides guidelines for modern Jewish families, and has contributed articles on that and other subjects to such publications as *Present Tense*, *Sh'ma* and *Menorah*. She also lectures widely.

Sharon Strassfeld is active in the Upper West Side Manhattan neighborhood where she lives and is on the board of Congregation Ansche Chesed.

BARBRA STREISAND

b. April 24, 1942
Singer; actress

Barbra Streisand's career is many a would-be performer's dream. An overnight success at the age of 19, the self-taught singer has matured into a stylist of extraordinary versatility, elegance and class. Now in her early 40s, Streisand has been featured in major screen roles and has directed original projects. In addition, she has become outspoken in her support of Jewish causes, including solidarity with Soviet Jews.

Barbara (the second *a* was dropped when she became a professional singer) Joan Streisand was born to Emanuel, who taught English, and Diana (Rosen) Streisand in Brooklyn. She grew up poor and unpopular in the Williamsburg section. For much of her childhood, she was fatherless—her own father died when she was 15 months old; her mother remarried six years later. She attended a Jewish religious school in Brooklyn, grew up in a kosher home and wanted to be an actress since the age of 4. Her mother wanted her to take secretarial courses "just in case," but instead she moved to Manhattan after graduating from Erasmus Hall High School in 1959 to pursue her career.

She began singing in Greenwich Village bars in the

early 1960s and, after winning a talent contest in one of them, received her first paid engagement at the Bon Soir, also in the Village. She also appeared, to rave reviews, in an otherwise mediocre show, *Another Evening with Harry Stoones* (1961). Streisand was slowly building a following.

But her first real break came when she was seen by David Merrick in a showcase performance at the Blue Angel in 1961. He signed her immediately for the role of Miss Marmelstein—the beleaguered secretary Streisand never became in real life—in Jerome Weidman's *I Can Get It for You Wholesale*. The show, which opened on March 22, 1962—Streisand was not yet 20—made her an instant success.

In the years that followed, Streisand lived up to her promise as a singer and an actress. Her style was spontaneous, earthy, sexy-yet-little-girlish, romantic. She has earned Gold Record Albums (more than 1 million sales) for almost all her albums, including *People* (1965), *My Name is Barbra* (1965), *Color Me Barbra* (1966), *Stoney End* (1971), *The Way We Were* (1974), *A Star Is Born* (1976) and *Superman* (1977).

After playing Miss Marmelstein, Streisand showed that she could play other roles, too—both comic and dramatic—and play them well. She created a new version of Fanny Brice in *Funny Girl* (1965), which she also played in the film version in 1968. She has also starred in the films *Hello, Dolly* (1969); *On a Clear Day You Can See Forever* (1970); *The Owl and the Pussycat* (1970); *What's Up Doc?* (1972); *Up the Sandbox* (1972); *The Way We Were* (1973); *For Pete's Sake* (1974); *Funny Lady* (1975); *A Star Is Born*, which she also co-produced (1976); and *The Main Event* (1978).

She has starred in numerous television specials for CBS, including "My Name Is Barbra" (1965), which received five Emmys, and "Color Me Barbra" (1966). Streisand received the Academy Award for Best Actress in 1968 for *Funny Girl* and a Grammy for best female vocalist and songwriter in 1978.

From obscure beginnings Streisand became the first performer to earn $100,000 a week in Las Vegas *(Cue* magazine, July 6, 1979). She was invited to the White House by the Kennedys in 1963 and has been in demand ever since. She is thought to be temperamental and difficult but is also reputed to be shy. Perhaps because of her stardom, it is difficult to know who the real Streisand is, and it is far easier to exploit a legend. An unauthorized but worshipful biography, *The Greatest Star* (New York, 1975), was written by Rene Jordan. Shortly afterward, a West Coast publishing group announced it would be creating a quarterly magazine devoted exclusively to the career of Streisand.

What does a Jewish girl from Brooklyn do with all her success? Streisand has used it to create her own production company and will produce the film version of Isaac Bashevis Singer's *Yentl*. She made a substantial contribution to an Orthodox synagogue, the Pacific Jewish Center, in Venice, California and donated $50,000 in 1981 for the funding at UCLA Hillel of a Streisand Center for Jewish Cultural Arts, which will sponsor a performance by a well-known personality in the arts each year. She has also lent her support to important liberal political candidates, including former New York congresswoman Bella Abzug.

If there's a key to the success of Barbra Streisand, it might be her absolute refusal to compromise. Despite the suggestions of her managers, she would not change her last name or fix her nose or teeth for the sake of appearance. But her mother, Mrs. Diane Kind, has a different version. In a *New York Times* interview (February 23, 1970), she describes how she kept tabs on the young Barbra: "I let her move to Manhattan and get an apartment. . . . I would call her all the time . . . and find out where she was living so I could bring her chicken soup."

ROGER STRAUS

b. January 3, 1917
Editor; publisher

Roger W. Straus Jr. is a distinguished editor and publisher. As a founder and currently as president of the prestigious New York publishing house Farrar, Straus and Giroux Inc., he has been responsible for publishing some of the most important works of literature, including many Nobel and Pulitzer Prize-winning books. Among those authors Straus has published and promoted are Aleksandr Solzhenitsyn, Hermann Hesse, T.S. Eliot and poets Pablo Neruda and Nelly Sachs.

Roger Straus was born in New York City, the son of Roger Williams and Gladys (Guggenheim) Straus. His grandfather, Oscar S. Straus, had written several books and was the American ambassador to Turkey during three presidential administrations. He also served as the secretary of commerce and labor in the cabinet of Theodore Roosevelt—the first Jew to earn such a high rank in American government. Straus's father was chairman of the board of the American Smelting and Refining Company and was a founder and past president of the National Conference of Christians and Jews. His mother was descended from the prominent Guggenheim family, which had settled in the United States in the 1850s to escape repression of the Jews in Switzerland. Her grandfather was first a peddler in the United States but later became active in mining and became the patriarch of one of the wealthiest families in America.

Straus attended Hamilton College from 1935 to 1937 and received a B.S. degree in journalism from the University of Missouri in 1939. But he had already begun a reporting career in 1936 with the White Plains (New York) *Daily Reporter*. From 1937 to 1939 he was an editorial writer and reporter for the *Columbian Missourian,* and then he returned for one year to the *Daily Reporter* to write features.

In 1940 Straus became an editorial assistant at *Current History* magazine and eventually became the associate editor, remaining until 1945. At the same time, Straus was an associate editor of *Forum* magazine and also served in the United States Naval Reserve. Furthermore, he initiated his first publishing venture, *Asterisk* magazine, which lasted for one year, and he was the president of Book Ideas Inc. from 1945 until 1946.

In 1941 Straus was the co-editor of three books based on World War II. They were *The Sixth Column, War Letters from Britain* and *The New Order,* all published in New York, and all personal reflections on the war.

Straus founded Farrar, Straus and Co. Inc., in 1945, which eventually became Farrar, Straus and Giroux Inc., and which has also published the works of Abraham Joshua Heschel, Bernard Malamud, Philip Roth and Isaac Bashevis Singer. He also began many of his own specialized book imprints, including L.C. Page & Co. in 1957, Noonday Press Inc. in 1960, Octagon Books in 1968 and Hill & Wang in 1971. He is particularly noted in the publishing world because of his staunch independence. Straus is critical of those publishers who bend to marketing trends and who have allowed themselves to be swallowed up by corporate owners that have pressured the publishers to compromise their goals. By remaining autonomous, Farrar, Straus and Giroux is not able to pay its authors the huge sums of money that other publishers can, yet many of its authors have remained loyal to the publishing house because of its integrity and dedication to literary values.

Straus has also been extremely active in the field of philanthropy and in the struggle for literary freedom around the world. He was a director of the Harry Frank Guggenheim Foundation at Manhattanville College from 1970 to 1976 and a director of the John Simon Guggenheim Foundation's Center for Inter-American Relations. He is also a vice president of the Fred L. Lavanburg Foundation.

From 1955 until 1965 Straus was on the publica-tions committee of the Union of American Hebrew Congregations. During those years he was also the chairman of the publishing board of *American Judaism* magazine. He is a director of the University of Missouri Press and was chairman of the advisory committee of *Partisan Review* magazine from 1959 until 1969.

He belongs to many professional organizations and associations, including PEN, the international writers' association; the Emerson Literary Society; and Sigma Delta Chi, the society of professional journalists.

ROBERT S. STRAUSS

b. October 10, 1918
Lawyer; politician

Robert Strauss, a leader in the Democratic Party, has served as chairman of the Democratic National Committee, U.S. ambassador to the Egyptian-Israeli talks on Palestinian autonomy and U.S. special trade representative. He is generally considered to be a brilliant organizer, fund raiser and mediator.

Robert Strauss was born in Lockhart, in south-central Texas, to Charles H., a German-Jewish immigrant who ran a dry goods store, and Edith (Schwartz) Strauss, whose family had lived in Texas since the 1850s. Strauss was reared in Stamford, Texas.

While a student at the University of Texas from 1937 to 1941, Strauss also worked as a clerk at the State Capitol in Austin. There he met John Connally, his first political contact in the Democratic Party, who later became governor of Texas and secretary of the treasury in the Nixon administration. In 1937 Strauss offered to work in Lyndon B. Johnson's first congressional campaign. Johnson was a strong supporter of the New Deal, and Strauss followed suit.

In 1941 Strauss received his Bachelor of Laws degree from the University of Texas. He joined the FBI and was therefore exempted from military service. He served as a special agent in Des Moines, Iowa; Columbus, Ohio; and Dallas, Texas. In 1946 after World War II ended, he founded the law firm of Akin, Gump, Strauss, Hauer, and Feld, specializing in corporate law. The partnership quickly grew into one of Dallas's largest and most respected law firms.

During the ensuing years Strauss earned a good deal of money investing in real estate and radio broadcasting stations. In 1962 he served as the major fund raiser for John Connally in his bid for the governorship of Texas. When Connally won, he rewarded Strauss with a seat on the State Banking Board, a position Strauss held for six years.

In 1968 Strauss managed the Humphrey-Muskie presidential campaign in Texas. He persuaded the feuding John Connally and Senator Ralph Yarborough to work together in the campaign, offering early evidence of his talent for reconciling people with divergent views. Throughout his career, in fact, Strauss has displayed the ability to bring disparate and conflicting political factions together to work for the common good.

Strauss became the treasurer of the Democratic National Committee in 1970. He was faced with the herculean task of reducing the huge multi-million dollar debt left from the Humphrey-Muskie campaign. When he took the job, he commented that if it was not going to be difficult to achieve his goal, the party would not have asked him to do it. He turned in a dazzling performance, reducing the debt by more than half in less than two years.

After Senator McGovern was nominated for the presidency in 1972, Strauss resigned his position as treasurer to allow a McGovern appointee to take his place. He remained loyal to the Democratic Party, however, and became the chairman of the National Committee to Re-Elect a Democratic Congress. In that capacity he raised more than $1 million for Democratic congressional candidates.

When McGovern was defeated in the 1972 election by Richard M. Nixon, Strauss was chosen by the divided Democratic Party to be chairman of the Democratic National Committee. As one who had backed Lyndon B. Johnson and the Vietnam War, Strauss was initially anathema to McGovern supporters, who believed he was the candidate of the "old guard." He quickly moved to assuage their doubts and conciliated the disparate elements in the Party, using persuasion and charm in addition to developing a well-managed organization. He named a black and a woman as committee vice chairpersons. He invited McGovern backers to help rewrite the party charter and set about to mend the wounds in the Democratic Party by talking to everybody in every wing of the party.

While he was chairman of the Democratic National Committee, Strauss brought suit against President Nixon's Committee to Re-Elect the President for burglarizing the Democratic Party's national headquarters in connection with the Watergate scandal. He won an award of $775,000 and an admission of guilt by the Republicans.

When Jimmy Carter was elected president in 1976, Strauss became the U.S. special trade representative, a position with the rank of cabinet officer, and the administration's chief troubleshooter. He served as special negotiator for the Middle East talks but left that position to become the campaign manager for President Jimmy Carter's unsuccessful bid for reelection in 1980.

In 1981 President Carter awarded Strauss the Medal of Freedom, the nation's highest civilian award.

ARTHUR OCHS SULZBERGER

b. February 5, 1926
Newspaper publisher

Under Arthur O. Sulzberger's leadership, *The New York Times* has become America's—if not the world's—most creative as well as the most influential daily newspaper. He has also made The New York Times Company into a public, highly profitable venture. In addition to the newspaper, it also owns several publishing companies and radio stations, a few newspapers outside of New York and two paper mills in Canada.

Arthur Ochs Sulzberger was born in New York City to Arthur Hays Sulzberger, the *Times'* publisher, and Iphigene (Ochs) Sulzberger, both descendants of very wealthy German-Jewish families that had settled in New York generations earlier. As a child he was nicknamed "Punch" to go with his next-older sister's "Judy"; the nickname stuck.

An undistinguished academic career in several private schools ended with Sulzberger's enlistment in the Army in 1944. He claims the military was good for him since it provided the discipline he lacked as a student. When he left the Army in 1946, he entered Columbia University and graduated with a B.A. degree in English in 1951. Following reserve duty in Korea, he joined *The New York Times* briefly in 1953 as a cub reporter and then spent one year with *The Milwaukee Journal*. When he returned to New York and the *Times* in 1954, he was there to stay. His positions ranged from reporter on the foreign news desk to stints as correspondent in London, Paris and Rome. In 1958 he returned again to New York and became assistant treasurer.

There was never any question that Sulzberger, the youngest of four children and the only son, would some day take over the *Times*. His grandfather, Adolph Ochs, had purchased the floundering paper in 1896 and turned it into a successful daily. His father, Arthur Hays Sulzberger, took the helm in 1935 and presided over the *Times'* ascent into New York's number one paper. The only real question about "Punch" Sulzberger's assuming the top post was when; it happened sooner than planned.

Upon Sulzberger's father's retirement in 1961, the

post of publisher and president went to Sulzberger's brother-in-law, Orville Dryfoos. Dryfoos' sudden death 2½ years later left an unexpected vacancy, which the younger Sulzberger was called to fill in 1963. He was only 37.

He rose to the occasion. Faced with a major strike (it lasted 114 days), Sulzberger proved an able manager and a shrewd negotiator. In the succeeding years he reorganized executive staffing and introduced many changes to the *Times*. Bringing in as executive editor A. M. Rosenthal, a distinguished journalist who had won many awards for overseas reporting with the *Times*, Sulzberger headed a paper that would sacrifice advertising revenues to print complete presidential speeches and judicial decisions as well as the entire text of the Warren Commission Report on the assassination of President Kennedy. Earlier, Sulzberger had resisted President Kennedy's pressure to transfer David Halberstam out of Vietnam because of the reporter's critical accounts of U.S. involvement there. Sulzberger was ultimately responsible for the publication of the Pentagon Papers in the *Times* in 1971, and it was he who sent Sydney Schanberg to Cambodia in 1976 during the mass evacuation of Cambodians from cities into the rural countryside—which resulted in mass death. Both efforts earned Pulitzer Prizes for the paper. Sulzberger also increased coverage of religion, sports and women's issues.

In 1976 he began a major overhaul of the *Times* "look," introducing the successful "Weekend" section, which appears on Friday. Eventually he led the innovation of a four-section daily newspaper, now copied by dailies throughout the United States, with special weekly sections devoted to sports, science, "living" and the home in addition to "Weekend." Consequently, the *Times'* circulation has grown consistently, as has advertising lineage, and it remains one of the most profitable newspapers in the world.

A history of *The New York Times*, including Sulzberger's early years there, is chronicled in Gay Talese's *The Kingdom and the Power* (New York, 1969) and Harrison Salisbury's *Without Fear or Favor* (New York, 1980).

DAVID SUSSKIND

b. December 19, 1920
Producer

The multi-talented, energetic David Susskind, known as an outspoken television talk show host and moderator, is also widely known as a producer of dozens of television programs, motion pictures and Broadway shows.

He is one of the most influential personalities in the media.

David Susskind was born in New York City to Benjamin, an insurance man, and Frances (Lear) Susskind. The oldest of three children, he grew up in Brookline, Massachusetts. After graduation from Brookline High School—where he edited the school paper—Susskind went to the University of Wisconsin, where he stayed for two years. In 1940 Susskind transferred to Harvard College, majoring in economics, government and history. He graduated cum laude with a B.S. degree in 1942.

In 1946, after serving in the United States Navy, he "settled on show business as the most dynamic and interesting field I could get into," he once explained. He became a press agent for Warner Brothers studio and in 1947 went to Universal in the same capacity. Soon frustrated by the demands of the field, Susskind decided to become a talent agent and, with Alfred Levy, formed Talent Associates Ltd., which produced programs for the new television industry. In 1952 he was hired as producer of the Philco TV Playhouse, a one-hour drama series.

From then on he began to amass a long list of television credits, which included works by some of America's major playwrights and adaptations of modern American literature. In many cases these were not popular works designed for a mass audience but highly sophisticated dramatic series or specials using top-notch actors and the highest production quality Susskind could get. Susskind's productions seldom attracted large audiences and high ratings, but they received much critical acclaim, and he won many awards. During the 1950s and 1960s, he produced the series *Kraft Theater*, *Armstrong Circle Theater*, *Kaiser Aluminum Hour* and *Play of the Week*. Some of the individual dramas Susskind produced for *Hallmark Hall of Fame* were Arthur Miller's *The Crucible* (1972), *The Price* (1971) and *Death of a Salesman* (1973). Others include *Look Homeward, Angel* (1972), *The Glass Menagerie* (1973), *Eleanor and Franklin* (which won 12 Emmy Awards in 1976), *Harry Truman: Plain Speaking* (1976), *Johnny We Hardly Knew Ye* (1977) and *The War Between the Tates* (1977).

Susskind produced his first motion picture, *Edge of the City*, starring Sidney Poitier and John Cassavetes, in 1959 and has followed with many others, such as *Raisin in the Sun* (1960), *Lovers and Other Strangers* (1970), *Alice Doesn't Live Here Anymore* (1974), *All Things Bright and Beautiful* (1976) and the controversial *Fort Apache—The Bronx* (1981). The latter film, which depicted the physical and human devastation of the South Bronx, aroused the ire of its residents, who claimed that the movie only portrayed one aspect of an otherwise lively, if struggling, community. On Broadway, Susskind has produced *A Very Special Baby* (1956), *Rashomon* (1959), *Kelly* (1965), *All in Good Time* (1965), *Brief Lives* (1967) and *Mr. Lincoln* (1980).

Despite all of his producing credits, Susskind is perhaps more famous as an opinionated television moderator. He was host of the popular talk show *Open End* from 1958 to 1967, where guests like Nikita Khrushchev, Bertrand Russell, Harry Truman and Adlai Stevenson made international headlines as Susskind continued to probe the famous with a series of provocative and irreverent questions. Since 1967 he has produced and hosted a televised discussion program, *The David Susskind Show,* in which all questions, especially those usually hidden from sight until recently—interracial marriage, sex, abortion, etc.—are discussed with candor.

In 1979 Susskind was at the center of a dispute with writer Eliot Asinof, who claimed that Susskind had bought the rights to a book by Asinof and intended to turn it into a television program in violation of an agreement with the author. A lawsuit followed, which resulted in Susskind's withdrawing from the project and a book by Asinof describing what happened, called *Bleeding Between the Lines* (New York, 1979).

Susskind is the recipient of numerous Television Critics Circle Awards and Sylvania Television Awards. He has also won the Peabody Television Award, the Robert Sherwood Award, the Newspaper Guild Award and the Christopher Award.

ELIZABETH SWADOS

b. February 5, 1951
Composer; writer; director

Since receiving a *Village Voice* Obie in 1971 at the age of 20 for her musical score for the off-off Broadway production of *Medea,* Elizabeth Swados has moved steadily toward a successful career as one of the most original and prolific composers, dramatists, directors and writers in non-traditional American theater. In addition to writing for other directors, she has also achieved renown as the creator of the 1978 show *Runaways,* which was a hit not only off-Broadway, but which also enjoyed a Broadway run, and *Haggadah* (1980), produced annually at Joseph Papp's Public Theater in New York City.

Elizabeth Swados was born in Buffalo, New York to Robert O., an attorney, and Sylvia (Maisel) Swados, an actress and poet. Music, art and literature were basic ingredients in her background; both parents were deeply committed to the arts, both professionally and as a

pastime, and the novelist and journalist Harvey Swados was a second cousin.

With the creativity, however, came intensity and anguish in Swados' family as she grew up. Her mother, who had abandoned an artistic career to raise her family, committed suicide when her daughter was quite young—but, as Swados later commented, "people in my family have gone both ways—off the deep end, or, like my father, using his energy to accomplish things, to be productive and giving. It's a fight. It's probably made me stronger than most people who come from sedate families."

Swados' penchant for creativity and experimentation appeared in early childhood, and she took piano and guitar lessons and wrote short stories. She entered Bennington College in 1967 majoring in writing and music, and while there studied Oriental musical forms. She also fell in with many of the trends of the late 1960s; her own early childhood rebelliousness flowered into a more political rebellion, and her lifestyle became one of constant change and experiment. According to one account, she tried drugs, communal living, spiritualism and vegetarianism. She also indulged her idealism, and spent time tutoring, organizing and working for several months in a poverty program in Appalachia as part of her college education.

But composing remained Swados' first love, and she left Bennington around 1970 to write for the experimental La Mama Experimental Theater Club in New York City's East Village. There she met the Rumanian-born director Andrei Serban, who became a mentor of sorts, and collaborated with him on an adaptation of *Medea.* Drawing on Serban's perception of the play, Swados created a score which required the actors to "sing" the play in ancient Greek and Latin, using rhythms and accents based on ancient patterns which added to the dramatic and ritualistic "feel" of the play. (Bennington later granted Swados a degree, after she submitted the *Medea* score as her senior thesis.)

Swados' debut as composer was auspicious; in 1971 her score earned for her a *Village Voice* Obie. But more than that, it paved the way for a broader and more visible career in avant-garde theater. Although Swados worked often with Serban at the beginning of her career, she also seized the opportunity to join other directors. For several months not long after she received her Obie, she toured Africa as musical director and composer with director Peter Brook's Paris-based International Theater Group and later worked with Hispanic troupes, Native Americans and the National Theater for the Deaf in the United States. In each instance, she picked up dramatic styles and influences which she used in her own work. She also rejoined Serban and composed scores for *Electra* in 1973, which premiered in Bordeaux, France, and *The Trojan Women* in 1974, for La Mama. Each new production incorporated amalgams of earlier musical experiences Swados had encountered. Actors working with her also had to expand their performing range as they inevitably were introduced to new languages, styles and sounds.

In 1976, after further collaboration with Serban, Swados created her own original production, *Nightclub Cantata,* a collection of songs and poetry, some original and some drawn from contemporary poets including Pablo Neruda and Sylvia Plath, and performed by a small musical ensemble in which she also performed. After a successful out-of-town debut, the show opened off-Broadway in New York in early 1977. Later that year Swados joined Serban once again, composing the score for a mounting of Chekhov's *The Cherry Orchard* and creating the music for a production of *Agamemnon.* Both plays, which were produced by Joseph Papp at the Vivian Beaumont Theater at Lincoln Center were received with mixed reviews. Apparently the avant-garde styles and inventive visions of Swados and Serban didn't work in an "establishment"-like theater such as the Beaumont.

Yet Swados persisted. With support from Papp, she created her first large-scale production, a show of songs and monologues called *Runaways* which was designed to capture the crises, anxiety, freshness, desolation, hopefulness and sometimes desperation of teenage existence. Using a mostly unprofessional cast which she personally recruited, Swados directed the show herself and explored such topics as drug use, child abuse and conflict with parents and loneliness. The show opened in Papp's Public Theater Cabaret in March 1978 to such critical acclaim that two months later it reopened on Broadway where larger audiences could be accommodated.

Runaways garnered five Tony nominations for Swados as well as a new following and the opportunity to create more original productions. Her next, opening in 1979, was an off-Broadway presentation of *Dispatches,* an adaptation of the Michael Herr book of the same name containing accounts of the fighting in Vietnam. That show, and the one that followed it, a 1980 production of *Alice in Concert,* loosely based on *Alice in Wonderland,* did not earn good reviews, as some critics complained her work was too complicated, obscure or unpredictable. A 1982 show, *Lullabye and Goodnight,* which explored the relationship between a prostitute and her pimp, likewise earned lukewarm reviews. *Haggadah* is a musical version of the events surrounding Passover, written and produced with imagination and verve.

In every way unconventional and adventurous, Swados took a new turn, and in 1982 published a first novel,

Leah and Lazar (New York), a semi-autobiographical account of a young writer's childhood and young adulthood, from its isolated beginnings in upstate New York and the constant conflicts with an older, sometimes mad and suicidal brother that affect almost everything she does, to her college years at Bennington and through a hippie life in her 20s in New York's East Village.

Swados has also written a children's book, *The Girl with the Incredible Feeling* (New York, 1977), which later became the title of a short film about Swados made by independent filmmaker Linda Fefferman.

MARIE SYRKIN

b. March 22, 1899
Writer; Zionist

Marie Syrkin is one of the world's most important Labor Zionists. A journalist, editor and poet, with strong pro-Israel views, she has been profoundly influenced by such preeminent Socialist Zionists as Ahad Ha'am, A.D. Gordon, Leon Pinsker, and her father, another noted Zionist.

Marie Syrkin was born in Bern, Switzerland to Nachman and Basya (Osnos) Syrkin. She immigrated with her family to America in 1907 and was naturalizd in 1915. Syrkin received her B.A. degree from Cornell University in 1920 and her M.A. degree in English, also from Cornell, in 1922.

From 1925 until 1950 Syrkin was an English teacher in New York City high schools. But it was as a Zionist that she became especially known; in fact, people say that Syrkin never *became* a Zionist because she was *born* one. Her father was one of Labor Zionism's founders and one of the great theorists of Socialist-Zionist ideology and the pioneers of the Second Aliyah in Palestine. She followed in his distinguished footsteps, but she made her own mark in Zionism and on Zionist thought in subsequent years and went far beyond merely being her father's daughter.

She has been a lifetime member of the Labor Zionist Organization of America and the Labor Zionist Alliance. She edited the *Jewish Frontier,* the journal of the Labor Zionists in America, for close to 25 years, starting in 1948. She has also been the confidante of Golda Meir and other Israeli leaders. From 1964 until 1968 she served on the executive board of the Jewish Agency and was also a member of the World Zionist Executive. She also serves on the editorial board of *Midstream,* the magazine published by the Herzl Foundation and a leading voice of Zionism in the United States.

In 1950, upon retiring from high school teaching,

Syrkin joined the faculty of Brandeis University as an associate professor of English. Brandeis, the first secular university sponsored by the Jewish community, was then only two years old. In 1966 she was named professor emeritus of humanities at the university.

Syrkin's books on Jewish subjects have always drawn on the passion of Jewish survival and the need to create a world free of hatred. (As a noted educator she has also written books about children and schools.) In 1947 she edited the diaries of Hannah Senesh, the Jewish World War II martyr, and wrote an introductory essay. They were published as *Blessed Is the Match* (New York, 1947), whose title comes from a line of a poem by Senesh extolling those whose lives are extinguished in the cause of liberty and freedom; in it Syrkin explored the resistance movement as a whole as well as the life of Senesh.

After Syrkin published *Way of Valor* (New York, 1955), about the early pioneers in Israel and particularly Golda Meir, she wrote two biographies. The first was a warm portrait of her father, *Nachman Syrkin: Socialist Zionist; A Biographical Memoir and Selected Essays* (New York, 1961). In 1964 Syrkin wrote the sympathetic *Golda Meir: Woman with a Cause* (New York). The book reflected Syrkin's intimate relationship with one of Israel's greatest leaders. Written before Meir returned to active political life in 1968, it was subsequently updated. Syrkin also edited *A Land of Our Own—Speeches of Golda Meir* (New York, 1973).

In 1978 Syrkin published *Gleanings* (Santa Barbara), a collection of her own poetry and essays. This volume was warmly received by critics and shows the breadth and depth of Syrkin's involvement with the Jewish community and with the world at large. She remains the respected elder stateswoman of Zionism.

For further information:

Syrkin, Marie. *The State of the Jews.* Washingto, D.C.: 1980.

THOMAS SZASZ

b. April 15, 1920
Psychiatrist; professor, writer

Throughout his controversial career as a psychiatrist, Thomas Szasz has been called everything from a "crank and a paranoid to a prophet and passionate humanitarian." His work in the defense of the civil rights of the mentally ill and his attempts to redefine the concept of illness so that people are not wrongfully and involuntarily committed to long hospitalizations have aroused the ire and praise of psychiatrists, politicians and groups on the left and right of the profession.

Thomas Tephen Szasz was born in Budapest, Hungary to affluent, landowning parents, Julius and Lily (Wellisch) Szasz. He attended the Royal Hungarian Training Institute, graduating in 1938. The Szasz family moved to the United States to escape the threat of nazism. Szasz attended the University of Cincinnati, graduating with a B.A. degree in 1941. He then studied at the College of Medicine there and was awarded an M.D. in 1944. He was at the top of his class. An internship in Boston was followed in 1945 by a return to Cincinnati, where he became the assistant resident at Cincinnati General Hospital.

Szasz's major work began in Chicago, where he relocated in 1946. There he trained in psychiatry and psychoanalysis at the Chicago Institute for Psychoanalysis and began formulating the theories that would place him in the center of the controversies that have continued to the present. Since 1956 Szasz has been at the Upstate Medical Center in Syracuse, New York, where he has a large following of students and fellow psychiatrists as well as a private practice.

Szasz has been controversial in medical circles because of his deliberate challenge to psychiatric traditions. In *The Ethics of Psychoanalysis: The Theory and Method of Autonomous Psychotherapy* (New York, 1965) he believes that the whole concept of psychotherapy must be changed from one where the patient is led and manipulated by the analyst to one where both patient and analyst are equal in a journey toward greater understanding and therefore toward freedom for the patient.

And in *The Myth of Mental Illness: Foundations of a Theory of Personal Conduct* (New York, 1961), he has raised the issue of drug use in treatment of mental illness by contending that what doctors refer to as "mental illness" is not "illness" or "disease" at all and therefore does not require medication.

"Mental illness" to Szasz is a secular myth. Just as witchcraft was dreamed up by a priestly class, so mental illness is fashioned by psychiatrists and allied professionals to rationalize society's persecution of the helpless. All the term does, he argues, is lend scientific respectability and alleged objectivity to their work. What he proposes is distinguishing between being sick and being a patient—one an abnormal psychological condition and the other a status. They are different, he contends. By ignoring the distinction, society can control its unorthodox and troublesome people.

In *Ceremonial Chemistry: The Ritual Persecution of Drugs, Addicts and Pushers* (New York, 1974), Szasz analyzes the drug problems through the roles of drug pushers and drug users within the context of modern society. But he also relates it to historical needs, in which addicts become scapegoats, just as medieval Inquisitors sought heretics, and the Nazis, in their turn, sought Jews. "The facts are," concludes Szasz the libertarian, "that some people want to take drugs which others do not want them to take."

As a result of his writing, teaching and practice, Szasz has also become a pioneer in the movement for the civil rights of mental patients and has been recognized by his supporters as one of the great humanists of the modern age.

In 1970 Szasz helped found the American Association for the Abolition of Involuntary Mental Hospitalization Inc. He is a member of the American Civil Liberties Union and the American Humanists Association. In 1968 he was on the board of governors of the International Academy of Forensic Psychiatry. He has received many awards for his contribution to humanistic improvement, and he lectures widely.

For further information:
Szasz, Thomas. *Ideology and Insanity: Essays on the Psychiatric Dehumanization of Man.* New York: 1970.
————. *The Insanity Plea and the Insanity Verdict.* New York: 1974.
————. *Law, Liberty and Psychiatry.* New York: 1963.
————. *The Manufacture of Madness.* New York: 1970.
————. *The Myth of Psychotherapy.* New York: 1978.
————. *Psychiatric Injustice.* New York: 1965.
————. *Psychiatric Slavery.* New York: 1977.
————. *The Theology of Medicine.* New York: 1977.

TAD SZULC

b. July 25, 1926
Journalist

A foreign affairs and diplomatic reporter for nearly 20 years with *The New York Times* before devoting himself to free-lance writing, Tad Szulc has used his journalistic skill and insights to demystify Latin America, Eastern Europe and even domestic intrigues for American readers. Because of the breadth of his experiences— Szulc was in Latin America during Fidel Castro's triumphant takeover of Cuba and was based in Czechoslovakia during the "Prague Spring" and turmoil of 1968—he has brought to his reporting an unusual first-hand knowledge of how oppressed people act under pressure, of what makes dictatorships flourish, and how political

leaders create new weapons—such as their manipulation of oil—as pawns in their power struggles.

Tad Szulc was born on July 25, 1926, in Warsaw, Poland, to Seweryn Szulc and Janina (Baruch) Szulc. His family left Poland and from 1943 to 1945, Szulc studied at the University of Brazil. His reporting career began in 1945, when he worked as an Associated Press reporter in Rio de Janeiro. In 1947 he came to the United States and from 1949 to 1953 he was United Nations correspondent for United Press International. He was naturalized in 1954.

Szulc joined the *Times* in 1953 and two years later became the paper's Latin American correspondent, a post he held through 1961. The boiler-pot quality of many Latin American nations led him, in addition to his extensive reporting, to write his first book, *Twilight of the Tyrants* (New York, 1959), a searching portrait of five South American dictators which predicted that their era of dominance was over. In 1962 Szulc coauthored with Karl E. Meyer a history of Castro's revolution in the Caribbean island, *The Cuban Invasion* (New York).

After leaving his Latin American post, Szulc joined the *Times'* Washington bureau, serving from 1961 to 1965 and later from 1969 to 1972. He went overseas in 1965, for three years as the correspondent in Spain and Portugal, and from 1968 to 1969 as a reporter in Eastern Europe. In addition to his dispatches from the Iberian peninsula, Szulc was one of several journalists who wrote book-length accounts of an incident in Spain in which a United States military jet literally lost an H-bomb somewhere off the Spanish coast. His account, which detailed the bizarre events leading to the ominous error, was entitled *The Bombs of Palomares* (New York, 1967).

But one of Szulc's most important books emerged from his experiences in Prague, during which he witnessed the dramatic liberalization of that Iron Curtain country under the daring but brief rule of Alexander Dubcek, who attempted to bring a semblance of democracy to the Czech people. But when the Russians invaded the country in 1968 and squelched all opportunities for freedom of expression and participation in political decision-making, Szulc was expelled for his detailed dispatches recounting the Russians' seizure of Prague. He later drew on his experiences to write *Czechoslovakia Since World War II* (New York, 1971), which, although a history, focused on the events of 1968.

In 1972 Szulc left the *Times* to become a free-lance writer and commentator on foreign policy, publishing articles in such periodicals as *The New Yorker, Foreign Policy, The New York Times* and others, and writing books, which ranged in subject from personality profiles to analyses of international and domestic politics.

One of these books was *The Compulsive Spy: The Strange Career of E. Howard Hunt* (New York, 1974), which used the biography of one of the most intriguing culprits in the Watergate break-in to frame a story of the events that led to this scandal.

The same year Szulc also published *The Energy Crisis* (New York), an exploration of the petroleum industry and its political uses, particularly during the oil shortage of 1973 and 1974. In another of his political analyses, *The Illusion of Peace: Foreign Policy in the Nixon Years* (New York, 1978), Szulc chronicled the exploits of the Nixon-Kissinger team in resolving the Vietnam and Middle Eastern conflicts during Nixon's administration, the events leading to and during summits in the Soviet Union and China, and the beginning of the SALT talks.

Szulc tried his hand at fiction writing in 1981, with the publication of his first novel, *Diplomatic Immunity* (New York). Set in a Latin American dictatorship and focusing on an American woman ambassador who finds herself drawn to a revolutionary leader in that country, the novel describes how the ambassador becomes tangled in a complicated web including the CIA, which supports the dictator, and the White House, which seeks his ouster.

Szulc's magazine articles reflect his mastery of complex political issues and his ability to explain them in clear and simple language. A Spring 1975 article in *Present Tense*, "Arms and Men in the Persian Gulf: Who's Doing What to Whom and Why?" described how, since early 1973, billions of dollars of war material swelled the armed forces—and tensions—in an already volatile region in which oil became what Szulc has called "the overwhelming factor in the Persian Gulf equation." He continued: "Virtually all the Persian Gulf countries are oil producers, and their new and spectacular wealth is based on the quadrupling of its prices since 1974. Oil pays for the extraordinary arms purchases by the Gulf nations and the control and protection of oil colors all Gulf politics." As part of the piece, Szulc presented analyses of the opposing roles of the Iranian government and the Saudis, and how their mutual antagonism reflected that of the Soviet Union and the United States. Because of recession which left many Americans jobless in America in 1974, Szulc speculated that the federal government might promote a defense buildup in the Persian Gulf as a means to strengthen the defense industry and create more employment opportunities. Already, he commented in the article, "the United States has become the world's leading arms merchant. The major countries of the Persian Gulf thirsting for more and more weapons, are its principal clients. The time has come to review the wisdom of this policy, or we may live to regret it. And the first test may well come in the Middle East if a new war erupts and Israel bears the brunt of attacks by Arabs armed with weapons Made in the USA."

In another, very different article, Szulc profiled Simon Wiesenthal, the elderly Nazi-hunter, concentration camp survivor and fighter for the rights of political prisoners regardless of religion, for a 1977 issue of *New York* magazine. "To be sure, Wiesenthal, who is almost 69 and has a bad heart, still hunts for Nazi criminals hiding around the world because, he says, this quest must never cease so long as the last of the killers remains alive," Szulc wrote. "Thus he still receives death threats, and when we recently met in Vienna, Wiesenthal matter-of-factly showed me the black snub-nosed pistol he always carries in the pocket of his gray overcoat. His house is protected by laser beams." Later Szulc quotes Wiesenthal in one of the most telling sentences of the story.

> I've met American Jews who say, "I'm not a survivor, but I'll support you." I answer: "You *are* a survivor. Hitler's program was to kill all the Jews. If he had won the war, it would have been the same in America as in Europe." Hitler said, "First, give me the Jews," and in every country there were people who gave him these Jews. The French police, the Croatian police, the Slovaks, and so on. And in your country such people would be found too. Because Hitler lost the war, you *are* a survivor. . . . Even those born after the war are survivors.

For further information:

Szulc, Tad. *Dominican Diary*. New York: 1965.
———. *Innocents at Home*. New York: 1974.
———. *Latin America*. New York: 1965
———. *Portrait of Spain*. New York: 1972.
———. *United States and the Caribbean*. Englewood Cliffs, N.J.: 1971.
———. *The Winds of Revolution*. New York: 1963 and 1965.

MARC TANENBAUM

b. October 13, 1925
Rabbi

Rabbi Marc Tanenbaum, director of interreligious affairs of the American Jewish Committee, is one of the nation's best-known and most influential religious leaders. Active in numerous human rights organizations, an ardent advocate of promoting dialogue between Christians and Jews, Tanenbaum has been described by *New York* magazine as "the foremost Jewish leader in the world today."

Marc Tanenbaum was born in Baltimore, Maryland to Abraham and Sadie (Siger) Tanenbaum, who operated a small general store. He received his B.A. degree in biological sciences from Yeshiva University in 1946 and his master's degree in Hebrew Literature and rabbinical ordination from the Jewish Theological Seminary of America in 1950. Tanenbaum was rabbi of the Northeast Hebrew Congregation in Washington, D.C. from 1951 to 1952 and the Jewish Center of the Mahopacs from 1952 to 1954 and was executive director of the Synagogue Council of America from 1954 to 1960. Since 1960 he has been director of interreligious affairs of the American Jewish Committee.

Long interested in humanitarian causes, he has supported the black Christians in Uganda, Biafra, the Sudan, South Africa and Rhodesia; the Vietnamese boat people and Indochinese refugees; the victims of the civil war in Northern Ireland; and the Jews in the Soviet Union—all of whom have been threatened by oppression and repression. "We Jews have learned one permanent universal lesson from the Nazi trauma," he says in one of hundreds of lectures he makes annually. "And that lesson is a paraphrase from the Book of Leviticus—'You shall not stand idly by while the blood of your brothers and sisters cries out to you from the earth.'"

Dedicated to building understanding between Jews and other religious groups, Tanenbaum is the founder and co-secretary of the Joint Vatican International Jewish Consultative Committee. He was the only rabbi at Vatican Council II in 1964, where he was consulted by Catholic and Protestant authorities during deliberations that led to the Vatican Declaration on Non-Christian Relations, which repudiated anti-Semitism and called for fraternal dialogue between Christians and Jews. In March 1979 he joined other world Jewish leaders in meeting with Pope John Paul II in Vatican City. But he also openly criticized the Pope, saying he thinks Pope John Paul II "needs a good basic course in Judaism." (The Vatican does not recognize Israel.)

Tanenbaum aroused a great deal of controversy in October 1980 when he met with the Reverend Jerry Falwell, the evangelical minister and leading spokesperson for the conservative Christian organization the Moral Majority, and has since maintained a regular dialogue with him. Explaining his move, Tanenbaum wrote:

My concern when Falwell started his movement in 1979 was that his first preachment was to start a Christian republic, which means to vote for born-again Christians only. I knew that if that was allowed to go on uncontested, and were to become institutionalized as the message of the movement, it could have been a disaster for the Jews and a greater disaster for America. Setting that up as a viable option for American life could have led to a kind of fascism.

As a result of his meeting with Falwell, at the latter's request, Falwell declared publicly that his group was opposed to the establishment of a Christian republic and that it did indeed support religious pluralism. He also asserted an abiding support for Israel. At the same time, however, Tanenbaum lent his name to Norman Lear's group, People for the American Way, which was formed specifically to combat the Moral Majority.

He has contributed articles to several books, including *American Religious Values and the Future of America* (Philadelphia, 1978), a collection of essays discussing the American religious experience, and *Torah and Gospel: Jewish and Catholic Theology in Dialogue* (New York, 1966), in which Tanenbaum asserts that the church and synagogue are major agencies of social reform and can provide Americans with a source of values and an awareness of moral responsibility.

In addition, he has edited a number of books, including *Speaking of God Today: Jews and Lutherans in Conversation* (Philadelphia, 1974), in which leading Jews and Lutheran scholars explore such issues as the Holocaust, law and grace in Judaism and Lutheranism, and concepts of "the promised land" and "the chosen people." Tanenbaum also edited (with A. James Rudin and Marvin Wilson) *Evangelicals and Jews in Conversation: On Scripture, Theology and History* (Grand Rapids, Michigan, 1978), in which he contends that Christians and Jews have a moral and social responsibility to establish on a global basis "a new humanism"—to restore biblical value to the "preciousness of each human life." He asserts that Christians and Jews should use their humanistic ideology to combat social injustice and to create a world of peace.

A pioneer in race relations, Tanenbaum helped found during the 1960s the National Conference on Race and Religion, which mobilized religious forces in the civil rights struggle. He has also served on various United Nations committees. He was vice chairman of the White House Conference on Children and Youth in 1960 and vice chairman of the White House Conference on Aging in 1961. He is a member of the Rabbinical Assembly of America.

A 1978 poll of the editors of America's religious newspapers published in the *Christian Century* voted Marc Tanenbaum "one of the 10 most respected and influential religious leaders in America"—after Billy Graham, Martin Marty and Jimmy Carter.

In conformity with that belief, he publicly criticized the Reverend Billy Graham, following the evangelist's 1982 visit to Moscow in which he said that he had not seen evidence of religious persecution in the USSR. Tanenbaum said Graham's "rambling, naive comments have hurt him and damaged his credibility."

HENRY TAUB

b. September 20, 1927
Business executive; Jewish communal leader

When Henry Taub became president of the American Jewish Joint Distribution Committee in 1980, he capped a lifetime of involvement in Jewish affairs. A highly successful businessman in addition to being a Jewish activist, he co-founded Automatic Data Processing Inc., an international company providing computer services to corporations.

Henry Taub was born in Paterson, New Jersey to Morris and Sylvia (Sievitz) Taub. He studied at New York University, where he received a B.S. degree in 1947, with training in accountancy. In 1949 he formed his own business, Automatic Payroll, Inc. in a Paterson, New Jersey storefront, in which he tabulated payrolls for area companies. The business grew steadily, and 12 years later Taub introduced computers to his operation. Automatic Data Processing, as the company was renamed, eventually expanded into the largest and most successful independent computer service bureau in the United States. With headquarters in Clifton, New Jersey, the company has 50 bureaus throughout the United States and overseas. Taub has shared management of ADP with Frank Lautenberg, a businessman who, like Taub, has been a major contributor to Jewish causes.

Taub's Jewish activism dates from his teen years, when he became vice chairperson of the Young Adult Division for the UJA campaign sponsored by the Paterson, New Jersey YM and YWHA. In those days he had few resources to contribute to Jewish causes besides time. In an interview he explained, "Like other young students, I couldn't give much more than my time, but those were the heady days of the birth of Israel, and the enormity of the Holocaust was fresh in our minds." But with the subsequent success of ADP, Taub was able to combine substantial philanthropy with activism. In addition to his JDC post, Taub is president of the Jewish Community Center of Englewood (New Jersey) and has held executive positions with the American Friends of

Hebrew University, the American Friends of the Technion and the national board of United Jewish Appeal.

The American Jewish Joint Distribution Committee, to which Taub has contributed so much effort, aids needy Jews in more than 30 countries around the world. Its programs include refugee aid to Soviet Jews during stopovers in Vienna and Rome en route to settlement in Israel or the United States and educational subsidies for Jewish schools in North Africa, Europe and Latin America. It also sponsors projects within Israel, including community center development throughout the country and delivery of social service aid in disadvantaged sectors within Jerusalem. The JDC/Brookdale Institute of Gerontology and Adult Human Development in Israel plans programs of long-term care for Israel's aged, and the JDC supports the development of services for the physically and mentally disabled.

Within Eastern Europe JDC has supervised kosher canteens in Rumania and food programs for the elderly and had aided Holocaust survivors and other Jews in small communities in Hungary and Yugoslavia. JDC also participates in support programs for the Falasha Jews in Ethiopia and has provided help for a small Jewish community in India and for four World War II survivors residing in China.

According to Taub, JDC programs are meticulously designed so that resources are used appropriately. "JDC never begins a program without planning for its completion or eventually handing it over to local authorities," he explained in an interview. "This phasing out enables JDC to keep responding to our needs. Thus, JDC acts as a catalyst."

Taub's humanitarian interests also extend beyond the Jewish sphere. He has been chairperson of the New York chapter of the Hemophilia Foundation, is a director of the New York Shakespeare Festival and is a trustee of his alma mater, New York University, and of the Interfaith Hunger Appeal.

EDWARD TELLER

b. January 15, 1908
Nuclear scientist

Edward Teller is known as the "father" of the hydrogen bomb. He was one of six nuclear scientists, including Albert Einstein, who wrote a letter to President Franklin Delano Roosevelt in 1939 urging that the atomic bomb development program be instituted, which led to the Manhattan Project.

Edward Teller was born in Budapest, Hungary, the

son of Max, an attorney, and Ilona (Deutch) Teller. He studied at the Institute of Technology in Budapest and received a degree in chemical engineering from the Institute of Technology in Karlsruhe, Germany in 1928. Excited by the new theory of quantum mechanics, Teller went to Munich to study physical chemistry. In Munich he lost a foot in a streetcar accident. In 1930 he received his Ph.D. from the University of Leipzig.

After being awarded a Rockefeller fellowship in 1934, Teller traveled to Copenhagen to study with Niels Bohr, the father of quantum mechanics. After a year, due to the rise of the Nazis in Germany, Teller went to lecture at the University of London and then became a visiting professor of molecular and atomic physics at George Washington University. He stayed at George Washington until 1941, when he joined the atomic energy research group under the direction of Enrico Fermi at Columbia University.

Teller worked on the atomic bomb project from 1941 until 1946. He stayed with the uranium pile aspect of the project when it moved to Chicago, and then he joined the theoretical studies group under the supervision of Dr. J. Robert Oppenheimer at the University of California at Berkeley. Finally, he moved to Dr. Hans Bethe's theoretical studies division at the atomic research laboratory at Los Alamos, New Mexico.

Teller announced in 1945 that he would only stay with the atomic research program if there were a commitment to test 12 fission weapons a year or if a complete thermonuclear program were instituted. When these demands were not met, he moved to the Nuclear Institute of the University of Chicago. In 1946 he became a professor of physics at the University of Chicago. After the first atomic bomb tests in the Bikini Islands, Teller predicted the eventual dangers of radioactive fallout, and in 1949 he met with English and Canadian scientists to discuss safeguards for nuclear reactors. Nevertheless, he is a strong advocate of nuclear power, for both domestic and military purposes, and is associated with groups such as the American Security Council urging the rearming of America and nuclear superiority over the Soviet Union.

In 1949, after the Russians had succeeded in detonating a nuclear device, Teller returned to Los Alamos to direct the program to develop the hydrogen bomb. He was primarily concerned with the theoretical aspects of the project and did not supervise the actual bomb construction.

Teller became the director of the Atomic Energy Commission research laboratory at Livermore, California in 1952. In 1975 he was made director emeritus of the laboratory and joined the Hoover Institution of War,

Revolution and Peace at Stanford University as a senior research fellow.

He has received honorary degrees from 18 universities and has won the Harvey prize in science and technology and the Albert Einstein award from the Technion. He is a member of the board of governors of Tel Aviv University. An avid supporter of Ronald Reagan during the 1980 election campaign, Teller is also a member of the International Conference for PEACE (an acronym for Preventing Emergence of Another Arab Country in Judea, Samaria and Gaza), a group supporting Israeli settlements on the West Bank and Gaza.

Teller has written four books. The first was called *The Structure of Matter* (New York, 1948). His latest book is *The Constructive Uses of Nuclear Explosives* (New York, 1969), an outline of some industrial uses for atomic power.

STUDS TERKEL

b. May 16, 1912
Oral historian

In his best-selling books oral historian Studs Terkel has been a unique recorder and dramatizer of the thoughts and emotions of thousands of anonymous Americans who might otherwise have been known only as statistics. By listening to those whose voices are rarely heard—blue-collar workers, former slaves, loggers and other less visible citizens—and by transcribing and publishing those tape-recorded conversations, Terkel, who has also been a radio and television personality, sports columnist, playwright, journalist, lecturer and music festival host, has contributed to a greater understanding of American life.

Louis Terkel was born in the Bronx, the third son of Samuel, a tailor, and Anna (Finkel) Terkel. When he was 11 years old, he moved with his family to Chicago, where—after his father became seriously ill—his mother managed a hotel. Terkel has fond memories of talking with local workers who used to meet there for a drink on Saturday nights, an experience that turned out to be the training ground for his later work.

Terkel attended the University of Chicago, where he received a Ph.B. degree in 1932 and a law degree from the same school two years later. Disenchanted with the law by the time he graduated, he took a government job in Washington, D.C. and relieved his boredom by acting in the Washington Civic Theater. In 1935 he returned to Chicago, where he acted in radio shows and theater productions and renamed himself "Studs" after Studs Lonigan, the hero of James T. Farrell's best-selling novel about Chicago's working Irish during the Depression.

From the 1940s to the mid-1960s, Terkel's career was centered in media. He became an established voice on radio, starred in a television program called *Stud's Place* (1950–53), and in the 1950s and 1960s wrote a jazz column for the *Chicago Sun-Times* and a book called *The Giants of Jazz* (New York, 1957). In 1959 he wrote a play, *Amazing Grace,* which drew mixed reviews.

Terkel is best-known for his books, which he describes as "simply the adventures of one man equipped with a tape-recorder and badgered by the imp of curiosity . . . trying to search out the thoughts of non-celebrated people . . . thoughts concerning themselves, past and present, the city, the society, the world." *Division Street: America* (New York, 1966) focuses on the feelings of despair among city people; *Hard Times: An Oral History of the Great Depression* (New York, 1970) consists of personal memories of the 1930s; *Working: People Talk About What They Do All Day and How They Feel About What They Do* (New York, 1974) explores Americans' attitudes toward their work. All his books seem to reexamine heroism and seek it among obscure Americans.

American Dreams: Lost and Found (New York, 1980) examines achievement and the loss of power. Here 100 people speak of their hopes and what happened to them. Several are prominent—Joan Crawford, Senator Jesse Helms, Bill Veeck—but the rest are anonymous Americans in all social and economic groups. What is most unsettling about their recollections is the collective sense of disillusionment and frustration about contemporary America, yet it also reveals grassroots struggles against injustice, such as the Kentuckian who battled strip mining and the grandson of a slave who demanded the right to vote in a particularly racist Mississippi district. Commented a former Ku Klux Klan "cyclops," now a union official, to Terkel: "I can understand why people join extreme right-wing or left-wing groups. They're in the same boat I was. Shut out. . . . Nobody listens, so we join these groups."

Terkel has won many awards, including the UNESCO East-West Values Award in 1962 for best radio program, the Prix Italiana and the Communicator of the Year award from the University of Chicago Alumni Association.

For further information:
Terkel, Studs. *Talking to Myself: A Memoir of My Times.* New York: 1977.

LAURENCE A. TISCH

b. March 5, 1923
Financier; businessman

Financier Laurence Tisch is believed to be one of the shrewdest analysts of the stock market in corporate America. A few hotels he owned were parlayed into a $4 billion corporation that includes Bulova Watch; CNA Financial Corporation; Kent, True and Newport cigarettes; more than 20 hotels; a movie theater group operating over 100 film screens in 26 cities; and a significant portion of the American Broadcasting Company.

Laurence Alan Tisch was born in New York City to Abraham Solomon and Sayde (Brenner) Tisch. The elder Tisch was probably responsible for his son's later string of business successes. Originally a garment manufacturer, Abraham Tisch entered the real estate business and brought his sons Laurence and Preston Robert into it. (Laurence Tisch has continued the family tradition, and two of his four sons work with him.) A high school graduate at 15, Tisch completed a B.A. degree at New York University by 1941 and one year later received a business degree from the University of Pennsylvania's Wharton School of Finance.

Tisch's partnership with his brother proved to be the beginning of a long string of moneymaking successes apart from their business with their father. Their first joint purchase in real estate, the Laurel-in-the-Pines resort in Lakewood, New Jersey, earned them early recognition in business and real estate circles. Good luck has since continued for the two men, who today head one of the country's largest corporations, Loew's, with Laurence Alan Tisch serving as chairman of the board and chief executive of the conglomerate.

Tisch came to Loew's in 1959 as a major stockholder in what was then called Loew's Theaters. He was soon named director of the movie theater chain, which had earlier split from MGM. Under Tisch's leadership Loew's began to move into new ventures including several New York hotels. Over the years the company shifted into its present major investments—tobacco; property, casualty and life insurance; travel; entertainment; and jewelry.

Lorillard, the tobacco arm of the Loew's empire, was acquired during the diversification plan under Tisch's sponsorship in 1968. This acquisition alone nearly quadrupled the revenues of a company whose annual income is in the low billions.

CNA Financial Corp., the property, casualty and life insurance branch of Loew's, was bought in 1974, after Loew's purchased for cash a 57 percent controlling interest—20 million shares—of the company. Tisch serves as chairman of CNA in addition to his chairmanship of the larger corporation.

Despite his always time-consuming responsibilities with Loew's, Tisch has found the time and energy over the past years to be involved with numerous business, civic, cultural and religious organizations. Tisch is a past president of the United Jewish Appeal of New York and of the UJA-Federation Joint Board. He is a member of the board of directors of the American Joint Distribution Committee and is on the American Jewish Committee's board, as well as being a trustee with the Federation of Jewish Philanthropies and president of the Jewish Community Relations Council of New York. Sackler Medical School, affiliated with Tel Aviv University, named Tisch a chairman of the school.

Other organizations with which Tisch is and has been involved include the Whitney Museum of American Art, where he is a trustee and chairman of the museum's finance committee; the American Technion Society, as past president; and the Automatic Data Processing Corp., as a member of the board. Tisch's undergraduate alma mater, New York University, has received numerous gifts from the brothers, one of which paid for the building of Tisch Hall, in memory of their father. Tisch is chairman of the board of trustees at NYU.

ALVIN TOFFLER

b. October 4, 1928
Writer

Alvin Toffler's book *Future Shock* (New York, 1970), which has appeared in 20 languages and sold almost 6 million copies and been applauded as "brilliant . . . prophetic . . . disturbing . . . stimulating . . . profound. . . ." could become the single most influential book in shaping popular notions of the future.

Alvin Toffler was born in New York City to Samuel, a sewing machine operator in the fur industry, and Rose (Albaum) Toffler, two Jewish immigrants from Poland. From his earliest years Toffler dreamed of writing. He received his B.A. degree from New York University in 1949 and then, with his new wife, Heidi, moved to the Middle West.

He worked in Ohio steel mills as a welder and as a millwright. He repaired machines in foundries, drove large trucks, built Chevrolets. His wife became a shop steward in an aluminum foundry. Later he wrote that

for two impressionable young people, the experience was a godsend, showing them firsthand how things were truly manufactured and how harsh the life of working people often was. He recalled:

> One day I carried a sixty-five year old woman out of a punch press in which she had just lost four fingers. She screamed, "Jesus and Mary, I'll never work again." In her agony, with four bleeding stumps, that was all she could think about. You never forget that.

Along the way, he wrote stories he failed to publish but finally succeeded in obtaining a sub-editor's job with a welding magazine. With this initial experience, he went to work for *Labor's Daily,* a daily national newspaper published by the International Typographical Union in West Virginia and later in Iowa as a labor-inspired competitor to the *Wall Street Journal.* The paper was often brilliant if short-lived as its editors and writers struck out time and again at racism and at George Meany, the president of the AFL-CIO. Armed with this added background as features editor, he went to work part-time in Washington, D.C. for a liberal, iconoclastic small town daily, the *York* (Pennsylvania) *Gazette and Daily.* Soon he was free-lancing for a wide variety of publications, such as *The Nation,* the *New Republic* and the *Washington Star.* Together with his regular articles and column for the *Gazette and Daily,* Toffler asserts the experience was "training me, sharpening my craft, preparing me to be a real magazine writer."

He continued to write, especially for *Fortune,* for which he worked and free-lanced as well, into the 1960s, when *Horizon* magazine asked him to write a piece on the future. It was titled "The Future as a Way of Life." In writing it he finally understood what had happened to him and to the culture in which he lived. During one interview he recalled an analogy: "If a person could be dislocated geographically in space, a person could, in effect, be dislocated in time: if one could have 'culture shock' one could also have 'future shock.' That analogy changed my life."

In *Future Shock* he cautioned about the "dizzying disorientation" of too-quick social change in technologically advanced nations. "We are creating a new society," he wrote, "one that will be an age of 'super-industrialism.' " How well that complex era is handled, the extent to which it will permit freedom and individual achievement, depends largely on the large degree of stress caused by assimilating and controlling change." This stress, or "future shock," he insists, is present now.

The Third Wave (New York, 1980) continues Toffler's

thesis in which he offers a measure of hope that despite the prevailing turmoil and chaos, a humane civilization could very well emerge, because of the coming and inevitable decline of the nation-state, the ensuing reconciliation between producer and consumer and the consequent return to production for local use. The *Zurich Neue Zurcher Zeitung* called the book "unquestionably a major work," and the *Washington Post,* in a "rave review," described it as "a magnificent piece of work."

For further information:
Toffler, Alvin. *The Culture Consumers.* New York: 1964.
————. *The Eco-Spasm Report.* New York: 1975.
————. *Learning for Tomorrow.* New York: 1973.
Toffler, Alvin, ed. *The Futurists.* New York: 1972.

BARBARA TUCHMAN

b. January 30, 1912
Historian

Barbara Tuchman, journalist and historian, has become prominent among academically unaffiliated historians. Much of her research is painstakingly amassed in the field as well as in libraries. Her meticulous work, combined with an elegant literary style, is typical of this two-time Pulitzer Prize winner, whose books have explored America's entry into World War I, early contacts with China and prewar European society.

Barbara Wertheim was born in New York City, the daughter of Maurice and Alma (Morgenthau) Wertheim. Her family was distinguished on both sides. Her father was a banker, publisher and eminent philanthropist and from 1941 to 1943 was president of the American Jewish Committee. Her maternal grandfather, Henry Morgenthau Sr., served as U.S. ambassador to Turkey; her uncle, Henry Morgenthau Jr., was Secretary of the Treasury under President Franklin D. Roosevelt; and a cousin, Robert M. Morgenthau, is New York City District Attorney.

Tuchman was graduated from the Walden School in New York and in 1933 received a B.A. degree from Radcliffe College. During her school and college years, she developed a keen interest in history and world affairs. Her honors thesis at Radcliffe was titled "The Moral Justification for the British Empire." Her first job was with the Institute of Pacific Relations; she worked in its office in Tokyo in 1935. Later that year she went to *The Nation,* a magazine that her father then owned, and reported on the Spanish civil war from Madrid in 1937. During the late 1930s she reported on events in the

United States for *The New Statesman and Nation* of London. From 1943 to 1945, the last two years of World War II, she worked on the Far Eastern desk of the Office of War Information.

Tuchman's first major book was *Bible and Sword* (New York, 1956), a detailed analysis of centuries of relations between Palestine and Great Britain, from the Bronze Age through the Crusades and the European Reformation, and on to the present. She contends that the 1917 Balfour Declaration to sanctify a Jewish homeland in Palestine was an attempt by the British to satisfy their conscience and ambition. Her next book, *The Zimmermann Telegram* (New York, 1958), recounts the events that led to America's entry into World War I in 1917. Apparently it was triggered by a telegram sent by German Foreign Minister Arthur Zimmermann proposing that the Mexican government join with Germany and attack the United States as a means of reclaiming Arizona, New Mexico and Texas. The telegram was intercepted by the British, who decoded it, then happily shared it with President Wilson.

Tuchman garnered her first Pulitzer Prize for *The Guns of August* (New York, 1962), a moving and dramatic account of the battles fought during the first 30 days of World War I. As in her previous works, the book evolved only after the most intensive research combined with visits to battle sites. An in-depth look at the factors leading to the Great War was the subject of *The Proud Tower: A Portrait of the World Before the War, 1890–1914* (New York, 1966). In this book Tuchman profiles Anglo-American and Western European society during the 25 years that preceded the calamitous First World War, taking a look at the English aristocracy, various political movements, such as the anarchists then active, and such critical events as the Dreyfus case. Her focus was limited to those experiences most directly related to American culture.

Tuchman received her second Pulitzer Prize for her 1971 book *Stilwell and the American Experience in China, 1911–1945* (New York). Using General Joseph Stilwell, whose dealings with the Chinese government spanned more than three decades, during which both the United States and China underwent immense internal political and social change, she created a model for more sensitive Western attitudes and approaches toward the East.

When Barbara Tuchman embarked on writing a history of 14th-century France, she began by traveling through Picardy and Normandy, retracing the routes that had been followed by her book's main character, the knight Enguerrand de Coucy, so that she could imbibe the sense of mission that had absorbed the knight.

She also followed the routes of the Crusaders, crossed the Alps and then traveled down the Danube to Istanbul, as de Coucy had done six centuries earlier. The resulting work, *A Distant Mirror: The Calamitous 14th Century* (New York, 1978), took Tuchman seven years to research and write and after publication became a critically acclaimed best seller.

Her career, her approaches to history and her technique as a historian are summed up in Tuchman's first book since *A Distant Mirror*. *Practicing History* (New York, 1981) is a collection of essays in which she describes her "Craft" (the first section of the book); her "Yield" (the middle section), a compilation of short pieces covering such subjects as China, Israel and the First World War; and "Learning from History" (the last section), a series of editorial writings drawing on American experiences with Watergate and Vietnam and on the need to look to history for guidance on the future. As in her full-length narrative histories, Tuchman in her essays focuses on the human element—especially human fallibility—as it influences the course of events leading to social upheavals and the catastrophic results of war.

Actively involved in organizations linked to her interests, Tuchman has served as president of the Society of American Historians, council member of the Smithsonian Institution, treasurer of the Authors' Guild and council member of the Authors' League. A winner of the Gold Medal for History of the American Academy and Institute of Arts and Letters in 1978, she became its first woman president in 1979.

ROSALYN TURECK

b. December 14, 1914
Pianist

The American pianist Rosalyn Tureck, the first woman to direct the New York Philharmonic Symphony, is world renowned as a major interpreter of the work of Johann Sebastian Bach and in fact has been dubbed "The First Lady of Bach."

Rosalyn Tureck was born in Chicago to Samuel and Monya (Lipson) Tureck, who came to the United States in the early 1900s. Her father was a Russian of Turkish descent—his original surname was "Turk"—and her mother was Russian-born. Both parents were descended from a long line of rabbis and cantors, and the entire family was very music-oriented. Rosalyn Tureck's musical training began early, and she studied piano, harpsichord, clavichord and organ. At age 4, after imitating her older sister on piano, she was recognized as a prodigy.

By the age of 9 she had made her public debut with two piano recitals in Chicago, and three years later she performed with the Chicago Symphony Orchestra. At 16 she won a four-year fellowship to study at the Juilliard School of Music in New York, where she graduated cum laude in 1935. She appeared in her first New York concert at Carnegie Hall that year, performing Brahms' Concerto in B-Flat Major with the Philadelphia Orchestra, and had her formal recital debut at New York's Town Hall the following year. In 1937 she began her annual concert tours of the United States and Canada.

From 1951 to 1955 Tureck was founder-director of Composers of Today (Society for the Performance of Contemporary Music). But her primary work has always been in presenting the music of Bach; since 1957 she has directed the Tureck Bach Players, and since 1968 she has headed the Institute for Bach Studies. She appears frequently as a soloist with nationally and internationally renowned symphony orchestras, including the Israel Philharmonic and Israel's Kol Israel Orchestra, and as a conductor with the London Philharmonic and New York Philharmonic, both in 1955; the Scottish National Symphony in 1963; the Washington National Symphony in 1970; the Rhode Island Philharmonic in 1977; and many others.

She first performed the complete Preludes and Fugues of Bach's "Well-Tempered Clavier" and the Goldberg Variations, for which she has become famous, in six concerts in Town Hall in 1937, when she was 22 years old. She plays Bach on organ, clavichord, Moog synthesizer and, of course, piano. She told a *New Yorker* writer:

> My piano performance does not imitate the harpsichord performance. However, the basic structure must stand undisturbed for its own sake on either instrument and it dictates the musical characteristics of each variation as well. Thus, in some variations, I retain the same concept on both instruments but achieve it by different means. . . . The idea is to etch the structure of the music, to achieve the quality of the composer's fantasy and vision and always to employ the instrument as a means and never as an end in itself.

She calls her concerts "double-headers" because she usually plays, besides piano, both the clavichord and harpsichord. When she presents the Goldberg Variations, she will often play them through on harpsichord. Then, following a long intermission, she will perform them again on piano.

Tureck realized she had a special talent for Bach while still a teen-ager. She developed a new keyboard technique for Bach centering on touch and phrasing dynamics. "I had to find every inch of the way myself," she has said, "a whole new pattern of thinking, an entirely different physical approach to the keyboard, entirely different ways of using the fingers, new ideals of color and articulation."

Since the mid-1930s Tureck has taught widely at conservatories in the United States and Great Britain. She is the author of the three-volume *An Introduction to the Performances of Bach* (New York, 1960) and numerous articles for such publications as *Current Musicology*, *Hi-Fi Magazine, Making Music* (London), *Music & Letters* (London) and others.

She is an honorary member of the Music Library in the Hebrew University of Jerusalem and the Societe Johann Sebastian Bach de Belgique. She is also the recipient of many awards, including the Phi Beta Kappa award and the Town Hall Endowment Award.

GUS TYLER

b. October 18, 1911
Labor union leader

Gus Tyler, veteran labor union official, is perhaps the most articulate and prolific writer in the union movement of the 20th century. Thoughtful, rooted in the American experience, Tyler continues to write on the future of the American economy and the role of the working class.

Gus Tilve was born in Brooklyn to Samson and Dora (Magid) Tilve, the "descendant of several generations of *magidim,* the unordained itinerant preachers who crisscrossed the east European countryside . . . to hold a dispersed Jewry together with a line of talk. . . ." Both parents were garment workers, his father a sewing machine operator, pattern maker and cutter and his mother a sewing machine operator who started working at the age of 11 and stopped when she married. Tyler was so imbued with working class and labor union loyalty that he wrote that on his bar mitzvah day he gave out literature on behalf of Robert M. LaFollette and Burton K. Wheeler, Progressive Party candidates for the presidency and vice-presidency in 1924.

Tyler graduated from New York University with a B.A. degree in English and mathematics in 1933, although his first love was economics and politics. He worked as an assistant labor editor for the Yiddish daily newspaper, the *Jewish Daily Forward,* and the *Socialist Call* in 1933 and 1934 and then in 1934 began his life's work with the International Ladies Garment Workers' Union where he helped establish a summer school for workers at the University of Wisconsin. In 1942 he left for the air force but once demobilized in 1945, returned to the ILGWU. Thereafter he held a series of jobs in the union

in its education and training departments and in 1963 was named assistant to the president.

Tyler has tried to explain the role of labor in many books and articles. In *The Labor Revolution: Trade Unionism in a New America* (New York, 1967), he outlined the various stages of labor's history—from the period of early craft unions, to the development of industrial unionism, to the efforts after 1960 to recruit the white collar and service trades. Tyler has long been skeptical of the thesis that excludes unionism from the American tradition. In *The Political Imperative: The Corporate Character of Unions* (New York, 1968), he asserts that unions are as much a part of that tradition as are corporations. In *Scarcity: A Critique of the American Economy* (New York, 1976) he blamed corporations and conglomerates for creating artificial scarcities for their own ends and urged increased government regulation, if need be, to control those multinational organizations.

In late November 1981 he began writing a series of articles for *The New Leader* called "Charting America's Future." In them he argued, among other things, that "maximum production, by itself desirable, is not sufficient to fulfill the potential of this country's greatness" and that "the economy has become so complex that it demands a grand design if it is not to degenerate into another Tower of Babel." What was also required to stimulate the economy in the decade ahead, he wrote, was a "redistribution of income and a reallocation of capital," to provide a more substantial home market, raise productivity and assist in "capital formation." For the contemporary working person is as much an investor as consumer. Therefore, legislation should be enacted to encourage middle income wage earners and salaried employees to invest more in banks, mutual funds, pensions and the like. Such a "redistribution of the national income to the people who form the foundation of our economic structure would ultimately provide a market —that indispensable market—for our market economy," Tyler concludes.

For further information:

Tyler, Gus. "Charting America's Future," *The New Leader.* A series of occasional articles beginning on November 30, 1981 and running through November 1982.
———. "Educating the Proletariat: The University and the Labor Union," *Change.* February 1979.
———. *Labor in the Metropolis.* New York: 1972.
———. *A Legislative Campaign for a Federal Minimum Wage: A Case Study in Practical Politics.* New Brunswick, N.J.: 1959.
Tyler, Gus, ed. *Organized Crime in America: A Book of Readings.* Ann Arbor, Mich.: 1962.

LEON URIS

b. August 3, 1924
Novelist; screenwriter

Leon Uris's knack for writing enormously popular historical novels, often with Jewish-based themes, has spelled "best seller" more than a half-dozen times. With his second novel, *Exodus* (New York, 1956), Uris achieved international fame. Largely self-taught—he never finished college—Uris has used his writing to promote his firm dedication to his Jewish roots and to his belief in Zionism.

Leon Marcus Uris—the name is an Anglicization of "Yerushalmi," "man of Jerusalem"—was born in Baltimore, Maryland to Wolf William, a Russian immigrant paperhanger and storekeeper, and Anna (Blumberg) Uris. He was raised in poor Jewish neighborhoods in Baltimore, Norfolk and Philadelphia. He attended Baltimore City College in 1941 but never graduated; his basic education seems to have been in the United States Marine Corps, in which he served from 1942 to 1946. Uris's first published article, following many rejections, was "The All-American Razzmatazz," an account of the selection of the All-American football team, which appeared in *Esquire* in January 1951. He then committed himself to a writing career and over the succeeding years produced approximately one novel every two or three years..

Battle Cry (New York, 1953) documented the psychological and emotional impact of barracks life and the battlefield for a troop of marines during World War II. Uris wrote a screen version for Warner Brothers, which released the film in 1955. *The Angry Hills* (New York, 1955) is a spy story based on the diary of an uncle who fought in Greece as part of the Palestine Brigade of the British Army. As Uris's first look at the founding of Israel, it became the springboard for further explorations into how the Jewish state came about and the people who made it happen. A movie version by MGM was released in 1959.

Exodus (New York, 1958) pulled everything together for Uris. Stirred by the Sinai campaign of 1956—Uris was caught up in it while living in Israel—he began research on the novel. An account of the unfolding of Israel from the birth of Zionism in Europe at the beginning of the 20th century to its founding in 1948, *Exodus* was ultimately translated into 35 languages and sold over 10 million copies. A film version by Otto Preminger was released by United Artists in 1960. (In 1971 an attempt at a Broadway musical based on *Exodus, Ari,* closed after 20 performances.) Uris followed

up *Exodus* shortly after its initial publication with *Exodus Revisited* (New York, 1960), a photo-documentary illustrating the places described in the novel.

Subsequent novels have fit into the historical-block-buster-thriller mold. *Mila 18* (New York, 1961) described the resistance movement in the Warsaw Ghetto. Uris interviewed many survivors for the novel. *Armageddon* (New York, 1963) detailed the crises in Berlin from the Second World War to the 1948 airlift. *Topaz* (New York, 1967) was a spy novel using the Cuban missile crisis as the setting for an intrigue about a cadre of Russians within the de Gaulle government. (A film version by Alfred Hitchcock was produced in 1969.) A libel suit was brought against Uris in 1964 by Dr. Wladislav Dering, who claimed that he had been incorrectly identified in *Exodus* as guilty of atrocities against prisoners in Auschwitz. It resulted in *QB VII* (New York, 1970), a novel about it, and a court award to Dering of one half-penny in damages. A made-for-television movie was aired in 1974.

Marriage in 1970 to photographer Jill Peabody gave Uris a new source for material. Together they produced *Ireland: A Terrible Beauty*, with photographs by Jill Uris and text by Leon Uris (New York, 1975), and a year later Uris's novel *Trinity* (New York, 1976) followed. *Ireland: A Terrible Beauty* was either loved or hated by critics. Jill Uris's photographs were universally admired, but Leon Uris's text upset the Jesuit weekly *America*, which called it the view of a "New York liberal." *Choice* wrote that "cliches that Irish historical research has worked to revise, to modify, to explain over the last forty years can be found here." All the same, many thoughtful critics also praised the book. "Both the pen and the camera are sympathetic" *(Critic)*, and it "captures . . . the beauty . . . but also the tragedy of conflict and war. . ." commented *Library Journal. Trinity* traces several generations in three Irish families from the 1840s through 1916. For these two works Uris received the John F. Kennedy Award of the Irish Institute.

Uris has written one original screenplay not related to his novels. *Gunfight at the OK Corral*, produced in 1957, is an "adult western" about Wyatt Earp. Uris was fired from writing the screenplays of his own *The Angry Hills* and *Exodus* (and says, sardonically, "I was fired from the screenplay because I didn't understand the characters of the novel").

He is widely criticized as a pulp writer whose characters are flat and predictable, and it is said that the quality of his novels fails to meet the literary standards of other authors who have used similar themes, such as John Hersey, Norman Mailer and James Jones. Nonetheless, Uris has attracted millions of readers to material that is often difficult to digest, and he has made it palatable without diluting its impact. As such, he is a novelist of some importance.

MELVIN UROFSKY

b. February 7, 1939
Historian; professor

Melvin Urofsky, whose specialty is American history with sub-specialties in American Jewish history and oral history, is as much a teacher as a scholar. He is an active participant in Jewish communal affairs and has written extensively about and spoken on Jewish subjects.

Melvin I. Urofsky was born in New York City to Philip, a bookkeeper, and Sylvia (Passow) Urofsky. He received a Bachelor of Arts degree with a major in history and minors in English and religion from Columbia College in 1961 and was a Columbia National Honor Scholar through his four years as an undergraduate. He then pursued graduate studies at Columbia University and completed an M.A. degree in American history in 1962 and a Ph.D. in 1968.

He taught at Columbia from 1961 to 1963 and at Ohio State University as a history instructor from 1964 to 1967. In 1967 Urofsky joined the faculty of the State University of New York at Albany, where, as assistant professor, he developed new courses on the history and political aspects of American education. From 1970 to 1972 he was head of the Office of Innovative Education, which, in addition to creating new programs at Albany, also paved the way for interaction among students, faculty and administration in policy determination; in the implementation of student-designed courses; in the establishment of a children's theater project and in the creation of a community service program. Urofsky returned to teaching in 1972 and became assistant to the dean at an experimental college within the university.

Since 1974 Urofsky has been chairperson of the history department at Virgina Commonwealth University in Richmond. Named associate professor when first appointed, he was elevated to full professor in 1976. In his new post he completely revised the history and geography curricula and has focused on upgrading teaching quality within the department.

In both Albany and Richmond, Urofsky was active in local synagogues and has also been involved in campus Jewish organizations. In Richmond he was founding member and first president of the Richmond Oral

History Association from 1974 to 1976, and since 1976 he has been on the academic council of the American Jewish Historical Society. From 1976 to 1978 he was co-chairperson of the American Zionist Ideological Committee and was responsible in part for formulating a statement regarding American Zionism and reconciling it with Israeli Zionism. Some of his other Zionist affiliations include membership on the Zionist Academic Council and on the board of governors of the Association of Reform Zionists of America from 1978 to 1981.

Urofsky's books reflect the breadth of his interests. *Big Steel and the Wilson Administration: A Study in Business-Government Relations* (Columbus, Ohio, 1969) traced the development of the liaison between the steel industry and the presidential administration of Woodrow Wilson —one of the first times in American history that industry became entwined with the federal government.

Urofsky's book-length studies of American Zionism include *American Zionism from Herzl to the Holocaust* (New York, 1975), certainly one of the central historical works dealing with the growing relationship between American Jewry and the Jewish State of Israel. In it Urofsky considers the impact of American institutions and American acculturation on the generation of Jewish leaders involved with the evolution of Zionism in this country and how Jews favoring Israel were able to develop and use their political power to support Israel. Primarily pragmatic, and therefore often quite different from the founding fathers of Zionism and Israel, the Americans were transformed dramatically by World War II and the Holocaust and became ardent supporters.

Urofsky is also the biographer of Rabbi Stephen S. Wise, the last of the "giants" among American Jewish leaders. In *A Voice That Spoke for Justice: The Life and Times of Stephen S. Wise* (Albany, N.Y., 1982), he considers sympathetically the man who was both a pacifist and a supporter of World War I, one of the leading proponents of American Zionism and the founder of the American and World Jewish Congresses and the Jewish Institute of Religion. Wise was a reformer and a friend of the powerful, especially President Franklin D. Roosevelt. In this book Urofsky seeks to defend Wise against those who censured him for "failing to act vigorously and effectively when learning the facts of the Nazi genocide" and for being FDR's accessory in turning his back on European Jewry. To these charges, Urofsky replies sharply that Wise could have done little to convince Americans—many of whom were very anti-Jewish —to aid Jewish victims. American Jews, Urofsky contends, were "powerless," with little political muscle. They represented but 3 percent of the population. Moreover, FDR was deeply involved in winning the war, and he (and Churchill) took the position that the best way to save the Jews was to defeat Hitler quickly. Nor does Urofsky accept the allegation that American Jewish leaders were "silent" during that period of history: "Wise, Abba Hillel Silver, Chaim Weizmann and others spoke frequently and loudly, but to no avail."

For further information:

Urofsky, Melvin I. *Louis D. Brandeis and the Progressive Tradition*. Boston: 1980.

———. *A Mind of One Piece: Brandeis and American Reform*. New York: 1971.

———. *We Are One!: American Jewry and Israel*. New York: 1978.

Urofsky, Melvin I., ed. *Perspectives in Urban America*. New York: 1973.

———. *Why Teachers Strike: Teachers, Rights and Community*. New York: 1970.

Urofsky, Melvin I., and Levy, David W., eds. *Letters of Louis D. Brandeis*. Albany, N.Y.: 1978.

ROMAN VISHNIAC

b. August 19, 1897
Photographer; scientist

Perhaps Roman Vishniac did not know he was a prophet when he traveled through Eastern Europe in the mid-1930's, risking his life several times to photograph Jewish communities. Today, in most cases, Vishniac's photographs are all that survive of the many cities and towns that were wiped out in the Holocaust. Vishniac is also an accomplished scientist as well as a photographer, but above all, when one considers the scope of his career and his contributions, he is a humanist.

Roman Vishniac was born near St. Petersburg, Russia —now Leningrad—to Solomon, owner of Russia's largest umbrella factory, and Maria (Alexandrov) Vishniac. Vishniac explains that his mother's maiden name means "Jew who is coming from this little village." His family had a home in Moscow, where Vishniac's grandfather had been one of only 100 Jews granted the right to live there and where Vishniac grew up. Even then, Vishniac said in an interview, the family had to bribe the police to keep them from interfering with their lives and from making arrests. Until he was 10, Vishniac was educated at home. His introduction to science occurred when he was 7 and received a microscope from his grandmother. Before long, he had devised a system of micrography using a box camera to photograph insect parts, and was on his way toward a career in biology.

After attending a private school for several years,

Vishniac entered Shanyavsky University in Moscow in 1914, where he studied biology and ultimately received an M.D. in 1918 and a Ph.D. in zoology in 1920. He also got a faculty appointment while still a teen-ager. From 1917 to 1920 Vishniac remained at the university to take a government-sponsored medical course aimed at filling the shortage of doctors created by World War I. However, growing anti-Semitism caused Vishniac to flee to Latvia immediately after completing his degree, and soon after he moved to Berlin, where his family had already emigrated in 1918.

In Berlin, faced with the need to support several members of his household, Vishniac combined portrait photography and a variety of odd jobs with postgraduate research and study in endocrinology, optics and oriental art. Upon completion of studies in the latter, he should have received a Ph.D. but did not because he was Jewish.

Vishniac then began his travels through Eastern Europe, wandering almost compulsively, through Poland, Lithuania, Latvia, Hungary and Czechoslovakia, taking more than 16,000 photographs during a seven-year period. Trying to explain what motivated him, he said once: "I read the book by Hitler, *Mein Kampf* . . . I wanted only, if I cannot save the people, I should save their memory." The pictures themselves are remarkable: a view into the old ghetto of Cracow, three young students in Heder reading *halakah;* a Bet Midrash library; a boy with earlocks; an elderly woman wrapped in a shawl; a gravestone in Hebrew with images of books—a record of a vital community totally obliterated.

Vishniac was arrested frequently and on two occasions detained in a concentration camp. The second time occurred in 1939, after his family had fled the Nazis and settled in France and he was interned by the Vichy government. Upon his release in 1940, he joined his family, now in Sweden, and they departed for New York.

The first years in America were precarious; despite his background and knowledge of eight languages, Vishniac did not speak English. Thus, to survive at the outset, he became a portrait photographer—he wanted to be a photojournalist but could not get an editor to give him an assignment because of the language barrier —catering primarily to the Russian emigre community. But he continued experiments with photomicrography and in 1950 turned to full-time free-lancing as a scientific photographer. He also became a professor of biological education at Yeshiva University and a lecturer at The Pratt Institute and was project director and cinematographer for the film series *Living Biology,* produced by the National Science Foundation.

Vishniac has lectured widely and has had numerous photography exhibits that have covered either his photographs of Eastern European Jews, which were collected in *Polish Jews: A Pictorial Record* (New York, 1947), or his scientific photographs, which in themselves—even without one's knowing what they are—are images of dramatic beauty. Discovering that they are glimpses into a microscopic world so mysterious to most of us adds a further dimension to them.

Because Vishniac's interests are so diverse, he refuses to call himself just a scientist or a photographer but prefers to explore the notion of human effort toward the achievement of some creative act. Creativity, Vishniac said, "is something that is triggering the intelligence of a person and his knowledge and, at the same time, is also the ability of adaptation of an order into one's activity."

Remaining active into his mid-80s, combining a lecture schedule with his exploration into photomicrography and research, Vishniac told a reporter once, quite simply, that he was in "the business of discovery."

ALBERT VORSPAN

b. February 12, 1924
Communal leader; writer

Albert Vorspan, vice president of the Union of American Hebrew Congregations, is a long-standing liberal who has played an active role in religious, cultural and political activities. He has written numerous works that emphasize Jewish commitment to social and ethical responsibility and point to ways in which Jewish ethics can be used to deal with larger, more universal questions. As director of the Commission of Social Action in Reform Judaism, he took a strong stand against the Vietnam War and for civil rights.

Albert Vorspan was born in St. Paul, Minnesota to Benjamin, a postal employee, and Fanny (Swidelsky) Vorspan. During World War II he served in the Navy as a gunnery officer on a destroyer escort in the Pacific. Following his discharge he returned to school and graduated from New York University with a B.A. degree in 1948 and then began pursuing graduate courses at the New School for Social Research n New York City, but received no degree. From 1946-53 he worked on the staff of the National Community Relations Advisory Council, now called the National Jewish Community Relations Advisory Council.

Vorspan, who has been vice president of the Union of American Hebrew Congregations (Reform) since 1953,

coauthored his first book, *Justice and Judaism: The Work of Social Action* with Rabbi Eugene J. Lipman (New York, 1959). The book, a text for adult education classes and study groups, demonstrates how Jewish ethical principles apply to controversial social issues, like civil rights, juvenile delinquency and capital punishment.

In *Giants of Justice* (New York, 1960), Vorspan profiled 14 dynamic Jewish figures who influenced American society in the 20th century, including Louis Brandeis, Albert Einstein and Henrietta Szold. The author points out that all these people shared a passion for social justice, a need to speak out and a dependence upon their Jewish heritage. Vorspan demonstrated his interest in intergroup relations in his book *A Tale of Ten Cities: The Triple Ghetto in American Religious Life,* which he edited with Rabbi Eugene J. Lipman (New York, 1962). The book is a major study on the changing relations among Protestants, Jews and Catholics in America's major cities and deals with questions like "Is religious bigotry receding?" "Upon what issues do the three religions cooperate?" "Upon what are they divided?"

Vorspan's other books include *Jewish Values and Social Crisis: A Casebook for Social Action* (New York, 1973), a text that uses the technique of case study and debate to examine issues like Vietnam, racial conflict, poverty, drugs, sex and family life in the light of Jewish ethics. In the preface he wrote: "I believe that the ethical values of Judaism, as they were tested and refined through Jewish history, have something sharp and important to say about these problems and to the real world in our time." Vorspan's *Great Jewish Debates and Dilemmas: Jewish Perspective on Moral Issues in the Eighties* (New York, 1980) examines Jewish liberalism from the vantage point of Jewish ethical heritage. It discusses whether the Jews have traded away their own interests for universal concerns. Jews, he wrote, carry the burden

> to face this world and its pain head on; to engage in endless study and moral debate; to cherish human life and to pursue justice; to enhance the life of the mind and to struggle, despite all complexity and despair, to be God's co-partners in repairing His broken and incomplete world.

With Rabbi Balfour Brickner, Vorspan coauthored *Searching the Prophets for Values* (New York, 1981), an exploration of biblical foundations for dealing with contemporary problems, such as abortion, intermarriage, capital punishment, nuclear war and others. Vorspan and Brickner assert that values are learned through proper teaching and then analyze how appropriate traditional Jewish values should be applied in the home, at work and elsewhere.

Vorspan has also been one of the Jewish leaders outspoken in his oppostition to the Moral Majority and similar Christian fundamentalist organizations, which he has publicly denounced, warning as he did in 1981 that "the climate of mutual tolerance and pluralism in America is being polluted by an ominous and potent campaign of religious absolutism . . . a fever of religious radicalism now sweeps America." In addition to his more serious publications, Vorspan has become one of the more prominent—if not *the* prominent—writers about humorous aspects of modern American Jewish life. *My Rabbi Doesn't Make House Calls: A Guide to Games Jews Play* (New York, 1969) is an oftimes hilarious book poking fun—lovingly but with sharp and sometimes dead aim—at the foibles and pretensions of his people. The book's dust jacket reveals what's ahead for the reader: a rabbi is on the phone to a congregant's wife saying, "Have him read the 'Song of Songs,' take a glass of wine and call me tomorrow." Each chapter heading "tells all" but especially noteworthy and too often true is the chapter entitled "How To Translate Public Relations." Two examples of Vorspan's humor: The press release says "A membership of approximately 50,000 members." The reality is 20,000 members. The press release says "Mr. Asa Shmendrick, chairman of the board, urged the organization to concentrate its energies and resources on the strengthing and deepening of Jewish identity and Jewish education." The reality is that "Shmendrick wants us to lay off civil rights."

For further information:
Vorspan, Albert. *I'm O.K., You're a Pain in the Neck.* New York: 1976.
———. *Mazel Tov! You're Middle Aged.* New York: 1974.
———. *So the Kids Are Revolting. . . ?* New York: 1970.
———. *You Packed the Cat in the Suitcase?!* New York: 1978.

GEORGE WALD

b. November 18, 1906
Biologist; professor

George Wald is a Nobel Prize-winning biologist and Harvard professor who has become one of America's leading humanists. An outspoken and early opponent of the Vietnam War, Wald has come to represent the scientist with a conscience, who has dedicated his work toward the betterment of humanity and who speaks out when he feels that science is being directed toward destructive purposes.

George Wald was born in Manhattan's Lower East Side to Isaac, an immigrant tailor, and Ernestine (Rosenmann) Wald. He received his B.S. degree from New York University in 1927 and an M.A. and Ph.D. in zoology from Columbia College in 1932. That year he was awarded a National Research Council Fellowship in biology. It was during his two-year fellowship that Wald, working in the laboratory of Otto Warburg in Berlin, identified vitamin A in the retina, the first person to do so. This important discovery would lead to a greater understanding of the role of proper nutrition in preserving good health and eyesight, particularly in some developing countries where poor nutrition made blindness a common occurrence among children. Wald left Berlin when Hitler rose to power in Germany and moved to Chicago.

Wald came to Harvard as a tutor in biochemistry in 1934 and remained until 1977. He became professor of biology in 1948, Higgins Professor in 1968 and Higgins Professor Emeritus in 1977. Throughout his career he was known as a distinguished teacher and researcher. He won numerous awards, including the Eli Lilly Award for Fundamental Research in Biochemistry in 1939 and the Proctor Medal of the Association for Research in Ophthalmology in 1955.

When he received the 1967 Nobel Prize in Physiology, which he shared with two other scientists, he said:

A scientist lives with all reality. There is nothing better. To know reality is to accept it, and eventually to love it. A scientist is in a sense a learned child. There is something of the scientist in every child. Others must outgrow it. Scientists can stay that way all their lives.

Wald is the author of two books, *General Education in a Free Society* (Cambridge, Mass., 1945) and *Twenty-Six Afternoons of Biology: An Introductory Laboratory Manual* (Reading, Mass., 1962). He was elected to the National Academy of Sciences in 1950 and to the American Philosophical Society eight years later. He spent the 1963–64 academic year at Cambridge University as a Guggenheim fellow.

In 1969 the politically conscious Wald called the Vietnam War "the most shameful episode in the whole of American history." He said in an address on March 4, 1969 at the Massachusetts Institute of Technology that "Our government has become preoccupied with death, with the business of killing and being killed. So-called defense now absorbs sixty per cent of the national budget, and about twelve per cent of the Gross National Product." In regard to nuclear weapons, he once said: "There is nothing worth having that can be obtained by nuclear war—nothing material or ideological—no tradition that it can defend. . . . Nuclear weapons offer us nothing but a balance of terror, and a balance of terror is still terror."

Since his retirement in 1977, Wald says he spends his time "trying to help keep the human species from self extinction" and often lectures about the dangers of nuclear weapons and an out-of-control arms race.

MIKE WALLACE

b. May 9, 1918
Television journalist

Television journalist Mike Wallace has carried on the old newspaper tradition of the abrasive, outspoken and fearless reporter who will not stop until he gets his story. As one of the original hosts of CBS-TV's hard-hitting, popular and award-winning news series 60 Minutes, Wallace is one of the most influential—and probably most controversial—personalities in television today.

Myron Leon Wallace was born of immigrant parents, Frank, an insurance broker, and Zina (Sharfman) Wallace—the name was altered from "Wallik" by an Ellis Island immigration official—and grew up in the Boston suburb of Brookline, Massachusetts. After graduating from high school in 1935, where he had immersed himself in debating activities, drama and reporting for the school newspaper—often at the expense of high grades—Wallace entered the University of Michigan, where he received a B.A. degree in 1939. His original plan was to study teaching, but he joined the college radio station and for the remainder of his life pursued that general occupation.

Armed with his bachelor's degree, he went to work in 1939 for a Grand Rapids, Michigan radio station; transferred in 1940 to Detroit, where he worked on such popular serials as The Green Hornet and The Lone Ranger; and then, on the eve of America's entry into World War II in 1941, worked for the Chicago Sun, performed on radio programs and announced the soap operas Ma Perkins and The Guiding Light. In 1943 he enlisted in the Navy and served aboard a submarine tender in the Pacific Ocean and later as an officer in charge of entertainment at the Great Lakes Naval Training Station near Chicago.

Discharged in 1946, Wallace returned to radio work and, with his then-wife Buff Cobb, introduced an irreverent and outspoken husband-and-wife talk show broadcast from the Chez Paree, a prominent Chicago nightclub. Eventually the show proved so successful it was moved to New York City, where it lasted until the Wallaces were divorced. Soon after, in 1955, he began reporting

news for the Dumont television station and with Ted Yates Jr. developed Night Beat, a weekly interview program that started in October 1956. The setting for Night Beat was stark and bare-bones: a ladder, cigarette smoke invariably curling toward the ceiling, the atmosphere of a third-degree session in a dingy detective squad room. The subjects interviewed were the very famous.

While his inquisitorial manner offended a good many viewers and critics, Wallace's interviewing technique brought him to the attention of the major TV networks, hungry for entertainment and ratings. In February 1963 he was hired by CBS News and soon became the star of CBS Morning News with Mike Wallace. He had other assignments as well, but none made him more prominent than when he teamed up with Harry Reasoner in 1968 for the premier of Don Hewitt's 60 Minutes, a television magazine patterned in part after the format of the Canadian Broadcasting Company's long-running and brilliant radio program.

In this format he interviewed the best-known celebrities of the day, from the Shah of Iran and Nguyen Cao Ky to Ronald Reagan and John Connally, as well as playwrights, Soviet dissidents, fraudulent businessmen and a deposed president. When he tried to develop a link between Henry Kissinger, the deposed Shah and the high price of crude oil, Kissinger refused to appear on camera with him. Civil libertarians criticized his manner by saying that his methods of detecting crooked businessmen often bordered on entrapment.

Wallace rarely if ever publicly identified with Jewish life. But three times he infuriated the American Jewish Congress, leading, in the first instance, to its protest that Wallace's February 1975 report on Syrian Jewry was "inaccurate and distorted." Some letter-writers charged Wallace was myopic because he declared that "life for Syria's Jews [was] better than it was in years past," although in fact their lives were severely restricted. Wallace nonetheless pledged to "take another look" at the problem, and in 1976 he went back to Damascus and then stated again that life was indeed improved "for all Syrians and for Syrian Jews among them." But one skeptical journalist has observed that the improvements, including the lifting of the ban on automobile ownership and university attendance, might, in fact, have been expedited by Wallace's interview with Syrian President Assad. Afterward, Wallace pointedly told the Christian Science Monitor: "But the fact is that there is not one Syrian Jew in jail today as a political prisoner."

In 1977 Wallace devoted a segment to an interview with Menachem Begin. At one point he suggested that Begin and Yasir Arafat, leader of the terrorist Palestine

Liberation Organization, were actually quite similar inasmuch as Begin had been a leader of the underground terrorist movement, Irgun Zevai Leumi, almost 30 years earlier in the 1948 Israeli War of Independence. This implication—and probably Wallace's provocative approach—created such heat between the two men that Israeli Defense Minister Ezer Weizmann, who arrived at the meeting just then, commented only half-jokingly that he'd heard the two men were having a "fist fight."

But Wallace's most stormy episode on a *60 Minutes* story on Israel occurred in 1980, when he attempted to profile the conditions of an Arab village in the Galilee. When the TV crew filmed an Arab boy stoning an Israeli military vehicle, Wallace and *60 Minutes* were accused of deliberately enticing the boy to do so. Although Wallace denied any involvement, the incident triggered further allegations about Wallace's biases as he set out to tell his story. The town was portrayed as impoverished and neglected, although a nearby Jewish town was clean, modern, in fact, rather luxurious. An Israeli journalist reported that major civic improvement projects in the Arab town that had been brought to Wallace's attention were simply never filmed, and that he had deliberately chosen to film only the most deteriorated sections. Jewish groups complained that Wallace failed to put his story in perspective—it would be like telling the story of New York City and only filming the most ravaged blocks in the South Bronx, they said, and further accused him of being a "self-hating Jew." Not so, responded Wallace, who told one reporter: "It's a matter of pride to me that I'm Jewish . . . I have had trees planted in memory of my family. I raised a lot of money for the cancer research institute at Hadassah Hospital. I've been going in and out of the country for 25 years."

Nonetheless, whether or not Wallace can satisfy his critics, in fact he keeps them and millions of other Americans riveted in front of their television sets every Sunday all year round. For years *60 Minutes* has been one of the highest-rated shows, dominated and characterized by the man *Time* magazine described as having "sharp eyes, alert and aggressive manner, quick and probing questions, and the grin of disbelief crossing his eyes as a quarry makes an unconvincing reply."

ELI WALLACH

b. December 7, 1915
Actor

Tony Award-winning actor Eli Wallach is a consummate performer. On the screen he has played heroes, lovers and villains. On television he is often seen on comedies, dramas and bank commercials. And on the stage he has appeared in some of the major shows of the American legitimate theater.

Eli Wallach was born in Brooklyn to Abraham and Bertha (Schorr) Wallach. He grew up in the predominantly Italian neighborhood of Red Hook in Brooklyn, where his parents owned and operated a candy store named "Bertha's." He graduated from Erasmus Hall High School, where he was a mediocre student, but it was during his teen-age years, through the local Boy's Club, that Wallach first began to act. He starred in a play, *Fiat Lux,* in the role of a 65-year-old man.

Wallach graduated from the University of Texas with a B.A. degree in 1936 and then, to please his parents, earned an M.S. degree in education from City College of New York in 1938. But unlike his brother and two sisters who became teachers, Wallach hated the profession. Instead, he studied acting at the Neighborhood Playhouse in New York from 1940 to 1941, where he was first exposed to the Stanislavski method. From 1941 to 1945 he served in the United States Army Medical Corps.

Discharged in 1945, Wallach started looking for jobs in acting. One of his first roles was in the Equity Library production of Tennessee Williams' one-act play *This Property Is Condemned.* In it he played opposite actress Anne Jackson, whom he married in 1948. Wallach made his Broadway debut in 1945 at the Belasco Theater as the crew chief in *Skydrift.* In 1946 he joined the American Repertory Theatre and played the coward in *Androcles and the Lion,* Cromwell in *Henry VIII* and minor roles in other plays, and began perfecting roles that ranged from irresistible warmth to displays of evil.

Though he was working, Wallach was unsatisfied. He had put in an application to become a postman when producer Joshua Logan asked him in 1949 to replace an actor as Stefanowski in the Broadway production of *Mister Roberts.* The part represented the turning point in Wallach's career, as he played the role for two years. In 1951 he was chosen to play the Sicilian lover in Tennessee Williams' *The Rose Tattoo* opposite Maureen Stapleton, a performance for which he received the 1951 Tony Award for best featured actor; the Donaldson Award; the Drama Critics Award and the Theater Award. His directness, the passion with which he projects his roles and his obvious mastery of acting have brought Wallach much recognition in his profession.

After *The Rose Tattoo* Wallach refused the role of Maggio in the film *From Here to Eternity* (the role that earned Frank Sinatra an Academy Award) in order to appear in Tennessee Williams' new play *Camino Real.* Although the 1963 play was a failure, Wallach's fine portrayal of Kilroy, the American boy, was hailed by critics. Wallach has appeared in numerous plays since, many of them in partnership with his wife, Anne Jackson. The couple have performed together in *Major Barbara* (1956); *Luv* (1961); *Rhinoceros* (1961); *The Typist* (1962); *The Tiger* (1962); *Waltz of the Toreadors* (1973); *The Diary of Anne Frank,* which also included one of their daughters (1978); and others.

His film credits include *The Tiger Makes Out* (1973), *Cinderella Liberty* (1973), *How to Steal a Million* (1973), *The Sentinel* (1976), *Nasty Habits* (1977), *The Domino Principle* (1977) and *Girlfriends* (1979).

He remains an actor of stature.

BARBARA WALTERS

b. September 25, 1931
Television journalist

Barbara Walters has turned the television interview into a unique art form, of which she is the undisputed queen. A newswriter and broadcaster who worked her way through the networks at a time when few opportunities existed for women, she now exercises carte blanche over the programs she produces and hosts and commands one of the highest salaries earned by a television journalist.

Barbara Jill Walters was born in Boston, Massachusetts to Lou, owner of the Latin Quarter and other nightclubs, and Dena (Selett) Walters. She was reared in New York and Miami. As a result of her father's work—he was a notable impresario—she came to know many celebrities when she was quite young. Thus, she was not intimidated by the fame of people she would later meet and in fact cultivated the diplomacy and tact that would later become her trademarks. She attended grade schools and high schools in New York and Miami and then entered Sarah Lawrence College in Bronxville, New York, where she received a B.A. degree in English in 1953. She then moved to New York City, where she planned to start a career in television.

Beginning at RCA-TV, the local affiliate of NBC, Walters was able to get some work in writing, producing and public relations. But her first break came in 1961, when she was invited by Dave Garroway, one of the earliest hosts of the long-running *Today* show, to join the staff as a writer. Once there, she demonstrated an acute news sense, which was recognized by the NBC staff. In fact, from time to time she was given on-air assignments; for example, she covered Jacqueline Kennedy's trip to India in 1962. However, slots for women to cover hard news stories were still virtually nonexis-

tent, and the best *Today* assignments invariably went to the show's male hosts. But, even then Walters proved to be a skilled interviewer, and she was increasingly permitted to continue conducting interviews of those personalities she was able to schedule for the show.

The interviews soon became a staple, and Walters won a reputation not only for her perseverance in getting the most noteworthy personalities of the time but for eliciting some extremely private and personal information from them in the most off-handed yet sensitive manner. "I have developed a particular type of interview," she once commented. "I'm good at drawing people out—there's a thin line between asking critical questions well and making someone mad."

At the outset of her career, Walters said she deferred to the male hosts of *Today* because she did not want to appear too aggressive, yet some viewers nonetheless complained that she was too pushy and abrasive. Still, her work was so successful and popular that in 1963 it became a regular feature on the show. She was able to interview presidents when other reporters could not and met with members of the Kennedy family and the widow and children of the late black leader Martin Luther King Jr. And Walters could be equally at ease with movie stars, transcending the glamor of their careers to probe their individual psyches and problems. By 1974 she was made co-anchor of *Today,* and her career soared.

In the mid-1970s the production of television news became more sophisticated technologically and more influential because of its ability to capture breaking news on the spot. Evening and late night news programs were significantly expanded, and with the expansion came the careers of many long-time television news broadcasters. Walters was no exception. In 1976 she was hired away from NBC to become the first woman news anchor on ABC's *Nightly News* program at a record-breaking salary of $1 million a year. Her appointment was not accepted well by her male peers, especially her coanchor, Harry Reasoner, and in an overhaul at ABC News within the year, Walters was forced out. (Reasoner had already departed for CBS.) Nonetheless, by 1977 Walters scored what is perhaps her greatest coup of all: She scheduled a joint interview with Egyptian President Anwar Sadat and Israeli Prime Minister Menachem Begin after their historic meeting in Jerusalem in November of that year.

Since then she has consistently interviewed the most important people making news in politics, show business or any other area that happens to be newsworthy. She visited Jimmy Carter in Plains, Georgia and interviewed black comedian Richard Pryor both before and after a tragic accident that nearly killed him. Walters herself is so newsworthy that even the dinner parties she gives are prestigious events, and the guest lists often include the most important leaders in American business and politics.

Since losing her anchor spot, Walters has continued as special correspondent with almost total control over the interview specials she airs from time to time, and she is still regarded as one of the most influential women in the country. Her many awards include Woman of the Year in Communications from *Ladies Home Journal* in 1974; the mass media award from the American Jewish Committee's Institute of Human Relations in 1975 and the Hubert H. Humphrey Freedom Prize from the Anti-Defamation League of B'nai B'rith in 1978.

For further information:
Walters, Barbara. *How to Talk with Practically Anybody About Anything.* New York: 1970.

MICHAEL WALZER

b. March 3, 1935
Social scientist

In theory and in practice, social scientist Michael Walzer supports a humane liberalism as the best approach to fostering the growth of personal liberties and improving material well-being. To that end, although his own life has been almost exclusively in the academic realm, Walzer has written extensively about the role of democratic political action in paving the way toward a just world.

Michael Walzer was born in New York City to Joseph P., who managed a jewelry store, and Sally (Hochman) Walzer. He attended Brandeis University, where he was a distinguished scholar and was president of the student government. Walzer also became involved in the burgeoning civil rights movement of the mid-1950s. He helped organize campus support for the 1954 Montgomery boycott and the picketing of northern counterparts of stores being picketed in the South.

After graduating with a B.A. degree from Brandeis in 1956, he studied at Cambridge University in England as a Fulbright scholar in 1957. Returning to the United States, Walzer completed a Ph.D. at Harvard University in 1961. He taught at Princeton University from 1962 to 1966 and then returned to Harvard, where two years later he was promoted to full professor—a remarkable achievement for his age and in so short a time. Among the courses he taught were "History of Modern Political Thought," "Problems in Contemporary Polit-

ical Philosophy," "Problems in Socialist Thought" and "The Political Theory of Nationalism." In 1980 Walzer left Harvard to accept a tenured faculty appointment in the School of Social Sciences at the Institute for Advanced Study in Princeton, New Jersey. In Walzer's current post, he is able to devote his time exclusively to writing and research.

Walzer has published many articles and six books of political and social history and theory. In *Obligations: Essays on Disobedience, War and Citizenship* (Cambridge, Mass., 1970), he wrote that since the governors derive their just powers from the consent of the governed, this meant certain obligations were incurred. But, he asked what if an oppressed minority is denied access to democratic processes? Does it have the right to rebel? To lead the mass of people? Walzer suggests the answer is yes and raises the larger question of precisely how repressed blacks can share in the benefits of a free society if they are denied all the opportunities available to others.

In *Just and Unjust Wars* (New York, 1977), Walzer tried to clarify the moral guilt of leaders and citizens. In his section on war crimes, for example, he writes "there can be no justice in war if there are not, ultimately, responsible men and women." Statesmen, he argues, *are* often responsible for provoking aggressive wars. Such wars include the Japanese invasion of China, the Italian and German intervention in Spain, the Nazi invasions, the Soviet invasion of Hungary and Czechoslovakia, the Egyptian attack on Israel in 1967 and the United States war in Vietnam. The latter, he continues, "was, first of all, an unjustified intervention, and it was, secondly, carried on in so brutal a manner that even had it initially been defensible, it would have to be condemned, not in this or that aspect, but generally."

Walzer's book *Radical Principles: Reflections of an Unreconstructed Democrat* (New York, 1980) is a collection of essays spanning the previous 15 years of his career. Among them he presents analyses of the welfare state as a necessary component of American democracy and predicts that surface support for "Reaganomics" will ultimately evaporate. The problems with liberalism that caused the downfall of Democratic Party politics in the United States in the early 1980s will lead to a retrenchment of liberal thinking and forces, Walzer believes, after which liberalism will come to the fore once again. Walzer feels that American social programs are useful and have, in fact, led to the creation of a growing and vibrant middle class among American minority groups. At the same time, he believes in a democratic socialism that would foster individual growth as well as collective participation in government. Many of his views are grounded in a humane vision, emphasized in this phrase from *Radical Principles:* "Man has both a mind and passion for society . . ."

On September 24, 1981 writing in *The New York Review of Books,* Walzer defended the struggle of Argentine-Jewish journalist and editor Jacobo Timerman against the oppression of the dictatorial regime of Argentina. In 1981, two years after Timerman's release from Argentine prisons, his subsequent move to Israel and the publication of memoirs relating his experiences of torture, which he claimed were motivated by anti-Semitism, American neo-conservatives lashed out against Timerman while Walzer criticized the neo-conservatives, whom he called "nervous liberals . . . nervous about liberalism." Walzer claimed that the neo-conservatives— many of whom had previously been liberal Democrats— felt threatened by advances made by poor people and minorities, advances they had in fact helped foster.

Walzer is also deeply committed to Israel and to Zionism, an involvement that began in the 1960s. He was supportive of the Camp David accords, which established a peace treaty between Egypt and Israel, although he was critical of President Jimmy Carter's apparent ambivalence about the pact. He also advocates the hardline anti-PLO stand of the Reagan administration at the United Nations as part of an international drive to stem terrorism.

In line with his sympathies, Walzer has become a member of the board of governors of Hebrew University, is on the faculty advisory cabinet of the United Jewish Appeal and participates in the International Affairs Committee of the American Jewish Congress.

Walzer is an editor of *Dissent,* a contributing editor to *The New Republic* and on the editorial board of *Philosophy and Public Affairs.*

In 1981, in honor of his achievements, Walzer received an honorary degree from Brandeis University—the first Brandeis alumnus to earn such recognition.

For further information:

Walzer, Michael. *Political Action.* New York: 1971.
————. *Regicide and Revolution.* Cambridge, Mass.: 1974.
————. *The Revolution of the Saints: A study in the Origins of Radical Politics.* Cambridge, Mass.: 1965.

ARTHUR WASKOW

b. October 12, 1933
Writer; theologian

Arthur Waskow's primary motivation and concern in his public life is *tikun olam,* literally "repairing the world," which has become a springboard for his social activism and progressive politics within the Jewish community. Whether the subject is world peace or the revitalization of American Jewish life, he has propounded many original, highly controversial and even radical ideas designed to invigorate Jewish religious and secular thought and action.

Arthur Waskow was born in Baltimore, Maryland to Henry B., a teacher, and Hannah (Osnowitz) Waskow. He earned his B.A. degree from Johns Hopkins University in 1954 and his M.A. degree and Ph.D. in 1956 and 1963 respectively from the University of Wisconsin.

From 1959 to 1961 Waskow worked as a legislative assistant at the United States House of Representatives. This was followed by a two-year stint at the Peace Research Institute. In 1963 Waskow joined the Institute of Policy Studies in Washington, D.C. as a senior staff member. The Institute of Policy Studies is a liberal-radical "think-tank" devoted to the study of public policy and the development of alternative strategies for dealing with such global concerns as hunger, nuclear proliferation and the problems of the third world.

In the mid-1960s Waskow became increasingly involved with the growing anti-Vietnam War movement, and afterward, following the fall of Saigon in 1975, he helped organize Trees for Vietnam, a group that collected money to replant huge areas of Vietnam defoliated during the war. By way of explanation, Waskow asserted that the tree was the traditional Jewish symbol for life and the project was an authentically Jewish way of expressing opposition to the conflict.

Seeking even more Judaic outlets for his activities, he turned then to the counterculture movement, or that aspect of it that was expressly Jewish. Waskow looks to Judaism for guidance in social and ethical issues, but he also feels that Judaism must be integrated into a person's everyday life rather than being a separate component. To that end, he believes that Jews must come together in small communities, based on the spiritual and ethical traditions of the past. Jewish identity stems from a sense of community, and morality flows from people actually living together, removing it from the realm of the abstract to the realm of the concrete. Each day, Waskow believes, must be devoted to *tikun olam,* and this is best done within the context of small communities where people actually live together as *haverim,* or "comrades." He studied the Torah, spent time in Israel and became kosher (also excluding food grown by nonunion workers or infested with damaging chemicals).

He was a key member of Jews for Urban Justice, which sought to rely on traditional Jewish concerns for social justice to bridge the growing gap between blacks and Jews in the Washington, D.C. area. He was a member of the executive board of the Jewish Peace

Fellowship, a pacifist organization founded in 1941 and dedicated to the Jewish nonviolent tradition. And he published *Freedom Seder* (New York, 1969), which tried in part to link the black struggle for equality and the antagonism to the war then raging in Southeast Asia with the Jewish freedom festival of Passover.

Soon after, he organized the Farbrangen Community, a community fellowship dedicated to living according to the precepts of Judaism, such as equality between the sexes, participating in positive social acts and attempting to be guided by the ethical precepts of the Prophets. The Farbrangen later became one of the models for the *havurah* movement, informal groups of committed Jews moved by common ideals.

In 1973 Waskow also joined the executive board of Breira, a dovish national organization that insisted on reordering the relationship of American Jewry and Israel and in the process criticized certain aspects of Israeli practices. Breira was then bitterly attacked and destroyed by critics, who charged it with lacking *ahavat Yisrael*, or a "sufficient love of Israel." He has, however, continued to call for peace and reconciliation between Palestinian Arabs and Israeli Jews. In 1973, following the Yom Kippur War, he wrote: "To Jews who have a specially poignant desire for peace and safety [for Israel] Jeremiah's prophecy [calling for justice] is that justice and safety do not stand in opposition, but reinforce each other."

In *The Bush Is Burning! Radical Judaism Faces the Pharaohs of the Modern Superstate* (New York, 1971), he reminded Garry Wills of his "resemblance to Dan Berrigan." The prophetic tradition was central to his thinking. A human being, wrote Waskow, foreshadows the sabbath by living it each day. Nonviolence was for Waskow a permanent interest: "The only means we may use are those that partake of the ends themselves, and to reject illegitimate means is not to postpone the revolution but to bring it nearer."

Waskow's most important work is *Godwrestling* (New York, 1978), a collection of sermonlike essays that contend with the human struggle to reconcile opposites and conflicts and reflect on the moral dimension of that struggle. Often using biblical stories—such as Esau and Jacob, Isaac and Ishmael, and Joseph and his brothers—Waskow asks the question "Why does it (the world, each person, the universe) have to be this way (not perfect)?" and then meditates on the possibilities of change and improvement. In essence, *Godwrestling* is a contemporary *midrash* (or way of interpreting scripture to emphasize particular lessons or morals), reinterpreting the past and seeking to make its lessons relevant to the present.

In the light of the reluctance of many Jewish organizations to take a stand on the nuclear arms race, and in the face of the support for a powerful and evergrowing nuclear force by Jews on the neo-Conservative right, Waskow has been in the vanguard of those urging American Jewry to actively oppose nuclear weaponry. "From where, if not from the Jewish people," he wrote in 1982, "should come not only the warning, but also the action to prevent a world thermonuclear holocaust?" He created the Rainbow Covenant, based on the divine pledge to Noah that life on Earth will never be completely destroyed again. He has also developed the Shalom Aleichem Statement, a call by well-known American Jews to "develop new approaches of mind and spirit in addressing the spirit of thermonuclear world disaster and the need for controlling and reversing the nuclear arms race."

For further information:
Waskow, Arthur. *From Race Riot to Sit In: 1919 and the 1960s.* New York: 1966.
———. *The Limits of Defense.* New York: 1962.
———. *The Worried Man's Guide to World Peace.* New York: 1963.
Waskow, Arthur, ed. *Menorah,* a newsletter of Jewish Renewal.

BEN J. WATTENBERG
b. August 26, 1933
Author; editor

Neo-conservative author and editor Ben Wattenberg has played an active role in political life since he was first appointed as aide and speechwriter for President Lyndon Johnson in 1956. As an essayist and host of a series of television weekly programs entitled *In Search of the Real America,* and as author of several significant books dealing with the social and political conditions in America, he has commented regularly on the conduct of foreign affairs.

Ben J. Wattenberg was born in New York City to Judah, an attorney, and Rachel (Gutman) Wattenberg, a dietician. He received a B.A. degree from Hobart College in 1955 and served in the Air Force from 1956 until 1958. From 1958 to 1965 he was editor and publisher of *Leisure* magazine and the president of Bold Face Books.

During this period he also collaborated with Richard M. Scammon to produce *This U.S.A.* (New York, 1965), a book that scrutinized the implications of the 1960 census. In it they discussed the broad range of material and concluded, among other points, that population growth posed no threat to the quality of life in this country.

Wattenberg was an aide and speechwriter for President Johnson at the White House from 1966 to 1968 and was a supporter of the Vietnam War. In 1970 he was an adviser in Senator Hubert Humphrey's race for the Senate and in 1972 and again in 1976 for Senator Henry Jackson's ill-fated try for the Democratic presidential nomination. He has twice, in 1972 and 1976 served on the 15-person Platform-Drafting Sub-Committee on the Democratic National Committee, helping to write the Democratic national platform. Wattenberg's book *The Real Majority,* on which he again collaborated with Scammon (New York, 1970), was hailed by some as a "bible" of the 1970 and 1972 elections and was used by both liberal Democrats and conservative Republicans in planning their strategies. The book analyzed present-day American voting trends by examining demographic data on past presidential primaries, public opinion polls and election results.

In 1977 Wattenberg was named to the Presidential Advisory Board on Ambassadorial Appointments by President Jimmy Carter. As a business consultant in Washington, he has also prepared for the National Association of Food Chains and *Family Circle* magazine the first major report on the declining birth rate in America: "The Birth Dearth and What It Means—the Demography of the 1970's."

Wattenberg was the essayist-narrator of a weekly 1981 Public Broadcasting Service television program, *In Search of the Real America,* based on his book *The Real America: A Surprising Examination of the State of the Union* (New York, 1974). The themes of his shows varied, but, in general, they celebrated such developments as bigness in industry, massive military rearmament and political freedom. Both in the PBS series and in his book, Wattenberg expresses his optimistic belief that the working and middle classes—blacks and whites and Hispanics included—have benefited tremendously since 1960.

Typical of his point of view in world affairs was his article ". . . And What Ronald Reagan Failed to Say" in *The Wall Street Journal* (April 23, 1982). Reflecting the widespread neo-conservative disillusionment in the spring of 1982 with Reagan's conduct of foreign policy, Wattenberg wrote that President Reagan had neither explained the situation nor shaped public opinion. What Wattenberg wanted the President to say was that the government of El Salvador (since defeated in elections) "began an unprecedented land reform" and that the guerrillas, not the government, have resorted to violence.

Very simply, guerillas, armed and supported by and through Cuba, are attempting to impose a Marxist-Leninist dictatorship on the people of El Salvador as part of a larger imperialistic plan. If we do not act promptly and decisively in defense of freedom, new Cubas will arise from the ruins of today's conflicts. We will face more totalitarian regimes, tied militarily to the Soviet Union; more regimes exporting subversion.

In 1972 Wattenberg was one of the founders of the Coalition for a Democratic Majority, a neo-conservative bloc within the Democratic Party that organized as a protest against the nomination of Senator George McGovern for the presidency. He is also a senior fellow at the conservative-oriented American Enterprise Institute and a co-editor of its *Public Opinion* magazine.

SIMON WEBER

b. May 4, 1911
Newspaper editor

Since he had his first Yiddish stories published in 1932, Simon Weber has become the leading force in Yiddish journalism as editor in chief of the *Jewish Daily Forward.*

Simon Weber was born in Staszow, Poland to Abraham Nochem, a merchant in Poland and Ford worker in Detroit, and Brayndl (Piasecki) Weber. He received a traditional Jewish education, first in *heder* and then at the hands of his maternal grandfather, who gave him lessons in the Bible and the Talmud. But he made an early break with the Hasidism of his family, attending a Polish school and reading modern literature in both Polish and Yiddish. It was in school as a teen-ager that Weber first started writing stories and poetry, using Polish as a medium.

Weber came to America in 1929, following his parents, who had emigrated because, in Weber's words, "it was miserable over there." At that time, America was in the depths of the Great Depression, and it was not easy for a young immigrant to find work. He held a variety of jobs, including stints as a house painter, paperhanger and garment presser. At the same time, he attended school, first to learn English and then to complete high school. He has never had any formal university training, although he studied with Yiddish poet Ezra Korman and others. In 1932 he began teaching Yiddish. That same year he had his first stories published in a Yiddish newspaper. Even as a schoolboy in Poland, Weber's writing had been singled out from that of his classmates as noteworthy. Now his efforts at English composition attracted the attention of his English teacher. Ironically, it was his teacher who suggested that he write in his native tongue—Yiddish.

He soon turned from fiction to journalism and started earning a living as a journalist in 1936. After a brief association with the now-defunct *Philadelphia Jewish World,* he joined the staff of the *Forward* in 1939. He worked first as a reporter and newswriter, later serving as city editor and editor of the paper's Sunday edition. He became managing editor in 1968 and served in that position until he became editor in chief in 1970.

As the *Forward's* editor in chief, Weber has maintained the paper's high literary standards. Writers such as Chaim Grade and Nobel Prize winner Isaac Bashevis Singer still appear regularly in its pages. He also introduced several new features, including the popular "Gems of Yiddish Poetry."

As editor, Weber expresses his views regularly in his column *Notes,* writing on such subjects as Soviet treatment of Jews, Israeli politics and international politics related to Israel, American politics and Yiddish itself. Under his direction the *Forward* has continued its strong support of Israel and its opposition to Soviet totalitarianism. It continues its traditional support for the American and Jewish labor movements as well.

In addition to his duties at the *Forward,* he is vice chairperson of the World Council for Jewish Culture, a member of the administrative committee of the Jewish Labor Committee and an active member of the Workmen's Circle. For many years he was a regular commentator on WEVD in New York City.

JAMES A. WECHSLER

b. October 31, 1915
Journalist

James Wechsler, editorial columnist of *The New York Post* and author of several important books on politics, is one of the country's respected editor-journalists. A life-long liberal, he has always been in the forefront of humane politics, defending freedom and diversity from authoritarian crusaders of the left and right.

James Arthur Wechsler was born in New York City to Samuel, a lawyer, and Anna (Weisberger) Wechsler. He graduated with a B.A. degree in 1935 from Columbia University, where, during his senior year, he was editor of *The Columbia Daily Spectator,* the school's daily newspaper. He was editor of *The Student Advocate,* a liberal student paper, from 1936 to 1937. A member of the Young Communist League from 1934 to 1937, Wechsler coauthored with the biographer Joseph Lash a book called *Revolt on the Campus* (New York, 1935), which explored the difficulties confronted by liberal student groups on college campuses in the 1930s. As an example he cites Reed Harris, who in 1932 was editor of *The Columbia Daily Spectator* and was expelled for writing candidly about lamentable conditions in the school cafeteria, college football, politics and other problems of the day.

Wechsler began his professional journalism career as assistant editor of *The Nation,* a position he held from 1938 to 1939. From 1940 to 1941 he worked at the liberal newspaper *PM* as assistant editor, and from 1942 to 1944 he was chief of its Washington bureau.

After spending 1944 to 1946 in the United States Army, Wechsler joined the staff of the *New York Post* in 1947 as a reporter for its Washington bureau. Two years later he became an editor at the *Post,* a position he kept until 1961, when he was made editorial columnist and wrote thousands of columns and editorials upholding the free, liberal tradition and the dignity of individuals, particularly the poor and helpless. He was strongly in favor of civil rights legislation in the 1960s, was an early and articulate opponent of the Vietnam War and often defended ordinary people frustrated by impersonal bureaucracies. In one instance in 1970 he urged that a black woman denied a New York City teaching license because she had once been jailed in Jacksonville, Florida for picketing a segregated movie theater be granted the right to seek a teaching job. That same year he defended a teacher suspended because of alleged homosexuality. In both instances, Wechsler's influence helped vindicate the accused persons.

Much respected for his principles, Wechsler has published *War Propaganda and the United States,* with Harold Lavine (New Haven, 1940), a study of propaganda used by different nations to attain support for the United States during World War II. He demonstrated his staunchly democratic views in *Labor Baron: A Portrait of John L. Lewis* (New York, 1944), which presents an unsympathetic portrayal of the union mining boss as a powerful broker out of place in a democracy. He has published two memoirs, *The Age of Suspicion* (New York, 1953) and *Reflections of an Angry Middle-Aged Editor* (New York, 1959), which depict his own political and journalistic career since his student activist days and include an account of the bigoted and biased McCarthy hearings, in which he was unjustly attacked for his political views by opportunistic and extremist politicians and their unscrupulous allies.

In a Darkness, which Wechsler coauthored with his wife and daughter (New York, 1972), is an account of his 26-year-old son Michael's bout with mental illness, his years of treatment with seven different doctors and his eventual suicide in 1969. The highly emotional book troubled many critics; some wondered if it was not merely Wechsler's attempt to admit his own guilt, while others blasted his attack on the psychiatric establishment. Even so, other critics praised the honesty and candor of the work and suggested that the book could be helpful to families in an similar situation.

Wechsler has long stood for a principled approach toward attacks on freedom. Thus he was associated with the Americans for Democratic Action from its inception in 1946 in defense of liberty everywhere, His newspaper articles of the time mirror those attitudes, including his persistent criticism of those still in thrall to the Soviet Union. He was also a strong opponent of the Vietnam War, although he continued to insist that attacks by radicals against liberalism were ill-informed and inaccurate. He has continued this approach, rejecting the views of right-wingers who demand that the Reagan White House ignore the economic recession and turn instead to "social issues" such as abortion and school prayers. At the same time, Wechsler strongly derides the neo-Conservatives who, as he wrote in the *New York Post* on May 26, 1982, "yearn for a return to the strident rhetoric of the anti-Boshevik crusade and worldwide leadership of a struggle to the death (preferably not but, if necessary, nuclear) with Moscow." Instead, Wechsler believes in the nuclear freeze movement and paring away "the traditional sanctity of swollen military budgets" as well as attending seriously to the social and economic needs of the Americans.

Wechsler has been a member of the American Civil Liberties Union since 1953 and won the Florence Lasker Civil Liberties Award in 1968.

MURRAY LEW WEIDENBAUM

b. February 10, 1927
Economist; educator

Murray Weidenbaum, chief economic adviser to President Ronald Reagan and formerly Assistant Secretary of the Treasury for Economic Policy under President Richard M. Nixon, is an expert on government regulation. He is a Mallinckrodt Distinguished University Professor of Economics at Washington University in St. Louis and author of several books on economics.

Murray Lew Weidenbaum was born in the Bronx to David, a cab driver, and Rose (Warshaw) Weidenbaum. He received his Bachelor of Business Administration degree from City College in 1948, his master's degree from Columbia University in 1949 and his Ph.D. in economics from Princeton University in 1958.

From 1949 to 1957 he worked for the federal government in Washington as an economist with the Bureau of the Budget. He was a corporate economist with the Boeing Company from 1958 to 1963 and in 1963 was hired as senior economist at the Stanford Research Institute, a position he held for one year, before moving to St. Louis.

Except for his years of government service, Weidenbaum has taught at Washington University since 1964. There he founded the Center for the Study of American Business, which is funded primarily by corporate grants. He has been a visiting scholar at the American Enterprise Institute, a conservative research organization, and is director of the American Council for Capital Formation.

As assistant secretary of the treasury for economic policy from 1969 to 1971, Weidenbaum was the first high-ranking official in the Nixon administration to publicly advocate a policy of restraining wages and prices. He made the proposal in June 1970, more than a year before President Nixon imposed a wage and price freeze. During that time he was also dubbed "Mr. Revenue Sharing" because of his support for that program created by Nixon.

He was appointed chairman of the Council of Economic Advisors by President Reagan in January 1981. The first Jew assigned to a high-level position by the newly inaugurated president, Weidenbaum is well known for his controversial assertion that federal regulation costs business about $100 billion a year. He has urged Reagan to impose legislation forcing agencies to give greater consideration to costs and benefits in deciding on regulations, and favors—like Reagan—the Kemp-Roth "supply side" economic proposal for a 30 percent, three-year tax cut for individuals. Because of his total support for the Reagan economic proposals, Weidenbaum was described by one unfriendly journalist as the president's "echo." Yet in July 1982 he resigned.

The Republican economist has written numerous books expressing his views on government regulation, including *Federal Budgeting: The Choice of Government Programs* (Washington, D.C., 1965), a critical analysis of the congressional budget; *Modern Public Sector* (New York, 1969), which offers new methods of doing government business; *Watching Needs and Resources: Reforming the Federal Budget* (Washington, D.C., 1973); *Government-Mandated Price Increases* (Washington, D.C., 1975); *Prospects for Reallocating Public Resources: A Study in Federal-State Fiscal Relations* (Washington, D.C., 1967); and *The Future of Business Regulation: Private Action and Public Demand* (New York, 1980), all of which examine federal budget reform and government regulation.

He is a fellow at the National Association of Business Economists and a member of the Association of Evolutionary Economists and the National Economists Club. He has been a consultant to various business firms and has served on the editorial board of the *Journal of Economic Issues*.

For further information:
Weidenbaum, Murray. "Winners and Losers." *Society*, November–December 1981.

TRUDE WEISS-ROSMARIN

b. June 17, 1908
Editor; writer

Trude Weiss-Rosmarin, founder and editor of *The Jewish Spectator*, is one of the Jewish establishment's greatest critics as well as a distinguished Talmudist and Hebraist, long-time Jewish feminist and an influential educator and writer.

Trude Weiss was born in Frankfurt, Germany to Jacob, a wholesale wine merchant, and Celestine (Mulling) Weiss. Her family was "religiously" but not "culturally" Jewish, she says. As a child she joined the Blau-Weiss group, a Zionist youth fellowship dedicated to enjoying outdoor life. When the philosopher Gershom Scholem criticized the group as "fascist" because their penchant for outdoor activity vaguely resembled certain far-right German nativist groups, Weiss-Rosmarin was alleged to have responded: "Scholem, I suppose, doesn't like physical exercise."

She studied at Franz Rosenzweig's Freie Juedische Lehrhaus where "the spirit" of Judaism was taught and disseminated. She became fluent in the Hebrew language, telling an interviewer decades later, "Look, you don't learn Hebrew to order breakfast in your hotel in Israel. Order your breakfast in English. But read Hebrew!"

In 1931 she emigrated with her husband to the United States and directed the School of the Jewish Woman in New York City from 1933 to 1939 under the sponsorship of Hadassah. Here she stressed equal opportunity and equal access to learning and jobs.

In 1936, now divorced, she began her magazine and embarked on her career as writer and lecturer. *The Jewish Spectator* is a unique publication and its pages have been adorned by such eminent thinkers and scholars as Franz Werfel, Jakob Wasserman, S. Y. Agnon, Israel Joshua Singer and the historian Cecil Roth, among others. Most notably, she has repeatedly criticized the Federations of Jewish Philanthropies which collect charitable contributions and then distribute them to various charities. Again and again, she has charged that Federation activities are unaccountable and that only a few insiders know for sure how and why the money is allocated. There has never been, she has written, a public accounting of the Federations.

Weiss-Rosmarin has also emphasized the duty when necessary to criticize Israel's policies, but more significantly the way American Jewish groups defer to Israel on virtually all matters. "There is no freedom of speech in Jewish publishing in America," she states. In "Israel: Facing Facts," in her Spring 1982 issue, she wrote that Breira (Hebrew for alternative)

> was hounded and starved out of existence by a vicious campaign of defamation. Now "The New Jewish Agenda" is being attacked as "subversive" and some of its early members and supporters have broken ranks because they "cannot afford" to express their convictions. . . .
> I am progressive and liberal—because the Jewish tradition is progressive and liberal. The imperatives of human rights, freedom, equality and social justice . . . are the legacy of the Hebrew Bible. . . .

She has long since concluded that Israel must make peace with Palestinians and other Arabs in order to survive. In her pamphlet "Toward a Jewish-Muslim Dialogue" (1967) she argued that Israel cannot absorb the increasing Arab population within its borders and that the nation and Zionist principles have been hurt by the reluctance of Jews to engage in physical work anymore, insisting instead that Arabs be employed for such purposes.

Weiss-Rosmarin relishes her role as a "Jewish maverick." At the National Conference for a New Jewish Agenda held in Washington, D.C. in 1980, she stated that according to the Jewish establishment, "whoever thinks independently, whoever does not toe the line, has no place in the Jewish community" and she added that such thinking is indeed a loss for American Jewish life since "it has been deprived of its idea-content."

She is the author of numerous books on American Jewish life, including *Religion of Reason: The Philosophy of Hermann Cohen* (New York, 1935); *The Hebrew Moses' New Light on the Bible* (New York, 1939); *Jewish Women Through the Ages* (New York, 1941); and *Judaism and Christianity* (New York, 1943). She has also written many reviews and articles. In her review of Roger Moser's book *Gotteserfahrun bei Martin Buber* (translated as "God-experience by Martin Buber") which appeared in *The Jewish Quarterly Review*, Volume LXX, April 1980, she wrote approvingly of Martin Buber's beliefs that "community—the prayer community of the minyan [quorum], the fate-community whose members are mutually pledged in responsible fealty in the everyday world—is what Jewishness is all about."

Weiss-Rosmarin's works have led Robert Gordis, editor of *Judaism* magazine and himself a widely-respected scholar-editor, to call her "the most Jewishly learned woman in the world." Indeed, she may rank among the most learned Jews anywhere, male or female.

VICTOR WEISSKOPF

b. September 19, 1908
Physicist

Ever since he witnessed the first nuclear explosion in 1943 and understood the potential for mass annihilation with the atomic bomb, physicist Victor Weisskopf has been in the forefront of the international movement to ban the production and proliferation of nuclear arms. He was a founder of the Federation of Atomic Scientists, an organization whose goal is to publicize the threats posed by nuclear war and to stress the use of nuclear power for peaceful purposes, and he has been a leader in the movement to internationalize scientific study.

Victor Frederick Weisskopf was born in Vienna to Emil, a corporate lawyer, and Martha (Gut) Weisskopf. He grew up under the Austro-Hungarian monarchy and through the turbulence of World War I. As a teenager, Weisskopf was drawn to physics, which was then a new field and one that his father considered impractical since there were few real jobs to be had for physicists. But that became Weisskopf's field of study at Vienna University, which he entered in 1926, and two years later he switched to an even newer subdivision of physics, quantum mechanics, which he studied at the University of Gottingen in Germany. Gottingen had many of the best young pioneers in this specialized area, and as Weisskopf later wrote in a 1973 essay entitled "My Life as a Physicist," "Every new Ph.D. thesis at that time opened up a new field." His own thesis, completed in 1931, was the result of a collaboration with a young instructor at Gottingen named Wigner and concerned the use of divergent integrals in the study of the natural width of spectral lines.

By 1931 Hitler had already become a major threat in Europe, and for the community of physicists, many of whom were Jewish, jobs were especially scarce. Weisskopf managed to get a postdoctoral slot to study with the physicist Werner Heisenberg in Leipzig in 1932, but in those days postdoctoral grants did not include living stipends, and Weisskopf remained dependent on his parents. After spending six months studying in Berlin and a year in Kharkov in the Soviet Union, Weisskopf received a Rockefeller fellowship in 1934 which enabled him to be self-supporting for one year and continue physics research in the place of his choice. He opted to go to Copenhagen for six months of work with the Nobelist Niels Bohr and then to finish his grant in Cambridge, England. The next three years consisted of further study and research with many of the top physicists of the time; Weisskopf also became renowned within his own specialization in quantum electrodynamics and elementary particle physics. But as a Jew, he found living and working in Europe increasingly difficult, and when Bohr, who had developed extensive contacts with physicists in America, arranged for him to teach at the University of Rochester in New York in 1937, he accepted the post. He was an instructor at Rochester from 1937 to 1939 and an assistant professor from 1939 to 1945.

During World War II, when many physicists were being recruited to do war-related research, Weisskopf began teaching at other universities near Rochester. But in 1943, the same year he was naturalized, he became part of the war effort himself, when the physicist J. Robert Oppenheimer invited him to participate in atomic bomb development in Los Alamos, New Mexico. As group leader and associate head of the theory division on the exploitation of nuclear energy, Weisskopf was privy to many significant scientific developments, and he witnessed the first-ever nuclear explosion in a New Mexico desert named, ironically, Jornado del Muerte, or "Journey of Death." The event so moved him that in 1944 Weisskopf became one of the first public opponents of nuclear weaponry. In addition to being a founder of the Federation of Atomic Scientists, he became involved in subsequent efforts to halt arms development, including creating networks with scientists around the world to forge an international community that would bridge political and social differences in an attempt to use science for constructive and humanistic purposes.

From Los Alamos, Weisskopf returned to Rochester, where he specialized in research in high-energy physics. In 1945 he joined the faculty at the Massachusetts Institute of Technology, heading the theory group at the Institute's Nuclear Science Lab, where many contributions were made toward the understanding of nuclear reactions and quantum electrodynamics. In 1949 he joined an emergency committee of scientists, headed by Albert Einstein, which fought for atomic weapons control and for greater interaction between Eastern and Western countries. The following year Weisskopf and 11 other physicists published a manifesto condemning the development of the hydrogen bomb by the American government, stating: "We believe that no nation has the right to use such a bomb no matter how righteous its cause. This bomb is no longer a weapon of war, but a means of extermination of whole populations. Its use would be a betrayal of all standards of morality and of Christian civilization itself."

By the mid-1950s Weisskopf had become internationally prominent in the movement to internationalize scientific research—he had headed the effort himself in 1950, when he became the first foreign physicist to teach at the Sorbonne in Paris—and in 1956 he helped coordinate the first Atoms for Peace conference in Geneva, which included participation by scientists from the Soviet Union. He was also instrumental in the planning of the Pugwash Conferences, the first of which was held in Nova Scotia in 1957 and which have since been held periodically in different locations so that scientists from all over the world could convene and discuss new developments in their respective fields.

At about this time, Weisskopf was also involved in planning the European Center for Nuclear Research (CERN) in Geneva. In 1960 he became CERN's director-general for five years, taking an extended leave from MIT. A year after his return, he was appointed institute professor of physics, one of MIT's most prestigious chairs, and from 1967 until his retirement in 1973, he headed the Department of Physics.

Even in retirement Weisskopf remained outspoken and active in the anti-nuclear arms movement and in the world of physics. From 1976 to 1979 he was president of the American Academy of Arts and Sciences, and in 1981 he headed a delegation of four American scientists—all Jews—to represent Pope John Paul II in a meeting with President Reagan to discuss the need to prohibit nuclear weapons use.

For further information:

Weisskopf, Victor. *Knowledge and Wonder: The Natural World as Man Knows It.* Cambridge, Mass.: 1979.

————. *Physics in the XX Century.* Cambridge, Mass.: 1972.

Weisskopf, Victor and Blatt, John M. *Theoretical Nuclear Physics.* Cambridge, Mass.: 1952.

DAVID "SONNY" WERBLIN

b. March 17, 1910
Sports executive

Throughout his career as a theater, broadcasting and sports entrepreneur, "Sonny" Werblin has displayed an intuitive talent for marketing with enormous success whatever product he was packaging. He was one of the pioneers in television programming in the 1950s, formulated the most dramatic deal in football history when he recruited an untried player named Joe Namath from the University of Alabama and turned an isolated swamp area in New Jersey into the successful Meadowlands sports complex.

David Abraham Werblin was born in the Flatbush section of Brooklyn, the son of Simon Abner, the owner of a paper bag company whose success enabled the family to live very comfortably, and Henrietta (Gross) Werblin, from whom Werblin got his nickname.

Werblin attended Erasmus Hall High School and graduated from James Madison High School in 1927. That year he entered Rutgers University in New Jersey, where he continued playing football, as he had in high school. But injuries forced him to quit during his freshman year, and he turned his extracurricular energies in other directions. He became a sports stringer for seven newspapers in New York and New Jersey and established the Rutgers Interscholastic Debating Leagues, which sponsored meets and competitions among New Jersey high schools. These early initiatives earned him substantial income—more, he later commented, than he earned during the first few years of working full-time after he received his B.A. degree from Rutgers in 1931.

For about a year he was a sports writer for a Brooklyn paper, which folded soon after, and worked as a copyboy for *The New York Times.* Then, in 1932 he joined the Music Corporation of America (MCA), earning $21 a week as a band manager for Guy Lombardo, Eddy Duchin and others and as booking and theatrical agent and promoter for such film and stage stars as Al Jolson, Frank Sinatra, Jackie Gleason, Abbott and Costello, Joan Crawford and Betty Grable.

As an agent, Werblin had a "Midas touch"; and by 1951, despite a heart attack some years earlier that had curbed his activities, he was named president of MCA television, where he supervised a host of series and specials that were then sold to the networks. Among his greatest innovations was to attract stage and film stars to television by giving them part-ownership in their own shows. By 1964 Werblin was labeled "the ultimate show business agent and the father of the package deal."

One year earlier, he had begun to move from show business to sports, where he utilized his special talents to turn sports into profitable audience entertainment with its own galaxy of stars, who would become as celebrated in media as many of the Broadway and television personalities he had managed. His first move was to buy a mediocre young professional football team, the New York Titans. He renamed them the New York Jets and in 1964 moved the team to Shea Stadium and hired as coach Weeb Ewbank, who had won a National

Football League championship with the Baltimore Colts. The following year he signed Joe Namath to the Jets after seeing him play in the Orange Bowl and engineered one of the most controversial deals in sports history when he offered the 21-year-old a three-year contract of $400,000—a mammoth sum at the time—with a new Lincoln Continental thrown in as an "extra." The rival National Football League reeled at Werblin's move as big money now became a fact of life in pro football and other big league sports. In January 1969 his underdog Jets won the Super Bowl, stunning the sports world.

In 1968 Werblin retired from sports when he sold his share of the New York Jets and moved to Florida. But the respite from management was temporary, as he joined with Johnny Carson and several other investors to form Raritan Enterprises, a holding company with investments in real estate, the leisure industry and entertainment. In 1971 Werblin was instrumental in negotiating a huge contract for Carson at NBC. And that year he also returned to sports when be became chairman of the New Jersey Sports and Exposition Authority. Under his aegis the huge Meadowlands Sports Complex in East Rutherford was completed in 1976 and currently houses a soccer team (the Cosmos), a football team (the Giants), a basketball team (the Nets), a hockey team (the Devils) and a racetrack.

In 1977 Werblin became president and chief executive officer of the Madison Square Garden Corporation, which includes a huge roster of sports and entertainment events as well as ownership of the New York Knicks basketball team and the New York Rangers hockey club.

Werblin's behind-the-scenes gift for promoting competition through astute packaging and use of media has played a major role in improving the quality of theatrical, television and sports presentations.

THEODORE H. WHITE

b. May 6, 1915
Journalist

Theodore H. White is best-known to Americans for his books on the four presidential campaigns from 1960 to 1972. With *The Making of the President 1960* (New York, 1961), he introduced a new approach to political journalism, viewing presidential candidates for office and their colleagues and the combined aspirations of everyone involved with an eye for detail and an insight into personalities that had never been explored before in quite the same way.

Theodore Harold White was born in a Jewish section of Boston to David, a lawyer, and Mary (Winkeller) White. From 1925 until 1929 he attended the Hebrew College of Boston. After his father's death during the Depression, White worked as a newsboy, and with a newspaper scholarship he entered Harvard College. He graduated from Harvard in 1938 with a B.A. degree in Chinese history and oriental languages.

White became China correspondent for *Time* magazine in 1939, covering the revolution and becoming *Time's* bureau head in Peking until his resignation in 1945. His first book, *Thunder Out of China*, coauthored with journalist Annalee Jacoby (New York, 1946), recounted his experiences in China and was critical of the government of Chiang Kai-shek. Virtually all reviewers praised the book's perceptive reportage. He was briefly an editor with *The New Republic* in 1947 but resigned to become a free-lance writer contributing to many major American magazines, which he continues to do today. At the same time, he edited *The Stilwell Papers* (New York, 1948), the World War II writings of a man he greatly admired, General Joseph Stilwell, who commanded the U.S. forces in China.

Following a reporting stint in Paris from 1948 to 1953, White wrote *Fire in the Ashes: Europe in Mid-Century* (New York, 1958), a description of postwar Europe. He then turned to novel-writing with *The Mountain Road* (New York, 1958), a tale of the evacuation of Chinese and American armed forces, and *The View from the Fortieth Floor* (New York, 1960), a semi-autobiographical account of his experiences at *Collier's* magazine in the mid-1950s. Although it was not a rousing success, actor Gary Cooper was interested enough to buy the movie rights from White. That income enabled him to embark on his first presidential campaign project.

The Making of the President 1964 (New York, 1965) duplicated the thorough and exhaustive empirical researching approach White had used four years earlier, but with somewhat less success: Other writers were now using similar styles, and he was no longer unique. *The Making of the President 1968* (New York, 1969) and *The Making of the President 1972* (New York, 1973) were best sellers. *The Making of the President* series had White following presidential candidates long before election time through the arduous process of announcing candidacies; formulating their identities as presidential aspirants; growing, changing, flubbing their way through campaigns. He not only reports on events, he explores emotional developments among his "characters." For example, *The Making of the President 1960* has White spending more than a year pursuing all seven aspirants across the United States from their first primaries in New Hampshire and Wisconsin through Inauguration day. He analyzes the meaning of John F. Kennedy's victory but relies heavily on detail and anecdote. The series became a prototype for later political journalists who attempted to ape White's style.

During the 12 years that he documented the presidential campaigns of 1960, 1964, 1968 and 1972, White also wrote television documentaries based on the histories he had written and a play, *Caesar at the Rubicon: A Play About Politics* (New York, 1968). But the presidential books made him—and almost unmade him. He was criticized for oversimplification of what had become increasingly complex issues and personalities with each successive campaign and for tending to adulate politicians. But at the same time, his command of politics, his eye for nuances and his very readable style brought him much recognition. Following the Nixon reelection in 1972 and his resignation less than two years later in the wake of the Watergate scandal, White published *Breach of Faith: The Fall of Richard Nixon* (New York, 1975), a chronicle and analysis of Nixon's entire political career.

He has often been described by his peers as a "political journalist's journalist." What many have in mind is his dedication to exhaustively pursuing all sides of whatever story he was investigating, his total absorption in the subject and his sense of history.

"Teddy" White has summed up his own career in an autobiography, *In Search of History: A Personal Adventure* (New York, 1978), in which he describes his experiences as a foreign correspondent and a historian of contemporary America. He received the Pulitzer Prize in 1962 for general nonfiction, more than 20 awards for journalism, the Benjamin Franklin award for magazine writing and several Emmys for his documentaries.

White had considered ending his series on the presidency with the election in 1980. Then, he said, "What I had been reporting in 1980 was more than a campaign . . . it simply had to be seen as a climactic episode in a much longer period of time than I had attempted to write of before." Thus, in *America in Search of Itself: The Making of the President 1956-1980* (New York, 1982), White looks backward and ahead and the result is a disillusioned White, saddened and depressed at what he believes has occurred in the United States since 1956. Still inordinately kind to virtually all politicians, White now castigates such statutes as the Civil Rights Act of 1964 because it "was a new departure. It undertook to regulate behavior." He blames liberalism, particularly the 89th Congress which enacted many of Lyndon B. Johnson's Great Society programs. In short, White sees the United States in very serious trouble, either at the beginning or the end of a daring experiment. The basic change in politics "has come, and will continue to come,

in the nature of the questions Americans ask of themselves." Can individual well-being be defended? Will the United States be "the last hunting ground of international predators as well as the refuge of the huddled poor?" Will politicians be able to sense the common national interest and act accordingly?

ELIE WIESEL

b. September 30, 1928
Writer

Elie Wiesel, writer, philosopher, novelist and playwright, is known throughout the world for his extraordinary efforts to rescue the Holocaust from historical and literary oblivion and to dramatize the plight of Soviet Jewry. To many, he is the conscience of the Holocaust.

Elie Wiesel was born in Sighet, a Hungarian-speaking town located in Transylvania near the Ukrainian frontier and ruled by Rumania. His father, Shlomo, a storekeeper, and his mother, Sarah (Feig) Weisel, lived quiet religious lives, while their only son, Elie, studied *Cabala* with Hasidic rabbis. But in 1944 all of Sighet's 12,000 Jews—about half the town's population—were sent to concentration camps. At Buchenwald, Wiesel watched his father die, a scene grippingly related in his first book, *Night* (New York, 1960), an autobiographical account of concentration camp experiences. His mother and younger sister and other relatives were also murdered at Auschwitz, and only two sisters survived. At the end of the war, he and other Jewish orphans were shipped to France to become wards of a French Jewish children's agency. There he learned to write French and met Francois Mauriac, the eminent Catholic philosopher, who encouraged him to write and who later wrote a searing and moving introduction to *Night*.

Between 1948 and 1951 Wiesel studied philosophy at the Sorbonne and worked simultaneously as a teacher of Hebrew and Bible, as choir director and as a stringer for the Tel Aviv *Yediot Achronot*. His doctoral dissertation, which he never completed, compared Jewish, Christian and Buddhist concepts of asceticism. In that period he visited India and also learned English.

Twelve years after he entered Buchenwald, he arrived in New York City, where he was employed by the *Jewish Daily Forward* and by *L'Arche,* the official publication of organized French Jewry. Seven years later, in 1963, he became an American citizen.

Night originally appeared in 1956 in Buenos Aires, Argentina in Yiddish as *Un di Velt Hot Geshvign* ("And the World Has Remained Silent") and was later rewritten in French for publication in France in 1958 as *La Nuit*. But when it was published in the United States in 1960, the effect was shattering. For nearly two decades surprisingly little had been written or said publicly about the Holocaust. *Night,* though, was the powerful story of Wiesel and his father incarcerated in a Nazi concentration camp. There the young Wiesel underwent a total loss of faith, and his book became an effort to bear witness before the world to what he and others had experienced. His struggles since then to reconcile the horrors of the past with present realities have provided the foundations for all of his subsequent work. "In *Night,*" Wiesel has since remarked:

> I wanted to show the end, the finality of the event. Everything came to an end—history, literature, religion, God. There was nothing left. And yet we begin again with *Night*. Only where do we go from there? Since then, I have explored all kinds of options. To tell you that I have now found a religion, that I believe—no. I am still searching. I am still exploring. I am still protesting.

As a result of the book's publication, not only did the Holocaust once again become a proper subject for public discussion by Jews, Christians and younger generations, it also transformed Wiesel into a major American and world Jewish hero, a conscience of world Jewry, a "modern Job" who would never permit the Holocaust to be forgotten again. Indeed, he visited Cambodia and Thailand in 1979 to assist suffering Cambodian refugees as a protest against allowing people to die, forgotten.

Dawn (New York, 1961), his first novel, tells the story of a camp survivor who joins the underground in pre-Israel Palestine and is ordered to murder a British officer in retaliation for the sentencing of a Jewish partisan to death. Wiesel uses the plot to examine the moral problem and concludes that all murder is suicide. In *The Accident* (New York, 1962), an immigrant Jewish journalist is hit by a cab and lies in critical condition in a hospital. (Wiesel himself was in a similar accident.) Pained by the guilt he feels because he is the sole survivor of his family, Wiesel's protagonist struggles against God but also tries to accept life and love as part of his existence.

Among Wiesel's other novels are *A Beggar in Jerusalem* (New York, 1970), a complicated and poetic tale of the Six-Day War in 1967 as viewed by a camp survivor, and *The Oath* (New York, 1973), which opens 20 years before the start of the death camps and examines what is doubtless his own life: the death of a Carpathian town and its Jewish inhabitants and the spiritual anguish of its only survivor.

Wiesel has also turned his attention to the plight of Soviet Jewry. In a series of pioneering articles in 1966 in the *Saturday Evening Post* and in a later book, *The Jews of Silence* (New York, 1966), he brought to light the fact that despite Stalinist terror and forced assimilation, Jewishness had not been destroyed in the Soviet Union. "How can it be explained?" he asked. "I don't know. The temptation to assimilate was tremendous."

His play *Zalman and the Madness of God* (1974) was performed on public television and in Washington and New York City. It told the story of the years 1948 to 1953, when Stalin decided to kill Jewish intellectuals and even exile all Soviet Jews to Siberia. Says Wiesel of the murdered intellectuals: "I am haunted by these people whose death was taken away from them. It's not part of Jewish history. We don't know what happened to them. That's what I'm trying to imagine."

In addition to his writing and activism, Wiesel has taught, first at the City College of New York, then at Boston University. He speaks widely and offers an annual feast of Hasidic tales at the 92nd Street Y in New York City.

Wiesel was named chairman of the United States Holocaust Memorial Council by President Jimmy Carter in 1978.

For further information:
Wiesel, Elie. *Ecstasy and Sadness: Further Tales of the Hasidic Masters.* New York: 1982.
———. *Five Biblical Portraits.* South Bend, Ind.: 1981.
———. *The Testament.* New York: 1981.

JEROME WIESNER

b. May 30, 1915
Electrical engineer; professor; former university president; presidential science adviser

Jerome Wiesner's expertise in military technology and his background as one of the first developers of radar led to his becoming one of the scientific community's first and most vocal proponents of nuclear disarmament and the need for a more humanistic view in scientific study. A former adviser to Presidents Kennedy and Johnson, he served as president of the Massachusetts Institute of Technology from 1971 to 1980.

Jerome Bert Wiesner was born in Detroit, Michigan to Joseph, a dry goods merchant, and Ida (Friedman) Wiesner. Raised in Dearborn, where he witnessed the labor strife that pitted auto workers against Ford management's "goon squad," Wiesner early on developed a sensitivity to social problems which would color the direction of his later scientific research, teachings and writings. He attended the University of Michigan, where he received a B.S. degree in engineering in 1937, an M.S. degree in 1938 and eventually a Ph.D. in 1950.

Wiesner served as associate director of the University of Michigan Broadcasting Service from 1937 to 1940. In 1940 he brought his skill in acoustical engineering to a post with the Library of Congress. As part of his job, he travelled across the United States with folklorist Alan Lomax, collecting and recording American folk music.

In 1942 he joined the radiation laboratory of the Massachusetts Institute of Technology, which introduced him to research in military technology. Except for one year of research at the University of California lab at Los Alamos from 1945 to 1946, Wiesner made his career at MIT. He was on the engineering faculty from 1946 to 1971, served as director of the electronics research lab from 1952 to 1961, headed the electrical engineering department from 1959 to 1960, was dean from 1964 to 1966 and was provost—second in command at the university—from 1966 to 1971. As provost Wiesner had academic responsibility for 2200 faculty members who taught in 23 departments or worked in 25 research and teaching labs.

During these years, Wiesner became a public figure, as much for his statements opposing the arms race as for articles and books he published. From 1956 to 1961 he served as an Eisenhower appointee on the Army Science Advisory Committee, an experience which convinced him of the uselessness of the arms race. As early as 1961 he was posing provocative questions to American readers about the need for immediate arms control. His thoughts were included in two books, *Arms Control, Disarmament and National Security,* edited by Donald G. Brennan (New York, 1961) and *Arms Control: Issues for the Public,* edited by Louis Henkin. (Englewood Cliffs, New Jersey, 1961). Wiesner's liberal political stance and his prominence in the scientific community brought him into early contact with the Kennedy circle. In 1961, taking leave of MIT, he went to Washington as science adviser and played an important role in developing the nuclear test ban treaty. He remained in Washington through part of 1964, serving in the administration of President Lyndon B. Johnson.

Returning to Cambridge, Wiesner published in 1965 a collection of papers and speeches, *Where Science and Politics Meet* (New York), which discussed the relationship of science and government as they pertained to science education and disarmament.

As Wiesner rose through the administrative ranks of MIT, he introduced some of his own ideas to the university's curriculum. As provost, for example, he expanded academic offerings in the humanities, arts and social sciences.

But his work as a scientific spokesperson against the arms race remained Wiesner's foremost mission. In 1969 he coauthored with scholar Abram Chayes *ABM: An Evaluation of the Decision to Deploy an Anti-Ballistic Missile* (New York). His views incurred the wrath of President Richard M. Nixon. Nixon was antagonistic to many Jews, especially liberal Jews, as the Watergate tapes and the memoirs of former aide John D. Ehrlichmann reveal. When Wiesner criticized Nixon's March 1969 ruling to deploy a limited antiballistic missile network, Ehrlichmann charged that in Henry Kissinger's presence, the president bitterly censured Wiesner, calling him "another one of those Jews."

In 1971 Wiesner was elected president of MIT, succeeding Dr. Paul E. Gray. Holding that post for nine years, he retired in 1980 to become president emeritus and Institute Professor. He remained throughout that period outspoken in his views against expansion of the arms race, regularly publishing bold, analytic articles discussing the futility of nuclear weapons build-ups and of what he called the "scare-mongering" common to presidential candidates during their quadrennial quest for the White House. In a 1980 Op-Ed piece in *The New York Times* entitled "We're Hearing It Again: Reds' Sails in the Sunset," Wiesner reminded readers of how, as early as 1948, Americans were being made to feel "terrified by the vision of a surprise attack by a Soviet bomber force, which eventually proved to be nonexistent, but not before billions of dollars had been spent augmenting an already vastly superior United States Air Force." Nearly two years later, as the antinuclear movement had blossomed into an international and nonpartisan endeavor, Wiesner contended that there was, indeed, "an easily structured, effective way to stop the escalating arms race." In a 1982 Op-Ed Page piece also in the *Times,* he wrote, "President Reagan should declare an open-ended unilateral moratorium, always subject to reversal, on the production testing and deployment of new nuclear weapons and delivery systems. He should invite the Russians to respond with a parallel declaration of purpose. If they did, it would result in a non-negotiated freeze." While a moratorium would not be the same thing as nuclear disarmament, Wiesner added that "it is a way of arresting the arms race. . . . What we ultimately do and how far we finally go beyond this easy initial stage depends upon how each side responds. The unilateral moratorium should be just a first step in global psychotherapy."

AARON WILDAVSKY

b. May 31, 1930
Professor; political scientist

Aaron Wildavsky is one of America's foremost scholars on the power of the American presidency and on the role of financial planning in the development of public policy on the domestic level and in foreign affairs. As economic considerations have taken a more dominant role in American politics, Wildavsky, who heads the Survey Research Center at the University of California at Berkeley, has stepped beyond academic circles to participate in government and private organizations concerned with policy formation.

Aaron Wildavsky was born in New York City to Sender, a bookbinder who also dabbled in real estate, and Eva (Brudnow) Wildavsky. His parents, refugees from Bolshevik Russia, were ardent Democrats, and as a teen-ager, Wildavsky became active in the local Democratic Club in Brooklyn, later working in the 1936 presidential campaign of Franklin D. Roosevelt. (He writes that he met his first "live" Republican when he was 14.)

At Brooklyn College, which Wildavsky entered in 1948, he became active in the New York state Liberal Party, feeling that it combined the best forms of welfare liberalism while rejecting the totalitarianism that characterized the Communist movement, then popular on college campuses. He served in the U.S. Army from 1950 to 1952, then returned to Brooklyn College, where he received a B.A. degree in 1954.

The following year Wildavsky studied political science at the University of Sydney in Australia as a Fulbright scholar. He then entered graduate school at Yale University planning to focus on Soviet politics, but after being influenced by the Yale scholar James Fesler, a specialist in government and public administration, he switched his focus and received an M.A. degree in 1957 and a Ph.D. in 1959.

Having "discovered" his vocation as a researcher and professor on the university level during his years at Yale—the background to which he provides in the introduction to his essay collection *The Revolt Against the Masses* (New York, 1971)—Wildavsky entered teaching. He spent 1958 to 1960 as an instructor of government at Oberlin College and was assistant professor when he left in 1962 to spend a year as a research fellow at Resources for the Future. In 1963 he accepted an appointment to the Berkeley faculty as assistant professor. He rose to associate professor in 1965 and was named full professor the following year. From 1966 to 1969 he served as department chair of the political

science department and from 1969 to 1977 was dean of the Graduate School of Public Policy.

Wildavsky has been a dedicated and prolific writer as well as a teacher, commenting in one essay that "writing is a process of self-discovery which sometimes leads you to say more than you knew was in you or carries you far from original intentions." In all he has written 15 books on public policy, budgeting and urban politics, and related studies that discuss the role of governments in determining spending priorities for their constituencies. He has also developed and edited 6 series of teaching materials on American federalism, the American presidency and U.S. foreign policy and is or has been on the editorial boards of 12 professional publications, including *Public Policy, Urban Studies, Journal of Contemporary Studies, Public Budgeting and Finance* and others. He has also written dozens of articles and contributed chapters to many books.

Although Wildavsky was attracted to left-wing politics as a youth, in later years as a professional, he espoused some apparently conservative views that essentially questioned traditional liberal government programs. Yet he indicates that overall he sees himself as "a representative of the passionate and committed center. Mostly I push hard for small changes compatible with the little knowledge and limited moral sensibility of mankind." Although he was drawn into a field that initially seemed far removed from the fervor of earlier interests in history and politics, he wrote that what he does is inherently valuable to the well-being of humankind, for which he sees a bleak and precarious future. In a 1971 essay he wrote that "My life and my work embody both a deep-seated pessimism about man's ability to control the evil in him and an abiding faith that it is worth trying to perfect his capacity for self-government."

For further information:

Wildavsky, Aaron. *Budgeting: A Comparative Theory of Budgetary Processes.* Boston: 1975.

———. *How to Limit Government Spending.* Berkeley, Calif.: 1980.

———. *The Politics of the Budgetary Process.* Boston: 1979.

———. *The Revolt Against the Masses and Other Essays on Politics and Public Policy.* New York: 1971.

———. *Speaking Truth to Power: The Art and Craft of Policy Analysis.* Boston: 1979.

Wildavsky, Aaron, and Heclo, Hugh. *The Private Government of Public Money.* London: 1981.

Wildavsky, Aaron; Levy, Frank; and Meltsner, Arnold. *Urban Outcomes.* Berkeley, Calif.: 1973.

Wildavsky, Aaron, and Tenenbaum, Ellen. *The Politics of Mistrust: Estimating American Oil and Gas Resources.* Beverly Hills, Calif.: 1981.

GENE WILDER

b. June 11, 1935
Actor; scriptwriter; director; producer

Gene Wilder has gained fame since the late 1960s as a madcap actor in film comedies, including Mel Brooks' *Blazing Saddles, The Producers* and *Young Frankenstein,* the latter of which he helped write. More recently Wilder has also established himself as a director and producer, shaping his films as satires of other films.

Jerome Silberman was born in Milwaukee, Wisconsin to William and Jeanne (Baer) Silverman. His father, a Russian immigrant, was an importer and manufacturer of souvenirs. His American-born mother had a heart attack and was left a partial invalid when Wilder was 6 years old. From an early age, Wilder enjoyed creating comedy skits to alleviate her depression. Wilder's parents sent him to Black Fox Military Institute in Hollywood, where, he once told a *Time* reporter, "I was the only Jew in school, and I got either beat up or insulted every day." After a very short and unhappy stay there, he transferred to high school in Milwaukee, from which he was graduated in 1951.

Wilder began studying acting in 1947 in Milwaukee and at age 13 made his first stage appearance at the Milwaukee Playhouse as Balthazar in *Romeo and Juliet.* At the University of Iowa, he acted in student plays and worked in summer stock. He graduated with a B.A. degree in 1955.

Upon graduating from college, Wilder attended the Old Vic Theatre School in Bristol, England with the apparent intention of studying classical acting technique. Instead, he took courses in judo, fencing, gymnastics and voice but left when he reached the acting class. After returning home, Wilder was drafted into the Army and assigned to the Valley Forge Hospital in Pennsylvania. On weekends he went to drama classes at the Herbert Berghof Studio in New York City. In 1961 he became a member of the Actors Studio and began to work with the famed Lee Strasberg. That same year he made his Broadway debut as the confused valet in Graham Greene's comedy *The Complaisant Lover,* a performance that won him the Clarence Derwent Award, given to a new performer in a secondary role.

In 1963 Wilder again appeared on Broadway, as the chaplain in Bertolt Brecht's *Mother Courage and Her Children.* Sharpening his craft, Wilder continued on Broadway in *One Flew over the Cuckoo's Nest* (1965), *Dynamite Tonight* (1965), *The White House* (1966) and several other plays. In 1967 he went to Hollywood to play the bewildered undertaker taken as a captive by the gang in *Bonnie and Clyde.* One year later, in 1968, Brooks created for Wilder the role of Leo Bloom, an anguished accountant, in Brooks' first film, *The Producers* (which starred Zero Mostel), a dazzling comedy of a crooked producer and his neurotic partner, Wilder. Wilder's portrayal won him an Oscar nomination for best supporting actor.

In many of Wilder's subsequent films—including *Start the Revolution Without Me* (1969), *Quackser Fortune Has a Cousin in the Bronx* (1970), *Willy Wonka and the Chocolate Factory* (1971), and *The Little Prince* (1973)—critics said Wilder's acting was much better than the scripts. But when he performed in Brooks' films, as the brazen Waco kid in *Blazing Saddles* (1973), a spoof of Hollywood westerns, and as Dr. Frankenstein, a brain surgeon trying to live down the stigma of his relative, in *Young Frankenstein* (1974), both the acting and the script were hailed as uproarious. "One look at Gene Wilder and you know that he's a funny guy. You can see it in his face," wrote a critic.

Wilder's successful collaboration in writing *Young Frankenstein* with Brooks encouraged him to write, on his own, *The Adventures of Sherlock Holmes' Smarter Brother,* a parody of the 19th century detective story. The film, released in 1975, was frantic and funny.

In his 1977 film *The World's Greatest Lover,* Wilder acted, wrote, directed and produced. He played a Milwaukee baker who is enticed to Hollywood in the 1920s by a movie studio's talent search for an actor to rival Rudolph Valentino.

Wilder, whose expressive blue eyes can make him look anything from meek to wild and near-hysterical, has also appeared in Woody Allen's *Everything You Always Wanted to Know About Sex* (1972)—as the man with a passion for sheep; *Silver Streak* (1976); *The Frisco Kid* (1979), a comedy that dealt with an Orthodox Jew traveling from his *shtetl* (East European Jewish village) to the American wild West; and *Stir Crazy* (1978) as well as such television films as *Home for Passover, Death of a Salesman* and *Thursday's Game.*

HAROLD WILLIAMS

b. January 5, 1928
Economist; managerial specialist

Harold Williams has had a distinguished career in the corporate world, the world of academe and government. He was dean of the Graduate School of Business and Management at UCLA when he was chosen by President Jimmy Carter to head the Securities and Exchange Commission. From that position he worked to restore an image of integrity to the business world, which had been rocked with foreign bribery scandals, and was instrumental in the passage in 1977 of the Foreign Corrupt Practices Act.

Harold Marvin Williams was born in Philadelphia, the son of Louis W., an accountant and insurance man, and Sophie (Fox) Williams. He received his B.A. degree from the University of California at Los Angeles in 1946 and then went to Harvard Law School, where he received his Bachelor of Laws in 1949. He did a year of postgraduate study at the University of Southern California Graduate School of Law from 1955 until 1956. He was admitted to the California bar in 1950.

After a year of law practice in 1950, Williams joined the United States Army and served until 1953, attaining the rank of first lieutenant. He then returned to private law practice until 1955, when he joined Hunt Foods and Industries in Los Angeles. Williams stayed at Hunt Foods and Industries from 1955 until 1968. In 1958 he became a vice president and two years later was appointed executive vice president. From 1964 until 1966 he was the general manager of Hunt-Wesson Foods, a subsidiary of Hunt Foods and Industries, and became president of Hunt-Wesson Foods in 1966. In 1968 he became president of Hunt Foods and Industries.

In 1959 Williams had joined the board of directors of Norton Simon Inc., another California conglomerate. From 1968 until 1970 Williams was the chairman of the finance committee of Norton Simon, and from 1969 to 1970 he was the chairman of the board of directors. He remained on the board of directors until 1977. In 1970 Williams became a professor of management and the dean of the Graduate School of Management at the University of California at Los Angeles.

In addition to his personal career, Williams has held a number of important governmental positions. He was co-chairman of the Public Commission on Los Angeles County Government. From 1971 until 1975 he served as the public member of the National Advertising Review Board. He was a member of the Commission for Economic Development of the state of California from 1973 until 1977, and for one year (1973–4) he was the energy adviser to the city of Los Angeles. In 1977 Williams was appointed by President Jimmy Carter to the chairmanship of the Securities and Exchange Commission.

While head of the SEC, Williams worked to improve accounting procedures so that they would reflect inflation. He also argued that corporate boards of directors should be independent of management and moved to relax regulations on small businesses.

He left the SEC on March 1, 1981 and became president and chief executive officer of the J. Paul Getty Museum in Malibu, California. In July 1981 Williams charged publicly before two Senate banking subcom-

mittees that the Reagan administration was trying to change the Foreign Corrupt Practices Act forbidding overseas bribes and payoffs.

HENRY WINKLER

b. October 30, 1945
Actor; producer

For actor Henry Winkler, his greatest success has also been his greatest frustration. As the character "Fonzie" in the television series *Happy Days,* which ran on ABC for seven seasons, he became so renowned to millions of American children and adults that the person underneath became secondary. Winkler's primary efforts are currently focused on establishing himself as a serious film actor as well as a producer and humanitarian.

Henry Franklin Winkler was born in New York City to Harry, president of an international lumber company, and Ilse Anna Maria (Hadra) Winkler. His parents were refugees from Nazi Germany who settled on New York's West Side, where Winkler was raised and where his parents remain today. He attended the McBurney School for Boys and alternated high school in New York with studies in Lausanne, Switzerland from 1959 to 1963. Although his father hoped Winkler, an only son, would follow him into his successful lumber business, Winkler knew early on that he wanted to be an actor. (His first role was as a tube of toothpaste in a school play when he was 6 years old.) He studied theater at Emerson College in Boston, receiving a B.A. degree in 1967. He then studied at the Yale School of Drama, receiving a Master of Fine Arts degree in 1970.

A period of acting with the Yale Repertory Theater in 1970 to 1971 was followed by a stint in New York, where Winkler acted in more than 25 commercials and in small parts in films (*The Lords of Flatbush* in 1972; *Crazy Joe* in 1974). He performed briefly in an improvisational troupe called Off the Wall as well in the Story Theater for children and two programs for public television, *Masquerade* and *The American Dream Machine.* He even had a Broadway debut in March 1973 in *42 Seconds from Broadway.* Unfortunately, the show closed after one performance.

But it was in October 1973 that Winkler finally got his first break. Some months earlier he had moved to Hollywood on the advice of an agent. He got small roles in several television programs (*The Mary Tyler Moore Show, Rhoda, The Paul Sand Show, The Bob Newhart Show*). However, as Arthur Fonzarelli—a high-school dropout-turned-garage mechanic who rides a motorcycle and has a select vocabulary consisting mostly of "AAayyyyy!"—Winkler found the role that "made" him. Initially a minor character in *Happy Days*, a show allegedly inspired by the movie *American Graffiti*, which glorified the 1950s, "the Fonz" became the great attention-grabber, especially of teen-age girls. The show, which had its debut in the 1974–75 season, peaked the following year. By then, it was reported that Winkler was receiving 50,000 fan letters a *week*.

Always aspiring to serious drama, Winkler made a television special, "William Shakespeare Meets Henry Winkler," in 1977. He also made two films, *Heroes*, about a confused soldier newly returned from Vietnam, and *The One and Only* (directed by Carl Reiner), about a would-be actor who tries to wrestle his way to stardom with unpredictable silly antics and doesn't quite make it. Too closely identified with "the Fonz," Winkler had difficulty establishing a new persona, and his films were not well received. Critics thought his acting superficial because he has been stereotyped.

In another area, however, Winkler is doing significantly better. As the founder of Fair Dinkum Productions, he produced a documentary called "Who Are the DeBolts and Where Did They Get 19 Kids?" This film describes a family with 13 adopted children, several of whom are severely handicapped. Winkler's interest in children—he minored in child psychology in college and occasionally does volunteer work—came through in the film.

Winkler has received many awards and honors, including Golden Globe Awards in 1976, 1977 and 1978. He is Honorary Youth Chairman of the Epilepsy Foundation. In 1977 he was named Entertainment Personality of the Year by the National Association of Theater Owners as well as King Bacchus for the New Orleans Mardi Gras.

In May 1979 Winkler received a special Champion of Youth Award from Los Angeles B'nai B'rith. He acknowledges his Jewish upbringing, describing his mother as "fixing breakfast for me—[serving] eggs, toast and guilt." Guilty or not, he returned to the West Side in 1978 to marry at Congregation Habonim, where he was a bar mitzvah.

ELMER LOUIS WINTER

b. March 6, 1912
Corporate official; Jewish and human rights leader

Elmer Louis Winter, co-founder and ex-president of Manpower Inc., the world's largest temporary employment agency, is an accomplished businessman, a former president of the American Jewish Committee and a well-known civil rights advocate. He is also the author of numerous practical books and a recognized painter and sculptor.

Elmer Louis Winter was born in Milwaukee, Wisconsin to Sigmund, an immigrant owner of a clothing store, and May (Kraus) Winter. He earned a B.A. degree from the University of Wisconsin in 1933 and a law degree from the same university two years later. Winter worked in a private law practice from 1936 to 1948, the year he and his brother-in-law co-founded Manpower Inc. with an initial investment of $7,000. The company, which was believed to be the first temporary employment service anywhere, grew to eventually include 700 offices in 34 nations. Through Manpower Inc., Winter sponsored a free nationwide summer job service in the 1960s called Youthpower, which, in a period of 10 years, placed over 100,000 young people in summer jobs. In 1976 Winter sold his firm to the Parker Pen Company for $28 million.

After selling his business, Winter turned immediately to public service and problem solving. He became chairman of the Committee for the Economic Growth of Israel, an organization devoted to expanding trade between the United States and Israel and encouraging American investment in Israel. Between 1973 and 1977 Winter served as president of the American Jewish Committee. During this period he helped to create the Elmer Winter Institute on the Social Concerns of Business to assist major corporations in solving urban social problems. He also promoted AJC's job-linked Housing Center, to help provide housing near jobs in suburbs and jobs in cities near available housing. Winter is also a fellow of Brandeis University and a member of the board of governors of Haifa University.

Dynamic and respected in his community, Winter has concentrated, in recent years, on finding jobs for the large number of jobless minority youths in Milwaukee. Having been active during the 1960s in civil rights and the organization of housing, school and employment programs, Winter tried to recapture that spirit in 1979 by founding Operation 4,000. The program took its name from the number of unemployed black youths in Milwaukee and is a modest version of Winter's earlier national Youthpower project.

Winter has also been instrumental in trying to restore life to the poor, devastated area of Upper 3rd Street in Milwaukee. "Now that I no longer have the primary responsibility for the success of Manpower, I'd like to be a 'bottom line man' of social responsibility. I've had a good life in Milwaukee. I feel I still owe some rent to the community."

Winter has also been involved in national programs. He was appointed by senators Charles Percy and Hubert Humphrey in 1977 to serve on the National Alliance to Save Energy, a position he held until 1980. According to Winter: "Conservation for most Americans is definitely tied to money motivation. We have to convince people to save money by saving energy. Then we can tie the two together."

A member of the National Alliance of Businessmen, Winter has written many books outlining how to succeed at work, including *Women at Work* (New York, 1967), *Your Future in Jobs Abroad* (New York, 1968), *A Complete Guide to Making a Public Stock Offering* (New York, 1973) and *The Successful Manager/Secretary Team* (New York, 1974).

A painter and sculptor, Winter has exhibited his art works at Milwaukee's Performing Arts Center, Wisconsin Modern Salon of Art, and the Wisconsin Painters and Sculptors Annual Exhibit. He is a member of the board of directors of the Milwaukee Art Center and the Wisconsin State Arts Foundation and Council.

SHELLY WINTERS

b. August 18, 1923
Actress

For close to 30 years, Shelly Winters has been a successful star of stage and screen. A very versatile actress, she has played both dramatic and comic roles as well as singing and dancing to entertain her many millions of fans. She has won an Academy Award and numerous nominations for both Academy and other awards in recognition of her talents.

Shirley Schrift was born in East St. Louis, Illinois. Her father, Johann, was a men's clothing designer, and her mother, Rose (Winter) Shrift, sang for the St. Louis Municipal Opera. Winters recalls that she first got on stage at an amateur show when she was 3 years old, and people couldn't get her off again. In 1934, her family moved to Brooklyn, where she later attended Thomas Jefferson High School and played in the Gilbert and Sullivan show *The Mikado*. She quit high school six months before her graduation in 1939 and began to model in New York's garment district.

In 1939 Winters studied acting at the New Theater School and performed in the chorus line at the La Conga Club. She also did some summer stock theater that year and changed her name to "Shelly Winter." It became "Winters" six years later. In 1939 she received a bit acting and singing role in *The Conquest of April*, and

three years later she played a supporting role in the operetta *Rosalinda*.

That performance led to a contract with Columbia Pictures at a salary of $150 a week. In 1944 and 1945 Winters had small parts in seven films produced by Columbia, but the contract was allowed to expire, and Winters returned to the stage. She had parts in *The Taming of the Shrew* and *Of Mice and Men*. She also began to study acting under the tutelage of Charles Laughton. After a series of unsuccessful screen tests, she finally received a small role in the film *The Gangster* in 1947.

The noted director George Cukor saw her in the film and cast her as a waitress who is killed by Ronald Coleman in *A Double Life* (1948). Her stellar performance led to her nomination for an Academy Award for the best supporting actress of the year. This was followed by another strong performance as a mobster's girl friend in *Larceny* (1948), a film made by Universal Pictures. Winters then signed a contract with Universal, and in 1949 she played her first featured role in the musical *South Sea Sinner*.

That same year, 1949, Winters played Alice Tripp, the factory working woman in the film *A Place in the Sun,* based on Theodore Dreiser's *An American Tragedy*. Once again she was nominated for an Academy Award but lost out to Vivien Leigh for the New York Critics' Circle Award as the best actress.

In 1951 Winters began to study acting, singing and dancing at the Actors Studio under the direction of Elia Kazan. After she won the Academy Award for best supporting actress for her role in *The Diary of Anne Frank,* her career was off and running. She has played in more than 31 films and six plays. Some of her more noted work has been in the movies *A Patch of Blue* (1965); *Alfie* (1965); and *Last Stop, Greenwich Village* (1976), directed by Paul Mazursky. On the stage she has done *Who's Afraid of Virginia Woolf* (1966) and *The Effects of Gamma Rays on Man-in-the-Moon Marigolds* (1972). Winters is a "method" actress with the uncanny ability to be appealing, obscene, self-centered, domineering and funny, all at once. She once joked that she had the "whore" and "mother" markets locked up.

In 1971 she wrote a play, *One Night Stands of a Noisy Passenger,* and nine years later, her biography, *Also Known as Shirley* (New York, 1980), which astounded people both with her near total recall of countless conversations and that she actually dared to recall some of them. As the book climbed the best-seller charts, Winters complained that nobody in her family was talking to her anymore. To make up for the book, she threw a party for all the people she had offended in it. More than 400 people came.

MAYNARD I. WISHNER

b. September 17, 1923
Business executive; communal leader

Maynard Wishner, the 18th national president of the American Jewish Committee—the oldest human rights organization in the United States—is a new kind of contemporary leader: self-made, the child of Eastern European immigrants, as fluent in Yiddish as he is in the arcane world of finance.

Maynard I. Wishner was born in Chicago to Hyman, a knitter of sweaters and Frances (Fisher) Wishner. He attended the University of Chicago, graduating in 1944 with a B.A. degree. Following service in the army in 1943, he earned a law degree from the University of Chicago Law School in 1947. He then became staff counsel and afterwards executive director of the Mayor's Commission on Human Relations for the City of Chicago. From 1952 to 1955 he served as an Assistant Corporation Counsel, acting as lawyer for different municipal departments and as head of the Ordinance Enforcement Division. His major work involved housing and urban renewal. Beginning in 1955 he was also Special Assistant Corporation Counsel to the City of Chicago. At that point, in 1955, he joined a private law firm (now Cole, Wishner, Epstein & Manilow), specializing in general business and corporate law. In 1963 he moved to Walter E. Heller & Company, the main commercial financing and factoring operating subsidiary of Walter E. Heller International Corporation. As a lawyer, Heller had been one of its clients.

Wishner has also been heavily involved with Jewish life in Chicago. During the 1970s he was honorary chairman of the Public Affairs Committee of the Jewish United Fund of Chicago, a group composed of nearly three dozen Jewish organizations seeking to act in a unified fashion on events concerning the Jewish community. He was also a member of the National Hillel Commission, serving college campus Jewish student life.

It was as president of the American Jewish Committee that he became nationally and even internationally known. Continuing the policies of his predecessors, he expanded the AJC's involvement in direct Jewish concerns. He helped the organization make the transition from its non-Zionist base to one more closely attuned to Israel and relationships between Israel and the American Diaspora. For example, in late 1981 he argued that to better comprehend Israel's air strikes against the P.L.O. in Lebanon "we must understand the nature of the dilemma Israel found herself in" inasmuch as a P.L.O. artillery and rocket barrage was causing massive "damage and disruption in the northern Galilee." And in early 1982 he wrote that the real story behind the Israeli withdrawal from the Sinai on April 25, 1982 was that the action was "virtually an unprecedented voluntary return of territory captured in retaliation for a surprise attack" and "ran totally counter to the widely held image of Israel's so-called 'intransigence' and 'unwillingness to negotiate.' "

Wishner has also turned his attention to other areas of interest. In mid-1981 he led the way in reporting and protesting a campaign to arouse anti-Jewish sentiments that was underway in Poland in connection with the country's efforts to destroy the Solidarity labor movement. And following an A.J.C. study of the extent of anti-Semitism in the United States he concluded that while the "manifestations of anti-Semitism give us reason to worry, the numerous confirmations of respect and acceptance give us reason to hope. The combination is endemic to the Jewish condition."

He addressed the 85th Anniversary luncheon of the *Jewish Daily Forward* in May 1982 and surprised everyone when he delivered his remarks in Yiddish. It was, for him, just an aspect of his intensely-felt Jewishness.

DAVID WOLPER

b. January 11, 1928
Film producer

"The three largest producers of documentary films for television are NBC, CBS and David Wolper," a *Time* magazine reporter once wrote. David Wolper, a motion picture and television executive and producer, is a dominant American independent television documentary producer. An expert at blending factual material and showmanship, he has created over 400 productions that explore every facet of contemporary American life.

David Lloyd Wolper was born in New York City to Irvin and Anna (Fass) Wolper. He attended Columbia Grammar School, graduating in 1945, and after one year (1946) at Drake University in Des Moines, Iowa, transferred to the University of Southern California, where he became business manager of the college humor magazine. Always interested in film production, Wolper formed Flamingo Films with his school friend Jim Harris, when he was 20. They created a television first by selling to television a feature motion picture called *Adventures of Mark Eden*. After a series of jobs, one of which involved selling features, shorts and cartoons to TV stations, he formed Wolper Productions in 1958. His first documentary, "Race for Space" (1959), which dealt with the struggle between America and the Soviet Union for space supremacy, was the first independently made documentary to be aired on television.

Wolper, who triggered a demand for factual programming and was the first to see a natural alliance between nonfiction and TV documentaries, is responsible for hundreds of documentary series and specials depicting major events. They include such famous series as *Biography, The Making of the President* (1960 and 1964), *The Undersea World of Jacques Cousteau* (beginning in 1965) and the historic, record-breaking mini-series *Roots* (1977), which traced one black American's quest for his African heritage and his American beginnings. It was so highly praised and successful that a sequel, *Roots: The Next Generations* (1980), followed. Wolper's famous specials include "D-Day" (1962); "Hollywood: The Fabulous Era" (1963); "Let My People Go" (1965), an account of the founding of the state of Israel; and "The Rise and Fall of the Third Reich" (1966), among others. He has also produced numerous prime-time entertainment shows, including such popular comedy series from the mid-1970s as *Chico and the Man* and *Welcome Back, Kotter.*

As the foremost independent maker of documentaries, Wolper has developed a style that combines information with entertainment. He is responsible for encouraging in television the Hollywood film production style—a breaking out of sound stages, the use of hand-held cameras, shooting on location. In his feature film *If It's Tuesday, It Must Be Belgium* (1969), he used material shot in 14 countries.

Wolper has won many awards, including 28 Emmys (and 93 Emmy nominations), 1 Oscar (and 11 Oscar nominations) and the Grand Prix for TV programming at the Cannes Film Festival in 1964 and again in 1971.

HERMAN WOUK

b. May 27, 1915
Writer

With his 1952 Pulitzer Prize-winning novel *The Caine Mutiny* (New York), Herman Wouk was transformed into a best-selling and highly acclaimed storyteller. Whether writing about World War II or Jewish-American life, he has significantly altered the way readers view those two phenomena.

Herman Wouk was born in New York City to Russian immigrant parents, Abraham, a laundry executive, and Esther (Levine) Wouk. He grew up in the Bronx.

After graduating from the elite Townsend Harris High School in 1932, he entered Columbia University, where he majored in comparative literature and philosophy, edited the college humor magazine and wrote two varsity shows. After graduation in 1936 with a B.A. degree, he worked as an advertising and radio scriptwriter.

Wouk enlisted in the United States Navy during World War II and, to ease the boredom of sea duty, wrote a novel, *Aurora Dawn* (New York, 1947). The book, chosen as a Book-of-the-Month Club selection, poked fun at the nervous, fast-paced, hokey atmosphere of radio advertising, with which Wouk was so familiar.

Wouk's early books were drawn, to some degree, from personal experience. *City Boy* (New York, 1948) portrays the adventures of a chubby Bronx boy at school and in summer camp. *The Caine Mutiny* (New York, 1951), his Pulitzer Prize-winning novel of World War II, while not autobiographical, drew in part on his naval experience on the destroyer *Zane*. It depicts a conflict of values between personal rights and duty when an erratic and psychotic ship's captain is removed from duty by his crew. *Marjorie Morningstar* (New York, 1955), which was enormously successful, is the story of a middle-class Jewish girl who falls in love with and becomes involved in show business but finally settles down to ordinary life as a suburban housewife. In *Don't Stop the Carnival* (New York, 1965), he depicts the alienation of a middle-aged Broadway press agent who buys a hotel on a Caribbean island but feels out of place as a Jew.

Wouk's three major novels—*The Caine Mutiny, The Winds of War* (Boston, 1971) and *War and Remembrance* (Boston, 1978)—are nothing less than an effort to recreate in fiction the sweep and meaning of World War II. "World War II," he once told *Publishers Weekly,* "was an Everest of human experience, and as always, you cannot see the mountains until you get some distance away. It started with a horse-drawn army moving into Poland and ended with the atom bomb. Its outcome was crucial to the human race and it is important to realize how close an outcome it really was."

An observant, Orthodox Jew, Wouk wrote *This Is My God* (New York, 1959) explaining his faith in the tenets of Orthodoxy. He wrote:

> Judaism is part of my life and of my family's life. . . .
> I believe it is our lot to live and serve in our old identity,
> until the promised day when the Lord will be one and his
> name one in all the earth. I think the extinction of Jewish learning and Jewish faith would be a measureless
> tragedy.

Wouk has actively supported synagogues and educational institutions in the United States and Israel. He has established a student scholarship at Bar-Ilan University in Israel in memory of his grandfather, Rabbi Mendel Leib Levin, and has been a member of the board of directors of the Orthodox Jewish Council of Congregations. He worships daily in an Orthodox synagogue in Washington and devotes time each day to the study of the Talmud.

For further information:
Wouk, Herman. *Youngblood Hawke.* New York: 1962.

WALTER S. WURZBURGER

b. March 29, 1920
Rabbi

During his tenure as president of the Rabbinical Council of America, Rabbi Walter Wurzburger became known for his efforts to make Orthodox Jewry more in tune with the demands of modern life. Currently spiritual leader of a synagogue in Far Rockaway, New York and a professor at Yeshiva University, Wurzburger is a highly regarded theological scholar who was once cited by Rabbi Gilbert Rosenthal in *Four Paths to One God* (New York, 1973) as "one of the young [thinkers who] have resuscitated Orthodox theology."

Walter Samuel Wurzburger was born in Munich, Germany to Adolph, a businessman, and Hedwig (Tannenwald) Wurzburger. He came to the United States in 1938 and was naturalized in 1944. Wurzburger received his B.A. degree magna cum laude from Yeshiva University in 1943, where he was greatly influenced by the scholar Rabbi Joseph D. Soloveitchick. He was ordained the following year. Pursuing graduate studies in philosophy at Harvard University, he completed an M.A. degree in 1946 and a Ph.D. in 1951.

While studying for his doctorate, Wurzburger also headed Congregation Chai Odom in Dorchester, Massachusetts, serving from 1944 to 1953. His next appointment took him to Toronto, Canada, where he was spiritual leader of Congregation Shaarei Shomayim. In 1967 he returned to New York, where he has been the rabbi of Congregation Shaaray Tefila in Far Rockaway and Lawrence, Long Island. Since that time he has also taught philosophy at Yeshiva University and from 1978 to 1980 was adjunct professor of Judaic studies at Brooklyn College of the City University of New York.

Since 1962 Wurzburger has edited *Tradition*, a magazine of Orthodox Jewish thought, and he has contributed articles to *Commentary, Sh'ma, Moment, Jewish Life* and many other Jewish publications.

He has also spoken widely, especially of the need to preserve Orthodox Jewish life and values, but in a modern context. He also feels it is important "to spread the influence of orthodoxy to the general Jewish community." In an interview he commented that he "never believed that traditional Jews should separate themselves from others. We should not feel that we solved our problems, that we, in our circle, saved our souls, or that we do not care about moving others closer to the world of Torah and Yiddishkeit. Quite the contrary."

His worry that Jewish observance was declining sharply led Wurzburger to reach out to younger Jews for participation on the decision-making level within the Orthodox hierarchy. "We must halt the alienation of our spiritually sensitive youth from our religious institutions," he told *The New York Times* in 1976, when he was elected to his second two-year term as president of the Rabbinical Council of America. (His first two-year term ran from 1962 to 1964.) "If religion is to emerge as a vibrant and dynamic force in the American scene, we cannot afford to squander the opportunities and spiritual energy provided by the quest for authenticity and spiritual meaning on the part of our young people."

In 1982 he became the first nationally known Orthodox rabbi to publicly associate himself with groups in the American Jewish community seeking to link opposition to the nuclear arms race to Jewish tradition.

In 1981 Wurzburger became president of the Synagogue Council of America. He is a member of the International Jewish Committee on Inter-religious Consultations in New York; is on the board of trustees of the Federation of Jewish Philanthropies and is a member of the National Rabbinic Council of United Jewish Appeal.

ROSALYN S. YALOW

b. July 19, 1921
Medical physicist

When Rosalyn Yalow won the Nobel Prize for Medicine in 1977, she was the first woman to do so since Gert Cori 30 years earlier and the second woman in the history of the prize.

Rosalyn Sussman was born in the Bronx to Simon, a small business man, and the former Clara (Zipper) Sussman. An excellent student, she developed a leaning toward science while at Walton High School and was encouraged to study physics at Hunter College of the City University of New York, in those days an outstanding free liberal arts institution for women. However, in her senior year at Hunter she was advised that if she intended to pursue graduate work in physics, she would have to support herself as a secretary. Yalow thus combined advanced physics courses with typing and shorthand and graduated with a Bachelor of Arts degree magna cum laude and Phi Beta Kappa.

Fortunately, she never had to type. Yalow instead received a teaching fellowship for graduate studies at the University of Illinois, where she was the only woman among 400 men in the engineering school. She received her M.S. degree in 1942 and in 1945 was only the second woman in the university's history to receive a Ph.D. in physics.

By now already married to Aaron Yalow, also a physicist, Rosalyn Yalow returned to New York, where for one year she worked as an electrical engineer for the Federal Telecommunications Lab, and then from 1946 to 1950 lectured in physics at Hunter.

In 1947 she was a consultant for the Bronx Veterans Administration Hospital and three years later was appointed to the post of physicist and assistant chief of the hospital's radioisotope service. That year Yalow also met Dr. Solomon A. Berson, a young internist with whom she began what would become a long-standing and complementary collaboration, which ended only when Berson died in 1972. Together they began the pioneering work on radioimmunoassay (RIA) that culminated in the Nobel award. Through RIA, radionuclides are used to measure minute amounts of various substances in the blood such as antibodies and hormones. Other uses suggested include the control of infectious diseases and measurement of endocrine levels in the brain, which Yalow conjectures will reveal more about what makes the brain work and how it controls body functions.

In 1968 Yalow was named acting chief of the radioisotope service at the VA and since 1969 has been chief of its radioisotope reference lab. In 1972 she became a VA senior medical investigator and was named director of the Solomon A. Berson Research Lab the following year. At the same time, Yalow was a professor at the department of medicine at Mt. Sinai Hospital and since 1974 has been distinguished professor of medicine at Mt. Sinai.

Recognition came for her development of radioimmunoassay, an application of nuclear physics to clinical medicine that permits scientists to utilize radioisotopic tracers to measure the concentration of hundreds of pharmacologic and biologic substances in the blood and other body fluids in animals and plants. The technique, first used by Yalow in 1959 in measuring the insulin level of diabetics, is currently widely used in screening blood in blood banks for contamination by the hepatitis virus and determining if a person has recently taken drugs, such as heroin, methadone or LSD.

She was the first woman to win the Albert Lasker Prize for Basic Medical Research in 1976. Among her other awards are the Torch of Learning, donated by the American Friends of Hebrew University, which she was granted in 1978. In 1980 she was presented with an honorary doctor of science degree by the University of Hartford in Connecticut. At the commencement she reflected on some of her early experiences as an aspiring scientist and her observations since then: "If we are to have faith that mankind will survive and thrive on the face of the earth, we are dependent on continued revolutions brought by science. These revolutions will set us free from hunger and disease and permit us to set our sights on the stars."

DANIEL YANKELOVICH

b. December 29, 1924
Pollster; sociologist

Daniel Yankelovich, head of one of the more eminent polling operations in the world, is also well-known as an analyst of social and political trends in this country.

Daniel Yankelovich was born in Boston to Frederick, a realtor, and Sadie (Mostow) Yankelovich. He graduated from Harvard in 1946 with a B.A. degree and received a master's degree in psychology, also from Harvard, in 1950. He did postgraduate work in philosophy and psychology at the Sorbonne in Paris from 1950 to 1952.

From 1952 to 1958 Yankelovich was vice president and director of research at Nowland and Company and in 1958 launched his own business and social research firm. The subjects of his research have included attitudes about unemployment, education, housing, crime, drugs and political figures. In 1969 he studied (for CBS News) the views of college and non-college youth about three television programs on American youth.

Yankelovich has also been a research professor of psychology at New York University (1973–77), a visiting professor of psychology at the New School for Social Research (1973–76) and a lecturer in psychiatry at Tufts Medical School (1967–77). He is the founder—with former Secretary of State Cyrus Vance—of the Public Agenda Foundation, a nonprofit organization designed to encourage public interest in and concern about issues of national significance.

In *New Rules: Searching for Self-Fulfillment in a World Upside Down* (New York, 1981), Yankelovich's most important work, he seeks to synthesize his empirical observations. He scrutinizes the recent abandonment of traditional values for freer sexual expression, divorce and abortion and the rise of opposing forces, such as the Moral Majority, which are attempting to revert to older mores and laws. Looking ahead, Yankelovich predicts that Americans will continue to pursue personal freedom and greater goals for themselves, but this time in the midst of a shrinking economy.

In that same year he announced the findings of his study of anti-Semitism in the United States, commissioned by the American Jewish Committee. His conclusion was that it had declined significantly since 1961. The reason, he stated, was "not primarily the result of changes in the views of individuals, but the result of generational changes." Since 1964, he stressed, "an older, more anti-Semitic generation has passed on, and has been replaced by a younger, less anti-Semitic one." Moreover, he commented that Americans "have grown increasingly tolerant of a variety of life-styles and beliefs," and "the increasing acceptance of Jews is, in part, a reflection of the more general trend toward increasing acceptance of social pluralism." This information was widely disseminated and occasionally questioned, inasmuch as many American Jews nonetheless felt—despite any documentary evidence to the contrary—that anti-Semitism was rising, often more steeply than in any decade since the end of World War II. But Yankelovich's study concluded otherwise on the basis of his lengthy study and questionnaires.

He has long studied national attitudes for the American Jewish Committee. In March 1977 (as in the years since 1974), he looked at American attitudes toward Israel and the Middle East and found that most Americans still favored Israel. One question his firm usually posed was: Do you think American Jews are more loyal to Israel or to the United States? Essentially, about half the respondents said they thought Jews were more loyal to this country than to Israel, although a third consistently take the opposite view. Still, in a 1979 Yankelovich poll, he found that the question of "Jewish power" was diminishing: Only 16 percent thought Jews "too powerful."

Looking ahead into the eighties, Yankelovich told the Council on Foundations in May 1982 that "the burning issue of this decade" will be the general insecurity Americans feel as a result of the nuclear arms race. "The possibility of nuclear annihilation of the United States has, for the first time, entered the American consciousness," he said. An "astonishing" 43 percent of the public fear that increased military expenditures will not bring peace. If this proves to be so, then the implications for the United States and the world may well be enormous.

For further information:
Yankelovich, Daniel. *The Changing Values on Campus.* New York: 1972.

———. *The New Morality: A Profile of American Youth in the Seventies.* New York: 1974.
———. *Students and Drugs.* Washington, D.C.: 1975.
———. *Work, Productivity and Job Satisfaction: An Evaluation of Policy-Related Research.* New York: 1975.

ADAM YARMOLINSKY

b. November 17, 1922
Lawyer; government official

During the liberal presidential administrations of John F. Kennedy and Lyndon B. Johnson, Adam Yarmolinsky was one of the more influential and controversial government figures in the formation of domestic programs.

Adam Yarmolinsky was born in New York City to intellectually prominent parents. His father, Avrahm Yarmolinsky, was an internationally recognized scholar of Slavonic and Jewish literature, and his mother, Babette (Deutsch) Yarmolinsky, was a renowned poet and author of books for juveniles. Yarmolinsky carried on the family literary tradition with editorial duties on his school papers at the prestigious Fieldston School, from which he graduated in 1939, and at Harvard University, where he received his B.A. degree in 1943. Yarmolinsky then spent three years in the Army Air Force. After his discharge, he attended Yale Law School, where he served as editor in chief of the Yale Law Journal before receiving his Bachelor of Laws in 1948.

He clerked on the United States Court of Appeals for a year and then entered private practice with Root, Ballantine, Harlan, Bushby and Palmer in New York City. From 1950 to 1951 he was clerk to Associate Justice Stanley Reed on the U.S. Supreme Court. From 1951 to 1955 he was an associate with the Washington law firm of Cleary, Gottlieb, Friendly and Ball before joining the Fund for the Republic Inc. as director. While there from 1955 to 1956, he supervised a study of federal security programs called *"Case Studies in Personnel Security,"* which was published. He then worked as public affairs director for Doubleday and Co., as special correspondent to the London *Economist* from 1956 to 1960 and as a consultant to several foundations before joining the Kennedy administration in 1961.

His first appointment was to the Defense Department, as one of Defense Secretary Robert McNamara's so-called whiz kids. One of Yarmolinsky's major projects as special assistant in the department was to supervise the fallout shelter program. As he became more influential, Yarmolinsky became involved in legal moves to desegregate southern military bases and to divert government work from contractors who practiced racial discrimination. His efforts proved successful, but as a result his own future in government service was jeopardized. Southern congressmen and senators from states affected by Yarmolinsky's actions were so angered that they refused to confirm his nomination for further government assignments. Thus, after serving in the Defense Department until 1964, and one year following as deputy director to the President's Anti-Poverty Task Force under Sargent Shriver and as principal deputy assistant secretary of defense for internal security (1965-66), he left government service.

He has since taught at Harvard's Law School and the John F. Kennedy School of Government. And since 1972 he has been Ralph Waldo Emerson University Professor at the University of Massachusetts. Yarmolinsky has, however, been a consultant to the government, first with the Office of Technical Assessment (1974-77) and then, from 1977 to 1979, with the U.S. Arms Control and Disarmament Agency.

A contributor to many periodicals, Yarmolinsky published a major book in 1971, *The Military Establishment: Its Impact on American Society* (New York), a thorough and critical analysis of the economic, social and political interactions between the military and society. Among the issues he explores are the relationship between the military and foreign policy; its role in domestic unrest; its increasing costs to taxpayers; its impact on racial mobility and higher education; and the growing alienation between the military establishment and the public.

For further information:
Yarmolinsky, Adam. *Recognition of Excellence.* New York: 1960.

ZEV YAROSLAVSKY

b. December 21, 1948
Politician

Since 1968 and while still in college, Zev Yaroslavsky has been a major public figure in Los Angeles. His leadership of that city's protest movement against the Soviet Union's treatment of its Jews, followed by a forceful presence in the Los Angeles City Council, has made him one of the most popular and effective young politicians in Southern California.

Zev Yaroslavsy was born in Los Angeles to David, a Jewish educator, and Minna Yaroslavsky, both immigrants from Russia and loyal Zionists. As a youth he was active in the Labor Zionist movement Habonim. Following graduation from Fairfax High School, he carried his interest to the University of California at Los Angeles, where he studied history and economics.

In 1968 he visited the Soviet Union and made contact with many Jews there who wanted to leave. On his return to the United States, Yaroslavsky founded the California Students for Soviet Jews and joined with the California Council for Soviet Jews in organizing rallies and demonstrations. His aggressive activism was evident even then: Yaroslavsky also staged several individual protests that resulted in his arrest, but he used the publicity to his advantage. Following graduation from UCLA, where he received a B.A. degree in 1971 and an M.A. degree in 1972, he became a staffer with the Community Relations Committee of the Jewish Federation Council, managing programs for Soviet Jews. He was later fired for his radical views, however. Even so, following the defeat of Democratic presidential candidate George McGovern, for whom Yaroslavsky had campaigned, he was hired as executive director of the Southern California Council for Soviet Jews.

Yaroslavsky's image as a provocateur and a "60s-type radical" began to undergo change, although his penchant for political activism did not. In 1974 he ran for the Los Angeles City Council seat from his home base of the Beverly-Fairfax district, a predominantly Jewish and mostly well-to-do community. With little money and an even smaller power base, he managed to win the seat after a close runoff election. In a short time he cultivated not only the broad range of Jewish interests within his own district but extended his visibility into other Los Angeles neighborhoods.

Reelected in 1977 for his first full term with 91 percent of the vote and only one opponent, and again in 1981 with no opponents, Yaroslavsky proved outspoken and effective as a reformer and legislator in all areas of city government. He engineered reforms in the City Charter that ended discriminatory hiring practices and eliminated unfair advantages to candidates for political office by ending automatic alphabetical listing on voting ballots. He spearheaded the movement to restructure electric rates so that all Los Angeles customers were treated equally and was similarly active in other areas of consumer rights, including the acquisition of credit. As the representative of an area with many elderly citizens, he instituted programs addressing crime prevention, special transportation needs and nutrition.

Following his 1981 reelection, Yaroslavsky became

chair of the prestigious Police, Fire and Public Safety Committee, a role particularly prized by politicos for its power and visibility. He conducted an inquiry into past abuses by the Los Angeles police, including alleged spying on himself while he was a student leader at UCLA. And he worked closely with the police force to monitor the goings-on of the so-called Israeli Mafia in Los Angeles, a small group that was reportedly involved in drug traffic, murder and extortion. He supported the involvement of Los Angeles's substantial Israeli community, estimated at 100,000, in the Jewish community at large, which numbers about a half million. Yaroslavsky's overall effectiveness, despite his reputation for abrasiveness, made him one of the city's most admired personalities.

HOWARD ZINN

b. August 24, 1922
Historian

Radical historian Howard Zinn has challenged the very underpinnings of historical scholarship in the United States. An advocate of civil disobedience, the civil rights movement and the anti-Vietnam War movement, Zinn has argued that history as it is written does not reflect the experience of groups in conflict with the privileged classes. His *A People's History of the United States* (New York, 1980) includes the experiences of neglected groups, such as women, blacks and laborers.

Howard Zinn was born in Manhattan, the son of Edward, a waiter, and Jenny (Rabinowitz) Zinn. When World War II erupted, he went to work in the Brooklyn Navy Yard and in 1943 joined the U.S. Army Air Corps. He served in Europe for two years, winning an Air Medal and battle stars for combat in Central Europe. He was discharged in 1945, having attained the rank of second lieutenant.

After his discharge from service, Zinn received his B.A. degree from New York University in 1951 and his M.A. degree in history from Columbia University the following year. He was awarded his Ph.D. degree by Columbia University in 1958.

He began his teaching career at Upsala College, a small institution in New Jersey, where he was an instructor from 1953 until 1956, and was a lecturer in history at Brooklyn College from 1955 to 1956. That year he became chairman of the History and Social Science department at Spelman College, an all-black private women's college in Atlanta, Georgia. While at Spelman he became deeply involved in the civil rights movement

and was an adviser to the Student Non-violent Coordinating Committee (SNCC), a newly created, southern-based black power organization. His political leanings and activism brought him into conflict with the administration at Spelman, and he was released in 1963 with a year's severance pay. That enabled him to write *The Southern Mystique* (New York, 1964) and *SNCC: The New Abolitionists* (Boston, 1964).

In *The Southern Mystique*, Zinn blended post-Freudian psychology, history and personal experience to dispute the popularly held concept that segregation was an unalterable southern state of mind and that blacks were somehow different from whites. He admitted that during his years at Spelman, he had slid back and forth across the barriers of race consciousness. In his book about SNCC, Zinn asserted that the black power movement was teaching Americans that they could not depend on government to remedy their grievances. Freely comparing black power advocates to the abolitionists, Zinn declared that changing the consciousnesses of the oppressed would change the circumstances of the ruling class.

After Zinn became a professor of government at Boston University in 1964, he maintained his attack on injustice, as he perceived it, in America. In *Disobedience and Democracy* (New York, 1968), Zinn outlined his strong belief in the virtues of civil disobedience. Civil disobedience, he contended, could only be weighed against the size of the evil it was intended to eliminate. Thus, civil disobedience in the name of civil rights or against the war in Vietnam was justified and necessary, and to prove his point, he defied a government ban on travel to North Vietnam and visited Hanoi in 1968 with the activist priest Daniel Berrigan to receive three newly released American prisoners of war. The following year he was one of the most prominent academics in the American Mobilization Committee and was involved with organizing work stoppages and moratoriums in universities across the country.

In his next book, *The Politics of History* (New York, 1970), Zinn critiqued the way history was then written, pointing out that injustices are buried by historians because historical accounts are based on the records of the upper classes. Therefore, he concluded, political history is written from the viewpoint of politicians; slavery from the viewpoint of plantation owners and so on. *A People's History of the United States* (New York, 1980) was aimed at rectifying the situation. Beginning with "the European invasion of Indian settlements of North America" and continuing with such topics as the American Revolution as seen by poor people and other chapters on American history as perceived by women, prisoners and other minorities, Zinn casts a cynical and negative light upon traditional histories and is most respectful of resisters of the establishment.

Zinn's history proved highly controversial. While Harvard historian Oscar Handlin lambasted the work, referring to "the deranged quality of his fairy tale in which the incidents are made to fit the legend," the *New Statesman* critic praised Zinn's success in "[revealing] much about the people who are usually missing from American history textbooks."

For further information:
Zinn, Howard. *Justice in Everyday Life.* New York: 1974.
————. *LaGuardia in Congress.* Ithaca, N.Y.: 1959.
————. *New Deal Thought.* New York: 1966.
————. *Post War America.* New York: 1973.
————. *Vietnam: The Logic of Withdrawal.* New York: 1967.

EUGENIA ZUKERMAN

b. September 25, 1944
Flutist; writer

Although for several years Eugenia Zukerman stood in the wings while her husband, violinist Pinchas Zukerman, forged a career as a top international performer and orchestra conductor, since the late 1970s she has gained recognition as a top-flight flutist and more recently as a novelist. Frequently performing in concerts with her husband and in special concerts with James Galway and Jean-Pierre Rampal, the world's best-known flutists, as well as in solo recitals, she has successfully managed a career that includes writing and appearing as a television commentator.

Eugenia Rich was born in Cambridge, Massachusetts to Stanley, a physicist and the inventor of sonar technology who taught at the Massachusetts Institute of Technology, and Shirley (Cohen) Rich, an executive assistant who was the first woman admitted to the engineering department at the City College of New York. Exposed to the arts as she grew up, Eugenia Rich began studying at age 10 and soon displayed a special talent and a serious commitment to music. By the time she was a senior at Hall High School in West Hartford, Connecticut, she had begun taking lessons with the well-known flutist Julius Baker and had spent several summers studying and performing at the Aspen Music Festival.

Upon high school graduation, Rich moved to New York City and entered Barnard College. But she left, ostensibly to write a novel, and then enrolled at the Juilliard School of Music, where she played first flute in the Juilliard student orchestra and in 1966 met Zukerman, a talented scholarship student from Israel. They were married in 1968. While fame loomed near for Pinchas Zukerman, who won the coveted Leventritt Competition in 1967 and shortly thereafter rose to prominence, Eugenia Zukerman continued playing flute, steadily developing a reputation of her own. In 1970 she was a winner in the prestigious Young Concert Artists International Auditions, which have served to launch the careers of many talented young musicians, and in 1971 she made her New York recital debut at Town Hall. She subsequently performed frequently at the Spoleto Festival, with the Chamber Music Society of Lincoln Center, and with many other orchestras and smaller ensembles in the United States, Europe and Israel. She has also, on occasion, been in the PDQ Bach Orchestra conducted by Peter Schickele, who for many years has written and performed widely acclaimed parodies of Bach's music.

During the mid-1970s Zukerman spent much of her time raising two young daughters, but she began to perform and to record regularly in the late 1970s. Among her recordings for CBS Masterworks are the complete Mozart works for flute and orchestra and works by Beethoven, C.P.E. Bach, Telemann, Vivaldi and Stamitz. She has also performed some rarely heard contemporary music for flute, including the Sonatine by Henri Dutilleux; *Ulloa's Ring,* a composition by a young American composer, Libby Larsen; and Jacque Ibert's Concerto for Flute. While Zukerman is not a flamboyant artist in the style of Galway, nor has she attained the stature of Rampal, she has nonetheless developed a wide following and has been praised for her clean, expressive tone.

But her urge to write never quite left her, and in addition to publishing articles in *The New York Times Magazine, Vogue, Esquire* and other periodicals, she finally completed her first novel, *Deceptive Cadence* (New York), in 1980. Based on Zukerman's firsthand knowledge of the international music world—but not at all autobiographical—*Deceptive Cadence* focuses on the plight of Tibor Szabo, a temperamental, philandering young Hungarian pianist on the verge of stardom, who, on the eve of an important concert, mysteriously disappears. In fact, he has deliberately "vanished" in order to take stock of his life as a musician whom others have tried to direct and as a man in control of his fate.

Being the wife of one of the world's top violinists had its pressures early in the marriage. "I'll never forget what it was like," she said, "seeing the world and hearing the world applaud Pinky, but I become more and more aware that I would have to do something with my own drives." Having since then risen to the top ranks among flutists performing today, Zukerman adds: "I feel fulfilled in so many ways. To have a happy relationship with the people in your life and be active in your work is already enough. Then if a modicum of success comes also, that's the icing on the cake."

PINCHAS ZUKERMAN

b. July 16, 1948
Violinist

Pinchas Zukerman, one of the world's most outstanding violinists, is also a conductor of growing eminence and influence.

Pinchas Zukerman was born in Tel Aviv, Israel to two concentration camp survivors, Yehuda, a onetime violinist in the Warsaw Philharmonic, and Miriam (Lieberman-Skotchilas) Zukerman. When Pinchas—known as "Pinky" to his friends—was 7, his father gave him a small violin and began instructing the boy. Before long, father and son were playing duets, and afterward Pinchas studied at the Israel Conservatory and the Academy of Music in Tel Aviv.

After Isaac Stern heard Zukerman during a visit to Israel in 1961, he arranged for the young violinist to study with Ivan Galamian at the Juilliard School of Music in Manhattan with the aid of an American-Israel Cultural Foundation scholarship. While studying at Juilliard, the Professional Children's School and the High School of Performing Arts from 1962 until 1966, Zukerman lived with pianist Eugene Istomin's family.

At Juilliard, Zukerman found it hard to adjust to being one among many gifted students. When Stern found out that Zukerman was often truant from school, "he did everything but punch me. He got me to see that music isn't a profession. It's a way of life," Zukerman told the *New York Daily News.*

Zukerman gave his initial New York performance at Town Hall on October 27, 1963. After co-winning the prestigious 1967 Leventritt International Competition, he signed a contract with impresario Sol Hurok, who had him tour the United States and Canada. In 1969 he first appeared with the New York Philharmonic and also performed with young Israeli pianist Daniel Barenboim at the Brighton (England) Festival. Since then he has performed with the finest symphonic orchestras.

Today, when people speak of eminent violinists, they always include "Pinky," frequently citing the complete Beethoven trios he recorded with Daniel Barenboim and the cellist Jacqueline de Pre. Still, he has not only tried to master the viola, too, but believes that to be really effective as a violinist, he had to become a conductor, the better to play the violin. "That's the ultimate," he told the *New York Daily News,* "to make your own sound. On the other hand, the total instrument, the total music-making is really in front of the orchestra. As a player there's a certain physical fulfillment that you can never have as a conductor." Yet his finest performances with the St. Paul Chamber Orchestra—which he has conducted since 1980—are when he is both conductor and soloist. "It's like playing large chamber music," he told inverviewer Stephen Rubin. "You don't have an intermediary."

A Selected Bibliography of American Jewish Life

Bellow, Saul. *Herzog*. New York: 1964.

Birmingham, Stephen. *Our Crowd*. New York: 1977.

———. *The Grandees: America's Sephardic Elite*. New York: 1971.

Blau, Joseph. *Judaism in America*. Chicago: 1976.

Cahan, Abraham. *The Rise of David Levinsky*. New York: 1970.

Cohen, Naomi. *American Jews and the Zionist Idea*. New York: 1975.

Feingold, Henry L. *The Politics of Rescue*. New Brunswick, N.J.: 1970.

———. *Zion in America: The Jewish Experience from Colonial Times to the Present*. New York: 1974.

Fuchs, Daniel. *The Williamsburg Trilogy*. New York: 1972.

Glazer, Nathan. *American Judaism*. Chicago: 1957.

Gold, Michael. *Jews Without Money*. New York: 1930.

Goodman, Saul, ed. *Faith of Secular Jews*. New York: 1976.

Goren, Arthur. *New York Jews and the Quest for Community*. New York: 1970.

Grinstein, Hyman B. *The Rise of the Jewish Community of New York, 1654-1860*. New York: 1975.

Halkin, Hillel. *Letters to an American Friend*. Philadelphia: 1977.

Heilman, Samuel C. *Synagogue Life*. Chicago: 1976.

Helmreich, William. *Wake Up! Wake Up! And Do the Work of the Creator*. New York: 1980.

Howe, Irving. *World of Our Fathers*. New York: 1977.

Kaplan, Mordecai M. *Judaism as a Civilization*. New York: 1957.

Korn, Bertram. *American Jewry and the Civil War*. New York: 1970.

Levin, Meyer. *The Old Bunch*. New York: 1973.

Lewisohn, Ludwig. *The Island Within*. New York: 1928.

Malamud, Bernard. *The Assistant*. New York: 1957.

Marcus, Jacob Rader. *The Colonial American Jew, 1492–1776*. 3 vols. Detroit: 1970.

Metzker, Isaac, ed. *A Bintel Brief*. New York: 1977.

Miller, Arthur. *Focus*. New York: 1945.

Nissenson, Hugh. *A Pile of Stones*. New York: 1965.

Ozick, Cynthia. *The Pagan Rabbi and Other Stories*. New York: 1976.

Plaut, W. Gunther. *The Growth of Reform Judaism*. New York: 1967.

Polner, Murray. *Rabbi: The American Experience*. New York: 1977.

Roth, Henry. *Call It Sleep*. New York: 1960.

Roth, Philip. *Goodbye, Columbus*. Boston: 1959.

———. *The Ghost Writer*. New York: 1979.

Sanders, Ronald. *The Downtown Jews*. New York: 1977.

Schappes, Morris U., ed. *A Documentary History of the Jews in the United States, 1654–1875*. New York: 1971.

Sklare, Marshall. *Conservative Judaism*. New York: 1976.

Snetsinger, John. *Truman, The Jewish Vote and the Creation of Israel*. Stanford, Calif. 1974.

Teller, Judd. *Strangers and Natives*. New York: 1968.

Urofsky, Melvin I. *American Zionism from Herzl to the Holocaust*. New York: 1975.

Wischnitzer, Mark. *To Dwell in Safety: Jewish Migration Since 1800*. Philadelphia: 1948.

Wyman, David. *Paper Walls*. Amherst, Mass.: 1969.

INDEX

INDEX